LAW AND BUSINESS OF THE SPORTS INDUSTRIES

Volume I

Professional Sports Leagues

LAW AND BUSINESS OF THE SPORTS INDUSTRIES

Volume I

Professional Sports Leagues

ROBERT C. BERRY
Boston College Law School

GLENN M. WONG
University of Massachusetts

Auburn House Publishing Company
Dover, Massachusetts • London

Library of Congress Cataloging in Publication Data
Berry, Robert C.
   Law and business of the sports industries.

   Bibliography: p.
   Includes index.
   1. Professional sports—Law and legislation—United
States. I. Wong, Glenn M. II. Title.
KF3989.B47   1986   344.73'009   82–22833
ISBN 0–86569–081–2   347.30499

Printed in the United States of America

CONTENTS

Introduction   ix

CHAPTER 1
Background on Professional Sports   1

The Development of Industries   1
1.10 Constituencies within the Industries   2
    1.11 Leagues or Associations   3
    1.12 Clubs and Owners   6
    1.13 The Commissioner   11
    1.14 Player's Associations   13
    1.15 Sports Attorneys and Agents   15
    1.20 Players   17
1.20 The Constituencies and Their Views on a
    Current Issue   20
1.30 Economics of Professional Sports   50
    1.31 Player Salaries   42
    1.32 League and Club Economic Profiles   51
    1.33 Broadcast Revenues   61

CHAPTER 2
Legal Structure of Professional Sports   65

2.00 Early Legal Skirmishes   65
    2.01 New Leagues, Ensuing Legal Battles   65
    2.02 Formative Eras in Sports Legal
    Developments   66
    2.03 The Big Three: Contracts, Antitrust,
    and Labor   66
2.10 Enforcement of Contracts   67
    2.11 The Initial Approaches and Setting of
    Standards   68
    2.12 Uniqueness and Irreparable Harm   73
    2.13 Clean Hands   80
    2.14 Scope and Duration of the Injunction   87

2.20 Application of Antitrust   90
    2.21 The Sherman and Clayton Acts   91
    2.22 Setting the Standards—Baseball   92
    2.23 Antitrust Applied to Other Sports   97
    2.24 Baseball's Continuing Exemption   100
2.30 Labor and Sports   107
2.40 Convergence of Antitrust and Labor
    Principles   111
    2.41 Nonsports Background   112
    2.42 Early Considerations of Player Freedom
    of Movement Complaints   116
    2.43 The Labor Exemption Applied to Sports   131

CHAPTER 3
Basic Agreements Controlling Sports   139

3.00 The Hierarchy of the Agreements   139
3.10 League Constitutions and Bylaws   140
3.20 Standard Player Contracts   141
    3.21 NBA Allowable Amendments   142
    3.22 Comparative Provisions: Other
    Leagues   155
    3.22-1 Injuries, Physical Examinations, and
        Suspensions Due to Injury   155
    3.22-2 Player Representatives   157
    3.22-3 Unauthorized Bonuses and Bribery   158
    3.22-4 Contract Assignments   158
    3.22-5 Contract Termination by Club   159
    3.22-6 Extensions   161
3.30 Collective Bargaining Provisions: Direct
    Application to Standard Contracts   161
    3.31 Required Use of the Standard Contract   162
    3.32 Salaries: Definitions, Individual Minimums,
    Maximum Reductions, and Deferred
    Compensation   162

3.33 NBA Maximum/Minimum Team
Salary 165
3.34 Severance and Termination Pay 169
3.35 Injuries and Medical Care 170
3.36 Assignments, Waivers, Releases 172
3.37 Benefits: Preseason, Moving, Travel,
Group Insurance and Others 174
3.38 Club Discipline 176
3.39 Future Actions 177
3.40 Collective Bargaining Provisions: Restrictions
on Player Mobility 177
3.41 Draft 178
3.42 Options 181
3.43 Free Agency 182
3.44 Right of First Refusal 185
3.45 Free Agent Compensation 190
3.46 Summary 194
3.50 The 1985 Baseball Collective Bargaining
Provisions 194

CHAPTER 4
Representing the Player 199

4.00 Functions of the Sports Representative 199
4.01 Negotiating 199
4.02 Counseling 200
4.03 Managing 200
4.04 Marketing 200
4.05 Resolving Disputes 201
4.06 Planning 201
4.10 Establishing the Attorney/Client Relationship 202
4.11 Legal Requirements 202
4.12 Ethical Constraints 213
4.13 Player Association Certification 217
4.14 Representative Player Agreements 223
4.20 Negotiation, Formation, and Interpretation of
Contracts in League Sports 228
4.21 Standard Contracts 228
4.21-1 Correct Terminology: Sports Terms and
Contract Usage 229
4.21-2 Waiver of Liability 230
4.22 The Negotiations: Preparation and
Execution 232
4.22-1 Knowing the Legal Background 233
4.22-1 Knowing the Factual Background 233
4.22-3 Knowing with Whom One Is
Dealing 234
4.22-4 Mapping a Negotiation Strategy 234

4.22-5 Following Through on the Negotiation
Strategy 234
4.22-6 Closing the Deal 234
4.23 Salaries and Tax Consequences 235
4.23-1 Tax Minimization 235
4.23-2 Tax Planning 240
4.24 Bonus Clauses 243
4.24-1 Types of Bonus Clauses 244
4.24-2 Disputes over Bonus Provisions 248
4.25 Formation Problems 253
4.26 Length of Contract 257
4.27 Guaranteed Contracts 260
4.28 Options 268
4.28-1 Exercisable by Player 268
4.28-2 Exercisable by Club 269
4.29 Duties in Light of Other Party's Breach 277
4.30 Problems in the Performance of Contracts 287
4.31 Player's Contract Is Terminated (For Other
Than Lack of Skill or Injury) 287
4.32 Player Is Injured 289
4.32-1 Procedural Issues 290
4.32-2 Special Contract Provisions 294
4.32-3 Determination of Injury 296
4.32-4 Worker's Compensation 303
4.33 Player Is Traded 305
4.34 Player Is Disciplined 306
4.35 Player Wants to Renegotiate 308
4.36 Player Needs Additional Monies 311
4.37 Player's Salary Is Reduced 312
4.40 Nonstandard Contracts 313
4.41 Side Deals in League Contracts 313
4.42 Individual Performer Sports 315
4.43 Foreign Leagues 318
4.50 Managing and Marketing the Athlete 321
4.51 League Provisions on Endorsements 321
4.52 Endorsement Contracts 322
4.53 Commercial Value in the Athlete's Name or
Image 326
4.53-1 Right of Publicity 327
4.53-2 Publicity Compared with Privacy 331
4.53-3 Trademark 339
4.53-4 Relinquishing Rights by Agreement 340
4.53-5 Rights Yielding to "News" 349
4.53-6 Libel 344
4.60 Constitutional Protections 345
4.70 Antitrust Protection for the Athlete 349
4.71 Eligibility Requirements 349
4.72 Suspensions and Blacklists 364

CHAPTER 5

Professional Sports Unions 371

5.00 Labor Law and Labor Relations 371
5.10 The Unit: Labor and Management 371
    5.11 Union Certification and Multiemployer
        Bargaining Unit 372
    5.12 Forcing Collective Bargaining 374
    5.13 Union Membership 378
5.20 Collective Bargaining: Enforcement
    Mechanisms 383
    5.21 The NLRB and Unfair Labor Practices 383
    5.22 Enforcing the *Robertson* Settlement
        in the NBA 393
5.30 Labor Arbitration 402
    5.31 Types and Procedures 402
    5.32 Arbitration on Vital Player-Owner
        Interests 407
5.40 Unresolved Issues Facing Sports Labor
    Unions 482
    5.41 Individual versus Collective Interests 429
    5.42 Drug Use by Players 436
5.50 Strikes in Professional Sports 441
    5.51 Unfair Labor Practices 442
    5.52 Salary Grievances Arising from Strikes 447

CHAPTER 6

*Management Perspectives on Sports Leagues
and Clubs* 461

6.00 Legal Status of the Sports League 461

6.10 Factors in Structuring a Sports Franchise 469
    6.11 Tax Considerations 469
    6.12 Control Considerations 476
    6.13 Right to Own a Club 477
    6.14 Right to Move a Franchise 481
6.20 Competing Leagues and Ensuing Problems 496
    6.21 Control of Geographical Markets 497
    6.22 Control over Player Markets 503
    6.23 Control over Stadiums 507
    6.24 Control of Television Markets 509
6.30 Role of the Commissioner 510
    6.31 General Powers 510
    6.32 Discipline 514
    6.33 Interclub Dealings 523
    6.34 Arbitration 526
6.40 League Controls Over Its Product 528
    6.41 Commercial Interference 528
    6.42 Government Interference 538
6.50 Sports and Related Industries 540
6.60 Operational Concerns at the Club Level 540
    6.61 Interferences with Contractual
        Relations 540
    6.62 Dealing with Consumer Interests 548
    6.63 Stadium Leases 552
    6.64 Concessions 554

Table of Cases 555

Index 563

INTRODUCTION

On October 1, 1961 Roger Maris belted homerun number 61, earning an immortal asterisk as the one to break Babe Ruth's single season record, but in 162 games, not 154. It was a beautiful fall afternoon with a cloudless sky as Maris stepped in to face Tracy Stallard of the Boston Red Sox. The shot at first looked catchable, but it sailed long and deep into Yankee Stadium's right field upper deck. Maris had bested the Babe, whatever the detractors said.

Less than 25 years later, in December 1985, Roger Maris died prematurely at age 51. For those who recall his one glorious season, it seems not so long ago that he sent the ball deep. Yet in sports time, much has changed. By their nature, sports heroes and sports records pass quickly. Though Maris's 61 still prevails, we await the inevitable. Next season may well produce the next phenom.

This work is only tangentially about sports heroes. While certain stars—and less than stars— are discussed in a business and legal context, the concentration is on the behind-the-scenes operatives—those in the trenches who make sports as a business survive and mostly succeed. Even so, as with sports heroes and the records they set, we must ask whether sports as a business has been transformed as well. Our initial impulse is to affirm.

In 1961, when Maris hit 61, the National Football League (NFL), with assistance from other leagues, successfully lobbied Congress to enact an exemption to the antitrust laws to allow league-wide television contracts. Prior to that time, the clubs were on their own, dealing with stations and networks as best they could. That single congressional enactment revolutionized sports as a business, and the developments of the past quarter century have propelled sports into new dimensions.

Collective bargaining was unknown in professional sports in 1961. There were players' associations in some sports, but their leaders carefully refrained from labeling their organizations "unions." In many respects, the advent of collective bargaining in the late 1960s has equalled in impact the growth of televised sports events and the burgeoning of television revenues.

Free agency for players—the ability to negotiate with whichever teams the player chooses—was nonexistent in 1961. In baseball, the last vestiges of free dealing expired with the institution of a draft of amateur players. All leagues now controlled the movement of players throughout the entirety of their professional careers. By 1961, while the courts had decreed that professional sports leagues, except baseball, were subject to the federal antitrust laws, there was no clear perception that these laws extended to restrict the player control devices used by the leagues. That was to come over a decade later.

Rival leagues had formed to challenge the established order before 1961, notably in baseball, but it was with the 1960s that a new wave of full-scale assaults commenced. The past quarter century has seen the American Football League (AFL), the World Football League (WFL), and the United States Football League (USFL) challenge the NFL. The National Basketball Association (NBA) has faced competitors in the American Basketball League (ABL) and the American Basketball Association (ABA). The World Hockey Association (WHA) took on the National Hockey League (NHL). Ironically, Major League Baseball with its National and American Leagues, challenged so many times in prior decades, has found no rivals in this quarter century, though rumors of leagues have surfaced from time to time.

The rival leagues in general were not notably successful, though the AFL in football, ABA in basketball, and WHA in hockey all persevered long enough to be absorbed, in whole or in part, by the established leagues. The partial success records have been enough to keep others interested in venturing into other new leagues. The prospects of a quick fix through television revenues and the availability of players from established leagues, now that free agency was more a reality, made new leagues feasible and infinitely more attractive. That many dreams were ill-conceived has not deterred entrepreneurs.

The sports agents, who now represent players in individual contract negotiations, were unknown in 1961. There had previously been a few "agent" types, such as the famous Cash-and-Carry Pyle, who wheeled and dealt in sports as far back as the 1920s, but sports agentry was not yet a business. The agents developed in the 1960s alongside the unions—and not always harmoniously.

In 1961 the one hundred thousand per year salary for a player was still the measure of stardom. Only a select few attained such status. We have since witnessed the million per year standard, which is today threatened by the two million mark of "greatness."

In professional sports, all aspects of the business and legal side have become more complex, seemingly more magnified in importance, and ever bigger and grander. Sports loom in our

society. The space and time devoted to the on and off the field maneuverings of sports leagues, teams, players, players' agents, and players' associations are remarkable. Often lost is the fact that it is men and women playing children's games. Of course, at the level at which the games are played, it is arguable that new art forms are created, but that is not the reason millions of dollars pour into sports each year. Professional sports are important components of the leisure-time entertainment industries. People want entertainment, and those who run sports have responded. Sports are cast in a business mold that gives the public what it wants, and then responds when asked for more.

This volume approaches the multifaceted problems of professional sports from two general perspectives. The first three chapters are explanations of the foundations of the industries, the table-setters for the particularized perspectives examined in the second set of chapters, 4 to 6. Between the two approaches emerges a relatively full explication of how the businesses came to develop and an examination of legal problems in the context of ongoing business dealings.

In Chapter 1 we examine the components of the professional sports industries, concentrating on team sports but with insights as to individual performer sports as well. We then present the voices of various professional sports interests as they plead their vantage points to a United States congressional committee. The vital issues are the control over the movement of franchises and the sharing of revenue among clubs in a league. At the base are questions of the essence of a league. Finally, basic economics about sports leagues are analyzed.

The major formative legal structures affecting professional sports are dissected in Chapter 2. The concentration is on contracts, antitrust, and labor laws. Other legal categories obviously have substantial impacts on the industries, but these three, chosen for their qualitative impacts and influences, are the initial focus. In later chapters, other legal categories such as tax, torts, corporations, rights of publicity and privacy, and trademark all weave into the contexts of transactional considerations.

The importance of the agreements forged between parties within the infrastructure of professional sports leagues is analyzed in detail in Chapter 3. These include the internal agreements among those who own teams within a league, largely manifested in league constitutions and by-laws; the collective bargaining agreements which are today the single most dominant determinant of league and player fortunes alike; and the individual contracts entered between clubs and players, dictated in large part by the collective bargaining provisions of the applicable league but permitting latitude in individual bargaining in profound respects. One begins to understand a sports league only by first becoming thoroughly acquainted with its agreements.

The first three chapters provide essential foundations for the transactional situations described in Chapters 4 to 6. The treatments in these chapters examine extensively those who represent professional athletes and the role they play (Chapter 4), those who are involved in labor relations (Chapter 5), and those who face the legal and business problems of league and club management (Chapter 6). These comprise the internal workings of professional sports leagues.

Where problems affect amateur as well as professional sports, the detailed analysis is generally left to Volume II, though mention of the issues is made at appropriate points in this volume. The discussions of certain aspects of sex discrimination (Vol. II, Chapter 3), torts (Vol. II, Chapter 4), criminal proceedings (Vol. II, Chapter 5), and sports and media (Vol. II, Chapter 6) are important to those closely involved in professional sports. Both volumes are essential reference sources.

Three other works that are cited at various points in both volumes should be mentioned as general resources: Berry, Gould, and Staudohar, *Labor Relations in Professional Sports* (Auburn House, 1986); Weistart and Lowell, *Law of Sports* (Michie Bobbs Merrill, 1979), with supplement; and Sobel, *Professional Sports and the Law* (Law Arts, 1976), with supplement. In particular, *Labor Relations in Professional Sports* provides additional background and insights.

In commencing a full-scale inquiry into professional sports—the business and legal structures, negotiation aspects, power balances, and dispute resolution mechanisms—it is important to recognize underlying themes that affect the mix. The sports industries do not exist in a vacuum. They are sensitive to the economy and exhibit many of the same fluctuations as other industries, particularly businesses depending on a consumer audience that dotes on luxuries. In addition, with the great publicity accorded professional sports as they have become media events, a political sensitivity has developed. The sports industries have entered the political arena, at times willingly, at other times reluctantly, attested by the recently published *Government and Sport: the Public Policy Issues,* edited by Johnson and Frey (Rowman & Allanheld, 1985).

It is no longer 1961. As we said, that year was simply one benchmark of many. A quarter century past 1961 the problems continue to develop. We believe the analyses which follow respond to these problems as they exist in the present and extend into the future.

Chapter 1

BACKGROUND ON PROFESSIONAL SPORTS

1.00   The Development of Industries

All sports have certain things in common. At the heart is an appeal to the competitive instinct — the desire to do one's best and to watch others succeed or fail. Organized sports have sought to capitalize on this instinct by putting out a product that will appeal to those who enjoy competition — its failure as well as its success. This has been no quick or easy task, particularly during the years when the so-called professionalization of sport attempted to take hold. For a variety of reasons, there was indifference and sometimes even resistance. Slowly, however, as our society became more entertainment conscious, the obstacles were overcome. Today, both professional and amateur sports enjoy a measure of prosperity surely not contemplated by early sports pioneers.

Baseball was the first sport to achieve professional status with the founding in 1876 of the National League. Even so, many decades passed before baseball evolved into what has become at present a major industry. In many respects, football, hockey, and basketball have had even more uncertain passages, suffering either from obscurity, regionalism, antipathy, or a combination of those conditions. The National Football League, for example, began in 1920,

but only the most perceptive would have forecast success based on the league's first few years. The National Hockey League began in Canada in 1918, and officially added the first U.S. team in 1924; the league, however, remained a closed, six-team affair until the 1960s. The history of professional basketball has been even more fragmented. Touring teams picked up competition where they could, and only a few of the major eastern metropolitan areas supported local leagues. Not until 1946 did the National Basketball Association's predecessor, the Basketball Association of America, put together an ultimately winning combination.

Today's sports leagues are basically creations of the social, political, and technological climate of post–World War II. This was a period when relatively small businesses turned into industries. As these small, isolated sports leagues evolved into major sports industries, the differences in their business operations have become more pronounced. There are still distinct similarities in their organizational bases — indeed, in most instances, a conscious copying of another league's successes has been the standard — but subtle differences among the various professional sports leagues have emerged. The problems each faces today may well be peculiar to that sport, and the economic potentials vary significantly. While commonalities remain, inviting examination across sports, there is always the need to step back and ask whether one sport's experiences are transferrable to another.

A starting point in viewing the development of sports industries is to consider carefully the multiple interests as professional leagues seek their share of profits from the business endeavors undertaken. There are the owners, of course, and the players. Individually, they have always been there, the interests of one versus the interests of the other. Today, however, there are collective interests, which are asserted through the leagues (or at times through a special creation often called a management council) and through players' associations. There are other interests as well, both within and outside the league. To understand these groupings, as well as to grasp the relationships, conflicts, and tensions among them, is to proceed toward a full analysis of the sports industries and their places in a legal regulatory scheme.

Chapter 1 concentrates more on industry characteristics than on the legal aspects of professional sports leagues. Although law and business cannot ultimately be separated, there are emphases on certain organizational, political, and economic structures that aid in the later examination of a more complete business-legal context.

The chapter first examines the constituencies that exist in almost all professional sports leagues and associations (see Section 1.10). This is done by examining how court decisions have described the inner workings of leagues, clubs, commissioners, and unions and the efforts of player-agents and the players themselves. The emphasis is on the descriptions of the constituencies. No attempt is made to set forth or discuss the legal issues of these cases. Those await later development. The focus is on what a court finds relevant as a factual matter.

Section 1.20 next examines a set of problems of relatively recent vintage and places them in a larger context than a single court decision would

likely attempt. The circumstances arise from proposed legislation before the United States Congress, which is largely favored by the various leagues and parties adversely affected by certain events that spurred the introduction of such legislation, and opposed by one particular club owner, the players' associations, and certain parties who had benefited from the same events. The perspectives that each constituency brings to the congressional hearings have been excerpted in this chapter in an effort to highlight the disparity of views. The testimony is revealing, not only regarding the precise issues addressed by the proposed legislation, but also regarding the interests and concerns of those constituencies in general.

The final introductory materials in this first chapter (see Section 1.30) are economic data about sports leagues, individual clubs, players, and other constituencies. The data are hardly exhaustive. One cannot build a workable economic profile for even one league from that which is presented. But that is not our purpose. Rather, a perspective is presented that will become important later on when legal-business problems are introduced and explored.

1.10   Constituencies within the Industries

The professional sports industries create multiple interests. Leagues and clubs align themselves on one side; players, unions, and player-agents congregate on the other side. Other interests are a little harder to read — for example, the commissioner or president of a league. Although usually allied with management, sometimes the commissioner must transcend such inclinations and act in the greater interests of the sport. Then there are the minor leagues for some sports. These are separate organizations; yet their close involvement with the sport makes them internal to the whole process. So it is, as well, with the officials who run the game — the referees, the umpires, and the others in the striped shirts. Finally, there are the related industries. All play key roles. For example, most professional sports teams do not own the stadiums or arenas in which they perform. The owners, whether they be from the public or private sector, are in the center of the action. And then there are the media — print, radio, and television.

The millions of dollars funneled into sports, particularly by television, makes a close examination of the relationships among sports-related interests compelling. Of course, not all aspects of the ways that the constituencies fit into the sports industries' grand scheme can be determined. Indeed, the entire book is devoted to unraveling that mystery. Rather, these introductory vignettes, taken in the main from actual court decisions that contain background information about a league, club, or player in order to address the legal issues involved, serve to uncover the nuts and bolts of professional sports. The legal issues are left for later.

1.11   Leagues or Associations

Professional sports leagues and associations have long intrigued both courts of law and interested observers. It is one thing to recount how they operate; it is another to pin down in legal terms just what they are — a monopoly or cartel, a joint venture, a partnership, or a group of competitors. There is little agreement on what the ultimate legal significance of their being comprises. The bylaws and constitution of a league mandate cooperation, but this is the theory, not the reality. Internal bickering is standard until there is an outside threat. Then the concentration shifts; until moved by legal edict, cooperation means freezing out opposing leagues, controlling one's own players to the greatest extent possible, and presenting a united front against unwanted intrusions.

A sports league divides up territories, allocating exclusive franchises and attempting to eliminate competition within the league for the same sports consumer's dollars. Leagues spread themselves as widely as possible, absorbing as many markets as is deemed economically feasible. One reason is to maximize profit and exposure; the beneficial side effect is that rival leagues are discouraged from forming. A paucity of open markets usually means there is little opportunity to challenge an established league. Many still try to challenge, of course, but only a few succeed.

Sports leagues share revenue, although the extent of sharing varies substantially from one league to another. The main sources of revenue are gate receipts and television rights. The National Football League shares gate revenue on a 60-40 basis, with the major share going to the home team. Exhibition gate receipts are shared 50-50. And, of course, the NFL's network television package, the richest in all of sports, is evenly split. The current package gives $14.5 million to each club per year. This is the high side of revenue sharing. Other leagues are less socialistic. Both Major League Baseball and the National Basketball Association (NBA) have television contracts that give equal shares to each club, but baseball only shares gate revenues on an 80-20 basis. The NBA does not share revenues at all. It should also be noted that local television packages in baseball and basketball vary substantially and are not shared. The National Hockey League (NHL) has no national television packages (although the Canadian clubs do share the revenues from "Hockey Night in Canada"). Nor does the NHL share gate revenues. Consequently, the economic bases of leagues differ substantially, particularly regarding club-by-club comparisons within the leagues.

Players are the major resource shared within a league. Although court and arbitration decisions, attended by later collective bargaining agreements, have made inroads on the degree to which leagues, and thus clubs, control player mobility, leagues still use numerous devices to share player wealth. Foremost among these is the dispersal draft of eligible amateurs. The player draft is discussed later, as are other player restriction devices, such as reserve and option clauses, player compensation, and rights of first refusal.

The elements of sports leagues are discussed in the following excerpts from two important cases. The first case concerns the challenge in the early 1970s by the World Hockey Association to become a rival major hockey league alongside the established National Hockey League. The excerpts merely describe the makeup of the NHL and its relationships with other hockey leagues. The second case also involves rival leagues within the same sport, but has different origins. After the American Basketball Association was formed as a rival of the established National Basketball Association, hard feelings between the leagues eventually turned into litigation. In addition, the players, particularly those in the NBA, determined to enter the act. A class action brought by leaders within the players' union — the NBA Players Association — sought injunctory relief preventing several actual and potential practices by the NBA. The excerpts focus on certain practices by the league vis-à-vis restrictions on a player's right to freely choose an employer.

Philadelphia World Hockey Club, Inc. v. Philadelphia Hockey Club Inc., 351 F.Supp. 462, 465–466, 474–475 (E. D. Pa. 1972)

In 1917, the National Hockey League was born with Montreal and Toronto as its only members. In 1924, Boston was added, followed in 1926 with Chicago, Detroit and New York. In 1967, Los Angeles, Philadelphia, Pittsburgh, California, Minnesota, St. Louis entered the League and in 1970 Buffalo and Vancouver. In 1972, Nassau (New York) and Atlanta joined this now famous League. Since 1966, the National Hockey League has received in excess of $36,000,000 for the sale of rights to play major league professional hockey in their league. When in 1970 the National Hockey League admitted Vancouver and Buffalo, each of these two new clubs paid in excess of $8,000,000 for the acquisition of the minor professional league clubs in their locality and for distribution to National Hockey League clubs.

Thus, from what in 1917 was a relatively minor sports attraction, the National Hockey League has skated into the 1970s to a position of substantial wealth, power, broad spectator interest, international recognition and many superstars, all crescendoing into huge profits for both its owners and players.

One writer observes: "What has happened is this: the intrinsic speed and excitement of hockey has made it the game of the second half of this century." . . .

The Structure of Professional Hockey and the Supply of Professional Players

35.   Prior to the formation of the WHA in 1971, the NHL was the only major league professional hockey association in North America. . . .

36.   In addition to the NHL, there are three other professional hockey leagues in North America. These are the American Hockey League (AHL), the Western Hockey League (WHL), and the Central Hockey League, formerly the Central Professional Hockey League (CHL), with a total of 24 teams . . . The best players are found in the NHL . . . , the next best in the American and Western Hockey Leagues, and the lowest level of professional players is in the Central Hockey League . . .

37.   The International and Eastern Hockey Leagues are amateur or at best semi-professional leagues. William Wirtz (NHL) testified that the International Hockey League is an amateur organization "[t]hat does have professional players that have sat out for a couple of years and come back and want their amateur status reinstated." . . .

38.   The NHL requires that each of its member teams must have an affiliation with a "player development team" . . . Thus, at least 16 of the 24 professional minor league teams are owned or operated by or affiliated with NHL teams. All of the teams in the CHL are owned by NHL teams . . . C. S. Campbell stated that in addition to the teams owned by NHL members, ". . . there are almost an unlimited number of affiliations and loaning arrangements of various kinds." . . .

39.   The National Hockey League is governed by a Board of Governors and a President selected by that Board, and each individual team defendant herein has a representative and a vote on the Board of Governors. . . .

42.   Unlike professional football and basketball, which can draw on an ample supply of talented players developed in competition at the

college level in the United States at no cost to the member clubs of the professional leagues, the NHL has never had such a ready-made source of talent. Accordingly, it has invested millions of dollars to help support a system of amateur league and minor league hockey in Canada and the United States which will give youngsters an opportunity to play hockey and develop their hockey skills and which will thus also provide a source of potential players of major league calibre. . . .

43. During the period June, 1967 through June, 1971 alone, the NHL made grants totaling $5,493,000 to amateur hockey associations for distribution to and support of amateur hockey leagues throughout Canada and the United States. . . .

44. In addition to the NHL's support of amateur hockey, the NHL clubs have invested large sums for the development and support of professional minor league hockey clubs in Canada and the United States, many of which could not continue to operate without the subsidies provided by the NHL clubs. . . .

Robertson et al. v. National Basketball Association, 389 F.Supp. 867, 872–874 (S.D.N.Y. 1975)

Defendants are the National Basketball Association (NBA) and the American Basketball Association (ABA). All the named plaintiffs, William Bradley, Joseph Caldwell, Archibald Clark, Melvin Counts, John Havlicek, Donald Kojis, Jon McGlockin, McCoy McLemore, Thomas Meschery, Jeffrey Mullins, Oscar Robertson, Westley Unseld, Richard Van Arsdale and Chester Walker were active players with, and the elected player representative of, one of the then 14 clubs of the NBA. Plaintiffs sue on behalf of themselves, all presently active players, those who were active at the time the action was originally commenced, and future players of the NBA . . .

This litigation began after reports in the spring of 1970 of a proposed merger between the NBA and the ABA. Plaintiffs' amended complaint charges defendants with conspiring to restrain competition for the services and skills of professional basketball players through such devices as the college draft, the reserve clause in the Uniform Player Contract (the Uniform Contract), the

compensation plan attached to the reserve clause, and various boycott and blacklisting techniques. The complaint further alleges that the NBA and the ABA seek to effectuate a non-competition agreement, merger or consolidation. . . .

The following practices are cited as making the means used by the NBA to effectuate and advance the underlying objectives of the conspiracy:

(1) *The College Draft* is allegedly designed to prevent competition among member NBA clubs for what is virtually the exclusive source of basketball talent in the country. The system operates so that each NBA club is given the exclusive right to choose specific college players with whom it desires to negotiate. If the college player does not wish to negotiate or play for the NBA club which "owns" his rights, the player may not negotiate with or for any other NBA club;

(2) *The Uniform Contract*, entitled the "National Basketball Association-Uniform Contract" must be signed by every college player who agrees to play with one of the NBA clubs after he is "drafted," and by every veteran player each year. The contract provides that the player shall play basketball for his club or its assignees exclusively until "sold" or "traded"; that the club has the absolute right to sell, exchange, assign or transfer the uniform Contract on the same terms to another club; and that if the player refuses to play, the club may either terminate the Uniform Contract or seek an injunction to prevent the player from playing basketball for anyone else;

(3) *The Reserve Clause* is a part of the Uniform Contract which, if a player refuses to sign the Uniform Contract for the next playing season, empowers the club unilaterally to renew and extend the Uniform Contract for one year on the same terms and conditions including salary. Any "traded" or "sold" player is bound to his new club by the reserve clause. Plaintiffs contend that the reserve clause gives the NBA clubs the express and unilateral right to keep renewing the Uniform Contract so long as the player refuses to execute the Uniform Contract, thus binding the player to one club for his entire playing career;

(4) *Boycotts, Blacklisting and Refusals to Deal* are allegedly utilized as well. Plaintiffs contend that no NBA club will negotiate with a player to play for another who has signed or refused to sign the Uniform Contract, and is thus under "reserve".

Nor will any NBA club negotiate for the services of a player who is voluntarily retired from another club, under suspension, in military service, disabled or injured. Any NBA club which contracts or negotiates with such a player is similarly boycotted, blacklisted or otherwise penalized;

(5) *The New League* is off-limits to NBA players. Plaintiffs assert that the NBA has used the practices summarized in (1) through (4) above to prevent the players not only from negotiating freely with member clubs of the NBA, but also from negotiating with or playing for clubs in any rival league.

1.12   Clubs and Owners

The relationship between a league and the clubs in that league is an intriguing phenomenon. We have noted a couple of important aspects of league rules, such as the sharing of gate and television revenues (see Section 1.11). In addition, clubs belonging to a league each have one vote, equal to the other clubs, whereby the league business and thus the business of the clubs as a collective unit must proceed by forging some sort of consensus among the owners. This is not always the means of doing business. The clubs may have delegated certain functions and authorities to the league commissioner or a special owner group. Even so, the basis of authority lies with the representational one vote per club. To that extent, being part of a league is central to the club's essence.

It must be remembered, however, that clubs are also individual entities. They take risks and are ultimately responsible only to themselves for turning a profit or incurring a loss. To only a very limited extent can a club look to a league for help in times of trouble. The more likely recourse for a foundering club is to seek new infusions of money and leadership, largely through the sale of the franchise to a new owner.

This duality in the being of a club leads to several dilemmas, both in the business and in the legal sense. In recent years, obvious tensions have resulted from a league wanting to characterize itself as a single business entity for certain purposes, and at the same time wanting to cling to an operation that washes its hands of responsibility for its member clubs on other issues. Leagues are finding it difficult to have it both ways. These problems are explored at length throughout this book, beginning with Section 1.20 in this chapter and discussed in greater detail in Chapter 6 where a gamut of concerns that test the single-versus-multiple business entity theories are presented from management perspectives. At this point in the analysis, the various theories are not vigorously pursued. However, certain observations about how sports clubs operate should be noted. While not necessarily applicable to all clubs, enough clubs or their owners share these traits so that the leagues are significantly affected.

1. The operations of many clubs are greatly influenced by the personalities of their owners. Forceful people own sports franchises, and they put indelible stamps on the operation. Doing business in this fashion spells likely conflicts with others, be it clubs, the league, players, or other involved parties.

2. Many clubs still operate more as sports enterprises than as bottom-line businesses. This may not be entirely bad, depending on one's perspectives, but it certainly does make for inconsistencies in approaches and results.

3. There is a high turnover in ownership of sports clubs, more in some leagues than others. Fast profits, tax advantages, cooling of ardor for being an owner, financial miscalculations, legal problems, personality conflicts — all these and more contribute to the turnover. Whatever the reasons, the results may spell instability, both for the league and the individual clubs.

4. Owners get restive and view new horizons with contemplative stares. For some owners, it takes little persuasion to consider relocating the franchise. As more and more markets have been filled, the process has slowed somewhat, at least for

the established leagues. But where it has occurred has meant major repercussions.

5. The number of clubs actually making a profit may be small. This fact, at the same time, may be somewhat misleading. As long as there are advantages to ownership, there will be willing buyers. This circumstance adds to the turnover process, however, and one must be uneasy about this.

6. Certain owners wish to involve themselves in multiple sports ventures. This can cause problems, since having interests in various ventures could give the appearance and actuality of a conflict of interest.

The following case, *North American Soccer League* v. *National Football League*, discusses this aspect of club ownership; it is revealing both for its comments about leagues and about the individuals who own and operate clubs within a league.

North American Soccer League v. National Football League, 505 F.Supp. 659, 664–666, 678–679 (S.D.N.Y. 1980)

III. *The Characteristics of Professional Team Sports Leagues*

No. 7: The NASL and the NFL are two of the major professional sports leagues in the United States. Each is composed of member teams located throughout the United States (and, in the case of the NASL, in parts of Canada) which compete on the playing field with each other and also operate jointly to promote attendance at and fan interest in the games which they play and to create and market professional athletic entertainment events in competition with other sports leagues (and other producers and marketers of sports and other entertainment events.)

No. 8: The NASL and NFL, along with the other major professional sports leagues in hockey, basketball and baseball, compete with each other in the entertainment industry.

No. 9: The NASL, the NFL and the other major professional sports leagues all compete in interstate commerce for fan interest, media attention, advertising revenues and network television revenues. The primary "products" sold to the public by the individual sports leagues and/or their member teams, including the NFL and NASL, are tickets for spectator viewing and the broadcast rights to games which the individual clubs play with other league members.

No. 10: In the case of ticket sales and sale of local radio/television broadcasting rights, this competition occurs within the metropolitan areas in which any two or more leagues have teams; in the case of network broadcasting and telecasting rights, it occurs in a market including the entire United States and some contiguous areas of Canada.

No. 11: The ways in which the NFL, the NASL and other professional sports leagues organize the activities to be carried out by a central league office, various committees and the member clubs individually vary from league to league. Professional team sports leagues like the NFL and NASL, as opposed to their individual member teams, are generally responsible for, *inter alia*: national promotional activities; the negotiation of network television contracts; the employment of referees; the structure and rules of competition for the sport; certain aspects of player relations; and the establishment and enforcement of rules governing league membership.

No. 12: The individual clubs which comprise the NASL, like those which make up the NFL, each require, *inter alia*:

(a) adequate capital investment to support operations;

(b) membership in a league in which the member teams are reasonably well matched in playing ability;

(c) the employment of a group of highly skilled players;

(d) location in a geographic area that is able to support the team by attendance at games sufficient to provide adequate revenues;

(e) the sale of radio, television and ancillary rights to the games which they play; and

(f) a share of league revenues or funds from other sources adequate to assure the ability to field a team which is reasonably well matched with others in the same league.

No 13: The economic success of each franchise in a professional sports league is dependent on the quality of sports competition throughout the league and the economic strength and stability of other league members.

No. 14: Damage to or the loss of any professional sports league member ordinarily damages the stability, success and operations of both the league and its individual members.

IV. *Markets in Which Professional Team Sports Leagues Compete with Each Other*

No. 15: As noted in Finding No. 8, *supra*, professional sports leagues compete with each other in the entertainment industry. The general entertainment market includes television, and identifiable submarkets such as professional sports, professional team sports, and specialized television sports programming.

No. 16: The NASL contends that the leagues also compete with each other in a market for "sports ownership capital and skill," whose boundaries are confined to individuals presently owning controlling interests in major league sports teams. I find, however, that to the extent a "sports ownership capital and skill" market exists, its boundaries are significantly wider than the NASL suggests. The market includes sports-minded, wealthy individuals who are not presently team owners, but would be receptive to an attractive investment opportunity in the field; and corporations of the type previously and presently involved in professional sports team ownership.

No. 17: As for individuals, the NASL's perception of a "sports ownership capital and skill" market is based upon an archetypal figure I came to know during the trial. I shall call him, for lack of a better word, the "sportsman." The sportsman has these distinguishing characteristics: love of sport; love of the limelight (or at least a willingness to be exposed to public view); substantial capital and a readiness to risk it in ventures with the potential for large short-term losses; and, in some cases, a familial affection for the city in which his teams perform. Sportsmen who testified during the trial included Lamar Hunt of Dallas; Joseph Robbie of Miami; Leonard Tose of Philadelphia; Edward Bennett Williams of Washington; Aaron Fogelman of Memphis; and Peter Pocklington of Edmonton. Just as some successful individuals turn for their extracurricular fulfillment to music (Avery Fischer Hall), rare books (the Beinecke Library), or fine art (the Frick Museum), so these

individuals, at various stages in their personal races through life, have turned to professional sports.

No. 18: The paths by which individuals come to professional sports team ownership vary, as do the individuals themselves. Hunt has for a number of years focused upon a variety of sporting ventures: controlling ownership of the NFL Kansas City Chiefs and the NASL Dallas Tornados, as well as a leading role in professional tennis tournaments. Williams acted as attorney for other individuals who owned the Redskins, eventually acquired a controlling ownership himself, and recently expanded his sports interests to ownership of the baseball Baltimore Orioles. Pocklington was a businessman (meat packing, car dealership, real estate development) who acquired his first sports ownership interest in the Edmonton Oilers (then of the now defunct World Hockey Association, now a National Hockey League team) as the result of a casual exchange with a friend. Tose is chairman of an interstate trucking company, who in 1969 acquired a minority interest in the Philadelphia Eagles, and now owns 99 percent of the team. These individuals illustrate the ways in which, from various walks of life, one can become a professional sports team owner, frequently without prior experience in the field.

No. 19: Corporate owners have been a significant factor in American professional team sports. The NFL's bylaws prohibit corporate ownership as a matter of policy, but the other four major leagues do not. Major league baseball currently has 10 corporate investors in control group positions; the NASL has 8 (including Molson Breweries' recent acquisition of the Philadelphia franchise); the National Basketball Association has 3; and the National Hockey League 8. Thus 29 corporations hold controlling interests in four major sports leagues. The industries most heavily represented among corporate sports owners are those involved in consumer products sold to sports fans (beer, soft drinks and other beverages, cigarettes, home building supplies), or in communications, which market sports. Many other corporations, not currently sports owners, fit this profile. There are also a number of corporations in other fields that are identified with a particular city's professional teams.

No. 20: Shifts between individual and corporate ownership occur. We have noted the sale of the Philadelphia NASL franchise by a limited partnership of individuals to a corporation. Conversely, I may judicially notice that some years ago, CBS, a communications corporation, sold the baseball New York Yankees to a group of individuals headed by George Steinbrenner, who conforms neatly to the "sportsman" profile described in Finding No. 17.

No. 21: The presence of potential individual or corporate investors in professional sports precludes an effort to confine the boundaries of a "sports ownership capital and skill" market to present major league sports owners. While the NASL has been relatively unsuccessful in recent years in attracting potential investors, that is because the league has lost increasing amounts of money over the years. In 1979, for the second consecutive year, every NASL team operated at a loss, with some teams losing in excess of $2,000,000; and the NASL teams showed an aggregate operating loss of over $20,000,000, the most in the NASL's history. By way of contrast, when the NFL, a consistently profitable league, expanded by adding the Seattle and Tampa Bay franchises in 1974, the league had no difficulty attracting competing bidders. The capital resources of potential sports investors are reasonably interchangeable with those of present investors. . . .

D. *The Nature of the Competition Between the NASL and NFL*

This question does not require extended discussion. Competition between the NASL and NFL in the entertainment industry is one on one: league against league. Judge Curtis was quite right in *San Francisco Seals* . . . when he said that the "main purpose" of a professional sports league is "producing sporting events of uniformly high quality," the member teams "acting together as one single business enterprise, competing against other similarly organized professional leagues." It is the league product — its sporting events — which competes against the comparable products of competing leagues. The NASL's product is NASL soccer. The NFL's product is NFL football. The other competing products are major league baseball, NHL hockey, and NBA basketball. The degree of competition grows greater as the traditional sports seasons expand under the influence of television marketing. When I was a

child, I played as a child: baseball in the summer, football in fall, hockey in winter. But now that commercial sports marketing has made me a man, I put away childish limitations, and sit before my television to watch hockey in late May, football in the heat of early August, and baseball in the chilly night winds of late October. Competition between the NASL and NFL has grown in recent years, in part because their seasons overlap. Increasingly, the seasons of all five major league sports overlap. The resulting competition is between sports events in the generic sense: professional football, soccer, baseball, basketball, and hockey. These are products which only the professional league, acting as a single entity, can manufacture.

This proposition is essentially undisputed. . . . [t]he parties agree that the primary economic competition in professional sports "occurs between and among the competing leagues."

The reality of league against league competition is recognized by Louis Guth, the NASL's expert witness. In Guth's view, "major professional team sports is a submarket of the general entertainment industry." . . . Within that entertainment industry submarket, all the major professional team sports leagues compete in at least three further submarkets:

(1) the major professional team sports market;

(2) the sports programming market;

(3) the market for sports ownership capital and skill.

NOTES

1. The substantive legal issues of *NASL* v. *NFL* are discussed in Section 6.20.

2. In the discussion above, the point is made that many owners fail to proceed in a fully businesslike manner. Numerous examples from the Boston professional sports scene substantiate this. The Carlton Fisk free agency, discussed in Section 4.30, is one example. A similar incident occurred in the early 1970s when the New England Patriots neglected to renew lineman Phil Olsen's contract, thus making him a free agent. The Patriots received no compensation when he signed elsewhere. The memorable John Y. Brown, for a short time the owner of the Boston Celtics and later the governor of Kentucky, took it upon himself to renegotiate a contract with the highly talented but deeply troubled Marvin Barnes. Neither party had counsel present. In the process, most forms of guarantees in Barnes's contract were removed. These could well have precipitated lengthy litigation when Barnes was later released. For accounts of some of these episodes, see McDonough,

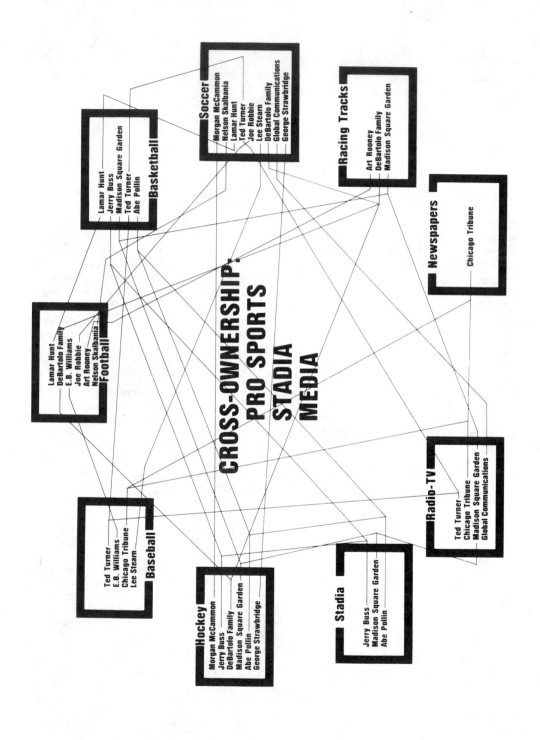

Exhibit 1-1   Cross-Ownership: Pro Sports Stadia Media

Source: National Football League Players Association, Position Pamphlet, 1981, p. 15

"Celtics Ax Barnes: Will They Pay Him?" *Boston Globe*, February 6, 1979, p. 41; Van Handle, "Players Ass'n. Backs Barnes," *Boston Globe*, February 9, 1979, p. 46.

3. Other tales of owner idiosyncracies and questionable maneuvers are highlighted in D. Kowet, *The Rich Who Own Sports* (New York: Random House, 1977). Kowet contrasts the approaches of the old-style owners such as Phil Wrigley and Art Rooney with the new breed — the Lamar Hunts and the Clint Murchisons, the ever-volatile Charlie Finley and his battles with almost everyone, and Ray Kroc, who once grabbed the mike to the public address system at his ballpark and publicly castigated both his players and the visiting team for their sloppy play. See also such disparate accounts as the following:

   (a) Ryan, "Sparky Sees Money Root of All Evil," *Boston Globe*, Dec. 7, 1976, p. 31.

   (b) Briner, "Making Sport of Us All," *Sports Illustrated*, Dec. 10, 1973, pp. 36–42.

   (c) McGraw, "Memo to Dilettante Owners: Sports Are Not a Joke," *New York Times*, January 22, 1978, sec. 5, p. 2.

   (d) Smith, "Charlie I and His subjects," *New York Times*, October 17, 1973, p. 49.

4. Squabbles among owners have become much more the rule than the exception. The following excerpt is from R. Kennedy, "Who Are These Guys?" *Sports Illustrated*, January 31, 1977, pp. 58, 60.

> As the tremors in professional sports continue, there is cause to question whether the leagues are equipped to cope. Small groups of owners that once found it difficult to agree on anything are now larger groups that agree on nothing. The incompatibility is built in. League meetings, in which men of strong wills and robust egos are asked to seek accord with their opponents in bidding wars, are often little more than stylized free-for-alls. Personal rivalries abound. Cliques clash. Says one combatant, "Off the record, dealing with my fellow owners is like trying to go around the world in a rowboat."

5. In analyzing the owners in baseball (circa 1983), one writer divided the owners into four groups — the baseball people, the business subsidiaries, the ego gratifiers, and the capital-gain seekers. In some instances, the author conceded there was overlap, since almost all owners were in it, in large part, for ego gratification. See P. Gammons, "Doing Their Owner Thing," *Boston Globe*, March 5, 1983, p. 25.

6. The cross-ownership problem, addressed in *North American Soccer League* v. *National Football League, supra*, raises problems of possible conflicts of interest. The diagram in Exhibit 1–1, introduced by the National Football League Players Association in connection with hearings before the United States Senate, illustrates how pervasive cross-ownership has become. See: Committee on the Judiciary. Ninety-Seventh Congress. Second Session. No. J-97-134. Aug. 16, 20, 29 (1982) at p. 108. The diagram was also included on page 15 of the NFLPA's position pamphlet, "Q. Why a Percentage of Gross? A. Because We Are the Game" (1981), published to present the association's position in the collective bargaining negotiations that subsequently occurred in 1982.

1.13   The Commissioner

Following the example set by Major League Baseball, each league as it has developed has used the model of having one person, designated as commissioner or, in the case of the National Hockey League, as president, to preside over the affairs of the league. In theory, the commissioner or president operates apart from the owner collective. From time to time, some commissioners have even maintained that they acted as a buffer between the owners and the players. Most concede, however, that they are part of management. The question is how much power do they actually receive under league constitutions and bylaws?

Since baseball was the first professional sport to adopt this method of league supervision, it is appropriate to examine a major dispute that developed between a baseball commissioner and one of the more controversial and colorful owners of the past few years. When Bowie Kuhn and Charlie Finley locked horns, which was frequently, the blood was sure to flow. Excerpts from one of their legal battles will explain how a commissioner came to be positioned to take on the challenge of an individual owner.

Charles O. Finley & Co., Inc. v. Kuhn, 569 F.2d 527, 531–535 (7th Cir. 1978)

> The defendant Bowie K. Kuhn is the Commissioner of baseball (Commissioner), having held that position since 1969. On June 18, 1976, the Commissioner disapproved the assignments of the contracts of Rudi, Fingers and Blue to the Red Sox and Yankees "as inconsistent with the best interests of baseball, the integrity of the game and the maintenance of public confidence in it." The Commissioner expressed his concern for (1) the debilitation of the Oakland club, (2) the lessening of the competitive balance of professional baseball through the buying of success by the more affluent

clubs, and (3) "the present unsettled circumstances of baseball's reserve system." . . .

Basic to the underlying suit brought by Oakland and to this appeal is whether the Commissioner of baseball is vested by contract with the authority to disapprove player assignments which he finds to be "not in the best interests of baseball." In assessing the measure and extent of the Commissioner's power and authority, consideration must be given to the circumstances attending the creation of the office of Commissioner, the language employed by the parties in drafting their contractual under-standing, changes and amendments adopted from time to time, and the interpretation given by the parties to their contractual language throughout the period of its existence.

Prior to 1921, professional baseball was gov-erned by a three-man National Commission formed in 1903 which consisted of the presidents of the National and American Leagues and a third member, usually one of the club owners, selected by the presidents of the two leagues. Between 1915 and 1921, a series of events and controversies contributed to a growing dissatisfaction with the National Commission on the part of players, owners and the public, and a demand developed for the establishment of a single, independent Commissioner of baseball.

On September 28, 1920, an indictment issued charging that an effort had been made to "fix" the 1919 World Series by several Chicago White Sox players. Popularly known as the "Black Sox Scandal," this event rocked the game of profes-sional baseball and proved the catalyst that brought about the establishment of a single, neutral Commissioner of baseball.

In November, 1920, the major league club owners unanimously elected federal Judge Kene-saw Mountain Landis as the sole Commissioner of baseball and appointed a committee of owners to draft a charter setting forth the Commissioner's authority. In one of the drafting sessions an attempt was made to place limitations on the Commissioner's authority. Judge Landis re-sponded by refusing to accept the office of commissioner.

On January 12, 1921, Landis told a meeting of club owners that he had agreed to accept the position upon the clear understanding that the owners had sought "an authority . . . outside of your own business, and that a part of that authority would be a control over whatever and whoever had to do with baseball." Thereupon, the owners voted unanimously to reject the proposed limitation upon the Commissioner's authority, they all signed what they called the Major League Agreement, and Judge Landis assumed the position of Commissioner. Oakland has been a signatory to the Major League Agreement continuously since 1940. The agreement, a contract between the constituent clubs of the National and American Leagues, is the basic charter under which major league baseball operates.

The Major League Agreement provides that "[t]he functions of the Commissioner shall be . . . to investigate . . . any act, transaction or practice . . . not in the best interests of the national game of Baseball" and "to determine . . . what preventive, remedial or punitive action is appropriate in the premises, and to take such action. . . ." Art. I, Sec. 2(a) and (b).

The Major League Rules, which govern many aspects of the game of baseball, are promulgated by vote of major league club owners. Major League Rule 12(a) provides that "no . . . [assign-ment of players] shall be recognized as valid unless . . . approved by the Commissioner."

The Major Leagues and their constituent clubs severally agreed to be bound by the decisions of the Commissioner and by the discipline imposed by him. They further agreed to "waive such right of recourse to the courts as would otherwise have existed in their favor." Major League Agreement, Art. VII, Sec. 2.

Upon Judge Landis' death in 1944, the Major League Agreement was amended in two respects to limit the Commissioner's authority. First, the parties deleted the provision by which they had agreed to waive their right of recourse to the courts to challenge actions of the Commissioner. Second, the parties added the following language to Article I, Section 3:

> No Major League Rule or other joint action of the two Major Leagues, and no action or procedure taken in compliance with any such Major League Rule or joint action of the two Major Leagues shall be considered or construed to be detrimental to Baseball.

The district court found that this addition had the effect of precluding the Commissioner from finding an act that complied with the Major

League Rules to be detrimental to the best interests of baseball.

The two 1944 amendments to the Major League Agreement remained in effect during the terms of the next two Commissioners, A. B. "Happy" Chandler and Ford Frick. Upon Frick's retirement in 1964 and in accordance with his recommendation, the parties adopted three amendments to the Major League Agreement: (1) the language added in 1944 preventing the Commissioner from finding any act or practice "taken in compliance" with a Major League Rule to be "detrimental to baseball" was removed; (2) the provision deleted in 1944 waiving any rights of recourse to the courts to challenge a Commissioner's decision was restored; and (3) in places where the language "detrimental to the best interests of the national game of baseball" or "detrimental to baseball" appeared those words were changed to "not in the best interests of the national game of Baseball" or "not in the best interests of Baseball."

The nature of the power lodged in the Commissioner by the Major League Agreement is further exemplified "[i]n the case of conduct by organizations not parties to this agreement, or by individuals not connected with any of the parties hereto, which is deemed by the Commissioner not to be in the best interests of Baseball" whereupon "the Commissioner may pursue appropriate legal remedies, advocate remedial legislation and take such other steps as he may deem necessary and proper in the interests of the morale of the players and the honor of the game." Art. I, Sec. 4.

The Commissioner has been given broad power in unambiguous language to investigate any act, transaction or practice not in the best interests of baseball, to determine what preventive, remedial or punitive action is appropriate in the premises, and to take that action. He has also been given the express power to approve or disapprove the assignments of players. In regard to nonparties to the agreement, he may take such other steps as he deems necessary and proper in the interests of the morale of the players and the honor of the game. Further, indicative of the nature of the Commissioner's authority is the provision whereby the parties agree to be bound by his decisions and discipline imposed and to waive recourse to the courts. . . .

1.14 Players' Associations

Players' associations are now recognized as unions, entitled to protection under the National Labor Relations Act. An accounting of the pivotal case that affirmed this protection is set forth in Section 2.30. Gaining such recognition and generally proceeding forward as a union were not accomplished without a struggle. The experience of the National Football League is a good example. In the late 1950s, the sports leagues other than baseball still had some hopes of obtaining exemption from the federal antitrust laws. When it appeared that their quest for such exemption would fail in the courts, the leagues looked to Congress for legislative relief. To improve the NFL's bargaining position in the fight for favorable legislative action, the NFL commissioner, Bert Bell, made the following statement to a House Subcommittee:

> Accordingly, in keeping with my assurance that we would do whatever you gentlemen consider to be in the best interest of the public, on behalf of the National Football League, I hereby recognize the National Football League Players Association and I am prepared to negotiate immediately with the representatives of that association concerning any differences between the players and the clubs that may exist. This will include the provisions of our bylaws and standard players' contract which have been questioned by members of this committee. [United States. Congress. House. Committee on the Judiciary. Antitrust Subcommittee. *Organized Professional Team Sports.* Hearing, 85th Congress, 1st Session. August 1, 1957, at pp. 2691–2692]

George Halas, owner of the Chicago Bears and one of the founders of the NFL, concurred, with reservations, in this recognition of the NFL Players' Association.

Despite these assurances given to a Congressional subcommittee, it was over ten years later in 1968 before the first collective bargaining agreement was effectuated in the NFL. Part of the difficulty lay with the players and their counsel. The players were fearful of declaring their organizations to be unions. Creighton Miller was for many years the counsel for the

National Football League Players Association (NFLPA). Throughout this period, he generally resisted labeling the NFLPA as a union. For example, in Krasnow and Levy, "Unionization and Professional Sports," 51 *Georgetown Law Journal* (1963), pp. 749, 773, the authors cite correspondence they had with Miller in which he was extremely reluctant to talk in terms of the NFLPA being a union.

Despite such reservations, the players' groups in all sports at length emerged as full-fledged labor organizations, and the umpires and referees in most of the sports were not far behind. These matters are discussed in much greater detail later in the book, particularly in Chapter 5. The important thing to note, though, is that the leagues have not quietly acquiesced to the notion that players' associations are here to stay. There is still great infighting within the leagues, and more than one charge has been leveled by players' associations that a league was out to "bust" the union. Thus, at this point, we consider the background of a lengthy battle waged in the late 1970s. Effective unionization was still at issue when a U.S. District Court determined to act in 1980. The case involved a relatively new league, the North American Soccer League, and its efforts to resist collective bargaining. This excerpt on the union's background efforts is instructive.

Morio v. North American Soccer League, 501 F.Supp. 633, 636–637 (S.D.N.Y. 1980)

Respondent, the North American Soccer League, is a non-profit association. It currently comprises about 24 professional soccer teams, 21 of which are located in the United States and three of which are located in Canada. The League's principal office is at 1133 Avenue of the Americas, County, City and State of New York, where it has been engaged in its operation as a non-profit association. Each of the constituent members is engaged primarily in the business of promoting and exhibiting professional soccer contests for viewing by the general public. Collectively, these clubs annually gross revenue in excess of half a million

dollars and purchase and cause to be imported in interstate commerce goods and materials valued in excess of $50,000. The Respondent League and its constituent member clubs constitute and have constituted at all times material herein joint employers for the purpose of collective bargaining.

The Union is an unincorporated association and is an organization of employees which exists for the purpose, in whole or in part, of dealing with employees concerning grievances, labor disputes, wages, rates of pay, hours of employment or conditions of employment. The Union maintains its principal offices at 1300 Connecticut Avenue, N.W., Washington, D. C. . . .

All professional soccer players, whether on loan or otherwise, employed by Respondent League and Respondent Clubs constitute a unit appropriate for the purposes of collective bargaining within the meaning of Section 9(b) of the Act. This unit includes players on the following eligibility lists: active, temporarily inactive, disabled, suspended, ineligible, and military. The unit does not include officials of Respondent League or managerial or executive personnel of Respondent League and Respondent Clubs or players employed by the Edmonton Drillers, Toronto Metos and Vancouver Whitecaps. All other employees and supervisors as defined in the Act are also included. Since September 1, 1978, the Union, by virtue of Section 9(a) of the Act has been and is now the exclusive representative of all the employees in the unit for the purpose of collective bargaining with respect to the rates of pay, wages, hours of employment and other terms and conditions of employment.

In this case Petitioner alleges that she has reasonable cause to believe that Respondent interfered with, restrained and coerced employees in the exercise of rights guaranteed them by Section 7 of the Act by engaging in the following acts and conduct:

1. On or about October 19, 1978, and continuing thereafter, Respondents unilaterally changed the employment conditions of the employees in the Unit by requiring them to obtain permission from their respective clubs whenever a particular brand of footwear, other than selected by each of Respondent Clubs, is desired by an employee.

2. On April 10, 1979, Respondent, acting

through their agents, Phil Woosman and Ted Howard, unilaterally changed the employment conditions of the employees in the unit by initiating plans for a new winter indoor soccer season which began in November, 1979, and ended in March, 1980.

3. On or about November 24, 1979, and continuing to the present, Respondents, acting through their agents, Phil Woosman and Ted Howard, and other agents presently unknown, unilaterally changed and are continuing to change the employment conditions of the employees in the unit by requiring them to play or otherwise participate in the winter indoor soccer season.

4. On or about October 16, 1979, Respondents, acting through the same agents named above, unilaterally changed the employment conditions of employees in the unit by initiating plans to increase the 1980 regular summer outdoor soccer season schedule by two games and two weeks over the 1979 format and by subsequently implementing said plans and maintaining them in full force and effect.

5. On or about October 16, 1979, Respondents, acting through their said agents, unilaterally changed the employment conditions of employees in the unit by initiating plans to reduce the maximum roster of all the Respondent Clubs during the regular outdoor summer season from 30 to 26 players and by subsequently implementing said plans and maintaining them in full force and effect.

6. Commencing on or about October 19, 1978, until on or about March, 1979, and continuing thereafter, Respondents by-passed the Union and dealt directly with employees in the unit. Respondents solicited employees to enter into individual employment contracts, negotiated individual employment contracts, and actually entered into individual employment contracts with employee members of the unit.

The evidence introduced at the hearing conducted by the court established that Petitioner has reasonable cause to believe that Respondents have entered into individual contracts with employees since September 1, 1978, and continue to do so and that these individual contracts constitute 96.8% of the existing individual contracts. The other 3.2%

of the current individual player contracts were entered into prior to the Union's certification on September 1, 1978.

1.15 Sports Attorneys and Agents

Large numbers of eager men (and a few women) have descended on professional sports with a vengeance in the past few years. They generally are called agents, although many refer to themselves as sports attorneys. The fact is some have legal training and are members of a bar, but many have no such training and are not lawyers under any definition. While Chapter 4, particularly Section 4.10, details the many functions that a sports attorney or agent fulfills, the following case of *Zinn* v. *Parrish* provides a good introduction and explains how these activities can lead to friction between the attorney/agent and the client. The legal issues of *Zinn* v. *Parrish* are also of significance and are discussed in Section 4.20.

Zinn v. Parrish, 644 F.2d 360, 361–362 (7th Cir. 1981)

For over two decades the appellant Zinn had been engaged in the business of managing professional athletes. He stated that he was a pioneer in bringing to the attention of various pro-football teams the availability of talented players at small black colleges in the South. In the Spring of 1970, Parrish's coach at Lincoln University approached Zinn and informed him that Parrish had been picked by the Cincinnati Bengals in the annual National Football League draft of college seniors, and asked him if he would help Parrish in negotiating the contract. After Zinn contacted Parrish, the latter signed a one-year "Professional Management Contract" with Zinn in the Spring of 1970, pursuant to which Zinn helped Parrish negotiate the terms of his rookie contract with the Bengals, receiving as his commission 10% of Parrish's $16,500 salary. On April 10, 1971 Parrish signed the contract at issue in this case, which differed from the 1970 contract only insofar as it was automatically renewed from year to year unless one of the parties terminated it by 30 days' written notice to the other party. There were no other restrictions placed on the power of either party to terminate the contract.

Under the 1971 contract, Zinn obligated himself to use "reasonable efforts" to procure pro-football employment for Parrish, and, at Parrish's request, to "act" in furtherance of Parrish's interest by: (a) negotiating job contracts; (b) furnishing advice on business investments; (c) securing professional tax advice at no added cost; and (d) obtaining endorsement contracts. It was further provided that Zinn's services would include, "at my request — efforts to secure for me gainful off-season employment," for which Zinn would receive no additional compensation, "unless such employment [was] in the line of endorsements, marketing and the like," in which case Zinn would receive a 10% commission on the gross amount. If Parrish failed to pay Zinn amounts due under the contract, Parrish authorized "the club or clubs that are obligated to pay me to pay to you instead all monies and other considerations due me from which you can deduct your 10% and any other monies due you. . . ."

Over the course of Parrish's tenure with the Bengals, Zinn negotiated base salaries for him of $18,500 in 1971; $27,000 in 1972; $35,000 in 1973 (plus a $6,500 signing bonus); and a $250,000 series of contracts covering the four seasons commencing in 1974 (plus a $30,000 signing bonus). The 1974–77 contracts with the Bengals were signed at a time when efforts were being made by the newly-formed World Football League to persuade players in the NFL to "jump" to the WFL to play on one of its teams. By the end of 1973 season Parrish had become recognized as one of the more valuable players in the NFL. He was twice selected for the Pro Bowl game, and named by Sporting News as one of the best cornerbacks in the league. Towards the end of the 1973 season, the Bengals approached Parrish with an offer of better contract terms than he had earlier been receiving. By way of exploring alternatives in the WFL, Zinn entered into preliminary discussions with the Jacksonville Sharks in early 1974, but decided not to pursue the matter once he ascertained that the Sharks were in a shaky financial position. In retrospect, Zinn's and Parrish's decision to continue negotiating and finally sign with the Bengals was a sound one, for the Sharks and the rest of the WFL with them

folded in 1975 due to lack of funds.

Shortly after signing the 1974 series of contracts, Parrish informed Zinn by telephone that he "no longer needed his services." By letter dated October 16, 1975 Parrish reiterated this position, and added that he had no intention of paying Zinn a 10% commission on those contracts. In view of its disposition of the case, the district court made no specific fact finding as to the amounts Parrish earned during the 1974–77 seasons. Zinn claims that the total was at least $304,500 including bonus and performance clauses. The 1971 contract by its terms entitled Zinn to 10% of the total amount as each installment was paid, and Zinn claims that he has only received $4,300 of the amounts due him. . . .

In addition to negotiating the Bengals contracts, Zinn performed a number of other services at Parrish's request. In 1972 he assisted him in purchasing a residence as well as a four-unit apartment building to be used for rental income; he also helped to manage the apartment building. That same year Zinn negotiated an endorsement contract for Parrish with All-Pro Graphics Inc., under which Parrish received a percentage from the sales of "Lemar Parrish" t-shirts, sweat-shirts, beach towels, key chains, etc. The record shows that Zinn made a number of unsuccessful efforts at obtaining similar endorsement income from stores with which Parrish did business in Ohio. He also tried, unsuccessfully, to obtain an appearance for Parrish on the Mike Douglas Show. Zinn arranged for Parrish's taxes to be prepared each year by H & R Block.

The evidence showed that, despite his efforts, Zinn was unable to obtain off-season employment for Parrish. In this connection, however, it was Zinn's advice to Parrish that he return to school during the off-season months in order to finish his college degree, against the time when he would no longer be able to play football. With respect to Zinn's obligation to provide Parrish with advice on "business investments," he complied first, by assisting in the purchase of the apartment building; and second, by forwarding to Parrish the stock purchase recommendations of certain other individuals, after screening the suggestions himself. There was no evidence that Zinn ever forwarded such recommendations to any of his other clients; he testified that he only did so for Parrish. In summing up Zinn's performance under the contract, Parrish testified as follows:

> Q: Did you ever ask Zinn to do anything for you, to your knowledge, that he didn't try to do?
>
> A: I shall say not, no.

1.16 Players

Borrowing from a quote used widely by the NFL Players Association as it rallied its members to move toward a strike during the 1982 football collective bargaining negotiations, "We (the players) Are the Game." This is true. They may not be the "be-all" as far as the industry is concerned, but the players are the game. They are what people see and remember. They are why people spend their money.

The ultimate focus is on the playing field or court or rink and on the talented young athletes who are at the top of their profession. The excerpts that follow underscore the unique position that athletes occupy, whether it be in sports lore as it invades a legal decision, in showing how uniqueness becomes of legal consequence, or in revealing some of the troubling aspects of too much notoriety and too little self-containment. Justice Blackmun delivered the opinion of the Court.

Flood v. Kuhn, 407 U.S. 258, 260–265 (1972)

I. The Game

It is a century and a quarter since the New York Nine defeated the Knickerbockers 23 to 1 on Hoboken's Elysian Fields June 19, 1846, with Alexander Jay Cartwright as the instigator and the umpire. The teams were amateur, but the contest marked a significant date in baseball's beginnings. That early game led ultimately to the development of professional baseball and its tightly organized structure.

The Cincinnati Red Stockings came into existence in 1869 upon an outpouring of local pride. With only one Cincinnatian on the payroll, this professional team traveled over 11,000 miles that summer, winning 56 games and tying one. Shortly

thereafter, on St. Patrick's Day in 1871, the National Association of Professional Baseball Players was founded and the professional league was born.

The ensuing colorful days are well known. The ardent follower and the student of baseball know of General Abner Doubleday; the formation of the National League in 1876; Chicago's supremacy in the first year's competition under the leadership of Al Spalding and with Cap Anson at third base; the formation of the American Association and then of the Union Association in the 1880s; the introduction of Sunday baseball; interleague warfare with cut-rate admission prices and player raiding; the development of the reserve "clause"; the emergence in 1885 of the Brotherhood of Professional Ball Players, and in 1890 of the Players League; the appearance of the American League, or "junior circuit," in 1901, rising from the minor Western Association; the first World Series in 1903, disruption in 1904, and the Series' resumption in 1905; the short-lived Federal League on the majors' scene during World War I years; the troublesome and discouraging episode of the 1919 Series; the home run ball; the shifting of franchises; the expansion of the leagues; the installation in 1965 of the major league draft of potential new players; and the formation of the Major League Baseball Players Association in 1966.

Then there are the many names, celebrated for one reason or another, that have sparked the diamond and its environs and that have provided tinder for recaptured thrills, for reminiscence and comparisons, and for conversation and anticipation in-season and off-season: Ty Cobb, Babe Ruth, Tris Speaker, Walter Johnson, Henry Chadwick, Eddie Collins, Lou Gehrig, Grover Cleveland Alexander, Rogers Hornsby, Harry Hooper, Goose Goslin, Jackie Robinson, Honus Wagner, Joe McCarthy, John McGraw, Deacon Phillippe, Rube Marquard, Christy Mathewson, Tommy Leach, Big Ed Delahanty, Davy Jones, Germany Schaefer, King Kelly, Big Dan Brouthers, Wahoo Sam Crawford, Wee Willie Keeler, Big Ed Walsh, Jimmy Austin, Fred Snodgrass, Satchel Paige, Hugh Jennings, Fred Merkle, Iron Man McGinnity, Three-Finger Brown, Harry and Stan Coveleski, Connie Mack, Al Bridwell, Red Ruffing, Amos Rusie, Cy Young, Smokey Joe Wood, Chief Meyers, Chief Bender, Bill Klem, Hans Lobert, Johnny Evers, Joe Tinker, Roy Campanella, Miller Huggins, Rube Bressler, Dazzy Vance, Edd Roush, Bill Wambsganss, Clark Griffith, Branch Rickey, Frank Chance, Cap Anson, Nap Lajoie, Sad Sam Jones, Bob O'Farrell, Lefty O'Doul, Bobby Veach, Willie Kamm, Heinie Groh, Lloyd and Paul Waner, Stuffy McInnis, Charles Comiskey, Roger Bresnahan, Bill Dickey, Zack Wheat, George Sisler, Charlie Gehringer, Eppa Rixey, Harry Heilmann, Fred Clarke, Dizzy Dean, Hank Greenberg, Pie Traynor, Rube Waddell, Bill Terry, Carl Hubbell, Old Hoss Radbourne, Moe Berg, Rabbit Maranville, Jimmie Foxx, Lefty Grove. The list seems endless.

And one recalls the appropriate reference to the "World Serious," attributed to Ring Lardner, Sr.; Ernest L. Thayer's "Casey at the Bat"; the ring of "Tinker to Evers to Chance"; and all the other happenings, habits, and superstitions about and around baseball that made it the "national pastime" or, depending upon the point of view, "the great American tragedy."

II.   The Petitioner

The petitioner, Curtis Charles Flood, born in 1938, began his major league career in 1956 when he signed a contract with the Cincinnati Reds for a salary of $4,000 for the season. He had no attorney or agent to advise him on that occasion. He was traded to the St. Louis Cardinals before the 1958 season. Flood rose to fame as a center fielder with the Cardinals during the years 1958–1969. In those 12 seasons he compiled a batting average of .293. His best offensive season was 1967 when he achieved .335. He was .301 or better in six of the 12 St. Louis years. He participated in the 1964, 1967, and 1968 World Series. He played errorless ball in the field in 1966, and once enjoyed 223 consecutive errorless games. Flood has received seven Golden Glove Awards. He was co-captain of his team from 1965–1969. He ranks among the 10 major league outfielders possessing the highest lifetime fielding averages.

Flood's St. Louis compensation for the years shown was:

1961	$13,500 (including a bonus for signing)
1962	$16,000
1963	$17,500
1964	$23,000
1965	$35,000
1966	$45,000
1967	$50,000
1968	$72,500
1969	$90,000

These figures do not include any so-called fringe benefits or World Series shares.

But at the age of 31, in October 1969, Flood was traded to the Philadelphia Phillies of the National League in a multi-player transaction. He was not consulted about the trade. He was informed by telephone and received formal notice only after the deal had been consummated. In December he complained to the Commissioner of Baseball and asked that he be made a free agent and be placed at liberty to strike his own bargain with any other major league team. His request was denied.

Flood then instituted this antitrust suit in January 1970 in federal court for the Southern District of New York. . . .

NOTE _____

1. The following were examples of the footnotes that Justice Blackmun felt he needed to include in the opening part of his decision:

(a) Millions have known and enjoyed baseball. One writer knowledgeable in the field of sports almost assumed that everyone did until, one day, he discovered otherwise:
"I knew a cove who'd never heard of Washington and Lee,
   Of Caesar and Napoleon from the ancient jamboree,
But, bli'me, there are queerer things than anything like that,
   For here's a cove who never heard of 'Casey at the Bat'!
   "Ten Million never heard of Keats, or Shelley, Burns or Poe;
   But they know 'the air was shattered by the force of Casey's blow';
They never heard of Shakespeare, nor of Dickens, like as not,
   But they know the somber drama from old Mudville's haunted lot.
"He never heard of Casey! Am I dreaming? Is it true?
   Is fame but windblown ashes when the summer day is through?
Does greatness fade so quickly and is grandeur doomed to die
   That bloomed in early morning, ere the dusk rides down the sky?"
"He Never Heard of Casey" Grantland Rice, The Sportlight, New York Herald Tribune, *June 1, 1926, p. 23.* [Flood *v.* Kuhn, *fn.4 at p. 263]*
(b)   "These are the saddest of possible words,
         'Tinker to Evers to Chance.'
      Trio of bear cubs, and fleeter than birds,
         'Tinker to Evers to Chance.'
      Ruthlessly pricking our gonfalon bubble,

Making a Giant hit into a double—
Words that are weighty with nothing but trouble:
'Tinker to Evers to Chance,' "
Franklin Pierce Adams, Baseball's Sad Lexicon. [Flood *v.* Kuhn, *fn. 5 at p. 264]*

Central New York Basketball, Inc. v. Barnett, 181 N.E.2d 506, 513 (Ohio C.P. 1961)

Plaintiff claims that defendant Barnett is a professional basketball player of great skill and whose talents and abilities as a basketball player are of special, unique, unusual and extraordinary character.

There is some disagreement in the testimony as to the ability and standing of Barnett as a basketball player. Daniel Biasone, the General Manager of the Syracuse club for the past 16 years, testified that (R. 47): "As of now I think Richard Barnett is one of the greatest basketball players playing the game." "[H]e is an exceptionally good shooter." (R. 48) "He is above average . . . with other foul shooters in the National Basketball Association and that he ranked 19th in the whole league (approximately 100 players) scoring, playing as a guard." (R. 48 and 49.) He further testified (R. 153):

"Q What is your opinion as to his ability, this is, as a guard, now, at driving?
"A Terrific.
"Q What is your opinion as to his ability as play making as a guard?
"A Good. He has all the abilities a good basketball player should have. He has all the talent of a great basketball player. He is terrific all the way around."

Mr. Biasone also testified on cross-examination that he would place Barnett in the group of some specifically-named nine or ten unusual and extraordinary players in the National Basketball Association. (R.109 and 110)

Mr. Biasone also testified that Barnett was a box office attraction and was asked on cross examination: "On what basis do you say he was a great box office attraction?" He answered (R. 128):

"A Because he, in my opinion, he is such a tremendous ball handler and he does things that have crowd appeal, he is noticeable. He appeals to the crowd because he does things extraordinary."

Coach McLendon of the Cleveland Pipers is not so generous in his appraisal. Barnett, in his opinion, is not in the class of the specifically named outstanding basketball players. McLendon concedes that both Barnett and Neuman, now playing for Syracuse in his first year as a professional, are both "pretty good." (R. 256)

The defendant Barnett was asked by his counsel (R. 195):

"Q Do you represent to this court that you have exceptional and unique skill and ability as a basketball player?
"A No.
"Q Do you represent to this Court that your services are of a special, unusual and extraordinary character?
"A No.
"Q You do represent to the Court that you are a professional basketball player; is that correct?
"A Yes.
"Q Do you think you are as good as Oscar Robertson?
"A No."

Erving v. Virginia Squires Basketball Club, 468 F.2d 1064, 1065–1067 (2nd Cir. 1972)

This case presents another chapter in the history of contract jumping by famous American athletes. As usual the amounts paid by the competing teams are fantastic. Julius W. Erving, we are told, was playing a remarkable game of basketball as an undergraduate at University of Massachusetts when, after his junior year, he agreed to turn professional and he signed a contract with the Virginia Squires to play exclusively for the Squires for four years commencing October 1, 1971 for $500,000.00. He made an extraordinary record in his first year as a pro, but he seems, for one reason or another, to have defected and in April, 1972 he signed a contract to play for the Atlanta Hawks. This contract with the Hawks is not before us but we were informed on the oral argument that it called for payments to Erving, or "Dr. J." as he was generally called by the fans, aggregating $1,500,000.00 or more. . . .

In view of the large sums of money involved, and the publicity generated by the reputation of "Dr. J." as a highly talented basketball player with a brilliant future, we need not be surprised at the amount of perhaps pardonable exaggeration and bombast in the claims of the respective parties. On the one hand we are assured that "Dr. J." was, as stated in the opinion below, "for all practical purposes" the Squires' "whole team," that he was featured in the Squires' advertisements as "fabulous" and that the fans were deserting in droves when told that "Dr. J." had switched to the Hawks. On the other hand we are told that there is no showing of irreparable harm to the Squires if "Dr. J." plays with the Hawks, and the charge of fraud in inducing this innocent collegian to leave college and play for the Squires for four years for the inadequate sum of $500,000.00 is repeated *ad nauseum*. We think, however, that irreparable damage to the Squires is plainly proved even if we assume that "Dr. J." is not the Squires' "whole team" and even if we doubt, as we do, that in the absence of "Dr. J." the Squires will collapse and with them the whole American Basketball Association.

Just as counsel for "Dr. J." repeat in various colorful phrases the claim that "Dr. J." was defrauded, counsel for Squires insist that this is just a plain, ordinary case of contract jumping to get more money, that the claim of fraud did not originate until two months or more after "Dr. J." had signed his contract with the Hawks, and that the whole sorry business is nothing more nor less than the usual maneuvering by a greedy young athlete to sell out to the highest bidder. . . .

1.20   The Constituencies and Their Views on a Current Issue

Even though the National Football League incurred its share of litigation in the early to mid-1970s, the league was still noted for its effective internal management. The owners stayed in line. Little dissent over the policies and positions of Commissioner Pete Rozelle surfaced. Many pointed to the NFL as a model for other leagues to emulate. But that was before Al Davis, the Oakland Raiders, and the Los Angeles Memorial Coliseum combined to give the league a monumental headache.

It began when the Los Angeles Rams announced they were moving from the Coliseum in Los Angeles to the perceived friendlier confines of Anaheim. Upon failing to obtain a substitute franchise to play in the Coliseum, the stadium brought a suit against the NFL, alleging monopoly, conspiracy, and other standard antitrust allegations. The suit was dismissed, the judge holding that no real controversy existed because the commission could not show it was in reality being denied a team for that locale (see *Los Angeles Memorial Coliseum* v. *NFL*, 468 F. Supp. 154 [C.D. Cal. 1979]).

It did not take long for the Coliseum to find its prospective tenant. Five hundred miles to the north, Al Davis, president of the Oakland Raiders, was restless. He could be wooed if the price was right. It was, and the contemplated move to Los Angeles was announced. When the National Football League acted to block the move, the Los Angeles Memorial Coliseum renewed its suit, joined by Al Davis and the Raiders. It was to be the start of many years of litigation in a host of federal and state courts.

Among the many intriguing aspects of the situation was a turn to Congress for assistance. This was hardly the first time that Congress was called upon to act in behalf of sports interests. Indeed, every year multiple bills are introduced into Congress that would directly affect the sports industries. Many of these are sponsored by the leagues themselves; others come from other sources. In this particular instance, several parties were at work, urging that bills be introduced and enacted with dispatch, and the National Football League was undoubtedly a chief proponent.

The *Los Angeles Memorial Coliseum* and related cases are discussed in Chapter 6. Here we turn instead to the hearings before the Senate Committee charged with considering two particular bills. Substantial excerpts from the testimony before the committee are reproduced for several purposes. The testimony provides valuable factual background on league stability, movement of franchises, and revenue sharing. Beyond that, the testimony lends special perspectives on what different sports constituencies view as their best interests. Legislation that is seemingly innocuous on its face can nevertheless excite and agitate affected parties. They will raise issues that others will dispute. So it is with these bills.

Presented are three sets of materials. First is the National Football League bylaws, pertaining to the procedures by which approval must be gained for the movement of a franchise. Second is the proposed legislation — two bills that take different routes in an attempt to effectuate a solution. Third is the testimony before the congressional committee, either in the form of live testimony or through prepared statements filed with the committee. The various parties emphasize issues important to their perspectives. Why the parties choose to focus on particular issues should be explored.

These two bills got no further than the Senate committee that heard the testimony. Why the proposed legislation got no further is a separate fascinating story of political maneuverings. What is clear is that the whole controversy has not ended. When Robert Irsay moved his Baltimore Colts to Indianapolis in early 1984, renewed calls for legislation to restrict such practices were again voiced. New bills, substantially similar to the old ones, were introduced. One Senate committee by a narrow vote actually approved one piece of legislation, but by the time it had been amended to appease various rival factions, the National Football League said it could no longer support the bill (See *New York Times*, June 14, 1984, p. D24). Its prospects for passage were conceded to be doubtful by the bill's sponsor.

The National Football League is not alone in its problems with "itchy-feet" owners. In 1984, Donald Sterling announced his NBA Clippers, located in San Diego, were moving to Los Angeles. Again, the Los Angeles Memorial Coliseum Commission was involved, since it operates the Los Angeles Sports Arena as well as the Coliseum. However, this time, the NBA and its new commissioner, David Stern, did not attempt to prohibit the move. They announced, instead, that the matter had been referred to the appropriate NBA owners' committee for study and evaluation. The Clippers pressed the move, however, and the NBA at length counterattacked by filing suit against the club and the Coliseum Commission. The NBA asked that a court declare that the league had the ability to terminate the franchise, since the Clippers had moved without league approval. Furthermore, according to Stern, the court was also asked to "confirm the NBA's right to evaluate the move under NBA franchise relocation procedures — and to approve or disapprove it after such evaluation." The NBA asked for $25 million in damages (see *Boston Globe*, June 16, 1984, p. 27).

From these ongoing episodes, it is clear the issues will not die. Both the courts and Congress will be asked to act. The discussions that follow allow us to see the issues as presented by the various affected interests.

Constitution and By-laws of the National Football League (Effective February 1, 1970, As Amended Through 1981)

ARTICLE III
Membership

Members

3.1 (a) Membership in the League shall be limited to the twenty eight (28) member clubs specified in Section 4.4 hereof and such new members as may be hereafter duly elected.

(b) The admission of a new member club, either within or outside the home territory of an existing member club, shall require the affirmative vote of three-fourths of the existing member clubs of the League.

Eligibility of New Members

3.2 Any person, association, partnership, corporation, or other entity of good repute organized for the purpose of operating a professional football club shall be eligible for membership except:

(a) No corporation, association, partnership or other entity not operated for profit nor any charitable organization or entity not presently a member of the League shall be eligible for membership. . . .

Transfer of Membership

3.5 No membership, or any interest therein, may be sold, assigned, or otherwise transferred in whole or in part except in accordance with and subject to the following provisions:

(a) Application for the sale, transfer or assignment of a membership or of any interest therein, must be made in writing to the Commissioner; upon receipt of such application, the Commissioner is empowered to require from applicant and applicant shall furnish such information as the Commissioner deems appropriate, including:

(1) The names and addresses of each of the buyers, transferees or assignees thereof.

(2) The price to be paid for such sale, transfer or assignment, and the terms of payment, including a description of the security for any unpaid balance, if any.

(3) A banking reference for each buyer, transferee, or assignee. . . .

(b) Upon receipt thereof, the Commissioner shall conduct such investigation as he deems appropriate. Upon the completion thereof, the Commissioner shall submit the proposed transfer to the members for approval, together with his recomendation thereon, and all information in respect thereto that the Commissioner deems pertinent. All sales, transfers or assignments except a transfer referred to in Section 3.5(c) hereof, shall only become effective if approved by the affirmative vote of not less than three-fourths or 20, whichever is greater, of the members of the League.

(c) If any person owning or holding a membership, or an interest therein, by stock ownership or otherwise dies, such membership or interest therein may be transferred to a member of the "immediate family" of the deceased without requiring the consent or approval of the members of the League or the Commissioner thereof; similarly, if any person owning or holding a membership or an interest therein, by stock ownership, or otherwise, seeks to transfer such membership or any interest therein, by gift, such membership or the interest therein may be transferred to the donee if the donee is a member of the "immediate family" of the donor; in such event, no consent to or approval of the members of the League or the commissioner shall be required to complete such transfer. . . .

Membership Fees and Assessments

3.10 Assessment. Whenever moneys are required to meet the expenses of the League, and League funds are not available for that purpose, then, upon demand by the Commissioner, each member shall be obligated to contribute equally its share of the required moneys.

Membership Covenants and Obligations

3.11 Each member club, and each and all of the owners, officers, stockholders, directors or partners therein, as well as any other person, owning any interest in such member club, assumes and agrees to be bound by the following obligations of membership in the League:

(a) They, and each of them, shall be bound by and will observe all decisions of the Commissioner of the League in all matters within his jurisdiction.

(b) They, and each of them, shall be bound by and will observe all decisions, rulings and action of the Executive Committee or the member clubs of the League in every matter within the jurisdiction of such Committee or such member clubs, as the case may be.

(c) They, and each of them, waive any and all claims or demands, whether for damages or otherwise, which they, or any of them, might now or hereafter possess against the Commissioner of the League, individually or in his official capacity, as well as against the League or any employee thereof, and against any member club or any officer, director, owner, stockholder, or partner thereof, or the holder of any interest therein, in connection with or by reason of any decision, ruling action of the Commissioner, the Executive Committee, or the League in reference to any matter within their respective jurisdictions.

(d) They, and each of them, shall include in every contract between any member club and its employees, including coaches and players, a clause wherein the parties to such contract agree to be bound by the Constitution and By-Laws of the League.

(e) That after becoming a member of the League, the primary purpose of the corporation, partnership or other entity operating the club shall at all times be and remain the operation of a professional football team as a member club of the

League, and such primary purpose shall not be changed.

(f) They, and each of them, consent to be bound by the provisions of the Final Judgment of the United States District Court for the Eastern District of Pennsylvania entered against the National Football League and certain of its member clubs on December 28, 1953, and as thereafter modified and for the purpose of said Judgment submit to the jurisdiction of said Court.

(g) They, and each of them, agree to be bound by all of the terms and provisions of the Constitution and By-Laws of the League as now or hereafter in effect.

(h) They, and each of them, agree to be represented at each and every meeting of the League and of the Executive Committee of the League by a representative duly authorized and empowered to cast the binding vote of the member club on all questions coming before such meeting.

ARTICLE IV
TERRITORIAL RIGHTS

Home Territory Defined

4.1 "Home Territory" with respect to any club means the city in which such club is located and for which it holds a franchise and plays its home games, and includes the surrounding territory to the extent of 75 miles in every direction from the exterior corporate limits of such city, except as follows:

(a) Whenever two member clubs, . . . are located and hold franchises for different cities within 100 miles of each other measured from the exterior corporate limits of such city, then the territorial rights of each of such clubs shall only extend to and include an area of one-half the distance between such cities.

(b) The "home territory" of the Green Bay Packers shall extend and include all of Milwaukee County, Wisconsin, despite the fact that portions of such County are outside the 75 mile limits from the exterior corporate limits of the City of Green Bay.

Rights within Home Territory

4.2 Each member shall have the exclusive right within its home territory to exhibit professional football games played by teams of the League except that:

(a) Whenever two club franchises in the League are located in the same city, then the owners of each of such franchises shall have equal rights within the home territory of such city. . . .

(c) Subject to the provisions of sections 4.2(a) and (b) above, no club in the League shall be permitted to play games within the home territory of any other club unless a home club is a participant.

League Control of Games

4.3 The League shall have exclusive control of the exhibition of football games by member clubs within the home territory of each member. No member club shall have the right to transfer its franchise or playing site to a different city either within or outside its home territory, without prior approval by the affirmative vote of three-fourths of the existing member clubs of the League.

Two Bills in the United States Senate

97th CONGRESS
2D SESSION

S.2784

To clarify the application of the antitrust laws to professional team sports leagues, to protect the public interest in maintaining the stability of professional team sports leagues, and for other purposes.

IN THE SENATE OF THE UNITED STATES

July 28 (legislative day, July 12), 1982
Mr. DeCONCINI (for himself, and Mr. HEFLIN, Mr. SIMPSON, Mr. HUDDLESTON, and Mr. BENTSEN) introduced the following bill; which was read twice and referred to the Committee on the Judiciary

---

A BILL

To clarify the application of the antitrust laws to professional team sports leagues, to protect the public interest in maintaining the stability of professional team sport leagues, and for other purposes.

Be it enacted by the Senate and House of Representatives of the United States of America in Congress assembled, That this Act may be cited as the "Major League Sports Community Protection Act of 1982".

FINDINGS AND DECLARATIONS

SEC. 2. The Congress finds and declares that the public has interest in preserving stability in the relationship between professional sports teams and the communities in which they operate and in encouraging professional team sports leagues to promote the economic and geographic stability of their member clubs: Therefore, be it enacted, that—

(1) It shall not be unlawful by reason of any provision of the antitrust laws for a professional team sports league and its member clubs —

(a) to enforce rules authorizing the membership of the league to decide that a member club of such a league shall not be relocated; or

(b) to enforce rules for the division of league or member club revenues that tend to promote comparable economic opportunities for the member clubs of such a league.

INAPPLICABILITY TO CERTAIN MATTERS

SEC. 3. Nothing contained in this Act shall —

(a) be deemed to change, determine, or otherwise affect the applicability or nonapplicability of the labor laws, the antitrust laws, or any other provision of law to the wages, hours, or other terms and conditions of player employment within any sports league, to any player employment matter within any sports league, or to any collective bargaining rights and privileges of any player union within any sports league;

(b) exempt from the antitrust laws any agreement to fix the prices of admission to sports contests;

(c) exempt from the antitrust laws any predatory practice or other conduct with respect to competing sports leagues which would otherwise be unlawful under the antitrust laws; or

(d) modify any existing Federal statutes relating to the television practices of sports leagues, or change, determine, or otherwise affect the applicability or non-applicability of the antitrust laws or communications laws to any form of joint dealing practices by sports leagues with respect to the sale of cable or subscription television.

FEDERAL PREEMPTION

SEC. 4. Notwithstanding any other provision of law, no State or political subdivision thereof shall establish, maintain, or enforce any regulation of commerce that imposes any limitation on the collective conduct of professional team sports leagues or their member clubs authorized by this Act.

APPLICABILITY TO PENDING ACTIONS

SEC. 5. (a) This Act shall apply to all actions commenced under the antitrust laws of the United States after the date of enactment of this Act.

(b) This Act shall also apply to all actions commenced under the antitrust laws of the United States prior to the date of enactment of this Act unless —

(1) the judgment in an action is final and unappealable on or before the date of enactment of this Act; or

(2) the court determines in an action involving collective conduct of a professional team sports league in which a release or covenant has been signed prior to the day of enactment of this Act that it would be manifestly unjust, in light of subsection (c) of this section and other circumstances, to apply this Act in such action to any unresolved claim of any party not a member club of such league.

(c) No agreement to settle, compromise, or release a claim which has been signed by the parties prior to the date of enactment of this Act may be rescinded, disapproved, reformed, or modified by the parties or by the court because of the application of the provisions of this Act, except upon the written consent of all the parties thereto.

DEFINITIONS

SEC. 6. For purposes of this Act, the term "professional team sports league" means the organized professional team sports of basketball, football, hockey, or soccer.

97TH CONGRESS
2D SESSION

S.2821

To protect the public interest and to clarify the application of antitrust laws with respect to the location of professional football teams.

IN THE SENATE OF THE UNITED STATES

AUGUST 9 (legislative day, JULY 12), 1982
Mr. SPECTER introduced the following bill; which

was read twice and referred to the Committee on the Judiciary.

A BILL

To protect the public interest and to clarify the application of antitrust laws with respect to the location of professional football teams.

Be it enacted by the Senate and House of Representatives of the United States of America in Congress assembled, That this Act may be cited as the "Professional Football Stabilization Act of 1982".

SEC. 2. (a) The Congress finds that —

(1) professional football teams achieve a strong local identity with the people of the cities and regions in which they are located, providing a source of pride to their supporters;

(2) professional football teams provide a valuable form of entertainment in the cities and regions in which they are located;

(3) substantial tax revenues and employment opportunities derive from the operation of professional football teams to the cities and regions in which they are located;

(4) the public, through a municipal stadium authority (which may be a city or county agency, or a municipal corporation) generally authorizes capital construction bonds to build a stadium, while the team's lease or use agreement generally sets rent to cover only operating costs of the stadium, without reimbursing the public for construction costs; and

(5) professional football teams are invested with a strong public interest.

(b) The Congress, therefore, finds and declares that professional football teams are affected with a strong public interest and that it is the national policy to discourage the relocation of professional football teams receiving local support.

SEC. 3. The Act of September 30, 1961 (75 Stat. 732; 15 U.S.C. 1291–1295), is amended —

(1) by redesignating section 4 as section 7 and striking out all after section 7, as redesignated;

(2) by inserting after section 3 the following:

"SEC. 4. No professional football team which has played its home games in a metropolitan area for six continuous years or more shall relocate unless —

"(1) one or more of the other parties to the stadium lease agreement fails to comply with a provision of material significance to the agreement, and such noncompliance cannot be remedied within a reasonable period of time;

"(2) the stadium in which the team wishing to move presently plays is inadequate for the purposes of properly and competitively operating the team, and the stadium authority demonstrates no intent to remedy such inadequacies; or

"(3) the team has incurred an annual net loss for at least three consecutive years immediately preceding the relocation, or has incurred losses in a shorter period that endangers the continued financial viability of the team.

"SEC. 5. The antitrust laws, as defined in section 1 of the Clayton Act, and the Federal Trade Commission Act, shall not apply to any joint agreement by or among persons engaging in or conducting the organized professional sport of football which restricts the movement of any member team in accordance with the criteria provided in section 4.

"SEC. 6. Any government authority in a metropolitan area from which a professional football team relocates may bring a civil action for damages and equitable relief if such relocation does not comply with the criteria provided in section 4.";

(3) by inserting after "section 1" in section 7, as redesignated, "and section 5";

(4) by inserting after section 7, as redesignated, the following:

"SEC. 8. For purposes of this Act:

"(1) The term 'persons' means any individual partnership, corporation or unincorporated association, or combination or association thereof.

"(2) The term 'relocate' means to change the location in which a team plays its home games from one metropolitan area to another.

"(3) the term 'governmental authority' means any unit of general local government, or other government agency, or authority which exercises regulatory authority with respect to a professional sports team.

"(4) the term 'metropolitan area' means a standard metropolitan statistical area."

Excerpts from Witnesses' Testimony

Prepared Statement of Pete Rozelle, Commissioner, National Football League

. . . I stress the precise and narrow limits of this bill, Mr. Chairman, because much of the criticism directed against it has been either midguided or intentionally misleading. This bill is not anti-player. It is not anti-union. It does not give the NFL a green light to move franchises at will. And it provides no incentive for us to shift from free network television to pay television.

The NFL's Policy on Team Stability

Mr Chairman, a review of the NFL's operations over the past thirty years plainly demonstrates the NFL's firm commitment to competitive and geographic balance, franchise stability, and protection of fan and community interests. The NFL fully supports a national policy of maintaining stable team-community ties. We believe that well-supported and financially successful clubs should not, except in the most extraordinary circumstances, be permitted to relocate outside of their home territories. . . .

It is worth emphasizing, I think, that the NFL's ability to conduct team operations on a nation-wide scale, in communities of vastly differing economic potential, and its ability to insist upon team-community stability is directly tied to the partnership structure of the League itself, including its revenue-sharing principles. Such revenue sharing is a further reason for affording leagues the right to determine whether successful team operations can be conducted in a given locale. Today, almost 60 percent of the revenue of the average NFL club comes from network television contracts; these revenues are shared *equally* among the 28 clubs. When 97 percent of League-wide revenues are broadly shared, as in the NFL, the advantages of the clubs in the largest population and media markets are to a large extent offset by their own contributions to the teams in smaller and medium-sized communities and markets. Next season, for example, the Green Bay Packers will receive $11.8 million in network television revenues from the 1982 season contracts. This network television distribution is likely to represent more than 60 percent of the Packers' total operating revenues. Without such League partnership practices, NFL franchises could not survive in many smaller and mid-sized communities, and franchise failures and contraction of the NFL itself would be most likely. . . .

We are proud of this record of league stability and believe it amply demonstrates our commitment to fan and community service. NFL fans know where NFL teams are and can identify with them locally, regionally, and nationally. Team stadium transfers during the last two decades have been strictly within a metropolitan area, have been made with local commuting and television patterns firmly in mind, and have resulted in superior facilities to better serve local fans. Today the League By-Laws require approval by the membership even for local stadium relocations. In short, the assertion that the Raiders should be permitted to abandon Oakland for a stadium 400 miles away because the Buffalo Bills now play in a modern stadium in Orchard Park, New York, or the Dallas Cowboys in Texas Stadium in Irving, Texas, is rhetoric without substance. . . .

Throughout the 1970s the Raiders were one of the League's best-supported and most financially successful franchises. In 1978, the year before they undertook secret negotiation to move to Los Angeles, the Raiders had profits of over $2 million. In 1979, while taking every possible step to avoid reaching a lease agreement in Oakland, their profits were nearly $1.5 million. This year, the Raiders' profits in Oakland would be substantially higher. That the Raiders earned profits of this magnitude is not surprising. For twelve consecutive seasons, the team sold out every home game it played in Northern California — a record of support virtually unmatched in professional sports. Its total revenues in 1978 and 1979 were squarely within the top 5 NFL clubs. In short, there is no possible argument that the Raiders have been experiencing losses that would "endanger the continued financial viability of the team."

The Raiders earned these revenues and profits while playing in the publicly-financed Oakland-Alameda County Coliseum. This modern facility was specifically constructed for the Raiders and made available in 1966. . . .

You may have heard that this is a personal dispute between the Raiders and myself. In fact, no issue in League history has so firmly unified the other 27 clubs of the League, which unanimously rejected the transfer and have accepted heavy treble damage exposure simply because they believe what the Raiders are doing is wrong — wrong in terms of the League's reputation, its obligations to Oakland fans, and its past commitments to Congress and the American public. I for one deeply regret that any club in the NFL should sacrifice so much in the way of good will, moral commitment, and fan loyalty for nothing more than an increase in its own profit potential. But such practices can become the order of the day in professional sports if this legislation is not enacted. This is my main concern as I speak to you today. . . .

Note: All excerpts of witness testimony appear in United States Senate. Hearings. Committee on the Judiciary. Ninety-Seventh Congress. Second Session. No. J-97-134. Aug. 16, 20, 29 (1982). Commissioner Rozelle's statement, appearing above, is at pp. 51, 55–56, 59, 68–69. Hereinafter, this will be cited as "Hearings."

Statement of Al Davis, Managing General Partner, Los Angeles Raiders, Accompanied by Joseph L. Alioto, Attorney, and Jim Otto, Ex-Raider, Hall of Fame Member

. . . In 1963, I went to Oakland, Calif., as the head coach and general manager. I stayed there for 3 years, and in 1966, we were members of a league called the American Football League. We were in great competition for players. We were in great competition for cities. We were in great competition as to who would dominate the American public as to which league was better.

The owners of the American Football League in 1966 asked me to give up coaching and become the commissioner of the American Football League. I did do that.

And within a period of 4 months, we had a merger with the National Football League which brought all these clubs together. I think that is the quickest expansion and the best expansion we have ever had in this country because the National Football League took nine of the American Football League teams into their league, and we all became one, and it was based on competition, and it was based on something that is inherent in the American way of life.

But to go further, I had the good fortune to go back to Oakland at that time and be the principal owner. I no longer was in coaching, but I was the principal owner.

Just about that time in 1966 Oakland built a new stadium called the Oakland-Alameda County Stadium. It was a complex for basketball and it was a complex for football.

And at that time, the Raiders signed a 5-year lease with the Oakland County Coliseum with five 3-year options, and within the confines of that lease were escape clauses which would allow us to leave.

We could leave if, by nature of the merger between the two leagues it was decided we should leave, we could leave. We could leave for other reasons, but in any event, we stayed.

We stayed the first 5 years. We exercised three of the 3-year options. So we were there in this Oakland-Alameda County Coliseum 14 years.

In the middle seventies I began to ask for certain improvements in the Oakland-Alameda County Coliseum. I thought it was necessary that we get these improvements because the Raiders had done well for the community.

We had the best record in professional football. The coliseum was selling out, but the Raiders did not have certain of the things that I thought were necessary to be competitive in the eighties, the things that other stadiums were getting that were being built.

And so I went to these people and asked for these things. I asked for improvements. For example, we talked about revenue sharing in the National Football League. I believe in revenue sharing, but I believe in sharing it equally.

We have certain teams that have individual contracts based on what we call luxury boxes where they get the money and they keep it. They do not share it with us. The revenue sharing on gate receipts is shared, but it is not shared equally.

There is a disparity of wealth between the top teams in the National Football League and some of the other teams of $4 or $5 million of income.

Now, we share television, and that is the only thing we share equally. Now, the Raiders in Oakland did not get parking or concessions. We did not have luxury boxes that a lot of these stadiums do, and there were many other features that we needed.

We were in a baseball configuration where we had to have actually two different seating arrangements for our fans based on baseball and based on football. For example, this year the league, in anticipation that we would be in Oakland, scheduled us for the first three games of the year on the road.

We had to open in San Francisco. We had to open in Atlanta this Sunday, and next week we open in San Diego on Sunday. And there is no other team in football that had to do this. They do it because of baseball, the problems there.

But in any event, and I could not help it, the Los Angeles Rams who were one of the most prosperous teams in football, if not the most prosperous, in the Los Angeles Coliseum decided to move to Anaheim.

Now, they had large crowds, and as I say, I think they led the league for the 3 years before they left in gate receipts. They had large crowds. They went to Anaheim based on a new stadium situation and a land deal.

I did not begrudge them for leaving to be quite frank. If that is what they wanted to do, it was their business. They did not get league approval when they announced they were moving, and if they wanted to go to Anaheim, fine.

Two things happened when they moved to Anaheim. The people in Los Angeles went to Pete Rozelle and asked for another franchise, an expansion franchise, and he said no, that he would not have another franchise there and that they would have to take their turn down the line if expansion was ever done.

So they went to court. Now, they went to court to sue the National Football League on the rule 4.3, and they also went one other place. They went out in the marketplace to try and get some teams.

And they went to Baltimore, and Baltimore used the Los Angeles Coliseum to get themselves a better deal in Baltimore, and the commissioner interceded and helped them.

Miami got a better deal in Miami by using the Los Angeles Coliseum as a wedge. And Minnesota in 1979, in March, out in Hawaii, the Minnesota Vikings were having trouble getting a new dome stadium in Minnesota. They did not have the vote. So Commissioner Rozelle announced publicly out of Hawaii that no team is locked into a city in perpetuity. Economics are not the only reason that keeps a team in a locale, and if Minnesota, in essence, did not get out of there, they were going to let the Minnesota Vikings move to Los Angeles.

Within about a month, it was committed to build a new dome stadium in Minneapolis, some $54 million, and it ended up costing approximately $74.

Now, Los Angeles started to pursue the Raiders because they knew our lease was up at the end of 1979. And in November 1979, Pete Rozelle came to the bay area for a press club. He was a featured speaker.

And I talked to him, and I said to him, "I want you to do one favor for me. Give me the same treatment you gave Minnesota," because I was having trouble with the people in the bay area in getting any commitment from them on the things that I thought were necessary to be competitive in the eighties, what our stadium needed.

We were one of the smallest stadiums in the league, the Oakland-Alameda County Coliseum. They still are. We had no luxury boxes. We needed moveable bleachers in the stadium which would give a configuration so we could play during the baseball season and play well.

And he would not do it for me. Even after the press club, all newspaper articles, and this was documented at the trial and documented in court, all newspaper articles said about Davis moving or the Raiders moving, everything, Rozelle said everything but no.

Now, other owners came into my community and said Davis cannot get the vote. He cannot move. The vote would be 27 to 1 against Davis. He cannot move. And so it became almost impossible to negotiate. [Hearings, pp. 310–313]

Prepared Statement of David J. Stern, Executive Vice President, National Basketball Association

. . . As a matter of current NBA practice, when a request is received for the relocation of a franchise, an analysis is undertaken to determine whether the current city of operation will be unfairly impacted by the move of the team. This analysis consists essentially of two components. First, the ownership of the franchise must demonstrate that, despite the investment of adequate funds to run the franchise, substantial losses have been incurred, and the financial situation is unlikely to improve. Second, we have made an effort to determine whether there is any interest among potential local investors to purchase the team in order to keep it at its present location and possibly turn its financial situation around. Recently, the approval of the transfer of our New Orleans franchise to Salt Lake City was withheld for several months while negotiations with a prospective investor identified by the League were conducted, in an effort to retain the franchise for the City of New Orleans.

Prior to the *Oakland Raider* decision, we thought that our approach was clearly within the guidelines set down in the *San Francisco Seals* litigation, about which Mr. Stein, Vice President of the National Hockey League, testified last week. We were considering all aspects of the issue of where NBA franchises should be located, including recognition of the special relationships that sport franchisees enjoy with their home cities.

Last June, however, following the *Oakland Raider* decision, we were faced with the following situation:

1. Our San Diego team signed an unconditional lease with the Los Angeles Coliseum Commission, to play its future games at the Los Angeles arena operated by the Commission.

2. While the NBA was preparing to meet to consider how to deal with the proposed relocation of a franchise from San Diego to Los Angeles, lawsuits were either commenced or threatened by San Diego interests, contending that the franchise should not be moved by the NBA.

3. Counsel for the Los Angeles Coliseum Commission, who was also retained, *at Coliseum Commission expense*, to represent our San Diego franchise, advised the NBA and its teams that (a) under the precedent of the *Oakland Raider* case, a sports league could exercise *no control whatever over the relocation* of a franchise, (b) that the NBA and its teams would be sued by the Coliseum Commission if we did not simply approve the move of San Diego without further consideration, and (c) in light of the resolve of the Coliseum Commission to attract our San Diego team, we should expect to incur legal fees in excess of $10,000,000 (in addition to tens of millions of dollars of antitrust liability) if we did not approve the transfer.

Despite this gun-at-the-head approach made possible by the legal aberration of the *Oakland Raider* case, the NBA Board of Governors concluded that as a business matter and in all fairness to all parties concerned, it would not approve such a move without adequate consideration, and appointed a Committee to study all aspects of the proposed transfer, including the impact of the move on the City of San Diego. In addition, in light of the legal uncertainties and threats, it sought, among other things, a declara-

tory judgment from a federal court as to what rights the NBA possessed to consider a franchise relocation.

Nevertheless, two days later, the Los Angeles Coliseum Commission commenced an antitrust action against the NBA in Los Angeles federal court, seeking damages of $120,000,000, because the NBA had voted to study the application to move, rather than approve it without any consideration.

After the commencement of the litigation, both the federal court in San Diego and the federal court in Los Angeles concluded that the appropriate forum for the litigation was in San Diego, which is the city in which the NBA meeting had occurred and the NBA had sought its declaratory judgment. Last week, the Coliseum Commission, having lost the "home court" advantage, about which so much has been written and said in connection with the conduct of the trial in the *Oakland Raider* case, notified the NBA that it was withdrawing its lawsuit. [Hearings, pp. 377–379]

Statement of Hon. Lionel Wilson, Mayor, Oakland California

. . . In my remaining time, Senator, I primarily intend to discuss why it is fully appropriate to apply any legislation to the transfer of the Oakland Raiders to Los Angeles.

Senator, it is both fair and critical to apply this bill to the Oakland Raiders' attempt to abandon our community. Both bills currently before the committee are intended to restore the Raiders to Oakland, and I applaud Senator Specter's nationally televised remarks in which he very eloquently explained why it is so unjust to break up the 22-year marriage of the Raiders and Oakland.

Let me offer these further thoughts for your consideration, sir. First the Raiders' economic survival is not at all an issue. In 1979, the year before the Raiders announced their intention to move, they had the third highest gate receipts in the National Football League.

In their last two seasons in Oakland, their profit had averaged approximately $1.8 million. They had the highest ticket prices in the National Football League and still had thousands more requests for season tickets than they could accommodate.

Every game at the Oakland-Alameda County

Coliseum for 12 consecutive seasons was sold out. I am told that in 1982 if the Raiders were in Oakland, their profits would be substantially higher than in 1978 and 1979.

If this is so, if the Raiders could be so profitable in Oakland, one might ask why we in the Oakland community did not work with the league itself to try and keep the Raiders in Oakland.

The answer is simple and I think most unfortunate. Our coliseum representatives did try to work directly with the National Football League, and when Mr. Davis learned of this, he told our coliseum representatives that if they did so, he would break off all negotiations to stay in Oakland.

This was at a critical time in early 1980, and faced with this threat from Mr. Davis, we could not, of course, take steps to seek assistance from the National Football League itself or from Commissioner Rozelle. [Hearings, pp. 352–354]

Prepared Statement of John Ziegler, President of the National Hockey League, Submitted by Gilbert Stein

Mr. Chairman, we believe that we bring a different perspective to this legislation than some of the other professional sports leagues. We have just successfully completed the difficult and painful process of a franchise relocation. The Colorado Rockies were sold and moved to the Brendan Byrne Arena in East Rutherford, New Jersey and are now called the Jersey Devils. I can assure you that that relocation was very difficult, effected as it was, under the shadow of the *Oakland Raiders* lawsuit in Los Angeles. Fortunately, the move was successfully concluded without resorting to our legal system, always a costly process both financially and in terms of fan relations. . . .

The NHL Position on Relocation

The National Hockey League's rule on the movement of clubs is simple. "Thou Shalt not." Our Constitution provides simply that "No member shall transfer its club and franchise to a different city." If a club wishes to move, the Constitution must be amended and this requires a unanimous vote. Every club must be convinced that a move is absolutely necessary. The League feels that strongly about movements and their effect on our relations with the communities and fans that support NHL clubs.

One of the objectives of the league has been stability. We have always made every effort to preserve an existing franchise which may have experienced financial difficulties. The league has expended millions of dollars in assisting ailing franchises, with the hope that they would survive and that the fans in that area would not be disappointed and left without a club.

In most cases we have been successful. In four instances, however, circumstances have required that NHL clubs be permitted to move from one city to another. All have occurred since 1976. In each case the moves involved new franchises that were having financial problems, not established clubs.

The Oakland Seals moved to Cleveland in 1976. That club was subsequently merged with the Minnesota North Stars. The Kansas City Barons moved to Denver in the same year and became the Colorado Rockies. As I indicated, that club moved this year to New Jersey. And, the Atlanta Flames moved to Calgary, Alberta in 1980.

I can assure you that in each instance a great deal of time and money was spent in order to avoid shifts to other cities. Every attempt was made to keep a club in its original location. In each instance, moves were permitted only because the club was losing substantial amounts of money, in some cases so much that there was a fear that personnel salary requirements might not be met. I can also assure you, that no club would be permitted to move — and it would take a unanimous vote to authorize relocation — were it being supported by fans in its city and financially viable. . . .

Revenue Sharing

The National Hockey League believes that in today's economic climate it is essential for a league's survival that its members have the freedom to agree to share common revenue sources.

In the NHL gate receipts are not shared by the member clubs, however, revenue from television broadcasting is. In addition, our member clubs and the NHL Players' Association are joint venturers in all international competition, and, as such, shared equally in the proceeds of such events. Without these revenue sources, and the freedom to share additional like revenue sources, the viability of a number of our member clubs would be in jeopardy. We accordingly support the concept of continuing to permit revenue sharing.

The NHL supports the right of each league to make its own determination freely regarding revenue sharing without the ghost of antitrust litigation and damages in the background. [Hearings, pp. 255, 256, 260]

Statement of Howard Cosell, Esq., Senior Producer, ABC Sports

... I should like to review very briefly, even as Senator Biden touched upon the history of franchise removals in this country.

The genesis is obvious. It is lodged in baseball. The touchstone point, the departure of the most profitable team for the 13 prior years in all of baseball, the Brooklyn Dodgers to Los Angeles. The reason for the departure, the acquisition for free of 295 acres in an area known as Chavez Ravine with the attendant oil rights thereunder. Chavez Ravine, choice acreage, closer to the Bonaventure Hotel in downtown Los Angeles than Time Square to the start of Central Park in New York, which is a matter of 17 blocks.

That having happened, there came the departure, with young people using money borrowed from Illinois banks, buying the Milwaukee Braves, and remember Walter O'Malley said I have to move to Los Angeles to compete with Milwaukee. Milwaukee went to advantage to compete with Los Angeles so they could get a better television contract and, subsequently, there was a move of musical chairs of franchises being played in baseball where owners could act free, exempt from the antitrust laws based on Mr. Justice Holmes' historic decision in 1922 that baseball was in fact intrastate rather than interstate commerce, and with Congress having failed to revoke that exemption, baseball could act, asserted by Senator Biden, at whim and caprice.

The final franchise removal in baseball was when Mr. Short took the Washington Senators to the great metropolis of Arlington, Tex., and since then there has not been a single baseball franchise removal.

It turned then to football, and if one reviews my testimony in 1972 when I supported Senator Cook's Federal Sports Acts, I noted that the prepossessing problem then was the impending departure in football of the then New York Football Giants with an unparalleled, or close to it,

profit in football. Never a season ticket for sale in Yankee Stadium. Perhaps the greatest strong safety in my lifetime in sports sits behind me. He remembers Yankee Stadium. He wore No. 40 out of the University of Colorado for the Miami Dolphins, the great unbeaten team; executed four interceptions in one game against the mighty, and Dick knows what the Giants meant to New York. Tickets went by way of inheritance only. The Giants, at the same time, in defiance of the free enterprise system in this country, were getting, based upon the merger exemption and the merger, $10 million in payments for "territorial rights." Those were the rights to New York, not East Rutherford, N.J.

That, by my precepts, was the clear intent of that agreement at the time of the merger with its last many exemptions by way of rider from the antitrust laws.

Subsequent to that, there came the Los Angeles removal to Anaheim.

Now, I know something about the history of Baltimore. . . .

But the National Football League's history in that city, sir, is another matter, and I look directly at you, Senator Heflin. It is another matter for this reason. First, the late Carroll Rosenbloom traded that franchise in a tax free exchange and gave the Baltimore Colts to Mr. Irsay, who then owned Los Angeles, the Colts in exchange.

Second, after the Rosenbloom removal to Anaheim, there developed a whole new tactic. First, the mere threat of removal, enough to bring a city to its knees. Examples: Baltimore. Irsay went to the great city of Jacksonville. 50,000 people stormed that stadium, screaming we want the Colts. Mr. Irsay said, and we showed it on national television on August 22, on ABC Sports Beat, now this will show the people of Baltimore they got to get off their duffs and do this kind of thing or else.

So they could have been the Jacksonville Colts. But 2 weeks later, he was in Memphis, and they could have been the Memphis Colts, and then 2 weeks later he was in Los Angeles where he went prospecting around, and they could have been the Los Angeles Colts. A study of the unbiased and objective sports reporting in Los Angeles at that time, because they would take anything they could get, any team — they had a story, 12 reasons was the headline why they should be the Los Angeles Colts.

Now, that was a beginning. There was another situation, Buffalo, N. Y. By my precepts, one of the major cities of this country. First, the taxpayers of Erie County renovated old War Memorial Stadium, at $1.5 million. Then Buffalo, in the very vogue of Mayor Schaefer's delivery before all of you, agreed to build and contracted for a $90 million all purpose stadium. One of the finest, most estimable gentlemen I know, very interested in thoroughbred racing, with a lovely wife, Ralph Wilson and Jane Wilson, said, no, I want my own football stadium. The Erie County taxpayers bought it, $14 million for Rich Stadium, which is a great football stadium, where I will be tonight, and where the Bills might beat the Vikings. Total cost to the taxpayers $1.5 million for the renovation of War Memorial, $90 million in potential damages for the contracts to build the dome, which was never built, and finally, $41 million for Rich Stadium. The mere threat of removal, because Ralph had said if I don't get my stadium, I have got to leave Buffalo.

Next case, the Minnesota Vikings. Tired of playing in the gloom and snow and darkness at Metropolitan Stadium, said, hey, we need a new dome built in the very heart of Minneapolis. Now, some might figure in the priorities and exigencies of our civilization today that there are more essential priorities in the governess of a great municipality, the essential services lodged in fire, police, energy, schools, housing, job opportunities. But, no, the enabling legislation, as the headlines read — it is dome time or doom time. The enabling legislation was passed and now there is the Metro Dome and indeed the Vikings beat the Buccaneers in the opening. And there are also in that dome stadium more than 100 luxury loges providing $3 million plus, nondividable with the visiting team, to go to the Minnesota Vikings, even as the Giants got when they went to New Jersey, not only the 10 million but nearly 70 luxury loges now providing $2 million a year, nondividable with the visiting team.

Now, let me show you how it actually works. I got a call, I was on assignment one day in Los Angeles, and I got a call at the Beverly Wilshire Hotel from one of the most brilliant men I know, the late Carroll Rosenbloom, extraordinary businessman. And he asked me to come over to his home in Belagio Drive in the Bel Air section of greater Los Angeles. I went with my wife, and we sat at poolside with Carroll as he talked in those carefully muted measured tones wearing his great suede slippers, no socks. It was Hollywood. The manicured gabardine slacks, the proper suede belt, the carefully tailored suede sport shirt, the silk ascot to envelop the otherwise open neck. And he tried me on for media size, and he said, Howard, what would be your on-air position if I moved the Rams to Anaheim? I said my position has never wavered; it has been the same before the Senate Commerce Committee, the House Select Committee, the Rodino Committee. I believe that franchise removal should be countenanced, apart from abridgement of the lease or another extraordinary matter, to the detriment of the tenant, should be predicated only upon the ability to show continuity of economic distress.

But, Howard, O'Malley did it, Mara did it. I can have the best of both worlds. I can have the land, indeed, options at a marvelous price for 95 acres, duly exercised, a subsequent deal with Gannett Realty in Boston, and more than 110 luxury loges producing into the area of $2½ million a year.

I said, Carroll, this just is not right. You asked me my position; you know it. You know where I stand.

But, Howard, it is legal; is it not?

Yes; it is legal, because Los Angeles would take whatever they could get. Los Angeles could not do the simple thing, go into a court of equity. As you know, courts of equity were established initially because there was no adequate remedy as to common law. Adequate remedy here for Los Angeles would be to go into a court of equity, seek an injunction, estop them from moving. They could not prove financial distress. Quite the converse.

But Los Angeles had filthy hands. They had taken the Rams from Cleveland, the Dodgers from Brooklyn, the Lakers from Minneapolis. So they had to take another tack, steal another team, and the whole history of franchise removal from baseball to football is the unseemly result it produces politically. That does not do other than stigmatize our politicians and our whole political process. It pits State against State, city against city, Senator against Senator.

Look back to the late Senator Russell and Senator Proxmire when Milwaukee moved to Atlanta. It was beneath, in my opinion, the dignity of the body.

So I agree essentially with Senator Biden. I am not willing, and this has nothing to do with my love of Monday Night football — we just got a record opening game share in our new 13-year history last Monday night, and I love that damn game and I love that league.

But that has got nothing to do with my feelings, my background, and my knowledge and my experience about such matters as the judicial process, the question of constitutional law involved in Senator DeConcini's bill. Other questions that relate in the future to revenue sharing which, and if one read a brilliant column by David Israel, who was once a reporter for the Washington Star who now writes cityside for the Los Angeles Herald Examiner, and his spoken feelings about the very matter that Senator Specter does not want to take up now, which I think is understandable. I am not prepared to leave this whole matter to the whim and caprice of an ownership that has in fact contributed, along with baseball, to the very problems that now exist.

Basically that is my position. I support Senator Specter's bill. I believe in those standards and guidelines and yardsticks. . . .

Senator Heflin. You mentioned potential of the provisions in the DeConcini bill relating to revenue sharing and that that poses a threat where you could have a monopolistic TV display of games. There has been raised the issue of pay television, that that poses a threat to the players, which I am not sure that I fully understand, assuming that they have the right to negotiate as revenues increase.

But would you elaborate on the dangers of pay television as you see it to the football game — to professional football?

Mr. Cosell. Only in terms of the antitrust laws and the past history of the motion picture industry. With regard to the players, that is a separate issue. The players will undoubtedly seek a return, if it goes to pay television, a part of that. Larry Fleisher has already testified to that before the Congress. He is the representative of the NBA players and, of course, baseball is already in a lawsuit with the players who are seeking a percentage of television revenues.

So that is a separate issue and that is a matter to be resolved through bargaining or in the courts of law.

My concern was a different one. Six years hence, in theory, the National Football League, and this relates to antitrust, could establish its own network. It is the sport for our time, for whatever reason. The very ratings share we got last Monday, in the midst of all of this turmoil, problems like the present one you are considering, the drug abuse problem, all of these things spilling out and over, the labor management problems, still it has not canceled the appetite for the public for this remarkable sport one bit. Six years hence, in my opinion, they would be the totally dominant sport in this country and they owe that, a lot of that, to the leadership of the commissioner, which has been utterly brilliant in his year in/year out leadership of this league.

Now, 6 years hence, what if they say, hey, we have got antitrust exemption, let us form our own network. We will bring in the other sports. They can be part of it but we will be the dominant one and they will become the producers, exhibitors and distributors in the whole new technology that may be existent 6 years hence, and based upon the temporary nature of cable, in whatever form, they would dominate the industry. That is what happened in the motion picture industry until the Federal court declared it a monopoly, in restraint of trade, and broke it up in 1949.

Senator Biden. Would you elaborate on the condition of the motion picture industry prior, if you can? I am not familiar with that.

Mr. Cosell. Well, the great motion picture companies got together. There were only a handful of them and they utterly controlled production, exhibition, and distribution. An independent could not get anywhere. Today it is different. Independents are producing some of the greatest movies we have.

Senator Heflin. How does that differ from the present day free network television?

Mr. Cosell. If you are suggesting, sir, that the three networks have a monopoly, the answer is yes. But we did not create that and we are in competition every single day. That is why rights acquisition costs are so totally , in my opinion, out of line. Because if we do not buy in, NBC might, CSB might, and indeed the very history of my company, sir, bespeaks of the fact — because we were once the third network until our president of news and sports took over sports and we could buy our way in. And then with his brilliance and leadership, we could become No. 1 in that area of the industry, and he is responsible for that.

Senator Heflin. Now, the Federal Communications Commission, which has the responsibility of licensing — would not their laws have to be changed before that fear would come into existence?

Mr. Cosell. With regard to cable?

Senator Heflin. With regard to cable TV and the football league being able to produce and to send out their own television system.

Mr. Cosell. I am not qualified to answer that, sir. [Hearings, pp. 232, 233–235, 242–243]

Prepared Statement of David Cunningham

I am David Cunnigham, Councilman of the City of Los Angeles since 1973. I am Chairman of the Grants, Housing and Community Development Committee, and I am on the Board of Directors of the National League of Cities. I have come before you today representing the three million people of Los Angeles and to delineate the City of Los Angeles' opposition to S.2764 and S. 2821.

The Retroactive Feature of the NFL Proposals

As an elected official I am all too familiar with the pressure that a special interest group can bring to bear on behalf of selfish legislation which is always grandly styled as being in the public interest. I am aware of no better recent illustration than the bills being considered here today. The "Major League Sports Community Protection Act" is a sham which in reality would offer no protection to communities but would in fact remove the last recourse municipalities would have against the already formidable power of Commissioner Rozelle.

Before I turn to the real motives behind the NFL's awesome lobbying campaign, I must stress that the most offensive portions of the bills which have been introduced are the provisions for retroactive effect. As members of the Committee on the Judiciary, you are naturally aware that a delicate balance exists between the legislative and judicial branches. It would be an unwarranted intrusion on the province of the courts for Congress to change the rules after the game has been played. In recent years, various losers in judicial antitrust battles have lined up outside your doors to plead for after-the-fact relief, I am thinking of soft drink bottlers, corrugated container manufacturers, and newspaper publishers,

among many others. It is bad public policy to grant such exemptions, and it only guarantees that the growing trickle of losers seeking congressional bail-outs will turn into a veritable flood.

I cannot help wondering what the public thinks when the NFL loses a long, highly publicized court battle, and far from accepting its loss in good grace, immediately unleashes a high pressure, big bucks lobbying effort to nullify its loss. For Congress to respond favorably to this campaign would surely reinforce the prevailing view that there is one type of justice for the average citizen and another for fat-cat special interests.

If a retroactivity provision were included in any legislation, it would simply guarantee another protracted court battle. There are serious questions as to the constitutionality of a bill which applies to a case which has already been tried and is pending on appeal. I can assure you that the Los Angeles Coliseum and the Raiders would vigorously contest the legality of any retroactive legislation, with the result that the final home of the Raiders would remain uncertain for years to come. . . .

For over three decades the people of Los Angeles strongly supported NFL football by attending Rams games in the Los Angeles Coliseum. Moreover, the Coliseum served as the home of the NFL's Pro Bowl game for 21 consecutive years and hosted two Super Bowl games, including the inaugural contest in 1967. Hardly a stadium "not fit" for pro football, as Commissioner Rozelle has claimed on a few occasions.

In point of fact, the Coliseum provided millions of dollars worth of improvements during the Rams' tenancy. However, when Carroll Rosenbloom acquired the Rams in 1972 by means of a tax-free exchange of his ownership in the Colts, it quickly became apparent that nothing would satisfy the new owner of the team. In material discovered during the recent Coliseum-NFL litigation we found that Mr. Rosenbloom was entertaining thoughts of moving the Rams out of Los Angeles as early as six months after he acquired title to the team. Some of these plans included land deals very similar to the one he ultimately pulled off for 95 acres of public property in Anaheim when he moved the Rams.

Throughout this entire period, the Coliseum Commission and the City of Los Angeles never received any assistance from Mr. Rozelle or the

NFL in its dealings with the ownership of the Rams. It is ironic that Mr. Rozelle tells this Committee of his great mediator role in helping the Colts in Baltimore, the Dolphins in Miami and the Vikings in Minnesota come to agreements with their communities. We in Los Angeles would like to know where Mr. Rozelle was when Rosenbloom put the Rams on the auction block in complete disregard for the welfare of the South-Central Los Angeles community. Mr. Rozelle stood idly by while Rosenbloom deserted a community that had supported his franchise over decades for a deal that conservatively was worth over 25 million dollars personally to Mr. Rosenbloom. Is it coincidental that Rosenbloom was instrumental in electing Rozelle to the Commissioner's job?

The NFL argument that the Rams move from Los Angeles to Anaheim, California is analogous to other moves of teams to outlying suburbs such as Pontiac, Michigan; Orchard Park, New York; and Irving, Texas is a farce. In 1973, in a study conducted by the Stanford Research Institute *on behalf of the National Football League* surveying areas for possible expansion, SRI identified Anaheim as the number one area in the country for an expansion team, even with the Rams located in Los Angeles. Attached to the written text of my testimony is a copy of the conclusion of that study. It is worth noting that while Anaheim is listed as the top area for a new team, nowhere does one find a listing for the communities of Pontiac, Orchard, Irving, East Rutherford, New Jersey, where the Giants now play or Foxboro, Massachusetts, the relatively new home of the Patriots. Quite simply, the move of the Rams to Anaheim was to an area that the NFL knew was separate and distinct from Los Angeles — an area with a completely separate financial, residential and business base. . . .

The true purpose of S.2784 is to carry on a personal vendetta of Pete Rozelle. This Committee should know that on the eve of trial of the Raiders' antitrust action, the NFL held a meeting in Phoenix. The owners voted 17–10 to approve the Judge's settlement proposal, which would permit Al Davis to own an expansion team in Los Angeles, while leaving the Raiders team in Oakland. The Los Angeles Coliseum and Davis had already agreed to such a proposal. Pete Rozelle literally threw a tantrum, threatening to resign if the owners did not reverse their vote. Since Rozelle

was putting the finishing touches on a 2 billion dollar television contract, the owners hastily acquiesced and staged a phony 27–0 vote against settlement.

Anyone who is close to the NFL knows that Mr. Rozelle is obsessed with waging a personal war against Al Davis, a man who has been a thorn in Rozelle's side since he was Commissioner of the rival American Football League in the mid-1960s. Does anyone doubt that Rozelle would have permitted the Raiders to move if someone else owned the franchise? Why would Rozelle reject a settlement that left the Raiders in Oakland, if not because of hatred for Davis?

In fact, if the expressions of concern for fan loyalty and community concern were sincere, Commissioner Rozelle would be busy arranging for an expansion team for Oakland. He cannot do that, of course, because he needs two expansion carrots to dangle before you in his crusade to force Al Davis back to Oakland. . . .

In conclusion I urge you to look through the lofty motives Mr. Rozelle ascribes to himself to see this legislation for what it is — an attempt to enact one man's personal grudge into the law of the land. [Hearings, pp. 264–267, 269]

Statement of a Panel Consisting of Edward R. Garvey, Executive Director, National Football League Players Association, and Gene Upshaw, President, National Football League Players Association, Accompanied by Benjamin L. Zelenko, Counsel.

Mr. GARVEY. I guess it is fair to say that we would not envy a Senator from the States that are considering expansion, or at least hoping to have an expansion NFL team in their particular States. There is enormous pressure on them to try to accommodate the NFL so that the NFL will indeed expand.

But in a real sense, I think what the NFL is saying to the Congress is what each team says to its city: "Unless you do certain things, we will move or we will do something else." For example, I see that the mayor of San Francisco will testify, and she endorsed the bill that Congressman Stark had introduced. And at the same time, the 49'ers and the San Francisco Giants are indicating that the city of San Francisco must build a domed stadium.

Really, what happens in that kind of situation is

that the city feels the enormous pressure of the possibility of losing a team unless it complies with what the NFL wants. And it seems to us that the question really is — and the only person who has focused on it thus far is yourself in the bill that you introduced — and that is a bill that will actually do what the NFL says it wants, and that is to protect the communities?

You have to set standards, and if you do not set standards, all you have to go on is what Pete Rozelle essentially said this morning; that is, "Trust us." Well, if we go back to the 1966 merger hearings, he said that the teams would stay in the same stadium locations in the same cities that they were in at the time of the merger. They also said they wanted nothing more than the exemption for the merger itself.

Yet, when we brought the *Mackey* case, we heard from Covington and Burling in court that when Congress exempted the merger, surely it must have exempted the Rozelle rule and other player restrictions.

So, I think a carefully drawn bill that would protect the cities is what everyone here is looking for. . . .

So, the real problem here is how do you protect the city? As far as the revenue sharing is concerned, there seems to be an underlying assumption that revenue sharing is good. And yet I do not know anyone who has put forward anything other than to say, "We are enormously successful, so trust us again with our pooling exemption."

We suggested to the House Committee on the Judiciary that it was time to take a long, hard look at revenue sharing, because it has hurt the player market pool and we do not see that it has helped competition. More importantly, it has given the NFL enormous power to make sure that other leagues could not form, and it allows them to decide when and where to expand.

There should be other teams in Los Angeles, Chicago, Philadelphia, and New York, but the NFL is able to stop that expansion simply because they have been given the opportunity and the power to share all their revenues equally. . . .

We also hear — and I am sure that Gene Upshaw will speak to this — that somehow or other the Commissioner of the National Football League is now a labor expert and they are very concerned to make sure that this bill does not in any way impact adversely on the players.

Anyone who looks at the antitrust laws and the history of sports litigation could not reach that conclusion, and they know that that is not the conclusion that they want to reach. If the Congress declares that this is a joint venture, then by really force of law, they will be able to successfully argue their way out of section 1 of the Sherman Act. They tried it in the *Los Angeles Coliseum* case. They have tried it every time they have had a case come before a court — also in the *Yazoo Smith* case, as Mr. Zelenko points out, here in Washington.

The courts have said, "Follow a rule of reason; come up with something less restrictive; negotiate with the union, and you have no problems." And, indeed, that is what has happened. Yet, if this bill passes, they know perfectly well that then they have an incentive not to reach agreement with the union, but to continue what they have been trying to do for years, and that is not to have a union at all.

And if you pass this legislation, essentially declaring them a joint venture, it is our concern that no player would ever be able to resort to the courts again to prevent them from unreasonable restrictions on movement, the draft, and the like. [Hearings, pp. 87, 88–89]

Prepared Statement of Edward Garvey

Organized professional team sports is big business today. Although individual NFL clubs do not qualify as members of the Fortune "500", the NFL as an aggregate — which the League likes to represent itself as — may well qualify in that exclusive grouping. In 1980, total gross revenues are estimated in excess of 400 million dollars. The new 5 year NFL network TV package of *2.1 billion dollars* guarantees each team an average of 14 million dollars each year. That means that all teams will collect almost 400 million dollars from network TV alone in 1982. If we were to lump together all of the major sports leagues including the NFL, Major League Baseball, the NBA, the NHL, the MISL, amd the NASL, the professional teams sports industry clearly ranks among the major businesses in America today. And with anticipated expansion of cable and subscription television revenues, sports business will be a lot bigger in the 1980s and '90s. Moreover, the policies and practices of these businesses are highly visible and of immediate interest and concern to millions of Americans who support professional sports, and to the communities in which they operate.

Not only is sports big business, it has always enjoyed and used monopoly powers to control player wages and mobility. The Sports Broadcasting Act of 1961 gave to the National Football League enormous powers to control or at least significantly influence selection of announcers and control over what they say on the air. The merger exemption legislation of 1966 confirmed "special status" onto the NFL. These acts of Congress conferred tremendous economic power to sports leagues in dealing with broadcast networks and stations, municipal governments, stadium authorities and athlete-employees. Indeed, the financial and political leverage these acts conveyed is virtually unparalleled in American history. With these powers, sports cartels engage in anticompetitive restraints to restrict a player's choice of employer and job mobility throughout his career; they limit expansion and/or sale of franchises; they establish exclusive territories and curtail off-field competition. And yet, despite its size and government granted powers, information about the economics of professional sports is extremely limited. We probably know more about the Soviet economy than we do about the NFL's finances. Data on the profitability of professional sports teams historically has been as secretly guarded as key national security files. Only when clubs allege losses or find it convenient in court or administrative proceedings, are any figures furnished. But even then, the NFL normally provides only meaningless averages. [Hearings, pp. 94–95]

Statement of Donald M. Fehr, General Counsel, Major League Baseball Players Association

. . . We think the issues raised in the bills before the committee are important and deserve very serious consideration.

In baseball, unfortunately, we have had long experience with what it means to give antitrust immunities to the people who own professional sports franchises. Baseball has had one on an unrestricted basis since the Federal baseball case in 1922.

What that has done is to allow baseball owners to operate that industry as an absolute cartel. It is the only industry in the country that we know of that is both free from antitrust restriction and also free from any form of Government regulation.

What does a cartel do? Well, in the sports industry, be it baseball, or others, baseball is a good example, it does, in essence, three things, and possibly a fourth. It divides the geographic market to prevent competition there. It divides the broadcast market to prevent competition there. It divides the player market to prevent competition there, and in the case of baseball, by virtue of interlocking agreements with all major league and minor league teams, it effectively controls access to the industry, because it controls all stadiums, and substantially all cities in the country.

Well, who is that benefiting? In our view, it has benefited only baseball owners. . . .

Finally, just a couple of words about revenue-sharing, and I will conclude.

We oppose the granting to professional sports leagues carte blanche authority to share revenues in any manner that they determine, regardless of the anticompetitive purpose or effect, that any particular revenue-sharing proposal might have.

It is important to remember that the NFL and the other people supporting this bill do not say that a given revenue-sharing formula ought to be immunized. What they say is any revenue-sharing formula adopted for any purpose ought to be immunized. We do not think so.

If the revenue-sharing plan cannot meet the standard of reasonableness, under the antitrust laws, it ought not to be allowed to stand.

Finally, Mr. Chairman, it has been suggested that athletes really have no interest in the revenue-sharing bill, and we would take strong issue with that. Because, contrary to the assertions made in support of S.2874, in our view, that bill would have significant anticompetitive effects on players, and that can be illustrated by a very simple example.

When a player has to sell his services, the more unique and talented those services are, theoretically the more valuable they are to someone wishing to employ him. The NFL owners could pass a revenue-sharing measure tomorrow, which provided that all revenues, from whatever source, would be shared equally, which is entirely proper under the DeConcini bill. At that point there would be absolutely no incentive for any professional sports team to hire an athlete, because they will share the benefits of his labors to the same percentage, one twenty-eighth, whether he plays in Los Angeles or Buffalo, or Washington, or where he does.

In other words, absolute revenue-sharing destroys the athlete's ability to argue to his team that he can, by playing there, be financially beneficial for that team. That would be a terrible anticompetitive effect on the players. [Hearings. pp. 381, 384]

Statement of Louis B. Schwartz, Professor of Law, University of Pennsylvania Law School

. . . Now, the rest of my presentation is divided into a set of general principles and a set of specific critiques of the two bills that are under consideration.

General principle No. 1 would be that you do not send the fox to guard the chicken coop. If there are municipalities and players and fans to be protected, you do not ask the owners of the teams to do that protecting. The conflict of interests is obvious. Principle No. 1 is directly derived from centuries of antitrust tradition. Going all the way back to Adam Smith in the 18th century and the 17th century statute of monopolies, it has always been recognized, as it was in the preambles of that 17th-century statute, that cartels and monopolies put themselves forward as protectors of the public interests. Adam Smith says that you cannot rely on gentlemen of the same profession getting together and protecting the public interest. They get together secretly for reasons that would animate all of us. They are not villains, but they get together to promote their interests. So I repeat the first principle is do not send the fox to guard the chicken coop.

Second, do not proceed on the theory that the league is an entity. We have heard a great deal of that in litigation and before this committee at some point. It is not an entity. A business entity recognized as such under the antitrust laws is an organization like a corporation or partnership which shares profits, which shares the liabilities, sustains the losses, has a single economic policy. That is simply not the situation here. These are separate enterprises that compete for personnel, for finances, for remunerative concession, contracts, and the like. They do not have a common front vis-à-vis the television networks. But the proper conception for such an arrangement is that of a joint venture or joint enterprise. That means these people are, of course, competitors but, for certain reasons, we are willing to allow them to collaborate in a limited area. The obvious limited area for a professional sports league is rules of play and scheduling. Now, there may be other things, but I am giving an illustration of what is meant by the proper definition of the scope of a joint enterprise and its distinction from a single business entity. [Hearings, pp. 410, 411]

Statement of Colin P. Flaherty, Chairman of the Stadium Committee, San Diego, California

. . . The testimony given so far has cited the large investment that cities have in their stadiums as one reason for this legislation. However there has been no testimony on the details of these investments. Our research on the nature of these investments and the different results that different cities have had protecting their investments have a direct bearing on the legislation being considered here today. We feel before the Congress considers how to protect local governments from the whims of a sports entrepreneur, you should first consider what they are doing to protect themselves. Anti-trust immunity, revenue sharing, and public investment in stadiums and other issues make this a very complex issue. Our testimony will be limited to the public investment in sports facilities.

The *first-thing* we found out is that in the Alice in Wonderland world of sports economics, many things are not always what they appear to be. For example, ask a public stadium operator what the financial condition of his stadium is and he may give you a figure and call it a surplus. Rarely does this figure include the annual payments on a bond debt. Thus a stadium with a so called surplus may end up making the city 1-2 million dollars poorer. A professional sports team, on the other hand, is given to making public statements about how much money they are losing. These "losses" are often the result of unusual tax allowances that no other industry in the world enjoys. An owner with millions of dollars of so called losses may have a million more dollars at the end of a season than at the beginning.

Thus the people that are making money claim they are losing it and the people who are losing money claim they are making it.

The *second* thing we found is what we couldn't

find out. Few of the nation's publicly operated stadiums keep adequate records of the use of their stadium. Very few of the stadium operators knew how many days a year their stadium was used, what percentage of the seats are filled or what other cities are doing with their stadiums.

Every stadium has unique agreements with its tenants governing revenue from concessions, rent, parking, etc. When the House Select Committee on Professional Sports made a request to see the lease revenue arrangements they received replies that were cryptic and even hostile. According to Parade magazine Arlington stadium claimed they were secret and accused the Committee of trying to destroy professional sports.

Our luck was not much better. A typical answer was the information we requested would take days to gather and they didn't have the time. . . .

The Total Costs of a Stadium

Since the costs to local governments is a major reason for this legislation we should take a closer look at the total costs of owning and operating a stadium. As the mayors testified last month the cities do have a large amount of money tied up in their stadiums. But the mayors were being uncharacteristically modest. The cost to taxpayers of operating a major stadium is much larger than they said. As you know the direct cost to local governments is the operating expense as well as the annual payment on the bond debt. At least 60-70% of the stadiums receive public subsidies to help it meet its bond debt.

The mayors ignored the indirect but very real costs that a stadium can inflict. I'll list a few:

1. Forgone use of the land.
2. Public improvements adjacent to a stadium such as streets lights, public utilities, etc.
3. Unusual tax breaks. Virtually all of the luxury skyboxes and many of the season tickets in a stadium are corporate owned and written off as a business expense for tax purposes.

Another unusual tax break that increases the public's cost for the operation of the stadium is a depreciation allowance for players wages. There is no other business in the world where wages are depreciated for tax purposes. . . .

4. Time is another expense. Because of its high visibility, local public officials spend a lot of time discussing stadium affairs. How much is the time

of all those public officials worth? Honest men disagree on that.

There are many major costs of a stadium that are indirect and never show up on a balance sheet.

But what about benefits? Previous witnesses have extolled the benefits to a community of a major league stadium and it's true there are many. Any Chamber of Commerce is more than willing to recite their *estimates* of the gross benefits that a professional team brings. But this too deserves a closer look.

It has *never*, I repeat *never*, been shown that the total benefits outweigh the total costs. *Never.* Not only are the net benefits overestimated, the ones receiving the benefits are not the ones bearing the cost.

Most cities have paid a very high price to subsidize their stadiums.

Virtually all of the more than 50 stadiums built in the last twenty years were supposed to make money for local governments. Instead stadiums are a burden to most cities. Some cities deserve special mention.

New York, for example. The City of New York bought Yankee Stadium and refurbished it. It cost $95.6 million, 4 times the original estimate. When it came time to collect the rent, the City was surprised to find that *they had to pay the Yankees $10,000.* They had negotiated a lease that permitted them to take so many deductions that the city ended up *paying them to play.* With the money they spent to improve the stadium they could have bought several baseball teams.

In Buffalo, the Bills demanded that their home stadium be *expanded.* The City of Buffalo enlarged War Memorial Stadium. That wasn't good enough. The owner of the Bills said, "He had *no alternative* to moving," unless given a new and bigger stadium. So Buffalo built another stadium. "The city now pays off bonds on an abandoned stadium that it improved expressly for the Bills, while the County pays on bonds for new Rich Stadium." . . .

The Louisiana Superdome stood out as the textbook example of how not to build or operate a stadium. The stadium cost $163 million to build, 5 times the original estimate. When their stadium was completed their problems were only beginning. The concessions were poorly located, slow and losing money. A promoter had to deal with as many as 12 different people. It was overstaffed. Bills weren't being paid on time, accumulating thousands of dollars in late charges. Maintenance was shoddy. There was a costly legal battle because the structure was literally sinking in the soft Louisiana soil. Public management of the Superdome was an administrative nightmare that was costing the taxpayers of Louisiana $6 million in operating deficits and $10 million in bond payment a year. . . .

Recommendations

We believe that before federal legislation is appropriate local authorities should take several steps:

1. The cities have to become more accountable for the operations of their stadiums. Our Committee believes that the only way for a city to become free from the threat of franchise movement is to sell their stadiums, then the marketplace could decide how important professional sports are. Only then would people who use the stadium be forced to pay for it. Who would buy them? Maybe the professional sports teams would. Bill Veek sums up the benefits, "I believe I'm the only one in baseball who has operated both ways; in a civic stadium in Cleveland and my own parks in St. Louis and here (Chicago). I wouldn't want to go back to saying, 'Please, can I do something to a ballpark?' And remember, we're on the tax rolls. *We're a giver and not a taker.*"

Because local officials don't want to lose control of their stadiums, no matter what the price, it isn't realistic to expect them to sell them. The San Diego Sports arena has been operating in the black for the last ten years, yet even as late as last month a San Diego Councilwoman was quoted as saying she was displeased with the arrangement at the Arena because the city had lost control over it. That is a bad attitude.

2. An alternative to the cities selling their stadiums or putting them under private management would be to form an association of local governments that would bargain as a unit with the pro sports leagues. Clearly, the threat of a franchise moving has been a powerful negotiating tool that has helped the franchise owners achieve contracts with the cities that are very beneficial to the owners. But there is also a tremendous gap in negotiation skills that has contributed to the many

one sided settlements. Men like Al Davis, Gene Klein, George Steinbrenner are some of the shrewdest and most successful businessmen in the country. When they go one on one with bureaucrats in negotiating contests you don't need Howard Cosell to tell you that it is no contest.

A union of professional sports league cities with professional negotiators bargaining as a unit could be a very effective bargaining tool for the cities who feel intimidated by franchise threats. [Hearings, pp. 446–452]

1.30   Economics of Professional Sports

The four major teams sports — football, baseball, basketball, and hockey — gross combined revenues in excess of $1 billion per year. The National Football League is the standard bearer, at close to $600 million. Baseball follows at just over $300 million, and the NBA, NHL, and now the USFL trail substantially behind. The great bulk of the revenues come from two sources — the gate and broadcast contracts. The NFL's revenues, for example, jumped nearly $200 million the year the current contract with the three television networks took effect (see Section 1.33). By any accounting, the professional sports leagues spell "big business."

The sports leagues, however, cannot be compared to any of several industries, nor even to companies. For example, Gulf & Western owns the Madison Square Garden Corporation, which in turn owns the New York Knicks and Rangers. As a single company, albeit a diversified one, G & W's gross profit is at least three times the gross of the combined totals for the professional sports leagues.

In grasping some of the basic economics about professional sports, it is easy to be influenced by media talk of the high salaries paid to players, the quick profits earned in the sale of franchises, the large amounts of monies coming from television rights, and the high-style, big-bucks atmosphere that generally surrounds professional sports. It is true that some of the salaries are high and that profits can be substantial in comparison to capital investment, but we are talking for the most part about a relatively few individuals, be they players or owners, and we are singling out the success stories.

Even so, the monies are substantial and rising. Precise figures are often unavailable, particularly as to league and club gross and operating revenues. Except for the Green Bay Packers, almost all professional sports clubs are either partnerships, sole proprietorships, or closely held corporations, and as such do not have to divulge income figures. While economic and other relevant data are becoming more available, reflected in part by some of the charts and tables that follow, there is still a substantial amount of information to which the outsider does not have immediate access. Therefore, it is difficult to assess exactly the financial health of several sports. What is safe to assume is that the stakes are substantial and the personal opportunities for gain are enticing, at least for the fortunate few.

Sports are characterized as growth industries, and the figures over time seem to substantiate this. Whether it be attendance figures, the size of the television and radio audiences, the amounts in rights fees paid at both the national and local levels, or generally the interest in sports, surveys show overall, if fluctuating, growth. A survey on attendance at major sports events, contrasting total attendance in 1974 with 1965, noted an increase of 33 percent in total attendance figures across sports. When the four team sports were combined with horse, dog, and auto racing, plus boxing, attendance figures at all events climbed 106 million in 1965 to 273 million in 1974. (See U.S. Congress. House. Final Report of the Select Committee on Professional Sports. House Report No. 94–1786. Jan. 3, 1977. Appendix I–1, at p. 177.)

It is a fair extrapolation to suggest that the past ten years have witnessed similar growth patterns. What is less certain is where precisely the growth in attendance has occurred. The 1965 to 1974 comparisons showed professional hockey (up 325 percent) and professional basketball (up 249 percent) as experiencing the largest increases. It is extremely doubtful that these two sports have maintained that pace. Hockey, indeed, may have slipped, while basketball may have witnessed modest gains. We do know that Major League Baseball has continued to set attendance records and stands at close to 50 million per year in the 1980s. The National Football League reported total attendance of 13.6 million for 1981, based on far fewer games than baseball. Attendance at sports events, overall, remains high. For some sports, however, such as the NFL, there appears to be a maximum, and growth in dollars will come not so much from attendance as from the other great source — broadcasting.

In total, the estimated dollars per year spent by Americans on spectator sports has risen with the attendance figures and has done so markedly since 1960. Estimates put total dollar expenditures at $300 million in 1960, less than half the current gross of the NFL alone. By 1980, total gross was in the range of $2.25 billion, a sevenfold increase in that 20-year period. By contrast, the expenditure in 1935 (some $100 million), compared with the $300 million in 1960, reflected only a threefold increase in the prior 25-year span. Accounting for inflation of the dollar, particularly since 1960, the seven-versus-three ratio shrinks, but it is impressive nonetheless. (These figures are based on an analysis of J. Markham & P. Teplitz, *Baseball Economics and Public Policy* (Lexington, Mass.: Lexington Books, 1981), p. 60. The figures include dollars spent attending amateur events, as well as professional events.)

Whether it be in representing management or players, or simply being an interested student of professional sports, analyzing certain economic data is necessary to understand the overall dynamics and potential of sports leagues, clubs, and player opportunities. While the following sections present only partial data, they do serve to suggest that several major economic sources can be consulted for study. Section 1.31 discusses player salaries, which gain most of the media attention. Then representative data on sports leagues and clubs are presented in Section

1.32. Finally, some overall figures on both network and local television and radio sports revenues are presented in Section 1.33.

NOTES _____

1. Studies of the sports industries that examine economic data run the risk of quickly becoming outdated. Inflation and other fluctuations make past years' dollar amounts seem insignificant. Some analyses, however, have stood up well over time. The following are worth consulting:

(a) J. Markham and P. Teplitz, *Baseball Economics and Public Policy* (Lexington, Mass.: Lexington Books, 1981).

(b) R. Noll, ed., *Government and the Sports Business* (Washington, D.C.: Brookings Inst., 1974).

(c) Neale, "The Peculiar Economics of Professional Sports," *Quarterly Journal of Economics* (February 1964), pp. 1–14.

(d) Quirk, "An Economic Analysis of Team Movements in Professional Sports," 38 Law and Contemporary Problems 42 (1973).

(e) Davis and Quirk, "The Ownership and Valuation of Professional Sports Franchises," California Institute of Technology, Social Science Working Paper #79, April 1975.

(f) Scully, "Pay and Performance in Major League Baseball," *American Economic Review* (December 1974), pp. 915–30.

(g) J. Durso, *The All-American Dollar: The Big Business of Sports* (Boston: Houghton-Mifflin, 1971). See particularly his account of growth of sports after World War II (pp. 47–66).

(h) Blum, "Valuing Intangibles: What Are the Choices for Valuing Professional Sports Teams?" *Journal of Taxation* (November 1976), p. 286.

(i) El-Hodiri and Quirk, "An Economic Model of a Professional Sports League," 79 *Journal of Political Economy* (1971), p. 1302.

(j) Jones, "The Economics of the National Hockey League," *Canadian Journal of Economics* (1969), pp. 1–10.

1.31   Player Salaries

For players who reach the top, the financial rewards are outstanding. This obvious statement becomes less obvious, however, when we add that the top can be defined in any of several ways, with varying levels of rewards. Simply making a major league roster in any of the sports and lasting a few years is, in a very real sense, making it to the top. The competition is sufficiently intense these days, so that only the hardiest and best survive. Thus, becoming an average salaried major league player, staying in the league long enough to obtain vested pension rights, and setting aside some of those quick earnings for long-term investments are ideals realizable by a substantial number of players. While these numbers are increasing, the truth is that many talented athletes never quite make it. For them, the financial rewards are slim. They perhaps make a comfortable living, for a short time, but life-long security they do not have. Consequently, the figures presented in the following tables must be accompanied by certain realities. The gaudy numbers must be countered by knowledge that figures can deceive.

The average major league life of an athlete in any of the team sports is between 4 and 5 years. While some players last 10 years in a league and a handful make it to 15 or 20 (the percentages varying significantly with the sport), the great majority of players are around for a short time only. The money may be very good to outstanding for 2 or 3 years, but that is it.

Exhibit 1–2 reports the top salaried professional athletes in the four major team sports, as of early 1984. In most instances, these are estimated figures, both from the standpoint that the exact figures are not available and because players' contracts are often constructed with several contingencies attached, particularly as to payouts. It is one thing to earn in excess of $1 million per year in up-front money. It is another to have much of the contract deferred or the salary earned only by meeting complicated performance requirements. It is difficult, therefore, to be precise as to the true worth of an athlete's contract, and one should always realize that some of the reported figures are "soft" as to an athlete's net worth.

Even with these reservations, one can see from Exhibit 1–2 that the top athletes do exceedingly well. For example, the figures for the National Hockey League, while they pale beside those of the other sports, particularly baseball and

Exhibit 1-2   Highest Salaried Players: Team Sports, 1984-1985

Major League Baseball

1. Mike Schmidt, third baseman, Philadelphia Phillies, $2,130,000
2. Jim Rice, outfielder, Boston Red Sox, $2,090,000
3. Ozzie Smith, shortstop, St. Louis Cardinals, $2,000,000
4. George Foster, outfielder, New York Mets, $1,950,000
5. Dave Winfield, outfielder, New York Yankees, $1,745,000
6. Gary Carter, catcher, New York Mets, $1,728,000
7. Dale Murphy, outfielder, Atlanta Braves, $1,600,000
8. Bob Horner, third baseman, Atlanta Braves, $1,500,000
9. Ricky Henderson, outfielder, New York Yankees, $1,470,000
10. Eddie Murray, first baseman, Baltimore Orioles, $1,380,000

Football (NFL and USFL)

1. Herschel Walker, running back, New Jersey Generals, $1,500,000
2. Doug Flutie, quarterback, New Jersey Generals, $1,450,000
3. Steve Young, quarterback, Los Angeles Express, $1,250,000
4. Warren Moon, quarterback, Houston Oilers, $1,100,000
5. John Elway, quarterback, Denver Broncos, $1,000,000
6. Joe Montana, quarterback, San Francisco 49ers, $860,000
7. Lynn Dickey, quarterback, Green Bay Packers, $850,000
8. James Lofton, wide receiver, Green Bay Packers, $845,000
9. Three tied at $800,000 (Jim Kelly, Houston Gamblers; Brian Sipe, Jacksonville Bulls; Billy Sims, Detroit Lions)

National Basketball Association

1. Larry Bird, forward, Boston Celtics, $1,800,000
2. Moses Malone, center, Philadelphia 76ers, $1,600,000
3. Jack Sikma, center, Seattle Sonics, $1,600,000
4. Kareem Abdul Jabbar, center, Los Angeles Lakers, $1,500,000
5. Julius Erving, forward, Philadelphia 76ers, $1,250,000
6. Ralph Sampson, forward, Houston Rockets, $1,200,000
7. Otis Birdsong, guard, New Jersey Nets, $1,075,000
8. Seven tied at $1,000,000 (Earvin Johnson, Los Angeles Lakers; Kevin McHale, Boston Celtics; Jim Paxon, Portland Trail Blazers; Mychal Thompson, Portland Trail Blazers; Wayne Rollins, Atlantic Hawks; Marques Johnson, Los Angeles Clipper; Isiah Thomas, Detroit Pistons)

National Hockey League

1. Wayne Gretzky, forward, Edmonton Oilers, $825,000
2. Mike Bossy, forward, New York Islanders, $610,000
3. Marcel Dionne, forward, Los Angeles Kings, $475,000
4. Dave Taylor, forward, Los Angeles Kings, $450,000
5. Bryan Trottier, forward, New York Islanders, $450,000
6. Denis Potvin, defenseman, New York Islanders, $425,000
7. Mike Liut, goalie, St. Louis Blues, $400,000
8. Barry Beck, defenseman, New York Rangers, $385,000
9. Gil Perreault, forward, Buffalo Sabres, $375,000
10. Kent Nilsson, forward, Calgary Flames, $360,000

Sources: Various published accounts and author's own records. Salaries include signings through early 1985 and thus include, in some cases, figures for 1985 seasons (baseball and football only).

basketball, indicate that life at the top of the top is quite lucrative.

During 1982–83, Moses Malone, under his contract with his new team, the Philadelphia 76ers, was reported to have earned $2.9 million. This does not make Moses Malone a $2.9 million player per year. The reported figure included a signing bonus, a guaranteed salary, and bonuses earned that year. Malone had a great season, led his team to the NBA championship, and was recognized for his efforts as the league's most valuable player (MVP). In many respects, he was indeed a $2.9 million ballplayer — but for that one season. The next year his salary plummeted. There was no signing bonus. There were few earned or performance bonuses. His earnings were closer to his reported guaranteed base of $1.6 million. Malone's salary of $1.6 million reported in Exhibit 1–2 must be understood to be a minimum. Over the term of his contract, Malone's earnings are more likely to be slightly in excess of $2 million per year.

In contrast, Exhibit 1–2 indicates that in 1984 Larry Bird was reportedly the highest paid player in the NBA at $1.8 million per year, on the basis of a new contract he signed with the Boston Celtics just prior to the 1983–84 season. The Celtics' faith in Bird was justified, as the Celtics won the 1984 NBA championship in seven hard-fought games against the Los Angeles Lakers. Bird was chosen the most valuable player for that championship series, capping a year in which he was also chosen league MVP for the season.

The question is, did Bird earn bonuses similar to those of Malone to cause Bird's total earnings to approach the $3 million mark? The answer is no. Bird's attorney, Bob Woolf, negotiated for Bird a straightforward, up-front, no-deferred, no-bonus arrangement — the way Bird (and Woolf) wanted it. The only unusual feature, and this is not altogether uncommon in sports, is that the contract did not really begin with the 1983–84 season. The Celtics do not normally tear up an old contract and start over. In Bird's case, they structured a seven-year deal to begin technically with the 1984–85 season, but added

a $1.2 million signing bonus, paid prior to the 1983–84 season that effectively raised his $600 thousand 1983–84 salary to the desired $1.8 million. It is "cash." Larry Bird would have gotten his $1.8 million if he had fallen flat on his face throughout the 1983–84 season, and he will continue to receive the same for the seven seasons thereafter. In sum, Larry Bird over the next several seasons may be earning more than Moses Malone. Then again he may not. It will depend on Malone's good fortunes and performance.

The analysis of the true worth of player contracts is important throughout the structure of professional sports. In many respects, it is even more vital for the marginal player. A club may not be willing to pay set numbers of dollars. Thus, the deal must be structured to provide for contingencies. The player who performs well gets paid more. Consequently, in looking at average salary figures, one must realize that there are alternative ways of reaching those figures.

The tables and figures presented in this section point to some of the many considerations that are important in analyzing player salaries. Some of these have to do with perspectives about the overall economic structure of the sports leagues. Others relate more to what one would consider if contemplating the negotiation of a contract on behalf of a player or of a club wishing to deal with the player.

A note about the sources and dates for the numbers should be added. We said earlier that accurate figures are difficult to obtain. Sports clubs have traditionally not made such information available. This policy has loosened somewhat, primarily through efforts of the players' associations, at least in some of the leagues. But even the players' groups face a dilemma. In one sense it is good to have the numbers made public. They can dispel rumors. On the other hand, the privacy of the players is also at issue, and full information about player salaries may be an unwelcome intrusion. In addition, salary data, as well as other club and league data (see Section 1.32), are not released every year; even when

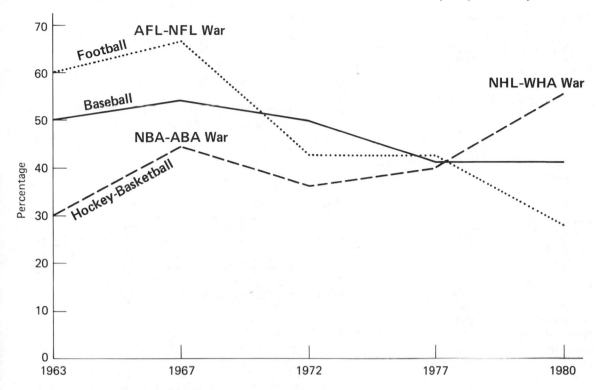

Exhibit 1-3   Player Percentage of Gross Receipts

Source: National Football League Players Association (from data compiled by U.S. Commerce Dept., U.S. Bureau of Census, and other players' associations).

they are, the information is normally for internal consumption and is not made public. Thus, the numbers that are presented, even though they are not always for the latest year, are only reasonable estimates of how matters stand as of the date of the publication of this book. They are numbers valuable for study and are representative of the current financial state of the professional sports leagues.

Instances in which some of the numbers have changed to a significant extent are noted, so that extrapolations on the numbers in the tables can be made. What has not been done is to tamper with the numbers presented by the source cited. As presented, these are not composite figures. Generally, they are single-source figures. While composites have value it was felt best where possible to present the numbers without alteration and to name the source. Realizing that the

numbers at times may not be completely accurate, depending on the source and purposes for which they are compiled, the tables we have selected seem sufficiently precise to include without major qualifications.

To expand on the theme that the figures presented are constantly undergoing change, nowhere is this more true than in discussing the top-salaried players in the professional sports leagues. Each superstar who signs a new contract attempts to vault over any predecessors at the bargaining table. For example, Exhibit 1–2 lists Herschel Walker as the top-salaried player. This is probably still true, but only because he renegotiated a new contract just one year after signing with the New Jersey Generals. Otherwise, he might well be behind Steve Young, whose contract with the Los Angeles Express of the USFL was reported as a $43

Exhibit 1-4   Percentage of Team Gross Revenue Allocated to Players

Base Salaries + Pre-Season Pay + Bonus Payments + Earned Compensation – Less Deferred Pay		1981 Team Salary Survey					
Team		Team	Average Salary*	Total Team Wage Compensation	Team	Average Salary*	Total Team Wage Compensation
Atlanta	23%	Atlanta	$ 69,740	$3,487,000	New England	$ 90,467	$5,156,600
Baltimore	31%	Buffalo	$ 89,664	$5,200,512	New Orleans	$ 80,402	$4,663,300
Buffalo	29%	Baltimore	$ 85,935	$4,640,500	N.Y. Giants	$ 75,738	$4,620,018
Chicago	37%	Chicago	$ 95,311	$5,432,700	N.Y. Jets	$ 78,263	$4,617,517
Cincinnati	37%	Cleveland	$ 87,602	$4,730,500	Oakland	$ 92,170	$4,885,000
Cleveland	26%	Cincinnati	$100,058	$5,203,016	Philadelphia	$ 83,063	$5,316,032
Dallas	31%	Denver	$106,028	$5,725,500	Pittsburgh	$104,282	$5,735,500
Denver	37%	Dallas	$ 90,491	$4,796,023	San Diego	$ 87,643	$4,908,008
Detroit	28%	Detroit	$ 78,655	$4,562,000	San Francisco	$ 76,310	$4,120,740
Green Bay	31%	Green Bay	$ 77,067	$4,624,000	St. Louis	$ 74,759	$4,186,500
Houston	26%	Houston	$ 71,502	$3,861,100	Seattle	$ 85,880	$4,465,750
Kansas City	22%	Kansas City	$ 64,859	$3,891,513	Tampa Bay	$ 76,761	$4,298,616
Los Angeles	26%	Los Angeles	$ 86,229	$5,087,500	Washington	$ 89,162	$5,706,350
Miami	26%	Miami	$ 80,225	$4,171,700			
Minnesota	27%	Minnesota	$ 71,028	$3,835,500	Totals	$ 83,811	131,928,863
New England	35%						
New Orleans	30%						
N.Y. Giants	28%						
N.Y. Jets	32%						
Oakland	33%						
Philadelphia	32%						
Pittsburgh	39%						
San Diego	31%						
San Francisco	28%						
St. Louis	30%						
Seattle	30%						
Tampa Bay	25%						
Washington	38%						
Average	30%						

*Average Salary = (Base Salary – Deferred Salary Payments)
+ (Bonuses – Deferred Bonus Payments)
+ (Deferred Compensation Received)
+ (Pre-Season Pay)

All salary information based on 1,574 contracts made available to the NFLPA by the National Football League.

Source: National Football League Players Association.

million deal. Since this amount is spread over multiple years, however, its current dollar value is probably less than what Walker is receiving. And Walker would certainly be behind his new teammate, Doug Flutie, were it not for Walker's renegotiated contract. Flutie's six-year deal for almost $9 million places him in the same lofty stratosphere as Walker, making these two currently the highest paid players in professional football.

Those are the top figures. Now let's consider the figures for the average player. The numbers are still impressive but not without qualifications. Exhibit 1–3 returns us to earth a bit. Instead of focusing on the high glamor of the big numbers, it focuses on something perhaps more important — the percentage of a league's gross revenues that go into player salaries. The graph in Exhibit 1–3 was prepared by the National Football League Players Association in late 1981

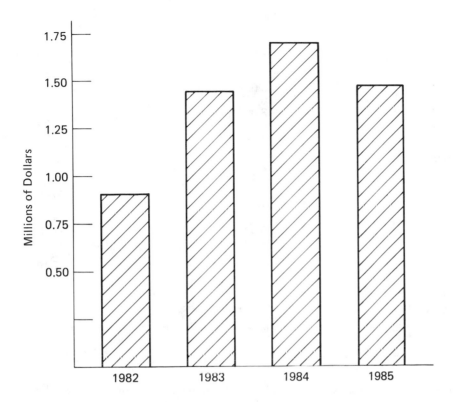

Exhibit 1-5   Salary Comparisons of NFL First-Round Draft Picks, 1982-1985 (Four-Year Salary Packages)

Source: Various published reports compiled by authors.

in anticipation of the association's struggle with the league to gain a new collective bargaining agreement. It was part of the advocacy presented to show that the players' share of the gross was disproportionately low. One should not focus on these figures, alone, however. It is important to realize that other costs and club profits are also involved.

Exhibit 1–4 presents a breakdown by team of the precentage of the gross allocated to NFL players. As one can see, the precentage varies considerably, from a low of 22 percent (Kansas City) to a high of 39 percent (Pittsburgh). The raw dollars spent on player salaries as a consequence also vary significantly, although the clubs do not necessarily have the same ranking as to percentage of the gross as they do for dollars spent, since team grosses vary (see Exhibit 1–19). In Exhibit 1–4, it can be seen that

in actual dollars Atlanta's payroll was the lowest, at slightly under $3.5 million, and Pittsburgh's the highest, in excess of $5.7 million. As club personnel mature, as was the case with the Pittsburgh Steelers in 1981, payrolls will naturally be higher. No lasting significance can be derived if these figures are taken in isolation, but if they are compiled over time, along with other data such as team performance, year after year, trends are discernible. In general, the richest perform the best and reward their players the most. Even though it does not always work that way, particularly in the short run, the correlation is stronger as more years are added.

What Exhibits 1–3 and 1–4 do not take into account is the creation of a rival to the NFL — that is, the United States Football League. Normally, one would have expected the percen-

Exhibit 1-6   Average Salaries, Major League Baseball, 1967–1983

Year	Minimum Salary	Average Salary
1967	$ 6,000	$ 19,000
1968[a]	10,000	N.A.
1969	10,000	24,909
1970	12,000	29,303
1971	12,750	31,543
1972	13,500	34,092
1973	15,000	36,566
1974	15,000	40,839
1975	16,000	44,676
1976	19,000	51,501
1977	19,000	76,066
1978	21,000	99,876
1979	21,000	113,558[b]
1980	30,000	143,756[b]
1981	32,500	185,651[b]
1982	33,500	241,497[b]
1983	35,000	289,194[b]
1984	40,000	329,408[b]

[a]First basic agreement between clubs and Major League Players Association.

[b]Salary figures have been discounted for salary deferrals without interest at a rate of 9% per year for the period of delayed payments.

Source: Major League Baseball Players Association.

tage of the gross for players in the NFL to have decreased in the years following the date for the data presented in Exhibits 1–3 and 1–4, mainly because of the substantial infusion of more dollars per team from the new television contracts that went into effect in the NFL in 1982. What was not anticipated, particularly after the largely unsuccessful NFL player strike in 1982, was that players could have effectively bargained for a large portion of the increased revenue coming to the clubs. In fact, although precise figures are not available, it appears as if the percentage of the gross has not declined. Player salaries have substantially escalated because of the emergence of the rival USFL, as can be seen in Exhibit 1–5 which compares the salaries of NFL players drafted in the first round in 1982, 1983, and 1984. Since there is no other plausible explanation, the presence of the USFL apparently caused the NFL owners to open their pocketbooks in an unprecedented fashion. However, in 1985, the USFL noticeably slackened its quest for the top college players, and the

NFL owners consequently signed their first round choices at figures closely approximating 1983 prices.

Having as precise salary information as possible is of course essential for those actually involved in the representation of the players or the clubs. The latter have always had access to salary information, but even clubs did not always fully share their contract specifics with other clubs. That has changed. Clubs now have full and complete access to all contract figures within the league.

For those representing the player, the story is not as happy. Depending on the league, great strides have been made in making more information available to athletes and their representatives. Except for Major League Baseball, however, the information is far from complete. Even though general figures revealing average salaries, often by position played, can be obtained for hockey, football, and basketball, the precise numbers for named players are readily available only in baseball. Player repre-

Exhibit 1-7   Average Salary vs. Years of Service, Major League Baseball, 1984

Service (through 1983)

At Least	But Less Than	No. of Players	Mean Salary*
15		22	705,352
14	15	6	674,573
13	14	15	625,435
12	13	22	512,591
11	12	25	618,793
10	11	27	570,518
9	10	31	607,672
8	9	37	472,929
7	8	37	562,126
6	7	44	536,722
5	6	45	422,540
4	5	51	412,050
3	4	57	310,054
2	3	69	200,251
1	2	83	103,234
0	1	158	51,908

*Salary figures have been discounted for salary deferrals without interest at a rate of 9 percent per year for the period of delayed payments.

Source: Major League Baseball Players Association.

sentatives can, through the players, receive from the Major League Baseball Players Association the contract figures of all players similarly situated to their client, in terms of position played and years in the league. This is regarded with flexibility, moreover, so that representatives can receive figures on players that may not be absolutely parallel in terms of career with their client, but that are arguably comparable.

Exhibits 1–6 through 1–9 all contain data released through the Major League Baseball Players Association. Although not as valuable as data on specific players' contracts, they are nevertheless quite useful in forming an overall view of salary trends and levels in the baseball major leagues. The data in Exhibit 1–6, for example, reveal a constant rise in salaries, without exception, since 1967. The great increases in average baseball salaries occurred after the Messersmith-McNally arbitration deci-

sion (see Chapter 5) and the consequent onset of baseball's form of player free agency.

The numbers are startling. Between 1976 and 1977, the average salary jumped from $51,501 to $76,066, an increase in that one year of 47.7 percent. The following year, 1978, the increase was to $99,876, a further percentage leap of 31.3 percent. Again, from 1981 to 1982, the figures reflect increases from $185,651 to $241,497, a huge raw dollar escalation of almost $55,000 per player and a percentage increase of 29.4 percent. An examination of Exhibit 1–6 makes it clear that the parties are faced with difficulties in figuring market value for the player over the five or so years to come when the present figures are increasing at such fluctuating rates. The other possibility, moreover, is that at some point the saturation point will be reached, and the increases will not continue.

Exhibit 1-8   Average Salaries vs. Position, Major League Baseball

Position[a]	No. of AL Players	1984 AL Mean[b]	No. of NL Players	1984 NL Mean[b]	1984 Major League Mean[b]	1983 Major League Mean[b]	1982 Major League Mean[b]
1st Base	13	377,818	9	737,950	525,145	572,105	461,234
2nd Base	13	438,612	10	303,800	379,998	322,363	321,419
3rd Base	13	457,084	6	914,701	601,595	511,751	362,137
Shortstop	11	303,620	10	578,311	434,425	386,823	328,409
Catcher	10	415,898	11	486,353	452,803	473,445	324,171
Outfielders	36	473,585	32	463,810	468,985	457,789	394,053
Designated Hitter (80 or more games)	13	447,334			447,334	443,209	386,291
Starting Pitcher (19 or more starts)	58	376,917	51	421,401	397,730	337,797	293,717
Relief Pitcher (10 or less starts; 25 or more relief appearances)	49	271,597	52	350,486	312,313	221,564	200,271

[a]100 or more games unless noted.

[b]Salary figures have been discounted for salary deferrals without interest at a rate of 9 percent per year for the period of delayed payments.

Source: Major League Baseball Players Association.

Exhibits 1–7 and 1–8 provide breakdowns for the figures in other insightful ways. The fact is that one's value in baseball is not only determined by the quality of one's play but also by position played and years in the league. The perceived star quality of the player is still most determinative by far; but the average salaries based on years and position played provide other guidelines. Finally, Exhibit 1–9 notes the total salaries paid per team in Major League Baseball. Although general in nature, it does give some feel for the present position of what clubs are paying their own players. As with the earlier discussion on NFL club salaries, much of the significance of these figures is understood only when studied in combination with other information, such as the relative seniority of players on one club as opposed to another. But the figures also reflect general club policies as to which clubs are willing or able to pay at what levels. As will be discussed in Section 4.22, this knowledge aids the negotiation process.

Exhibit 1-9   Salaries per Team, Major League Baseball, 1984 (With 1981-1983 Comparison Salaries)

1983 Rank	1984 Rank	Club	1984[a] Mean	1983[a] Mean	1982[a] Mean	1981[a] Mean	No. of Players
1	1	Yankees	458,544	463,687	411,988	309,855	29
12	2	White Sox	447,281	291,114	247,673	192,658	25
3	3	California	431,431	389,833	423,403	259,404	32
14	4	Chicago Cubs	422,194	268,947	220,662	125,117	28
7	5	Atlanta	402,689	347,620	209,492	195,449	30
2	6	Philadelphia	401,476	442,165	390,370	289,971	30
6	7	Milwaukee	385,215	352,061	330,965	243,882	31
15	8	Oakland	384,027	266,815	266,335	148,065	28
4	9	Houston	382,991	364,825	306,565	260,789	28
17	10	Detroit	371,332	263,899	174,134	160,561	26
5	11	Montreal	368,557	353,357	299,192	195,958	27
11	12	Baltimore	360,204	305,305	242,558	169,919	27
8	13	Pittsburgh	330,661	314,769	251,234	206,359	30
13	14	Los Angeles	316,530	288,555	216,332	192,104	29
18	15	San Diego	311,199	261,820	137,946	103,106	26
16	16	Boston	297,878	264,883	247,513	223,252	28
23	17	Toronto	295,632	212,087	127,860	97,271	26
9	18	Kansas City	291,160	309,962	258,091	112,910	29
19	19	St. Louis	290,886	259,393	237,533	207,654	27
10	20	New York Mets	282,952	306,253	263,539	201,303	28
20	21	San Francisco	282,132	248,204	198,438	185,939	29
22	22	Cincinnati	269,019	239,068	203,532	201,557	27
24	23	Texas	247,081	180,848	186,424	178,131	26
26	24	Minnesota	172,024	97,980	67,335	85,736	28
25	25	Seattle	168,505	118,875	114,405	95,263	28
21	26	Cleveland	159,774	242,134	216,000	186,396	27
		Mean Salary	329,408	289,194	241,497	185,651	729

[a]Salary figures have been discounted for salary deferrals without interest at a rate of 9 percent per year for the period of delayed payments.

Source: Major League Baseball Players Association.

Exhibit 1–10 presents data from the National Hockey League, which provides a contrast with the high baseball figures. Further breakdowns on averages per position played and years in the league are available through the NHL Players Association.

1.32   League and Club Economic Profiles

The leagues exist to conduct competition among the clubs and to make the many parts operate as efficiently as possible. As separate economic entities, however, the leagues are not "major

Exhibit 1-10   Salary Survey, National Hockey League Players' Association, October 1984

Salary Range (000's)	Forwards No. Players	Defensemen No. Players	Goalies No. Players	Total No. Players	Percent
Under 50					
51 – 60	—	1	—	1	0.2%
61 – 70	5	4	—	9	2.0%
71 – 80	19	9	4	32	7.0%
81 – 90	41	21	3	65	14.3%
91 – 100	32	16	7	55	12.1%
101 – 110	28	10	1	39	8.6%
111 – 120	21	5	2	28	6.2%
121 – 130	15	13	3	31	6.8%
131 – 140	11	12	5	28	6.2%
141 – 150	15	12	6	33	7.2%
151 – 160	9	5	—	14	3.1%
161 – 170	16	7	—	23	5.1%
171 – 180	11	5	2	18	4.0%
181 – 190	3	—	1	4	0.9%
191 – 200	11	1	4	16	3.5%
201 – 300	23	14	3	40	8.8%
Over 300	11	5	1	17	4.0%
Total	271	140	42	453	100.0%
Median Salary	$114,700	$123,500	$132,000	$120,000	
Average Age	24.7	24.9	26.2	25.0	
Average Yrs. Pro	4.6	4.7	6.2	4.8	
Nos. in Option Yr.	34.0	20.0	6.0	60.0	13.2

Note: 453 players from 21 clubs responded to this survey by the NHL Players' Association.

league." Illustrative of this is Exhibit 1–11, which sets forth a statement of operations for a year's budget for the league offices of the National Basketball Association. The total income is under $6 million, and the disbursements are for three items: officiating, operations (which means largely the running of the league's central office in New York City), and legal expenses. The league's office performs several functions, including the central handling of the relationships among clubs, television contracts, and publicity. Note that its total operations require less expenditure than what Moses Malone earns in a good year (see Section 1.31).

The same can be said of officiating. The $2.5 million yearly budget for officiating, only half of which is for salaries (see Exhibit 1–12), has risen with the new agreement the NBA signed with its referees in late 1983; it is still, however, miniscule when placed beside players' salaries in the league.

The NBA's operations budget is replicable in the other professional sports leagues. One would expect to find somewhat larger budgets for the National Football League and for baseball's American and National Leagues, but only at best proportional rises related to the leagues' gross revenues. In total, no more than 5 percent of a league's gross actually goes to league expenses. The rest, such as revenue from network television receipts, goes directly to the clubs. It is, in reality, club income, not league income.

Exhibit 1-11   Statement of Operations, National Basketball Association, Year Ending May 31,1981

	Current Year Estimated	Prior Year	Current Year Over/(Under) Prior Year
Receipts:			
Gate Share	$ 5,042,678	$ 4,775,188	$ 267,490
Capital Contributions			
Annual	138,000	132,000	6,000
Dallas	31,018		31,018
Additional (Properties Royalties)	432,496	140,000	292,496
Exhibition Games	127,500	102,500	25,000
Interest Income	35,096	74,605	(39,509)
Total Receipts	$ 5,806,788	$ 5,224,293	$ 582,495
Disbursements:			
Officiating (page 9)	$ 2,548,502	2,014,014	$ 534,488
Operations (page 11)	2,635,278	2,408,201	227,077
Legal	375,933	474,737	(98,804)
Total Disbursements	$ 5,559,713	$ 4,896,952	$ 662,761
Cash receipts Over/(Under) cash disbursements	$ 247,075	$ 327,341	$ (80,266)
Fines	$ 108,320	$ 107,325	$ 995
Charitable contributions	97,041	60,150	36,891
Net	$ 11,279	$ 47,175	$ 35,896

Source: National Basketball Association.

Exhibit 1-12   Officiating Expenses, Actual vs. Prior Year, National Basketball Association, Year Ending May 31, 1981

	Current Year Estimated	Prior Year	Current Year Over/(Under) Prior Year
Salaries	$1,264,731	$1,026,415	$ 238,316
Travel	568,921	496,078	72,843
Maintenance	211,844	168,287	43,557
Camps & clinics/on the job training	44,740	35,558	9,182
Pension Plan	142,000	87,934	54,066
Other leagues — including travel	125,679	27,874	97,805
Uniforms & miscellaneous	18,737	26,499	(7,762)
Life/medical insurance	57,661	72,449	(14,788)
Workmen's compensation/ unemployment/disability	62,197	33,809	28,388
Payroll taxes (FICA)	51,992	39,111	12,881
Total	$2,548,502	$2,014,014	$ 534,488

Source: National Basketball Association.

Exhibit 1-13   Paid Attendance, National Basketball Association, 1980-81 and 1979-80

	1980-81	No. of Games	Average	1979-80	No.of Games	Average	Increase/ Decrease	Percent
Atlanta	327,230	41	7,981	415,697	41	10,139	−88,467	−21.28
Boston	564,641	41	13,772	560,194	41	13,663	+4,447	+0.79
Chicago	358,828	41	8,752	338,957	41	8,267	+19,871	+5.86
Cleveland	171,946	41	4,194	259,108	41	6,320	−87,162	−33.64
Dallas	278,632	41	6,796				+278,632	+0.00
Denver	351,935	41	8,584	454,985	41	11,097	−103,050	−22.65
Detroit	132,565	41	3,233	244,576	41	5,965	−112,011	−45.80
Golden State	361,257	41	8,811	286,790	41	6,995	+74,467	+25.97
Houston	314,534	41	7,672	362,341	41	8,838	−47,807	−13.19
Indiana	367,666	41	8,967	382,663	41	9,333	−14,997	−3.92
Kansas City	268,960	41	6,560	331,698	41	8,090	−62,738	−18.91
Los Angeles	501,444	41	12,230	542,581	41	13,234	−41,137	−7.58
Milwaukee	429,186	41	10,468	430,396	41	10,497	−1,210	−0.28
New Jersey	288,485	41	7,036	251,594	41	6,136	+36,891	+14.66
New York	495,610	41	12,088	495,728	41	12,091	−118	−0.02
Philadelphia	421,959	41	10,292	443,623	41	10,820	−21,664	−4.88
Phoenix	453,709	41	11,066	462,805	41	11,288	−9,096	−1.97
Portland	495,996	41	12,097	500,984	41	12,219	−4,988	−1.00
San Antonio	338,537	41	8,257	363,657	41	8,870	−25,120	−6.91
San Diego	217,341	41	5,301	325,012	41	7,927	−107,671	−33.13
Seattle	642,006	41	15,659	855,500	41	20,866	−213,494	−24.96
Utah	265,874	41	6,485	273,244	41	6,664	−7,370	−2.70
Washington	306,149	41	7,467	399,996	41	9,756	−93,847	−23.46
Totals	8,354,490	943	8,859	8,982,129	902	9,958	−627,639	−6.99

Source: National Basketball Association.

Exhibits 1–13 and 1–14 point to differences in paid attendance experienced by the NBA clubs in two different years. Note the disparities for the 1980–81 season among the top teams in attendance, such as Boston, Los Angeles, New York, Portland, and Seattle, and the lowest — Detroit, Cleveland, and San Diego. If projected over ten-year periods, the disparities would no doubt even out somewhat. Detroit, for example,

witnessed substantial attendance leaps after the date of the table, particularly for the 1983–84 season. Even so, others over the ten-year period will stay consistently high or steadily low, and this causes chronic problems for the league. Of the major team sports, only the National Football League is able, by and large, to avoid this malady.

In examining the NFL, several data sets are

Exhibit 1-14 Gate Receipts, National Basketball Association, 1980-81 and 1979-80

	1980-81	No. of Games	Average	1979-80	No. of Games	Average	Increase/ Decrease	Percent
Atlanta	$2,254,265	41	$54,982	$2,587,591	41	$63,112	$-333,326	-12.88
Boston	5,053,465	41	123,255	3,882,306	41	94,690	+1,171,159	+30.17
Chicago	2,478,697	41	60,456	2,402,431	41	58,596	+76,266	+3.17
Cleveland	1,434,174	41	34,980	1,936,337	41	47,228	-502,163	-25.93
Dallas	2,606,673	41	63,577				+2,606,673	+0.00
Denver	2,731,137	41	66,613	3,477,942	41	+84,828	-746,805	-21.47
Detroit	776,045	41	18,928	1,544,859	41	37,679	-768,814	-49.77
Golden State	2,766,538	41	67,720	2,323,563	41	56,672	+452,975	+19.49
Houston	2,141,225	41	52,225	2,348,892	41	57,290	+207,667	+8.84
Indiana	2,357,986	41	57,512	2,159,412	41	52,669	+198,574	+9.20
Kansas City	1,849,673	41	45,114	2,194,493	41	53,524	-344,820	-15.71
Los Angeles	5,873,729	41	143,262	4,128,586	41	100,697	+1,745,143	+42.27
Milwaukee	3,527,046	41	86,026	2,945,901	41	71,851	+581,145	+19.73
New Jersey	2,533,879	41	61,802	2,058,542	41	50,208	+475,337	+23.09
New York	5,183,274	41	126,421	5,010,662	41	122,211	+172,612	+3.44
Philadelphia	3,250,027	41	79,269	2,988,333	41	72,886	+261,694	+8.76
Phoenix	3,517,652	41	85,796	3,187,347	41	77,740	+330,305	+10.36
Portland	4,473,982	41	109,122	4,371,035	41	106,611	+102,947	+2.36
San Antonio	2,290,239	41	55,859	2,370,513	41	57,817	-80,817	-3.39
San Diego	1,587,662	41	38,723	2,714,256	41	66,201	-1,126,594	-41.51
Seattle	4,703,015	41	114,708	4,662,944	41	113,730	+40,071	+0.86
Utah	1,795,481	41	43,792	1,861,826	41	45,410	-66,345	-3.56
Washington	2,039,841	41	49,752	2,524,825	41	61,581	-484,984	-19.21
Totals	$67,235,705	943	$71,300	$63,682,596	902	$70,602	$3,553,109	+5.58

Source: National Basketball Association.

Exhibit 1-15 Attendance and Gate Receipts, National Football League, 1981

1981 Home Games	Tickets Sold	Net Receipts	Visitors' Share
American Football Conference (AFC)	$ 6,651,020	$ 78,954,769	$ 26,844,625
National Football Conference (NFC)	6,955,970	76,930,747	26,156,447
1981 NFL Totals (224 Games)	13,606,990	155,885,516	53,001,072
1980 NFL Totals (224 Games)	13,392,230	143,581,377	48,793,017
Increase (December) over 1980	214,760	12,304,139	4,208,055
Percent increase (December) over 1980	1.60%	8.57%	8.62%
1981 average per game (224 games)	60,745	695,917	236,612
1980 average per game (224 games)	59,787	640,988	217,826
Increase (December) over 1980	958	54,929	18,788
Percent increase (December) over 1980	1.60%	8.57%	8.62%

Source: National Football League.

presented. Exhibit 1–15 presents total attendance and gate receipts for 1981. Exhibit 1–16 is an economic profile of a typical NFL club, put together by the NFL Players Association. Such a profile was undoubtedly prepared following the Los Angeles Memorial Coliseum's suit against the NFL, wherein such clubs as the Los Angeles Rams were compelled to disclose their financial statements. The Rams' 1980 financial statement is presented in Exhibit 1–17. Even this disclosure did not remove all skepticism. The NFL Players Association, which circulated the Rams' financial statement in pamphlets designed to advance the association's case for a larger percentage of the gross for NFL players, constantly questioned the accuracy of the figures. For example, the association noted that coaching and operations expenses seemed inordinately high (see the notes in Exhibit 1–17). The association could not come up with any breakdown that would account for why expenses in those categories ran that high.

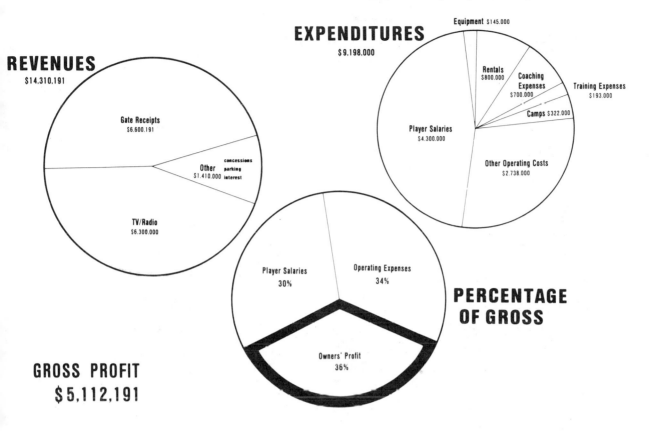

Exhibit 1-16 Economic Profile of an Average NFL Club

Source: National Football League Players Association (1980 figures).

Exhibit 1–18 contains gate revenues for the NFL, broken down on a club-by-club basis. For purposes of comparison, Exhibit 1–18 can be contrasted with Exhibit 1–14 and similar data for NBA teams. The first thing of note is that club revenues are higher in the NFL, even though far fewer games are played. Stadium sizes and prices per ticket are the obvious keys. Another factor is that the lowest team in gate receipts (Green Bay at $4.9 million) has income generated from this source that is 56 percent of what the top team (Los Angeles Rams at $8.8 million)

received. While this disparity is notable, a comparable look at NBA figures presents even more striking differences. The lowest team (Detroit at $776 thousand) received only 13 percent of that of the highest team (Los Angeles Lakers at almost $5.9 million). When the large television monies received by the NFL, in contrast to the NBA, are factored in, the ratio between the highest and the lowest in the NFL shrinks much further than in the NBA. This point is illustrated for the NFL in Exhibit 1–19, which presents overall profiles of NFL clubs.

Exhibit 1-17 Rams' 1980 Financial Statement

Revenues		*Expenditures*	
Gate Receipts	$ 8,700,000[a]	Player Salaries	$ 4,200,000
TV and Radio	6,600,000	Non-Salary Payments to Players	2,200,000[b]
Luxury boxes	1,300,000	Coaching Expenses	1,470,000[c]
Pro! Magazine	172,000	Equipment	186,000
Parking	238,000	Training	157,000
Interest and Other Revenue	1,390,000	Trainers	91,000
Total	$18,400,000	Off-Season Camp	23,000
		Mini-camp	28,000
Reconciliation		Pre-Season Camp	362,000
Revenue	$18,400,000	Regular Season Expenses	1,744,000
Less Expenses	14,034,000	Other Operating Expenses	3,573,000
Profit	$ 4,366,000	Total	$14,034,000

[a]1980 playoff revenues of $374,000 are not included in this item. Even when the Rams' post-season share is added in, the resulting total fails to tally with League-produced data showing gate revenues of all teams.

[b]We have no detailed explanation of this item. We presume it represents deferred compensation for previous years and signing bonuses.

[c]Coaching expenses seem inordinately high. Assuming an average coaching salary of $45,000 and $100,000 for the head coach, salaries would be $505,000. Where the other $965,000 went is not explained. Possibly salaries to Georgia Frontierre, Don Klosterman and other front office personnel are included in this item.

[d]It is impossible to believe that football operations cost this much. We are seeking a breakdown of this figure.

Source: National Football League Players Association (based on figures presented in *Los Angeles Memorial Coliseum Commission v. NFL*).

Exhibit 1-18 Teams Ranked by 1980 Gate Revenue

Team	*Revenue*	*Team*	*Revenue*
1. Los Angeles Rams	$8,834,623	15. Detroit Lions	6,480,428
2. Dallas Cowboys	7,715,383	16. New Orleans Saints	6,397,941
3. Seattle Seahawks	7,579,146	17. Houston Oilers	6,370,855
4. Tampa Bay Buccaneers	7,412,612	18. Chicago Bears	6,322,202
5. San Diego Chargers	7,303,185	19. New York Jets	6,283,804
6. New England Patriots	7,154,416	20. San Francisco 49ers	6,261,037
7. Philadelphia Eagles	7,151,369	21. Pittsburgh Steelers	6,124,970
8. Atlanta Falcons	7,067,784	22. St. Louis Cardinals	6,084,718
9. Denver Broncos	6,933,861	23. Miami Dolphins	6,070,268
10. Washington Redskins	6,933,860	24. Minnesota Vikings	5,748,111
11. Buffalo Bills	6,805,821	25. Kansas City Chiefs	5,342,488
12. Cleveland Browns	6,737,396	26. Cincinnati Bengals	5,223,621
13. Oakland Raiders	6,725,669	27. Baltimore Colts	5,222,573
14. New York Giants	6,568,221	28. Green Bay Packers	4,921,277

Source: National Football League Players Association.

Exhibit 1-19   Team-by-Team Analysis of 1981 Gross Income

Team & Owner	Purchase Date	Price (Millions or Thousands)	Average Ticket Price	Average Home Attendance	Average Road Attendance	Gate Income (Millions) +	Luxury Loge Income +	Con-cession/ Parking +	Broadcast Income (Millions) +	Misc. Income (Millions) +	Team Income (Millions)
Atlanta Rankin Smith	6/65	8.5 M	$12.00	52,400	61,800	$6.91 M	$135,000		$6.55 M	$1.29 M	$14.89 M
Baltimore Robert Irsay	7/72	$19 M	$12.00	36,200	62,000	$5.9 M		$1.45 M	$6.55 M	$1.29 M	$15.19 M
Buffalo Ralph Wilson, Jr.	10/59	$25,000	$12.00	75,600	52,700	$8.05 M	$850,000	$1.51 M	$6.55 M	$1.29 M	$18.25 M
Chicago George Halas	9/20	$100	$11.50	54,600	56,000	$6.84 M			$6.55 M	$1.29 M	$14.68 M
Cincinnati Paul Brown	9/67	$7.5 M	$ 9.50	52,800	48,300	$5.82 M		$486,000	$6.55 M	$1.29 M	$14.15 M
Cleveland Art Modell	3/61	$3.9 M	$ 9.50	75,200	59,400	$7.3 M	$2.57 M	$397,000	$6.55 M	$1.29 M	$18.11 M
Dallas Clint Murchison, Jr.	1/60	$600,000	$12.00	62,700	62,900	$7.58 M		$752,000	$6.55 M	$1.29 M	$15.42 M
Denver Edgar Kaiser, Jr.	2/81	$35 M	$10.50	75,800	59,500	$7.73 M			$6.55 M	$1.29 M	$15.58 M
Detroit William Clay Ford	1/64	$8 M	$12.50	75,500	57,800	$8.21 M			$6.55 M	$1.29 M	$16.05 M
Green Bay Non-Profit Corp.	9/21	$250	$ 9.30	53,700	60,600	$6.23 M			$6.55 M	$1.29 M	$14.70 M
Houston Bud Adams, Jr.	8/59	$25,000	$11.80	44,400	61,300	$6.39 M	$550,000		$6.55 M	$1.29 M	$14.78 M
Kansas City Lamar Hunt	10/59	$25,000	$ 9.70	63,300	56,900	$66.9 M	$1.25 M	$1.52 M	$6.55 M	$1.29 M	$17.30 M
Los Angeles Georgia Frontiere	7/72	$23 M	$14.30	60,500	59,300	$9.17 M	$1.6 M	$1.21 M	$6.55 M	$1.29 M	$19.81 M
Miami Joe Robbie	8/65	$7.5 M	$10.50	61,300	57,800	$6.88 M		$1.03 M	$6.55 M	$1.29 M	$15.75 M
Minnesota Max Winter	1/60	$1 M	$12.00	45,200	60,400	$6.4 M		$108,000	$6.55 M	$1.29 M	$14.35 M
New England Billy Sullivan	11/59	$25,000	$12.60	52,000	51,700	$6.74 M			$6.55 M	$1.29 M	$14.58 M
New Orleans John Mecom, Jr.	12/66	$8.5 M	$12.00	55,100	56,300	$6.89 M	$960,000		$6.55 M	$1.29 M	$15.69 M
N.Y. Giants Wellington Mara	1925	$2,500	$ 9.75	69,000	55,800	$6.97 M	$1.58 M		$6.55 M	$1.29 M	$16.39 M
N.Y. Jets Leon Hess	3/63	$1 M	$11.50	53,600	58,000	$6.77 M			$6.55 M	$1.29 M	$14.61 M
Oakland Al Davis	7/72	$2 M	$13.45	46,000	61,700	$6.88 M			$6.55 M	$1.29 M	$14.72 M
Philadelphia Leonard Tose	5/69	$16.2 M	$12.20	68,500	60,400	$7.87 M	$525,000	$247,000	$6.55 M	$1.29 M	$16.49 M
Pittsburgh Art Rooney, Jr.	7/33	$2,500	$11.00	52,600	60,400	$6.87 M			$6.55 M	$1.29 M	$14.71 M
San Diego Eugene Klein	8/66	$10 M	$13.30	51,500	61,100	$7.20 M	$350,000	$686,000	$6.55 M	$1.29 M	$16.08 M
San Francisco Edward Debartolo, Jr.	3/77	$17 M	$11.60	54,400	54,700	$6.79 M			$6.55 M	$1.29 M	$14.63 M
Seattle Nordstrum Family	6/72	$12 M	$12.80	56,700	50,500	$7.07 M			$6.55 M	$1.29 M	$14.91 M
St. Louis William Bidwill	2/72	$6 M	$11.50	48,100	53,100	$6.34 M			$6.55 M	$1.29 M	$14.18 M
Tampa Bay Hugh Culverhouse	12/74	$16 M	$11.35	66,500	58,600	$7.68 M	$520,000	$1.004 M	$6.55 M	$1.29 M	$17.04 M
Washington Jack Kent Cooke	1961	$300,000	$13.50	52,000	56,600	$7.14 M			$6.55 M	$1.29 M	$14.98 M

In examining Exhibit 1–19, note that the only major corrections that need be made in updating the 1981 figures are that ticket price increases have undoubtedly inflated gate receipts by 15 to 20 percent, and more significantly, the new network television contracts for the NFL have pushed the total broadcast income from $6.55 million to at least $15 million per club. Thus, income per NFL club totals more in the $20- to $26-million ranges than in the $14- to $19-million ranges stated in the 1981 figures.

A final note should be added about the value of franchises. These are a remarkable phenomenon in the sports industries. Exhibit 1–19 notes the latest reported prices paid for NFL franchises, ranging from the $100 paid by George Halas for his original franchise in 1920 (which was then the Decatur Staleys and only later the Chicago Bears), to the $19 million paid by Robert Irsay for the then Baltimore Colts, to the $35 million coming from Edgar Kaiser for the Denver Broncos. Even this latter figure has paled in recent years.

Spurred by the 1982 television contracts, NFL franchises have spiraled rapidly. Two events in early 1984 underscore this point. The Dallas Cowboys were sold for a reported $60 million, and Kaiser turned his Broncos over at 100 percent profit, reaping some $70 million.

NFL franchises command the steepest prices. In this case, figures do not lie. Largely through television revenues, NFL clubs accumulate by far the most revenue. Until the USFL challenge, NFL costs (referring mainly to player salaries) were relatively low. While that has changed somewhat as of 1984, it is evident that prospective NFL buyers regard the USFL challenge as a short-run cause of player-salary escalation. The long run, by conventional wisdom, is a rosy one.

Other sports have also witnessed increases in franchise purchase prices. One would have predicted that the franchise costs would be at much lower levels for sports other than football — more at the $20 to $25 million for baseball, $10 to $15 million for basketball (with perhaps a couple of higher exceptions), and at $10 million or so for hockey. However, these are all hard to predict. In June 1984, a sale of baseball's Minnesota Twins was announced that had the Griffith family's 52 percent share going for an unexpectedly high $42 million. It was also reported that a buyout of the other 48 percent might be made for $11 million (the difference in price obviously geared to controlling versus noncontrolling interests). This would mean baseball franchises might now be in the $50 million range. While part of this is tied into baseball's new television pacts (see Exhibit 1–20 in Section 1.33), the figures for a shaky franchise such as the Twins are still impressive.

In a word as to franchise prices, there is more than the coldly analytic at work. Some people just want to be owners.

Methodology

Gate Income = (average home attendance x 8 home games x average ticket price minus 35% visitor share) + (average road attendance x 8 road games x $12 average league-wide ticket price x 35% visitor share) + ($1.14 million average preseason gate) + ($416,000 average share of gross payoff gate revenues).

Broadcast Income = $6 million national television contract share + $330,000 average preseason + $220,000 average radio.

Miscellaneous Income = $189,000 average share of PRO magazine income + $1.1 million from interest earned on short-term notes and other sources.

Average salary excludes post-season pay.

Source: National Football League Players Association.

Exhibit 1-20   Television Revenues, Combined Networks and National Cable

Professional Leagues	Term of Contract	Total in Millions	Per Year Average	No. of Clubs	Club Share Per Year
NFL	5 yr; 1982-1986	2,000 million (2 billion)	400 million	28	14.2 million
	4 yr; 1978-1981	650 million	162.4 million	28	5.8 million
	1977	61 million	61 million	28	2.2 million
Baseball	5 yr; 1984-1988	1,125 million (1.125 billion)	187.5 million	26	7.2 million
	4 yr; 1980-1983	190 million	47.5 million	26	1.8 million
	4 yr; 1976-1979	92.8 million	23.2 million	26	.9 million
NBA	4 yr; 1983-1986 network	88 million	27.75 million	23	1.2 million
	2 yr; 1983-84 Cable	11.5 million 99.5 million total			
	4 yr; 1979-1982 network	74 million	18.8 million	23	.82 million
	1982 Cable	.8 million (800 thousand) (74.8 million total)			
USFL	2 yr; 1983-1984 option 1985	33 million	16.5 million	12	1.4 million
	(network)	14 million	14 million	1984-18	$950,000
	ABC option 1986 - ABC	18 million	18 million		
NHL	2 yr; 1982-1983	8.8 million	4.4 million	21	.2 million
	1 yr; 1981	1.1	1.1	21	.052 million (52 thousand)

1.33   Broadcast Revenues

Television has been called the salvation of modern professional sports. For at least some sports, the figures seem to substantiate this claim. It is the perception that a new sports league, to survive, must attract substantial broadcast revenues, particularly the large television contract. On the other hand, as the National Hockey League has shown, success is relative. The NHL would undoubtedly prefer the lucrative network contract, but it gets along without it. Whether that can be true for a league such as the USFL, which faces severe competition in its own sport from the established, powerful, and wealthy NFL, is another story altogether. Consequently, it is necessary to examine the numbers.

Exhibit 1–20 is the central data set that should be examined. The figures are drawn from several

Exhibit 1-21   Local Baseball Broadcast Revenue

AMERICAN LEAGUE EAST			NATIONAL LEAGUE EAST		
Team	1985 rights	1984 rights	Team	1985 rights	1984 rights
Baltimore Orioles	4,000,000	3,500,000	Chicago Cubs	3,600,000	3,600,000
Boston Red Sox	4,200,000	4,000,000	Montreal Expos	7,500,000	7,500,000
Cleveland Indians	3,400,000	3,400,000	New York Mets	12,100,000	10,900,000
Detroit Tigers	4,000,000	3,700,000	Philadelphia Phillies	8,500,000	8,000,000
Milwaukee Brewers	2,200,000	2,700,000	Pittsburgh Pirates	3,000,000	3,000,000
New York Yankees	14,000,000	11,700,000	St. Louis Cardinals	3,100,000	2,600,000
Toronto Blue Jays	6,500,000	5,000,000			
AMERICAN LEAGUE WEST			**NATIONAL LEAGUE WEST**		
California Angels	4,200,000	4,000,000	Atlanta Braves	3,100,000	2,100,000
Chicago White Sox	4,000,000	4,000,000	Cincinnati Reds	2,300,000	2,300,000
Kansas City Royals	2,400,000	1,800,000	Houston Astros	3,200,000	3,100,000
Minnesota Twins	2,000,000	1,500,000	Los Angeles Dodgers	4,000,000	3,500,000
Oakland A's	2,500,000	2,000,000	San Diego Padres	2,750,000	2,400,000
Seattle Mariners	1,600,000	1,200,000	San Francisco Giants	2,750,000	2,400,000
Texas Rangers	6,000,000	5,500,000			

AL total	$ 61,000,000	$ 54,000,000
NL total	$ 55,900,000	$ 51,400,000
Majors total	$116,900,000	$105,400,000

Source: Broadcasting Magazine, March 4, 1985, p. 60.

sources because no one source supplied sufficient information. But the figures are accurate as far as can be verified. Two points are immediately suggested. First, the NFL and now Major League Baseball do well by their latest national contracts. In the case of those two sports, the amounts listed are almost entirely network contracts. The NFL has not ventured into cable at all, and baseball does so on a local basis.

Second, although the national contracts have been rising steadily for football and have been less so but still significant for baseball, they must be regarded as a disappointment for the NBA and a disaster for the NHL. As solace, however, both the NBA and the NHL have been looking to cable for important supplementary support. The NBA has found at least some substantial help.

Not reflected in Exhibit 1–20 is the NBA's 1984 contract with Ted Turner's superstation in Atlanta, which will pay some $70 million over a three-year period, resulting in $1 million per year per team from cable, basically matching the amount they receive from their network contract. Because of these two sources, the NBA is moving up somewhat on the national scale.

Added to national television revenues are the local monies derived from regular and cable television, and radio. Since the NFL features all of its regular season games through the network contracts, its local revenues are limited to radio and preseason telecasts. These account for tidy sums, but are not the tipping points in an NFL club's balance sheet.

This is not true for the other sports. Exhibit 1–21 underscores this point as it presents figures

Exhibit 1-22 Advertising Costs, Professional Football, 1983

Event	Cost per 30-sec. spot
Super Bowl	$400,000 per 30 sec.
NFL Regular Season	165,000 per 30 sec.
USFL Telecast	35,000 per 30 sec.
Average Prime Time Telecast (non-sports)	90,000 per 30 sec.

Exhibit 1-23 Advertising Costs, Super Bowls, 1974-1983

Year	Cost per 30-sec. spot
1974	$107,000
1975	110,000
1976	125,000
1977	162,000
1978	185,000
1979	222,000
1980	275,000
1981	324,300
1982	345,300
1983	400,000

Exhibit 1-24 Advertising Costs, Baseball

Baseball	Cost per 30-sec. spot 1983	1982
World Series	$210,000	$185,000
All Star Game	180,000	135,000
Primetime Playoffs	122,500	110,000
Weekend Playoffs	70,000	55,000
Weekday Playoffs	40,000	37,500
Primetime Regular Season	62,500	58,000
Saturday Afternoon	33,500	32,000

on local baseball broadcast revenue. Though the figures vary sport by sport, it is nevertheless true that local broadcast revenues are vital for clubs in sports other than football. Exhibit 1–21 also illustrates, however, that the income from local broadcasting varies from locale to locale by tremendous degrees. One can contrast the $8.1 million going to the Montreal Expos with the $1.0 million going to the Milwaukee Brewers, Kansas City Royals, and Seattle Mariners. The $7.1-million disparity spells potential problems when one considers baseball's free-agent market and the bidding for players' services.

The final three exhibits (1–22, 1–23, and 1–24) represent the other consideration in telecasting sports events. That is, in order to pay the leagues and clubs such high rights fees, the networks must turn around and charge top dollar to sponsors (Exhibit 1–22). The Super Bowl is a prime example; in 1983 a 30 second spot went for $400,000. In 1985, that figure was $500,000, or $1 million per minute. Even at those prices, there is still no dearth of sponsors. For an event such as the Super Bowl, potential advertisers wait in line. Obviously, as reflected in Exhibit 1–23, the growth of a single event such as the Super Bowl has prompted rights fees and thus advertising costs to escalate sharply over the past ten years.

Exhibit 1–24 presents contrasting figures for baseball. Compared with the Super Bowl, the World Series at $210,000 per 30 seconds is a bargain. Of course, when that amount is realized on a four- to seven-game series as opposed to one game, the total revenues exceed those of the Super Bowl.

The bottom line concerning television revenues is that they must keep coming if professional sports leagues are to continue to prosper as they do today. Over half the revenue realized by the NFL comes from television. A prolonged drop in the ratings, therefore, could spell disaster. Although not likely to occur, some disturbing signs appeared in the beginning of 1983. A drop in ratings is something to which all sports leagues must be prepared to react. With few exceptions, ratings rule future television opportunities. One thing is certain: Television will not carry a declining product indefinitely. So it is that those who run sports must continually worry not only about spectators in the stands, but also viewers in front of TV sets.

Chapter 2

LEGAL STRUCTURE
OF PROFESSIONAL SPORTS

2.00 Early Legal Skirmishes

Sports legal problems are often thought of as being exclusively of recent vintage. That is a misconception. Legal authorities, particularly in the federal and state courts, were at an early date in the "life" of professional sports called upon to resolve controversies. Even though the past 20 years have witnessed ever-increased legal activity, the roots of it all lie in the late 1800s.

Two themes in the history of sports litigation can be identified. The first is competition between leagues. As soon as a league or association appeared to achieve economic viability, and thus the potential for profit, outsiders immediately attempted to get in on the action. As competition developed, leagues tried to invade each others' territories — the predictable response of established businesses trying to maintain supremacy and suppress competition. The second theme concerns the legal responses made over time to nonsports business and industrial problems. By and large, no special laws have been enacted just for sports; rather, general legal principles (as of contracts and remedies) were applied in most situations. Questions have been and are posed — and rightfully so — as to whether general legal principles are properly applicable to specific sports business situations. Are sports problems special? Even today, this question is debatable. It is a question pursued by the inquiries posed in this and succeeding chapters.

2.01 New Leagues, Ensuing Legal Battles

For the first several decades after professional team sports were first successfully organized, as, for example, with the founding of baseball's National League in 1876, the legal problems that reached the courts mainly resulted from the competition of rival leagues with established leagues. With few exceptions, not until the 1960s and into the 1970s was this pattern disrupted. Thus, as each new league formed, it inevitably challenged an existing league, and before long, both parties headed for the courts. The National League, for example, found itself doing legal battle over competition from the American Association in 1882, the Union Association in 1884, the Players League in 1890, the American League in 1900, and, of course, others into this century. By the same token, the National Football League, the National Hockey League, and the National Basketball Association all were able to proceed pretty much as they willed until rival leagues emerged in these sports.

Even today, one can predict that a new league will increase the work of the courts and lawyers.

The established National Football League, for example, is carefully considering the tactics it might have to employ in dealing with the latest rival league — the United States Football League. The stakes are raised and litigation looms.

Exhibit 2–1 illustrates the correlation between the emergence of rival leagues and resulting litigation. As stated earlier, until the 1960s, this was undoubtedly the chief cause for legal activity. In recent years, team owners within a league have entered the picture, so that now they are fighting each other over the spoils. Nor are the players sitting still. Largely through players' associations, players and their agents are pressing their interests. Rival leagues, however, still are identified with increased litigation and, potentially, regulatory legislation. The cases listed in Exhibit 2–1 are only a representative sampling.

2.02   Formative Eras in Sports Legal Developments

Two time periods stand out in considering the most important developments in sports legal principles. The first was the era from 1890 to 1922. During this period, as exemplified by the cases presented later in this chapter, certain basic contract principles, applicable to professional sports situations, were established. These years also marked the first forays into the antitrust area. Even though the antitrust laws at that time did not apply to professional sports, at least to baseball, the initial inquiries did set a course for the industry. For the next 25 years after 1922, the sports scene was relatively peaceful, if not necessarily happy. No rival leagues emerged in any of the sports, and only occasional outbursts occurred, mainly on the part of certain baseball owners who were unhappy with the actions of their iron-fisted commissioner, Judge Kennesaw Mountain Landis.

After World War II, legal activity in the sports world began to increase, but not until the late 1950s did the second formative era in the development of sports legal principles emerge. What followed, in rapid succession, was the

application of antitrust laws to all sports except baseball, the formation of viable players unions, the application of the labor laws, the beginnings of collective bargaining, new looks at contract problems through litigation, and, much later, arbitration. Matters in the sports world were never to be the same.

2.03   The Big Three: Contracts, Antitrust, and Labor

Legal problems in sports came at length to revolve around three general legal areas: contracts, antitrust, and labor. The succeeding applications of new legal principles to professional sports did not mean that earlier applications were replaced or that later applications could be considered in isolation from the earlier. Today, these three legal areas influence each other, although it would appear that labor law and labor relations are at least the catalysts, and possibly the predominate influences.

These three legal areas provide the base for a sports legal structure. This hardly means they are the only legal concerns. As with other complex industries, a full panoply of legal principles affect the sports industry, including tort and property concepts. While perhaps not central to the actual way in which the sports leagues are structured, they are vital elements in the legal concerns.

Another legal area of note is tax. Federal and state tax laws have a strong influence on the ways leagues and clubs are organized. Player contracts often respond to the latest tax nuances, thereby affecting a club's economic posture as well. Overall, there is impact on the legal framework of sports. Moreover, tax laws are sufficiently complicated that special expertise is needed to explore their applications and ramifications, something this book cannot possibly accomplish. Some discussions of tax problems are presented in Chapter 4, from the perspective of the player, and from the perspective of management in Chapter 6. These discussions are introductory, however, and not exhaustive.

Even so, in the structure of sports law, the

Exhibit 2-1   Rival Leagues and Resulting Litigation

Year(s)	Sport	Established League(s)	Rival League	Sampling of Cases*
1882–84	Baseball	National	American Ass'n.	Bennett
1884	Baseball	National American Ass'n.	Union	Wise Mullane
1890	Baseball	National American Ass'n.	Players	Ward Ewing Pickett Hallman
1900-03	Baseball	National	American	Lajoie McGuire
1914-15	Baseball	National American	Federal	Fed. Baseball Weegham Chase Marsans
1946-49	Football	National (NFL)	All-American (AAFC)	Radovich
1946-47	Baseball	National American	Mexican	Gardella Martin Kowalski
1961-63	Basketball	National (NBA)	American (ABL)	Barnett
1960-66	Football	NFL	American (AFL)	Robinson Cannon AFL v. NFL Harris NY Giants Neely
1967-76	Basketball	NBA	American (ABA)	Robertson Sharman Hudson Lemat/Barry Capitols/Barry Cunningham

concentration is primarily on the interrelationships of contract, antitrust, and labor principles. The materials that follow introduce these principles and explore some of their interlocking impacts. This is particularly true of the final section of this chapter, which examines the labor exemption to the antitrust laws.

2.10   Enforcement of Contracts

As soon as rival leagues appeared (in the case of

baseball, the rival American Association was formed in 1882), offers to players to leave their present teams and go with the new league became irresistible. A player's contract that had run out was one thing. A contract still in force, however, was quite another, and understandably, clubs losing players moved to protect their own interests.

Damages for breach of contract is the usual remedy in the jurisprudence of this country. Such a solution was hardly satisfactory in a sports setting, however, since it is exceedingly difficult to gauge just what one player on a team is worth when that player defects. The obvious response would be to force the player to stay with the old team. But again, well-established legal principles both here and in our English background, dictate that ordering specific performance of a contract is an extraordinary remedy and that when the services under the contract are personal in nature, a court should not attempt to coerce relations between the parties.

That still left open the possibility of other responses. One of these was the negative injunction — an order to a party not to engage in activities that are detrimental to the interests of the other party, when such interests arise out of the contract between the two. Since this might mean prohibiting a party from engaging in his or her livelihood, the negative injunction is obviously not something that should be lightly or improvidently ordered. Standards would have to be devised to consider under what circumstances and with what limitations the negative injunction could be obtained. This did not remove all possibilities of other types of relief, such as damages, but the negative injunction came to be the usual remedy; its parameters directly affected the structure of sports leagues and, ultimately, the legal overlay which controlled them.

The early courts had to look for assistance in determining whether or not a negative injunction should issue. One theme of this book is that today's sports industries are a special part of the overall entertainment industry. To underscore

this, one can point to the 1800s and how the courts looked to other parts of the entertainment field for guidance.

2.11   The Initial Approaches and Setting of Standards

The English courts in the mid-1850s first began to issue the so-called negative injunction in cases that dealt with entertainers, who were certainly analogous to the sports figures to come under judicial scrutiny in this country. One could not be forced to remain in the employ of another, but one could be restrained from going elsewhere, particularly to a competitor of the current employer. The famous case of *Lumley* v. *Wagner*, 1 DeG.M. & G 604, 42 Eng. Rep. 687 (1852), is the standard-bearer for this proposition. It was quickly followed by cases such as *Webster* v. *Dillon*, 30 L.T.R.O.S. 71, 3 Jan. N.S. 432 (1857), and *Montague* v. *Flockton*, 42 L.J.R.N. 677, 16 Eq. 189 (1873). Two early cases in the United States, taking the lead from their English brethren, also embraced the notion of the negative injunction, at least in theory. (See *Daly* v. *Smith*, 38 N.Y. Super. Ct. 158 [1874], and *Mapleson* v. *Del Puente*, 13 Abb. N.C. 144). When considering the applicability of the negative injunction to the sports setting, the courts placed direct reliance on these precedents.

Certain features about the sports contracts, however, distinguished them from the entertainment agreements scrutinized in *Lumley* and the other cases. A central feature of the sports contract was the authority the club had to terminate the contract if it so chose. Another feature was the reserve clause, which reportedly made its appearance as early as 1879, just three years after the founding of the National League. This meant that a club could renew a player's contract at the end of the season and extend it at the will of the club for one more year. Thus, in contrast to the entertainment contracts, in which the term of the contract was for a specified period of time and the alleged breach would occur during that time, many of the sports cases involved a time period after the expiration of the original contract. The club would hold the players to an additional term by invoking the reserve clause in the old contract.

It is safe to assume, at least in the early cases such as *Ewing, Ward,* and *Lajoie,* which are discussed below, that the courts believed they had to go beyond the inquiries that were relevant to the entertainment cases. Consequently, as these cases suggest, early concern was expressed over the mutuality of obligation in the sports contracts, as well as over problems of definiteness. Eventually, these concerns were overcome and replaced by other considerations, such as uniqueness and irreparable harm, problems of clean hands, and the scope and duration of the injunction. Since the early cases were the precedent setters, however, an examination of their standards is an appropriate place to begin.

NOTES

1. For more specific information about the early entertainment cases, such as *Lumley* v. *Wagner,* see Tannebaum, "Enforcement of Personal Service Contracts in the Entertainment Industry," 42 *California Law Review* 18 (1954). These cases are also discussed for background purposes in Berry and Gould, "A Long, Deep Drive to Collective Bargaining: Of Players, Owners, Brawls and Strikes," 31 *Case Western Law Review* 685 (1981).

2. In *Lumley* v. *Wagner,* a young opera singer, Joanna Wagner, had left the employ of one opera company in London to go with a competitor in the same city. As is often the case, it may not have been Wagner who initiated the actions leading to this attempted defection. Often the rival is the one who is avidly seeking to obtain the services of the star. Consequently, a second action against the rival promoter or club often accompanies an action for a negative injunction against the entertainer or the athlete. So it was in the *Wagner* situation. A companion action was started and is recorded in *Lumley* v. *Gye,* 2 El. & Bl. 216, 118 Eng. Rep. 749 (1853). The action was for tortious interference with an advantageous relationship. Several similar actions have been initiated in the sports context. These are considered in Chapter 6 of this book.

Metropolitan Exhibition Co. v. Ewing, 42 F. 198 (S.D.N.Y. 1890)

Plaintiff baseball club brought this action to enjoin defendant ballplayer from playing the

upcoming season with another team. The plaintiff contended that under the contract it had with the player, a right of reservation, when fully exercised, obligated the ballplayer to play the upcoming season for them only. The right-of-reservation clause, as it appeared in the contract, mentioned only a minimum salary in reference to the subsequent year's contract terms. The plaintiff argued that the remainder of the terms carried over from the original contract.

The court began its inquiry by examining what would be required for a court to grant an injunction to enforce a negative convenant. The requirements were as follows:

1. The breach must be one for which damages would be inadequate compensation.
2. The party seeking the injunction must have "clean hands."
3. The injunction sought must not be unduly oppressive to the defendant.
4. The contract must have mutuality or be founded on adequate consideration.
5. The terms of the contract must be definite.

Because the plaintiff failed to satisfy this last requirement — that of definiteness — the court denied relief.

The court held that the right of reservation was not adequately defined in the contract. The clause mentioned a minimum salary, but even reference to the other parts of the contract could not fill in the other terms to be used in the second year of the contract. Reference was attempted to usage of trade but also to no avail. The court also discounted the importance of any course of dealing between the parties. In its view, the right of reservation was merely an agreement to agree and as such could not support either an action for damages or an injunction should the player not agree to a new contract.

Metropolitan Exhibition Co. v. Ward, 9 N.Y.S. 779 (Sup. Ct. 1890)

Plaintiff baseball club sought to restrain defendant ballplayer from playing the upcoming season for anyone except plaintiff. This right to an injunction was claimed under a right-of-reservation clause, similar to that contested in *Metropolitan Exhibition Co.* v. *Ewing,* and merely directed that the club had the right to reserve the ballplayer for the ensuing season at not less than the present season's salary.

The court resolved at first the right of a party to seek an injunction in a court of equity to enforce a negative convenant. Baseball players of peculiar fitness and skill, like actors and actresses, can be so enjoined from performing elsewhere. But before a court will grant such an injunction at a point preliminary to a trial on the issues, as was sought here, it must be satisfied that the plaintiff has a strong probability of prevailing on the ultimate issues of law. Furthermore, the court must be satisfied that "a contract exists which is reasonably definite and certain, and that for a breach thereof no adequate remedy exists at law. . . " and if "sufficiently definite, is it entirely conscionable, wanting neither in fairness or mutuality?"

In measuring this contract against these requirements, the court found that it failed both for indefiniteness and for lack of mutuality. As to the former, the court's interpretation of the reserve clause rendered it an agreement by the ballplayer to allow the club to reserve him upon terms to be negotiated thereafter. Without any of the terms or conditions of this subsequent contract explained, the contract was lacking for definiteness.

The court then explained that if it were to accept the argument of the plaintiff that the contract terms were to be continued once the right of reservation was exercised, then the contract must fail and an injunction be denied for lack of mutuality. To so interpret the contract would permit the ball club to reserve the player in perpetuity while it also reserved the right to terminate the player's rights on ten days notice. Such concentration of power in one party could lead to its complete control over the terms of any future contract, since it could wait to terminate until the player had nowhere else to seek

employment. The club would thus have no obligation to employ the player even if it reserved the player. Therefore, mutuality did not exist.

For either of these reasons — definiteness or mutuality — the request for a preliminary injunction must fail.

NOTES

1. The *Ward* decision considered whether or not a preliminary injunction should issue. There was never, evidently, a full trial on the matter; thus, there is no definitive holding that the contract was lacking in mutuality. However, the decision does express great doubts that plaintiff ball club would succeed on the merits (see 9 N.Y.S. at 784). Similar reservations were expressed in *Ewing* as well, as when the court states:

The law implies that the option of reservation is to be exercised within a reasonable time; but when this has been done the right to reserve the player becomes the privilege, and the exclusive privilege, as between the reserving club and the other clubs, to obtain his services for another year if the parties can agree upon the terms. As a coercive condition which places the player practically, or at least measurably, in a situation where he must contract with the club that reserved him, it is operative and valuable to the club. But, as the basis for an action for damages if the player fails to contract, or for an action to enforce specific performance, it is wholly nugatory. In a legal sense, it is merely a contract to make a contract if the parties can agree [42 F. at 204]

2. Often in these cases the preliminary injunction stage is a crucial one. The parties can generally discern from the court's ruling how the ultimate merits will likely be decided. This is particularly true when, as in *Ward,* there is no jury and the full trial may well be before the same judge. Accordingly, a large percentage of the injunction cases are settled after the hearing on the preliminary injunction and before the trial on the merits.

3. The *Ewing* and *Ward* cases revolved around a situation unique in sports annals—that is, an attempt by the athletes to form their own league, called, appropriately enough, the Players League. They had a fair chance for success and might have prevailed had they not been undercut by investors brought in to help get the league started. Further accounts about the Players League are detailed in H. Seymour, *Baseball: The Early Years* (Oxford University Press, 1960), pp. 228–229 and 240–250.

4. In addition to *Ewing* and *Ward,* other lawsuits were brought against players who left the National League and the American Association to head for the Players League. Most attempts to retain the players were unsuccessful (see, for example, *Philadelphia Ball Club* v. *Hallman,* 8 Pa. County Ct.

57 [1890]). In only one case was the club successful, at least in the courts. John Pickett, who had been playing for the American Association's Kansas City club, was ordered not to play for any other team. However, Pickett evidently was able to ignore the injunction. He is reported to have played second base for the Philadelphia Players League club (see Seymour, *Baseball: The Early Years*, p. 237).

Philadelphia Ball Club, Limited v. Lajoie, 51 A. 973 (Pa. 1902)

Opinion by Mr. Justice Potter, April 21, 1902:

The defendant in this case contracted to serve the plaintiff as a baseball player for a stipulated time. During that period he was not to play for any other club. He violated his agreement, however, during the term of his engagement, and in disregard of his contract, arranged to play for another and a rival organization.

The plaintiff by means of this bill, sought to restrain him, during the period covered by the contract.

The court below refused an injunction, holding that to warrant the interference prayed for, "The defendant's services must be unique, extraordinary, and of such a character as to render it impossible to replace him; so that his breach of contract would result in irreparable loss to the plaintiff." In the view of the court, the defendant's qualifications did not measure up to this high standard. The trial court was also of opinion that the contract was lacking in mutuality; for the reason that it gave plaintiff an option to discharge defendant on ten days' notice, without a reciprocal right on the part of defendant.

The learned judge who filed the opinion in the court below, with great industry and painstaking care, collected and reviewed the English and American decisions bearing upon the question involved, and makes apparent the wide divergence of opinion which has prevailed.

We think, however, that in refusing relief unless the defendant's services were shown to be of such a character as to render it impossible to replace him, he has taken extreme ground.

It seems to us that a more just and equitable rule is laid down in Pomeroy on Specific Performance, page 31, where the principle is thus declared: "Where one person agrees to render personal services to another, which require and presuppose a special knowledge, skill and ability in the employee, so that in case of a default the same service could not easily be obtained from others, although the affirmative specific performance of the contract is beyond the power of the court, its performance will be negatively enforced by enjoining its breach. . . . The damages for breach of such contract cannot be estimated with any certainty, and the employer cannot, by means of any damages, purchase the same service in the labor market."

We have not found any case going to the length of requiring as a condition of relief, proof of the impossibility of obtaining equivalent service. It is true that the injury must be irreparable, but as observed by Mr. Justice Lowrie, in Commonwealth v. Pittsburg, etc., Railroad Company, 24 Pa. 160, "The argument that there is no 'irreparable damage' would not be so often used by wrongdoers if they would take the trouble to discover that the word 'irreparable' is a very unhappily chosen one, used in expressing the rule that an injunction may issue to prevent wrongs of a repeated and continuing character, or which occasion damages which are estimated only by conjecture, and not by any accurate standard."

We are therefore within the term whenever it is shown that no certain pecuniary standard exists for the measurement of the damages. . . .

The court below finds from the testimony that "the defendant is an expert baseball player in any position; that he has a great reputation as a second baseman; that his place would be hard to fill with as good a player; that his withdrawal from the team would weaken it, as would the withdrawal of any good player, and would probably make a difference in the size of the audiences attending the game."

We think that in thus stating it, he puts it very mildly, and that the evidence would warrant a stronger finding as to the ability of the defendant as an expert ballplayer. He has been for several years in the service of the plaintiff club, and has been re-engaged from season to season at a constantly increasing salary. He has become thoroughly familiar with the action and methods of the other players in the club, and his own work is peculiarly meritorious as an integral part of the team work which is so essential. In addition to these features which render his services of peculiar and special value to the plaintiff, and not easily replaced, Lajoie is well known, and has great reputation among the patrons of the sport, for ability in the position which he filled, and was thus a most attractive drawing card for the public. He may not be the sun in the baseball firmament, but he is certainly a bright, particular star.

We feel therefore that the evidence in this case justifies the conclusion that the services of the defendant are of such a unique character, and display such a special knowledge, skill and ability as renders them of peculiar value to the plaintiff, and so difficult of substitution, that their loss will produce irreparable injury, in the legal significance of that term, to the plaintiff. . . .

But the court below was also of the opinion that the contract was lacking in mutuality of remedy, and considered that as a controlling reason for the refusal of an injunction. The opinion quotes the nineteenth paragraph of the contract, which gives to the plaintiff a right of renewal for the period of six months beginning April 15, 1902, and for a similar period in two successive years thereafter. The seventeenth paragraph also provides for the termination of the contract upon ten days' notice by the plaintiff. But the eighteenth paragraph is also of importance, and should not be overlooked. It provides as follows: "18. In consideration of the faithful performance of the conditions, covenants, undertakings and promises herein by the said party of the second part, inclusive of the concession of the options of release and renewals prescribed in the seventeenth and nineteenth paragraphs, the said party of the first part, for itself and its assigns, hereby agrees to pay to him for his services for said term the sum of $2,400, payable as follows," etc.

And turning to the fifth paragraph, we find that it provides expressly for proceedings, either in law or equity, "to enforce the specific performance by the said party of the second part, or to enjoin said party of the second part from performing services for any other person or organization during the period of service herein contracted for. And nothing herein contained shall be construed to prevent such remedy in the courts in case of any breach of this agreement by said party of the second part, as said party of the first part, or its assigns, may elect to invoke."

We have then at the outset, the fact the paragraphs now criticised and relied upon in defense, were deliberately accepted by the defendant, and that such acceptance was made part of the inducement for the plaintiff to enter into the contract. We have the further fact that the contract has been partially executed by services rendered, and payment made therefore; so that the situation is not now the same as when the contract was wholly executory. The relation between the parties has been so far changed, as to give to the plaintiff an equity arising out of the part performance, to insist upon the completion of the agreement according to its terms by the defendant. This equity may be distinguished from the original right under the contract itself, and it might well be questioned whether the court would not be justified in giving effect to it by injunction, without regard to the mutuality or nonmutuality in the original contract. The plaintiff has so far performed its part of the contract in entire good faith, in every detail; and it would, therefore, be inequitable to permit the defendant to withdraw from the agreement at this late day. . . .

In the contract now before us, the defendant agreed to furnish his skilled professional services to the plaintiff for a period which might be extended over three years by proper notice given before the close of each current year. Upon the other hand, the plaintiff retained the right to terminate the contract upon ten days' notice, and the payment of salary for that time, and the expenses of defendant in getting to his home. But the fact of this concession to the plaintiff is distinctly pointed out as part of the consideration for the large salary paid to the defendant, and is emphasized as such. And owing to the peculiar nature of the services demanded by the business, and the high degree of efficiency which must be maintained, the stipulation is not unreasonable. Particularly is this true when it is remembered that the plaintiff has played for years under substantially the same regulations.

We are not persuaded that the terms of this contract manifest any lack of mutuality in remedy. Each party has the possibility of enforcing all the rights stipulated for in the agreement. It is true that the terms make it possible for the plaintiff to put an end to the contract in a space of time much less than the period during which the defendant has agreed to supply his personal services; but mere difference in the rights stipulated for, does not destroy mutuality of remedy. Freedom of contract covers a wide range of obligation and duty as between the parties, and it may not be impaired, so long as the bounds of reasonableness and fairness are not transgressed. . . .

. . . . The defendant sold to the plaintiff for a valuable consideration the exclusive right to his professional services for a stipulated period, unless sooner surrendered by the plaintiff; which could only be, after due and reasonable notice and payment of salary and expenses until the expiration. Why should not a court of equity protect such an agreement until it is terminated? The court cannot compel the defendant to play for the plaintiff, but it can restrain him from playing for another club in violation of his agreement. No reason is given why this should not be done, except that presented by the argument that the right given to the plaintiff to terminate the contract upon ten days' notice destroys the mutuality of the remedy. But to this it may be answered, that as already stated, the defendant has the possibility of enforcing all the rights for which he stipulated in the agreement, which is all that he can reasonably ask; furthermore, owing to the peculiar nature and circumstances of the business, the reservation upon the part of the plaintiff to terminate upon short notice, does not make the whole contract inequitable.

In this connection another observation may be made, which is that the plaintiff by the act of bringing this suit, has disavowed any intention of exercising the right to terminate the contract on its own part. This is a necessary inference from its action in asking the court to exercise its equity power to enforce the agreement made by the defendant not to give his services to any other club. Besides, the remedy by injunction is elastic and adaptable, and is wholly within the control of the court. If granted now, it can be easily dissolved whenever a change in the circumstances or in the attitude of the plaintiff should seem to require it. The granting or refusal of an injunction or its continuance is never a matter of strict right, but is always a question of discretion to be determined by the court in view of the particular circumstances.

Upon a careful consideration of the whole case, we are of opinion that the provisions of the contract are reasonable, and that the consideration is fully adequate. . . .

The specifications of error are sustained, and the decree of the court below is reversed, and the bill is reinstated. And it is ordered that the record be remitted to the court below for further proceedings in accordance with this opinion.

NOTES

1. The American League officially started in 1900. In fact, it developed from a minor league, the Western. Under the leadership of Ban Johnson, it determined to go major and changed its name in October 1899 to give itself a national image. Many reports have chronicled this league's successful challenge to the established National League. In particular, see L. Allen, *The American League Story* (Hill Wang) (1962) and R. Smith, *Baseball* (New York: Simon & Schuster), (1947).

For the 1900 season, the American League did little in the way of player raids on the National League. In fact, Ban Johnson promised there would be no such actions. The promise lasted for only one year. In a short time, several national league players had defected, among the most notable, Napoleon Lajoie.

2. Although the Philadelphia National League Club obtained an injunction against Lajoie, its victory was a shallow one. Lajoie was forthwith traded to another American League club in Cleveland. When the Philadelphia Nationals sought to obtain injunctive relief in Ohio, the result went the other way. Lajoie never returned to Philadelphia or to the National League. See *Philadelphia Baseball Club* v. *Lajoie,* 13 Ohio Dec. 504 (1902).

3. After *Lajoie,* the courts moved away from concerns over the mutuality of obligations in the player contracts. As the following materials attest, much greater scrutiny was placed on issues of uniqueness and irreparable harm, "clean hands," and undue harshness. However, at least one case, *Weegham* v. *Killifer,* adhered to the traditional mutuality approach (see Section 2.13). Another case, *Connecticut Professional Sports Corporation* v. *Heyman* (see Section 2.12), on the special facts of that case, also was concerned about a lack of mutuality.

2.12 Uniqueness and Irreparable Harm

Cincinnati Exhibition Co. v. Marsans, 216 F. 269 (E.D. Mo. 1914)

A suit in equity brought against Armando Marsans sought an injunction against Marsans from rendering his services to another club in violation of a term in the contract in which Marsans covenanted to render exclusive services to plaintiff. The court ruled that a refusal of the injunction would cause irreparable injury to the plaintiff; defendant's services were unique and extraordinary and could not be rendered by another. The court considered an injunction proper to prevent defendant from violating his negative convenant. The contract, which was for a specified period at a fixed compensation, was not invalid because of a ten-day notice provision which allowed plaintiff to discharge the defendant. The court ruled that because the defendant entered upon the performance of the contract and received compensation as valuable consideration, the contract was valid. Equity demanded that defendant would not be allowed to render his services to any other club until the final decision of the case.

Long Island American Ass'n. Football Club, Inc. v. Manrodt, 23 N.Y.S. 2d 858 (Sup. Ct. 1940)

This action was brought by a professional football club to restrain certain players from breaching a provision in their contracts against playing for any other club. Defendants Spencer Manrodt and George Lenc signed contracts to play professional football for the Long Island Indians. They later signed contracts to play for the New York Yankees football team. The Yankees denied any knowledge that the players were already signed and further claimed the players' contracts with the Indians were void for lack of consideration.

The court issued an injunction restraining the players from breaching the contract and the Yankees from procuring such breaches, conditioned upon the continued performance of the Long Island club of its contract obligations with the players. The court noted special and peculiar factors involved in the organization of a new football team, such as competition from established clubs and brevity of the season, and said the players possessed such extraordinary ability as football players to render their services irreplaceable. The court held the club would suffer irreparable harm if the players breached the contract.

The court further ruled that a provision allowing the club to terminate the contracts on three days written notice did not render the contract void for lack of mutuality. The court's rationale was that mutuality of obligation was not lacking because the provisions made the

contract binding on the plaintiff at least until notice was given, that there was no requirement of mutuality of remedy, and that the injunction granted was conditioned upon plaintiff's performance of the contracts.

Winnipeg Rugby Football Club v. Freeman and Locklear, 140 F. Supp. 365 (N.D. Ohio 1955)

This action was brought by Winnipeg, a Canadian football club, to enjoin performance of contracts between the Cleveland Browns and two football players, R.C. Freeman and Jack Locklear, who had previously contracted to play for Winnipeg. The players signed contracts on January 8, 1955, to play for Winnipeg. Part of their contracts read that they could not play with another team during the life of the contract. On February 6, 1955, they signed with Cleveland and never reported to the Winnipeg team. The Browns had heard rumors that the players were already under contract with the Canadian team.

The court granted the preliminary injunction. The contracts between the players and Winnipeg were valid and were for services of special merit, which were of peculiar and particular value to Winnipeg. Despite testimony by Paul Brown of Cleveland that the players were merely good, not extraordinary players, the court ruled that a standard of special skill and ability must have some relation to the class and character of play. The Canadian Football League had a lower standard of play, and it could easily be found that the players were of exceptional value to Winnipeg. Winnipeg was willing and able to perform its obligations, and the defendant players should have to perform theirs.

Spencer v. Milton, 287 N.Y.S. 944 (Sup. Ct. 1936)

Plaintiff baseball club applied for an injunction, during the pendency of the action, to restrain defendant baseball player from playing for any other person or association for the year 1936, other than the Albany Black Sox Athletic Association, or its assignees.

The New York Supreme Court, at Special

Term, denied plaintiff's motion for an injunction during the pendency of the action. The court reasoned that two tests govern an action to enjoin the violation of the negative covenant of an agreement by an employee that he will not work for another. The first is that the employee's services must be of a unique and unusual character, and the second is that the agreement must contain mutuality of obligation.

With regard to the second test, the court noted that the obligation that the plaintiff's association incurred with regard to the defendant by the agreement between the parties was expressed by the provision stating "the club will pay the players a salary for skilled services during the season of 1936 on the percentage basis, 60 percent for all the players composing the team, to be divided equally after each game played." The court held that this provision did not clearly fix the obligation of the plaintiff association to the defendant.

The court based its conclusion on the fact that it was not agreed that defendant would receive a pro rata share with the other players of 60 percent of the profits of each game or of the receipts of each game, that it was not provided precisely what the obligation of the plaintiff's association with respect to defendant's compensation would be, and that the obligation of the defendant "to render to the plaintiff the services which it is sought to prevent his rendering to another" was not clearly nor precisely fixed. The agreement merely provided that defendant would "faithfully serve the club in conformity with the agreement above recited." Defendant agreed to keep himself in good physical condition, to conform to certain standards of conduct, and to surrender a uniform or uniforms furnished him by the plaintiff's association, not to engage in any game or exhibition except for the club, and to report for practice and to participate in such exhibitions as may be arranged by the club for a period of 30 days prior to the playing season.

The court found that the agreement did not expressly require that the defendant should play on the baseball team of the plaintiff's association and that unless the contract were to be construed largely by implication, it was doubtful it could be enforced in an action at law against defendant for damages arising from a refusal by defendant to play.

The court further held that the requirement that the employee's services be of a "unique" and unusual character" was not satisfactorily established. Although the complaint described the defendant as having "particular and special qualifications to play the position of first base" and "special proficiency and wide reputation," the court held neither statement to be sufficient. The description of defendant in plaintiff's affidavit as being "an especially proficient and able first baseman," and that his playing with the team tended to "increase the attendance at games" was held by the court to be insufficient proof that plaintiff could not resort to an action at law as an adequate remedy for a breach of the defendant's contract.

Connecticut Professional Sports Corporation v. Heyman, 276 F. Supp. 618 (S.D.N.Y. 1967)

This diversity action was brought by Connecticut Professional Sports Corporation (the Club) to obtain an injunction to prevent Arthur Heyman from playing professional basketball with the New Jersey Americans (New Jersey) of the American Basketball Association (ABA) or any other professional basketball team except the Hartford Capitols (Hartford) of the Eastern Professional Basketball League (EPBL).

Heyman had been rated as one of the top 50 basketball players of the century while at Duke University. However, he was unable to succeed in the National Basketball Association, and his contract was purchased from the Wilmington Blue Bombers of the EPBL for $1,500. On October 20, 1966, Heyman and the Club entered an exclusive contract for Heyman to play basketball for a one-year period ending August 31, 1967. Heyman was to play as many games as the Club required, giving his best and most skillful performance at all times. Heyman was to be paid $125 and $50 in expenses for each regular season and playoff game actually played. The agreement acknowledged that Heyman's special talents were of a unique character, which had to be maintained to meet the competitive requirements of the EPBL and the public. An option clause was part of the agreement, which provided the Club with the right to renew the contract for one year at an agreed salary. If no agreement was reached, the Club could fix compensation. This option could be exercised by the Club only by serving Heyman with written notice prior to August 31, 1967. In addition, the Club had the right to terminate Heyman's services by written notice at any time. Heyman would then be free of all obligations to the Club.

Heyman also agreed that the Club could seek injunctive relief if he played professional basketball with any other team without written permission. The Club was also entitled to receive $100 per game in liquidated damages for each regularly scheduled game at which Heyman failed to appear.

During the 1966–67 season, Heyman met all the obligations required by the Club and was the league's leading scorer. In March 1967, Heyman learned that a new professional basketball league was being formed (the ABA) and signed to play for New Jersey during the 1967–68 season for $15,000. Upon discovering Heyman's defection, the Club exercised its option to renew Heyman's contract, with an increased salary. The Club contacted New Jersey and informed them of the Club's renewal rights under Heyman's contract. The Club indicated a willingness to settle, but no settlement was reached. This action was commenced by the Club to obtain injunctive relief.

In discussing injunctive relief, the court noted that the type of relief sought, which would preclude an athlete from practicing his trade, was an extraordinary remedy to be granted only when the equities favored the plaintiff. Also, the damage to the plaintiff must be irreparable, outweighing the harm to the defendant. The court noted that this type of relief had to be made on a case-by-case basis after careful analysis of the contractual terms to see whether they were unduly harsh or one-sided.

The primary reason for denying relief in this instance was that the contract the Club sought to enforce permitted the Club to terminate it at will, while binding Heyman for a one-year period. Further, the contract entitled Heyman, as a matter of right, to play in games only when his services were requested by the Club. Heyman was then compensated only for games actually played. If Heyman were injured, he would receive no compensation but would be obligated to play for the Club once he recovered. The contract also failed to provide for a minimum number of games to be played, resulting in the potential of limiting Heyman's meager salary even more.

The court noted that the Club had not enforced any of these one-sided provisions and had helped Heyman supplement his income by finding him an insurance agent's job. These actions were insufficient, however, to permit the court to enforce a contract that could have been used to prevent Heyman from earning a living at playing basketball. Thus, the court exercised its discretion and denied granting the negative injunctive relief sought. The court also pointed out that it was aware of the necessity of economic protection of new organizations, so that sufficient competition against rival leagues would be possible. However, enforcing negative injunctive relief of one-sided bargains would serve the Club's interest only at the expense of one with even less economic power.

NOTE _____

1. The foregoing *Spencer* and *Heyman* cases dealt with minor league players, arguably distinguishable in terms of uniqueness from major league athletes. A "minor league" boxer also benefited from the same type of analysis. In *Safro* v. *Lakofsky,* 238 N.W. 641 (Minn. 1931), the defendant boxer appealed from an order granting a temporary injunction for breach of a contract held to be an employment contract for purposes of the action, in which plaintiff agreed to act as boxing manager for defendant and defendant agreed that during the life of the contract (five years) he would not engage in any fights except those procured by plaintiff. The court held that the contract was one for

personal services, the services provided by the defendant were not unique, and the defendant was not peculiarly qualified above others to render them. Plaintiff was not irreparably damaged by defendant's breach of his negative convenant not to engage in any matches not procured by plaintiff.

Dallas Cowboys Football Club, Inc. v. Harris, 348 S.W. 2d 37 (Tex. Civ. App. 1961)

Appellant Dallas Cowboys Football Club of the NFL brought this action against James B. Harris seeking an injunction to restrain Harris from playing professional football for anyone except the Cowboys. Appellant alleged that defendant Harris was bound by the terms of a written contract to play football for the Cowboys and no one else, but that in violation of his contract he was playing football for the Dallas Texans Football Club of the AFL. The suit was for an injunction only. No money judgment was sought.

After a hearing and upon execution of a $15,000 injunction bond, a temporary injunction was granted to the Cowboys on July 19, 1960. Prior to submission of his appeal from the temporary order, Harris filed a motion to dismiss his appeal on the grounds that the appeal had become moot, as the temporary injunction had necessarily been dissolved by the entry of the judgment on the merits denying the club a permanent injunction. The court overruled Harris's motion to dismiss his appeal. The court reasoned that the temporary injunction did not expire under its own term but remained in effect pending final determination, which means final determination on appeal.

In the meantime, the trial court had reached the main suit for trial on the merits, and on September 21, 1960, returned a judgment favorable to Harris. The Cowboys appealed.

In June 1958, Harris signed a one-year, $8,000 standard player contract to play football and to engage in activities related to football for the Los Angeles Rams, a member of the NFL. The contract, which extended until May 1, 1959, included the following clause:

10. On or before the date of expiration of this contract, the Club may, upon notice in writing to the Player, renew this contract for a further term until the first day of May following said expiration on the same terms as are provided by this contract, except that (1) the Club may set the rate of compensation to be paid by the Club to the Player during said period of renewal, which compensation shall not be less than ninety percent (90%) of the amount paid by the Club to the Player during the preceding season, and (2) after such renewal this contract shall not include a further option to the Club to renew the contract;. . .

Should Player . . . retire from football prior to the expiration of this contract or any option contained herein, and subsequently . . . return to professional football, then . . . the date lapsed between . . . his retiring from professional football and his return thereto, shall be considered as tolled, and the term of his contract shall be considered as extended for a period beginning with the player's . . . return to professional football . . . and ending after a period of time equal to the portion of the term of his contract which was unexpired at the time the Player . . . returned from professional football; and the option contained herein shall be considered as continuously in effect from the date of this contract until the end of such extended term.

Harris and the Rams both fulfilled the terms of the primary contract. However, a controversy as to the Rams's exercise of the option clause arose, and as a result, Harris chose not to play professional football during the 1959 season. Instead, he enrolled as a student at the University of Oklahoma, where he also held the position of assistant football coach. In April 1960, Harris signed a contract with the Dallas Texans Football Club of the AFL for the 1960 season.

On June 22, 1960, Harris's contract with the Rams was assigned to the Dallas Cowboys of the NFL. The Cowboys immediately instituted this action to restrain Harris for playing football for anyone other than the Cowboys.

The Cowboys contended that Harris was bound to play football only for the Cowboys for an additional year by the terms of the 1958 contract and its option. Harris contended that the lower court found that Harris did not have exceptional and unique knowledge, skill, and ability as a football player. However, the court of appeals found that the evidence was "insufficient" to support the jury verdict in the lower court — that is, the finding was so against the overwhelming weight and preponderance of the evidence as to be manifestly wrong. The court reasoned that the definition of the word "unique" introduced in evidence was too narrow and limited. Relying on *Philadelphia Ball Club* v. *Lajoie*, 202 Pa. 210, 51 A. 973, the court held that in granting an injunction, it is not necessary that defendant's services be shown to be of such character as to make it impossible to replace him. The better test, the court reasoned, was whether in the case of a default the same service could not easily be obtained from others. On the basis of Harris's own testimony and that of other witnesses, the court ruled that the evidence was insufficient to support the fact finding of the jury to the effect that Harris did not possess exceptional and unique knowledge, skill, and ability as a football player.

Harris contended that, even setting aside the jury's finding, the injunctive relief sought by the Cowboys should be denied because the contract was not valid, having expired by its own terms, and because Harris had not retired from activities related to football. Harris argued that the Cowboys invalidly exercised its option in that the renewal contract tendered Harris itself contained an option clause, although the original contract expressly provided that the renewal contract should not contain an option clause. The court, however, rejected this argument, ruling that by later proposing a new and different contract the Club did not waive or abandon its earlier exercise of its option under the first contract. Harris also argued that because he had not retired from activities related to football, the contract provision providing that the running of time on the option agreement should be tolled did not apply. The court rejected this argument as well, noting that Harris did not play professional football during the 1959–60 season but rather was a student and employed as an assistant football coach during that time.

In his appeal from the order granting the Club a temporary injunction, Harris argued, inter alia, that the trial court erred in granting the temporary injunction because the Club was thereby afforded all the relief to which it would be entitled upon a final hearing of the case, that that contract violated antitrust laws, and that the contract sued on was unreasonably harsh and unenforceable in equity.

The court upheld the granting of the injunction by the trial court, holding that there was no abuse of the court's discretion in granting the order. The court reasoned that the granting of the temporary injunction did not conclude the controversial issues between the parties or afford the Club all the relief it could obtain in a trial on the merits. The right of Harris to play for the Dallas Texans or any other club after a finding for Harris on the merits would have been unimpaired. The court also held that no antitrust question was involved. The issue was which of the two contracts that Harris signed was he obligated to. Finally, the court found that there was no support for the contention that the contract was so unreasonable or harsh as to be unenforceable in equity.

The judgement on the merits was reversed and the cause remanded for a new trial; the order granting the temporary injunction was affirmed.

NOTE _____

1. In holding that no viable antitrust claim was raised in this situation, the court said: "The contract sued on here does not violate the anti-trust laws of the State of Texas and of the United States . . . Harris is not being black-listed or boycotted. Quite the contrary, at least two professional football teams are eager to employ his services. His trouble is that he has signed with both of them and the only difficulty is to determine under which of them Harris is obligated" (348 S.W. 2d at 47). Harris may have been just a few years early with his antitrust complaint. The football cases in the 1970s litigating the antitrust claims of such as Joe Kapp and Jim "Yazoo" Smith were heard by judges much more sympathetic to the players. See Section 2.40.

Central New York Basketball, Inc. v. Barnett and Cleveland Basketball Club, Inc., 181 NE 2d 506 (Ohio C.P. 1961)

Richard Barnett attempted to jump from the Syracuse Nationals of the National Basketball Association to the Cleveland Pipers of the American Basketball Association before the expiration of his NBA contract. Central New York Basketball, Inc. (CNYB), which owned and operated the Syracuse team, brought this action, seeking to enjoin Barnett from playing for the Cleveland team and to enjoin the Cleveland team from interfering with the performance of Barnett's contract with Syracuse. Judgment was rendered for the plaintiff on all counts.

Barnett played for Syracuse in his rookie year (1959–60) after being selected as the team's first-round draft choice in 1959. He contracted with Syracuse for a second year (1960–61) for a salary of $8,500. The contract contained a renewal clause so that Barnett's services could be retained beyond the one-year provision of the contract. In order to exercise the renewal clause, Syracuse had to tender a contract to Barnett by September 1. If the parties were unable to agree on the terms of the contract by November 1, Syracuse had to notify Barnett in writing within ten days that the option had been executed. All terms would be the same as the preceding year, except that the club could fix the salary, provided it was at least 75 percent of the salary figure of the prior year.

Plaintiff alleged that terms were discussed and agreed upon between Barnett and Syracuse for the 1961–62 season and that a salary advance was sent to Barnett. Defendant admits that he requested and received the advance, which remained in its envelope, but denies that terms were reached for a new contract. Since the defendant did not sign and return the contract sent to him for the 1961–62 season, which called for a salary increase of $3,000, CNYB exercised its option to renew the Barnett contract as called for in the original agreement. In its letter of notification, CNYB informed Barnett that "[i]t is our position that your 1960–61 contract with

us was renewed when we came to terms and we sent you an advance. However, to abide by the letter of the contract and to make the position of the Syracuse Nationals absolutely clear, we hereby notify you that pursuant to Paragraph 22(a) of said contract, we hereby renew the same for the period of one year ending October 1, 1962. The amount payable to you under such renewed contract is hereby fixed at $11,500."

During the time between the issuance of the contract for Barnett to sign (May 26, 1961) and the exercise of the renewal clause (November 6, 1961), Barnett was involved in negotiations with the Cleveland team. They reached an agreement for the 1961–62 season.

Defendant claimed that Barnett's contract with Syracuse was void because the renewal clause called for perpetual option that the Club could exercise, thus holding Barnett forever. The plaintiff interpreted the renewal clause as a one-year option only. The court decided that the plaintiff's claim was the proper interpretation because "if the language of a contract is susceptible of two constructions, one of which will render it valid and give effect to the obligation of the parties, and the other will render it invalid and ineffectual, the former construction must be adopted."

Defendant also challenged the renewal provisions on the grounds that they lacked mutuality. The court held for plaintiff, relying on *Philadelphia Ball Club* v. *Lajoie* 51 A. 973 (Pa. 1902), in which case the court found that "mere differences in the rights stipulated for does not destroy mutuality of remedy." Thus, the court found that the renewal clause was valid and enforceable because there was sufficient consideration granted to the defendant in the way of salary to justify the existence of the renewal clause. Mutuality is unimpaired. The court determined that there was a valid and binding contract between Syracuse and Barnett for the 1961–62 season.

Finally, the court relied on several factors to arrive at its conclusion concerning Barnett's worth to Syracuse, such that his loss would cause irreparable harm. The contract Barnett signed in both leagues explicitly stated:

> [T]he player represents and agrees that he has exceptional and unique skill and ability as a basketball player; that his services to be rendered hereunder are of a special, unusual and extraordinary character which gives them peculiar value which cannot be reasonably or adequately compensated for in damages at law, and that the player's breach of this contract will cause the Club great and irreparable injury and damage. The player agrees that in addition to other remedies, the Club shall be entitled to injunctive and other equitable relief to prevent a breach of this contract by the player. . . .

Despite this clause, the Cleveland Pipers coach testified that he found Barnett to be a "pretty good" player but not in a class with the top players in professional basketball. Barnett testified that he was "a professional basketball player" but not of unique and exceptional skill and ability and not such that his services were of a special, unusual, and extraordinary character. However, the court found that "it would seem that mere engagement as a basketball player in the NBA or ABL carries with it recognition (of a player's) excellence and extraordinary abilities." The paragraphs in the contracts were given heavy weight. The court ruled that the testimony of the Cleveland coach was that of an interested party and that it was contradictory to the offer of $13,000 made for Barnett's services. Barnett's testimony also was from an interested witness, and understandable embarrassment tempered his opinions of his own abilities.

The general manager of the Syracuse Nationals testified that he thought Barnett was "one of the greatest basketball players playing the game." He also placed Barnett among the group of the top players in pro basketball. Additional evidence pertaining to Barnett's abilities as a pro basketball player included the following: he was a number one draft choice; he was the 19th leading scorer in the NBA during the 1960–61 season; he was not, however, among the players chosen for the East-West All Star Game in 1961; nor was he among the players named in the U.S. Basketball Writers' All-NBA Team for 1961.

Once again, the court recognized that the witness was not disinterested. Nevertheless, the court determined that "[t]he increase of salary from $8,500 to $11,500 agreed to by the plaintiff, the Cleveland Basketball Club's willingness to pay $13,000, and the latter's eagerness to secure [Barnett's] services, all point to a high regard for his playing abilities. Whether Barnett ranks with the top basketball players or not, the evidence shows that he is an outstanding professional basketball player of unusual attainments and exceptional skill and ability, and that he is of peculiar and particular value to plaintiff."

In concluding, the court summarized by stating:

> Professional players in the major baseball, football, and basketball leagues have unusual talents or skills or they would not be so employed. Such players, the defendant Barnett included, are not easily replaced.
>
> The right of the plaintiff is plain and the wrong done by the defendants is equally plain, and there is no reason why the Court should be sparing in the application of its remedies.
>
> The Court finds in favor of the plaintiff on all issues joined and permanent injunctions as requested for the 1961–62 basketball playing season are decreed. Thereafter the said injunctions shall be dissolved.

NOTE ———————————————————

1. Excerpts from the trial testimony regarding the uniqueness of Dick Barnett as a professional basketball player are reported in Section 1.16.

2.13   Clean Hands

Numerous cases and all the standard treatises on equitable remedies set forth the basic proposition that "he who comes into equity must have clean hands." Since the primary remedy available to a club to prevent a player from defecting to another club or league is the equitable negative injunction, the possible application of the "clean hands" doctrine is always present. Since, in addition, there is in the sports world the inevitable desire to get a jump on a competitor and to do so by means that are of questionable ethics at best and of outright illegality at worst, the invocation of the doctrine has been a reality on several occasions.

The discussions which follow begin with the 1914 case of *Weegham* v. *Killefer*. The case sets a standard that makes it clear that the conduct complained of need not necessarily be illegal. Unethical conduct may suffice as well.

After that, matters become more confusing, as attempts must be made, however unsatisfactorily, to reconcile the *New York Giants* and *Houston Oilers* cases, and then the *Minnesota Muskies* and *Washington Capitols* cases. Both sets of cases raise distinctive possible applications of the "clean hands" doctrine. What approach in each set of cases should prevail is a matter for careful analysis.

Weegham v. Killefer, 215 F. 168 (W.D.Mich. 1914)

Plaintiffs Charles Weegham and the Chicago Federal League Baseball Club brought a suit in equity against William Killefer and the Philadelphia National Club to enjoin them from executing a contract which called for Killefer to play for Philadelphia for three years.

Killefer was under contract to play for Philadelphia in 1913. Twenty-five percent of his salary was in consideration of Killefer's obligation to contract with and continue in the services of Philadelphia for the 1914 season at a salary to be determined by the parties. Killefer agreed to play for Philadelphia, then negotiated a contract with Chicago; twelve days later he negotiated yet another contract with Philadelphia.

The court decided there were two main issues in the case. The first was whether the 1913 contract with Philadelphia relative to the reservation of the player for the succeeding season was valid and enforceable. Second, if the contract was invalid, were the plaintiffs by their own conduct barred from seeking relief in a court of equity?

The court found that Killefer was a ballplayer of unique, exceptional, and extraordinary skill

and that the 1913 contract with Philadelphia, though founded on sufficient consideration, was unenforceable for lack of mutuality. The employer (Philadelphia) was expressly authorized to terminate the contract at any time on ten-day's notice. Executory contracts of this nature cannot be enforced in equity, because they are lacking in the necessary qualities of definiteness, certainty, and mutuality. However, the court also ruled that plaintiffs were *not* entitled to relief. Knowing Killefer was under a moral, if not legal, obligation to Philadelphia, plaintiffs induced him to enter into a contract with them by offering him a larger salary. Any misconduct which is wrongful, even though not punishable as a crime, is sufficient to bar relief in equity. The court concluded that a basic principle of equity is that good faith is required to bring a suit. A party must come into equity with clean hands. Equity only acts when conscience demands; otherwise one must resort to remedy at law. Therefore, the injunction was denied because the actions and conduct of the plaintiffs in procuring the contract upon which their right to relief was founded did not square with vital and fundamental principles of equity. It was not because the 1913 contract with Philadelphia was enforceable.

New York Football Giants, Inc. v. Los Angeles Chargers Football Club, Inc., 291 F. 2d 471 (5th Cir. 1961)

This was an equitable action brought by the New York Giants (National Football League) against the L.A. Chargers (American Football League) and Charles Flowers. In 1959, Flowers was an outstanding football player on the University of Mississippi team. In December of that year, Flowers met with a Giants official to discuss signing a contract for the 1960 and 1961 seasons. Flowers's college team, however, was scheduled to play in the postseason Sugar Bowl game on January 1, 1960, and college conference and national rules expressly excluded from participation in intercollegiate games any player who had signed a contract with a professional team. Above all else, Flowers wanted to play in the Sugar Bowl game. To enable him to do so, the New York Giants owner, Wellington Mara, suggested that Flowers sign the contract and that the signing be kept confidential until after the January 1 game. Flowers signed the contract and received checks totaling $3,500 as a signing bonus. The contract, the standard form contract of the National Football League, contained a provision stating that the agreement would be valid only on approval of the commissioner. As part of the agreement with Flowers, Mara had agreed not to submit the contract to the commissioner until after the Sugar Bowl game. When, on December 5, Flowers attempted to withdraw from the contract, the Giants promptly filed the contract with the commissioner; he "approved" it on December 15. At Mara's request, the commissioner withheld announcement of his approval until after January 1.

On December 29, after negotiations with the L.A. Chargers, which resulted in a better offer than the one with the Giants, Flowers wrote to the Giants and informed them that he was withdrawing from the deal and returning the uncashed checks for the bonus money. Flowers played in the Sugar Bowl game, after which he formally executed his contract with the Chargers.

Relying on the doctrine that "he who comes into equity must come in with clean hands," the court of appeals upheld the trial court's decision for the defendants. Equity requires that its suitors shall have acted fairly and without fraud or deceit as to the controversy in issue; the court reasoned that this "clean hands" doctrine not only prevents a wrongdoer from enjoying the fruits of his transgression but averts an injury to the public. Because plaintiff admittedly took from Flowers what it claimed to be a binding contract, but which it agreed with Flowers it would represent was not in existence in order to deceive others who had a very important and material interest in the subject matter, the court ruled that the plaintiff's suit should have been dismissed on the trial level on the basis of the

"clean hands" doctrine. If, the court continued, there had been a straightforward execution of the document, followed by its filing with the commissioner, none of the legal problems presented by this suit would have arisen.

The court held that no party has the right to create such problems by its devious and deceitful conduct and then approach a court of equity with a plea that the pretended status which it has foisted on the public be ignored and its rights be declared as if it had acted in good faith throughout.

Houston Oilers, Inc. v. Neely, 361 F. 2d 36 (10th Cir. 1966)

This suit was brought by the Houston Oilers, Inc., operators of a professional football team in the American Football League, pursuant to a contract that the team had with Ralph Neely, a University of Oklahoma football player, for a judgment declaring Houston's contract with Neely to be valid and enforceable, and for an injunction restraining Neely from playing professional football with any team other than Houston.

Neely, in his senior year at the University of Oklahoma, was recognized as one of the nation's most outstanding collegiate football players. Upon completion of the regular football schedule at the University of Oklahoma on November 28, 1964, the right to contract for Neely's services was awarded under a draft process to the Houston Oilers in the American Football League and to the Baltimore Colts in the National Football League. On November 30, Neely met with representatives of the Houston team: The club offered Neely a four-year contract, which contained a "no-cut" clause for the seasons 1965–1968 and provided for a $25,000 bonus and an annual salary of $16,000. In addition, Houston agreed to secure employment for Neely with a local real estate firm at a guaranteed annual income of not less than $5,000, and also to convey to Neely by special warranty deed a "conventional Phillips '66 Service Station." Neely accepted Houston's offer on December 1, 1964. The Standard Players Contracts were prepared and executed by the parties but left undated; the letter agreement for additional employment, the filling station agreement, and the bonus check were dated December 1, 1964, and were executed and delivered on that date. Neely, for tax reasons, had insisted that the bonus money be paid in 1964, and further, that the signing of the contract and the acceptance of the bonus money be kept secret to prevent him from being declared ineligible to participate in the postseason Gator Bowl game on January 1, 1965, to which the University of Oklahoma had accepted an invitation. According to the rules of the NCAA and the Big Eight Conference, of which the University of Oklahoma was a member, by signing a professional football contract and receiving money therefor, Neely would consequently become ineligible to participate in the postseason game. To enable Neely to continue to assert his amateur status, all parties agreed that the contract transactions would remain confidential, with no public announcement until after the Gator Bowl game.

After negotiations between the parties were completed, however, Houston's general manager inserted the date "December 1, 1964" on the Standard Players Contracts and filed copies with the AFL commissioner. Neely testified that he understood the arrangement to mean that the contracts would not be effective or filed until after the postseason game. However, the contracts provided in plain language that they should be valid and binding immediately upon execution and that a copy should be filed with the league commissioner within ten days thereafter. The AFL rules also required the filing of all player contracts within ten days after execution.

Also, subsequent to his negotiations with Houston, Neely learned that the Dallas Cowboys had obtained Baltimore's draft rights and desired contract discussions with him. After Dallas attorneys examined Neely's contracts, they prepared letters, which Neely signed, dated December 29, 1964, and addressed to the president and general manager of the Houston club, advising that Neely did not consider himself bound by the contracts and was withdrawing therefrom; the $25,000 bonus check was returned.

Due to publicity concerning his signing with Houston, Neely was informed on December 31, 1964, that he was ineligible to participate in the Gator Bowl game. On January 1, 1965, Neely signed with Dallas for the 1965 through 1968 seasons, whereupon Houston brought this action. The trial court denied Houston the relief sought, finding that the contract was tainted with fraud and violative of the Texas Statute of Frauds. On appeal, the court of appeals reversed the trial court's decision and held that a valid and enforceable contract existed between the parties.

The court of appeals held that although there are many dismal indications to the contrary, athletes, amateur or professional, are bound by their contracts to the same extent as anyone else and should not be allowed to repudiate them at their pleasure. The court explained that while they did not condone the ruthless methods employed by professional football teams in their contest for the services of college football players, it must be conceded that there is no legal impediment to contracting for the services at any time, and conduct such as that involved in this situation, while regrettable, does not furnish athletes with a legal excuse to avoid their contracts for reasons other than the temptations of a more attractive offer.

The court then addressed itself to the trial court's apparent application of the equitable maxim that "he who comes into equity must come with clean hands." The court ruled the doctrine does not exclude all wrongdoers from a court of equity, nor should it be applied in every case where the conduct of a party may be considered unconscionable or inequitable. Rather, the court held, the maxim admits of the free exercise of judicial discretion in the furtherance of justice. The court ruled that it could not accept the argument that because Houston participated in a scheme to conceal the fact that Neely was ineligible for postseason play, a court of equity should not intervene to assist in the enforcement of the contract. The court recognized that Neely was free to surrender his amateur status and that Houston was not under any legal duty to publicize the contract or to keep it secret. Houston's agreement to keep secret that which it had a legal right to keep secret, cannot, the court held, be considered inequitable or unconscionable as those terms are ordinarily used in contract negotiation. The court expressed its opinion that this case was distinguishable from *New York Football Giants* v. *Los Angeles Chargers* (discussed earlier). However, the court stated, if the rule announced in that case was intended to apply to every instance in which a contract is entered with a college football player before a postseason game with an understanding that it be kept secret to permit that player to compete in the game, then it would have to disagree with the conclusion of that case.

The case was reversed and remanded with instructions to grant the injunction.

Minnesota Muskies, Inc. v. Hudson, 294 F. Supp. 979 (M.D. N.C. 1969)

This action was brought by the Miami Floridians of the American Basketball Association (formerly the Minnesota Muskies) against Lou Hudson of the Atlanta Hawks (formerly the St. Louis Hawks) to enjoin Hudson from playing for any team other than the plaintiff.

Hudson, after graduating from the University of Minnesota, signed to play with the St. Louis Hawks of the NBA for the 1966–67 season for a $15,000 salary and a $4,000 signing bonus. He signed a Uniform Player Contract, which included a reserve clause that stated a club may tender to the player a contract for the next succeeding season by mailing the same to the player at player's address; the contract would then be deemed to be renewed and extended even if not returned by the player. Under these terms, the player promised not to play for any other team except the existing club or its assignees. Hudson also borrowed $4,000 from

St. Louis; it was agreed the money would be repaid out of his salary for the 1967–68 season.

Hudson enjoyed a fine rookie season and was named NBA rookie-of-the-year. While still playing for St. Louis in the NBA playoffs, he was contacted by the Minnesota Muskies of the recently established American Basketball Association. The Muskies and Hudson's agents were aware of the reserve clause in the St. Louis contract. While they were uncertain as to the legal effect of the reserve clause, they expected St. Louis to exercise its option under the clause. Therefore, they drafted a contract taking that fact into consideration. The contract, drafted and signed by Hudson in May of 1967, was for three years at $37,500 for year one, $42,500 for year two, and $47,500 for year three; it also included a $7,500 bonus for signing. This contract included a provision saying that if Hudson was unable to play for the Muskies for the first year of the contract, he would receive $25,000 for that year and would play for the Muskies the remaining years. The club reserved the right to enjoin him by appropriate injunction proceedings against playing for any other club.

St. Louis brought an action against the Muskies and the ABA, and against Hudson, seeking an injunction against Hudson from playing for any other club. However, in June of 1967, Hudson, persuaded by friend and teammate Bill Bridges, signed a contract with St. Louis for five years at $34,000 per year, plus a $15,000 signing bonus, and tendered back the bonus given him by the Muskies. The Muskies refused this tender. In August of 1967, Hudson entered the armed services; he played part-time for St. Louis, but in January of 1968, he resumed full-time playing with the Hawks. The Muskies took the position that Hudson was entitled to play for St. Louis for the 1967–68 season, because it was his option year; they asserted, however, that they expected him to start playing for the Muskies during the 1968–69 season. In May of 1968, the Hawks were sold to new owners in Atlanta (Hudson's NBA contract was included), and in July 1968 the Muskies were sold to new owners in Miami (likewise, Hudson's ABA contract was included). Hudson announced his intention to play for Atlanta and did so.

The court concluded that the sole question for discussion was whether plaintiffs were entitled to an injunction restraining Hudson from playing basketball with any team other than Miami under the terms of the contract he signed with the Muskies in May 1967.

The court concluded that the Muskies, now Miami, had "soiled its hands" in negotiating its contract with Hudson while he was still bound by his contract with St. Louis. While recognizing that generally a court of equity is empowered negatively to enforce performance of an agreement by enjoining its breach, especially when that agreement is for personal services of unique skill and ability as was the case here, the court ruled that relief is denied when the party comes into court with unclean hands. Even if the reserve clause was of doubtful validity, Hudson had a moral obligation to perform for St. Louis during the option 1967–68 season. Plaintiff, by inducing Hudson to repudiate his obligation with St. Louis, was so tainted with unfairness that the court, exercising its broad range of discretion, withheld injunctive relief. Any claim that the Hawks were also guilty of unfairness was irrelevant.

Washington Capitols Basketball Club, Inc. v. Barry, 304 F. Supp. 1193 (N.D. Cal. 1969)

This action was commenced by the assignee of a contract with a professional basketball player for declaratory and equitable relief and for damages. The assignee, asserting breach of the contract, sought a preliminary injunction to restrain the player from playing basketball with defendant basketball club; player and defendant club moved to increase the amount of bond as security for the issuance of the preliminary injunction.

On June 19, 1967, Richard F. Barry granted to Charles E. Boone and S. D. Davidson an option to acquire his services as a professional basketball player for the 1967–68 season, and received

an assignment for the transfer of a certain undivided interest in the Oakland franchise of the ABA. On the same date, Boone executed an agreement guaranteeing, among other things, certain earnings to Barry for his services and also agreeing to cause Oakland Basketball, Inc. (Oaks) to indemnify and hold Barry harmless from any and all liability Barry might incur by reason of his execution of the option. The indemnity agreement was executed on September 29, 1967 by Barry, Boone, Davidson, and the Oaks.

Pursuant to the option, Barry signed an ABA Uniform Player Contract with the Oaks; he also signed an amendment to the ABA contract, dated October 31, 1967, which provided that the term of the employment of Barry would be for three years, commencing October 2, 1967. The agreement, as amended, provided "for a salary of $75,000 per year plus an amount equal to the lesser of (a) 5% of all gross gate receipts received by the club per year in excess of the sum of $60,000 plus Player's compensation, or (b) $15,000." (While the original contract said $60,000, the later executed option stipulated the sum to be $600,000.) The agreement also stipulated that the club should have "the right to sell, exchange, assign and transfer this contract to any other professional basketball club in the Association and the Player agrees to accept such assignment and to faithfully perform and carry out this contract with the same force and effect as if it had been entered into by the Player with the assignee Club instead of with this Club."

On August 28, 1969, the Washington Capitols Basketball Club, Inc. entered into an agreement of purchase with the Oaks by which the Oaks agreed to sell and Washington to buy all of the Oaks' property and assets connected with its basketball team, including all of the Oaks' rights and interests in and contracts with all professional basketball players, as well as the Oaks' rights and interest to players not under contract with the club. A bill of sale from the Oaks to Washington, dated September 8, 1969, was executed by the president and secretary of the Oaks, and an assignment from the Oaks to

Washington as of the same date was similarly executed.

On August 29, 1969, Barry entered into a contract to play professional basketball with defendant San Francisco Warriors of the NBA for a term of five years, commencing October 2, 1969 and terminating October 1, 1974. Washington brought this action to obtain a preliminary injunction to enjoin Barry from playing professional basketball with any team other than plaintiff "for so long as Barry remains in default under his contract with plaintiff."

The court, in deciding whether to grant the preliminary injunction, prefaced its opinion with a discussion of the factors that determine when such relief will be given. Injunctive relief, being a matter of equitable jurisdiction, will be granted when a court determines it essential to restrain an act contrary to equity and good conscience. The court noted that the purpose of the preliminary injunction is to maintain the status quo between the litigants pending final determination of the case. In order for plaintiff to succeed in its motion for a preliminary injunction, it is fundamental that it show first, a reasonable probability of success in the main action, and second, that irreparable damage would result from a denial of the motion.

The court held the status quo to be the last, peaceable, uncontested status between the parties which preceded the present controversy. The status quo of the parties to this action, the court held, was that peaceable state of affairs existing when Barry was under contract to the Oaks and, prior to his injury, playing professional basketball for that team during the 1968–69 season. The court reasoned that although Barry could not then play basketball for the Oaks, their assets having been sold to Washington, the assignment of Barry's contract to Washington made his obligations to them the closest to the status quo that could be attained.

As to the probability of success on the merits, the court held that although it was uncertain whether plaintiff would prevail at the trial, a plaintiff need not prove its case with absolute certainty prior to the trial in order to succeed in its motion for a preliminary injunction. The court reasoned that the burden of showing probable success is less when the balance of hardship tips decidedly toward the party requesting the temporary relief, and that it will ordinarily be enough that the plaintiff has raised questions going to the merits so serious, substantial, difficult and doubtful, as to make them a fair ground for litigation and more deliberate investigation. The court noted that the precedents for granting injunctive relief against "star" athletes "jumping" their contracts (defendants did not deny that Barry is a unique "star" athlete) are numerous.

As to the requirements of a showing of irreparable injury, the court held that irreparable injury is that which is certain and great and cannot be adequately compensated for by the award of money damages, and that such injury exists when an athletic team is denied the services of an irreplaceable athlete. The court held that, considering Barry's awards and statistics, the player fit within this category.

Addressing the merits of the case, the court held that contrary to defendants' arguments as to the validity of the contract and assignment, the facts of the case warranted the granting of a preliminary injunction. The court reasoned that Barry's contract with the Oaks clearly provided for an assignment of the contract, that the language of the contract was clear and unambiguous, and that the assignment was not contrary to public policy or the law of the state. Although defendants argued that the assignment of Barry's contract from Oakland to Washington diluted Barry's 5 percent "gate interest" and rendered null his ownership interest, the court held the contract was not breached by the assignment. Barry was still obligated to perform. The court noted that although Washington's seating capacity was less than in Oakland, the Oaks' average attendance for the preceding season was far less than Washington's capacity. Neither could the assignment be defeated as nullifying Barry's ownership interest, since the Oaks had ceased to exist, and Barry was entitled to a proportionate share of any amount realized on the sale of the club's assets.

Defendants also contended that the doctrine of clean hands barred injunctive relief in favor of Washington on the basis that since Washington's predecessor in interest, Oakland, was guilty of misconduct at an earlier time, Washington must be tainted similarly by imputation. The inducement by the Oaks of Barry to contract with the Oaks in 1967, while he still had a year to play under his contract "option" year with the Warriors, was the particular misconduct ascribed to the Oaks. The court held, however, that even if such conduct by Oakland would have been sufficient to invoke the defense of unclean hands were the Oaks a party to this suit, it was inapplicable to defeat the claim of Washington. The court reasoned that in order for defendants successfully to invoke the clean hands doctrine, they would have had to show that it was the plaintiff in this action (Washington) who was tainted. The court held that defendants had not made this showing and that Washington was not tainted by the acts of Oakland, even though Washington was aware of the malfeasance of its predecessor.

The court also reasoned that the maxim of clean hands will not be invoked unless the inequitable conduct sought to be attributed to plaintiff is referable to the very transaction which is the source of the instant controversy. The court held that in the instant case the transaction which is the subject matter of the suit is the offer by the Warriors to Barry of a contract which provides that Barry play basketball for the Warriors, while Barry was still under contract to play basketball for the Oaks. Any misconduct for which the Oaks were responsible by reason of entering into a contract with Barry while he was under his original contract with the Warriors, the court held, was at most a case of misconduct that was remote or misconduct that affected the instant case only indirectly. The court distinguished *Minnesota Muskies* v. *Hudson,* noting that in that case the plaintiff in the

action for an injunction was the original party which induced Hudson's breach of contract.

NOTE _____

1. In *Munchak Corp.* v. *Cunningham,* 457 F. 2d 721 (4th Cir. 1972), the court held that owners of an ABA professional basketball club (Carolina Cougars) were not barred under the clean hands doctrine because they had agreed to pay the player, Billy Cunningham, $80,000 if he did not play for his old club, the Philadelphia 76ers, during the option year of his contract with the 76ers. Cunningham's contract with the ABA club was not to take effect until after his contract with the 76ers expired. In addition, the court noted that Cunningham could not be required under specific performance to play the option year. He thus had the right to sit out that year. It also appeared that, in fact, Cunningham would have elected to play the option year for the 76ers and that the $80,000 was not actually owed. For these reasons, the Cougars were not barred under the clean hands doctrine from seeking injunctive relief when Cunningham decided not to honor his contract with them.

2.14 Scope and Duration of the Injunction

Even if other matters indicate that a negative injunction should issue, a court will hesitate to issue an order if it feels the injunction will be unduly harsh or burdensome to the defendant. Exactly what constitutes an undue or unreasonable burden depends on the facts of the particular case, of course, but we can generalize by saying that the court will be influenced by the length of time the injunction is to run, the extent of geographical area in which the defendant is to be prohibited from seeking alternative employment, and the types of activities specifically prohibited under the requested injunction.

The actual time left to run under the original contract is important, and normally, in the absence of an express agreement to be bound beyond the contract period, a court will limit the injunction to a time no longer than the original running of the contract. This solution is not always satisfactory, since the contract may provide for a tolling of the contract, such as occurs in *Dallas Cowboys* v. *Harris* (see Section 2.12), but in most situations this is a significant limitation, as the following cases attest.

Lemat Corporation v. Barry, 275 Cal. App. 2d 671 (1969)

Suit was brought by Lemat Corporation, sole general partner operating the San Francisco Warriors of the NBA, against Rick Barry for injunctive relief, alleging Barry's breach of the option clause of his contract.

Barry signed a one-year contract with the Warriors for the 1966–67 season, with a one-year option clause. After the 1966–67 season, Barry signed with the Oaklands Oaks of the ABA. Lemat brought suit against Barry upon discovering that he had signed with the Oaks, and after Barry had rejected the properly mailed and delivered option contract binding him to play for the Warriors during the 1967–68 season. On August 8, 1967, Lemat obtained an injunction preventing Barry from playing for the Oaks during the 1967–68 season.

At the expiration of that year, Lemat then claimed it was entitled to a permanent injunction for seven years, based on a California Labor Code provision that limited personal services contracts to that duration. The court dismissed that assertion, stating that the option clause controlled and that clause called only for a one-year extension. Additionally, the court stated that because the contract in question was an adhesion contract, it should be construed strictly against Lemat. Thus, any agreement that restricts a person's ability to follow his or her vocation must be similarly so construed.

The court, however, did state that the option provision of Barry's contract calling for renewal on the same terms and conditions as the first year, except for salary, was "eminently reasonable." It upheld the imposition of the lower court's injunction for the option year.

The court rejected Lemat's claim for damages due to Barry's absence from the Warriors, estimated by plaintiff as in excess of $350,000. Summarily, the court rejected as unsupported by authority Lemat's contention that it was entitled to both injunctive relief and damages. Generally, a plaintiff in an injunctive action is entitled only to an injunction from future injury and damages

for past injury. Procedurally, the court pointed out that Lemat's pleadings were in the alternative, and no effort was made to amend the pleadings. Injunctive relief thus preempted damage awards. Furthermore, damages were practically impossible to ascertain because of Barry's unique talents and the particular situation.

Machen v. Johansson, 174 F. Supp. 522 (S.D. N.Y. 1959)

Plaintiff, Eddie Machen, brought this action to enjoin the defendant, Ingemar Johansson, from engaging in a boxing match with heavyweight champion of the world, Floyd Patterson, until the plaintiff and the defendant had engaged in a rematch. Machen claimed that Johansson had agreed to a rematch with Machen. Johansson, it was argued, had also agreed not to engage in any fights in the United States, particularly with Floyd Patterson, until the rematch had taken place. Eddie Machen was recognized by several authorities as the premier challenger for the heavyweight title. Ingemar Johansson was the European heavyweight champion and ranked as sixth or eighth challenger in the world.

Plaintiff and defendant entered negotiations for a boxing match to take place in Sweden. Machen's manager, Sid Flaherty, and Swedish promoter Edwin Ahlquist conducted the negotiations. After the preliminary negotiations, the plaintiff mailed a letter to Ahlquist containing Machen's terms for the match. A portion of the letter stated, "one of the conditions of Eddie Machen meeting Ingemar Johansson is, that should Johansson win then he agrees to a rematch with Machen, said rematch to take place in San Francisco at a date to be agreed upon when we arrive in Sweden." Flaherty did not receive a response and telegraphed for an answer later that month.

Serious differences as to the facts developed at this point. Ahlquist insisted that he mailed a letter of reply between June 12 and 15, 1958. Ahlquist's alleged letter stated that Johansson would not agree to a rematch provision. Flaherty never received this letter, though a copy was produced at trial. Ahlquist claimed that he had handwritten the letter and given it to an employee to type and mail.

On July 18, 1958, Ahlquist sent a telegram, agreeing to arrange a match pursuant to the terms in the previous letter. Subsequent letters resulted in a match agreement. This agreement contained no provision for a rematch. Machen claimed that such a provision between a manager and promoter was unnecessary, since Ahlquist was also acting as Johansson's manager and agent and that the rematch agreement was part of Ahlquist's July 18 telegram. The defendant argued that this last agreement contained all of the terms agreed to and that the absence of a rematch provision indicated that it was never agreed upon.

The plaintiff arrived in Sweden in late August for the match, scheduled for September 14, 1958. Flaherty claimed that he approached Ahlquist the day he arrived about working out the details of the proposed rematch. Ahlquist, however, introduced testimony showing that Flaherty's first demand was made on September 12, 1958, two days before the fight. Ahlquist claimed that Flaherty used coercion and duress to get him to agree to a rematch. Flaherty threatened, according to Ahlquist, to take Machen and leave if a rematch was not accepted.

Flaherty admitted telling Ahlquist that there might be no fight unless a rematch was agreed upon. Ahlquist argued that cancellation of the fight would have meant financial ruin and that he had signed the agreement on September 13, 1958 as agent for Johansson. The fight was held on September 14, 1958. Johansson knocked out Machen in the first round. Johansson attained instant prominence and was ranked as the number one challenger. At the end of January 1959, Johansson and Patterson agreed to a match.

Johansson refused to honor the alleged rematch agreement for several reasons. He said Ahlquist was never his agent and had no authority to make such an agreement and that Flaherty had been specifically informed that Johansson would not agree to a rematch. He claimed the agreement was obtained by coercion and duress, that the agreement was void and unenforceable due to a lack of consideration, and that the terms were uncertain and indefinite.

In deciding that it would not issue the injunction, the court found that a decision concerning Ahlquist's authority was not necessary. Even if the law permitted granting equitable relief, the court in its discretion would not do so. The court first pointed out that even when a contract is valid, it may not provide a basis for equitable relief. The usual form of redress in a breach of contract action is money damages. It would have to be a unique situation before a court would restrain a defendant completely from practicing his trade. To do so would require a showing by the plaintiff that the right to such relief was clear, reasonable and well defined.

It was determined that the parties intended in the September 13, 1958 agreement for Johansson to perform the affirmative provision of the contract, the rematch, at the end of February 1959 and that failure to do so would be a breach of his obligation.

The negative covenant preventing Johansson from boxing in the United States, particularly against Floyd Patterson, or anywhere in the world, was included in the agreement. If the plaintiff was entitled to the injunction, it would flow from this negative covenant. The court noted that the covenant provided no time limitation on the restrictions contained in it. It was determined that the restrictions were intended to stay in effect until the rematch had occurred. The contract, according to the court, was open to two possible interpretations: (1) the negative covenant was in effect until a rematch was scheduled but no later than February 14, 1959; or (2) it could run indefinitely, unless a rematch was held or Machen rejected a rematch.

The court concluded that the parties never intended the negative covenant to run beyond February 14, 1959. The court pointed out that the plaintiff's interpretation of the covenant could run indefinitely. This would make it unduly restrictive and indefinite. Also, it was unlikely that Ahlquist, if he was defendant's agent, would agree to a provision that might permanently prevent Johansson from the beneficial enjoyment that would result from beating Machen. It was held that the parties did not intend the negative covenant to run past February 14, 1959.

In refusing to grant the injunction, the court felt that to do so would be to rely on a negative covenant that was unreasonable and would result in serious injury to Johansson, while failing to provide Machen with the desired protection. Concerning the reasonableness of the covenant, the court pointed out that injunctive relief was granted only sparingly and usually when covenants were clearly defined concerning time and place. The covenant in question was incredibly broad in terms of geography. The result would be an unreasonable restraint on Johansson's right to further his career in the most lucrative domain for prize fighting, the United States.

The remedy was determined to be ineffective since Johansson could return to Europe for the duration of the injunctive period — that is, one year — then contract with Patterson to fight. Machen's reputation would not be safeguarded since there would be no guarantee of the rematch he sought.

To implement a longer injunctive period, such as two or three years, might result in irreparable damage. Johansson would be unable to advance his career in the United States for a period which might represent a relatively large portion of his effective ring career. The benefit to Machen would be small, since he could and did engage in other fights that would have an impact, positively or negatively, on Machen's career. Machen's standing in the boxing world would be evaluated on the basis of those engagements and not upon Johansson's matches in any way. Thus, any effect on Machen's career, from his defeat by Johansson, would be of short duration.

The application for injunctive relief was denied.

2.20 Application of Antitrust

The development of principles leading to the invocation of negative injunctions to enforce sports contracts has occurred more or less continuously since Metropolitan Exhibition Company sought restraining orders against Buck Ewing and John Montgomery Ward in 1890. As the previous materials illustrate, denial of relief has been accompanied by a declaration that something was basically amiss with the contractual terms. At the heart, the provisions were deemed to be overly repressive — too much the product of a league and its clubs, with all the power imposing burdensome requirements on the relatively disadvantaged player.

Most of the time the clubs and leagues have prevailed. The general doubts about the enforceability of the contracts expressed in the early cases gave way to the equally general proposition that the contracts would be enforced, even by the extraordinary remedy of the negative injunction, unless special circumstances intervened. This did not mean, from the players' perspectives, that the contracts were less onerous or one-sided. It meant that they would have to look elsewhere for relief. That "elsewhere" was a long time in coming, as the following cases reveal.

Ironically, Congress made its first moves against concentrated power in the commercial world the same year as the Metropolitan Exhibition Company attempted to assert its rights against Ewing and Ward. The year was 1890, and the congressional legislation was the Sherman Act, a codification of common law principles designed to control monopolistic practices and unfair restraints of trade, at least as affected interstate commerce. Additional proscriptions were forthcoming in 1914 in the Clayton Act. Many of the basic principles still guiding antitrust activity today were derived from these two acts. U.S. statutes regulating trade and commerce have undergone numerous amendments and additions. Several of these are potentially applicable to the sports industries and a few are explicitly so. Other pertinent statutes are discussed at later points in this book, particularly in Volume II, Chapter 6. Here we examine some of the basic provisions of the Sherman and Clayton acts.

2.21 The Sherman and Clayton Acts

The following excerpts are from the Sherman and Clayton acts, as codified in volume 15, United States Code. Section references are to 15 U.S.C. and not the original section numbers under the two acts.

Section 1. Trusts, etc., in restraint of trade illegal; exception of resale price agreements; penalty

Every contract, combination in the form of trust or otherwise, or conspiracy, in restraint of trade or commerce among the several States, or with foreign nations, is declared to be illegal. . . .

Every person who shall make any contract or engage in any combination or conspiracy declared by sections 1 to 7 of this title to be illegal shall be deemed guilty of a misdemeanor, and, on conviction thereof, shall be punished by fine not exceeding fifty thousand dollars, or by imprisonment not exceeding one year, or by both said punishments, in the discretion of the court.

Section 2. Monopolizing trade a misdemeanor; penalty

Every person who shall monopolize, or attempt to monopolize, or combine or conspire with any other person or persons, to monopolize any part of the trade or commerce among the several States, or with foreign nations, shall be deemed guilty of a misdemeanor, and, on conviction thereof, shall be punished by fine not exceeding fifty thousand dollars, or by imprisonment not exceeding one year, or by both said punishments, in the discretion of the court. . . .

Section 4. Jurisdiction of courts; duty of United States attorneys; procedure

The several district courts of the United States are invested with jurisdiction to prevent and restrain violations of sections 1 to 7 of this title; and it shall be the duty of the several United States attorneys, in their respective districts, under the direction of the Attorney General, to institute proceedings in

equity to prevent and restrain such violations. . . .

Section 15. Suits by persons injured; amount of recovery

. . .[A]ny person who shall be injured in his business or property by reason of anything forbidden in the antitrust laws may sue therefor in any district court of the United States in the district in which the defendant resides or is found or has an agent, without respect to the amount in controversy, and shall recover threefold the damages by him sustained, and the cost of suit, including a reasonable attorney's fee. . . .

Section 17. Antitrust laws not applicable to labor organizations

The labor of a human being is not a commodity or article of commerce. Nothing contained in the antitrust laws shall be construed to forbid the existence and operation of labor, agricultural, or horticultural organizations, instituted for the purposes of mutual help, and not having capital stock or conducted for profit, or to forbid or restrain individual members of such organizations from lawfully carrying out the legitimate objects thereof; nor shall such organizations, or the members thereof, be held or construed to be illegal combinations or conspiracies in restraint of trade, under the antitrust laws.

Section 18. Acquisition by one corporation of stock of another

No person engaged in commerce or in any activity affecting commerce shall acquire, directly or indirectly, the whole or any part of the stock or other share capital and no person subject to the jurisdiction of the Federal Trade Commission shall acquire the whole or any part of the assets of another person engaged also in commerce or in any activity affecting commerce, where in any line of commerce or in any activity affecting commerce in any section of the country, the effect of such acquisition may be substantially to lessen competition, or to tend to create a monopoly.

No person shall acquire, directly or indirectly, the whole or any part of the stock or other share capital and no person subject to the jurisdiction of the Federal Trade Commission shall acquire the whole or any part of the assets of one or more persons engaged in commerce or in any activity affecting commerce, where in any line of commerce or in any activity affecting commerce in any section of the country, the effect of such acquisition, of such stocks or assets, or of the use of such stock by the voting or granting of proxies or otherwise, may be substantially to lessen competition, or to tend to create a monopoly.

This section shall not apply to persons purchasing such stock solely for investment and not using the same by voting or otherwise to bring about, or in attempting to bring about, the substantial lessening of competition. Nor shall anything contained in this section prevent a corporation engaged in commerce or in any activity affecting commerce from causing the formation of subsidiary corporations for the actual carrying on of their immediate lawful business, or the natural and legitimate branches or extensions thereof, or from owning and holding all or a part of the stock of such subsidiary corporations, when the effect of such formation is not to substantially lessen competition. . . .

Section 25.   Restraining violations; procedure

The several district courts of the United States are invested with jurisdiction to prevent and restrain violations of this Act, and it shall be the duty of the several United States Attorneys, in their respective districts, under the direction of the Attorney General, to institute proceedings in equity to prevent and restrain such violations. . . . Whenever it shall appear to the court before which any such proceeding may be pending that the ends of justice require that other parties should be brought before the court, the court may cause them to be summoned whether they reside in the district in which the court is held or not, and subpoenas to that end may be served in any district by the marshal thereof.

Section 26. Injunctive relief for private parties; exception; costs

Any person, firm, corporation, or association shall be entitled to sue for and have injunctive relief, in any court of the United States having jurisdiction over the parties, against threatened loss or damage by a violation of the antitrust laws, including sections 13, 14, 18 and 19 of this title when and under the same conditions and princi-

ples as injunctive relief against threatened conduct that will cause loss or damage is granted by courts of equity, under the rules governing such proceedings, and upon the execution of proper bond against damages for an injunction improvidently granted and a showing that the danger of irreparable loss or damage is immediate, a preliminary injunction may issue. . . .

2.22   Setting the Standards — Baseball

Even though the Sherman Act was passed in 1890 — the same year the Players League formed in baseball — 20 years passed before any attempts were made to apply the act's provisions to a sports setting. Three separate actions accompanied the formation of the Federal League, yet another in a long line of baseball rival leagues. The two cases with published opinions are set forth below. The *Federal Baseball* case is the most important since it set the standards that were to prevail for years to come and, in fact, still dictate baseball's exemption from the federal antitrust statutes.

Federal Baseball was not the first of the cases. Federal League owners also initiated a suit against the established National and American leagues, charging them with monopolistic practices designed to drive the Federal League out of existence. The U.S. District Court judge assigned to hear the dispute was none other than Kennesaw Mountain Landis, later to become the first commissioner of baseball when that office was created in 1920 in the aftermath of the Black Sox scandal. There is little doubt that Judge Landis's demeanor in the earlier case involving Federal League versus the established leagues caused him to be regarded with favor by the owners in 1920. His actions were simple; he sat on the case and failed to act, thus giving the two sides ample opportunity to come to a resolution of the matter. This they did.

The Federal League lasted but two seasons, and most Federal League owners were assuaged by being allowed to join in the ownership of clubs in the National and American leagues. One owner, however, felt aggrieved by these activities. Ned Hanlon of the Baltimore Terrapins eventually brought suit against both the National and American league owners *and* against many of his former Federal League compatriots. Although this suit eventually reached the United States Supreme Court and is now referred to as the famous *Federal Baseball* case, one cannot ignore the earlier dispute which Judge Landis failed to decide, since it could well have changed things had he acted adversely to the interests of the established leagues. Before considering *Federal Baseball,* we will examine an earlier case, *American League Baseball Club of Chicago* v. *Chase.* Hal Chase was a star first baseman and former manager of the New York Yankees' forerunners, the Highlanders. When he chose to defect to the new Federal League, suit was filed against him in the traditional mold of seeking a negative injunction. However, he fought back, raising questions of both state and federal antitrust law.

American League Baseball Club of Chicago v. Chase, 149 N.Y.S. 6 (Sup. Ct. 1914)

Plaintiff Baseball Club of Chicago sought to enjoin Harold Chase, its star first baseman, from playing for any other team during the period of his contract. The court had granted a temporary injunction, and now faced Chase's motion to dissolve the injunction.

Chase signed a standard form Player's Contract with the plaintiff club on March 26, 1914. On June 15, 1914, Chase gave notice to the club that he would not perform his part of the agreement and, on June 20, 1914, signed a contract to play for the Buffalo team of the Federal League. The court's temporary injunction against Chase was granted five days later.

The court continually referred to the scheme of "organized baseball" under which Chase had been employed. This scheme consisted of the so-called National Agreement, a written agreement among 40 major and minor leagues, the Rules of the National Commission, adopted to implement the National Agreement, and the standard form Player's Contract which Chase has signed with plaintiff. (The Federal League in

which Chase sought employment was the only league of importance which was not a party to the National Agreement.)

The National Agreement, for example, provided that "no nonreserve contract shall be entered into by any club operating under [this agreement]." To enforce this provision, a Rule of the National Commission stated that "a nonreserve clause in the contract of a major league player . . . shall not be valid." Accordingly, the Player's Contract signed by Chase contained the following:

> The player agrees to perform for no other party during the period of this contract . . . The player will, at the option of the club, enter into a contract for the succeeding season upon all the terms and conditions of this contract . . . and the salary to be paid the player . . . shall be the same . . . unless it be increased or decreased by mutual agreement.

The court first considered whether it could specifically enforce the negative covenant in Chase's contract. It noted the general rule that equity will not specifically enforce a personal service contract, but recognized the well-known exception "where services contracted for are of a special, unique, and extraordinary character, and a substitute for the employee cannot readily be obtained who will substantially answer the purpose of the contract." The court found that the services of Chase, "generally regarded as the foremost first baseman in professional baseball," were sufficiently unique to give equity jurisdiction to enforce the negative covenant "providing the contract does not lack mutuality and is not part of an illegal scheme or combination."

The court then examined whether the contract was a mutual one "furnish[ing] consideration for the negative covenant sought to be enforced." This part of the court's opinion analyzed in detail the three instruments referred to above which constituted "the general agreement or plan regulating the employment and conduct of the defendant as a National Agreement player." Under the scheme, a team could terminate all its obligations under the Player's Contract with only ten days written notice. On the other hand, the Player's Contract provided for an option year, the option exercisable by the team only. A team could require a player to stay with it indefinitely by continually insisting on contracts with option years available. The National Agreement provided further that the "right and title of a major league club to its players shall be absolute . . ." When a player refused to sign such a contract, his only alternative was to seek another vocation.

The court held that, under this scheme, there was an "absolute lack of mutuality," and equity would grant no injunctive or other relief. The court stated the general rule that a negative covenant in a personal service contract would not be enforced where the party seeking the injunction could terminate or revoke the contract on notice. The contract was without mutuality since if the team did terminate the contract, the player would be remediless, unable to acquire specific performance or damages in an action at law. The court added, conversely, that the breach of the negative covenant by Chase would have been enjoined had there been no contractual provision for the club's termination upon notice. This was sufficient to grant Chase's motion to dissolve the injunction.

The court analyzed further whether the Player's Contract "was part of an illegal scheme or combination." It concluded that "organized baseball" did not violate the Sherman Antitrust Act. Despite finding that "a monopoly of baseball as a business has been ingeniously devised and created," the court reasoned that baseball was not interstate commerce or trade subject to the Sherman Act, since baseball dealt not with players as commodites or articles of merchandise but with their services.

The court determined, however, that "organized baseball" was an illegal combination "in contravention of the common law." The court made it clear that the issue of the dissolution of this combination was not before it but made its analysis "for the purpose of ascertaining whether or not this plaintiff comes into a court of equity with clean hands. . . ." Organized baseball was found to be "as complete a

monopoly. . . as any monopoly can be made," in contravention of the common law for three reasons: it invaded the right to labor as a property right, it abridged the right to contract as a property right, and it was a combination restraining the exercise of a profession or calling. For this reason, as well as the "mutuality" issue, Chase's motion to vacate the preliminary injunction was granted.

Federal Baseball Club of Baltimore, Inc. v. National League of Professional Baseball Clubs, et al., 259 U.S. 200 (1922)

Mr. Justice Holmes delivered the opinion of the court.

This is a suit for threefold damages brought by the plaintiff in error under the Anti-Trust Acts of July 2, 1890, c. 647, § 7, 26 Stat. 209, 210, and of October 15, 1914, c. 323, § 4, 38 Stat. 730, 731. The defendants are The National League of Professional Base Ball Clubs and The American League of Professional Base Ball Clubs, unincorporated associations, composed respectively of groups of eight incorporated base ball clubs, joined as defendants; the presidents of the two Leagues and a third person, constituting what is known as the National Commission, having considerable powers in carrying out an agreement between the two Leagues; and three other persons having powers in the Federal League of Professional Base Ball Clubs, the relation of which to this case will be explained. It is alleged that these defendants conspired to monopolize the base ball business, the means adopted being set forth with a detail which, in the view that we take, it is unnecessary to repeat.

The plaintiff is a base ball club incoporated in Maryland, and with seven other corporations was a member of the Federal League of Professional Base Ball Clubs, a corporation under the laws of Indiana, that attempted to compete with the combined defendants. It alleges that the defendants destroyed the Federal League by buying up some of the constituent clubs and in one way or another inducing all those clubs except the plaintiff to leave their League, and that the three persons connected with the Federal League and named as defendants, one of them being the President of the League, took part in the conspiracy. Great damage to the plaintiff is alleged. The plaintiff obtained a verdict for $80,000 in the Supreme Court and a judgment for treble the amount was entered, but the Court of Appeals, after an elaborate discussion, held that the defendants were not within the Sherman Act. The appellee, the plaintiff, elected to stand on the record in order to bring the case to this Court at once, and thereupon judgment was ordered for the defendants. 50 App. D. C. 165; 269 Fed. 681, 688. . . .

The decision of the Court of Appeals went to the root of the case and if correct makes it unnecessary to consider other serious difficulties in the way of the plaintiff's recovery. A summary statement of the nature of the business involved will be enough to present the point. The clubs composing the Leagues are in different cities and for the most part in different States. The end of the elaborate organizations and sub-organizations that are described in the pleadings and evidence is that these clubs shall play against one another in public exhibitions for money, one or the other club crossing a state line in order to make the meeting possible. When as the result of these contests one club has won the pennant of its League and another club has won the pennant of the other League, there is a final competition for the world's championship between these two. Of course the scheme requires constantly repeated travelling on the part of the clubs, which is provided for, controlled and disciplined by the organizations, and this it is said means commerce among the States. But we are of opinion that the Court of Appeals was right.

The business is giving exhibitions of base ball, which are purely state affairs. It is true that, in order to attain for these exhibitions the great popularity that they have achieved, competitions must be arranged between clubs from different cities and States. But the fact that in order to give the exhibitions the Leagues must induce free persons to cross state lines and must arrange and pay for their doing so is not enough to change the character of the business. According to the distinction insisted upon in *Hooper* v. *California*, 155 U.S. 648, 655, the transport is a mere incident, not the essential thing. That to which it is incident, the exhibition, although made for money would not be called trade or commerce in the commonly accepted use of those words. As it is put by the defendants, personal effort, not related to production, is not a subject of commerce. That which in its

consummation is not commerce does not become commerce among the States because the transportation that we have mentioned takes place. To repeat the illustrations given by the Court below, a firm of lawyers sending out a member to argue a case, or the Chautauqua lecture bureau sending out lecturers, does not engage in such commerce because the lawyer or lecturer goes to another State.

If we are right the plaintiff's business is to be described in the same way and the restrictions by contract that prevented the plaintiff from getting players to break their bargains and the other conduct charged against the defendants were not an interference with commerce among the States.

Judgment affirmed.

Gardella v. Chandler, 172 F.2d 402 (2d Cir. 1949)

Gardella (appellant) violated the reserve clause of his contract with the National Exhibition Company (owner of the New York baseball Giants) by playing professional baseball in Mexico. Pursuant to an edict by the commissioner of baseball, appellant was barred from playing in the two major leagues, the American and National, or in the minor leagues. (By agreement among the major league teams, Commissioner of Baseball Albert Chandler had been given supervisory and disciplinary powers over the major league teams and players. A major-minor league agreement gave him similar powers over minor league teams and players.) Appellant brought this action against Chandler, individually and as commissioner of baseball, and against others involved in "organized baseball," seeking treble damages under the Sherman and Clayton Antitrust acts. He alleged that the reserve clause and the various mechanisms to enforce it created a scheme in restraint of trade or commerce. The District Court dismissed the complaint on the ground that it had no jurisdiction of the cause of action since "organized baseball" did not constitute "trade or commerce." Gardella appealed.

Judge Chase, writing first, dissented. He felt that *Federal Baseball Club* v. *National League*, 250 U.S. 200 (1922), controlled, that "major league ball clubs were not engaged in interstate commerce within the scope of the anti-trust laws." Judge Chase recognized that the Supreme Court had been broadening the reach of Congress under the Commerce Clause, but could not distinguish the present case from *Federal Baseball Club* and felt that "our duty as a subordinate court is to follow. . ." The rationale of Federal Baseball Club had been that baseball was a *local* activity and the interstate travel necessary to the leagues was merely *incidental* to such activity.

Although Judge Frank severely questioned the vitality of *Federal Baseball Club,* he agreed with Judge Chase that they should not declare the prior case "an impotent zombie." He felt, however, that the prior case was distinguishable from the suit brought by appellant Gardella. Frank felt that *Federal Baseball Club* should be distinguished, if possible, (thus bringing the reserve clause within the prohibition of the Sherman Act) since organized baseball constituted a monopoly "shockingly repugnant to moral principles" resulting in something resembling peonage of the baseball player.

Construing the complaint in a light most favorable to appellant, Frank found "that the facts of the instant case significantly differ from those in the Federal Baseball case, because here the defendants have lucratively contracted for the interstate communication, by radio and television, of the playings of the games." Frank then distinguished the function of interstate travel from that of interstate communication. In *Federal Baseball Club,* the Supreme Court had found the interstate travel necessary to organized baseball "a mere incident, not the essential thing." But Frank felt that the interstate communication changed the nature of the game itself, changed the local nature of baseball: "the traveling was but a means to the end of playing games which themselves took place intrastate; here the games themselves, because of the radio and television, are, so to speak, played interstate as well as intrastate." Frank later analogized to stage-plays being monopolized and then broadcast via radio and television to other states.

While *Federal Baseball Club* involved interstate communication via telegraph accounts of the games, Frank reasoned that by not mentioning this fact in its opinion the Supreme Court had restricted its finding to interstate travel. Further, Frank felt the telegraph accounts distinguishable; ". . . persons in other states received . . . mere accounts of the games as told by others, while here we have the very substantially different fact of instant and direct interstate transmission, via television, of the games as they are being played. . . ." Also, while the Supreme Court in *Federal Baseball Club* had said that oganized baseball involved services, which were not "trade or commerce," Frank pointed out that such a restrictive interpretation of "trade or commerce" had been "undeniably repudiated in later Supreme Court decisions."

Having decided that organized baseball did constitute interstate commerce, Frank next considered (a) whether Congress could constitutionally regulate the interstate part of organized baseball and (b) whether Congress via the Sherman Act did in fact exercise its constitutional power to regulate organized baseball.

Frank cited Supreme Court decisions which, he said, "leave little doubt that the Constitutional power of Congress, under the commerce clause, extends to such a situation." Under the decisions, for example, Congress may exercise its commerce power over an enterprise even though its activities affecting interstate commerce are but a small percentage of its total activities; thus the small percentage of defendant's activities represented by its radio and television contracts were sufficient to constitute engagement in interstate commerce.

Further, the Supreme Court had indicated that Congress in the Sherman Act had intended to use all the Constitutional power given it by the commerce clause, and that the scope of the Constitutional power and the Sherman Act were identical. Defendant's activities were, therefore, intended by Congress to be within the prohibitions of the Sherman Act.

Finally, Judge Frank rejected defendant's argument that the reserve clause was necessary to the survival of organized baseball as irrelevant: "the public's pleasure does not authorize the courts to condone illegality." The case was reversed and remanded.

NOTES _____

1. The *Gardella* decision was not appealed. The Major League owners decided to settle, rather than appeal. The blacklist was lifted, and, with others, Gardella was allowed to return to the majors, however briefly.

2. *Martin* v. *National League Baseball Club,* 174 F. 2d 917 (2d Cir. 1949), involved another case of a player jumping to the Mexican League. This was decided adverse to the player's claim; however, because of the settlement referred to in Note 1, the issue became moot.

Toolson v. New York Yankees, 346 U.S. 356 (1953)

Per Curiam.

In *Federal Baseball Club of Baltimore* v. *National League of Professional Baseball Clubs,* 259 U.S. 200 (1922), this Court held that the business of providing public baseball games for profit between clubs of professional baseball players was not within the scope of the federal antitrust laws. Congress has had the ruling under consideration but has not seen fit to bring such business under these laws by legislation having prospective effect. The business has thus been left for thirty years to develop, on the understanding that it was not subject to existing antitrust legislation. The present cases ask us to overrule the prior decision and, with retrospective effect, hold the legislation applicable. We think that if there are evils in this field which now warrant application to it of the antitrust laws it should be by legislation. Without re-examination of the underlying issues, the judgments below are affirmed on the authority of *Federal Baseball Club of Baltimore v. National League of Professional Baseball Clubs, supra,* so far as that decision determines that Congress had no intention of including the business of baseball within the scope of the federal antitrust laws.

Affirmed.

Mr. Justice Burton, with whom Mr. Justice Reed concurs, dissenting.

Whatever may have been the situation when the *Federal Baseball Club* case was decided in 1922, I am not able to join today's decision which, in effect, announces that organized baseball, in 1953, still is not engaged in interstate trade or commerce. In the light of organized baseball's well-known and widely distributed capital investments used in conducting competitions between teams constantly traveling between states, its receipts and expenditures of large sums transmitted between states, its numerous purchases of materials in interstate commerce, the attendance at its local exhibitions of large audiences often traveling across state lines, its radio and television activities which expand its audiences beyond state lines, its sponsorship of interstate advertising, and its highly organized "farm system" of minor league baseball clubs, coupled with restrictive contracts and understandings between individuals and among clubs or leagues playing for profit throughout the United States, and even in Canada, Mexico and Cuba, it is a contradiction in terms to say that the defendants in the cases before us are not now engaged in interstate trade or commerce as those terms are used in the Constitution of the United States and in the Sherman Act.

NOTE _____

1. Two other contemporary cases also challenged certain practices imposed by Major League Baseball on players. However, unlike *Gardella,* and in line with *Toolson,* the lower courts adhered to the *Federal Baseball* rationale and dismissed the complaints. See *Kowalski* v. *Chandler,* 202 F.2d 413 (6th Cir. 1953), and *Corbett* v. *Chandler,* 202 F.2d 428 (6th Cir. 1953). Both decisions were affirmed in the foregoing *Toolson* decision.

2.23 Antitrust Applied to Other Sports

With the reaffirmation of the antitrust exemption for baseball that was established by the *Toolson* decision in 1953, it might have seemed that owners in other sports could have looked forward to similar treatment. Of course, few other professional team sports were in existence at the time of the decision in *Federal Baseball* in 1922. The National Hockey League had formed in 1917 but had not even added a U.S. team by 1921. The National Football League had started in 1920, immediately almost went bankrupt, and was reconstituting itself at the princely sum of $50 per franchise in 1921. Professional basketball consisted of individual teams forming and challenging each other. Semblances of leagues existed for a year or so, but many years passed before the National Basketball Association appeared. Even so, the professional sports map had changed by 1953 and the *Toolson* decision. So the question was: Are the other sports leagues, like baseball, immune from antitrust scrutiny?

Several developments ultimately affected the other leagues' positions. First and foremost, other entertainment industries, particularly motion pictures, were growing. With growth came predatory practices, which in turn drew challenge from the U.S. government under the Sherman and Clayton acts. The decisions almost unanimously held that these other entertainment industries were subject to the antitrust laws, as evidenced by such decisions as *Binderup* v. *Pathe Exchange*, 263 U.S. 291 (1923); *Paramount Famous Lasky Corporation* v. *United States*, 282 U.S. 30 (1930); *Interstate Circuit, Inc.* v. *United States*, 306 U.S. 208 (1939); *United States* v. *Crescent Amusement Co.*, 323 U.S. 173 (1944); *United States* v. *Griffith* 334 U.S. 100 (1948); and *United States* v. *Paramount Pictures Inc.*, 334 U.S. 131 (1948), among others.

With *Federal Baseball* and *Toolson* on one side, and the entertainment cases on the other, the U.S. Supreme Court was then called on to determine the applicability of the federal antitrust laws to both professional boxing and to the legitimate theater. In *United States* v. *Shubert*, 348 U.S. 222 (1955), the Court determined that the federal antitrust laws extended to both the production and operation of legitimate theatrical productions throughout the United States. Decided at the same time was *United States* v. *International Boxing Club of New York, Inc.*, 348 U.S. 236 (1955). The complaint alleged that the defendants had entered into a conspiracy to restrain and monopolize the promotion, exhibition, broadcasting, telecasting and filming of professional championship boxing contests in the United States. In reversing the trial court's dismissal of the complaint, the Supreme Court

held that the defendants' multistate promotion of championship contests and sale of boxing rights to telecast as an interstate transmission constituted "trade or commerce among the several states" within the meaning of the Sherman Act, even though the boxing match itself was a local affair. The government had stated a cause of action and was entitled to an opportunity to prove its allegations.

After *International Boxing*, the sports world wondered if professional sports leagues other than baseball would be subject to the antitrust laws in line with the *International Boxing* decision, or would the court follow *Toolson*? The answer — not long in coming — was contained in *Radovich* v. *National Football League*, 352 U.S. 445 (1957).

Radovich v. National Football League, 352 U.S. 445 (1957)

Mr. Justice Clark delivered the opinion.

This action for treble damages and injunctive relief, brought under § 4 of the Clayton Act, tests the application of the antitrust laws to the business of professional football. Petitioner Radovich, an all-pro guard formerly with the Detroit Lions, contends that the respondents entered into a conspiracy to monopolize and control organized professional football in the United States, in violation of §§ 1 and 2 of the Sherman Act; that part of the conspiracy was to destroy the All-America Conference, a competitive professional football league in which Radovich once played; and that pursuant to agreement, respondents boycotted Radovich and prevented him from becoming a player-coach in the Pacific Coast League. Petitioner alleges that respondents' illegal conduct damaged him in the sum of $35,000 to be trebled as provided by the Act. The trial court, on respondents' motion, dismissed the cause for lack of jurisdiction and failure to state a claim on which relief could be granted. The Court of Appeals affirmed, 231 F. 2d 620, on the basis of *Federal Baseball Club* v. *National League*, 259 U.S. 200 (1922), and *Toolson* v. *New York Yankees, Inc.*, 346 U.S. 356 (1953), applying the baseball rule to all "team sports.". . . .

I.

Since the complaint was dismissed its allegations must be taken by us as true. It is, therefore, important for us to consider what Radovich alleged. Concisely the complaint states that:

1. Radovich began his professional football career in 1938 when he signed with the Detroit Lions, a National League club. After four seasons of play he entered the Navy, returning to the Lions for the 1945 season. In 1946 he asked for a transfer to a National League club in Los Angeles because of the illness of his father. The Lions refused the transfer and Radovich broke his player contract by signing with and playing the 1946 and 1947 seasons for the Los Angeles Dons, a member of the All-America Conference. In 1948 the San Francisco Clippers, a member of the Pacific Coast League which was affiliated with but not a competitor of the National League, offered to employ Radovich as a player-coach. However, the National League advised that Radovich was black-listed and any affiliated club signing him would suffer severe penalties. The Clippers then refused to sign him in any position. This black-listing effectively prevented his employment in organized professional football in the United States.

2. The black-listing was the result of a conspiracy among the respondents to monopolize commerce in professional football among the States. The purpose of the conspiracy was to "control, regulate and dictate the terms upon which organized professional football shall be played throughout the United States" in violation of §§ 1 and 2 of the Sherman Act. It was part of the conspiracy to boycott the All-America Conference and its players with a view to its destruction and thus strengthen the monopolistic position of the National Football League.

3. As part of its football business, the respondent league and its member teams schedule football games in various metropolitan centers, including New York, Chicago, Philadelphia, and Los Angeles. Each team uses a standard player contract which prohibits a player from signing with another club without the consent of the club holding the player's contract. These contracts are enforced by agreement of the clubs to black-list any player violating them and to visit severe penalties on recalcitrant member clubs. As a further "part of the business of professional football itself" and "directly tied in and connected" with its football exhibitions is the transmission of the games over radio and television into nearly every State of the Union. This is accomplished by contracts which produce a "significant portion of the gross receipts" and without which "the business of operating a professional football club would not be profitable." The playing of the exhibitions themselves "is essential to the interstate transmission by broadcasting and television" and the actions of the respondents against Radovich were necessarily related to these interstate activities.

In the light of these allegations respondents raise two issues: They say the business of organized professional football was not intended by Congress to be included within the scope of the antitrust laws; and, if wrong in this contention, that the complaint does not state a cause of action upon which relief can be granted.

II.

Respondents' contention, boiled down, is that agreements similar to those complained of here, which have for many years been used in organized baseball, have been held by this Court to be outside the scope of the antitrust laws. They point to *Federal Baseball* and *Toolson, supra,* both involving the business of professional baseball, asserting that professional football has embraced the same techniques which existed in baseball at the time of the former decision. They contend that *stare decisis* compels the same result here. True, the umbrella under which respondents hope to stand is not so large as that contended for in *United States* v. *International Boxing Club, supra,* nor in *United States* v. *Shubert,* 348 U.S. 222 (1955). There we were asked to extend *Federal Baseball* to boxing and the theater. Here respondents say that the contracts and sanctions which baseball and football find it necessary to impose have no counterpart in other businesses and that, therefore, they alone are outside the ambit of the Sherman Act. In *Toolson* we continued to hold the umbrella over baseball that was placed there some 31 years earlier by *Federal Baseball* than in upholding a ruling which at best was of dubious validity. . . .

The Court was careful to restrict *Toolson's* coverage to baseball, following the judgment of *Federal Baseball* only so far as it "determines that Congress had no intention of including the business of baseball within the scope of the federal antitrust laws." 346 U.S., at 357. The Court reiterated this in *United States* v. *Shubert, supra,* at 230, where it said, "In short, *Toolson* was a narrow application of the rule of *stare decisis.*" And again, in *International Boxing Club,* it added, "*Toolson* neither overruled *Federal Baseball* nor necessarily reaffirmed all that was said in *Federal Baseball....Toolson* is not authority for exempting other businesses merely because of the circumstance that they are also based on the performance of local exhibitions."348 U. S., at 242. Furthermore, in discussing the impact of the *Federal Baseball* decision, the Court made the observation that that decision "could not be relied upon as a basis of exemption for other segments of the entertainment business, athletic or otherwise.... The controlling consideration in *Federal Baseball* ... was ... the degree of interstate activity involved in the particular business under review." *Id.,* at 242-243. It seems that this language would have made it clear that the Court intended to isolate these cases by limiting them to baseball, but since *Toolson* and *Federal Baseball* are still cited as controlling authority in antitrust actions involving other fields of business, we now specifically limit the rule there established to the facts there involved, *i.e.,* the business of organized professional baseball....

If this ruling is unrealistic, inconsistent, or illogical, it is sufficient to answer, aside from the distinctions between the businesses, that were we considering the question of baseball for the first time upon a clean slate we would have no doubts. But *Federal Baseball* held the business of baseball outside the scope of the Act. No other business claiming the coverage of those cases has such an adjudication. We, therefore, conclude that the orderly way to eliminate error or discrimination, if any there be, is by legislation and not by court decision....

III

We now turn to the sufficiency of the complaint....

Petitioner's claim need only be 'tested under the Sherman Act's general prohibition on unreasonable restraints of trade," *Times-Picayune Publishing Co.* v. *United States,* 345 U. S. 594, 614 (1953), and meet the requirement that petitioner has thereby suffered injury. Congress has, by legislative fiat, determined that such prohibited activities are injurious to the public and has provided sanctions allowing private enforcement of the antitrust laws by an aggrieved party. These laws protect the victims of the forbidden practices as well as the public....

We think that Radovich is entitled to an opportunity to prove his charges. Of course, we express no opinion as to whether or not respondents have, in fact, violated the antitrust laws, leaving that determination to the trial court after all the facts are in.

Reversed.

NOTE _____

1. The language used by the Court in *Radovich* made it fairly clear that the sports of professional basketball and hockey were subject to the antitrust laws. The matter was contested by the NBA and NHL, but unsuccessfully. See, *Robertson* v. *National Basketball Association,* 389 F.Supp. 867 (S.D.N.Y. 1975), and *Philadelphia World Hockey Club, Inc.* v. *Philadelphia Hockey Club Inc.,* 351 F. Supp. 462 (E.D. 1972). After these decisions, baseball truly stood alone as an industry bestowed with special status.

2.24   Baseball's Continuing Exemption

While the other sports did battle with the antitrust laws, baseball continued to move forward under the assumption it alone among the major team sports was immune from the reach of the federal antitrust laws. Indeed, it also received additional insulation when the Wisconsin Supreme Court held that state laws could no longer reach baseball, contrary to the holding in *Chase.* (See *State of Wisconsin* v. *Milwaukee Braves,* 144 N.W.2d 1 [Wisc. S.C. 1966]).

It is true there were possible disruptions. Baseball's umpires successfully argued that the nation's labor laws could control relations between the major leagues and the umpire's union (see *American League* etc., Section 2.30). Although ultimately the *American League* case significantly advanced the interests of both umpires and players, at the time, around 1970, the outcome was not fully evident; the focus was still on whether or not baseball would be with the other leagues brought in line on antitrust matters. This was to be tested in *Flood* v. *Kuhn*.

Justice Blackmun's opening comments, describing the pastoral history of baseball, as well as many of the background facts that promped Curt Flood to file suit, were set forth in Chapter 1, Section 1.16. The attention now turns to the merits of Flood's complaint and whether the court would adhere to the line of precedent-granting baseball antitrust immunity or whether it would hold that precedent must yield to modern interpretations of the commerce clause. Not unexpectedly, the court split on the issue.

Flood v. Kuhn, 407 U.S. 258 (1972)

Mr. Justice Blackmun delivered the opinion of the Court.

. . . The defendants (although not all were named in each cause of action) were the Commissioner of Baseball, the presidents of the two major leagues, and the 24 major league clubs. In general, the complaint charged violations of the federal anti-trust laws and civil rights statutes, violation of state statutes and the common law, and the imposition of a form of peonage and involuntary servitude contrary to the Thirteenth Amendment and 42 U. S. C. § 1994, 18 U. S. C. § 1581, and 29 U. S. C. §§ 102 and 103. Petitioner sought declaratory and injunctive relief and treble damages. . . .

III
The Present Litigation

. . .Trial to the court took place in May and June 1970. An extensive record was developed. In an ensuing opinion, 316 F. Supp. 271 (SDNY 1970), Judge Cooper first noted that:

> Plaintiff's witnesses in the main concede that some form of reserve on players is a necessary element of the oganization of baseball as a league sport, but contend that the present all-embracing system is needlessly restrictive and offer various alternatives which in their view might loosen the bonds without sacrifice to the game. . . .

> Clearly the preponderance of credible proof does not favor elimination of the reserve clause. With the sole exception of plaintiff himself, it shows that even plaintiff's witnesses do not contend that it is wholly undesirable; in fact they regard substantial portions merito-rious. . . . 316 F. Supp., at 275-276.

He then held that *Federal Baseball Club* v. *National League,* 259 U. S. 200 (1922), and *Toolson* v. *New York Yankees, Inc.,* 346 U.S. 356 (1953), were controlling; that it was not necessary to reach the issue whether exemption from the antitrust laws would result because aspects of baseball now are a subject of collective bargaining; that the plaintiff's state-law claims, those based on common law as well as on statute, were to be denied because baseball was not "a matter which admits of diversity of treatment," 316 F.Supp., at 280; that the involuntary servitude claim failed because of the absence of "the essential element of this cause of action, a showing of compulsory service," 316 F.Supp., at 281-282; and that judgment was to be entered for the defendants. Judge Cooper included a statement of personal conviction to the effect that "negotiations could produce an accommodation on the reserve system which would be eminently fair and equitable to all concerned" and that "the reserve clause can be fashioned so as to find acceptance by player and club." 316 F.Supp., at 282 and 284.

On appeal, the Second Circuit felt "compelled to affirm." 443 F. 2d 264, 265 (1971). . . .

We granted certiorari in order to look once again at this troublesome and unusual situation. 404 U.S. 880 (1971).

IV
The Legal Background

A. *Federal Baseball Club* v. *National League,* 259 U.S. 200 (1922), was a suit for treble damages instituted by a member of the Federal League (Baltimore) against the National and American Leagues and others. The plaintiff obtained a verdict in the trial court, but the Court of Appeals reversed. The main brief filed by the plaintiff with this Court discloses that it was strenuously argued, among other things, that the business in which the defendants were engaged was interstate com-merce; that the interstate relationship among the several clubs, located as they were in different

States, was predominant; that organized baseball represented an investment of colossal wealth; that it was an engagement in moneymaking; that gate receipts were divided by agreement between the home club and the visiting club; and that the business of baseball was to be distinguished from the mere playing of the game as a sport for physical exercise and diversion. See also 259 U.S., at 201-206.

Mr. Justice Holmes, in speaking succinctly for a unanimous Court, said:

> The business is giving exhibitions of base ball, which are purely state affairs. . . . But the fact that in order to give the exhibitions the Leagues must induce free persons to cross state lines and must arrange and pay for their doing so is not enough to change the character of the business. . . .

B. *Federal Baseball* was cited a year later, and without disfavor, in another opinion by Mr. Justice Holmes for a unanimous court. The complaint charged antitrust violations with respect to vaudeville bookings. It was held, however, that the claim was not frivolous and that the bill should not have been dismissed. *Hart v. B. F. Keith Vaudeville Exchange*, 262 U.S. 271 (1923). . . .

In the years that followed, baseball continued to be subject to intermittent antitrust attack. The courts, however, rejected these challenges on the authority of *Federal Baseball*. In some cases stress was laid, although unsuccessfully, on new factors such as the development of radio and television with their substantial additional revenues to baseball. For the most part, however, the Holmes opinion was generally and necessarily accepted as controlling authority. And in the 1952 Report of the Subcommittee on Study of Monopoly Power of the House Committee on the Judiciary, H. R. Rep. No. 2002, 82d Cong., 2d Sess., 229, it was said, in conclusion:

> On the other hand the overwhelming preponderance of the evidence established baseball's need for some sort of reserve clause. Baseball's history shows that chaotic conditions prevailed when there was no reserve clause. Experience points to no feasible substitute to protect the integrity of the game or to guarantee a comparatively even competitive

struggle. The evidence adduced at the hearings would clearly not justify the enactment of legislation flatly condemning the reserve clause.

C. The Court granted certiorari, 345 U.S. 963 (1953), in the *Toolson, Kowalski,* and *Corbett* cases and, by a short *per curiam* (Warren, C. J., and Black, Frankfurter, Douglas, Jackson, Clark, and Minton, J.J.), affirmed the judgments of the respective courts of appeals in those three cases. *Toolson v. New York Yankees, Inc.,* 346 U.S. 356 (1953). *Federal Baseball* was cited as holding "that the business of providing public baseball games for profit between clubs of professional baseball players was not within the scope of the federal antitrust laws," 346 U.S., at 357, and:

> Congress has had the ruling under consideration but has not seen fit to bring such business under these laws by legislation having prospective effect. The business has thus been left for thirty years to develop, on the understanding that it was not subject to existing antitrust legislation. The present cases ask us to overrule the prior decision and, with retrospective effect, hold the legislation applicable. We think that if there are evils in this field which now warrant application to it of the antitrust laws it should be by legislation. Without re-examination of the underlying issues, the judgments below are affirmed on the authority of *Federal Baseball Club of Baltimore* v. *National League of Professional Baseball Clubs, supra,* so far as that decision determines that Congress had no intention of including the business of baseball within the scope of the federal antitrust laws. *Ibid.*

This quotation reveals four reasons for the Court's affirmance of *Toolson* and its companion cases: (a) Congressional awareness for three decades of the Court's ruling in *Federal Baseball,* coupled with congressional inaction. (b) The fact that baseball was left alone to develop for that period upon the understanding that the reserve system was not subject to existing federal antitrust laws. (c) A reluctance to overrule *Federal Baseball* with consequent retroactive effect. (d) A professed desire that any needed remedy be provided by legislation rather than by court decree. The emphasis in *Toolson* was on the determination, attributed even to *Federal Baseball,* that Congress had no intention to include baseball within the reach of the federal antitrust laws. Two Justices (Burton and Reed, JJ.) dissented, stressing the factual aspects, revenue sources, and the absence of an express exemption of organized baseball from the Sherman Act. . . .

D. *United States* v. *Shubert*, 348 U. S. 222 (1955), was a civil antitrust action against defendants engaged in the production of legitimate theatrical attractions throughout the United States and in operating theaters for the presentation of such attractions. The District Court had dismissed the complaint on the authority of *Federal Baseball* and *Toolson*. 120 F.Supp. 15 (SDNY 1953). This Court reversed. Mr. Chief Justice Warren noted the Court's broad conception of "trade or commerce" in the antitrust statutes and the types of enterprises already held to be within the reach of that phrase. He stated that *Federal Baseball* and *Toolson* afforded no basis for a conclusion that businesses built around the performance of local exhibitions are exempt from the antitrust laws. 348 U.S., at 227. He then went on to elucidate the holding in *Toolson* by meticulously spelling out the factors mentioned above:

> In Federal Baseball, the Court, speaking through Mr. Justice Holmes, was dealing with the business of baseball and nothing else. . . . The travel, the Court concluded, was "a mere incident, not the essential thing". . . .
>
> In *Toolson*, where the issue was the same as in *Federal Baseball*, the Court was confronted with a unique combination of circumstances. For over 30 years there had stood a decision of this Court specifically fixing the status of the baseball business under the antitrust laws and more particularly the validity of the so-called "reserve clause." During this period, in reliance on the *Federal Baseball* precedent, the baseball business had grown and developed. . . . And Congress, although it had actively considered the ruling, had not seen fit to reject it by amendatory legislation. Against this background, the Court in *Toolson* was asked to overrule *Federal Baseball* on the ground that it was out of step with subsequent decisions reflecting present-day concepts of interstate commerce. The Court, in view of the circumstances of the case, declined to do so. But neither did the Court necessarily reaffirm all

that was said in *Federal Baseball*. Instead, "[w]ithout re-examination of the underlying issues," the Court adhered to *Federal Baseball* "so far as that decision determines that Congress had no intention of including the business of baseball within the scope of the federal antitrust laws." 346 U.S., at 357. In short, *Toolson* was a narrow application of the rule of *stare decisis*.

. . . If the *Toolson* holding is to be expanded — or contracted — the appropriate remedy lies with Congress, 348 U.S., at 228-230.

E. *United States* v. *International Boxing Club*, 348 U.S. 236 (1956), was a companion to *Shubert* and was decided the same day. This was a civil antitrust action against defendants engaged in the business of promoting professional championship boxing contests. Here again the District Court had dismissed the complaint in reliance upon *Federal Baseball* and *Toolson*. The Chief Justice observed that "if it were not for *Federal Baseball* and *Toolson*, we think that it would be too clear for dispute that the Government's allegations bring the defendants within the scope of the Act." 348 U.S., at 240-241. He pointed out that the defendants relied on the two baseball cases but also would have been content with a more restrictive interpretation of them than the *Shubert* defendants, for the boxing defendants argued that the cases immunized only businesses that involve exhibitions of an athletic nature. The Court accepted neither argument. It again noted, 348 U.S., at 242, that "*Toolson* neither overruled *Federal Baseball* nor necessarily reaffirmed all that was said in *Federal Baseball*." It stated:

> The controlling consideration in *Federal Baseball* and *Hart* was, instead, a very practical one — the degree of interstate activity involved in the particular business under review. It follows that *stare decisis* cannot help the defendants here; for, contrary to their argument, *Federal Baseball* did not hold that all businesses based on professional sports were outside the scope of the antitrust laws. The issue confronting us is, therefore, not whether a previously granted exemption should continue, but whether an exemption should be granted in the first instance. And that issue is for Congress to resolve, not this Court. 348 U.S., at 243. . . .

F. The parade marched on. *Radovich* v. *National Football League*, 352 U.S. 445 (1957), was a civil Clayton Act case testing the application of the antitrust laws to professional football. The District Court dismissed. The Ninth Circuit affirmed in part on the basis of *Federal Baseball* and *Toolson*. The court did not hesitate to "confess that the strength of the pull" of the baseball cases and of *International Boxing* "is about equal," but then observed that "[f]ootball is a team sport" and boxing an individual one. 231 F.2d 620, 622.

This court reversed with an opinion by Mr. Justice Clark. He said that the Court made its ruling in *Toolson* "because it was concluded that more harm would be done in overruling *Federal Baseball* than in upholding a ruling which at best was of dubious validity." 352 U.S., at 450. He noted that congress had not acted. He then said:

All this, combined with the flood of litigation that would follow its repudiation, the harassment that would ensue, and the retroactive effect of such a decision, led the Court to the practical result that it should sustain the unequivocal line of authority reaching over many years.

[S]ince *Toolson* and *Federal Baseball* are still cited as controlling authority in antitrust actions involving other fields of business, we now specifically limit the rule there established to the facts there involved, i.e., the business of organized professional baseball. As long as the Congress continues to acquiesce we should adhere to — but not extend — the interpretation of the Act made in those cases. . . .

If this ruling is unrealistic, inconsistent, or illogical, it is sufficient to answer, aside from the distinctions between the businesses, that were we considering the question of baseball for the first time upon a clean slate we would have no doubts. But *Federal Baseball* held the business of baseball outside the scope of the Act. No other business claiming the coverage of those cases has such an adjudication. We, therefore, conclude that the orderly way to eliminate error or discrimination, if any there be, is by legislation and not by court decision. Congressional processes are more accommodative, affording the whole industry hearings and an opportunity to assist in the formulation of

new legislation. The resulting product is therefore more likely to protect the industry and the public alike. The whole scope of congressional action would be known long in advance and effective dates for the legislation could be set in the future without the injustices of retroactivity and surprise which might follow court action. 352 U.S., at 450-452. . . .

G. Finally, in *Haywood* v. *National Basketball Assn.*, 401 U.S. 1204 (1971), Mr. Justice Douglas, in his capacity as Circuit Justice, reinstated a District Court's injunction *pendente lite* in favor of a professional basketball player and said, "Basketball . . . does not enjoy exemption from the antitrust laws." 401 U.S., at 1205.

H. This series of decisions understandably spawned extensive commentary, some of it mildly critical and much of it not; nearly all of it looked to Congress for any remedy that might be deemed essential.

I. Legislative proposals have been numerous and persistent. Since *Toolson* more than 50 bills have been introduced in Congress relative to the applicability or nonapplicability of the antitrust laws to baseball. A few of these passed one house or the other. Those that did would have expanded, not restricted, the reserve system's exemption to other professional league sports. . . .

V

In view of all this, it seems appropriate now to say that:

1. Professional baseball is a business and it is engaged in interstate commerce.

2. With its reserve system enjoying exemption from the federal antitrust laws, baseball is, in a very distinct sense, an exception and an anomaly. *Federal Baseball* and *Toolson* have become an aberration confined to baseball.

3. Even though others might regard this as "unrealstic, inconsistent, or illogical," see *Radovich*, 352 U.S., at 452, the aberration is an established one, and one that has been recognized not only in *Federal Baseball* and *Toolson*, but in *Shubert, International Boxing*, and *Radovich*, as well, a total of five consecutive cases in this Court. It is an aberration that has been with us now for half a century, one heretofore deemed fully entitled to the benefit of *stare decisis*, and one that has survived the Court's expanding concept of inter-

state commerce. It rests on a recognition and an acceptance of baseball's unique characteristics and needs.

4. Other professional sports operating interstate — football, boxing, basketball, and, presumably, hockey and golf — are not so exempt.

5. The advent of radio and television, with their consequent increased coverage and additional revenues, has not occasioned an overruling of *Federal Baseball* and *Toolson.*

6. The Court has emphasized that since 1922 baseball, with full and continuing congressional awareness, has been allowed to develop and to expand unhindered by federal legislative action. Remedial legislation had been introduced repeatedly in Congress but none has even been enacted. The Court, accordingly, has concluded that Congress as yet has had no intention to subject baseball's reserve system to the reach of the antitrust statutes. This, obviously, has been deemed to be something other than mere congressional silence and passivity. Cf. *Boys' Markets, Inc.* v. *Retail Clerks Union,* 398 U.S. 235, 241-242 (1970).

7. The Court has expressed concern about the confusion and the retroactivity problems that inevitably would result with a judicial overturning of *Federal Baseball.* It has voiced a preference that if any change is to be made, it come by legislative action that, by its nature, is only prospective in operation.

8. The Court noted in *Radovich,* 352 U.S., at 452, that the slate with respect to baseball is not clean. Indeed, it has not been clean for half a century.

This emphasis and this concern are still with us. We continued to be loath, 50 years after *Federal Baseball* and almost two decades after *Toolson,* to overturn those cases judicially when Congress, by its positive inaction, has allowed those decisions to stand for so long and, far beyond mere inference and implication, has clearly evinced a desire not to disapprove them legislatively.

Accordingly, we adhere once again to *Federal Baseball* and *Toolson* and to their application to professional baseball. We adhere also to *International Boxing* and *Radovich* and to their respective applications to professional boxing and professional football. If there is any inconsistency or illogic in all this, it is an inconsistency and illogic of long standing that is to be remedied by the

Congress and not by this court. If we were to act otherwise, we would be withdrawing from the conclusion as to congressional intent made in *Toolson* and from the concerns as to retrospectivity therein expressed. Under these circumstances, there is merit in consistency even though some might claim that beneath that consistency is a layer of inconsistency.

The petitioner's argument as to the application of state antitrust laws deserves a word. Judge Cooper rejected the state law claims because state antitrust regulation would conflict with federal policy and because national "uniformity [is required] in any regulation of baseball and its reserve system." 316 F.Supp., at 280. The Court of Appeals, in affirming, stated, "[A]s the burden of interstate commerce outweighs the states' interests in regulating baseball's reserve system, the Commerce Clause precludes the application here of state antitrust law." 443 F. 2d, at 268. As applied to organized baseball, and in the light of this Court's observations and holdings in *Federal Baseball,* in *Toolson,* in *Shubert,* in *International Boxing,* and in *Radovich,* and despite baseball's allegedly inconsistent position taken in the past with respect to the application of state law, these statements adequately dispose of the state law claims.

The conclusion we have reached makes it unnecessary for us to consider the respondents' additional argument that the reserve system is a mandatory subject of collective bargaining and that federal labor policy therefore exempts the reserve system from the operation of federal antitrust laws. . . .

The judgment of the Court of Appeals is

Affirmed.

Mr. Justice Douglas, with whom Mr. Justice Brennan concurs, dissenting.

This Court's decision in *Federal Baseball Club* v. *National League,* 259 U.S. 200, made in 1922, is a derelict in the stream of the law that we, its creator, should remove. Only a romantic view of a rather dismal business account over the last 50 years would keep that derelict in midstream. . . .

Baseball is today big business that is packaged with beer, with broadcasting, and with other industries. The beneficiaries of the *Federal Baseball Club* decision are not the Babe Ruths, Ty Cobbs, and Lou Gehrigs.

The owners, whose records many say reveal a proclivity for predatory practices, do not come to us with equities. The equities are with the victims of the reserve clause. I use the word "victims" in the Sherman Act sense, since a contract which forbids anyone to practice his calling is commonly called an unreasonable restraint of trade. . . .

If congressional inaction is our guide, we should rely upon the fact that Congress has refused to enact bills broadly exempting professional sports from antitrust regulation. . . .

The only statutory exemption granted by Congress to professional sports concerns broadcasting rights. 15 U.S.C. §§ 1291-1295. I would not ascribe a broader exemption through inaction than Congress has seen fit to grant explicitly. . . .

Mr. Justice Marshall, with whom Mr. Justice Brennan joins, dissenting.

Petitioner was a major league baseball player from 1956, when he signed a contract with the Cincinnati Reds, until 1969, when his 12-year career with the St. Louis Cardinals, which had obtained him from the Reds, ended and he was traded to the Philadelphia Phillies. He had no notice that the Cardinals were contemplating a trade, no opportunity to indicate the teams with which he would prefer playing, and no desire to go to Philadelphia. After receiving formal notification of the trade, petitioner wrote to the Commissioner of Baseball protesting that he was not "a piece of property to be bought and sold irrespective of my wishes," and urging that he had the right to consider offers from other teams than the Phillies. He requested that the Commissioner inform all of the major league teams that he was available for the 1970 season. His request was denied, and petitioner was informed that he had no choice but to play for Philadelphia or not to play at all.

To non-athletes it might appear that petitioner was virtually enslaved by the owners of major league baseball clubs who bartered among themselves for his services. But, athletes know that it was not servitude that bound petitioner to the club owners; it was the reserve system. The essence of that system is that a player is bound to the club with which he first signs a contract for the rest of his playing days. He cannot escape from the club except by retiring, and he cannot prevent the club from assigning his contract to any other club. . . .

This is a difficult case because we are torn between the principle of *stare decisis* and the knowledge that the decisions in *Federal Baseball Club* v. *National League,* 259 U.S. 200 (1922), and *Toolson* v. *New York Yankees, Inc.,* 346 U.S. 356 (1953), are totally at odds with more recent and better reasoned cases. . . .

Has Congress acquiesced in our decisions in *Federal Baseball Club* and *Toolson?* I think not. Had the Court been consistent and treated all sports in the same way baseball was treated, Congress might have become concerned enough to take action. But, the Court was inconsistent, and baseball was isolated and distinguished from all other sports. In *Toolson* the Court refused to act because Congress had been silent. But the Court may have read too much into this legislative inaction.

Americans love baseball as they love all sports. Perhaps we become so enamored of athletics that we assume that they are foremost in the minds of legislators as well as fans. We must not forget, however, that there are only some 600 major league baseball players. Whatever muscle they might have been able to muster by combining forces with other athletes has been greatly impaired by the manner in which this court has isolated them. It is this Court that has made them impotent, and this Court should correct its error. . . .

Accordingly, I would overrule *Federal Baseball Club* and *Toolson* and reverse the decision of the Court of Appeals.

This does not mean that petitioner would necessarily prevail, however. Lurking in the background is a hurdle of recent vintage that petitioner still must overcome. In 1966, the Major League Players Association was formed. It is the collective-bargaining representative for all major league baseball players. Respondents argue that the reserve system is now part and parcel of the collective-bargaining agreement and that because it is a mandatory subject of bargaining, the federal labor statutes are applicable, not the federal antitrust laws. The lower courts did not rule on this argument, having decided the case solely on the basis of the antitrust exemption.

This Court has faced the interrelationship between the antitrust laws and the labor laws before. The decisions make several things clear. First, "benefits to organized labor cannot be utilized as a cat's-paw to pull employer's chestnuts out of the antitrust fires''. . . .

Second, the very nature of a collective-bargaining agreement mandates that the parties be able to "restrain" trade to a greater degree than management could do unilaterally. . . . Finally, it is clear that some cases can be resolved only by examining the purposes and the competing interests of the labor and antitrust statutes and by striking a balance.

It is apparent that none of the prior cases is precisely in point. They involve union-management agreements that work to the detriment of management's competitors. In this case, petitioner urges that the reserve system works to the detriment of labor. . . .

It is true that in *Radovich* v. *National Football League, supra,* the court rejected a claim that federal labor statutes governed the relationship between a professional athlete and the professional sport. But, an examination of the briefs and record in that case indicates that the issue was not squarely faced. The issue is once again before this Court without being clearly focused. It should, therefore, be the subject of further inquiry in the District Court. . . .

NOTE _____

1. Ever since *Flood* v. *Kuhn,* there have been repeated court challenges to the baseball antitrust exemption. All have been unsuccessful. See, for example: *Charles O. Finley & Co.* v. *Kuhn,* 569 F.2d 527 (7th Cir. 1968); *Portland Baseball Club, Inc.* v. *Kuhn,* 491 F.2d 1101 (9th Cir. 1974); and *Boise Baseball Club, Inc.* v. *Kuhn,* 49 U.S.L.W. 3824 (U.S. May 4, 1981). On the other hand, when a baseball club asserted antitrust violations against another business — one holding the concession franchise at the club's ballpark — the antitrust exemption was not successfully raised by the concessionaire. See *Twin City Sportservice, Inc.* v. *Charles O. Finley & Co.,* 512 F.2d 1264 (9th Cir. 1975).

2.30　Labor and Sports

Players' associations, asserting status as labor unions, are very much a part of professional sports today. Although popularly regarded as a recent phenomenon, players' associations can trace their roots for unionization back a century.

The National Brotherhood of Professional Baseball Players organized in 1885 and became an actual bargaining union one year later when the National League owners adopted a $2,000 *maximum* salary. Concern over the salary issue, as well as concern over what was the forerunner of the reserve clause, eventually led the Brotherhood to start its own Players League. Earlier considerations of the *Ewing* and *Ward* cases in Section 2.11 included notes on the quick demise of the Players League. With the league also died the union movement, at least for a time.

Although there were other attempts to join players, particularly in baseball, into collective associations for the united presentation of positions and demands, not until the late 1950s did anything resembling a viable labor organization appear. Even then two questions remained unanswered. First was whether the associations could gain sufficient clout to force collective bargaining on the leagues. By the late 1960s the associations finally did achieve a degree of power which was gained through a combination of perservance, legal pressures, and fortuitous circumstances. The second question was whether the sports unions could gain recognition under the National Labor Relations Act (NLRA). This point was crucial, particularly for unions in baseball, since they were denied the ability to proceed against the leagues and owners on antitrust grounds.

Congressional power to control labor relations is based on the commerce clause, article 1, section 8 of the U.S. Constitution, the same clause relied on by Congress to enact various antitrust statutes. Thus, if the courts or other duly authorized agencies were to proceed in matters of labor relations in baseball, the process by which an exemption was fashioned in antitrust matters would have to be reversed. It would have to be argued successfully that Congress could reach baseball through the commerce clause and that Congress intended to do so by the scope of its coverage in the NLRA.

The decisive resolution of the matter came in an opinion on a labor dispute before the National Labor Relations Board. It dealt, not with players, but with umpires. It was to be the ultimate breakthrough.

The American League of Professional Baseball Clubs. Case 1-RC-10414, 180 N.L.R.B. 189 (1969)

... Upon a petition duly filed under Section 9(c) of the National Labor Relations Act, as amended, a hearing was held before Hearing Officer Francis V. Paone. The Hearing Officer's rulings made at the hearing are free from prejudicial error and are hereby affirmed.

Upon the entire record in this case, including the briefs, the National Labor Relations Board finds:

1. The Petitioner seeks an election in a unit of umpires employed by the American League of Professional Baseball Clubs (hereinafter called the Employer or the League). The Employer, while conceding the Board's constitutional and statutory power to exercise jurisdiction herein, nevertheless urges the Board, as a matter of policy, not to assert jurisdiction pursuant to Section 14(c) of the Act.

The Employer is a nonprofit membership association consisting of 12 member clubs located in 10 states and the District of Columbia. Operating pursuant to a constitution adopted and executed by the 12 member clubs, the Employer is engaged in the business of staging baseball exhibitions and, with its counterpart the National League of Professional Baseball Clubs, constitutes what is commonly known as "major league baseball." The Employer currently employs, among other persons, the 24 umpires requested herein, and one umpire-in-chief.

The Employer stipulated the following commerce data for the year 1958:

(1) The business of the Employer was conducted substantially in interstate commerce.

(2) The Employer's net share of the revenue derived from the national radio and television contracts of Major League Baseball (Game-of-the-Week, World Series and All-Star Game) was a sum in excess of $3,000,000.

(3) Employer's member clubs derived revenue from gate receipts ranging from over $1,000,000 to over $2,250,000; and the League office's share of such total receipts was a sum in excess of $1,000,000.

(4) The Employer expended a sum in excess of $500,000 in maintaining its staff of umpires, such sum including umpires' salaries, travel and other expenses.

(5) The average revenue derived by each member club of the Employer from local radio and television contracts was a sum in excess of $900,000.

(6) The total revenue derived by the Employer from concession sales was a sum in excess of $500,000, a substantial portion of which resulted from interstate purchases.

(7) The total amount expended by the Employer for equipment and supplies was a sum in excess of $500,000, a substantial portion of which was made through interstate commerce.

(8) The total amount expended by the Employer for travel (mostly interstate) was a sum in excess of $500,000.

(9) In connection with working arrangements between the Employer's member clubs and their minor league affiliates, substantial portions of the operating expenses of such affiliates were paid by such clubs; and the total of all such payments was a sum in excess of $1,000,000.

The Board's jurisdiction under the Act is based upon the commerce clause of the Constitution, and is coextensive with the reach of that clause. In 1922 the Supreme Court in *Federal Baseball Club of Baltimore* v. *National League of Professional Baseball Clubs,* 259 U.S. 200, although characterizing baseball as a "business," ruled that it was not interstate in nature, and therefore was beyond the reach of the nation's antitrust laws. However, subsequent Supreme Court decisions appear to proceed on the assumption that baseball, like the other major professional sports, is now an industry in or affecting interstate commerce, and that baseball's current antitrust exemption has been preserved merely as a matter of judicial *stare decisis.* Thus, in both the *Toolson* and *Radovich* decisions the Supreme Court specifically stated that baseball's antitrust status was a matter for Congress to resolve, implying thereby that Congress has the power under the commerce clause to regulate the baseball industry. Since professional football and boxing have been held to be in interstate commerce and thus subject to the antitrust laws, it can no longer be seriously contended that the Court still considers baseball alone to be outside of interstate commerce. Congressional deliberations regarding the relationship of baseball and other professional team sports to the antitrust laws likewise reflect a Congressional assumption that such sports are subject to regulation under the commerce clause. It is, incidentally, noteworthy that these deliberations reveal Congressional concern for the rights of employees such as players to bargain collectively and engage in concerted activities. Additionally, legal scholars have agreed, and neither the parties nor those participating as *amici* dispute, that professional sports are in or affect interstate commerce, and as such are subject to the Board's jurisdiction. Therefore, on the basis of the above, we find that professional baseball is an industry in or affecting commerce, and as such is subject to Board jurisdiction under the Act.

Section 14(c)(1) of the National Labor Relations Act, as amended, permits the Board to decline jurisdiction over labor disputes involving any "class or category of employers, where, in the opinion of the Board, the effect of such labor dispute on commerce is not sufficiently substantial to warrant the exercise of its jurisdiction. . . ." The Employer and other employers contend that because of baseball's internal self-regulation, a labor dispute involving The American League of Professional Baseball Clubs is not likely to have any substantial effect on interstate commerce; and that application of the National Labor Relations Act to this Employer is contrary to national labor policy because Congress has sanctioned baseball's internal self-regulation. The employer also contends that effective and uniform regulations of baseball's labor relations problems is not possible through Board processes because of the sport's international aspects.

The Petitioner and other employee representatives contend, on the other hand, that Section 14(c) precludes the Board from declining jurisdiction, as any labor dispute arising in this industry will potentially affect millions of dollars of interstate commerce and have nationwide impact. They assert that baseball's self-regulation is controlled entirely by employers, and therefore has not and will not prevent labor disputes from occurring in this industry. Additionally, it is submitted that Congressional intent does not preclude, and national labor policy requires, Board jurisdiction — for without a national forum for uniform resolution of disputes, the industry might be subject to many different labor laws depending upon the State in which any particular dispute arises.

We have carefully considered the positions of the parties, and the *amicus* briefs, and we find that it will best effectuate the mandates of the Act, as well as national labor policy, to assert jurisdiction over this employer. We reach this decision for the following reasons:

Baseball's system for internal self-regulation of disputes involving umpires is made up of the Uniform Umpires Contract, the Major League Agreement, and the Major League Rules, which provide, among other things, for final resolution of disputes through arbitration by the Commissioner. The system appears to have been designed almost entirely by employers and owners, and the final arbiter of internal disputes does not appear to be a neutral third party freely chosen by both sides, but rather an individual appointed solely by the member club owners themselves. We do not believe that such a system is likely either to prevent labor disputes from arising in the future, or, having once arisen, to resolve them in a manner susceptible or conducive to voluntary compliance by all parties involved. Moreover, it is patently contrary to the letter and spirit of the Act for the Board to defer its undoubted jurisdiction to decide unfair labor practices to a disputes settlement system established unilaterally by an employer or group of employers. Finally, although the instant case involves only umpires employed by the League, professional baseball clubs employ, in addition to players, clubhouse attendants, bat boys, watchmen, scouts, ticket sellers, ushers, gatemen, trainers, janitors, office clericals, batting practice pitchers, stilemen, publicity, and advertising men, grounds keepers and maintenance men. *Congressional Hearings, supra,* footnote 8. As to these other categories, there is no "self-regulation" at all. This consideration is of all the more consequence for of those employees in professional baseball whose interests are likely to call the Board's processes into play, the great majority are in the latter-named classifications.

We can find, neither in the statute nor in its legislative history, any expression of a Congressional intent that disputes between employers and employees in this industry should be removed from the scheme of the National Labor Relations Act. In 1935, 1947, and again in 1959, Congress examined the nation's labor policy as reflected in the National Labor Relations Act; and Congress has consistently affirmed the Act's basic policy, as expressed in Section 1, of encouraging collective bargaining by "protecting the exercise by workers of full freedom of association, self-organization, and designation of representatives of their own choosing." Nowhere in Congress' deliberations is there any indication that these basic rights are not to be extended to employees employed in professional baseball or any other professional sport. We do not agree that Congress, by refusing to pass legislation subjecting the sport to the antitrust laws when it considered the regulation of baseball and other sports under the antitrust statutes, sanctioned a governmentwide policy of "noninvolvement" in all matters pertaining to baseball. Indeed, to the extent that Congressional deliberation on the antitrust question has reference to the issue before us, it indicates agreement that players' rights to bargain collectively and engage in concerted activities, are to be protected rather than limited.

There is persuasive reason to believe that future labor disputes — should they arise in this industry — will be national in scope, radiating their impact far beyond individual State boundaries. As stated above, the Employer and its members are located and conduct business in 10 States and the District of Columbia. The stipulated commerce data establishes that millions of dollars of interstate commerce are involved in its normal business operations. The nature of the industry is such that great reliance is placed upon interstate travel. Necessarily, then, we are not here confronted with the sort of small, primarily intrastate employer over which the Board declines jurisdiction because of failure to meet its prevailing monetary standards. Moreover, it is apparent that the Employer, whose operations are so clearly national in scope, ought not have its labor relations problems subject to diverse state labor laws.

The Employer's final contention, that Board processes are unsuited to regulate effectively baseball's international aspects, clearly lacks merit, as many if not most of the industries subject to the Act have similar international features.

Accordingly, we find that the effect on interstate commerce of a labor dispute involving professional baseball is not so insubstantial as to require withholding assertion of the Board's jurisdiction, under Section 14(c) of the Act, over Employers in that industry, as a class. As the annual gross revenues of this employer are in excess of all of our prevailing monetary standards, we find that the Employer is engaged in an industry affecting commerce, and that it will effectuate the policies of the Act to assert jurisdiction herein.

2. The Employer at the hearing denied that the Petitioner was a labor organization within the meaning of Section 2(5) of the Act. The record shows, however, that the Petitioner is an organization in which employees participate, and which exists for the purpose of dealing with employers concerning wages and other conditions of employment. Accordingly, we find that the Petitioner is a labor organization within the meaning of Section 2(5) of the Act.

3. A question affecting commerce exists concerning the representation of certain employees of the Employer within the meaning of Sections 9(c)(1) and 2(6) and (7) of the Act.

4. The Employer contends that the petition should be dismissed on the ground that the umpires sought to be represented are supervisors as defined in Section 2(11) of the Act. It is not contended that umpires have authority to hire, fire, transfer, discharge, recall, promote, assign, or reward. We think it equally apparent that umpires do not "discipline" or "direct" the work force according to the common meaning of those terms as used in the Act.

The record indicates that an umpire's basic responsibility is to insure that each baseball game is played in conformance with the predetermined rules of the game. Thus the umpire does not discipline except to the extent he may remove a participant from the game for violation of these rules. Testimony shows that after such a removal the umpire merely reports the incident to his superiors, and does not himself fine, suspend, or even recommend such action. As the final arbiter on the field, the umpire necessarily makes decisions which may favor one team over another, and which may determine to some extent the movements of various players, managers, and other personnel on the ball field. The umpire does not, however, direct the work force in the same manner and for the same reasons as a foreman in an industrial setting. As every fan is aware, the umpire does not — through the use of independent judgment — tell a player how to bat, how to field, to work harder or exert more effort, nor can he tell a manager which players to play or where to play them. Thus, the umpire merely sees to it that the game is played in compliance with the rules. It is the manager and not the umpire who directs the employees in their pursuit of victory.

Accordingly, we find that the umpires are not supervisors, and thus the employer's motion to dismiss on this ground is hereby denied. We further find that the following employees of the employer constitute a unit appropriate for the purposes of collective bargaining within the meaning of Section 9(b) of the Act:

> All persons employed as umpires in the American League of Professional Baseball Clubs, but excluding all other employees, office clerical employees, guards, professional employees and supervisors as defined in the Act. . . .

[Member Jenkins dissented.]

2.40 Convergence of Antitrust and Labor Principles

The importance of the players and umpires/ referees in baseball and the other sports banding into effective labor groups cannot be over-emphasized. Gaining the protections under federal labor law, as witnessed by the foregoing umpire's case, has had sweeping effects, not so much by the instances in which successful recourse was sought before the National Labor Relations Board, but as a goal toward realizing full collective bargaining over a whole range of issues, including those deemed most important to the players. Coming to the forefront in collective bargaining have been the issues related to so-called player mobility. As discussed previously (see Section 1.11), the leagues have long used restrictive devices whereby the rich resource of players was divided among the clubs. Drafts, reserves, options and other restrictions have prevented players from moving to perceived richer fields.

Chapter 3 sets forth many of the current collective bargaining provisions pertaining to player mobility (see particularly Sections 3.40–3.46). Before examining these provisions, one further piece to the legal structure must be analyzed. It is a specific exemption recognized under the antitrust laws that certain labor activities are not subject to sanction under the antitrust statutes. Representative of a convergence of antitrust and labor principles, this exemption has as its statutory base volume 15, United States Code, section 17, set forth earlier in Section 2.21.

As the cases reveal, there is both a statutory and a nonstatutory exemption. The latter is a creation by the courts, deemed essential in order for the statutory exemption to obtain its full purpose. For example, under 15 U.S.C., Sec. 17, if labor organizations alone are immune from antitrust attack, then who will deal with them? Certainly, management would be loath to join in any agreement whereby it would soon find itself in the courts on antitrust charges. Thus, protections for both labor and management were fashioned — up to a point.

To discover the outer reaches of the labor exemption and then to apply these limits to sports problems, it is necessary to begin with nonsports cases, which are presented in Section 2.41. The next step is to examine the background of cases in which the exemption was considered, but rejected, by the courts. This occurred with a series of player-mobility cases in the early to mid-1970s (see Section 2.42). The final step is to consider the few opportunities the courts have had to weigh the labor exemption in sports settings in which bona fide, arm's-length bargaining has taken place (see Section 2.43).

As a result of these decisions, collective bargaining regarding player-mobility issues must be viewed as a two-edged sword. It has obtained for players greater freedoms than previously enjoyed, but to the extent that restrictions remain (and Sections 3.40–3.46 show this to be the case), continued antitrust challenge to such limitations has been curtailed.

2.41   Nonsports Background

Allen Bradley Co. v. Local Union No. 3, (IBEW), 325 U.S. 797 (1945)

The plaintiffs, manufacturers of electrical equipment located outside of New York City, brought this action for declaratory and injunctive relief against the defendant union (located in N.Y.C.), which had established closed-shop agreements with the New York City electrical equipment manufacturers and contractors' union. These agreements provided that the contractors would only buy from manufacturers with closed-shop agreements with defendant union. In turn, the manufacturers agreed to sell only to contractors with closed-shop agreements with defendant union. In the course of time these union-employer agreements became industrywide understandings and included price and market controls. Agencies composed of union, contractor, and manufacturer representatives agreed to boycott noncomplying local contractors and manufacturers as well as to bar equipment manufactured out of New York City from use in the city. These combinations gave the three parties a complete monopoly within New York City.

The district court held that the combination violated the Sherman Act and granted an injunction against the union. The Circuit Court of Appeals for the Second Circuit reversed, holding that "combinations of unions and business men which restrained trade and tended to monopoly were not a violation of the Act where the bona fide purpose of the unions was to raise wages, provide better working conditions, and bring about better conditions of employment for their members."

However, the Supreme Court reversed the circuit court, holding that the union activity violated the Sherman Act and could be enjoined to the extent the union joined "with any person, firm or corporation which is a non-labor group. . . ."

The court phrased the issue as follows:

> . . . whether it is a violation of the Sherman Anti-trust Act for labor unions and their members, prompted by a desire to get and hold jobs for themselves at good wages and under high working standards, to combine with employers and with manufacturers of goods to restrain competition in, and to monopolize the marketing of, such goods.

The Court, in its review of the Sherman Act, Clayton Act, and Norris La Guardia Act, along with relevant court decisions, found these statutes, when jointly considered, to enunciate two separate and sometimes conflicting policies. First, there is the policy of preserving a competitive business economy. Second, there is the policy of preserving "the rights of labor to organize to better its conditions through the agency of collective bargaining."

When viewed in this light, if the union in the present case had acted independently, the Court felt that its actions would be immune from the antitrust laws regardless of their anticompetitive effect. However, the union could not "aid non-labor groups to create business monopolies and to control the marketing of goods and services . . ." In other words, the same labor union activities may or may not be in violation of the Sherman Act, depending on whether the union acts alone or in combination with business groups.

The test is twofold. First, the plaintiff must be able to show an illegal combination or conspiracy, among nonlabor groups. Second, to get an injunction against the union, there must be shown union participation in the combination or conspiracy: "A business monopoly is no less such because a union participates, and such participation is a violation of the Act."

Local Union No. 189, Amalgamated Meat Cutters, and Butcher Workmen of North America v. Jewel Tea Company, 381 U.S. 676 (1965)

The case arose out of a suit by Jewel Tea

Company, a supermarket chain, against the defendant union and a trade association which was a competitor of Jewel's, charging a conspiracy to violate the antitrust laws. The dispute centered on the 1957 collective bargaining negotiations between the defendant union and multi-employer unit composed of many Chicago retailers of fresh meat. The union rejected employer requests to relax the current contracted restriction on marketing hours for fresh meat, which forbade the sale of meat before 9 A.M. and after 6 P.M. in most markets. The restriction was kept in the final collective bargaining agreement, which Jewel at first refused to sign. It eventually signed only after a union vote authorized a strike. Jewel then instituted this suit.

The trial court rejected the claims of conspiracy against the defendant trade association because of a lack of evidence. As to the union, the trial court found that it had acted within its self-interest and thus qualified for the labor exemption from the antitrust laws. The court of appeals reversed both holdings and found that the union and the trade association had "entered into a combination or agreement which constituted a conspiracy" in restraint of trade.

The Supreme Court reversed the court of appeals, finding the union fell within the labor exemption to the antitrust laws. However, the Court split into three separate groups in making its decision. Justice White wrote the plurality opinion. Justice Goldberg wrote a concurring opinion, joined by Harlan and Stewart, and Justice Douglas wrote a dissent, joined by Justices Black and Clark.

The White opinion began by rejecting the union's contention that the case turned on whether the operating hours restriction is a term or condition of employment and as such that the Court should defer primary jurisdiction to a pending action before the National Labor Relations Board. First, the Court believed that "courts are themselves not without experience in classifying bargaining subjects as terms or conditions of employment." Thus, there was no need to defer to the board on the basis of a claim

that it had a special competency in this area. The Court went on:

> Secondly, the doctrine of primary jurisdiction is not a doctrine of futility; it does not require resort to "an expensive and merely delaying administrative proceeding when the case must eventually be decided on a controlling legal issue wholly unrelated to determinations for the ascertainment of which the proceeding was sent to the agency."

The Court next addressed the issue of the union's claimed exemption from the antitrust laws. Justice White set forth the ground rules explicitly. He was not concerned with a case in which the union had entered a conspiracy with a nonlabor group against the plaintiff.

> . . . We have a situation where the unions, having obtained a marketing hours agreement from one group of employers, have successfully sought the same terms from a single employer, Jewel, not as a result of a bargain between the unions and some employers directed against other employers, but pursuant to what the unions deemed to be in their own labor union interests.

This is the distinction from both the *Allen Bradley* and *Pennington* cases, in which in each instance a conspiracy of employers existed separate and apart from union actions.

Justice White saw the issue as

> . . . whether the marketing hours restriction, like wages, and unlike prices, is so intimately related to wages, hours and working conditions that the union's successful attempt to obtain that provision through bona fide, arm's-length bargaining in pursuit of their own labor policies, and not at the behest of or in combination with nonlabor groups, falls within the protection of the national labor policy and is therefore exempt from the Sherman Act.

The Court answered in the affirmative.

On the first point, the Court found that the hours of the day and the days of the week during which employers shall work are mandatory bargaining subjects. This conclusion does not make an agreement on these items exempt from antitrust laws but "weighs heavily in favor of antitrust exemption for agreement on these subjects." When the Court coupled this conclusion with its finding that the marketing restrictions were truly in pursuit of the unions' labor policy, the labor exemption arose. No employer conspiracy was present, as in both *Allen Bradley* and *Pennington*, to negate the unilateral action of the union, and in this respect the three cases are consistent.

Mr. Justice Douglas's dissent claimed this case fell squarely within the rules enunciated in *Allen Bradley*. Douglas found the *Allen Bradley* requirement of a nonlabor conspiracy which the union had joined in the collective bargaining agreement itself. Consistent with a footnote to his concurring opinion in *U.M.W.* v. *Pennington*, Douglas felt that, when competitors agree to a plan, whether it be as a part of a collective bargaining agreement or not, if the result of the plan is to restrain trade, then an unlawful conspiracy under the Sherman Act exists. The collective bargaining agreement containing these anticompetitive features would be strong evidence of the conspiracy.

Mr. Justice Goldberg in his concurring opinion agreed with the result in *Jewel Tea* but for different reasons, and dissented from the Court's reversal in *Pennington*. According to Justice Goldberg, both cases presented instances of unions bargaining over mandatory bargaining issues in accord with long-held union policies and based on the self-interest of the members of the unions. In his view, this was enough to make the union exempt from antitrust law violation. To hold otherwise would severely limit the ability of unions to bargain on mandatory bargaining issues, which is the core of our national labor policy.

He also took issue with the opinions of both White and Douglas in that they would let courts inquire as to the unions' and the employers' motives and purposes in reaching an agreement on mandatory subjects of bargaining. Douglas's opinion would presume the conspiracy simply from the fact that a collective bargaining agreement was entered into between a union and a multi-employer unit. To Goldberg, this would mean that no multi-employer bargaining agreement could avoid antitrust regulation. It was his belief that such inquiry into the economic motive behind bargaining on mandatory issues is improper for the courts to engage in and properly left to the parties alone.

His decision lists two limits to his labor exemption. The first is when the union and employers agree on *non*mandatory bargaining issues. In such cases the union does not have a direct and immediate interest as it does in wages, terms, and conditions of employment. The exemption also does not extend to situations in which the union is not acting as a union but as a business. In both of these situations, the congressional policy in favor of collective bargaining over the essential labor-management relationships is not at issue, and therefore the antitrust laws should not be prevented from taking effect.

United Mine Workers of America v. Pennington, 381 U.S. 657 (1965)

The trustees of the United Mine Workers Welfare and Retirement Fund (UMW) brought suit against defendant coal company to recover royalty payments plaintiff claimed were owed to it under the National Bituminous Coal Wage Agreement of 1950. The defendant answered and cross-claimed, alleging a conspiracy between the UMW, the trustees of its Welfare and Retirement Fund, and the large coal operators, to violate the antitrust laws.

The conspiracy was allegedly contained in the National Bituminous Coal Wage Agreement of 1950, which had been entered into by the UMW and the large coal operators as an overall solution to the problems plaguing the coal industry. The agreement provided for the union to

abandon its efforts to control the working time of the miners, agreed not to oppose the rapid mechanization of the mines which would substantially reduce mine employment, agreed to help finance such mechanization and agreed to impose the terms of the 1950 agreement on all operators without regard to their ability to pay. The benefit to the union was to be increased wages as productivity increased with mechanization, these increases to be demanded of the smaller companies whether mechanized or not. Royalty payments into the welfare fund were to be increased also, and the union was to have effective control over the fund's use. The union and large companies agreed upon other steps to exclude the marketing, production, and sale of nonunion coal.

The net effect of this agreement was to eliminate the smaller coal companies from the market, leaving control solely to the larger companies.

At the trial court level the jury returned a verdict for the defendant against both the UMW and the trustees. The trial court set aside the verdict as to the trustees only. Its decision was affirmed by the court of appeals.

The Supreme Court, through Justice White, first addressed the question of whether the UMW was exempt from liability under the antitrust laws. It found no such exemption in this case:

> If the UMW in this case, in order to protect its wage scale by maintaining employer income, had presented a set of prices at which the mine operators would be required to sell their coal, the union and the employees who happened to agree could *not* successfully defend this contract provision if it were challenged under the antitrust laws. . . . In such a case, the restraint on the product market is direct and immediate, is of the type characteristically deemed unreasonable under the Sherman Act and the union gets from the promise nothing more concrete than a hope for better wages to come.
>
> Likewise, if as is alleged in this case, the union became a party to a collusive bidding arrangement designed to drive . . . [defendant] . . . and others from the . . . market, we think any claim to exemption from antitrust liability would be frivolous at best.

The Court answered claims that this agreement concerned wages, a compulsory collective bargaining subject, and that as such the agreement entered into by the union and a multi-employer bargaining unit was exempt from the antitrust laws. In the Court's view, a truly unilateral policy decision by the union as to wages was exempt from the antitrust laws, and the union could impose its policy on multi- or single-employer bargaining units. However, when the union agreed with all or part of the employers of the unit to impose a certain wage scale on other employers, the union's exemption was lost. The test thus seems to be a direct result of *Allen Bradley.* First, does there exist an employer conspiracy to violate the antitrust laws? If so, then did the union join in this conspiracy? If both questions are answered in the affirmative, the union cannot assert antitrust exemption. It becomes irrelevant what the subject of the agreement is or how it was entered into (see language at 381 U.S. 664—666).

> We think it beyond question that a union may conclude a wage agreement with the multi-employer bargaining unit without violating the antitrust laws and that it may as a matter of its own policy and not by agreement with all or part of the employers of that unit, seek the same wages from other employers.
>
> This is not to say that an agreement resulting from union employer negotiations is automatically exempt from Sherman Act scrutiny simply because the negotiations involve a compulsory subject of bargaining regardless of the subject or the form and content of the agreement. . . . But *there are limits to what a union or an employer may offer or extract in the name of wages, and because they must bargain does not mean that the agreement reached may disregard other laws* . . . [emphasis added]
>
> . . .We have said that a union may make wage agreements with a multi-employer bargaining unit and may in pursuance of its own union interests seek to obtain the same terms from other employers. No case under the antitrust laws could be made out on evidence limited to such behavior. . . . [There must be additional direct or indirect evidence of the conspiracy.] . . . But we think a union forfeits its exemption from the antitrust laws when it is clearly shown that it has agreed with one set of employers to impose a certain wage scale on other bargaining units. *One group of employers may not conspire to eliminate competitors from the industry and the union is liable with the employers if it becomes a party to the conspiracy* . . . [emphasis added]

Having dispelled the union's notions of exemption, the Court then moved to a question which now encompasses the so called *Noerr-Pennington* doctrine. The trial court had allowed the jury to consider evidence of the union's intent and purpose in seeking to influence the secretary of labor and the TVA as part of the overall scheme to drive the small coal producers out of the market. The Supreme Court found this reversable error. Under the *Noerr* case, the intent or purpose of the union or the employers is irrelevant if the conduct is an effort to influence public officials.

> Joint efforts to influence public officials do not violate the antitrust laws even though intended to eliminate competition. Such conduct is not illegal, either standing alone or as part of a broader scheme itself violative of the Sherman Act.

In a concurring opinion, Justices Douglas, Black and Clark set out their understanding of the majority's opinion. They felt that if there was "an industry-wide collective bargaining agreement the union agreed on a wage scale that exceeded the financial ability of some operators to pay and that it was made for the purpose of forcing some employers out of business, the union as well as the employers who participated in the arrangement with the union should be found to have violated the antitrust laws." They further felt that "an industry-wide agreement containing those features is prima facia evidence of a violation." The conspiracy requirement would be fulfilled by the employers' acceptance of the agreement, the necessary consequence of which would be a restraint of interstate commerce.

Justices Goldberg, Harlan, and Stewart joined in the reversal but dissented from the Court's opinion because they felt that collective bargaining activity concerning a mandatory subject of bargaining is exempt from the antitrust laws. (This opinion is coupled with their concurrence in the *Jewel Tea* case.)

NOTE _____

See also, *Connell Construction Co.* v. *Plumbers & Steamfitters, Local Union 100,* 421 U.S. 616 (1975).

2.42   Early Considerations of Player Freedom of Movement Complaints

In tackling the labor exemption as it applies to professional sports, it is important to assess the full chronology of cases that erupted in the early 1970s. In these initial cases, even though the exemption was unsuccessfully raised, the possibilities it held for future resolution of issues without resort to litigation was seized upon by the courts. An exhortation to try to solve the problems through collective bargaining was made, as excerpts from the trial court decision in *Flood* v. *Kuhn,* cited below, make clear. The general question was to what extent collective bargaining agreements can legalize practices which otherwise would be violative of antitrust strictures. The opinions by scholars ranged from the cautious to the sweeping.

An early voice arguing for a sweeping application of the labor exemption was raised in an article by Michael Jacobs and Ralph Winter, "Antitrust Principles and Collective Bargaining by Athletes: Of Superstars in Peonage," 81 *Yale Law Journal* 1 (1971). It is appropriate to consider their arguments, then contrast them with the judicial handling of such problems as exhibited in the several cases discussed in this section.

In their article, Jacobs and Winter start with the basic proposition that the dispute raging in professional athletics concerning the allocation of players has too long focused on antitrust issues. Instead, they believe the focus should shift to the employment relationship and that collective bargaining in terms of the National Labor Relations Act should determine the legitimacy of the provisions in professional sports contracts which currently allocate players among teams. The article was written after the Supreme Court granted certiorari in the *Flood* case but before any decision had been rendered. The article is thus a recommendation to the Court to declare that its certiorari was improvidently granted and that the issues should be resolved at the bargaining table.

We would welcome the overruling of *Toolson.*

[But] the antitrust issue is a straw man, deserving the space we devote to it only because so many eminent persons, including some who have much to lose, mistake straw for flesh and blood. . . . The terms and conditions of employment of professional athletes in baseball, basketball and football are no longer governed solely by individual contracts but have been supplanted in part by collective bargaining between the leagues and player unions. As a result, national labor policy, rather than antitrust law, is the principal and pre-eminent legal force shaping relationships in professional sports.

. . . The "right" to exercise individual bargaining power without restraint, which Flood claims, is explicitly denied to employees with a bargaining representative recognized under the National Labor Relations Act. Furthermore, the reserve clause in baseball and the common draft in basketball raise questions, not of group boycott or merger law, but of the scope of the duty to bargain and the freedom of contract between parties to collective bargaining. To us, therefore, the question is no longer whether professional sports are entitled to a special exemption from the antitrust laws where their employment relationships are involved, but whether unions of professional athletes are entitled to special help from the courts and Congress in bargaining with their employers. [pp. 6-7]

The authors' analysis begins with the accepted principle that once a bargaining unit is chosen and a majority of the employees vote to be represented by a union, as they have in most professional sports, the individual employees lose their right to bargain individually. Instead, the union becomes the exclusive representative of the employees. Should an employee want to control his employment destiny, he is required to work through the union. Of course, the union is, by way of *Steele* v. *Louisiana & N.R.R.*, under a duty to represent all members of the bargaining unit fairly. However, this will not prevent what has happened in many other industries from also occurring here. For example, the most talented employees (here the superstars) will have to forego many of the benefits they could achieve through individual bargaining in order to accommodate the needs of the majority of players in the bargaining unit.

The next step in the authors' labor law approach is that the reserve or option clauses, because they are contractual provisions "intimately connected with determining the team for which an athlete will play and what salary and other benefits he may extract through individual bargaining" are mandatory subjects of bargaining, demanding good faith bargaining by both the owners and the unions. The National Labor Relations Act still recognizes freedom of contract and does not obligate the parties to make concessions or to reach an agreement, even on mandatory bargaining issues. Either or both parties may use all of its economic force to influence the other side, including the players' right to strike. But it is contended that the government should not interfere via judicial opinion or legislative enactment in the writing of the substantive contract terms. By judicially or legislatively outlawing reserve or option clauses, the government would be interfering on the employee side, a move for which the owner would have to find compensation by stronger demands on the other bargaining issues.

> There is not a shred of justification for outlawing the reserve system and leaving the players with the right to strike. If government is to intervene, it should do so as a substitute for, rather than a supplement to, collective bargaining — which is to say professional athletes should not be covered by the National Labor Relations Act and should not have the right to strike. [p. 29]

In addition to the reserve and option clauses, the authors see many other issues as requiring mandatory bargaining, including the proposed common draft and merger in basketball. This idea emerges from comparison with *Fibreboard Paper Products Corp.* v. *NLRB*, which held an employer must bargain about the "contracting out" of work for the bargaining unit. Since a common draft and merger would affect the extent to which persons outside the unit would do the work of the unit and since this would thus reduce revenues for those in the unit, the issues are mandatory bargaining items.

When analyzed in these terms, the reserve and option clauses are not illegal and can be bargained over. Even a reserve clause, which is the strongest case for those advocating that there are unreasonable restraints on an individual's freedom to seek employment, would expire at the end of each bargaining agreement. It is not an unreasonable contract term. There is sufficient evidence of its necessity in maintaining evenly balanced teams, which, in turn, is a necessity for the survival of competition in professional sports.

Finally, the authors find that the antitrust laws should not apply to the matters which are subject to collective bargaining unless and until the owners combine with the union to the detriment of a third party who may maintain an antitrust action. Otherwise, the actions of the union and the owners should be immune from the antitrust laws.

These are ideas advanced by Jacobs and Winter. An examination of the cases should be made to determine the acceptance of their position by the courts.

Flood v. Kuhn, 316 F.Supp. 271 (S.D.N.Y. 1970)

The Conflicts Are Reconcilable

Before concluding this opinion, we wish to unburden ourselves of two strong and related convictions which we took away from this trial. First, despite the opposing positions of plaintiff and the Major League Baseball Players' Association on the one hand, the present management and club owners of organized baseball on the other, we found the witnesses appearing on behalf of both sides in the main credible and of high order; they have a genuine enthusiasm for baseball and with constancy have the best interests of the game at heart.

Second, we are convinced that the conflicts between the parties are not irreconcilable and that negotiations could produce an accommodation on the reserve system which would be eminently fair and equitable to all concerned — in essence, what is called for here is continuity with change.

This issue is not so unique or complex and the parties are not at such loggerheads that negotia-tions could not succeed. What we have already said under "The Reserve System, A Necessity?" effec-tively supports this conclusion. Trial testimony developed several proposed modifications that could serve as bases from which negotiations might proceed toward an accommodation of the valid interests of both sides. . . .

Plaintiff's witnesses expressed a belief that this matter was capable of being resolved by good faith bargaining between the parties. Thus, Mr. Miller, executive director of the Major League Baseball Players' Association, recited the various modifica-tions suggested by the players and declared a continuing desire to resolve this dispute . . . He summed up the Association's bargaining position at the various meetings held with management regarding the reserve system as follows:

> Basically . . . it was our position that the reserve rule system was illegal in that its restrictions were just about total, that it was inconceivable to us that you could have a game of baseball with no rules, but that it seemed quite reasonable to us that modifications which were less restrictive than the present system could be made, were practical, and presumably could make the system safe from attack in terms of its illegality.

. . . The Major League Baseball Players' Associa-tion, organized in 1954, has proved a particularly effective bargaining representative obtaining since 1966 highly significant benefits for the players in such areas as pensions, life and disability insur-ance, health care, minimum salary, arbitration of grievances, expense allowances, maximum per-missible salary cut, termination pay, representa-tion at individual salary negotiations, negotiation of rule changes affecting player benefits or obligations, due process in player discipline. . . . Both management and the Players' Association recognize the reserve system to be a mandatory subject of collective bargaining. The National Labor Relations Board asserted jurisdiction over organized baseball in December, 1969.

The history of negotiations to date does not appear to us to establish, as plaintiff appears to contend, that organized baseball refuses to bargain with regard to the reserve system and will accept no modification of its structure unless forced to do so by the courts or by Congress. In the first place, several of the benefits mentioned above are directed at alleviating some of the undesirable side effects of the reserve system. Moreover, serious negotiations aimed at the core of this system are of quite recent origin and the failure to reach a quick accord should not be seen, in our opinion, as indicating intransigence on either or both sides.

While it is true the owners have continued to support the status quo of the reserve system and have been critical of the various proposals by the Players' Association for its elimination or modification, they have not closed the door entirely on various suggestions made during negotiations in the immediate past in efforts to ameliorate the objectionable features of the reserve clause. Indeed, Commissioner Kuhn in his testimony at this trial indicated that, "changes that could be made are changes that are best bargained out between parties that are involved here . . ." And representatives of the club owners expressed substantially similar views.

In such matters as labor relations and family disputes, to name just two, Congress (in the case of collective bargaining) and the courts have determined that such disputes as do arise therein are best resolved by the parties without outside interference and that resort to a court-imposed solution should be a matter of last resort. This is almost invariably the case whenever two parties must continue to work together amicably toward a common end after the dispute is settled. This is not to hold that the court should adopt a similar hands-off approach toward this case. Nevertheless, we believe that here, as well, the parties themselves are best able to reach a satisfactory accord, and that all avenues toward such an approach certainly have not yet been fully exhausted.

From the trial record and the sense of fair play demonstrated in the main by the witnesses on both sides, we are convinced that the reserve clause can be fashioned so as to find acceptance by player and club.

Far more complicated matters accompanied by an exclusive self-centered concern and by seemingly hostile and irreconcilable attitudes, frequently find their way to amicable adjustment and the abandonment of court claims. Why not here — with the parties positive and reasonable men who are equally watchful over a common objective, the best interests of baseball?

Philadelphia World Hockey Club Inc. v. Philadelphia Hockey Club, Inc., 351 F.Supp. 462 (E.D. Pa. 1972)

III
The Labor Exemptions of the Sherman Act

A preliminary issue is whether the National Hockey League is entitled to invoke the labor exemptions from the Sherman Act authorized by §§6 and 20 of the Clayton Act, 15 U.S.C. § 17, 29 U.S.C. § 52. For reasons which hereinafter follow, I conclude that the labor exemptions are not applicable and the National Hockey League is subject to the operations of the anti-trust laws.

Initially, the status of the National Hockey League Players' Association (hereinafter referred to as "Players' Association") must be considered to ascertain if it qualifies as a "labor organization" under § 2(5) of the National Labor Relations Act, 29 U.S.C. § 152(5). The record indicates that on June 7, 1967, a "Recognition Agreement" was executed between the owners of the National Hockey League and the Players' Association, whereby the Association would be regarded as the official representative of the players in their dealings with the member teams of the National Hockey League. The record, however, does not disclose whether the designation of the Players' Association complied with the provisions of § 8 of the National Labor Relations Act, 29 U.S.C. § 159. I cannot definitively conclude that the National Labor Relations Board has actually certified the Players' Association as the approved collective bargaining representative.

But even if the Court assumes, *arguendo,* a duly authorized collective bargaining representative exists, labor-employer activities are not entirely immune from the anti-trust laws. The history of labor exposure to anti-trust liability has not been ideologically and homogeneously consistent, but certain standards have been articulated by the courts which can be applied to the present factual context. *See generally,* 7 J. O. von Kalinowski, Anti-Trust Laws and Trade Regulation, §§ 48.01 et seq., pp. 41-1 to 82 (1971), and the references cited therein.

In United States v. Hutcheson, 312 U.S. 219, 61 S.Ct. 463, 85 L.Ed. 788 (1941), the Supreme Court sought to adumbrate the outer perimeters wherein labor unions would not be prosecuted under and insulated from the regulations of the Sherman Act. In order not to lose this exemption, the two caveats imposed by the Court were that the "union acts in its self-interest and does not combine non-labor groups." 312 U.S. at 232, 61 S.Ct. at 466.

The latter limitation enunciated in *Hutcheson* was reinvigorated in Allen Bradley v. Local Union No. 3, 325 U.S. 797, 65 S.Ct. 1533, 89 L.Ed. 1939, re-hearing denied, 326 U.S. 803, 66 S.Ct. 11, 90 L.Ed. 489 (1945). In *Allen Bradley,* the Supreme Court declared the union activities to be in contravention of the Sherman Act when the union combined with all local contractors and manufacturers to restrain trade in and monopolize the supply of electrical equipment in the New York City area. While undoubtedly the "hot cargo" clause contained in the collective bargaining agreement furthered the union interests, the Court held that ". . . Congress never intended that unions could, consistently with the Sherman Act, aid non-labor groups to create business monopolies and to control the marketing of goods and services." 325 U.S. at 808, 65 S.Ct. at 1539. Moreover, the Court continued, ". . . when the unions participated with a combination of business men who had complete power to eliminate all competition among others, a situation was created not included within the exemptions of the Clayton and Norris-LaGuardia Acts." 325 U.S. at 809, 65 S.Ct. at 1540. Finally, the Court remarked:

> The primary objective of all the Anti-trust legislation has been to preserve business competition and to proscribe business monopoly. It would be a surprising thing if Congress, in order to prevent a misapplication of that legislation to labor union, had bestowed upon such unions complete and unreviewable authority to aid business groups to frustrate its primary objective. For if business groups, by combining with labor unions, can fix prices and divide up markets, it was little more than a futile gesture for Congress to prohibit price fixing by business groups themselves.[325 U.S. at 809-810, 65 S.Ct. at 1540.]

The Supreme Court was again presented the opportunity to examine the *Allen Bradley* doctrine in United Mine Workers v. Pennington, 381 U.S. 657, 85 S.Ct. 1585, 14 L.Ed.2d 626 (1965). The Court reaffirmed the labor exemption position previously adopted in *Allen Bradley* and made it indisputably clear that ". . . [a collective bargain-

ing] agreement resulting from union-employer negotiations is [not] automatically exempt from Sherman Act scrutiny simply because the negotiations involve a compulsory subject of bargaining, regardless of the subject or the form and content of the agreement." 381 U.S. at 664-665, 85 S.Ct. at 1590.

In invalidating the wage scale the union sought to impose on all the coal mine operators in *Pennington,* the Court further stated "there are limits to what a union or an employer may offer or extract in the name of wages, and because they must bargain does not mean that the agreement reached may disregard other laws." (Emphasis added.) 381 U.S. at 665, 85 S.Ct. at 1591. Unions (and derivatively, employers) will not be shielded from the enforcement of anti-trust legislation against them when they do not act alone and function in concert with nonlabor groups to effectuate their labor goals and policies. See also, Ramsey v. United Mine Workers, 265 F.Supp. 388 (E.D.Tenn.1967), aff'd 416 F.2d 655 (6th Cir. 1969) (en banc), rev'd on other grounds 401 U.S. 302, 91 S.Ct. 658, 28 L.Ed.2d 64 (1971); South-East Coal Co. v. Consolidation Coal Co. 434 F.2d 767 (6th Cir. 1970), cert. denied 402 U.S. 983, 91 S.Ct. 1662, 29 L.Ed.2d 149 (1971), rehearing denied 404 U.S. 877, 92 S.Ct.28, 30 L.Ed.2d 124 (1971).

While the Union activities in Meat Cutters Local Union 189 v. Jewel Tea Co., 381 U.S. 676, 85 S.Ct. 1596, 14 L.Ed.2d 640 (1965), were held to be outside the scope of the Sherman Act, the National Hockey League (the employer) is not a beneficiary of that decision in behalf of the union. First, the Court in *Jewel Tea* noted there was no claim raised of union-employer conspiracy, and, second, the collective bargaining dispute related to an area in which the union had forcefully negotiated:

> Thus the issue in this case is whether the marketing-hours restriction, like wages, and unlike prices, is so intimately related to wages, hours and working conditions that the unions' successful attempt to obtain that provision through *bona fide, arm's-length bargaining in pursuit of their own labor union policies, and not at the behest of or* in combination with nonlabor groups, falls within the protection of the national labor policy and is therefore exempt from the Sherman Act. (emphasis added) [381 U.S. at 689-690, 85 S.Ct. at 1602.]

The crucial determinant is not the form of the agreement — e.g., prices or wages — but its *relative impact on the product market and the interests of union members.* (emphasis added) [Footnote 5, 381 U.S. at 690, 85 S.Ct. at 1602.]

From my examination of the foregoing cases, several conclusions can be drawn. First, those cases all involved situations where the union had been sued for its active, conspiratorial role in restraining competition of a product market, and the union, not the employer, sought to invoke the labor exemptions. Here there is no evidence that the Players' Association was a joint-conspirator with the National Hockey League in creating and retaining the reserve clause. The evidence establishes the Players' Association's persistent opposition to the present form of reserve system. The reserve clause, in fact, was more than a sturdy teenager when the Players' Association was born. The reserve clause was fathered by the NHL, and the Players' Association has repeatedly sought to exclude it in its present form.

Second, the cases cited above pertained to issues which furthered the interests of the union members and on which there had been extensive collective bargaining. Again, that is not true in this litigation. The National Hockey League has not come forward with any substantial evidence which could warrant this Court finding that the reserve clause — as it presently operates in conjunction with the other interlocking agreements — was ever a subject of serious, intensive, arm's-length collective bargaining. When the Players' Association was recognized in 1967, some variation of the reserve system had existed for probably sixteen years prior thereto. Subsequent efforts by the Association to markedly revamp the reserve system have been continually rebuffed by the NHL. The discussions revolving around the Arbitration Agreements related only to resolving salary disputes, and did not in any way alter or affect the basic perpetual option of the reserve system.

Finally, even if, *arguendo,* there had been substantial arm's-length collective bargaining by the National Hockey League and the Players' Association to revise the perpetual option provision of the reserve clause (see, e.g., Exhibits D-59-64; D-2 ¶10, App. A; and D-129, p. 50), those negotiations would not shield the National Hockey League from liability in a suit by outside competitors who sought access to players under

the control of the National Hockey League.

A stronger argument might be made by a newly-formed league that a collective agreement between an established league and players' union which, for example, permitted suits for injunction against players who attempted to "jump" leagues, was designed to prevent the new league from gaining access to the best players and to consign it permanently to second class status. This claim is similar to the one which succeeded in Allen Bradley: a union-employer combination to exclude entry by newcomers. [Jacobs and Winter, "Antitrust Principles and Collective Bargaining by Athletes: Of Superstars in Peonage," 81 Yale L.J. 1, 28 (1971)]

Even if the benefits of the labor exemptions can be extended to encompass the employer's activities, that outcome is not changed merely because the employer is a member of a multi-employer association. A multi-employer group will not be accorded any greater protections than a single employer. Though a multi-employer organization will be insulated from unfair labor practice prosecutions only if it acts in good faith and takes only the limited steps necessary to protect itself, see, e.g., NLRB v. Truck Drivers Local 449, 353 U.S. 87, 77 S.Ct. 643, 1 L.Ed.2d 676 (1957), however, restraining, anti-competitive acts will not be immunized from the Sherman Act. Cf. Kennedy v. Long Island R.R., 319 F.2d 366, 370-373 (2nd Cir. 1963), cert. denied. 375 U.S. 830, 84 S.Ct. 75, 11 L.Ed.2d 61 (1963); Prepmore Apparel, Inc. v. Amalgamated Clothing Workers of America. 431 F.2d 1004, 1007 (5th Cir. 1970), cert. dismissed by consent, 404 U.S. 801, 92 S.Ct. 21, 30 L.Ed.2d 34 (1971). While the employer activities in the two latter cases were not subject to the Sherman Act, the Courts clearly intimated that employer efforts to monopolize a particular product market would not be similarly treated.

In providing a special exemption from Sherman Act regulations for labor unions and employers who in good faith negotiated with those unions, Congress attempted to accommodate what frequently were conflicting public policies; the fostering and preservation of competitive business conditions in a free enterprise system on one hand, counterbalanced by a legitimate concern in improving and bettering the working conditions of laborers and the reduction of industrial strife through vigorous union organization and collective bargaining. The labor exemption which could be defensively utilized by the union and employer as a shield against Sherman Act proceedings when there was bona fide collective bargaining, could not be seized upon by either party and destructively wielded as a sword by engaging in monopolistic or other anti-competitive conduct. The shield cannot be transmuted into a sword and still permit the beneficiary to invoke the narrowly carved out labor exemption from the antitrust laws. To allow and condone such conduct would frustrate Congress' carefully orchestrated efforts to harmoniously blend together two opposing public policies.

In sum, the National Hockey League, as it stands before me in the instant action, is not the most ideal candidate to be a beneficiary of the labor exemptions. The National Hockey League itself was primarily responsible for devising and perpetuating a monopoly over the product market of all professional hockey players via the reserve system. Not only did it enforce and implement its restraints against players and member clubs of the National Hockey League, but, moreover, it sought to enforce it against outside competitors who wanted to enter the competition at the professional level.

I reject the argument that an employer (National Hockey League) can conspire with or take advantage of a union to restrain competition and seriously impair the business dealings and transactions of competitors. To grant the National Hockey League an exemption in this proceeding would undermine and thwart the policies which have evolved over the years in disposing of labor-management and antitrust disputes. I cannot compatibly reconcile the National Hockey League's monopolistic actions here with the labor exemptions from the Sherman Act. The NHL can do no more than could the employers and union in *Allen Bradley, supra.* Even if the National Hockey League was primarily concerned about the welfare of its players, its purported good intentions would be insufficient to insulate its actions. As the Supreme Court so aptly stated over twenty years ago:

> [B]enefits to organized labor cannot be utilized as a cat's-paw to pull employers' chestnuts out of the antitrust fires. [*United States* v. *Women's*

Sportswear Mfg. Ass'n., 336 U.S. 460, 464, 69 S.Ct. 714, 716, 93 L.Ed. 805 (1949)]

For the foregoing reasons, the National Hockey League cannot invoke the labor exemptions and is thus subject to a prosecution under the Sherman Act. . . .

NOTE

1. Several other suits were brought in connection with the defection of NHL players to the newly formed World Hockey Association. Principal among these were *Nassau Sports* v. *Hampson,* 355 F.Supp. 733 (D. Minn. 1972); *Nassau Sports* v. *Peters,* 352 F.Supp. 870 (E.D. N.Y. 1972); and *Boston Professional Hockey Association, Inc.* v. *Cheevers,* 348 F. Supp. 261 (D. Mass. 1972) (rev'd) 472 F.2d 127 (1st Cir. 1972).

At issue in *Nassau Sports* v. *Hampson* was clause 17 of the NHL Standard Player Contract which bound the parties to the contract to further obligations for a period of one year following the expiration of the original contract. Hampson contended that the effect of the clause was to act as a contract in perpetuity; he argued that clause 17 was renewed in each succeeding contract and continued therefore to bind the player year after year. The court adopted a four-test approach in resolving whether plaintiff hockey club should be granted an injunction: (1) probability of success on the merits, (2) irreparable injury, (3) interests of others impaired, and (4) the effect on the interests of the public.

The court believed plaintiffs failed to show probability of success on the merits, since the court concluded that clause 17 was a violation of the Sherman Act in that it was part of a scheme that restrained trade in professional hockey. Furthermore, the interests of Hampson and his family would be impaired if they were forced to move from Minnesota to where his NHL contract had been assigned, and the public interest would be better served if the new league, which Hampson wished to join, could increase economic competition by improving the caliber of its product through signing established hockey professionals. Although the court ruled that plaintiffs would suffer irreparable injury due to the loss of the services of Hampson, this was not enough to overcome the countervailing considerations.

Mackey v. National Football League, 543 F.2d 606 (8th Cir. 1976)

The appeal by the National Football League (NFL), twenty six (26) of its member clubs and NFL Commissioner Pete Rozelle followed a district court ruling that the Rozelle Rule violated section 1 of the Sherman Act and an injunction of its enforcement.

The rule provided that when a player signed with a different club after his contractual obligation to his team had expired, the signing club had to provide compensation to the player's former team. If the teams were unable to reach a satisfactory agreement, the commissioner could award compensation in the form of one or more players and/or draft choices that he deemed fair and equitable.

John Mackey and other players brought the action under sections four (4) and sixteen (16) of the Clayton Act and section one (1) of the Sherman Act. The players charged that the rule was an illegal combination and conspiracy in restraint of trade denying professional football players the right to freely contract for their services. The players sought injunctive relief and treble damages.

The district court found that enforcement of the rule was a concerted refusal to deal and a group boycott and therefore a per se violation of the Sherman Act. Alternatively, the district court also concluded that the evidence did not support a finding that the rule was necessary to the successful operation of the NFL. The evidence, instead, failed to justify the restrictive effects of the rule and was invalid under a Rule of Reason. The district court also rejected the NFL's argument that the rule had antitrust immunity since it had been the subject of collective bargaining between the club owners and the NFL Players Association.

The issues raised on appeal were (1) whether the so-called labor exemption to the antitrust laws immunized the NFL's enforcement of the Rozelle Rule from antitrust liability; and (2) if not, whether the rule and the manner in which it had been enforced violated the antitrust laws.

The labor exemption has its source in the Clayton Act and provides that labor unions are not combinations or conspiracies in restraint of trade. It specifically exempts certain union activities, such as secondary picketing and group boycotts, from the antitrust laws. The statutory exemption was created to insulate legitimate collective activity by employees and extends to legitimate labor activity undertaken by a union in furtherance of its own interests. The protection does not extend to concerted actions or agreement between unions and nonlabor groups. To promote free competition in business, however, certain union-employer agreements are given limited nonstatutory exemption from antitrust sanctions.

The players claimed that only employee groups should be entitled to the labor exemption, not employer groups. The court disagreed on the basis that the nonstatutory exemption was to promote the national policy favoring collective bargaining, that the benefits had to inure to both parties, and that a nonlabor group may avail itself of the labor exemption.

The NFL claimed the exemption, arguing that the Rozelle Rule was the subject of an agreement with the association and therefore should have been immune from antitrust law. The players argued that the NFL was not entitled to assert the exemption because the rule was the result of unilateral action by the clubs.

The district court determined that neither the 1968 nor 1970 collective bargaining agreements embodied an agreement concerning the rule and further that the association had never agreed to the rule. The court, however, found that the 1968 agreement incorporated by reference the NFL constitution and bylaws, of which the rule is a part and that the free agent rules were not to be changed. Thus, the court concluded that the 1968 agreement required the rule to govern a player who played out his option and signed with another team. The court assumed that the 1970 agreement embodied a similar understanding.

The court had to determine whether these agreements fell within the scope of the nonstatutory labor exemption. The court also had to determine whether the federal labor policy deserved preeminence over federal antitrust policy under the circumstances of the particular case.

The court deduced three principles that governed the proper accommodation of the competing labor and antitrust interests involved: (1) if the restraint on trade primarily affects only the parties to the collective bargaining agreement, the labor policy favoring these agreements may prevail over antitrust laws; (2) the federal labor policy is implicated sufficiently to prevail only where the agreement to be exempted concerns a mandatory subject of collective bargaining; (3) the labor policy must be furthered to a point necessary to override the antitrust laws only when the agreement to be exempted is the product of bona fide arm's-length bargaining. The court found, in applying the principles, that only the parties to the agreement were affected by the alleged restraint on trade which resulted from the Rozelle Rule.

Whether the rule was a mandatory subject of collective bargaining had to be determined by federal labor law. Under section 8(d) of the National Labor Relations Act, the subjects were wages, hours, and other terms and conditions of employment. The practical effect of the agreement determined whether it concerned a mandatory subject of bargaining. On its face, the rule was not a mandatory subject of bargaining, but the court held it to be such a subject based on the district court's finding that the rule operated to restrict a player's ability to move from one team to another and depressed salaries.

The court found that there was substantial evidence to support the district court finding that there was no bona fide arm's-length bargaining over the rule preceding either the 1968 or 1970 agreements. Thus, the court held that the agreements between the clubs and the players which embodied the rule did not qualify for the labor exemption.

The Sherman Act, section one (1), declares illegal "every contract, combination . . . or conspiracy, in restraint of trade or commerce among the several States." The district court found the Rozelle Rule to be a per se violation and violative of the Rule of Reason standard of the antitrust laws.

On the issue of the product market, the NFL argued that the rule only affects the market for players' services and that the restriction of competition for players' services was not the type of restraint proscribed by the Sherman Act. The court dismissed the NFL argument and pointed out that the Sherman Act had been unhesitantly applied to owner-imposed restraints on competition for players' services. It held accordingly that the restraints on competition within the market for players' services fell within the scope of the Sherman Act.

In reviewing the per se violation determination made by the district court, the court pointed out that the Sherman Act was broad enough to render almost every business agreement illegal. The standard, however, established that only those agreements which were an unreasonable restraint on trade were within the scope of the Sherman Act. Courts have found certain types of agreements to be so consistently unreasonable that they are held to be illegal per se, without any inquiry into their purported justification, because they have such a pernicious effect on competition while lacking any redeeming value. Group boycotts and concerted refusals to deal have been held illegal per se. Concerted refusal to deal was defined as an agreement not to deal or to deal only on specified terms by two or more persons. A group boycott was a refusal to deal or pressure on others not to deal with a business.

The lower court held that the rule was a per se violation of the Sherman Act because it had the effect of significantly deterring clubs from dealing with and signing free agents and thus a group boycott and concerted refusal to deal.

On appeal, the court disagreed and rejected the per se violation determination, because the case presented unusual circumstances requiring an inquiry into the purported justifications for the rule.

The court found that prior holdings dealing with per se violations generally involved agreements between business competitors. The court agreed with the NFL argument that, unlike traditional per se violations, they assumed only some joint venture characteristics, since each club was interested in the other clubs' success, not their demise. It was also pointed out that mere characterization of an operation as a joint venture is insufficient, alone, to avoid the antitrust laws. In this case, it was the unique nature of professional football, as well as the fact that the alleged restraint did not completely eliminate competition for players' services, that resulted in the mechanical application of the per se rule being inappropriate. Instead, the court held that the appropriate test for the validity of the Rozelle Rule was the Rule of Reason doctrine.

The necessary elements of the test under a Rule of Reason require a showing that the imposed restraint be justified by legitimate business purposes and that it be no more restrictive than necessary.

The district court had found that the restraint on competition for players' services (1) significantly deterred clubs from dealing with and signing free agents; (2) substantially deterred players from playing out their options to become free agents; (3) significantly reduced a player's bargaining strength in contract negotiations; (4) players thus could not sell their services in the open and free market; (5) the absence of competitive bidding reduces players' salaries; and (6) in the absence of the Rozelle Rule there would have been more player movement among the clubs. The court of appeals found there was substantial evidence to support those findings.

The NFL contended that the rule was not unreasonable and asserted several justifications: (1) that star players would migrate to the economically strong teams, resulting in a destruction of the competitive balance; (2) that the rule protected club investment in developing and scouting players; (3) that a truly competitive team required players to play together for a substantial period of time, and eliminating the rule would undermine that; (4) that all this would result in detriment to the clubs, players, and NFL.

These justifications were inadequate to hold the rule reasonable. Player development expenses were ordinary. Costs of doing business were similar to those faced by any business, with no right to compensation for such investment. Elimination of the rule was found to affect all teams equally and would not destroy player continuity or the quality of play. The rule was also found to have no material effect on the competitive balances of the NFL. Even if the rule did aid competitive balance, other more reasonable means were available. Elimination of the rule would have no disruptive effect, in the short or long term, in professional football. Thus, the court concluded that the rule was an unreasonable restraint of trade. It was overly broad (little concern was evidenced at trial for average player movement, only that of the better players, but the rule applied to every player regardless of ability), unlimited in duration (the rule operated as a perpetual restriction on a player's ability to sell his services in a competitive market), unaccompanied by procedural safeguards (a player had no input into the process to determine fair compensation) and further that it was employed in conjunction with anticompetitive practices such as the draft, Standard Player Contract, option clause, and the no-tampering rules.

Kapp v. National Football League, 586 F.2d 644 (9th Cir. 1978)

Former professional football quarterback Joe Kapp originally brought this action against the National Football League (NFL) and its 26 member clubs, alleging that certain NFL rules violated the antitrust laws and resulted in his unlawful expulsion from professional football. Kapp also claimed that the New England Patriots had breached an alleged contract with him.

After the District Court held that the challenged rules violated the antitrust laws, the jury returned a verdict against Kapp on all issues. The jury found that Kapp was unable to prove he had been damaged. This appeal followed and was based on a claim that the instructions to the jury were erroneously stated.

Kapp challenged the following NFL rules:

1. *The Draft rule* (contained in Article 14 of the NFL Constitution). At an annual meeting of the member clubs, prospective

players were selected principally from colleges and universities. This rule had the effect of preventing any other club from negotiating with that player, even if the offer was unacceptable to the player.

2. *The Tampering Rule,* which prevented any club from interfering with the selecting club's rights to the players (drafted or active). Thus, under Article 9.2 of the NFL constitution, no other club could negotiate or make an offer to another club's player.

3. *Standard Player Contract,* which had to be signed before a player could participate in the NFL. The contract bound the player to the constitution and bylaws, the rules of the league, of the club and the decision of the league commissioner. Salary, contract period, and other matters were incorporated into the Standard Player Contract for each player.

4. *The Option Rule,* which provided the player's club, at its option, to renew the player's expired contract for an additional year, at no less than 90 percent of the player's salary of the previous year. The purpose was to induce the player to renew and not become a free agent.

5. *The Rozelle Rule.* The new club could not employ the free agent until there was compliance with Article 12.1(H) of the Constitution. The Rozelle Rule required that the former and new clubs reach a satisfactory arrangement concerning the player. In the event such arrangements were not possible, the commissioner held nonreviewable power to "award" one or more players to the former club from the new club's active, reserve, or selection list.

The district court held that these rules were, taken together, patently violative of the antitrust laws under the "reasonableness" standard. Specifically, the Rozelle Rule was held to be an unreasonable restraint of trade under any legal test. The Draft Rule was also found unreasonable. And the Tampering Rule and the Standard

Player Contract were found unreasonable, but only to the extent they were used to enforce other NFL rules. The Option Rule was not found unreasonable.

The NFL based its defense on the proposition that all of the challenged rules were a part of the 1968 and 1970 collective bargaining agreements between the NFLPA and the NFL. By this, the NFL was attempting to invoke the labor exemption (see *Mackey* v. *NFL,* 543 F.2d 606 [8th Cir. Ct. 1976]). However, the district court held that no collective bargaining agreement was in effect when Kapp was allegedly forced out of football. The 1968 collective bargaining agreement had expired and the new one had not been signed until June 1971. The issue then facing the jury was whether enforcement of the NFL provisions, found to have violated the antitrust laws, caused damages to Kapp.

Kapp's career was reviewed at trial. Kapp had been drafted out of the University of California by the Washington Redskins of the NFL, but he decided to play in the Canadian Football League (CFL). The Redskins retained their rights to Kapp by keeping him on their reserve list. Kapp, at the end of his CFL career, negotiated and contracted with the Houston Oilers of the then American Football League (AFL). This contract was subsequently invalidated on the basis of an agreement between the NFL, AFL, and CFL that prohibited players from negotiating during their contract periods, in an attempt to change leagues.

The Minnesota Vikings then signed Kapp to a two-year contract after managing his release from both the CFL and the Redskins. Kapp played for the Vikings for two years, and then a third year after the club exercised its option right. At the end of Kapp's option year, two teams expressed an interest in him but failed to make a firm offer. Kapp argued that the Rozelle Rule restrained these teams because of the "ransom" they would have had to pay the Vikings. A third team, the New England Patriots, obtained the rights to Kapp's services for a future draft choice and a player. Kapp played for the Patriots for the 1970 season. The

Patriots sent Kapp a Standard Players Contract for the 1971–72 season. Kapp, however, refused to sign the 1971–72 contract. Since under the NFL constitution a player could not play or practice with his team until he signed the standard contract, Kapp was dismissed from the Patriots.

The court of appeals held that the district court had properly instructed the jury on the applicable law. The court pointed out that damages could not be based solely on a finding that the antitrust laws had been violated. The Clayton Act requires proof of injury. There must have been a direct causal relationship between the illegality and the damages suffered. Kapp had to prove that he had been injured "by reason of" one of the unlawful practices. The injury had to be the type that the antitrust laws were designed to prevent. Thus, the injury had to reflect the anticompetitive effect, either of the violation or of anticompetitive acts made possible by the violation.

The NFL argued that Kapp decided against playing professional football to pursue a career as an entertainer and only attempted to collect the financial losses that had resulted from his own choice not to play. The jury evidently agreed with the NFL position. Since both the Patriots and the NFL urged Kapp to sign the Standard Player Contract with the right reserved to challenge the rules if they were applied to him, the court held it could be found that Kapp's main concern was not in playing professional football.

Concerning the issue of breach of contract by the Patriots, Kapp argued that the decision determining the existence of a contract was not within the jury's domain. The Court, however, pointed out that only if there was no factual dispute would the determination, as a matter of law, be for the court to decide. Where a factual dispute existed, as to whether the parties intended that the terms of the initial agreement be included in the Standard Player Contract was for the jury to decide.

Thus, the court held that Kapp failed to prove damages, even if the challenged rule violated the antitrust laws.

Smith v. Pro-Football, Inc., 420 F.Supp. 738 (D.D.C. 1976)

Plaintiff Smith brought this action against Pro-Football, Inc. (Washington Redskins) and the NFL to recover treble damages under the Sherman Antitrust Act, 15 U.S.C., Sections 1, 2 and 3, and the Clayton Act 15 U.S.C., Section 4. Smith contended that he was damaged in his business or property — i.e., his ability to market his unique skills — on the grounds that the player selection draft of the NFL constitution and bylaws constituted a group boycott under the antitrust laws. As a result, Smith argued that he was unable to negotiate a contract reflecting the free market or true value of his service, and he could not obtain one with sufficient guaranteed protections against loss of income from injuries.

For this proceeding, the district court held that the Canadian Football League offered no significant competition for American college football players. Therefore, the relevant market was professional football in the United States, and the NFL was the sole purchaser of the product Smith sought to market.

Before discussing the issues, the court outlined the player selection draft process, noting that the team with the worst NFL win-loss record chose first, with the Super Bowl champion selecting last. Various changes in the selecting process resulted through trading particular choices in particular rounds to other teams for future choices or established players.

The restraints imposed by the NFL constitution and bylaws prohibited any team from negotiating (or signing) a player with draft eligibility and from negotiating with any player selected by another NFL team. This resulted in giving exclusive negotiating rights, as to any given player, to one particular team at a particular time. If no satisfactory agreement was reached with the drafting team, in absence of a trade, that player could not play in the NFL, the only market place for his services. If an agreement was reached, the player was required to sign an NFL Standard Player Contract, which bound him to the NFL constitution and bylaws.

Compensation and benefits agreements were signed with the team. In 1968 the NFL Players Association (the Union) became the exclusive agent and representative of the NFL players. Also in that year the union and the NFL owners negotiated their first collective bargaining agreement. The events giving rise to this action preceded that agreement. Even so, the Redskins argued that the NFL draft was a subject of mandatory collective bargaining between the NFL and the union and was therefore exempt under the antitrust laws under the so-called "labor exemption."

United States Supreme Court decisions concerning the applicability of the exemption resulted in rules and guidelines which the court applied to the defendants' arguments. The defendants claimed that arrangements concerning mandatory collective bargaining subjects, prior to their inclusion in an agreement, fall within the exemption merely because they pertain to mandatory subjects — a sort of automatic exemption. The case decisions relied on by the defendants were based on the existence of a collective bargaining agreement, and since none was in existence at the time Smith signed, the defendants' arguments were unsupported. The court noted that agreements resulting from union-employer negotiations are not automatically exempt from the antitrust law merely because they involved a mandatory bargaining subject, regardless of the subject or form and content of the agreement. If, therefore, a completed agreement is not exempt from antitrust scrutiny, then a mandatory subject, about which no agreement has been reached, cannot be exempt. Indeed, the purpose of the exemption — to permit unfettered progress in the collective bargaining process — would be undermined by applying the exemption to unilaterally imposed employer arrangements simply because they could be settled by mandatory collective bargaining in the future. Thus, a plan serving the employers' interests and otherwise violative of the antitrust law is not entitled to the exemption unless and until it becomes part of the collective bargaining agreement negoti-

ated by the union while serving its own best interest. The plaintiff, the court held, was entitled to the protection of the antitrust law since he contracted with the Redskins prior to the time when the initial collective bargaining agreement was reached between the league and the union. The court found that Smith's cause of action accrued before the exemption could have been considered operative under any interpretation of the law.

The court also discussed the exemption, making the assumption for the purpose of argument that the draft had been included in the collective bargaining agreement. The court again concluded that no automatic exemption for the draft would result. The court noted that it must first be shown that the draft constituted an agreement on mandatory subjects of bargaining. To the court, the draft appeared to inherently involve such mandatory subjects (wages, hours, and other terms and conditions of employment) and therefore seemed notable that each feature of the draft would be considered a term or condition of employment. Once it was shown that the draft was agreed to as a result of genuine arm's-length bargaining and was not "thrust upon" a weak players' union by the owners, it would then qualify for the labor exemption.

On the antitrust issue, the plaintiff contended that the NFL draft and consequent restrictions constituted a per se violation of the antitrust laws. The draft was an agreement between team owners that negotiation rights to all players drafted in the seventeen (17) rounds of the draft would go to only one team, prohibiting any other team from dealing with that player. The court held that this scheme was a group boycott in its classic form, a device long condemned as a per se violation of antitrust law. The owners argued that the league would not survive the competition for players within the draft. Defendants further argued that if the antitrust laws applied, the draft would be permitted under the Rule of Reason standard. The court, however, precluded application of the Rule of Reason because of the naked restraints of the group boycott. The court also stated that even if the rule was applicable, the defendants would not be saved from liability. For the draft to be lawful under the Rule of Reason, it would be necessary for the court to find that the draft was a reasonable way of pursuing legitimate business interests and that it did not have the purpose or effect of unreasonably restraining competition.

Central to the defendants' argument was the position that the draft and other NFL rules were indispensable in maintaining a competitive balance in the league — that is, that teams were sufficiently equal in playing strength to keep spectator interest aroused. The defendants claimed that in the absence of this reasonably equitable distribution of new player talent, the competitive balance would be irretrievably lost, since the better players would migrate to the teams in cities of glamor and money. The evidence at trial was at best equivocal and offered no substantial support for the defendants' position. Most importantly, the defendants failed to prove that there was any correlation between drafting early and an improvement in team performance. In fact, the proof revealed that the strong teams remained front runners for the Super Bowl. Also, there was no evidence that revealed movement of players to glamor cities and teams.

Even if there were compelling reasons for a draft, the court held that the current one was significantly more restrictive than necessary — in fact, the most restrictive possible. Thus, since less restrictive alternatives were available, the system that existed was not protected by the Rule of Reason.

After supplying several examples of less restrictive alternative drafting systems and pointing out that the owners were well aware of the negative impact on players' salaries (as compared to salaries in a free market) and that the owners had not attempted to change the system to a less restrictive system, the court held that the draft system that existed was not "reasonable" within the meaning of the antitrust law.

On the issues of damages, the court pointed out that the absence of a free market for valuing a player's services prevented exact calculation of Smith's damages, and that only a reasonable estimate was possible. Smith was considered a "blue-chip" player — that is, expected to make "all-pro" and the starting lineup in his rookie season, which he did. Players like Smith would have had great bargaining strength in a free market as opposed to more marginal players. Thus, the court examined top players' salaries in the market at that time, particularly those playing the same position, in the league and on his team. It also examined what free-agent compensation had been given by the Redskins. The evidence revealed that, in the absence of owner-imposed restraints, top players were able to negotiate long-term contracts, including such guarantees as full payment for the entire term of the contract even if the player was injured. These contracts were known as "fully vested." The court concluded that Smith could have negotiated such a contract if it had not been for the illegal restraints imposed on him and that the primary reason that Smith was unable to obtain a fully vested contract was a lack of bargaining power inherent in a free market. Thus, the court held that Smith's damages were equal to the difference between what he would have earned under a three-year contract with injury protection (which the court found to be a fair estimate in a free market of Smith's talents at his position during that time) and what the Redskins actually paid him. The court found that Smith had a three-year worth of $162,000 in a free market at the time of the negotiations. His actual salary of $69,800 was subtracted. Thus, his actual damages were $92,200, and a judgment for $276,600 (treble damages) was entered.

Smith v. Pro Football, Inc., 593 F.2d 1173 (D.C. Cir. 1978)

Antitrust action for treble damages was brought by former professional football player (a defensive back) against professional football club (the Washington Redskins) and professional football league (NFL). The claim of unlawful restraint was lodged against the player draft and its surrounding restrictions. In granting judgment for the plaintiff, the district court had held that the player draft was a per se violation of the antitrust laws, constituting a group boycott, and that player, who was permanently injured during the last game of the season, was entitled to recover the difference between his salary under the draft and what he could have negotiated in a competitive market. Plaintiff contended he could have negotiated a contract containing a guarantee of three years' full salary, regardless of injury, at a level equal to that received by an eight-year veteran defensive back who had just signed with the Redskins. The district court accepted this contention.

The court of appeals held that the player draft was not a per se violation of antitrust laws. The nature of professional football, in which clubs operate basically as a joint venture in producing an entertainment product, is such that the draft does not constitute a classic "group boycott." Clubs which have "combined" to implement the draft are not competitors in any economic sense and have not combined to exclude potential competitors from the market. Even so, the draft is illegal under the Rule of Reason in that it purposely restricts competition among clubs for the services of graduating college players, and it is significantly anticompetitive in its effect by forcing each player to deal with one, and only one, club. This deprives the players, as in any monopolistic market, of any real bargaining power. In remanding for recomputation of damages, the court of appeals held that it was not wrong to use the salary of an eight-year veteran, who signed as a free agent, in determining what plaintiff's salary would have been in a competitive market. The district court's decision to use it was not clearly erroneous. However, there was simply no evidence that plaintiff, in the absence of the draft, would have been able to negotiate a contract containing a guarantee of three years' full salary, regardless of injury, especially since no such contract had ever been negotiated by any defensive back in the NFL history. Consequently, there must be a new trial.

NOTES

1. In *Smith* v. *Pro Football Inc.,* the principal notation is to the district court opinion because of its extensive discussion of the labor exemption. It should also be noted, however, that *Smith* at the district court level fashions a very interesting measure of damages. This was modified, of course, at the appellate level. The final result was that Yazoo Smith, after several years of litigation, ended up with a small fraction of the amount originally awarded him.

2. At the present time, despite such decisions as *Smith* v. *Pro Football, Inc.,* there are no explicit provisions in either the Baseball Basic Agreement or the National Hockey League Agreement relating to the draft of amateurs. In these two sports, this evidently remains solely a management prerogative. In the NFL's collective bargaining agreement (see Section 3.41), the number of rounds of the draft and certain other details are made explicit, but no definitions as to who is eligible for the draft are included. Possible ramifications should be considered in conjunction with the *Haywood* case (*Denver Rockets* v. *All-Pro Management*), discussed in Section 4.72.

3. Challenges have been launched against the essential concepts of a draft in one other sport — tennis. By the time the case was decided, the original version of World Team Tennis (WTT) was on its way out, and the particular franchise named as defendant in the suit was defunct; the plaintiff, nevertheless, gained a preliminary court victory. In *Drysdale* v. *Florida Team Tennis, Inc.,* 410 F.Supp. 843 (W.D.Pa. 1976), Cliff Drysdale alleged a failure by the Florida club to pay salary owed. He also named the league in the suit, claiming it had warranted the solvency of its franchises and had also acted in restraint of trade in its use of a player draft.

Florida Team Tennis defaulted when it failed to answer the complaint. The WTT, however, attacked Drysdale's claim on several grounds, including his standing to bring an antitrust action under 15 U.S.C. Sec. 15. The league contended he was not directly damaged by any alleged antitrust violation. Drysdale had contended that as a direct result of the WTT draft, he was denied free bargaining and was forced to sign with a financially unstable franchise, leading to a $600,000 injury when Drysdale was not paid. The court held that Drysdale's claim fell within the "target area" test, which required the injury to be within the area intended to be protected by Congress, since the draft stifled competition and created limitations on what a player might earn.

The court held further that genuine issues of fact existed which precluded a dismissal based on defendant's argument that the WTT had not guaranteed a salary payment or that the plaintiff had failed to allege any reliance or consideration for any such guarantee. Thus, defendant WTT's motion to dismiss was denied.

2.43   The Labor Exemption Applied to Sports

The principal foregoing cases all rejected the applicability of the labor exemption in the contexts of the facts presented to the courts on those occasions. In general, the feeling was there had not been bona fide, arm's-length bargaining. At times, such as in the *Mackey* and *Smith* decisions, it seems the courts were influenced by the weakness of the union, a questionable position to take under labor law principles. Equally clear, though, was that the courts were waiting to be convinced that collective bargaining on the issues of player mobility was a reality in the professional sports leagues.

To date, there have been only two clear opportunities for a court to face this reality. In *Reynolds* v. *NFL,* discussed below, the court is not called on to focus directly on the legality of the player-mobility provisions embodied in the 1977 National Football League collective bargaining agreement. Instead, the issue is the propriety of the settlement reached between the league and the players of the *Mackey* suit and its companion case, *Alexander* v. *NFL.* However, as the discussion by the court makes clear, the labor exemption in all probability insulates the player-mobility provisions from successful attack.

The second case in which the court squarely faces the labor exemption is *Dale McCourt* v. *California Sports and the Los Angeles Kings.* It is the primary source, to date, to consult concerning the likely applicability of the labor exemption to collective bargaining provisions in sports.

Reynolds v. National Football League, 584 F.2d 280 (8th Cir. 1978)

Gibson, Chief Judge.

In these cases, fifteen active and one inactive National Football League players object to the settlement of an action brought on behalf of 5,706 former and present professional football players. The class action was prosecuted to secure monetary damages and other relief for the players from the National Football League, individual teams and other defendants for violations of the antitrust laws. The settlement approved by the District Court will provide a total of $13,675,000 for distribution to members of the plaintiff class. After carefully considering the record and the briefs and oral arguments of the parties and the objecting class members, we affirm the order of the District Court approving the settlement.

The present suit is an outgrowth of this court's decision in *Mackey* v. *National Football League,* 543 F.2d 606 (8th Cir. 1976), cert. dismissed, 434 U.S. 801, 54 L.Ed.2d 59 (1977). In Mackey, the Rozelle Rule was challenged as a violation of Section 1 of the Sherman Act. The Rozelle Rule, we noted,

> . . . essentially provides that when a player's contractual obligation to a team expires and he signs with a different club, the signing club must provide compensation to the player's former team. If the two clubs are unable to conclude mutually satisfactory arrangements, the Commissioner may award compensation in the form of one or more players and/or draft choices as he deems fair and equitable.
> [543 F.2d at 609, n.1]

The District Court in *Mackey* had concluded that the Rozelle Rule was a *per se* violation of the Sherman Act. A panel of this court concluded that it was not a *per se* violation of the Sherman Act, but was a violation when considered under the standard of reasonableness, as being more restrictive than reasonably necessary to meet legitimate business needs. We also noted that the matter of restrictions on player movement was a subject of mandatory collective bargaining under Sec. 8(d) of the National Labor Relations Act, 29 U.S.C. Sec.158(d). Had the Rozelle Rule been a result of bona fide arm's-length bargaining between the National Football League Players Association (Players Association) and the league teams, it would have qualified for the labor exemption from antitrust scrutiny. Since there was evidence to support the District Court's decision that the Rozelle Rule had not been the result of arm's-length bargaining, we concluded that the labor exemption did not apply.

The National Football League applied to the Supreme court for certiorari in *Mackey.* That petition was not acted upon prior to its being withdrawn by the football league as a part of the settlement of present action. Thus, the court's decision in *Mackey* stands as the final decision regarding the antitrust implications of the Rozelle Rule.

Following our decision in *Mackey*, the Players Association is the bargaining representative for the seeking damages and other relief. The Players Association is the bargaining representative for the National Football League players. They supplied financial support for this action, which was commenced by seventy-eight named players or retired players. The class was represented by Edward M. Glennon of the firm of Lindquist & Vennum of Minneapolis. Lindquist & Vennum had represented and continues to represent the Players Association.

The course of this class action litigation is set out in detail in the District Court's findings of fact and conclusions of law. Essentially, the National Football League, the Players Association, and the class action counsel proceeded to negotiate a collective bargaining agreement between the National Football League teams and the Players Association and a settlement of the class action between the National Football League and the other defendants and the plaintiff class. This approach was eminently practical in that it was obvious that the antitrust liability suggested by our decision in *Mackey* placed a potentially crippling strain on the resources of professional football. To have ignored this and the possibly devastating effect of operating without a means of compensating teams that lost premium players would have been irresponsible. It would have endangered the availability of any recovery for the players allegedly damaged by the Rozelle Rule and would have endangered the continued employment prospects of professional football players.

We do not say that the collective bargaining agreement that resulted and the class action settlement constituted a single entity. The evidence fully supports the District Court's conclusion that the collective bargaining agreement was not part of the consideration for the class action settlement, though there was not any great incentive to settle the class action absent some agreement on the procedural rules governing player movement. Thus the inquiry to be made by the District Court in reviewing the proposed settlement and by this court in reviewing the District Court's approval of that settlement is limited to the settlement itself rather than the labor agreement contained in the collective bargaining document.

As we stated in *Grunin* v. *International House of Pancakes*, 513 F.2d 114, 123 (8th Cir.), *cert. denied*, 423 U.S. 864 (1975):

> Our review of the settlement approved by the District Court in this case is guided by the principle that: "Such a determination is committed to the sound discretion of the trial judge. Great weight is accorded his views because he is exposed to the litigants and their strategies, positions and proofs. He is aware of the expense and possible legal bars to success. Simply stated, he is on the firing line and can evaluate the action accordingly" (*Ace Heating and Plumbing Co.* v. *Crane Co.*, 453 F.2d 30, 34 [3rd Cir. 1971]). Only upon the clear showing that the District Court abused its discretion will this court intervene to set aside a judicially approved class action settlement. . . .

Appellant-objectors' primary complaint relates to Article XV of the collective bargaining agreement denominated First/First Refusal/Compensation Rule, which replaced the discarded Rozelle Rule. The objectors, in argument, viewed the new rule as a perpetual option rule more restrictive in thwarting freedom of movement than the old Rozelle Rule. The record, however, does not support the objectors' complaint, as 168 players played out their options in two years under the present rule as contrasted with 176 players who played out their option during eleven years under the Rozelle Rule.

It appears from the objectors' brief and argument that they desire complete, unrestricted freedom of movement from club to club, offering their services to the highest bidder. This position ignores the structured nature of any professional sport based on league competition. Precise and detailed rules must of necessity govern how the sport is played, the rules of the game, and the acquisition, number and engagement of players. While some freedom of movement after playing out a contract is in order, complete freedom of movement would result in the best franchises acquiring most of the top players. Some leveling and balancing rules appear necessary to keep the various teams on competitive basis, without which public interest in any sport quickly fades. This, of course, is the crux of most of the past restrictive rules and those now in force. Professional sports are set up for the enjoyment of the paying customers and not solely for the benefit of the owners or the benefit of the players. Without public support any professional sport would soon become unprofitable to the owners and participants.

Although a collective bargaining agreement more favorable to the objectors as above average players might have been obtained, this is no reason for the court to enter into the picture and pass upon the merits of any collective bargaining agreement. In other words, the issue here is not whether the optimum collective bargaining agreement has been obtained. The objectors are few in number: 15 out of 1,500 active players and one retired player out of 4,300. This certainly does not indicate any substantial dissatisfaction with the settlement agreement. No settlement agreement arrived at between antagonists can provide the best possible world to all members of a relatively large class. Pragmatically, the settlement here appears fair, reasonable and substantial.

Covenant Not To Sue

The objector-appellants apparently also contend that the wording of a Covenant Not To Sue contained in the settlement serves to insulate the collective bargaining agreement from judicial challenge. The District Court seems to have accepted that premise and conducted hearings into the collective bargaining agreement and made findings of fact giving limited approval to the agreement. While the District Court findings on this matter seem amply supported by the evidence, it is not necessary for us to add any stamp of approval or disapproval to the collective bargaining agreement.

In the unlikely event that any class member were to bring suit against the National Football League or the other defendants for antitrust violations resulting from the Rozelle Rule, the defendants will be able to rely on the *res judicata* effect of this case. A.C. Wright and A. Miller, *Federal Practice and Procedure*, Sec. 1789 (1972). On the other hand, if a member of the present class were to sue alleging antitrust violations in the current collective bargaining agreement, our decision in *Mackey* would entitle the defendants to assert the labor exemption to liability. *Mackey* v. *National Foot-*

ball League, 543 F.2d. 606, 623 (8th Cir. 1976). Although we need not decide the question, it appears to be a near certainty that the collective bargaining agreement was the result of "bona fide arm's-length negotiations." We are satisfied that the Covenant Not to Sue is superfluous insofar as the matters properly before the District Court in this class action are concerned. To the extent that other suits are purported to be precluded by it, the disputes will have to be resolved through the machinery set up in the collective bargaining agreement or available under general principles of labor or constitutional law.

Supervision of the Collective Bargaining Agreement

Although the collective bargaining agreement was negotiated contemporaneously with the settlement of this class action, it was not before the District Court except as a circumstance bearing on the fairness of the settlement and the advisability of injunctive relief. The District Court was not required to decide whether the collective bargaining agreement satisfied the requirements stated in *Mackey, supra*, for exemption from the antitrust laws. Nor are we required to make this inquiry although it does appear that the *Mackey* requirements were met.

Despite this, the plaintiff class has urged that the District Court erred in failing to retain jurisdiction for purposes of supervising the collective bargaining agreement. Prior to oral argument in this case, the plaintiff class filed a motion for remand of the case or a stay of the appeal proceedings. They contended that newly discovered evidence and a change in the factual circumstances made this disposition appropriate. The only "new evidence" or "change in circumstance" is that the National Football League and its member clubs have interpreted the collective bargaining agreement in a manner different from that of the Players Association. This is precisely the kind of dispute to be resolved by arbitration and the normal channels of labor dispute resolution. Without deciding whether the plaintiff class followed the correct procedures in raising the issue, we hold that the District Court correctly refused to exercise supervisory jurisdiction over the collective bargaining agreement in this class action. The motion to remand or stay the appeal is denied.

Conclusion

We have considered the other arguments raised in the appellant-objectors' briefs and in the brief of the plaintiff class seeking remand of the case, and find them to be without merit. The findings of fact made by the District Court are not clearly erroneous and it applied correct principles of law. The District Court carefully guarded the rights of absent class members. *Grunin* v. *International House of Pancakes,* 513 F.2d 114, 123 (8th Cir. 1975). There was no abuse of discretion in approving this substantial settlement and the necessarily complicated distribution formula.

We emphasize today, as we did in *Mackey, supra,* that the subject of player movement restrictions is a proper one for resolution in the collective bargaining context. When so resolved, as it appears to have been in the current collective bargaining agreement, the labor exemption to antitrust attack applies, and the merits of the bargaining agreement are not an issue for court determination. The bargaining agreement is subject to change from time to time as it expires and is up for renegotiation.

The order approving the class action settlement is affirmed.

McCourt v. California Sports, Inc., 600 F.2d 1193 (6th Cir. 1979)

Engel, Circuit Judge:

The reserve system, in professional athletics, has been the subject of exhaustive and spirited discussion both in the sports and in the legal world. Its supporters urge that it stimulates athletic competition between the teams of a sports league; its opponents urge that it stifles economic competition among those same teams. We have no doubt that there is a measure of truth in both claims. . . .

Involved in this appeal is the validity, under federal antitrust laws, of the reserve system currently in effect in the National Hockey League. In its present form, the system has been termed a "modified Rozelle Rule" because it closely resembles the rule promulgated for the National Football League by its commissioner, Pete Rozelle, but has been modified to the extent that arbitration is not by the commissioner himself but by a professional and independent arbitrator.

At the heart of the NHL reserve system is By-Law Section 9A. This section provides the rules governing the acquisition of free agents of other clubs in the league and is specifically made applicable to the players in the league by paragraphs 17 and 18 of the Standard Players Contract, which each player in the NHL is required to sign. Further the Standard Player Contract, expressly including Paragraph 17, was approved by both the NHL team owners and the National Hockey League Players Association (NHLPA) in the current collective bargaining agreement, Sections 9.03(a) and (b).

As can be seen from its terms, By-Law Section 9A mandates that when a player becomes a free agent and signs a contract with a different club in the league, his original club has the right under the By-Law to exact an "equalization payment" from the acquiring club. That payment may be by the assignment of contracts of players, by the assignment of draft choices, or "as a last resort," by the payment of cash. If mutual agreement is not reached, each club submits a proposal to a neutral arbitrator, selected by majority vote of the Board of Governors of the League, who then must select, without change, one of the two proposals submitted. . . .

On October 10, 1977, Dale McCourt, a 21-year-old hockey player from Canada, signed an NHL Standard Players Contract (1974 form) with the Detroit Hockey Club, Inc. to play professional hockey for three years with the Detroit Red Wings. McCourt was to be paid $325,000 over three years. He subsequently played his rookie year, 1977-78, with the Red Wings and was the leading scorer.

Rogatien Vachon had been a star goaltender for the Los Angeles Kings for six years when he became a free agent in 1978. After rejecting a substantial offer by the Kings, Vachon entered into a contract with the Red Wings at a salary of $1,900,000 for five seasons. By signing Vachon, the Red Wings obligated itself to make an equalization payment under By-Law Section 9A to the Kings and, when no agreement was reached, each club submitted to arbitrator Houston a proposal pursuant to By-Law Section 9A.8. The Red Wings offered two of its players as compensation and the Kings proposed that McCourt's contract be assigned to it. The arbitrator selected the King's proposal and accordingly, the Red

Wings assigned McCourt's contract to Los Angeles. Rather than report to the Kings, however, Dale McCourt brought suit in the United States District Court for the Eastern District of Michigan. . . .

On September 19, 1978, following an extensive evidentiary hearing, the district court entered a preliminary injunction restraining the defendants from enforcing the arbitration award and from penalizing McCourt for refusing to play professional hockey with the Los Angeles Kings pursuant to the award. This appeal followed. . . .

The trial court and the parties before us in this appeal have all relied upon *Mackey* as properly enunciating the governing principles in determining whether the non-statutory labor exemption applies to the reserve system provisions of a collective bargaining agreement in professional sports. *Mackey* v. *National Football League*, 543 F.2d 606 (8th Cir. 1976), *cert. dismissed*, 434 U.S. 801, 98 S.Ct. 28, 54 L.Ed.2d 59 (1977). There Judge Lay set forth three broad principles:

> We find the proper accommodation to be: First, the labor policy favoring collective bargaining may potentially be given pre-eminence over the antitrust laws where the restraint on trade primarily affects only the parties to the collective bargaining relationship. . . . Second, federal labor policy is implicated sufficiently to prevail only where the agreement sought to be exempted concerns a mandatory subject of collective bargaining. . . . Finally, the policy favoring collective bargaining is furthered to the degree necessary to override the antitrust laws only where the agreement sought to be exempted is the product of bona fide arm's-length bargaining. . . .

543 F.2d at 614–15 (footnotes omitted).

We see no reason to disagree with the judgment of the district court and of the attorneys on both sides that the proper standards are set out in *Mackey*. In short, it was proper to apply *Mackey*'s standards; the issue is whether those standards were properly applied. . . .

We have little difficulty in determining that the first two policy considerations favor the exemption. Clearly here the restraint on trade primarily affects the parties to the bargaining relationship. It is the hockey players themselves who are primarily affected by any restraint, reasonable or not.

Second, the agreement concerning the reserve system involves in a very real sense the terms and conditions of employment of the hockey players both in form and in practical effect. As *Mackey* correctly points out, the restriction upon a player's ability to move from one team to another within the league, the financial interest which the hockey players have and their interest in the mechanics of the operation and enforcement of the rule strongly indicate that it is a mandatory bargaining subject within the meaning of the National Labor Relations Act, Section 8(d), 29 U.S.C. § 158(d) (1976).

The issue, therefore, in our judgment is narrowed to whether, upon the facts of this case, the agreement sought to be exempted was the product of bona fide arm's-length bargaining. The court in *Mackey* held under the circumstances before it that such arm's-length bargaining was missing. So did the district court here. The underlying facts in the two cases, however, are quite different.

In *Mackey* it was shown that the National Football League Players Association, at least prior to 1974, had stood in a relatively weak position with respect to the clubs. The Rozelle Rule had remained unchanged in form since it was unilaterally promulgated in 1963, even before the Players Association was formed. The Eighth Circuit specifically found that the Rozelle Rule was not bargained over in the negotiations leading to the 1968 or 1970 collective bargaining agreements. . . .

Returning to the area of professional hockey, we find its history well chronicled by Judge Higginbotham in *Philadelphia World Hockey Club, Inc.* v. *Philadelphia Hockey Club, Inc.*, 353 F.Supp. 462 (E.D. Pa. 1972). The district judge's opinion in the instant case picks up the history of the reserve system and the National Hockey League where Judge Higginbotham left it in *Philadelphia World Hockey Club, Inc.* The district judge here stated:

> Mr. John Ziegler, President of the National Hockey League, testified that in March 1973, after discussions between the NHL and the NHLPA, the Board of Governors authorized a special committee to negotiate a new reserve clause. NHL Exh. 1 at 2–4. At a meeting on March 19, 1973, the owners and player representatives tentatively agreed upon a new reserve clause pending ratification by the

players. NHL Exh. 2 at 3. The tentative agreement provided, among other things, that a player with five or more years in the NHL could elect to become a free agent. See NHL Exh. 3 for the full text of the proposed reserve clause. In June 1973, the NHLPA rejected the proposed reserve clause. Thereafter, the NHLPA, on advice of counsel, refused to attend a meeting on August 28, 1973 to further discuss the proposed reserve clause. Plaintiff Exh. 2 at 3. The NHLPA elected instead to await the final outcome of the World Hockey Association's suit attacking the old reserve clause. *See Philadelphia Hockey Club, Inc., supra.* When the positions of the parties solidified, the NHL unilaterally adopted bylaw 9A on November 27, 1973. Plaintiff Exh. 2 at 3.

Several months later, in February 1974, the district court approved a consent decree in the World Hockey Association suit. The NHLPA then threatened to file its own antitrust action to challenge the validity of bylaw 9A. To forestall that suit, the NHL agreed on July 9, 1975, that it would not assert laches or equitable estoppel as a defense. *See* Plaintiff Exh. 3 at 1; Exh. 4 at 1. At a subsequent meeting, on August 13, 1975, Mr. Ackerman, counsel for the NHL, implied that there would be no collective bargaining agreement until the dispute over bylaw 9A was resolved. The NHLPA, however, persisted in its refusal to negotiate on the clause. Plaintiff Exh. 5 at 1–2. The NHLPA's threat of an antitrust suit did not alter the NHL's firm position on bylaw 9A. On August 15, 1975, the members of the owner-players' council were advised that:

> Mr. Eagleson stated that the commencement of this type of action was still being considered. I replied that decision was, of course, up to them, but that the owners would not negotiate from fear of that possibility. Pl. Exh. 5 at 2.

On May 4, 1976, the NHL and the NHLPA signed their first collective bargaining agreement retroactive from September 15, 1975. Collective Bargaining Agreement (CBA) § 2.01. The collective bargaining agreement provides that paragraph 17 of the Standard Player's Contract and bylaw 9A are "fair and reasonable terms of employment." CBA § 9.03(b).

460 F.Supp. at 910–11.

We believe that in holding that the reserve system had not been the subject of good faith, arm's-length bargaining, the trial court failed to recognize the well established principle that nothing in the labor law compels either party negotiating over mandatory subjects of collective bargaining to yield on its initial bargaining position. Good faith bargaining is all that is required. That the position of one party on an issue prevails unchanged does not mandate the conclusion that there was no collective bargaining over the issue. *NLRB* v. *American National Insurance Co.*, 342 U.S. 395, 404, 72 S.Ct. 824, 96 L.Ed. 1027 (1952).

In a case where the collective bargaining negotiations proceeded much like those on By-Law Section 9A, our circuit followed *American National Insurance Co.* to hold that good faith bargaining did not require the employer to alter its position. *NLRB* v. *United Clay Mines Corp.*, 219 F.2d 120 (6th Cir. 1955). . . .

Contrary to the trial judge's conclusion, the very facts relied upon by him in his opinion illustrate a classic case of collective bargaining in which the reserve clause system was a central issue. It is apparent from those very findings that the NHLPA used every form of negotiating pressure it could muster. It developed an alternate reserve system and secured tentative agreement from the owner and player representatives, only to have the proposal rejected by the players. It refused to attend a proposed meeting with the owners to discuss the reserve system further. It threatened to strike. It threatened to commence an antitrust suit and to recommend that the players not attend training camp.

For its part, the NHL, while not budging in its insistence upon By-Law Section 9A, at least in the absence of any satisfactory counter proposals by the players, yielded significantly on other issues. It agreed as a price of By-Law Section 9A to the inclusion in the collective bargaining agreement of a provision that the entire agreement could be voided if the NHL and the World Hockey Association should merge. The undisputed reason for this provision was player concern that with a merger of the two leagues, the reserve system would be rendered too onerous because the players would, by the merger, lose the competitive advantage of threatening to move to the WHA. Likewise, the NHL team owners obtained a provision voiding the entire agreement should the reserve system be invalidated by the courts.

The trial court, while acknowledging that the new collective bargaining agreement contained significant new benefits to the players, held that they were not "directly related to collective bargaining on bylaw 9A." This observation and the trial court's conclusion that "the NHLPA never bargained for bylaw 9A in the first instance" typifies its approach. It is true that the NHLPA did not "bargain for" By-Law Section 9A; it bargained "against" it, vigorously. That the trial judge concluded the benefits in the new contract were wrung from management by threat of an antitrust suit to void the By-Law merely demonstrates that the benefits were bargained for in connection with the reserve system, although he opined that the threat of a suit was a more effective bargaining tool than the threat of a strike. And while we agree with the trial judge that inclusion of language in the collective bargaining agreement that the reserve system provisions were "fair and reasonable" would not immunize it from antitrust attack, it is manifest from the entire facts found by the court that there was no collusion between management and the players association. Thus, the trial court found that "[t]he NHLPA agreed to include bylaw 9A in the collective bargaining agreement only after the NHL conceded that the NHLPA could terminate the entire agreement if the NHL merged with the World Hockey Association." 460 F.Supp. at 911. The trial court also credited the testimony of John Ziegler that "the owners took a strong stand toward equalization, that they believed bylaw 9A was fair, and that they wanted it incorporated into the collective bargaining agreement. . . ." Finally, the trial court found that "[t]he NHLPA's acceptance of bylaw 9A was essential to get the parties off dead center. The players had no other alternative. The Standard Player's Contract required them to accept all the bylaws adopted by the NHL." 460 F.Supp. at 911.

From the express findings of the trial court, fully supported by the record, it is apparent that the inclusion of the reserve system in the collective bargaining agreement was the product of good faith, arm's-length bargaining, and that what the trial saw as a failure to negotiate was in fact simply the failure to succeed, after the most intensive negotiations, in keeping an unwanted provision out of the contract. This failure was a part of and not apart from the collective bargaining process, a process which achieved its ultimate objective of an agreement accepted by the parties. . . .

Assuming without deciding that the reserve system incorporated in the collective bargaining agreement was otherwise subject to the antitrust laws, whether the good faith, arms-length requirement necessary to entitle it to the non-statutory labor exemption from the antitrust laws applies is to be governed by the developed standards of law applicable elsewhere in the field of labor law and as set forth in *Mackey, supra*. So viewed, the evidence here, as credited by the trial court, compels the conclusion that the reserve system was incorporated in the agreement as a result of good faith, arm's-length bargaining between the parties. As such it is entitled to the exemption, and the trial court's conclusion to the contrary must be deemed clearly erroneous. . . .

Edwards, Chief Judge, dissenting.

I respectfully dissent. My basic disagreement with the majority opinion is planted on the proposition that if sports clubs organized for profit are to be exempted from the antitrust laws, this should be accomplished by statutory amendment, in accordance with the Constitution of the United States. Any such amendment would necessarily follow extensive hearings on the possible implications of the exemption, not only on organized sports, but also on the whole of the American economy — a process not available to the Judicial Branch.

The essence of the restriction on competition involved in this case is an agreement between all National Hockey League clubs not to hire any hockey player who has become a free agent (by refusing reemployment contract terms offered by his previous club) without undertaking to "equalize" the loss to his former club by agreed on or arbitrated transfer of player or cash.

The restriction by its terms is upon the NHL constituent clubs. Its impact, however, is clearly upon star hockey players. Clause 9A.6 obviously diminishes the hockey star's bargaining power, both with his previous employer and any prospective employer. It also may require any player who is transferred under the equalization clause to live in a city and play for a club against his professional (or private) best interests.

The legal question posed by this case is whether an association of employers may in the organized sports industry (here it is hockey) gain exemption from the antitrust laws for an agreement among themselves to restrict otherwise free competition in employment of hockey players by imposing their employer-devised agreement upon a union representing that class of employees through use of economic inducement or compulsion. Before we give judicial sanction to such a practice as consistent with the antitrust and labor-management laws of this country, we should take a long hard look at the implications for sections of the national economy other than organized sports.

Superstars whose services are at a high premium can be found in many areas of industry and commerce other than the world of sports. Is there any distinction to be drawn between Clause 9A and similar restrictions in, for example, the field of dress manufacturing for the services of highly talented engineers, designers, or die shop leaders, or the entertainment field for highly talented personnel, or in the publishing field for highly talented writers?

Such a restriction on freedom of competition (and human freedom in choice of employment), in the interest of promotion or maintenance of business profits, has a distinctly predatory ring. While the majority opinion declines to answer the question as to whether, without benefit of an exemption, Clause 9A would be violative of the Sherman Act, I believe that 9A does violate the antitrust laws and that no "labor union exemption" or nonstatutory exemption is applicable. . . .

I do reject one feature of the *Mackey and Reynolds* decisions upon which the majority relies. The fact that a particular provision restricting competition is a mandatory subject of collective bargaining and has been agreed upon by management and labor in a collective bargaining contract does not necessarily exempt the restriction from the Sherman Act. The antitrust laws were adopted to protect the free enterprise system and the general public. It is easy to postulate situations where the profit interests of capital and the wage-hour interests of labor could be mutually served by introducing into collective bargaining agreements restrictions upon competition which are greatly contrary to the public interest and have nothing to do with the labor interests protected by the Clayton and Norris-LaGuardia Acts. . . .

I simply see no way that the restrictive practices we deal with in Clause 9A can be held to "promote competition" (unless, of course, we turn from economic competition to competition on ice). Clause 9A is clearly an unreasonable restraint of trade.

NOTE _____

1. For a thorough discussion of the several issues raised in the foregoing sections (2.40–2.43), see Berry and Gould, "A Long, Deep Drive to Collective Bargaining: Of Players, Owners, Brawls and Strikes," 31 *Case Western Law Review* 685 (1981). See particularly, pp. 754–775.

Chapter 3

BASIC AGREEMENTS CONTROLLING SPORTS

3.00   The Hierarchy of the Agreements

Every major team sports league is now unionized. The overwhelming vote in early 1984 by players in the United States Football League to certify a union affiliated with the NFL Players Association meant that the NFL, NBA, Major League Baseball, NHL, NASL, MISL, and now the USFL had or would soon have collective bargaining agreements. Under our federal laws, this simple fact substantially alters the primacy of agreements used by sports leagues. A few short years ago, the constitution and bylaws of a league were the ultimate authority; today, the union movement in sports has drastically altered the hierarchy.

In scrutinizing and comparing the basic agreements for each league, it is imperative to keep in mind the relative authority of each agreement. First and foremost, a duly entered collective bargaining agreement that addresses an issue is the primary source. Under our nation's labor laws, rules or provisions that conflict with the collective agreement must yield. This is not as simple as it sounds, since many collective bargaining agreements allow for parties to add certain items through individual agreement. Even so, when conflict arises, the labor agreement prevails.

Most of the current sports agreements incorporate a standard player contract which gives that contract the force of the collective agreement. Consequently, unless provided otherwise, it will prevail over a league's constitution and bylaws. As we shall see upon further examination, however, standard contracts are capable of modification, but only up to certain limits. Often a standard form itself (and, remember, it is part of the collective bargaining agreement) states that an impermissible amendment is one that runs counter to the league bylaws. So something of a circle manifests itself.

Despite these twists, it is possible to describe the hierarchy. The ultimate authority is the collective bargaining agreement, including the standard contract if incorporated. Next in importance are the league constitution and bylaws, assuming no conflict with the collective agreement. Of least significance are amendments to the standard contracts, when those amendments are not expressly authorized by the collective agreement.

With this hierarchy in mind, we need to examine the various types of agreements utilized by professional sports leagues. Since these documents tend to be lengthy, we will present selected examples. Of course, the complete documents would have to be available for inspection and reference in an actual sports league case. The examples, while substantial, are not sufficient for actual decision making. They are presented here for purposes of analysis — to give insight to the concepts under which sports leagues operate.

Section 3.10 briefly mentions certain issues that deal with league bylaws. Section 3.20 focuses on standard player contracts. Although only one contract form is reproduced in its entirety — that of the National Basketball Association — Section 3.20 also analyzes some of the types of amendments often made to a standard player contract and examines some comparative clauses from other standard contracts.

The concluding two major sections of this chapter relate to collective bargaining agreements from the various team sports, with some emphasis on the NFL, NBA, and Major League Baseball. One consideration relates to provisions within collective agreements that directly affect the individual contract that a player has with a club (Sections 3.30–3.39). The other consideration expands on the antitrust cases considered in the previous chapter and describes how collective bargaining provisions have forged new ideas about player mobility, from the amateur draft to rights of first refusal to free agent compensation (See Sections 3.40–3.46). These provisions are vitally important to sports leagues. Many of the traditional restrictions were thrown out by the courts in the 1970s as evidenced in the cases previously considered (see Section 2.42). These restrictions have been replaced by different approaches. Whether they significantly alter the ways in which leagues operate is a question to examine.

The collective bargaining provisions set forth in Chapter 3 are from the following agreements, unless otherwise noted: Major League Baseball, the 1980 agreement (the 1981 amendments are noted as such); the National Football League, the 1982 agreement; and the National Basketball Association, the 1980 agreement (again with the 1983 amendments being specially

noted). Reference is also made to the revised National Hockey League provisions of 1982. A special section (3.50) has been added that highlights the recent provisions in the 1985 Major League Baseball settlement.

3.10   League Constitutions and Bylaws

The internal organization of a league is structured according to its constitution and bylaws. In matters not covered in the collective bargaining agreement between the league (or its stand-in) and the players' association, the league constitution and bylaws reign supreme. This is particularly true regarding the legal nature of the relationship among the clubs and the relationship between the league and the clubs.

In light of the earlier examination in Chapter 1 of some of the turmoil over moving franchises (see Section 1.20), it may seem optimistic or even delusionary to describe the constitution and bylaws of a league as "reigning supreme." Even so, once the antitrust questions are resolved, assuming leagues are given clear guidelines as to the extent of control that can be exercised over an individual club, the leagues will again look to the constitution and bylaws as primary authority.

Just what is included in a league's collective bargaining agreement varies from league to league. There may even be potentially bargainable issues that are not addressed or resolved through the collective bargaining process. Thus, one collective agreement might address the number of players that must be on a squad, while another agreement might bypass that issue, treating it as a decision to be made by management, or a so-called "management prerogative." Only through a careful reading of a league's collective bargaining agreement *and* of that same league's constitution and latest bylaws can one determine just which documents are the source to consult. In many situations, both have to be examined.

For example, many aspects of player contracts

in major league baseball are clearly and conclusively covered by the collective bargaining agreement and incorporated standard player contract. But this is clearly not the whole story. In the first place, baseball has a minor league system, and there is the Professional Baseball Agreement, attended by the Professional Baseball Rules, that governs much of the shuffling back and forth between the majors and minors experienced by many young or marginal ballplayers. There is also the Major League Agreement, with its Major League Rules, that not only affects what goes on on the playing field, but also what goes on in contract negotiations.

Consider the following two provisions from Rule 3, Player Contracts, of the Major League Rules of baseball:

> No contract shall be approved by the President of the league that shall provide for the giving of a bonus for playing, pitching or batting skill; or which provides for the payment of a bonus contingent on the standing of the club at the end of the championship season.
>
> No Club or Club official shall make any payment or convey anything of value to any firm or person for legal, representational or other such services provided by such firm or person to a player in connection with the negotiation of a contract between such Club and player.

Surely these two provisions affect the player contract negotiation process. They are "add-ons" to the provisions of both the collective bargaining agreement and the standard player contract. They are important and cannot be ignored.

All the agreements and rules of professional baseball are included in the *Baseball Blue Book*, a new edition of which is published annually. The constitution and bylaws of other leagues are also printed and are generally available, although their availability varies from league to league, as does the availability of a league's collective bargaining agreement. Despite the possible difficulties in obtaining basic league rules, they are essential as a source of reference and guidance.

3.20 Standard Player Contracts

Standard forms for player contracts have been used by sports leagues since the late 1800s. They are almost as much a part of the game as the ball, glove, basket, or goal post. Over the years, each league's forms have come to look remarkably similar and for good reason. One league studies what is in another league's form, particularly if problems with the language in its own form develop. Of course, that does not mean that all provisions are identical. One league's concerns may not be those of another league and consequently, the form of the second league may not include a particular issue. And, too, slight changes in language may produce different legal effects, as evidenced in court and arbitration decisions.

Exhibit 3–1 is a reproduction of one of the three standard forms used by the National Basketball Association, the "Rookie or Veteran — Two or More Seasons" form. Actually, it is identical to one of the other forms, "Veteran — Single Season." Only the third form, "Rookie — Single Season," varies, but in only one detail. It includes an option clause, so that the rookie player who signs for a single season is committed to the club for an additional year if the club chooses to exercise the option. This variation is the result of collective bargaining. Under the 1980 NBA Collective Bargaining Agreement, options are deleted from all contracts except for the single-season-rookie contract. Options can still be included in other contracts in the NBA, but if so done, they must be separately negotiated and must provide separate consideration. In actual practice, except for the single-season rookies, options have largely disappeared from NBA contracts. In this respect, this league differs from the NFL and NHL.

The NBA single-season rookie contract is not one normally signed by the top draft picks. It is more often utilized for the rookie who is not likely to make the squad. First- or second-round draft choices in the NBA — the players who will probably make it if any rookies do — will typically agree to a multiyear pact. That will change somewhat with the recently imposed salary cap in the NBA, since clubs over the maximum team salary will be able to sign first-round choices for one year only, with no option, at $75,000 and other choices at the league minimum, currently $65,000, for one year and no option (see Section 3.33).

The NBA standard form has one other feature that is peculiar to that league — that is, the clauses that can be changed by individual negotiation are designated in the agreement, and the wording for the changes, if made, is similarly specified. In other sports contracts, there is something of a guessing game as to what is negotiable and what is not. This is not true of an NBA player contract. Indeed, in the detailing of the NBA's allowable amendments, which appear in Section 3.21, note that for certain clauses there are variations on the allowable amendments. More than one possible alternative to a particular provision exists. Even so, except for a few instances in which the parties are free to devise their own language, an amendment to a standard form provision must use exactly the alternative language set forth in the allowable amendment.

What follows, then, are the NBA Uniform Player Contract (Exhibit 3-1), the allowable amendments to the NBA form (Section 3.21), and, as a contrast, some selected provisions from other leagues' contract forms (Section 3.22). As stated above, these other forms do not, as a rule, present major changes, but certain nuances must be recognized.

3.21   NBA Allowable Amendments

The allowable amendments appearing below relate only to a few provisions in the foregoing NBA Uniform Player Contract. Most of the provisions are considered to be final, the result of collective bargaining between the league and the Players Association. Obviously left open are the salary and the length of the contract. As can be seen from the allowable amendments, the other terms deemed negotiable include the

specifics of player requirements relating to dress and conduct, the right to engage in other sports, failure by the club to meet its obligations, guarantees as to player salaries (with several variations thereon), and termination of the contract by the player. In addition, the club and player can agree to an option, either in favor of the club or of the player, but no standard language is mandated for the option.

Other important additions that can be made to an NBA contract and other league contracts are not included in this section, since they are additions, and not amendments, to a contract. These include bonuses, loans, the amount of deferred compensation, and particular fringe benefits such as additional insurance, home or apartment, car, investment opportunities, outside employment, and so forth. These possibilities are explored further in Chapter 4, Section 4.20. Note should also be made of collective bargaining provisions relating to certain fringes. For these, see Section 3.37.

Allowable Amendments to Uniform Player Contract (UPC), Paragraph 5

5.   The Player agrees (a) to report at the time and place fixed by the Club in good physical condition; (b) to keep himself throughout the entire season in good physical condition; (c) to give his best services, as well as his loyalty to the Club, and to play basketball only for the Club and its assignees; . . . and (d) not to do anything which is detrimental to the best interests of the Club or of the Association.

Allowable Amendment to UPC, Paragraph 17

[For use when player and club agree that player may participate in sports or activities otherwise proscribed by paragraph 17.]

Notwithstanding the provisions of paragraph 17, the Player and the Club agree that the Player need not obtain the consent of the Club in order to engage in [*insert agreed-upon sports or activities*], and that the Player shall not be subject to fine or suspension by the Club if he engages in such sport[s] or activity[ies].

NATIONAL BASKETBALL ASSOCIATION

UNIFORM PLAYER CONTRACT

(Rookie or Veteran—Two or More Seasons)

THIS AGREEMENT made this .... day of ...., 19...... by and between .... (hereinafter called the "Club"), a member of the National Basketball Association (hereinafter called the "Association") and .... whose address is shown below (hereinafter called the "Player").

WITNESSETH:

In consideration of the mutual promises hereinafter contained, the parties hereto promise and agree as follows:

1. The Club hereby employs the Player as a skilled basketball player for a term of .... year(s) from the 1st day of September 19....... The Player's employment during each year covered by this contract shall include attendance at each training camp, playing the games scheduled for the Club's team during each schedule season of the Association, playing all exhibition games scheduled by the Club during and prior to each schedule season, playing (if invited to participate) in each of the Association's All-Star Games and attending every event (including, but not limited to, the All-Star Game luncheon and/or banquet) conducted in association with such All-Star Games, and playing the playoff games subsequent to each schedule season. Players other than rookies will not be required to attend training camp earlier than twenty-eight days prior to the first game of each of the Club's schedule seasons. Rookies may be required to attend training camp at an earlier date. Exhibition games shall not be played on the three days prior to the opening of the Club's regular season schedule, nor on the day prior to a regularly scheduled game, nor on the day prior to and the day following the All-Star Game. Exhibition games prior to each schedule season shall not exceed eight (including intra-squad games for which admission is charged) and exhibition games during each regularly scheduled season shall not exceed three.

2. The Club agrees to pay the Player for rendering services described herein the sum of $........, per year, (less all amounts required to be withheld from salary by Federal, State and local authorities and exclusive of any amount which the Player shall be entitled to receive from the Player Playoff Pool) in twelve equal semi-monthly payments beginning with the first of said payments on November 1st of each season above described and continuing with such payments on the first and fifteenth of each month until said sum is paid in full; provided, however, if the Club does not qualify for the playoffs, the payments for the year involved which would otherwise be due subsequent to the conclusion of the schedule season shall become due and payable immediately after the conclusion of the schedule season.

Exhibit 3-1   NBA Uniform Player Contract

Source: National Basketball Association.

3.   The Club agrees to pay all proper and necessary expenses of the Player, including the reasonable board and lodging expenses of the Player while playing for the Club "on the road" and during training camp if the Player is not then living at home.   The Player, while "on the road" (and at training camp only if the Club does not pay for meals directly), shall be paid a meal expense allowance as set forth in the Agreement currently in effect between the National Basketball Association and National Basketball Players Association. No deductions from such meal expense allowance shall be made for meals served on an airplane.   While the Player is at training camp (and if the Club does not pay for meals directly), the meal expense allowance shall be paid in weekly installments commencing with the first week of training camp.   For the purposes of this paragraph, the Player shall be considered to be "on the road" from the time the Club leaves its home city until the time the Club arrives back at its home city.   In addition, the Club agrees to pay $50.00 per week to the Player for the four weeks prior to the first game of each of the Club's schedule seasons that the Player is either in attendance at training camp or engaged in playing the exhibition schedule.

4.   The Player agrees to observe and comply with all requirements of the Club respecting conduct of its team and its players, at all times whether on or off the playing floor.   The Club may, from time to time during the continuance of this contract, establish reasonable rules for the government of its players "at home" and "on the road," and such rules shall be part of this contract as fully as if herein written and shall be binding upon the Player.   For any violation of such rules or for any conduct impairing the faithful and thorough discharge of the duties incumbent upon the Player, the Club may impose reasonable fines upon the Player and deduct the amount thereof from any money due or to become due to the Player during the season in which such violation and/or conduct occurred.   The Club may also suspend the Player for violation of any rules so established, and, upon such suspension, the compensation payable to the Player under this contract may be reduced in the manner provided in the Agreement currently in effect between the National Basketball Association and National Basketball Players Association. When the Player is fined or suspended, he shall be given notice in writing, stating the amount of the fine or the duration of the suspension and the reason therefor.

5.   The Player agrees (a) to report at the time and place fixed by the Club in good physical condition; (b) to keep himself throughout each season in good physical condition; (c) to give his best services, as well as his loyalty to the Club, and to play basketball only for the Club and its assignees; (d) to be neatly and fully attired in public and always to conduct himself on and off the court according to the highest standards of honesty, morality, fair play and sportsmanship; and (e) not to do anything which is detrimental to the best interests of the Club or of the Association.

6.   (a)   If the Player, in the judgment of the Club's physician, is not in good physical condition at the date of his first scheduled game for the Club, or if, at the beginning of or during any season, he fails to remain in good physical condition (unless such condition results directly from an injury sustained by the Player as a direct result of participating in any basketball practice or game played for the Club during such season), so as to render the Player, in the judgment of the Club's physician, unfit to play skilled basketball, the Club shall have the right to suspend such Player until such time as, in the judgment of the Club's physician, the Player is in sufficiently good physical condition to play skilled basketball. In the event of such suspension, the annual sum payable to the Player for each season during such suspension shall be reduced in the same proportion as the length of the period during which, in the judgment of the Club's physician, the Player is unfit to play skilled basketball, bears to the length of such season.

(b)   If the Player is injured as a direct result of participating in any basketball practice or game played for the Club, the Club will pay the Player's reasonable hospitalization and medical expenses (including doctor's bills), provided that the hospital and doctor are selected by the Club, and provided further that the Club shall be obligated to pay only those expenses incurred as a result of continuous medical treatment caused solely by and relating directly to the injury sustained by the Player. If, in the judgment of the Club's physician, the Player's injuries resulted directly from playing for the Club and render him unfit to play skilled basketball, then, so long as such unfitness continues, but in no event after the Player has received his full salary for the season in which the injury was sustained, the Club shall pay to the Player the compensation prescribed in paragraph 2 of this contract for such season. The Club's obligations hereunder shall be reduced by any workmen's compensation benefits (which, to the extent permitted by law, the Player hereby assigns to the Club) and any insurance provided for by the Club whether paid or payable to the Player, and the Player hereby releases the Club from any and every other obligation or liability arising out of any such injuries.

(c) The Player hereby releases and waives every claim he may have against the Association and every member of the Association, and against every director, officer, stockholder, trustee, partner, and employee of the Association and/or any member of the Association (excluding persons employed as players by any such member), arising out of or in connection with any fighting or other form of violent and/or unsportsmanlike conduct occurring (on or adjacent to the playing floor or any facility used for practices or games) during the course of any practice and/or any exhibition, championship season, and/or play-off game.

7. The Player agrees to give to the Club's coach, or to the Club's physician, immediate notice of any injury suffered by him, including the time, place, cause and nature of such injury.

8. Should the Player suffer an injury as provided in the preceding section, he will submit himself to a medical examination and treatment by a physician designated by the Club. Such examination when made at the request of the Club shall be at its expense, unless made necessary by some act or conduct of the Player contrary to the terms of this contract.

9. The Player represents and agrees that he has extraordinary and unique skill and ability as a basketball player, that the services to be rendered by him hereunder cannot be replaced or the loss thereof adequately compensated for in money damages, and that any breach by the Player of this contract will cause irreparable injury to the Club and to its assignees. Therefore, it is agreed that in the event it is alleged by the Club that the Player is playing, attempting or threatening to play, or negotiating for the purpose of playing, during the term of this contract, for any other person, firm, corporation or organization, the Club and its assignees (in addition to any other remedies that may be available to them judicially or by way of arbitration) shall have the right to obtain from any court or arbitrator having jurisdiction, such equitable relief as may be appropriate, including a decree enjoining the Player from any further such breach of this contract, and enjoining the Player from playing basketball for any other person, firm, corporation or organization during the term of this contract. In any suit, action or arbitration proceeding brought to obtain such relief, the Player does hereby waive his right, if any, to trial by jury, and does hereby waive his right, if any, to interpose any counterclaim or set-off for any cause whatever.

10. The Club shall have the right to sell, exchange, assign or transfer this contract to any other professional basketball club and the Player agrees to accept such sale, exchange, assignment or transfer and to faithfully perform and carry out this contract with the same force and effect as if it had been entered into by the Player with the assignee club instead of with this Club. The Player further agrees that, should the Club contemplate the sale, exchange, assignment or transfer of this contract to another professional basketball club or clubs, the Club's physician may furnish to the physicians and officials of such other club or clubs all relevant medical information relating to the Player.

11.   In the event that the Player's contract is sold, exchanged, assigned or transferred to any other professional basketball club, all reasonable expenses incurred by the Player in moving himself and his family from the home city of the Club to the home city of the club to which such sale, exchange, assignment or transfer is made, as a result thereof, shall be paid by the assignee club.   Such assignee club hereby agrees that its acceptance of the assignment of this contract constitutes agreement on its part to make such payment.

12.   In the event that the Player's contract is assigned to another club the Player shall forthwith be notified orally or by a notice in writing, delivered to the Player personally or delivered or mailed to his last known address, and the Player shall report to the assignee club within forty-eight hours after said notice has been received or within such longer time for reporting as may be specified in said notice. If the Player does not report to the club to which his contract has been assigned within the aforesaid time, the Player may be suspended by such club and he shall lose the sums which would otherwise be payable to him as long as the suspension lasts.

13.   The Club will not pay and the Player will not accept any bonus or anything of value for winning any particular Association game or series of games or for attaining a certain position by the Club's team in the standing of the league operated by the Association as of a certain date, other than the final standing of the team.

14.   This contract shall be valid and binding upon the Club and the Player immediately upon its execution.   The Club agrees to file a copy of this contract with the Commissioner of the Association prior to the first game of the schedule season or within forty-eight (48) hours of its execution, whichever is later; provided, however, the Club agrees that if the contract is executed prior to the start of the schedule season and if the Player so requests, it will file a copy of this contract with the Commissioner of the Association within thirty (30) days of its execution, but not later than the date hereinabove specified.   If pursuant to the Constitution and By-Laws of the Association, the Commissioner disapproves this contract within ten (10) days after the filing thereof in his office, this contract shall thereupon terminate and be of no further force or effect and the Club and the Player shall thereupon be relieved of their respective rights and liabilities thereunder.

15.   The Player and the Club acknowledge that they have read and are familiar with Section 35 of the Constitution of the Association, a copy of which, as in effect on the date of this Agreement, is attached hereto.   Such section provides that the Commissioner and the Board of Governors of the Association are empowered to impose fines upon the Player and/or upon the Club for causes and in the manner provided in such section.   The Player and the Club, each for himself and itself, promises promptly to pay to the said Association each and every fine imposed upon him or it in accordance with the provisions of said section and not permit any such fine to be paid on his or its behalf by anyone other than the person or club fined.   The Player authorizes the Club to deduct from his salary payments any fines imposed on or assessed against him.

16.   Notwithstanding any provisions of the Constitution or of the By-Laws of the Association, it is agreed that if the Commissioner of the Association shall, in his sole judgment, find that the Player has bet, or has offered or attempted to bet, money or anything of value on the outcome of any game participated in by any club which is a member of the Association, the Commissioner shall have the power in his sole discretion to suspend the Player indefinitely or to expel him as a player for any member of the Association and the Commissioner's finding and decision shall be final, binding, conclusive and unappealable. The Player hereby releases the Commissioner and waives every claim he may have against the Commissioner and/or the Association, and against every member of the Association, and against every director, officer, stockholder, trustee and partner of every member of the Association, for damages and

for all claims and demands whatsoever arising out of or in connection with the decision of the Commissioner.

17. The Player and the Club acknowledge and agree that the Player's participation in other sports may impair or destroy his ability and skill as a basketball player. The Player and the Club recognize and agree that the Player's participation in basketball out of season may result in injury to him. Accordingly, the Player agrees that he will not engage in sports endangering his health or safety (including, but not limited to, professional boxing or wrestling, motorcycling, moped-riding, auto racing, sky-diving, and hang-gliding); and that, except with the written consent of the Club, he will not engage in any game or exhibition of basketball, football, baseball, hockey, lacrosse, or other athletic sport, under penalty of such fine and suspension as may be imposed by the Club and/or the Commissioner of the Association. Nothing contained herein shall be intended to require the Player to obtain the written consent of the Club in order to enable the Player to participate in, as an amateur, the sport of golf, tennis, handball, swimming, hiking, softball or volleyball.

18. The Player agrees to allow the Club or the Association to take pictures of the Player, alone or together with others, for still photographs, motion pictures or television, at such times as the Club or the Association may designate, and no matter by whom taken may be used in any manner desired by either of them for publicity or promotional purposes. The rights in any such pictures taken by the Club or by the Association shall belong to the Club or to the Association, as their interests may appear. The Player agrees that, during each playing season, he will not make public appearances, participate in radio or television programs or permit his picture to be taken or write or sponsor newspaper or magazine articles or sponsor commercial products without the written consent of the Club, which shall not be withheld except in the reasonable interests of the Club or professional basketball. Upon request, the Player shall consent to and make himself available for interviews by representatives of the media conducted at reasonable times. In addition to the foregoing, the Player agrees to participate, upon request, in all other reasonable promotional activities of the Club and the Association.

19. The Player agrees that he will not, during the term of this contract, directly or indirectly entice, induce, persuade or attempt to entice, induce or persuade any player or coach who is under contract to any member of the Association to enter into negotiations for or relating to his services as a basketball player or coach, nor shall he negotiate for or contract for such services, except with the prior written consent of such member of the Association. Breach of this paragraph, in addition to the remedies available to the Club, shall be punishable by fine to be imposed by the Commissioner of the Association and to be payable to the Association out of any compensation due or to become due to the Player hereunder or out of any other moneys payable to him as a basketball player. The Player agrees that the amount of such fine may be withheld by the Club and paid over to the Association.

20. (a) In the event of an alleged default by the Club in the payments to the Player provided for by this contract, or in the event of an alleged failure by the Club to perform any other material obligation agreed to be performed by the Club hereunder, the Player shall notify both the Club and the Association in writing of the facts constituting such alleged default or alleged failure. If neither the Club nor the Association shall cause such alleged default or alleged failure to be remedied within five (5) days after receipt of such written notice, the National Basketball Players Association shall, on behalf of the Player, have the right to request that the dispute concerning such alleged default or alleged failure be referred immediately to the Impartial Arbitrator in accordance with Article XXI, Section 2(h), of the Agreement currently in effect between the National Basketball Association and National Basketball Players Association. If, as a result of such arbitration, an award issues in favor of the Player, and if neither the Club nor the Association complies with such award within ten (10) days after the service

thereof, the Player shall have the right, by a further written notice to the Club and the Association, to terminate this contract.

(b) The Club may terminate this contract upon written notice to the Player (but only after complying with the waiver procedure provided for in subparagraph (f) of this paragraph (20) if the Player shall do any of the following:

(1) at any time, fail, refuse or neglect to conform his personal conduct to standards of good citizenship, good moral character and good sportsmanship, to keep himself in first class physical condition or to obey the Club's training rules; or

(2) at any time, fail, in the sole opinion of the Club's management, to exhibit sufficient skill or competitive ability to qualify to continue as a member of the Club's team (provided, however, that if this contract is terminated by the Club, in accordance with the provisions of this subparagraph, during the period from the fifty-sixth day after the first game of any schedule season of the Association through the end of such schedule season, the Player shall be entitled to receive his full salary for said season); or

(3) at any time, fail, refuse or neglect to render his services hereunder or in any other manner materially breach this contract.

(c) If this contract is terminated by the Club by reason of the Player's failure to render his services hereunder due to disability caused by an injury to the Player resulting directly from his playing for the Club and rendering him unfit to play skilled basketball, and notice of such injury is given by the Player as provided herein, the Player shall be entitled to receive his full salary for the season in which the injury was sustained, less all workmen's compensation benefits (which, to the extent permitted by law, the Player hereby assigns to the Club) and any insurance provided for by the Club paid or payable to the Player by reason of said injury.

(d) If this contract is terminated by the Club during the period designated by the Club for attendance at training camp, payment by the Club of the Player's board, lodging and expense allowance during such period to the date of termination and of the reasonable travelling expenses of the Player to his home city and the expert training and coaching provided by the Club to the Player during the training season shall be full payment to the Player.

(e) If this contract is terminated by the Club during any playing season, except in the case provided for in subparagraph (c) of this paragraph 20, the Player shall be entitled to receive as full payment hereunder a sum of money which, when added to the salary which he has already received during such season, will represent the same proportionate amount of the annual sum set forth in paragraph 2 hereof as the number of days of such season then past bears to the total number of days of such schedule season, plus the reasonable travelling expenses of the Player to his home.

(f) If the Club proposes to terminate this contract in accordance with subparagraph (b) of this paragraph 20, the applicable waiver procedure shall be as follows:

(1) The Club shall request the Association Commissioner to request waivers from all other clubs. Such waiver request must state that it is for the purpose of terminating this contract and it may not be withdrawn.

(2) Upon receipt of the waiver request, any other club may claim assignment of this contract at such waiver price as may be fixed by the Association, the priority of claims to be determined in accordance with the Association's Constitution or By-Laws.

(3) If this contract is so claimed, the Club agrees that it shall, upon the assignment of this contract to the claiming club, notify the Player of such assignment as provided in paragraph 12 hereof, and the Player agrees he shall report to the assignee club as provided in said paragraph 12.

(4) If the contract is not claimed, the Club shall promptly deliver written notice of termination to the Player at the expiration of the waiver period.

(5) To the extent not inconsistent with the foregoing provisions of this subparagraph (f) the waiver procedures set forth in the Constitution and By-Laws of the Association, a copy of which, as in effect on the date of this agreement, is attached hereto, shall govern.

(g) Upon any termination of this contract by the Player, all obligations of the Club to pay compensation shall cease on the date of termination, except the obligation of the Club to pay the Player's compensation to said date.

21. In the event of any dispute arising between the Player and the Club relating to any matter arising under this contract, or concerning the performance or interpretation thereof (except for a dispute arising under paragraph 9 hereof), such dispute shall be resolved in accordance with the Grievance and Arbitration Procedure set forth in the Agreement currently in effect between the National Basketball Association and the National Basketball Players Association.

22. Nothing contained in this contract or in any provision of the Constitution or By-Laws of the Association shall be construed to constitute the Player a member of the Association or to confer upon him any of the rights or privileges of a member thereof.

23. This contract contains the entire agreement between the parties and there are no oral or written inducements, promises or agreements except as contained herein.

EXAMINE THIS CONTRACT CAREFULLY BEFORE SIGNING IT

IN WITNESS WHEREOF the Player has hereunto signed his name and the Club has caused this contract to be executed by its duly authorized officer.

WITNESSES:

....

By ....
          Title:

....

....
          Player

Player's Address...

MISCONDUCT OF OFFICIALS AND OTHERS

35. (a) The provisions of this Section shall govern all members, and officers, managers, coaches, players and other employees of a member and all officials and other employees of the Association, all hereinafter referred to as "persons." Each member shall provide and require in every contract with any of its officers, managers, coaches, players or other employees that they shall be bound and governed by the provisions of this Section. Each member, at the direction of the Board of Governors or the Commissioner, as the case may be, shall take such action as the Board or the Commissioner may direct in order to effectuate the purposes of this Section.

(b) The Commissioner shall direct the dismissal and perpetual disqualification from any further association with the Association or any of its members, of any person found by the Commissioner after a hearing to have been guilty of offering, agreeing, conspiring, aiding or attempting to cause any game of basketball to result otherwise than on its merits.

(c) Any person who gives, makes, issues, authorizes or endorses any statement having, or designed to have, an effect prejudicial or detrimental to the best interests of basketball or of the Association or of a member or its team, shall be liable to a fine not exceeding $1,000, to be imposed by the Board of Governors. The member whose officer, manager, coach, player or other employee has been so fined shall pay the amount of the fine should such person fail to do so within ten (10) days of its imposition.

(d) If in the opinion of the Commissioner any other act or conduct of a person at or during a pre-season, championship, playoff or exhibition game has been prejudicial to or against the best interests of the Association or the game of basketball, the Commissioner shall impose upon such person a fine not exceeding $1,000 in the case of a member, officer, manager or coach of a member, or $10,000 in the case of a player or other employee, or may order for a time the suspension of any such person from any connection or duties with pre-season, championship, playoff or exhibition games, or he may order both such fine and suspension.

(e) The Commissioner shall have the power to suspend for a definite or indefinite period, or to impose a fine not exceeding $1,000, or inflict both such suspension and fine upon any person who, in his opinion, shall have been guilty of conduct prejudicial or detrimental to the Association.

(f) The Commissioner shall have the power to levy a fine of $1,000 upon any Governor or Alternate Governor who, in the opinion of the Commissioner, has been guilty of making statements to the press damaging to the Association.

(g) Any person who, directly or indirectly, entices, induces, persuades or attempts to entice, induce, or persuade any player, coach, trainer, general manager or any other person who is under contract to any other member of the Association to enter into negotiations for or relating to his services or negotiates or contracts for such services shall, on being charged with such tampering, be given an opportunity to answer such charges after due notice and the Commissioner shall have the power to decide whether or not the charges have been sustained; in the event his decision is that the charges have been sustained, then the Commissioner shall have the power to suspend such person for a definite or indefinite period, or to impose a fine not exceeding $5,000, or inflict both such suspension and fine upon any such person.

(h) Any person who, directly or indirectly, wagers money or anything of value on the outcome of any game played by a team in the league operated by the Association shall, on being charged with such wagering, be given an opportunity to answer such charges after due notice, and the decision of the Commissioner shall be final, binding and conclusive and unappealable. The penalty for such offense shall be within the absolute and sole discretion of the Commissioner and may include a fine, suspension, expulsion and/or perpetual disqualification from further association with the Association or any of its members.

(i) Except for a penalty imposed under subparagraph (h) of this paragraph 35, the decisions and acts of the Commissioner pursuant to paragraph 35 shall be appealable to the Board of Governors who shall determine such appeals in accordance with such rules and regulations as may be adopted by the Board in its absolute and sole discretion.

EXCERPT FROM BY-LAWS OF THE ASSOCIATION

3.07 *Waiver Right.* Except for sales and trading between Members in accordance with these By-Laws, no Member shall sell, option or otherwise transfer the contract with, right to the services of, or right to negotiate with, a Player without complying with the waiver procedure prescribed by these By-Laws.

3.08 *Waiver Price.* The waiver price shall be $1,000 per Player.

3.09 *Waiver Procedure.* A Member desiring to secure waivers on a Player shall notify the Commissioner, and the Commissioner, on behalf of such Member, shall immediately notify all other Members of the waiver request. Such Player shall be assumed to have been waived unless a Member shall timely notify the Commissioner by telegram and telephone of a claim to the rights of such Player. Once a Member has notified the Commissioner to attempt to secure waivers on a Player, such notice may not be withdrawn. A Player remains the financial responsibility of the Member placing him on waivers until the waiver period set by the Commissioner has expired.

3.10 *Waiver Period.* If the Commissioner distributes notice of request for waiver at any time during the Season or within four weeks before the beginning of the Season, any Members wishing to claim rights to the Player shall do so by giving notice by telephone and telegram of such claim to the Commissioner within 48 hours after the time of the Commissioner's notice. If the Commissioner distributes notice of request for waiver at any other time, any Member wishing to claim rights to the Player shall do so by sending notice of such Claim to the Commissioner within ten days after the date of the Commissioner's notice. A team may not withdraw a claim to the rights to a Player on waivers.

3.11 *Waiver Preferences.* In the event that more than one Member shall have claimed rights to a Player placed on waivers, the claiming Member with the lowest team standing at the time the waiver was requested shall be entitled to acquire the rights to such Player. If the request for waiver shall occur between Seasons or prior to midnight November 30th, the standings at the close of the previous Season shall govern.

If the won and lost percentages of two claiming Teams are the same, then the tie shall be determined, if possible, on the basis of the Championship Games between the two teams, during the Season or during the preceding Season, as the case may be. If still tied, a toss of the coin shall determine priority. For the purpose of determining standings, both conferences of the Association shall be deemed merged and a consolidated standing shall control.

3.12 *Players Acquired Through Waivers.* A Member who has acquired the rights and title to the contract of a Player through the waiver procedure may waive such rights at any time, but may not sell or trade such rights for a period of 30 days after the acquisition thereof, provided, however, that if the rights to such Player were acquired between schedule Seasons, the 30 day period described herein shall begin on the first day of the next succeeding schedule Season.

3.13 *Additional Waiver Rules.* The Commissioner or the Board of Governors shall from time to time adopt such additional rules (supplementary to these By-Laws) with respect to the operation of the waiver procedures as he or it shall determine. Such rules shall not be inconsistent with these By-Laws and shall apply to but shall not be limited to the mechanics of notice, inadvertent omission of notification to a Member and rules of construction as to time.

Allowable Amendment to UPC, Paragraph 18

18. The Player agrees to allow the Club or the Association to take pictures of the Player, alone or together with others, for still photographs, motion pictures or television, at such times as the Club or the Association may designate, and no matter by whom taken may be used in any manner desired by either of them for publicity or promotional purposes. The rights in any such pictures taken by the Club or by the Association shall belong to the Club or to the Association, as their interests may appear. . . . Upon request, the Player shall consent to and make himself available for interviews by representatives of the media conducted at reasonable times. In addition to the foregoing, the Player agrees to participate, upon request, in all other reasonable promotional activities of the Club and the Association.

Allowable Amendment to UPC, Paragraph 20(b) (1)

[For use when Club agrees to pay salary for entire term of contract despite failures by player to conform to certain of the standards set forth in paragraph 20(b) (1).]

Notwithstanding the provisions of paragraphs 20(b) (1), 20(d), 20(e) and 20(g), the termination of this Contract by the Club on account of [the Player's failure, refusal or neglect to conform his personal conduct to standards of good citizenship] and/or [the Player's failure, refusal or neglect to conform his personal conduct to standards of good sportsmanship] and/or [the Player's failure, refusal or neglect to obey the Club's training rules] shall in no way affect the player's right to receive the sums payable pursuant to paragraph 2 in the amounts and at the times called for by said paragraph.

The foregoing shall not require the Club to continue the Player as a member of the Club's team, Active List, or Roster; nor shall it afford the Player any right to continue or to be deemed as having continued, as such member for any purpose.

Note: Allowable amendment may include all or any one or more of bracketed phrases.

Allowable Amendment to UPC, Paragraph 20(b) (1)

[For use when Club agrees to pay salary for part of term of contract despite failures by player to conform to certain standards set forth in paragraph 20(b) (1).]

Notwithstanding the provisions of paragraphs 20(b) (1), 20(d), 20(e) and 20(g), the termination of this Contract by the Club on account of [the Player's failure, refusal, or neglect to conform his personal conduct to standards of good citizenship] and/or [the Player's failure, refusal or neglect to conform his personal conduct to standards of good sportsmanship] and/or [the Player's failure, refusal or neglect to obey the Club's training rules] shall in no way affect the player's right to receive the sums payable pursuant to paragraph 2 for the [*insert seasons or contract years covered by the guarantee*] in the amounts and at the times called for by said paragraph.

The foregoing shall not require the Club to continue the Player as a member of the Club's team, Active List, or Roster; nor shall it afford the Player any right to continue, or to be deemed as having continued, as such member for any purpose.

Note: Allowable amendment may include all or any one or more of bracketed phrases.

Allowable Amendment to UPC, Paragraph 20 (b) (2)

[For use when Club agrees to pay salary for entire term of contract despite player's lack of skill.]

Notwithstanding the provisions of paragraphs 20(b) (2), 20(d), 20(e) and 20(g), the termination of this Contract by the Club on account of the Player's failure to exhibit sufficient skill or competitive ability shall in no way affect the player's right to receive the sums payable pursuant to paragraph 2 in the amounts and at the times called for by said paragraph.

The foregoing shall not require the Club to continue the Player as a member of the Club's team, Active List, or Roster; nor shall it afford the Player any right to continue, or to be deemed as having continued, as such member for any purpose.

Allowable Amendment to UPC, Paragraph 20(b) (2)

[For use when Club agrees to pay salary for part of term despite player's lack of skill.]

Notwithstanding the provisions of paragraphs 20(b) (2), 20(d), 20(e) and 20(g), the termination of this Contract by the Club on account of the Player's failure to exhibit sufficient skill or competitive ability shall in no way affect the Player's right to receive the sums payable pursuant to paragraph 2 for the [*insert seasons or contract years covered by guarantee*] in the amounts and at the times called for by said paragraph.

The foregoing shall not require the Club to continue the Player as a member of the Club's team, Active List, or Roster; nor shall it afford the Player any right to continue, or to be deemed as having continued, as such member for any purpose.

Allowable Amendment to UPC, Paragraph 20(b) (3)

[For use when Club agrees to pay salary for part of term despite death of player.]

Notwithstanding the provisions of paragraphs 20(b), 20(c), 20(d), 20(e) and 20(g), the termination of this Contract by the Club on account of the Player's failure to render his services hereunder, if such failure has been caused by the Player's death, shall (provided that, at the time of such failure, the Player is not in material breach of this contract) in no way affect the Player's (or his estate's or duly-appointed beneficiary's) right to receive the sums payable pursuant to paragraph 2 for the [*insert seasons or contract years covered by guarantee*] in the amounts and at the times called for by said paragraph.

By virtue of the foregoing, the Player shall not be deemed as having continued to be a member of the Club's team, Active List, or Roster for any purpose.

Allowable Amendment to UPC, Paragraph 20(b) (3)

[For use when Club agrees to pay salary for entire term of contract despite mental disability suffered by player.]

Notwithstanding the provisions of paragraphs 20(b), 20(c), 20(d), 20(e) and 20(g), the termina-tion of this Contract by the Club on account of the Player's failure to render his services hereunder, if such failure has been caused by the Player's mental disability, shall (provided that, at the time of such failure, the Player is not in material breach of this Contract) in no way affect the Player's (or his duly-appointed legal representative's) right to receive the sums payable pursuant to paragraph 2 in the amounts and at the times called for by said paragraph.

By virtue of the foregoing, the Player shall not be deemed as having continued to be a member of the Club's team, Active List, or Roster for any purpose.

Allowable Amendment to UPC, Paragraph 20(b) (3)

[For use when Club agrees to pay salary for part of term despite mental disability suffered by player.]

Notwithstanding the provisions of paragraphs 20(b), 20(c), 20(d), 20(e) and 20(g), the termina-tion of this Contract by the Club on account of the Player's failure to render his services hereunder, if such failure has been caused by the Player's mental disability, shall (provided that, at the time of such failure, the Player is not in material breach of this Contract) in no way affect the Player's (or his duly-appointed legal representative's) right to receive the sums payable pursuant to paragraph 2 for the [*insert seasons or contract years covered by guarantee*] in the amounts and at the times called for by said paragraph.

By virtue of the foregoing, the Player shall not be deemed as having continued to be a member of the Club's team, Active List, or Roster for any purpose.

Allowable Amendment to UPC, Paragraph 20(b) (3)

[For use when Club agrees to pay salary for entire term of contract despite death of player.]

Notwithstanding the provisions of paragraphs 20(b), 20(c), 20(d), 20(e) and 20(g), the termina-tion of this Contract by the Club on account of the Player's failure to render his services hereunder, if such failure has been caused by the Player's death, shall (provided that, at the time of such failure, the Player is not in material breach of this Contract) in no way affect the Player's (or his estate's or duly-appointed beneficiary's) right to receive the sums payable pursuant to paragraph 2 in the amounts and at the times called for by said paragraph.

By virtue of the foregoing, the Player shall not be deemed as having continued to be a member of the Club's team, Active List, or Roster for any purpose.

Allowable Amendment to UPC, Paragraphs 20(b) (1) and/or 20(b) (2) and/or 20(b) (3)

[Comprehensive "guarantee" form — for use when club agrees to pay salary for part of term of contract despite player's failure to conform to certain 20(b) (1) standards, lack of skill, death, and mental disability. The following is a combination of Exhibits AA–9, AA–11, AA–13, and AA–15, and any one or more of the numbered paragraphs and bracketed phrases may be included or excluded.]

The termination of this Contract by the Club—

(1)   On account of [the Player's failure, refusal or neglect to conform his personal conduct to standards of good citizenship] and/or [the Player's failure, refusal or neglect to conform his personal conduct to standards of good sportsmanship] and/or [the Player's failure, refusal or neglect to obey the Club's training rules]; or

(2)   On account of the Player's failure to exhibit sufficient skill or competitive ability; or

(3)   On account of the Player's failure to render his services hereunder, if such failure has been caused by the Player's death (provided that, at the time of such failure, the Player is not in material breach of this Contract); or

(4)   On account of the Player's failure to render his services hereunder, if such failure has been caused by the Player's mental disability (provided that, at the time of such failure, the player is not in material breach of this Contract) —

shall in no way affect the Player's (or his estate's, or duly-appointed beneficiary's, or duly-appointed legal representative's, as the case may be) right to receive the sums payable pursuant to paragraph 2 for the [insert seasons or contract years covered by the guarantee] in the amounts and at the times called for by such paragraph.

The foregoing shall not require the Club to continue the Player as a member of the Club's team, Active List, or Roster; nor shall it afford the Player any right to continue, or (unless the Club and the Player have otherwise agreed) to be deemed as having continued as such member for any purpose.

Allowable Amendment to UPC, Paragraphs 20(b) (1) and/or 20(b) (2) and/or 20(b) (3)

[Comprehensive "guarantee" form — for use when club agrees to pay salary for entire term of contract despite player's failure to conform to certain 20(b) (1) standards, lack of skill, death, and mental disability. The following is a combination of Exhibits AA–8, AA–10, AA–12, and AA–14 and any one or more of the numbered paragraphs and bracketed phrases may be included or excluded.]

The termination of this Contract by the Club —

(1)   On account of [the Player's failure, refusal or neglect to conform his personal conduct to standards of good citzenship] and/or [the Player's failure, refusal or neglect to conform his personal conduct to standards of good sportsmanship] and/or [the Player's failure, refusal or neglect to obey the Club's training rules]; or

(2)   On account of the Player's failure to exhibit sufficient skill or competitive ability; or

(3)   On account of the Player's failure to render his services hereunder, if such failure has been caused by the Player's death (provided that, at the time of such failure, the Player is not in material breach of this Contract); or

(4)   On account of the Player's failure to render his services hereunder, if such failure has been caused by the Player's mental disability (provided that, at the time of such failure, the Player is not in material breach of this Contract) —

shall in no way affect the Player's (or his estate's or duly-appointed beneficiary's, or duly-appointed representative's, as the case may be) right to receive the sums payable pursuant to paragraph 2 in the amounts and at the times called for by such paragraph.

The foregoing shall not require the Club to continue the Player as a member of the Club's team, Active List, or Roster; nor shall it afford the Player any right to continue, or (unless the Club and the Player have otherwise agreed) to be deemed as having continued as such member for any purpose.

Allowable Amendment to UPC, Paragraph 20 (g)

20(g). Upon any termination of this contract by the Player, all obligations of the Club to pay compensation shall cease on the date of termination, except the obligation of the Club to pay the Player's compensation to said date and to pay, when due, any deferred compensation earned by the Player as of said date.

Allowable Amendments to UPC Providing for Club and/or Player Option

1. A club and a player may amend a Veteran Uniform Player Contract or a Rookie Uniform Player Contract (which is for a stated term of more than one year) by including therein an option clause, provided such clause meets the requirements set forth in Article XXII, Section 1(b) of the collective bargaining agreement. (This is in addition to the option clause which is a standard provision in Rookie–Single Season Uniform Player Contract.)

2. A club and a player may amend a Veteran Uniform Player Contract or a Rookie Uniform Player Contract (which is for a stated term of more than one year) by including therein an option in favor of the player.

Note: No standard-form language has been provided for either of the above.

3.22 Comparative Provisions: Other Leagues

The fact that leagues borrow ideas about contract provisions from each other does not result in identical language in league contracts. There is sufficient disparity that certain factual circumstances could result in different legal consequences. The provisions that follow do contain language, and thus approaches, that vary somewhat from the NBA provisions. Some of these provisions are mentioned elsewhere in the text.

The provisions set forth at this point relate to injuries and physical examinations (Section 3.22–1), player representations (Section 3.22–2), unauthorized bonuses and bribery (Section 3.22–3), contract assignments (Section 3.22–4), contract termination by club (Section 3.22–5),

and extensions of the contract (Section 3.22–6).

3.22–1 Injuries, Physical Examinations, and Suspensions Due to Injury

Injuries are an inevitable part of sports competition. This is particularly true on the professional level, as athletes push to become ever quicker and stronger. The collisions of bodies and the extensions beyond normal body abilities cause the injury rates to climb. Contract provisions relating to injuries are important to all parties, perhaps amendable to a degree, but largely to be included in a player's contract as prescribed by the league's standard form.

National Football League

8. Physical condition. Player represents to Club that he is and will maintain himself in excellent physical condition. Player will undergo a complete physical examination by the Club physician upon Club request, during which physical examination Player agrees to make full and complete disclosure of any physical or mental condition known to him which might impair his performance under this contract and to respond fully and in good faith when questioned by the Club physician about such condition. If Player fails to establish or maintain his excellent physical condition to the satisfaction of the Club physician, or make the required full and complete disclosure and good faith responses to the Club physician, then Club may terminate this contract.

9. Injury. If Player is injured in the performance of his services under this contract and promptly reports such injury to the Club physician or trainer, then Player will receive such medical and hospital care during the term of this contract as the Club physician may deem necessary, and, in accordance with Club's practice, will continue to receive his yearly salary for so long, during the season of injury only and for no subsequent period, as Player is physically unable to perform the services required of him by this contract because of such injury. If Player's injury in the performance of his services under this contract results in his death, the unpaid balance of his yearly salary for the season of injury will be paid to his stated

beneficiary or, in the absence of a stated beneficiary, to his estate.

13. Injury Grievance. Unless a collective bargaining agreement in existence at the time of termination of this contract by Club provides otherwise, the following injury grievance procedure will apply: If Player believes that at the time of termination of this contract by Club he was physically unable to perform the services required of him by this contract because of an injury incurred in the performance of his services under this contract, Player may, within a reasonably brief time after examination by the Club physician, submit at his own expense to examination by a physician of his choice. If the opinion of Player's physician with respect to his physical ability to perform the services required of him by this contract is contrary to that of the Club's physician, the dispute will be submitted within a reasonable time to final and binding arbitration by an arbitrator selected by Club and Player or, if they are unable to agree, one selected by the League Commissioner on application by either party.

National Hockey League

5. Should the Player be disabled or unable to perform his duties under this contract he shall submit himself for medical examination and treatment by a physician selected by the Club, and such examination and treatment, when made at the request of the Club, shall be at its expense unless made necessary by some act or conduct of the Player contrary to the terms and provisions of this contract or the rules established under Section 4.

If the Player, in the sole judgment of the Club's physician, is disabled or is not in good physical condition at the commencement of the season or at any subsequent time during the season (unless such condition is the direct result of playing hockey for the Club) so as to render him unfit to play skilled hockey, then it is mutually agreed that the Club shall have the right to suspend the Player for such period of disability or unfitness, and no compensation shall be payable for that period under this contract.

If the Player is injured as the result of playing hockey for the Club, the Club will pay the Player's reasonable hospitalization until discharged from the hospital, and his medical expenses and doctor's bills, provided that the hospital and doctor are selected by the Club.

It is also agreed that if the Player's injuries resulting directly from playing for the Club render him, in the sole judgment of the Club's physician, unfit to play skilled hockey for the balance of the season or any part thereof, then during such time the Player is so unfit, but in no event beyond the end of the current season, the Club shall pay the Player the compensation herein provided for and the Player releases the Club from any and every additional obligation, liability, claim or demand whatsoever. However if upon joint consultation between the Player, the Club's physician and the Club General Manager, they are unable to agree as to the physical fitness of the Player to return to play, the Player agrees to submit himself for examination by an independent medical specialist and the Parties hereto agree to be bound by his decision. If the Player is declared to be unfit for play he shall continue to receive the full benefits of this Agreement. If the Player is declared to be physically able to play and refuses to do so he shall be liable to immediate suspension without notice.

If upon joint consultation between the Player, the Club's Physician and the Club General Manager, they are unable to agree upon the physical fitness to return to play following an injury not resulting directly from playing for the Club, the Player agrees to submit himself for examination by an independent medical specialist and the Parties hereto agree to be bound by his decision. If the Player is declared to be fit for play, he shall be entitled to receive the full benefits of this agreement. If he is declared to be not physically able to play, he shall not be entitled to the benefits of this agreement until he has been declared to be physically fit to play by the independent medical specialist.

Major League Baseball

2. The Player, when requested by the Club, must submit to a complete physical examination at the expense of the Club, and if necessary to treatment by a regular physician or dentist in good standing. Upon refusal of the Player to submit to a complete medical or dental examination the Club may consider such refusal a violation of this

regulation and may take such action as it deems advisable under Regulation 5 of this contract. Disability directly resulting from injury sustained in the course and within the scope of his employment under this contract shall not impair the right of the Player to receive his full salary for the period of such disability or for the season in which the injury was sustained (whichever period is shorter), together with the reasonable medical and hospital expenses incurred by reason of the injury and during the term of this contract; but only upon the express prerequisite conditions that (a) written notice of such injury, including the time, place, cause and nature of the injury, is served upon and received by the Club within twenty days of the sustaining of said injury and (b) the Club shall have the right to designate the doctors and hospitals furnishing such medical and hospital services. Failure to give such notice shall not impair the rights of the Player, as herein set forth, if the Club has actual knowledge of such injury. All workmen's compensation payments received by the Player as compensation for loss of income for a specific period during which the Club is paying him in full, shall be paid over by the Player to the Club. Any other disability may be ground for suspending or terminating this contract at the discretion of the Club.

3.22–2 Player Representations

A club's exclusive rights to a player's services was discussed in Chapter 2, Section 2.10. The clauses below are attempts by clubs to have it acknowledged in the contract that player possesses unique skills and abilities, thus setting the stage for injunctive relief, should player breach the contract and attempt to play for another professional sports team. As we saw in Section 2.10, the inclusion of a "unique skills" clause is not conclusive that the player in fact is unique. In addition, the failure to include such a clause does not preclude enjoining a player from jumping to another club. Even so, standard form contracts in team sports routinely contain these clauses, for whatever evidenciary weight a court might give them. The clauses below also contain representations as to player's physical condition.

National Football League

3. Other Activities. Without prior written consent of Club, Player will not play football or engage in activities related to football otherwise than for Club or engage in any activity other than football which may involve a significant risk of personal injury. Player represents that he has special, exceptional and unique knowledge, skill, ability and experience as a football player, the loss of which cannot be estimated with any certainty and cannot be fairly or adequately compensated by damages. Player therefore agrees that Club will have the right, in addition to any other right which club may possess, to enjoin Player by appropriate proceedings from playing football or engaging in football-related activities other than for Club or from engaging in any activity other than football which may involve a significant risk of personal injury.

National Hockey League

5. The Player represents and agrees that he has exceptional and unique knowledge, skill and ability as a hockey player, the loss of which cannot be estimated with certainty and cannot be fairly or adequately compensated by damages. The Player therefore agrees that the Club shall have the right, in addition to any other rights which the Club may possess, to enjoin him by appropriate injunction proceedings from playing hockey for any other team and/or for any breach of any of the other provisions of this contract.

Major League Baseball, Player Representations

Ability. 4.(1) The Player represents and agrees that he has exceptional and unique skill and ability as a baseball player; that his services to be rendered hereunder are of a special, unusual and extraordinary character which gives them peculiar value which cannot be reasonably or adequately compensated for in damages at law, and that the Player's breach of this contract will cause the Club great and irreparable injury and damage. The Player agrees that, in addition to other remedies, the Club shall be entitled to injunctive and other equitable relief to prevent a breach of this contract by the Player, including, among others, the right to enjoin the Player from playing baseball for any other person or organization during the term of his contract.

Condition. 4.(b)   The Player represents that he has no physical or mental defects known to him and unknown to the appropriate representative of the Club which would prevent or impair performance of his services.

Interest in Club. 4.(c)   The Player represents that he does not, directly or indirectly, own stock or have any financial interest in the ownership or earnings of any Major League Club, except as hereinafter expressly set forth, and covenants that he will not hereafter, while connected with any Major League Club, acquire or hold any such stock or interest except in accordance with Major League Rule 20(e).

3.22–3   Unauthorized Bonuses and Bribery

The integrity of the game being played is vital to sports leagues. If there is a loss of confidence in the honesty of the effort and outcome, fan interest will die. All team sports league contracts contain provisions against gambling, cheating, and bribery. Their approaches vary somewhat, however, and should be examined and compared.

National Football League

15.   Integrity of Game. Player recognizes the detriment to the League and professional football that would result from impairment of public confidence in the honest and orderly conduct of NFL games or the integrity and good character of NFL players. Player therefore acknowledges his awareness that if he accepts a bribe or agrees to throw or fix an NFL game; fails to promptly report a bribe offer or an attempt to throw or fix an NFL game; bets on an NFL game; knowingly associates with gamblers or gambling activity; uses or provides other players with stimulants or other drugs for the purpose of attempting to enhance on-field performance; or is guilty of any other form of conduct reasonably judged by the League Commissioner to be detrimental to the League or professional football, the Commissioner will have the right, but only after giving Player the

opportunity for a hearing at which he may be represented by counsel of his choice, to fine Player in a reasonable amount; to suspend Player for a period certain or indefinitely; and/or to terminate this contract.

National Hockey League

It is mutually agreed that the Club will not pay, and the Player will not accept from any person, any bonus or anything of value for winning any particular game or series of games except as authorized by the league By-Laws.

Major Indoor Soccer League

Section 5.1 Prohibited Conduct. Player agrees to comply with all reasonable provisions of the By-Laws and Regulations of the League applicable to players and with decisions of the League's officers. Player acknowledges that if he accepts a bribe or agrees to fix a League game; fails to promptly report a bribe offer; bets on a League game; or is guilty of any other form of conduct reasonably judged by the Commissioner to be detrimental to the League or professional soccer, the Commissioner has the right, after giving Player the opportunity for a hearing, to fine Player in a reasonable amount; to suspend Player for a period certain or indefinitely; and/or to terminate this contract.

3.22–4   Contract Assignments

Clubs trade players in attempts to improve. This is an accepted way of doing business in professional sports. In other industries, assignments of personal services contracts are rare. In sports, they are commonplace. However, since personal services are involved, an assignments clause must be included in the contract if such can be unilaterally done by a club. Such clauses appear in all standard sports forms. The examples below illustrate both the simple version (NFL) and the more detailed (Major League Baseball).

The assignments clauses in the standard contracts must be considered in conjunction with provisions in a league's collective bargaining agreement concerning assignments. Between the standard form and the collective agreement, the rights and duties of both clubs and players are specified. (See examples of collective bargaining provisions on assignments in Section 3.36.)

It should also be noted that most sports leagues allow the deletion of assignments clauses and the substitution of the so-called "no trade" provisions. Only the NBA, by its collective bargaining agreement, insists that the assignments clauses must be included in the player contract.

National Football League

15. Assignment. Unless this contract specifically provides otherwise, Club may assign this contract and Player's services under this contract to any successor to Club's franchise or to any other Club in the League. Player will report to the assignee club promptly upon being informed of the assignment of his contract and will faithfully perform his services under this contract. The assignee club will pay Player's necessary traveling expenses in reporting to it and will faithfully perform this contract with Player.

Major League Baseball

Assignment. 6.(a)   The Player agrees that this contract may be assigned by the Club (and reassigned by any assignee Club) to any other Club in accordance with the Major League Rules and the Professional Baseball Rules. The Club and the Player may, without obtaining special approval, agree by special covenant to limit or eliminate the right of the Club to assign this contract.

No Salary Reduction. 6.(b)   The amount stated in paragraph 2 and in special covenants hereof which is payable to the Player for the period stated in paragraph 1 hereof shall not be diminished by any such assignment, except for failure to report as provided in the next subparagraph (c).

Reporting. 6.(c)   The Player shall report to the assignee Club promptly (as provided in the Regulation) upon receipt of written notice from the Club of the assignment of this contract. If the Player fails so to report, he shall not be entitled to any payment for the period from the date he receives written notice of assignment until he reports to the assignee Club.

Obligations of Assignor and Assignee Clubs. 6.(d)   Upon and after such assignment, all rights and obligations of the assignor Club hereunder shall become the rights and obligations of the assignee Club; provided, however, that

(1) The assignee Club shall be liable to the Player for payments accruing only from the date of assignment and shall not be liable (but the assignor Club shall remain liable) for payments accrued prior to that date.

(2) If at any time the assignee is a Major League Club, it shall be liable to pay the Player at the full rate stipulated in paragraph 2 hereof for the remainder of the period stated in paragraph 1 hereof and all prior assignors and assignees shall be relieved of liability for any payment for such period.

(3) Unless the assignor and assignee Clubs agree otherwise, if the assignee Club is a National Association Club, the assignee Club shall be liable only to pay the Player at the rate usually paid by said assignee Club to other Players of similar skill and ability in its classification and the assignor Club shall be liable to pay the difference for the remainder of the period stated in paragraph 1 hereof between an amount computed at the rate stipulated in paragraph 2 hereof and the amount so payable by the assignee Club.

6.(f)   All references in other paragraphs of this contract to "the Club" shall be deemed to mean and include any assignee of this contract.

3.22–5   Contract Termination by Club

All standard player contracts provide for termination rights exercisable by a club if player fails to perform at acceptable levels. The examples which follow accentuate the fact that a professional sports career is an uncertain one, capable of being ended at any time if the club feels someone else can do a better job. There is little recourse if the club feels the player is not sufficiently skilled, although a few cases have found that a club improperly invoked the skills provisions and in fact attempted to terminate a player's contract for other reasons. (See Chapter 4, Section 4.31.)

A club's right to terminate can be modified. This is done by negotiating salary guarantees into the contract. These are complicated provisions, not to be done without a great deal of planning. (Complications relating to salary guarantees are discussed in Chapter 4, Section 4.27.)

National Football League

11. Skill, Performance and Conduct. Player understands that he is competing with other players for a position on Club's roster within the applicable player limits. If at any time, in the sole judgment of Club, Player's skill or performance has been unsatisfactory as compared with that of other players competing for positions on club's roster, or if Player has engaged in personal conduct reasonably judged by Club to adversely affect or reflect on Club, then Club may terminate this contract.

12. Termination. The rights of termination set forth in this contract will be in addition to any other rights of termination allowed either party by law. Termination will be effective upon the giving of written notice, except that Player's death, other than as a result of injury incurred in the performance of his services under this contract, will automatically terminate this contract. If this contract is terminated by Club and either Player or Club so requests, Player will promptly undergo a complete physical examination by the Club physician.

National Hockey League

13. The Club may terminate this contract upon written notice to the Player (but only after obtaining waivers from all other League clubs) if the player shall at any time:

(a) fail, refuse or neglect to obey the Club's rules governing training and conduct of players,

(b) fail, refuse or neglect to render his services hereunder or in any other manner materially breach this contract.

In the event of termination under sub-section (a) or (b) the Player shall only be entitled to compensation due to him to the date such notice is delivered to him or the date of the mailing of such

notice to his address as set out below his signature hereto.

In the event that this contract is terminated by the Club while the Player is "away" with the Club for the purpose of playing games the installment then falling due shall be paid on the first week-day after the return "home" of the Club.

Major League Baseball

By Club. 7.(b) The Club may terminate this contract upon written notice to the Player (but only after requesting and obtaining waivers of this contract from all other Major League Clubs) if the Player shall at any time:

(1) fail, refuse or neglect to conform his personal conduct to the standards of good citizenship and good sportsmanship or to keep himself in first-class physical condition or to obey the Club's training rules; or

(2) fail, in the opinion of the Club's management, to exhibit sufficient skill or competitive ability to qualify or continue as a member of the Club's team; or

(3) fail, refuse or neglect to render his services hereunder or in any other manner materially breach this contract.

7.(c) If this contract is terminated by the Club, the Player shall be entitled to termination pay under the circumstances and in the amounts set forth in Article VIII of the Basic Agreement between the Major League Clubs and the Major League Baseball Players Association, effective January 1, 1976. In addition, the Player shall be entitled to receive an amount equal to the reasonable traveling expenses of the Player including first-class jet air fare and meals en route, to his home city.

Procedure. 7.(d) If the Club proposes to terminate this contract in accordance with subparagraph (b) of this paragraph 7, the procedure shall be as follows:

(1) The Club shall request waivers from all other Major League Clubs. Such waivers shall be good for six (6) days only. Such waiver request must state that it is for the purpose of terminating this contract and it may not be withdrawn.

(2) Upon receipt of waiver request, any other Major League Club may claim assignment of this contract at waiver price of $1.00, the priority of claims to be determined in accordance with the

Major League Rules.

(3) If this contract is so claimed, the Club shall promptly and before any assignment, notify the Player that it had requested waivers for the purpose of terminating this contract and that the contract had been claimed.

(4) Within 5 days after receipt of notice of such claim, the Player shall be entitled, by written notice to the Club, to terminate this contract on the date of his notice of termination. If the Player fails so to notify the Club, this contract shall be assigned to the claiming Club.

(5) If the contract is not claimed, the Club shall promptly deliver written notice of termination to the Player at the expiration of the waiver period.

7.(e) Upon any termination of this contract by the Player, all obligations of both Parties hereunder shall cease on the date of termination, except the obligation of the Club to pay the Player's compensation to said date.

3.23–6   Extensions

Two professional leagues (NFL and MISL) provide for a player's contract to be extended in time if player fails or refuses to perform under the contract. This is often called "tolling the contract" and effectively extends the contract by the period of time equal to the period in which player fails to perform. Theoretically, this could mean several years, although no court case has ultimately held that a player is still bound to a contract after a multi-year tolling period had run. For an example of the tolling provision in effect, see *Dallas Cowboys Football Club, Inc.* v. *Harris,* 348 S.W.2d 37 (Tex. Civ. App. 1961), discussed in Chapter 2, Section 2.12.

National Football League

16. Extension. If Player becomes a member of the Armed Forces of the United States or any other country, or retires from professional football as an active player, or otherwise fails or refuses to perform his services under this contract, then this contract will be tolled between the date of Player's induction into the Armed Forces, or his retirement, or his failure or refusal to perform, and the later date of his return to professional football. During

the period this contract is tolled, Player will not be entitled to any compensation or benefits. On Player's return to professional football, the term of this contract will be extended for a period of time equal to the number of seasons (to the nearest multiple of one) remaining at the time the contract was tolled. The right of renewal, if any, contained in this contract will remain in effect until the end of any such extended term.

Major Indoor Soccer League

Section 9.5 Extended Term. This Agreement shall, at the option of the Club, be extended for that number of days in which Player (during the term of this Agreement): (a) is prevented from entering the United States because of immigration laws, regulations or rulings, or (b) is ineligible to play soccer in the League because of his being on the Voluntarily Retired, Restricted, Ineligible or Military Lists (provided in the League Regulations). The renewal clause contained in this Agreement shall remain in effect during such extended term. Player shall not be entitled to any compensation for any such period in which he is prevented from entering the United States or is ineligible to play soccer in the League.

3.30   Collective Bargaining Provisions: Direct Application to Standard Contracts

The range of collective bargaining provisions from the various leagues that directly affect terms and conditions in the standard player contract is broad. The selected samples in this section illustrate the significance of what is provided before one even contemplates negotiating an individual player contract. Since the terms are provided through collective bargaining, they generally cannot be waived during the negotiating process. Under labor law principles, additional benefits can be accorded the employee (player) in individual contracts, with exceptions, but benefits cannot be deleted.

The first step in the process of contract negotiations is to become thoroughly familiar with the terms of the standard player contract. Then the collective bargaining agreement should be carefully scrutinized for further delineation of guarantees and other provisions. The next steps are described in Chapter 4; for now, we will focus only on the collective bargaining provisions.

The following subsections note a depth of coverage in collective bargaining agreements, including mandated use of the standard form (Section 3.31); salary definitions and minimums (Section 3.32); the NBA's recently implemented salary cap (Section 3.33); severance and termination pay (Section 3.34); injury provisions and medical care (Section 3.35); assignments, waivers, and releases (Section 3.36); a variety of benefits relating to preseason travel during the season, moving, pensions, insurance, and other fringes (Section 3.37); club discipline (Section 3.38); and provisions relating to present concerns that may lead to future joint action by management and labor (Section 3.39).

3.31   Required Use of the Standard Contract

Leagues require that all players sign a standard player contract that includes only permissible amendments and additions. Normally, a player cannot attend a regular preseason camp without having signed an agreement. Most certainly, a player who has not signed such an agreement cannot compete in any preseason or regular season games. The NFL provision below is typical of most standard player contracts.

National Football League, Article XII, NFL Player Contract

Section 1. Form: The NFL Player Contract form will be used for all player signings. This form cannot be amended without NFLPA approval. In connection with the NFLPA's exclusive right to represent all players in its bargaining unit in negotiations with NFL clubs under Article XXII, Section 2 of this Agreement on Salaries, it is agreed and understood that: (a) copies of all individual player contracts signed by rookie and veteran players before the date of execution of this Agreement covering the 1982 and future seasons will be provided to the NFLPA within 30 days of

the execution of this Agreement; (b) copies of all contracts signed by rookie and veteran players after the date of execution of this Agreement covering the 1982 and future seasons will be provided to the NFLPA within 10 days of their execution; and (c) all information in such contracts will be made available to all clubs by the Management Council.

Section 2. Changes: Notwithstanding Section 1 above, changes may be made in a player's contract or contracts consistent with the provisions of this Agreement and with the provisions of the NFL Constitution and Bylaws not in conflict with this Agreement.

3.32   Salaries: Definitions, Individual Minimums, Maximum Reductions, and Deferred Compensation

Leagues have minimum salaries, many of which are noted below. Few players other than marginal rookies sign for the minimum. Unlike other industries in which the full wage scale is established through collective bargaining, sports leagues opt for minimum structures, explicitly leaving the final salary figures open to individual negotiation.

The NFL has an elaborate minimum wage scale, based on years of service in the league. Because the minimum salary increases for each additional year played in the NFL, more players are near the minimum than in other leagues. As of 1984, however, the presence of the rival USFL had driven NFL salaries to such heights that most NFL players received salaries in excess of the minimum prescribed for their years' service.

The NBA is another league with a somewhat variant approach. Its salary cap (see Section 3.33) undoubtedly forces additional players to sign at or near the minimum. This is explicitly true for rookies drafted by teams at the Maximum Team Salary. As set forth in Section 3.33, these players have to sign a one-year, no-option contract at the league minimum, or in the case of first-round draft picks, at $75,000.

Defining what constitutes salary can be important. Major League Baseball's definition is included here, since an earlier failure to have such a definition led to an important arbitration involving the Atlanta Braves and Bobby Horner (see Chapter 4, Section 4.28–2).

Leagues have recently worried about a growing trend that has led to large percentages of the amount named in the player contract being taken as deferred compensation. This has been a particularly bothersome problem in the NBA; it appears that several clubs are saddled with substantial amounts of long-term debt of this nature. The NBA's response, set forth below, has been to limit the amount of a player's contract that can be paid through deferred compensation.

National Football League, Article XXII, Salaries

Section 1. Salaries: Effective after the execution of this Agreement, the salary of a rookie player will be not less than $20,000 and the salary of any player who makes a club's Active List at any time during the regular season will be not less than the following [see table below].

For purposes of this Article, a player's salary under any contract in existence at the time of execution of this Agreement will include the amount of any signing or reporting bonus, prorated over the full number of years of the contract or contracts executed on the same date (including any option year). A player's salary under any contract executed after the time of execution of this Agreement will not include the prorated amount of any signing or reporting bonus. No other type of incentive bonus will be included at any time in the computation of a player's salary under this Article. The length of service of a player will be determined by crediting one year of service for each year the player has been on the Active List of a club for at least three regular season games.

Section 2. Other Compensation: A player will be entitled to receive a signing or reporting bonus, additional salary payments, incentive bonuses and such other provisions as may be negotiated between his club (with the assistance of the Management Council) and the NFLPA or its agent. The club and the NFLPA or its agent will negotiate in good faith over such other compensation; provided, however, that a club will not be required to deal with the NFLPA or its agent on a collective or tandem basis for two or more players on that club. Nothing in this Section will be affected by Article II, Section 1 of this Agreement.

Major League Baseball, Article V, Salaries

Individual player salaries shall be those as agreed

Length of Service	1982	1983	1984	1985	1986
Rookie	$ 30,000	$ 40,000	$ 40,000	$ 50,000	$ 50,000
2nd Year	40,000	50,000	50,000	60,000	60,000
3rd Year	50,000	60,000	60,000	70,000	70,000
4th Year	60,000	70,000	70,000	80,000	80,000
5th Year	70,000	80,000	80,000	90,000	90,000
6th Year	80,000	90,000	90,000	100,000	100,000
7th Year	90,000	100,000	100,000	110,000	110,000
8th Year	100,000	110,000	110,000	120,000	120,000
9th Year	110,000	120,000	120,000	130,000	130,000
10th Year	120,000	130,000	130,000	140,000	140,000
11th Year	130,000	140,000	140,000	150,000	150,000
12th Year	140,000	150,000	150,000	160,000	160,000
13th Year	150,000	160,000	160,000	170,000	170,000
14th Year	160,000	170,000	170,000	180,000	180,000
15th Year	170,000	180,000	180,000	190,000	190,000
16th Year	180,000	190,000	190,000	200,000	200,000
17th Year	190,000	200,000	200,000	200,000	200,000
18th Year & Above	200,000	200,000	200,000	200,000	200,000

upon between a Player and a Club, as evidenced by the execution of a Uniform Player's Contract, subject to the following:

A. Definition of Salary

The term "salary" for the purposes of interpretation and application of the maximum salary cut, contract tender, signing and renewal rules shall be determined by applying the following principles:

(1) Multi-year contract providing for current salary only (no up-front payment or deferred compensation);

(a) If the annual salary payment schedule *satisfies* the maximum salary cut rule, the salary specified for the last year of the contract shall be the base for applying the maximum salary cut rule to the year following the expiration of the contract.

(b) If the annual salary payment schedule *does not satisfy* the maximum salary cut rule, that rule shall not be applicable during the term of the contract and the aggregate salary payment provided by the contract shall be averaged and the average annual salary shall be the base for applying the maximum salary cut rule to the year following the contract's expiration.

(2) Multi-year contract including up-front payments and/or deferred compensation which is *specifically allocated* to one or more years of the contract:

Treat as in (1) above with the allocated up-front or deferred amounts included as specified as part of the salary for each year.

(3) Multi-year contract including up-front payments and/or deferred compensation which is *not specifically allocated* to certain years of the contract:

Average the aggregate of such payments, include the annual average as part of the salary for each year, and then treat as in (1) above.

(4) If any deferred compensation is included in the base determined as described above, it may be payable as deferred on the same terms, or the Club and Player may elect to substitute the discounted present value of such deferred amount.

(5) Performance Bonuses:

Regardless of whether or not any portion of a performance bonus is earned, the Club has the option of either: (i) including the entire bonus (both earned and unearned portions) in the salary base or (ii) excluding it from the base but repeating

the performance bonus on the same terms.

(6) Other forms of additional compensation, including but not limited to the following, are not addressed herein and are to be determined according to the facts in each situation:

(i) payments for performing services for a Club in addition to skilled services as a baseball player;

(ii) cash, lump sum, payments made in accordance with agreed upon special covenants to compensate for trading a Player, releasing a Player, etc.;

(iii) the value of individual property rights granted to a Player by a Club;

(iv) any compensation for post active Major League Baseball playing career employment;

(v) other payments not specifically made for performance as a Major League Baseball Player; provided that any amounts payable upon the occurrence of specific event or events shall not be included in the definition of "salary" if such event or events fail to occur within the specified period.

(7) Disputes:

In the event of a dispute regarding a contract tender, signing or renewal with respect to any form of additional compensation referred to in paragraph (6) above, either the Player or Club may file a Grievance in order to obtain a determination with respect thereto as the exclusive means of resolving such dispute, and both parties shall be bound by the resulting decision. The contract tender, signing or renewal shall be altered as necessary to conform to the decision, and such tender, signing or renewal shall remain valid.

B. Minimum Salary

(1) The minimum rate of payment to a player for each day of service on a Major League Club shall be as follows:

1980 — at the rate of $30,000 per season

1981 — at the rate of $32,500 per season

1982 — at the rate of $33,500 per season

1983 — at the rate of $35,000 per season

(2) Effective beginning with the 1981 Championship Season, for all Players (a) signing a second Major League contract (not covering the same season as any such Player's initial Major League

contract) or a subsequent Major League contract, or (b) having at least one day of Major League Service, the minimum salary shall be as follows:

(i) for Major League service: at a rate not less than the Major League minimum salary;

(ii) for National Association service: at a rate not less than the following:

1981 — at the rate of $14,000 per season

1982 — at the rate of $14,000 per season

1983 — at the rate of $16,000 per season

C. Maximum Salary Reduction

(1) No Player's contract shall be renewed pursuant to paragraph 10(a) of the Uniform Player's Contract in any year for a salary which constitutes a reduction in excess of 20% of his previous year's salary or in excess of 30% of his salary two years previous. For the purposes of this section, the "salary" of a Player with a salary stipulated in paragraph 2 of his Major League contract of less than the then applicable Major League minimum salary shall be deemed to be the greater of either (1) the total amount of his actual baseball salary earnings from Major League Clubs (and for National Association Clubs, if any) in that season or (2) the amount stipulated in paragraph 2 of his Major League contract for that season.

(2) The term "salary" shall include any salary amounts which were not paid to a Player for the season by reason of any fine or suspension which may have been imposed on the Player, or by reason of any other deduction from salary;

(3) In tendering a contract to a Player pursuant to paragraph 10(a) of the Uniform Player's Contract, no Major League Club shall offer a salary which constitutes a reduction in excess of 20% of the Player's previous year's salary or in excess of 30% of his salary two years previous.

Major League Baseball, 1981 Memorandum

(i) *Minimum Salary: Article V.* The minimum rate of payment to a player for each day of service on a Major League Club shall be at the rate of $40,000 for the 1984 season.

The National Association minimum salary set forth in Article V B(2) shall be at the rate of $17,500 for the 1984 season.

National Basketball Association, 1983 Memorandum of Agreement

P. Article XV of the prior collective bargaining agreement shall be amended to provide that no NBA Team may sign a Player Contract with any player which provides for deferred compensation of more than 30%. All Player Contracts entered into after the date hereof shall specify the season(s) to which any deferred compensation is applicable. For purposes of determining Team Salary only, any Salary attributable to a playing season covered by a Player Contract after the player is 35 years old shall be deemed to be deferred compensation, provided, however, that this sentence shall not apply to the first three years of any Player Contract.

3.33   NBA Maximum/Minimum Team Salary

In 1983, the owners and the union in the NBA set on a course not previously attempted in professional sports — that is, the so-called salary cap, a device by which teams are limited as to the total dollars each can spend on player salaries. The basic concept is that within the cap a club can choose how much it will spend on any single player, but the total must not exceed the maximum established for that team.

Several initial points should be emphasized. First, the actual caps vary from team to team. The general concept is that each year's team maximum is 53 percent of the league gross (divided by 23 teams) or a set dollar amount (in the $3.6 to $4.0 million range, depending on the year), whichever is greater; the reality is that many teams have higher maximums, which are established by their prior salary commitments. These higher amounts are, in fact, those teams' maximums. Second, the exceptions are numerous, in that a team can pay salaries over its supposed maximum when it acts to keep one of its own players who might otherwise be moving to a new team under free agency. Third, there is also a minimum salary. A team must pay, in total, a certain dollar amount, figured year to year on league grosses and other complicated considerations. Just what the final results should be are still disputed. Even so, the principle of a team minimum, as well as a maximum, was established in the 1983 accord.

The NBA salary cap provisions are presented here in essentially full detail. The concept of a salary cap is an important experiment in the sports world and will obviously be closely monitored. In 1984, the North American Soccer League moved toward a salary cap by establishing a team maximum salary of $850,000, with a requirement that teams currently over the maximum must gradually reduce their salary commitments to meet that standard. This move by NASL was not enough to save the league, as it announced it would not operate in 1985. Even so, the implementation of a salary cap was viewed a move that needed to be made.

The baseball owners were the next to suggest a salary cap. Their concept of a cap was introduced into the collective bargaining negotiations during the summer of 1985. The cap as proposed would restrict all clubs from signing free agents that were over the average team salary for the two leagues. This would effectively remove one-half of the teams each year from entering the free agent bidding. The players quickly rejected the proposal, saying it would undermine free agency; but as the negotiations dragged on, the idea of some type of salary cap was still proposed.

NOTE _____

1. An extensive discussion of the NBA salary cap and its many complications can be found in Chapter Six of Berry, Gould, and Staudohar, *Labor Relations in Professional Sports* (Dover, Mass.: Auburn House, 1986).

National Basketball Association, 1983 Memorandum of Agreement

III. Revenue Sharing for NBA Players and Minimum Team Salary and Maximum Team Salary

The successor collective bargaining agreement to be executed by the parties shall contain a new Article, providing as follows:

A. The NBA and each NBA Team shall in good faith act and use their best efforts so as to maximize Defined Gross Revenues for each playing season during the term of this Memorandum.

B. (1) For the 1983–84 playing season, there shall be no limitation on the Team Salary of any NBA Team, other than the five Teams referenced below . . .

(2) With respect to the 1983–84 playing season, each of the following five NBA Teams may not have a Team Salary that exceeds the amounts set forth below, except pursuant to the provisions of paragraph C(2) below:

Los Angeles Lakers	$5,200,000.
New Jersey Nets	$3,750,000.
New York Knickerbockers	$4,600,000.
Philadelphia 76ers	$4,450,000.
Seattle SuperSonics	$4,600,000.

(3) With respect to the 1984–85, 1985–86 and 1986–87 playing seasons, the Maximum Team Salary of the five above-referenced Teams shall be the greater of the amounts set forth in paragraph B(2) above or the Maximum Team Salary computed in accordance with paragraph C(1) below. . . .

C.(1) Subject to the provisions of paragraphs B(2) and (3) above, for the 1984–85, 1985–86 and 1986–87 playing seasons, there shall be a Maximum Team Salary equal to the greater of:

(a) $3.6 million in 1984–1985; $3.8 million in 1985–1986; $4.0 million in 1986–1987; or

(b) 53% of Defined Gross Revenues, less Benefits (as adjusted pursuant to paragraph (5) (b) below), divided by the number of Teams in the NBA as of July 31 of each year;

(2) A Team may have a Team Salary that exceeds the Maximum Team Salary only in one or more of the following situations:

(a) A Team will be permitted to exceed the Maximum Team Salary to the extent of contractual commitments in effect as of the end of the 1983–1984 season. The five above-referenced Teams will be permitted to exceed the Maximum Team Salary to the extent of contractual commitments in effect as of the end of the 1982–83 season;

(b) Commencing with the day following the last playoff game of the 1982–83 season, a Team may enter into a new Player Contract or exercise its Right of First Refusal with respect to any Veteran Free Agent who last previously played for that Team, without regard to the Maximum Team Salary; provided, however, that any Team that does so enter into a new Player Contract or formalizes a Player Contract after exercising its Right of First Refusal with respect to such Veteran Free Agent shall be entitled to any of the exceptions set forth in subparagraphs C(2) (c), (d) and (e) below with respect to that Player only to the extent of (i) the amount of Salary permitted by the applicable exception or (ii) 100% of the Salary last paid to the Player under his prior Player Contract, whichever is less;

(c) A Team with a Team Salary at or over the Maximum Team Salary may replace (i) a player who retires; or (ii) a player whose contract has been terminated in accordance with the NBA's waiver procedure, by entering into a Player Contract with a replacement player calling for a Salary no greater than 50% of the Salary last paid to the player being replaced or an amount that brings the Team Salary up to the Maximum Team Salary, whichever is greater, provided, however, that this exception shall not apply so as to allow a Team to replace any player who entered into a Player Contract after the last day of a regular season and which Player Contract was terminated in accordance with the NBA's waiver procedure prior to the first day of the next regular season;

(d) A Team with a Team Salary at or over the Maximum Team Salary may replace a player whose Player Contract has been assigned to another NBA Team with a player or players whose Player Contract(s) call(s) for a Salary no greater than 100%, in the aggregate, of the Salary last paid to the assigned player;

(e) A Team with a Team Salary at or over the Maximum Team Salary may replace a Veteran Free Agent who last previously played for that Team but who does not enter into a new Player Contract with that Team by entering into a Player Contract with a replacement player calling for a Salary no greater than 100% of the Salary last paid to the player being replaced; (i) A player replaced pursuant to either subparagraph C(2) (c) or (e) above may not be re-signed by the Team for which he last previously played if the result would be to increase the Team Salary above the Team Salary at the time the replacement player entered into his Player Contract. . . .

(f) A Team with a Team Salary at or over the Maximum Team Salary may enter into a one-year Player Contract, without an option clause, with a player selected in the College Draft at the minimum player salary then applicable in the NBA; and

(g) (i) A Team with a Team Salary at or over the Maximum Team Salary may replace a player who, due to injury or illness, has been temporarily removed from that Team's Active List by entering into a Player Contract with a replacement player calling for the minimum player salary then applicable in the NBA, pro-rated over the length of the contract entered into by the replacement player; (ii) In the event that a physician designated by the NBA determines that a player, due to injury or illness occurring before the fifty-sixth day after the first game of a scheduled season, will be unable to render his services for the remainder of that season, a Team with a Team Salary at or over the Maximum Team Salary may replace that player by entering into a Player Contract with a replacement player calling for a Salary of no more than 50% of the Salary last paid to the player being replaced. Notwithstanding such a determination, a player who, in fact, recovers from his injury or illness prior to the end of the season, may be restored to the Team's Active List.

(3) With respect to each of the 1984–85, 1985–86 and 1986–87 playing seasons, there shall be a guaranteed Minimum Team Salary designed to result in NBA teams being obligated to pay, in Salary and Benefits (as adjusted pursuant to paragraph C(5) below), 53% of Defined Gross Revenues. The Minimum Team Salary will be computed in accordance with the formula set forth in Exhibit A, annexed hereto. [Note: Exhibit A is not included in these materials.]

(4) (a) . . . On or before the July 31st following the conclusion of the 1983–84, 1984–85, 1985–86 and 1986–87 playing seasons, the NBA will provide to the Players Association a Special Purpose Letter by an independent auditor certifying the Defined Gross Revenues and Benefits of each NBA Team for the immediately preceding season. For purposes of computing the Maximum Team Salary and the Minimum Team Salary for each of the 1984–85, 1985–86 and 1986–87 playing seasons, Defined Gross Revenues and Team Salary shall be projected as follows: Defined Gross Revenues shall be projected to be the Defined Gross Revenues for the immediately preceding season, adjusted to reflect any reduction

or increase in the number of Teams in the NBA, increased by 10%. Team Salary for each Team shall be projected to be the Team Salary for the immediately preceding season, increased by 10%, taking into account all Team and individual performance bonuses actually earned.

(b) For purposes of determining a Team's Team Salary, the Maximum Team Salary and the Minimum Team Salary, any amounts which may be earned as a bonus, relating in any way to the performance of an individual player, shall be included in Team Salary only if such bonus is likely to be earned. Any bonus relating to a Team's performance shall be included in Team Salary, or not included in Team Salary, as the case may be, on the basis of the assumption that the Team's performance will be identical to its performance in the immediately preceding season. . . .

(6) For purposes of this Memorandum, in the case of any NBA player whose salary is paid for any playing season during the term of this Memorandum by more than one NBA Team, the Team for which such player is then playing or has last played, as the case may be, shall be deemed to be paying the entire salary in determining its Team Salary. However, all sums paid as Benefits for, to or on behalf of an NBA player shall be attributable to the NBA team actually paying such sums.

(7) For purposes of this Memorandum, any signing bonus received by any NBA player or contained in a Player Contract shall be allocated, pro rata, over the number of "guaranteed" playing seasons covered by such contract.

(8) A Team with a Team Salary at or over the Maximum Team Salary may not (a) renegotiate an existing Player Contract with any of its players if such renegotiation would serve to increase its Team Salary but may, except in the case of a first year player then signed to a Player Contract, extend any of its Player Contracts without regard to the Maximum Team Salary; or (b) enter into a new Player Contract with a first year player then signed to a Player Contract, until he becomes a Veteran Free Agent. A Team with a Team Salary below the Maximum Team Salary may not renegotiate an existing Player Contract with any of its players if the result would be to increase its Team Salary over the Maximum Team Salary but may, except in the case of a first year player then signed to a Player Contract, extend any of its Player Contracts without regard to the Maximum

Team Salary. In the event that the term of a Player Contract is extended, no salary payable pursuant to the extended term may be paid during the original term of the Player Contract, including, without limitation, signing bonuses . . .

(9) Neither the parties hereto, nor any Team or player shall enter into any agreement, Player Contract, Offer Sheet or other transaction which includes any terms that are designed to serve the purpose of defeating or circumventing the intention of the parties as reflected by (a) the provisions of this Memorandum with respect to Defined Gross Revenues, Maximum Team Salary and Minimum Team Salary and (b) those terms and provisions of the Settlement Agreement which remain in full force and effect as provided in Article I, paragraph D, above. . . .

(11) Article I, Sections 4(a) and (b) of the prior collective bargaining agreement shall be deleted and replaced with the following:

(a) Except as provided in Article I, Section 11, no Player Contract covering a player's playing season shall provide for compensation of less than the following: (1) For the 1983–84 season: $40,000; (2) For the 1984–85 season: $65,000; (3) For the 1985–86 season: $70,000; (4) For the 1986–87 season: $75,000.

(b) Notwithstanding the foregoing, for the 1984–85 through 1986–87 seasons, no Player Contract for a player selected in the first round of the immediately preceding College Draft shall provide for compensation of less than $75,000 for each playing season covered by the Player Contract.

(12) The NBA may conduct the annual College Draft at any time between April 29th and June 15th (or a later date if approved by the Players Association) of each year during the term of this Memorandum. . . .

(14) From the last day after a season during the term hereof until the day prior to the first day of the next regular season, each Team, without regard to the Maximum Team Salary, may enter into Player Contracts, without any guarantees or salary protection. No Player Contract entered into pursuant to this subparagraph may provide for any bonus of any kind, including a signing bonus, or any advance, which is or may be earned prior to the first day of the next regular season. No later than the day prior to the first day of the next regular season, any Team that has entered into any Player

Contract(s) permitted under this subparagraph must reduce its Team Salary to the level at which it would have been in the absence of any such contract(s). Any Player Contract entered into pursuant to this provision may be terminated by the Team to comply with the Maximum Team Salary.

3.34 Severance and Termination Pay

The NFL severance pay provisions which follow are unique to that league. Severance pay provisions were first established in the 1982 NFL collective bargaining agreement. Players who retire or are retired receive a payment based on years of credited service in the league, a provision to be distinguished from other termination pay provisions set forth, which contemplate termination for a variety of other reasons.

National Football League, Article XXXV, Termination Pay

Section 1. Payment: Effective after the execution of this Agreement, any player who has completed the season in which his fourth year or more of Credited Service under the Bert Bell NFL Player Retirement Plan has been earned, and is released from the Active List, Inactive List or Injured Reserve List of his club after the commencement of the regular season schedule, but prior to the Thursday before the eighth regular season game, is entitled to claim and receive, after the end of the regular season schedule, termination pay in an amount equal to the unpaid balance of the initial 50% of his salary, exclusive of deferred compensation, but not less than an amount equal to one week's salary, up to a maximum of $6,000; provided, however, that (a) the player will not be entitled to such termination pay if he has signed a contract with another club for that same season; and (b) a player will not be entitled to such termination pay more than once during his playing career in the NFL.

Section 2. One Week: Any player who otherwise qualifies for terminational pay under Section 1 above, but is released during the regular season after the time he would be entitled to the unpaid balance of the initial 50% of his salary, will receive termination pay in an amount equal to one week's salary, up to a maximum of $6,000.

National Football League, Article XXIV, Severance Pay

Section 1. Amount: Effective November 16, 1982, any player who has earned two (2) or more Credited Seasons under the Bert Bell NFL Player Retirement Plan and leaves the National Football League, will be entitled to receive from the last NFL club to which he was under contract a severance payment in accordance with the schedule below.

Major League Baseball, Article VIII, Termination Pay

A. Off-Season
Effective with contracts tendered after the signing of this Agreement, a Player who is tendered a

Credited Seasons	Last NFL Season 1982, 1983 or 1984	Last NFL Season 1985 or 1986
Two	$ 5,000	$ 10,000
Three	20,000	30,000
Four	60,000	70,000
Five	70,000	80,000
Six	80,000	90,000
Seven	90,000	100,000
Eight	100,000	110,000
Nine	110,000	120,000
Ten	120,000	130,000
Eleven	130,000	140,000
Twelve or more	140,000	150,000

Major League contract which is subsequently terminated by a Club during the period between the end of the championship season and prior to the beginning of the next succeeding spring training under paragraph· 7(b)(2) of the Uniform Player's Contract for failure to exhibit sufficient skill or competitive ability, shall be entitled to receive termination pay from the Club in an amount equal to thirty (30) days payment at the rate stipulated in paragraph 2 of (1) his Contract for the next succeeding championship season, or (2) if he has no contract for the next succeeding championship season, in an amount equal to thirty (30) days payment at the rate stipulated in Paragraph 2 of the contract tendered to him by his Club for the next succeeding championship season.

B. Spring Training

A Player whose Contract is terminated by a Club during spring training under paragraph 7(b)(2) of the Uniform Player's Contract for failure to exhibit sufficient skill or competitive ability, shall be entitled to receive termination pay from the Club in an amount equal to thirty (30) days payment at the rate stipulated in paragraph 2 of his Contract.

C. In-Season

A Player whose Contract is terminated by a Club during the championship season under paragraph 7(b)(2) of the Uniform Player's Contract for failure to exhibit sufficient skill or competitive ability, shall be entitled to receive termination pay from the Club in an amount equal to the unpaid balance of the full salary stipulated in paragraph 2 of his Contract for that season. . . .

E. Non-Duplication

The foregoing provisions of this Article VIII shall be applied regardless of the number of times a Player may be released during a year, subject to the following limitations:

(1) The maximum amount of termination pay which a Player shall be entitled to receive for any year shall not exceed the amount by which

(a) the salary stipulated in the Player's original Contract for such year exceeds

(b) the aggregate amount which the Player earns during that year from any Club or Clubs, including amounts deferred to later years, if any, and bonuses.

(2) In the event a released Player refuses to accept a reasonable Major League Contract

offered by a Club other than the Club which released him, such Player shall forfeit that portion of the termination pay which would not have been payable if such Contract had been accepted.

3.35   Injuries and Medical Care

The rules of all sports leagues provide that a player cannot be released from his contract if he is injured and received the injury through his employment with the club. While injured, players are entitled to both reimbursement for medical care and salary. However, there are limits, and these must be carefully studied by the person representing the athlete. Examples of such limits are set forth below as they pertain to Major League Baseball and to the NFL. Other leagues structure their injury benefits somewhat differently; so these examples should not be accepted as necessarily applicable to other leagues.

Major League Baseball, Article VIII

D. Injury

If a Player's Contract is terminated by a Club by reason of the Player's failure to render his services due to a disability resulting directly from injury sustained in the course and within the scope of his employment under the Contract, and notice is received by the Club in accordance with Regulation 2 of the Uniform Player's Contract, the Player shall be entitled to receive from the Club the unpaid balance of the full salary for the year in which the injury was sustained, less all workmen's compensation payments received by the Player as compensation for loss of income for the specific period for which the Club is compensating him in full.

National Football League, Article X, Injury Protection

Section 1. Qualification: A player qualifying under the following criteria will receive an injury protection benefit in accordance with Section 2 below:

(a) The player must have been physically unable, because of a severe football injury in an NFL game or practice, to participate in all or part of his club's last game of the season of injury, as certified by the club physician following a physical examination after the last game; or the player must have undergone club-authorized surgery in the off-season following the season of injury; and

(b) The player must have undergone whatever reasonable and customary rehabilitation treatment his club required of him during the off-season following the season of injury; and

(c) The player must have failed the pre-season physical examination given by the club physician for the season following the season of injury because of such injury and as a result his club must have terminated his contract for the season following the season of injury. The past understanding of the parties concerning a club releasing a player who otherwise qualifies under (a) and (b) above prior to the pre-season physical examination, will be continued during the term of this Agreement.*

Section 2. Benefit: Effective after the execution of this Agreement, a player qualifying under Section 1 above will receive an amount equal to 50% of his contract salary for the season following the season of injury, up to a maximum payment of $65,000, unless he has individually negotiated more injury protection into that contract. A player will receive no amount of any contract covering any season subsequent to the season following the season of injury, except if he has individually negotiated injury protection into that contract. The benefit will be paid to the player in equal weekly installments commencing no later than the date of the first regular season game, which benefit payments will cease if the player signs a contract for that season with another NFL club. A player will not be entitled to such benefit more than once during his playing career in the NFL.

Section 3. Disputes: Any dispute under this Article will be processed under Article VII of this Agreement, Non-Injury Grievance.

* This understanding is recited in a letter from the Management Council, dated June 29, 1977, which states, ". . . it was agreed that a player who qualifies for 'Injury Protection' under subsections (a) and (b) may be waived prior to being given a pre-season physical examination, but the waiving club would retain 'Injury Protection' liability unless and until the player signed a contract with and passed the physical examination of another NFL club. In other words, a club cannot evade 'Injury Protection' liability by early waiving."

National Football League, Article XXXI, Players' Rights to Medical Care and Treatment

Section 1. Club Physician: Each club will have a board certified orthopedic surgeon as one of its club physicians. The cost of medical services rendered by Club physicians will be the responsibility of the respective clubs. If a Club physician advises a coach or other Club representative of a player's physical condition which could adversely affect the player's performance or health, the physician will also advise the player.

Section 2. Club Trainers: All full-time head trainers and assistant trainers hired after the date of execution of this Agreement will be certified by the National Athletic Trainers Association. All part-time trainers must work under the direct supervision of a certified trainer.

Section 3. Players' Right to a Second Medical Opinion: A player will have the opportunity to obtain a second medical opinion. As a condition of the responsibility of the Club for the costs of medical services rendered by the physician furnishing the second opinion, the player must (a) consult with the Club physician in advance concerning the other physician; and (b) the Club physician must be furnished promptly with a report concerning the diagnosis, examination and course of treatment recommended by the other physician.

Section 4. Players' Right to a Surgeon of His Choice: A player will have the right to choose the surgeon who will perform surgery provided that: (a) the player will consult with the Club physician as to his recommendation as to the need for, the timing of and who should perform the surgery; and (b) the player will give due consideration to the Club physician's recommendations. Any such surgery will be at Club expense; provided, however, that the Club, the Club physician, the Club trainers and any other representative of the Club will not be responsible for or incur any liability (other than the cost of the surgery) for or relating to the adequacy or competency of such surgery or other related medical services rendered in connection with such surgery.

Section 5. Standard Minimum Pre-Season Physical: Beginning in 1983, each player will undergo a standardized minimum pre-season physical examination, outlined in Appendix D, which will be conducted by the Club physician. If either the Club or the player requests a post-season physical examination, the Club will provide such an examination and player will cooperate in such examination.

Section 6. Chemical Dependency Program: The parties agree that it is the responsibility of everyone in the industry to treat, care for and eliminate chemical dependency problems of players. Accordingly, the parties agree to jointly designate Hazelden Foundation, Center City, Minnesota or its successor if such becomes necessary, to evaluate existing facilities to assure the highest degree of care and treatment and to assure the strictest observance of confidentiality. Any treatment facility which does not meet standards of adequacy will be eliminated and a successor facility in the same metropolitan area chosen solely by Hazelden. Hazelden will be responsible for conducting an ongoing educational program for all players and Club personnel regarding the detection, treatment and aftercare of chemically dependent persons. The cost of retaining Hazelden will be paid by the clubs.

Section 7. Testing: The club physician may, upon reasonable cause, direct a player to Hazelden for testing for chemical abuse or dependency problems. There will not be any spot checking for chemical abuse or dependency by the club or club physician.

Section 8. Confidentiality: All medical bills incurred by any player at a local treatment facility will be processed exclusively through Hazelden which will eliminate all information identifying the patient before forwarding the bills to any insurance carrier for payment. Details concerning treatment any player receives will remain confidential within Hazelden and the local chemical dependency facility. After consultation with Hazelden and the player, the facility will advise the club of the player's treatment and such advice will not in and of itself be the basis for any disciplinary action. No information regarding a player's treatment will be publicly disclosed by Hazelden, the facility, or the club.

3.36   Assignments, Waivers, Releases

Previously set forth in comparative contract provisions were several examples relating to contract assignment. (See Section 3.22–4.) The

impact that collective bargaining provisions can have on the standard contract clauses is illustrated by the important modifications on a right to assign contained in Major League Baseball's collective agreement, detailed below.

In addition, the excerpts from collective agreements below also specify waiver and release procedures. The examples chosen are those for Major League Baseball and the NFL. These excerpts introduce a flavor of the procedures but should not be considered exhaustive.

Major League Baseball, Article XVII, Assignment of Player Contracts

A. Consent to Assignment

(1) The contract of a Player with ten or more years of Major League service, the last five of which have been with one Club, shall not be assignable to another Major League Club without the Player's written consent.

(2) The contract of a Player with five or more years of Major League service, not including service while on the Military List (or with seven or more years of Major League service, including service while on the Military List), shall not be assigned otherwise than to another Major League Club, without the Player's written consent.

B. Assignment to National Association Club

When a Player's contract is assigned from a Major League Club to a National Association Club, the rights and benefits of such Player that do, and do not, follow him to the National Association shall be in accordance with past practices. Additionally, such a Player shall retain the right, if any, to become a free agent, or to require the assignment of his contract, which he possessed under his then current Major League contract . . .

C. Disabled List — Assignment to National Association Club

There shall be no assignment of a Player by a Major League Club to a National Association Club while such Player is on a Major League Disabled List; provided, however, that with the Player's written consent, a copy of which shall be forwarded to the Players Association, and with the approval of the League President, a Player on the Disabled List may be assigned to a National Association Club for up to a maximum of twenty days for the purpose of rehabilitation. . . .

F. Waivers

Major League waiver requests on any one Player shall not be withdrawn by the same Club more than once in the period beginning November 11 in one calendar year and ending November 10 in the following calendar year. When waivers are asked for a second time on a Player whose contract has been claimed previously in one of the periods referred to above, the waiver request shall state that this is the second request by the asking Club and is irrevocable. . .

H. Interleague Trading

An additional interleague trading period will be provided under Major League Rule 10(a) during which a Major League Club may assign a Player's contract to a Club of the other League, without waivers, in the period starting 12:01 A.M., Pacific Coast Time, February 15 and ending at midnight, April 1, Pacific Coast Time . . .

I. Unconditional Release

Notwithstanding anything to the contrary provided in Major League Rule 8 and paragraph 7(d) of the Uniform Player's Contract, the following procedure may be used to give notice to a Player in connection with his unconditional release.

At the same time the Club advises a Player in writing that the Club has requested waivers for the purpose of unconditional release, and the date on which the waiver request will expire, the Player shall advise the Club in writing of the address and telephone number to which the Club should telephone or telegraph notice of termination to the Player upon the expiration of the waiver period. If the Player fails to supply a telephone number or address, the Club may use the most recent address or telephone number the Player has supplied the Club.

Upon the expiration of the waiver period, the Club shall either give notice to the Player by telephone or by sending a telegraph notice of termination to the Player. In addition the Player may make a collect telephone call to the Club to determine whether his contract has been claimed . . .

National Football League, Article XVI, Waiver System

Section 1. Release: Whenever a player who has completed the season in which his fourth year or more of Credited Service under the provisions of the Bert Bell NFL Player Retirement Plan has been earned is placed on waivers, claimed and would be awarded, the club having requested waivers will immediately advise the player of such fact, provided the waiver request has taken place within the time period of February 1 to the end of the NFL trading period. Within 24 hours after receipt of such information, the player may, at his option, given written notice to the club having requested waivers that he desires to terminate his contract or contracts and obtain his unconditional release. However, should the player fail to give such notice within the 24-hour period, his contract will be awarded to the claiming club in accordance with the rules prescribed in the NFL Constitution and Bylaws. In the event the player requests his unconditional release, the player and the NFLPA will be advised promptly by the NFL which clubs claimed the player.

Section 2. Contact: Coaches or any other persons connected with another NFL club are prohibited from contacting any player placed on waivers until such time as the player is released by the waiving club.

Section 3: Ineligibility: Any NFL player who is declared ineligible to compete in a pre-season, regular season or post-season game because of a breach of waiver procedures and regulations or any other provision of the NFL Constitution and Bylaws by any NFL club by whom he is employed will be paid the salary or other compensation which he would have received if he had not been declared ineligible, which, in any event, will be a minimum of one week's salary and, when applicable, expense payments.

Section 4. Notice of Termination: The Notice of Termination form attached as Exhibit E will be used by all clubs. If possible, the Notice of Termination will be personally delivered to the player prior to his departure from the team. If the Notice of Termination has not been personally delivered to the player prior to his departure from the team, the Notice of Termination will be sent to him by certified mail at his last address on file with the club.

NOTICE OF TERMINATION

...., ...

TO: ....

You are hereby notified that effective immediately your NFL Player contract(s) with the Club covering the .... football season (s) has been terminated for the reason(s) checked below:

[   ] You have failed to establish or maintain your excellent physical condition to the satisfaction of the Club physician.

[   ] You have failed to make full and complete disclosure of your physical or mental condition during a physical examination.

[   ] In the judgment of the Club, your skill or performance has been unsatisfactory as compared with that of other players competing for positions on the Club's roster.

[   ] You have engaged in personal conduct which, in the reasonable judgment of the Club, adversely affects or reflects on the Club.

....

Club

By: ....

3.37 Benefits: Preseason, Moving, Travel, Group Insurance and Others

Major League Baseball, Article VI, Expenses and Expense Allowances

A. Transportation and Travel Expenses

Each Club shall pay the following expenses of Players:

(1) All proper and necessary traveling expenses of Players while "abroad," or traveling with the Club in other cities, including board, and first-class jet air and hotel accommodations, if practicable.

Each Club shall give written notice to the team's Player Representative and the Players Association, prior to February 1 of each year, of the in-season hotels the Club intends to utilize during the next succeeding season.

On regularly scheduled commercial flights, when first-class accommodations cannot practicably be provided and Players travel in the coach section the Club shall provide three seats for each two Players and first-class meals.

(2) First-class jet air fare and meals en route, of Players to their homes at the end of the season, regardless of where the Club finishes its season. . . .

(3) All necessary traveling expenses, including first-class jet air fare and meals en route of Players from their home cities to the spring training place of the Club, whether they are ordered to go there directly or by way of the home city of the Club.

(4) In the case of assignment of a Player's contract during the championship season or during spring training, all traveling expenses, including first-class jet air fare and meals en route, of the Player as may be necessary to enable him to report to the assignee Club.

(5) In the case of termination by the Club of a Player's contract during the championship season or during spring training, reasonable traveling expenses, including first-class jet air fare and meals en route, to the Player's home city . . .

B. In-Season Meal and Tip Allowance

(1) During the championship season, each Player shall receive a daily meal and tip allowance for each date a Club is on the road and for each traveling day. No deductions will be made for meals served on an airplane.

(2) If, when a Club departs from the home city, departure is scheduled prior to 12:00 Noon, Players will receive the full daily allowance for that date; if departure is after 12:00 Noon, Players will receive one-half of the daily allowance for that date. Returning to the home city, if arrival is later than 6:00 P.M., Players will receive the full daily allowance; if arrival is prior to 6:00 P.M., Players will receive one-half of the daily allowance. The Club may require the Player to sign checks for meals at a hotel in lieu of the cash meal allowance.

(3) During the 1980 championship season, the daily allowance shall be $33.50. During the 1981, 1982 and 1983 championship seasons, the daily allowance shall be a base of $33.50 plus a cost of living adjustment to the nearest $.50, provided, however, that the cost of living adjustment shall not reduce the daily allowance below $33.50 . . .

C. Spring Training Allowances

[These are weekly allowances, escalating each year of the term of the agreement, and varying depending on whether the Player lives at the club's headquarters or in his own accommodations.]

D. Single Rooms On The Road

A Player may elect prior to the commencement of the championship season to have single rooms in the Club's hotels on all road trips. The cost of such rooms shall be paid by the Player except that the Club shall pay a portion of the cost equal to 50% of the Club's usual rate for a double room at the hotels involved. In the event the Player elects to have single rooms, the Club shall arrange to have such rooms made available to him at the Club's usual rate for single rooms at the hotels involved. Nothing herein shall prohibit the Clubs from making or continuing agreements with individual Players which provide more favorable arrangements for such Players.

E. All-Star Game

A Player who is a member of his League's All-Star team shall, in addition to being reimbursed in accordance with past practice, be reimbursed by the League for the first-class jet air fare within the continental United States and Canada to and from the site of the All-Star Game for one guest, and for hotel accommodations for a maximum of three days for such guest.

Major League Baseball, Article VII, Moving Allowances

A. If a Player's contract is assigned by a Major League Club to another Major League Club during the championship season, the assignee Club shall pay the Player, for all moving and other expenses resulting from such assignment the sum of $300 if the contract is assigned between Clubs in the same zone; the sum of $600 if the contract is assigned between a Club in the Eastern Zone and a Club in the Central Zone; the sum of $900 if the contract is assigned between a Club in the Central Zone and a Club in the Western Zone; and the sum of $1,200 if the contract is assigned between a Club in the Eastern Zone and a Club in the Western Zone . . .

B. A Player may elect, within one year after the date of the assignment of his contract, regardless of when his contract is assigned or whether the assignment is between Major League Clubs or a Major League Club and a National Association club, to be reimbursed for (1) the reasonable and actual moving expenses of the Player and his immediate family resulting therefrom, including first-class jet air transportation for the Player and his immediate family, and (2) all rental payments for living quarters in the city from which he is transferred (and/or spring training location, if applicable), for which he is legally obligated after the date of assignment and for which he is not otherwise reimbursed. Such rental payments shall not include any period beyond the end of a season or prior to the start of spring training. The Club paying reimbursement for rent shall have use and/or the right to rent such living quarters for the period covered by the rental reimbursement . . .

C. If a Player's contract is assigned by a Major League Club to another Major League Club during the championship season, the assignee Club shall pay to the Player an in-season supplemental moving allowance, for the Player's first seven days in the assignee Club's home city, up to a maximum of $500.00. This in-season supplemental allowance will reimburse the Player, based upon valid expense vouchers or receipts, for the following expenses:

(i) car rental and/or local transportation
(ii) motel/hotel lodging
(iii) meals

National Football League, Article XXXIII, Group Insurance

Section 1. Life: Effective after the execution of this Agreement, group insurance coverage will be increased to $50,000 for a rookie player, and a veteran player's coverage will be increased by $10,000 for each Credited Season under the Bert Bell NFL Player Retirement Plan to a maximum of $100,000.

Section 2. Major Medical: Effective after the execution of this Agreement, the group major medical maximum for a player and his family will be increased to $1,000,000, and, subject to the $25 deductible, 80% of the first $3,000 and 100% of the excess eligible medical expenses for a player will be reimbursed.

Section 3. Dental: Effective after the execution of this Agreement, there will be a 75% increase, not to exceed reasonable and customary charges, in the dental benefit schedule; the dental maximum will be increased to $2,000 per year per person subject to the $25 deductible . . .

National Basketball Association, Article V, Travel Accommodations, Locker Room Facilities and Parking

Section 1. Each Member agrees to use its best efforts to make the following arrangements for its players while they are "on the road":

(a) To have their baggage picked up by porters.

(b) To have them stay in first class hotels.

(c) To have extra-long beds available to them in each hotel.

Section 2. Each Member agrees to provide first class transportation accommodations on all trips in excess of one hour, except when such accommodations are not available.

Section 3. Each Member agrees to use its best efforts to improve locker room facilities and to stabilize the temperature in locker rooms to make it consistent with the temperature on playing courts.

Section 4. Each Member agrees to make parking facilities available to its players without charge in connection with games and practices conducted at the facility regularly used by such Member for home games and/or practices.

3.38   Club Discipline

Professional sports leagues and clubs feel it necessary to set guidelines for player conduct on and off the playing field. While these rules often emanate from management policies, today the normal procedure is to base the authority for imposing disciplinary rules on agreement between management and union in the league's collective bargaining agreement. The NFL provisions below illustrate this approach. The same result is reached in the NBA contract, appearing earlier in this chapter as Exhibit 3–1. In the NBA, management rules included in the league's constitution and by-laws are incorporated into the league's collective bargaining agreement and attached to the NBA's Uniform Player Contract.

National Football League, Article VI, Club Discipline

Section 1. Maximum Discipline: The following maximum discipline schedule will be applicable for the duration of this Agreement:

Overweight — maximum fine of $25 per lb./per day.

Unexcused late reporting for mandatory off-season training camp, team meeting, practice, transportation, curfew, scheduled appointment with club physician or trainer, or scheduled promotional activity — maximum fine of $100.

Failure to promptly report injury to club physician or trainer — maximum fine of $100.

Losing, damaging or altering club-provided equipment — maximum fine of $100 and replacement cost, if any.

Throwing football into stands — maximum fine of $100.

Unexcused late reporting for or absence from pre-season training camp — maximum fine of $1,000 per day.

Unexcused missed mandatory off-season training camp, team meeting, practice, curfew, bed check, scheduled appointment with club physician or trainer, or scheduled promotional activity — maximum fine of $500.

Unexcused missed team transportation — maximum fine of $500 and transportation expense, if any.

Loss of all or part of playbook, scouting report or game plan — maximum fine of $500.

Ejection from game — maximum fine of $500.

Conduct detrimental to club — maximum fine of an amount equal to one week's salary and/or suspension without pay for a period not to exceed four (4) weeks.

Discipline will be imposed uniformly within a club on all players for the same offense; however, the club may specify the events which create an escalation of the discipline, provided the formula for escalation is uniform in its application.

The club will promptly notify the player of any discipline; notice of any club fine in the $1,000 maximum category and of any "conduct detrimental" fine or suspension will be sent to the NFLPA.

Section 2. Published Lists: All clubs must publish and make available to all players at the commencement of pre-season training camp a complete list of the discipline which can be imposed for designated offenses within the limits set by the maximum schedule referred to in Section 1 above.

Section 3. Uniformity: Discipline will be imposed uniformly within a club on all players for the same offense; however, the club may specify the events which create an escalation of the discipline, provided the formula for escalation is uniform in its application. Any disciplinary action imposed upon a player by the Commissioner pursuant to Article VII of this Agreement will preclude or supersede disciplinary action by the club for the same act or conduct.

Section 4. Disputes: any dispute involved in club discipline may be made the subject of a non-injury grievance under Article VII of this Agreement, Non-Injury Grievance.

Section 5. Deductions: Any club fine will be deducted at the rate of no more than $250 from each pay period, if sufficient pay periods remain; or, if less than sufficient pay periods remain, the fine will be deducted in equal installments over the number of remaining pay periods. This will not apply to a suspension.

3.39 Future Actions

Matters are seldom stable in the sports industries. New concerns arise and must be addressed. A provision from the 1983 NBA Agreement illustrates some current concerns that will probably require future action, not only by the affected parties in the NBA but likely in other leagues as well. These concerns are hardly exhaustive of what lies ahead for resolution, but their importance is underscored by their inclusion in at least one league's collective bargaining agreement.

National Basketball Association, 1983 Memorandum of Agreement, Article IV

L. The NBA and the Players Association agree to create joint committees which shall meet and negotiate in good faith with respect to:

(1) continued education for NBA players who have not graduated from college;

(2) outplacement and career counselling for retiring NBA players;

(3) procedures for the conduct of off-season exhibition games;

(4) drug and alcohol abuse.

3.40 Collective Bargaining Provisions: Restrictions on Player Mobility

As the foregoing collective bargaining excerpts illustrate, security for the professional athlete has been a priority of the players' associations in all the major sports leagues. Pension plans, minimum salaries, benefits such as life and medical insurance, and other fringes deemed essential to putting some sense of stability into careers that might last anywhere from a couple of years to a couple of decades were the first orders of business. As these benefits were realized, other issues came to the fore.

At the top of the list have been the player mobility issues. Players have long contended that the key to increased prosperity lies in free agency — the ability of the player at the end of a contract to bargain with and move to other clubs. Since the late 1800s, owners have employed numerous devices that consign a player to a given club, permanently, unless the player is traded, waived, or released. Systems utilizing a draft of eligible amateurs, contracts with options and reserve clauses, rights of first refusal, and compensation provisions when a player does move to a new club have all impeded a free and open player market.

The current collective bargaining agreements, spurred by concerted union activity and the forces of favorable antitrust (see Section 2.40) and arbitration (see Section 5.30) decisions, have moved significantly away from the traditional restraints. Even so, leagues still impose limitations on the ability of a player to freely market himself.

The nature and extent of the restraints vary from one league to another. These variations significantly alter the bases for dealings in the different leagues. The excerpts which follow do not set forth all the nuances of the various approaches, but they do illustrate the major concepts. The subsections examine the draft, options, grounds for free agency, rights of first refusal, and free agent compensation. Within each subsection, the league differences are noted. Extensive excerpts from the current collective bargaining agreements are included for analysis, although in actual practice the full text must be consulted. Finally, a summary chart compares the approaches of the different leagues and sports.

Collective bargaining provisions of the NHL relating to player movement have not been included in the examples set forth in the following subsections. The NHL provisions, however, are discussed in the introductory text to the subsections and are summarized in the table in Section 3.46.

3.41 Draft

The NFL and NBA both detail provisions for the draft of eligible players in the leagues' respective collective bargaining agreements. One significant difference between the two, however, is that the NFL agreement does not specify eligibility rules for potential draftees, while the NBA does detail the basis for eligibility. The absence of such provisions in the NFL agreement has led to speculation as to whether the NFL can continue to impose stringent eligibility requirements on players with remaining college eligibility. (See Chapter 4, Section 4.71 for further analysis of this problem.)

The NHL and Major League Baseball do not include draft provisions in their collective agreements. With baseball's continuing antitrust exemption, few problems arising from this omission are posed. (See Chapter 2, Sections 2.22 and 2.24.) The NHL is not similarly blessed, however, and that league cannot rely on the labor exemption to immunize its drafting procedures. (See Chapter 2, Section 2.43.)

National Football League, Article XIII, College Draft

Section 1. Time of Draft: Commencing with the college draft to be held on or about May 1, 1983, and with respect to the college draft to be held on or about May 1 each year thereafter, through at least 1992, the following principles will apply; provided, however, that commencing in 1984 the clubs will have the right during the term of this Agreement to move the date of the draft from on or about May 1 to on or about February 1 of the same year, but no later than six days after the Pro Bowl game or, in the absence of a Pro Bowl game, ten days after the Super Bowl game.

Section 2. Number of Choices: There will be no more than 336 selection choices in any college draft (in the event of NFL expansion, there will be an addition 12 selection choices per expansion club, except in the first year of expansion, when the expansion clubs may be given additional choices) . . .

Section 3. Exclusive Right: A club which drafts a player will, during the period from the date of such college draft (hereinafter "initial draft") to the date of the next college draft (hereinafter "subsequent draft"), be the only NFL club which may negotiate for or sign a contract with such player. If, within the period between the initial and subsequent draft, such player has not signed a contract with the club which drafted him in the initial draft, such club loses the exclusive right, which it obtained in the initial draft, to negotiate for a contract with the player and the player is then eligible to be drafted by another NFL club in the subsequent draft.

Section 4. Subsequent Draft: A club which, in the subsequent draft drafts a player who (a) was drafted in the initial draft, and (b) did not sign a contract with such first NFL club prior to the subsequent draft, will, during the period from the date of the college draft held in the following year, be the only NFL club which may negotiate for or sign a contract with such player. If such player has not signed a contract within the period between the subsequent draft and the next college draft with the club which drafted him in the subsequent draft, that club loses its exclusive right, which it obtained in the subsequent draft, to negotiate for a contract with the player, and the player is free to sign a contract at any time thereafter with any NFL club, and any NFL club is then free to negotiate for and sign a contract with such player, without any compensation between clubs or first refusal rights of any kind.

Section 5. No Subsequent Draft: If a player is drafted by an NFL club in an initial draft and (a) does not sign a contract with an NFL club prior to the subsequent draft and (b) is not drafted by any NFL club in such subsequent draft, the player is free to sign a contract at any time thereafter with an NFL club, and any NFL club is then free to negotiate for and sign a contract with such player, without any compensation between clubs or first refusal rights of any kind.

Section 6. Other Professional Team: If a player is hereafter drafted by an NFL club in an initial draft and, during the period in which he may sign a contract with only the club which drafted him, plays for a professional football team not in the NFL under a contract that covers all or part of at least the season immediately following said initial draft, then such NFL club will retain the exclusive NFL rights to negotiate for and sign a contract with the player for the period ending four years from the date of the initial draft, following which four-year period the player is free to sign a contract with any NFL club, and any NFL club is free to negotiate for and sign a contract with such player, subject to Section 7 below.

Section 7. Return to NFL: If a player who hereafter signs a contract with a professional football team not in the NFL desires to return to the NFL four or more years following the date of his initial draft, the NFL club which had drafted the player will have no right of compensation under Article XV, but will have a right of first refusal under the applicable terms and conditions of that Article . . .

Section 9. Assignment: In the event that the exclusive right to negotiate for a player or the right of first refusal under Section 7 above is assigned by an NFL club to another NFL club, the NFL club to which such right has been assigned will have the same, but no greater, right to negotiate for such player or to exercise the right of first refusal as is enjoyed by the club assigning such right, and such player will have the same, but no greater, obligation to the NFL club to which such right has been assigned as he had to the club assigning such right . . .

National Basketball Association, Article XXII

(1) Under present NBA rules, a Team which drafts a player in a College Draft is the only Team with which such player may negotiate and sign a Player Contract. The present NBA rules place no time limitation on the duration of the exclusive right of a Team, obtained in the College Draft, to negotiate with such player.

(2) Commencing with the College Draft which is to be held between April 29, 1976 and June 10, 1976, and with respect to the College Draft to be held each year thereafter in the period March 1 to June 10, up to and including the College Draft to be held in 1986:

(a) A Team which drafts a player shall, during the period from the date of such draft (hereinafter "initial draft") to the date of the next College Draft (hereinafter "subsequent draft"), be the only Team with which such player may negotiate or sign a Player Contract, provided that, on or before the September 5 immediately following the initial draft, such Team has tendered to such player a Player Contract in the form prescribed . . .

(i) A Player Contract with a stated term of no more than one year, which contract must call for at least the minimum salary, if any, then applicable in the NBA, and may contain an Option Clause of one year, exercisable once for at least the same salary; or

(ii) A Player Contract with a stated term of four years, calling for a salary in years one through four, respectively, of at least $75,000, $90,000, $100,000 and $110,000, and providing that in the event the contract is terminated by the team in accordance with Paragraph 20(b)(2) or 20(c) of the Uniform Player Contract, the team shall nevertheless be obligated to pay the player the guaranteed amount of $120,000 . . .

(iii) A Player Contract with a stated term of five years, calling for a salary in years one through five, respectively, of at least $75,000, $90,000, $100,000, $110,000 and $125,000, and providing that in the event the contract is terminated by the team in accordance with Paragraphs 20(b)(2) or 20(c) of the Uniform Player Contract, the team shall nevertheless be obligated to pay the player the guaranteed amount of $165,000 . . .

(b) A Team which, in the subsequent draft, drafts a player who (i) was drafted in the initial draft, (ii) received a required tender from the Team which drafted him in the initial draft and (iii) did not sign a Player Contract with such first Team prior to the subsequent draft, shall, during the period from the date of the subsequent draft to the date of the College Draft held in the following year, be the only Team with which such player may negotiate or sign a Player Contract, provided such Team has made a required tender. If such player has not signed a Player Contract within the period between the subsequent draft and the next College Draft with the Team which drafted him in the subsequent draft, that Team loses its exclusive right, which it obtained in the subsequent draft, to negotiate with the player, and the player is free to negotiate and sign a Player Contract at any time thereafter with any Team, and any Team is then free to negotiate and sign a Player Contract with such player, without any penalty or restriction, including, but not limited to, compensation between Teams or first refusal rights of any kind.

(c) If a player is drafted in an initial draft and (i) receives a required tender, (ii) does not sign a Player Contract with a Team prior to the subsequent draft and (iii) is not drafted by any Team in such subsequent draft, the player is free to negotiate and sign a Player Contract at any time thereafter with any Team . . .

(d) If a player is drafted by a Team and that Team does not make a required tender to such player, the player is free to negotiate and sign a Player Contract with any Team on the September 6 following such draft and at any time thereafter, and any Team is then free to negotiate and sign a Player Contract with such player, without any penalty or restriction, including, but not limited to, compensation between Teams or first refusal rights of any kind.

(e) If a player is drafted by a Team in either an initial or subsequent draft and, during a period in which he may negotiate and sign a Player Contract with only the Team which drafted him, signs a player contract with a professional basketball team not in the NBA that covers at least the season immediately following said initial or subsequent draft, then such Team shall retain the exclusive NBA rights to negotiate with and sign the player for the period ending one year from the earlier of the following two dates: (i) the date the player notifies such Team that he is available to sign a Player Contract with such Team immediately, provided that such notice will not be effective until

the player is under no contractual or other legal impediment to sign with such Team, or (ii) the date of the College Draft occurring in the twelve-month period from September 1 to August 30 in which the player notifies such Team of his availability and intention to play in the NBA during the season immediately following said twelve-month period, provided that such notice will not be effective until the player is under no contractual or other legal impediment to play with such Team for said season. If during said one-year period the player signs a player contract with a team in another professional basketball league and (a) the player has not made a bona fide effort to negotiate a Player Contract with the Team with the exclusive NBA rights to negotiate with and sign such player or (b) if such bona fide effort is made and such Team makes a bona fide offer of a Player Contract to such player, then such Team shall retain the exclusive NBA right to negotiate with and sign the player for additional one-year periods as measured in the preceding sentence, but if the player has made such bona fide effort and such Team fails to make a bona fide offer of a Player Contract to such player, then in no event shall said exclusive NBA right be retained . . .

(f) A person whose high school class has graduated shall become eligible to be selected in a College Draft if he renounces his intercollegiate basketball eligibility by written notice to the NBA at least 45 days prior to such draft. If such person is selected in such draft by a Team, the following rules apply:

(i) If the player does not thereafter play intercollegiate basketball, then the Team which drafted him shall, during the period from the date of such draft to the date of the draft in which the player would, absent renunciation of intercollegiate eligibility, first have been eligible to be selected, be the only team with which the player may negotiate or sign a Player Contract, provided that such Team makes a required tender to the player each year. For purposes hereof, the draft in which such player would, absent renunciation of such intercollegiate eligibility, first have been eligible to be selected, will be deemed the "subsequent draft" as to that player, and the rules applicable to a player who has been drafted in a subsequent draft will apply. If the player, having been selected in a draft for which he was eligible by virtue of renunciation of intercollegiate eligibility, has not signed a Player Contract with the Team which drafted him in such draft following required tenders by that Team and is not drafted in the draft in which he would, absent renunciation of intercollegiate eligibility, first have been eligible to be selected, he is free, at any time thereafter, to negotiate and sign a Player Contract with such player, without any penalty or restriction, including, but not limited to, compensation between Teams or first refusal rights of any kind.

(ii) If the player does thereafter play intercollegiate basketball, then the Team which drafted him shall, during the period from the date of such draft to the date of the draft in which the player would, absent renunciation of intercollegiate eligibility, first have been eligible to be selected, be the only Team with which the player may negotiate or sign a Player Contract, provided that such Team makes a required tender to the Player each year . . .

NOTE

1. In the 1983 NBA Memorandum Agreement, the league and players' association agreed to delete subsections (i), (ii) and (iii) of (2) (a) appearing above. Instead of the detailed minimum salaries that must be tendered rookies under certain conditions, the following language was substituted: "A Player Contract with a stated term of one year, which contract must call for at least the minimum salary then applicable in the NBA." See Memorandum of Understanding, Article III (C) (10).

3.42 Options

The traditional sports contract in the various leagues invariably provided that a club could retain the player's services for an additional year if the club chose to exercise an option running in its favor. This approach supplanted the earlier perpetual reserve clauses, when the latter were declared illegal in all sports except baseball.

At the present time, even the option has undergone substantial modifications. The NFL and NBA provisions emphasize that, at least for many players in those leagues, options are not automatically included. The option must be individually negotiated. As a consequence, while options are still used in both leagues, they are not

used with the frequency that once existed. This is particularly true for NBA contracts.

The NHL has a complicated dual option system, but this is detailed in the league's uniform contract and does not appear separately in the league's collective bargaining agreement.

Options have become relatively rare in baseball, though some are still individually negotiated. The collective bargaining agreement and standard player contract for Major League Baseball are silent concerning options.

National Football League, Article XIV, Option Clause

Section 1. Vested Players: Any contract or series of contracts signed by a veteran player who has completed the season in which his fourth year or more of Credited Service under the Bert Bell NFL Player Retirement Plan has been earned will not include an option year, unless an option clause has been negotiated for the player for a specific consideration other than compensation for the player's services.

Section 2. Rookies and Non-Vested Players: Any one-year contract signed by a rookie player must include an option year; any other contract or series of contracts signed by a rookie player may include an option year; and any contract or series of contracts signed by a veteran player who has not completed the season in which his fourth year of Credited Service under the Bert Bell NFL Player Retirement Plan has been earned may include an option year.

Section 3. Compensation: The option will be exercised by the club at no less than 110% of the player's salary provided in his contract for the previous year, excluding any signing or reporting bonus. Player will receive 100% of performance bonus provisions where the bonus is earned in the option year.

National Basketball Association, Article XXII

(6) From April 29, 1976 to the end of the 1986-1987 season, Player Contracts entered into shall not contain any Option Clause except that:

(a) There may be an Option Clause in a Player Contract signed by a Rookie, but only if such contract has a stated term of not more than one year, subject to Section 6(b) below. Such Option Clause may authorize the extension of such contract for no more than one year beyond the stated term, may be exercisable only once, and shall provide that the compensation payable with respect to the option year shall be no less than 100% of the total compensation payable with respect to the stated one-year term of the contract and that all other non-monetary terms contained in such Player Contract shall be applicable in the option year.

(b) There may be an Option Clause in (i) a Veteran's contract or (ii) a Rookie's contract which is for a stated term of more than one year, provided that such Option Clause is specifically negotiated between such Veteran or Rookie and a Team, authorizes the extension of such contract for no more than one year beyond the stated term, is exercisable only once and provides that the compensation payable with respect to the option year is no less than 100% of the total compensation payable with respect to the last year of the stated term of such contract and that all other non-monetary terms applicable in the last year of the stated term of such contract shall be applicable in the option year. Any Player Contract for a Veteran or such a Rookie may contain an option in favor of the player. Other than the Uniform Player Contract to be used for a Rookie to be employed for a single season, no Option Clause may appear in a Uniform Player Contract.

3.43   Free Agency

Major League Baseball requires that a player has six full years of credited major league service before he can become a free agent. Since many baseball players in their early years go back and forth between the major and minor leagues, more than six playing seasons are often required to obtain free agent status. The requirements for the other major team sports are less stringent but nevertheless contain limitations on the ability of a player to obtain or retain free agent status. The collective bargaining excerpts below illustrate some of the approaches.

National Football League, Article XV, Right of First Refusal/Compensation

Section 17. Re-Signing: If no offer to sign a contract or contracts with a new NFL club pursuant to this Article is received by a player, and his old club advises the NFLPA in writing by June 1 that it desires to re-sign him, the player may, at his option within 15 days sign either (a) a contract or contracts with his old club at its last best written offer given on or before February 1 of that year, or (b) a one-year contract (with no option year) with his old club at 110% of the salary provided in his contract for the last preceding year (if the player has just played out the option year the rate will be 120%). If the player's old club does not advise the NFLPA in writing by June 1 that it desires to re-sign the player, he will be free on June 2 to sign a contract or contracts with any NFL club, and any NFL club will be free to negotiate for and sign a contract or contracts with such player, without any compensation between clubs or first refusal rights of any kind.

National Basketball Association, Article IV, 1983 Amendments

C. A Player who withholds his playing services during the last season of his Player Contract shall be deemed not to have "complet[ed] his Player Contract by rendering the playing services called for thereunder." Accordingly, such player shall not be a Veteran Free Agent and shall not be entitled to negotiate or sign a contract with any other professional basketball team unless and until the Team for which the player last previously played expressly agrees otherwise . . .

Major League Basketball, Article XVIII, Reserve System

A. Reservation Rights of Clubs
Subject to the rights of Players as set forth in this Agreement, each Club may have title to and reserve up to 40 Player contracts. A Club shall retain title to a contract and reservation rights until one of the following occurs:

(1) The Player becomes a free agent, as set forth in this Article;

(2) The Player becomes a free agent as a result of

(a) termination of the contract by the Club pursuant to paragraph 7(b) thereof,

(b) termination of the contract by the Player pursuant to paragraph 7(a) thereof,

(c) failure by the Club to tender to the Player a new contract within the time period specified in paragraph 10(a) of the contract, or

(d) failure by the Club to exercise its right to renew the contract within the time period specified in paragraph 10(a) thereof . . .

B. Free Agency . . .

(2) *Player Contracts Executed On or After August 9, 1976.* Following completion of the term of the contract as set forth therein, any Player with 6 or more years of Major League service who has not executed a contract for the next succeeding season shall become a free agent, subject to the provisions of Section C below, by giving notice as hereinafter provided within the 15 day period beginning on October 15 (or the day following the last game of the World Series, whichever is later). Election of free agency shall be communicated by telephone or any other method of communication by the Player to the Players Association. Written notice of free agency shall then be given within the specified time limits by the Players Association, on behalf of the Player, to a designated representative of the Player Relations Committee, and shall become effective upon receipt.

C. Reentry Procedure

The procedure set forth in this Section C shall apply to Players who become free agents pursuant to Section B above. Players who otherwise become free agents under this Agreement shall be eligible to negotiate and contract with any Club without any restrictions or qualifications . . .

(1) *Negotiation Rights Selection Procedure*

(a) A Selection Meeting of the Major League Clubs shall be convened by the Commissioner during the period between November 1 and November 15 of each year for the Clubs to select rights to negotiate and contract with free agent Players. Such Players shall be listed on an "Eligible List" certified by the League Presidents and the Players Association. Selections shall be made from the Eligible List.

(b) At the Selection Meeting, Clubs shall select in inverse order of their standing in the championship season just concluded. . . .

(d) If less than 2 Clubs select negotiation rights to a particular Player, the Player immediately will be free to negotiate and contract with any Major League Club, without restrictions or qualifications applicable to either the Player or the Club, in the same manner as a Player who becomes a free agent other than by virtue of Section B above.

(e) Any Player who, under these procedures, is unsigned on January 15 may elect, within 7 days after that date, to resubmit himself to a new drawing of lots by the Clubs for the selection of negotiating rights with him. The new drawing shall be held within 3 days after communication of the Player's election. Negotiating rights shall be granted to 4 Clubs determined by lot from Clubs which indicate at the time of the drawing that they are interested in signing such Player. The Player's former Club shall not be eligible to acquire negotiating rights pursuant to this paragraph . . .

(2) *Contracting With Free Agents*

(a) Regardless of the number of Players for whom they have drafted negotiation rights, Clubs shall be limited in the number they may subsequently sign to contracts. The number of signings permitted shall be related to the number of Players on the Eligible List. If there are 14 or less players on the Eligible List no Club may sign more than one Player. If there are from 15 to 38 Players on the Eligible List, no Club may sign more than 2 Players. If there are from 39 to 62 Players on the Eligible List, no Club may sign more than 3 Players. If there are more than 62 Players on the Eligible List, the Club quotas shall be increased accordingly.

(b) Irrespective of the provisions of paragraph (a) above, a Club shall be eligible to sign at least as many Players as it may have lost through Players having become free agents at the close of the season just concluded. . . .

(d) When a Player and one of the Clubs which has selected negotiation rights to him reach agreement on terms, the Club will immediately notify its League Office of that fact together with a summary of the terms to which the Player has agreed. The Players Association will then be advised by the League Office of these facts and will promptly seek confirmation of them by the Player. Upon obtaining such confirmation, the Players Association shall notify the League Office, and all other Clubs holding negotiation rights to that Player shall be advised that the Player has come to terms and is no longer a free agent.

(3) *Conduct of Free Agents and Clubs Prior To Selection Meeting*

(a) During the period beginning on the day the Player becomes a free agent and ending 3 days before the Negotiation Rights Selection Meeting, any Club representative and any free agent or his representative may talk with each other and discuss the merits of the free agent contracting, when eligible therefore, with the Club, provided, however, that the Club and the free agent shall not negotiate terms or contract with each other. The following subjects are among those which may properly be discussed between any Club and such player:

— The player's interest in playing for the Club, and the Club's interest in having the player play for it.
— The Club's plans about how it intends to utilize the player's services (as a starting pitcher or reliever, as a designated hitter or not, platooning, etc.)
— The advantages and disadvantages of playing for the Club: the nature of the organization, the climate of the city, availability of suitable housing, etc.
— Length of contract.
— Guarantee provisions.
— No-trade or limited no-trade provisions.

Notwithstanding the foregoing, the free agent and his previous Club may engage in negotiations and enter into a contract during said period. Should they enter into a contract during said period, the free agent shall be deemed not to have exercised his rights of free agency for purposes of Section F of this Article XVIII, and the Club shall be deemed not to have signed a free agent for purposes of the quota provisions of this Article. . . .

(4) *Miscellaneous*

(a) Any Club selecting negotiation rights to and signing a contract with a Player under this Section C may not assign his contract until after the next June 15. However, notwithstanding the foregoing, such contract may be assigned for other Player contracts and/or cash consideration of $50,000 or less prior to the next June 16 if the Player gives written consent to such transaction. . . .

(c) There shall be no restriction or interference with the right of a free agent to negotiate or contract with any baseball club outside the structure of organized baseball, nor shall there be any compensation paid for the loss of a free agent except as provided for in this Agreement. . . .

F. Repeater Rights

(1) *Free Agency.* Any Player who becomes a free agent pursuant to Section B of this Article or whose contract was assigned as a result of a trade required pursuant to Section E of this Article shall not subsequently be eligible to exercise his right to become a free agent until he has completed an additional 5 years of Major League service. . . .

G. Outright Assignment to National Association Club

(1) *Election of Free Agency.* (a) Any Player who has at least 3 years of Major League service and whose contract is assigned outright to a National Association Club may elect, in lieu of accepting such assignment, to become a free agent. (b) In the event that such Player does not elect free agency in lieu of accepting such assignment, he may elect free agency between the end of the then current Major League season and the next following October 15, unless such Player is returned to a Major League roster prior to making such election.

(2) A Player who becomes a free agent under this Section G shall immediately be eligible to negotiate and contract with any Club without any restrictions or qualifications. Such Player shall not be entitled to receive termination pay. . . .

H. Individual Nature of Rights

The utilization or non-utilization of rights under this Article XVIII is an individual matter to be determined solely by each Player and each Club for his or its own benefit. Players shall not act in concert with other Players and Clubs shall not act in concert with other Clubs.

Major League Baseball, 1981 Amendments

2. *Reentry Draft for Ranking Players*

The following procedure shall apply: There shall be a reentry draft for all players as set out in the 1980 Basic Agreement; except that ranking players shall be determined solely by statistics as provided in Paragraph 1, there shall be no limit on the number of clubs which may select negotiation rights to any player, and a ranking player selected by less than four clubs shall be free to negotiate and contract with any club.

3.44   Right of First Refusal

The NFL and NBA collective bargaining provisions give clubs a right of first refusal that allow them to retain the services of their free agent players by matching any offer made by another club. This important right significantly limits the actual movement of an NFL or NBA free agent to another club. As combined with significant free agent compensation provisions (see Section 3.45), the right of first refusal has been particularly effective in restricting free agent movement in the NFL.

Neither Major League Baseball nor the NHL provides for rights of first refusal in their collective agreements. Any attempt to insert such a proviso in an individual contract would undoubtedly bring charges that such cannot be done in contravention of established labor policy. (See, generally, Chapter 5 for further analysis of what are allowed as contract add-ons under existing labor law principles.)

National Football League, Article XV, Right of First Refusal/Compensation

Section 1. Applicability: For players who play out the option in their contracts or whose contracts otherwise expire (hereinafter referred to as "Veteran Free Agents") the following principles will apply; provided, however, that in the event the clubs make a determination during the term of this Agreement to move the date of the draft from on or about May 1 to on or about February 1 of the same year, any compensation under Section 12 of this Article XV will be in the next subsequent college draft.

Section 2. Contract Expiration Date: The expiration date of all player contracts will be February 1. After February 1, any NFL club will be free to negotiate for a contract with a veteran free agent.

Section 3. Offer Sheet: When the NFLPA receives an offer from a new club to sign a contract or contracts, which is acceptable, the NFLPA will on or before April 15 give to the player's old club a completed Offer Sheet substantially in the form of Exhibit A attached hereto, signed by the player and by the chief operating officer of the new club which will contain the "principal terms" (as defined in Section 7 below) of the new club's offer. Subject to Section 10 below, the player's old club, upon receipt of the Offer Sheet, may exercise its "right of first refusal," which will have the consequences set forth in Section 4 below.

Section 4. First Refusal Exercise Notice: Subject to Section 18 below, if, within seven days from the date it receives an Offer Sheet, the veteran free agent's old club gives to the NFLPA a First Refusal Exercise Notice substantially in the form of Exhibit B attached hereto, such player and his old club will be deemed to have entered into a binding agreement, which will be promptly formalized in an NFL Player Contract(s); containing all the "principal terms" of the Offer Sheet and those terms of the NFL Player Contract(s) not modified by the "principal terms."

Section 5. No First Refusal Exercise Notice: Subject to Sections 6 and 10 below, if, within seven days from the date it receives an Offer Sheet, the veteran free agent's old club does not give the NFLPA a First Refusal Exercise Notice, the player and the new club will be deemed to have entered into a binding agreement, which will be promptly formalized in an NFL Player Contract(s), containing all the "principal terms" of the Offer Sheet, those terms of the NFL Player Contract(s) not modified by the "principal terms," and the non-principal terms offered by the new club.

Section 6. One Offer Sheet: There may be only one Offer Sheet signed by both a club and a veteran free agent outstanding at any one time. An Offer Sheet, before it is given to the veteran free agent's old club, may be revoked or withdrawn only upon the written consent of the new club and the NFLPA. An Offer Sheet, after it is given to a veteran free agent's old club, may be revoked or withdrawn only upon the written consent of the old club, the new club and the NFLPA. In either of such events, any NFL club will be free to negotiate for a contract with such player, subject only to his old club's renewed right of first refusal.

Section 7. Principal Terms: For purposes of this Article, the "principal terms" will include the following: (a) the salary the new club will pay to the veteran free agent and/or his designees, currently and/or as deferred compensation in specified installments on specified dates, in consideration for his services as a football player under the contract or contracts; (b) any signing or reporting bonus the new club will pay to the veteran free agent and/or his designees, currently and/or deferred, and the terms thereof; and (c) any modification of and/or addition to the terms contained in the NFL Player Contract form requested for the veteran free agent and acceptable to the new club, which relate to terms of the player's employment as a football player (which will be evidenced by a copy of the NFL Player Contract form, marked to show changes).

Section 8. Non-Principal Terms: For purposes of this Article, the "principal terms" will not include any of the following: (a) any loan the new club will make to the veteran free agent and/or his designees under the contract or contracts, and the terms thereof and security therefor, if any; (b) any performance bonus the new team will pay to the veteran free agent under the contract or contracts; (c) a description of any property other than money which the new club will provide or make available to the veteran free agent and/or his designees under the contract or contracts; (d) any investment opportunity which the new club will provide or make available to the veteran free agent and/or his designees; (e) any money and/or property the new club will pay, provide or make available to the veteran free agent and/or his designees in consideration for services by him or others; (f) any intangible benefits or advantages that might accrue to the veteran free agent as a consequence of living and playing in the geographic area of the new club; (g) any promise by the new club of a try-out, audition or introduction for the possibility of performing services or earning income other than that as a football player; and (h) any other terms not included within the "principal terms" set forth in Section 7 above.

Section 9. Qualifying Offer: For purposes of Section 10, 11, and 12 of this Article, a "qualifying offer" will include the sum of: (a) the total amount of salary to be paid under the contract or contracts, averaged over the full number of years of the contract or contracts, but no more than five years; and (b) any signing or reporting bonus to be paid under the contract or contracts, prorated over the full number of years of the contract or contracts,

but no more than five years.

Section 10. Qualification for First Refusal: Anything above in this Article to the contrary notwithstanding, in order for a veteran free agent's old club to be entitled to a right of first refusal, the old club must have given a "qualifying offer" in writing to the NFLPA on or before February 1, to be represented by an Offer Sheet, in the following amounts: (a) $60,000 ($75,000 in 1985 through 1987) or more if the player has not yet completed the season in which his 3rd year of Credited Service under the Bert Bell NFL Player Retirement Plan has been earned; (b) $70,000 ($85,000 in 1985 through 1987) or more if the player has not yet completed the season in which his 4th year of Credited Service has been earned; (c) an increase of $10,000 for each year of Credited Service thereafter, in accordance with the graphs portrayed in Exhibits C and D attached hereto.

National Basketball Association, Article XXII

Section 1. . . .(d) *Right of First Refusal*

(1) No compensation obligation, rule, practice, policy, regulation or agreement of any kind shall be applicable to any Veteran Free Agent during the period from the day following the last NBA playoff game of the 1980–1981 season to the last day of the 1986–1987 season. During the aforesaid period, a Veteran Free Agent may negotiate and sign a Player Contract with any Team and any Team may negotiate and sign a Player Contract with any Veteran Free Agent without any penalty or restriction, subject only to the prior Team's Right of First Refusal . . .

(2) When a Veteran Free Agent receives an offer to sign a Player Contract from a Team (the new Team) other than the prior Team, which he desires to accept, he shall give to the prior Team a completed certificate substantially in the form of Exhibit C (the "Offer Sheet"), signed by the Veteran Free Agent and the new Team, which shall contain the "Principal Terms" (as defined below) of the new Team's offer. The prior Team, upon receipt of the Offer Sheet, may exercise its Right of First Refusal, which shall have the legal consequences hereinafter set forth below in this Section 1(d)(2).

(a) If, within fifteen (15) days from the date it receives an Offer Sheet, the prior Team gives to the Veteran Free Agent a "First Refusal Exercise

FIRST REFUSAL OFFER SHEET

Name of Player: Date:
Address of Player: Name of New Club:

National Football League   Name of Old Club:
Players Association
1300 Connecticut Avenue, N.W.
Washington, D.C. 20036

Principal Terms of NFL Player Contract or Contracts
With New Club:

(Supply Information on this Sheet or on Attachment)

(a) Salary, including deferred compensation:

(b) Signing or reporting bonus, if any:

(c) Modifications and additions to NFL Player Contract(s):
     [attached marked-up copy of NFL Player Contract(s)]

Player: New Club:
By .... By ....
                                                         Chief Operating Officer

FIRST REFUSAL EXERCISE NOTICE

Name of Player: Date:
Address of Player: Name of Old Club:

National Football League   Name of New Club:
Players Association
1300 Connecticut Avenue, N.W.
Washington, D.C. 20036

The undersigned member club of the NFL hereby exercises its Right of First Refusal under the Collective Bargaining Agreement dated .... so as to create a binding agreement with the player named above containing the "principle terms" set forth in the First Refusal Offer Sheet, a copy of which is attached hereto, and those terms of the NFL Player Contract(s) not modified by such "principal terms."

                                                         Old Club
                                                         By ....
                                                         Chief Operating Officer

Notice" substantially in the form of Exhibit D, such Veteran Free Agent and the prior Team shall be deemed to have entered into a binding agreement, which they shall promptly formalize in a Player Contract, containing (i) all the Principal Terms (subject to Section 1(d)(6) below), (ii) those terms of the Uniform Player Contract not modified by the Principal Terms, and (iii) such additional terms, not less favorable to the Veteran Free Agent than those contained in the Offer Sheet, as may be agreed upon between the Veteran Free Agent and the prior Team.

(b) If the prior Team does not give the First Refusal Exercise Notice within the aforementioned fifteen (15) day period, the player and the new Team shall be deemed to have entered into a binding agreement, which they shall promptly formalize in a Player Contract . . .

(c) There may be only one Offer Sheet signed both by a Team and a Veteran Free Agent outstanding at any one time. An Offer Sheet, before it is given to the prior Team, may be revoked or withdrawn only upon the written consent of the new Team and the Veteran Free Agent. An Offer Sheet, after it has been given to the prior Team, may be revoked or withdrawn only upon the written consent of the prior Team, the new Team and the Veteran Free Agent. In either of such events, a Veteran Free Agent shall again be free to negotiate and sign a Player Contract with any Team, and any Team shall again be free to negotiate and sign a Player Contract with such Veteran Free Agent, subject only to the prior Team's renewed Right of First Refusal.

(3) For purposes of this Section 1(d), the Principal Terms shall include, without limitation, the matters covered by Sections 1(d)(3)(a)–1(d)(3)(e) below:

(a) the money the new Team will pay (and lend, on described terms) to the Veteran Free Agent and/or his designee (currently and/or as deferred compensation in specified installments on specified dates) in consideration for his services as a basketball player under the Player Contract ("Money") and the security therefor, if any, and if the amount of Money is variable and/or is subject to calculation, a description of the variation and the method of calculation;

(b) a description of property other than Money which the new Team will pay, provide or make available to the Veteran Free Agent and/or his designees in consideration of his services as a basketball player under the Player Contract ("Property);

(c) a description of investment opportunities (including financing terms thereof, if any) which the new Team will provide or make available to the Veteran Free Agent and/or his designees ("Investments");

(d) modifications of and additions to the terms contained in the Uniform Player Contract requested by the Veteran Free Agent and acceptable to the new Team, which relate to non-compensation terms of the Veteran Free Agent's employment as a basketball player (which shall be evidenced either by a copy of the Uniform Player Contract, marked to show changes, or by a brief written summary contained on or attached to the Offer Sheet),

(e) Money, Property and Investments the new Team will pay, provide or make available to the Veteran Free Agent and/or his designees, in consideration for described services by him or others, other than as a basketball player.

(4) If any item of Property or Investments or the Principal Terms contained in an Offer Sheet is such that its fair market value cannot readily be estimated by the prior Team, the Veteran Free Agent and/or the new Team shall commence an arbitration (the "Valuation Arbitration"). . . . The prior Team and the NBA shall not be entitled to notice of or to participate in the Valuation Arbitration. . . .

(6) If the prior Team gives a First Refusal Exercise Notice, the Player Contract created thereby shall be deemed to contain the following additional provisions:

(a) The prior Team shall not be obligated to pay, provide or make available to the Veteran Free Agent and/or his designees, in kind, any terms within the Principal Terms which are unique or otherwise cannot be obtained or duplicated by the prior Team without unreasonable effort or expense ("Unique Terms");

(b) The prior Team shall be obligated to pay, provide or make available to the Veteran Free Agent and/or his designees, and the Veteran Free Agent shall be obligated to accept, in substitution for Unique Terms, substantially equivalent terms or, if substantially equivalent terms cannot be obtained by the prior Team without unreasonable effort or expense, cash equal to the fair market value of the Unique Terms, in either case payable to the Veteran Free Agent and/or his designees at the same or approximately the same time as would have been payable by the new Team pursuant to the Offer Sheet. . . .

(8) A Veteran Free Agent shall have no less than 165 days from the last playoff game of the preceding season to give an Offer Sheet to the prior Team. However, notwithstanding any other provision of this Section 1(d), a Veteran Free Agent shall not be entitled to give an Offer Sheet to the prior Team during the 200 day period commencing with the 166th day after the last NBA playoff game of the preceding season if all of the following

conditions have been met by the prior Team:

(a) the prior Team tendered a Player Contract to such Veteran Free Agent on or before the 150th day after the last playoff game of the preceding season with the condition that it could be accepted by the Veteran Free Agent up to and including the 165th day after such last playoff game of the preceding season; and

(b) such Player Contract had a stated term of only the next season (whether or not the next season already commenced prior to the tender); and

(c) the compensation stated to be payable in the tendered Player Contract was no less than 100% of the compensation payable to the Veteran Free Agent with respect to the last season in which he played, to be reduced, if applicable, pro rata to reflect the number of regular season games played by the Team prior to acceptance, if any, by the Veteran Free Agent of such Player Contract; and

(d) the tendered Player Contract contained all other non-monetary terms contained in the Veteran Free Agent's contract for the last season in which he played.

If all of such conditions were met by the prior Team and if the Veteran Free Agent does not accept the prior Team's tendered Player Contract by the 165th day after the last playoff game of the preceding season, the Veteran Free Agent shall not play for any other Team during that season but shall be free to negotiate and sign a Player Contract with any Team commencing with the next succeeding season, without any penalty or restriction, subject only to the prior Team's renewed Right of First Refusal, including the provisions of this Section 1(d) (8).

(9) (a) Unless otherwise specifically negotiated by a Veteran Free Agent, no right of first refusal rule, practice, policy, regulation or agreement shall apply to the signing of a player contract with or the playing with any team in any professional basketball league other than the NBA by any Veteran Free Agent.

Section 2, Additional Undertakings

(a) From April 29, 1976 until the last day of the 1986–1987 season, no Member, alone or by reason of any express or implied Agreement or understanding, shall fail or refuse to negotiate with, or enter into a Player Contract with any NBA player who is free to negotiate and sign a Player

Contract with any Team, on any of the following grounds:

(i) the player has previously been subject to the exclusive negotiating rights obtained by another Member in a College Draft; or

(ii) the player has previously been subject to the option of another Team; or

(iii) the player has previously refused or failed to enter into a Player Contract containing an Option Clause; or

(iv) the player has become a Veteran Free Agent; or;

(v) the player is or has been subject to the Right of First Refusal described in Section 1(d) above.

(b) From the last day of the 1980–1981 season until the last day of the 1986–1987 season, no Member shall directly or indirectly communicate or disclose to any other Member or to the NBA (other than as provided in Section 1(d)(10) above) that it has negotiated with or is negotiating with any Veteran Free Agent who is subject to the Right of First Refusal unless and until an Offer Sheet shall have been given to the prior Team.

(c) From the last day of the 1980–1981 season until the last day of the 1986–1987 season,

(i) no Member shall make an offer to a Veteran Free Agent subject to the Right of First Refusal which includes any Principal Terms which are (a) designed to serve the purpose of defeating the prior Team's ability to evaluate and meet the new Team's offer, and (b) not intended to be bona fide terms offered by the new Team to the Veteran Free Agent; and

(ii) no player who has become a Veteran Free Agent subject to the Right of First Refusal shall induce any new Team or cause any new Team to be induced to make an offer which violates the undertaking in Subsection (i) immediately above.

National Basketball Association, 1983 Memorandum of Agreement

(15) Article XXII, Section 2(c) of the prior collective bargaining agreement shall be amended by the addition of the following:

(iii) The parties expressly agree that any term in an Offer Sheet that (a) provides for a substantial bonus based upon attendance or gate receipts or team performance or composition and (b) as of the time of the Offer Sheet is demonstrably more likely to be paid by the prior team than the new team, shall be deemed a violation of Subsection (i) above.

North American Soccer League, Article XLIII, First Refusal: Rookie Player

A player without previous professional experience who signs his first contract with an NASL club, shall be required to sign a Club-Player Agreement for a term ending November 15 and for a period of no less than six months and no more than two years. The contract shall also contain a double option permitting the Club to renew the contract for two successive 12 month periods following the expiration of the initial term.

A rookie who has completed his first base term shall receive a 10 percent increase in the option year but shall not have his contract guaranteed beyond the provisions set forth in Article XX(c), unless so negotiated. In the second year, Article XXX Section (c) shall apply.

After the second option year has expired, the Club shall have the right of first refusal on any professional soccer contract offered to the player by a club from either within or outside of the United States and Canada. Such right may be exercised after a copy of the final executed bona fide contract offered to the player by another soccer club has been submitted to the NASL Club (or the assignee) which entered into the initial contract with the player. This right shall expire one year after the expiration of his second option.

Should a dispute arise as to whether the Club has matched the offer submitted, the question shall be resolved under Article II of this Agreement.

Should a player refuse to play after the club has exercised either of the options, the Club shall retain the exclusive rights to the player for the remaining option periods.

3.45   Free Agent Compensation

The NBA provides for a right of first refusal that limits the ability of players to move to a new club. (See Section 3.44.) If an NBA club does not exercise this right, it loses the player. There is thereafter no compensation to the club losing a free agent. The NBA is the only major professional sports league that does not provide for some sort of compensation to the free agent's old club. The NFL, Major League Baseball, and the NHL all have complicated free agent provisions. Those for baseball and football are reproduced below. Those for the NHL are summarized in the table in Section 3.46.

National Football League, Article XV, Right of First Refusal/Compensation

Section 11. Qualification for Compensation: In order for a veteran free agent's old club to be entitled to a right of compensation, the old club must have qualified for a right of first refusal under Section 10 above and the new club must have given a "qualifying offer" in writing to the NFLPA on or before April 15, to be represented by an Offer Sheet, in the following amounts: (a) $80,000 ($100,000 in 1985 through 1987) or more if the player has not yet completed the season in which his 3rd year of Credited Service under the Bert Bell NFL Player Retirement Plan has been earned; (b) $90,000 ($110,000 in 1985 through 1987) or more if the player has not yet completed the season in which his 4th year of Credited Service has been earned; and (c) an increase of $10,000 for each year of Credited Service thereafter, in accordance with the graphs portrayed in Exhibits C and D attached hereto. Anything in Subsections (a) through (c) to the contrary notwithstanding, the "qualifying offer" with respect to veteran free agent quarterbacks will increase by $5,000 for each year of Credited Service if the player has not yet completed the season in which his 8th year of Credited Service has been earned and thereafter.

Section 12. Amount of Compensation: Subject to Section 10 above, if, within seven days from the date it receives an Offer Sheet, a veteran free agent's old club, which is entitled to a right of first refusal or a right of compensation, chooses not to exercise its right of first refusal, then the player and the new club will be deemed to have entered into a binding agreement as provided in Section 5 above, and the player's old club will receive the following compensation: (a) the new club's 3rd round selection choice or a better 3rd round choice obtained by assignment from another NFL club, in the next immediate college draft: (i) if the player has not completed the season in which his 3rd year of Credited Service under the Bert Bell NFL Retirement Plan has been earned and if the "qualifying offer" is $80,000 or more but less than $95,000 ($100,000 and $120,000 in 1985 through 1987); (ii) if the player has not completed the season in which his 4th year of Credited Service has been earned and if the "qualifying offer" is $90,000 or more but less than $105,000 ($110,000 and $130,000 in 1985 through 1987); and (iii) an increase of $10,000 for each year of Credited Service thereafter, in accordance with the graphs portrayed in Exhibit D attached hereto [Exhibit 3–2]; (b) the new club's 2nd round selection choice or a better 2nd round choice obtained by assignment from another NFL club, in the next immediate college draft: (i) if the player has not completed the season in which his 3rd year of Credited Service has been earned and if the "qualifying offer" is $95,000 or more but less than $110,000 ($120,000 and $140,000 in 1985 through 1987); (ii) if the player has not completed the season in which his 4th year of Credited Service has been earned and if the "qualifying offer" is $105,000 or more but less than $120,000 ($130,000 and $150,000 in 1985 through 1987); and (iii) an increase of $10,000 for each year of Credited Service thereafter, in accordance with the graphs portrayed in Exhibits C and D attached hereto; (c) the new club's 1st round selection choice or a better 1st round choice obtained by assignment from another NFL club in the next immediate college draft: (i) if the player has not completed the season in which his 3rd year of Credited Service has been earned and if the "qualifying offer" is $110,000 or more but less than $150,000 ($140,000 and $180,000 in 1985 through 1987), (ii) if the player has not completed the season in which his 4th year of Credited Service has been earned and if the "qualifying offer" is $120,000 or more but less than $160,000 ($150,000 and $190,000 in 1985 through 1987), and (iii) an increase of $10,000 for each year of Credited Service thereafter, in accordance with the graphs portrayed in Exhibits C and D attached hereto; (d) the new club's 1st and 3rd round selection choices, or better 1st and 3rd round choices obtained by assignment from other NFL clubs in the next immediate college draft: (i) if the player has not completed the season in which his 3rd year of Credited Service has been earned and if the "qualifying offer" is $150,000 or more but less than $200,000 ($180,000 and $230,000 in 1985 through 1987); (ii) if the player has not completed

the season in which his 4th year of Credited Service has been earned and if the "qualifying offer" is $160,000 or more, but less than $210,000 ($190,000 and $240,000 in 1985 through 1987); and (iii) an increase of $10,000 for each year of Credited Service thereafter, in accordance with the graphs portrayed in Exhibits C and D attached hereto; (e) the new club's 1st round and 2nd round selection choices or better 1st and 2nd round choices obtained by assignment from other NFL clubs in the next immediate college drafts: (i) if the player has not completed the season in which his 3rd year of Credited Service has been earned and if the "qualifying offer" is $200,000 or more but less than $250,000 ($230,000 and $280,000 in 1985 through 1987); (ii) if the player has not completed the season in which his 4th year of Credited Service has been earned and if the "qualifying offer" is $210,000 or more but less than $260,000 ($240,000 and $290,000 in 1985 through 1987); and (iii) an increase of $10,000 for each year of Credited Service thereafter, in accordance with the graphs portrayed in Exhibits C and D attached hereto; (f) the new club's 1st round selection choices or better 1st round choices obtained by assignment from other NFL clubs, in the next immediate two college drafts: (i) if the player has not completed the season in which his 3rd year of Credited Service has been earned and if the qualifying offer is $250,000 or more ($280,000 in 1985 through 1987), (ii) if the player has not completed the season in which his 4th year of Credited Service has been earned and if the "qualifying offer" is $260,000 or more ($290,000 in 1985 through 1987); and (iii) an increase of $10,000 for each year of Credited Service thereafter, in accordance with the graphs portrayed in Exhibits C and D attached hereto. Anything in Subsections (a) through (f) to the contrary notwithstanding, the "qualifying offer" with respect to veteran free agent quarterbacks will increase by $5,000 for each year of Credited Service if the player has not yet completed the season in which his 8th year of Credited Service has been earned and thereafter.

Section 13. Absences of Choice: A club not having the future selection choice or choices necessary to provide compensation in the event the veteran free agent's old club chooses to exercise its right of compensation, if any, may not sign an Offer Sheet as provided in Section 3 above.

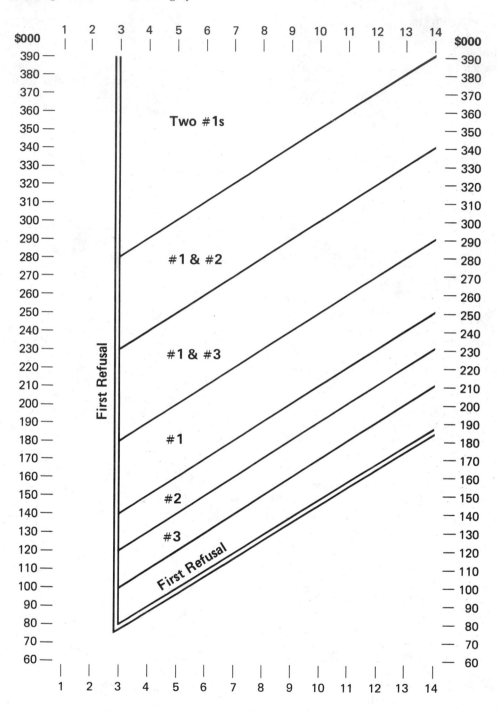

Exhibit 3-2   First-Refusal Compensation, 1985-1986-1987

Major League Baseball, 1981 Amendments

1. Definition of Ranking Player. The statistical system of ranking players shall be used to define ranking players. Ranking players shall be the top 30% of each respective position group using statistics based on a two-year average. Type A ranking players shall be the top 20%. Type B ranking players shall be from 20% to 30%.

The following players shall not be ranking players regardless of their standing in their position groups:

(a) players who have previously been free agents through reentry and completed the repeat rights period; or

(b) players with 12 or more years of credited service. . . .

4. Pool for Professional Player Added Compensation. If a ranking player becomes a free agent, compensation shall be made to the player's former club as set out below.

(a) Type A Ranking Players. For Type A ranking players, compensation shall be an amateur draft choice of the signing club in the June Major League Rule 4 Amateur Player Draft as set forth in Article XVIII of the Basic Agreement and . . . the contract of a professional player selected from the pool described below.

All clubs (except for certain "excluded clubs" as described below) shall make players available to the pool for selection as compensation as follows:

(i) A Club which does not sign a Type A ranking player shall participate in the pool (and shall be entitled to protect 26 players from its organization) until it loses a player from the pool, and then it need not participate in the pool (unless it signs a Type A ranking player) for the following two years:

(ii) A club which does sign one or more Type A ranking players shall be eligible to lose players from the pool as follows:

(a) a club which signs one Type A ranking player shall be eligible to lose one player from the pool in that year (and shall be entitled to protect 24 players from its organization);   (b) a club which signs more than one Type A ranking player shall be eligible to lose one player from the pool in the year of signing and shall also be so eligible in the next following years, up to a maximum of two additional years, one year for each Type A ranking player signed in excess of one (with a protected list of 24 in each such year); and

(iii) In no event shall a club be eligible to lose more than one player from the pool in any one year

All players in a participating club's organization who are not included in the protected list are available in the pool for selection as compensation; provided, however, that free agent players who have just participated in the Reentry Procedure and have signed with a club are ineligible for selection from the pool and need not be protected. All players with no-trade clauses and those whose consent is required by the Basic Agreement to the assignment of their contract must be included in a club's protected list.

Prior to each reentry selection meeting, the Player Relations Committee shall advise the Players Association of which clubs, if any, to a maximum of five shall not select nor sign any Type A ranking players; and these clubs shall be "excluded clubs" as referred to above. Any club designated as an "excluded club" shall not so select nor sign for three consecutive years . . .

(b) Type B Ranking Players. For Type B ranking players the compensation shall be an Amateur Draft Choice of the signing club in the June Major League Rule 4 Amateur Player Draft as set forth in Article XVIII of the Basic Agreement and an added Amateur Draft Choice which choice shall be a special choice awarded immediately following the first complete round of the draft and preceding the commencement of the second round. Clubs which have lost Type B ranking players shall make such choices in reverse order of their won-lost percentage in the preceding season. Ties shall be broken by lot . . .

5. Substitute Compensation for Type A Ranking Players Beyond the Maximum Limitation. Clubs which lose a Type A ranking player who is beyond the maximum limitation set forth in Paragraph 3 shall receive as added compensation, in lieu of a professional player, an Amateur Draft Choice in the June Major League Rule 4 Amateur Player Draft, which choice shall be a special choice awarded immediately following the first round of the draft and preceding the commencement of the second round.

6. Non-Ranking Players. There shall be compensation for non-ranking players selected by 4 or more clubs in the reentry draft in the form of an Amateur Draft Choice of the signing club in the June Major League Rule 4 Amateur Player Draft as

set forth in Article XVIII of the Basic Agreement. There shall be no compensation for players selected by less than 4 clubs.

7. Payment to Certain Clubs which lose Players from Pool as Compensation. A payment of $150,000 shall be made to a club which loses a player from the pool for the first time. No such payment shall be made if that club loses a player or players from the pool during the following two years. . .

3.46 Summary

The foregoing materials have detailed most, but not all, of the collective bargaining provisions pertaining to player mobility in Major League Baseball, NFL, and NBA. Exhibit 3–3 summarizes the provisions for these three leagues, as well as the NHL. The table graphically depicts the substantially different approaches utilized by the leagues at this point. Most of the differences have occurred through the collective bargaining process, reflecting the individual economic and political pressures experienced by the various leagues.

3.50   The 1985 Baseball Collective Bargaining Provisions

Highlights of the 1985 settlement agreement between the Major League Baseball owners and players are set forth below. These have obvious impacts on provisions discussed earlier in this chapter and elsewhere in Volume I. The 1985 agreement was reached after the players had gone on strike in early August. The strike ended swiftly, as both sides compromised on their earlier demands.

The 1985 agreement builds on the 1980 and 1981 accords, adding several provisions and modifying earlier approaches. Only selected portions of the 1985 agreement are here reproduced, but these should be carefully considered in conjunction with other parts of this book, including termination pay (see Section 3.34), minimum salaries (see Section 3.32), certification of agents (see Section 4.13), salary

arbitration (see Section 5.31), free agent draft and free agent compensation (see Sections 3.43 and 3.45), contributions to pension fund, actually derived from broadcast revenues (see, generally, Section 1.33), and funding of deferred compensation (see Section 3.32).

NOTE _____

1. Background and analysis of the 1985 baseball negotiations, strike and settlement agreement can be found in R. Berry, W. Gould and P. Staudohar, *Labor Relations in Professional Sports* (Dover, Mass.: Auburn House, 1986), Chapter 9.

_____

Major League Baseball, Memorandum of Settlement, August 7, 1985

ARTICLE VIII: Termination Pay
  Revise paragraph *B. Spring Training:*
  A Player whose contract is terminated by a Club under section 7 (b) (2) during spring training shall receive 30 days payment at the rate stipulated in paragraph 2 of his Contract, plus an additional day's payment for each day before the date of his outright unconditional release which is subsequent to the 16th day prior to the start of the championship season. The maximum termination pay for a Section 7 (b) (2) release during spring training shall be 45 days payment at the rate stipulated in paragraph 2 of the Player's Contract.

MINIMUM SALARIES
  A. Major League minimum salary shall be $60,000 in 1985 and 1986, with a COLA adjustment prior to the 1987 season (with the same adjusted minimum applicable to the 1988 season), and a subsequent COLA adjustment prior to the 1989 season.
  B. The Split minimum salary shall be $20,000 effective as of the 1986 championship season and shall thereafter be increased in each year so as to be equal to one-third ($1/3$) of the Major League minimum salary.

EXHIBIT A: Agents and Contract Approvals
. . . 3. Insert a new Article IV to read as follows:
ARTICLE IV: Negotiation and Approval of Contracts
A Player, if he so desires, may designate an agent to

Exhibit 3-3   Summary of Collective Bargaining Provisions Pertaining to Player Mobility (as of 1985)

	NBA	NFL	Major League Baseball	NHL
Draft of Amateurs	1) Provided in CBA 2) Eligibility requirements detailed in CBA	1) Provided in CBA 2) Eligibility requirements *not* detailed in CBA	Not in CBA	Incorporated by reference in CBA (In league by-laws)
Options	1) Required in rookie one-year contracts 2) Individually negotiated in all other contracts	1) Options in standard form may be deleted 2) Options in contracts of veterans (4 or more yrs.) must be individually negotiated	Not in CBA	Dual option system (detailed in standard contract)
Free Agency	End of contract term — few exceptions	End of contract term — player must get offer from another club in certain time period or rights revert to old club	Must have six full years of credited major league service *and* come to end of contract terms. Other exceptions	End of contract term
Right of First Refusal	Yes	Yes	No	No
Free Agent Compensation	No Compensation	1) Draft choices — choices improve as player's new salary increases 2) No compensation if new salary below certain level	Depending on free agent's status — 1) Draft choices *or* 2) No compensation	Depending on free agent's age and new salary — 1) Draft choices *or* 2) Final offer arbitration *or* 3) No compensation

conduct on his behalf, or to assist him in, the negotiation of an individual salary or Special Covenants to be included in his Uniform Player's Contract with any Club, provided such agent has been certified to the Clubs by the Association as authorized to act as a Players' agent for such purposes.

A Club may require a Player's physical presence only once during contract negotiations. This limitation shall not apply to telephone conference calls, at reasonable times, with a Player and his certified agent. A Player required to be physically present during negotiations shall be entitled to be paid by the Club for round-trip first class transportation and first class hotel costs.

Upon execution of a Uniform Player's Contract by the Club and Player, the Club promptly shall submit the Contract, in duplicate, to the appropriate League President for approval. Within 20 days of receipt, the League President shall approve or disapprove the Contract, or provide the Association with a written explanation of why the contract has not been approved. This period is extended to 30 days if a contract is received by the League President between February 15 and April 15. Within ten days after the League President is to provide an explanation of why a contract has not been approved, the League President shall approve or disapprove the contract.

EXHIBIT E: Salary Arbitration
1. Beginning in 1987, the eligibility reference to two years of Major League Service in Section (1) shall be changed to three years.
2. Section (12), "Criteria," shall be amended to add the following language:

Effective with the 1987 Championship Season, the arbitrator shall, except for a Player with five or more years of Major League Service, give particular attention, for comparative salary purposes, to contracts of players with Major League Service not exceeding one annual service group above the Player's annual service group. Nothing herein shall limit the ability of a Player, because of special accomplishment, to argue the equal relevance of salaries of Players without regard to service, and the arbitrator shall give whatever weight to such argument as he (or she) deems appropriate.

EXHIBIT F: Salary Arbitration
Amend Section (6) to provide that if a Player *wins* an award in excess of 50% of his prior years salary, the club may, if the Player appeals to arbitration again in the following year, submit a salary figure without regard to the maximum salary reduction provisions of the Basic Agreement.

EXHIBIT G: Article XVIII, Reserve System, Free Agency:
A *Eligibility*. No change in eligibility requirements or in the method of election of free agency.

B. *Re-Entry Draft.* The re-entry draft shall be abolished, and each free agent player shall be entitled to negotiate and sign with any Club.

C. *Compensation to Free Agent's Former Club.* The parties shall negotiate a provision which will provide that amateur draft choice compensation will be given with regard to a similar proportion of players as existed under the prior system. An additional, newly created draft choice shall be awarded to the former club of each free agent ranking in the top $\frac{1}{3}$ of his statistical category, in the manner set forth for "Type B" ranking players in the 1981 strike settlement agreement. Professional player compensation shall be abolished.

D. *Quota.* The parties shall negotiate a provision which will provide that players not subject to the quota will exist in similar proportions as under the prior system.

E. *Repeater Rights.* PA proposal to eliminate repeater rights restrictions is withdrawn. The parties shall negotiate a provision which provides that repeaters rights restrictions will apply to a similar proportion of players as under the prior system.

F. *Rights of Former Club to Sign Free Agent.* Within 30 days following the close of the free agency filing period, the former club of a free agent shall advise the player in writing whether it will agree to salary arbitration for the next following season. If it shall not so agree, the free agent player's former club shall not be entitled to negotiate with or sign the free agent. The player may accept such offer to arbitrate by filing for arbitration within the time periods set forth in Article V of the Basic Agreement. Should the player file for arbitration, he shall be deemed to be signed for the following season, subject to the salary arbitration process, in the same manner as currently provided for salary arbitration players. Any such player who files for arbitration shall be deemed not to have exercised his free agency rights. If the player does not file for salary arbitration, the former club shall not be permitted to sign the player after the expiration of the salary arbitration filing period.

EXHIBIT H: PENSION AND HEALTH AND WELFARE BENEFITS
The Clubs contribution to the Benefit Plan shall be as follows:

1984	$25 million
1985	$33 million
1986	$33 million
1987	$33 million
1988	$33 million
1989	$39 million

The PA has suggested the following changes in Pension and Health and Welfare Benefits. Such changes shall be subject to consultation with the PRC, actuarial analysis and availability within the agreed upon contribution.

1. Class VIII will remain as currently constituted.

2. Class VIII retirement benefits will be increased in accordance with a schedule provided by the PA.

3. The current medical expense limit ($250,000) will be increased to at least $1,000,000. The medical deductible will be reduced to $1,000 per person per year. The retired members' death benefit will be increased to $25,000.

4. Health care coverage will be extended to all individuals on the 40-man roster.

5. The pension benefit for all former players in Classes III through VII will be substantially increased. The PA will work in close consultation with the PRC concerning the percentage increase.

6. The future widow's benefit will be substantially increased. The PA will work in close consultation with the PRC concerning the percentage.

7. Disability benefits will be increased 100%.

8. Newly created benefits will be retroactive to April 1, 1984, in accordance with the 1981 Strike Settlement Agreement. The 9.5 million additional benefit contribution for 1984 is subject to the retroactivity provisions of the 1981 Strike Settlement Agreement, except that the clubs' obligation with respect thereto is reduced by 50%.

9. The PA and PRC will work closely with the Plan Administrator and Plan actuaries in changing the Plan in the manner described above. See also the Major League Baseball Players Benefit Plan Benefit Study, September, 1984, prepared by the Plan Administrator.

10. The PA and PRC will promptly consider the administrative changes recommended by the Plan Administrator.

EXHIBIT I: Deferred Compensation

1. The limitations on deferred compensation set forth below shall apply only to Player Contracts executed after December 31, 1985.

2. There shall be no limit on the amount or percentage of compensation which can be deferred during the term of a Player's Contract.

3. Subject to the limitations set forth in paragraph 4 below, a Club must fully fund a deferred compensation obligation calculated at present value within four calendar years from the year in which the deferred compensation is earned. The year in which the deferred compensation is earned shall be considered a calendar year for the purposes of this provision.

4. A club shall be entitled to a deductible amount of deferred compensation which need not be funded. The deductible amount for the term of this agreement shall be $2 million of the present value of the aggregate deferred compensation owed to all players commencing only with contracts executed after December 31, 1985. Notwithstanding the requirements of paragraphs 3 above, no funding shall be required unless and until the aggregate present value of such deferred compensation obligations assumed in contracts executed after December 31, 1985 for a club exceed $2 million.

5. The present value of all deferred compensation shall be discounted at the following rate: the total of the Chemical Bank prime rate each November 1 plus 1% (rounded to the nearest full percentage point).

6. The Clubs may fund deferred compensation obligations in any manner in which they choose. They shall certify to the Player Relation Committee and to the Players Association, no later than January 31 of each year, the manner in which such deferred compensation has been funded during the previous calendar year. The records of the Clubs relating to such deferred compensation funding arrangements shall be made available to the Player Relations Committee and/or to the Players Association in the event that there is a question as to deferred compensation funding.

Chapter 4

REPRESENTING
THE PLAYER

4.00 Functions of the Sports Representative

Attorneys and agents who represent professional athletes are called on to render a wide variety of services for their clients. The diversity of services, in fact, is such that it is unreasonable to expect one individual to master all the knowledge and skills necessary to accomplish the tasks demanded. Among other realities, this has led to a separation of the law and management functions, and sports representatives are examining a number of devices that would allow them to use full-service operations. As is seen later in this chapter (Section 4.12), this can raise a number of legal and ethical questions. Even so, with the demands for the full ranges of services coming to the fore, pressures are mounting to set up a business organization that will respond to the plethora of needs.

Sections 4.01 through 4.06 describe the major functions that a sports representative of professional athletes must contemplate. A note at the end of Section 4.06 presents a sample brochure that describes how one management company attempts to handle its services. This, of course, is only one model. Other individuals and groups approach the representational functions either by simplifying — that is, not attempting to

provide a full range of services — or by internalizing — namely, providing in-house persons who are capable of handling special functions, such as investments, taxes, insurance, and so forth.

Whichever model is chosen, the point to remember is that the sports representative is in a business that demands a number of services. Before proceeding with other considerations, such as the legal and ethical constraints placed on sports representatives, the functions themselves must be considered.

4.01 Negotiating

The significance of negotiating is a central inquiry of this chapter. Getting the necessary background, mapping appropriate strategies, and having the flexibility to counter alternatives that are proposed all call for a variety of skills and abilities. These are rarely inherent but must be learned.

One important fact to remember in the sports context is that, in a sense, one rarely stops negotiating. The signed contract is usually only the first step. A number of occurrences during the term of the contract may call for even greater skill on the part of the negotiator, a point emphasized by the problems set forth in Section 4.40.

A second important fact points to the interconnections between the negotiating function and the functions described below. One cannot, and should not, attempt to isolate completely one from the others. As noted above, a single individual cannot effectively handle all functions, at least not in the great majority of situations. So, knowing how to deal with the overlaps while dividing the functions efficiently calls for careful thought, planning, and organizational structure.

4.02   Counseling

Counseling is an often overlooked function of vital importance, both during negotiations and after the contract is signed. Making certain the client understands what is at stake in a professional sports contract may prevent later disillusionments.

For the nonsuperstar, the contract may be largely illusory, in that it exists only if the player makes the team. There are no guarantees. Such rudimentary facts are not always grasped by the client. Making the team and contract rights are not always paired in the client's mind. Such information must be conveyed.

After the contract is signed, other problems call for counseling. Section 4.40 illustrates some of the situations. For example, the player makes the team but is sitting on the bench. Personal frustrations become predominant. In this and many other contexts, the counseling function is crucial.

4.03   Managing

Many athletes come out of college with little self-discipline and an almost total lack of knowledge about financial matters. The money soon disappears if the client is left unsupervised.

Not all sports representatives get into money management, and those who do not should advise the client as to where such assistance can be obtained. An ongoing relationship between the representative and a firm that deals in management and investments should be explored.

4.04   Marketing

There is a prevailing attitude, although a mistaken one, that most professional athletes do well because of lucrative endorsements and other types of outside income. In truth, such wealth is largely reserved for the top stars. Other athletes do what they can to supplement their income with personal appearances at local clubs, dinners, commercial establishments, and other less-than-top-dollar affairs. Even so, the possibilities for some types of outside income do exist. How aggressively they are sought on behalf of the client varies with the representative, but some willingness on the part of the representative to assist the client in seeking supplementary income is demanded. With that in mind, a few rules and regulations should be noted.

First, chances are that either the player's contract with the club or the league's collective bargaining agreement will have some provisions regarding endorsements. These should be reviewed before any action is taken (see Section 4.51). Second, the other side of the marketing issue is being vigilant about protecting the player's name and image. These are property rights capable of protection under a variety of legal theories, including rights of privacy and publicity. Instances in which athletes have had to resort to the courts over alleged infringements are many, although in more than one case the player was held to have signed away his rights through the broad grant contained in an earlier contract. Noting these should be fair warning to the sports representative about the careless granting of rights.

Cases in this area continue to appear, as athletes are more and more often viewed as celebrities whose names and images have commercial potential. Together with the ever-growing number of cases dealing with the rights of celebrities in other entertainment areas, these cases have brought about a substantial body of law revolving around rights of privacy and publicity. These cases are considered in detail in Section 4.53.

4.05   Resolving Disputes

When things have gone awry under an existing contract, and the other side is believed to have done something that must be redressed legally, the athlete's representative basically has two possibilities for action — arbitration and litigation. Arbitration has preempted litigation in many situations in professional sports. A sports representative must thus be aware of these instances because the time period in which complaints under arbitration must be filed is often short. Rights are easily waived. The arbitration process, which is usually initiated through the players' association, is specified in the collective bargaining agreements between the association and the league. This document has become indispensible in the sports representative's library. (See Chapter 5, Section 5.31, for examples of collective bargaining provisions pertaining to arbitration.) Litigation is a feasible alternative in some situations. Alleged antitrust violations by a league or a club, for example, are still the province of the courts, although the leagues have become increasingly insulated from attack by the labor exemption existing under the Sherman and Clayton acts. Even so, the cases still come up (see Section 4.70).

4.06   Planning

An athlete's career lasts but a short time. The average career for professional athletes, assuming they make the team in the first place, is in the four- to five-year range, varying only slightly by the sport played. Thus, for many, there is never anything beyond the first contract. For this reason the sports representative must prepare the client for what will occur in the not-too-distant future. Such a task is easy to describe but hard to carry out.

Athletes may claim that they realize theirs will not be a long career, but it is hard to grasp just how short a career can be. Most players are not really prepared for the end. Their attitude is invariably — "next year, perhaps, but not now."

The sports representative may be unable to cushion the psychological blow completely. The hope is that the client has had sufficient time to produce enough income so that at least some preparations can be made for the financial transition. Achieving this goal relates to the managing function, but it adds the future ingredient of careful planning. The sports representative needs to obtain professional assistance in order to maximize the client's financial resources so that a bridge can be built to span the time period needed to get the athlete into a new career. A sports representative in this business for any period of time will find this a problem to be confronted.

NOTE _____

1. The following excerpts are from an information pamphlet that was sent to prospective professional athletes by a sports consulting firm that was attempting to establish itself.

What we do

Contract negotiation: We deal directly with management to obtain the maximum commitment regarding salary, benefits and contract provisions.

Endorsements and appearances: We will seek to supplement our client's regular income by promoting product endorsements and personal appearances. We will both pursue appearance possibilities and negotiate on our client's behalf for endorsement fees.

Investments: We will review investment recommendations and proposals with out Investment Consultants. In addition, we will draw upon investment research from several investment banking and brokerage firms to augment our investment consultants.

Financial planning, insurance, legal and tax matters. We will also:

1. Evaluate our client's financial condition and establish a proper plan to insure maximum use of present and future earnings.
2. Have outside insurance consultants analyze our client's insurance programs and make recommendations as to adequacy of individual and group life, health and accident and disability

insurance programs. We will make recommendations to our clients according to their needs after reviewing our consultants' proposals.

3. Provide complete legal advice in all areas of general law as they may affect our clients' needs.

4. Prepare personal Federal, State and other necessary tax returns — and — provide complete professional advice on Foreign Tax Matters, Tax-Sheltered Investments and other areas of tax specialization.

Our policy will be to care for the normal needs of the client and this effort will be incorporated into the negotiation fee.

Our clientele will be normally drawn from those who are not superstars and it is our feeling that we should not charge them excessively. We are sure that our fees are at least ½ to ⅓ of those fees charged by other people in the athletic representative field.

We want to establish a feeling of honesty and fairness with our clients. We are sure that from our clients will come superstars with whom we will become more involved. But, we will always maintain a policy of providing low cost and honest service to the average professional athlete.

In most cases, our advice to the athletes will be to let their money grow in savings or in AAA bonds. Then, when they have reached superstar status and/or have a large enough cash base, we will have them diversify their investments.

Outside Consultants

Investment advisers. We will receive investment advice from professional investment counselors and investment banking and brokerage firms. Our investment counselors include:

> Investment Banking and Brokerage Houses.
> We work closely with several brokerage houses including [names of firms].
> Investment research and recommendations which are acted upon by us will realize brokerage commissions to those firms. Therefore, there will be no outside fee expense in conjunction with such investments.

Attorneys and tax specialists. We receive legal and tax advice from several major law firms.

Insurance, pensions, profit sharing, etc.. Our insurance consultants include representatives and managers of several major Insurance Companies — to include: [names of firms].

Advertising consultants. Our Advertising Consultants are creative directors, artists and copy writers at several Advertising Agencies and provide leads of client firms seeking professional athletes as well as advice on public relations, fee schedules and promotions.

4.10 Establishing the Attorney/Client Relationship

A good deal of notoriety has surrounded the relationship between sports agents and their athlete clients. The publicity concerning those who represent players has been far from favorable. As a result, increasing scrutiny is being directed toward the sports representative, leading, in some instances, to legal and other constraints being placed on the representative, obviously having an effect on the client relationship. This section summarizes some of the activities that have taken place and notes the trend toward standardizing the agreements forged between the representative (at times referred to in this section as a contract advisor) and the client.

4.11 Legal Requirements

California is one state that has enacted legislation directed at so-called athlete agencies. Under Sec. 1500, et seq., of the California Labor Code, registration, bonding, and other requirements are imposed. However, the code's description of an athlete agency "does not include any employee of a professional sport team, and does not include any member of the State Bar of California when acting as legal counsel for any person." Just who constitutes "legal counsel" can obviously be tricky, particularly for the sports attorney who wishes to go beyond contract negotiation into some of the other activities discussed in the preceding section. Clearly at least for some activities, the attorney would be moving into nonlegal functions that would qualify the attorney as an "athlete agency."

Sports representatives have also been questioned about their activities in connection with other legal restrictions. *Zinn* v. *Parrish*, discussed below, raises the possibility of an agent being in violation of federal securities laws. Though the issue was ultimately resolved in favor of the agent, the message of the case sounds a warning. See also, *Detroit Lions and Billy Sims* v.

Jerry Argovitz and Houston Gamblers.

Clearly, legislatures and courts are placing increased scrutiny on the actions of sports representatives.

California Legislature — 1981–82 Regular Session, Assembly Bill No. 440

. . .The people of the State of California do enact as follows:

Section 1. Chapter 1 (commencing with Section 1500) is added to Part 6 of Division 2 of the Labor Code, to read:

Chapter 1. Athlete Agencies
Article 1. Definitions

1500. The following definitions shall govern the construction of this chapter:

(a) ~~"Person" means any individual, company, corporation, association, partnership, or their agents or employees.~~

(b) "Athlete agency" means any person who, ~~as an independent contractor,~~ directly or indirectly, recruits or solicits any person to enter into any agency contract or professional sport services contract, or procures, offers, promises, or attempts to obtain employment for any person with a professional sport team.

"Athlete agency" does not include any employee of a professional sport team, and does not include any member of the State Bar of California ~~when acting as legal counsel for any person.~~

(c) "Agency contract" means any contract or agreement pursuant to which a person authorizes or empowers an athlete agency to negotiate or solicit on behalf of such person with one or more professional sport teams for the employment of such person by one or more professional sport teams.

(d) "Professional sport services contract" means any contract or agreement pursuant to which a person is employed or agrees to render services as a participant or player on a professional sport team.

Article 2. Registration

1510. No person shall engage in or carry on the occupation of an athlete agency without first registering with the Labor Commissioner.

1511. A written application for registration shall be made to the Labor Commissioner in the form prescribed by him or her and shall state:

(a) The name and address of the applicant.

(b) The street and number of the building or place where the business of the talent agency is to be conducted.

(c) The business or occupation engaged in by the applicant for at least two years immediately preceding the date of application.

(d) If the applicant is other than a corporation, the names and addresses of all persons, except bona fide employees on stated salaries, financially interested, either as partners, associates, or profit sharers, in the operation of the athlete agency in question, together with the amount of their respective interests.

If the applicant is a corporation, the corporate name, the names, residential addresses, and telephone numbers of all officers of the corporation, the names of all persons exercising managing responsibility in the applicant or registrant's office, and the names and addresses of all persons having a financial interest of 10 percent or more in the business and the percentage of financial interest owned by such persons.

The application must be accompanied by affidavits of at least two reputable residents, who have known or been associated with the applicant for two years, of the city or county in which the business of the athlete agency is to be conducted that the applicant is a person of good moral character or, in the case of a corporation, has a reputation for fair dealing.

1512. Upon receipt of an application for a registration, the Labor Commissioner may cause an investigation to be made as to the character and responsibility of the applicant and of the premises designated in such application as the place in which it is proposed to conduct the business of the athlete agency.

1513. The commissioner, upon proper notice and hearing, may refuse to grant a license. The proceedings shall be conducted in accordance with Chapter 5 (commencing at Section 11500) of Part 1 of Division 3 of Title 2 of the Government Code, and the commissioner shall have all the power granted therein.

1514. No registration shall be granted to conduct the business of an athlete agency to a person whose registration has been revoked within three years from the date of application.

1515. The registration when first issued shall

run to the next birthday of the applicant, and each license shall then be renewed within the 30 days preceding the licensee's birthday and shall run from birthday to birthday. In case the applicant is a partnership, such license shall be renewed within the 30 days preceding the birthday of the oldest partner. If the applicant is a corporation, such license shall be renewed within the 30 days preceding the anniversary of the date the corporation was lawfully formed. Renewal shall require the filing of an application for renewal, a renewal bond, and the payment of the annual license fee, but the Labor Commissioner may demand that a new application or new bond be submitted.

If the applicant or licensee desires, in addition, a branch office license, he shall file an application in accordance with the provisions of this section as heretofore set forth.

1516. All applications for renewal shall state the names and addresses of all persons, except bona fide employees on stated salaries, financially interested either as partners, associates, or profit sharers, in the operation of the business of the talent agency.

1517. A filing fee of twenty-five dollars ($25) shall be paid to the Labor Commissioner at the time the application for issuance of an athlete agency license is filed.

In addition to the filing fee required for application for issuance of an athelete agency license, every athlete agency shall pay to the Labor Commissioner annually at the time a license is issued or renewed:

(a) A license fee of one hundred fifty dollars ($150).

(b) Fifty dollars ($50) for each branch office maintained by the athlete agency in this state.

1518. A filing fee of twenty-five dollars ($25) shall be paid to the Labor Commissioner at the time application for consent to the transfer or assignment of an athlete agency registration is made but no fee shall be required upon the assignment or transfer of a registration.

The location of an athlete agency shall not be changed without the written consent of the Labor Commission.

1519. An athlete agency shall also deposit with the Labor Commissioner, prior to the issuance of renewal of a registration, a surety bond in the penal sum of ten thousand dollars ($10,000).

1520. Such surety bonds shall be payable to the people of the State of California, and shall be conditioned that the person applying for the registration will comply with this chapter and will pay all sums due any individual or group of individuals when such person or his representative or agent has received such sums, and will pay all damages occasioned to any person by reason of misstatement, misrepresentation, fraud, deceit, or any unlawful acts or omissions of the registered athlete agency, or its agents or employees, while acting within the scope of their employment.

1521. If any registrant fails to file a new bond with the Labor Commissioner within 30 days after notice of cancellation by the surety of the bond required under Section 1519, the registration issued to the principal under the bond is suspended until such time as a new surety bond is filed. A person whose registration is suspended pursuant to this section shall not carry on the business of an athlete agency during the period of such suspension. . . .

1527. The Labor Commissioner may revoke or suspend any registraton when any one of the following is shown:

(a) The registrant or his agent has violated or failed to comply with any of the provisions of this chapter.

(b) The registrant has ceased to be of good moral character.

(c) The conditions under which the registration was issued have changed or no longer exist.

1528. Before revoking or suspending any registration, the Labor Commissioner shall afford the holder of such registration an opportunity to be heard in person or by counsel. The proceedings shall be conducted in accordance with Chapter 5 (commencing at Section 11500) of Part 1 of Division 3 of Title 2 of the Government Code, and the commissioner shall have all the powers granted therein.

Article 3. Operation and Management

1530. Every athlete agency shall submit to the Labor Commissioner a form or forms of contract to be utilized by such agency in entering into written contracts with persons for the employment of the services of the agency by such persons, and secure the approval of the Labor Commissioner thereof. Such approval shall not be withheld as to any proposed form of contract unless such proposed form of contract is unfair, unjust, and oppressive to the person. Each such form of contract, except under the conditions specified in Section 1544, shall contain an agreement by the agency to refer any controversy between the person and the agency relating to the terms of the contract to the Labor Commissioner for adjustment. There shall be printed on the face of the contract in prominent type the following: "This athlete agency is registered with the Labor Commissioner of the State of California."

1531. Every person engaged in the occupation of an athlete agency shall file with the Labor Commissioner a schedule of fees to be charged and collected in the conduct of such occupation. Changes in the schedule may be made from time to time, but no change shall become effective until seven days after the date of filing thereof with the Labor Commissioner.

1532. Every athlete agency shall keep records approved by the Labor Commissioner, in which shall be entered the following:

(a) The name and address of each person employing the athlete agency.

(b) The amount of fee received from such person.

(c) Other information which the Labor Commissioner requires.

No agency, its agent or employees, shall make any false entry in any such records.

1533. All books, records, and other papers kept pursuant to this chapter by any athlete agency shall be open at all reasonable hours to the inspection of the Labor Commissioner and his agents. Every agency shall furnish to the Labor Commissioner upon request a true copy of such books, records, and papers or any portion thereof, and shall make such reports as the Labor Commissioner prescribes.

1534. The Labor Commissioner may, in accordance with the provisions of Chapter 3.5 (commencing at Section 11340) of Part 1 of Division 3 of Title 2 of the Government Code, adopt, amend, and repeal such rules and regulations as are reasonably necessary for the purpose of enforcing and administering this chapter and as are not inconsistent with this chapter.

1535. No registrant shall sell, transfer, or give away any interest in or the right to participate in the profits of the agency without the written consent of the Labor Commissioner. A violation of this section shall constitute a misdemeanor, and

shall be punishable by a fine of not less than one hundred dollars ($100) nor more than five hundred dollars ($500), or imprisonment for not more than 60 days, or both.

1536. No athlete agency shall knowingly issue a contract containing any term or condition which, if complied with, would be in violation of law, or attempt to fill an order for help to be employed in violation of law.

1537. No athlete agency shall publish or cause to be published any false, fraudulent, or misleading information, representation, notice, or advertisement. All advertisements of an agency by means of cards, circulars, or signs, and in newspapers and other publications, and all letterheads, receipts, and blanks shall be printed and contain the registered name and address of the agency and the words "athlete agency." No athlete agency shall give any false information or make any false promises or representations concerning any employment to any person.

1538. No athlete agency shall knowingly secure employment for persons in any place where a strike, lockout, or other labor trouble exists, without notifying the person of such conditions.

1539. No athlete agency shall divide fees with an employer, an agent, or other employee of an employer.

1540. In the event that an athlete agency shall collect from a person a fee or expenses for obtaining employment, and the person shall fail to procure such employment, or the person shall fail to be paid for such employment, the agency shall, upon demand therefor, repay to the person the fee and expenses so collected. Unless repayment thereof is made within 48 hours after demand therefor, the agency shall pay to the person an additional sum equal to the amount of the fee.

1541. All actions brought in any court against any registrant may be brought in the name of the person damaged upon the bond deposited with the state by the registrant, and may be transferred and assigned as other claims for damages. The amount of damages claimed by plaintiff, and not the penalty named in the bond, determines the jurisdiction of the court in which the action is brought. . . .

1543. In cases of controversy arising under this chapter the parties involved shall refer the matters in dispute to the Labor Commissioner, who shall hear and determine the same, subject to an appeal within 10 days after determination, to the superior court where the same shall be heard de novo. To stay any award for money, the party aggrieved shall execute a bond approved by the superior court in a sum not exceeding twice the amount of the judgment. In all other cases the bond shall be in a sum of not less than ten thousand dollars ($10,000) and approved by the superior court. . . .

1544. Notwithstanding Section 1543, a provision in a contract providing for the decision by arbitration of any controversy under the contract or as to its existence, validity, construction, performance, nonperformance, breach, operation, continuance, or termination, shall be valid:

(a) If the provision is contained in a contract between an athlete agency and a person for whom the agency under the contract undertakes to endeavor to secure employment,

(b) If the provision is inserted in the contract pursuant to any rule, regulation, or contract of a bona fide labor union regulating the relations of its members to an agency,

(c) If the contract provides for reasonable notice to the Labor Commissioner of the time and place of all arbitration hearings, and

(d) If the contract provides that the Labor Commissioner or his authorized representative has the right to attend all arbitration hearings.

Except as otherwise provided in this section, any such arbitration shall be governed by the provisions of Title 9 (commencing with Section 1280) of Part 3 of the Code of Civil Procedure.

If there is such an arbitration provision in such a contract, the contract need not provide that the agency agrees to refer any controversy between the person and the agency regarding the terms of the contract to the Labor Commissioner for adjustment, and Section 1543 shall not apply to controversies pertaining to the contract.

A provision in a contract providing for the decision by arbitration of any controversy arising under this chapter which does not meet the requirements of this section is not made valid by Section 1281 of the Code of Civil Procedure.

1545. (a) An athlete agency shall, prior to communicating with or contacting in any manner any student concerning an agency contract or a professional sport services contract, file with the postsecondary educational institution at which the student is enrolled a copy of the registration certificate of the athlete agency.

(b) An athlete agency shall file a copy of each agency contract and professional sport services contract made with any student, with the postsecondary educational institution at which the student is enrolled, within five days after such contract is signed by the student party thereto.

(c) Filing of the copies required by subdivisions (a) and (b) shall be made with the president or chief administrative officer of such postsecondary educational institution, or the secretary of such officer, or by registered or certified mail, return receipt requested, directed to such officer.

1546. Any agency contract and professional sport services contract which is negotiated by any agency who has failed to comply with Section 1545 is void and unenforceable.

1547. Any person, or agent or officer thereof, who violates any provision of this chapter is guilty of a misdemeanor, punishable by a fine of not less than one thousand dollars ($1,000) or imprisonment for period of not more than 60 days, or both. . . .

NOTES

1. The senate of the California legislature has a Select Committee on Licensed and Designated Sports, whose staff has been active in assessing the impact of the foregoing California legislation. Many are of the opinion that the statute, as originally passed, suffered from ambiguity and arguable underinclusion. Thus, the committee in 1984 proposed amendments to the California law that would change the current registration system to a licensing system. The most significant change would seem to be in defining what "agents" must be licensed — in particular, the new category characterized as "attorney agent." Though the amendments were not approved in 1984, their chances of eventual passage are strong. Accordingly, the definitional language is included here for analysis. Proposed new language appears in italics.

Section 1. The heading of Chapter 1 (commencing with Section 1500) of Part 6 of Division 2 of the Labor Code is amended to read:
CHAPTER 1. ATHLETE AGENCIES *AGENT*
SEC. 2. Section 1500 of the Labor Code is amended to read:
1500. The following definitions shall govern the construction of this chapter:

(a) "Person" means any individual, company, corporation, association, partnership, or their agents or employees.

(b) "Athlete agency" *agent*" means any person who, as an independent contractor, directly or indirectly, recruits or solicits any person to enter into any agency *agent* contract or professional sport services contract, or for a fee procures, offers, promises, or attempts to obtain employment for any person with a professional sport team.

"Athlete agency" *agent*" does not include any employee of a professional sport team, and does not include any member of the State Bar of California when acting as legal counsel for any person.

(b) *"Attorney agent" means any member of the State Bar of California who, as an independent contractor, or in conjunction with a firm, directly or indirectly recruits or solicits any person to enter into an agent contract or professional sport services contract, or for a fee procures, offers, promises, or attempts to obtain employment for any person with a professional sport team.*

(c) "Agent" means both athlete agent and attorney agent.

(c) "Agency

(d) "Agent contract" means any contract or agreement pursuant to which a person authorizes or empowers an athlete agency *agent* to negotiate or solicit on behalf of such *the* person with one or more professional sport teams for the employment of such *the* person by one or more professional sport teams.

(e) "Professional sport services contract" means any contract or agreement pursuant to which a person is employed or agrees to render services as a participant or player on a professional sport team.

2. Discussion of the California legislation, as originally enacted, can be found in the following articles:

(a) Fox, "Regulating the Professional Sports Agent: Is California in the Right Ballpark?" 15 *Pacific Law Journal* 1231 (1984).

(b) Sobel, "The Regulation of Player Agents," *Entertainment Law Reporter* (March, 1984), p.3.

3. In 1979, in the aftermath of the Richard Sorkin incident (see note 1 after *Zinn* v. *Parrish, infra*), there was concerted activity in the New York legislature to enact legislation somewhat along the lines of that subsequently adopted in California. The bill introduced by Senator Marino generated substantial publicity but was not enacted. See State of New York, In Senate, No. 5972, 1979–80 Regular Sessions, May 15, 1979.

4. Boxing managers have long been licensed in a number of jurisdictions. Cases dealing with contracts between a manager and boxer should be considered in their own right, as well as for the purpose of suggesting certain problems that might arise in other sports.

(a) *In Rosenfeld* v. *Jeffra*, 1 N.Y.S. 2d 388 (Sup.Ct. 1937), plaintiff manager sought an injunction to prevent defendant boxer from engaging in a contest arranged by defendant Blaustein, in violation of a contract between the manager and boxer which provided that only the manager could arrange exhibitions on behalf of the boxer. The defendants moved for dismissal on the grounds that plaintiff was not licensed as a manager by the New York State Athletic Commission. The court upheld the motion, stating that a contract made by an unlicensed manager is void, and the provisions of the contract will not be upheld in the state of New York.

(b) In *Zwirn* v. *Galento*, 43 N.E. 2d 474 (N.Y.Ct.App. 1942) plaintiff administrator for the estate of a boxing manager sought recovery for completion of a contract whereby the manager was to receive 33 percent of defendant boxer's earnings. Joe Jacobs and defendant entered into a contract on March 20, 1939, whereby defendant agreed to render his exclusive services to manager Jacobs. In exchange for Jacobs using his best efforts to secure remunerative boxing contests for defendant, defendant promised to pay Jacobs 33 percent of his earnings. The contract also stipulated that it would not be valid unless (1) the New York State Athletic Commission approved the contract and (2) the manager was duly licensed by the commission to act as manager. It was undisputed that the contract was never approved by the commission and that Jacobs was never duly licensed as manager.

In March 1940, Jacobs procured a contract for defendant to fight Max Baer in Jersey City, New Jersey, on May 28, 1940. Jacobs died on April 24. Although the fight was postponed until July 2, 1940, the agreement initiated by Jacobs remained intact and unchanged. Defendant earned $33,571 for the bout, plus additional unknown sums for radio and movie rights. Plaintiff sought recovery of 33 percent of these sums.

Defendant moved for and was granted a dismissal at the trial level on the grounds that since the contact was never approved by the Athletic Commission, and since Jacobs was not duly licensed, the contract was unenforceable. But the court of appeals held that the condition of the contract had been waived, since the fight took place outside the state of New York. The court found that the contract between Jacobs and Galento was valid in its origin, valid on its face, and had no illegal objective. Further, a reasonable interpretation of the agreement led to the conclusion that the conditions precedent (licensing and the commission's approval) applied only to exhibitions to be held in New York.

The court continued by declaring that the contract was not invalid as contrary to the public policy of New York. Further, injustice would prevail if plaintiff were denied the right to recover for services which plaintiff's intestate rendered in obtaining a contract for defendant.

This case was held to differ in one major respect from the case of *Rosenfeld* v. *Jeffra* — that is, in *Zwirn* v. *Galento* the fight took place and the contract was executed in New Jersey. The New York licensing regulations were therefore inapplicable.

(c) *Trammel* v. *Morgan*, 158 N.E. 2d 541 (Ohio Ct.App. 1957) was an action brought by plaintiff manager on the basis of an agreement entered with defendant's father, which provided for plaintiff to manage defendant's boxing career until November 15, 1955. On October 9, 1955, plaintiff and defendant entered into an agreement for plaintiff to manage defendant for an additional five years, and further, for plaintiff to purchase a home for defendant, suitable for his family, at a fair price to be paid out of defendant's earnings. On November 17, 1955, defendant entered into an agreement with a third party for the latter to manage defendant for a period of five years.

The court of appeals held that the purchase of the house was a condition precedent to the agreement becoming effective as a binding contract, and therefore, the agreement was too indefinite for enforcement. Further, the court found no consideration was rendered by the plaintiff, thus causing the contract to fail.

(d) In a case dealing with California statutes regulating professional boxing in the state, a federal district court found that the failure of a boxing manager to comply with several regulations under the statutes rendered the boxer-manager contract unenforceable. However, under the circumstances of the case, the court declined to void the contract as it had the power to do. Instead, because of the manager's good faith efforts on the boxer's behalf, the court used its equity powers to fashion a remedy that reimbursed the manager for money advanced under the agreement. See *George Foreman Associates, Ltd.* v. *Foreman*, 389 F.Supp. 1308, *affd.* 517 F.2d 354 (9th Cir. 1975). In reaching its conclusions the trial court relied heavily on *Baksi* v. *Wallman*, 65 N.Y.S.2d 894, *affd.* 74 N.E.2d 172 (N.Y. 1947).

Zinn v. Parrish, 644 F.2d 360 (7th Cir. 1981)

Agent Leo Zinn and professional football player Lemar Parrish of the Cincinnati Bengals entered into a multiyear personal management contract in 1971. Under the terms of the agreement, Zinn was obligated to use "reasonable efforts" to procure professional football employment for Parrish and to act in Parrish's professional interests. Specifically, Zinn was required to negotiate job contracts, furnish advice on business investments, secure professional tax advice, and obtain endorsement contracts. Zinn also agreed to use reasonable efforts to secure off-season employment at Parrish's request. In return, Parrish agreed to pay Zinn 10 percent of his salary and endorsement contracts as agent fees. The contract was automatically renewed each year unless one of the parties terminated it by 30 days' notice.

From 1971 to 1974, Zinn successfully negotiated Parrish's football contract with the Bengals, obtaining increasingly lucrative amounts; Parrish's salary rose from $18,500 in 1971 to $250,000 covering the four seasons from 1974 to 1977, including a $30,000 signing bonus. With respect to Zinn's obligation to assist Parrish financially, Zinn arranged for Parrish's taxes to be professionally prepared, and he assisted Parrish in purchasing a residence and an apartment building for rental income. Zinn also obtained one endorsement contract for Parrish, but failed with a number of similar deals; nor was he able to obtain off-season employment for Parrish. Finally, and crucial to this action, Zinn forwarded to Parrish stock recommendations, which were prepared by others but screened by Zinn.

Parrish adequately compensated Zinn from 1971 through 1973, but shortly after signing the 1974 contracts, Parrish informed Zinn that he no longer needed his services and stopped payment. Zinn thus sought to recover, as his agent fees, the 10 percent commission on the 1974–1977 Bengals' contracts.

The appeals court overturned the district court's ruling that the personal management contract was void under the 1940 Employment Agency Act (15 U.S.C., Sec.80b–3[a]), which required Zinn to register and obtain a license before he disseminated investment advice. The court held that Zinn's screening of the securities for Parrish was an isolated transaction and merely incidental to the main purpose of the management contract to negotiate football contracts. Additionally, Zinn did not hold himself out as an investment advisor, either by advertisement or word of mouth. For these reasons, Zinn's conduct did not fall under the activity regulated by the 1940 act, and the contract could not be voided.

The court next considered whether Zinn fulfilled the terms of the contract to use reasonable efforts to procure professional football employment. Noting that Parrish never objected to Zinn's performance for the first three years and that Zinn performed substantial services in negotiating the 1974–1977 contracts with the Bengals, the court could not find "any basis for Parrish to complain." With respect to Zinn's other obligations, the court found that while Zinn failed to obtain jobs or contracts in many cases, it was not a failure to perform. The court, relying on the district court's finding that Zinn acted in good faith at all times, held that Zinn was entitled to a percentage of all amounts earned by Parrish under the 1974, 1975, 1976, and 1977 Bengals' contracts.

NOTES

1. Some agents have been accused of going far beyond the activities which resulted in the defenses raised by Lemar Parrish against Leo Zinn. Charges of outright fraud or embezzlement have been made and, at least in one instance, have been substantiated. Consider the following: Richard Sorkin's 1978 conviction for grand larceny represents an example of an agent misappropriating client funds. Sorkin allegedly misappropriated money from approximately 50 professional athletes he was representing, totaling more than $1.2 million. Acting as their agent and handling their funds, Sorkin had easy access to the athlete's monies and squandered their funds for his own uses, either through mob gambling or bad personal investments. See: *People* v. *Sorkin*, No. 46429 (Nassau County, N.Y., Nov. 28, 1977), *sentence aff'd*, 407 N.Y.S.2d 772 (App.Div.2d Dept., July 24, 1978). See also, "The Spectacular Rise and Ignoble Fall of Richard Sorkin, Pros' Agent," *New York Times*, October 9, 1977, Sec. 5, p.1; *New York Times*, February 2, 1978, Sec. 4, p. 15.

2. Los Angeles Raiders running back, Greg Pruitt, filed a $2.4 million lawsuit in July 1984, charging his former investment advisor with securities fraud, racketeering, and embezzlement. Pruitt claimed that the advisor embezzled about $150,000 by forging Pruitt's name on checks and withdrawing money from Pruitt's account. Pruitt charged that some 156 checks were forged over a three-year period and that the advisor had made investments of Pruitt's money that yielded exceedingly low returns. The company for whom the advisor worked settled with Pruitt in late November 1984, and the suit was dropped. See *San Francisco Chronicle*, November 30, 1984, p. 87.

3. One other case involving a professional athlete suing his former agent, which resulted in a finding for the player, was *Burrow* v. *Probus Management Inc.*, Civil No. 16840 (N.D. Ga., Aug.9, 1973) (unpublished order).

Detroit Lions, Inc. and Sims v. Argovitz, 580 F.Supp. 542 (E.D.Mich. 1984)

DeMascio, District Judge.

The plot for this Saturday afternoon serial began when Billy Sims, having signed a contract with the Houston Gamblers on July 1, 1983, signed a second contract with the Detroit Lions on December 16, 1983. On December 18, 1983, the Detroit Lions, Inc. (Lions) and Billy R. Sims filed a complaint in the Oakland County Circuit Court seeking a judicial determination that the July 1, 1983, contract between Sims and the Houston Gamblers, Inc. (Gamblers) is invalid because the defendant Jerry Argovitz (Argovitz) breached his fiduciary duty when negotiating the Gamblers' contract and because the contract was otherwise tainted by fraud and misrepresentation. Defendants promptly removed the action to this court based on our diversity of citizenship jurisdiction.

For the reasons that follow, we have concluded that Argovitz's breach of his fiduciary duty during negotiations for the Gamblers' contract was so pronounced, so egregious, that to deny recision would be unconscionable.

Sometime in February or March 1983, Argovitz told Sims that he had applied for a Houston franchise in the newly formed United States Football League (USFL). In May 1983, Sims attended a press conference in Houston at which Argovitz announced that his application for a franchise had been approved. The evidence persuades us that Sims did not know the extent of Argovitz's interest in the Gamblers. He did not know the amount of Argovitz's original investment, or that Argovitz was obligated for 29 percent of a $1.5 million letter of credit, or that Argovitz was the president of the Gamblers' Corporation at an annual salary of $275,000 and 5 percent of the yearly cash flow. The defendants could not justifiably expect Sims to comprehend the ramifications of Argovitz's interest in the Gamblers or the manner in which that interest would create an untenable conflict of interest, a conflict that would inevitably breach Argovitz's fiduciary duty to Sims. Agovitz knew, or should have known, that he could not act as Sims' agent under any circumstances when dealing with the Gamblers. Even the USFL Constitution itself prohibits a holder of any interest in a member club from acting "as the contracting agent or representative for any player."

Pending the approval of his application for a USFL franchise in Houston, Argovitz continued his negotiations with the Lions on behalf of Sims. On April 5, 1983, Argovitz offered Sims' services to the Lions for $6 million over a four-year period. The offer included a demand for a $1 million interest-free loan to be repaid over 10 years, and for skill and injury guarantees for three years. The Lions quickly responded with a counter offer on April 7, 1983, in the face amount of $1.5 million over a five-year period with additional incentives not relevant here. The negotiating process was working. The Lions were trying to determine what Argovitz really believed the market value for Sims really was. On May 3, 1983, with his Gamblers franchise assured, Argovitz significantly reduced his offer to the Lions. He now offered Sims to the Lions for $3 million over a four-year period, one-half of the amount of his April 5, 1983, offer. Argovitz's May 3rd offer included a demand for $50,000 to permit Sims to purchase an annuity. Argovitz also dropped his previous demand for skill guarantees. The May 10, 1983, offer submitted by the Lions brought the parties much closer.

On May 30, 1983, Argovitz asked for $3.5 million over a five-year period. This offer included an interest-free loan and injury protection insurance but made no demand for skill guarantees. The May 30 offer now requested $400,000 to allow Sims to purchase an annuity. On June 1, 1983, Argovitz and the Lions were only $500,000 apart. We find that the negotiations between the Lions and Argovitz were progressing normally, not laterally as Argovitz represented to Sims. The Lions were not "dragging their feet." Throughout the entire month of June 1983, Mr. Frederick Nash, the Lions' skilled negotiator and a fastidious lawyer, was involved in investigating the possibility of providing an attractive annuity for Sims and at the same time doing his best to avoid the granting of either skill or injury guarantees. The evidence establishes that on June 22, 1983, the Lions and Argovitz were very close to reaching an agreement on the value of Sims' services.

Apparently, in the midst of his negotiations with the Lions and with his Gamblers franchise in hand, Argovitz decided that he would seek an offer from the Gamblers. Mr. Bernard Lerner, one of Argovitz's partners in the Gamblers, agreed to negotiate a contract with Sims. Since Lerner admitted that he had no knowledge whatsoever about football, we must infer that Argovitz at the very least told Lerner the amount of money required to sign Sims and further pressed upon Lerner the Gamblers' absolute need to obtain Sims' services. In the Gamblers' organization, only Argovitz knew the value of Sims' services and how critical it was for the Gamblers to obtain Sims. In Argovitz's words, Sims would make the Gamblers' franchise.

On June 29, 1983, at Lerner's behest, Sims and his wife went to Houston to negotiate with a team that was partially owned by his own agent. When Sims arrived in Houston, he believed that the Lions organization was not negotiating in good faith; that it was not really interested in his services. His ego was bruised and his emotional outlook towards the Lions was visible to Burrough and Argovitz. Clearly, virtually all the information that Sims had up to that date came from Argovtiz. Sims and the Gamblers did not discuss a future contract on the night of June 29th. The negotiations began on the morning of June 30, 1983, and ended that afternoon. At the morning meeting, Lerner offered Sims a $3.5 million five-year contract, which included three years of skill and injury guarantees. The offer included a $500,000 loan at an interest rate of 1 percent over prime. It was from this loan that Argovitz planned to receive the $100,000 balance of his fee for acting as an agent in negotiating a contract with his own team. Burrough testified that Sims would have accepted that offer on the spot because he was finally receiving the guarantee that he had been requesting from the Lions, guarantees that Argovitz dropped without too much quarrel. Argovitz and Burrough took Sims and his wife into another room to discuss the offer. Argovitz did tell Sims that he thought the Lions would match the Gamblers' financial package and asked Sims whether he (Argovitz) should telephone the Lions. But, it is clear from the evidence that neither Sims nor Burrough believed that the Lions would match the offer. We find that Sims told Argovitz not to call the Lions for purely emotional reasons. As we have noted, Sims believed that the Lions' organization was not that interested in him and his pride was wounded. Burrough clearly admitted that he was aware of the emotional basis for Sims' decision not to have Argovitz phone the Lions, and we must conclude from the extremely close relationship between Argovitz and Sims that Argovitz knew it as well. When Sims went back to Lerner's office, he agreed to become a Gambler on the terms offered. At that moment, Argovitz irreparably breached his fiduciary duty. As agent for Sims he had the duty to telephone the Lions, receive its final offer, and present the terms of both offers to Sims. Then and only then could it be said that Sims made an intelligent and knowing decision to accept the Gamblers' offer.

During these negotiations at the Gamblers' office, Mr. Nash of the Lions telephoned Argovitz, but even though Argovitz was at his office, he declined to accept the telephone call. Argovitz tried to return Nash's call after Sims had accepted the Gamblers' offer, but it was after 5 p.m. and Nash had left for the July 4th weekend. When he declined to accept Mr. Nash's call, Argovitz's breach of his fiduciary duty became even more pronounced. Following Nash's example, Argovitz left for his weekend trip, leaving his principal to sign the contracts with the Gamblers the next day, July 1, 1983. The defendants, in their supplemental trial brief, assert that neither Argovitz nor Burrough can be held responsible for following Sims' instruction not to contact the Lions on June 30, 1983. Although it is generally true that an agent is not liable for losses occurring as a result of following his principal's instructions, the rule of law is not applicable when the agent has placed himself in a position adverse to that of his principal.

During the evening of June 30, 1983, Burrough struggled with the fact that they had not presented the Gamblers' offer to the Lions. He knew, as does the court, that Argovitz now had the wedge that he needed to bring finality to the Lions' negotiations. Burrough was acutely aware of the fact that Sims' actions were emotionally motivated and realized that the responsibility for Sims' future rested with him. We view with some disdain the fact that Argovitz had, in effect, delegated his entire fiduciary responsibility on the eve of his principal's most important career decision. On July 1, 1983, it was Lerner who gave lip service to Argovitz's conspicuous conflict of interest. It was Lerner, not Argovitz, who advised Sims that Argovitz's position with the Gamblers presented a conflict of interest and that Sims could, if he wished, obtain an attorney or another agent. Argovitz, upon

whom Sims had relied for the past four years, was not even there. Burrough, conscious of Sims' emotional responses, never advised Sims to wait until he had talked with the Lions before making a final decision. Argovitz's conflict of interest and self-dealing put him in the position where he would not even use the wedge he now had to negotiate with the Lions, a wedge that is the dream of every agent. Two expert witnesses testified that an agent should telephone a team that he has been negotiating with once he has an offer in hand. Mr. Woolf, plaintiff's expert, testified that an offer from another team is probably the most important factor in negotiations. Mr. Lustig, defendant's expert, believed that it was prudent for him to telephone the Buffalo Bills and inform that organization of the Gamblers' offer to Jim Kelly, despite the fact that he believed the Bills had already made its best offer to his principal. The evidence here convinces us that Argovitz's negotiations with the Lions were ongoing and it had not made its final offer. Argovitz did not follow the common practice described by both expert witnesses. He did not do this because he knew that the Lions would not leave Sims without a contract and he further knew that if he made that type of call Sims would be lost to the Gamblers, a team he owned.

On November 12, 1983, when Sims was in Houston for the Lions game with the Houston Oilers, Argovitz asked Sims to come to his home and sign certain papers. He represented to Sims that certain papers of his contract had been mistakenly overlooked and now needed to be signed. Included among those papers he asked Sims to sign was a waiver of any claim that Sims might have against Argovitz for his blatant breach of his fiduciary duty brought on by his glaring conflict of interest. Sims did not receive independent advice with regard to the wisdom of signing such a waiver. Despite having sold his agency business in September, Argovitz did not even tell Sims' new agent of his intention to have Sims sign a waiver. Nevertheless, Sims, an unsophisticated young man, signed the waiver. This is another example of the questionable conduct on the part of Argovitz, who still had business management obligations to Sims. In spite of his fiduciary relationship he had Sims sign a waiver without advising him to obtain independent counseling.

Argovitz's negotiations with Lustig, Jim Kelly's

agent, illustrates the difficulties that develop when an agent negotiates a contract where his personal interests conflict with those of his principal. Lustig, an independent agent, ignored Argovitz's admonishment not to "shop" the Gamblers' offer to Kelly. Lustig called the NFL team that he had been negotiating with because it was the "prudent" thing to do. The Gamblers agreed to pay Kelly, an untested rookie quarterback, $3.2 million for five years. His compensation was $60,000 less than Sims', a former Heisman Trophy winner and a proven star in the NFL. Lustig also obtained a number of favorable clauses from Argovitz; the most impressive one being that Kelly was assured of being one of the three top paid quarterbacks in the USFL if he performed as well as expected. If Argovitz had been free from conflicting interests he would have demanded similar benefits for Sims. Argovitz claimed that the nondisclosure clause in Kelly's contract prevented him from mentioning the Kelly contract to Sims. We view this contention as frivolous. Requesting these benefits for Sims did not require disclosure of Kelly's contract. Moreover, Argovitz's failure to obtain personal guarantees for Sims without adequately warning Sims about the risks and uncertainties of a new league constituted a clear breach of his fiduciary duty.

The parties submitted a great deal of evidence and argued a number of peripheral issues. Although most of the issues were not determinative factors in our decision, they do demonstrate that Argovitz had a history of fulfilling his fiduciary duties in an irresponsible manner. One cannot help but wonder whether Argovitz took his fiduciary duty seriously. For example, after investing approximately $76,000 of Sims' money, Argovitz, with or without the prior knowledge of his principal, received a finder's fee. Despite the fact that Sims paid Argovitz a 2 percent fee, Argovitz accepted $3800 from a person with whom he invested Sims' money. In March 1983, Argovitz had all of his veteran players, including Sims, sign a new agency contract with less favorable payment terms for the players even though they already had an ongoing agency agreement with him. He did this after he sold his entire agency business to Career Sports. Finally, Argovitz was prepared to take the remainder of his 5 percent agency fee for negotiating Sims' contract with the Gamblers from monies the Gamblers

loaned to Sims at an interest rate of 1 percent over prime. It mattered little to Argovitz that Sims would have to pay interest on the $100,000 that Argovitz was ready to accept. While these practices by Argovitz are troublesome, we do not find them decisive in examining Argovitz's conduct while negotiating the Gamblers' contract on June 30 and July 1, 1983. We find this circumstantial evidence useful only insofar as it has aided the court in understanding the manner in which these parties conducted business.

We are mindful that Sims was less than forthright when testifying before the court. However, we agree with plaintiff's counsel that the facts as presented through the testimony of other witnesses are so unappealing that we can disregard Sims' testimony entirely. We remain persuaded that on balance, Argovitz's breach of his fiduciary duty was so egregious that a court of equity cannot permit him to benefit by his own wrongful breach. We conclude that Argovitz's conduct in negotiating Sims' contract with the Gamblers rendered it invalid.

Conclusions of Law

1. This court's jurisdiction is based on diversity of citizenship and, therefore, Michigan's conflict of laws rules apply.

2. The Michigan courts would apply the law of Texas because all of the contracts giving rise to a claim of fraud or breach of fiduciary duty occurred in Texas. Moreover the parties have stipulated to the application of Texas law.

3. The relationship between a principal and agent is fiduciary in nature, and as such imposes a duty of loyalty, good faith, and fair and honest dealing on the agent.

4. A fiduciary relationship arises not only from a formal principal-agent relationship, but also from informal relationships of trust and confidence.

5. In light of the express agency agreement, and the relationship between Sims and Argovitz, Argovitz clearly owed Sims the fiduciary duties of an agent at all times relevant to this lawsuit.

6. An agent's duty of loyalty requires that he not have a personal stake that conflicts with the principal's interest in a transaction in which he represents his principal . . .

7. A fiduciary violates the prohibition against

self-dealing not only by dealing with himself on his principal's behalf, but also by dealing on his principal's behalf with a third party in which he has an interest, such as a partnership in which he is a member . . .

8. Where an agent has an interest adverse to that of his principal in a transaction in which he purports to act on behalf of his principal, the transaction is voidable by the principal unless the agent disclosed all material facts within the agent's knowledge that might affect the principal's judgment . . .

9. The mere fact that the contract is fair to the principal does not deny the principal the right to rescind the contract when it was negotiated by an agent in violation of the prohibition against self-dealing . . .

10. Once it has been shown that an agent had an interest in a transaction involving his principal antagonistic to the principal's interest, fraud on the part of the agent is presumed. The burden of proof then rests upon the agent to show that his principal had full knowledge, not only of the fact that the agent was interested, but also of every material fact known to the agent which might affect the principal and that having such knowledge, the principal freely consented to the transaction.

11. It is not sufficient for the agent merely to inform the principal that he has an interest that conflicts with the principal's interest. Rather, he must inform the principal "of all facts that come to his knowledge that are or may be material or which might affect his principal's rights or interests or influence the action he takes."

12. Argovitz clearly had a personal interest in signing Sims with the Gamblers that was adverse to Sims' interest — he had an ownership interest in the Gamblers and thus would profit if the Gamblers were profitable, and would incur substantial personal liabilities should the Gamblers not be financially successful. Since this showing has been made, fraud on Argovitz's part is presumed, and the Gamblers' contract must be rescinded unless Argovitz has shown by a preponderance of the evidence that he informed Sims of every material fact that might have influenced Sims' decision whether or not to sign the Gamblers' contract.

13. We conclude that Argovitz has failed to show by a preponderance of the evidene either: 1) that he informed Sims of the following facts, or 2)

that these facts would not have influenced Sims' decisions whether to sign the Gamblers' contract:

a. The relative value of the Gamblers' contract and the Lions' offer that Argovitz could be obtained.

b. That there was significant financial differences between the USFL and the NFL not only in terms of the relative financial stability of the Leagues, but also in terms of the fringe benefits available to Sims.

c. Argovitz's 29 percent ownership in the Gamblers; Argovitz's $275,000 annual salary with the Gamblers; Argovitz's five percent interest in the cash flow of the Gamblers.

d. That both Argovitz and Burrough failed to even attempt to obtain for Sims valuable contract clauses which they had given to Kelly on behalf of the Gamblers.

e. That Sims had great leverage, and Argovitz was not encouraging a bidding war that could have advantageous results for Sims.

14. Under Texas law, a nonbinding prior act cannot be ratified, and the right to seek recision cannot be waived, unless the party against whom these defenses are asserted had full knowledge of all material facts at the time the acts of ratification or waiver are alleged to have occurred.

15. At no time prior to December 1, 1983, was Sims aware of the material nondisclosures outlined above; accordingly, the defenses of ratification and waiver must be rejected.

16. Defendants' asserted defenses of estoppel and latches are also without merit.

17. As a court sitting in equity, we conclude that recision is the appropriate remedy. We are dismayed by Argovitz's egregious conduct. The careless fashion in which Argovitz went about ascertaining the highest price for Sims' service convinces us of the wisdom of the maxim: no man can faithfully serve two masters whose interests are in conflict.

Judgment will be entered for the plaintiffs rescinding the Gamblers' contract with Sims.

It is so ordered.

(Case citations were omitted.)

4.12 Ethical Constraints

The sports representative who is also an attorney faces the constraints imposed by the canons of ethics. This can be particularly troublesome when competing with nonlawyers, who do not face similar requirements. Issues relating to solicitation are foremost among these concerns.

Another ethical area is somewhat more subtle. This relates to dealing with athletes who still have remaining college athletic eligibility. Under the NCAA rules, any number of activities involving the athlete with a prospective representative may cause forfeiture of the athlete's remaining eligibility. While these regulations do not impose restrictions directly on the sports representative, they do raise ethical issues for that person. It is also possible that a court might view a representative's activities, whereby the representative causes an athlete to lose eligibility, as constituting "unclean hands." This could affect the representative's legal remedies in certain situations.

American Bar Association: Code of Professional Responsibility

CANON 1: A Lawyer Should Assist in Maintaining the Integrity and Competence of the Legal Profession

Ethical Considerations

EC 1-5   A lawyer should maintain high standards of professional conduct and should encourage fellow lawyers to do likewise. He should be temperate and dignified, and he should refrain from all illegal and morally reprehensible conduct. Because of his position in society, even minor violations of law by a lawyer may tend to lessen public confidence in the legal profession. Obedience to law exemplifies respect for law. To lawyers especially, respect for the law should be more than a platitude.

CANON 2: A Lawyer Should Assist the Legal Profession in Fulfilling its Duty to Make Legal Counsel Available

Ethical Considerations

EC 2–3   Whether a lawyer acts properly in volunteering advice to a layman to seek legal services depends upon the circumstances. The giving of advice that one should take legal action could well be in fulfillment of the duty of the legal profession to assist laymen in recognizing legal problems. The advice is proper only if motivated by a desire to protect one who does not recognize that he may have legal problems or who is ignorant of his legal rights or obligations. Hence the advice is improper if motivated by a desire to obtain personal benefit, secure personal publicity, or cause litigation to be brought merely to harass or injure another. Obviously, a lawyer should not contact a non-client, directly or indirectly, for the purpose of being retained to represent him for compensation.

EC 2-4   Since motivation is subjective and often difficult to judge, the motives of a lawyer who volunteers advice likely to produce legal controversy may well be suspect if he received professional employment or other benefits as a result. A lawyer who volunteers advice that one should obtain the services of a lawyer generally should not himself accept employment, compensation or other benefit in connection with that matter. However, it is not improper for a lawyer to volunteer such advice and render resulting legal services to close friends, relatives, former clients [in regard to matters germane to former employment], and regular clients.

EC 2-8   Selection of a lawyer by a layman often is the result of the advice and recommendation of third parties — relatives, friends, acquaintances, business associates, or other lawyers. A layman is best served if the recommendation is disinterested and informed. In order that the recommendation be disinterested, a lawyer should not seek to influence another to recommend his employment. A lawyer should not compensate another person for recommending him, for influencing a prospective client to employ him or to encourage future recommendations.

Disciplinary Rules

DR2-102 . . .(E) A lawyer who is engaged both in the practice of law and another profession or business shall not so indicate on his letterhead, office sign, or professional card, nor shall he identify himself as a lawyer in any publication in connection with his other business.

DR2-103 Recommendation of Professional Employment

(A) A lawyer shall not recommend employment,

as a private practitioner, of himself, his partner, or associate to a non-lawyer who has not sought his advice regarding employment of a lawyer.

(B) A lawyer shall not compensate or give anything of value to a person or organization to recommend or secure his employment by a client, or as a reward for having made a recommendation resulting in his employment by a client, except that he may pay the usual and reasonable fees or dues charged by any of the organizations listed in DR 2-103(D) . . .

Principles for the Conduct of Intercollegiate Athletics (from NCAA Constitution, Article Three)

Section 1. Principle of Amateurism and Student Participation. An amateur student-athlete is one who engages in a particular sport for the educational, physical, mental and social benefits derived therefrom and to whom participation in that sport is an avocation. . .

(a) An individual shall not be eligible for participation in an intercollegiate sport if the individual:

(1) Takes or has taken pay, or has accepted the promise of pay, in any form, for participation in that sport, including the promise of pay when such pay is to be received following completion of the intercollegiate career; or

(2) Has entered into an agreement of any kind to compete in professional athletics in that sport or to negotiate a professional contract in the sport; or

(3) Has directly or indirectly used athletic skill for pay in any form in that sport; however, a student athlete may accept or have accepted scholarships or educational grants-in-aid administered by an eductional institution which do not conflict with the governing legislation of this Association, and may receive compensation authorized by the United States Olympic Committee to cover financial loss occurring as a result of absence from employment to prepare for or participate in the Olympic Games. . . .

(b) Any individual who signs or who has ever signed a contract or commitment of any kind to play professional athletics in a sport, regardless of its legal enforceability or the consideration (if any) received; plays or has ever played on any professional athletic team in a sport, or receives or has ever received, directly or indirectly, a salary, reimbursement of expenses or any other form of financial assistance from a professional organization in a sport based upon athletic skill or participation, except as permitted by the governing legislation of this Association, no longer shall be eligible for intercollegiate athletics in that sport.

(1) A student-athlete shall be eligible although, prior to enrollment in a collegiate institution, the student-athlete may have tried out at his or her own expense with a professional athletic team in a sport or received not more than one expense-paid visit from any one professional organization in a sport, provided such a visit did not exceed 48 hours and any payment or compensation in connection with the visit was not in excess of actual and necessary expenses.

(2) A student-athlete shall not try out with a professional athletic team in a sport during any part of the academic year (i.e., from the beginning of the fall term through completion of the spring term, including any intervening vacation period) while enrolled in a collegiate institution as a regular student in at least a minimum full-time academic load, unless the student-athlete may try out with a professional organization in a sport during the summer or during the academic year while not a full-time student, provided the student-athlete does not receive any form of expenses or other compensation from the professional organization.

(c) Any individual who contracts or who has ever contracted orally or in writing to be represented by an agent in the marketing of the individual's athletic ability or reputation in a sport no longer shall be eligible for intercollegiate athletics in that sport. An agency contract not specifically limited in writing to a particular sport or particular sports shall be deemed applicable to all sports. Securing advice from a lawyer concerning a proposed professional sports contract shall not be considered contracting for representation by an agent under this rule unless the lawyer also represents the student-athlete in negotiations for such a contract. Any individual agency or organization representing a prospective student-athlete for compensation in placing the prospect in a collegiate institution as a recipient of athletically related financial aid shall be considered an agent or organization marketing the athletic ability or reputation of the individual.

(d) An individual may participate singly or as a

member of a team against professional athletes; but if the individual participates or has ever participated on a team known to the individual or which reasonably should have been known to the individual to be a professional team in that sport, that individual no longer shall be eligible for intercollegiate athletics in that sport. . . .

0.1. 3. A professional team shall be any organized team which is a member of a recognized professional sports organization, which is directly supported or sponsored by a professional team or professional sports organization, which is a member of a playing league that is directly supported or sponsored by a professional team or professional sports organization or on which there is an athlete receiving directly or indirectly payment of any kind from a professional team or professional sports organization for the athlete's participation.

0.1. 4. A noncollegiate amateur team or playing league which receives financial support from a national amateur sports administrative organization or an administrative equivalent, either of which receives developmental funds from a professional team or professional sports organization, shall not be considered a professional team or league.

0.1. 5. An individual may compete on tennis or golf teams with persons who are competing for cash or a comparable prize, provided the individual does not receive payment of any kind for such participation.

(e) Subsequent to becoming a student-athlete . . . an individual shall not be eligible for participation in intercollegiate athletics if the individual accepts any remuneration for or permits the use of his or her name or picture to directly advertise, recommend or promote the sale or use of a commercial product or service of any kind or receives remuneration for endorsing a commercial product or service through the individual's use of such product or service.

(1) If a student-athlete's appearance on radio or television is related in any way to athletic ability or prestige, the student-athlete shall not receive under any circumstances remuneration for that appearance; nor shall the student-athlete make any endorsement, expressed or implied, of any commercial product or service. The student-athlete may, however, receive legitimate and normal expenses directly related to such an appearance.

(2) It is permissible for a student-athlete's name or picture or the group picture of an institution's athletic squad to appear in an advertisement of a particular business, commercial product or service provided the advertisement does not include a reproduction of the product with which the business is associated or any other item or description identifying the business or service other than its name or trademark; there is no indication in the makeup or wording of the advertisement that the squad members, individually or collectively, or the institution endorse the product or service of the advertiser, and the student-athlete has not signed a consent or release granting permission to use the student-athlete's name or picture in a manner inconsistent with the requirements of this paragraph.

(f) Compensation may be paid to a student-athlete only for work actually performed and at a rate commensurate with the going rate in that locality for services of like character. Such compensation may not include any remuneration for value or utility which the student-athlete may have for the employer because of the publicity, reputation, fame or personal following the student-athlete has obtained because of athletic ability. A student-athlete who receives compensation prohibited under this legislation no longer shall be eligible for participation in intercollegiate athletics, unless the compensation is authorized by the United States Olympic Committee to cover financial loss occurring as a result of absence from employment to prepare for or participate in the Olympic Games.

(1) A student-athlete may serve as a coach or an instructor for compensation in a physical education class outside of the student-athlete's institution in which the student-athlete teaches sports techniques or skills or both, but a student-athlete shall not be so employed if the employment is arranged by the student-athlete's institution or a representative of its athletic interests.

(2) A student-athlete may not receive compensation for teaching or coaching sports skills or techniques in the student-athlete's sport on a fee-for-lesson basis.

(3) A student-athlete may be employed by his or her institution to work in the institution's summer camp unless otherwise restricted by the provisions of the bylaws and interpretations relating to playing and practice seasons and

summer camps.

(4) A student-athlete may officiate games or contests for compensation except those involving teams which are members of or affiliated with a recognized professional sports organization. . . .

4.13 Player Association Certification

Largely through the impetus of player unions, various sports leagues are moving to control the player-representative relationship. Baseball has for some time required that a signed authorization by the player be filed with a club before the club will deal with that player's chosen representative.

Even more stringent requirements now exist in the National Football League, as a result of provisions inserted into the 1982 collective bargaining agreement. The NFL Players Association, pursuant to those provisions, has imposed registration and other requirements, including maximum fee schedules, on all who wish to act as contract advisors for NFL players. Because of the importance of these requirements in the representation of NFL players and because of the possible precedent this may set for other sports leagues, the NFLPA regulations are here reproduced in essentially full form. The suggested "Standard Representation Agreement between NFLPA Contract Advisor and Player" is set forth in Section 4.14.

NFLPA Regulations Governing Contract Advisors (Adopted September 4, 1983)

The Board of Representatives of the National Football League Players Association hereby adopts the following Regulations to govern the representation of NFL players in individual contract negotiations with the employer/clubs of the National Football League. This action is taken pursuant to the authority and duty conferred upon the NFLPA as the exclusive bargaining representative of NFL players under Section 9(a) of the National Labor Relations Act, which states:

Representatives designated or selected for the purposes of collective bargaining by the major-

ity of the employees in a unit appropriate for such purposes, shall be the *exclusive* representatives of *all* the employees in such unit for the purposes of collective bargaining in respect to *rates of pay, wages,* hours of employment, or other conditions of employment.

The authority and duty to promulgate these Regulations are also based upon Article XXII, Section 2 of the 1982 Collective Bargaining Agreement between the NFLPA and the NFL Management Council, which states in relevant part:

A player will be entitled to receive a signing or reporting bonus, additional salary payment, incentive bonuses and such other provisions as may be negotiated between his club (with the assistance of the Management Council) and the NFLPA or *its agent.*

Persons serving or wishing to serve as the NFLPA's "agent" pursuant to this provision, which persons are herein referred to as "Contract Advisors," shall be governed by these regulations.

Section 1: Scope of Regulations

No person shall be entitled to represent an NFL player in individual contract negotiations with NFL clubs unless he or she is first certified as an NFLPA Contract Advisor pursuant to these Regulations, and thereafter remains certified through compliance with these Regulations.

The following shall be considered activities or conduct of Contract Advisors which are governed by these Regulations:

A. Negotiating compensation and other benefits for player-clients in individual contract negotiations with NFL clubs;

B. Negotiating and drafting of special provisions which are inserted into the player contract form signed by individual players;

C. The giving of advice, counsel and information to individual players and the NFLPA in the context of negotiating with or preparing for negotiations with NFL clubs, or in enforcement of the contracts which the Contract Advisor negotiates;

D. The handling of player funds paid to or on behalf of players as compensation for NFL playing services; and

E. Any other activity or conduct which directly

bears upon the Contract Advisor's integrity, competence, or ability to properly represent individual NFL players and the NFLPA in individual contract negotiations.

Section 2: Requirements for Certification

A. *Application.* Any person desiring to obtain certification from the NFLPA as a Contract Advisor must file a verified Application for Certification . . . Certification shall be granted hereunder only to individual persons, and not to any firm, company, corporation or other entity.

B. *Compliance with Regulations.* Upon the filing of an Application for Certification, the applicant shall be deemed to have agreed with the NFLPA that:

(1) He or she will be bound by and shall conform with these Regulations, and shall not evade, violate, or circumvent, either directly or indirectly, these Regulations; and

(2) Any Certification issued by the NFLPA hereunder may be revoked if it is discovered that the application contained false or misleading statements of a material nature.

C. *Action on Application.* Within thirty days of the filing of an Application for Certification, the NFLPA shall determine whether Certification shall be granted to the applicant. This period may be extended for an additional 30 days upon written notification to the applicant within the initial 30-day period. Grounds for denial of Certification shall include, but not be limited to, the following:

(1) Failure of the applicant to have substantially complied with the Interim Authorization System for Agents used by the NFLPA from December 11, 1982 to the effective date of these Regulations;

(2) Prior conduct of the applicant involving fraud, misrepresentation, embezzlement, misappropriation of funds, or theft;

(3) Making false or misleading statements of a material nature in the Application for Certification or in the applicant's previously filed "NFLPA Information Sheet";

(4) Any other conduct which adversely affects the competence, credibility, or integrity of the applicant in serving as an NFLPA Contract Advisor.

In the event that an application is denied by the NFLPA pursuant to this Section, the applicant may appeal such action to the Arbitrator appointed pursuant to Section 7 of these Regulations. Such appeal shall be made by filing written notice of appeal with the NFLPA and the Arbitrator within 30 days of his or her receipt of the notice denying the Application for Certification.

Such appeal shall be decided in accordance with the procedures outlined in Section 7 of these Regulations.

D. *Representation of Players Pending Granting or Denial of Initial Certification.* The NFLPA may, in its discretion, authorize any person who has filed an Application for Certification to engage in individual contract negotiations for a specific player pending the granting or denial of Certification, in the event that such action is deemed to be in the best interests of the player. However such authorization shall be revocable, limited to the individual negotiation in question, and shall not be deemed as a waiver of the NFLPA's right to deny Certification under these Regulations.

E. *Form of Certification.* Upon approval of an applicant's Application for Certification as an NFLPA Contract Advisor, the Contract Advisor shall receive a written Certification. . . . Such Certification, however, shall not be considered in any way as conferring liability upon the NFLPA for any acts or conduct of the person certified, whether or not such acts or conduct fall within the activities governed by these Regulations.

Section 3: Participation by Certified Contract Advisor in Individual Negotiations

Any person who has been granted Certification pursuant to Section 2 above shall be permitted to thereafter act as a Contract Advisor in individual negotiations with NFL clubs for any player who requests him or her to act in such capacity and verifies such request to the NFLPA. The authority of the Contract Advisor to continue to act in such capacity, however, shall be subject to his or her continued compliance with these Regulations. The Contract Advisor shall be solely responsible and liable for, and shall hold the NFLPA harmless from, any damages or claims arising from his or her activities as a Contract Advisor.

Section 4: Agreements Between Contract Advisors and Players; Maximum Fees

A. *Standard Form.* Any Contract Advisor who is requested by an NFL player to act as the NFLPA's agent in individual contract negotiations with any

NFL club shall first sign a written agreement with the player ...* Upon and after signing, the Contract Advisor shall be the exclusive representative for negotiating the player contract(s) in question, subject to the player's right to terminate as contained in the form agreement. A copy of the executed agreement shall be mailed to the NFLPA within five (5) days of execution. A player may make an agreement with a Contract Advisor which is more, but not less, favorable to him than the form of contract. . . . No deviation, addition, or deletion shall be made in the form contract without the approval of the NFLPA.

All agreements between a Contract Advisor and a player which are not in writing or which are not in compliance with these Regulations shall be of no force and effect, and no Contract Advisor shall have any right to assert any claim for compensation on a basis other than what is specified in his or her written agreement with the player. The existence of a valid agreement between the Contract Advisor and an NFL player under these Regulations is conditioned upon the Contract Advisor becoming and remaining certified by the NFLPA for the term of such agreement.

B. *Existing Agreements.* Any agreement in existence between an NFL player and a Contract Advisor as of the effective date of these Regulations shall be deemed modified in accordance with these Regulations, except as such agreements pertain to the Contract Advisor's fees for the negotiation of NFL Player Contracts signed on or before September 4, 1983. To the extent that such existing agreement is less favorable to the NFL player than the provisions of these Regulations, these Regulations shall control insofar as they apply to the negotiation of the player's contract with an NFL club. Provisions of existing agreement(s) which apply to matters other than the negotiation of the player's contract may be considered severable and not affected by these Regulations. Any dispute concerning the proper application of these Regulations to existing agreements shall be resolved through the Arbitration procedures set forth in Section 7 of these Regulations.

C. *Contract Advisor's Compensation.* The maximum fee which may be charged or collected by a Contract Advisor shall be as follows:

(1) First contract year. A fee of no more than ten per cent (10%) of the compensation received by the player in *excess of the minimum salary applicable* to the player's years of service category for his services in the first year of the contract, or $1,000, whichever is greater, plus

(2) *Second contract year.* A fee of no more than five per cent (5%) of the compensation received by the player in excess of the minimum salary applicable to the player's years of service category for his services in the second year of the contract, plus

(3) *Third Contract year.* A fee of no more than two per cent (2%) of the compensation received by the player in excess of the minimum salary applicable to the player's years of service category for his services in the third year of the contract.

(4) *Guarantees.* In the event that the Contract Advisor negotiates provisions which *guarantee* payment to the player of any compensation attributable to the second and/or third years of the player's contract(s), the maximum fee percentage under sub-sections (2) and (3) above shall be increased from five per cent (5%) to seven per cent (7%) and from two per cent (2%) to three per cent (3%), respectively, of the compensation amounts which are so guaranteed.

(5) *Minimum salary contracts.* In the event that the Contract Advisor fails to negotiate compensation for the player in excess of the applicable minimum salary for any year covered by the contract(s) in question, the maximum fee which may be charged by the Contract Advisor shall be the lesser of:

(a) $125.00 for each hour spent by the Contract Advisor in negotiation of the contract; or

(b) The sum of $1,000.00.

Such fee shall not be payable, however, until and unless the player has been on the club's Active List under such contract for at least one regular season game.

As used in this subsection C, the term *compensation* shall be deemed to include only salary, signing bonus, or reporting bonus payments received by the player and attributable to the base year(s) of the contract(s) (i.e. not option year). For example, and without limitation, the term *compensation* shall not include any incentive or performance bonuses, any collectively bargained benefits or payments provided for in the player's individual

---

* The NFLPA suggested form appears in Section 4.14.

contract, or any compensation or benefits of any kind received for a player's services in the option year.

It is the intent of this subsection to prohibit a Contract Advisor from receiving any fee for his or her services until and unless the player receives the compensation upon which the fee is based. Accordingly, any portion of a fee based on player compensation which is deferred may not be collected by the Contract Advisor until and unless the deferred compensation is received by the player.

Notwithstanding the maximum fee provisions of this Section, a Contract Advisor may be entitled to receive a fee in excess of the maximum hereunder in cases of exceptional achievement on behalf of the player in negotiation of the player's contract(s), or in cases where an extraordinary amount of additional time was necessary to effectively complete the negotiation in question. The payment or amount of any such additional fee, however, shall be determined by the NFLPA upon application by the Contract Advisor and approved by the player involved.

Section 5: Requirements Concerning Contract Advisor's Conduct

It is of utmost concern to the NFLPA and the players it represents that persons serving as Contract Advisors hereunder conduct themselves in a manner which will:

(1) Assure the most effective representation possible in individual contract negotiations; and

(2) Avoid any conflict of interest which could potentially compromise the best interests of NFL players.

A. *General*

Therefore, a Contract Advisor shall be required to:

(1) Disclose upon request all information relevant to his or her qualifications to serve as a Contract Advisor, including educational background, special training, experience in negotiations, past representation of professional athletes, and relevant business associations or memberships in professional organizations;

(2) Maintain the highest degree of integrity and competence in individual negotiations with NFL clubs;

(3) Become and remain sufficiently educated in the areas of league structure and economics, applicable Collective Bargaining Agreements and other governing documents, basic negotiating techniques, and developments in sports law and related subjects;

(4) Fully comply with applicable state and federal laws;

(5) Fully comply with these Regulations and amendments hereto; and

(6) Attend at least once annually, an NFLPA briefing on individual contract negotiations.

B. *Prohibited Conduct*

An NFLPA Contract Advisor is prohibited from:

(1) Holding or seeking to hold, either directly or indirectly, a financial interest in any professional football team;

(2) Failing to disclose in writing to a player prior to accepting representation of such player, the names and current positions of any NFL management personnel whom he or she has represented or is representing in matters pertaining to their employment by or association with any NFL team;

(3) Engaging in any other activity which creates an actual or potential conflict of interest with the effective representation of NFL players;

(4) Negotiating and/or agreeing to any provision in a player contract which directly or indirectly violates or jeopardizes collectively bargained benefits or other provisions in any applicable documents which are designed to protect the working conditions of NFL players;

(5) Negotiating and/or agreeing to any provision in a player contract which directly or indirectly violates any stated policies, rules, or requirements established by the NFLPA;

(6) Failing to keep the NFLPA informed on a periodic basis of the developments in negotiation with NFL clubs involving individual players, or concealing material facts from the NFLPA or the player involved which relate to the subject of the individual negotiations in question, or failing to report to the NFLPA any known violations by an NFL club of a player's individual contract or a player's rights under other applicable documents; and

(7) Engaging in unlawful conduct and/or conduct involving material dishonesty, fraud, deceit, misrepresentation, or other conduct which reflects adversely on his or her fitness as a Contract Advisor or jeopardizes the effective representation of NFL players.

C. *Solicitation.* An NFLPA Contract Advisor is also prohibited from:

(1) Providing or offering to provide anything of significant value to a player in order to become the Contract Advisor for such player;

(2) Providing or offering to provide anything of significant value to any other person in return for a personal recommendation of the Contract Advisor's selection by a player;

(3) Providing materially false or misleading information to any person in the context of solicitation for selection as the Contract Advisor for any player;

(4) Using titles or business names which imply the existence of professional credentials which he or she does not actually possess; and

(5) Soliciting or accepting anything of value from any club or other NFL management personnel for his or her personal use or benefit.

Section 6: Oversight and Compliance Procedure

A. *Disciplinary Committee.* The President of the NFLPA shall appoint a three-person Disciplinary Committee which shall be charged with the responsibility of initiating disciplinary procedures against certified Contract Advisors who violate these Regulations. The Disciplinary Committee shall consist of active or retired NFL players chosen at the discretion of the President. The Staff Counsel of the NFLPA shall serve as a non-voting advisor to the Committee.

B. *Complaint; Filing.* Disciplinary proceedings against any certified Contract Advisor shall be initiated by the filing of a written Complaint against the Contract Advisor by the Disciplinary Committee. Such Complaint shall be based upon verified information received by the Disciplinary Committee from any person having knowledge of the action or conduct of the Contract Advisor in question, including players, other Contract Advisors, NFLPA staff, or other persons associated with professional football. The Complaint shall be sent to the Contract Advisor by prepaid certified mail addressed to the Advisor's business office, or may be hand-delivered to the Advisor personally at his or her business address. The Complaint shall contain a specific description of the action or conduct giving rise to the Complaint, and make reference to the Regulation(s) alleged to have been violated.

A Complaint must be filed by the Disciplinary Committee within one year from the date of the occurrence of the facts which give rise to the Complaint, or within one year from the date on which the facts became known to the Disciplinary Committee, whichever is later.

C. *Answer.* The Contract Advisor against whom the Complaint has been filed shall have twenty (20) days in which to file a written Answer to the Complaint. Such Answer shall be personally delivered to the offices of the NFLPA or sent by prepaid certified mail in care of the NFLPA Staff Counsel. The Answer must contain admissions or denials as to the facts alleged in the Complaint, and shall also assert any facts or arguments which the Contract Advisor wishes to state in his or her defense.

D. *Disciplinary Action.* Within ten (10) days after receipt of the Answer, the Disciplinary Committee shall inform the Contract Advisor in question as to the nature of the discipline, if any, which the Committee intends to impose, which discipline may include one or more of the following:

(1) Issuance by the Committee of an informal order of reprimand to be retained in the Contract Advisor's file at the NFLPA offices;

(2) Issuance of a formal letter of reprimand which may be made public through any NFLPA publication;

(3) A fine of not more than $5,000 (payable to a designated charity) and/or payment of a specific sum to any player represented by the Contract Advisor in an amount equal to any loss sustained by such player as a result of the Contract Advisor's action found to be in violation of these Regulations;

(4) Suspension for a time certain of the Contract Advisor's right to represent the NFLPA in individual contract negotiations for any NFL player; and

(5) Revocation of the Contract Advisor's Certification hereunder.

The Disciplinary Committee may extend the time for determining disciplinary action beyond the ten-day period referred to above by providing written notification to that effect to the Contract Advisor; provided, however, that the Disciplinary Committee must inform the Contract Advisor of its intended disciplinary action no later than the 30th day following the NFLPA's receipt of the Answer.

E. *Appeal.* The Contract Advisor against whom a Complaint has been filed under this Section may appeal the Disciplinary Committee's disciplinary action to the outside Arbitrator by filing written Notice of Appeal with the Arbitrator within twenty (20) days following his or her receipt of notification of the disciplinary action. The filing of an appeal shall result in an automatic stay of any disciplinary action. The outside Arbitrator shall be the same person used for resolution of disputes under Section 7 of these Regulations. Within thirty (30) days of receipt of the Notice of Appeal, the Arbitrator shall set a time and place for a hearing on the Appeal, which hearing shall take place in Washington, D.C. or New York unless the convenience of the parties involved, in the sole discretion of the Arbitrator, compels selection of a different site for the hearing.

F. *Conduct of Hearing.* At the hearing of any appeal, the NFLPA shall first present, through testimony or otherwise, any evidence concerning the Contract Advisor's action or conduct alleged to be in violation of these Regulations. The Contract Advisor shall then have the opportunity to respond with any evidence, either through testimony or otherwise, in support of his or her defense. Such hearing shall be conducted in accordance with the hearing procedures used by the American Arbitration Association.

At the close of the hearing or within ten (10) days thereafter, the Arbitrator shall issue a decision on the appeal, which decision shall either affirm, vacate, or modify the action of the Disciplinary Committee. No modification of such discipline, however, may result in more severe discipline than is contained in the Disciplinary Committee's action.

The decision of the Arbitrator will constitute full, final and complete disposition of the dispute, and will be binding upon the Contract Advisor involved, and the NFLPA. However, the Arbitrator will not have the jurisdiction or authority to add to, subtract from, or alter in any way the provisions of these Regulations or any other applicable document, and no decision of the Arbitrator shall prevent or preclude subsequent amendment of these Regulations in a manner which would compel a different result in subsequent disciplinary cases.

G. *Time Limits; Costs.* Each of the time limits set forth in this Section may be extended by mutual written agreement of the parties involved.

The fees and expenses of the Arbitrator and transcript costs, if any, will be borne by the NFLPA. Each party will bear the cost of its own witnesses, counsel, and the like. If and when the Arbitrator compels payment of money by the Contract Advisor, such payment shall be made within ten (10) days of receipt of the Arbitrator's Award.

Section 7: Arbitration Procedure

A. *Disputes Between Contract Advisors and Players.* Any dispute between an NFL player and a Contract Advisor concerning: (1) The conduct of individual negotiations by a Contract Advisor, (2) The payment of fees due or allegedly due by any player to a Contract Advisor, or (3) Other activities of the Contract Advisor within the scope of these Regulations, shall be resolved exclusively in accordance with the procedures set forth in this Section. All time limitations in this Section may be extended by mutual agreement of the parties involved.

B. *Filing.* The Arbitration of a dispute under this Section shall be initiated by the filing of a written grievance by an NFL player, or a certified Contract Advisor. Any such grievance must be filed within six months from the date of the occurrence or non-occurrence upon which the grievance is based or within six months from the date on which the facts of the matter became known or reasonably should have become known to the grievant, whichever is later. A player need not be under contract to an NFL club at the time a grievance relating to him hereunder arises or at the time such grievance is initiated or processed.

A player may initiate a grievance against a Contract Advisor by sending the written grievance by prepaid certified mail to the Contract Advisor's business address or by personal delivery at such address, and a Contract Advisor may initiate a grievance against a player by sending a written grievance by certified mail to the player and furnishing a copy thereof to the NFLPA, or by personal delivery of the grievance to the player with a copy to the NFLPA. The written grievance shall set forth the facts and circumstances giving rise to the grievance and a description of the relief sought. If a grievance is filed by a player hereunder without a copy being provided to the NFLPA, the Contract Advisor must promptly send a copy thereof to the NFLPA.

C. *Answer.* The party against whom a grievance has been filed will answer in writing by certified mail or personal delivery within ten (10) days of receipt of the grievance. The Answer will set forth admissions or denials as to the facts alleged in the grievance and shall also recite the position or arguments of the respondent in defense of his or her position. The respondent must provide a copy of the Answer to all other parties, and the NFLPA. Once the Answer is filed, the NFLPA shall promptly provide the Chairman of the Arbitration Panel with copies of the grievance and Answer and all other relevant documents.

D. *Mediation.* Once an answer is filed, the NFLPA shall undertake an investigation of the grievance and attempt to mediate the dispute. Such investigation and mediation shall be on an informal basis and the parties shall not be required to attend any meetings or hearings in connection therewith.

E. *Appeal.* If the grievance is not resolved through mediation within thirty (30) days of receipt by the NFLPA of the respondent's Answer, either party to the grievance may appeal to Arbitration by filing a written Notice of Appeal with the Arbitrator. Any case which is not appealed within ninety days (90) of the receipt of the Answer, however, shall be considered withdrawn and dismissed.

F. *Arbitrator.* The Executive Committee of the NFLPA shall select a person with sufficient experience in arbitration of issues in either the sports or entertainment business to serve as the outside Arbitrator hereunder.

G. *Hearing.* After receipt of a Notice of Appeal pursuant to this Section, the Arbitrator shall select a time and place for a hearing on the dispute, giving due consideration to the convenience of the parties involved and the degree of urgency for resolution of the dispute. At such hearing, all parties to the dispute and the NFLPA will have the right to present, by testimony or otherwise, any evidence relevant to the grievance. At the close of the hearing or within thirty days thereafter, the Arbitrator shall issue a written decision. Such decision shall constitute full, final and complete disposition of the grievance, and will be binding upon the player and the Contract Advisor involved, provided, however, that the Arbitrator will not have the jurisdiction or authority to add to, subtract from, or alter in any way the provisions of these Regulations or any other applicable document.

H. *Costs.* Each party will bear the costs of its own witnesses and counsel. Costs of arbitration, including the fees and expenses of the Arbitrator, will be borne equally between the parties to the grievance; provided, however, that the arbitrator may assess some or all of a party's costs to an opposing party if he or she deems the grievance or appeal to be frivolous in nature. If the Arbitrator grants a money award, it shall be paid within ten (10) days.

NOTE _____

1. The foregoing NFLPA regulations were adopted by the executive board of the union after substantial study and review. In the process of review, an advisory board drawn from entertainment and sports people outside the NFLPA were asked for comments and input. Models adopted from other entertainment union mechanisms for control of agents were studied. The Advisory Board consisted of the following: Ed Asner, president of the Screen Actors' Guild; Ellen Burstyn, president of Actors' Equity and her representative, Randy Barber; Bud Woolf, executive secretary of American Federation of Television and Radio Artists; Tony Chursky, president of the NASL Players Association; John Kerr, staff director of the Soccer Unions; Donald Dell, founder of American Tennis Professionals, and sports attorney; Bill Carpenter, general counsel of International Management Group; Robert Berry, professor of law, Boston College; Wayne Hooper, sports attorney. In addition, labor attorneys Ron Rosenberg and Chip Yablonski were overall advisors on the new system. See Garvey, *The Agent Game* (Washington, D.C.: Federation of Professional Athletes, 1984), p. 20.

4.14 Representative Player Agreements

The relationship established between the sports representative and the client has traditionally varied greatly in terms of the formality of any agreement effectuated between the parties. The agreement has ranged from a handshake to a letter of understanding to a detailed contract. Increasingly, interested parties within professional sports are urging that greater formality and detail be introduced into the relationship in order to safeguard the rights of both parties. For example, the NFLPA has suggested a contract form that might be used. Other groups, such as the Association for Representatives of Professional Athletes (ARPA), have also produced model forms (Exhibits 4–1 and 4–2).

Exhibit 4-1   NFLPA Suggested Contract

Standard Representation Agreement
Between
NFLPA Contract Advisor and Player

This Agreement is made this _____ day of _____ , 19_____ by and between
_____ , hereinafter "Player," and _____ ,
(name of player)   (name of Contract Advisor)
hereinafter "Contract Advisor," pursuant to and in accordance with the NFLPA Regulations Governing Contract Advisors, as adopted May 5, 1983 and amended from time to time thereafter. In consideration of the promises made by each to the other, Player and Contract Advisor agree as follows:

1. *Contract Negotiation Services.* Contract Advisor hereby warrants and represents that he has been duly ceritified as an NFLPA Contract Advisor pursuant to the NFLPA Regulations Governing Contract Advisors. Player hereby retains Contract Advisor to represent, advise, counsel, and assist Player in the negotiation, execution, and enforcement of his playing contract(s) in the National Football League. Such services are to be rendered by Contract Advisor pursuant to and in full compliance with the NFLPA Regulations Governing Contract Advisors. Contract Advisor, serving in a fiduciary capacity, shall act in such manner as to protect the best interests of Player and assure effective representation of Player in individual contract negotiations with NFL clubs. Contract Advisor shall not have the authority to bind or commit Player to enter into any contract without actual execution thereof by the Player.

2. *Contract Advisor's Compensation.* If Contract Advisor succeeds in negotiating an NFL Player Contract or contracts acceptable to Player and signed by Player during the term hereof, Contract Advisor shall be paid a fee equal to the following:

Note: Such fee may be less than but may not exceed the maximum fee for Contract Advisors provided in Section 4 of the NFLPA Regulations Governing Contract Advisors, and, in accordance with that Section, such fee shall not be due and payable to Contract Advisor unless and until Player receives the compensation provided for in the player contract(s) negotiated by Contract Advisor.

3. *Expenses.* Player shall reimburse Contract Advisor for all reasonable and necessary communication expenses (i.e., telephone and postage) actually incurred by Player's NFL Contract(s). Player shall also reimburse Contract Advisor for all reasonable and necessary travel expenses actually incurred by Contract Advisor during the term hereof in the negotiation of Player's NFL Contract(s), but only if such expenses and the approximate amounts thereof are approved in advance by Player. Player shall promptly pay all such expenses upon receipt of an itemized, written statement thereof from Contract Advisor.

4. *Disputes.* Any disputes between Player and Contract Advisor involving the interpretation or application of this Agreement or the obligations of the parties hereunder shall be resolved exclusively through the Arbitration Procedures set forth in Section 7 of the NFLPA Regulations Governing Contract Advisors. If Contract Advisor constitutes or represents an "athlete agency" governed by the Labor Code of the State of California, Contract Advisor shall provide reasonable notice to the Labor Committee of the State of California of the time and place of any arbitration hearing to be held under said Arbitration Procedures, and said Labor Commissioner or his authorized representative shall have the right to attend all arbitration hearings thereunder.

5. *Disclaimer of Liability.* Player and Contract Advisor, by virtue of entry into this Agreement, agree that they are not subject to the control or direction of any other person with respect to the timing, place, manner or fashion in which individual negotiations are to be conducted (except to the extent that Contract Advisor shall comply with NFLPA Regulations) and that they will save and hold harmless NFLPA, its officers, employees and representatives from any liability whatsoever with respect to their conduct and activities relating to or in connection with such individual negotiations.

6. *Term.* Except as provided otherwise in this Paragraph, the term of this Agreement shall begin on the date hereof and continue for the term of any player contract or series of contracts negotiated by Contract Advisor on Player's behalf and signed by Player within one year of the date of this Agreement. Player may terminate this Agreement at any time if:

a. Contract Advisor fails to disclose in writing to Player, prior to accepting representation of Player hereunder or continuing to represent Player hereunder, as the case may be, the names and positions of any NFL management personnel whom Contract Advisor has represented or is representing in matters pertaining to their employment by any NFL club; or

b. Contract Advisor substantially fails or refuses to negotiate in good faith on Player's behalf in individual contract negotiations with the NFL club(s) desiring Player's services.

Such termination shall be effective upon the Player's giving written notice to such effect, either personally delivered or sent by prepaid mail to Contract Advisor's business address.

In the event that Contract Advisor fails to negotiate an NFL Player Contract acceptable to Player and signed by him on or before the date which is one year after the date Player signs this Agreement, this Agreement shall automatically terminate as of such later date.

The revocation or suspension of Contract Advisor's Certification as an NFLPA Contract Advisor pursuant to the NFLPA Regulations Governing Contract Advisors shall automatically terminate this Agreement.

In the event that Player has an opportunity to negotiate a new player contract in the NFL at any time prior to the termination of the contract or series of contracts negotiated by Contract Advisor hereunder, Player shall not be obligated to retain Contract Advisor or use Contract Advisor's services for such negotiation, and Contract Advisor shall not be entitled to any fee for such negotiation unless Player retains Contract Advisor through the signing of a new Representation Agreement.

7. *Filing.* A copy of this Agreement shall be filed by Contract Advisor with the NFLPA within ten days of execution. Any deviation, deletion, or addition in this form shall not be valid until and unless approved by the NFLPA. Approval shall be automatic unless, within ten days after receipt of this Agreement by the NFLPA, the NFLPA notifies the parties either of disapproval or of extension of this ten-day period for investigation or clarification.

8. *Entire Agreement; Governing Law.* This Agreement, along with the NFLPA Regulations Governing Contract Advisors, governs the relationship between the parties hereto and can not be modified or supplemented orally. This Agreement supercedes all prior agreements between the parties on the same subject matter.

This Agreement shall be interpreted in accordance with the laws of the State of

_____ .

EXAMINE THIS CONTRACT CAREFULLY
BEFORE SIGNING IT

In witness whereof, the parties hereto have hereunder signed their names as hereinafter set forth.

_____

Contract Advisor

_____

Player   Date

_____

Parent or Guardian if Player is under 21 years of age

Exhibit 4-2   ARPA Suggested Contract

REPRESENTATION AGREEMENT

AGREEMENT made this _____ day of _____ , 19_____ , by
_____ (herein called the Representative) and _____
(herein called the Player).

WITNESSETH:

In consideration of the mutual promises made in this agreement, the parties agree as follows:

1. *Term*

The term of this Agreement shall commence on the date of its execution and shall continue during the term of any player contract negotiated by Representative on behalf of Player pursuant to this Agreement. This Agreement shall be considered automatically renewed unless terminated by either party by written notice. The Agreement shall be deemed terminated twenty (20) days after the notice of termination is sent pursuant to paragraph 8 of this document.

2. *Representative Services*

During the term of this Agreement, Representative shall have the exclusive right to represent, advise, counsel and assist Player as follows:

   (a)   Negotiation of any and all professional athletic contracts on behalf of the Player;

   (b)   Consultation and advice with respect to finances, taxes and tax planning;

   (c)   Preparation of income tax returns due during the term of this agreement;

   (d)   Collection of income due Player and maintenance of commercial and other bank accounts under Player's name at such bank or banks as Player may designate;

   (e)   Payment of Player's accounts due during the term of this agreement;

   (f)   Engagement of services of an investment advisor to provide investment advice to Player at no additional cost. . . .

4. *Compensation*

Player shall pay to Representative for services rendered pursuant to this Agreement a sum equal to the greater of either (a) the sum of standard hourly rate charged by Representative for such services up to a maximum of $_____ per hour multiplied by the hours spent on those services by Representative, or (b) _____ percent (_____%) of the gross amount of all monies received by Player or on Player's behalf as the result of any player contract, including any substitutions, additions, modifications, renewals or extensions thereof, the negotiation of which commenced during the term of this agreement regardless of whether such income is received during the term of this agreement or after the termination of such term, except that it shall not include bonuses that are payable to any player in the league by reason of participation in extra-season or post-season events such as playoffs, all star games or other similar events. Unless otherwise expressly agreed in writing by the parties to this Agreement, the Player shall make all such compensation payments to Representative within fifteen (15) days of receipt of a salary payment under any aforesaid player contract or in such annual installments as may be agreed between Player and Representative. No such compensation shall directly or indirectly be made payable or be paid to Representative by Player's professional athletic team or league, and the amount of such compensation shall neither be agreed upon nor discussed by Representative with such professional athletic team or league.

5. *Expenses*

Player agrees to reimburse Representative for travel expenses actually incurred by Representative in the performances of his services under this Agreement in an amount up to, but not exceeding, One Thousand Dollars ($1,000) for negotiation for each separate player contract pursuant to this Agreement. Player shall promptly pay all such expenses upon receipt of an itemized statement from Representative.

6. *Standards and Practices*

In the performance of the services pursuant to this Agreement, Representative shall abide by and conform to the Code of Ethics adopted by the Association of Representatives of Professional Athletes.

7. *Disputes*

The parties shall submit all disputes arising out of or relating to this Agreement to binding arbitration before the American Arbitration Association, and under the rules of that Association. The costs of the arbitration shall be paid as the arbitrators may direct. The award shall be rendered in such form that a judgement may be entered thereon.

8. *Notices*

All notices pursuant to this Agreement shall be effective if sent by certified or registered mail, postage prepaid, return receipt requested, to the following addresses:

To Representative:

To Player:

9. *Entire Agreement*

This document sets forth the entire agreement between the parties and replaces or supersedes all prior agreements between the parties relating to the same subject matter. This Agreement cannot be changed orally.

10. *Successors and Assigns*

This Agreement shall be binding upon and inure to the benefit of each party and their respected successors, assigns, heirs and personal representatives, as the case may be.

11. *Governing Law*

This Agreement shall be construed, interpreted and enforced according to the laws of the State of _____ .

12. *Severability*

In the event any provision of this Agreement shall be for any reason rendered illegal or unenforceable, the same shall not affect the validity or enforceability of the remaining provisions.

_____
Representative

_____
Player

READ THIS CAREFULLY BEFORE SIGNING IT

NOTE _____

1. For further information on the problems of those who represent the professional athlete, see the following articles and books:

(a) Garvey, *The Agent Game* (Washington, D.C.: Federation of Professional Athletes, 1984).

(b) Ruxin, *An Athlete's Guide to Agents* (Bloomington, Ind.: Indiana University Press, 1983).

(c) "Agents of Professional Athletes," 15 *New England Law Review* 545 (1980).

(d) Hearings Before the House Select Committee on Professional Sports, 94th Cong., 2d Sess. (1976).

(e) Weistart and Lowell, *The Law of Sports* (Indianapolis: Bobbs-Merrill, 1979). Note particularly, pp. 319–333.

(f) Gallner, *Pro Sports: The Contract Game*, 1975.

(g) Woolf, *Behind Closed Doors* (New York: Atheneum, 1976).

(h) Jones, ed., *Current Issues In Professional Sports* (Durham, N.H.: University of New Hampshire, 1980). Note particularly Shepherd, "Establishing the Contractual Relationship Between the Representative and the Athlete," pp. 13–29.

(i) Blackman and Gershon, chr., *Counseling Professional Athletes and Entertainers* (New York: Practicing Law Institute, 1970)

(j) Needham, ed., *Counseling Professional Athletes and Entertainers*, 3rd ed. (New York: Practicing Law Institute, 1971).

(k) Gershon and Blackman, chr., *Counseling Professional Athletes and Entertainers* (New York: Practicing Law Institute, 1972).

(l) Blackman and Gershon, chr., *Counseling Professional Athletes and Entertainers* (New York: Practicing Law Institute, 1974).

(m) Blackman, chr., *Representing the Professional Athlete* (New York: Practicing Law Institute, 1976).

(n) "Do Agents Exploit Athletes?" *Professional Sports Journal*, Nov.–Dec. 1979, p. 20.

(o) Blackman and Hochberg, *Representing Professional Athletes and Teams* (New York: Practicing Law Institute, 1980).

4.20   Negotiation, Formation, and Interpretation of Contracts in League Sports

All professional sports leagues use standard contract forms. Indeed, there is a substantial uniformity among forms from league to league and sport to sport. As indicated in Chapter 3 (Sections 3.20–3.23), certain clauses are deemed basic and recur in the forms. There are differences, however, and part of the analysis that follows examines the variances among league practices as well as the commonalities.

The prior sections (4.10–4.14) discussed the establishment of the attorney/player relationship and its many dimensions. The appearance of attorneys or agents on behalf of the player has become routine. Few players attempt to negotiate on their own behalf. Some leagues, in fact, go so far as to guarantee in the league's collective bargaining agreement that a player can get help during negotiations with a club. For example, baseball's basic agreement provides: "A Player may be accompanied, if he so desires, by a representative of his choice to assist him in negotiating his individual salary with his employing Club" (Art. V, para. D).

The negotiation of the contract, as noted earlier (Sections 4.00–4.06, is only one part of the representational efforts undertaken by most attorneys/agents. After further considerations of negotiation and contract formation in this section and its subparts, the rest of this chapter explores other dimensions in the representational function.

4.21   Standard Contracts

Leagues require a player to sign the league's standard contract form before the player can participate in the activities of a club. Only rarely has that requirement been waived, and in one notable case in which a temporary relaxation occurred, litigation resulted (see *Kapp* v. *NFL,* in Chapter 2, Section 2.42). The requirements for use of a standard player contract are usually specified in the league's collective bargaining agreement with the players' association (see: Major League Baseball, Art. III; NFL, Art. XII; and NBA, Art., Sec. 1). Under normal circumstances, the player must sign the form contract, with whatever modifications and additions that can be negotiated, before even being allowed to participate in the club's preseason training camp. A minor exception is noted in Section 4.21–2, which deals with waivers-of-liability forms for certain types of pre-preseason activities.

Many of the following considerations focus on the negotiation function as well as on special contract terms that may be included as special covenants appended to a standard player contract. Before proceeding with these examinations, two preliminary points should be mentioned. The first concerns contract language. Terms peculiar to sports have developed, some of which are useful; others, however, are ambiguous. The next section (4.21–1) considers the latter. The second preliminary point concerns special waivers-of-liability. These are discussed in Section 4.21–2.

4.21–1 Correct Terminology: Sports Terms and Contract Usage

The following excerpts are taken from materials compiled for a seminar sponsored by the National Football League. The attendees were club general managers and other club personnel who deal with the drafting of provisions in player contracts. Although the message of this seminar was aimed at clubs, the cautionary policies contained in the materials are equally applicable to player representatives. Neither side benefits from ambiguous language. The potentials for later misunderstandings and eventual disputes should be realized and avoided. Other examples of poor drafting dealing with bonus provisions are excerpted from these materials and appear in Section 4.24.

National Football League, Contract Language Discussion, Negotiations Seminar, Harvard University, Feb. 10–12, 1981

Common Mistakes in Contract Language

Following are several words, terms, and procedures which frequently cause problems in player contracts. Clubs would do well to avoid them completely.

Cut (used either as a verb or noun)

This informal term, used as a verb, usually means *terminated through the waiver system*. But *cut*, by itself, is too imprecise to write into contracts, because no one is ever certain whether it means the end result of a waiver request or the mere action of being placed on waivers, in which case the player could just as easily be *assigned* as *terminated*. The word *released* is only slightly better. Stick to *terminated through the waiver system*.

As a noun, *cut* means one of the mandatory reductions in a club's Active List that occur each year in the preseason. Here again the word leaves much to be desired. Occasionally there may be some justification for the word *cutdown*, but a better one is *reduction,* as in *... if Player is a member of the Club's 45-man Active List at the final roster reduction before the regular season.*

No-Cut

Most of us have a general idea of what this means, but in a contract — as in *This is a no-cut contract* — it's extremely bad form. The apparent intent is to create some sort of guarantee. Yet too much is left unsaid: guarantee against what? Lack of skill? Injury? What about an offset? Does the guarantee cover more than one year? For appropriate language, see pp. 10–15 in the player personnel section of the *1980 GUIDE for MEMBER CLUBS/Administration.*

League or Championship (used adjectivally before *season* or *game*)

Misleading. The commonly accepted term is *regular season* to denote those 16 games played after the preseason and before the postseason. The term is routinely employed in the *NFL Player Contract* form, the *Constitution and Bylaws*, and the *Collective Bargaining Agreement*.

Assigned

When you mean trade, say *trade*; when you mean assigned through the waiver system, say so. The use of *assigned*, with no clarification, can cover either of these transactions and can cause a great deal of confusion.

Starter, Regular, or First-Stringer

Despite the familiarity of these terms and the assumption by many who use them that they all mean the same thing, a closer look raises questions. Is a *starter* really a *regular*? What if the player starts on special teams but nowhere else? What if someone else is in on the first play from scrimmage but the player in question participates most of the rest of the game? What about players who shuttle at the same position, e.g., backs or tight ends? Nebulous descriptions like *first-string* not only create headaches for the clubs that use them, they also can be burdens to assignee clubs if the player moves on.

Standard Player Contract

This term went out of fashion five years ago. The official document is *NFL Player Contract*.

Deletion of words, sentences, or paragraphs from the *NFL Player Contract* form

This practice almost never is handled correctly. The usual intent is to fashion some form of a guarantee by deleting the section on termination or on skill, performance, and conduct. Often other essential language is deleted in the process, resulting in a dilemma in which there is no way to remove the player from your roster, even though you are willing to pay him his guaranteed salary . . . The deletion of 17 ("RENEWAL") is, of course, acceptable if there is to be no option on the player's services for a future year . . . But for all other purposes there are better ways to accomplish your goal than by removing sections of the contract.

NOTE _____

1. In the above materials note that the correct terminology in the NFL is to refer to the *regular season,* and not the *league* or the *championship* season. However, other leagues may use the latter terminology. The league's standard player contract undoubtedly uses one of these terms, be it *regular, league,* or *championship.* Conformity to the league's particular terms is desirable. To like effect, the above materials say the correct term is *NFL Player Contract.* Other leagues, however, use other terminology; *Uniform Player Contract,* for example, is often employed.

4.21–2   Waiver of Liability

In most sports leagues, players must sign uniform player contracts before they can attend any type of regular preseason camp. However, some leagues hold special try-out camps for players who have little chance of eventually making the team. In some instances, given the

many players and the small likelihood of any of them succeeding, players are not signed to regular league contracts. For them to attend the try-out camp, though, protection must be accorded the club. The normal approach is to require the aspiring player to sign a release and waiver form.

Exhibit 4–3 shows a form used by several NBA clubs. There is no standard form prescribed by the league, but the provisions contained in the exhibit are closely tracked in other clubs' forms. As is evident, the player signs the release and waiver and proceeds to camp very much at his own risk.

_____

In the Matter of Arbitration between National Basketball Association (Cleveland Cavaliers) and National Basketball Players Association (Ronald Cox), Sept. 11, 1978, Peter Seitz, Arbitrator

Paragraph 6(b) of the Uniform Player Contract obligates a club to pay full-season salary to a player who is rendered unfit to play for the season as a result of an injury sustained while playing for the club. Ronald Cox signed a Uniform Contract with the Cavaliers prior to the start of rookie camp in September 1977. An amendment to paragraph 6(b) of his contract limited Cleveland's full salary liability to injuries sustained after the start of the regular season, October 18, 1977. Cox suffered an injury during rookie camp which disabled him for the season.

The critical question was whether Cox had waived a benefit in violation of Article I, Section 3 of the collective agreement. Cleveland and the NBA argued that Cox never possessed the benefit of the waiver. Players are not legally required to sign Uniform Player Contracts until before the start of the regular training camp. Cox had no right to a full season salary because he was injured during rookie camp. The Players Association claimed that the amendment in Cox's contract was illegal and Cox was entitled to full salary for the 1977–78 season. Otherwise, they argued, a club would be permitted to lock a

Exhibit 4-3

RELEASE & WAIVER

STATE OF _____

COUNTY OF _____

For and in consideration of *[team name]* a *[state]* Limited Partnership inviting and permitting the undersigned to attend and participate in the *[team]* Rookie/Free Agent Tryout Camp for the 1978-'79 basketball season and for and in the further consideration of round trip travel expenses, hotel room, per diem and travel from the hotel to the tryout facility, I, the undersigned individual, being of lawful age, now and forever, fully and finally, for myself, my heirs, my administrators, executors, successors, and assigns, agree to waive all claims of whatever nature, and forever release, remise, acquit, discharge, and hold harmless the *[team name]* and *[name of facility]* and any other facility used for this Rookie/Free Agent Tryout Camp, and their respective officers, agents, employees, successors, assigns, and assureds, and all other persons, firms, corporations, associations or partnerships associated therewith, for all claims, demands, actions or causes of action arising out of any losses or injuries to my person or property, or both, which may result, be sustained, or be received by me as a result of my attending and participating in the above Rookie/Free Agent Tryout Camp for the 1978-'79 basketball season.

The undersigned fully understands that by executing this Release and Waiver, he agrees to completely release, acquit, discharge and hold harmless forever the *[team name]* and *[name of facility]* and any other facility used for this Rookie/Free Agent Tryout Camp from all claims of whatever kind, nature and description arising in any manner whatever from his attendance and participation in the aforementioned Rookie/Free Agent Tryout Camp, or from any travel or other activity associated therewith.

The undersigned further understands that by signing this Release and Waiver, he covenants and agrees that he, as well as his heirs, executors, administrators, successors, and assigns, will never institute any suit or action at law or otherwise against the *[team name]* or *[name of facility]* or any other facility used for this Rookie/Free Agent Tryout Camp, or in any way aid in the institution or prosecution of any claim, demand, action or cause of action for damages, costs, loss of services, expenses or compensation for or on account of any damage, loss or injury either to his person, property or both, which may result from the undersigned's attendance and participation at the aforementioned Rookie/Free Agent Tryout Camp, or any travel or other activity associated therewith.

The undersigned acknowledges that by attending the abovementioned Rookie/Free Agent Tryout Camp he voluntarily assumes all risks and dangers known or unknown, foreseen or unforeseen, attendant to his attendance and participation in said Camp. The undersigned further declares and represents that no promise, inducement or agreement not herein expressed has been made to the undersigned, and that this release contains the entire agreement between the parties to this release and that the terms of this release are contractual and not a mere recital.

The undersigned has read the foregoing release and fully understands it.

Witness my hand and seal this _____ day of _____ , 1978.

SWORN to and Subscribed before me   Signature _____

this _____ day of _____   Address _____

_____   _____

NOTARY PUBLIC

player in for the season at a minimum salary while avoiding obligations imposed by the Uniform Player Contract.

Article I, Section 6 of the collective agreement prohibits players from attending "the *regular* training camp of any member unless he is a party to a Player Contract then in effect." Cleveland and the NBA conceded that Cox would have been entitled to his salary if his injury had occurred before Oct. 18 at regular training camp, because of the requirement that he be under contract before that time. Although the Uniform Player Contract and the collective agreement do not distinguish between rookie and regular training camp, the arbitrator was convinced of the difference. Cox did not have to sign a contract before rookie training camp.

Article I, Section 3 prohibits only the waiver of benefits and sacrifice of rights "to which the player is entitled by virtue of a Uniform Player Contract or this Agreement." To the extent that the contract Cox signed departed from the Uniform Player Contract, it was *not* a Uniform Player Contract. The arbitrator found that his waiver was not in violation of the agreement. The benefit would not have been contractually conferred upon Cox until the start of regular training camp.

With the appropriate waiver forms or amendments to the Uniform Player Contract, any club can avoid full-season liability to a player injured in rookie training camp.

Timeliness. The arbitrator chose not to dismiss the grievance on the ground that it was untimely filed. He referred to its analysis on the *Poquette* case of the difficulties forced by the Players Association in gathering information from around the country, which would alert them to possible contract or agreement violations. Contracts are not routinely filed with the Players Association. The arbitrator's position suggested that Article XV, Sections 2(a) and (c) would not be strictly enforced against grievances filed by the Players Association until more efficient procedures and administrative rules are adopted.

4.22   The Negotiations: Preparation and Execution

Negotiations with professional sports clubs are usually circumscribed affairs. There is, to begin with, the standard player contract that is not easily changed. The contract "price" is open for negotiation somewhat, and there are several approaches than can be taken on that. However, as to other wording modifications sought by a player's representative, it will be an uphill battle the entire way.

On the other hand, the standard form does allow for concentration on the key considerations that go into most individual sports contract negotiations. Keeping these firmly in mind allows for planning and the establishment of priorities.

Key considerations addressed in any sports contract negotiations include the following:

1. Length of the contract (including options).
2. Basic salary per year (or season).
3. Signing bonus (perhaps a reporting bonus as well).
4. Incentive or performance bonuses.
5. Guarantees.
6. Trade provisions (contract assignment).
7. Additional injury protection.
8. Fringes and special benefits.
9. Personal conduct provisions.

Not all contract negotiations involve the entire list. Guarantees (except for signing bonus), restrictive trade provisions, additional injury protection, fringes beyond those already guaranteed by the league's collective bargaining provisions, and modifications of other standard provisions may all be wan hopes. They can be suggested; but obtaining affirmative results is unlikely except for the established player or the very high draft choice.

However, with the above list in mind, one can begin the process that leads to the actual negotiations. What follows are brief descriptions of what needs to be done, and how one goes about doing it.

4.22–1 Knowing the Legal Background

A costly mistake in dealing with clubs is not to know the precise provisions of a league's standard player contract and collective bargaining provisions. Some knowledge of league rules, as they are applicable to the standard contract, is also important.

Chapter 3 contained examples of standard player contracts and comparative clauses. These are only the initial forms to consult when preparing to deal with sports contracts.

The collective bargaining provisions pertaining to player benefits and rights are also integral to the negotiation process. Substantial excerpts from the collective agreements also appeared in Chapter 3. These were examples of collective bargaining provisions that help explain, as well as control, the standard player agreement. Many other provisions guarantee benefits for the player and are stipulated through collective bargaining and need not be sought through negotiation. Also, under applicable labor laws, provisions guaranteed under the collective bargaining agreement generally cannot be waived by the player. The representative must know exactly what is assured and what is not, what can be bargained over and what cannot be waived.

In each league, the matters bearing on the individual contract that are covered in the collective bargaining agreement are substantial. Items such as transportation and travel expenses, preseason pay and allowances, termination pay, playoff pools, parking facilities, and pension and insurance plans are among provisions usually detailed. Players and sports representatives alike should become familiar with these provisions, not only for the initial contract negotiations but also for the duration of the contract.

There may be special wrinkles, league by league. For example, in the National Basketball Association Contract that was reproduced in Chapter 3, there is set forth exactly what parts of the standard player contract are negotiable. It also provides for the precise language that can be substituted, if any modifications are to be made. Except in rare instances, other language is not acceptable.

The Major League Baseball Players Association lists the following publications as necessary for representation of a Major League Baseball player:

1. The Basic Agreement: contains the Uniform Players Contract.
2. Baseball Blue Book: contains major league and professional agreements and rules.
3. Official Baseball Guide: contains major and minor league player statistics.
4. Official Baseball Register: contains season-by-season records of all active players.

In the same fashion, similar lists of publications should be compiled for each of the sports leagues. They are necessary working tools for the sports representative.

4.22–2 Knowing the Factual Background

Awareness of the economics of sports leagues, particularly as to precise salary figures, is important in preparing for negotiations. Examples of general salary data for various leagues are set forth in Chapter 1 (Section 1.31). In some leagues, more precise data are obtainable through the players' association, but in others information is shared among sports representatives. Compiling salary profiles for the club to be involved in the negotiations and for the league, particularly for players similarly situated to that of the client, is essential.

Performance statistics for the client and for other players of comparable background (position played, years in league, etc.) are also important. Learning to deal with statistics, both as an affirmative tool and as a counter to assertions made by the other side, is a necessary feature of the negotiator's work.

4.22–3   Knowing with Whom One Is Dealing

Learning as much as one can about the club and the individuals who will be on the other side of the negotiations is helpful. Advance knowledge can prevent the sports representative from falling into certain traps or wandering down fruitless paths.

A club may have certain policies regarding salary structures, types of bonuses routinely offered or always refused, and other restrictions placed unilaterally on the negotiation process. This does not mean that the other side cannot be budged; in the absence of considerable leverage, however, it may be best to avoid concentrating on possibly hopeless pursuits and instead to find other ways to satisfy the client's needs and desires.

Individual idiosyncrasies of the representative negotiating for the club should be noted Different people have different styles, and knowing these can work to the advantage of the athlete's representative.

4.22–4   Mapping a Negotiation Strategy

A sports representative hopefully does not enter into negotiations unprepared or on the defensive. Meticulous planning of what will be asked of the club and the order in which the items will be addressed should be determined in advance. Priorities must be set, and decisions must be made about which points to press all the way and which points to hold for possible compromise. Indeed, inserting some initial demands into the process for the sole purpose of later compromise or abandonment is a frequent negotiation tactic. If not overdone, it can be effective.

Optimism mixed with realism is a healthy approach for a negotiator. The idea is to make a deal. The methods are many. The negotiator needs to map the different ways a deal can come to fruition.

Anticipation of what the other side is likely to do in the course of the negotiations is quite important. Although one can be wrong, the chances of being out-guessed are less if the strategy of the opposition is thought out ahead of time.

Finally, there is need to devise a plan for keeping control of the flow of the negotiations and keeping the focus in constant sight. A sports representative should expect the unexpected and be prepared to deal with it.

4.22–5   Following Through on the Negotiation Strategy

The best-laid plans often go astray in contract negotiations for reasons not wholly explainable. To keep the negotiations under control, a delicate balance may have to be forged. All negotiations demand flexibility but how to allow for this without sacrificing basic strategies is the problem. The answer comes back time and time again to anticipation. If there is the need to shift strategy, having anticipated this in advance should make the new strategy more effective.

If the flexibility demanded means scrapping the original plans, then new strategies must be devised. Letting things float and get out of control can only lead to disaster. Finally, as a cautionary policy that is all too often ignored in the heat of negotiation, the client's needs are paramount. Sports representatives who let their own ego interfere with the best interests of their clients are doing a disservice to the client and to themselves.

4.22–6   Closing the Deal

Knowing when to close the deal is something that the sports representative must learn through experience. It means knowing the temperaments of the other side as well as the representative's own strengths (and weaknesses). Knowing when to bring the negotiations to a close by saying, "Okay, it's a deal," is probably the single toughest aspect of negotiation. The best representatives in the business are those who know when to stop maneuvering and demanding and when to start agreeing.

4.23   Salaries and Tax Consequences

Average annual salaries for NBA and Major League Baseball players topped $300,000 as of 1984. At the same time, NFL average salaries were approaching $150,000 a year, and NHL averages were around $120,000. In all sports, except hockey, a "millionaires club" of players earning in excess of one million dollars per year has continued to increase in size.

The growth in player salaries the past ten years has, indeed, been extraordinary. It has been attended, however, by an ever greater need for the athlete's attorney or agent to recognize the potential pitfalls in handling the fortunes of the suddenly rich client. The tax consequences of salaries at this level are the first matters to address. An attorney or agent must realize that no steps can be taken without highly competent tax advice. If the person directly representing the athlete is not an accomplished tax expert, the first thing to do in representing the highly paid player is to obtain assistance in tax minimization and planning.

The short review which follows cannot, of course, sufficiently equip anyone to attempt to engage in tax planning. It is included only to illustrate the depth of the problems and how essential is expert advice. To provide the materials necessary to give full information about tax consequences when dealing with highly paid performers would require a volume in and of itself. This brief section is introductory, intended to suggest warning signals.

4.23–1   Tax Minimization

Under the Internal Revenue Code, a number of allowable techniques exist for taking advantage of tax savings. Three are mentioned here, since they have engendered past litigation involving athletes: deductible items, income averaging, and income splitting. All have significant potentials for the right client at the right time. As the cases reveal, however, all also contain — if used improperly — potentials for a finding of tax deficiencies.

4.23–1(a)   Deductible Items

Professional athletes travel a great deal and receive various types of special awards. The travel can be a basis for deductions from one's personal gross income, assuming it is not reimbursed by a club or other sponsor. Even so, what for some individuals would be deductible travel expenses may not be for the athlete, where the travel includes going to and from his permanent residence to where his employer is located. In addition, awards can be nice, but they may also be taxable. One-time Dodger shortstop Maury Wills learned the facts of tax life as related to deductions and awards.

In *Wills v. Commissioner of Internal Revenue*, 411 F.2d 537 (9th Cir., 1969), the issues before the court were whether there were deficiencies in Maury Wills' income taxes paid for 1962 and 1963. The court held that the deductions for travel, meals, and lodging in the Los Angeles area were not allowable as business expenses and that the fair market value of an automobile and a special Hickock belt awarded to Wills were taxable as ordinary income.

Crucial to the first issue was the factual determination of the locale of Wills' "tax home," since Wills maintained a residence in Spokane, Washington, and rented while in Los Angeles, playing for the Dodgers. The court found that since Los Angeles was his principal place of business and his reasons for the Spokane residence were purely personal, Los Angeles was his home for the purposes of the Internal Revenue Code definition. His expenses thus incurred while living in Los Angeles were not deductible.

The court next determined that the automobile and the belt received by Wills as awards for his popularity and skill did not fall under any exceptions to the classification of prizes and awards as gross income under 26 U.S.C. Section 74. Wills' achievements could not be classified as either civic or artistic. The court felt this interpretation was supported by the actions of Congress when it had refused to add the word "athletic" to the list of exempted prizes.

The court felt its decision was required by law, but noted this was an inequitable result. However, both the problem and the remedy lie with Congress and not the courts.

4.23–1(b)　Income Averaging

Every advisor to a professional athlete should be aware of the Internal Revenue Code's provisions relating to income averaging, Sections 1301–1305. Quite often an athlete earns little income for several years and then suddenly becomes highly compensated. For purposes of income averaging, however, there is a significant difference between the athlete who comes directly out of college into a high-salaried status, as opposed to one who struggles through several years of minor league play or is otherwise at the low end of the salary structure before making it with the big contract. Only the latter can, in all likelihood, take full advantage of income averaging. The general requirement is that the taxpayer have been self-supporting for all of the years calculated in the base period. As the cases below indicate, a college player on an athletic scholarship will have a hard time convincing a court that he or she was self-supporting.

Where income averaging is available, it can be a substantial tax saver. The athlete who has been earning $20,000 a year for several years and now will earn $200,000 a year can substantially reduce the tax bite under the new contract. There are formulae for figuring the exact amounts, but in rough form the tax will be calculated on the total salaries earned over five years, as if an equal amount had been earned in each year of the base period. Thus, instead of paying on $20,000 for four years and then on $200,000 the fifth, the tax will be calculated as having been on $56,000 for each of the five years. This is an optional method of calculation, and each time both the straight and alternative income averaging methods should be used to determine which is most favorable to the individual. Income averaging is not limited to a one time use. It can be repeated for however long it is beneficial to do so.

It should be noted that the purpose of Sections 1301–1305 is to provide relief from the hardship of a sudden jump in income and the resulting effects of the graduated income tax. Therefore, these provisions — as with all tax relief — are carefully scrutinized and are strictly construed. This is particularly true as to eligibility to use income averaging, as the following court decisions reveal.

Heidel v. Commissioner of Internal Revenue, 56 T.C. 95 (1971)

In 1960 James Heidel concluded his career as a high school football star in Yazoo City, Mississippi. He applied to the University of Mississippi for a Southeastern Conference (S.E.C.) athletic scholarship, which he received, commencing September 1961. During 1961 Heidel's parents paid over $900 toward their son's support, while Heidel furnished just over $700. Heidel's parents claimed him as an exemption in 1961, and Heidel did not file an income tax return. While at the University of Mississippi, Heidel observed the prescribed training rules, attended daily practice in season, trained himself to improve, and played at the varsity level for most of his time there.

In December 1964, Heidel was drafted by the New York Jets of the AFL and the St. Louis Cardinals of the NFL as a defensive back. He ultimately chose to sign with St. Louis, and in December 1965 he received a bonus of $50,000. He was to play for St. Louis for the 1966 and 1967 seasons.

In his income tax return for 1965, Heidel elected to compute his income tax liability under the income averaging provisions of Sections 1301–1305 of the Internal Revenue Code. The commissioner disallowed the use of that method, claiming Heidel was not an "eligible individual" within the meaning of Section 1303.

The major factors considered by the court were whether the value of the S.E.C. scholarship received by Heidel constituted support furnished by him within the meaning of Section 1303(c)(1) and whether the $50,000 bonus received from St. Louis in 1965 was income attributable to work performed in substantial part during two or more of the base period years 1961–1964, as defined by Section 1303(c)(2)(B).

The court held that Heidel was not an "eligible individual," that the athletic scholarship did not constitute support furnished by Heidel in 1961, and that he failed to prove that the $50,000 bonus was income attributable to work performed in substantial part in the required base period years.

Under Section 1303(c), an individual is not eligible for income averaging for any base year where the individual furnished less that half of his support unless more than half of the individual's adjusted taxable income for the computation year was attributable to work performed by him in substantial part in two or more of the base period years. The court concluded that 1961 was the key year. If Heidel furnished half or more of his support that year, he would qualify for income averaging. Even if he did not, he could still qualify if the $50,000 bonus in 1965 was attributable in substantial part to work performed during two or more of the base years.

Heidel claimed that he performed services to maintain his scholarship, that his parents therefore did not have to expend any additional funds to support him, and that this constituted support furnished by him. The court rejected this contention, focusing on the fact that income averaging is a tax relief provision, to be strictly interpreted. One of the concerns of Congress in providing for income averaging was that income during the entire base period be subject to tax. The scholarship was not. In addition, the court concluded that a scholarship should not be considered income for services rendered, since it is not necessary that an athlete play to receive it.

Finally, the court opined that the bonus was not attributable to work performed during two or more of the base period years. Despite Heidel's contention that it should be attributed to the earlier period during which he was preparing himself to perform at a level qual-

ifying him for such rewards, the court instead viewed the bonus as an inducement to him to play with the Cardinals in the future.

Frost v. Commissioner of Internal Revenue, 61 T.C. 488 (1974)

William Frost graduated from high school in 1963 and received a scholarship to play baseball at the University of California at Berkeley. In 1966 Frost was a number one pick of the San Francisco Giants in a special phase of Major League Baseball's draft. The Giants made Frost an offer, which he accepted on June 14, 1966. Under his contract, Frost was to receive a $30,000 signing bonus and $15,000 salaries for each of 1966 and 1967.

The court was faced with the determination of whether Frost was an "eligible individual" in 1966 within the meaning of Section 1303 of the Internal Revenue Code, thereby entitling him to the benefit of income averaging. Since Frost was not eligible under Section 1303(c), the question was whether he was otherwise qualified because the signing bonus was income attributable to work performed by Frost in substantial part during two or more of the base period years 1962–1965. The court concluded that Frost could not utilize the income averaging provisions. He was not an "eligible individual" under Section 1303 and the exception was not applicable.

Frost's argument was that pitching is a marketable product developed over a number of years and that payment was in fact attributable to previous work as well as to future contributions. Although the court cited the *Heidel* decision, discussed above, the court stated that the earlier opinion had not really resolved the issue of what constituted "work" within the meaning of Section 1303 (c)(2)(B). The fact that the bonus was paid as an inducement should not necessarily preclude a finding it was also attributable in substantial part to work performed earlier. The court again noted that the purpose of income averaging is to provide tax relief and that it should therefore not be subjected to a liberal interpretation. The exception was designed to insure that those who perform some work of a substantial nature over a period of years are eligible for income averaging.

The court concluded that, for the purposes of Section 1303(c)(2)(B), work means gainful employment which generates income. Frost was not paid. A scholarship is to defray educational costs; it is not payment in the employment sense. Thus no "work" was performed.

NOTES _____

1. In considering income averaging, Revenue Ruling 75–40 should be consulted.

2. For an argument that the income averaging provisions should be either broadened legislatively or more liberally construed by the courts, see Thomas, "Income Averaging and the Professional Athlete: A Re-Examination," 19 *New England Law Review* 335 (1983–1984).

4.23–1(c)   Income Splitting

In concept, income splitting proceeds much as income averaging. It is a tax savings, used to counter the fact that higher amounts of income are taxed at higher marginal rates. At the heart of tax splitting is the question of who or what is the proper taxable unit.

For example, a parent will receive potential tax savings if he or she finds some means of shifting taxable income to a child's lower income bracket. Sophisticated trusts have been developed to accomplish this objective. In an attempt to unify treatment among the states, Congress enacted Section 73 of the Internal Revenue Code, which states that "amounts received in respect of the services of a child shall be included in his gross income and not in the gross income of the parent, even though such amounts are not received by the child."

In professional sports, it may well be the child who is the large wage earner. Shifting income from him or her to a parent or other relative is no easy task. The following cases illustrate the difficulties encountered in income shifting. The finding of unique circumstances in the *Hundley* case must be noted, and the question whether such circumstances justified the different tax result should be asked.

_____

Hundley v. Commissioner of Internal Revenue, 48 T.C. 339 (1967)

Randy Hundley was a professional baseball player, at the time of trial a catcher for the Chicago Cubs. Hundley's father was a former semiprofessional baseball player and coach. The senior Hundley had developed a one-handed method of catching, which was unique and unorthodox. In 1958, when Randy Hundley was still in high school, he and his father entered an agreement where the father would devote substantial efforts to training Randy and would also act as his business agent and publicity director. As compensation, the father would receive 50 percent of any bonus Hundley might later receive for signing a professional baseball contract. Randy could not sign a contract while still a minor without his parents' consent.

The father taught his son the one-handed method of catching. According to the findings, this required a great amount of time and effort by both parties. The father gave batting tips and met with scouts. He also met with the press and handled all negotiations. This required the father to be away from his business at times.

On June 16, 1960, shortly after graduation from high school, Randy Hundley signed a contract with the San Francisco Giants. The contract provided for a bonus of $110,000 payable over a five-year period. His father negotiated the deal. The Giants knew of the arrangement whereby the father was to receive half of the bonus, some $11,000 a year for the five-year period.

For the court, the issue was the portion, if any, of the $22,000 cash bonus earned by Randy in 1960 that was deductible as the reasonable value of services actually performed by his father. Both sides in the litigation agreed that, under Internal Revenue Code, Section 73, the entire bonus should be included in Randy Hundley's gross income, even though not received by him. The question then was one of whether he could deduct for the amount paid his father. The court held that the deduction should be allowed, citing Internal Revenue Code, Sections 162 and 212.

Under Section 162, a deduction is allowed for an ordinary and necessary expense paid during the taxable year in carrying on any trade or business, including a reasonable allowance for compensation for personal services actually rendered. The father spent considerable time in coaching, training, and representing Randy. The father handled all negotiations. He also lost income because he spent less time on his construction business. While the agreement between the father and son did not possess the arms length character that usually exists in most commercial contracts, the particular facts in this situation met every test. The father should not be expected to handle all of his son's dealings without some assurance of financial return. This was evidenced by the pre-existing agreement.

The next question was whether the son was actually in a trade or business, a necessity in order to qualify for the deduction. The commissioner claimed Randy was merely preparing to enter a trade or business. The court held, however, that young Hundley was engaged in a trade or business in the taxable year in which the expenses were incurred, paid, and deducted. The deduction was thus allowed, even though the payment was for services rendered prior to the commencement of the trade or business. It was in essense a joint venture through which the son received a contract to play professional ball. His expenses were ordinary and necessary under the circumstances.

Allen v. Commissioner of Internal Revenue, 50 T.C. 466 (1968)

The commissioner determined deficiencies in the income tax of Richard Allen in 1961, 1962, and 1963. Allen was born in 1942 in Wampum, Pennsylvania, one of eight children. His mother, who was separated from his father, provided all the support for her children. Allen was a star baseball and basketball player in high school and acquired a statewide reputation. John Ogden, a scout for the Philadelphia Phillies, became aware of Allen during Allen's junior year in high school. Ogden felt Allen was the greatest prospect he had ever seen. Allen wanted to play professional baseball, but his mother desired that he first graduate from high school. The issue was settled by the fact that, while the Phillies would have signed him immediately, the club could not do so under league rules until Allen graduated from high school.

Ogden kept in constant touch with the Allen family. The Phillies signed one brother to play baseball and another brother as a scout in the Philadelphia organization. All negotiations regarding Richard were conducted through his mother. She made all the decisions.

One hour after he graduated from high school, Richard Allen signed a contract to play baseball for the Phillies. Being a minor, his mother's consent was necessary. One of the principal items of the contract was a $70,000 signing bonus. Of this amount, under the contract which Allen signed, the mother was to receive $40,000, and Richard $30,000, both to be paid over a five-year period. Each party subsequently reported receipt of their monies on their income tax returns. Mrs. Allen felt that she was entitled to the $40,000 because she was responsible for Richard's success through her hard work.

The court held that the portion of the bonus paid directly to the mother was taxable to the son. He was not entitled to deduct from his gross income any part of the bonus payments made to his mother during the years in issue. The court concentrated on whether the bonus payments constituted "amounts received in respect of the services" of Richard Allen, as defined in Internal Revenue Code, Section 73. If the amounts were for his services, they must be included in his gross income.

Allen's mother claimed that the $40,000 represented compensation for services performed by her and for influencing her son to sign the contract. The court found that no such evidence existed. Instead, it found that the bonus was paid and the amount determined was solely by Allen's ability to play baseball and for his future prospects as a player.

The purpose of Section 73 is to achieve uniform tax treatment for income earned by a minor. All amounts received in respect of the services as a child shall be included in his income. The bonus payments were paid by the Phillies as an inducement to obtain Allen's services as a professional baseball player, and they constituted amounts received in respect of his services.

Allen argued in the alternative that, even if they were includable in his income, he should still be allowed to deduct the bonus payments received by his mother as an ordinary and necessary expense in carrying on his trade as a professional baseball player, relying on the *Hundley* decision as authority for this position. The court, however, noted the special facts in *Hundley.* The court noted that there was an agreement two years before the contract was signed and that Randy Hundley's father served as coach and agent. These facts warranted the conclusion that the amounts paid were a bona fide expense incurred in Hundley's trade. These special facts were found not to exist in the situation of Richard Allen and his mother.

4.23–2   Tax Planning

One of the central philosophies of tax planning is to remove income from present taxable status and postpone tax consequences to a later, more beneficial time. Two principal methods of delaying tax consequences are through deferred compensation arranged by contract and through qualified pension and profit sharing plans. Both can be used by the professional athlete, but both at the same time have serious consequences if done improperly.

4.23–2(a)   Deferred Compensation by Contract

When the tax rates on personal income ranged as high as 90 percent in the top bracket, there were obvious advantages to deferring substantial amounts of income. This was particularly true for the professional athlete, whose peak earning years are few. The postponement of taxable income until later years when the athlete would almost inevitably be in a lower tax bracket made eminent sense.

Recent revisions in the tax laws have changed that picture. The maximum tax rate today is 50 percent on personal income. In addition, the distinction between earned and other income, such as interest and dividends, has been dropped. When a 50 percent maximum tax is combined with the fact that a top professional athlete may be able to extend indefinitely the years at which he can expect earnings that place him at or near the 50 percent maximum rate, the tax advantages of deferred compensation are considerably less than they were.

This is still an individual situation, however, and it must not be assumed that all tax advantages from deferred compensation arrangements have disappeared. For a great many professional athletes, the potential advantages may be there. It takes someone with ability to calculate earning potential to determine whether deferred compensation makes sense from a tax perspective.

In addition, there are other advantages to deferring compensation through agreement with the club, promoter, and others. It is a financial planning device that assures a steady source of income to the client and removes the temptation to spend it all as it is earned during the playing years. In other words, assessing whether the client is likely to be frugal with the income as it comes in is a necessary exercise.

In considering deferred compensation proposals, one must carefully analyze the actual economic implications. It is only too easy to be misguided by the asserted total dollar amounts. Of crucial importance are whether the deferred compensation will accrue interest over the years before payout and whether the payments are postponed for exceedingly long periods of time in the future. Examples of deferred compensation arrangements have revealed too often that the person in question would never receive as much money as he or she would have if the money had been paid immediately, the 50 percent maximum tax paid, and the balance after expenses invested. Again, competent people can calculate the earning potentials under each available alternative.

There are legal pitfalls relating to deferred compensation. One is the "constructive receipt" doctrine. In Revenue Ruling 60–31, the Internal Revenue Service agreed to the basic rule relating to deferred compensation, that the taxpayer is not taxed until the year in which he is paid. There are exceptions to this, however. Example 4 under the ruling cites a football player who enters a two-year contract with a team. Under the contract, he received a signing bonus, one that could have been received when he signed. The contract, though, calls for the bonus to be paid to an escrow agent, with a pay-out to the player over five years. The Internal Revenue Service will rule that the total amount of the bonus is includable in the year the contract was signed because the club had unconditionally paid the bonus to the player's designee. The player has exercised control over the funds. The general rule, then, is that anything more than a personal guarantee by the owner, the club, or some other party is an attempt to give the player control over the money. This makes all such amounts immediately taxable.

The following case, dealing with a boxer and fight promoter, illustrates other problems with deferred compensation arrangements.

Robinson v. Commissioner of Internal Revenue, 44 T.C. 20 (1965)

In the 1950s, Sugar Ray Robinson was an internationally known boxer and substantial gate attraction. Robinson entered into a contract with the International Boxing Club (IBC) of New York to fight Carmen Basilio on September 23, 1957, in Yankee Stadium for the middleweight championship of the world. Robinson was the current champion.

The IBC was responsible for all promotion of the fight. Under its contract with Robinson, the boxer was to receive 45 percent of all gate receipts and motion picture rights. The payments were to made over a three-year period. The contract was approved by the New York State Athletic Commission.

The commissioner contended that the entire amount should be included in Robinson's taxable income for 1957. First, the commissioner contended that Robinson and the IBC had engaged in a joint venture and that the income was currently taxable. The court rejected this argument, stating that it is not sufficient that two parties have agreed to act in concert to achieve some stated objective. The venture here was the promotion of the bout, and the IBC was solely responsible for this, not Robinson. In addition, the IBC dealt and contracted separately with Robinson and Basilio.

The commissioner also maintained that Robinson had constructively received the income in 1957, because receipt of the income was not subject to substantial limitations. In addition, the IBC would have been willing to pay the money immediately. The court noted, however, that even though the IBC might have been willing to contract to pay the income at an earlier date, it did not agree to do so. Once the contract was signed, Robinson's money was commingled with other IBC funds and no separate escrow account was established. Robinson's contractual arrangement with IBC avoided the constructive receipt doctrine because he was a general creditor and took the risk of loss.

NOTE _____

1. Sugar Ray Robinson won his battle with the Internal Revenue Service; he lost the fight and his title to Basilio.

4.23–2(b) Qualified Pension and Profit Sharing Plans

Until recently, substantial tax savings could be accomplished through forming a personal corporation, with the athlete as the sole or primary stockholder. This enabled the athlete, then, to take advantage of the many qualified pension and profit sharing plans available to corporations and their employees but not to individuals. In contrast, individuals and Subchapter S corporations were restricted to use of the so-called Keogh plans, which allowed only much more modest sums to be put into the plans.

It was always the case that one must take care in setting up a personal corporation. Section 4.32–3, which follows, suggests some of the traditional difficulties. Even so, if done properly, substantial tax advantages accrued through the ability to implement pension and profit sharing plans.

Much of this changed with Congress passing the Tax Equity and Fiscal Responsibility Act of 1982 (TEFRA). Important parts of that act call for an equalization of the amounts that can be put in qualified plans under either the corporate or indivdiual approach. The amounts that could go into Keogh plans were increased, and it was mandated that corporate plans must decrease to equal the level of the Keoghs.

There is still the need to consider qualified pension and profit sharing plans. These are complicated devices, requiring expert assistance in creating and maintaining. But the type of business organization for the individual, be it corporation or not, should no longer be dictated by the tax benefits to be gained from the corporate pension and profit sharing plans.

4.23–2(c)   Incorporation of the Athlete

As explained in Section 4.32–2(b) above, the most significant tax advantages of incorporating have been removed by act of Congress. There are other considerations, however, that must be weighed in reaching a decision as to whether still to go for the corporate structure for a professional athlete.

First, if the corporation is to attempt to contract out a player's services to a club as well as be the recipient of other monies earned by the player, a real question exists as to whether the club will deal with the player corporation. In the NBA, such is forbidden by terms of the 1983 collective bargaining agreement. In the NFL, all clubs traditionally have refused to deal with a personal corporation. Major League Baseball clubs have a varying response; some will contract with the corporation, others refuse. The NHL still retains a separate standard form for dealings between a club and a personal corporation. This does not necessarily mean an individual club will want to do business in that manner.

Even if a player's club will not or cannot deal with the player as a corporation, there may still be advantages to incorporating the player where there are other substantial sources of revenue, such as endorsement income. This, then, leads to other considerations.

One important decision that must be made is that, if a personal corporation is formed, it must be structured and operated as a real corporation. If created sloppily or if the corporate form is then ignored, a court may by-pass the corporation and declare all income as taxable to the individual. Very instructive are the factual circumstances elaborated in *Patterson* v. *Commissioner of Internal Revenue*, 25 T.C.M. 1230 (1966), and *Johnson* v. *U.S.*, 698 F. 2d 372 (9th Cir. 1982).

In *Patterson*, the court held that the corporation performed no meaningful business function. Supposedly, it was formed to exploit the ancillary rights accruing from heavyweight boxer Floyd Patterson's matches. In reality, the corporate structure often was ignored, with monies earned from ancillary rights being paid directly to Patterson. The corporation merely served as an instrument by which income and expenses could be arbitrarily allocated to serve the tax interests of Patterson. The factual depiction in the court's decision is almost a textbook as to how *not* to incorporate an athlete.

The *Johnson* case concentrated on the fact that former NBA player Charles Johnson had formed his corporation *after* signing a personal services contract with the San Francisco Warriors. He then assigned the Warriors' contract to his corporation, and the club sent his salary checks to the corporation. The court enunciated a two-part test. The first was whether the corporation controlled the player; the second was whether the corporation had a contract with the purchaser of the player's services. Despite the assignment, the court held that no contract existed between Johnson's corporation and the Warriors. All income was attributable to Charles Johnson as an individual.

Further insights on the perils of forming a corporation for an individual can be found in related cases from the entertainment field. Noteworthy are such as *Commissioner of Internal Revenue* v. *Laughton*, 113 F. 2d 103 (9th Cir.1940), and *Borge* v. *Commissioner of Internal Revenue*, 405 F. 2d 673 (2d Cir. 1968).

There is also a new section of the Internal Revenue Code, Section 269A, to contend with as a result of TEFRA's enactment in 1982. This section provides that where a corporation essentially has only one customer, such as a club, tax benefits to the corporation may be denied. It may be found that the corporation serves "no meaningful business purpose." This would not apply where the corporation receives revenues from several sources, such as would be realized from multiple endorsement contracts.

Despite losing the substantial tax benefits derived through qualified pension and profit sharing plans, there are still potential advantages to incorporating the athlete. These would include deductible life insurance and accident and health insurance plans, medical reimbursement plans, possibly business deductions for other purposes that would be harder to prove if in an individual's name, and using a different tax year.

The disadvantages relate to formation and filing fees, additional social security taxes, other state taxes, legal and accounting fees, and the dangers attending improper formation or implementation. A final disadvantage is that it is likely that the corporation will be deemed a personal holding company for tax purposes. This means that any undistributed income is subject to a personal holding company tax rate of 70 percent. This is in addition to the normal corporate tax, which will have been paid before the amount of undistributed income is calculated. Thus, to avoid this onerous tax, it is essential that almost all income "flow through" the corporation each year. For further understanding of the consequences of a personal holding company, one should consult Internal Revenue Code, Section 543 (particularly Section 543 (a)(7)) and such as Revenue rulings 75–67, 75–249, and 75–250. See also *Kurt Frings Agency, Inc* v. *Commissioner of Internal Revenue*, 42 T.C. 472 (1964).

4.24   Bonus Clauses

Bonuses of a wide variety are used throughout the sports industries in player contracts. Although there are differences from league to league in the types of bonuses most generally employed, the bonus clause in sports is nevertheless a staple. In certain instances, it is not only acceptable but, from the perspective of both sides, also desirable. For example, the worth to the team of a player with unproved potential is a matter for speculation — particularly if the parties are contemplating a multiyear contract. Thus, certain types of bonuses can be drafted to provide for the contingency that the player will be worth more than current accomplishments or prospects indicate. To do this properly takes careful foresight, but it can be done. In other words, the bonus can be a form of salary adjustment.

The adjustment aspect is not the only reason for including a bonus. Some are given to lure a player to sign, particularly in cases in which the signing team faces competition for the player's services from other teams. The signing bonus should be regarded as being quite different in concept and purpose from other types of bonuses. When a bonus is not so much a lure vis-à-vis other teams but is more of an assurance to the player, it can provide up-front money that may be the only reward a marginal player receives under the contract. If released before the regular season begins because of failure to make the team, the player gets to keep the signing bonus, but the rest of the contract becomes illusory.

Providing for the many uncertainties and contingencies that exist for the player in professional sports is essential for proper representation of the player's interest. So, too, is structuring bonuses to allow proper salary escalation if the player fulfills or exceeds current prospects. Before examining the types of bonuses and some of the pitfalls arising from poor drafting of bonuses, a brief review of the use of bonus provisions on a sport-by-sport basis should be made.

Bonus clauses are widely used in baseball contracts, particularly at the major league level. One restriction that the Major League Rules provide is that "No contract shall be approved . . . that shall provide for the giving of a bonus for playing, pitching or batting skill; or which provides for the payment of a bonus contingent on the standing of the club at the end of the championship season" (Major League Rule 3[a]). Consequently, bonuses cannot be based on pitcher wins or saves, batter home runs, average, runs batted in, or the like. This had led to heavy reliance on bonus provisions related to the volume of play — that is, the number of games pitched, plate appearances, and games played. Baseball does allow for certain types of other bonuses, such as those based on attendance and other special circumstances. These are discussed later.

Both the NFL and the USFL allow for statistically based bonus provisions. Consequently, these are widely used, at least at the so-called "skill" positions, when official statistics can be compiled. The performances of quarterbacks, running backs, wide receivers, most defensive positions, punters, and kickers are all subject to statistical comparison. Except for a club's own system (which probably should not be relied on for bonus awards), offensive linemen are not the beneficiaries (or perhaps victims) of this process. It makes a great difference, then, as to what position a football player has when structuring a bonus. In addition, the player who is young and relatively untried may be moved around from one position to another — for example, from defense or offense to special teams.

Basketball. Bonus clauses are not as widely used in the National Basketball Association as in the other sports leagues. The salaries for most players are sufficiently high that the base is more than enough. The greater debate between a player representative and the club may be over how much up-front money is coming in each year of the contract, and how much is being deferred. Even so, bonus provisions are used, including statistical bonuses, and these will be noted.

Hockey. Statistical bonus clauses are allowed in hockey. They vary substantially in structure, according to the position played. In general, bonus clauses are widely used.

In soccer, the MISL does not use performance bonuses (statistical or quantitative) on a very wide basis. Estimates are that only about 25 percent of the players have such clauses.

With this background, consideration can now be given to the types of bonus provisions. What follows is only a sampling. The inventive minds of player representatives keep coming up with new ones, which is fine if they are done carefully; the careless approach, however, causes problems.

4.24–1 Types of Bonus Clauses

Different leagues attach different names to the same types of bonus clauses, and what is common parlance in one instance may sound foreign in another. We attempt to include in the types mentioned here any alternate terminology, but omissions may occur. Our breakdown examines bonuses based on status (Section 4.24–1[a]), statistical performance (Section 4.24–1[b]), volume of play (Section 4.24–1[c]), awards or honors (Section 4.24–1[d]), and other contingencies (Section 4.24–1[e]).

NOTE

1. An exhaustive treatment of bonus provisions could constitute almost a volume in and of itself. An extensive examination of the provisions is contained in R. Woolf and R. Berry, *Sports Contracts*, one volume of a series titled, *Sports and Entertainment Contracts* (forthcoming).

4.24–1(a) Status Bonus

The most widely employed bonus provision that relates to a player's status with the team is the signing bonus, witnessing the initial commitment that the player makes to either play for the team or at least attempt to make the team. Exhibit 4–4 is a reproduction of one of several forms used for a signing bonus. Note that it provides for several payments rather than just one. In addition, the conditions in the last two paragraphs place restrictions on what the bonus means in terms of later circumstances. All of these items are negotiable.

In addition to the signing bonus, status bonuses are also at times employed for such occasions as making the player roster at the start of the season or at some point later in the season. There are also so-called reporting bonuses, which are generally payable when the player appears for preseason camp.

4.24–1(b) Statistical Performance Bonus

Statistical performance bonuses are often re-

Exhibit 4-4   An Example of a Status Bonus

SIGNING BONUS

Between _____ and _____ .
               (Club)   (Player)

As additional consideration for the execution of NFL Player Contract(s) for the year(s) _____ , and for the Player's adherence to all provisions of said contract(s), Club agrees to pay Player the sum of $_____ .

The above sum is payable as follows:

    $_____ upon execution of this rider (Player acknowledges receipt of said sum); and

    $_____ on _____ 19____ ; and

    $_____ on _____ 19____ ; and

    $_____ on _____ 19____ .

It is expressly understood that no part of the bonus herein provided is part of any salary in the contract(s) specified above, that said bonus will not be deemed part of any salary in the contract(s) specified above if Club exercises an option for Player's services in a season subsequent to the final contract year, and that such obligations of Club are not terminable if such contract(s) is (are) terminated via the NFL waiver system.

In the event Player, in any of the years specified above or an option year, fails or refuses to report to Club, fails or refuses to practice or play with Club, or leaves Club without its consent, then, upon demand by Club, Player will return to Club the proportionate amount of the total bonus not having been earned at the time of Player's default.

Date: _____

Club: _____ Player: _____

   By: _____

ferred to as just plain performance or incentive bonuses. Their variety is boundless, except in baseball, where they are not allowed. At the same time, the provisions for statistically based performance bonuses are often carelessly worded, thrown into the "special covenants" section of the uniform player contract in abbreviated fashion. For this reason, and to avoid future misunderstandings and disputes, regard for the lessons contained in Section 4.24–2 should be heeded. Keeping in mind these cautionary notes, we will now examine several samples from actual statistical bonus provisions in those sports that allow them. Some are included deliberately because they contain potential language problems.

Football

Quarterback:

250 passing attempts	$
150 completions	$
Pass 1,000 yards	$
Pass 1,500 yards	$
Pass 2,000 yards	$
Pass 5 touchdowns	$
Pass 10 touchdowns	$

Running Back:

Rushes for 400 yards	$
Catches over 40 passes	$
Scores 6 touchdowns	$
Scores 5 touchdowns rushing	$
Scores 3 touchdowns rushing	$
Leads NFC or AFC in scoring	$

Defense:

Leads team in total tackles	$
Leads team in assists	$
Leads NFL in tackles	$
Leads NFC in tackles	$
Leads or ties linebackers in interceptions	$
Returns interception for touchdown (each)	$
Leads or ties team in tackles for loss	$
Fumble recoveries (each recovery)	$
Ties or leads team in interceptions	$
Leads NFL in interceptions	$
Leads NFC in interceptions	$
Leads or ties team linebackers for quarterback sacks	$
Quarterback sacks (each sack)	$

Basketball

In addition to other monies Player shall receive the following, if such are attained in any year under this contract:

For averaging over 20 points per game, the sum of $_____.

For leading the team in scoring, the sum of $____.

For leading the NBA in assists or steals, the sum of $_____.

For being in the top five in the NBA in scoring, the sum of $_____.

Hockey

30 goals or 65 points — $_____	, and
35 goals or 75 points — $_____	, and
40 goals or 85 points — $_____	, and
45 goals or 95 points — $_____	, and
50 goals or 105 points — $_____	.

4.24–1(c)   Volume of Play Bonus

Volume-of-play bonus provisions are particularly popular in Major League Baseball, with its ban on statistical bonuses. The need for some type of salary adjustment, particularly for younger players whose swings in performance are so pronounced from year to year and whose trips to and from the minors are so numerous, causes teams and agents alike to turn to volume of play as a meaningful barometer for additional monies. In baseball, the position played in terms of distinguishing pitchers from everyone else is crucial. The volume of play for the pitcher is either games started, game appearances, or innings pitched. Obviously, whether the pitcher is a starter or reliever may be crucial in judging volume of play. When there is uncertainty as to just what role the pitcher will play, the bonus usually contains alternative measures by which the bonus can be earned. In addition, the bonus provision is often made incremental — for each additional level of game appearances or innings pitched or games started, additional rewards will flow. For others than pitchers, the chief indicators are games played (which include partial games, even pinch hits) or plate appearances. The example that follows illustrates how these provisions might be structured.

Other sports also utilize volume-of-play bonuses, particularly in football where bonus provisions revolve around the percentage of playing time that the athlete is on the field. In that instance, great care must be placed on wording, since the base against which the percentage is to be compared can be tricky in a sport like football, with a constant shifting of personnel on and off the field.

Pitcher

In addition to other compensation, Player shall receive the following bonuses if player's record of performance during the regular playing season (and not including the League Championship Series or World Series) for [each of] the year(s)____ equals or exceeds any or all of the following:

a) If player appears in [____ games], or [starts ____ games], or [has ____ innings pitched], player shall receive $____;

b) If player appears in [____ games], or [starts ____games], or [has ____ innings pitched], player shall receive $____, which shall be an amount in addition to that which he is entitled to receive in clause a) above;

c) If player appears in [____ games], or [starts ____ games], or [has ____ innings pitched], player shall receive $____, which shall be an amount in addition to that which he is entitled to receive in clauses a) and b) above.

Non-pitcher

In addition to other compensation, Player shall receive the following bonuses if player's record of performance during the regular playing season (and not including the League Championship Series or World Series) for [each of] the year(s) ____ equals or exceeds any or all of the following:

a) If player appears in [____ games], or [has ____ plate appearances], player shall receive $____;

b) If player appears in [____ games], or [has ____ plate appearances], player shall receive ____, which shall be an amount in addition to that which he is entitled to receive in clause a) above;

c) If player appears in [____ games], or [has ____ plate appearances], player shall receive $____, which shall be an amount in addition to that which he is entitled to receive in clauses a) and b) above.

4.24–1(d)   Awards or Honors Bonus

All leagues allow for bonuses that recognize a player's achievements, such as being named All-League, or Gold Glove, or Fireman of the Year. The major deficiency in the drafting of these provisions, as illustrated by the decisions in arbitrations appearing in Section 4.24–2, is pinpointing exactly which all-star teams and which selectors are to form the basis for determining whether the award or honor has been achieved. Contrast the following provisions and note that some are sufficiently specific, while others are not.

Basketball

In addition to other monies Player shall receive under this contract, Player shall also receive the following, if such are attained in any year under this contract:

For being named the NBA Most Valuable Player, the sum of $____.

For playing in the NBA All-Star Game, the sum of $____.

For making the All-NBA first team, as selected at the end of the season, the sum of $____.

Football

Player shall receive the additional sum of ____ Dollars (____) if he is named "Rookie of the Year" by AP or UPI.

Player shall receive the additional sum of ____ Dollars (____) if he is selected for a Rookie team by either Sporting News, Pro Football Weekly or the AP.

Player shall receive the additional sum of ____ Dollars (____) if he is selected for and participates in the Pro Bowl game following the current regular season.

Baseball

If Player attains any of the following honors, Player shall receive the following:

Gold Glove, the sum of $_____.

Louisville Slugger award, the sum of $_____.

Rolaid's Fireman of the Year, the sum of $_____.

Selected to play in the All-Star game at midseason, the sum of $_____.

4.24–1(e)   Other Contingencies

This catchall section simply lists some of the other approaches occasionally used for bonus clauses. It makes no attempt to detail all the drafting problems, though a general caution is that the greater the intangible nature of what determines a bonus or not, the more potentials for later disputes. For example, one provision that is sometimes inserted, particularly in baseball contracts, is that the player will receive a bonus "if in the judgment of the Club, player has contributed to the team's success." Even though this provision is clearly ambiguous and invites trouble, it is nevertheless used.

Other bonus provisions add monies to the player's income if the club attains certain attendance levels. Some clubs give a bonus if the player is traded or if the club fails to exercise an option to renew the player's contract. Still other provisions nudge the player toward attaining some level of physical condition greatly desired for the club, the most popular of these being a "make weight" clause. Instead of fining the player for reporting to camp overweight, the player is instead rewarded for making and retaining the desired weight.

4.24–2   Disputes over Bonus Provisions

Prior considerations have repeatedly referred to the possibilities for dispute if bonus provisions are not carefully conceived and drafted. The following two examples explore these problems further. The first example contains excerpts from materials compiled for the NFL to use at a seminar for NFL club personnel. (Earlier excerpts on contract language were discussed in Section 4.21.) The second example contains arbitration decisions that deal with disputes over bonus provisions.

National Football League, Contract Language Discussion, Negotiation Seminars, Harvard University, February 10–12, 1981

Pitfalls in Performance Bonuses

The most pernicious and widespread disease in player contracts is faulty language — either ambiguous expression or outright obscurity. In examining contracts at the League office it is sometimes impossible to determine what the parties meant when the agreement was struck. Nowhere is this deficiency more evident than in so-called performance bonuses. Because the game of football does not result in easily documented statistics for all players — e.g., batting averages, pitching records, or basketball figures such as points, assists, rebounds — and because very few limitations are placed on our clubs' imaginative attempts to quantify performance and reduce it to dollar goals, player contracts often become a jumble of agreements that carry extemely high potential for dispute.

Below we explore many types of performance bonuses and offer discussion on their faults. All of the examples actually appeared in contracts filed in the League office by NFL clubs. The names of clubs and players have been omitted.

The Shorthand Syndrome

Too often, when a club writes performance bonuses, such clauses are tossed off in a shorthand style as if they were items on a grocery list and as if the lingo used in football circles were sufficient to be understood in a legal instrument. Here's a verbatim example from a 1980 contract:

Ex. 1 $2000 — First Official Cut; $1000 — Second Official Cut; $3000 — Third Official Cut.

In addition to the problem posed by the word *cut* (see previous section of this notebook), other questions would immediately be raised by a reader who is unfamiliar with football. Does the language mean that one of the parties will receive money for doing something? Who? The player? What must he do? Presumably it has to do with this cryptic term

Official Cut. And are the amounts listed here cumulative? Even a person familiar with the NFL's system would ask: what status must the player be in to receive the money? Active List? Is Injured Reserve good enough?

The Verbosity Syndrome

The opposite of being too informal and brief, of course, is the sin of writing windy, unessential language:

Ex. 2 Notwithstanding the compensation provided for in Paragraph 5 above, it is expressly understood between Club and Player that should Player achieve any of the goals specified below in various incentive clauses, Player shall receive such moneys, over and above those called for in Paragraph 5, that are earned under such incentive clauses, and no such moneys for earned incentive clauses shall be construed to be any part of that compensation called for in Paragraph 5. [After which the performance bonuses are listed.]

None of this is needed. Paragraph 5 of the NFL Player Contract provides for payment not only of base salary but of "such earned performance bonuses as may be called for in Paragraph 24 of or any attachment to this contract."

"Leader" Bonuses

Among the most frequently used incentives are those which reward the player for leading his club, conference, or the League in a statistical category.

Ex. 3 Player shall receive a bonus in the amount of $_____ if he leads the Conference in punt returns.

Looks reasonably harmless. But there are lots of ways to rate punt returners: average return, number of returns, total yardage, etc. We assume, of course, that a clause like the one above aims to reward the player for leading in *average* return. If so, it should clearly state that fact.

Ex. 4 The player shall receive a bonus in the amount of $_____ if he is in the top three in NFC in kick-off or punt returns during the 1980 regular season.

Same problem but compounded by expanding the bonus to two different return categories and dipping as low as third place in each.

Ex. 5 Player shall receive a bonus in the amount of $_____ if player ranks first in the NFL (net average).

Here the problem is turned upside down. We know a little bit more about the statistical measurement — it's net average (average what? yards, we presume) — but now we don't have the overall category. We don't know what the player is supposed to rank first *in*. The player's position might give us a clue. But if he's both a receiver and a special teams kick returner, we remain in the dark.

Ex. 6 Said player shall receive a bonus in the amount of $_____ if he is one of the top three kickers in the National Football Conference.

In addition to not making the statistical category clear (e.g., total vs. average yardage), the drafter of this language doesn't bother to tell us what kind of kicker the player is — field goal kicker, punter, combined FG/PAT man for purposes of the overall scoring statistics?

Ex. 7 Top 3 punters NFL $5000.

The Shorthand Syndrome revisited. We get the idea, but a little care might prevent grief later on if this punter is among the top three in *total number of punts* and seeks to collect.

Ex. 8 If player is the top punter in the NFC during the 1980 League Season, net or gross, he shall receive an additional $_____.

Net or gross what? For punters the *NFL Record Manual* lists net punts, gross yards, gross average yards, net average yards.

Ex. 9 $_____ bonus if player is among the top three receivers in yardage gained by receptions.

The statistical category is unambiguous, but we aren't told whether this performance is to be achieved on a club, conference, or League level.

Ex. 10 Player shall receive the additional sum of $_____ if he gains 1000 yards during the regular League season.

An extremely common mistake. One thousand yards by what means? Rushing? Receiving? Punt returns? Kickoff returns? A combination? . . .

Ex. 13 If Player among AFC statistical leaders in QB rankings, Player will receive the specified non-cumulative amount according to following distribution:

1st – $____; 2nd – $____; 3rd – $____; 4th – $____; 5th – $____.

Following is an excerpt of the letter sent to the club by the League office, asking for clarification of the above clause:

> Although there is no statistical category known as "QB rankings" (quarterbacks appear in several different statistical tables: passing, rushing, fumbles, etc.), we assume that you meant to focus only on the *offical passing statistics*. If that is the case, you should be aware that the NFL maintains passing statistics on *all* passers, regardless of the number of passes each has attempted. Therefore it is conceivable that a player may achieve a high number of rating points yet throw very few passes. On the other hand, in order to be listed among the so-called "qualifiers" for the conference or League passing championship, a passer must have attempted a minimum average of 12 passes for each of his team's regular-season games. If it was the parties' intention that [player] be required to meet the eligibility standards for a "qualifier," such should be specified.
>
> We fail to understand the meaning of "non-cumulative" as used in [the bonus clause]. Since [player] is only one passer, he cannot occupy more than one spot on any list of individual passers in a given season."

Specialized "Club Awards"

Occasionally performance bonuses tied exclusively to achievements on a particular club cause problems for that club or for an assignee.

Ex. 14   Player is to receive a bonus in the amount of ____ if [club name] *wins 8 or more games.*

Quite apart from the failure to tell us whether these are regular-season games or some other type, the writer of this clause overlooks the possibility that the player might be with some other club (through trade or the waiver system) or even terminated while his former club wins eight games. Was the intent to pay him anyway? We assume it was not.

Ex. 15   Player shall receive a bonus in the amount of $____ if he is named local rookie-of-the-year.

Unassignable (unless, of course, the assignee club is foolish enough to accept it), unspecific, and unwise. If local Volunteer Fire Co. no. 39, which includes several drinking buddies of our hero, decides to name him rookie-of-the-year — despite his having barely hung on as the 45th man on the roster all year — do we have the ingredients for a dispute? Obviously it could be argued that any grievance centering on such a claim should be labeled frivolous, but there's no doubt the award will have been truly "local." . . .

Ambiguous or Nonexistent Achievements

It is one thing to write a bonus clause based on a performance that only the club can measure, e.g., leading the team in quarterback "sacks"; it is quite another to broaden such imprecise achievements to a League level.

Ex. 17   If player leads his conference in quarterback sacks as listed on official records, Player will receive $____.

The amount of the bonus in this case runs to five figures. Yet if a dispute arises between the player and club there are no *official records* to consult. Quarterback sacks (or assists, or partial sacks) achieved by individual players are not recorded and compiled officially on a conference or League basis. It is true that a number of clubs maintain unofficial defensive statistics for their own purposes, but even here only a few of the clubs double-check through game films the sacks that are recorded on the spot in the press box. Further, some clubs do not release information on defensive statistics.

Ex. 18   Player shall receive the sum of $____ if he leads NFL in tackles for the 1980 regular season.

Again there is nothing indisputably official with which to test this clause. . . .

Roster Bonuses and Percentage of Playing Time

Two of the most prevalent devices used to reward the efforts of players who don't easily accumulate offensive or defensive statistics are the so-called "roster bonus," i.e., compensation for making the team at some point, and a similar reward for participating in a certain percentage of plays or for a portion of playing time. The roster bonus is seen, of course, in a great number of contracts of younger players.

Ex. 21   Player shall receive a bonus in the amount of $_____ if he is a member of the roster after the cutdown to 50 players.

The word *roster* is imprecise. There is an Injured Reserve "roster," too. If *Active List* is meant, please say so.

Ex. 22   Player shall receive a bonus in the amount of $_____ if he makes final roster for the 1980 season.

Is this the Active List on the day of the final mandatory reduction or as of the first regular-season game? (Remember, these two things are very different; Active Lists can undergo considerable change in that period of about six days.) Or perhaps Example 22 means the *final* (i.e., the 16th) regular-season game?. . .

Honor Teams and Individual Awards

In its Labor-Management section of the *GUIDE for MEMBER CLUBS/Administration,* the Management Council offers recommended language on most of the types of performance bonuses discussed in this notebook. Among them are bonuses for being named to various honor teams or for receiving individual honors. Please review this section. The most common mistake is that particular news agencies are cited in many contract clauses, but those agencies often do *not* make the selections on which the clauses focus. Here are some other problems:

Ex. 29   If player is a member of All Rookie team by nationally accredited selection body player will receive $_____.

Who decides what a *nationally accredited selection body* is?

Ex. 30   If player is All NFL by any news media the player will receive $_____ 1st or 2nd Team.

The player in this case might want to get chummy with the people who put out his old high school's newpaper.

Ex. 31   Said player shall receive a bonus in the amount of $_____ if is "Defensive Rookie of the Year".

Apparently this award doesn't even have to be made by *any news media* or a *nationally accredited selection body*. . . .

Ex. 35   The Club agrees to pay the player $_____ as a bonus if in the opinion of the coaches he has had a good season during this year.

The mystery of who is offering the opinion is cleared up. But the criterion for earning the money grows murkier. . . .

Defining Your Terms

Many of the errors in performance bonuses can be reduced to a simple lack of care in defining routine terms such as *season* or the name of a particular postseason game or the status of the player (see examples above which fail to specify Active List; also the discussion in the first section on *starter* and *regular*). Similarly, clubs often draft groups of related bonuses (e.g., X dollars for gaining 500 yards, X dollars for gaining 750, etc.) but neglect to state whether the amounts are cumulative or whether the player will collect only for his *highest* achievement. Here are a few clauses where definition of terms is a potential problem.

Ex. 38 $_____ bonus if Player plays in 50% of the offensive or defensive plays during the regular League season (excluding special teams).

Ex. 39 $_____ bonus if Player plays in 75% of the offensive or defensive plays during the regular League season (excluding special teams).

If the player plays in at least 75 per cent, will he receive the dollars for that bonus in addition to the dollars under Ex. 38? Also, bonuses of this type should include the words a *minimum of* or *at least* [50% of the . . .] so that there is no confusion about what the player must do. This same player had a third bonus for starting in 8 regular-season games and a fourth for starting in 12. We have to assume that if he starts in 10 he will receive the money cited in the bonus for 8. But could the player argue — because the clause appears to focus on an *exact* number instead of a minimum — that a sliding scale for all games between 8 and 12 is implied and that he should be paid an additional amount equal to half the difference between the bonus for 8 and 12?

Ex. 40   Player is to receive an additional $_____ if he reports to camp weighing 225 pounds.

Unless we know the player's habits, we don't know if he's too heavy or too light. Is it possible that the club literally meant an exact 225 pounds — no more, no less?

Ex. 41   If the player participates in a minimum of 40 per cent of the total offensive plays of the playoff game and the Club participates in a Conference playoff game, then player will receive as additional compensation for his services the sum of $_____.

There are four levels of the postseason leading to the NFL championship: First Round Playoffs (commonly known as Wild Card games), Divisional Playoffs, Conference Championships, and Super Bowl. Example 41 might be interpreted to mean any of the first three. . . .

NOTE _____

1. The National Football League Players Association has also voiced concerns about the wording and use of incentive or performance bonuses. The following are excerpts from an outline distributed by the NFLPA in connection with one of a series of seminars it has sponsored for the education of present and prospective agents and attorneys.

H. Incentive Bonuses.

1. Incentive clauses are used widely in the NFL, probably more than any other sport.

a. They are often used as a means of compromising player's salary demands vs. the club's offer.

b. Some clubs use them more than others — consistent winners use them less than "building" teams.

2. Clubs can control the player's opportunity to earn them, so their financial risks can be minimized.

3. Nevertheless, they are very important to many players.

4. Types of Incentive Clauses:

a. Statistical achievements.

(1) Player gets $X if he is leading rusher in AFC.

(2) Player get $X if he has 40 or more unassisted tackles.

b. Team Bonuses.

(1) Player gets $X if team wins the divisional championship.

(2) Player gets $X if defense gives up 200 points or less.

(3) Player gets $X if quarterback is sacked less than 10 times.

c. Individual Honors.

(1) Player gets $X if selected All-Conference by the Associated Press.

(2) Player gets $X if selected as most valuable player on the team.

(3) Player gets $X if he is selected for the Pro Bowl.

d. Others.

(1) Player gets $X if he makes the team.

(2) Player gets $X if in the opinion of the head coach, he has a good year.

5. Problem areas to keep in mind.

a. A player can be traded at any time.

(1) If player to get $X "if he makes the final squad of the San Francisco 49ers," will he get it if he is traded to Denver the week before the season begins?

(2) If player to get $X from NFC team for leading the conference in unassisted tackles, what happens if he is traded to AFC team? (AFC does not publish defensive statistics.)

(3) If player to get $X for grading 90% or higher, what if he is traded to team that doesn't have grades?

b. Injuries will affect the player's opportunity to earn them.

(1) Player to get $X if he starts at least half the games — what if he starts first six games and is then injured for the rest of the year?

(2) Player to get $X if he makes the squad at the beginning of the regular season — what if he's injured but comes back to play last half of the season?

(3) Player to get $X if team wins division — what if he's injured in the pre-season and out for the year?

c. Some terms aren't well defined, and clubs benefit by ambiguity.

(1) *All-Pro or All-Conference* — could mean first team, second team, Associated Press, UPI, Ray Nitschke's Packer Report.

(2) *Beginning of the regular season* — is it the final cut-down date or kick-off time of first League game?

(3) If player to get $X if defense gives up 200 or less points, does this include points scored on punt returns, interceptions for touchdowns, or kick-off returns?

(4) If player to get $X if he plays "50% of the time," is this minutes, plays, or games?

(5) If player to get $X if team wins division, what about a tie or wild card?

In the Matter of Arbitration Between Alan Page and the Minnesota Vikings, July 23, 1973. Com. Rozelle, Arb.

In Alan Page's Standard Player contract for 1972, a clause was inserted that read, "said player shall receive a bonus in the amount of $2,500 if he is selected 'All Pro' by any of the following: AP, UPI, PFW, or the Sporting News." When Page was selected to the AP's second team all-NFL squad and was chosen as one of the two defensive tackles on the all-NFC teams selected by UPI and The Sporting News, he requested payment of the bonus from the Minnesota Vikings.

The controversy centered on the interpretation of "All-Pro." Jim Finks of the Minnesota Vikings, who worded the clause in question, testified that All-Pro signified to him that a player was selected as the very best performer in his position in the entire league. In contrast, Page believed that any honorary selection, including honorable mention, would entitle him to a bonus.

Commissioner Pete Rozelle ruled that "All-Pro" did not have the sweeping connotation that Page ascribed to it. However, the Vikings had specifically designated the UPI and *The Sporting News* as agencies whose selections would determine Page's eligibility. These two agencies did not select a true All-Pro (i.e., All-NFL) team, but chose two All-Conference teams. Since Page, named to the All-NFC team, was selected to the highest honorary plateau that a player could reach under the agencies' formats, and because the Vikings had themselves designated these agencies, Rozelle held that Page was entitled to his bonus, and ordered payment of the $2,500.

NFLPA and Russ Bolinger v. Detroit Lions, PCRC Decision (1977)

At issue were the following two incentive bonus clauses in Bolinger's 1976 contract with the Lions:

> 26. Player shall receive a bonus of $3,500.00 if he starts seven (7) games as an offensive player, excluding special teams, during the 1976 regular season.

> 28. Player shall receive a bonus of $3,500.00 if he is named to the official All-Rookie Team by either the AP, UPI or NEA news services in the 1976 season.

Bolinger's position was that he had earned the "games-started" bonus because he started six regular season games as an offensive lineman and a seventh regular season game, the last one of the season, as a member of the goal-line offensive team on the first offensive play of the game following the kick-off reception by the Lions. The Lions' position was that he started only six regular season games as

an offensive player and that the seventh game was excluded because the goal-line offense is a "special team."

Bolinger's position on the "All-Rookie" bonus was that he earned it because he was chosen to the second team of the All-Rookie Team selected by the Professional Football Writers of America. The Lions' position was that second team selection was not being named to an official "All-Rookie Team"; and in any event, Bolinger was not picked to an All-Rookie Team by AP, UPI, or NEA, as specified in the bonus clause.

After discussion, the PCRC resolved the grievance by mutual agreement, as follows:

1. Bolinger is entitled to the $3,500 "games-started" bonus. He started seven (7) regular season games as an offensive player. A goal-line offense may be considered a special circumstance but is not a "special team" within the meaning of the exception to the bonus clause.

2. Bolinger is not entitled to the $3,500 "All-Rookie Team" bonus. "All-Rookie Team" within the meaning of the bonus clause applies only to first team selection. In any event, Bolinger was named to the second team by Pro Football Writers of America and not by AP, UPI or NEA.

In accordance with Section 5 of Article VII, this resolution by the PCRC constitutes full, final, and complete disposition of the grievance and is binding on Bolinger, the Lions, the NFLPA, and the Management Council.

4.25   Formation Problems

Parties have difficulties formulating precise contract terms in the sports world as elsewhere. At times, the formation of the contract itself is jeopardized. The circumstances by which a contract fails in formation are varied. Sometimes one of the parties presses too hard to provide all advantages to his side, while leaving an "out" if matters are not as anticipated. In other instances, parties are unwilling to agree to terms where future events are unknown; the contingencies left for future agreement are then deemed essential to the existence of a contract. As a result, there is no contract.

The cases discussed below illustrate only a few of the circumstances that cause a contract to collapse. In the first two situations, a term in the

NFL contract is held to create a condition precedent, and no contract is formed until that condition is fulfilled. The decisions in these cases caused the NFL and most other leagues to change the language in their standard forms. For example, in conjunction with the discussion of the *Robinson* and *Cannon* cases, comparison should be made with present language in the NBA contract, set forth in Chapter 3, Exhibit 3–1, at paragraph 14.

The other two cases presented below deal with individually negotiated "contracts." Each is instructive on ways in which parties at times fail to agree or, if there is later breach, fail to move to remedy the situation in timely fashion.

Detroit Football v. Robinson, 186 F. Supp. 933 (E.D. La. 1960)

The basic issue presented was whether the standard player's contract signed by Robinson with the Detroit Club constituted a valid and binding agreement upon him. While in his last year of college, Robinson signed an agreement with Detroit. Paragraph 13 of the agreement provided that the commissioner's signature would make the agreement valid and binding upon each party.

As worded, paragraph 13 of the then NFL standard player contract read: "This agreement shall become valid and binding upon each party hereto only when, as and if it shall be approved by the Commissioner." The club gave Robinson an advance percentage of his agreed-upon salary. However, prior to the commissioner's approval, Robinson was approached by the Dallas Club of the AFL and later signed with them. He notified Detroit. In the sequence of events, Robinson returned the advanced funds after the commissioner's approval of the contract. Detroit refused to accept the funds and filed to enforce the contract.

The agreement was characterized by the court as an offer by Robinson to Detroit. Since the commissioner's approval was a condition precedent to the existence of the contract, the court concluded that Detroit's acceptance was conditional and that Robinson could rightfully revoke his offer before such acceptance became binding. Robinson's acceptance of the advanced funds did not preclude his subsequent withdrawal.

The court inferred that if the advanced funds were in consideration of holding Robinson's option to play for them open, it was possible the offer could not be revoked. However, in the absence of an express stipulation, such an argument could not be pressed.

Los Angeles Rams v. Cannon, 185 F.Supp. 717 (S.D.Ca. 1960)

Prior to the draft and defendant Billy Cannon's last intercollegiate game, the Los Angeles Rams contacted him. The player and club signed NFL player contracts covering 1960, 1961, and 1962. Cannon received two checks, for $10,000 and $500, respectively. The Rams sent the 1960 contract to the acting commissioner of the NFL for his signature pursuant to paragraph 13. Later, Cannon was approached by the Houston Club of the American Football League and subsequently signed with them. On December 30, 1959, Cannon notified the Rams, purportedly revoking his acceptance. However, prior to such revocation, the commissioner had approved the 1960 contract on December 1.

The court first considered the issue of the provision relating to the commissioner's signature. It found the language in the provision unequivocal in declaring that the commissioner's approval was essential to the formation of the contract. Hence, in substance, the signed "agreement" was an offer by Cannon and a conditional acceptance by the Rams. Since the 1960 agreement was the only one approved by the commissioner, only it could be binding upon the player. The 1961 and 1962 offers were revocable.

Looking at the totality of the circumstances, the court determined the terms of the offer. The court concluded that Cannon's offer was to play for three years, commencing in 1960 and ending in 1962. However, Commissioner Rozelle's submission of the 1960 contract alone was determined a counteroffer. Since Cannon's offer was for three years, not one, the Rams clearly did not accept this offer. Acceptance of the offer was necessary to the formation of the contract. Hence, the court concluded that the 1960 agreement, as well, was not binding upon the player.

The Rams further argued that Cannon's taking possession of the check constituted an acceptance of the counteroffer of the Rams. The court reasoned that Cannon knew he could not accept the payment until after the January 1 Sugar Bowl game. Furthermore, he had not endorsed the check. The court determined that accepting possession of the check did not constitute acceptance of payment. As such, Cannon did not accept the counteroffer of the Rams to play in 1960 only.

The last line of attack by the Rams was the contention that the $10,000 bonus check was consideration for holding open the offer of Cannon for a reasonable time. Since the keeping of the check was conditioned upon Cannon's appearing at spring training camp (if he did not, it would have to be returned), the court found the bonus characterization of a consideration for an option illusory. The agreements signed by Cannon were revocable.

Eckles v. Sharman, 548 F. 2d 905 (10th Cir. 1977)

A breach of contract action was brought by Mountain State Sports, owner of the Utah Stars (Utah) of the American Basketball Association (ABA), against Bill Sharman, their former coach. Plaintiff also filed suit against California Sports Inc., owner of the National Basketball Association (NBA) team, the Los Angeles Lakers (Los Angeles), for a tortious interference with plaintiff's contract with Sharman.

In 1968, Sharman was hired by the Los Angeles Stars of the ABA for seven years at $55,000, with annual increases of 5 percent. The provisions of the agreement pertinent to the case included the following: (1) Sharman had an option to purchase 5 percent of the club at a price to be agreed upon between him and the owner; (2) Sharman was to participate in an undefined pension plan; and (3) the invalidity of any one paragraph would not cause the invalidity of the agreement, which would then be interpreted as if the invalid provision had been omitted.

In 1970, the Los Angles Stars were sold to Mountain State Sports of Colorado. An addendum to the sale agreement provided for no obligation to assume Sharman's contract unless he agreed to transfer to the team's new city. Sharman did move to Salt Lake City with the team, which became known as the Utah Stars, and led them to the ABA championship during the 1970–71 season.

While the team was in Los Angeles, no agreements were reached regarding pension and option provisions. The general manager of Utah assured Sharman that the pension agreement would be worked out; however, after numerous communications, there was still no final agreement. Sharman resigned as coach of Utah in June of 1971 and signed a contract to coach the Los Angeles Lakers.

The court ruled that California law applied in the case. The first trial was declared a mistrial. In the second trial, the judge directed a verdict against the defendants. The jury returned an award of $250,000 against Sharman and $175,000 against California Sports. By the directed verdict, the court held that as a matter of law the contract between the Los Angeles Stars and Sharman was valid and enforceable, the contract was validly assigned to Mountain States Sports, and the option and pension provisions of the contract were severable from it.

The court of appeals disagreed and held that the option clause was unenforceable since it was nothing more than an agreement to agree. The pension clause was ambiguous because it failed to state the pension amount, the manner of its funding, and the age of commencement. The court of appeals reasoned that a fatally ambiguous contract could not be made valid and enforceable merely by negotiating in good faith concerning various terms of the agreement. The parties must have agreed on the essential and material terms of a contract for it to be enforceable. A contract would be legally cognizable, in spite of any uncertainties, if the contract had been agreed to and all that remained was clarification of nonessential terms. The question facing the court was whether the pension and option clauses were so essential to the contract that failure to agree on the pertinent terms made the contract unenforceable.

The court held that the severability clause was only an aid to construction and that the crucial question was whether the potentially severable clauses were essential to the contract. Whether they are essential was to be determined by the parties' intent. On the question of intent, the evidence was not conclusive. The court ruled that the directed verdict was in error, since such a verdict was proper only if the evidence pointed all one way and was not susceptible to reasonable inferences favoring the party against whom it is directed.

The liability of California Sports depended on the validity of Sharman's contract with the L.A. Stars and whether it was enforceable by Utah against Sharman. California Sports was not liable for interference if Sharman's contract with the L.A. Stars was invalid and was unenforceable by Utah. The court reversed the decision against California Sports, since the trial court had erred in directing a verdict against Sharman.

As to damages, the defendants argued that they were not liable for lost profits and that damages should be measured by either the increased replacement expense or, if Sharman was unique and irreplaceable, by the increased pay he would have received in the open market. The defendants pointed out that Sharman's replacements were paid lower salaries and his salary from the Lakers was basically the same that Utah had paid him.

The court stated that damages for contract breach must place the plaintiff in the position it would have been in if the contract had been completed. The court noted that lost profits could be recovered if the employer showed that the parties had reason to believe that such losses would result from a breach.

Recovery for consequential damages, such as lost profits, is appropriate in a breach of employment contract. The court held that recovery could be had only if Sharman were unique and irreplaceable. The evidence in this regard was conflicting. In the absence of an instruction to that effect the trial court had erred.

The court of appeals criticized the trial court judge for showing a strong personal bias and prejudice to the plaintiff. Indications of this one-sidedness were the pyramiding of losses for inducement on top of damages for breach of contract. The court of appeals compared the total award to plaintiffs of $425,000 with the sale price of the franchise of $345,000 a little more than one year before the breach.

The court reversed the trial court decision and remanded the case for a new trial by a judge from outside the District of Utah.

NOTE _____

1. The specific language of the court regarding the issue of excessive damages should be noted:

. . . The failure of the court to instruct the jury that to award consequential damages the jury must find that the claimed losses were reasonably foreseeable at the time when the contract was made may explain how the jury awarded $250,000 in damages against Sharman. The entire franchise of the Los Angeles Stars had been sold to the plaintiff a little more than a year before the breach for $345,000. The sale contract included the players and attributed no value to the services of Sharman.

The jury verdicts awarded a recovery of $250,000 from Sharman and $175,000 from California Sports. The judgment of the court reads that the plaintiff "recover against defendants, William Sharman and California Sports, Inc., jointly and severally, the sum of $250,000" and against California Sports individually $175,000. The judgment is inconsistent with the verdicts and cannot stand. It may be that damages for inducement may not be less than damages for breach. We know of no law which permits the pyramiding of losses for inducement on top of damages for breach. The pyramiding action of the court is indicative of the atmosphere in which the trial was conducted. [548 F.2d at 910–911]

4.26   Length of Contract

Although it might seem that the length of a contract should not cause problems in uniform player contracts, such is not always the case. The two cases that follow reflect a practice still utilized by many NFL clubs — that is, instead of a single contract for a period of years, the NFL clubs insist that a player sign a series of successive contracts. This practice supposedly limits the club's liability if the player is injured in the early years of the successive contracts. Salary for the entire time is avoided, as was held in the *Sample* case below. Particular facts, however, may alter the result, as the *Chuy* case demonstrates. Other allegations raised in these two interesting cases, although not germane to the topic of length of contract, are also discussed.

Sample v. Gotham Football Club, 59 F.R.D. 160 (S.D. N.Y. 1973)

This action was brought by a professional football player, Johnny Sample, against the New York Jets, seeking to recover for breach of a personal services contract.

The parties had entered into contracts for the 1968, 1969, and 1970 seasons. Plaintiff was allegedly injured in August 1969 in a preseason game. His 1969 contract was later terminated. He brought this action for (1) a breach of the 1969 contract, (2) a breach of the 1970 contract, and (3) injury to his reputation.

Plaintiff contended he was arbitrarily dismissed because defendant had unsuccessfully sought to obtain waivers or trade him to another team, and when they had failed, they dismissed him. Plaintiff also contended he was entitled to recover under the injury-benefit clause of the 1970 contract. His theory was that, notwithstanding the three separately executed documents, his intention was to enter into one three-year contract. He claimed he was deceived because of his lack of sophistication in legal matters and his unequal bargaining position and that he subjectively believed he had entered into one contract. Plaintiff further alleged the wrongful dismissal caused an injury to his good name and reputation and to other business pursuits. He based this claim on the *manner* in which the termination was carried out, claiming the club's press releases were wanton and malicious in suggesting that plaintiff was unwilling or unable to play apart from his injury.

Defendant denied all of plaintiff's allegations. It claimed as an affirmative defense that plaintiff's wrongful dismissal allegation was barred by his failure to comply with the exclusive procedures contained in the contract for remedies based on a claim of an injury preventing performance. Paragraph 14 of the contract stated there must be an injury sustained during performance of services pursuant to the contract, that written notice of that injury must be given to the team physician within 36 hours, and once declared physically able to play, the player had 72 hours to get an examination by a physician of his choice. Defendant claimed this procedure was the only limitation on its unqualified right to terminate plaintiff's contract, salary, or both. Defendant's answer to plaintiff's second allegation was that the objective intent of the parties illustrated that the agreements between plaintiff and defendant were three separate and distinct contracts, each pertaining to a single football season. Defendant claimed that plaintiff's third cause of action was not cognizable in actions based on breach of employment contracts.

The court, ruling on both parties' motions for summary judgment, held that a substantial fact issue existed whether plaintiff met the prerequisites of paragraph 14, which limited defendant's right to terminate, and therefore summary judgment was precluded. The court did allow defendant summary judgment as a matter of law concerning plaintiff's claim to recovery under the injury benefits clause of the 1970 contract. The court said the contracts related to different subject matter and called for performance at different times; thus, they were separate. The injury-benefit provision was only operative during the relevant contract period; therefore, only if the injury was during the 1970 season could plaintiff have invoked the provision. As for the third cause of action, the court said it was not cognizable in an action for breach of contract, but because plaintiff's claim was also based on the manner in which he was terminated, and that discovery had been suspended, he should have been given sufficient opportunity to present his claim. The court ordered a continuance of this part of defendant's motion.

Chuy v. Philadelphia Eagles Football Club, 595 F.2d. 1265 (3rd Cir. 1979)

Don Chuy joined the Philadelphia Eagles in 1969 after six years with the Los Angeles Rams. In a meeting with the Eagles' general manager, Chuy negotiated three National Football League standard form player contracts covering the 1969, 1970, and 1971 football seasons.

The contracts each contained the standard NFL injury benefit provision, which stated that a player injured in the performance of his services was entitled to his salary "for the term of the contract." Chuy sustained a serious shoulder injury during the 1969 season. During hospitalization, his diagnosis indicated a blood clot on his lung, thus ending his professional athletic career. Notifying the Eagles of his intention to retire, Chuy requested payment for the remaining two years of what he asserted to be a three-year contract.

Chuy was then examined by a physician of the Eagles' choosing, who concluded Chuy suffered from an abnormal blood condition. Eagles' General Manager Pete Retzlaff informed a sports columnist that Chuy had been advised to quit football due to a blood-clot condition. Brown, the columnist, telephoned the Eagles' team physician for further information. Brown then published a column stating that Chuy suffered from a blood disease. The press services picked up the story and reported that Chuy had been "advised to give up football and professional wrestling because of a blood condition." They quoted Dr. Nixon, the Eagles physician: "Chuy is suffering from polychythemia vera, which is a threat to form blood clots."

Chuy testified he panicked upon reading these articles and called his personal physician, who told him that while the disease was fatal, his records did not show Chuy to have the disease. Chuy testified that despite these assurances, he became apprehensive, avoided people, and had difficulty coping with daily activities. Although his personal physician's tests disproved the presence of the disease, he continued to be apprehensive. Among other matters, marital difficulties developed.

Chuy's suit against the Eagles and the NFL alleged antitrust violations, breach of contract, intentional infliction of emotional distress, and defamation. The district court dismissed the antitrust claim. See 407 F. Supp. 717 [E.D. Pa. 1976]. The remaining claims were submitted to the jury by special interrogatories, with a finding for the plaintiff on all but the defamation claim. After entry of judgment against the Eagles in the aggregate amount of $115,590.96, both parties appealed — the Eagles appealing the contract and intentional infliction of emotional distress claims, and Chuy appealing dismissal of the defamation claim. The court of appeals affirmed on all counts.

The Eagles contended that the three contracts Chuy signed were three separate, consecutive, one-year contracts. They asserted the 1970 and 1971 contracts required Chuy to comply with paragraph 6, providing for a complete physical and the right of the club to terminate if the "player" fails to establish excellent physical condition. The Eagles' position was that in the absence of a "no-cut" or "no-release" provision, Chuy was entitled only to the balance of his 1969 salary and that the district court should have given effect to this unambiguous construction without resort to parol evidence as to party intent and understanding.

Judge Becker for the district court had concluded the three contracts were susceptible to ambiguity as to the phrase "term of the contract" and that the jury should resolve this ambiguity predicated on pertinent parol evidence. The jury found, under established NFL practice, that the club is liable for subsequent salary covered by "multiple" season contracts.

The cardinal rule of contract construction is that the intent of the parties at the time they contracted is controlling. Under Pennsylvania law, intent is determined by the written instrument if its words are "clear and unambiguous." If ambiguous, parol evidence is admissible to resolve the ambiguity.

Coverage and compensation per season were covered in paragraph 14 of Chuy's contract, which provided that in event of injury the club will "continue during the term of this contract to pay Player his salary as provided in paragraph 3 . . . if and so long as it is the opinion of the Club Physician that Player, because of such injury, is unable to perform the services required of him by the contract."

The standard player contract adopted by the professional football leagues sets forth the obligations of player, club, and league. Individualized negotiations are required only as to the term of the contract and the amount of compensation. The date of execution of each contract was June 16, 1969; paragraph one of the contracts, respectively, created a one-year contract for the 1969 season, a two-year contract for the 1969–1970 seasons, and a three-year contract for the 1969–1971 seasons and as such rendered paragraph 14 ambiguous. Thus, the district court did not err in admitting parol evidence to clarify the intent of the parties as to the term of the contract.

The Eagles relied on *Sample* v. *Gotham Football Club, Inc.,* which the court distinguished from the instant case.

Both parties testified as to their intent regarding the term of the contract. The jury found that both Chuy and Retzlaff "manifested by words and intent" to have the Eagles liable for salary to Chuy for 1970 and 1971 in the event he sustained a football-related injury in 1969 which rendered him incapable of playing in 1970 and 1971.

On appeal, viewing the evidence most favorably to the plaintiff (as one must on appeal from denial of motion for judgment notwithstanding the verdict), we conclude there is sufficient

evidence for the jury to have found intent to compensate Chuy for the three-year term of his contract.

Plaintiff's recovery of damages for emotional distress was based on Section 46 of the Restatement (Second) of Torts (1965) providing:

> One who by extreme and outrageous conduct intentionally or recklessly causes severe emotional distress to another is subject to liability for such emotional distress, and if bodily harm to the other results from it, for such bodily harm.

The court had to determine, as a matter of law, whether there was sufficient evidence for reasonable persons to find extreme or outrageous conduct. The district court ruled that if Dr. Nixon, the Eagles' physician, advised sportswriter Brown that Chuy suffered from polycythemia vera, knowing that Chuy did not have the disease, such conduct could reasonably be regarded as extreme and outrageous.

The Eagles next contended that the district court erred in charging the jury on intent and recklessness. Reckless conduct causing emotional distress renders an actor liable as if he has acted intentionally. If Dr. Nixon's statements were intentional, he need not have been aware of the natural and probable consequences of his words. It is sufficient that Chuy's distress was substantially certain to follow Dr. Nixon's rash statements. The jury was properly charged as to these elements and reasonably could have found the requirements of Section 46, as to intent, to have been met.

The Eagles asserted that Chuy's reaction to these statements was exaggerated and unreasonable. Chuy's refusal to undergo tests and failure to communicate with the Eagles' physician to verify the reports are cited as unreasonable conduct precluding their liability. The jury was asked to determine whether the "natural and probable" impact of Dr. Nixon's statements rendered the statements beyond the bounds of decency; the jury responded affirmatively. Implicit in this ruling is that Chuy did not feign his mental anxiety. No cases cited require plaintiff to alleviate his distress by seeking immediate medical treatment or verification. The district court instructed the jury that failure to minimize damages could reduce plaintiff's damage award.

The Eagles contended that even if Dr. Nixon had committed a tort, they should not be held vicariously liable on a master-servant theory. A master is liable for the torts of his servant if the latter's tortious conduct was within the scope of his employment. The jury found the Eagles controlled the substance of Dr. Nixon's press statements. The jury's focus was to be only on Dr. Nixon's role as a press spokesman, relating to a player's medical status. His statements thus fell within his scope of employment, and the Eagles could be held vicariously liable for Dr. Nixon's tortious statement to Brown.

The district court instructed the jury that punitive damages could be awarded to penalize and deter. The Eagles argued that since compensatory damages were based on outrageous and extreme conduct, enhancing a verdict by punitive damages is double punishment. Predicating compensatory damages upon a finding of outrageous conduct does not preclude a separate assessment of punitive damages to punish past and deter future tortious conduct. There is nothing special about the tort of intentional infliction of emotional distress to limit its victims only to compensatory damages.

The court concluded that the Pennsylvania Supreme Court, in light of the noncompensating purposes promoted by punitive damages, would sanction an award of punitive damages in appropriate cases of tortious infliction of emotional distress.

The Eagles argued that no punitive damages should be assessed a principal who does not participate in or approve his agent's tortious conduct. With the absence of managerial participation in or approval of Dr. Nixon's statements, the Eagles claimed punitive damages were inappropriate. The Eagles relied on Section 217C of the Restatement (Second) of Agency (1958), which circumscribes employers' or principals' liability for punitive damages. However, Pennsylvania follows a less restrictive rule requiring "the conduct of the agent be rather clearly outrageous to justify the vicarious imposition of exemplary damages upon the principal." The court concluded the Pennsylvania courts would adopt a standard of vicarious liability for punitive damages which would encompass the conduct of Dr. Nixon found by the jury to be outrageous.

Chuy appealed the district court's denial of his motion for a new trial on the defamation count. The jury, in answer to a specific interrogatory, found that Dr. Nixon intentionally told Brown that Chuy was suffering from polycythemia vera, and that Nixon's statements tended to injure Chuy's reputation. The jury also found that Brown did not know Dr. Nixon's statements would tend to injure Chuy's reputation. Pennsylvania law, which requires the recipient (Brown) to understand the communication as defamatory, compelled the court, as per the jury's finding, to enter a verdict for the Eagles on the defamation claim.

To prove defamation, Chuy was required to show Dr. Nixon's remarks were capable of defamatory meaning. To decide this question, Chuy's public status was crucial. As a professional athlete of some renown, the court held as a matter of law that Chuy was a public figure. Applying the standard of *New York Times Co. v. Sullivan*, proof of actual malice was needed to prove defamation.

In carefully scrutinizing the comments attributed to Dr. Nixon, the court perceived no basis for Chuy's contention that the statements were defamatory per se. There was absolutely nothing in Dr. Nixon's statements that could be construed as defamatory.

4.27   Guaranteed Contracts

Players are always after the "no-cut" contract. We have seen that the term "no-cut" is really inappropriate (Section 4.21–1). What is really sought is a guaranteed salary, whether the player stays on the team or not. But what is meant by a guarantee? That term is only slightly less ambiguous. Is the salary guaranteed even if the player defaults and refuses to play? Obviously, no club would agree to such one-sidedness. Thus, there is a need to specify under what circumstances the salary will be paid, and under what conditions it will not. The National Basketball Association has set forth different approaches in its Allowable Amendments to the Uniform Player Contract (Chapter 3, Section 3.22). These guides should be consulted when contemplating the various possibilities. But even those provisions may not anticipate all grounds for dispute. The decisions that follow illustrate that a guarantee is not easy to define — nor are its consequences always clear.

In the Matter of Arbitration Between National Basketball Association (Houston Rockets) and National Basketball Players Association (John S. Vallely), Peter Seitz, Arbitrator, October 2, 1974

In May 1970 Vallely signed a three-season contract with the Atlanta Hawks. A rider attached to his uniform player contract stipulated, in part, that he accept employment "on a *no-cut* guaranteed basis." After one and a quarter seasons, Vallely was traded to the Houston Rockets, which assumed his contract. In September 1972, Houston informed Vallely that his services were no longer required. The club continued to pay his salary even though he was removed from the roster. Vallely's presence on a team roster for three years would have automatically qualified him for the pension plan. This arbitration dealt with Vallely's appeal from the commissioner's decision that he was ineligible to participate in the pension plan. At issue was whether the club and the league denied pension credits to Vallely in violation of the collective bargaining agreement.

Both sides based their arguments on their interpretation of the "no-cut" guarantee. The club maintained that a no-cut contract guaranteed only that a player's salary would not be terminated if the player was removed from the squad at the option or initiative of the club without fault on the player's part. The Player's

Association argued that a club could not relieve itself of any obligations due a player under a no-cut contract by removing the player from the team roster. Accordingly, they claimed that the Rockets could not extinguish Vallely's right to credit the remainder of his contract term for the purpose of completing the three-year pension eligibility requirement.

Seitz felt that the club failed to offer any persuasive reason why the application of the no-cut provision should be limited to salary compensation and not other collateral benefits. In his view, a no-cut provision assures a player that the club cannot cut him from the team, so long as he has not breached, and deny him *whatever* the contract provided as benefits. The theory of entitlement to salary, based on the notion of the player's constructive presence on the team, applies as well to the player's right to accumulate additional pension credits.

Seitz disagreed with the club's claim that Vallely had waived his rights by accepting the club's decision to dispense with his continued services under the contract. Also, the club could have restricted the application of the no-cut provision in the contract. In fact, another provision of the rider gave assurance that the no-cut provision would not affect other benefits in the uniform player contract.

Seitz did not wish to establish a binding precedent concerning the meaning of all no-cut contract provisions. He did sustain the grievance. Vallely was deemed to have been on the roster and active list of the club on February 2, 1973, and, thus, eligible to participate in the pension plan.

In the Matter of Arbitration between National Basketball Association (Denver Nuggets) and National Basketball Players Association (Rudy Hackett), Peter Seitz, Arbitrator, Sept. 27, 1977

Rudy Hackett entered into a one-year contract for the 1975–76 basketball season with the Denver Nuggets. Section 2 of his uniform player contract called for payment of $40,000 as compensation for services; an "addendum to

Section 2, page one" was typed in and stated that the "Club hereby agrees to guarantee salaried compensation to player in the amount of $20,000 for the 1976–77 season."

Hackett reported to the Nuggets' training camp and received an advance payment of $575. In October, the Nuggets conditionally assigned Hackett's contract to the New York Nets, with the agreement that if Hackett were on the Nets roster after November 1, 1976, the Nets would assume liability for $10,000 of the $20,000 guarantee; after December 1, the Nets would assume the entire guarantee. Prior to November 1, however, the Nets reassigned Hackett's contract to the Nuggets and paid him $2,093.04 for his services. The Nuggets then exercised its powers pursuant to Section 20(b)(2) of the agreement to terminate the contract.

Hackett next contracted with the Indiana Pacers for a salary of $30,000 for the remainder of the season. One month later, Hackett was released and paid $5,232.55 for his services.

The dispute centered on the $20,000 guarantee under the contract. The Nuggets, who had tendered $12,099.41 after the hearing, argued that they could properly take credit for, or "offset" against the $20,000 guarantee, the monies received from the Indiana Pacers in the amount of $5,232.55. The Players Association, on behalf of Hackett, conceded the amount received from the Nets ($2,093.04) on the theory that this was a payment under the Nuggets' contract which had been assigned to the Nets, but viewed the payment by the Pacers as inapplicable to the guarantee since the contract with the Nuggets was no longer in effect.

At the hearing, Carl Scheer, president and general manager of the Nuggets, testified that Hackett's agent, Dan Cronson, and he had orally agreed that if Hackett was signed by another team, his compensation from that team should reduce the guarantee pro tanto. This was supported by an affidavit submitted by Nugget coach Larry Brown. Cronson, on the other hand, had also submitted an affidavit stating that there was no discussion about whether Denver would be permitted to set off any other salary amounts earned by Hackett.

The arbitrator declined to decide the relative credibility of Scheer, Cronson, and Brown, especially in light of the absence of confrontation and cross-examination of Cronson and Brown. Instead, the arbitrator relied on the integration clause of the uniform player contract (paragraph 23), which stated that the contract "contains the entire agreement between the parties and there are no oral or written inducements, promises, or agreements except as contained therein." The failure to do so would create a precedent opening the door to clubs and players and would encourage litigiousness and chaotic relationships.

The arbitrator could not find any ambiguity in the guarantee clause that would allow the parol evidence of the circumstances of the negotiation: "If the Club desired to condition its obligation under the guarantee, it should have done so, expressly, in the contract. Having failed to do so, I must assume that the obligation assumed was absolute and unqualified."

The arbitrator also failed to give substance to the club's argument that Hackett had a duty to mitigate his damages for the breach of the contract and that the club was entitled to offset any earnings achieved. The arbitrator found that Hackett's services were not terminated wrongfully and hence no question of whether the employer or employee should bear the burden of the period of unemployment during the time of litigation. Damages were known and certain; there was no discernible basis for claiming offsets.

The arbitrator thus ordered the Denver Nuggets to pay Hackett the sum of $20,000 without offset or credit for personal services performed by him but not covered under the Nugget contract.

In the Matter of Arbitration between the National Basketball Association (Golden State Warriors) and the National Basketball Players Association (Charles Johnson), Peter Seitz, Arbitrator, July 26, 1978

At issue was whether the Golden State Warriors had the right to offset against monies payable under the Johnson-Golden State Player Contract for the 1977–1978 season monies received by Johnson in that season from the Washington Bullets.

Johnson's salary for 1977–78 was $100,000. The Warriors placed him on waivers on January 5, 1978. On January 9, 1978, he cleared waivers. Pursuant to paragraph 20(b) (2), Johnson was entitled to receive his full compensation for the 1977–78 season because he was cut after December 16, 1977. In February, Johnson first signed a ten-day contract and then later signed a contract for the rest of the 1977–78 season with the Bullets. The Bullets agreed to pay Johnson $13,104 for the season.

Seitz decided that the Warriors were not entitled to deduct $13,104 from the monies owed Johnson. The contract made no reference to set-offs. When the Johnson-Warriors' contract was terminated, all rights and duties of the parties were extinguished except for the Warriors' obligation to pay Johnson full compensation. The Warriors would have been entitled to a set-off if their contract with Johnson had been sold or assigned to another club.

The Warriors elected to terminate Johnson's contract by placing him on waivers after December 16, thereby assuming the obligation to pay his full salary when he cleared waivers: "The fact that Johnson received compensation from another Club under another contract has no more significance than if he had rendered those services to a broadcasting company as a television announcer."

NOTE _____

1. NBA player Bob Love had had his guaranteed contract terminated by the New Jersey Nets before either the foregoing *Hackett* or *Johnson* arbitrations were decided. Since he later signed with another NBA club, the Nets had reduced the payments to Love by the amount he received from the new club. Love grieved the issue, claiming he filed in timely fashion after learning of the *Hackett* and *Johnson* awards. Arbitrator George Nicolau denied the grievance "on the ground that he [Love] has not complied with the time limits of the Agreement. . ." Nicolau stated further (at p. 11): "If Love had felt aggrieved by the Nets' refusal to pay him, it was his responsibility, if he wanted to contest that action under the collective bargaining agreement, promptly to issue his challenge, whether he knew he could win at the time or not or even thought victory possible." See, In the Matter of Arbitration between National Basketball Association (New Jersey Nets) and National Basketball Players Association (Robert Love), Nicolau, Arbitrator, May 1, 1980.

_____

In the Matter of Arbitration Between the National Football League Players Association and Dante Pastorini, Jr., and the National Football League Management Council and the Oakland Raiders, Kagel, Arbitrator, May 30, 1984

. . . Based on the grievance and the response, the specific issue in this case is whether the Oakland/Los Angeles Raiders Club is entitled to offset against its guaranteed salary obligations to Pastorini the amounts he received from other NFL Clubs after his release by the Raiders in September of 1981. . . .

On March 17, 1980, as the result of a trade between the Houston Oilers and the Oakland team, Pastorini was under a contract to the Oakland Raiders for the 1980–1983 seasons.

In 1981, when training camp opened, Pastorini passed the pre-season physical examination. The Raiders did not terminate Pastorini within 36 hours of that physical examination, although they had the right to do so.

Pastorini played with the Oakland Raiders until September 1, 1981.

The Raiders placed Pastorini on waivers and released him in the final cut in accordance with the provision in his contract, specifically Paragraph 11, that his "skill or performance" was "unsatisfactory" as compared with that of other players competing for a position on the Raiders' roster. Thereafter, demand was made upon the Raiders, in accordance with Paragraph 24-B(2) of Pastorini's 1981 through 1983 contracts, that the Raiders pay Pastorini his salary even if his skill or performance was judged to be unsatisfactory.

After that, Pastorini signed with the Los Angeles Rams on September 25, 1981, and then the Raiders informed Pastorini's attorney that the Raiders were no longer liable for any further salary payment to Pastorini, and the position taken by the Raiders is noted hereinabove in its answer to the grievance. Pastorini was released by the Rams, and he then played for the Philadelphia Eagles during the 1982 and 1983 football seasons.

Basically, as noted in the issue, it is the contention of the Raiders that they are entitled to an offset of Pastorini's earnings when he played with the Rams and the Philadelphia Eagles, as against the salary guarantees set forth in the Raiders' agreements of 1981, 1982 and 1983. . . .

Both Parties have made reference to certain cases within the NFL, each contending that these cases support its respective position, the Association claiming that they do not provide for a recognition of offsets, and the Management Council contending that they do.

Charles Smith v. *Oakland Raiders and San Diego Chargers:*

In that case, Smith had an agreement with the Raiders for the 1975 season which provided for a full guaranteed salary of $45,000. The agreement provided that the Raiders would ". . . pay player the full salary provided in Paragraph 3 hereof even though player does not display sufficient skill to play professional football for the club." (Jt. Ex. 10)

In mid-September of 1975, Smith was released by the Oakland Raiders. He then signed with the San Diego Chargers and played for a five-week period.

As a result of the grievance filed by Smith against the Oakland Raiders and the San Diego Chargers, this case was heard by the Player-Club Relations Committee (PCRC) on March 10, 1978. The PCRC Decision states Smith's position on his salary claim as follows: "Smith's position was that he was entitled to be paid his full $45,000 salary for 1975 by Oakland, less the $10,714.25 paid by San Diego — a sum of $34,285.75." And Smith contended, contrary to Oakland's position, that the $15,000 signing bonus paid by San Diego should not be offset against Oakland's liability.

There was a further difference between Oakland and San Diego as to the amount of offset Oakland should receive from Smith's employment with San Diego.

The PCRC made a unanimous decision which reads, in part:

> Since Smith had a "guaranteed salary" contract with Oakland for 1975, that club owes him $45,000 even though he was released for "lack of skill." The $15,000 signing bonus paid

by San Diego to Smith five weeks or so after he was released by Oakland cannot be considered an off-set against salary since the bonus rider specifically provided that "the bonus shall not be deemed to be a part of the salary for the year 1975." Oakland's $45,000 liability should be reduced by $10,714.25 rather than $16,666.65. . . . [Jt. Ex. 10]

The PCRC granted the exact relief which Smith had requested in his grievance, namely that the Oakland Raiders pay him the $45,000 less the salary he had received from the Chargers in the same season. Specifically, the Committee rejected the offset argument advanced by the Raiders, namely that Smith's signing bonus in San Diego should offset the guaranteed salary obligation, and granted Smith the exact salary payment he sought in his grievance.

It is significant that the League, after and as a result of the *Smith* case, recommended a form dealing with offsets. Joel Bussert, Director of Personnel for the National Football League, testified that subsequent to the *Smith* case, the League distributed the following form:

> Club's obligation under this guarantee will be reduced by the amount of any and all compensation, including salary and signing, reporting and/or incentive bonuses, earned, or that reasonably could have been earned by Player from such other football organization during the unexpired term covered by this guarantee. [Tr. 82] . . .

Anthony Davis v. *Houston Oilers:*

This case was decided by the Players Club Relations Committee (PCRC) in March of 1980 (Jt. Ex. 11).

Davis had signed a series of contracts in 1978 with the Houston Oilers calling for a salary of $80,000 in the 1979 season. The 1979 contract provided that the Club "absolutely and unconditionally" guaranteed payment of one-half of that amount, even if Davis were removed from the Club's roster during or before the 1979 season.

Davis was waived and released by the Oilers in November of 1978 and then was signed as a free agent by the Los Angeles Rams where he played the remainder of the 1978 season. He returned to the Rams in 1979, was injured and later released from the Rams' injured reserve list on September 20, 1979. Thereafter, Davis asked for payment of his $40,000 guarantee from the Oilers. The Oilers refused to pay anything more than the difference between the $40,000 and the amount he received from the Rams in 1979.

In the PCRC Decision there apears the following:

... Pat Peppler stated on behalf of the club, "We have been under the impression that we are entitled to an offset," apparently relying on alleged custom and practice in the League. Davis argued through counsel that there was no language in his contract permitting an offset, and stressed that his $40,000 was "absolutely and unconditionally guaranteed to be paid by Club" meaning Houston and no other club. It was further argued that the *Charles Smith* v. *Oakland Raiders* case considered by the PCRC in March of 1978 was distinguishable, because the grievant in that case had different contract language and his grievance asked only for the difference between the guaranteed amount and the amount paid by the other club. [Jt. Ex. 11, p.2]

The PCRC, which was composed of two representatives of Management and two of the Players, reached a unanimous decision which reads as follows:

Since the language of Davis' guarantee clause was clear and unmistakable, providing that the Club "absolutely and unconditionally" guaranteed payment of 50% of his $80,000 salary, the Houston Oilers are not entitled to an offset for salary received by Davis from the Los Angeles Rams during the 1979 season. There was no language in Davis' contract supporting Houston's right to such an offset, and the clear meaning and intent of that contract required payment of the $40,000 whether or not monies were earned from any other club in the year in question. Houston is therefore ordered to pay Davis $40,000 less applicable deductions. [Jt. Ex. 11]

It should be noted that the PCRC, in *Anthony Davis* v. *Houston Oilers,* heard the argument that the *Smith* case considered in March of 1978 was "distinguishable because the Grievant in that case had different contract language and his grievance

asked only for the difference between the guaranteed amount and the amount paid by the other club." And, the PCRC accepted that posture of the *Smith* case. If it had considered that *Smith* recognized salary offsets, then its Decision in *Davis* would have had to comport with that principle. Further, the PCRC noted that there was "... no language in Davis' contract supporting Houston's right to such an offset. . . ." Similarly, there is no language in Pastorini's contract supporting the Raiders' right to an offset; and, as will be noted herein, the Raiders, when they wanted the right of an offset, provided for such contract language, as they did in Plunkett's contract. . . .

League Policy:

Joel Bussert, a witness for the Management Council, who is the Director of Personnel for the National Football League, testified as to what he contends is the past practice of the League on the question of offsets. He testified on direct examination as follows:

A. The League's policy, as I attempted to say earlier, was that when a player was released from a guaranteed contract and signed with a second club, that any amounts earned from that second club would be offset against the guaranteed amounts he was entitled to receive from the first club. [Tr. 69]

On cross-examination, Bussert testified as follows:

Q. (Mr. BERTHELSEN, Players' Counsel): Have you ever communicated to the NFL Players Association in written form or any other form this policy that you testified to about what the custom and practice of the League is?

A. No. [Tr. 84]

He further testified on cross-examination:

Q. Could you indicate for us what written information there may be as to this policy of offsets that you testified about? Is it in the Constitution By-Laws?

A. It's not in the Constitution By-Laws.

Q. Is it in the Rules and Regulations of the League?

A. No . . .

Q. Where is it?

A. As I attempted to explain earlier, it's been the policy of the League.

Q. But it's not in writing anywhere?

A. No . . .

Again, on cross-examination, Bussert testified:

Q. When you talked to the Los Angeles Rams about the requirement that Dan Pastorini be offered a commensurate amount of money, did you call him and tell him the same thing?

A. No.

Q. Did you call his agent or his lawyer or anybody representing him and tell them the same thing?

A. No.

Q. Did you call the Players Association and tell them?

A. No . . .

Mitigation:

The Raiders argue that Pastorini had a duty to mitigate damages as an offset to a terminated guaranteed contract under common law and California case law. In this regard, they cite *Parker* v. *Twentieth Century-Fox Film Corp.*, 474 P.2d 689 (Cal. 1970).

The Court in that case stated a rule which is cited in the Raiders' brief, as follows:

The general rule is that the measure of recovery by a wrongfully discharged employee is the amount of salary agreed upon for the period of service, less the amount which the employer affirmatively proves the employee has earned or with reasonable effort might have earned from other employment.

That rule is not applicable in the Pastorini case. There is no claim that Pastorini was "wrongfully discharged." In fact, Pastorini was not discharged — he was waived, an action *authorized* by the contract. The Raiders had a right to waive Pastorini but it also had an obligation to pay the salaries provided for in the contracts which they assumed from Houston.

This case does not concern itself with an alleged breach of the contracts between the Raiders and Pastorini at the time of waiver; it is not a case seeking damages; but it is an action on the contracts themselves for the agreed-upon compensation which is set forth in the contracts between the Raiders and Pastorini. What Pastorini is seeking is the payment of a debt owed to him by the Raiders as a result of the contracts and the concept of offset by way of mitigation is not applicable in this instance.

Summary:

The record shows with reference to so-called "custom and practice," that whatever that custom and practice is claimed to have been, as among the Clubs themselves regarding offsets in guarantee cases, no such custom or practice was considered by the Management Council and the Players Association in the *Davis* and *Smith* PCRC decisions.

Again, whatever the "custom and practice" might be with reference to the League's recommendations to the Clubs, it is not part of the Collective Bargaining Agreement since it was not accepted by both Parties to the Collective Bargaining Agreement.

The record establishes that when an offset is intended, the League and Management Council have provided for such language in Paragraph 10 of the NFL Player Contract form. Paragraph 10 of that form thus sets forth a specific offset against the Player's salary or any Workers' Compensation benefits received by the Player.

The Collective Bargaining Agreement also provides specific language dealing with offsets, such as the provision which limits a Club's liability for certain benefits once a released Player has re-signed with another NFL Club, as Pastorini did. In Article X, the Parties have provided that injury protection payments to a released Player will stop when he signs with another NFL Club. In Article XXXV, the Agreement provides that a Player will not get his termination pay, a collectively bargained "skill" guarantee, if he resigns with another Club for the same season. . . .

It must be concluded that in Pastorini's case his contracts do not provide for an offset, nor does League "policy," nor do PCRC decisions insert offset provisions into his contracts; and, the concept of "mitigation" does not apply to Pastorini's case.

Decision:

The Oakland/Los Angeles Raiders are hereby directed to pay to Dante (Dan) Pastorini the salary provided for in his 1981, 1982 and 1983 contracts between the Raiders and Pastorini. Such payment shall be made in accordance with the terms of those contracts and past payments now due shall be made forthwith, with payments thereafter being made in accordance with the specific terms of the contracts.

NFLPA and Bob Lee v. Minnesota Vikings, June, 1977, PCRC Decision

At a meeting held at the Conrad Hilton Hotel in Chicago, Illinois, on June 9, 1977, the PCRC considered the non-injury grievance filed on May 17, 1977 by the NFLPA and Bob Lee against the Minnesota Vikings. Representing Lee was attorney Wayne Hooper and representing the Vikings was general manager Mike Lynn. In attendance for the NFLPA was Ed Garvey and for the Management Council were Sargent Karch and Terry Bledsoe. All four members of the PCRC — Len Hauss, Gene Upshaw, Wellington Mara, and Dan Rooney — were present.

The grievance involved interpretation of the following portion of article XV, section 17 of the Collective Bargaining Agreement on "Re-Signing":

> If a veteran free agent receives no offer to sign a contract or contracts with a new NFL club pursuant to this Article, and his old club advises him in writing by June 1 that it desires to re-sign him, the player may, at his option within 15 days, sign . . . (b) a one-year contract (with no option year) with his old club at 110% of the salary provided in his contract for the last preceding year. . . .

Lee's 1976 contract had no option clause, hence he became a veteran free agent upon expiration of that contract on March 1, 1977. He received no offer to sign a contract with a new NFL club pursuant to Article XV, and the Vikings advised him in writing before June 1, 1977, that it desired to re-sign him. The Vikings' position was that if Lee chose to sign at option (b) of Section 17, the one-year contract would be at 110% of $50,000, or $55,000, since the face amount of Paragraph 3 of his 1976 contract with the Vikings was $50,000. Lee's position was that if he chose to sign at option

(b), the one-year contract would be at 110% of $110,000, or $121,000, since in addition to the $50,000 called for in Paragraph 3 of the 1976 contract with the Vikings, he earned $60,000 in 1976 as deferred salary payable by the Atlanta Falcons.

After discussion, the PCRC resolved the grievance by mutual agreement, as follows:

1) The one-year contract under option (b) of section 17, article XV, will be at 110% of $110,000, or $121,000. The reason is that the 1976 contract Lee had with the Atlanta Falcons, which was guaranteed, called for compensation of $110,000, $50,000 payable during the 1976 regular season and $60,000 in deferred payments. When Lee signed a new 1976 contract with the Vikings for $50,000, the Falcons remained responsible under a separate agreement for the $60,000 in deferred compensation. Thus, Lee's "salary provided in his contract for the last preceding year" under Section 17 was actually $110,000, even though the Vikings were responsible only for $50,000.

2) Since the Vikings sent Lee notice of its desire to re-sign him under the belief that his option (b) would be at 110% of $50,000, the club will be permitted until 4:00 P.M. EDT on Monday, June 13, 1977, to decide whether or not it desires to give him the option of re-signing at 110% of $110,000. If the club does not notify Lee in writing by that time that it desires to give him that option, then he will be free to negotiate and sign a contract with any NFL club, and any NFL club will be free to negotiate and sign a contract with him, without any compensation between clubs or first refusal rights of any kind.

3) Since Lee's 1976 contract was guaranteed, if the Vikings notify him by June 13 of a desire to re-sign him at 110% of $110,000, and Lee exercises such option, his 1977 contract will also be guaranteed on the same basis as the 1976 one. The reason is that by giving notice of a desire to re-sign a club is, in effect, exercising a collectively bargained "renewal option" at 110% of the salary in the last preceding contract (if the player chooses that alternative). Therefore, the principal terms of the last preceding contract (except for the 110% of salary) are included in the renewal.

In accordance with Section 5 of Article XV, this resolution by the PCRC constitutes full, final and complete disposition of the grievance and is binding on Lee, the Vikings, the NFLPA and the Management Council.

4.28   Options

There are several types of options in sports contracts. Most operate in favor of a club, but occasionally one may be put in a contract exercisable by the player. This is more likely to happen with individual performers than with players of team sports. Even so, as the *Community Sports* case, which follows, indicates, a team performer may be able to exact an option under appropriate circumstances as well.

In those instances in which the club has the option, the nature of that option should be carefully considered. A court's interpretation of the formalities to be observed in exercising the option may vary, depending on whether the option was secured through a general collective bargaining provision and attending uniform player contract, or whether it was individually negotiated, with real value for the option flowing from the club to the player. In the latter case, a court might hold a club to a less stringent standard of exercise. It is hard to generalize on that likelihood, however; thus it is imperative to examine the "option" cases one by one. In doing so, consideration should also be focused on the *Tidrow* arbitration (see Chapter 5, Section 5.42).

4.28–1   Exercisable by Player

Options can take various forms, some favorable to a player. If an option in a player's favor is included in a contract, it is likely to be a provision that allows the player to opt for an early release from the contract. This is the type of option that allowed basketball player Bill Walton to become a free agent in 1985, even though he had signed a four-year contract with the Los Angeles Clippers only one year earlier. When the Clippers failed to make the NBA playoffs, this triggered a provision that allowed Walton to elect to be released from his contract. The legality of the option providing for early release is discussed in the following case.

Community Sports, Inc. v. Denver Ringsby Rockets, 240 A.2d 832 (Pa. 1968)

Plaintiffs were owners of an Eastern Professional Basketball League team. They sought to enjoin the defendant Larry Jones from playing for defendant Denver Rockets, an American Basketball Association team.

In September 1966, Jones and one of the plaintiff owners of the Wilkes-Barre Barons entered a written agreement for the 1966–67 Eastern League season. It was an exclusive performer contract, with a one-year option in favor of the club, if exercised no later than October 31, 1967. On the same day as the two signed the first contract, they also entered a second agreement, which gave Jones an absolute right to "jump" to another league if Jones had the opportunity to better himself by playing in the National Basketball Association or some other major league basketball league.

The court held that this second agreement, which effectively could be used by Jones as a release, was a part of the first contract. The court rejected several arguments by plaintiffs, including (1) that the one owner had no legal authority to grant Jones permission to elect to go to a higher league, (2) that the release was not properly in evidence, and (3) that Jones's reaffirmation of his employment with the Barons precluded his reliance on the release.

Plaintiffs argued further that on July 5, 1967, Jones agreed to pay plaintiffs $1,500 as consideration for the latter's permission to let Jones play for the Los Angeles Lakers of the NBA, assuming he made the team, and that this agreement proved that Jones did not consider the release enforceable. However, the court here concluded that Jones, without legal advice, may not have realized that he could leave the Barons without having to pay to do so. The court held that the release was still valid. Jones could "jump" to Denver without paying anything to the Wilkes-Barre club.

NOTE

1. The Eastern Basketball League was founded in 1946, the same year the Basketball Association of America was

founded, which with its absorption of most National Basketball League teams, became the NBA in 1949. The Eastern Basketball League later changed its name to the Continental Basketball Association and continues in existence at the present time.

4.28–2 Exercisable by Club

Options in sports contracts generally are for the benefit of clubs rather than players. Even so, the method by which a club exercises an option is circumscribed by procedures that are established by the league's collective bargaining agreement or by the terms of the individual contract. A club's failure to comply with the precise procedures can be costly, as the *Carlton Fisk* arbitration, discussed below, indicates. In addition, disputes over the interpretation of what was included in the earlier contract cause the exercise of an option to be far from simple.

In the Matter of Arbitration between California Sports, Inc. (Lakers) and Wilton N. Chamberlain, Seitz, Arbitrator, December 4, 1973

At issue was whether the Los Angeles Lakers had properly exercised the option provided in Section 22 of the NBA Uniform Player Contract to retain the services of Wilt Chamberlain for the 1973–74 basketball season.

On June 10, 1968, California Sports Inc. (CSI) and Chamberlain entered into a "Letter Agreement," which outlined special financial considerations to be included as compensation for Chamberlain's services as a member of the Lakers. On September 26, 1968, Chamberlain signed an NBA Uniform Player Contract for three years at a salary of $200,000 per year. CSI agreed to provide ventures to shelter his salary from taxes and arranged a stock investment scheme. Chamberlain signed a promissory note for $100,000 and became the equitable owner of $100,000 worth of stock purchased and held by Jack Kent Cooke (sole shareholder of CSI) as security for payment of the note. Chamberlain was entitled to whatever value the stock had in excess of the "loan" on or before the due date of

the note, which was December 31, 1971. He would not be liable for the difference if the stock declined in value.

On September 9, 1971, Chamberlain signed another NBA Uniform Player Contract for the 1971–72 and 1972–73 seasons at $200,000 per year, plus other considerations — that Cooke extend the due date on the note to December 31, 1973, that Cooke agree to purchase the remaining shares of stock (now Teleprompter Corporation) at player's election, and that player might elect to pay the balance of the note and receive the security in exchange.

The parties signed an addendum on October 16, 1972, which stipulated that "Any reference to the 1972–73 season in the 1971 agreement shall be deleted; $230,000 shall be added to his $200,000 salary for 1971–72; and compensation for the 1972–73 season shall be at the rate of $450,000." The addendum deleted all references to tax shelters and stock investment schemes and stated that there was no further obligations between Cooke or Chamberlain with respect to the stock investment scheme.

In fact, Chamberlain's indebtedness was extinguished on March 28, 1972, when Cooke repurchased the remainder of the Teleprompter shares which he held as security. Chamberlain received a check for $69,777.83.

Section 22 of the Uniform Player Contract was revised on August 4, 1971. Compensation offered by a club for a player's additional option year had to be at least 100 percent of the compensation payable to the player for the last season covered by the contract.

The Lakers tendered a player contract to Chamberlain for 1973–74, offering compensation of $450,000. It made no reference to any stock option rights.

Seitz accepted the argument that "compensation" referred to in Section 22 could embrace the kind of secured loan and pledged stock transaction which took place in 1968, as well as a stated salary figure. The question for Seitz boiled down to whether the $69,777.83 check paid to Chamberlain in 1972 represented compensation for the last playing season covered by his contract.

Chamberlain did not accept the tender of the contract. He claimed that he should have received stock option rights in addition to the $450,000 offered for 1973–74. Seitz concluded that the $69,000 check represented compensation from the 1968 and 1971 deals. Any additional stock rights were extinguished by the addendum of October 16, 1972. CSI's tender, including the compensation figure of $450,000, did conform to the requirements of Section 22 of the Uniform Player Contract, signed by CSI and Chamberlain on September 9, 1971 (as modified or amended).

In the Matter of Arbitration Between Major League Baseball Player Relations Committee (Atlanta National League Baseball Club, Inc.) and Major League Baseball Players Association (James Robert Horner) Panel Dec. No. 39, Goetz, Chairman, June 6, 1979

The salary negotiations between Horner and the Atlanta Braves for the 1979 season led to the filing of three grievances consolidated in this decision. At the center of the dispute was whether the term salary consisted of bonuses, educational expenses, and other payments for the purposes of determining what the Braves must tender to Horner in order to prevent him from becoming a free agent. Under Article V(B) of the Collective Bargaining Agreement, a club must not offer a salary of less than 80 percent of the player's salary for the previous year. The Brave's position was that Article V(B) required only a tender of $21,000, while Horner and his agent believed the amount was $146,400.

Horner's 1978 contract provided for payment at the rate of $21,000 in equal, semi-monthly installments, with a special covenant providing for a bonus of $75,000 upon contract approval by the president of the National League and an additional $75,000 payment on January 5, 1979. The contract also provided for a payment of $5,000 for educational expenses and $7,500 for participation in the Incentive Bonus Plan. Concurrently with the signing of this contract,

the Braves signed a separate contract with Horner's father, employing him as a baseball scout. The Braves, believing that "salary" excluded all amounts other than the $21,000, nevertheless tendered Horner a contract for $146,400 under protest, stating that this amount was subject to any adjustment which may be appropriate as a result of the decision by the arbitration panel, and promptly filed a grievance.

Horner never signed the proposed contract presented by the Braves. The Players Association, in response to the Braves' grievance, took the position that it was not arbitrable under Article X of the Basic Agreement. In addition, the Players Association contested the Braves' claim that the maximum salary reduction provisions would permit tender of $21,000.

The Players Association made the next move and on January 24, 1979, filed a grievance on behalf of Horner, asserting that the Braves failed to tender a 1979 contract in compliance with paragraph 10(a) of Horner's 1978 contract and that he was therefore a free agent pursuant to Article XVII, paragraph A(2)(c) of the Basic Agreement. The Braves denied this allegation and refused to remove Horner from the club's reserve list. On March 9, 1979, the Braves sent Horner a letter renewing the 1978 contract but stating that the $146,400 was still under protest and subject to reimbursement should the arbitration panel decide in the club's favor. The Players Association then filed another grievance, claiming that this renewal attempt was invalid and that it provided a further basis for Horner's free agency by virtue of Article XVII, paragraph A(2)(d). Alternatively, the Players Association asked that if Horner was determined not to be a free agent, that the terms and conditions of his 1979 contract be clarified.

The arbitration panel first determined that the grievance filed by the Braves was arbitrable. The Players Association had argued that because the grievance had not alleged any action in violation of the Basic Agreement, it was in effect asking for a declaratory judgment concerning the obligations of the club itself. The panel examined

Article X and found that the provisions did not confine grievances to challenges that one party is in violation of the agreement, but was broad enough to encompass any disputed interpretation of the Basic Agreement or the Uniform Player Contract. Furthermore, at the time the Braves filed the grievance, an actual controversy existed between Horner and the club. As a practical necessity, the Braves had to take this action by offering the full amount under protest to avoid losing Horner to free agency. Thus, there was "an on-going dispute" in which resolution was essential for the possible protection of the club's interest in retaining Horner and the determination of Horner's compensation.

The grievance filed by the Players Association claimed that Horner became a free agent pursuant to paragraph A(2)(c) of Article XVII of the Basic Agreement, which provides: "The player becomes a free agent as a result of . . . failure by the Club to tender to the Player a new contract within the true period specified in paragraph 10(a) of the contract." The association contended that the contract submitted to Horner on December 15, 1978, failed to qualify as a contract tender because (1) it was conditional and (2) it was too indefinite.

The panel held that while the contract was conditional, based on the club's intention to limit or qualify the amount by any reduction the arbitration panel might find, the condition related only to the extent of the Braves' commitment, rather than to any compensation that would be paid. The Braves offered $146,400, the amount Horner claimed would be sufficient, and consequently, there was no way Horner could be paid less than the required minimum. The panel found that as a matter of contract law, the salary provision was in such form that acceptance by Horner would have resulted in formation of a contract.

The compensation provisions also did not fail for indefiniteness. All that was required was that the terms be reasonably certain so that they would provide a basis for determining the existence of a breach and for giving an appropriate remedy. Here, the existence of

breach and basis for remedy would be determined by the arbitration panel, or, if the panel declined jurisdiction, would be based on the $146,400 amount. Even though Horner could not determine in advance what his 1979 compensation would be, the offer was not purely within the discretion of the club and was a sufficient tender, precluding Horner from becoming a free agent.

A closely related question was whether the Braves' letter of March 9, 1979, to Horner constituted a proper renewal. The association took essentially the same position as it did regarding the December 15 tender — that it was invalid because it was conditional and indefinite. The panel held the contract tender was less indefinite than the tender because the renewal required "on the same terms" as the predecessor contract, and thus the bonuses which were the subject of dispute in the salary-reduction area were clearly within the amount payable to Horner in 1979. Accordingly, since Horner's 1978 contract was properly renewed for 1979, the panel held that he could not possibly become a free agent.

The panel then turned to the application of the maximum salary-reduction provisions of paragraph B of Article V of the Basic Agreement, which states:

> No Player's contract shall be renewed pursuant to paragraph 10(a) of the Uniform Player Contract in any year for a salary which constitutes a reduction in excess of 20% of his previous year's salary or in excess of 30% of his salary two years previous. For the purposes of this section, the "salary" of a Player with a salary stipulated in paragraph 2 of his Major League contract of less than the then applicable Major League minimum salary shall be deemed to be the greater of either (1) the total amount of his actual baseball salary earnings from Major League Clubs (and from National Association Clubs, if any) in that season or (2) the amount stipulated in paragraph 2 of his Major League contract for that season. (See also Attachment 3).

Attachment 3 referred to in this provision states:

> This will set forth the understanding of the parties

regarding Article V, Section B, of the Basic Agreement:

(1) The term "salary" shall include any salary amounts which were not paid to a Player for the season by reason of any fine or suspension which may have been imposed on the Player, or by reason of any other deduction from salary;

(2) In tendering a contract to a Player pursuant to paragraph 10(a) of the Uniform Player Contract, no Major League Club shall offer a salary which constitutes a reduction in excess of 20% of the Player's previous year's salary or in excess of 30% of his salary two years previous.

The primary question was whether the "salary" should be limited to the sum of $21,000 inserted in the first sentence of paragraph 2 of Horner's 1978 contract, as claimed by the Braves, or whether it should include additional payments provided for in the special covenants as asserted by the Players Association. The panel examined Horner's contract, the Basic Agreement, the practical application by the parties, the Major League Rules, and surrounding circumstances and purposes to ascertain the meaning of salary.

Horner's contract, on balance, provided some support for the association's position, but was "hardly conclusive" in the panel's opinion. Both paragraph 2 of the Uniform Player Contract and the contract renewal provision were cited for their surprising lack of use of the word "salary." Instead, the "amount payable" was referred to as the amount not less than specified by the maximum cut. From the use of this term, it appeared to the panel that the parties contemplated the possibility of the maximum cut, including "amounts" other than the same monthly installment payments that might normally be deemed salary.

The panel found support for the Braves' position in the ordinary meaning of the word "salary," which was defined as compensation being fixed in advance and paid regularly. This would rule out the Incentive Bonus Plan, but the other payments would still be disputed. As to the Basic Agreement, the panel concluded that the term *salary* broadly encompassed all forms of compensation in the salary-reduction provisions

and negotiation provision. Because negotiating by agents centers on bonuses and deferred payments, these were deemed to be included within salary as used in paragraph C of Article V, immediately following the salary-reduction paragraph.

The panel next looked to the practical interpretation and application by the parties as a further expression of the meaning to be given to their written expression. The panel viewed conflicting evidence concerning preparation of tabulations of all major league salaries, but found that a special footnote explaining the special covenants seemed to indicate that the special covenants were an integral part of a player's compensation for salary arbitration purposes and thus seemed deserving of protection under the maximum salary cut.

The language of Major League Rule 4(j) distinguished salary from bonus, but the panel found this not controlling since under paragraph 9(a) of the Uniform Player Contract a player agrees to abide by the rules only if they are consistent with the player's contract or the Basic Agreement.

The panel gave considerable weight to the surrounding circumstances, including the purpose or object to be accomplished by the contract. The purpose of the maximum salary reduction provisions was self-evident — to protect the player against drastic reduction in compensation from one year to the next. In view of this purpose, the panel asked, "Why should the maximum cut apply only to his semimonthly installment payments at the rate of $21,000?" This was purely a nominal amount — the bare minimum required for any major league player. The amount did not bear a reasonable relationship to the value to the Braves of the services of this sought-after player: "To hold that a player such as Horner who earned well in excess of $150,000 for playing baseball for less than one full season could be cut to $21,000 by the Braves the following season would make a mockery of the protection meant to be afforded by the maximum salary reduction provisions."

Thus, the panel sustained the Players Association's interpretation of salary with a few minor adjustments. The $7,500 in payments to Horner under the Incentive Bonus Plan was excluded because, as conceded by the association, the payments were dependent on contingencies that could not possibly occur more than once. Likewise, the panel excluded the $5,000 educational expenses analogizing it to an expense reimbursement and not part of a player's regular compensation. Also excluded was the $7,500 paid to Horner's father under a separate contract since it was not an amount payable to Horner under his contract.

The panel thus concluded that the maximum cut was therefore 20 percent of the $171,000, or $136,800.

In the Matter of Arbitration Between Major League Baseball Players Association (Carlton E. Fisk) and Major League Baseball Players Relations Committee, Inc. (Boston Red Sox), Panel Decision No. 45, Grievance No. 80–35, Goetz, Chairman, February 12, 1981

The issue in this case is whether Carlton E. Fisk, a player who has been under contract with the Boston Red Sox, became a free agent as of December 20, 1980, by virtue of Article XVII A(2)(c) of the Basic Agreement, which provides:

A. Reservation Rights of Clubs

Subject to the rights of Players as set forth in this Agreement, each Club may have title to and reserve up to 40 Player contracts. A Club shall retain title to a contract and reservation rights until one of the following occurs: . . .

(2) The Player becomes a free agent as a result of . . .

(c) failure by the Club to tender to the Player a new contract within the time period specified in paragraph 10(a) of the contract, or . . .

Paragraph 10(a) of Fisk's individual contract with the Red Sox dated August 4, 1976, covering the years 1976, 1977, 1978, 1979, and 1980, is identical to the corresponding paragraph of the Uniform Player's Contract set forth as Schedule A of the Basic Agreement. It provides:

Renewal

10.(a) Unless the Player has exercised his right to become a free agent as set forth in the Basic Agreement between the Major League Clubs and the Major League Baseball Players Association, effective January 1, 1976, the Club may, *on or before December 20* (or if a Sunday, then the next preceding business day) in the year of the last playing season covered by this contract, tender to the Player a contract for the term of the next year by mailing the same to the Player at his address following his signature hereto, or if none be given, then at his last address of record with the Club . . .

There is no dispute about the fact that the Club failed to tender Fisk a new contract for the 1981 season on or before the December 20, 1980, date specified in Article XVII A(2)(c) of the Basic Agreement and paragraph 10(a) of his Player's contract. On December 22, 1980, Red Sox Vice President and General Manager Haywood C. Sullivan mailed Fisk a new contract with the following letter:

As you probably know, these past few weeks have been most hectic for us in baseball and as a result, I have not had the opportunity to commence negotiations relative to an extension of your present contract. However, you can rest assured that I will be talking with Jerry Kapstein immediately after the holidays . . .

This letter and the accompanying contract were both dated Friday, December 19, 1980, but actually were not prepared and mailed until Monday, December 22. (The postmark on the mailing envelope is December 22, and the club itself admits to that mailing date.) Sullivan testified that he dated the letter and contract December 19 "just to get it in that week's business," along with all other Players' contracts that had been mailed by the Club on December 17, 18, and 19, in accordance with the Club's normal procedure each year. He explained that a new contract had not been tendered to Fisk on or before December 20 because he (Sullivan) then was under the impression that no such tender was necessary for renewal of Fisk's contract. He based this impression on Sections II and XI of the Addendum to Fisk's contract dated August 4, 1976, which provide:

II. "Option Year" Salary and Right of First Refusal

If, at the expiration of the 1980 Championship Season, Club and Player are unable to agree upon a new Major League Baseball Contract for the 1981 Championship Season, and *if Club elects to renew Player's contract no later than March 11, 1981 for the year 1981, under Paragraph 10(a) of this contract,* then Club guarantees that if this contract is renewed, that compensation shall be fixed by the Club at a sum not less than the salary received by Player for the 1980 Championship Season as set forth under the section of this addendum titled "Payment Schedule," and that Player shall be paid the said sum, even though Player may be "unsigned" and may be playing out his option during the 1981 Championship season. If Club elects not to renew Player's contract, then Club shall have no further salary obligations whatsoever to Player and Player will have Free-Agent Status. . . .

XI. Supercession

The provisions of this Addendum to this contract control, supercede and take precedence over any other clause or clauses within this total contract.

On December 10 or 11, 1980, while attending the annual winter meeting of Major League and Minor League Clubs in Dallas, Sullivan had been advised by Albert Curran, Legal Counsel for the Red Sox who was there with him, that the above-quoted portions of the Addendum to Fisk's contract eliminated any necessity for a December 20 contract tender as a pre-requisite to contract renewal by the Club. This advice was given in response to a question from Sullivan about the effect of substantially identical clauses in the contracts of Fred Lynn and Richard Burleson, as well as Fisk, all of whose contracts Sullivan had with him at the meeting. Based on this advice, Sullivan made no contract tender to either Fisk or Lynn on or before December 20 although contracts were tendered before that date to all other Players the Club intended to retain on its reserve list. No tender was made to Burleson because his contract had been assigned to the California Angels immediately following the meeting in Dallas. . . .

The optional renewal provisions of the Addendum to the contracts of Fisk, Lynn, and Burleson for 1976 through 1980 had been inserted at the request of Jerry Kapstein, who was acting as agent for each of them and had been engaged in protracted negotiations of the terms of their 1976–1980 contracts with the Red Sox. His purpose in insisting on this clause was to make certain that if the Club exercised its right under paragraph 10(a) of the Player's contract to renew for an additional year beyond the contract term, the salary for the renewal year would be the same as for the preceding year. In the absence of such stated salary for the so-called "option year," the contract could be renewed for a salary reduced by as much as 20%, the maximum cut permitted under paragraph 10(a) together with Article V B of the Basic Agreement.

The phraseology of Section II of the Addendum to Fisk's contract was taken almost verbatim from a contract Kapstein had negotiated with the New York Yankees for Kenneth Holtzman executed on July 25, 1976, a copy of which was presented to Red Sox officials by Kapstein in the closing stages of the negotiation of Fisk's contract on August 2, 1976. . . .

All parties agree that the subject of tender was not discussed during the negotiation of the option renewal clause in Fisk's contract. Justin Morreale, then Counsel for the Club, testified that on August 3, 1976, he was called to the Club offices to assist in drafting language to express the terms of special covenants that had been agreed upon for Fisk's contract. Morreale testified that the words "under Paragraph 10(a) of this contract" were included in Section II of the Addendum because he had asked what the authority was to have a right to renew for the sixth year and suggested that paragraph 10(a) be referred to as providing that authority. He further testified that it was "kind of an enabling provision" intended to modify the word "renew." He could not recall looking at any document other than the Blue Book of Major League Rules and the Basic Agreement, but conceded that several lines of the option clause had been written before he arrived. . . .

The Club's basic argument that the necessity for tender of a contract to Fisk on or before December 20 was eliminated by Sections II and XI of the Addendum to his contract is unpersuasive for several reasons.

Section II does *not* by its terms say that the

preliminary step of tender is to be eliminated. It says absolutely nothing about tender. Not only was the word "tender" not used, but the subject was not even discussed in connection with its negotiation or drafting. With all the care that was taken to draft this provision and the amount of time spent on it on August 3, 1976, surely the parties would have expressly stated that renewal could be effectuated without any preliminary tender if that actually had been their intention. The plain fact is that there was no outward manifestation of intent to that effect.

Actually, the wording used negates any intent to eliminate the tender step. The key phrase is "if the Club elects to renew Player's contract no later than March 11, 1981, for the year 1981, *under Paragraph 10(a) of this contract.*" (Emphasis added.) Undoubtedly, the underscored portion of this clause was meant to modify the verb "renew" which precedes it, as the Club points out. But these underscored words are just another way of stating that such renewal is to be effectuated "in accordance with" the procedures set forth in paragraph 10(a). When one turns to the referenced paragraph to find *how* renewal is accomplished, it becomes clear that the right to renew 10 days after March 1 is provided for only in the context of a preceding contract tender on or before December 20. To renew "under Paragraph 10(a)" therefore, the Club would have to follow the procedures outlined therein, one of which is tender. Consequently, Section II did not establish a self-contained mechanism for renewal, as the Club maintains. Specific mention of tender in Section II of the Addendum was unnecessary to *retain* a step set forth in the paragraph to which reference was made. Express provision would have been necessary to eliminate it.

The drafting history of the reference to paragraph 10(a) in Section II of the Addendum militates against the Club's contention that it was inserted by Counsel for the Club merely to evidence contractual authority for the Club's right to renew. On this point, the recollection of Morreale must be in error. There can be no doubt that this provision was taken from the Holtzman contract almost verbatim. Morreale made only a few accommodating changes, none of which involved the phrase "under Paragraph 10(a) of this contract," which was found in the Holtzman contract in those very words at the same location. In the Holtzman contract, their only apparent

purpose would have been to provide a cross-reference to the procedure for renewal — which, as has been explained, includes tender.

A cardinal rule of contract interpretation is that ambiguous wording should be interpreted in the light of the parties' principal purpose. The primary purpose of the first paragraph of Section II of the Addendum, as evidenced by the testimony of Kapstein and the surrounding circumstances, was to guarantee Fisk a salary equal to that of the preceding year in the event the Club should choose to exercise its option to renew for 1981. This limited purpose of Section II is borne out in the heading: "Option Year Salary and Right of First Refusal." Without this salary provision, renewal could — under paragraph 10(a) of Fisk's contract and Article V B of the Basic Agreement — be at a salary reduced as much as 20% from the prior year. This purpose of protecting Fisk from a salary cut on renewal could be fully accomplished without any necessity for eliminating the contract tender step.

On the other hand, there is no evidence of any reason why the parties would have wanted to eliminate the tender step. From the Club's standpoint, such elimination might have simplified the renewal procedure to some extent, but from Fisk's standpoint, tender or knowledge of lack thereof would fulfill an important function. Receipt of tender would provide some indication the Club was interested in retaining his services; more important, non-receipt would put him on notice that the Club had no intention to renew. He then could immediately start negotiations with other Clubs. Under the Club's interpretation, he would have to wait until March 10 before he could determine the practicality of looking elsewhere. Since the effect attributed to Section II by the Club would go beyond its purpose, as well as its wording, it cannot be sustained. . . .

For all these reasons, the "supercession" clause in Section XI of the Addendum, on which the Club relies to eliminate the tender provision from paragraph 10(a), is of no significance in this regard. Since nothing in Section II eliminates the necessity for tender as a prelude to renewal, the tender provision in paragraph 10(a) cannot possibly be superceded. . . .

The Club argues that even if Section II of the Addendum to Fisk's contract was not effective to eliminate the necessity for contract tender, Article XVII A(2) (c) of the Basic Agreement should not be given its stated effect in this case because the delay was slight, no harm was suffered by Fisk, and a substantial forfeiture to the Club would result. Disposition of this argument requires some review of the operation of conditions under general principles of contract law.

To begin with, it must be kept in mind that the Club has no *duty* to tender a contract to any Player. Paragraph 10(a) of the Player's contract states only that the Club "may" on or before December 20 tender to the Player a contract for the next year. Article XVII A(2) (c) of the Basic Agreement is not a *promise or covenant* on the part of the Club that such tender shall be made. Instead, it makes such tender an *express condition* to the Club's retention of title to the Player's contract and failure to tender a condition to the Player's free agency. For our purposes here, it is not important whether tender is considered a "condition precedent" to the Player's duty to remain under contract with the Club for the succeeding season, or whether failure to tender is considered a "condition subsequent" that extinguished the club's right to retain title to the contract and the Player's duty to perform for the Club the following year. In either event, tender or non-tender constitutes an event that qualifies the rights and duties of the parties. See *Restatement of Contracts,* Section 250.

This distinction between a covenant and a condition has a crucial legal effect. Covenants are subject to the doctrine of "substantial performance." Even though under a bilateral contract, each party's duty to perform usually is *constructively* conditional on performance by the other, *substantial* performance will satisfy the condition. Put another way, failure to perform by one party under a bilateral contract will discharge the duty of the other only if the non-performance is *material.* *Restatement of Contracts*, Sections 268(2) and 274.

This doctrine of substantial performance, however, does *not* apply to express conditions, such as the one established by Article XVII A(2) (c). As noted in *Murray on Contracts*, Section 169 (1974), the landmark case of *Jacobs & Young, Inc.* v. *Kent*, 230 N.Y. 239, 129 N.E. 889, 891 (1921), recognized that "parties may include an express condition to the duty of either party and the non-occurrence of that condition would result in failure to activate the duty to which it is attached thereby ultimately discharging that duty, *notwith-*

standing possible forfeiture to the obligee." (Emphasis added.) Similarly, *Restatement of Contracts Second*, Section 262, commen (d) (Tent. Draft No. 8 1973) states: "If, however, the parties have made an event a condition of their agreement, there is no mitigating standard of materiality or substantiality applicable to the non-occurrence of that event."

The *Restatement of Contracts Second* does, however, recognize the possibility of relief in the case of express conditions only through the possibility of *excuse* of the condition in the very limited circumstances described in Section 250:

> To the extent that the non-occurrence of a condition would cause extreme forfeiture, a court may excuse the non-occurrence of a condition unless its occurrence was a material part of the agreed exchange.

Clearly in the case at hand, the condition of tender was not a "material part of the agreed exchange" that would make this principle inapplicable. The only question is whether non-occurrence of this condition would cause "extreme forfeiture" of the type contemplated. . . .

Even though loss of the right to renew the contract of a Player of Fisk's stature undoubtedly would cause hardship to the Red Sox, this does not seem to be the type of "extreme forfeiture" required for excuse of the condition under this rule. This is because there will be no denial or loss of compensation for prior performance or preparations by the Club. The Red Sox have already received, in exchange for past salary payments to Fisk, his performance for the years 1976 through 1980. His performance for 1981 was contingent on the Club's exercise of the option, for which the Club has made no separate payment. . .

Prior decisions of this Panel are consistent with this conclusion. In Panel Decision No. 30 (Chairman Porter) dated May 4, 1977, the Panel held that a Player became a free agent under Article XVII A(2) (d) because of failure of the Club properly to renew the contract within the time period specified in paragraph 10(a), even though the Club attempted to make an effective renewal on March 21 by correcting the salary amount in the original renewal contract of March 10 to conform to the maximum salary reduction limitation. Also analogous is Panel Decision No. 23 (Chairman Seitz) dated December 13, 1974, in which the Panel ordered free agency for the Player under paragraph 7(a) of the Player's Contract. It is significant that following this Decision the parties added subparagraph (8) to Article X F of the Basic Agreement, thereby limiting termination by a Player under paragraph 7(a) of the Player's Contract to "defaults or failures to perform which are material in nature." In the case at hand, the Club seems to be asking the Panel to write a similar limitation into Article XVII A(2) (c) of the Basic Agreement, which of course would be beyond the Panel's authority.

Thus, while free agency for Fisk is indeed an unfortunate consequence for the Club in comparison to the minor inconvenience to him flowing from the belated contract tender, that is the inevitable effect of the condition to which the parties agreed in Article XVII A(2) (c), which the Panel is powerless to deviate from.

NOTE

1. Earlier considerations have contrasted options and rights of first-refusal provisions (see Sections 3.42 and 3.44). The two are not identical, but often result in basically the same circumstance — that is, for some period of time a player is still bound to his old club. Thus, in analyzing option situations, comparison should be made with the right of first refusal. In early 1984, a U.S. District Court judge ruled that Joe Cribbs, a running back for the NFL Buffalo Bills, could jump to the United States Football League and the Birmingham Stallions of the USFL. The main issue was a right-of-first-refusal clause that appeared in Cribbs's Buffalo contract, which had expired at the conclusion of the 1983 NFL season. The Bills contended this gave them the ability to match any offer by any other professional football team. Cribbs and the USFL argued that the clause only extended to matching offers from other NFL clubs, particularly since the USFL was not even in existence when Cribbs signed the earlier contract with the Bills in 1980. The court held that the clause was "slightly ambiguous," but concluded that it cannot "have any effect on any teams outside the National Football League." See *New York Times*, February 24, 1984, p. A20.

4.29   Duties in Light of Other Party's Breach

Many of the earlier considerations in these past few sections have dealt with alleged breach of one's contractual obligation. When the player alleges breach, the sought-after remedy is usually termination of the contract, which, of course, translates into free agency for the player. A notable case in which this strategy was employed successfully, thus setting a standard of sorts, was the dispute between Jim "Catfish" Hunter and Charlie Finley, discussed below. The facts were peculiar to that case. Certainly, in terms of precedent, it is without the sweep of some of the antitrust, freedom-of-movement cases considered earlier (see, for example, Section 2.42) or baseball arbitrations (see *Messersmith* v. *McNally*, Section 5.32). Even so, it was a significant step for players, particularly in baseball, and its background is worth repeating.

The *Hunter* case is attended by another baseball arbitration involving Jim Bibby and the Cleveland Indians. Since the case concerns the failure of the Indians to pay Bibby earned bonuses in a timely fashion, it might have been discussed in Section 2.42. However, because its message addresses the extreme consequences that can flow from relatively minor actions, we have included it in these considerations.

The final discussions in the section focus not so much on obtaining free agency as on investigating duties that may still exist, even where the other party is in breach. The cases dealing with a defunct franchise (in this instance one from the World Football League) and whether players who signed with that franchise are relieved of contractual obligations because of the club's prospective inability to pay involve important considerations. The bonuses advanced the players earlier come in for significant deliberations by the courts. How the courts describe the legal significance of the bonus should be compared with the arbitration decision in *Horner* (Section 4.28).

An Early Confrontation: James Hunter v. Charles O. Finley

In December 1974, Oakland player Jim "Catfish" Hunter was baseball's most successful and celebrated pitcher. As the current Cy Young Award winner, Hunter had finished the previous season with the Athletics with an impressive

25-12 won-lost record. The 28-year-old pitcher had been a 20-game winner for four consecutive seasons and had compiled a total of 88 wins during his four years with Oakland.

Hunter's salary with the Athletics was $100,000 a year. The previous winter, Hunter and Charles O. Finley, owner and operator of the Oakland team, had agreed on a two-year contract, whereby $50,000 of Hunter's salary was to be paid to him as direct salary and the remaining $50,000 was to be paid to a deferment plan of Hunter's choosing. Hunter had requested a specific deferred-payment provision phrased in such a way as to avoid current tax liability on the money. Finley, having agreed to the provision, only later discovered that he, Finley, would incur tax liability for the money. Finley then insisted that the contract clause did not require him to assume this increased burden.

Hunter, in the 1974 season, routinely received the portion of his salary that was to be paid directly to him; the deferred payments, however, were not made to the investment company that Hunter had designated to receive the money. The season ended with the deferred payments still not made, despite several requests by Hunter that this be done. Hunter claimed that the failure to make the deferred payments constituted a breach of contract by Finley and allowed the pitcher to exercise his right to terminate his contract; Hunter maintained that Finley's failure to pay him in the agreed manner allowed Hunter to exercise this right, which was explicitly granted under the terms of the pitcher's contract with Finley. Hunter then announced that since he had no contract, he was a free agent. Finley insisted that no free-agent question was involved, that the only dispute was about the method of payment; he claimed there had not been a violation of the contract but merely a difference of interpretation. He offered the other $50,000 to Hunter as direct payment, but Hunter rejected the proposal as not being in accord with the agreement between the parties.

The case was then submitted to arbitration, pursuant to the collective bargaining agreement then in force in Major League Baseball. The arbitrator, Peter Seitz, decided the dispute in Hunter's favor, ruling that there was no ambiguity about the club's obligations, its failure to carry them out, or about Hunter's right to terminate the contract for such failure. The arbitrator ruled that Hunter no longer had a valid contract with the Oakland team and was a free agent able to entertain offers from any major league club.

Finley claimed that the arbitration ruling making Hunter a free agent was not valid. He obtained a hearing on January 3, 1975, before an Alameda County judge. Finley argued that the arbitration panel exceeded its authority by ruling that Hunter could invoke the termination provision before the case was heard. He contended that the panel was empowered only to decide how the payment clause should be interpreted, and that it could not go beyond that to grant Hunter free agency. In addition, Finley argued that the fact that he failed to pay to the investment company the $50,000 deferred income due Hunter did not result in breach until the arbitrator determined so on December 13, and that from the start of that date, Finley had ten days to correct the situation. Thus, claimed Finley, Hunter was in no way free to negotiate with others before December 23, and payment by Finley before that date would have served to reinstate Hunter's original two-year contract with the Oakland team. The court rejected Finley's contentions.

NOTES

1. On December 31, 1974, Hunter accepted an offer from the New York Yankees, which was comprised of a $100,000 bonus, $150,000 salary per year for five years, and $500,000 worth of life insurance. Only later, in March 1976, was it learned that the bidding for Catfish had progressed much higher than the Yankees' offer of $2,850,000. In a suit brought by former quarterback Joe Kapp, who contended that he was forced out of the National Football League in 1971 after refusing to sign a standard player contract, it was disclosed that Hunter had rejected a $3,800,000 offer from the Kansas City Royals. In the Kapp action, the testimony of

Hunter's lawyer concerning the bids was allowed for the limited purpose of showing how open competition for players could affect their salaries.

2. The full text of the arbitration award is set forth in: In the Matter of the Arbitration Between American and National Leagues of Professional Baseball Clubs (Oakland Athletics) and Major League Baseball Players Association (James A. Hunter), Decision No. 23, Grievance Nos. 74–18 and 74–20, Seitz, Impartial Chairman of Panel, December 13, 1974.

In the Matter of Arbitration between Major League Baseball Clubs (Cleveland Indians) and Major League Baseball Players Association (James B. Bibby), Decision No. 36, Grievance No. 78–3, Porter, Impartial Chairman of Panel, April 3, 1978

This grievance presents a claim by the Association, on behalf of Player James B. Bibby, that under Paragraph 7(a) of the Uniform Player Contract Bibby properly terminated his contract with the Cleveland Indians Club by a written notice of termination, dated December 21, 1977, which is said to have been dispatched after the Club allegedly defaulted in paying Bibby an end of season bonus, was sent a written notice of such default on November 2, 1977, and failed to remedy the default until after Bibby notified the Club he was terminating the contract. . . .

The main facts underlying the case are undisputed. On March 9, 1977, Player Bibby and the Cleveland Club entered into a two-year contract for the 1977 and 1978 playing seasons, consisting of the Uniform Player Contract and certain Special Covenants. One of the Special Covenants provided that Bibby, a pitcher, would receive an additional ("bonus") sum of Five Thousand Dollars ($5,000.00), if he started 20 games or pitched 180 innings during a season, and would receive a further Five Thousand Dollars ($5,000.00) bonus (i.e., a total of $10,000.00), if he started 30 games during a season. . . Finally, the Special Covenant provided: "All payments earned pursuant to the above provisions *will be paid at the end of the respective seasons* (emphasis added)."

Bibby, did, in fact, start 30 games in the 1977 season, thereby earning the $10,000.00 bonus. The Club's season ended on October 1 or 2, 1977.

The Club did not pay the bonus at the end of the season. After a month had elapsed, Bibby's attorney, Richard M. Hull of Dallas, Texas, wrote a letter, dated November 2, 1977, to Phillip D. Seghi, Vice President and General Manager of the Club. The letter reads as follows:

Dear Phil:

Jim Bibby earned a $10,000 bonus during the 1977 baseball season as a result of 30 starts. This bonus was to be paid at the end of the baseball season. I have not received this money and I would appreciate it if you would look into this matter and see that a check is sent to me promptly. You may deduct from the check the amount of expenses Jim owes the Indians, the bill for which is enclosed. . . .

Seghi did not answer Hull's letter, although, as will appear, he claims he talked to Hull on the phone some weeks after the November 2nd letter was received. As will also appear, Hull has a different recollection. It is undisputed, however, that the bonus remained unpaid as of December 21, 1977, when Hull sent the following Mailgram to Seghi:

Pursuant to Section 7(A) of the 1977 Contract (the "Contract") dated March 9 1977 between Cleveland Indians Co (the "Club") and James B. Bibby, I on behalf of Mr. Bibby notify the Club that the Contract is terminated by reason of the failure of the Club to pay Mr. Bibby the additional payments of $10,000.00 provided for under "Special Covenants" provision of the Contract and the letter dated March 8 1977 from the Club to Mr. Bibby. Ten days written notice of such default was given to the Club pursuant to my letter dated November 2, 1977 to Phillip D. Seghi.

By reason of such default (I) Mr. Bibby is now a free agent; and (II) I on behalf of Mr. Bibby hereby notify the Club that the additional payments of $10,000.00 and the deferred amount of $18,000.00 under the contract are now due to Mr. Bibby. These amounts should be sent to me immediately.

A letter to the above effect follows.

Seghi received the Mailgram on December 22 and dispatched a check for $10,000.00 to Bibby that same day. The check was sent to Hull with a covering letter, dated December 22, 1977. . . .

In addition to the foreoging chronology of essentially undisputed facts, the record contains testimony or other evidence regarding certain other matters which either are disputed or, if undisputed, are peripheral to the central issue. In no particular sequence, these include the following.

Bibby's 1976 contract with Cleveland contained a bonus provision similar to but more restricted than the 1977–78 bonus provision, whereby he was to be paid a bonus of $5,000 if he had 20 starts in the 1976 season. Like the 1977–78 bonus, the 1976 bonus was to be paid at the end of the season. Bibby earned the bonus by starting more than 20 games in 1976. The bonus was not, in fact, paid until December 15, 1976.

In 1976, unlike 1977, Bibby's salary and bonus payments were made directly to him rather than to his attorney, Hull. Accordingly, Hull was unaware that the bonus had not been paid when he wrote a letter to Seghi on October 25, 1976 congratulating the General Manager on his good faith in enabling Bibby to obtain the requisite 20 starts and earn the $5,000 bonus. Hull discovered the Club's delay in paying the bonus sometime between October 25 and January 11, 1977, when he again wrote to Seghi in connection with the Club's proposal for a 1977 contract for Bibby. . . .

With regard to the 1977 bonus, it appears that Bibby was sent to the bull pen toward the end of the season, apparently because his services were needed there. Whatever the reason for his assignment to the bull pen, Bibby had had only 29 starts as the end of the season approached. Seghi states that he intervened with the field manager to urge that Bibby be given one more start in order to enable him to earn the $10,000 bonus for 30 starts and Bibby actually received his 30th start in the last game of the season.

As to the Club's failure to respond to Hull's letter of November 2 regarding the non-payment of the bonus, Seghi explained on direct examination that he had not understood the letter to be a "notice" of a "7(a) violation"; that he simply filed the letter in Bibby's file; and that he took no action "because it seemingly was an exchange of letters between Dick (Hull) and I and in telephone conversations we always appeared friendly and I thought that was just a general reminder by Mr. Hull that there was some money due." The general manager further stated that it was the Club's "policy" to pay bonuses at the end of the calendar year; and he cited the cases of two other players who "were due bonuses" in 1977 and as to whom "there was an exchange and an agreement was made that we would pay them and we paid them and it was after January" (1978). . . .

Turning to the merits, the issue to be decided is whether or not, under Paragraph 7(a) of the Uniform Player's Contract, Bibby properly terminated his contract with Cleveland under the circumstances set forth above. Paragraph 7(a) reads as follows:

> 7.(a) The Player may terminate this contract, upon written notice to the Club, if the Club shall default in the payments to the Player provided for in paragraph 2 hereof or shall fail to perform any other obligation agreed to be performed by the Club hereunder and if the Club shall fail to remedy such default within ten (10) days after the receipt by the Club of written notice of such default. The Player may also terminate this contract as provided in subparagraph (d)(4) of this paragraph 7.

It will be apparent that at least three discrete events must occur before a Player may terminate his contract under Paragraph 7(1):

1. The Club must "default in the payments to the Player provided for in paragraph 2" of the Uniform Player's Agreement or "fail to perform any other obligation agreed to be performed by the Club hereunder."
2. The Club must "fail to remedy such default within ten (10) days after the receipt by the Club of written notice of such default."
3. The Player must elect to terminate and send a written notice of termination.

The bulk of the evidence and argument herein has been directed to point 2, the focal question being whether Hull's November 2 letter constituted sufficient "written notice of such default" within the meaning of Paragraph 7(a). In the process, the question of whether or not under point 1 the Club had actually "defaulted" in payment of the bonus and whether or not under point 3 the Player had sent a notice of termination on December 21 tended to get lost in argument regarding the "default notice."

For clarity's sake, the Panel believes it necessary to consider the three points separately. Taking point 1 (the default question) first, the Association argues that the Club was in default when the end of the season came on or about October 1 or 2 and the Club failed to pay Bibby his bonus. Under the contract the Club had obligated itself to pay Bibby the bonus at the end of the season, if Bibby had earned it. There was no dispute that he had earned it, hence, payment was clearly due him and the Club simply failed to pay it, thereby defaulting in its obligation, the Association concludes.

The Club argues that the contract's requirement of payment "at the end of the season" did not establish a specific date and, hence, "the past practice of the parties must be the basis for determining the obligation of the Club with respect to that bonus." Since Bibby had had a similar "end of the season" bonus provision in his 1976 contract and was paid that bonus on December 15, 1976, the payment of his 1977 bonus on December 22, 1977 is said to have been consistent with the payment practice followed under the prior year's contract. Thus, in the Club's view, it was not in default.

The Panel majority cannot accept the Club's argument that "the end of the season" standard lacks sufficient specificity to establish a date on which payment was due under the contract. To be sure, the Club's season could arguably be said to end upon the completion of the regular scheduled season of 162 games; upon the Club's elimination for the playoffs, if it had qualified for them; or upon the end of the World Series, if Cleveland had reached the Series. However, the term "season" or "Playing season" is used to determine all manner of rights and obligations of the parties under the Uniform Player's Contract, including salary payments under Paragraph 2, and the parties themselves obviously consider the commencement and end of the season to be clearly definable events. There is no dispute herein that Cleveland's season ended with the last game played by the Club in Toronto, the game on which Bibby made his 30th start. No one at the hearing could recall with certainty whether this game was played on October 1 or 2, but there is no doubt the season ended for Cleveland when that last game had been played.

There is also no dispute that Bibby earned the $10,000.00 bonus and that, under the contract, the bonus was due to be paid at the end of the season. When it was not paid to him, the Club was clearly in default under the terms of the Agreement.

Turning to point 2, the major issue in this dispute, the question to be determined, the Club's default having been established, concerns the sufficiency of Hull's November 2 letter as a "written notice of such default," within the meaning of Paragraph 7(a). The Association argues that the first three sentences of the November 2 letter contain all the necessary elements of such a notice. . . . In the Association's view, a default notice need do no more than recite that the bonus money of a specified amount to be paid under the contract was, in fact, earned; that payment is due; and that payment has not been received. Hull's November 2 letter contained all of these elements plus a request for payment "promptly."

The Club contends a notice of default must contain language which clearly and concisely sets forth not only the elements cited by the Association above but some further statement plainly indicating that it is a "default" notice under Paragraph 7(a). . . .

Finally, the Club, joined by Counsel for the Major League Baseball Clubs, stresses the critical nature of this issue under Paragraph 7(a) for baseball as a whole. Citing *Corkins*, both argue that this Panel has previously recognized that forefeiture [termination under Paragraph 7(a)] is an extraordinary remedy to be applied strictly. Strict application means in the present context that a Player or his agent acting on his behalf must make clear he is claiming a default pursuant to Paragraph 7(a); and, unless the Club remedies the default within 10 days, it risks forfeiting the contract. If anything less is permitted, they argue, the result will be chaos, because the Major League Clubs receive "literally hundreds" of letters from the Association or from Players or their agents claiming money or asking the Clubs to "look into" a matter. If such letters are to be deemed default notices triggering the machinery of Paragraph 7(a), the Clubs will be confronted with a choice of acceding to every such request or risking forfeiture if they do not accede and are proven wrong in a subsequent arbitration. Counsel for the Clubs observes that it usually takes more than 10 days either to resolve the issue or to pay the Player.

In response to this last line of argument, which it characterizes as the "floodgate" argument, the

Association notes that, in the wake of *Corkins* and *Hunter,* the parties in 1976 did seek to limit the application of Paragraph 7(a) by negotiating a new provision of the Basic Agreement, Article X,F(8). Article X,F(8) provides, in most pertinent part:

> (8) During the term of this Agreement, the right of a Player to terminate his Uniform Player's Contract pursuant to the provisions of the first sentence of paragraph 7(a) of such contract shall be limited to defaults or failures to perform which are *material in nature. . . .* (emphasis added)

In the Association's view, this provision will suffice to eliminate most of the potential claims of contract termination which the Clubs, under their floodgate argument, fear may flow from a decision sustaining the validity of Hull's November 2 letter as a valid notice of default in the circumstances of this case. As to those defaults or failures to perform which *are* "material in nature," the Association asserts, the Clubs have an obligation to respond by remedying the default when it is called to their attention.

However overdrawn it may be, the concern expressed in the Clubs' floodgate argument is clearly not lacking in substance. The parties, themselves, plainly recognized the legitimacy of this concern when, following the *Corkins* and *Hunter* decisions in 1974, they negotiated Article X,F(8) limiting a player's right to terminate under Paragraph 7(a) to "material" breaches. The latter provision has taken care of most of the Player claims for money — claims regarding items such as travel, hotel accommodations, and other matters which are not "material in nature." It clearly did nothing, however, to change the notice requirements of Paragraph 7(a). If the present provision is not adequate, the parties have an opportunity now to negotiate an agreed-upon form of notice.

There is no contention by the Club herein that Bibby's claim should be denied on the ground that the default, if established, is not "material in nature." The Club's default having already been established by the Panel, the question remains whether Hull's letter of November 2 was a sufficient "written notice of such default."

In answering the latter question it may be well to begin by reviewing the circumstances surrounding Hull's dispatch of the November 2 letter and the Club's response. The Panel has already noted that there is no contention herein that the claimed default, if proven, is not "material in nature." Similarly, although the Club sought afterward to claim that Bibby's $10,000 bonus was not "due" at the end of the season, it made no such claim at the time of the November 2 letter and, in any event, the Panel has now rejected the Club's belated argument that the bonus was not, in fact, due. The Club has never claimed that the bonus was not "owed."

As to the Club's response to the letter of November 2, assuming, for the moment, that it was a sufficient notice, the fact is that the Club made no response whatever to the November 2 letter. To the contrary, Seghi arrogantly disregarded the November 2 letter, disdaining to reply not only to Hull's request for payment of the overdue $10,000 bonus but to his further requests for information as to the club's 1977 attendance and information regarding the possibility of working out a new bonus provision in the event the Club intended to use Bibby as a relief pitcher. In the circumstances, it is difficult to avoid the conclusion that Seghi was simply stalling on paying a financial obligation which he was well aware was overdue.

The latter statement foreshadows the Panel majority's conclusion that Hull's November 2 letter was fully adequate to notify the Club of its default in meeting its obligation to pay Bibby the $10,000 bonus which he had admittedly earned and which the contract plainly provided was to be paid "at the end of the season." To be sure, the notice was sufficient only to inform the Club of its default; it did not signify an intent to terminate the contract, did not say it was a "default" notice under Paragraph 7(a), and did not say the Club had 10 days to remedy the default or risk termination of the contract by Bibby.

The question, then, is whether a notice of default must contain one or more of the latter elements in order to be a sufficient "written notice of such default" under Paragraph 7(a). In a case such as this one, where there was and is no question that the payment was owed and due, the Panel majority can find no foundation in the language of Paragraph 7(a) for requiring a Player to do anything more than give the Club written notice sufficient to apprise it of a "default" in payment of an obligation which is due and owing under the contract. . . .

Finally, with respect to this "point 2" issue, the

Panel notes that a Club confronted by a default notice is not necessarily confronted by a choice of paying under protest within the 10-day period allowed or risking forfeiture. If a Club has a problem living up to its agreement or a genuine question as to whether or not it owes the obligation on which it has allegedly defaulted, its proper recourse is to contact the Association and the Player Relations Committee and lay the problem on the table. Much of the real fault in this case stems from the lack of the kind of communication between management and union which is a normal component of a mature labor-management relationship. If, instead of filing away his player's legitimate request for moneys due him under the contract, Seghi had written to the Association and the Player Relations Committee saying the Club had a payment problem, the outcome of this matter might well have been different. . . .

The grievance is sustained. James B. Bibby's Contract for services to be performed during the 1978 season no longer binds him and he is a free agent.

Alabama Football, Inc. v. Stabler, 319 So.2d 678 (Ala. 1975)

Professional football player Ken Stabler sought a declaratory judgment to relieve him from terms of an agreement with Alabama Football, Inc., a World Football League franchise. On April 1974, Stabler signed an agreement with Alabama Football Inc. (AFI) which would pay Stabler a $50,000 signing bonus, an additional $50,000 in the latter part of 1974, $100,000 in 1975, and $135,000 per year through 1980, for a total of $875,000. Stabler was paid $50,000 upon execution of the contract, and the parties entered into an agreement to set up a pay schedule to cover the balance of $50,000 owed to Stabler in 1974. Stabler received $20,000 but when the final $30,000 was due, AFI did not have the funds to pay him. Stabler subsequently filed suit seeking cancellation of the contract, and a temporary restraining order preventing the use of his name by AFI.

Stabler argued that AFI had breached the contract by refusing to pay him amounts owed under the agreement, that AFI had used Stabler's name in promotions and prevented him for negotiating with other pro football teams, and that financial problems prevented AFI from living up to the contract. AFI argued that they were trying to straighten out their financial problems and that they should be given the opportunity to live up to the contract. But the court, finding that AFI was in debt in excess of $1,600,000, ruled that AFI was in breach.

AFI argued further that since Stabler had not offered to return any of the money he had received, the contract could not be rescinded. However, the court ruled that since AFI had used Stabler's name in promoting ticket sales and enticing other players to "jump" to the WFL, and since Stabler was prohibited from negotiating with other teams while under contract with AFI, the defendant had received benefits under the contract. The balancing of equities did not require Stabler to return the money he had received.

AFI also argued that notice of rescision is a condition to such an action and that Stabler had delivered no such notice. But the court dismissed this argument, holding that the conduct of the parties — that is, Stabler's repeated demands for payment and the defendant's refusal — was sufficient notice.

Alabama Football, Inc. v. Greenwood, 452 F. Supp. 1191 (W.D. Pa. 1978)

Alabama Football, Inc. (AFI), which operated the Birmingham Americans of the World Football League (WFL), brought action against L. C. Greenwood when he failed to play for the Americans in abrogation of his contract with them. AFI sought recovery of general damages, as well as a $50,000 bonus paid to Greenwood. The court ruled against AFI. In order for AFI to recover against Greenwood, it had to prove it would have had the willingness and ability to perform its end of the contract had the defendant not repudiated the contract. AFI failed to show this.

AFI and Greenwood entered into a contract on May 31, 1974, in which it was agreed that

Greenwood would play for the Birmingham Americans starting in the 1975 season. Greenwood was still under contract to his present club, the Pittsburgh Steelers, of the National Football League, for the 1974 season. The Americans' contract covered a three-year period. In addition to salaries for each year, Greenwood was to receive three $25,000 bonuses: one upon signing; one in September 1974; and the third in April 1975. Under the agreement, Greenwood granted AFI the right to use his name, likeness, and biographical sketch for promotions and publicity for the team and league.

Greenwood received his first two bonuses as per the agreement. During the 1974 season, AFI ran into financial difficulties and was found in default on its payment to the league in mid-October. The WFL Board of Governors apparently canceled AFI's league membership on January 16, 1975. On February 13, 1975, the board confirmed and approved the ruling of default against AFI.

About this time, Greenwood repudiated his contract with AFI, and on March 18, Greenwood and the WFL executed a mutual release. This agreement was based on the assumption that AFI had defaulted on its contract with Greenwood.

Two weeks later, the WFL informed Greenwood that it was of the impression that AFI had not failed on its contract to Greenwood, and the league was ready to assume his contract based on a clause in the original agreement. In mid-April, AFI contacted Greenwood, telling him it still intended to operate a WFL team in 1975 and regarded his contract as valid and binding. Even so, the bonus due in April was not paid, due to the questionable status of Greenwood. On June 18, Greenwood signed a new contract with the Steelers for the 1975 season. AFI did not operate a team in 1975, and the entire WFL folded before the end of the 1975 season.

Because of AFI's tremendous financial problems, the revocation of its membership in the WFL, and its failure to provide a team in 1975, the court concluded that AFI had not proved that at the time of Greenwood's repudiation it had the ability to perform substantially its responsibilities under the contract.

The court found that AFI's dire financial condition would have "absolutely" prevented it from performing its duties, particularly in light of cancellation of the franchise. Termination of the franchise frustrated the object of AFI's contract with Greenwood. The court noted that AFI's insolvency was not caused by Greenwood and that neither party contemplated or assumed the risk of a franchise termination when the contract was executed.

The court held that the "parties are excused from further performance" in compliance with the contract when "performance of the remaining unexecuted" portion is "impossible." AFI is precluded from recovery since it was unable to perform at the time of repudiation.

The court noted that AFI could pursue an action for restitution of the consideration paid to Greenwood. Greenwood contended that restitution was not available, since the payment was a signing bonus. The physical act of signing was the performance required which, Greenwood argued, corresponded to the bonus payment. Greenwood relied on the customary use of the term, signing bonus, as used in professional sports to mean a bonus paid to the player for merely executing the contract. Greenwood submitted as evidence notations on two checks given to Greenwood at the time of signing. The notation on one (made out to a third party on behalf of Greenwood) read "part bonus for signing contract (L. C. Greenwood)," and the second notation was "bonus for contract." AFI argued that the contract could not be apportioned but was one entire contract calling for total compensation of $375,000 for the three years of service.

The court examined the contract between AFI and Greenwood. The portion dealing with the compensation terms read in part:

$ 25,000.00	Bonus due upon signing
$ 25,000.00	Due Sept. 1, 1979
$ 25,000.00	Balance due on Bonus April 1, 1975
$ 90,000.00	1975
$100,000.00	1976
$110,000.00	1977

Based on these figures and other provisions of the WFL contract, the court concluded that the parties had apportioned the salary as designated. The court also noted that provisions 7 and 12 clearly indicated that if Greenwood failed to perform, "the agreed performances of the parties would be apportioned on a season-by-season or game-by-game basis."

AFI contended that the payment to Greenwood was an "advance" on Greenwood's salary. The court dismissed this argument, pointing out that if the payment had been an advance, to be returned if Greenwood failed to perform, the parties had failed to express that intention in the contract.

The court found "significant legal authority which demonstrate(d) that an interpretation (as Greenwood contended) in professional sports contract (is both common and equitable)." The court quoted Corbin on *Contracts* (St Paul: West, 1972) to support its position that bonuses are a common practice used to induce players to sign. Corbin stated that "when the player attached his signature to the service contract he had performed an act that constituted the full agreed equivalent of the 'bonus' (the money payment)."

AFI, according to the court, benefited from Greenwood signing the contract to play in Birmingham for the 1975–77 seasons. For example, Greenwood had appeared at the opening game in July of 1974 and at a publicity reception. In addition, AFI had nonexclusive rights to use Greenwood's name for publicity. AFI exercised this right by advertising Greenwood's name in each game program, along with other future WFL players. The court found "that the mere execution of the contract by an established player such as Greenwood had

promotional value which AFI was able to exploit." The court concluded that Greenwood's execution of the contract "more than a year before he was to begin playing football for AFI" and "the use of his name for promotional" reasons "constituted adequate consideration to support the bonuses paid to Greenwood."

In concluding that Greenwood did not breach his obligation under the contract and that AFI was not entitled to recover, the court said:

> Where a specific portion of a defendant's performance, such as the execution of the contract, has been apportioned as the equivalent of a part of plaintiff's performance, such as payment of the bonus, plaintiff is not entitled to restitution if the defendant has rendered the apportioned consideration in full.

NOTE

1. In yet another case involving the ill-fated Alabama Football, Inc., a U.S. District Court in Dallas held:

> [I]t is undisputed that the dissolve of Alabama [Football, Inc.]'s team and the World Football League has made performance of the remaining unexecuted four-fifths of the contract impossible. Accordingly, the parties are excused from further performance in compliance with the contract. [*Alabama Football, Inc.* v. *Wright*, 452 F.Supp. 182, 185 (N.D.Tex. 1977)]

Madison Square Garden Boxing, Inc. v. Muhammad Ali, 430 F. Supp. 679 (N.D. Ill. 1977)

Madison Square Garden Boxing, Inc. (MSGB) brought action against Muhammad Ali (Ali), heavyweight champion of the world at the time, for breach of a contract to fight Duane Bobick in Madison Square Garden. MSGB sought damages and injunctive relief.

Ali's contract to fight Bobick was executed on November 26, 1976, shortly after his successful title defense against Ken Norton in September of 1976, and was to be completed between February 14 and 28, 1977. After signing the contract, however, Ali announced his retirement. Despite this, Teddy Brenner, president and promoter for

MSGB, contacted Herbert Muhammad (Muhammad), Ali's manager, in an attempt to reinstate the contest between Bobick and Ali. Muhammad told Brenner that the decision to fight was entirely Ali's.

By mid-November 1976, Brenner was now attempting to arrange a Bobick–Norton fight. These negotiations reached an impasse, and Brenner approached Bobick's manager to indicate his belief that an Ali–Bobick contest could still be arranged. Bobick's manager was skeptical but was told by Muhammad that there was always a possibility that Ali might box again. Norton's manager responded to this development by executing an agreement for Norton to fight Bobick. Two conditions to this agreement were made: (1) if the Ali–Bobick contest was arranged, Norton would step aside; and (2) in the event Bobick won, he would contract with Norton for his first title defense. This agreement was executed on November 17, 1976.

Brenner then met with Ali's attorney, who had held Ali's power of attorney. Ali had authorized his attorney to make a deal for the Ali–Bobick fight for $2,500,000. A letter was sent to Ali for his signature, as a letter of intent, and was not claimed to be a binding contract. Ali verbally indicated his assent to the contest and signed the letter. A deposit of $125,000 was made to seal the agreement. Final arrangements for the Ali–Bobick contest were made, including the agreement for Norton to step aside. Ali executed that document on November 26, 1976 in Brenner's presence.

Shortly after Ali executed the Ali–Bobick agreement, he was approached by promoter Don King about fighting the South African Champion, Schutte. Ali agreed and executed an agreement for this fight after informing King of his fight with Bobick. King penciled in on his agreement that it would not be valid without Muhammad's signature. Muhammad's attorney signed the Ali–Schutte agreement for Muhammad. This agreement acknowledged the Ali–Bobick fight.

At the end of November, however, further retirement stories about Ali began to circulate.

Official notification followed, and MSGB decided to announce the Bobick–Norton contest. Ali participated in a press conference by telephone in which he announced his retirement and aided in promoting the Bobick–Norton fight. Subsequent to the press conference, Muhammad and Ali had not discussed boxing with Brenner, whose attitude was that the matter was finished.

In the middle of December, however, Muhammad contacted Brenner by letter stating that Ali was prepared to fight in accordance with the terms of the previous letter of intent. Muhammad also stated that in the event that MSGB was committed to the Bobick–Norton fight that Ali would fight Bobick within four months of that contest. Muhammad's letter also stated that if an agreement wasn't signed by December 24, 1976, the $125,000 payment would be returned by Ali. MSGB never responded to Muhammad's letter, and in late January of 1977 the money was returned to and accepted by MSGB.

Ali raised four separate defenses to the allegation of breach of contract: (1) the contract was invalid because Ali lacked capacity to enter a contract without his manager's approval; (2) there was no breach; (3) MSGB was unable to perform; and (4) if the contract existed, it was mutually abandoned.

The court disposed of Ali's first contention by pointing out that the November 26 contract clearly established mutuality of obligation and was supported by adequate consideration. Muhammad had clearly indicated his desire that Ali alone decide. Muhammad's conduct revealed his approval. Ali's claim that there was no breach also failed, since his announced retirement was a stated intention to refuse performance and was at least anticipatory breach. MSGB at that point had grounds to sue for breach.

MSGB failed to bring an action at the time of Ali's breach, and the court examined MSGB's conduct to determine whether mutual abandonment had occurred. The court held that mutual abandonment had occurred when MSGB took no action after notice that Ali was going to retire. MSGB also revived the Bobick–Norton contest. Ali was asked to help promote this and did so. The court also noted that Brenner believed and acted as though the matter was finished. This was supported by MSGB's acceptance of the money and their failure to respond to Muhammad's letter. Finally, the court noted MSGB's failure to bring suit until the time for performance had passed.

The court held that there had been a binding contract, that the anticipatory breach by Ali provided MSGB with the right to sue but that mutual abandonment of the contract had occurred.

4.30   Problems in the Performance of Contracts

So the deal is made, the player is under contract to a team, the salary is guaranteed, and the bonuses are substantial. The attorney/agent can relax. Right? Wrong.

In many areas, and particularly so in sports, the signing of the contract is often only the start as far as the attorney or agent is concerned. The career for the professional athlete is a tenuous one, beset by constant uncertainties and setbacks. Things look great when the contract is signed, but it is only a short time before new problems arise. The following subsections examine only a few of the problems that will cause the phone to start ringing and the headaches to multiply.

While concentration is on the legal response to a problem, often through arbitration under the applicable league procedures, the real-life response is often that of counseling the client and hopefully negotiating a resolution with the perceived offender. When those fail, then the grievance or complaint may be necessary.

4.31   Player's Contract Is Terminated (For Other than Lack of Skill or Injury)

When the player's contract is not guaranteed, the long-range forecast for that player's tenure with a club is uncertain, at best. It was long assumed, in fact, that a club could be rid of a player for any reason because of the existence of the right-to-terminate clauses in the player contract. That unlimited ability to release has been challenged, as the following arbitration decisions reveal. However, these are relatively unique circumstances, and generalization is difficult. In addition, the grievance is not always successful, as the *Sharockman* decision underscores.

In the Matter of Arbitration Between Detroit Lions and Mitchell Hoopes, Scearce, Arbitrator, September 2, 1978

At issue was whether (1) the Detroit Lions had violated Article XXXIV, section 5 of the Collective Bargaining Agreement (CBA) when the head coach publicly criticized Hoopes or (2) the club had violated the NFL Player Contract when it terminated his 1977 contract.

Hoopes, a punter, was claimed off waivers by the Detroit Lions on September 12, 1977. Following his first appearance for the Lions in a preseason game against Chicago on September 18, 1977, the former head coach, Hudspeth, severely criticized Hoopes's performance at a postgame critique and a press conference. He blamed the loss on Hoopes and said that Hoopes had "choked completely."

On September 22, Hudspeth informed Hoopes that he was being placed on waivers because "too much pressure" had been put on him because of criticism that he had kicked inadequately. Hudspeth said he had put Hoopes "into such a hole" that Hoopes could not do the job. He was not claimed by any other club for the 1977 season.

According to Hoopes, the tension created by the coach's remarks could be relieved only by a public retraction or his removal from the club. Hoopes claimed that the coach violated his contractual rights by removing him from the team for a reason not cited in his player contract. Hoopes also argued that the coach's public criticism was a violation of Article XXXIV, section 5 of the CBA on Public Statements.

The club claimed it had acted within its authority by exercising its unilateral right to evaluate a player's skill and/or performance. The coach had the right to determine which players could and would be retained. The club also argued that Article XXXIV, section 5 neither absolutely prohibits public criticism by a coach nor provides for any penalties.

Article XXXIV, section 5 does not explicitly prohibit management and players from expressing criticism publicly. Its intent is to mitigate such public comments but it merely requires that the NFL Players Association and the Management Council use their "best efforts" to curtail critical public comments. With no showing that the NFLPA or the council were in a position to exert any influence in this instance, Scearce concluded that the club was not in violation of the CBA Article XXXIV, section 5.

Three sections of the NFL Player Contract address grounds upon which a player may be waived or released from a team; physical condition, personal conduct, and skill or performance. Only the provisions of section 11, dealing with skill or performance, were relevant to this dispute.

Scearce did not question the coach's right to release Hoopes because of inadequate skill or performance. He concluded, however, that the club's actions were not motivated solely by its assessment of Hoopes's skill and performance. Hudspeth's explanation to Hoopes was that he had "put too much pressure on him." His assurance to the new punter, Wilbur Sumners, that "there was no pressure on him," highlights the significance which the coach placed on the results of his public criticism of Hoopes. Thus, the club had violated section 11 of the NFL Player Contract.

Scearce directed the Club to pay Hoopes the remainder of monies due to him under his 1977 Player Contract.

In the Matter of Arbitration Between National Basketball Association (Atlanta Hawks) and National Basketball Players Association (Ken Charles), Seitz, Arbitrator, June 22, 1978

At issue was whether the Atlanta Hawks had satisfied the conditions of paragraph 20(b) of Charles's player contract, which lists grounds for termination, when they terminated his contract.

Charles had signed a three-year, $132,000 per year contract with Atlanta on September 7, 1976. Atlanta placed him on waivers on December 8, 1977. Upon clearing waivers on December 12, 1977, his contract was terminated.

Paragraph 20(b) provides in part that:

> The Club may terminate this contract upon *written notice* to the Player (after complying with the waiver procedure) if the Player shall do any of the following: . . . (2) at any time, fail, in the sole opinion of the Club's management, to exhibit sufficient skill or competitive ability to qualify to continue as a member of the Club's team . . .

Great weight must be given to the club's appraisal of the player's skills and ability; his failure to measure up is determined by "the sole opinion of the Club's management." Seitz noted, however, that a club must be able to establish and demonstrate a rational basis for its opinion that a player deserves to be terminated.

The club failed to give Charles written notice of any kind. Written notice issued on December 8, 1977, stating the reasons for the termination, would have been evidence that on that date the club was of the opinion that Charles did not possess the skills and ability necessary to remain under contract. Without anything in writing, Seitz had to rely on testimony concerning conversations and statements to the media.

Charles claimed that the club was motivated by considerations not mentioned in the paragraph 20(b)(2). Atlanta's general manager, Mike Gearon, told Charles and a sports columnist that his contract was terminated for financial reasons. An Associated Press story called it an "economic move." Gearon testified that he made these remarks in order to minimize harm to Charles.

Apparently Gearon told Robert Woolf, Charles's lawyer, that the reasons were not financial. but were related to Charles's shooting only 39 percent. In Seitz's view, even this statement fell short of an unequivocal declaration that Charles had failed to exhibit sufficient skills or competitive ability. Moreover, Gearon told Woolf that Atlanta had an "austerity program" and would give consideration to a renegotiated Charles contract at a minimum figure.

Atlanta also argued that Charles did not fit into the team's revised structure and new running style of play. Seitz was wary of this type of argument. If the skills and ability of a veteran player, although not diminished, cease to be useful to a club because of its revised style of play, the player could be traded. Without strong proof, it would be difficult to justify that such circumstances justify contract termination.

Coach Hubie Brown testified that Charles did a good job in 1976–1977. In 1977–78 Charles started in 21 of 22 games. Nothing was said to Charles prior to December 8, 1977, to indicate that he was playing under par.

Seitz found the evidence insufficient for him to conclude that Charles had failed "to exhibit sufficient skills or competitive ability to qualify to continue as a member of the Club's team."

The facts on the record supported Charles's contention that Atlanta was motivated by other considerations, primarily economic. Also, the new team structure and style-of-play arguments were not made until the arbitration hearing and were not supported by sufficient evidence.

Seitz sustained the grievance and ordered Atlanta to pay Charles all monies to which he was entitled under his contract. The contract was declared to have continued in full force and effect.

In the Matter of Arbitration Between NFL Players Association (Ed Sharockman) and NFL Management Council (Minnesota Vikings), Rozelle, Arbitrator, July 27, 1973

The NFL Players Association filed a grievance against the Minnesota Vikings asserting that a club "releases" a player by putting the player on waivers; hence, Ed Sharockman was entitled to termination pay. Sharockman had played the first seven regular season games of the 1972 season with the Vikings but was placed on waivers on October 30. On November 1, Sharockman was claimed, and his contract was awarded to the Philadelphia Eagles. The following day, Sharockman notified Philadelphia that he had decided to retire from pro football to become a stockbroker; he never reported to the Eagles. The Eagles subsequently placed him on reserve, listing him as "Did Not Report, Retired."

Commissioner Pete Rozelle found that section 18.1(A) of the constitution and bylaws outlining the waiver system compelled a ruling that a player cannot be released by a club until the player clears waivers without having his contract claimed by and awarded to another club. The pertinent language read: "Clubs desiring to release players must first give written notice to Commissioner of said intention." The commissioner was then to notify each club of the waiver request. Only if the player was not claimed was the club in a position to release him.

Rozelle also looked at the negotiating history of the termination pay principle and found that it was intended for veterans who found their football careers involuntarily terminated when other employment positions such as school teaching were largely foreclosed. No evidence was found to suggest that the provision was intended to apply to players who voluntarily retire when their contracts are transferred to another club. There likewise was no evidence of any attempt to broaden the provision during the 1970 negotiation to include situations such as Sharockman's when continuing employment as a player was still available within the league. Sharockman's grievance was thus denied.

4.32 Player Is Injured

No single circumstance causes as many disputes as injuries. Any player in any sport who performs as a professional is eventually going to suffer an injury. If nothing else, the wear on the body will cause it to break down. Drawing the line between sports-incurred injuries and those resulting from the aging process is difficult, if not almost impossible. Even so, in the sports legal arena, such must be done all the time. In most sports, a player cannot be released while injured. Consequently, the team often insists that the player is all right; the player, of course, will assert he is disabled. The makings for a dispute are at hand.

Even when an injury is fully evident, the collective bargaining agreements and standard player contracts in the various sports leagues provide the injured player with only fairly minimal protection. There are insurance provisions for medical expenses and guaranteed salary stipulations — up to a point. The standard provision says that the player will receive full salary for the season in which the injury is sustained, but nothing beyond. In addition, the injury must result directly from job activities that are within the scope of employment. Workers' compensation received for loss of income will proportionately reduce the club's obligation to the player.

The National Football League goes slightly beyond the other leagues in providing salary protection. Under Article X of its collective agreement, a player who was physically unable to play in the last game of the prior season because of a "severe football injury" or who had to have off-season surgery, and who after rehabilitation still fails the physical examination at the start of the next season's preseason camp, shall be entitled to compensation in an amount equal to 50 percent of his contract salary, up to a maximum of $65,000.

There are three responses to the minimal types of protection that are afforded. First, the agent may purchase additional insurance for a client. This option is costly and will hardly be appealing to the client. Second, the agent can negotiate for extended protection. Today, most "guaranteed" contracts specify that in case of disabling injury the salary for the entire period of the contract is payable. The wording of these provisions is crucial and must be drafted with care. The third response is to allege that the player was released while still injured and should be compensated for the full length of the contract. These contentions were traditionally handled through litigation. At the current time, collective bargaining provisions are likely to stipulate that arbitration is the exclusive method for resolving the dispute. Even so, in the analysis that follows, certain court cases are discussed for the interpretations given on important contract terms.

In the first subsection that follows, the NFL's "Injury Grievance" procedures are set forth, as well as NFL and other leagues' arbitration decisions relating to procedural issues (see Section 4.32–1). This is followed by disputes over special contract provisions (Section 4.32–2), problems of determining whether the player was disabled at the time of release (Section 4.32–3), and a brief look at workers' compensation issues (Section 4.32–4).

4.32–1   Procedural Issues

Some leagues establish only one set of arbitration grievance procedures. Other leagues, such as the NFL, deem injuries and grievances arising therefrom so much a part of the league's operation, and so complex, that separate grievance procedures are specified for injury and noninjury disputes. The player and his representative must be aware of the appropriate method of pressing the grievance in the particular league in question.

The NFL injury grievance procedures are detailed below. Following the procedures are two arbitration decisions, one from the NBA and one from the NFL, which underscore the importance of protecting the player's rights by observing all procedural requirements.

National Football League, Collective Bargaining Agreement, 1982

Article IX: Injury Grievance

Section 1. Definition: An "injury grievance" is a claim or complaint that, at the time an NFL player's Standard Player Contract or NFL Player Contract was terminated by a club, the player was physically unable to perform the services required of him by that contract because of an injury incurred in the performance of his services under that contract. All time limitation in this Article may be extended by mutual agreement of the parties.

Section 2. Filing: Any NFL player and/or the NFLPA must present an injury grievance in writing to a club, with a copy to the Management Council, within 20 days from the date it became known or should have become known to the player that his contract had been terminated. The grievance will set forth the approximate date of the alleged injury and its general nature. If the player passes the physical examination of the club at the beginning of the pre-season training camp for the year in question, having made full and complete disclosure of his known physical and mental condition when questioned by the club physician during the physical examination, it will be presumed that such player was physically fit to play football on the date he reported.

Section 3. Answer: The club to which an injury grievance has been presented will answer in writing within five days. If the answer contains a denial of the claim, the general grounds for such denial will be set forth. The answer may raise any special defense, including but not limited to the following:

(a) That the player did not pass the physical examination administered by the club physician at the beginning of the pre-season training camp for the year in question. This defense will not be available if the player participated in any team drills following his physical examination or in any pre-season or regular season game; provided, however, that the club physician may require the player to undergo certain exercises or activities, not team drills, to determine whether the player will pass the physical examination;

(b) That the player failed to make full and complete disclosure of his known physical or mental condition when questioned during the physical examination;

(c) That the player's injury occurred prior to the physical examination and the player knowingly executed a waiver or release prior to the physical examination or his commencement of practice for the season in question which specifically pertained to such prior injury;

(d) That the player's injury arose solely from a non-football related cause subsequent to the physical examination;

(e) That subsequent to the physical examination the player suffered no new football-related injury;

(f) That subsequent to the physical examination the player suffered no football-related aggravation of a prior injury reducing his physical capacity below the level existing at the time of his physical examination as contemporaneously recorded by the club physician.

Section 4. Neutral Physician: The player must present himself for examination by a neutral physician within 20 days from the date of the grievance. This time period may be extended by mutual consent if the neutral physician is not available. Neither club nor player may submit any medical records to the neutral physician, nor may the club physician or players physician communicate with the neutral physician. The player will notify the club of the identity of the neutral physician by whom he is to be examined as soon as possible subsequent to a selection by the player. The neutral physician will not become the treating physician nor will the neutral physician examination involve more than one office visit without the prior approval of both the NFLPA and Management Council.

Section 5. List: The NFLPA and the Management Council will maintain a jointly-approved list of neutral physicians, including at least two orthopedic physicians in each city in which an NFL club is located. The list will be subject to review and modification every 12 months, at which time either party may eliminate any two neutral physicians from the list by written notice to the other party. Each physician should be willing and able to examine NFL players promptly.

Section 6. Appeal: A grievance may be appealed to an arbitrator by filing of written notice of appeal with the chairman of the arbitration panel within 30 days from the date of receipt of the neutral physician's written report. There will be a panel of five (5) arbitrators, whose appointment must be accepted in writing by the NFLPA and the Management Council. The parties have designated Pat Fisher as the chairman of the panel. Either party to this Agreement may discharge a member of the arbitration panel by serving written notice upon the arbitrator and the other party to this Agreement between December 1 and 10 of each year, but at no time shall such discharges result in no arbitrators remaining on the panel.

Section 7. Hearing: Each arbitrator shall designate a minimum of one hearing date each month for use by the parties to this Agreement. Upon being appointed, each arbitrator will, after consultation with the Chairman, provide to the NFLPA and the Management Council specified hearing dates for each of the ensuing 12 months, which process will be repeated on an annual basis thereafter. The parties will notify each arbitrator 30 days in advance of which dates the following month are going to be used by the parties. The designated arbitrator will set the hearing on his or her next reserved date and, after consultation with the parties, designate a convenient place for hearing such grievance. If a grievance is set for hearing and the hearing date is then cancelled by a party within 30 days of the hearing date, the cancellation fee of the arbitrator will be borne by the cancelling party unless the arbitrator determines that the cancellation was for good cause Should good cause be found, the parties will share any cancellation costs equally. If the arbitrator in question cannot reschedule the hearing within 30 days of the postponed date, the case may be reassigned by the Chairman to another panel member who has a hearing date available within the 30 day period. At the hearing, the parties to the grievance and the NFLPA and Management Council will have the right to present, by testimony or otherwise, any evidence relevant to the grievance. All hearings shall be transcribed. Post-hearing briefs must be submitted to the arbitrator postmarked no later than thirty (30) days after receipt of the last day's transcript. The arbitrator will, if at all possible, considering the arbitrator's schedule and other commitments, issue a written decision within 30 days of the submission of briefs. The arbitrator may issue the decision after 30 days have passed from the date of receipt of the last day's transcript regardless of the failure of either party to submit a brief. His decision will be final and binding; provided, however, that no arbitrator will have the authority to add to, subtract from, or alter in any way any provision of this Agreement or any other applicable document.

Section 8. Miscellanous: The arbitrator will consider the neutral physician's findings conclusive with regard to the physical condition of the player and the extent of an injury at the time of his examination by the neutral physician. The arbitrator will decide the dispute in light of this finding and such other issues or defenses which may have been properly submitted to him. The club or the Management Council must advise the grievant and the NFLPA in writing no later than seven days before the hearing of any special defense to be raised at the hearing. The arbitrator may award the player payments for medical expenses incurred or which will be incurred in connection with an injury.

Section 9. Expenses: Expenses charged by a neutral physician will be shared equally by the club and the player. All travel expenses incurred by the player in connection with his examination by a neutral physician of his choice will be borne by the player. The parties will share equally in the expense of any arbitration engaged in pursuant to this Article; provided, however, the respective parties will bear the expenses of attendance of their own witnesses.

Section 10. Pension Credit: Any player who receives payment for three or more regular season games during any year as a result of filing an injury grievance or settlement of a potential injury grievance will be credited with one year of Credited Service for the year in which injured under the Bert Bell NFL Player Retirement Plan as determined by the Retirement Board.

Section 11. Payment: If an award is made by the arbitrator, payment will be made within twenty (20) days of the receipt of the award to the player or jointly to the player and the NFLPA provided the player has given written authorization for such joint payment. The time limit for payment may be extended by mutual consent of the parties or by a finding of good cause for the extension by the arbitrator.

In the Matter of Arbitration Between National Basketball Association (Portland Trail Blazers) and National Basketball Players Association (Bob Davis), Seitz, Arbitrator, June 19, 1975

This dispute was decided on procedural grounds rather than on the merits. Davis signed a three-year, guaranteed, no-cut contract in April 1972 for a total of $225,000 after his agent assured the Trail Blazers that Davis's knee problem was "OK." When his knee required surgery on June 12, 1972, Trail Blazers' manager Glickman informed his agent that he thought the club had been misled. Davis signed a modification of his contract giving the club the authority to cut Davis within 30 days following the start of the 1973–74 training camp if Davis was unable to perform as the result of his knee surgery. The club decided to terminate his contract for that reason on October 3, 1973. Davis claimed that he was able to play and that the club's evaluation was in error. He sought $175,000 plus interest.

Article XVI of the Collective Bargaining Agreement between the NBA and the Players Association requires a party to discuss a disputed matter with the opposing party before initiating a grievance. The grievance must be initiated within 20 days from the date of the occurrence or within 20 days from the date on which the facts of the matter became known or reasonably should have become known.

Seitz rejected Davis's argument that the 20-day period did not begin until October 23, 1973, which was the date Davis received an independent doctor's report. He knew about his termination on October 3, 1973. The provision cannot mean that a grievance need not be initiated until a player collects sufficient witnesses and evidence to support his claim.

In fact, Davis's agent admitted that their first communication to the club, by letter dated November 1, 1973, wasn't an attempt to raise a grievance under the procedures of the CBA. There wasn't even any mention of the CBA in the letter.

Rather than contest the club's response, which alleged that no timely or bonafide grievance existed according to the procedures outlined in the CBA, Davis filed a civil suit in federal court. The court stayed the action pending a determination by the deputy commissioner on the merits and the procedural requirements. The commissioner ruled in favor of the club.

In effect, Davis did not initiate a grievance until September 25, 1974, almost one year after October 3, 1973. Noncompliance with the timeliness requirements of the agreement is permissible only when the parties mutually agree to extend the limits or a party decides to waive its complaint concerning the other's noncompliance. The Trail Blazers objected from the beginning.

Seitz felt that it was his clear duty to require adherence to the agreement's procedural provisions. He did not reach the question of whether Davis was able to perform as a player under the terms of their Modification Agreement. The grievance was denied on the ground that Davis had not followed the procedures nor complied with the time limits prescribed by the collective agreement.

In the Matter of Arbitration Between NFL Management Council (Tampa Bay Buccaneers) and NFL Players Association (Jim Peterson), Scearce, Arbitrator, November 4, 1978

Peterson signed three contracts with the Tampa Bay Buccaneers for 1976, 1977, and 1978. A special clause was included in his 1977 Player Contract to ensure payment of his compensation in the event he became unable to play due to a football-related injury. The club would not be obligated unless the club physician certified that Peterson was unable to play in 1977 and/or 1978.

Peterson injured his left knee in the third game of the 1976 season. After two bouts with knee surgery and rehabilitation programs, he reported to training camp on July 11, 1977. The club doctor assigned him a risk factor of 5 (50/50) chance of significant injury but did not certify him unfit to play. On July 22, 1977, Peterson was cut from the team and placed on waivers.

On August 5, 1977, Peterson filed an injury grievance in accordance with Article IX of the CBA seeking compensation for 1977 and 1978. That claim was still assigned to Arbitrator Marlin Volz at the time of this decision. The NFL Players Association came into the picture on February 17, 1978, when it filed a noninjury grievance against the club based on Article VII of the CBA. The association maintained that its letter of February 17 was merely a "redirecting" of the original grievance from Article IX to Article VII.

The arbitrator never reached the merits of the case. He agreed with the club's contention that the provisions for filing injury and noninjury grievances are expressly and procedurally different. The burden of meeting timeliness requirements falls upon a grievant, his representative, and the association.

Section 2 of Article VII requires that a grievance be initiated within 60 days from the date of the event or nonevent upon which the grievance is based or within 60 days from the date on which the facts of the matter became known or reasonably should have become known to the grievant.

The association's February 17, 1978, letter to the club was filed after the 60-day deadline. Thus, Scearce dismissed the grievance as offered under Article VII. He referred to the provision of Article VII, which prevents an arbitrator from adding to, subtracting from, or altering in any way the provisions of the CBA.

NOTES _____

1. In *Spain* v. *Houston Oilers, Inc.,* 593 S.W. 2d 746 (Tex. Civ. App. 1979), an allegedly injured professional football player sued his football club to recover his salary for the duration of the season. The court of civil appeals, in reversing the district court's dismissal, held that the club's unreasonable delay in submitting the claim to arbitration as required by the contract (negotiated via collective bargaining by the NFL Players Association) operated as a waiver of arbitration rights as to allow suit in state court on the claim.

2. In *Tillman* v. *New Orleans Saints Football Club,* 265 So.2d 284 (La. Ct. App. 1972), plaintiff football player was signed by the club under a standard form contract, which stated that if the player was injured the contract would remain in full force. However, it further stipulated that when a player is physically able to perform services under the contract, the club shall have the right to activate the player and require him to perform. Plaintiff suffered a knee injury and was operated on by the team physician. Some weeks later, on October 24, 1967, plaintiff was declared fit to play by the physician despite some residual disability. Plaintiff was activated, then released by the club, with the club alleging it was relieved of any further contractual obligations. One month later plaintiff obtained another physician's opinion, declaring plaintiff unfit to play. The plaintiff then

claimed that defendant had to allow a third opinion from an independent source. However, defendant contended that plaintiff failed to meet the 72-hour limit allowed to gain a second opinion after the team physician's ruling. The court allowed defendant's contention, pointing to language of the contract providing for these time limits. Plaintiff was denied recovery.

4.32–2 Special Contract Provisions

The injury provisions in the standard player contracts and the grievance procedures in the collective bargaining agreements are not perfectly drafted clauses. At times, players appear to fall "between the cracks" of the provisions. The stakes are high, since often involved is whether the club must pay the player's salary after release of the player. In the two opinions below, Bill Stanfill wins and Charlie Hennigan loses. Stanfill succeeds, but only after his grievance is shifted to a noninjury classification. In Charlie Hennigan's case, the reasoning by the court suggests that the player's representative must be watchful that the client's rights do not fall in an area where no protection is afforded.

In the Matter of Arbitration Between NFL Players Association (William Stanfill) and NFL Management Council (Miami Dolphins), Scearce, Arbitrator, October 31, 1977

Stanfill suffered a severe head injury in an exhibition game on August 9, 1975. He was hospitalized, placed in traction, and experienced temporary paralysis in his upper body. After a program of rehabilitation, he played during the 1975 season. Another neck injury in July 1976 required hospitalization and sleeping in traction. Still, he played for the club in 1976.

With Coach Shula's approval, Stanfill sought another medical opinion in January 1977. An independent doctor suggested that his life would be in danger if he continued to play football. The club doctor determined that Stanfill was fit to play. Stanfill filed a grievance. The Player-Club Relations Committee permitted him to seek another independent medical opinion. This opinion suggested that possible death or permanent injury would result if he played football. With Shula's permission he left camp. The club then terminated his salary payments.

The association argued that the Dolphins should not be able to disregard the findings of independent medical experts. The Dolphins have customarily used outside medical consultation. Stanfill was injured playing for the club. He was too injured to play and thus entitled to his salary for 1977 and 1978.

Scearce agreed with the club's observation that Stanfill's grievance could not be raised as an injury grievance since he had not been cut (Article IX) and had not failed the physical (Article X). He found, however, that the dispute was properly raised under Article VII as a noninjury grievance. While Stanfill's physical condition was relevant, the central issue was whether the club owed him compensation. The dispute involved the interpretation of a provision added to Stanfill's standard player contract: "It is the intention of the parties that the payments provided by the contract are guaranteed only against Player *being cut* from the team for lack of skill or an injury incurred while playing football for the club."

A literal interpretation of the provision would leave a player like Stanfill in limbo — unable to play due to an injury but not compensated if the club chose not to cut him. In Scearce's view, Stanfill suffered an injury while playing for the club and should have been protected against being cut for that reason. Although the club physician found him fit to play, the contrary evaluations and assessments of independent experts were germane and should not have been ignored.

Scearce was not persuaded that the independent opinions were conclusive, but he worked out a "compromise" award in Stanfill's favor. He directed that Stanfill not be required to play football but be required to perform reasonable "activities related to football" referred to in section 2 of the standard player contract. Stanfill was to receive the compensation he had signed for, continue therapy and rehabilitation, and decide on his own whether he was able to play.

Scearce retained jurisdiction over the case, directing the club to compensate Stanfill for salary owed when he left camp unless it was established that Shula had not given his permission.

Scearce also limited the precedential value of his decision to the parameters of this grievance.

Hennigan v. Chargers Football Co., 431 F.2d 308 (5th Cir. 1970)

Charles T. Hennigan, a professional football player, brought an action to recover salary allegedly due him under the injury clause of his contract with defendant, the San Diego Chargers. The district court awarded summary relief to plaintiff, from which judgment defendant brought an appeal.

The facts of the case were not in dispute. On March 19, 1964, Hennigan signed an AFL Standard Players Contract for three years with the Houston Oilers, Inc. The contract included among its provisions an "injury" clause, guaranteeing the player his salary if injured while performing services under the contract; a "no-cut" clause, by which the Oilers agreed not to terminate the contract before May 1, 1967, on certain conditions; and a "renewal" clause, by which the Oilers had the option of renewing the contract for a period of one year provided certain conditions were satisfied.

Hennigan performed fully his obligations to play professional football for the Oilers under the contract for three seasons. He sustained injuries to his right knee during both the 1965 and 1966 seasons. In March 1967, the Oilers exercised its right of assignment under the contract and assigned Hennigan's contract to the defendant, whereupon defendant exercised the "renewal" option by giving notice to plaintiff.

When Hennigan reported for training in July 1967, the defendant's team physician determined that his knee condition rendered him incapable of playing, and defendant therefore terminated the contract under the termination clause in the contract. Plaintiff performed no services for the defendant during the 1967 season as a result, and he brought suit for the salary which he claimed was owed him on the alternative grounds of the "injury" clause and the "no-cut" clause. The trial court ruled that the defendant was bound by both of these clauses and therefore awarded summary relief to the plaintiff.

Reversing the trial court's decision, the appellate court concluded that summary judgment was proper in the case but that such relief should have gone to the defendant, not to the plaintiff. In the court's view, the injury clause in the original contract set forth a condition precedent which had to occur before the Oilers or their assignees were obligated to pay the salary under the clause. Since the plaintiff's injury in this instance had occurred prior to the exercise of the renewal option by defendant, the central question was whether the renewal contract was an extension of the original contract, as contended by plaintiff, or a new contract, as contended by defendant: "This case, ultimately, turns upon the meaning that should be ascribed to the term 'renewal' and its variations as they appear in the AFL Contract signed by Hennigan with the Houston Oilers in 1964."

The issue thus categorized as a problem of interpretation and construction of the contract, the court went about a detailed analysis of the meaning of "renewal" as used by the parties. Said the court:

> Our analysis of the AFL Contract leads us to the conclusion that, when the Chargers exercised the "renewal" option granted the Club by paragraph 10, in essence a new contract was established to set the rights and obligations of the Club and the player during its "further term" as distinguished from the previous term during which the player rendered services.

The court concluded:

> From our conclusion that the exercise of its option on Hennigan's services by the Chargers had the effect of making a new contract with the player for a term of one year, it follows that Hennigan was not entitled to compensation for the 1967 football

season from the Chargers. He suffered no injury while in performance of any services required of him after the option was exercised. Consequently, he is not entitled to payment [under the injury clause]. He was terminated for his inability to pass the physical examination. Because . . . this inability was not excused by [the injury clause] his disabling injury not having occurred during the option year, the "no-cut" clause did not protect Hennigan from termination, and the proviso in this clause was inapplicable. Moreover, the "no-cut" clause, by its terms, expired on May 1, 1967. Therefore, summary judgment should have been granted in favor of the Chargers.

One judge dissented from the court's decision on the grounds that (1) the majority's interpretation of the meaning of the terms "renew" and "extend" was supportive of the trial court's view rather than contradictory, and (2) that even if the premise in (1) was not accepted, then the contract was at least ambiguous and it was therefore improper to overturn the trial court's construction: "As I read the words of the document, the continuation of the contract by the exercise of this option continued the injury clause in the same manner that it continued the restriction on Hennigan's activities."

NOTES _____

1. In *Houston Oilers* v. *Floyd,* 518 S.W.2d 836 (Tex. Civ. App. 1975), the player in question purported to sign a general release of all claims against the club. However, the court construed the release in a narrow fashion, saying it was not a release as to the club's contract obligations.

2. In *Schultz* v. *Los Angeles Dons,* 238 P.2d 73 (Cal. Ct. App. 1951), plaintiff, a professional football player, was twice examined by defendant's trainer and physician, was declared fit to play, and signed a contract. During training he complained of numbness and was determined to be suffering a herniated disc. Defendant claimed plaintiff was not in proper physical condition as called for by the contract. The court ruled the club had all the information necessary to determine the plaintiff's physical condition, chose to sign him to a contract, and therefore had to pay plaintiff the rest of his salary.

4.32–3 Determination of Injury

In injury-related grievances, the most difficult issue is the one on the merits: Was the player handicapped by a sports-induced injury when released? The several following opinions only begin to explore the many dimensions of this perplexing inquiry. The factual investigations are complex and troublesome.

In the Matter of Arbitration Between NFL Players Association (Eric Harris) and NFL Management Council (St. Louis Cardinals and New Orleans Saints), Smith, Arbitrator, 1972

This dispute involved interpretation of the intent and meaning of Article XI (Injury Grievance Procedure) of the Collective Bargaining Agreement.

Harris signed three, one-year contracts with the St. Louis Cardinals in 1970. During training for the 1971 season, Harris pulled his left hamstring muscle. After some rehabilitation, he reinjured the same leg. The team physician examined Harris on August 29, 1971, and advised him not to run for some time. Dr. Reynolds next saw Harris on September 11. He testified that Harris was about healed at that time and almost ready to return to practice. On September 14, Harris was "cut" by being placed on waivers. He again sought an opinion from Dr. Reynolds, who said that Harris was able to practice and might be able to play in about two weeks. His contract was awarded to the New Orleans Saints. The Saints terminated his contract after Harris failed to pass their physical due to the hamstring injury.

On November 2, 1971, a neutral physician concluded that Harris had essentially recovered from his injury. Harris sought payment of his $20,000 salary from the Cardinals, the Saints, or both. He claimed that Article XI imposes such an obligation on the Club which terminated his services when he was physically incapable of playing professional football as the result of a football injury.

The Cardinals disclaimed liability on several grounds. They claimed the right to cut or waive a player because of his inability to compete for a spot on the team, even if he happens to be injured at the time. They argued that Harris was physically capable within the meaning of Article XI and, alternatively, that Harris became physically capable two weeks subsequent to his termination, limiting their liability to pay for two games.

The Saints disclaimed any liability because of their unqualified right to terminate the contract of a player who fails a team's physical examination.

The arbitrator recognized an important but unanswerable question in this case — would Harris have made the team if he had not been injured? In the arbitrator's view, Article XI gives a player a right to damages if he is terminated by a club when he is suffering a football injury disability which may reasonably be held to have been a factor contributing to the decision to terminate him. In the absence of a showing by the club of grounds for termination wholly independent of the injury or its consequences (i.e., effect on the player's ability), Article XI provides a type of contract insurance for an injured football player, even during training camp.

The arbitrator chose not to distinguish between "cutting" or "waiving" and terminating a player. He held that primary responsibility for any liability rests on the club which first cut or terminated the injured player. It was further held that the measure of damages under Article XI is the player's monetary loss subject to his duty of mitigation. However, an arbitrator can exercise broad discretion in fixing a limit to the amount of relief awarded.

The arbitrator found no evidence on the record to support the Cardinals' claim that Harris was cut for reasons independent of his injury. He concluded that Harris was entitled to damages under Article XI, since he was unable to play under game conditions due to his injury at the time he was "cut." Though avoiding a determination of which team terminated Harris's contract, the arbitrator ordered the Cardinals to pay the award. He awarded Harris only one-half of his contract salary ($10,000), because it was not clear that Harris would have "made the team" had he not suffered the injury.

In the Matter of Arbitration Between NFL Players Association (Keith Lewis and Ezekial Moore) and NFL Management Council (Houston Oilers), Smith, Arbitrator, August 30, 1982

Arbitrator Russell A. Smith agreed to reconsider the relevance of the "skill defense" in this separate decision, reserving for further determination the merits of the other claims in the *Lewis* and *Moore* arbitrations. The skill defense, as applied in *Satterwhite* v. *Baltimore Colts* (February 4, 1981), permitted a club to assert that a player who was physically unable to perform nonetheless lacked the requisite skill for the position and could be released without the club's incurring any liability for his salary. The NFL Players Association had argued in *Satterwhite* that this kind of defense was irrelevant, but the arbitrator, relying on his past decision in *Harris* v. *St. Louis Cardinals and New Orleans Saints,* in which the skill defense was considered, concluded that the issue was settled. He agreed, however, to reconsider the matter upon a full review of pertinent collective bargaining history.

The NFL Players Association began its presentation of the collective bargaining history by pointing out that the substantive basis which grants injury protection has always been contained in the standard contract. Therefore, the relevant bargaining history focuses on the negotiating of the injury clause into the standard contract and the extent to which it has been modified by subsequent collective bargaining.

Creighton Miller, the lawyer who organized the NFL Players Association, testified in a deposition that the insertion of an injury protection clause in the standard player contract was one of the first priorities for the NFL in 1956. Despite strenuous opposition from management, the injury protection clause (then paragraph 15) was inserted in the player contract. It included an explicit recognition that the failure of a player to perform services because of an injury in the performance of services under the contract constituted an exception to the right of a club to terminate a player's salary or contract.

In the 1968 collective bargaining negotiating session, among the proposals suggested were revisions of the injury protection clause to remove the commissioner from any role in choosing the neutral physician. During these negotiations, there was no mention by management of any skill defense, and likewise, management never contended in any injury grievances that the club was exempt from liability because the player was not good enough to make the team.

In 1970, the negotiations centered on the grievance procedures and certain defenses that the clubs could assert. Ed Garvey testified that the association at this time contended that the clubs would continue to be strictly liable and that the council never suggested applying a skill defense. In 1977, negotiations concerned the extent of injury protections in contract years after the injury. The association again contended that during this period, management admitted that the clubs had strict liability for players who were injured.

For its part, the NFL Management Council agreed that the past decision in *Harris* was correct. *Harris* expounded the principle that for a player to recover under an injury claim, the injury had to be a "contributing factor" in the determination of the player's skill and capabilities at the time of termination. The council presented evidence that in 1970, the parties first provided four special itemized defenses to the injury claim in the collective bargaining agreement. In addition, it was clearly stated that the club could also raise other, "nonitemized" defenses. With no evidence that the parties intended otherwise, the arbitrator Smith in *Harris* determined that the skill defense was indeed available to a club. After *Harris* was decided in 1972, the association had the opportunity to argue that the arbitrator was wrong in *Harris* or to bargain a provision in the new collective bargaining agreement to make it clear that the defense in *Harris* was no longer available; the association, however, failed to do so. The council contended that this behavior demonstrated that the parties did not intend to make the "noncontributing factor" injury defense no longer available.

The arbitrator phrased the issue as whether the collective bargaining history indicated that the parties, in negotiating the 1970 agreement, intended that the skill defense was not to be available and hence the interpretive principle in *Harris* was clearly wrong. The arbitrator found that in neither of the negotiations of the 1970 or 1977 agreements was the specific question of the availability of the skill defense discussed.

Despite the inclusion in the 1970 agreement of the provision permitting other defenses to be raised, the parties implicitly agreed or understood that the skill defense was not to be available. The inclusion of this defense would surely have been raised in the negotiations, but instead, the parties concentrated on matters relating to the injury itself, such as nonfootball injuries.

While the arbitrator stated that the association's failure to raise the skill defense issue during the 1977 negotiation was difficult to understand in light of *Harris* and other decisions containing the interpretive principle which had been handed down, he concluded that this failure did not require the conclusion that it had become available.

In summary, the arbitrator held that prior to the period of negotiations for the 1970 agreement, the injury clause was an exception to the club's general right of termination of a player for lack of skill or failure to stay in excellent physical condition. This entitled a player who became disabled from playing because of a football-related injury to continue to receive a salary.

In the Matter of Arbitration Between NFL Players Association (Steven Manstedt) and NFL Management Council (New Orleans Saints), Fisher, Arbitrator, 1978

While playing for the New Orleans Saints during a preseason game in 1977, Manstedt suffered a neck injury. He underwent treatment by the team trainer until November 14, when his contract was terminated.

Following his injury, Manstedt was examined by Dr. J. Kenneth Saer, the team physician, who prescribed medication and the use of a cervical collar. Thereafter, Manstedt underwent daily treatments under the supervision of the team trainer. He was placed on the injured reserve list on August 9. The cervical collar was discontinued on August 21. Manstedt was last examined by Dr. Saer on September 28, 1977, at which time Dr. Saer concluded that Manstedt was capable of playing football. However, Dr. John J. Wentzberger, a neutral physican, found that Manstedt's neck had a restriction in extension and lateral bend to both sides and that all ranges of motion caused some discomfort in the posterior neck region. Manstedt continued to take treatments until he was cut by the team on November 14. No physical examination was given at the time of Manstedt's release in November.

Patrick J. Fisher, impartial arbitrator, found that Manstedt was physically incapable of the service required of him by his player's contract and, hence, entitled to the balance due on his contract. Fisher found that Dr. Wentzberger's findings were not inconsistent with those of the team physician. Though there were no objective physical findings demonstrating that Manstedt was unable to play professional football, an injury to the soft tissue is not as obvious as a broken bone, nor as discernible on x-rays. During his September 28 examination, Dr. Saer noted that there was a 50 percent restriction in the movement of Manstedt's neck. Because no examination was made at the time of his release, no presumption can be made that his condition improved. In addition, Fisher noted as odd that although on September 28 Manstedt was capable of playing professional football, the treatments for his neck were continued for seven additional weeks.

In the Matter of Arbitration Between National Basketball Association (Atlanta Hawks) and National Basketball Players Association (Michael Sojourner), Seitz, Arbitrator, June 14, 1978

At issue was (1) whether the Atlanta Hawks had the right to suspend Sojourner and withhold his compensation on the grounds that he had injured his knee during an out-of-season "game or exhibition" of basketball, which is prohibited under paragraph 17 of the Uniform Player Contract; and (2) whether the Hawks had the right to maintain Sojourner's suspension because of his mental and emotional condition.

Sojourner broke his kneecap executing a slam-dunk while practicing informally at the University of Utah in August 1977. Seitz rejected Atlanta's claim that Sojourner had violated paragraph 17. There was no evidence that slam-dunking is a "dangerous activity." The practice occurs during regular pro-basketball games. The injury did not occur while Sojourner was playing for another team or in an exhibition game. Acceptance of Atlanta's argument would subject any player who practices basketball between seasons to grave risks. In fact, paragraph 5 requires players to maintain their physical condition and basketball skills in the off-season.

Under a Standard Uniform Player Contract, Atlanta might have avoided an obligation to pay Sojourner his salary because his physical disability did not occur while "playing for the Club." Sojourner's contract, however, had been amended to guarantee him salary payments as long as a physical disability was due to a "basketball related" injury. The arbitrator found that Sojourner's injury met that condition.

The club sent written notice to Sojourner on November 3, 1977, stating he was suspended because he had injured his knee in an unauthorized game. Atlanta claimed that it made no mention of Sojourner's psychotic condition out of concern for his mental health. At the hearing, Atlanta argued that Sojourner's condition could justify its decision to suspend him. The arbitrator did not agree. He indicated that a player deserves written notice of his suspension, detailing the grounds, as a matter of fundamental fairness: "A player has a right to look to the reasons articulated by the Club for his suspension and should not be bound by subjective motivations unexpressed."

Dr. Apple had determined on January 12, 1978, that Sojourner was physically ready to resume conditioning. Thus, Seitz ordered Atlanta to pay Sojourner his contract compensation for the 1977–78 season up to January 12, 1978.

In three separate episodes, Sojourner had required hospitalization and medication for psychotic schizophrenia. Although there was evidence that Sojourner's condition was remitting, Seitz found that his mental and emotional state warranted the withholding of his salary from January 13, 1978, to the end of the 1977–78 season. If permitted to play, Sojourner might have done damage to himself and others. Also, his mental and emotional illness was not due to playing basketball.

Seitz refused to rule on the contractual obligations of the parties for the 1978–79 and 1979–80 seasons, the two remaining years in Sojourner's contract, until psychiatric examinations could be held shortly before the 1978–79 season. The interlocutory award that resulted from this arbitration can be summarized as follows:

1. Sojourner, who had been placed on Atlanta's suspended list without cause, was removed from that list.
2. Atlanta was ordered to pay Sojourner his contract salary for the 1977–78 season up to January 13, 1978.
3. Compensation for the rest of the 1977–78 season was not awarded.
4. Re the 1978–79 and 1979–80 seasons: (a) Atlanta was entitled to conduct psychiatric examinations of Sojourner in advance of the 1978–79 season; (b) Sojourner was to be subjected to psychiatric and medical examinations during training camp; (c) On application of

either party, Seitz was to preside over an adjourned hearing for a determination of 1978–79 contract obligations.

In the Matter of Arbitration Between National Basketball Association (Seattle Supersonics) and National Basketball Players Association (Gerald Edwards), Seitz, Arbitrator, May 9, 1978

At issue was whether the Supersonics violated the player contract or the collective bargaining agreement when they terminated Edwards's contract shortly after he received an injury in training camp.

Edwards had failed to appear at the original arbitration hearing scheduled for June 1, 1976. Seitz denied the club's applications to dismiss the case because of Edwards's "default." He used his discretion to accommodate Edwards as he has accommodated NBA clubs with delayed hearings in the past.

Edwards claimed that the injury to his Achilles' tendon prevented him from properly demonstrating his basketball skills, which would have enabled him to be retained. Paragraph 20(c) of the Uniform Player Contract entitles a player whose contract is terminated because of an injury sustained in the course of employment to full salary for the season, less worker compensation and club insurance benefits.

The club argued that Edwards's contract was legally terminated under paragraph 20(b)(2), which provides for termination if the player shall "at any time fail, in the *sole opinion* of the Club's management to exhibit sufficient skill or competitive ability to qualify to continue as a member of the Club's team . . ."

Seitz's decision was influenced by factual considerations. Edwards, a rookie, was not a veteran player whose basketball skills were well recognized and established in the NBA. He returned to training exercises five days after the injury and never complained to the coaches that his ankle hindered his performance. Also, head coach Russell testified that his evaluation of Edwards ("not good enough for the NBA") was

based on observations before and after the injury.

Judgment as to the level of skill and ability of players is accorded to the club management. The impartial arbitrator cannot interfere with that judgment unless it is demonstrated that the decision to terminate a contract "was clearly without rational basis, was invidiously discriminatory, or that the termination was motivated by some other wrongful or improper design or pretext." The evidence failed to show that Edwards' injury was the basis for the termination of his contract. The club's actions appeared to have been in good faith and based on good reasons, in their "sole opinion."

Edwards also argued that the club's failure to give him written notice barred his termination without pay. Seitz refused to take such a technical view; Edwards knew he was cut and why. Seitz did warn, however, that the absence of written notice of termination might (1) affect a party's ability to sustain burden of proof, (2) bring the good faith of a party into question, and (3) raise a problem of fairness of procedure.

Nevertheless, Edwards's grievance was denied.

In the Matter of Arbitration Between National Basketball Association (New Orleans Jazz) and National Basketball Players Association (Toby Kimball), Seitz, Arbitrator

Part I: March 3, 1975

At issue was whether the club acted within its legal rights in terminating Kimball's Uniform Player Contract. The association charged that the club was obliged to pay Kimball his salary, since it had terminated his contract while he was disabled due to an injury suffered in the course of a regular season game.

Kimball had an arthritic condition in his right knee but had played for eight seasons in the NBA prior to the 1974–75 season. He had an arthrotomy and a medial meniscectomy in 1967. Since 1968, Kimball had been examined and evaluated yearly by Dr. Bauer of the San Diego Rockets.

During the third game of the season, Kimball experienced a sharp pang in his knee, which became progressively more painful. The club physician, Dr. Saer, noted no significant new injury and claimed that he believed Kimball would have been able to play after a week or two. Dissatisfied with Dr. Saer's evaluation, Kimball received permission and expenses to visit Dr. Bauer in San Diego. On October 24, Dr. Bauer concluded that something other than arthritic degeneration had caused Kimball's knee to lock. By phone he recommended to the club's general manager of operations, Phil Bertka, that Kimball be placed on the injured list.

Bertka authorized Bauer to send a telegram to the deputy commissioner placing Kimball on the injured list. Dr. Bauer sent a report to Dr. Saer suggesting that Kimball would probably not be able to play for any extended period of time that season due to his injury. Four days later, on November 8, 1974, without any further examination of Kimball's condition and without notice to Kimball, the club removed him from the injured list. On November 12, they placed him on waivers and subsequently terminated his contract.

The club maintained that Kimball had not been waived because of his disability, that the disability had not resulted from an injury suffered in the course and scope of his employment but was a degenerative condition, and that the club could terminate a player's contract before December 2 without the obligation to pay compensation due according to paragraph 20(b)(2) of the Uniform Player Contract. There were evidentiary problems because Dr. Saer was not available for questioning, but Seitz was persuaded that the club sought to avoid its monetary obligations to Kimball by removing him from the injured list and terminating his contract before December 2. He found that Kimball's locked knee was the immediate and direct consequence of "something" that happened during the game in question and thus

during the course of Kimball's employment. He agreed with the association's argument that the club was obliged to pay Kimball's full salary for the season as outlined in sec. 20(c) and sec. 6 of the Uniform Player Contract.

The club also argued that compensation under sec. 20(c) was dependent upon the sole judgment of the club's physician concerning a player's condition. Seitz concluded, however, that Dr. Bauer was, in effect, substituted for Dr. Saer in this instance as the club's designated physician. The club had paid for Kimball's travel expenses to San Diego and had authorized Dr. Bauer to place Kimball on the injured list. Seitz sustained Kimball's grievance and ordered the club to pay any compensation due him for the 1974–75 season.

At the outset of the hearing, the club objected that the hearing should be conducted before three impartial arbitrators as set out in the Collective Bargaining Agreement. Seitz observed that all prior arbitrations had been held by him alone. He decided that the club should have made its request earlier and denied the club's request to convene a tripartite arbitration panel.

Part II: June 23, 1975 (Before J. Fine, Supreme Court, New York County)

The petitioners' motion to confirm their award in arbitration was denied. Respondents cross-motion to vacate the award was granted on the grounds that the arbitrator, Peter Seitz, had acted improperly when he denied the club's request to be heard before a tripartite panel rather than before Seitz alone.

The club had not waived its right, as outlined in Article XVI, section 1(b) of the NBA collective bargaining agreement, to be heard by a panel of three arbitrators: "The fact that in prior arbitrations such procedure was followed [Seitz alone] did not deprive them of the right to have the arbitration proceed pursuant to the Contract."

Part III: July 21, 1975 (Seitz, Arbitrator)

Subsequent to the court order which required a

new hearing before a tripartite arbitration panel, the New Orleans club moved to have Peter Seitz remove himself from that panel. Seitz denied the motion, finding no sufficient reason why he should disqualify himself.

Seitz found that the club had no standing to challenge his qualifications. He was designated chairman of the arbitration panel by the parties who signed the Collective Bargaining Agreement, the NBA, and the Players Association. While the club was a member of the NBA, it was not a signatory to the Collective Bargaining Agreement. In his view, only a party who had signed the agreement could seek to remove him on grounds of prejudice. Allowing a club to determine who shall or shall not arbitrate would constitute a disruptive and disturbing precedent in the arbitration of labor disputes.

The club argued that a footnote in the Kimball award of March 3, 1975 (see Part I), since vacated, demonstrated Seitz's animosity and prejudice toward their attorney, Mr. Beychok. Beychok had filed his brief three days after Seitz's deadline. The footnote called attention to the delayed filing of the brief because of the growing usage of submitting tardy briefs. Seitz also wanted to assure the club that its brief had been fully considered anyway. He found this argument groundless and unreasonable.

Beychok cited other incidents as "evidence" of Seitz's prejudice against the club: Seitz sent copies of his original decision to the Players Association and the NBA but not the club; Seitz sent only a courtesy copy of the mailgram announcing the date of the hearing before the tripartite panel to Beychok; and Seitz did not respond to Beychok's letter of March 10.

Seitz's actions were based on an understanding he had reached with counsels for the NBA and the Players Association. Since they represented the principal parties in the dispute because they were the parties who signed the collective agreement, Seitz communicated with them and expected the association counsel to contact Kimball and the NBA counsel to contact the club through Beychok. Seitz also felt that correspondence with the club after his decision

had been issued on March 3 would have been inappropriate.

Part IV: October 23, 1975 (Arbitration Panel, Seitz, Chair)

Pursuant to the federal court order vacating Kimball's March 3, 1975, award (see Part II), his grievance was heard by a panel of three arbitrators on September 17, 1975.

Seitz was careful to preface his opinion with the declaration that the conclusions and findings of the panel were based solely on the record made before it. His reasoning, analysis, and conclusions were identical to the original opinion. The panel sustained Kimball's grievance.

By their actions, the club had designated Kimball's physician, Dr. Bauer, the club physician for the purposes of sec. 6 and sec. 20 of the Uniform Player Contract. Kimball was unable to play because of an injury sustained while playing for New Orleans. With the club's authorization, Dr. Bauer placed Kimball on the injured list. Although Kimball was still disabled, the club waived him and then terminated his contract.

The panel ordered the club to pay Kimball the unpaid balance of the compensation due to him for the 1974–75 season.

4.32–4 Worker's Compensation

Sports injuries, since they are employment-related, are subject to worker's compensation laws. These rules and regulations vary dramatically state by state. No treatment of the issues can be exhaustive unless presented as a separate study. But some indications of how worker's compensation rights are tied to individual contract rights should be examined.

Ellis v. Rocky Mountain Empire Sports, Inc., 602 P.2d 895 (Colo. Ct. App., 1979)

An action was brought by the plaintiff, a former professional football player, against his team, head coach, team physician, and orthopedic clinic, alleging that he was required to engage in contact football drills before he had fully recovered from an off-season injury. The district court granted the team and coach's motions for summary judgment, holding (1) that Ellis's claim was barred by his failure to comply with mandatory contract arbitration requirements; and (2) that Ellis's exclusive remedy for his negligence and intentional tort claims was under the Workmen's Compensation Act, sec. 8–41–105, C.R.S., 1973. Ellis appealed the summary judgment.

Ellis injured his knee while playing basketball during the off-season in April of 1975. After being traded to the Denver Broncos in May of 1975, Ellis underwent knee sugery, and he began a rehabilitation program under the guidance of the Bronco organization. On August 1, 1975, Ellis reinjured his knee in a contact practice drill with the other players. He was unable to play during the 1975 season, and after failing the Bronco physical in the spring of 1976, Ellis was placed on waivers.

Ellis alleged that Bronco coach Ralston and the Broncos required him to engage in football drills before he had fully recovered, and that this activity caused further damage to his knee, as a result of which he was entitled to compensatory and exemplary damages. Ellis also claimed that he was owed additional money under contracts for the 1975 and 1976 football seasons.

The Colorado Court of Appeals, in affirming the district court, held that the arbitration clause in the Standard Player Contract was enforceable against Ellis. While Ellis argued that enforcement of the arbitration clause would be unconscionable, the court of appeals noted that, as in the instant case, arbitration clauses which were arrived at through collective bargaining are favored in Colorado. Further, the court observed that there was not a serious disparity of bargaining power between the Players Association and the NFL.

Ellis also argued that the arbitration clause should not be enforced because it would be inequitable to allow Commissioner Rozelle, who is selected by and serves at the pleasure of the club owners, to be the arbitrator. But the court of appeals, in concurring with the lower court, ruled that Ellis had the option to use one of the other arbitrators as provided in the 1977 Collective Bargaining Agreement, which was retroactive to 1974.

The court of appeals also agreed with the district court by holding that Ellis's sole remedy was in worker's compensation. Ellis sought to avoid this result by contending that the Broncos and Ralston had committed the intentional torts of intentional infliction of emotional distress and outrageous conduct, and that intentional torts were not covered by the Workmen's Compensation Act. But the court held that intentional torts are covered under the acts, and compensation awards may be made for injuries suffered from intentional acts of co-employees.

Sielicki v. New York Yankees, 388 So.2d 25 (Fla.Dist.Ct. App. 1980)

John Sielicki, a pitcher for the New York Yankees baseball club, appealed an order which denied his worker's compensation claim. The lower court held that Sielicki failed to show his disability resulted from an accident on April 7, 1978, the last day he played for the Yankees. The district court of appeal reversed and remanded the proceeding.

Sielicki underwent surgery on his left elbow in 1974 for an injury suffered while pitching for the San Francisco Giants. Between the time of the surgery and April of 1978, Sielicki experienced some tendonitis in his left arm, although he had no elbow problems. Sielicki pitched three innings in an exhibition game for the Yankees on April 7, 1978. While he experienced no pain during the game, Sielicki felt tightness in his left elbow and muscle spasms the following morning. Shortly thereafter, a Yankee vice-president called Sielicki into his office and unconditionally released him.

The Yankees argued, and the lower court agreed, that Sielicki was not entitled to worker's compensation because no unusual, unexpected damage occurred suddenly to Sielicki. But the district court of appeal held that such proof of an accident is not necessary to uphold Sielicki's claim. Citing *Festa* v. *Teleflex, Inc.*, 382 So. 2d 122 (Fla. 1st. DCA 1980), the court ruled that injuries resulting from repeated trauma were compensable. In order to prove repeated trauma, a claimant must show prolonged exposure the cumulative effect of which is injury or aggravation of a preexisting condition, and exposure to a hazard greater than that to which the general public is exposed. The court held that Sielicki, upon the strength of his expert's testimony, had proven his injury was the result of repeated trauma. Accordingly, the court of appeal reversed and remanded for further proceedings.

Harrington v. New Orleans Saints Football, 311 So. 2d 555 (La.Ct.App. 1975)

Harrington, a professional football player, brought suit against the New Orleans Saints for total and permanent disability benefits under the Workmen's Compensation Act. The Saints argued that the suit was premature because they had already given him $14,000, which was in excess of any amount that might yet be due him under the Workmen's Compensation Act. Harrington argued that the act provided that such voluntary payments as the Saints had given him should be deducted from the last weekly payments which would be due and that, hence, payments would be currently due him.

The court held that the question whether or not such monies shall be deducted from the first weeks due or the last was irrelevant. Harrington's contract with the Saints provided that "the club shall be entitled to be reimbursed the amounts thereof out of any award of compensation." The court concluded, therefore, that since the amount the club should be reimbursed could not be determined until a worker's compensation award was made, Harrington's suit was not premature.

4.33 Player Is Traded

The assignment of a player's contract is a frequent occurrence in professional sports. Earlier discussions (see Chapter 3, Sections 3.22–4 and 3.36) have examined the individual contract and collective bargaining provisions pertaining to contract assignments. This section examines the complications where a contract provides for special compensation when a player is traded. These provisions appear in many players' contracts and are enforceable if properly drafted.

In the Matter of Arbitration Between NFL Players Association (Henry Childs) and NFL Management Council (New Orleans Saints and Washington Redskins), Kagel, Arbitrator, August 18, 1982

In 1979, Henry Childs signed a series of five, one-year contracts with the NFL's New Orleans Saints. The following provision was an addendum to the NFL Standard Player Contract:

> 24. Special Provisions.
>
> F. In the event that the Player shall be traded or sold by the New Orleans Saints Football Club to a club other than the New Orleans Saints Football Club, the player shall be paid a bonus upon reporting to play for such other Club of $25,000 in consideration for his reporting to play for such football club other than the New Orleans Saints.

In 1981, four of the five original contracts were assigned to the Washington Redskins, and two days later the Redskins traded Childs to the Los Angeles Rams. Childs filed this grievance in September of 1981, asking for a decision ordering either the New Orleans Saints or the Washington Redskins to pay him the $25,000 bonus. The National Football League Players Association filed to amend the grievance to claim an award of costs and fees and punitive damages, alleging the Management Council's actions amounted to a violation of the Collective Bargaining Agreement and was an unjustified denial of the player's rights.

The arbitrator began by absolving the Redskins of responsibility for the bonus because of an express provision contained in the trade agreement. The provision stated: "It is further agreed that the Saints will absolve the Washington Redskins of any responsibility relative to paragraph 24(F) of his 1981 contract."

The arbitrator then addressed the issue that Childs himself had precipitated his trade by threatening to breach his contract and the Saints should therefore be relieved from compliance.

The evidence examined was a series of letters between Child's agent, William Session, and the administrative assistant of the Saints regarding the meaning of Session's statement that Childs would do anything and everything to see that a trade would occur.

The arbitrator found that the club retained its exclusive right to determine whether or when it would trade Childs through the clarification of Session's statement to mean cooperation and through the Saints' assertion in a letter that coach Phillips had no intention of trading him. When coach Phillips made the decision to trade him, he made no attempt to ascertain whether Childs would refuse to play to the best of his ability if he did not receive a change in the agreements.

The Saints next alleged that a $20,000 loan made to Childs was now due and owing, and if it was found that the Saints were obligated to pay the $25,000 bonus, the award should be reduced by the amount of the loan. The arbitrator held that this loan, not filed with the league office, nor a part of the actual contracts, was a private matter and would have to be decided in a different forum. Finally, the NFLPA's amendment was held not to be a part of this arbitration. The arbitrator denied the award of punitive damages, costs, and fees, since nothing in the agreement gave him such authority.

4.34 Player Is Disciplined

Earlier examinations of provisions relating to player discipline (see Chapter 3, Exhibit 3–1 and Section 3.38) have noted the powers of both a league's commissioner and the individual club to take action against a player in the form of a fine, suspension, or even contract termination. The ability to discipline finds its basis in the league's collective bargaining agreement, either as detailed in that document or as ceded as a power to the league or clubs to implement by specified rules.

The alleged offense giving rise to the attempted disciplinary action is often disputed. The procedures by which the action can be challenged must be scrupulously followed.

In the Matter of Arbitration Between NFL Players Association (Dick Cunningham) and NFL Management Council (Philadelphia Eagles), Rozelle, Arbitrator, December 23, 1974

The grievance arose out of a confrontation between player Dick Cunningham and head coach Mike McCormack of the Philadelphia Eagles. Cunningham had been on the inactive list for two weeks and had made plans to be in Buffalo the weekend the Eagles played in San Francisco. He alleged that he needed to take care of personal and business problems. When McCormack informed Cunningham that he would be going to San Francisco, Cunningham responded with "Do I have to go?" A few hours later on the practice field, a heated argument ensued between the two, and as a result, Cunningham was placed on the club's reserve list as suspended.

The arbitrator, Pete Rozelle, held that the confrontation was a fundamental misunderstanding between McCormack and Cunningham, complicated by the outside factors troubling Cunningham and the pressures of a head coach's position. Cunningham's conduct never rose to the level of actual or prospective refusal to fulfill his duties to the Eagles. Rozelle ordered the Eagles to remit the amount of the game salary that Cunningham was deprived of by his suspension.

John Dutton v. Baltimore Colts, Player-Club Relations Committee Decision, April 7, 1978

The Player-Club Relations Committee considered the grievance of *John Dutton* v. *Baltimore Colts* at its March 10, 1978, session in San Francisco, California, and its April 3, 1978, session in Washington, D.C. At the March 10 session, John Dutton appeared with his attorney, Frank DeMarco. Dutton was absent from the 1977 Baltimore Colts' training camp from July 25, 1977, to September 14, 1977, a period of 52 days. The Colts assessed a fine of $26,000 for 52 days of being "absent without permission" at the rate of $500 per day. According to a telegram from the team, the fine was "in accordance with the fine schedule agreed upon between the NFLMC and NFLPA for 1977." The Colts proceeded to withhold amounts from Dutton's salary checks thereafter, with the result that $26,000 was taken from Dutton's checks during the 1977 season.

At the March 10 session, Dutton provided the Committee with copies of what purported to be the Baltimore Colts Fine List for 1977. That document, entitled "Baltimore Colt Fine Schedule — 1977," provided in relevant part as follows:

> In accordance with the Collective Bargaining Agreement, the maximum fine for conduct detrimental to the club is the amount equal to one week's salary and/or suspension without pay for a definite time period.
>
> The club also considers to be conduct detrimental to the club offenses including but not limited to the following for which fines will be levied in the listed amounts: . . .
>
> $400.00 per day — Failure to report or unauthorized leaving of training camp for first days.
>
> $500.00 per day — Continued unauthorized absence from training camp after two days.
>
> $1,000.00 per day — Continued unauthorized absence after six days.

Colts' Vice-President and General Counsel, Michael Chernoff, appeared at the March 10 session. Mr. Chernoff said the Colts were entitled to fine Dutton pursuant to the "Maximum Club Discipline Schedule" agreed to by the NFLPA and the NFLMC pursuant to the March 1, 1977, Collective Bargaining Agreement. That schedule provides: "Unexcused late reporting for or absence from pre-season training camp — maximum fine of $500.00 per day." The Maximum Club Discipline Schedule does not contain any reference to a maximum fine of one week's salary for absence from training camp.

After hearing presentations from both parties at the March 10 session, the Committee concluded that a decision should be held in abeyance until such time as the Baltimore Colts could either confirm or deny that the "Baltimore Colts Fine Schedule" submitted by Dutton at the hearing was in fact used by the Colts in 1977. At the April 3 session in Washington, the Management Council reported that the Colts had confirmed that the "Baltimore Colts Fine Schedule" was given to Dutton in 1977. The Committee then unanimously ruled that the Colts could fine Dutton no more than one week's salary for his absence from training camp in the 1977 preseason because the Colts' fine schedule contained that limitation. The committee concluded, however, that the $26,000 fine would have been proper had the club's fine list not contained the provision concerning the one-week salary limitation.

The Baltimore Colts were ordered to return to John Dutton the amount of $19,582.68. This amount was determined by subtracting one week's salary, or $6,417.32 (1/14 × 90% of Dutton's 1977 salary of $99,825) from the $26,000 previously withheld.

In the Matter of Arbitration Between National Basketball Association (Atlanta Hawks) and National Basketball Players Association (Bill Willoughby), Seitz, Arbitrator, July 15, 1977

Willoughby was drafted directly out of high school by the Atlanta Hawks in 1975. He was one of the subjects of a *TV Guide* article (March 19–25, 1977), concerning the difficult transition from high school to pro basketball. In the article,

Willoughby spoke of his disappointment and disillusionment, stating in part: "The coach continues not to play me for no reason."

Coach Brown notified Willoughby that $500 had been deducted from his paycheck as a fine "for comments made to news media detrimental to team morale." In support of its action, the club relied on provisions of the Uniform Player Contract, which states: "The player agrees to comply with the Club's requirements concerning player conduct and not to do anything detrimental to the best interests of the Club; the Club is allowed to establish reasonable rules for governing its players and to impose reasonable fines upon the player for violations of such rules or for conduct detrimental to the Club's best interests." The rule allegedly violated by Willoughby was communicated orally to the players by Coach Brown at a team meeting on September 21, 1976. He had announced that any player would be fined $500 for speaking publicly in detriment of the coach or the club.

The question for the arbitrator was whether the club had acted lawfully and reasonably in establishing the rule and fining Willoughby.

Seitz observed initially that a rule involving a possible $500 fine should be in writing. While not basing his decision on this point, he noted that the content of rules orally communicated may be difficult to prove in the face of a direct challenge by a live witness.

The club did not identify what portions of the article were objectionable as detrimental to team morale; nor did it indicate how or why the morale of the team was affected. Seitz recognized that public airing of a team's internal difficulties could have a deleterious effect on an NBA franchise, but he could not conclude, without facts on the record, that team morale was impaired by Willoughby's statements.

His decision to overturn the fine and have the club reimburse Willoughby was based primarily on the unreasonably broad scope and uncertain nature of the rule in question and the unreasonably mechanical application of the fine in this instance. Under the rule, a player could be automatically fined $500 for any statement deemed to be detrimental to team morale. The fixed fine has no rational relationship to the nature of the statement, the degree of detriment, the professional personality and career history of the player, or any mitigating circumstances that might have motivated its utterance. Seitz felt that Willoughby's immaturity (youngest player in NBA) and transitional problems should have been considered by the club. Seitz concluded that the rule was unfair and should not be enforced. Even if the rule were sustained, its mechanical application without regard to relevant mitigating circumstances made it unreasonable.

NOTE _____

1. Other instances of attempted disciplinary actions by clubs, the commissioner, or other league officials are examined throughout the book. See, for example, Sections 3.38, 4.72, 5.43 and 6.32.

4.35   Player Wants to Renegotiate

A refrain often heard in professional sports occurs after a player has a good year: He "wants to renegotiate." Suddenly, the player feels underpaid. One cannot dismiss the possibility that this is factually correct, if one gauges salaries on an objective comparative basis. (Of course, at the same time, many other players are overpaid.)

When a player is dissatisfied with his contract and demands a renegotiation, the club's response will often be to wait out the player. It then becomes a question as to which side has the greatest leverage. In a small percent of the situations, one side feels it has some legal basis either to press for a renegotiation or to force a cessation of the demand that this occur. At this point, the dispute leaves the negotiating arena and enters the legal realm.

In the Matter of Arbitration Between National Basketball Association (Chicago Bulls) and National Basketball Players Association (Robert Love), Seitz, Arbitrator, February 6, 1975

The issue for decision before the arbitrator was

whether the Chicago Bulls had an oral understanding to renegotiate its contract with Bob Love. If so, the issue was whether Love became a free agent because of the Bulls' failure to renegotiate in good faith.

Irwin Wiener, Love's agent, alleged that Pat Williams, then general manager of the Bulls, had promised to renegotiate Love's contract at the end of the 1973 season. Williams denied he had promised anything to Wiener beyond meeting with him to discuss Wiener's concerns. Williams testified that he considered it his official duty to be concerned with what his players and their agents wished to convey to him. The record of the case contained only two letters written by Wiener expressing his self-serving statement of what he believed Williams had agreed to, rather than Williams's statement of the objectives or what had occurred. In fact, Williams made no responses to either letter. Williams later left the Bulls but before leaving met with the new general manager, Dick Motta, and told him that there was "trouble on the horizon with Love."

The arbitrator, based on the evidence presented, failed to find that Williams promised to reopen Love's contract. He stated that there was a great danger in holding that Williams's agreement to meet was an agreement to renegotiate. It would mean that any time a club representative sat down with a player's agent to discuss an existing contract, the club would run the risk of being charged with an agreement "in good faith" to modify the contract or substitute a new one. This would severely inhibit any discussions between clubs and players.

In addition to the insufficiency of proof of the promise alleged by Wiener, problems were raised by the law of contracts as to the enforceability of such a promise. Under the Illinois Statute of Frauds (Ill. Rev. Stat., ch. 56, sec. 1), an oral modification of a contract which itself is required to be in writing, is unenforceable. Moreover, there was no sharing of consideration for the alleged promise; Love was not obliged to do anything that he was not already obliged to do under the 1972 five-year contract.

Subsequent events were examined on the theory that they might furnish independent grounds for holding that the club made a promise to renegotiate. Wiener, in September of 1973, asserted to Motta that Motta was under an obligation to continue the renegotiations begun by Williams, and apparently some salary figures were discussed. However, the arbitrator found this unpersuasive as proof of a promise to engage in renegotiation. In fact, Motta's letter of September 11, 1973, flatly asserted to Love that he would be expected to live up to the terms of the 1972 contract and that Love could not expect to reopen negotiations whenever he changed agents.

The next event was the grievance before Commissioner Kennedy scheduled for October 8, 1973. Shortly before this meeting, Motto invited Love to his home and offered Love terms more advantageous if he did not appear at the hearing. This proposal was more for the purpose of dissuading Love from attending the hearing rather than an endeavor to fulfill any commitment previously made by Williams. As to the hearing before Commissioner Kennedy, all that was agreed to was an understanding that at the end of the season, Motta and Wiener would meet. Wiener was to be given the opportunity to sit down with Motta and express his views regarding why and how the 1972 contract should be amended. It was not an obligation by the Bulls to void the existing contract. When the meeting did occur in September of 1974, no agreement between the parties was reached.

The arbitrator then expressed his view that had Williams or Motta by word of mouth or by letter, in a timely fashion, sharply delineated the terms and conditions under which they would meet with Wiener, and expressed unequivocally their desire to hold Love to his present contract, the case would probably have not come to arbitration. As the arbitrator designated by the parties for all disputes arising under the Collective Bargaining Agreement, he felt under a duty to guide the parties to future conduct in order to avoid the expense, delay and uncertainty caused by arbitration.

Finally, the fines levied by the club on Love for

missed practices, games, and exhibitions were held within the club's authority, but special circumstances that existed led the arbitrator to reduce the amounts. Among the special circumstances were the club's ambiguous and equivocal actions, which led Love to believe over a considerable period of time that he may have had rights, which, in fact, he did not possess.

National Football League Management Council v. John Hannah and Leon Gray, PCRC Decision, September 29, 1977

New England Patriots John Hannah and Leon Gray staged a walkout during the early part of the 1977 season because their demands for an extension of their contracts had not been met. Both men had over two years and an option year remaining on their contracts. According to the agent who represented both players, Howard Slusher, the issue was simply one of money. The NFL Management Council filed a grievance against the two men, citing violations of the Collective Bargaining Agreement. Under the 1977 agreement, the grievance was submitted to the Player-Club Relations committee (PCRC), consisting of two owner representatives and two player representatives. The panel convened just two weeks later to consider the charges that the players (1) violated their contracts, (2) violated the bonus agreements in the contracts, (3) violated the no-strike, no work-stoppage section of the Collective Bargaining Agreement, and (4) violated the section of the agreement which prevented an agent from representing players as a package deal. The following are the findings of the PCRC.

Findings

The Player-Club Relations Committee, established under the Collective Bargaining Agreement between the NFL Management Council and the NFL Players Association, heard testimony in the matter of the *Management Council* v. *Leon Gray and John Hannah* for nearly 7 hours. All facets of the contract negotiations between the Patriots and these players were explored, including the contract prior to the ones now in question. The New England Patriots were represented by counsel, as were the two players. The findings and conclusions were reached unanimously by this committee.

1. The Committee finds that there is a binding, legally enforceable contract between the New England Patriots and Leon Gray and between the New England Patriots and John Hannah. These contracts were entered into freely by the parties. There was no allegation nor is there any finding that the players were induced by fraud to enter into the contracts. This was Gray's third contract and he was represented by an agent as well as a law student; this was Hannah's third contract and he too was represented by an agent. There may well have been oral representations made by representatives of the New England Patriots that were misunderstood by the players, but the Committee does not find any bad faith on the part of the Patriot officials when they negotiated the contracts.

In the case of Leon Gray, he alleges that a Patriot official, when asked what would happen if Leon Gray made the Pro Bowl, suggested that Gray would "be deserving of a new contract." Even if this statement was made, we find that this falls far short of any fraudulent inducement to sign the contract in the belief that if the player worked hard and made the Pro Bowl that he would have a right to cancel his existing contract. Nevertheless, the Committee can sympathize with Mr. Gray, who may well have misunderstood the significance of oral representations at the time of contract signing. It is hoped by this Committee that management and players alike, throughout the League, will learn from this experience. Oral representations are not to be considered part of a contract.

As for Mr. Hannah, he signed his contract in the midst of the 1974 player strike. In fact, the contract was signed one day before the players' union called for a cooling-off period. There was considerable confusion on the part of management, the players, the union and everyone else concerning the 10 percent pre-season pay package. That particular provision became the subject of extensive litigation before the National Labor Relations Board and was a focal point of the 44-day hearing before Judge Schneider. It is understandable that the Patriot management and John Hannah were confused about the future of the 10 percent provision. Nevertheless, the contract of Hannah is clearly set forth and there should not have been sufficient confusion to justify any breach of contract. The uncertainty came about because of union-management contract negotiations, not Patriot-Hannah negotiations.

2. The Committee finds, therefore, that the players are in violation of their Standard Player Contracts by virtue of the fact that they left the team prior to the last pre-season game and have failed to report to the team as of this date.

3. The Committee also finds that the New England Patriots did not have any obligation to renegotiate the existing Standard Player Contracts. Nor did the Patriots have an obligation to negotiate an "extension" of the existing contracts; nevertheless, the Patriots chose to venture into negotiations on an extension. Once having made that decision, they were under the obligation of the Collective Bargaining Agreement to negotiate in good faith.

4. Both Hannah and Gray were represented by the same agent. The Patriots were notified at the same time that both players had hired the same agent; the agent sent virtually identical letters to the Patriots concerning both players, urging negotiations for "extensions" of the existing contracts; contract demands for both players were at times identical and at other times different only because of the varying length of the existing contracts; both decided to leave the New England Patriots on the same day. It would be naivete in the extreme for this Committee to believe that there was anything but coordinated bargaining by the two players through the same agent.

5. Finally, the Committee, having had an opportunity to meet extensively with Leon Gray and John Hannah, could not help but find that both are outstanding young men who believe that a wrong was committed.

Conclusions

1. The Committee believes that for this matter to drag on throughout the season would be a disservice to the fans of the New England Patriots, the two players, the other players of the New England Patriots, as well as management. In some cases finality is as important as anything else. We believe that this is such a case. Therefore, we have adopted the following conclusions:

A. We urge the players Hannah and Gray to return to work immediately.

B. We order the New England Patriots to reinstate the players as soon as the players report to

perform under their existing Standard Player Contracts.

C. Should the players not report by Tuesday, at 5:00 P.M. Eastern Standard Time, October 4, the New England Patriots are ordered to place the players on the retired list under the NFL Constitution and Bylaws, Sec. 17.16, which would mean that they would not be eligible to return to play in the National Football League during the 1977 regular or post-season.

D. Because the parties have demonstrated their good faith in coming to the hearing and cooperating fully with this Committee, and because it is reasonable to believe that all parties may have misunderstood various representations, the Committee denies the New England Patriot claim for a return of the signing or reporting bonus and orders the Patriots not to assess fines the club would otherwise be entitled to assess as a result of the players' actions. The Patriots have no obligation to compensate the players for the period of their absence.

E. We direct the players to negotiate their contracts separately and individually. This Committee cannot dictate, nor can the club, the agent or lawyer chosen to represent the player; nevertheless, the Collective Bargaining Agreement clearly states that a club should not be forced to bargain with more than one player at a time. We feel that the problems in this case have been brought about in large measure because of the decision of the agent to violate Article XXII, Section 9 of the Collective Bargaining Agreement by taking a coordinated bargaining approach in the case of these two players.

F. At the end of the 1977 season all parties shall engage in good faith contract negotiations.

G. The Player-Club Relations Committee directs all parties to cease and desist from further derogatory public comments.

H. The Player-Club Relations Committee will retain jurisdiction over this matter to insure that the directives of this Committee are carried out by the parties.

4.36 Player Needs Additional Monies

Clubs deal with their players in many matters that are not included in the basic contract between club and player. One instance is where the player needs extra monies to meet current pressing expenses. An advance against salary is made by the club — or is it an advance? The parties need to specify in writing the nature and consequences of the tendering of money. A failure to do so is an invitation to a future dispute.

In the Matter of Arbitration Between NFL Players Association (Rickie Harris) and New England Patriots, Rozelle, Arbitrator, December 11, 1973

When the parties failed to settle this noninjury grievance amicably, Harris appealed to NFL Commissioner Pete Rozelle.

Harris, under contract to the Patriots in 1971, wanted a $3,500 loan from the club to put a down payment on a new house. Harris and Upton Bell, general manager, executed a 1972 player contract on January 19, 1972, which stipulated and acknowledged Harris's receipt of a $3,500 advance in salary. The amount of his salary was to be negotiated after the 1971 game films were graded. John Wooten began salary negotiations on behalf of Harris with Bell in April of 1972. They executed a new contract on August 10, 1972, which contained a typed notation: "This contract supersedes the 1972 contract dated January 19, 1972." The August contract contained no specific reference to the $3,500 Harris had previously received from Bell.

Wooten testified that Bell had agreed to let Harris keep all monies previously advanced in return for a lower salary figure. Bell did not recall such an arrangement. The Patriots made systematic deductions from Harris's checks totalling $3,500. Wooten wrote to Bell reiterating their agreement that Harris was supposed to keep the $3,500. He received no response. The club's position, that they would not return the salary deductions, was not communicated to Harris until March 9, 1973, at an off-season Patriot's camp.

Rozelle did not uphold the Management Council's claim that the grievance was untimely filed. The club had lulled Harris into foregoing other recourse by failing to make its position clear until March of 1973.

Rozelle reasoned that the best evidence of the parties' unclear and imprecise intentions was in the written contracts. While the January contract characerized the $3,500 as a salary advance, the August contract made no reference to the $3,500. Most importantly, the parties took care to emphasize that the August contract completely superseded the January agreement. The commissioner viewed the August contract as an expression of the Patriot's intention to cancel the advance that had been specifically incorporated in the January contract.

The club could have included reference to the $3,500 advance in the August contract. The commissioner could not read into Harris's August contract terms favorable to the club that do not appear in the Standard Player Contract itself or any addendum thereto.

Rozelle, accordingly, directed the New England Patriots to remit $3,500 to Rickie Harris.

4.37   Player's Salary Is Reduced

Players' salaries in professional sports seem always to increase. In rare circumstances, though, the player is asked, persuaded, or coerced to take a pay cut. The player may be willing to do so, if not enthusiastically, because his job is on the line. The league's players' association will respond differently. The association does not like the precedent this may set and accordingly grieves the matter.

In the Matter of Arbitration Between National Basketball Association (Detroit Pistons) and National Basketball Players Association (Ben Poquette), Seitz, Arbitrator, July 24, 1978

The National Basketball Players Association filed a grievance claiming that the Pistons had violated paragraph 20(b)(2) of the Uniform Player Contract, which does not permit the termination of a contract solely because of economic or financial considerations. The second issue was whether the grievance was timely filed.

Poquette had signed with the Pistons for

$48,500 for the 1977–1978 season. Near the end of training camp, Detroit conveyed its disappointment with his performance and informed Poquette that he would be placed on waivers unless he agreed to a restructuring of his contract and a reduction of his salary to $35,000.

Paragraph 20(b)(2) allows a club to terminate a player's contract after complying with the waiver procedure if the player fails "to exhibit sufficient skill or competitive ability . . ." The association argued that the retention of Poquette on the roster demonstrated that he possessed sufficient skill and thus that the Pistons could not have properly terminated his contract pursuant to 20(b)(2). Therefore, the association claimed, Detroit's threat to terminate his contract (via waivers) was improper.

Seitz, the arbitrator, appeared to agree that Detroit's motivation was economic in nature. He concluded, however, that the club had not violated paragraph 20(b)(2) since Poquette was not placed on waivers nor was his contract terminated.

Seitz also concluded that the agreed-to salary reduction had not been extracted by illegal duress or coercion Poquette could have called Detroit's "bluff" and challenged the propriety of the club's action under 20(b)(2) if it had placed him on waivers.

Since Seitz denied the grievance, he did not need to reach the issue of timeliness. He did recommend that new rules and procedures be adopted to ensure a more timely filing of grievances for similar cases in the future. The Players Association had not become aware of the revised contract until it was allowed to conduct one of its periodic reviews of contracts filed with the NBA. Such delays could prejudice the interest of the Players Association, the NBA, and clubs.

4.40   Nonstandard Contracts

The preceding two sections (4.20 and 4.30) largely emphasized contract dealings in league

sports. The uniform player contract was the starting point, with collective bargaining mechanisms for dispute resolution through arbitration being of significant importance. Though the focus now shifts away from standard contract considerations, certain common problems are still observable. Even so, the inquiry expands to include other types of deals that professional athletes may contemplate entering.

The first consideration (Section 4.41) concerns the so-called "side deal," entered by the player with one or more of the team owners. A second area (Section 4.42) considers players in individual performer sports. Finally, Section 4.43 sets forth a sample contract form for foreign leagues. The problems that occur in any of these areas go well beyond what can be covered in these sections. The analysis can focus on only a sampling — such as types of contracts and certain legal and business problems that arise.

4.41   Side Deals in League Contracts

We have previously considered many devices that help make a contract more attractive for a player. These have included various bonus provisions, contract guarantees, and increased fringe benefits. At times, however, even those do not match the income that might be generated by getting in on some "outside action." Typically, an owner will suggest that the player might participate in some business venture not directly related to the team. For that reason, it may well be inappropriate to contemplate detailing the terms of this arrangement in the "Special Covenants" part of the Uniform Player Contract. Outside deals may be barred by league rules, but even when allowed, they obviously should be approached with caution. The following guidelines should be followed:

1. The deal should be able to stand on its own merits. It should not be mere sweetener to the standard contract.
2. The negotiation must be at "arm's

length." The fact that a relationship already exists does not lessen the need for basic business caution.

3. Provisions for the resolution of any disputes that might arise should be anticipated in the side agreement, if at all practicable. As the *Bethea* arbitration which follows reveals, the deal probably will be regarded as separate and distinct from the players contract with the club. Thus, whether the arbitration mechanisms provided in the collective agreement can be used is doubtful.

In the Matter of Arbitration Between NFL Players Association (Elvin Bethea) and NFL Management Council (Houston Oilers), Scearce, Arbitrator, April 17, 1978

Bethea, a premier defensive lineman for the Houston Oilers, was paid a total of $111,500 in 1975, including All-AFC and All-Pro bonuses. He commenced negotiations with club owner K. S. Adams in 1976, seeking a three-year contract at $150,000 per season, plus a signing bonus and a paid annuity for his children.

Bethea signed three contracts for 1976, 1977, and 1978 for a base yearly salary of only $110,000. He agreed to the lower salary after head coach Phillips, Assistant General Manager Williams, and Adams encouraged him to participate as a partner in a cattle-feeding operation. The partners in the "Oiler Partnership" were Adams, Phillips, and Bethea. Bethea was to share in 10 percent of the profits or losses. Their discussions produced expectations of profits for Bethea of $20,000 in 1977, $40,000 in 1978, and $60,000 in 1979. Had those profits materialized, Bethea would have received the $450,000 he sought for the three-year period.

The partnership lost money and was dissolved by Adams and Phillips. They offered Bethea a $700 check for "public relations services" to offset his $628 share of the loss. Bethea refused the check and skipped training camp for six to eight days. He was notified of a $500-per-day absence fine. On August 1, 1977, Bethea initiated a noninjury grievance, claiming that the club was liable to him for the $20,000, $40,000, and $60,000 for 1977, 1978, and 1979. He also sought immediate payment of all salary monies previously deferred.

The union argued that Bethea, at the height of his bargaining power in 1976, was induced not to play out his option (1976) and to reduce his salary demands. According to the union, the assurances and representations of Phillips, Williams, and Adams concerning the potential of the cattle-feed operation were guarantees.

The union claimed that Bethea could retract the salary deferral amendments because they were written for his benefit. They also argued that Bethea should not be fined because the club was in breach of contract, via the dissolution of the partnership, at the time of his absence.

Scearce agreed with the club's contention that the "Oiler Partnership" was not a valid subject for consideration under section 1 of Article VII of the Collective Bargaining Agreement. Although the two principal partners were owner/president and general manager/head coach, they were acting as individuals and not as or on behalf of the Houston Oilers. Bethea's mistake was his failure to refer to the partnership in his player contracts. Other circumstances worked against him. The partnership was established over a month before his player contracts and not as a package deal. The agreement did not set forth as a condition that Bethea would have to sign his player contracts. Also, neither the agreement nor conversations contained an express guarantee of returns from the partnership. Thus, Scearce found that the partnership agreement was not part of the NFL Player Contract and the club was not in breach of contract or in violation of Article XIX.

The club did not have to pay deferred monies upon Bethea's request. Whether or not the amendments were for Bethea's benefit, they were mutually agreed to and executed in good faith.

Scearce also agreed with the club and council that the matter of the fines imposed was not a proper subject for arbitration because it was first discussed at the arbitration hearing.

Although he denied the grievances, Scearce made note of the vast difference between Bethea's expectations and the club's obligations. He suggested that the club drop the fines, try to accelerate the payment of deferred monies, and examine, with Bethea, the possibility of reaching a special agreement on the annuity for his children.

4.42 Individual Performer Sports

The sports worlds of tennis, golf, boxing, track, horse and auto racing, and other events that largely have the athlete competing as an individual, rather than on a team in a league, present far different vistas than those that have been considered to this point. The possibilities for exploration of issues are so great, in fact, that no attempt is made in this brief aside other than to suggest a few of the important considerations.

Obviously, the basic contract starting points differ. Gone, for example, is the uniform player contract. Even so, its influences are not missing. After all, in tennis and golf, there are players' associations — perhaps not unions in the full sense as in the league sports but important in terms of giving their blessings to certain activities, including the types of contracts tendered players. Thus, when it comes to tennis and golf tournaments, the Sponsor-Player Contract assumes great uniformity as to many of the terms.

Endorsement contracts are staples in individual performer sports. These are not discussed at this point, except to note their prevalence and importance. But they can comfortably be considered in tandem with league player endorsements (see Section 4.52).

Finally, for many of the individual performer sports, there are clubs or resorts that wish to have a player's name associated with the facility. Any of a number of deals are possible, ranging from straight money payments to other enticements. One of the latter approaches is used in the sample contract that follows.

Dear Mr.
The purpose of this letter is to set forth the understanding between   *   ("Company") and   with respect to the relationship for the promotion of Company's club, ("Club"). The understanding is set forth in the following twelve numbered paragraphs.

1. During the term of this agreement,   agrees that   shall register out of   in all tennis exhibitions and tournaments in which   plays in the states of Maryland, West Virginia, Kentucky, Virginia, North Carolina, Tennessee, South Carolina, Georgia, Alabama and Florida and the District of Columbia.   further agrees that   will make every reasonable effort to publicize and advertise Club during   travels as a professional tennis player.

2. During the term of this agreement, Company may designate   as Club's "Director of Tennis" and may use the name of   in its advertisements and other promotional material, but agrees that it will not use nor permit the use of any such advertisement and/or promotional material without prior approval thereof by   .   agrees that such material submitted to   for approval hereunder at the address set forth in paragraph 9 hereof may be deemed by Club to have been approved by   if the same is not disapproved in writing within ten (10) days after receipt thereof by   .   agrees that   will not unreasonably disapprove any such material submitted to   and will, in the event of any disapproval, advise Company of the specific reasons therefor.

3.   agrees that, at the request of Company,   shall place Club's name and/or logo on such items used by   in connection with the game of tennis as   reasonably deems to be appropriate under the circumstances such as, by way of example, warm-up suits and blazers, it being understood that any such logo or name shall be provided by Company.

4. For the purposes hereof, a "Contract Year" shall mean a fiscal year commencing on any September 1st during the term of this agreement except that the first Contract Year shall commence on the date of acceptance set forth below and conclude   . During each Contract Year,   agrees that   will, at Company's request and

* Blank spaces throughout this sample contract denote information to be filled in by the parties to the agreement.

upon adequate notice, visit Club for at least fourteen (14) days on at least four (4) separate occasions, upon days reasonably convenient to the schedules of both Company and   . Such visits shall be no less than three (3) nor more than four (4) days in duration. Visits made during said fourteen (14) days are hereinafter called "Official Visits." In addition to Official Visits,   or her authorized representatives, shall have the right to spend an additional thirty-five (35) days at Club during each Contract year at no charge. The services to be rendered by   during Official Visits shall be such as   and Company may agree upon. Company agrees that such services will make only reasonable demands upon   and   agrees that   will not unreasonably object to proposals of Club with respect thereto. During Official Visits, Company may schedule tennis exhibitions and/or tennis clinics by   at Club for the benefit of guests of Club.

5. During the visits by   referred to in paragraph 4 hereof and in the event that the "Town House" referred to in paragraph 6 hereof has not been fully constructed and furnished, Club shall provide   and her immediate family with first-class accommodations and food. In addition thereto, with respect to Official Visits only, Club shall reimburse   for the round-trip transportation expense of   and   immediate family from that location on   itinerary next preceding such visit to that location on   itinerary next succeeding such visit, it being understood that no such location shall be ouside the continental limits of the United States.

6. Company agrees that it will cause to be constructed a condominium-type town house (the "Town House") the construction for which will be completed on or before   . The Town House will be at a location at Club approved by   and will have a fair market value of at least $. Company agrees that Company will, at its own expense, fully and completely furnish the Town House with furnishings selected by   .
     agrees that during all visits by   to Club, or during all visits to Club by   authorized representatives as herein provided,   or such representatives, will stay at the Town House. It is agreed that Company will furnish the Town House for   with kitchen appliances, such as a dish-washer, garbage disposal, refrigerator and stove, along with wall to wall carpeting. It is

understood that these named items will belong to   along with any "fixtures" constituting a part of the Town House and will be thought of as part of   Town House. It is also understood that   will be allowed to choose up to   worth of furnishings at retail value, but that these items will belong to Company rather than to   It is contemplated that   might very well choose to spend more than $ on furnishings and any amount   spends over $ will be at   expense, but will be, of course, for goods that   owns rather than the Company.

7. During the term of this agreement, Company will exercise its best efforts to rent the Town House during periods when   or   authorized representatives are not using it and agrees that with respect to each Contract year it will pay   a sum which is $720 less than 80% of the gross rents received as the result of rental of the Town House during such year. Such payments shall be made to   as and when the rents on which they are based are received by Company. On or before thirty (30) days after the conclusion of each Contract Year, Company shall pay   the amount, if any, by which   exceeds all amounts theretofore paid to   with respect to such Contract Year pursuant to this paragraph 7, the first such payment to be made on or before October 1, 1973, it being understood that such payments shall be made without regard for the status of construction of the Town House.

8. On or before each first day of July and until such time as the entire right, title and interest have been conveyed to   , Company shall convey to   in the manner hereinafter provided an undivided one-fifth (1/5) interest in the Town House. Such conveyances shall grant to   an interest as a tenant in common and not as a joint tenant and the only other person or entity to have an interest in the Town House shall be Company (other than a mortgagee). Such conveyances shall be by general warranty deed. Company shall be responsible for properly and promptly recording each such conveyance and providing   with suitable evidence of such recordation. Until such time as Company shall have conveyed to   the entire right and title in and to the Town House, Company shall, itself, be responsible for all taxes, assessments and maintenance charges (including utilities) with respect to the Town House. Coincidentally with the last such conveyance (which

shall convey to   the entire right, title and interest in and to the Town House), Company shall pay all delinquent taxes, including penalties and interest which are a lien on the closing date of such last conveyance prorated to that date and computed, if undetermined, on the basis of the last available tax rate and valuation. Company shall also pay all assessments which are a lien on said closing date and shall pay all costs involved in such last closing. On such last closing date, Company shall, at Company's expense, furnish   with a policy of title insurance in the amount of the value of the Town House on that date or $, whichever is greater, said policy to insure in Court good and merchantable title in fee simple, free and clear of all liens and encumbrances excepting restrictions, conditions and utility easements created or reserved as a part of a general plan for the subdivision in which the Town House is located and zoning ordinances and all legal highways. If, on said last closing date, the title to the Town House is defective or unmerchantable or if any part of the property is subject to liens, encumbrances, easements, conditions or restrictions other than those mentioned in this paragraph 8, Company shall have a reasonable time, not to exceed thirty (30) days after written notice thereof, within which to remedy or remove any such defect, lien, encumbrance, easement, condition or restriction. If Company is unable to remedy or remove, or to secure title insurance against, such defect, lien, encumbrance, easement, condition or restriction within said thirty (30) day period, Company shall pay to   the value of said Town House in cash, or $, whichever is greater.

9.   hereby designates   as authorized agent for all purposes hereunder. All notices and/or submissions to be made or delivered by Club to   pursuant to the terms hereof shall be delivered to   marked to the attention of   . All payments to be made to   pursuant to the terms hereof shall be made by check drawn to the order of   and delivered to   at said address.

10. The term of this agreement shall commence on the date of acceptance set forth below and shall conclude on   , it being understood that any uncompleted obligations of Company pursuant to the provisions of paragraph 7 hereof shall survive the termination of the term of this agreement.

11. At any time after   ,   shall have the right to elect to require Company to purchase all of her then right, title and interest in and to the Town House for a purchase price of $. Such election shall be exercised by   by so notifying Company in writing, such writing to designate an escrow agent for the closing of such purchase which escrow agent shall be a national or state chartered financial institution in or around   Coincidentally with such notice,   shall deliver to such escrow agent a deed which conveys all of then right, title and interest in and to the Town House to Company. On or before thirty (30) days after receipt of   election, Company shall deposit with said escrow agent the sum of $ plus such sum as may be necessary to pay for such closing costs as are to be a charge against Company's escrow account pursuant to the provisions of this paragraph 11. Company and   agree that said escrow agent may charge only the following costs to   escrow account:

(a) one-half (1/2) of the escrow agent's fee;
(b) the cost of discharging any mortgage against the Town House which mortgage has been secured by   personally;
(c) the amount necessary to prorate taxes and assessments against the Town House to the date of closing, it being understood that   shall not be responsible for any taxes or assessments or for any proration thereof to any date which precedes the filing of the last conveyance to   pursuant to the provisions of paragraph 8 hereof.

All other closing costs including real estate commissions, if any, shall be a charge against Company's account with said escrow agent.

12. Company agrees that until the recordation of the last conveyance to   pursuant to the provisions of paragraph 8 hereof, Company shall be responsible for insuring the Town House against fire and other casualty and shall cause the insurance company or companies issuing such policy or policies of insurance to execute and affix to said policy or policies a rider or riders which shall insure Company and   "as their interests may appear." Company shall cause said insurance carrier or carriers to issue a certificate of said insurance to   which certificate shall provide that such insurance shall not be cancelled by said carrier or carriers until   has received at least ten (10) days prior written notice.

If the foregoing twelve numbered paragraphs

accurately set forth our understanding, will you please sign the two xerox copies enclosed and return them to me for final approval by   and the return of a fully executed copy to you whereupon this letter will constitute the memorandum of the agreement.

Sincerely yours,

A legal inquiry that is raised but not pursued in this part of the book is whether individual performer sports require variant legal standards in some instances. For example, is injunctory relief available when the athlete fails to honor a contract? (see, *Machen* v. *Johansson* in Chapter 2, Section 2.14). When the specific situation is relevant in a court fashioning the relief to be awarded, it may be that a performer in individual sports stands in a position that is different from that of a team player. If so, that must be anticipated in the drafting of the initial agreements.

4.43   Foreign Leagues

Limited alternatives are available to United States athletes to play "professionally" in foreign countries. In football, there is the Canadian Football League, where salaries are approximately two-thirds of those in the NFL. For baseball players, Japan offers opportunities, generally for ex-major leaguers. In basketball and hockey, leagues exist across Europe, with the quality of play varying substantially from country to country.

All foreign leagues limit the number of noncitizens who can play on any one team. This makes the scramble for spots by United States players an intense one, particularly in the better leagues. For example, the Italian basketball league is considered the strongest outside the United States. Top players can earn as much as $150,000 a year, even though the league is classified as amateur under international rules. (For NBA purposes, it is considered professional. See the *David Batton* case, Chapter Five, Section 5.22.) Each Italian team is severely limited as to how many foreign players can make

a squad. It takes a top U.S. player, one just below the NBA level, to secure a contract, unless the player can somehow claim Italian citizenship.

Produced below is a contract form used by several Italian clubs. There is no standard form for the league, but all clubs use basically this or a similar agreement. There can be additions and modifications. A highly sought-after-player can command several extras, in terms of bonuses and other benefits. Comparison should be made between this form and the standard NBA contract (see Chapter 3, Exhibit 3–1).

Lega Societa Pallacanestro (Italian Basketball League)

This Agreement made and entered into as of * , by   and between   (hereinafter referred to as the "Club") and   (hereinafter referred to as the "Player").

In consideration of the mutual promises hereinafter set forth, the parties hereto agree as follows:

1. The Club does hereby engage the Player as a skilled basketball player for a term which shall begin on the   August 1981 and end on   and for a term which shall begin on the   and end on   . The Player's engagement during the playing years covered by this Agreement shall include attendance and participation in regular season games and any and all exhibitions, playoff, tournament and cup games scheduled or entered into by the Club, whether the same are scheduled prior, during or subsequent to the regular season schedule.

2. The Club agrees to pay the Player the sums necessary to cover his living expenses and to prepare himself for a profession which he will practice when he shall cease to be active as a basketball Player.

Therefore during the period of his agreement, the Club agrees to pay the Player the sum of USA Dollars for the first year, . . . or its equivalent in Italian Lire at the rate of exchange which exists at the time payments are due.

3. During the period of this Agreement, the Club shall provide the Player with the appropriate

---

* Blank spaces throughout this sample contract denote information to be filled in by parties to the agreement.

certificate of tax credit indicating that all required income taxes due in Italy on the aforesaid sums have been paid and such certificate shall be in such form so as to assure that the Player receive a United States tax credit for such payment. The Club shall have no responsibility to pay any tax obligations of the Player in the United States.

However the Club agrees to cooperate with the Player to minimize the tax consequences of the Player's expense compensation.

4. The Basic expense payments due to the Player under Paragraph 2 of this Agreement shall be paid directly to the Player or such other designee as he designates in writing.

5. During the period of this Agreement, the basic expense compensation due to the Player shall be guaranteed by the Lega Societa Pallacanestro Serie "A" (hereinafter referred to as the "League") provided, however, that this Agreement has been filed in the office of the League at Via Fontanina 2, Bologna, Italy.

6. During the period of this Agreement, the Club will provide the Player with the use of a car and provide for car insurance covering injuries to the Player or to the person or property of others. It is expressly understood, however, that the Player shall be responsible for his own gas, oil and repair costs.

7. During the period of this Agreement, the Club will provide the Player with the use of a furnished apartment reasonably suitable to the Player's needs and the Player will pay all telephone, gas, electric and water charges and the Club shall pay all other expenses associated with the use of the apartment. The Player shall also be responsible for any damage to the apartment or any of its contents.

8. During the period of this agreement, the Club shall provide the Player with   round-trip economy class airline tickets between   and

9. The Club agrees to pay all proper and necessary expenses of the Player including reasonable board and lodging expenses of the Player while playing for the Club "on the road" and during training camp if the Player is not then living at home.

10. During the period of this Agreement, the Club shall provide the Player with all medical and dental services (other than those of an aesthetic nature) required for the Player while he resides in Italy, provided the same are caused by injury or disease, and, provided further that the same do not occur as a result of the gross misconduct and/or gross negligence of the Player outside of his basketball playing as set forth in paragraph 12 of this agreement.

11. In this regard the Player agrees that he will become a member of the Club and will, at all times during the period of this Agreement, remain a member in good standing. In this regard the Player agrees that he will, to the best of his ability, maintain himself in physical condition sufficient to play skilled basketball on a world class level at all times during the period of this agreement, and that he will report for training camp and/or practice sessions in Italy in such physical condition. All expenses incurred in regards to these activities shall be paid by the Club.

The Player also agrees to give his best services, as well as his loyalty, to the Club and to be neatly attired in public and always to conduct himself on and off the court according to appropriate standards of honesty, morality, and sportsmanship giving due consideration to the nature of his membership in the Club.

12. The fact that the Player may not perform as a basketball player hereunder because of a lack of playing ability or because of illness or injury or death, other than that caused by his own gross misconduct or negligence as set forth in paragraph 13, shall in no way affect the Player's right to receive the payments specified in paragraph 2.

However, the Player agrees to make himself available for insurance examinations and to do all other things which may be necessary in order to allow the Club to purchase a policy of disability insurance, or to receive payments on claims made against the policy.

13. The Player agrees that any injury to himself which is caused by his own gross misconduct and/or complete disregard of his responsibility as a basketball player, which injury prevents him from performing his obligations under this contract, will constitute a breach of contract entitling the Club to rescind the contract upon ten (10) days' written notice after the date of the occurrence of such injury and, thereafter, the Club shall have no obligation to make any further payment of any sums owing to the Player as of the date of such notice. This same right of rescission shall apply in the event the Player is suspended by the Federazione Italiana Pallacanestro (hereinafter referred to as the "Federation") for a period in excess of one month due to his own misconduct. No rescission

shall be effective until the Player has had a hearing with respect thereto.

14. The Player agrees to observe and comply with all requirements of the Club respecting conduct of the team and the players, at all times whether on or off the playing floor. The Club may, from time to time during the continuance of this contract, establish reasonable rules for the governance of its players "at home" and "on the road," and such rules shall be part of this contract as fully as if herein written and shall be binding upon the Player. Player shall be given a complete set of such rules translated into the English language.

For any violation of such rules or for any conduct impairing the faithful and complete discharge of the duties incumbent upon the Player, the Club may impose reasonable fines upon the Player and deduct the amount thereof from any amount due or to become due to the Player. The Player understands that he must also obey the rules of the League and the Federation and that violations of such rules by him may result in fines against him or against the Club by the Federation. Any such fines caused by the Player shall be his responsibility and the Club may deduct the amount thereof from any amount due or to become due to the Player.

The Player also understands that the Federation may disqualify him for his misconduct for one or more games but less than an entire season and, that, in such case the Club has the right to make application for the reinstatement of the Player upon payment of such sums as may be required by the Federation. The Player agrees that the Club shall have the sole right to determine if this application should be made and, if the Club decides to make such application, the Player agrees to be responsible for all payments and costs incurred by the Club to obtain his reinstatement, provided, however, that the total amount of such payments and costs shall not exceed the sum of 1,250 (one thousand two hundred fifty) USA Dollars for each disqualification. The Player also agrees that the Club may deduct these sums from any amount due or to become due to the Player.

When the Player is fined or disqualified he shall be given notice in writing stating the amount of the fine or disqualification and the reason therefor and the Player shall have the right to appeal such fine or disqualification according to the rules of the Club, the League or the Federation, at his expense.

15. The Player understands and agrees that he must abide by all rules of the Federation International Basketball Amateur (hereinafter referred to as F.I.B.A.) as a condition of this agreement as if said rules were fully set forth herein.

16. The Player represents and agrees that he has extraordinary and unique skill and ability as a basketball player, that the services to be rendered by him hereunder cannot be replaced or the loss thereof adequately compensated for in money damages, and that any breach by the Player of this contract will cause irreparable injury to the Club and to its assignees. Therefore, it is agreed that in the event it is alleged by the Club that the Player is playing, attempting or threatening to play, or negotiating for the purpose of playing, during the term of this contract, for any other person, firm, corporation or organization without the consent of the Club, the Club and its assigness (in addition to any other remedies that may be available to them judicially or by way of arbitration) shall have the right to obtain from any court or arbitrator having jurisdiction, such equitable relief as may be appropriate, including a decree enjoining the Player from any further breach of this contract, and enjoining the Player from playing basketball for any other person, firm, corporation or organization during the term of this contract.

In any suit, action or arbitration proceeding brought to obtain such relief, the Player does hereby waive his right, if any, to trial by jury, and does hereby waive his right, if any, to interpose any counterclaim or set-off for any cause whatever.

17. The Player agrees that he will not enter into any agreements to advertise his use of any product, nor use any product while participating as a member of the Club, if such advertisement or use would, in any way, conflict with existing agreements of the Club or the League.

18. The Player agrees that all obligations of the Club under this agreement are expressly contingent upon the Player's ability to pass the standard medical examination for basketball players under stress prior to the commencement of each training camp before each season under this agreement. Such examination shall be conducted by a doctor selected by the Club.

19. The Player also agrees that all obligations of the Club under this agreement are expressly contingent upon the Player's ability to obtain all necessary documents, particularly travel permits,

which are required under the rules of F.I.B.A. before he can participate in the League.

20. The Player also agrees that the Club shall have the right to terminate this agreement at any time without cause, provided, however, that in such case the Player shall be entitled to receive the full sum specified in paragraph 2 and shall further be entitled to receive the use of the car and apartment as specified in paragraph 6 and 7 for a period of fifteen (15) days after he has received notice of the Club's intention to terminate under this paragraph.

21. This agreement contains the entire agreement between the parties, and there are no oral or written documents or promises except as contained herein.

22. The terms hereof shall inure to the benefit of and be binding on (a) the Player, his heirs and assigns, and (b) the Club, and its successors and assigns.

23. The parties hereto agree to submit themselves to the jurisdiction of the Courts and the laws of the U.S.A should any litigation arise out of this agreement.

IN WITNESS WHEREOF, the parties have caused this agreement to be executed and by their signatures they agree to be bound thereto as of the day and year first above written.

_____   _____

(Player)   (Club)

4.50 Managing and Marketing the Athlete

The income derived by a player from a sports team (or, in the case of individual performer sports, from tournament sponsors) may be only the base for other lucrative opportunities. In the past 20 years, players have become "hot" items for advertising and other types of endorsements. Although the opportunities are not simply there for the taking, at least not for the majority of professional athletes, there are substantial rewards for a great many. Individual sports performers are in general more avidly sought by sponsors than team players. Part of this has to do with the individual focus they receive, being out

on the court or on the course in full and splendid isolation for two or three hours, under full glare of television and live audiences. Even so, the stars in team sports reap their rewards as well. Larry Bird and Julius Erving have as much to say as John McEnroe and Jack Nicklaus about what the American public should wear, eat, and enjoy.

This section does not give advice on how to obtain lucrative endorsements for a client. Rather, it concentrates on the legal pitfalls and protections that prevail in this important area. Subsection 4.51 briefly addresses players in league sports. Restrictions are often imposed on players either by the league's collective bargaining agreement or by the provisions of the league's standard player contract.

Subsection 4.52 examines the growing legal problem of a celebrity indiscriminately endorsing products without verifying what is said about the product. The final subsection, 4.53, focuses on the legal protections that can be asserted against unauthorized intrusion on or misappropriation of the player's name or image. This raises questions of rights of publicity, invasions of privacy, unfair competition, libel, and other legal safeguards. Although the legal concerns are too complex for comprehensive analysis in this work, they are dealt with in the following cases and materials to an extent that a lawyer can be alerted to the opportunities available for protecting a client's best interests.

4.51 League Provisions on Endorsements

In all likelihood, either the player's contract with the club or the league's collective bargaining agreement will include provisions regarding publicity for the club and restrictions on a player's ability to make endorsements. For example, consider the following paragraph 3(c) which appears in all Major League Baseball contracts:

Pictures and Public Appearances

3.(c) The Player agrees that his picture may be taken for still photographs, motion pictures or television at such times as the Club may designate and agrees that all rights in such pictures shall belong to the Club and may be used by the Club for publicity purposes in any manner it desires. The Player further agrees that during the playing season he will not make public appearances, participate in radio or television programs or permit his picture to be taken or write or sponsor newspaper or magazine articles or sponsor commercial products without the written consent of the Club, which shall not be withheld except in the reasonable interests of the Club or professional baseball.

Similar provisions appear in NBA and NFL contracts. While alterations of these provisions are possible through the negotiation process, in reality only minor revisions are usually made.

Some leagues' collective bargaining agreements address the matter of endorsements, while others are silent. The 1982 NFL pact, for example, specifies only that "no club may arbitrarily refuse a player to endorse a product" (Article XXXVII, Sec. 1). Alleged infractions of this nebulous standard would have to be tested through arbitration. The NBA and Major League Baseball, at present, have no provisions in their collective bargaining agreements concerning endorsements.

The National Hockey League is the most specific about endorsements, and spells out the following provisions in Article XXIV of its collective bargaining agreement:

24.01. No player shall be involved in any endorsement of alcoholic beverages and/or tobacco products.

24.02. When a player obtains an endorsement for himself, he shall receive the entire fee therefor and may mention the name of his Club for identification purposes only. A player shall not use the sweater or Club insignia without the consent of the Club which shall not be unreasonably withheld, and if consent is granted, Section 24.04 shall be applicable.

24.03. In the case of a team endorsement, the proceeds shall be divided one-half to the players and one-half to the Club.

24.04. In the case of a single player wearing the sweater or identified with the insignia of the Club in connection with an endorsement, 2/3 of the fee thereof shall be paid to the player, and 1/3 shall be paid to the Club.

24.05. An accounting between each club and its players for endorsement fees, if any, provided for in this Article shall be made at Christmas and at the conclusion of the regular season.

4.52   Endorsement Contracts

The endorsement contract in Exhibit 4–5 is not presented as the ultimate in drafting or in providing fairness for all parties to an endorsement transaction. It is included here because it is typical of the form contracts used by advertising agencies and other parties seeking athlete's endorsements. Like all endorsement contracts, it should be approached with caution by all concerned.

One legal problem area must be noted. For a long time many people assumed that one could endorse a product by saying about anything one chose. No matter how outrageous an endorsement statement, it was considered the buyer's responsibility to be forewarned of the likely puffery involved. That circumstance is changing, as noted by such cases as *Cooga Mooga, Inc.,* FTC Docket No. C-2925, Oct. 1978.

In May 1978, the FTC issued a complaint against the Cooga Mooga company in connection with its advertising and marketing a product sold mainly through the mails. The product supposedly cured acne. The entertainer Pat Boone, along with his daughter Debbie, had endorsed the product for a fee, which was based on a return for each unit of the product sold over a certain period of time.

In October 1978, the FTC accepted an agreement containing a consent decree with Boone and the company, Cooga Mooga Inc. Under this order, Pat Boone was potentially liable for substantial sums. Although the final consent decree limited his liability to $5,000, as opposed to $60,000 for the advertising agency and $175,000 for the manufacturer, the action could signal problems for athletes and entertain-

Exhibit 4-5 ENDORSEMENT AGREEMENT

AGREEMENT, made and entered into this _____ day of _____, 19_____, by and between Player and Company Athletic Products (hereinafter referred to as "Company").

WITNESSETH:

WHEREAS, Player is recognized and widely known throughout the world as a professional basketball player; and

WHEREAS, Player's name, by virtue of his ability and experience, has acquired a meaning in the mind of the purchasing public important to the advertising, promotion, and sale of athletic equipment, particularly basketballs; and

WHEREAS, Company is engaged in the manufacture, distribution, and sale of basketballs and is desirous of acquiring the exclusive right to utilize Player's name in connection with the advertisment, promotion, and sale of basketballs.

NOW, THEREFORE, in consideration of the mutual covenants set forth herein and for other good and valuable consideration, it is agreed as follows:

1. DEFINITIONS

As used herein, the terms set forth below shall be defined as follows:

A. "Player's Endorsement" shall include the right to use the name, nickname, initials, autograph, facsimile signature, photograph, likeness and/or endorsement of Player.

B. "Endorsement Products" shall refer only to basketballs bearing the Player's Endorsement which are manufactured and/or distributed by Company or its licensees. Company shall have the right to manufacture and/or distribute as many models of basketballs bearing the Player's Endorsement as it chooses.

C. "Contract Territory" shall mean the entire world.

D. "Contract Term" shall mean that period of time commencing _____ and concluding _____ unless sooner terminated within the terms and conditions hereof.

E. The first contract year shall mean a $\frac{\text{twelve (12)}}{\text{seventeen (17)}}$ month period of time. The second and third contract years shall mean a twelve (12) month period of time, each contract year commencing on each first day of _____ during the contract term.

2. GRANT OF ENDORSEMENT RIGHTS

Subject to the terms and conditions set forth herein, Player grants to Company the exclusive right and license during the Contract Term and within the Contract Territory to use the Player's Endorsement in connection with the advertisement, promotion, and sale of Endorsed Products. Player warrants that he has not granted to others any right to use the Player's Endorsement in connection with the advertisement, sale, or promotion of the Endorsed Products during the Contract Term. Player further represents to Company that he has the full right, power, and authority to grant the Endorsement contained herein.

3. PROMOTIONAL APPEARANCES

A. If requested to do so by Company, Player agrees to make himself available once in each Contract Year for photographs for use in Company's advertising.

B. If requested to do so by Company, Player shall make one (1) public appearance in each Contract Year for the purpose of promoting endorsed products.

C. If no photo sessions are required by Player in a given Contract Year, then he shall make two (2) public appearances in that year.

D. For each photo session or public appearance described in subparagraphs A – C above:

(1) Company agrees to pay all reasonable out-of-pocket expenses incurred by Player in connection with such session or appearance;

(2) Company shall give Player not less than fourteen (14) days notice of the time and place Company desires Player to appear;

(3) Company shall not schedule any such session or appearance at a time which would conflict with Player's performance of his obligations as a professional basketball player.

4. GUARANTEED COMPENSATION

For the rights and benefits granted to Player pursuant to the terms of this Agreement, Company agrees to compensate Player on a graduated basis as follows:

Contract Year	Compensation
FIRST	$_____
SECOND	$_____
THIRD	$_____

The Annual Guarantee owing to Player in each contract year during the contract term shall be payable in four (4) equal installments on/or before the first day of May, August, November, and February in each contract year.

5. ROYALTIES

A. Company agrees to pay Player a royalty equal to _____ percent (____%) of all net sales of Endorsement Products. The term "net sales" is defined as the gross sales less normal cash and trade discounts, quantity discounts and returns, but no deduction shall be made for uncollectable accounts. No costs incurred in the manufacture, sale, distribution, or exploitation of the Endorsed Product shall be deducted from any royalty compensation payable by Company to Player.

B. Within forty-five (45) days following the conclusion of each Contract Year, Company shall furnish Player an itemized statement setting forth the total number of Endorsed Products sold by Company during the preceeding Contract Year on which Player is entitled to royalty compensation as set forth in sub-paragraph A. above. Simultaneously, with the delivery of such statement to Player, Company shall pay to Player the appropriate royalties due under this paragraph, provided, however, that the full amount of the royalty paid to Player shall be first credited against the amount of guaranteed compensation due, under paragraph 5 above. For example, if the royalties due and payable to Player under paragraph 5.A. above do not exceed $_____ for the first Contract Year, the Player shall receive the sum of $_____ (guaranteed compensation), but shall not receive additional royalties for the first Contract year. If, in any Contract Year, the royalties due under sub-paragraph 5.A. are greater than the guaranteed compensation as set forth in paragraph 4. for that Contract Year, the difference between the guaranteed compensation and the royalties due shall be paid to Player at the time of delivery of the itemized statement referred to above.

6. PERFORMANCE BONUSES

In addition to the guaranteed compensation and royalties provided in paragraphs 4. and 5. herein, Company shall pay bonuses to Player based upon the following performance achievements by Player during each Contract Year:

A. A bonus payment for Player's final NBA regular season league scoring ranking in accordance with the following schedule;

Player's Scoring Ranking	Bonus Payment
Number 1	$_____
2 – 5	$_____
6 – 10	$_____

B. A bonus of $_____ if Player is selected as the Most Valuable Player of the NBA as recognized in the offical NBA Guide.

C. A bonus of $_____ if Player is selected to the NBA First Team All Pro as chosen by the writers and broadcasters designated by the NBA.

D. A bonus of $_____ if Player is selected to the first team All Star Team in his league as chosen by the writers and broadcasters designated by the NBA.

E. A bonus of $_____ if Player is selected to be the NBA rookie of the year as chosen by the writers and broadcasters designated by the NBA.

7. PAYMENTS TO PLAYER

All payments are to be made to Player at such address as is designated in writing to Company from time to time by Player.

8. ENDORSED PRODUCTS FOR PLAYER'S USE

During the Contract Term, Company shall supply the Player at no charge, such amounts of Endorsed Products as Player may reasonably request for his own personal use or for distribution in connection with clinics approved by Company.

9. LABELING OF ENDORSED PRODUCTS

Each of the Endorsed Products which is distributed or sold in the Contract Territory shall have some part or all of the Player's endorsement affixed thereto or imprinted thereon.

10. RETENTION OF ENDORSEMENT RIGHTS

Subject to the terms of this Agreement, Player shall retain all rights in and to his name and endorsement and, whether during the Contract Term or any extension thereof, Player shall not be prevented from using or permitting or licensing others to use his name or endorsement in connection with the advertisement, promotion, and sale of any product or service other than the Endorsement Products. Company and Player agree that they shall take all necessary steps during the Contract Term to protect the Player's Endorsement in connection with the advertisement, promotion, and sale of Endorsed Products.

11. SPECIAL RIGHT OF TERMINATION BY PLAYER

Player shall have the right to terminate this Agreement upon thirty (30) days prior written notice to Company in the event of the appearance of any of the following contingencies:

A. If Company is adjudicated insolvent, declares bankruptcy, or fails to continue its business of selling Endorsed Products; provided, however, that nothing contained in this Agreement shall obligate Company to sell any specific quantities of Endorsed Products during the Contract Term; or

B. If Company fails to make payment to Player of any sums due pursuant to this Agreement within thirty (30) days that such payment is due.

12. SPECIAL RIGHT OF TERMINATION BY COMPANY

Company shall have the right to terminate this Agreement upon thirty (30) days prior written notice to Player or his legal representative in the event of the occurrence of any of the following contingencies:

A. If Player retires as an NBA player; or

B. If, at any time during the NBA regular season, Player fails for a period of forty (40) consecutive NBA professional basketball games to be on an NBA roster. For the purpose of this Agreement, the status of "Injured Reserve" shall be included in the definition of NBA roster; or

C. If Player has engaged in illegal or immortal conduct resulting in a felony conviction, or if he has otherwise conducted himself in a manner which is not reasonable in keeping with the standards of professional athletics.

13. RIGHT TO USE ENDORSEMENT UPON TERMINATION

Upon termination of this Agreement for any reason whatsoever, Company shall have no right to continue to use the Player's Endorsement except as provided below:

A. Player agrees that Company shall, for a period of one hundred eighty (180) days following the effective date of termination, have the right to continue to sell Endorsed Products bearing the Player's endorsement which were manufactured or ordered prior to the effective date of termination; provided that Company delivers to Player within fourteen (14) days following the date of termination, an itemized statement setting forth the total number of Endorsed Products bearing the Player's Endorsement in its closing inventory.

B. Player further agrees that Company shall have the right, for a period of ninety (90) days following the effective date of termination, to dispose of all advertising and promotional materials bearing Player's Endorsement which were printed or ordered prior to the effective date of termination.

C. For any period during which Company shall continue to sell the Endorsed Product, Company shall pay Player his share of the royalty as set forth in paragraph 5.

14. EMPLOYER/EMPLOYEE RELATIONSHIP

Player's performance of services for Company hereunder is in his capacity as an independent contractor. Accordingly, nothing contained in this Agreement shall be construed as establishing an Employer/Employee, a Partnership, or a joint venture relationship between Player and Company.

15. ASSIGNMENT

Player shall not assign this Agreement but shall have the right to assign his financial benefits hereunder and Company hereby consents to such assignment.

---

ers who endorse products without first verifying the claims they make about the product.

In a statement accompanying the action taken vis-à-vis Boone, the FTC bureau of consumer protection emphasized that failure to make reasonable efforts at independent evaluation of a product could result in personal liability for the endorser.

NOTE _____

1. For more extensive discussions of this problem, see Jones, "Protecting and Promoting the Commercial Value of the Professional Athlete," in Jones (ed.), *Current Issues in Professional Sports* (Durham, N.H.: University of New Hampshire, 1980), pp. 96–105.

4.53 Commercial Value in the Athlete's Name or Image

One of the primary concerns of the attorney representing the celebrity (athlete or entertainer) is the outsiders who seek to capitalize on the client's fame. Posters or T-shirts bearing the celebrity's likeness often appear, having been manufactured without permission. If the problem is one of copyright, trademark, or patent infringement, the legal response is straightforward. But often the "borrowing" is not of a tangible work product; instead it involves the unauthorized use of a name or image. In these cases, the legal response is more uncertain.

Because of the inconsistent nature of the rights in one's name or image, resort must be made to any number of concepts. The first efforts concentrated on the right to privacy — the right to be left alone and free from intrusion. However, when applied to the outgoing and newsworthy celebrity, this approach seemed false. Thus, some jurisdictions fashioned a right of publicity — the ability to exploit one's own name for personal gain and the concomitant right to prevent others from invading this "property" interest. The concept is simple enough, but legal principles do not always develop logically or consistently. Certain jurisdications have resisted a right of publicity, insisting that the rights of an individual be in traditional rights of privacy, or not at all. Other states are more explicit in recognizing the right of publicity. A third approach holds that which concept is advanced really does not matter — a right exists and will be enforced.

In this mix, one cannot ignore other legal concepts — notably, unfair competition and libel. Although different in origin and application, each is available to aid the individual from unwanted misappropriation or misrepresentation. At times, the two concerns converge, as some of the later cases in this section reveal.

The cases that follow do not always fit into one neat category. However, by analyzing the cases, one can gain perspectives on the various legal approaches. The right of publicity is examined first in Section 4.53–1; then it is compared with the right of privacy in Section 4.53–2. Trade names are discussed in the *Hirsch* case (Section 4.53–1), which should be compared with trademarks (Section 4.53–3). Libel and unfair competition are mentioned from time to time but are highlighted in the last subsection (4.53–6). It is also important to note how rights can be relinquished through prior agreement (Section 4.53–4), or must yield to rights under concepts of free speech and press to report the "news" (Section 4.53–5). In total, these cases provide a substantial breadth of legal concepts and principles.

4.53–1 Right of Publicity

The concept that a right of publicity is a distinct and separate property right was first articulated in the *Haelan Laboratories* case, set forth below. By its opinion, the Second Circuit Court of Appeals, in interpreting New York law, started what has become an avalanche of inquiry. Some jurisdictions still do not recognize a separate right of publicity. If the facts constituting a publicity right are recognized at all in these jurisdictions, they are subsumed under a right of privacy.

Even where the right of publicity is recognized, it is unclear just how extensive the right is. The following cases and notes indicate the breadth of the problems opened by the Second Circuit in its 1953 opinion.

Haelan Laboratories, Inc. v. Topps Chewing Gum, 202 F.2d 866 (2d Cir. 1953)

Frank, Circuit Judge.

After a trial without a jury, the trial judge dismissed the complaint on the merits.[1] The plaintiff maintains that defendant invaded plaintiff's exclusive right to use the photographs of leading baseball-players. Probably because the trial judge ruled against plaintiff's legal contentions, some of the facts were not too clearly found.

1. So far as we can now tell, there were instances of the following kind:

(a). The plaintiff, engaged in selling chewing-gum, made a contract with a ball-player providing that plaintiff for a stated term should have the exclusive right to use the ball-player's photograph in connection with the sales of plaintiff's gum; the ball-player agreed not to grant any other gum manufacturer a similar right during such term; the contract gave plaintiff an option to extend the term for a designated period.

(b). Defendant, a rival chewing-gum manufacturer, knowing of plaintiff's contract, deliberately induced the ball-player to authorize defendant, by a contract with defendant, to use the player's photograph in connection with the sales of

---

[1] We think the New York decisions recognize such a right. . .

defendant's gum either during the original or extended term of plaintiff's contract, and defendant did so use the photograph.

Defendant argues that, even if such facts are proved, they show no actionable wrong, for this reason: The contract with plaintiff was no more than a release by the ball-player to plaintiff of the liability which, absent the release, plaintiff would have incurred in using the ball-player's photograph, because such a use, without his consent, would be an invasion of his right of privacy under Section 50 and Section 51 of the New York Civil Rights Law; this statutory right of privacy is personal, not assignable; therefore, plaintiff's contract vested in plaintiff no "property" right or other legal interest which defendant's conduct invaded.

Both parties agree, and so do we, that, on the facts here, New York "law" governs. And we shall assume, for the moment, that, under the New York decisions, defendant correctly asserts that any such contract between plaintiff and a ball-player, in so far as it merely authorized plaintiff to use the player's photograph, created nothing but a release of liability. On that basis, were there no more to the contract, plaintiff would have no actionable claim against defendant. But defendant's argument neglects the fact that, in the contract, the ball-player also promised not to give similar releases to others. If defendant, knowing of the contract, deliberately induced the ball-player to break that promise, defendant behaved tortiously. . . .

[We] must consider defendant's contention that none of plaintiff's contracts created more than a release of liability, because a man has no legal interest in the publication of his picture other than his right of privacy, i.e., a personal and non-assignable right not to have his feelings hurt by such a publication.

A majority of this court rejects this contention. We think that, in addition to and independent of that right of privacy (which in New York derives from statute), a man has a right in the publicity value of his photograph, i.e., the right to grant the exclusive privilege of publishing his picture, and that such a grant may validly be made "in gross," i.e., without an accompanying transfer of a business or of anything else. Whether it be labelled a "property" right is immaterial; for here, as often elsewhere, the tag "property" simply symbolizes

the fact that courts enforce a claim which has pecuniary worth.

This right might be called a "right of publicity." For it is common knowledge that many prominent persons (especially actors and ball-players), far from having their feelings bruised through public exposure of their likenesses, would feel sorely deprived if they no longer received money for authorizing advertisements, popularizing their countenances, displayed in newspapers, magazines, busses, trains and subways. This right of publicity would usually yield them no money unless it could be made the subject of an exclusive grant which barred any other advertiser from using their pictures.

Uhlaender v. Henricksen, 316 F. Supp. 1277 (D. Minn. 1970)

Neville, District Judge.

Presented to the court is the question as to whether some several hundred Major League Baseball Players, appearing in this action by one such individual player and by an unincorporated association of major league baseball players have a proprietary or property interest in their names, sporting activities and accomplishments so as to enable them to enjoin the use thereof for commercial purposes by private entrepreneurs engaged in the manufacture of parlor or table games which employ and use their names and sports accomplishments. Diversity jurisdiction is clear, and no challenge is made as to the sufficiency of the parties plaintiff.

Defendants manufacture and sell games called "Negamco's Major League Baseball" and "Big League Manager Baseball." These employ the names and professional statistical information such as batting, fielding, earned run and other averages of some 500 to 700 major league baseball players, identified by team, uniform number, playing position and otherwise. . . .

It is clear to the court that the use of the baseball player's names and statistical information is intended to and does make defendants' games more salable to the public than otherwise would be the case. Counsel for plaintiff Association of Major League Baseball Players, an unincorporated association, testified that the association was formed in 1966 to represent the major league baseball players' common interest and that this association is authorized by all but a handful of major league baseball players to act for them in marketing and licensing the use of group names or for group endorsement purposes. The Association does not represent players insofar as they desire to make or have made individual product or other endorsements. The Association now represents over 850 major league baseball players and to date it has issued some 27 different licensing contracts or agreements for group licenses, including four or five other parlor game manufacturers, calling for payments of 5% of gross sales with a minimum royalty of $2,500 per year. These agreements generated over $400,000 income in 1969, all of which is distributed equally, and not according to prominence or excellence in accomplishments, to the various player members. As far back as January, 1967 the plaintiff association wrote defendants notifying them that they were exploiting a claimed property right and offering to enter into a licensing agreement. Defendants have consistently refused so to do. . . .

Defendants do not deny that they are using the names as alleged. They assert, however, (1) that there is nothing offensive nor demeaning about the way the names are used, which both witnesses Kaat and Perry acknowledged; (2) that the names and statistics concerning sports achievements used in the game are readily available to anyone at Major League offices on inquiry, are published with some regularity in the newspapers and news media and are thus in the public domain; (3) baseball players seek and are anxious for publicity which defendants' games tend to further; (4) the plaintiff association by insisting on a minimum of $2,500 from each licensee tends "to keep little people out of the business" constituting in some way a conspiracy in violation of the antitrust laws.

The defendants insist upon characterizing this action as one involving an alleged invasion of the right of privacy. The complaint however does not predicate its claim for relief upon any assertion of a right to be let alone. Instead, plaintiffs' claim "misappropriation and use for commercial profit of the names of professional major league baseball players without the payment of royalties." The distinction between these two legal theories is important to the disposition of the case. . . .

It is this court's view that a celebrity has a legitimate proprietary interest in his public perso-

nality. A celebrity must be considered to have invested his years of practice and competition in a public personality which eventually may reach marketable status. That identity, embodied in his name, likeness, statistics and other personal characteristics, is the fruit of his labors and is a type of property.

Defendants' contention has no merit that by the publication in the news media and because of the ready availability to anyone of the names and statistical information concerning the players, such information is in the public domain and the players thus have waived their rights to relief in this case. Such argument may or may not have some weight against a right of privacy claim, but in an appropriation action such as in the case at bar the names and statistics are valuable only because of their past public disclosure, publicity and circulation. A name is commercially valuable as an endorsement of a product or for use for financial gain only because the public recognizes it and attributes good will and feats of skill or accomplishments of one sort or another to that personality. To hold that such publicity destroys a right to sue for appropriation of a name or likeness would negate any and all causes of action, for only by disclosure and public acceptance does the name of a celebrity have any value at all to make its unauthorized use enjoinable.

It seems clear to the court that a celebrity's property interest in his name and likeness is unique, and therefore there is no serious question as to the propriety of injunctive relief. Defendants have violated plaintiffs' rights by the unauthorized appropriation of their names and statistics for commercial use. The remedy at law, considering particularly the difficulty in determining and measuring damages, past or future, is inadequate.

Hirsch v. S. C. Johnson & Son, Inc., 280 N.W. 2d 129 (Wisc. 1979)

Elroy Hirsch, a sports figure of national prominence, sought damages from the unauthorized use of his nickname "Crazylegs" on a shaving gel for women manufactured by S. C. Johnson & Son.

Hirsch first gained notoriety as "Crazylegs" in 1942, when, as a freshman for the University of Wisconsin, he wobbled 62 yards along the sidelines for a touchdown. The nickname stuck throughout Hirsch's college and professional career, and as a football player with the Los Angeles Rams, Hirsch appeared as Crazylegs in a number of advertisements.

The defendants successfully brought a motion in the trial court to dismiss at the close of plaintiff's evidence for failure to spell out a cause of action under common law. The two issues before the court were legal questions: (1) whether under Wisconsin law a cause of action existed for the appropriation of a person's name for commercial use and (2) whether the plaintiff had established a prima facie case of trade-name infringement when he failed to assert that his name had ever been used to identify a product or service.

The court first differentiated between an invasion-of-privacy action, which protects one's mental interest in being left alone, and an appropriation tort, which protects the property interest in the publicity value of one's name. The court found that under Wisconsin law, the right to control the exploitation of one's name was not controlled by the cases which explicitly refused to recognize a common-law cause of action for the invasion of privacy.

The record attempted to show that Hirsch devoted time and energy to cultivate a reputation of sportsmanship and that Hirsch was protective of his name; he refused to advertise cigarettes and had a beer commercial withdrawn when he became athletic director at the University of Wisconsin. Supported by public-policy considerations such as the need to control the effect of the commercial use on one's reputation and to prevent the unjust enrichment of those who benefit from the publicity value of another's identity, the court found sufficient grounds to recognize a cause of action to protect the right of publicity.

The court then ruled that the trial court erred by ruling that there was no cause of action for trade-name infringement unless it was alleged and proved that "Crazylegs" had been used by Hirsch to identify goods or services. A trade name is a designation used to identify a person's business, vocation, or occupation; it does not require an identification with specific goods or services. Thus, to establish a cause of action for trade-name infringement, it was sufficient to allege that "Crazylegs" designated Hirsch's vocation as a sports figure and that the use of the phrase by the defendants created confusion with respect to the sponsorship of the shaving gel.

Finally, the court issued a caveat that its decision only established that a cause of action did exist and that the plaintiff still faced substantial problems of proof. Because Hirsch's action was dismissed prior to the determination of factual issues by a jury, the case was remanded.

NOTES

1. Extensive writings address the factual and legal areas considered in this subsection. The most handy source for thorough analysis of the four areas of unfair competition, privacy, publicity, and libel can be found in T. Selz and M. Simensky, *Entertainment Law*, vol. 2, Chps. 17–20 (1983).

2. Other articles to note include the following:

(a) "First Amendment Does Not Privilege Violation of Right of Publicity — *Zacchini* v. *Scripps-Howard Broadcasting Co.*, 31 *Rutgers Law Review* 269 (1978).

(b) Gordon, "Right of Property in Name, Likeness, Personality and History," 55 *Northwestern Law Review* 553 (1961).

(c) "Intellectual Property — Performer's Style — A Quest for Ascertainment, Recognition, and Protection," 52 *Denver Law Journal* 561 (1975).

(d) Kalven, "Privacy in Tort Law — Were Warren and Brandeis Wrong?" 31 *Law and Contemporary Problems* 326 (1966).

(e) "Lugosi v. Universal Pictures: Descent of the Right of Publicity," 29 *Hastings Law Journal* 751 (1978).

(f) Nimmer, "The Right of Publicity," 19 *Law and Contemporary Problems* 203 (1954); 62 *Yale Law Journal* 1123 (1953); and 41 *Georgetown Law Journal* 583 (1953).

(g) Prosser, "Privacy," 48 *California Law Review* 383 (1960).

(h) "The Right of Publicity — Protection for Public Figures and Celebrities," 42 *Brooklyn Law Review* 527 (1976).

(i) "Transfer of the Right of Publicity: Dracula's Progency and Privacy's Stepchild," 22 *UCLA Law Review* 1103 (1975).

(j) Treece, "Commercial Exploitation of Names, Likenesses and Personal Histories," 51 *Texas Law Review* 637 (1973).

(k) Warren and Brandeis, "The Right to Privacy," 4 *Harvard Law Review* 193 (1890).

(l) Weinstein, "Commercial Appropriation of Names or Likenesses: Section 3344 and the Common Law," 52 *Los Angeles Bar Journal* 430 (1977).

4.53–2   Publicity Compared with Privacy

The cases in the prior section discuss various ways in which a right of publicity and related property concepts have been formulated in certain jurisdictions. The cases which follow either adhere to a privacy concept or dismiss the importance of any distinction between publicity and privacy. The discussions in *Ali* v. *Playgirl* and *Motschenbacher* v. *R. J. Reynolds Tobacco Co.* are of particular importance in determining to what extent distinctions between privacy and publicity should be drawn.

O'Brien v. Pabst Sales Co., 124 F.2d 167 (5th Cir. 1942)

Hutcheson, Circuit Judge.

Plaintiff, in physique as in prowess as a hurler, a modern David, is a famous football player. Defendant, in bulk, if not in brass and vulnerability, a modern Goliath, is a distributor of Pabst beer. Plaintiff, among other honors received during the year 1938, was picked by Grantland Rice on his Collier's All American Football Team. Defendant, as a part of its advertising publicity for 1939, following its custom of getting out football schedule calendars, placed an order with the Inland Lithographing Company, to prepare for and furnish to it, 35,000 Pabst 1939 football calendars. The calendars were to carry complete schedules of all major college games; professional schedules; and pictures of Grantland Rice's 1938 All American Football Team, the Inland Company to furnish photographs and necessary releases.

At the top of the calendar, as thus printed and circulated, were the words "Pabst Blue Ribbon." Directly underneath were the words "Football Calendar, 1939"; to the left of these words was a photograph of O'Brien in football uniform characteristically poised for the throw; to the right of them was a glass having on it the words "Pabst Breweries, Blue Ribbon Export Beer"; and to the right of the glass still, a bottle of beer, having on it "Pabst Blue Ribbon Beer." Directly below these was the intercollegiate football schedule for 1939, and in the center of the calendar were pictures, including that of O'Brien, of Grantland Rice's All American Football Team for 1938. Near the bottom was the schedule of the national football league and on the very bottom margin, were the words "Pabst Famous Blue Ribbon Beer."

Claiming that this use of his photograph as part of defendant's advertising was an invasion of his right of privacy and that he had been damaged thereby, plaintiff brought this suit.

The defenses were three. The first was that if the mere use of one's picture in truthful and respectable advertising would be an actionable invasion of privacy in the case of a private person, the use here was not, as to plaintiff, such an invasion, for as a result of his activities and prowess in football, his chosen field, and their nationwide and deliberate publicizing with his consent and in his interest, he was no longer, as to them, a private but a public person, and as to their additional publication he had no right of privacy. The second defense was that plaintiff, in his own interest and that of Texas Christian University, had posed for and had authorized the publicity department of T. C. U. to distribute his picture and biographical data to newspapers, magazines, sports journals and the public generally, and that the particular picture whose use is complained of had been in due course obtained from and payment for it had been made to the T. C. U. publicity department. Third, no injury to appellant's person, property or reputation had been or could be shown and there was therefore no basis for a recovery. The testimony fully supported these defenses. It showed that plaintiff, then 23 years old, had been playing football for 14 years, four years of that time with Texas Christian University, and two with the Philadelphia Eagles, a professional football team. During that period he had received many and distinguished trophies and honors as an outstanding player of the game. He had in fact been the recipient of practically every worthwhile football trophy and recognition, being picked by Grantland Rice on his Collier's All American Football Team, and by Liberty on their All Players All American Team, and many other so-called All American Football Teams. Plaintiff testified that he had not given permission to use his picture, indeed had not known of the calendar until some time after its publication and circulation; that he was a member of the Allied Youth of America, the main theme of which was the doing away with alcohol among young people; that he had had opportunities to sell his endorsement for beer and alcoholic beverages and had refused it; and that he was greatly embarrassed and humiliated when he saw the calendar and realized that his face and name was associated with publicity for the sale of beer. But he did not, nor did anyone for him, testify to a single fact which would show that he had suffered pecuniary damage in any amount. In addition, on cross-examination he testified; that he had repeatedly posed for photographs for use in publicizing himself and the T. C. U. football team; that Mr. Ridings, director of publicity and news service of T. C. U. without obtaining particular, but with his general, approval and consent, had furnished numberless photographs to various people, periodicals and magazines; and that the pictures of those composing Grantland Rice's All American Football Team which appeared on the calendar, including his own picture, were first publicized in Collier's magazine, a magazine of widest circulation.

On defendants' part, it was shown that following the instructions given by the defendant, the calendar company had written to the T. C. U. Director of publicity for, and obtained from him, the photograph for use in the calendar, paying him $1 therefor, and that the photograph had been used in the belief that the necessary consent to do so had been obtained. The proof that plaintiff had posed for many football pictures for the publicity department of T. C. U. for the purpose of having them widely circulated over the United States was overwhelming and uncontradicted. Mr. Riding, director of publicity, testified that Davey O'Brien was perhaps the most publicized football player of the year 1938–39; that it was the function of his office to permit and increase the publicity of football players; that his office had furnished some 800 photographs of plaintiff to sports editors, magazines, etc.; that if anybody made a request for a picture of O'Brien he would ordinarily grant the request without asking what they were going to do with it; that the picture in the upper left hand corner of the calendar is a very popular picture of O'Brien and perhaps his most famous pose, and that the publicity department had general author-

ity to furnish plaintiff's pictures for publicity purposes but had never knowingly furnished any for use in commercial advertising except with O'Brien's consent and approval. . . .

The District Judge agreed with defendant that no case had been made out. He was of the opinion: that considered from the standpoint merely of an invasion of plaintiffs right of privacy, no case was made out, because plaintiff was an outstanding national football figure and had completely publicized his name and his pictures. He was of the opinion too, that considered from the point of view that the calendar damaged him because it falsely, though only impliedly, represented that plaintiff was a user of, or was recommending the use of, Pabst beer, no case was made out because nothing in the calendar or football schedule could be reasonably so construed: every fact in it was truthfully stated and there was no representation or suggestion of any kind that O'Brien or any of the other fooball celebrities whose pictures it showed were beer drinkers or were recommending its drinking to others; the business of making and selling beer is a legitimate and eminently respectable business and people of all walks and views in life, without injury to or reflection upon themselves, drink it, and that any association of O'Brien's picture with a glass of beer could not possibly disgrace or reflect upon or cause him damage. He directed a verdict for defendant. . . .

Assuming then, what is by no means clear, that an action for right of privacy would lie in Texas at the suit of a private person, we think it clear that the action fails; because plaintiff is not such a person and the publicity he got was only that which he had been constantly seeking and receiving; and because the use of the photograph was by permission, and there were no statements or representations made in connection with it, which were or could be either false, erroneous or damaging to plaintiff. Nothing in the majority opinion purports to deal with or express an opinion on the matter dealt with in the dissenting opinion, the right of a person to recover on quantum merit, for the use of his name for advertising purposes. That was not the case pleaded and attempted to be brought. The case was not for the value of plaintiff's name in advertising a product but for damages by way of injury to him in using his name in advertising beer. Throughout the pleadings, the record and the brief, plaintiff has uniformly taken the position that he is not suing for the reasonable value of his endorsement of beer, on the contrary, the whole burden of his pleading and brief is the repeated asseveration, that he would not and did not endorse beer, and the complaint is that he was damaged by the invasion of his privacy in so using his picture as to create the impression that he was endorsing beer.

The judgement was right. It is affirmed.

Holmes, Circuit Judge (dissenting).

There is no Texas statute or decision directly in point, but I think, under the Texas common law, the appellant is entitled to recover the reasonable value of the use in trade and commerce of his picture for advertisement purposes, to the extent that such use was appropriated by appellee. . .

Palmer v. Schonhorn Enterprises, Inc., 232 A.2d 458 (N.J. Sup.Ct. 1967)

Professional golfers (Arnold Palmer, Gary Player, Doug Sanders, and Jack Nicklaus) sought an injunction and damages with respect to the use of their names by defendant corporation in conjunction with a game manufactured by the defendant.

Defendant corporation manufactured a game on golf. The cover of the box in which the game was contained had a picure of a golfer and a caddy and writing that said the profiles and playing charts of 23 famous golfers were inside. The names were not advertised on the lids of the box; the customer would have to purchase the box first to find out who the golfers were. The information contained about the plaintiffs was admittedly accurate. It was the kind of information readily available and was frequently reproduced by magazines. At the same time, the use of plaintiff's names admittedly enhanced the marketability of the game. The issue was whether the use of plaintiffs' names and biographical data was a violation of their right to privacy.

The court held that the defendant was not permitted to commercially exploit or capitalize on the many accomplishments of the plaintiffs. Appropriation is a component of the right to privacy, a right recognized in New Jersey. While

for public figures, the right to privacy is more limited than for the average citizen, public figures are entitled to relief when their names are used to advertise or enhance the sale of a product without their consent. Plaintiffs can receive great sums of money for their endorsements and have the right to enjoy the fruits of human industry, free from unjustified interference.

Ali v. Playgirl Inc. et al., 447 F.Supp. 723 (S.D.N.Y. 1978)

Gagliardi, District Judge.

Plaintiff Muhammad Ali, a citizen of Illinois and until recently the heavyweight boxing champion of the world, has brought this diversity action for injunctive relief and damages against defendants Playgirl, Inc., a California corporation, Independent News Company ("Independent"), a New York corporation, and Tony Yamada, a California citizen, for their alleged unauthorized printing, publication and distribution of an objectionable portrait of Ali in the February, 1978 issue of Playgirl Magazine ("Playgirl"), a monthly magazine published by Playgirl, Inc., and distributed in New York State by Independent. The portrait complained of depicts a nude black man seated in the corner of a boxing ring and is claimed to be unmistakably recognizable as plaintiff Ali. Alleging that the publication of this picture constitutes, *inter alia,* a violation of his rights under Section 51 of the New York Civil Rights Law (McKinney 1976) and of his related common law "right of publicity," Ali now moves for a preliminary injunction pursuant to Rule 65, Fed.R.Civ.P., directing defendants Playgirl, Inc. and Independent to cease distribution and dissemination of the February, 1978 issue of Playgirl Magazine. to withdraw that issue from circulation and recover possession of all copies presently offered for sale, and to surrender to plaintiff any printing plates or devices used to reproduce the portrait complained of. For the reasons which follow and to the extent indicated below, plaintiff's motion for a preliminary injunction is granted. . . .

On January 31, 1978, plaintiff Ali commenced this action by order to show cause seeking a preliminary injunction and the issuance of a temporary restraining order pending the hearing on the preliminary injunction. Rule 65(b), Fed.R. Civ.P. The temporary restraining order was issued on January 31 and the matter was set for a hearing on February 2, 1978.

At the preliminary injunction hearing on February 2, counsel stated that the February issue of Playgirl containing the allegedly unlawful portrait of Ali was then scheduled to go "off sale," that is, to be removed from newsstand circulation on February 4. Defendant Independent, through counsel, represented to the court that it was scheduled to conduct the removal of the remaining issues on that date and that thereafter Independent would not be involved in any further distribution of the magazine. . . .

As to defendant Playgirl, Inc. however, the circumstances were substantially different. It contended, through counsel, that there would be no further domestic distribution of the issue containing the allegedly offensive picture (Tr. 7), but advised that it did intend to distribute the magazine in England (Tr. 7–8). Plaintiff therefore renewed his application for a preliminary injunction as to Playgirl Inc., restraining any further publication or circulation of the disputed copies. In this regard all parties agree that the court, on the basis of the portrait and accompanying descriptive legend, is fully competent to decide the question of the issuance of a preliminary injunction without holding further evidentiary hearings. . . .

This court concludes that plaintiff has satisfied the standard established in this Circuit for determining whether a preliminary injunction should issue. *Sonesta International Hotels* v. *Wellington Associates*, 483 F.2d 247 (2d Cir. 1973). The familiar alternative test formula is that

> a preliminary injunction should issue only upon a clear showing of either (1) probable success on the merits *and* possible irreparable injury, *or* (2) sufficiently serious questions going to the merits to make them a fair ground for litigation *and* a balance of hardships tipping decidedly toward the party requesting the preliminary relief.

Id. at 250 (emphasis in original). . .

In determining the issues of probable success on the merits or sufficiently serious questions going to the merits of this action, it is agreed that this court must look to the substantive law of New York. *Erie Railroad Co.* v. *Tompkins*, 304 U.S. 64, 58 S.Ct. 817, 82 L.Ed. 1188 (1938). To be considered are plaintiff's claims that his statutory "right of privacy" under Sec. 51 of the New York Civil Rights Law and his common law "right of publicity" have been violated.

Section 51 of the New York Civil Rights Law provides in pertinent part:

> Any person whose name, portrait or picture is used within this state for . . . the purposes of trade without the written consent [of that person] may maintain an equitable action . . . against the person, firm or corporation so using his name, portrait or picture, to prevent and restrain the use thereof; and may also sue and recover damages for any injury sustained by reason of such use . . .

Defendants do not, and indeed cannot, seriously dispute the assertion that the offensive drawing is in fact Ali's "portrait or picture." This phrase, as used in sec. 51, is not restricted to photographs, *Eians* v. *Vitagraph, Co.*, 210 N.Y. 51, 57, 103 N.E. 1108 (1913), but generally comprises those representations which are recognizable as likenesses of the complaining individual. *Negri* v. *Schering Corp.*, 333 F.Supp. 101, 104 (S.D.N.Y. 1971). Even a cursory inspection of the picture which is the subject of this action strongly suggests that the facial characteristics of the black male portrayed are those of Muhammad Ali. The cheekbones, broad nose and widest brown eyes, together with the distinctive smile and close cropped black hair are recognizable as the features of the plaintiff, one of the most widely known athletes of our time. In addition, the figure depicted is seated on a stool in the corner of a boxing ring with both hands taped and out-stretched resting on the ropes on either side. Although the picture is captioned "Mystery Man," the identification of the individual as Ali is further implied by an accompanying verse which refers to the figure as "the Greatest." This court may take judicial notice that plaintiff Ali has regularly claimed that appellation for himself and that his efforts to identify himself in the public mind as "the Greatest" have been so successful that he is regularly identified as such in the news media.

It is also clear that the picture has been used for the "purpose of trade" within the meaning of sec. 51. In this regard it is the established law of New York that the unauthorized use of an individual's picture is not for a "trade purpose," and thus not violative of sec. 51, if it is "in connection with an item of news or one that is newsworthy.". . .

In the instant case there is no such informational or newsworthy dimension to defendants' unauthorized use of Ali's likeness. Instead, the picture is a dramatization, an illustration falling somewhere between representational art and cartoon, and is accompanied by a plainly fictional and allegedly libellous bit of doggerel. Defendants cannot be said to have presented "the unembroidered dissemination of facts" or "the unvarnished, unfictionalized truth.". . . The nude portrait was clearly included in the magazine solely "for purposes of trade — e.g., merely to attract attention." . . .

Finally, defendants concede that Ali did not consent to the inclusion of his likeness in the February, 1978 Playgirl Magazine (Tr. 2). Defendants contend, however, that even if their use of Ali's likeness is determined to be unauthorized and for trade purposes within the meaning of sec. 51, the statutory right of privacy does not extend to protect "someone such as an athlete . . . who chooses to bring himself to public notice, who chooses, indeed, as clearly as the plaintiff here does to rather stridently seek out publicity" (Tr. 5). Defendants are plainly in error in disputing liability on the basis of Ali's status as a public personality. Such a contention

> confuses the fact that projection into the public arena may make for newsworthiness of one's activities, and all the hazards of publicity thus entailed, with the quite different and independent right to have one's personality, even if newsworthy, free from commercial exploitation at the hands of another . . . That [plaintiff] may have voluntarily on occasion surrendered [his] privacy, for a price or gratuitously, does not forever forfeit for anyone's commercial profit so much of [his] privacy as [he] has not relinquished. [citations omitted]

Booth *v.* Curtis Publishing Co., 15 A.D.2d 343, 351–52, 223 N.Y.S.2d 737, 745 (1st Dept.), aff'd, 11 N.Y.2d 907, 228 N.Y.S.2d 468, 183 N.E.2d 812 (1962). . . .

Accordingly, this court is satisfied that plaintiff Ali has established probable success on the merits of his claimed violation of privacy under sec. 51 of the New York Civil Rights Law.

The foregoing discussion also establishes the likelihood that plaintiff will prevail on his claim that his right of publicity has been violated by the publication of the offensive portrait. This Circuit has long held that New York recognizes the common law property right of publicity in addition to, and distinct from, the statutory right under sec. 51. *Haelan Laboratories, Inc.* v. *Topps Chewing Gum, Inc.*, 202 F.2d 866, 868 (2d Cir.), *cert. denied*, 345 U.S. 816, 74 S.Ct. 26, 98 L.Ed. 343 (1953). . . .

It must be noted, however, that the courts of New York do not regularly distinguish between the proprietary right of publicity, discussed *infra*, and the sec. 51 right of privacy. The latter has been characterized as establishing and limiting the right of a person "to be left alone" and protecting "the sentiments, thoughts and feelings of an individual . . . from [unwanted] commercial exploitation," *Flores* v. *Mosler Safe Co., supra,* 7 N.Y.2d at 280, 196 N.Y.S.2d at 977–78, 164 N.E.2d at 855, but numerous cases blend the concepts together and expressly recognize a right of recovery under sec. 51 for violations of an individual's property interest in his likeness or reputation. See, e.g., *Redmond* v. *Columbia Pictures Corp.*, 277 N.Y. 707, 14 N.E.2d 636 (1938). . . .

The distinctive aspect of the common law right of publicity is that it recognizes the commercial value of the picture or representation of a prominent person or performer, and protects his proprietary interest in the profitability of his public reputation or "persona." See *Zacchini* v. *Scripps-Howard Broadcasting Co., supra,* 433 U.S. at 573, 97 S.Ct. 2849. As held by this Circuit, New York State recognizes that, independent of his sec. 51 rights, "a man has a right in the publicity value of his photograph, i.e., the right to grant the exclusive privilege of publishing his picture." . . .

Accordingly, this right of publicity is usually asserted only if the plaintiff has "achieved in some degree a celebrated status." *Price* v. *Hal Roach Studios, Inc, supra,* 400 F.Supp. at 847, quoting Gordon, *Right of Property in Name, Likeness, Personality and History*, 55 NW. U.L.Rev. 553, 607 (1960). In the instant case, it is undisputed that plaintiff Ali has achieved such a "celebrated status" and it is clear to this court that he has established a valuable interest in his name and his likeness. . . .

It is established that plaintiff must make a showing of irreparable injury. . . .

As has been noted, in the course of his public

career plaintiff has established a commercially valuable propietary interest in his likeness and reputation, analogous to the good will accumulated in the name of a successful business entity. To the extent that defendants are unlawfully appropriating this valuable commodity for themselves, proof of damages or unjust enrichment may be extremely difficult. . . .

In virtually identical circumstances it has been observed that "a celebrity's property interest in his name and likeness is unique, and therefore there is no serious question as to the propriety of injunctive relief." *Uhlaender* v. *Henricksen, supra,* 316 F.Supp. at 1283. Furthermore, defendants appear not only to be usurping plaintiff's valuable right of publicity for themselves but may well be inflicting damage upon his marketable reputation. As described previously, the "likeness" of Ali which has been published is a full frontal nude drawing, not merely a sketch or photograph of him as he appears in public. Damages from such evident abuse of plaintiff's property right in his public reputation are plainly difficult to measure by monetary standards. . . .

Defendant Playgirl, Inc. contends that under New York law any injunction which issues cannot extend to prohibit publication or distribution of the portrait complained of beyond the boundaries of New York State, citing *Rosemont Enterprises, Inc.* v. *Urban Systems, Inc.,* 42 A.D.2d 544, 345 N.Y.S.2d 17 (1st Dept. 1973). Consequently, Playgirl, Inc. takes the position that, although it is subject to the *in personam* jurisdiction of this court and has announced its intention to distribute the issue of Playgirl Magazine containing the offensive picture throughout England, the court is without authority to restrain that distribution. This court cannot agree.

Although the issue is not entirely free from question, this court agrees that, under the rule of *Erie Railroad Co.* v. *Tompkins,* it is to be guided by applicable state law in determining the geographical scope of any injunction it issues in aid of state law rights. . . .

The New York case relied on by defendants for the proposition that any injunction issued by this court must not extend beyond New York, *Rosemont supra,* 42 A.D.2d 544, 345 N.Y.S.2d 17, restricts the extent of sec. 51 injunctive relief in certain circumstances due to a concern for possible conflicts between the law of New York and the

applicable law of other jurisdictions. In that regard this court is clearly bound by the law of New York. . . .

However, defendant Playgirl, Inc., misconstrues the rationale of *Rosemont* and its applicability to the facts of the instant action. That case arose from a suit brought under sec. 51 of the Civil Rights Law by Howard Hughes. The lower court held that the defendants' unauthorized marketing and distribution of "The Howard Hughes Games," a board game based on plaintiff Hughes' career, constituted an appropriation of plaintiff's property rights in his name and career in violation of sec. 51. *Rosemont Enterprises, Inc.* v. *Urban Systems, Inc.,* 72 Misc.2d 788, 790–91, 340 N.Y.S.2d 144, 146–47 (Sup.Ct. N.Y.Co. 1973). . . .

Careful examination of this holding in light of the lower court injunction compels the conclusion that the Appellate Division did not intend to establish a flat prohibition against *any* sec. 51 injunction extending beyond the limit of New York State. Rather, reviewing an injunction which declared plaintiff's rights under sec. 51 to be equitably protected as "against all the world," the Appellate Division recognized that, as a practical matter, such global restraint would plainly involve intrusions into unknown foreign jurisdictions of such numbers and varieties of substantive law that no conflict-of-law analysis concerning the law of privacy could be undertaken. Consequently, the reviewing court exercised its discretion under the facts before it to note simply that "[i]n other jurisdictions, the law with respect to the right of privacy *could* have other efficacy with respect to a public figure" 42 A.D.2d at 544, 345 N.Y.S.2d at 18 (emphasis added; citations omitted), and to restrict application of the injunction to New York.

In the present case, by contrast, this court is not faced with factual circumstances involving the necessity of equitable relief running throughout numerous indeterminable jurisdictions. Defendant Playgirl, Inc., has represented its intention to distribute overseas only in England. For purposes of the motion for preliminary relief and compliance with the second branch of the *Sonesta* test, this court concludes that the law of England with respect to plaintiff's right of privacy, at least insofar as it includes his proprietary right of publicity and reputation, is such that under it there exist "sufficiently serious questions going to the merits to make them a fair ground for litigation."

Sonesta International Hotels v. *Wellington Associates, supra,* 483 F.2d at 250. . . .

Furthermore, the balance of hardships tips decidedly toward Ali in this matter, for defendant Playgirl, Inc. is merely being restrained from further distribution and is not being affirmatively ordered to undertake new or unduly burdensome obligations. Since all the parties and legal contentions are presently before this court, to require plaintiff to commence a new action in England would subject him to unnecessary and avoidable hardship. Finally, as discussed previously, plaintiff has satisfied this court that there is a strong possibility of irreparable injury absent the issuance of a preliminary injunction. For the foregoing reasons, the preliminary injunction shall extend to restrain defendants' activities with respect to all copies of the magazine containing the disputed portrait in England as well as New York.

A hearing on the issue of a permanent injunction shall be scheduled promptly. Among the issues there to be determined is whether or not the privacy or publicity law of England does in fact "have other efficacy with respect to a public figure." *Rosemont Enterprises* v. *Urban Systems, Inc., supra,* 42 A.D.2d at 544, 345 N.Y.S.2d 18. *See* Rule 44.1, Fed.R.Civ.P. In addition, plaintiff will maintain the burden of establishing that there is a likelihood of recurrent violations of his rights. *United States* v. *W. T. Grant, supra.* Accordingly, plaintiff's request for preliminary relief pursuant to Rule 65 is granted. . . .

Motschenbacher v. R. J. Reynolds Tobacco Co., 498 F.2d 821 (9th Cir. 1974)

Koelsch, Circuit Judge:

Lothar Motschenbacher appeals from the district court's order granting summary judgment in favor of defendants in his suit seeking injunctive relief and damages for the alleged misappropriation of his name, likeness, personality, and endorsement in nationally televised advertising for Winston cigarettes. . . .

The "facts" on which the district court rendered summary judgment are substantially as follows: Plaintiff Motschenbacher is a professional driver of racing cars, internationally known and recognized in racing circles and by racing fans. He derives part of his income from manufacturers of commercial products who pay him for endorsing their products.

During the relevant time span, plaintiff has consistently "individualized" his cars to set them apart from those of other drivers and to make them more readily identifiable as his own. Since 1966, each of his cars has displayed a distinctive narrow white pinstripe appearing on no other car. This decoration has adorned the leading edges of the cars' bodies, which have uniformly been solid red. In addition, the white background for his racing number "11" has always been oval, in contrast to the circular backgrounds of all other cars.

In 1970, defendants, R. J. Reynolds Tobacco Company and William Esty Company, produced and caused to be televised a commercial which utilized a "stock" color photograph depicting several racing cars on a racetrack. Plaintiff's car appears in the foreground, and although plaintiff is the driver, his facial features are not visible.

In producing the commercial, defendants altered the photograph: they changed the numbers on all racing cars depicted, transforming plaintiff's number "11" into "71"; they "attached" a wing-like device known as a "spoiler" to plaintiff's car; they added the word "Winston," the name of their product, to that spoiler and removed advertisements for other products from the spoilers of other cars. However, they made no other changes, and the white pinstriping, the oval medallion, and the red color of plaintiff's car were retained. They then made a motion picture from the altered photograph, adding a series of comic strip-type "balloons" containing written messages of an advertising nature; one such balloon message, appearing to emanate from plaintiff, was: "Did you know that Winston tastes good, like a cigarette should?" They also added a sound track consisting in part of voices coordinated with, and echoing, the written messages. The commercial was subsequently broadcast nationally on network television and in color.

Several of plaintiff's affiants who had seen the commercial on television had immediately recognized plaintiff's car and had inferred that it was sponsored by Winston cigarettes.

On these facts the district court, characterizing plaintiff's action as one "for damages for invasion of privacy," granted summary judgment for defendants, finding as a matter of law that

. . . [t]he driver of car No. 71 in the commercial (which was plaintiff's car No. 11 prior to said change of number and design) is anonymous: that is, (a) the person who is driving said car is unrecognizable and unidentified, and (b) a reasonable inference could not be drawn that he is, or could reasonably be understood to be plaintiff, Lothar Motschenbacher, or any other driver or person. . . .

Since the Winston commercial was broadcast on television throughout the United States, our initial inquiry in determining the correct legal standards to be applied on the motion for summary judgment is directed at the proper choice of law. In a diversity case, a federal court must follow the substantive law of the state in which it sits. . . .

In this case, we believe that California courts, under Reich v. Purcell, 67 Cal.2d 551, 63 Cal.Rptr. 31, 432 P.2d 727 (1967), would apply California local law. By the same token, noting the novelty of the factual situation presented and recognizing that the parties have each cited general case law in support of their respective positions, we think that California courts would not hesitate to consider relevant precedent from other jurisdictions in determining California local law.

In California, as in the vast majority of jurisdictions, the invasion of an individual's right of privacy is an actionable tort. . . .

California courts have observed that "[t]he gist of the cause of action in a privacy case is not injury to the character or reputation, but a direct wrong of a personal character resulting in injury to the feelings without regard to any effect which the publication may have on the property, business, pecuniary interest, or the standing of the individual in the community." . . .

It is true that the injury suffered from an appropriation of the attributes of one's identity may be "mental and subjective" — in the nature of humiliation, embarrassment, and outrage. . . . However, where the identity appropriated has a commercial value, the injury may be largely, or even wholly of an economic or material nature. Such is the nature of the injury alleged by plaintiff.

Some courts have protected this "commercial" aspect of an individual's interest in his own identity under a privacy theory. *See e.g.,* Palmer v. Schonhorn Enterprises, Inc., 96 N.J.Super. 72, 232

A.2d 458 (1967); *see generally* Treece, Commercial Exploitation of Names, Likenesses, and Personal Histories, 51 Texas L.Rev. 637 (1973). . . .

Others have sought to protect it under the rubric of "property" or a so-called "right of publicity." *See e.g.,* Ettore v. Philco Television Broadcasting Corp., 229 F.2d 481, 485–493 (3d Cir. 1956), cert. den., 351 U.S. 926, 76 S.Ct. 783, 100 L.Ed. 1456 (1956); Haelan v. Topps Chewing Gum, 202 F.2d 866, 868 (2d Cir. 1953), cert. den. 346 U.S. 816, 74 S. Ct. 26, 98 L.Ed. 343 (1953), *noted in* Nimmer, The Right of Publicity, 19 Law & Contempt.Prob. 203 (1954), 62 Yale L.J. 1123 (1953), *and* 41 Geo.L.J. 593 (1953). . . .

Prosser synthesizes the approaches as follows:

> Although the element of protection of the plaintiff's personal feelings is obviously not to be ignored in such a case, the effect of the appropriation decisions is to recognize or create an exclusive right in the individual plaintiff to a species of trade name, his own, and a kind of trade mark in his likeness. It seems quite pointless to dispute over whether such a right is to be classified as "property"; it is at least clearly proprietary in its nature. Once protected by the law, it is a right of value upon which the plaintiff can capitalize by selling licenses. (footnotes omitted)

Law of Torts (4th ed. 1971), at 807.

So far as we can determine, California has no case in point; the state's appropriation cases uniformly appear to have involved only the "injury to personal feelings" aspect of the tort. Nevertheless, from our review of the relevant authorities, we conclude that the California appellate courts would, in a case such as this one, afford legal protection to an individual's proprietary interest in his own identity. We need not decide whether they would do so under the rubric of "privacy," "property," or "publicity"; we only determine that they would recognize such an interest and protect it.

We turn now to the question of "identifiability." Clearly, if the district court correctly determined as a matter of law that plaintiff is not identifiable in the commercial, then in no sense has plaintiff's identity been misappropriated nor his interest violated.

Having viewed a film of the commercial, we

agree with the district court that the "likeness" of plaintiff is itself unrecognizable; however, the court's further conclusion of law to the effect that the driver is not identifiable as plaintiff is erroneous in that it wholly fails to attribute proper significance to the distinctive decoration appearing on the car. As pointed out earlier, these markings were not only peculiar to the plaintiff's cars but they caused some persons to think the car in question was plaintiff's and to infer that the person driving the car was the plaintiff.

Defendant's reliance on *Branson* v. *Fawcett Publications, Inc.,* 124 F.Supp. 429 (E.D.Ill.1954), is misplaced. In *Branson,* a part-time racing driver brought suit for invasion of privacy when a photograph of his overturned racing car was printed in a magazine without his consent. In ruling that "the photograph . . . does not identify the plaintiff to the public or any member thereof," 124 F.Supp. at 433, the court said:

> [T]he automobile is pointed upward in the air and the picture shows primarily the bottom of the racer. The backdrop of the picture is not distinguishable. No likeness, face, image, form or silhouette of the plaintiff or of any person is shown. From all that appears from the picture itself, there is no one in the car. Moreover, no identifying marks or numbers on the car appear. . . . Plaintiff does not even assert that the car he was driving was the same color as that which appears in the colored reproduction. 124 F.Supp. at 432.

But in this case, the car under consideration clearly has a driver and displays several uniquely distinguishing features.

The judgment is vacated and the cause is remanded for further proceedings.

(Opinion footnotes are omitted.)

4.53–3 Trademark

The right of publicity is a common law property right that arises from a person's name, image, and reputation. Closely aligned is the idea of a tradename or trademark. Going beyond a right of publicity, the trademark requires an infringement by another party that is likely to mislead or confuse the public.

In the example of *Ashe* v. *Pepsico,* discussed below, the possibility of conflict arises between the right to use one's own name and the possible trademark involving that name that is owned by another party. Obviously, a right to market oneself in a particular manner can be curtailed if there has been any relinquishment of the right to another.

Ashe v. *Pepsico, Inc.,* 205 USPQ 451 (S.D. N.Y. 1979)

Professional tennis player Arthur Ashe sought a declaratory judgment that his use of the term "Advantage Ashe" did not infringe on the rights of the defendant, doing business as Wilson Sporting Goods Company, to its trademark "Advantage," used for tennis rackets and other sporting goods.

Beginning in 1971, Ashe began using the title "Advantage Ashe" for a tennis column. In 1974, he published a recommendation in his column that yellow-lensed eyeglasses should be used while playing tennis indoors or on cloudy days. Based on the article, the American Optical Corporation researched and tested the product, and, endorsed by Ashe, began marketing the Advantage Ashe glasses in 1976. Over 32,000 pairs were sold through 1978 when the licensing agreement expired.

Meanwhile, in 1973, Wilson had applied for and was granted a trademark registration for "Advantage," used to denote their tennis rackets. The mark was later expanded to include golf clubs, golf balls, and racquetball rackets. When Ashe and American Optical applied for registration of the trademark "Advantage Ashe," they were denied because the term "Advantage" was already being used in the general field of tennis equipment. The key question before the court was whether there was any likelihood that an appreciable number of ordinary, prudent purchasers were likely to be misled or simply confused as to the source of the eyeglasses.

The court first held that the strength of the mark "Advantage" was intrinsically weak and required imagination to reach a conclusion as to the nature of Wilson's rackets. The two terms were also dissimilar; Ashe's well-known name predominated over the word "advantage." The phrase was made even more identifiable with Ashe because of its adjoining picture of him on the logo. In contrast, Wilson's "Advantage" products predominantly featured the Wilson logo. Furthermore, while the meaning of advantage used by Wilson meant edge or upper hand, when it was combined with Ashe, it took on the meaning of a tennis score.

The court next found a significant competitive distance between the glasses as accessories and the racket as necessary equipment to the game. Because the buyers were generally sophisticated consumers, they were probably not confused as to the source of these separate goods.

Finally, the court found that Ashe had adopted the mark in good faith, with no attempt to ride on the coattails of Wilson's reputation. While Wilson's sale of its rackets could not be expected to fall because of the use of Ashe's mark for tennis glasses, the court held that Ashe did have a significant interest in retaining the goodwill developed through the use of his name in conjunction with advantage. Therefore, the court allowed the trademark to stand.

4.53—4   Relinquishing Rights by Agreement

Rights accruing to an individual can be contractually relinquished. The *Cepeda* case in particular details the consequences of careless and overbroad grants of rights. Those who wish to capitalize on the fame of the celebrity will always press for the broadest possible grants. The celebrity's representative must safeguard the client's interests by restricting the grant to the limited purposes specifically discussed in the negotiations.

Cepeda v. Swift and Company, 415 F.2d 1205 (8th Cir. 1969)

Mehaffy, Circuit Judge.

Orlando Cepeda, a citizen of Puerto Rico and a famous major league baseball player, brought this suit in state court against Swift and Company. Upon timely removal to federal court by Swift, Cepeda filed an amended complaint, joining as an additional defendant Wilson Sporting Goods Company. The action was grounded upon the asserted unauthorized use of plaintiff's name, likeness, photograph, signature and good will by Swift in an advertising campaign utilized by one of its divisions in the promotion of sales of meat products, namely Mayrose franks and bacon.

The complaint alleged that plaintiff has become a widely renowned athlete and, as a result, his right to associate his name through endorsement of products and in connection with promotions and sales of products is an asset of great value; that his right of privacy has been invaded and infringed by defendants in their unauthorized use of his name, photograph, etc.; that this unauthorized use has unjustly enriched defendant Swift; and that plaintiff is entitled to compensatory and punitive damages. In the second count of the complaint, plaintiff asserts that on April 30, 1963 he entered into an agreement with defendant Wilson through which Wilson acquired the right to use plaintiff's name, facsimile signature, initials, portrait, or any nickname popularly applied to him, in connection with the sale of baseballs, baseball shoes, baseball gloves and baseball mitts and to license others to do the same. The contract period was for two years with an option to renew for an additional period of one, two or three years. On March 29, 1965, defendant Wilson notified plaintiff of its execution of its option to renew for a period of two years. Plaintiff further alleged that in 1967 Wilson, in disregard of plaintiff's rights, entered into an agreement with Swift by the terms of which Wilson sold baseballs to Swift and agreed that Swift could conduct an advertising campaign employing plaintiff's name and picture with the promotion and sale of Swift's meat products.

Swift did not advertise that Cepeda endorsed its meat products but merely offered Cepeda baseballs at a special price to those forwarding with their order a specified portion of the wrapper from certain products. The campaign was carried out and employed extensively by radio, television, newspapers, magazines and other advertising media in Missouri, Illinois and elsewhere. Plaintiff contends that the gist of Swift's advertising campaign was to associate plaintiff's name and good will inherent in it with defendant's products, asserting that Wilson at no time had his consent to use or assign his name in connection with the promotion and sale of meat products.

The pertinent part of the contract between plaintiff and Wilson reads as follows:

> 1. Cepeda grants to Wilson the exclusive world right and license to manufacture, advertise and sell baseballs, baseball shoes, baseball gloves and baseball mitts identified by his name, facsimile signature, initials, portrait, or by any nickname popularly applied to him, and to license others so to do. During the term of this agreement Cepeda agrees not to grant any similar right or license to any other person. Cepeda shall sign all lawful documents which may be necessary to enable Wilson to secure federal state or foreign registration of trade marks or trade names for products identified as herein provided.

The consideration for the contract was that Wilson should pay plaintiff a royalty of $1.00 per dozen on baseball catcher's or basemen's mitts, 60¢ per dozen on baseball gloves and 10¢ per dozen on baseballs sold by Wilson or its licensees, provided that the royalties should not be less than $50.00 per year nor more than $500.00 per year. When the contract was renewed, the maximum royalty was raised to $1,000 per year, but in no year have the royalties reached said maximum amounts. It is not in dispute that Wilson paid plaintiff all of the royalties for the Cepeda products manufactured and sold by it.

The thrust of plaintiff's argument is that the contract conveyed to Wilson the right to use his name only in connection with the sale of certain baseball products and that nowhere in the contract does plaintiff authorize his name to be used in connection with meat products or the promotion of meat products as was done here. We disagree. The contract plainly grants to Wilson the exclusive world right to manufacture, advertise and sell baseballs, baseball shoes, baseball gloves and baseball mitts identified by plaintiff's name, facsimile signature or picture, and the right to license others so to do. The contract nowhere contains any restriction on the manner in which baseballs could be advertised or sold. Plaintiff's argument is rooted in the concept that the intent of the parties was to restrict the advertising and sale

of products. To accept plaintiff's interpretation of the contract would require a rewriting and the interpolation of words into the contract. This we cannot do when the language of the contract is so clear. The contract, being unambiguous as it is, needs no interpretation except to give the plain and simple words their plain and simple meaning. . . .

It is perfectly clear to us that plaintiff contracted with Wilson and granted to it the exclusive world right and license to manufacture, advertise and sell baseballs. Wilson was also authorized to contract its rights to others and this is exactly what was done in this case. We further find that Swift did not exceed the authority granted to it by Wilson. The advertising material that Swift used was an offer to sell Orlando Cepeda baseballs for only $1.00 with the words "Special Offer" taken from a package of Mayrose franks or bacon. A number of the advertisements contained a picture of plaintiff in his baseball uniform either swinging a bat or catching a ball along with a picture of the baseball offered, a picture of the Mayrose products, and an explanation of the "Special Offer." However, as hereinbefore mentioned, a survey of all the advertisements reflects that Swift did not in any fashion attempt to indicate that plaintiff used or endorsed its meat products but simply offered for sale Cepeda baseballs for $1.00 when accompanied with a portion of the wrapper from one of its meat products.

We find that the interpretation of the contract by the district court is correct and that the defendants did not exceed their contractual authority.

The judgment of the district court is affirmed.

Sharman v. C. Schmidt & Sons, Inc., 216 F.Supp. 401 (E.D. Pa. 1963)

Claimant professional basketball player brought action for libel and invasion of privacy as a result of his picture being used in an advertisement for beer.

In 1960, Bill Sharman was a basketball player with the Boston Celtics. In an attempt to capitalize on his fame, he hired an agent to procure advertisements and endorsements for him. His picture was taken, and his agent sent it to various advertising agencies. One agency, Ted Bates & Co., selected his picture for a Schmidt

Beer campaign (apparently without knowing who Sharman was). They had Sharman pose in a bowling shirt, holding a bowling ball. There were no other props. Sharman signed a release granting unrestricted permission to the use of his picture. He received compensation of $125. At no time was he told the picture would be used in a beer commercial.

A beer bottle was later engraved onto the photograph, and it was used in Schmidt's advertising campaign. Sharman claimed Schmidt knew he was an athlete and was taking unfair advantage of him. He claimed he was the object of ridicule and criticism because of the photograph and that he would be harmed by it when seeking further endorsements. Furthermore, it would be harmful to his coaching career because it is detrimental to an athlete to be associated with liquor.

The court denied recovery. Even though Sharman had not specifically consented to participate in a beer commercial, he had signed the release and received compensation. Consent to an invasion is a complete defense to the appropriation of plaintiff's likeness to sell products. Only if the use exceeds the consent granted could there by recovery. Here, plaintiff knew and wanted the picture to be used in some sort of ad; the court did not see that a beer advertisement exceeded the consent granted. While the court had sympathy for Sharman, since his agent obviously took advantage of him, it could not grant relief.

NOTE _____

1. One interesting case shows how technological innovations may affect signed waivers that grant permission to other parties to portray one's activities. In *Ettore* v. *Philco Television Broadcasting Corp.*, 229 F.2d 481 (3rd Cir. 1956), a prizefighter brought an action against television stations and sponsors to recover damages for telecast of a motion picture of an old prize fight without his consent.

Albert Ettore fought Joe Louis in 1936 and was knocked out in the fifth round. He had consented to motion pictures being taken of the fight and had received compensation. In 1949 and 1950, the National Broadcasting Corporation broadcast the fight as one in a series called the "Greatest Fights of the Century." Plaintiff claimed he had not

consented to these broadcasts (there was no television in 1936) and said the broadcasts subjected him to ridicule among his friends. (The court noted plaintiff knew of broadcasts and only got upset when the third round, his best, was cut from the show.) The broadcasts were seen in New York, New Jersey, Pennsylvania, and Delaware.

The question was whether there was an injury to plaintiff's property right — his contract of services. (The court noted it was not a violation of a right to privacy.) The defendant claimed the plaintiff waived his property right by sale of motion picture rights. While this view is considered correct by some, this court ruled that such picture rights may not be used for a purpose not contemplated at time of creation. Since television was not in existence, plaintiff could not have contemplated such use. Therefore, the case was remanded to determine the facts in light of the Court of Appeals' decision.

4.53–5   Rights Yielding to "News"

Significant tensions exist between the individual's rights of publicity and privacy and the rights of the press and others to report the news. The discussions in this section introduce the conflicts. More extensive analysis appears in the considerations of sports and the media in Volume Two, Chapter 6, Section 6.40.

_____

Namath v. Sports Illustrated, 371 N.Y.2d 10 (N.Y. App. Div. 1975)

Capozzoli, Justice:

Plaintiff sought substantial compensatory and punitive damages by reason of defendants' publication and use of plaintiff's photograph without his consent. That photograph, which was originally used by defendants, without objection from plaintiff, in conjunction with a news article published by them on the 1969 Super Bowl Game, was used in advertisements promoting subscriptions to their magazine, Sports Illustrated.

The use of plaintiff's photograph was merely incidental advertising of defendants' magazine in which plaintiff had earlier been properly and fairly depicted and, hence, it was not violative of the Civil Rights Law (*Booth* v. *Curtis Publishing Co.*, 15 A.D.2d 343, 223 N.Y.S.2d 737, aff'd, 11 N.Y.2d 907, 228 N.Y.S.2d 468, 182 N.E.2d 812).

Certainly, defendants' subsequent republication of plaintiff's picture was "in motivation, sheer advertising and solicitation. This alone is not determinative of the question so long as the law accords an exempt status to incidental advertising of the news medium itself." (*Booth* v. *Curtis Publishing Co., supra,* p. 349, 223 N.Y.S.2d p. 744.) Again, it was stated, at 15 A.D.2d p. 350, 223 N.Y.S.2d p. 744 of the cited case, as follows:

> Consequently, it suffices here that so long as the reproduction was used to illustrate the quality and content of the periodical in which it originally appeared, the statute was not violated, albeit the reproduction appeared in other media for purposes of advertising the periodical.

Contrary to the dissent, we deem the cited case to be dispositive hereof. The language from the Namath advertisements relied upon in the dissent, does not indicate plaintiff's endorsement of the magazine Sports Illustrated. Had that been the situation, a completely different issue would have been presented. Rather, that language merely indicates, to the readers of those advertisements, the general nature of the contents of what is likely to be included in future issues of the magazine. . . .

Kupferman, Justice (dissenting):

It is undisputed that one Joseph W. Namath is an outstanding sports figure, redoubtable on the football field. Among other things, as the star quarterback of the New York Jets, he led his team to victory on January 12, 1969 in the Super Bowl in Miami.

This feat and the story of the game and its star were heralded with illustrative photographs in the January 20, 1969 issue of Sports Illustrated, conceded to be an outstanding magazine published by Time Incorporated and devoted, as its name implies, to the activities for which it is famous. Of course, this was not the first nor the last time that Sports Illustrated featured Mr Namath and properly so.

The legal problem involves the use of one of his action photos from the January 20, 1969 issue in subsequent advertisements in other magazines as promotional material for the sale of subscriptions to Sports Illustrated.

Plaintiff contends that the use was commercial in violation of his right of privacy under sections 50 and 51 of the Civil Rights Law. See, in general, "The Muddled State of Law of Privacy" by J. Irwin

Shapiro, N.Y.L.J., May 16 and May 19, 1975, p. 1, col. 3. Further, that because he was in the business of endorsing products and selling the use of his name and likeness, it interfered with his right to such sale, sometimes known as the right of publicity. *Haelan Laboratories* v. *Topps Chewing Gum,* 202 F.2d 866 (2nd Cir. 1953). Defendants contend there is an attempt to invade their constitutional rights under the First and Fourteenth Amendments by the maintenance of this action and that, in any event, the advertisements were meant to show "the nature, quality and content" of the magazine and not to trade on the plaintiff's name and likeness.

Initially, we are met with the determination in a similar case, *Booth* v. *Curtis Publishing Co.,* 15 A.D.2d 343, 223 N.Y.S.2d 737 (1st Dept.) *aff'd without op.,* 11 N.Y.2d 907, 228 N.Y.S.2d 468, 182 N.E.2d 812 (1962) relied on by Baer, J., in his opinion at Special Term dismissing the complaint.

The plaintiff was Shirley Booth, the well-known actress, photographed at a resort in the West Indies, up to her neck in the water and wearing an interesting chapeau, which photo appeared in Holiday Magazine along with photographs of other prominent guests. This photo was then used as a substantial part of an advertisement for Holiday.

Mr. Justice Breitel (now Chief Judge Breitel) wrote:

> Consequently, it suffices here that so long as the reproduction was used to illustrate the quality and content of the periodical in which it originally appeared, the statute was not violated, albeit the reproduction appeared in other media for purposes of advertising the periodical. [15 A.D.2d at p. 350, 223 N.Y.S.2d at p. 744]

However, the situation is one of degree. A comparison of the Booth and Namath photographs and advertising copy shows that in the Booth case, her name is in exceedingly small print, and it is the type of photograph itself which attracted attention. In the Namath advertisement, we find, in addition to the outstanding photograph, in Cosmopolitan Magazine (for women) the heading "The Man You Loves Loves Joe Namath," and in Life, the heading "How to get Close to Joe Namath." There seems to be trading on the name of the personality involved in the defendants' advertisements. . . .

The complaint should not have been dismissed as a matter of law.

NOTES _____

1. In *Virgil* v. *Time, Inc.*, 527 F.2d 1122 (9th Cir. 1975), the Ninth Circuit upheld the right of a California bodysurfer to recover damages against a sports magazine. An article in the magazine had detailed certain bizarre incidents relating to the plaintiff's lifestyle. The plaintiff had initially cooperated in the interviews leading up to the article; but he later withdrew his permission for the magazine to publish facts about him. He claimed he had originally understood the article would be concerned only with bodysurfing. The court held that the magazine pried into the strictly private affairs of the plaintiff, reporting on details that were not in any sense "news." Consequently, the truth of the depictions was no defense to plaintiff's suit for an invasion of privacy.

2. In *Neff* v. *Time, Inc.*, 406 F. Supp. 858 (W.D.Pa. 1976), a U.S. District Court refused to award damages to a football spectator who was shown in a national sports magazine on top of a dugout, "hamming it up," with his fly unzipped. The court concluded that the picture was taken with the plaintiff's active encouragement, although without his express consent. The article was deemed to be of legitimate public interest. "Of course we are concerned that Neff's picture was deliberately selected by an editorial committee from a number of similar pictures and segregated and published alone. If his picture had appeared as part of the general crowd scene of fans at a game, even though embarrassing, there would be no problem. Although we have some misgivings, it is our opinion that the publication of Neff's photograph, taken with his active encouragement and participation, and with knowledge that the photographer was connected with a publication, even though taken without his express consent, is protected by the Constitution." [At 862]

3. In *Zacchni* v. *Scripps-Howard Broadcasting Co.*, 433 U.S. 562 (1977), the U.S. Supreme Court held that a television station could not successfully assert First Amendment rights, protecting it from suit brought by a "human cannonball," where the TV station insisted on showing the plaintiff's entire act (all 15 seconds worth) on the nightly news. Stressing that the station had depicted the entire act, and not just a segment, the Court held the news function did not extend this far. Four justices dissented. Substantial portions of the Court's opinion and Justice Powell's dissent are set forth in Volume II, Chapter 6, Section 6.40.

4.53–6   Libel

The case of *Johnston* v. *Time, Inc.*, discussed below, is included at this point to underscore (1)

the nexus between issues of publicity, privacy, and libel, and (2) the problems that one representing the athlete or any other party in professional sports encounters in guarding against unwise public utterances. As the *Johnston* case indicates, one cannot assume that the rigorous standards for libel relating to public figures are applicable, even where the individual involved is a sports figure. The more traditional tests relating to false statements may be the standards applied by a court.

For more on libel involving celebrities, see also Volume Two, Chapter 6, Section 6.40, in particular the case of *Spahn* v. *Julian Messner Company*.

_____

Johnston v. **Time, Inc.**, 321 F. Supp 837 (M.D.N.C. 1970)

Plaintiff pro-basketball player Neil Johnston sought recovery from Time, Inc., coach Red Auerbach, and author George Plimpton for libel which allegedly ended his career. The statements appeared in the December 28, 1968, *Sports Illustrated* cover story on Bill Russell. Boston coach Auerbach was reported as saying that Russell "destroyed" Johnston psychologically, because Johnston played so ludicrously that players on the bench laughed at him, and subsequently Johnston was run out of organized basketball.

The first motion before the court was defendant Time's motion to dismiss for lack of jurisdiction over the person. The court held that North Carolina provided means for obtaining jurisdiction of foreign corporations under G.S. Sec. 55–145. First, compared with the case *Putnam* v. *Triangle Publications Inc.*, 245 N.C. 432, 96 S. E. 2d 445 (1957), Time had sufficient minimum contacts to establish jurisdiction: Time solicited subscriptions within the state, sold advertising space to North Carolina businesses, and owned property within the state. Secondly, under G. S. Sec. 55–145(a)(4), a single tort was sufficient to confer jurisdiction. Assuming for the purposes of this question that the article was libelous, the court held that a tortious act was committed in North Carolina each time the article was read.

The next question was whether the *in personam* reach of the state conflicted with the due process clause of the Fourteenth Amendment. The standard was whether minimum contacts with the state existed so that the suit did not offend traditional notions of fair play and substantial justice. The court relied on the closely analogous case of *Curtis Publishing Company* v. *Golino,* 383 F.2d 586 (1967), which held that it would not comport with notions of fair play and substantial justice to allow a national magazine which relies on exploitation of the national market to insulate itself from suits in other states by minimizing physical contacts with foreign states. Since a significant portion of *Sports Illustrated*'s revenue came from its North Carolina sales, the court held Time's presence within the state was sufficient to meet the due process requirements. Time argued that there should be a greater showing of contact because of First Amendment guarantees, but the court held that this consideration had been minimized in light of recent cases and that more than the bare essentials of the minimum contacts were present in this case.

The court next heard motions for summary judgment. Viewing the evidence most favorable to the plaintiff, the court held that the article was libelous per se. A jury could find that since Johnston was a basketball coach at Wake Forest University, the article impeached him in his trade. The qualified privilege sometimes extended to material written in good faith about a matter of public interest was not applied since North Carolina had not extended this doctrine to the field of sports reporting. Even if it were applicable, the court held that a jury would have a reasonable basis for finding malice, which would surmount the protection that the privilege affords.

The court held that plaintiff and defendant were not entitled to a summary judgment based on federal constitutional principles except on the limited grounds that there was no actual malice

or reckless conduct on the part of the defendant. Time argued that Johnston was a public figure and that the matter was of public interest — both grounds for barring recovery for the plaintiff. The court held that Johnston, while a public figure in the 1950s, was not one at the time of the suit and was in no position to refute the statements. Moreover, the topic was not a matter of public interest. The article dealt with Bill Russell being named Sportsman of the Year and "[t]hat which is interesting to the public may not always be in the public interest."

Accordingly, both plaintiff's and defendant's motions for summary judgment were denied.

4.60 Constitutional Protections

Most disputes between professional athletes and their clubs, leagues, or associations do not involve constitutional questions. However, some athletic events are sanctioned under the auspices of a state-created body. The requirements of due process and equal protection are accordingly imposed. Muhammad Ali used these circumstances to his advantage in contesting the denial of a boxing license by the New York state authorities.

Ali v. State Athletic Commission of New York, 316 F.Supp. 1246 (S.D.N.Y. 1970)

Mansfield, District Judge.

In this action for a declaratory judgment and injunction, plaintiff, Muhammad Ali, popularly known as Cassius Clay, has moved for a preliminary injunction restraining defendants from denying him a license to box in the State of New York. For the reasons stated below the motion is granted.

The essential facts are not in dispute. From 1961 until April, 1967, Ali was licensed to box in New York, where he was recognized as the World Heavyweight Champion. On April 28, 1967, the New York State Athletic Commission ("Commission" herein) suspended his license because of his refusal to submit to induction in the Armed Forces of the United States. On September 30 of the same year, Ali's license automatically expired pursuant to N.Y. Unconsolidated Laws sec. 8910, which provides that all such licenses are for one year's duration and automatically expire on that date.

On June 20, 1967, Ali, after a jury trial, was convicted in the United States District Court for the Southern District of Texas of the federal felony of refusing to submit to induction into the Armed Forces, 50 U.S.C. App. sec. 462(a), and was sentenced to a term of five years imprisonment. The sentencing judge indicated that he might be disposed to consider a reduction of the sentence if the conviction should be affirmed. The conviction was affirmed by the Fifth Circuit Court of Appeals, *Clay* v. *United States,* 397 F.2d 901 (5th Cir. 1968), but the Supreme Court remanded the case to the district court on March 24, 1969, to determine whether the conviction was tainted by evidence obtained through unlawful electronic surveillance. The district court, after holding hearings, decided that the conviction did not rest upon such evidence, and its determination was recently affirmed by the Fifth Circuit, *United States* v. *Clay,* 430 F.2d 165 (5th Cir. July 6, 1970). Ali is now in the process of petitioning the Supreme Court for certiorari.

During all of these proceedings in his criminal case, Ali has been at liberty upon a $5,000 bond. On September 22, 1969, he applied to the Commission for renewal of his license to box in New York. On October 14, 1969, the Commission unanimously denied his application because his "refusal to enter the service and [his] felony conviction in violation of Federal law is regarded by this Commission to be detrimental to the best interests of boxing, or to the public interest, convenience or necessity.". . .

Approximately four months after the Texas district court's reaffirmation of Ali's conviction the present action was begun. Invoking our jurisdiction under 28 U.S.C. sections 1343(3) and 1332(a), the complaint as originally drawn charged that the defendants' action in denying Ali a license because of his conviction for refusing to serve in the Armed Services violated his First and Fourteenth Amendment rights and constituted cruel and unusual punishment in violation of the Eighth Amendment thus giving rise to a claim of 42 U.S.C. sec. 1983. Ali's Due Process claim was based on his general charge that defendants' action

was arbitrary and capricious, his contention being that a conviction for draft evasion had no rational relationship to the regulated activity of boxing and was therefore irrelevant to defendants' proper exercise of their functions. . . .

On January 27, 1969 . . . plaintiff amended his complaint to make the following charge:

E. Defendants have arbitrarily, capriciously and invidiously refused to renew plaintiff's professional boxer's license in violation of plaintiff's right to equal protection of the laws guaranteed by the Fourteenth Amendment. Although defendants have denied plaintiff a boxer's license on the basis of his refusal to submit to induction and consequent conviction, defendants have on other occasions licensed professional boxers who had been convicted of crimes involving moral turpitude to wit: (1) Jeff Merritt, who currently holds a New York State boxer's license, has been convicted of robbery; (2) Joey Giardello, who was granted a New York State boxer's license on August 4, 1965, had been convicted of assault; (3) Rocco Barbella, also known as Rocky Graziano, who was licensed to box in New York State from approximately 1942 to 1947, and from May, 1949, to an unknown date, had been twice convicted of petty larceny and in addition was court martialed while serving in the United States Army and convicted of being absent without leave and of disobeying orders and sentenced to one year at hard labor and a dishonorable discharge. In addition, on October 3, 1962, defendants recognized Sonny Liston, who had been convicted of armed robbery and of assault with intent to kill, as heavyweight boxing champion in the State of New York. On information and belief, defendants have in their possession records of all professional boxers licensed in New York State which reveal other instances in which individuals convicted of a crime of moral turpitude have nonetheless been licensed to box in the State of New York.

On August 18, 1970, Judge Frankel denied defendants' motion to dismiss the complaint as thus amended.

Forced as we are to assume jurisdiction over this federalized dispute, *Eisen* v. *Eastman,* 421 F.2d 560 (2d Cir. 1969); *Houghton* v. *Shafer,* 392 U.S.

639 (1968), even though we would prefer that Ali invoke New York state court procedures (e.g., an Article 78 proceeding) rather than risk exacerbation of our relations with the state and its agency, the Athletic Commission, we must now decide whether plaintiff has adduced sufficient evidence to demonstrate a strong likelihood that the Commission's action violated his equal protection rights and that he will suffer irreparable injury unless preliminary relief is granted. . . .

Following the filing of the amended complaint, Ali's counsel, exercising his rights of pretrial discovery, investigated the Commission's current files for the purpose of determining whether it had licensed other boxers who had been convicted of crimes or military offenses. The fruits of this investigation are rather astounding. The commission's records reveal at least 244 instances in recent years where it has granted, renewed or reinstated boxing licenses to applicants who have been convicted of one or more felonies, misdemeanors or military offenses involving moral turpitude. Some 94 felons thus licensed include persons convicted for such anti-social activities as second degree murder, burglary, armed robbery, extortion, grand larceny, rape, sodomy, aggravated assault and battery, embezzlement, arson and receiving stolen property. The misdemeanor convictions, 135 in number, were for such offenses as petty larceny, possession of narcotics, attempted rape, assault and battery, fraud, impairing the morals of a minor, possession of burglar's tools, possession of dangerous weapons, carrying concealed weapons, automobile theft and promotion of gambling. The 15 military offenses include convictions or dishonorable discharges for desertion from the Armed Forces of the United States, assault upon an officer, burglary and larceny. On the basis principally of these undisputed records, plaintiff now seeks preliminary injunctive relief. . . .

The legislature has authorized the Commission to grant licenses to engage in public boxing exhibitions only if the "character and general fitness" of an applicant are such that his participation in boxing "will be consistent with the public interest, convenience or necessity and that the best interests of boxing . . . generally and in conformity with the purposes of this act," Unconsolidated Laws sec. 8912. In addition it is specifically provided that the Commission may "refuse to

renew or issue a license, if it shall find that the applicant . . . has been convicted of a crime in any jurisdiction," Unconsolidated Laws sec. 8917.

The state's power to deny a license because of the applicant's prior conviction has usually been upheld on the ground that the conviction relates directly to the standards of character and conduct properly demanded of a person engaged in certain activities affecting the public, such as the practice of law, . . .

Although conviction of a crime involving moral turpitude should have little or no effect upon a boxer's athletic skill or physical prowess in the ring it could bear upon his proclivity to corruption or upon the general reputation of professional boxing as a sport. For these reasons the action of a state or its agency in barring convicted persons from certain types of employment affecting the public has been upheld as constitutional. *DeVeau* v. *Braisted,* 363 U.S. 144, 80 S.Ct. 1146, 4 L.Ed.2d 1109 (1960) (service as officer of longshoremen's union).

Although the state possesses broad powers to regulate boxing, however, it may not exercise those powers in such a way as to deny to an applicant the equal protection of the state's laws, which is guaranteed to him by the Fourteenth Amendment. A deliberate and arbitrary discrimination or inequality in the exercise of regulatory power, not based upon differences that are reasonably related to the lawful purposes of such regulation, violates the Fourteenth Amendment. . . .

In determining whether there has been such an arbitrary denial of equal protection, the acts of the state's duly constituted Athletic Commission or similar agency are deemed to be those of the state itself. *United States* v. *Guest,* 383 U.S. 745 (1966); . . . In short, the exercise of state power by a state agency in the issuance or refusal of licenses to engage in a regulated activity should not represent the exercise of mere personal whim, caprice or prejudice on the part of such agency. *Yick Wo* v. *Hopkins,* 118 U.S. 356 (1886); . . .

If the Commission in the present case had denied licenses to all applicants convicted of crimes or military offenses, plaintiff would have no valid basis for demanding that a license be issued to him. But the action of the Commission in denying him a license because of his refusal to serve in the Armed Forces while granting licenses to hundreds of other applicants convicted of other crimes and military offenses involving moral turpitude appears on its face to be an intentional, arbitrary and unreasonable discrimination against plaintiff, not the even-handed administration of the law which the Fourteenth Amendment requires. . . . It is not suggested that any rational basis exists for singling out the offense of draft evasion for labelling as "conduct detrimental to the interests of boxing" while holding that all other criminal activities such as murder, rape, arson, burglary, robbery and possession of narcotics are not so classified. All other things being equal, the convicted murderer, burglar, rapist, or robber would seem to present a greater risk of corruptibility as a licensed boxer, and a greater likelihood of bringing boxing into disrepute, than would the person who openly refused to serve in the Armed Forces. We find it even more difficult to detect any rational basis for distinguishing between a deserter from the Armed Forces, to whom a boxing license has been granted by the Commission, and a person who frankly refuses in the first place to serve.

Nor do we see any rational basis for denying Ali a license because his conviction is "recent" (June 20, 1967), and he has not yet served his sentence. The Commission's contention that the recentness of Ali's conviction provides an adequate basis for denying him a license is without merit. Although a distinction between recent and older convictions is reasonable in the abstract, the Commission's own records reveal that it has not made such a distinction in its disposition of other applications. The Commission's records reveal numerous instances where a license has been issued either in the same year as, or within a year or two after, the applicant's conviction of a serious crime.

The Commission further argues that in the case of applicants who have served their sentences the interests of society would best be served by permitting them to assume their normal places in society, notwithstanding the conviction. The Commission has viewed the license of such persons as part of the rehabilitative process "after they had paid their debt to society." On the other hand, argues the Commission, since plaintiff's conviction is current and "has not yet spent its full force," and since he must "yet serve a substantial prison sentence," it has refused him a license.

First of all, this tenuous distinction apparently overlooks the line of reasoning by which prior convictions are normally deemed relevant to licensing decisions. The assumption is that the convicted person might fail to meet standards of conduct considered appropriate in the licensed activity, whether or not his sentence has "spent its full force." . . . The records of the Commission show that 28 individuals have been licensed to box while on probation, and 26 while serving their sentences on parole. It is settled beyond dispute that a prisoner released on parole, although outside prison walls, continues to be in the legal custody of the warden of the prison from which he is released and is subject to being retaken and returned to actual custody until the expiration of the term of his sentence. . . . The 26 parolees who were awarded licenses by the Commission, like the plaintiff in this case, had sentences still to serve, some for as long as nine years. Moreover, plaintiff has furnished from the Commission's files 19 recent instances where the Commission has licensed a boxer or renewed his license when it knew that a serious criminal charge was pending against him or where it took no action to suspend a boxer's license upon learning of his arrest or even of his conviction of a crime. . . .

We are equally unable to accept the Commission's asserted solicitude for the "rehabilitative" process as a reason for deferring the issuance of a license until plaintiff has served his sentence. Such action proceeds on the theory that rehabilitation cannot commence until after confinement, whereas most penologists take the view that rehabilitation should be commenced at the earliest possible moment.

The suggestion that it is useless to issue a license because plaintiff's use of the license may soon be terminated by a long term of confinement, during which he will be unable to engage in public boxing exhibitions, poses a matter that has not apparently been of any concern to the Commission in the issuance of licenses to others. Its records reveal at least 16 cases in which it has issued a license that would expire automatically within less than 30 days pursuant to N.Y. Unconsolidated Laws sec. 8910. Furthermore, the argument ignores the possibilities that the plaintiff's conviction may yet be reversed or, if affirmed, that his sentence may be reduced.

Upon the record before us, therefore, plaintiff demonstrates a strong likelihood of success on the merits and the evidence compels us to find that the

Commission's action in denying him a boxing license because of his conviction and refusal to serve in the Armed Forces constituted an arbitrary and unreasonable departure from the Commission's established practice of granting licenses to applicants convicted of crimes or military offenses. Thus the Commission has denied Ali his right under the Fourteenth Amendment to equal protection of the laws of the State of New York. . . .

4.70 Antitrust Protections for the Athlete

Considered at length earlier were the cases that dealt with the basic applicability of the federal antitrust laws to professional sports. The eventual conclusions were that professional sports, in almost all aspects, are today interstate commerce. Save for the anomaly of baseball, granted antitrust immunity in *Federal Baseball Club of Baltimore v. National League of Professional Baseball Clubs*, 259 U.S. 207 (1922), which immunity under principles of *stare decisis* has been carried forward to the present, all professional sports leagues are seemingly subject to controls under the antitrust statutes. Three cases in particular made this clear. For football, it was *Radovich v. National Football League*, 352 U.S. 445 (1957); for hockey, *Philadelphia World Hockey Club v. Philadelphia Hockey Club*, 351 F.Supp. 462 (E.D. Pa. 1972); and for basketball, *Robertson v. National Basketball Association*, 389 F.Supp.867 (S.D.N.Y. 1975).

The earlier considerations focused on cases from the 1970s that struck such decisive blows for greater freedom of movement for professional athletes, as evidenced by the restrictive provisions in several sports — most notably the National Football League — that were declared illegal in several precedent-setting cases, such as *Kapp v. National Football League*, 586 F.2d 644 (9th Cir. 1978); *Mackey v. National Football League*, 543 F.2d 606 (8th Cir. 1976); and *Smith v. Pro-Football*, 593 F.2d 1173 (D.C.Cir. 1978).

The attention in this section shifts to the sports

leagues' exclusionary rules, where for some reason a league (and thus its clubs) either refuse to deal with a player or suspend that player because of supposed infractions. The cases that follow present a variety of concerns, but ultimately, all face the same inquiry: Under what circumstances, and to what extent, can a sports league or club deny to an athlete the opportunity to earn a living in that league?

The first category of exclusionary rules deals with exclusion because of a person's status — such as age, educational attainment, physical condition, or objectified standard of skill. The second category concentrates on exclusion because of a person's activities — engaging in alleged gambling or cheating, for example. The two categories are not totally exclusionary of each other; however, the courts evoke enough disparate reactions to separate the two for purposes of analysis. Section 4.71 examines exclusions because of status, and Section 4.72 scrutinizes suspensions and blacklists for alleged improper behavior.

4.71 Eligibility Requirements

Sports associations and leagues establish guidelines for determining who is eligible to join the organization's ranks and who is excluded. Obviously, not everyone who wishes to be a professional athlete can do so. There must be limits. But setting limits cannot be done in an arbitrary or anticompetitive manner.

The eligibility rules of several leagues and associations are examined in this section. The inquiries focus on (1) whether the rules are to be subjected to a per se or rule of reason antitrust analysis, and (2) if it is a rule of reason test, whether the eligibility rules can be justified as fair and competitive ways of doing business.

Deesen v. Professional Golfers' Ass'n. of America, 358 F.2d 163 (9th Cir. 1966)

Hamley, Circuit Judge:

Herbert C. Deesen brought this action against

the Professional Golfers' Association of America (PGA) and a number of individuals to recover damages and obtain injunctive relief for alleged violations of sections 1 and 2 of the Sherman Act. Damages were claimed in the sum of $70,000, trebled to $210,000. Jurisdiction in the district court was asserted under sections 4 and 16 of the Clayton Act.

In his complaint, as modified by the pretrial orders, Deesen, who is a professional golfer, claimed that PGA and its members have combined and conspired to monopolize the business of tournament golf professionals in violation of section 2 of the Sherman Act. He also claimed that, as evidenced by PGA's rules and regulations governing the eligibility of entrants into PGA sponsored and co-sponsored tournaments, defendants have combined and conspired to restrain, unreasonably, the business of tournament golf professionals, and to boycott plaintiff, in violation of section 1 of the Sherman Act.

After a trial without a jury, judgment was entered for defendants. Plaintiff appeals. In the following paragraphs we summarize the findings of fact entered by the trial court, amplified to include certain undisputed facts stated in the second pretrial order but not carried forward into the findings of fact.

PGA is an association of some 4,300 golfers, founded in 1916 as a voluntary unincorporated non-profit association. The named individual defendants are persons who were, at the time the complaint was filed on April 23, 1959, officers and employees of PGA and members of its tournament committee.

PGA sponsors or co-sponsors substantially all of the professional golf tournaments held in the United States. In order to compete in these golf tournaments, a player must either be a member of PGA, or an approved tournament player, or one of a limited number of participants who may be designated or invited by the local sponsor. Because of the increasing popularity of professional tournament golf, the increasing number of golfers, and the increasing number of persons eligible to enter PGA sponsored tournaments, and because the limitations of time and space make it impossible to play a full tournament with a field of more than 150 or 160 golfers, some means had to be found to limit the number of golfers who could enter these tournaments. PGA rules limiting entry

to PGA members, approved tournament players and a few others, and defining the qualifications necessary for non-member entrants, were intended to accomplish this purpose.

In order to become a PGA member a person must have five years experience, either in the employ of a golf club as a professional or in the employ of a professional, as an assistant at a golf club, or (in recent years) as a tournament player under an agreement with PGA, playing a minimum of twenty-five tournaments per year, or any combination of these methods for a period of five years. Deesen was at all times, and now is, unwilling to become employed by a golf club as a professional or as an assistant to a professional at a golf club.

An approved tournament player must be approved first by a local committee of PGA, then by PGA's tournament and executive committees. Approval is given if the applicant has, in the opinion of each of these committees: (1) the ability to play golf and finish in the money in tournaments in which he competes, (2) the financial responsibility to undertake the golf tours, and (3) moral character and integrity. There are no issues herein as to Deesen's financial responsibility or his character and integrity.

There are no exact or definite standards set up to determine ability to play. The nature of golf is such that no precise standard of ability can be established other than by comparison of scores and ability to finish in the money in tournaments. In order to enter PGA sponsored and co-sponsored tournaments, PGA members are not required to meet the standards set for PGA-approved tournament players.

Deesen is a professional golfer who was eligible to compete as a PGA-approved tournament player in PGA sponsored and co-sponsored tournaments under contract with PGA from 1952 to 1958. Pursuant to PGA rules and regulations and the tournament player's agreement that Deesen signed, he was required to compete in a minimum of fifteen PGA sponsored tournaments each year and maintain an ability to finish in the money in such tournaments. The requirement of competing in fifteen tournaments a year was later reduced to ten. During this period Deesen was active as a professional golf tournament player, and he placed in the money three times, earning $240.35. Some of his scores were better than some of the PGA members' scores playing in the same tournaments. . . .

During this time he was otherwise unemployed. However, during part of this period he had a partnership arrangement with his parents to support him while he was thus engaged as a professional golfer. His expenses during the period from 1952 to 1958, were approximately $13,500. In 1958, Deesen sustained an injury which affected his playing ability and prevented him from competing in ten tournaments that year. PGA's tournament field supervisor was informed of this injury prior to September 1, 1958. . . .

In 1958, PGA's national tournament committee undertook to terminate the approved tournament player status of a number of professional golfers. The committee designated Harvey Raynor, J. Edwin Carter, and Lou Strong, PGA members and employees, to select the players whose contracts were to be terminated. As a result of their recommendations PGA terminated the contracts of fifty-seven professional golfers, including Deesen. His status as an approved tournament player was terminated by PGA on September 1, 1958. This was done on the grounds that his playing ability was not sufficient in the opinion of the PGA tournament committee, and for failure to compete in the requisite number of tournaments. . . .

After this action was commenced, Deesen again applied to PGA for reinstatement. Pursuant to an agreement reached between the parties at the first pretrial conference in this case, Deesen played a number of "test" rounds of golf with various professionals in the San Francisco Bay Area. His scores on these rounds ranged from seventy-five to eighty-four and averaged over seventy-eight. On this showing, reinstatement was denied. . . .

On the basis of these facts, the trial court further found as follows: Deesen has not shown that the PGA rules were applied to him in a manner different in any way from that in which they were applied to any other approved tournament player or non-member of PGA. The fact that members are entitled to play in PGA sponsored and co-sponsored tournaments without the qualifications required of non-PGA members is not an improper discrimination since membership in PGA is open to all persons on the same conditions.

The district court also found: Deesen has failed to prove the existence of any agreement, combination, or conspiracy entered into for the specific purpose of keeping him personally out of PGA tournaments or for preventing him from making a living as a professional golfer. The evidence shows that admission to the status of an approved tournament player is and has always been open to all persons on the same terms. PGA has not excluded Deesen and other non-PGA members from tournament golf play in an arbitrary and unreasonable manner. The evidence does not establish that Deesen possessed such ability as a golfer that it is unreasonable to bar him from entering PGA tournaments. Deesen has suffered no financial loss as a result of not having been permitted to play in PGA sponsored or co-sponsored tournaments.

On these findings, the trial court concluded that Deesen had not established any violation of sections 1 or 2 of the Sherman Act. . . .

Deesen argues, in effect, that under the established facts it must be held that PGA's rules and regulations concerning eligibility to participate in PGA sponsored tournaments are unreasonable restraints in violation of section 1 of the Sherman Act.

In support of this position appellant first contends that PGA rules and regulations are so indefinite as to be incapable of non-discriminatory enforcement and are thus unreasonable. Deesen attacks the method of processing applications for standing as an approved PGA tournament player. Pointing to the fact that such applications must receive the approval of a local PGA section, the sectional executive committee and the national tournament committee, Deesen argues that the standards applied are inadequate and are in any event subject to being disregarded in favor of personal bias. . . .

Deesen argues that the personal dislike of just one member of a local section could result in denial of an application. However, no evidence has been called to our attention indicating that an individual member can control the action of a local section, or that applications are ever denied because of personal dislike unassociated with the standards referred to above.

In general the same standards are applied by the sectional executive committee and the national tournament committee, based on the results of the local section's inquiry and test rounds. Deesen argues, in effect, that these latter committees have uncontrolled discretion to deny applications for personal reasons entirely disassociated from the indicated standards. But, again, appellant does not call attention to any evidence which the trial court was required to accept, indicating that these top committees have discriminated against applicants on such a basis. It is true that Deesen testified, in effect, that he had been discriminated against in connection with his applications for reinstatement, but the trial court was not required to accept his appraisal of PGA's motivation.

The basic purpose of PGA in requiring persons who seek approved tournament standing to meet certain standards and obtain committee approval appears to be a reasonable one, insofar as the evidence before us indicates. That purpose is to insure that professional golf tournaments are not bogged down with great numbers of players of inferior ability. The purpose is thus not to destroy competition but to foster it by maintaining a high quality of competition.

The means PGA has chosen to accomplish this purpose also appear to be reasonable insofar as this record reveals, having in view the national scope of the activity and the practical problems which had to be met. The trial court did not err in holding that, in these respects, Deesen did not establish a violation of section 1 of the Sherman Act.

Deesen also attacks the PGA tournament entry rules on the additional ground that they are not applied uniformly to members and non-members, asserting that the rules are therefore unreasonable on their face. Appellant's specific grievance here is that a PGA member may play in any PGA tournament regardless of his average score, or his ability to finance himself, or the number of tournaments entered, or his ability to finish in the money regularly. Non-PGA members, on the other hand, may not play unless they obtain standing as PGA tournament players. . . .

In *Chicago Board of Trade* v. *United States*, 246, U.S. 231, 238, 38 S.Ct. 242, 244, 62 L.Ed. 683, the Supreme Court said:

> The true test of legality is whether the restraint imposed is such as merely regulates and thereby perhaps promotes competition or whether it is such as may suppress or even destroy competition. To determine that question the court must ordinarily consider the facts peculiar to the business to which the restraint is applied; its condition before and after the restraint was imposed; the nature of the restraint and its effect, actual or probable. The history of the restraint, the evil believed to exist, the reason for adopting the particular remedy, the purpose or end sought to be attained, are all relevant facts.

Measured by the test spelled out in *Chicago Board of Trade* v. *United States,* the indicated differentiation between PGA and non-PGA members with regard to the right to participate in sponsored tournaments was not, on this record, shown to be for the purpose of suppressing or destroying competition, nor did it have that effect. The trial court did not err in so ruling.

Deesen contends that the trial court erred in failing to hold that PGA and its members have monopolized the business of tournament golf professionals in violation of section 2 of the Sherman Act.

Appellant premises this argument on three assertions of fact: (1) PGA sponsors and co-sponsors substantially all professional golf tournaments in the United States; (2) to compete in these tournaments a player must either be a member of PGA or a PGA approved tournament player; and (3) PGA has the power to exclude any applicant for participation in these tournaments for any reason whatsoever. Appellant states that, in view of these asserted facts, appellees have monopolized the business of tournament golf professionals in violation of section 2 of the Sherman Act.

The last of these assertions of fact is critical to Deesen's argument, but as worded, it is inconclusive. It is true that generally speaking, any association that undertakes to sponsor a contest of any kind has power to exclude any applicant from participation for any reason whatsoever, unless such power is curtailed by operation of law. The pertinent inquiry, however, is whether an association intends to use that power in a manner which tends to suppress or destroy competition.

Mere size, unaccompanied by unlawful intent or conduct in the exercise of the power gained through size, does not constitute a violation of section 2 of the Sherman Act. *United States* v. *Swift & Co.*, 286 U.S. 106, 116, 52 S.Ct. 460, 76 L.Ed. 999. It is the existence of monopoly power coupled with the intent to use it for anticompetitive purposes or with inevitable anticompetitive effects that establishes the offense of monopolization. *United States* v. *Griffith,* 334 U.S. 100, 107, 68 S.Ct. 941, 92 L.Ed. 1236.

No finding nor evidence has been called to our attention which indicates that PGA has used, or intends to use, its position as the sponsor or co-sponsor of a substantial number of tournaments to preclude sponsorship of tournaments by others, to exclude golfers from access to PGA sponsored tournaments, or to suppress or eliminate competition in professional tournament golf. . . .

Finally, Deesen argues that PGA and its members have combined and conspired to monopolize the business of tournament golf professionals and to boycott and exclude Deesen therefrom in violation of sections 1 and 2 of the Sherman Act.

Under this heading, appellant shifts his attack from the charge of actual monopolization, boycott and restraint to an accusation that PGA has at least combined and conspired to accomplish those results.

Granting that not only actual monopolization and restraint is condemned by the Sherman Act, but also combinations and conspiracies intended to bring about those results, the established facts of this case support one charge no more than the other.

With particular reference to the boycott charge, Deesen's tournament record over a period of several years provided an ample basis for the striking of his name from the list of approved tournament players. Similarly, his showing made during the test rounds arranged after this action was commenced warranted PGA in denying reinstatement to that list. Deesen could still engage in such tournaments if he chose to become a golf teacher employed by a golf club.

PGA is entitled to adopt reasonable measures for holding the tournaments to a manageable number. It was required to treat Deesen as well as it treated others in the same category but it was not compelled to give him special treatment merely because he did not wish to accept PGA tournament entry rules and regulations. . . .

Nilon v. Philadelphia Section Professional Golfers' Ass'n., Civil Action No. 79–3013 (E.D.Pa. 1979)

Plaintiff professional golfer Michael J. Nilon challenged a regulation of a professional golfers' association that excluded professional golfers from participating in certain regional tournaments. Nilon sought a preliminary injunction to enjoin the defendant from excluding him from regional competitions, charging that his exclusion was a per se illegal group boycott. The district court held that the defendant's regulation was neither a per se illegal boycott nor an unreasonable restraint because it was based on the distinction between a professional golfer and a club professional.

The defendant, the Professional Golfers' Association of America, Philadelphia Section Inc., is a nonprofit organization in Pennsylvania whose operations cover a three-state area. The defendant's regulation provides that "Any PGA Tour Member who has played in more than 12 PGA Tour events in the preceding twelve months is *only* eligible for Philadelphia Section Championship events . . ." The tournament in question was not a "Philadelphia Section Championship event."

That Nilon had participated in 20 PGA events in 1979 was undisputed. Nilon contended that the exclusionary regulation which prevented him from competing in 75 percent of defendant's sectional tournaments was a per se violation of the Sherman Act, 15 U.S.C., section 1. Nilon argued that the officers and executive committee of the defendant acted in concert to exclude plaintiff and others similarly situated so that they as individuals would be more likely to win the prize money in the 30 tournaments from which Nilon had been excluded.

The district court, in holding that defendant's regulation was not a per se violation of the antitrust laws, ruled that the instant case, because it arose in a sports context, lacked the requisite "pernicious effect on competition" and had no real negative impact on consumers. The court, in applying a rule-of-reason analysis, found that defendant's contention that there is a distinction between a professional golfer and a club professional to be persuasive. The court noted that the duties of club professionals make it impossible for them to hone their skills to the same extent as touring professionals. For these reasons, the court ruled that club professionals may exclude from some tournaments professional golfers who have elected to compete on the national tour. Accordingly, Nilon's request for a preliminary injunction was denied.

Denver Rockets v. All-Pro Management, Inc., 325 F.Supp. 1049 (C.D. Ca. 1971)

Memorandum Opinion Granting Partial Summary Judgment

Ferguson, District Judge

A part of this litigation is an antitrust claim brought by Spencer Haywood, a professional basketball player, against the National Basketball Association (hereinafter NBA), one of two major basketball leagues in the United States. Haywood filed a motion for partial summary judgment seeking an order of this court declaring Sections 2.05 and 6.03 of the by-laws of the NBA to be illegal under Section 1 of the Sherman Antitrust Act. 15 U.S.C. sec. 1.

Section 2.05 of the by-laws of the NBA provides as follows:

> *High School Graduate, etc.* A person who has not completed high school or who has completed high school but has not entered college, shall not be eligible to be drafted or to be a Player until four years after he has been graduated or four years after his original high school class has been graduated, as the case may be, nor may the future services of any such person be negotiated or contracted for, or otherwise reserved. Similarly, a person who has entered college but is no longer enrolled, shall not be eligible to be drafted or to be a Player until the time when he would have first become eligible had he remained enrolled in college. Any negotiations or agreements with any such person during such period shall be null and void and shall confer no rights whatsoever; nor shall a Member violating the provisions of this paragraph be permitted to acquire the rights to the services of such person at any time thereafter.

Section 6.03, while included in the bylaws as a part of the draft provisions, further defines eligibility for the NBA and reinforces the rule that a player cannot sign with an NBA team prior to four years after the graduation of his high school class. Section 6.03 provides as follows:

> *Persons Eligible for Draft.* The following classes of persons shall be eligible for the annual draft:
> (a) Students in four year colleges whose classes are to be graduated during the June following the holding of the draft;
> (b) Students in four year colleges whose original classes have already been graduated, and who do not choose to exercise remaining collegiate basketball eligibility;
> (c) Students in four year colleges whose original classes have already been graduated if such students have no remaining collegiate basketball eligibility;
> (d) Persons who become eligible pursuant to the provisions of Section 2.05 of these By-laws.

Except for Section 6.03, the other provisions of the player draft are not challenged by this partial summary judgment motion.

The NBA is an unincorporated association organized to operate, and engaged in the business of operating, a league of professional basketball teams. The NBA has 17 member teams, each located in a major metropolitan area. The NBA teams are engaged in the business of staging professional basketball exhibitions, and their principal source of revenue arises from the sale of admission tickets and from the sale of the right to broadcast games by radio and television. Each of the member teams has agreed, in writing, to be bound by the provisions of the NBA constitution and by-laws.

Spencer Haywood is now a professional basketball player. Following graduation from high school in 1967, he attended Trinidad Junior College, where he was a junior college "All-American" during the 1967–68 season. In the summer of 1968, he played in the United States Olympic basketball games and led the United States team to a gold medal. In the fall of 1968, Haywood enrolled at the University of Detroit, where he played basketball during the 1968–69 season and was named an "All-American."

In the fall of 1969, Haywood entered into a contract with the Denver Rockets, a professional basketball team in the American Basketball Association (hereinafter ABA), pursuant to a "hardship" exemption from the ABA's four-year college rule. He played as a member of the Denver team during the 1969–70 season and was named "Rookie of the Year," and "Most Valuable Player in the ABA" for that season. Early in the 1970–71 season, a dispute arose between Denver and Haywood with regard to their contractual relations, and Haywood stopped playing for the Denver team. The status of the Denver-Haywood contract is presently the subject of litigation in this court.

Claiming that he had validly rescinded his Denver contract, Haywood signed a contract to play basketball with the Seattle Supersonics, a professional basketball team in the NBA. Walter Kennedy, the Commissioner of the NBA, disapproved Haywood's Seattle contract on the ground that Haywood was not yet eligible under the four-year college rule, and threatened sanctions by the NBA should he attempt to play. Haywood is presently playing basketball for the Seattle team under the provisions of a preliminary injunction issued by this court against the NBA pending final determination of this action.

. . .[T]he Supreme Court has held that all professional sports, with the exception of baseball, are governed by the antitrust laws. . . .

Stated simply, Section 2.05, in conjunction with Section 6.03, provides that no person is eligible as a player or for the draft, under any circumstances, until four years after his original high school class graduated. Applied to Spencer Haywood, these rules make him ineligible to play in the NBA until the commencement of the 1971–72 playing season, *i.e.* four years after his 1967 high school graduation.

Haywood alleges that the effect of this provision is a group boycott on the part of the NBA and its teams against himself and other qualified players who come within those terms. The provisions prevent Haywood, a qualified professional basketball player, from contracting with any NBA team, even though he does not desire to, or may not be eligible to, attend college and even though he does not desire to, and is ineligible to, participate in collegiate athletics.

Haywood also challenges the so-called "reserve clause" and the college draft, among other NBA provisions, as being similarly violative of the antitrust laws. However, those allegations are not subject to this partial summary judgment motion,

and the court expresses no view with regard to the legality of those practices.

It should be pointed out initially that this case does not involve the question of whether Spencer Haywood is qualified to play basketball at the high level of competency required of NBA players. It is uncontested that he is so qualified. In fact, Haywood is now playing for the Seattle team. The sole question involved here is whether the NBA can prevent Haywood from playing in the NBA pursuant to his contract with Seattle until four years after his high school class graduated.

Application of the four-year college rule constitutes a "primary" concerted refusal to deal wherein the actors at one level of a trade pattern (NBA team members) refuse to deal with an actor at another level (those ineligible under the NBA's four-year college rule).

The harm resulting from a "primary" boycott such as this is threefold. First, the victim of the boycott is injured by being excluded from the market he seeks to enter. Second, competition in the market in which the victim attempts to sell his services is injured. Third, by pooling their economic power, the individual members of the NBA have, in effect, established their own private government. Of course, this is true only where the members of the combination possess market power in a degree approaching a shared monopoly. This is uncontested in the present case. . . .

In response to Haywood's motion for partial summary judgment, the NBA argues three points: (1) There are disputed issues of material fact which make summary judgment improper; (2) summary judgment denies the NBA its right to a jury trial; and (3) this action is governed by the "rule of reason" and the NBA is entitled to prove that the rules involved do not "unreasonably restrain trade". . . .

The NBA . . . argues that whether Haywood will suffer irreparable injury is a contested issue of material fact. The law governing the issuance of a permanent injunction in antitrust cases such as this requires the application of traditional equitable principles. 15 U.S.C. sec. 26. Therefore, if the NBA could show that Haywood had an adequate remedy at law a permanent injunction would not properly issue in this case. It therefore seems clear that this is a disputed issue of material fact, and a trial will be required to properly determine this issue. This does not, of course, bar partial summary judgment on the narrow issue presented here.

The NBA's second major argument is that even assuming *arguendo* that the by-laws are undisputed in their terms and in their application to Haywood and that a group boycott is *per se* illegal, Haywood is still not entitled to the requested partial summary judgment. The NBA bases this argument on its right to a jury trial. However, it has long been held that a summary judgment does not infringe upon the right of a party to a jury trial. *See, e.g., Fidelity & Deposit Co. v. United States,* 187 U.S. 315, 23 S.Ct. 120, 47 L.Ed. 194 (1902). Where no material fact is controverted, there is no issue triable by a jury and a summary judgment is proper.

Finally, the NBA argues that the "ultimate facts" concerning the four-year college rule, as alleged by Haywood, do not "constitute a group boycott and a *per se* restraint of trade." This argument is so intertwined with the "legal" issue of determining the antitrust law which is properly applicable in this case, that it must be discussed in that context.

Before a concerted refusal to deal can be illegal under Section 1 of the Sherman Act, two threshold elements must be present: (1) There must be some effect on "trade or commerce among the several States," and (2) there must be sufficient agreement to constitute a "contract, combination . . . or conspiracy." 15 U.S.C. sec. 1.

It is uncontested that both of these elements are present in the instant case. The NBA operates teams in seventeen of the major metropolitan areas of the United States. It schedules games in numerous states, and receives television and radio revenue from nationwide broadcasts of its games. It is thus clear that the NBA conducts its business in such a manner as to constitute interstate commerce. Furthermore, the members of the NBA have agreed, through their constitution and by-laws, not to deal with those persons described by Sections 2.05 and 6.03 of their by-laws.

Very early in the history of the anti-trust laws, the Supreme Court was forced to decide whether the antitrust laws should be used to regulate the use of private aggregations of power or to prevent their existence altogether. Despite the fact that the literal language of Section 1 of the Sherman Act declares "every" combination in restraint of trade to be illegal, the Supreme Court, in *Standard Oil Co. v. United States,* 221 U.S. 1, 31 S.Ct. 502, 55 L.Ed. 619 (1911), ruled that the Sherman Act should be construed in the light of reason; and, as so construed, it prohibits only contracts and combinations which amount to an unreasonable or undue restraint of trade in interstate commerce. Thus, the "rule of reason" became the standard by which antitrust violations would be measured, and the Court undertook to regulate rather than prohibit private combinations.

The primary disadvantages of the "rule of reason" are that it requires difficult and lengthy factual inquiries and very subjective policy decisions which are in many ways essentially legislative and ill-suited to the judicial process. For instance, in the present case, a complex economic inquiry would be required to determine the economic necessity of action of this type. In addition, the court would be required to determine a standard which could be used to weigh the various public policy goals which might be alleged as justification by the NBA. The court would further be forced to determine whether the boycott was genuinely motivated by the purposes given, or by other reasons. Frequently, these motives are closely intertwined.

The Supreme Court has on numerous occasions recognized these difficulties and has declared that with regard to certain practices the problems of making adequate economic determinations and setting appropriate guidelines are so complex that they simply outweigh the very limited benefits deriving from those practices and have declared them to be illegal *per se*. A group boycott is one such practice.

> [T]here are certain agreements or practices which because of their pernicious effect on competition and lack of any redeeming virtue are conclusively presumed to be unreasonable and therefore illegal without elaborate inquiry as to the precise harm they have caused or the business excuse for their use. This principle of *per se* unreasonableness not only makes the type of restraints which are proscribed by the Sherman Act more certain to the benefit of everyone concerned, but it also avoids the necessity for an incredibly complicated and prolonged economic investigation into the entire history of the industry involved, as well

as related industries, in an effort to determine at large whether a particular restraint has been unreasonable — an inquiry so often wholly fruitless when undertaken. Among the practices which the courts have heretofore deemed to be unlawful in and of themselves are price fixing, *United States* v. *Socony-Vacuum Oil Co.,* 310 U.S. 150, 210; division of markets, *United States* v. *Addyston Pipe & Steel Co.,* 85 F. 271, aff'd. 175 U.S. 457; group boycotts, *Fashion Originators' Guild* v. *Federal Trade Comm'n,* 312 U.S. 457; and tying arrangements, *International Salt Co.* v. *United States,* 332 U.S. 392, *Northern Pacific* v. *United States,* 356 U.S. 1, 5, (1957).

In *Fashion Originators' Guild* v. *F.T.C.,* 312 U.S. 457, 61 S.Ct. 703, 85 L.Ed. 949 (1941), a combination of manufacturers of women's garments and manufacturers of textiles used in garment making, sought to suppress competition by others who copied their designs. They did this by registering their designs and refusing all sales to manufacturers and retailers of garments who dealt in the copies. The Supreme Court affirmed the "cease and desist" order entered by the Federal Trade Commission. In doing so, the Court found no error in the refusal of the Commission to hear evidence on the reasonableness of the methods pursued by the combination. . . . The Court went on to note that even if systematic copying of dress designs was tortious under the laws of all states, that circumstance would not justify a group boycott.

In *Klor's* v. *Broadway-Hale Stores,* 359 U.S. 207, 79 S.Ct. 705, 3 L.Ed.2d 741 (1959), Klor's, a retail appliance dealer, brought a treble damage suit against a competing retailer, Broadway-Hale, and several manufacturers and distributors of appliances, alleging that Broadway-Hale had used its buying power to induce the others to stop dealing with the plaintiff. The defendants responded that it was purely a "private quarrel" between Klor's and the others and submitted affidavits to show that the boycott had no discernible effect on competition. The Supreme Court held that the concerted boycott by defendants violated the Sherman Act. The Court noted that "[g]roup boycotts, or concerted refusals by traders to deal with other traders, have long been held to be in the forbidden category." 359 U.S. at 212, 79 S.Ct. at 709.

These two cases have been frequently cited for the proposition that a concerted refusal to deal cannot be justified by any motive or ultimate goal, however reasonable. . . .

The possibility that all concerted refusals to deal were not *per se* illegal was given considerable impetus in *Silver* v. *New York Stock Exchange,* 373 U.S. 341, 348–349, . . . (1963), where the Court recognized that a "justification derived from the policy of another statute or otherwise" might save a collective refusal to deal from *per se* illegality.

Silver, a securities dealer, while not a member of the New York Stock Exchange, maintained direct private telephone and tickertape connections with several member firms. Pursuant to Exchange rules, the member firms involved applied for approval of the connections. After granting temporary approval, the Exchange disapproved the applications and under the Exchange's constitution the member firms were then required to discontinue the services. This they did. Silver brought a treble damage suit, alleging that the cut-off was a concerted refusal to deal. The district court granted summary judgment in Silver's favor. The Second Circuit Court of Appeals reversed, on the grounds that the Securities Exchange Act, which gave the Commission the power of self regulation, had exempted the Exchange from the restrictions of the Sherman Act.

The Supreme Court began by noting that "absent any justification derived from the policy of another statute or otherwise," the action of the Exchange would constitute a group boycott, *per se* illegal under the Sherman Act. The Court then stated that the exemption of the Exchange did not extend to section which could not "be justified as furthering legitimate self-regulative ends." In concluding that the self-regulation involved was not justified, the Court focused on the absence of notice and hearing prior to Exchange action.

Thus, *Silver* seems to envision the application of the *per se* rule to group boycott cases, with one narrow exception. A factual situation falling into this exception would be governed by the "rule of reason." To qualify for this exception it would have to be shown that:

(1) There is a legislative mandate for self-regulation "or otherwise." In discussing the history of the New York Stock Exchange in *Silver,* the Court suggests that self-regulation is

inherently required by the market's structure. From this basis, it has been argued that where collective action is required by the industry structure, it falls within the "or otherwise" provision of *Silver*. Note, Trade Association Exclusionary Practices: An Affirmative Role for the Rule of Reason, 66 Colum.L.Rev. 1486 (1966).

(2) The collective action is intended to (a) accomplish an end consistent with the policy justifying self-regulation, (b) is reasonably related to that goal, and (c) is no more extensive than necessary.

(3) The association provides procedural safeguards which assure that the restraint is not arbitrary and which furnishes a basis for judicial review.

The question then arises as to whether this court can, without a lengthy factual inquiry and a complex balancing of values, determine whether the present fact situation falls into the narrow exception which is governed by the "rule of reason." The importance of this question is obvious. If a trial court cannot do this, it will be required to evaluate all of the evidence and make all of the value judgments necessary to apply the "rule of reason" in order to determine whether the case falls into the exception. This would destroy the benefits of the *per se* approach.

This is, primarily, a question of the administration of the antitrust laws. For this reason, it should be remembered that the *per se* rule and the "rule of reason" constitute polar opposites on the spectrum of possible approaches.

The answer to this question is found in the Court's reasoning in *Silver*. There the Court focused on the issue of notice and hearing. According to the Court, the requirement of a hearing will, in itself, act as check on illegitimate self-regulation. In addition, it will provide the antitrust court with a record from which it can determine whether the self-regulation is justified, necessary and sufficiently limited. "Hence the affording of procedural safeguards not only will substantively encourage the lessening of anticompetitive behavior outlawed by the Sherman Act but will allow the antitrust court to perform its function effectively." 373 U.S. 363, 83 S.Ct. 1260.

The *Silver* ruling explains the apparent inconsistency between the two ninth circuit decisions most similar factually to the present case. In

Deesen v. *Professional Golfers' Ass'n,* 358 F.2d 165 (9th Cir.), cert. denied, 385 U.S. 846, 87 S.Ct. 72, 17 L.Ed.2d 76 (1966), the circuit held that the Professional Golfers' Association's eligibility requirements for professional golf tournaments did not violate the antitrust laws. The PGA had terminated Deesen's approved tournament status only after a committee reassessed his performance against established standards; opportunities were also provided for Deesen to apply for reinstatement and to play "test rounds" in an effort to prove he was qualified for tournament play. The court found (a) that eligibility requirements were required by the industry structure, (b) that the requirements in question were intended to meet this goal, not improperly motivated, flexible and reasonably limited, and (c) that the procedural safeguards mentioned above were present.

On the other hand, in *Washington State Bowling Prop. Ass'n* v. *Pacific Lanes, Inc.,* 356 F.2d 371 (9th Cir.), cert. denied, 384 U.S. 963, 86 S.Ct. 1590, 16 L.Ed.2d 674 (1966), the court applied a *per se* rule to invalidate the regulatory scheme of the Bowling Proprietors Association of America. In this case, there was no provision for a hearing comparable to that found in *Deesen*. BPAA eligibility rules required that tournament bowlers restrict their league and tournament bowling to member establishments. The ostensible purpose was to prevent "sandbagging" — the inclusion of substandard scores in computing a bowler's average to gain a larger handicap. In holding the rules illegal, the court specifically rejected the defendant's argument that the *per se* rule applied only to commercial boycotts.

With regard to the facts of the instant case it can readily be determined that the case does not fall within the "rule of reason" exception provided by *Silver*. It is clear from the constitution and by-laws of the NBA that there is no provision for even the most rudimentary hearing before the four-year college rule is applied to exclude an individual player. Nor is there any provision whereby an individual player might petition for consideration of his specific case. Due to the lack of any such provisions, this court must conclude that on the basis of undisputed facts, the NBA rules in question fall outside the *Silver* exception and are subject to the *per se* rule normally applicable to group boycotts.

In addition, it is uncontested that the rules in

question are absolute and prohibit the signing of not only college basketball players but also those who do not desire to attend college and even those who lack the mental and financial ability to do so. As such they are overly broad and thus improper under *Silver*. Summary judgment for violations of the antitrust laws is proper where less restrictive means than those used could have been employed. . . .

Throughout the briefs and affidavits of the NBA, there is the suggestion that the purpose of the rules in question removes those rules from the normal coverage of the antitrust laws. Three reasons have been suggested for having the four-year college rule. First, the NBA has suggested that it is financially necessary to professional basketball as a business enterprise. It seems clear from *Klor's* that this does not provide a basis for exemption from the antitrust laws with regard to group boycotts, unless it qualifies under the ruling of *Silver*. As discussed earlier, *Silver* does not exempt the present rules from illegality.

A second reason given by the NBA is that this type of regulation is necessary to guarantee that each prospective professional basketball player will be given the opportunity to complete four years of college prior to beginning his professional basketball career. However commendable this desire may be, this court is not in a position to say that this consideration should override the objective of fostering economic competition which is embodied in the antitrust laws. If such a determination is to be made, it must be made by Congress and not the courts.

Finally, Haywood has suggested that at least one of the reasons for the four-year college rule is that collegiate athletics provides a more efficient and less expensive way of training young professional basketball players than the so-called "farm team" system, which is the primary alternative. Even if this were true, it would not, of course, provide a basis for antitrust exemption. . . .

Pursuant to the provisions of Rule 58, a judgment shall be entered as follows:

1. Sections 2.05 and 6.03 of the by-laws of the National Basketball Association are declared to be illegal under Section 1 of the Sherman Act. 15 U.S.C. sec. 1.

2. The preliminary injunction granted by this court on February 2, 1971, will remain in full force and effect pending final determination of all matters raised by the crossclaim. That injunction reads as follows:

IT IS ORDERED AND ADJUDGED that Cross-defendant NBA, its members, officers, agents, servants, employees, attorneys and all persons in active concert or participation with them, pending the final hearing and decision in this action, are enjoined from applying the Constitution, By-laws, Rules and Regulations of the NBA in any manner so as to prevent or interfere with, or from taking any other action, directly or indirectly, to prevent or interfere with Cross-claimant Haywood playing professional basketball as a player on the playing roster of the Seattle Supersonics. Nothing in this order shall prevent the NBA from sanctioning Haywood in the normal manner for improper behavior unrelated to the subject matter of this suit.

3. The court retains jurisdiction to enforce the provisions of this judgment, for the purpose of issuing orders to clarify, modify, or amend any of the provisions hereof, and for all other purposes.

Linseman v. World Hockey Ass'n., 439 F.Supp. 1315 (D. Conn. 1977)

Ruling on Motion for a Preliminary Injunction

Clarie, Chief Judge

The plaintiff Kenneth S. Linseman is a nineteen year old amateur Canadian hockey player, who is challenging the validity of a regulation of the World Hockey Association (hereinafter "WHA"), prohibiting persons under the age of 20 from playing professional hockey for any team within their association, on the ground that the restriction constitutes an unreasonable restraint of trade in violation of sec. 1 of the Sherman Act. 15 U.S.C. sec. 1. The plaintiff, who is under contract to play professional hockey for the Birmingham Bulls (hereinafter "Bulls") in the 1977–78 season, requests a preliminary injunction during the pendency of this action to restrain the WHA from applying said regulation in any manner which would prevent Linseman from playing pursuant to the terms of his contract. The Court finds that there is good cause for awarding relief and therefore grants the preliminary injunction. . . .

The defendant WHA has alleged that if Linseman is permitted to play, the league will suffer a loss in revenue in excess of two and one half million dollars. The defendant represents that this result will occur because the WHA has scheduled professional hockey games between member teams of the association and teams representing Russia, Czechoslovakia, Sweden and Finland to be played in the United States and Canada during the 1977–1978 season. The approval of the Canadian Amateur Hockey Association (hereinafter "CAHA") is required in order for the WHA teams to compete against these European teams in Canada. That organization has indicated that it would not approve those contests if the twenty-year old rule — which is the result of an agreement between the WHA and the CAHA — is violated. . . .

The Second Circuit has adopted two alternative tests for determining when a preliminary injunction should issue. In *Sonesta International Hotels Corp.* v. *Wellington Associates,* 483 F.2d 247 (2d Cir. 1973) the court ruled:

> The settled rule is that a preliminary injunction should issue only upon a clear showing of either (1) probable success on the merits *and* possible irreparable injury, or (2) sufficiently serious questions going to the merits to make them a fair ground for litigation *and* a balance of hardships tipping decidedly toward the party requesting the preliminary relief. *Id.* at 250 (emphasis in original).

Some courts have added a third requirement to the showing of irreparable injury and probable success, the "balancing of equities." *See e.g., Heldman* v. *United States,* 354 F.Supp. 1241, 1249–1250 (S.D.N.Y.1973). This third factor means, in essence, that preliminary relief is not warranted unless the court finds that the importance of the injunction to the plaintiff is such that it outweighs the inconvenience which will be visited upon the defendant from the issuance of the injunction. *Id.* at 1250. The addition of this third factor is consistent with the teaching of the Supreme Court in *Doran* v. *Salem Inn, Inc.,* 422 U.S. 922, (1975). . . .

These three factors are interdependent, so that if a plaintiff makes a strong showing of irreparable injury and a likelihood of success on the merits, he

may be granted preliminary relief even though the defendant has alleged that the granting of the preliminary injunction will subject him to serious harm. *Heldman* v. *United States Lawn Tennis Association,* 354 F.Supp. 1241, 1250 (S.D.N.Y. 1973). . . .

If the preliminary relief is denied, Linseman will be unable to compete in the WHA for the 1977–1978 season. Despite the defendant's assertion to the contrary, the damage he will suffer as a consequence cannot be adequately compensated with monetary damages. The plaintiff will forfeit more than the salary he has coming to him under the contract with the Bulls, if he is denied permission to play in the WHA for the current season. The career of a professional athlete is more limited than that of persons engaged in almost any other occupation. Consequently the loss of even one year of playing time is very detrimental. . . .

In a case which is very similar to the one *sub judice* a basketball player was granted a preliminary injunction to permit him to continue playing for the team of his choice despite his ineligibility under the league rules. . . . *Denver Rockets* v. *All-Pro Management, Inc.,* 325 F.Supp. 1049, 1057 (C.D.Cal.1971).

A professional football player was also granted preliminary relief in a similar situation, where the court found that his inability to play would cause him irreparable injury. *Bowman* v. *National Football League,* 402 F.Supp. 754, 756 (D.Minn.1975). The considerations which led those courts to find that a professional football or basketball player would suffer irreparable injury, if he were not granted preliminary relief, are equally applicable to a professional hockey player.

The practice of which Linseman complains in this case is known as a group boycott or a concerted refusal to deal. The WHA and its member teams have agreed not to deal with Linseman solely for the reason that he will not have attained the age of 20 before December 31, 1977. A group boycott, or a concerted refusal to deal, has been long and consistently classified as a *per se* violation of the Sherman Act. *Fashion Originators' Guild* v. *Federal Trade Commission,* 312 U.S. 457, 468, 61 S.Ct. 703, 85 L.Ed. 949 (1941); *Klor's* v. *Broadway-Hale Stores,* 359 U.S. 207, 212, 79 S.Ct. 705, 3 L.Ed.2d 741 (1959). . . .

The twenty-year old rule of which plaintiff complains in the instant case constitutes a "primary" boycott wherein the actors at one level of trade (the WHA and its member teams) refuse to deal with an actor at another level (Linseman). A threefold harm results from a primary boycott. First, the victim of the boycott (Linseman) is excluded from the market he desires to enter. Second, competition in the market in which the victim attempts to sell his services (hockey players in the WHA) suffers. Third, by pooling their economic power, the individual members of the WHA have substituted their own private government for the rule of the marketplace. *Denver Rockets* v. *All-Pro Management, Inc.,* 325 F.Supp. 1049, 1061 (C.D.Cal.1971). . . .

[T]he attention of the Court has not been directed to any valid purpose for the twenty-year old rule. The major thrust of defendant's argument has been that the WHA itself did not initiate the rule, but was coerced by the threat of a boycott against its member teams by the foreign teams with which it has scheduled contests if the WHA teams did not agree to the twenty-year old rule. Courts have uniformly rejected any defense that an antitrust violation was "forced" onto the defendant. The Supreme Court has held that "acquiescence in an illegal scheme is as much a violation of the Sherman Act as the creation and promotion of one." *United States* v. *Paramount Pictures,* 334 U.S. 131, 161, 68 S.Ct. 915, 931, 92 L.Ed 1260 (1948). . . . Another reason suggested for the twenty-year old rule is that the Canadian junior hockey league, from which the WHA and National Hockey League draw much of their talent, would fail if the most talented teenagers were signed by professional teams. If these Canadian junior teams failed to draw spectator support, the pool of talent relied upon by the professional leagues would dry up. The hockey leagues lack an organized farm system or an adequate number of college teams as a source from which to draw their players. Regardless of whether this chain of events may come to pass in the future, if the twenty-year old rule is abrogated, that is no justification for an organized restraint of trade. The antitrust laws do not admit of exceptions due to economic necessity. . . . If the WHA needs a training ground for its prospective players, the principles of the free market system dictate that it bear the cost of that need by establishing its own farm system. As to the argument that the Canadian league is unable to survive without the twenty-year old rule, the

Sherman Act does not permit a failing enterprise to be buoyed up with an illegal agreement to restrain trade. . . .

Defendant argues that the instant case is distinguishable from *Denver Rockets* in that sec. 8.2 of the WHA By-Laws provides a procedure whereby a player may submit to the Executive Committee or to the full Board of Trustees of the WHA any objection to the disapproval of a player contract, and argues that plaintiff should have pursued his remedies under that section before litigating in this Court. Despite this appeal procedure, Operating Regulation 17.2(a) is unequivocal. There is no provision for any exceptions to this rule, as in the case with the American Basketball Association's "hardship" exception to its four-year college rule. Therefore if Linseman had appealed to the Executive Board or the Board of Trustees, those bodies would have been powerless to alter the rule. Consequently, Linseman comes to this Court as if he had no appeal procedure available to him at all; the law will not require an individual to perform a meaningless act.

The greatest distinction between the case at bar and *Deesen* is that the rule in the present case is completely arbitrary. While the rule in *Deesen* excluded players only after their skill had been assessed, the present rule is a blanket restriction as to age without any consideration of talent. The Court may take judicial notice of the fact that many teenagers have played in the professional ranks with distinction. Darryl Dawkins, Moses Malone, Bobby Orr and Gordon Roberts are a few names which come readily to mind. . . .

Having found that Linseman will suffer irreparable injury, if he is denied the preliminary relief he seeks, and that there is a great probability that he will prevail in a trial on the merits, the Court now turns to a discussion of the balance of equities. As noted above, in balancing the equities, the Court must weigh the importance of the preliminary relief to the plaintiff against the potential harm to the defendant should the relief be granted. The Court finds that the importance of the interim relief to Linseman outweighs any harm that may result to the WHA.

The WHA has submitted that it stands to lose in excess of $2.5 million if Linseman is permitted to play in the current season. This loss will result from the refusal of the CAHA to sanction any hockey contests scheduled between WHA teams and teams from foreign countries. It is not at all certain that the WHA will in fact suffer this loss. In the first place, this figure represents the projected ticket sales revenue from all 36 contests scheduled between WHA member teams and foreign teams to be played in both the United States and Canada. While it has been alleged that the CAHA, which must sanction the contests to be played in Canada, will withhold its approval if Linseman plays, there is nothing in the record to suggest that the AHAUS, responsible for games scheduled in the United States, will similarly deny approval. Secondly, the WHA's projection of average attendance at these games of 11,000 with an average ticket price of seven dollars, which was used to arrive at the total of potential lost revenue, may be somewhat optimistic. Third, defendant's counsel conceded that he did not know whether the CAHA's position might be altered by the fact that Linseman was playing pursuant to a court order rather than from a voluntary breach of the agreement between the WHA and the CAHA by the WHA.

More importantly, however, even if the Court were convinced that the WHA would lose $2.5 million, there is no reason to permit a violation of the antitrust laws by the defendant to prevent the issuance of a preliminary injunction to the plaintiff. The Court has already determined that there exists a great likelihood that the WHA's twenty-year old rule will be held at trial to be a classic case of a *per se* illegal concerted boycott, which is not redeemed by either the act of state doctrine or the economic compulsion argument. . . .

NOTE

1. Mentioned in the foregoing *Linseman* decision is *Bowman* v. *National Football League*, 402 F.Supp. 754 (D. Minn. 1975). When the World Football League expired in 1975, National Football League club representatives issued a joint resolution barring the signing of "any player who has been under a 1975 contract as a player or coach in another major professional football league" for the remainder of that season. A class action was brought on behalf of all WFL players. It was alleged that this resolution constituted a concerted illegal boycott against the affected class. The trial court agreed, and a preliminary injunction was issued.

Boris v. United States Football League, U.S. Dist. Ct., C.D. Ca., No. CV 83–4980 LEW (Kx), Feb. 28, 1984

Order Specifying Facts which Appear to be Without Substantial Controversy

Waters, District Judge

This matter is before the Court on the motion of plaintiff Robert F. Boris ("Boris") for an order adjudicating and declaring the defendants United States Football League ("USFL") and the Arizona Wranglers ("Wranglers") liable to Boris under Count One of the complaint for damages and Count Two of the complaint for an injunction.

Count One of the complaint alleges that defendant USFL and Wranglers violated section one of the Sherman Act (15 U.S.C. sec. 1) and seeks damages for that breach under section four of the Clayton Act (15 U.S.C. sec. 15).

Count Two of the complaint alleges that defendants USFL and Wranglers violated section one of the Sherman Act (15 U.S.C. sec. 1), and seeks a preliminary and permanent injunction under section 16 of the Clayton Act (15 U.S.C. sec. 26). . . .

Having considered the pleadings and other papers on file and the parties' briefs, and evidence submitted in connection with this motion for summary judgment, and having ruled on the motion, the Court hereby finds that there is no genuine issue as to the following material facts:

1. Plaintiff Boris was a varsity football player at the University of Arizona during the 1980–81 and 1981–82 seasons and for the first three games of the 1982 season.

2. After the third game of the 1982 season, Boris voluntarily withdrew from the University of Arizona.

3. Boris is not currently eligible to nor is he playing college football.

4. Boris will not be eligible to play college football in the fall of 1984 or any time thereafter under the rules and regulations of the NCAA. . . .

9. The USFL and its member teams have agreed with each other to abide by an "Eligibility Rule" which provides:

No person shall be eligible to play or be selected as a player unless (1) all college football eligibility of such player has expired, or (2) at least five (5) years shall have elapsed since the player first entered or attended a recognized junior college, college or university or (3) such player received a diploma from a recognized college or university.

10. The USFL and all of the USFL member teams, including defendant Wranglers, have agreed among themselves to adhere to and to enforce the Eligibility Rule quoted in the paragraph above.

11. The reasons advanced by the defendants in support of the Eligibility Rule, as it existed relative to the USFL's 1983 football season, are (in summary): The Eligibility Rule promotes on-field competitive balance among USFL teams; very few college-age athletes are physically, mentally, or emotionally mature enough for professional football; abolition of the Eligibility Rule will not benefit the college athlete; the Eligibility Rule promotes the concept of the importance of a college education; the Eligibility Rule promotes the efficient operation of the USFL by strengthening the sport at the college level so that the USFL does not have to develop players at that level; the Eligibility Rule is not inflexible; since 1983 was the USFL's first season of play, competitive conditions required it to adopt and enforce the same Eligibility Rule previously adopted and enforced by the two powerful and established existent major professional football leagues (the National Football League and the Canadian Football League), if it cannot enforce the Eligibility Rule, its very existence will be threatened, and the best chance that college football players have for increased remuneration (viz, interleague economic competition) will be gone.

12. The Court finds that although the above listed reasons may have varying degrees of merit, the principal reason for the adoption by the USFL and its member teams of the Eligibility Rule was to respond to apparent demands made by college football programs and thereby to gain better access to these programs towards the end of selecting the best college players available.

13. The Eligibility Rule of the USFL, as it existed relative to the USFL's 1983 football season, involved combining for the primary purpose of coercing or excluding third parties, and did in fact have the effect of coercing or excluding those third party individuals deemed ineligible by the Rule. *Joseph E. Seagrams & Sons, Inc. v. Hawaiian Oke and Liquors Ltd.,* 416 F.2d 71 (9th Cir. 1969).

14. While in certain areas cooperation and not competition among professional sports teams is required and thus the USFL might in some respects be considered to be an economic entity, as measured against issues presented in this case the Court finds that the USFL teams are economic competititors. *Los Angeles Memorial Coliseum, Inc.* v. *National Football League,* 468 F.Supp. 154 (C.D. Cal. 1979).

Order re Plaintiff's Motion for Partial Summary Judgment

Plaintiff's motion for partial summary judgment having come on regularly for hearing before this Court on January 30, 1984, the Court having read all of the papers filed by the parties in connection therewith and having considered the oral arguments presented at the hearing,

It is hereby ordered:

1. Plaintiff's motion for partial summary judgment is granted in part in that the Court finds that the "Eligibility Rule" of the United States Football League ("USFL"), as it existed in 1983, and which provided as follows:

> No person shall be eligible to play or be selected as a player unless (1) all college football eligibility of such player has expired, or (2) at least five (5) years shall have elapsed since the player first entered or attended a recognized junior college, college or university or (3) such player received a diploma from a recognized college or university.

as it was applied to plaintiff Robert F. Boris, constituted a "group boycott," and was, therefore, a *per se* violation of section one of the Sherman Act (15 U.S.C. sec. 1). Pursuant to 28 U.S.C. sec. 1292(b), the Court is of the opinion that the foregoing order involves a controlling question of law as to which there is substantial ground for difference of opinion and that an immediate appeal from this order may materially advance the ultimate termination of the litigation. . . .

Neeld v. National Hockey League, 594 F.Supp. 1297 (9th Cir. 1979)

Belloni, District Judge:

Appellant, Gregory Neeld, is a one-eyed hockey player. Appellee, the National Hockey League, maintains a by-law which prevents Neeld from playing in the League. Neeld has appealed from a summary judgment holding that the League's by-law does not violate the Sherman Act. Neeld has also sought a remand to the District Court for the purpose of pleading various other claims not asserted below. For the reasons below, we affirm the District Court and deny in its entirety the motion for remand. . . .

The National Hockey League is composed of franchised member professional hockey teams. Consequently, Neeld argues the by-law in question constitutes a *per se* illegal boycott. The many cases he cites for this proposition are not on point.

Not all concerted action is judged by the rule of *per se* illegality. Fundamental to the *per se* rule is the rationale that the facts underlying certain conduct such as price fixing, *United States v. Socony-Vacuum Oil Co.*, 310 U.S. 150, 60 S.Ct. 811, 84 L.Ed. 1129 (1940); division of markets, *United States* v. *Addyston Pipe & Steel Co.*, 175 U.S. 211, 20 S.Ct. 96, 44 L.Ed. 136 (1899); group boycotts, or concerted refusals to deal, *Klor's* v. *Broadway-Hale Stores*, 359 U.S. 207, 79 S.Ct. 705, 3 L.Ed.2d 741 (1959); and other "naked restraints of trade with no purpose except stifling of competition," *White Motor Co.* v. *United States*, 372 U.S. 253, 263, 83 S.Ct. 696, 702, 9 L.Ed.2d 738 (1963); *Joseph E. Seagram & Sons, Inc.,* v. *Hawaiian Oke & Liquors, LTD.*, 416 F.2d 71, 76 (9th Cir. 1969) need not be examined on a case by case basis. These types of agreements or practices "because of their pernicious effect on competition and lack of any redeeming virtue are conclusively presumed to be unreasonable and therefore illegal. . . ." *Northern Pacific R. Co.* v. *United States*, 356 U.S. 1, 5, 78 S.Ct. 514, 518, 2 L.Ed.2d 545 (1958). Additionally, particularly apparent in cases where the *per se* rule is applicable is the fact that the exclusionary or coercive conduct, for example, is a direct affront to competition rather than merely an incidental effect.

Here, however, the record amply supports the reasonableness of the by-law. We agree with the District Court's conclusion that the primary purpose and direct effect of the League's by-law was not anticompetitive but rather safety.

Neeld argues that if the rule of reason is applied then summary judgment was inappropriate because of alleged material issues of fact. Specifically, he contends the affidavits establish a disputed issue of fact whether a certain "safety mask" (designed especially for Neeld) would adequately protect Neeld from further injury. . . .

Even assuming for purposes of argument that the adequacy of the "safety mask" for Neeld's protection is disputed, summary judgment was still appropriate since that fact alone would not affect the outcome of this case.

The by-law is not motivated by anti-competitiveness and Neeld does not actually contend that it is. Further, any anticompetitive effect is at most *de minimis, see Gough* v. *Rossmoor Corp.*, 585 F.2d 381, 386, 389 (9th Cir. 1978), and incidental to the primary purpose of promoting safety, both for Neeld, who lost his eye in a hockey game, and for all players who play with or against him. We take judicial notice that ice hockey is a very rough physical contact sport, and that there is bound to be danger to players who happen to be on Neeld's blind side, no matter how well his mask may protect his one good eye. Also of some importance and legitimate concern to the League and its members is the possibility of being sued for personal injuries to Neeld himself or to others, if Neeld is permitted to play. *See National Society of Professional Engineers* v. *United States*, 435 U.S. 679, 696 N.22, 98 S.Ct. 1355, 55 L.Ed.2d 637 (1978). . . .

4.72   Suspensions and Blacklists

Severe sanctions can be, and are, imposed against athletes for alleged infractions of league or association disciplinary rules. The cases below detail antitrust challenges to actions taken against an athlete. Except in the *Blalock* case, the challenges were unsuccessful. Consequently, it is important that the cases in this section be considered in conjunction with other methods of disputing disciplinary actions (see Sections 3.38, 4.34, 5.43, and 6.32).

Molinas v. **National Basketball Association**, 190 F.Supp. 241 (S.D.N.Y. 1961)

Irving R. Kaufman, District Judge.

Plaintiff, Jack Molinas, is a well-known basketball player. In 1953, upon his graduation from

Columbia University he was "drafted" by the Fort Wayne Pistons, then a member of the defendant National Basketball Association (now the Detroit Pistons). Subsequently, in the fall of 1953, he signed a contract to play with the Pistons. In January of 1954, however, he admitted, in writing, that he placed several bets on his team, the Pistons, to win. The procedure he followed was that he contacted a person in New York by telephone, who informed him of the "point spread" on the particular game in question. The plaintiff would then decide whether or not to place a bet on the game. The plaintiff admitted that he received some $400 as a result of these wagers, including reimbursement of his telephone calls to New York. After the plaintiff admitted this wagering, Mr. Podoloff, the president of the league, acting pursuant to a clause (Section 15) in plaintiff's contract, and a league rule (Section 79 of the League Constitution) prohibiting gambling, indefinitely suspended the plaintiff from the league. This suspension has continued until the present date. Since the suspension, plaintiff has made several applications, both oral and written, for reinstatement. All of these have been refused, and Mr. Podoloff has testified that he will never allow the plaintiff to re-enter the league. He has characterized the plaintiff as a "cancer on the league" which must be excised.

In the meantime, plaintiff attended and graduated from the Brooklyn Law School, and was then admitted to the New York State Bar. He has also been playing basketball for Williamsport and Hazelton of the Eastern Basketball League.

In 1954, shortly after the suspension, plaintiff brought an action in the New York State Supreme Court, alleging that he had been denied notice and hearing prior to the suspension, and that there was no authority for the indefinite suspension imposed by Mr. Podoloff. The court, after a trial, found against the plaintiff, holding that since he had engaged in reprehensible and morally dishonest conduct, he was not entitled to seek the aid of an equity court. The court also found that even if a hearing was required by league rules, it would have been a futile formality in this case, since the plaintiff had admitted violations of his contract and the league rules. An appeal was taken to the Appellate Division but was subsequently dismissed.

In the action presently before the court, the plaintiff alleges that the defendant National Basketball Association has entered into a conspiracy with its member teams and others in restraint of trade, and thus has violated the antitrust laws. It is alleged that the operation of the so-called reserve clause, by which players are allocated among the league teams, and through which a team holding a player's contract is given an option to renew it each year, is an unreasonable restraint of trade in violation of the anti-trust laws. It is further alleged that the suspension of the plaintiff by the league, and its subsequent refusal to reinstate him, is the result of a conspiracy in violation of these laws. Finally, plaintiff charges that the league has, through this conspiracy, imposed certain collateral restraints upon him, affecting his opportunities to play in "exhibition games" against league personnel.

Plaintiff seeks treble damages in the sum of three million dollars, an injunction against the conspiracies alleged, and reinstatement to the league.

It is well established that the plaintiff has the burden of proving, by a preponderance of the evidence, that there has been a violation of the anti-trust laws which has injured him. This burden clearly has not been met in the instant case. Plaintiff has not established any violation of the anti-trust laws which has in any way injured him, and thus his complaint must be dismissed.

The law is clear that, in order for a private plaintiff in a civil anti-trust suit to recover, he must establish a clear causal connection between the violation alleged and the injuries allegedly suffered. . . . With respect to the plaintiff's contention based on the so-called reserve clause, no causal connection whatsoever has been established between the reserve clause and any damage which he may have sustained. Plaintiff has not shown that he suffered any damage at the time he signed his contract with the Fort Wayne Pistons, in the fall of 1953, following the so-called college draft. It does not appear that Molinas was in any way displeased over playing for the Pistons, and were it not for his suspension in January of 1954, it is likely that he would have continued to play for them without complaint. Following the suspension, the refusal of the league or its member clubs to deal with the plaintiff was clearly due to the suspension, rather than the reserve clause. These teams would obviously have refused to deal with the plaintiff even if the reserve clause had never existed. Thus, the plaintiff has not sustained his burden of proof on this claim.

With respect to plaintiff's suspension from the league in January of 1954, and the subsequent refusal by the league to reinstate him, plaintiff has patently failed to establish an unreasonable restraint of trade within the meaning of the anti-trust laws. A rule, and a corresponding contract clause, providing for the suspension of those who place wagers on games in which they are participating seems not only reasonable, but necessary for the survival of the league. Every league or association must have some reasonable governing rules, and these rules must necessarily include disciplinary provisions. Surely, every disciplinary rule which a league may invoke, although by its nature it may involve some sort of a restraint, does not run afoul of the anti-trust laws. And, a disciplinary rule invoked against gambling seems about as reasonable a rule as could be imagined. Furthermore, the application of the rule to the plaintiff's conduct is also eminently reasonable. Plaintiff was wagering on games in which he was to play, and some of these bets were made on the basis of a "point spread" system. Plaintiff insists that since he bet only on his own team to win, his conduct, while admittedly improper, was not immoral. But I do not find this distinction to be a meaningful one in the context of the present case. The vice inherent in the plaintiff's conduct is that each time he either placed a bet or refused to place a bet, this operated inevitably to inform bookmakers of an insider's opinion as to the adequacy or inadequacy of the point-spread or his team's ability to win. Thus, for example, when he chose to place a bet, this would indicate to the bookmakers that a member of the Fort Wayne team believed that his team would exceed its expected performance. Similarly, when he chose not to bet, bookmakers thus would be informed of his opinion that the Pistons would not perform according to expectations. It is certainly reasonable for the league and Mr. Podoloff to conclude that this conduct could not be tolerated and must, therefore, be eliminated. The reasonableness of the league's action is apparent in view of the fact that, at that time, the confidence of the public in basketball had been shattered, due to a series of gambling incidents. Thus, it was absolutely necessary for the sport to exhume gambling from its midst for all times in order to survive.

The same factors justifying the suspension also serve to justify the subsequent refusal to reinstate. The league could reasonably conclude that in order to effectuate its important and legitimate policies against gambling, and to restore and maintain the confidence of the public vital to its existence, it was necessary to enforce its rules strictly, and to apply the most stringent sanctions. One can certainly understand the reluctance to permit an admitted gambler to return to the league, and again to participate in championship games, especially in light of the aura and stigma of gambling which has clouded the sports world in the past few years. Viewed in this context it can be seen that the league was justified in determining that it was absolutely necessary to avoid even the slightest connection with gambling, gamblers, and those who had done business with gamblers, in the future. . . .

NOTE

1. The action pursued by Jack Molinas in the New York courts, alluded to in the foregoing federal court decision, is *Molinas* v. *Podoloff*, 133 N.Y.S.2d 743 (1954). The New York court took special note of the publicity accorded sports, assessing that a scandal in one sport puts suspicion on others, causes injuries to players, and shakes the confidence of the public and the morale of youth. The court, further noting that basketball had been inflicted with bribery and the fixing of games, stated every effort to eliminate suspicion of dishonest competition must be made. Plaintiff's admission meant that a hearing would inevitably result in a suspension. The court said equity demanded that what ought to be done should be done; accordingly, one who admits a violation does not come into court with clean hands. The court thus concluded that Molinas, with or without a hearing, was properly suspended.

Shortly after the 1961 federal court suit, Jack Molinas was implicated in the new outbreak of fixing charges in college basketball that resulted in the suspension of several players in the college ranks and their blacklisting by the NBA on the professional level. One such blacklisted player was Connie Hawkins, whose later antitrust suit against the NBA was eventually settled, leading to his admittance into the league after several years' exclusion. For an account of the Hawkins story, arguing largely for his innocence, as well as of the role played by Jack Molinas in the 1960s scandals, see D. Wolf, *FOUL! The Connie Hawkins Story* (1973).

Manok v. Southeast District Bowling Association, 306 F.Supp. 1215 (C.D. Ca. 1969)

This action was brought by Ralph Manok, a

professional bowler, against the American Bowling Congress (ABC) and it local association for suspending him as a member and for restricting the sale of a bowling device called "Mono-Grip," which he had invented. He claimed relief under the Sherman Antitrust Act (sections 1–6) and the Clayton Act (sections 15 and 16) charging that the defendants restrained trade through unreasonable restrictions on membership and readmittance to the association, and that they discriminated against him through vague, unfair, and unequal rules.

Manok had been a member in good standing of the defendant association, which was a nonstock membership corporation of male bowlers. The association provided uniform conditions and methods of playing "ten pin" bowling, maintained and enforced rules, and conducted and governed leagues and tournaments. It was financed by membership dues. Rules 26(b) and 29 provided for suspension of membership for participation in unsanctioned leagues, or for participating under an assumed name. All persons involved in the prohibited conduct could be suspended.

Manok was suspended from the ABC for knowingly bowling in tournaments with a partner who was using an assumed name and for collecting prize money from those tournaments. He claimed association officers treated him unfairly by making malicious statements about associating with blackballed members and by prejudicing association members from patronizing his place of business and from using his invention.

The court adopted its general policy for refusing to review suspension proceedings of members from voluntary associations without a clear showing of bad faith. The court held Manok was not entitled to relief in absence of a showing of the existence of a combination of the ABC and the local association with the intent and purpose of restricting trade. The size and strength of the ABC only would become material if it was linked to some conspiracy by individuals to restrict competition and control prices. The court ruled Manok failed to present any

substantial evidence on the issue and therefore granted defendants' motion for summary judgment.

Blalock v. Ladies Professional Golf Association, 359 F.Supp. 1260 (N.D. Ga. 1973)

Plaintiff, Barbara Jane Blalock, a successful professional woman golfer, brought this suit against other professional women golfers, the Ladies Professional Golf Association (hereinafter LPGA, of which plaintiff and individual defendants were active members), and the LPGA Tournament Players Corporation (hereinafter LPGATPC, a Texas Corporation organized to carry on LPGA business). Individual defendants, who were both officers of LPGA and player-competitors of plaintiff, comprised the executive board of LPGA, which directs the policies, business, and affairs of the association. Plaintiff moved for partial summary judgment on the grounds that her one-year suspension from the LPGA constituted a group boycott and thus was illegal under Section 1 of the Sherman Antitrust Act, 15 U.S.C. Sec. 1. The facts leading to Blalock's suspension were as follows:

Four observers were appointed on May 5, 1972, by the defendant-tournament director of LPGA to observe plaintiff in the tournament's second round. The observers thereafter claimed that plaintiff illegally moved her ball. In a May 20, 1972, meeting, at which plaintiff was not present, the executive board of LPGA decided to disqualify plaintiff as to that tournament, to place her on probation for the rest of the season, and to fine her $500 for cheating. She was summoned before the executive board on May 26, 1972, and informed of this decision.

On May 28, 1972, the executive board reconvened; absent were two board members of the first meeting and present were two nonmembers, co-competitors with plaintiff and tournament committee representatives. At this meeting, two of the board members related certain statements made by plaintiff on May 20, 1972, when informed of the board's decision, which they considered to be admissions of wrong-doing. Suspension of plaintiff for one year was discussed and agreed to by the present board members, who in turn were able to contact and explain the discussion to one of the two missing board members, who also voted to suspend plaintiff. Plaintiff was not present at this meeting.

On May 30, 1972, plaintiff was again summoned before all members of the board. After extensive discussion with plaintiff, the board informed her that she was suspended for one year, as agreed to by all board members.

In granting plaintiff's motion for partial summary judgment on the ground that her one-year suspension from the LPGA constituted a group boycott and *per se* restraint of trade, the court first noted, by citing dicta in *Flood* v. *Kuhn,* 407 U.S. 258, 92 S.Ct. 2099, 32 L. Ed. 2d 728 (1972), that professional golf is subject to the antitrust laws.

Next the court stated the two threshold elements necessary before there can be a 15 U.S.C. 1 concerted refusal to deal: (1) there must be effect on interstate commerce, and (2) there must be agreement equivalent to a contract, combination or conspiracy. The court found both elements were met in this case. First, LPGA tournaments are held in several states and rights for their interstate broadcast are sold. Second, individual and association defendants agreed not to deal with plaintiff by imposing the one-year suspension pursuant to the association constitution and bylaws.

The court next briefly stated the Rule of Reason under the Sherman Antitrust Act: those arrangements which merely regulate and thereby promote competition are legal; and those which suppress or destroy it are illegal. *Chicago Board of Trade* v. *United States*, 246 U.S. 231, 238, 38 S.Ct. 242, 244, 62 L.Ed.2 683 (1918). The court then discussed group boycotts as illegal per se (and an exception to the Rule of Reason test) in being arrangements which by virtue of their obvious and necessary effect on competition are presumed to be unreasonable restraints on trade. See *Northern Pacific Ry.* v.

United States, 356 U.S. 1, 5, 78 S.Ct. 514, 518, 2 L.Ed. 2d 545 (1958).

The court listed three categories of group boycotts: (1) horizontal combinations in which traders at one level of distribution act to exclude direct competitors from the market; (2) vertical combinations, in which traders at different marketing levels act to exclude from the market direct competitors of some members of the combination; and (3) combinations in which traders at one level act to coerce the trade practices of boycott victims rather than to eliminate them as competitors. The common thread running through each of these combinations, which makes them illegal per se, is the presence of exclusionary or coercive conduct with a purpose and effect equivalent to a naked restraint of trade.

The court determined that the purpose and effect of plaintiff's one-year suspension from the LPGA was not only exclusion from this immediate market, but also (considering that plaintiff is an LPGA member and LPGA bylaws provide that members may not compete for money in *any* tournament not sponsored or approved by the LPGA), "total exclusion" from the market of professional golf. That this severe discipline was imposed without hearing from the plaintiff, after an initial lesser discipline of only a fine and probation, and that it was rendered by plaintiff's competitors who could gain financially from the plaintiff's exclusion, further supported the court's finding this arrangement to be a per se illegal restraint of trade. As a per se violation, the question of the reasonableness of the suspension did not have to be addressed.

Defendants argued that a Rule of Reason test was the proper standard to apply on the grounds that the suspension was pursuant to a valid exercise of self-regulation. The court's reply to this argument was that this "self-regulation" was not equivalent to the type enunciated by the Supreme Court in *Silver* v. *New York Stock Exchange,* 373 U.S. 341, 83 S.Ct. 1246, 10 L.Ed.2d 389 (1963), to be an exception to the *per se* rule, as relied on by defendants. Unlike the self-regulation in *Silver,* the present actions were not pursuant to a statute justifying such concerted actions.

The court granted plaintiff's motion for summary judgment to the limited extent that the plaintiff's suspension was violative of Section 1 of the Sherman Antitrust Act, but did not rule on those self-regulating acts of the LPGA which have less than exclusionary effect.

Because the plaintiff's supension had expired by its own terms by the time of this decision, the court gave no further injunctive relief, dissolved the heretofore granted preliminary injunction, and awarded plaintiff those winnings acquired during the period of her purported (because it was heretofore enjoined) suspension.

Chapter 5

PROFESSIONAL
SPORTS UNIONS

5.00   Labor Law and Labor Relations

Chapter 4 concentrated on the role of the person who represents professional athletes and how that role contrasts with the role of those who represent the players' associations. The dichotomy between the two was noted as early as Chapter 1. It is now imperative that we investigate just what the union can, should, or must do in the context of labor law and labor relations. At the core is understanding how unions in sports came to play the key roles they do today.

There are many reasons for the growth and development of players' associations and their attendant collective agreements. Increasingly, the players felt the need for united action. Fortunately there were people available to tell them where and how such help could be obtained. In addition to the growing awareness of the possible strengths of collective efforts, three other concerted actions developed the muscle of collective bargaining and action in sports: (1) the strike weapon; (2) antitrust litigation; and (3) arbitration of grievances — an outgrowth of collective bargaining. While antitrust litigation and labor arbitration have garnered the most obvious gains, strikes and threats of strikes should not be underestimated.

Chapter 5 not only examines the muscle of players' associations but also their makeup. Because the professional athlete's career is not long, union membership is in constant flux. Thus the chapter begins with an investigation of who constitutes the unit, from the perspective of management as well as from labor.

5.10   The Unit: Labor and Management

All sports unions have struggled for recognition. For years, the debate was over whether player groups were really unions, capable of recognition under the National Labor Relations Act. Even when recognition was assured, battles continued. Management procrastinated at the bargaining process. Spokespersons for the union were contested.

The major cases which follow all arise from soccer, which from an economic standpoint is not one of the major sports in this country. Perhaps this is why the battles are so protracted. The two principal soccer leagues questioned the unions' existence from the beginning; only the intervention of the labor laws forced true collective bargaining.

The three cases presented for primary analysis examine the many aspects of a union fighting for recognition — having to fight for a definitive statement as to who in management is in the employer unit, and having to find out what protections under the labor laws can be invoked to force meaningful bargaining.

5.11 Union Certification and Multiemployer Bargaining Unit

Most professional sports leagues are nonprofit associations. The members of the association are the individual clubs. In collective bargaining, the problem is to determine just who in management is part of the multiemployer bargaining unit. It sounds simple, but it is not.

For example, the National Football League owners in the early 1970s formed the NFL Management Council (NFLMC), a separate owners' group. This was done to keep the league and commissioner's offices out of direct participation in collective bargaining. The move was successful in obtaining this result.

In general, owners would prefer to force players unions to deal just with the clubs. The players want the league directly accountable. At times, as with the NFLMC, a compromise is reached. In other instances, such as with the North American Soccer League, the NLRB and ultimately the federal courts have to decide the issue.

North American Soccer League v. National Labor Relations Board, 613 F.2d 1379 (5th Cir. 1980)

Roney, Circuit Judge

The correct collective bargaining unit for the players in the North American Soccer League is at issue in this case. Contrary to our first impression, which was fostered by the knowledge that teams in the League compete against each other on the playing fields and for the hire of the best players, our review of the record reveals sufficient evidence to support the National Labor Relations Board's determination that the League and its member clubs are joint employers, and that a collective bargaining unit comprised of all NASL players on clubs based in the United States is appropriate.

Finding petitioners' due process challenge to be without merit, we deny the petition for review and enforce the collective bargaining order on the cross-application of the Board.

The North American Soccer League is a non-profit association comprised of twenty-four member clubs. The North American Soccer League Players Association, a labor organization, petitioned the NLRB for a representation election among all NASL players. The Board found the League and its clubs to be joint employers and directed an election within a unit comprised of all the soccer players of United States clubs in the League. Excluded from the unit were players for the clubs based in Canada, because the Board concluded its jurisdiction did not extend to those clubs as employers.

Players in the unit voted in favor of representation by the Association. After the League and its clubs refused to bargain, the Board found them in violation of Sections 8(a)(1) and (5) of the National Labor Relations Act, 29 U.S.C.A. sec. 158(a)(1) and sec. (5), and ordered collective bargaining. The League and its member clubs petitioned this Court for review. The Board's cross-application seeks enforcement of that order.

The settled law is not challenged on this petition for review. Where an employer has assumed sufficient control over the working conditions of the employees of its franchisees or member-employers, the Board may require the employers to bargain jointly. The Board is also empowered to decide in each case whether the employee unit requested is an appropriate unit for bargaining. The Board's decision will not be set aside unless the unit is clearly inappropriate. Thus the issues in this case are whether there is a joint employer relationship among the League and its member clubs, and if so, whether the designated bargaining unit of players is appropriate.

Joint Employers

Whether there is a joint employer relationship is "essentially a factual issue," and the Board's finding must be affirmed if supported by substantial evidence on the record as a whole.

The existence of a joint employer relationship depends on the control which one employer exercises, or potentially exercises, over the labor relations policy of the other. In this case, the record supports the Board's finding that the League exercises a significant degree of control over essential aspects of the clubs' labor relations, including but not limited to the selection, retention, and termination of the players, the terms of individual player contracts, dispute resolution and player discipline. Furthermore, each club granted the NASL authority over not only its own labor relations but also, on its behalf, authority over the labor relations of the other members clubs. The evidence is set forth in detail in the Board's decision and need be only briefly recounted here. . . .

The League's purpose is to promote the game of soccer through its supervision of competition among member clubs. Club activities are governed by the League constitution, and the regulations promulgated thereunder by a majority vote of the clubs. The commissioner, selected and compensated by the clubs, is the League's chief executive officer. A board of directors composed of one representative of each club assists him in managing the League.

The League's control over the clubs' labor relations begins with restrictions on the means by which players are acquired. An annual college draft is conducted by the commissioner pursuant to the regulations, and each club obtains exclusive negotiating rights to the players it selects. On the other hand, as the Board recognized, the League exercises less control over the acquisition of "free agent" players and players "on loan" from soccer clubs abroad.

The regulations govern interclub player trades and empower the commissioner to void trades not deemed to be in the best interest of the League. Termination of player contracts is conducted through a waiver system in accordance with procedures specified in the regulations.

The League also exercises considerable control over the contractual relationships between the clubs and their players. Before being permitted to participate in a North American Soccer League game, each player must sign a standard player contract adopted by the League. The contract governs the player's relationship with his club, requiring his compliance with club rules and the League constitution and regulations. Compensation is negotiated between the player and his club, and special provisions may be added to the contract. Significantly, however, the club must seek the permission of the commissioner before signing a contract which alters any terms of the standard contract.

Every player contract must be submitted to the commissioner, who is empowered to disapprove a contract deemed not in the best interest of the League. The commissioner's disapproval invalidates the contract. Disputes between a club and a player must be submitted to the commissioner for final and binding arbitration.

Control over player discipline is divided between the League and the clubs. The clubs enforce compliance with club rules relating to practices and also determine when a player will participate in a game. The League, through the commissioner, has broad power to discipline players for misconduct either on or off the playing field. Sanctions range from fines to suspension to termination of the player's contract.

Although we recognize that minor differences in the underlying facts might justify different findings on the joint employer issue, the record in this case supports the Board's factual finding of a joint employer relationship among the League and its constituent clubs.

Having argued against inclusion of the Canadian clubs in the NLRB proceeding, petitioners contend on appeal that their exclusion renders the Board's joint employer finding, encompassing 21 clubs, inconsistent with the existence of a 24-club League. The jurisdictional determination is not before us on appeal, however, and the Board's decision not to exercise jurisdiction over the Canadian clubs does not undermine the evidentiary base of its joint employer finding.

Even assuming the League and the clubs are joint employers, they contend that *Greenhoot, Inc.*, 205 N.L.R.B. 250 (1973), requires a finding of a separate joint employer relationship between the League and each of its clubs, and does not permit all the clubs to be lumped together with the League as joint employers. In *Greenhoot*, a building management company was found to be a joint employer separately with each building owner as to maintenance employees in the buildings covered by its contracts. The present case is clearly distinguishable, because here each soccer club exercises through its proportionate role in League management some control over the labor relations of other clubs. In *Greenhoot*, building owners did not exercise any control through the management company over the activities of other owners.

Appropriate Unit

The joint employer relationship among the League and its member clubs having been established, the next issue is whether the leaguewide unit of players designated by the Board is appropriate. Here the Board's responsibility and the standard of review in this Court are important.

The Board is not required to choose *the most* appropriate bargaining unit, only to select a unit appropriate under the circumstances. The determination will not be set aside "unless the Board's discretion has been exercised 'in an arbitrary or capricious manner.' "

Notwithstanding the substantial financial autonomy of the clubs, the Board found they form, through the League, an integrated group with common labor problems and a high degree of centralized control over labor relations. In these circumstances the Board's designation of a leaguewide bargaining unit as appropriate is reasonable, not arbitrary or capricious.

In making its decision, the Board expressly incorporated the reasons underlying its finding of a joint employer relationship. The Board emphasized in particular both the individual clubs' decision to form a League for the purpose of jointly controlling many of their activities, and the commissioner's power to disapprove contracts and exercise control over disciplinary matters. Under our "exceedingly narrow" standard of review, no arguments presented by petitioners require denial of enforcement of the bargaining order.

Thus the facts successfully refute any notion that because the teams compete on the field and in hiring, only team units are appropriate for collective bargaining purposes. Once a player is hired, his working conditions are significantly controlled by the League. Collective bargaining at that source of control would be the only way to effectively change by agreement many critical conditions of employment. . . .

5.12   Forcing Collective Bargaining

A constant complaint about the national labor laws is that their procedures are cumbersome and relief is slow and uncertain. The fight by players in the North American Soccer League to gain recognition as a certified union and then to obtain a collective bargaining agreement with

the league and clubs is often cited as an example of how long it can take for a union to force good faith bargaining. While this is largely an accurate portrayal of the soccer players' plight, the following case (*Morio* v. *NASL*) also illustrates some of the more sweeping and powerful weapons that can ultimately be used to resolve labor disputes. The Section 10(j) (injunction) is issued only in extreme cases, but as *Morio* reveals, the sanctions when applied will be effective.

Morio v. North American Soccer League, 501 F.Supp. 633 (S.D.N.Y. 1980)

Findings of Fact and Conclusions of Law

Motley, District Judge

This is an action brought by Petitioner, the Regional Director, Region 2, National Labor Relations Board, for and on behalf of the National Labor Relations Board (the Board) in which she seeks a temporary injunction pursuant to Section 10(j) of the National Labor Relations Act, as amended (the Act), pending the final disposition of matters presently pending before the Board. Respondents in this action are the North American Soccer League and its 21 constituent member clubs in the United States. The action is now before the court upon the issuance of an order to show cause why the temporary injunctive relief prayed for by Petitioner should not be granted. Petitioner filed her order to show cause for a temporary injunction, verified complaint, affidavits and brief in support of her application on July 30, 1980. Respondents' answer was served on August 5, 1980. A hearing was held on August 6 and 7, 1980. The North American Soccer League Players Association (the Union) was permitted to intervene in the action and to participate in the hearing. . . Upon the entire record, the court finds and concludes that Petitioner has reasonable cause to believe and there is reasonable cause to believe that Respondents have engaged in unfair labor practices and that Petitioner is entitled to the temporary injunctive relief sought in this action.

On August 16, 1977, the Union filed a petition for an election under Section 9(c) of the Act alleging that the League and each of its affiliated members constituted a single employer for purposes of collective bargaining. Hearings were held from September 8 to September 30, 1977, and briefs were submitted on the unique and complex issues of the appropriate unit in the professional soccer industry. On June 30, 1978, exactly nine months later, the Board issued a decision and direction of election among the soccer player employees of those teams listed in the petition as well as other employers who had been granted franchises by the League and commenced operations of teams during the intervening period.

On or about July 27, 1978, through August 4, 1978, the employees of Respondent Clubs participated in a secret ballot election conducted under the supervision of the Board, wherein a majority of the valid votes counted were cast for the Union. On September 1, 1978, the Union was certified as the exclusive collective bargaining representative of the employees of Respondent Clubs.

Subsequent to the certification, Respondents refused to bargain with the union and contested the Board's determination of a single "League wide unit" as being appropriate for collective bargaining. The Union filed an unfair labor practice charge on October 30, 1978, in Case No. 2-CA-15966. The General Counsel issued a complaint on November 24, 1978, against Respondents which alleged, *inter alia,* that Respondents had failed and refused to recognize and bargain with the Union in violation of Section 8(a)(1) and (5) of the Act. Following a summary judgement proceeding, the Board, on April 30, 1979, issued an order directing Respondents to bargain with the Union (241 NLRB No. 199). The Respondents appealed the Board's order to the United States Court of Appeals for the Fifth Circuit.

On March 21, 1980, the United States Court of Appeals for the Fifth Circuit issued its decision enforcing the Board's Order (103 LRRM 2976) and on May 14, 1980, issued its mandate. The mandate contained language directing the Respondents to recognize and bargain with the Union as exclusive collective bargaining representative of Respondent's professional soccer players. . . .

Respondents conceded that they have unilaterally changed the conditions of employment by requiring employees to obtain permission from their respective clubs before wearing a particular brand of footwear other than that selected by each

Respondent Club; that they have changed the conditions of employment by initiating plans for a new winter indoor soccer season which began in November, 1979, and ended in March, 1980; that they unilaterally changed conditions of employment by requiring employees to play or otherwise participate in the winter indoor soccer season; that they unilaterally changed conditions of employment by initiating plans to increase the 1980 summer outdoor soccer season by two games and two weeks over the 1979 format, which is presently in operation; and that they unilaterally changed employment conditions by initiating plans to reduce the maximum roster of all the Respondent Clubs during the regular summer outdoor season from 30 players to 26 players beginning on or about October 16, 1979, and continuing to the present.

Petitioner has therefore established that she has reasonable cause to believe that the Respondents have engaged in the foregoing unfair labor practices and is, therefore, entitled to temporary injunctive relief, pending the final determination of these charges presently pending before the Administrative Law Judge and the Board, as provided by Section 10(j) of the Act.

The court therefore finds and concludes that there is reasonable cause to believe Respondents have engaged in unfair labor practices in violation of the Act and that Petitioner is entitled to temporary injunctive relief as prayed for in the petition. . . .

The unilateral changes which Respondents admit have occurred since September 1, 1978, in the terms and conditions of employment, may violate the employer's obligations to bargain with the exclusive bargaining representative of the players. The duty to bargain carries with it the obligation on the part of the employer not to undercut the Union by entering into individual contracts with the employees. . . .

It is undisputed that Respondents have since September 1, 1978, refused to bargain with the Union. Respondents claim that they had the right to refuse to bargain with the Union since they were pursuing their right to appeal the Board's determination that all of the players referred to above constitute a unit for collective bargaining purposes. Respondents' duty to bargain with the Union arose from the time the Union was certified as the exclusive bargaining representative of the players—September 1, 1978. The fact that Respondents were pursuing their right to appeal did not, absent a stay of the Board's order, obviate their duty to bargain with the Union and does not constitute a defense to an application for relief under Section 10(j) of the Act where, as here, Respondents have apparently repeatedly refused to bargain with the Union and have continued to bypass the Union and deal directly with employees. *Lebus* v. *Manning, Maxwell & Moore, Inc.*, 218 F.Supp. 702 (W.D.La.1963). As Petitioner says, Respondents could have bargained subject to later court decision adverse to Petitioner and the Union and can do so now. Negotiations between Respondents and the Union were scheduled to commence August 12, 1980, notwithstanding Respondents' petition for a writ of certiorari.

Respondents' most vigorous opposition comes in response to Petitioner's application for an order requiring Respondents to render voidable, at the option of the Union, all individual player contracts, whether entered into before or after the Union's certification on September 1, 1978. Respondents' claim that such power in the hands of the Union, a non-party to this action, would result in chaos in the industry and subject Respondents to severe economic loss and hardship since these individual contracts are the only real property of Respondents.

It should be noted, at the outset, that the relief requested by Petitioner is not a request to have all individual contracts declared null and void. It should be emphasized that Petitioner is not requesting that the "exclusive rights" provision of the individual contracts, which bind the players to their respective teams for a certain time, be rendered voidable. Moreover, the Board seeks an order requiring Respondents to maintain the present terms and conditions in effect until Respondents negotiate with the Union — except, of course, for the unilateral changes — unless and until an agreement or a good faith impasse is reached through bargaining with the Union. Petitioner does not, however, seek to rescind that unilateral provision which provided for the *present* summer schedule. The Board has consciously limited its request for relief to prevent any unnecessary disruption of Respondents' business. The Board is seeking to render voidable only those unilateral acts taken by the Respondents, enumerated above, which Respondents admit have in fact occurred.

These unilateral changes appear to modify all existing individual contracts entered into before September 1, 1978, in derogation of the Union's right to act as the exclusive bargaining agent of all employees in the unit.

The court finds that Petitioner is entitled to the temporary injunctive relief which it seeks with respect to all of the individual contracts. The individual contracts entered into since September 1, 1978, are apparently in violation of the duty of the Respondents to bargain with the exclusive bargaining representative of the players. The Act requires Respondents to bargain collectively with the Union. The obligation is exclusive. This duty to bargain with the exclusive representative carries with it the negative duty not to bargain with individual employees. *Medo Photo Supply Corp.* v. *NLRB*, 321 U.S. 678, 64 S.Ct. 830, 88 L.Ed. 1007 (1944); *NLRB* v. *Acme Air Appliance Co.*, 117 F.2d 417 (2d Cir. 1941); *see* 29 U.S.C. sec. 159(a).

With respect to the individual contracts entered into prior to September 1, 1978, Petitioner is entitled to an injunction enjoining Respondents from giving effect to these individual contracts of employment or any modification, continuation, extension or renewal thereof "to forestall collective bargaining." *J. I. Case Co.* v. *NLRB*, 321 U.S. 332, 341, 64 S.Ct. 576, 582, 88 L.Ed. 762 (1944). The evidence adduced at the hearing disclosed that Respondents have refused to recognize that only the Union has the right to waive, if it so desires and to the extent it so desires, its right to be the exclusive bargaining representative. Respondents had also refused to negotiate with the Union since September 1, 1978, pending resolution of their appeal.

In *National Licorice Co.* v. *NLRB*, 309 U.S. 350, 60 S.Ct. 569, 84 L.Ed. 799 (1940), the Supreme Court held that the Board has the authority, even in the absence of the employees as parties to the proceeding, to order an employer not to enforce individual contracts with its employees which were found to have been in violation of the NLRA. Petitioner is seeking temporary relief to this effect as to those individual contracts entered into before September 1, 1978, as well as relief with respect to those contracts entered into prior to September 1, 1978. The evidence discloses that Petitioner has reasonable cause to believe that Respondents have used, and will continue to use, the individual contracts entered into prior to

September 1, 1978, to forestall collective bargaining.

With such contracts in place, Petitioner has reasonable cause to believe that Respondents' determination not to bargain with the Union has been well fortified and that there simply is no incentive for Respondents to bargain with the Union with those contracts in place. Petitioner has reasonable cause to believe that the ability of Respondents to enter into individual contracts and to continue to enforce them is to bypass and to undermine support for the Union. The court therefore finds that there is reasonable cause to believe that Respondents have used the individual contracts entered into prior to September 1, 1978, to forestall collective bargaining.

The Board is, therefore, entitled to the relief which it seeks requiring Respondents to render voidable certain provisions in the existing individual contracts which the Union requests, as set forth above. The Union has been permitted by the court to intervene in this action as a party petitioner. The court finds that it is not the intent of the Petitioner, as Respondents claim, to visit punitive actions on Respondents and that the requested relief with respect to the individual contracts has been carefully tailored to avoid chaos in Respondents' industry and to avoid any economic hardship to Respondents.

Finally, the court finds that under the circumstances of this case a temporary injunction would be just and proper. . . .

Morio v. North American Soccer League, 632 F.2d 217 (2d Cir. 1980)

Per Curiam:

We affirm on Judge Motley's thorough findings of fact and conclusions of law, 80 Civ. 4332 (S.D.N.Y. Aug. 18, 1980).

For the purpose of clarifying our holding, we note that the remedies imposed in this case — the revocation of certain unilateral changes in employment conditions and authorization for the North American Soccer League Players Association (Union) to rescind, at their option, any or all provisions of any current player contract, except for the "exclusive rights" provisions — is not without precedent. This form of relief was "just and proper," 29 U.S.C. sec. 160(j) (1976), and

within the trial court's discretion, *Kaynard* v. *Palby Lingerie, Inc.,* 625 F.2d 1047, 1051 (2d Cir. 1980). There was sufficient evidence that the North American Soccer League's (League) practices threatened "to render the N.L.R.B.'s processes 'totally ineffective' by precluding a meaningful final remedy." *Kaynard* v. *Mego Corp.,* 633 F.2d 1026 at —— (2d Cir.1980), citing *Seeler* v. *Trading Port, Inc.,* 517 F.2d 33 (2d Cir. 1975). The Union's prestige and legitimacy with its members has been severely eroded by the League's conduct during the past two years. Although the League finally approached the bargaining table in August 1980, in compliance with the Fifth Circuit's recent order to bargain in a related case, this injunction frees the Union from the severe contractual restraints imposed by the allegedly unlawful actions of the League, and thereby prevents the frustration of the remedial purposes of the Act.

Aggressive remedial relief is necessary in appropriate labor cases. We have granted an injunction ordering an employer to bargain with a union that did not win an election. *Seeler, supra.* The Union in this case, of course, prevailed in a representation election conducted more than two years ago. And, the Board in unfair labor practices proceedings has frequently voided contracts negotiated by the employer with individual employees. *J. I. Case Co.* v. *N.L.R.B.,* 321 U.S. 332, 64 S.Ct. 576, 88 L.Ed. 762 (1944); *National Licorice Co.* v. *N.L.R.B.,* 309 U.S. 350, 60 S.Ct. 569, 84 L.Ed. 799 (1940); *KXTV,* 139 N.L.R.B. 93 (1962); *Cascade Employers Association,* 126 N.L.R.B. 1014 (1960). Unilateral changes in the conditions of employment also have been rescinded by the Board. *Fibreboard Paper Prod. Corp.* v. *N.L.R.B.,* 379 U.S. 203, 85 S.Ct. 398, 13 L.Ed.2d 233 (1964).

Where, as in this case, an equity court has "reasonable cause" to believe that particularly flagrant unfair labor practices have been committed, the court's fashioning of those remedies typically framed by the Board in an unfair labor practice proceeding is "just and proper," even though a final decision by the Board is pending. . . .

NOTE ———————————————————

1. For the possible application of Section 10(j) in another sports setting, see the analysis in Lock, "Section 10(j) of the

National Labor Relations Act and the 1982 National Football League Players Strike," 1985 Arizona State Law Journal 113.

5.13   Union Membership

A union will experience difficulty in determining who is eligible for union membership when there is a high turnover among the workforce. In professional sports, the turnover problem is exacerbated. Professional careers in most leagues average only four to five years. A great many players are drafted and signed to contracts, but only a relative few make the team. Players from other leagues are signed. In some instances, players are shuttled daily back and forth between major and minor league franchises. Veterans become free agents, expecting to play in the league the following season, but with no assurance this will occur.

When an important issue arises in a sports context that requires union members' participation, a fight may well develop as to which players are union members at the time and eligible to vote. Determining membership in a sports union is a complex task.

In addition, the lingering tension between a sports union and the agents who represent athletes in individual contract negotiations is evidenced when agents threaten to challenge a union's authority. Only once has a challenge actually resulted in a full-scale hearing before a legal tribunal. However, that one instance gives insights into the seriousness of the potential schism between unions and agents.

Major Indoor Soccer League and Professional Soccer Players Association (Prospa) and MISL Players Association, Decision and Direction of Election, Before NLRB Regional Director, Louis J. D'Amico, November 15, 1983

. . . The petition in Case 5–RC–11987 was filed by Major Indoor Soccer League Players Association, affiliated with Federation of Professional Athletes, AFL–C1O (herein referred to as the "Association"). The petition in Case 5–RC–12001 was filed by Professional Soccer Players Association (herein referred to as "PROSPA"). Neither Petitioner stipulated that the other Petitioner is a labor organization within the meaning of the Act. The Association states that PROSPA was formed and is controlled by certain persons who are engaged in the business of representing professional soccer players as agents for the purpose of negotiating individual employment contracts with professional soccer teams. The Association asserts that the status of these persons as agents for individual players constitutes a conflict of interest which disqualifies PROSPA from serving as a collective-bargaining representative. On the other hand, PROSPA contends that the Association is not a statutory labor organization because (a) it has not filed LM–1 and LM–2 reports with the Department of Labor as required by the Labor Management Reporting and Disclosure Act, and because (b) the Association is the *alter ego* of another organization, the North American Soccer League Players Association (herein referred to as "NASLPA") which represents professional soccer players within the NASL, and therefore the Association does not and cannot represent MISL soccer player–employees in its own right.

The Association

Concerning the Association, the record reveals the following: in 1979, MISL voluntarily recognized the Association as the bargaining representative for professional soccer players employed by the MISL constituent teams. The first collective-bargaining agreement between the Association and MISL was effective for the term October 8, 1979 to June 1, 1982; there was a succeeding collective agreement for the period November 6, 1982 to August 1, 1983. The Association admits to membership individuals who are employed as professional soccer players by the various constituent teams within MISL. Policy matters of the Association are determined by a board of player representatives who, along with alternate representatives, are elected by the employee/members of the Association; one representative and one alternate are selected from each team. The board of player representatives elects a negotiating committee and that committee has negotiated with the MISL the two above-mentioned collective-bargaining agreements, which were ratified by the professional soccer players. The Association has a constitution adopted by a vote of player-members, who also adopt bargaining goals and participate in committees. The Association has processed grievances on behalf of player/members, arising out of work-related disputes with various soccer teams. The Association, with other organizations, is a member of the Federation of Professional Athletes (herein "Federation"), an umbrella organization chartered by the AFL-CIO, which has as its purpose, *inter alia,* the support of collective bargaining among professional athletes. One of the other organizations affiliated with the Federation is the NASLPA; John Kerr, staff director of the Association, is a member of the Federation's board as well as the director of the NASLPA. Kerr testified that the NASLPA, as is the case with the Association, is governed by a board of player representatives elected by player/members from the various NASL teams. Kerr also testified that these respective boards of player representatives do not have a policy role with respect to actions of the other organization. Based on these facts I find and conclude that the Association is a labor organization within the meaning of Section 2(5) of the Act. . . . Moreover, there is no evidence supporting the contention that the Association is incapable of, or unwilling to represent, MISL soccer players, because of the Association's relationship with either NASLPA or the Federation, or because Kerr is also a board member of the Federation and a director of NASLPA, or because the Association is affiliated with the Federation.

PROSPA

PROSPA was formed in March 1983, by Alan Herman and by Scott Simpson. At this time Herman is PROSPA's executive director and Simpson is its West Coast liaison representative. PROSPA has retained an attorney as its chief counsel and Herman maintains an office for PROSPA which is located within the offices of its chief counsel. PROSPA does not have any elected officers, it has not collected any dues or membership fees, and it does not have a constitution or bylaws. Both Herman and Simpson are self-employed as agents of professional athletes and among their clients are professional soccer players employed by MISL teams. As agents, Herman and Simpson represent individual professional athletes

in negotiating individual contracts with the teams employing those athletes. Herman testified that PROSPA admits to membership professional soccer players employed by MISL teams, and that some of these MISL players have become PROSPA members. Although PROSPA does not have a constitution, it has established a committee, composed of two players from each of the MISL teams, which at the time of the hearing was drafting a constitution. Herman testified that PROSPA was formed for the purpose of representing MISL soccer players as their collective-bargaining representative in dealings with the MISL owners and managers.

Based upon the facts noted above, I find that PROSPA satisfies the statutory requirements of Section 2(5) of the Act. *Alto Plastics Manufacturing Company, supra.* That PROSPA lacks certain structural formality in that it has no constitution or bylaws, has not collected dues or membership fees, and has no elected officers, does not compel a contrary conclusion. *Butler Manufacturing Company,* 167 NLRB 308.

The Association, nevertheless, argues that PROSPA must be disqualified because Herman and Simpson serve as principals of a labor organization while simultaneously engaging in the business, for profit, of representing individual players in the negotiation of individual employment contracts. The Association contends that such an agent/union official may compromise the bargaining interests of the collective group of employees in favor of the interests of the few, individual players whom he simultaneously represents as an agent. The Association also argues, in support of its contention that PROSPA must be disqualified, that PROSPA was formed only to further the personal business interests of Herman and Simpson; that Herman and Simpson are also engaged, for profit, in placing players with MISL teams; and that as agents, Herman and Simpson have a personal business incentive not to represent aggressively and successfully unit employees in collective bargaining.

In this regard the record shows that the collective-bargaining agreements between MISL and the Association have established a minimum salary level for soccer players. The Association agreed with MISL that individual players and their teams may negotiate salary, certain benefits, and other forms of compensation which exceed those established by the collective-bargaining agreements. All contracts negotiated between a player and his team must be submitted to and approved by the MISL commissioner, and the Association has the right to challenge through arbitration any player's contract which conflicts with the terms of the collective-bargaining agreement. In negotiating an individual contract with his team, a player may choose to be represented by an agent. Herman was employed by the MISL's New York Arrows team in 1978 and 1979 in a managerial capacity; since that latter date he has held no managerial position with, nor any ownership interest in, any MISL team. At this time Herman is a principal of A.G.H. Management Services, Inc., and he is engaged in the business of representing professional athletes, including approximately 35 MISL players. Simpson held positions with the NASLPA as well as with the National Football League Players Association (herein "NFLPA") prior to the formation of MISL. Simpson has no managerial position with, nor any ownership interest in, any professional soccer team. Since early 1981, he has been the sole owner of Simpson Management Company, based in San Diego, California, and like Herman he represents professional athletes, including MISL soccer players as well as professional football players. The number of MISL players whom Simpson represents is not disclosed by this record. . . .

When representing individual players in contract negotiations with a team, agents such as Herman and Simpson typically negotiate with a team's general manager or its owner. In collective-bargaining negotiations between the Association and the MISL, the MISL is represented by a management council, consisting of a selected number of owners and general managers from some of the MISL teams. Simpson testified that some of the various team owners and managers with whom he has negotiated contracts as an agent for individual players have also served as members of MISL's management council in collective-bargaining negotiations with the Association.

In contending that there is no disqualifying conflict of interest between the personal business of agents such as Herman and Simpson and their roles in forming and establishing PROSPA, PROSPA maintains that officers in other labor organizations representing professional athletes also represent individual players as agents. Thus

Herman testified that the chief counsel of the National Basketball Association's players' union, and the director of the National Hockey League's players' association, have continued to represent individual athletes as agents while simultaneously holding the above-noted positions with those players' unions. The Association, on the other hand, presented evidence that yet other unions representing professional athletes, such as NASLPA and NFLPA, prohibit their staff members from acting as paid agents for individual players for the purpose of negotiating individual contracts, and that the purpose of such policy is to avoid entangling an agent's financial interest in representing an individual player-client with a union representative's handling of collective-bargaining affairs on behalf of all unit employees.

The Association further argues that Herman and Simpson formed PROSPA in order to protect and further their personal businesses as player agents by opposing the Association's possible future policy concerning the establishment of a comprehensive wage-scale. The purpose of PROSPA, it is argued, is to preserve individualized contract negotiation of player salaries and, hence, perpetuate the system under which agents such as Herman and Simpson are compensated. PROSPA, on the other hand, maintains that opposition to the negotiation of a comprehensive wage-scale was merely one of a number of factors cited by MISL players as alleged reasons for dissatisfaction with the Association. I find nothing in the record establishing that Herman or Simpson formed PROSPA solely to protect and promote their own personal business enterprises. PROSPA or the Association are free to establish their own philosophies and policies concerning collective bargaining. The fact that the Association and PROSPA may, at this point, differ as to the relative merits of one form of player compensation rather than another does not, in itself, serve as a basis for disqualifying PROSPA.

The disqualification of a labor organization from representing employees is a matter which the Board carefully scrutinizes. Employees have the essential right, guaranteed in Section 7 of the Act, to bargain collectively through representatives of their own choosing. . . .

Thus in the lead case in this area, *Bausch & Lomb Optical Company*, 108 NLRB 1555, the Board disqualified the union from representing the employer's employees because the union established and began operating a company engaged in the manufacture and distribution of eyeglasses, in direct competition with the employer's business enterprise. The basis for the disqualification of a union from serving as bargaining representative is not because a union is in the same business as the employer, but rather because the union's business activities interfered with the union's "single-minded purpose of protecting and advancing the interests of the employees." *Bausch & Lomb Optical Company, supra*, at 1559. . .

Initially, I find no merit in the Association's contention that PROSPA must be disqualified because PROSPA is nothing more than the activities of Herman and Simpson themselves, or because it was formed to advance the personal business of its founders. It is also evident that PROSPA, as an entity, does not operate a business enterprise which competes with MISL or any MISL constituent team, nor does PROSPA control or dominate a business enterprise which engages in business with MISL or any MISL constituent team. Thus there is no basis in this record for disqualifying PROSPA because of any business activity in which it is engaged. *Bausch & Lomb, supra; Visiting Nurses Association*, 254 NLRB 49.

A more difficult question is presented, however, concerning the personal business enterprises of Herman and Simpson and their role in a potential collective-bargaining relationship of MISL and PROSPA. In this context, it is clear that the business in which Herman and Simpson are personally engaged is reasonably and intimately related to the business in which the MISL and each of its constituent member teams are themselves engaged, i.e., the employment of professional soccer players. Agents deal with individual MISL teams in a business relationship, and the agent's own compensation for his services, although not paid directly to the agent by the MISL team, is directly related to the amount of financial compensation which the agent is able to obtain from that team on behalf of his player-client. I thus find . . . that agents such as Herman and Simpson have personal financial and business interests which require them to engage in direct business transactions with various MISL teams. I also find that if agents such as Herman and Simpson continue in their personal business enterprises while simultaneously serving in collective-

bargaining positions on behalf of PROSPA, they ". . . may be tempted to make demands, or grant concessions, not in the interests of the employees [PROSPA] seeks to represent, but to further [their] own interests. . . . In reaching this conclusion I attach no significance to PROSPA's argument that other labor unions representing professional athletes have permitted their officers to represent individual players as their agents. That such persons may hold positions within their respective labor unions while simultaneously maintaining personal business enterprises as agents for player–clients does not establish that the potential for a conflict-of-interest is nonexistent. . . .

In view of the fact that PROSPA has not engaged in any collective-bargaining activities on behalf of any employees, there is no record evidence upon which to assess the extent, if any, in which either Herman or Simpson would be involved in any collective-bargaining activity on PROSPA's behalf. Simpson expressly testified that in the event PROSPA were to be certified by the Board he intends to terminate his relationship with PROSPA, and to resume his personal business of representing professional athletes as an agent. Herman also testified that he intends to continue in his personal business as an agent for professional athletes in the event PROSPA is certified by the Board. Moreover, in its post-hearing memorandum to the undersigned, PROSPA represents that in the event a disqualifying conflict-of-interest would be found by the Board Herman would resign from his position in PROSPA.

Therefore, in light of my conclusions that PROSPA itself is not disqualified from representing the employees involved herein but that there exists the protential for a disqualifying conflict-of-interest between the personal business activities of Herman and Simpson and PROSPA's obligation to represent all unit employees collectively, and in light of PROSPA's representation that both Herman and Simpson will resign their positions within PROSPA in the event a disqualifying conflict-of-interest is found to exist, I shall allow PROSPA to appear on the ballot in the election directed herein. However, to assure the integrity of any collective-bargaining activity that may ensue should PROSPA receive a majority of the valid votes cast in such election, I shall direct that PROSPA not be certified so long as either Alan Herman, Scott Simpson (or any other person who also is employed as an agent for professional soccer players of the MISL) holds any role, position or consultative capacity within PROSPA regarding its collective-bargaining affairs. . .

The MISL's rules require that a player execute a Standard Player Agreement before being eligible to compete on an MISL team. Between 30 percent and 40 percent of the players in the 1982/1983 season had signed multi-year or multi-season contracts and were therefore contractually obligated to their respective teams for the coming 1983/1984 season. The rest of the players were subject to contracts which were effective only for the duration of the 1982/83 season. The Standard Player Agreement also contains an option provision. Under the option provision, a team which has employed a player under a Standard Player Agreement has the right to tender to that player a contract to be effective for the succeeding season; by tendering such a contract the team is said to "exercise its option" on that player, and the player is thereby obligated to the tendering team for the succeeding season. Veteran free agents, therefore, are those players who were once contractually obligated to an MISL team but whose contracts have expired, who are not subject to the right of a team to obligate them to an option-year contract, and who have not signed a new contract for the succeeding season of play. During the period of free agency the player is allowed to market his skills to and sign a contract with any MISL team. Although MISL conducts an annual draft of college soccer players, veteran free agents are not eligible to be drafted.

MISL contends that there is no evidence within the record establishing that free agents have a reasonable expectation of reemployment within the MISL during the season following their becoming free agents. The Association, on the other hand, strongly maintains that it has always represented the veteran free agents during their periods of free agency, and that its collective-bargaining agreements delineate the basis for negotiations between a free agent and any MISL team. Thus the Association notes that its most recent collective-bargaining agreement contains language requiring the MISL teams to deal in good-faith bargaining with free agents, and that the limitations contained within the collective-bargaining agreement concerning individual negotiations between players and teams have been

applied to negotiations between teams and free agents. The Association also points to record evidence showing that the Board has certified unions of professional athletes to represent bargaining units which include players who are free agents: *National Football League,* Case 18–RC–8308 and *American Soccer League,* Case 2–RC–18949. MISL contends, however, that these cases do not have precedential value inasmuch as the inclusion of free agents was not litigated in either of those cases. . . .

In urging that veteran free agents be excluded from the unit the MISL relies upon *Major League Rodeo, Inc.,* 246 NLRB 743, and *The North American Soccer League,* 236 NLRB 1317. Free agents in *Major League Rodeo* were free to negotiate contracts with any other team in the league, and unlike the MISL the free agents in *Major League Rodeo* were subject to the league's annual player draft; if drafted, rodeo athletes could only sign a contract with the selecting team. The Board agreed with the employer's contention and excluded free agents, although it noted that the league had only completed its first season at the time of the hearing therein, that all players were still employed under their initial contracts, that the player draft had not been held, and that hiring practices with respect to free agents had not had sufficient time to develop. The Board also found that there was no record evidence permitting a determination of the degree to which a player who played out his option contract had a reasonable expectation of further employment for succeeding seasons. In *The North American Soccer League,* the unit inclusion of players on the league's military and ineligible lists was in dispute, inasmuch as the employer contended that players on those lists were not under the control of a team during the course of a season. The Board included such players, however, finding that while on either list players could remain under a contractual obligation to their teams and that they could return to active play subject to rules and regulations established by the league itself.

Applying these cases to the facts herein, I conclude that veteran free agents should be excluded from the bargaining unit. Free agents are able to negotiate a contract with any MISL team, and they are not subject to the draft procedures which limit a player's right to negotiate with MISL teams. During the period of free agency these players are not covered by various provisions in the MISL-Association collective-bargaining agreement, such as union security, insurance coverage and grievance and arbitration procedures. Further, it is most significant that during the period of free agency a player is not subject to the control or direction of any MISL team or of the MISL itself. Neither class of players, free agents or those under contractual obligation to a particular team, have any guarantee that they will be selected to the roster of a team and participate as an active player during the succeeding season. Moreover, there is no evidence in the record showing how many veteran free agents have ultimately been signed to contracts by MISL teams after they became free agents, nor is there any evidence establishing how many free agents have even attempted to compete for places on MISL teams after they have become free agents. In light of record evidence establishing that veteran free agents are not subject to any control or contractual obligation to any MISL team or the MISL itself, nor to the MISL's disciplinary powers, and in the absence of probative evidence that free agents have a reasonable expectation of re-employment, I shall *exclude* them from the bargaining unit herein. . . .

5.20   Collective Bargaining: Enforcement Mechanisms

From the union perspective, forcing meaningful and eventually fruitful collective bargaining is essential. This requires leverage. The union may have to litigate, arbitrate, or strike. The choices depend on the circumstances; the right choices may be crucial.

The following two subsections (5.21 and 5.22) examine two enforcement mechanisms. One is standard in labor law and relations; the second is a special byproduct of particular litigation. To understand labor law is to fathom when an appeal can be made to the National Labor Relations Board under charges of unfair labor practices. The board, despite its frequent delays and ponderous tendencies, does possess significant corrective powers. Whether it can be induced to deploy these is, of course, the question. The inquiries in Section 5.21 provide

no definitive answers, but the cases do suggest parameters.

The second set of cases are special in that they relate to circumstances peculiar to the National Basketball Association. The Players Association of that league, in the mid-70s, sought to prevent an unauthorized merger of the NBA and the rival ABA. Other antitrust violations were alleged, including complaints against many of the league's restrictions on player mobility. The end result was that the NBA was effectively restrained from negotiating any type of accommodation with its rival, the ABA, in the absence of court approval, which would have allowed for full argumentation against any such moves by the NBA Players Association. Eventually, the NBA absorbed four of the viable ABA clubs, but this was pursuant to what has become known as the *Robertson* settlement. Under this settlement, initiated and maintained by the players' union in the NBA, two principles were established: (1) the first collective bargaining agreement reached after the settlement (in 1976) had to achieve court approval to ensure that it was in accord with the settlement; and (2) future actions by the league, for the next ten years, were to be under the jurisdiction of the U.S. District Court to ensure continued compliance with the settlement. From the labor perspective, the union achieved a major goal — immediate access to an effective enforcement mechanism.

As a contrast to the NLRB activities in professional sports, Section 5.22 explores some of the controversies that have surfaced since the *Robertson* settlement. The problems are intriguing, diverse, and challenging.

5.21   The NLRB and Unfair Labor Practices

When collective bargaining negotiations become heated, both union and management hurl charges and countercharges about the other side's failure to negotiate in good faith. Often, as it happens, the charges are later forgotten, as a new agreement is reached and labor peace is restored. If the negotiations are protracted however, one side, or both, may seek redress before the National Labor Relations Board and ultimately the courts. Even then, the matters may be dropped and remedies not pursued once an agreement is reached.

The opinions that have been issued, even if they have not always been implemented, are instructive on (1) the labor weapons each side has in protesting the other side's activities, (2) the issues that are bargainable in a sports context, and (3) the factual data that a union can demand in preparing for negotiations with management.

National Football League Players Ass'n. v. National Labor Relations Board, 503 F.2d 12 (8th Cr. 1974)

Heaney, Circuit Judge

The National Football League Players Association [Union] petitions this Court to review an order of the National Labor Relations Board dismissing a complaint against the Employers, consisting of the National Football League [Owners] and the National Football League Management Council [Council]. The complaint alleged that Employers violated sec. 8(a)(5) and (1) of the National Labor Relations Act, 29 U.S.C. sec. 151 et seq., by unilaterally establishing a rule that "any player leaving the bench area while a fight is in progress on the field will be fined $200." The Board's decision and order is reported at 203 N.L.R.B. No. 165 (1973).

We emphasize at the outset that the wisdom of the rule is not at issue here. The sole question before us is whether the Board erred in dismissing the complaint on the ground that the rule was adopted and promulgated by the Commissioner of the NFL rather than by the Employers. A brief discussion of the facts is necessary to an understanding of the issue.

On January 22, 1971, the Union was certified by the NLRB as the exclusive bargaining representative for the professional football players employed by the NFL and its member clubs. A collective bargaining agreement was signed by the Union, council's predecessor . . . and each of the member clubs on June 17, 1971, effective February 1, 1970. The Agreement expired on January 31, 1974.

In early 1971, the NFL Commissioner, Pete Rozelle, discussed with his staff the problem of injuries to players through violence on the football field. He directed a member of the NFL staff to discuss this problem with the competition committee (consisting of four Owners or their representatives) to deal with the effect of proposed changes in policy on the competitive aspects of football. The committee recommended that a rule be established to fine players who left the bench during a fight on the field. At the March 25th meeting of the Owners, the Commissioner explained the proposal to the clubs. The Owners then adopted a rule which read:

> Any player leaving the bench area while a fight is in progress on the field will be fined $200.

Rozelle subsequently fined thirty-four players for leaving the bench while a fight was in progress during the Minnesota-San Diego exhibition game on August 4, 1971, fifty-eight players for doing the same thing during the Atlanta-San Francisco game on August 15th, and fourteen players for identical conduct during the Chicago-New Orleans game on October 10th.

On September 30th, the Union's Executive Director, Edward Garvey, wrote to the Commissioner requesting information with respect to the fines imposed as a result of the Minnesota-San Diego incident. On October 18th, Garvey again wrote to the Commissioner. He appealed the imposition of the fines on players who had left the bench during the Minnesota-San Diego and Atlanta-San Francisco games. He did so on the grounds that the players had not been notified of the new rule and that the rule imposing the fines was violative of the Collective Bargaining Agreement, which provided that:

> . . . any change in current practices affecting employment conditions of the players shall be negotiated in good faith.

Commissioner Rozelle replied to the two letters on October 21st. He wrote:

> While still considering your letter of September 30 regarding player fines I am now in receipt of your October 18 letter on the same subject.
> *The action taken as the result of the player fights was done so under a resolution passed by the member clubs last March.* It reads:

"Any player leaving the bench area while a fight is in progress on the field will be fined $200.". . .

It has been the long-standing policy of this office to most certainly accord any disciplined players the right of appeal to the Commissioner, either through writing or hearing, but I have serious doubts whether the [Union] has jurisdiction in the area of player fines for misconduct during the course of a game. Therefore, I believe I must request written argument from the [Union] and the [Council] on this issue before I can entertain any grievance initiated by the [Union]. (Emphasis added.). . .

The Union filed an unfair labor practice charge with the Board on December 10, 1971, alleging that the Employers' unilateral adoption of the rule was a refusal to bargain. Amended charges were filed on February 11 and May 10, 1972. The General Counsel of the N.L.R.B. issued a complaint on May 12, 1972. It alleged that the Employers violated sec. 8(a)(5) of the Act by unilaterally promulgating and implementing a new rule providing for an automatic $200.00 fine against any player leaving the bench area during a fight or altercation on the football field during the game.

The Employers denied the Union's allegations, taking the position that the fines were Commissioner fines rather than Owner fines and that the Employers had not violated sec. 8(a)(5) because they had not instituted the rule change. They contended, alternatively, that the action was taken more than six months prior to the filing of the charges by the Union and hence was barred by sec. 10(b) of the Act, and that the Collective Bargaining Agreement contained grievance and arbitration mechanisms for resolution of the issue and that the Board should stay its hand in deference to those mechanisms. . . .

We understand the Board to have made the following findings: (1) that the Union conceded that the Commissioner had a right to adopt the bench-fine rule; (2) that the bench-fine rule had in fact been promulgated by the Commissioner rather than the Owners and that the Owners engaged in no meaningful or substantial conduct with respect to its adoption or promulgation; and (3) that, as a matter of law there is no substantive difference between the Commissioner's imposing individual fines for conduct detrimental to the game after notice and hearing and promulgating the bench-fine rule — thus, promulgation of the rule was within the authority of the Commissioner.

(1) The record does not support the Board's finding that the Union conceded that the Commissioner had the right under the Collective Bargaining Agreement to adopt and promulgate the bench-fine rule; to the contrary, the Union denied that he had such a right. The Union agreed only that the Commissioner had a right pursuant to the Agreement to fine a player for conduct detrimental to the League or professional football after *notice* and *hearing*. The distinction is a meaningful one to the Union and also to us. If the Commissioner's power is limited in the manner the Union suggests, each player who has been notified that he is being charged with conduct detrimental to the game can at the hearing attempt to prove that the conduct in question is not, in fact, detrimental and to prove that he did not engage in the proscribed conduct. . . .

(2) Nor does the record support the Board's finding that the bench rule was adopted by the Commissioner without meaningful or substantial conduct on the part of the Owners.

(a) The Commissioner stated in his letter of October 21, 1971, that the action was taken pursuant to a resolution passed by the member clubs. He was not called by the Employers to qualify that statement. Thus, it is fair to say that the Commissioner viewed the rule as one adopted and promulgated by the Owners and the individual fines as being levied pursuant to that rule.

(b) The Commissioner did discuss with his staff "his feeling that from now on if a player left the bench area during a fight, he felt he would have to fine him." But, he was obviously concerned about the reaction of the Owners to such a course of action and instead of announcing that such would be his policy or simply imposing a fine when an occasion occurred, he asked a member of the staff of the NFL to discuss the matter with the competition committee of the League — a committee in which only management is represented. When that committee indicated its approval, the Commissioner still wasn't satisfied. He had the committee bring a recommended resolution to the Owners for their approval. It was only when Owners voted twenty-four to two that the rule should be put into effect that the Commissioner had a press release sent out indicating that the bench-fine rule was now in effect.

(c) At no time prior to the press release did the Commissioner discuss the problem of players leaving the bench during fights with the Union. If, as the Employers contend, the Commissioner is the agent of both the Employers and the Union, and promulgated the rule as their agent, one must assume a serious breach of ethics by the Commissioner if he talked to only one of his principals. And, no one suggests that the Commissioner is an unethical man.

To summarize, every fact and inference supports the administrative law judge's conclusion that the rule was adopted and promulgated by the Owners.

(3) Finally, the Board held that because the Commissioner had the power to promulgate the bench-fine rule, he exercised that power. The premise is doubtful, . . . and the conclusion a *non sequitur*. While the Board is permitted to draw inferences from the facts in the record and while we are required to accept such inferences when supported by facts we are not required to adopt inferences or conclusions that are totally lacking in factual support.

We hold that the Employers, by unilaterally promulgating and implementing a rule providing for an automatic fine to be levied against any player who leaves the bench area while a fight or an altercation is in progress on the football field, have engaged in unfair labor practices within the meaning of Section 8(a)(5) and (1) of the Act.

We remand to the Board with instructions to it to adopt a remedy consistent with this opinion. . . .

[Footnotes are omitted; Judge Matthes wrote a separate concurring opinion.]

NOTE _____

1. As collective bargaining negotiations become heated, it is not at all unusual for one or both sides to file charges of unfair labor practices before the NLRB. Appearing below are two examples, both filed by the NFLPA during the long summer of 1982 against the league. As often happens, both complaints were later dropped when union and management finally reached agreement on a new bargaining accord in December 1982.

(a) Filed July 8, 1982:

Since on or about February 16, 1982, constituent member clubs of the National Football League (NFL), the names and addresses of which are attached hereto as Appendix A, by its officers, agents and representatives, including the National Football League Management Council (NFLMC), have failed and refused to bargain with the National Football League Players Association (NFLPA) in violation of Section 8(a)(1) and (5) of the Act by, *inter alia:*

(1) Designating as their bargaining representatives individuals who lack sufficient authority to negotiate an agreement with the Union;

(2) Failing and refusing to make counterproposals;

(3) Refusing to meet and bargain for an entire month, just prior to the expiration of the current collective bargaining agreement;

(4) Engaging in other dilatory and evasive tactics to avoid good faith bargaining;

(5) Engaging in a campaign to undermine the NFLPA and its leadership in an effort to destroy its effectiveness as the bargaining representative of the players;

(6) Failing and refusing to furnish the Union with bargaining information which it had agreed to provide;

(7) Engaging in surface bargaining in an attempt to justify imposing unilateral terms and conditions of employment upon their employees; [and]

(8) Following a predetermined course not to reach an agreement with the Union.

(b) Filed July 19, 1982:

Since on or about May 1, 1982, the Constituent Member Clubs of the National Football League, by their officers, agents and representatives including Commissioner Pete Rozelle and the NFL Management Council, have violated Section 8(a)(1) and (5) of the Act by:

(1) Unilaterally implementing and/or expanding programs at the club level regarding possible drug or alcohol abuse by players without bargaining with the NFLPA;

(2) Bypassing the Union and dealing directly with players on the club level with regard to such programs;

(3) Unilaterally implementing urinalysis testing of players to detect use of drugs without bargaining with the NFLPA;

(4) Refusing to bargain in good faith with the NFLPA on the subject of a player counseling service dealing in part with the subject of possible drug or alcohol abuse; and

(5) Attempting to undermine the Union leadership by public statements to the effect that it can not be "trusted" in dealing with such subjects.

The Constituent Member Clubs of the National Football League, and their Agent, National Football League Management Council, and National Football League Players Association, National Labor Relations Board, New York Branch, Case No. 2-CA–18267, Cohn, Administrative Law Judge, September 27, 1982

... Upon a charge filed August 11 and served August 12, 1981, by National Football League Players Association, herein called Union or NFLPA, the Regional Director for Region 2 issued a complaint on April 19, 1982, alleging that the Constituent Member Clubs of the National Football League; and their agent, National Football League Management Council, herein called Respondent or NFLMC, violated Section 8(a)(1) and (5) of the Act by failing and refusing to furnish the Union with copies of player contracts, and copies of the non-monetary terms of so-called media contracts. It is alleged that such documents and information is necessary and relevant to the Union in the performance of its function as the exclusive bargaining representative of employees in an appropriate unit. Respondent filed an answer denying the commission of unfair labor practices. . . .

The salient facts are relatively brief and basically uncontroverted.

The Union was certified in 1971 as the exclusive bargaining representative of the employees in an appropriate unit. The Respondent and the Union have been parties to collective bargaining agreements, the most recent running from March 1, 1977 to July 15, 1982. Prior to the execution of that agreement, certain events occurred which provide a necessary background for the consideration of the issues involved herein. The Union and Respondent had been involved in litigation both in the courts and before the NLRB. Thus in 1975 there was a lengthy hearing before Administrative Law Judge Charles W. Schneider culminating in his Decision finding a number of violations on the part of Respondent. Of relevance to this matter is Judge Schneider's findings that Respondent violated Section 8(a)(5) of the Act by its failure to furnish to the Union copies of player contracts. While Judge Schneider's Decision was pending before the Board on exceptions, the parties executed the 1977 contract and also agreed to settle all outstanding litigation between them including the Board case. Respondent and the Union signed a non-Board settlement agreement of that case which, among other things, purported to dispose of the Union's request for copies of player contracts. Interpretation of paragraph 4 of that agreement, particularly with regard to Respondent's defense herein, is an issue in this proceeding, and it states:

4. The NFLMC agrees to provide to the NFLPA and to its Member Clubs once annually on or about October 1, a compilation of salary information which shall set forth the average salary for all players then under contract to the Member Clubs, including current and deferred compensation and any signing or reporting bonus, compiled by team positions and years of service of the players. This information shall also include the highest and lowest salary for each team position, by years of service of the number of such contracts containing "no-cut," "no-trade" or "guarantee" provisions. It is understood that this information shall not include either names of players or names of teams. It is further understood that the NFLPA shall be entitled to publish this information for the benefit of its members.

The NFLMC further agrees to make available at Management Council offices, upon reasonable notice and at reasonable times, a copy of all individual contracts of players currently under contract to the Member Clubs for inspection by the Executive Director or legal counsel of the NFLPA. It is understood that such inspection shall be on a confidential basis, and in pursuance of the NFLPA's statutory duty of policing the Collective Bargaining Agreement and properly representing its membership. Upon reasonable request by the NFLPA, the NFLMC will send copies of specific individual contracts, where said request relates to the NFLPA's statutory duty of policing the Collective Bargaining Agreement.

By letter dated May 13, 1981, Edward Garvey, Executive Director of the Union requested, for purposes of collective bargaining, that Respondent furnish certain detailed information. Among those demands are the items which provide the basis for this proceeding. They are as follows:

1. A copy of the current network television and/or radio contracts between the NFL and CBS; between the NFL and NBC; and between the NFL and ABC, and a copy of the immediately preceding contracts with each network (including radio). Any memoranda of agreement or other written evidence of agreements or proposed agreements regarding any future contractual arrangements between the NFL and any radio or television network.

2. A copy of any memoranda of agreements, or other written evidence of agreements or proposed agreements for the showing of NFL games through transmission other than free television broadcasts, including any form of pay TV, cable, or other means or media, and also including any agreements for sale, marketing, or distribution of any film or tape of NFL games, including video tapes, cassettes, video discs, films, and the like.

3. A copy of any and all television or radio contracts between any member club of the NFL and any other entity entered into during, or contemplating telecasts or broadcasts of games during the term of the current CBA (March 1, 1977 to the present).

4. Copies of any and all player contracts (referred to as "Standard Player Contract" or "NFL Player Contract") entered into between any member of the bargaining unit and any of the NFL teams.

Jack Donlan, Executive Director of NFLMC, replied to Garvey's letter on July 8. With regard to the request for player contracts, Donlan referred to two previous letters he had written to Garvey in which the Respondent maintained that the Union was not entitled to copies of the player contracts, having waived its rights to same pursuant to paragraph 4 of the Settlement Agreement of the prior Board case. As to the request for the television and radio contracts set forth in items No. 1 to 3 above, Donlan stated that the media contracts are not relevant or necessary to the Union for purposes of collective bargaining. He also noted that Respondent has not claimed nor does it intend to claim inability to pay during the collective bargaining which will take place. In this respect it must be borne in mind that while the Union had requested that Respondent furnish copies of the media contracts in toto, the complaint alleges violation only insofar as Respondent refused to furnish the non-monetary portions of those contracts.

Some additional background should be noted concerning the player contract system and the manner in which Section 4 of the Settlement Agreement was carried out. Under the collective-bargaining agreement, the Union waived its right to bargain as to individual player contracts but did bargain with Respondent concerning minimum pay scales and other terms and conditions of employment. However the clubs and the players individually bargained concerning the players' salary and other benefits as the case may be. Thus all players signed a standard form contract, but in addition, many of them had an addendum to the standard form which set forth special terms each had agreed upon. Copies of all agreements are maintained in the League office, and, as needed for inspection, they are sent over to the office of the NFLMC. Each time the Union wished to view any contracts, arrangements had to be made to visit the office of NFLMC in New York, the Union's office being in Washington, D.C. The Union could only view contracts for one year, despite the fact that players often signed contracts for more than one year, or a series of contracts extending for a period of years. Copies were not permitted to be made, but the Union representatives could take notes by hand of the contracts it was inspecting. Moreover the agreement restricted access to the contracts only to the Union's executive director or counsel. Apparently some of these restrictions were eased in one period just prior to the hearing herein. Nevertheless it is clear that Respondent's position is unchanged and is to the point that it is only obliged to permit the Union to view these contracts in accordance with the terms of paragraph 4 of the Settlement Agreement.

In his testimony Garvey outlined a number of items and subjects presumably covered in the media contracts which he believed would impinge upon working conditions of the players. Thus there would probably be provisions for scheduling of games on certain days of the week which would determine the amount of time between games for players' recovery from injuries or rest for those not hurt. Undoubtedly the contracts provided for the starting time of games, and in that regard, Garvey cited examples of when weather conditions created a considerable difference as to whether a game should be played during the day or night. Garvey said he would like to know about the length of time-outs and whether they were stipulated in the media contracts, since this had some relationship to the time available for a trainer or doctor to take care of an injured player. The point Garvey made was that the Union had to know what the constraints are as provided in the television contracts. In addition to the length of any particular time-out, he was also concerned as to whether there were any limitations on the total number of time-outs.

Garvey also mentioned provisions regarding pre-and post-game interviews of individual players, noting that a player who just completed a game may be exhausted, and whether he may be subject to discipline if he failed to appear for an interview. He also noted that there could be a possibility that the club is being paid for the players' interviews and perhaps the players should be the one getting the money or some of it. Garvey stated that there may be provisions with respect to the length of the game, that in the event the networks have a time problem and could not run beyond a certain point, they may be able to put pressure to move the game along, and eliminate time-outs, for example.

Other subjects that may have been included in the media contracts are, according to Garvey, the number of restrictions, if any, imposed by the media on injury time-outs; the maximum time of the game; the status of a network official on the field who signals when commercials are finished; the total number of games whether preseason or regular season, arguing in this connection that if a preseason game is nationally televised there may be requirements from the network that a certain percentage of veterans perform; whether the contracts provide for time between the end of the game and the beginning of the overtime period; whether contractual provisions determine the placement of cameras and network personnel on the sidelines or near the playing area which may be a possible source of danger to the players.

Garvey further testified that there may be some problems as to NFL Films, a wholly owned subsidiary of Respondent, which makes films and video tapes of NFL games, and other features. It is his belief that the media contracts may contain provisions with respect to resale rights to discs, video tapes, and films which may impact on the players' rights to try to market resale rights. Apart from the information as to the possible amount of money involved in the sale by Respondent to the networks of these rights, not sought by General Counsel, Garvey believes that the question as to whether or not these matters are included in the contract is relevant to the Union's bargaining position, in that they may desire to take certain positions relative thereto.

The union was also interested to learn whether the media contracts contained provisions concern-

ing promotional announcements and whether time is alloted for public service announcements. He believes that the Union may wish to negotiate about these matters because it impacts on players' images and reputations. Finally Garvey stated that contractual provisions as to the appointment or removal of announcers or color men, may impact on player working conditions because statements by announcers as to management's position in collective bargaining, and the appearance of the Commissioner who expresses his views on Court cases, affect the position of the Union. Garvey's statement is to the effect that all of the matters referred to above, are or may be contained in either the network contracts or in letters, memoranda, or other communications.

Pete Rozelle, Commissioner of the National Football League, testified that the media contracts contained provisions for some of the items referred to by Garvey in his testimony. Thus he stated that the League is required on Sundays to provide a 4:00 p.m. game for either CBS or NBC, and a starting time of 9:00 p.m. on the Monday night game. Starting times for play-off games are arranged at the time of the play-offs, when the League sets the time after consultation with the network. The amount of commercial minutes are incorporated in the media contracts which provide for a certain amount of such time. In the recent contracts these amounts have been increased. The total number of games to be televised, including the recent change from 14 to 16, are provided for in the media agreements. The media contracts also stipulate the length of the half-time intermission, but he doesn't recall anything in the agreements as to the length of time between the end of regulation play and the beginning of an overtime period in the event of a tie game.

Rozelle stated that there are no contractual provisions for the placement of camera men and other media personnel on the field during the game but these matters are worked out in advance with each home club. He did not recall whether local agreements between the clubs and networks included this subject. The contracts also contain provisions allowing the networks to use video tapes for news and for promotional purposes. On the other hand he did not believe there is anything in the contracts as to providing player likenesses, nor is there any provision for player interviews, either pre-game or post-game.

Jack Donlan, Executive Director of NFLMC, testified with respect to relevance, that Respondent has never taken any position in collective bargaining because of the provisions of the media contract. Donlan stated that he had never seen the television or radio contracts with the networks. Moreover he said in the event the Union and Respondent reached agreement on some matter which was contradictory of a provision in the media contracts, the Commissioner and the networks would have to change their agreements. . . .

It is well settled that the duty of an employer to bargain in good faith includes the obligation to disclose to its employees' collective bargaining representative data that are relevant and reasonably necessary to its role as bargaining agent. The Supreme Court has stated "there can be no question of the general obligation of an employer to provide information that is needed by the bargaining representative for the proper performance of its duties." *N.L.R.B.* v. *Acme Industrial Co.*, 385 U.S. 432, 435 (1967). The Courts and the Board have gone even beyond the purview of the instant case in which the Union has requested information for the purpose of collective bargaining, by holding that an employer's disclosure obligation relates not only to issues that may be raised at the bargaining table, but also to those raised during the administration of the collective bargaining contract.

It is thus necessary to determine whether the Union's request for information pertains to a bargaining issue. Then, according to the Supreme Court, the scope of the employer's disclosure obligation is measured by a "discovery type standard" of relevance, which requires only a "probability that the desired information is relevant, and that it would be of use to the Union in carrying out its statutuory duties and responsibilities" *N.L.R.B.* v. *Acme Industrial Co., supra*, at 437 . . .

In its May 13, 1981, letter to Respondent, the Union had requested copies of the contracts of those players in the bargaining unit. Following the above cited principles, it is clear that this information with respect to employees' wages is presumptively relevant and therefore specific relevance need not be shown. This situation is slightly different from the normal in that most of the players receive salaries above the minimums set forth in the collective bargaining agreement and

the Union has waived its right to bargain with Respondent concerning the salaries of the individual players. However, that question is not novel as the Board has held that information as to wages of individual employees is relevant even where a contract establishes a minimum rate; nor does the Union's waiver of the right to bargain for individual players' salaries above the contractually established minimum, operate as a waiver of the Union's right to receive the wage rate information. . . .

Respondent's principal argument with regard to the players' contract is to the effect that the Union waived its right to obtain copies of the players' contracts by virtue of paragraph 4 of the settlement agreement in the 1977 case, as quoted above. At the outset I find no merit to Respondent's contention that the provision in that paragraph for an annual survey of players' salaries to be submitted by Respondent to the Union on October 1 of each year is sufficient for the union's informational purposes. Assuming Respondent had adhered to and complied with this provision, and there is some dispute as to that, the salary survey in and of itself does not provide the complete information necessary for a union's functions in collective bargaining. It only dealt with salaries and not with any of the other matters in player contracts which define the terms and conditions of employment.

As previously noted the settlement agreement involved here purported to settle pending litigation before the Board. Also noted is that the Board was not a party to this non-Board settlement pursuant to which the Charging Party withdrew its charge. The pertinent part of the agreement, Section 4 quoted above, sets forth a process for providing information concerning the player contracts to the Union. Thus it was agreed that the Union by its Executive Director or legal counsel could inspect individual player contracts at the NFLMC offices, that such inspection shall be on a confidential basis, and "in pursuance of the NFLPA's statutory duty of policing the collective-bargaining agreement and properly representing its membership." The agreement further stated that upon reasonable request NFLMC would send copies of specific contracts where such requests relate to the NFLPA's statutory duties of policing the collective-bargaining agreement. A reading of this paragraph does not indicate any words of specific waiver of the Union's right to obtain copies of the contract for purposes of collective bargaining. Indeed, the repetition of the words "policing the collective-bargaining agreement" indicates, as testified by Garvey, that the parties, who had just executed a five year collective-bargaining agreement, intended to settle outstanding litigation, and also by paragraph 4 to provide a procedure to assist the Union in its obligation of policing the agreement.... Also noteworthy is that express words of waiver were utilized in the drafting of other portions of the settlement agreement not applicable to the instant case.

It is well settled that a waiver "is not to be readily inferred and it should be established by proof that the subject matter was consciously explored and that a party has 'clearly and unmistakably waived its interest in the matter' and has 'consciously yielded' its rights." *Tucker Steel Corp.*, 134 NLRB 323, 332 (1961). I find from the facts as set forth above and the record herein that the Union has not "consciously waived its rights" to obtain the players' salary contracts in this case....

Accordingly I find that by its refusal to furnish the Union copies of player contracts, Respondent violated Section 8(a)(1) and (5) of the Act....

Although the Union requested that Respondent furnish copies of network television and radio contracts and other materials as set forth in detail above, the complaint alleges violation of the Act by reason of Respondent's failure to turn over the non-monetary terms of these agreements and documents. Both Garvey and Rozelle testified to a number of subjects dealt with in the media contracts which would be relevant to the working conditions of the players. Thus Rozelle conceded specifically that the contracts provided for starting times, amount of commercial minutes, number of games to be televised, length of half-time breaks, use of game film for news or promotional purposes, NFL public service announcements, and the days of the weeks of which games are scheduled. In addition other matters such as pre- and post-game interviews carried in the broadcasts, and the use of tapes by NFL films for further broadcasts would clearly have relevance to conditions of employment and collective bargaining. This would be true despite Respondent's contentions regarding the unsettled condition of the law as to whether players would be entitled to remuneration for interviews and rebroadcasts, or

the fact that some of these matters may be provided for in individual player contracts. Based on the clear relevance provisions described by Rozelle, and other areas noted by Garvey which have a "probability of relevance," (see *Acme Industrial, supra*), I find that the non-monetary provisions of the media contracts have relevance to the Union's preparation for collective bargaining and, indeed, for other purposes to enable the Union to discharge its duty of representation....

Having found that Respondent has engaged in certain unfair labor practices, I shall recommend that it be ordered to cease and desist therefrom and to take certain affirmative action designed to effectuate the policies of the Act.

As I have found that Respondent has not made available, pursuant to the request of the Union, the individual player contracts, and the current and previous television and radio network contracts and related memoranda as more particularly described in that request, I shall recommend that Respondent be ordered to turn over copies of said documents to the Union. This Order shall apply only to the non-monetary provisions of the so-called media contracts....

NOTES

1. An NLRB administrative law judge, Bernard Ries, held that the Seattle Seahawks of the NFL unlawfully terminated the contract of one of its players, Sam McCullum, because of his union activities. The action occurred in September 1982, as the NFLPA and its members were about to call a strike against the NFL. Ries ordered Seattle to reinstate McCullum at full back pay. However, also noting that McCullum had signed with the Minnesota Vikings four days after being released by Seattle, Ries ordered the Seahawks to reimburse the player for any costs he had incurred in moving to his new team. See "Court: Seahawks Cut McCullum Illegally," *Los Angeles Times*, November 26, 1983, pt III, p.7. See also, "Discriminatory Discharge in a Sports Context: A Reassessment of the Burden of Proof and Remedies Under the National Labor Relations Act," 53 Fordham Law Review 615 (1984–85).

2. In the foregoing 1982 NLRB opinion by Administrative Law Judge Cohn, reference is made to a dispute in the NFL arising in connection with previous collective bargaining. Although the complaints by the players association against management were later dropped when a new agreement was reached, it is instructive to consider the scope of Administrative Law Judge Schneider's 1976 order.

In *National Football League Management Council and the Constituent Member Clubs of the National Football*

League and National Football League Players Association, National Labor Relations Board, Washington, D.C., Case No. 2-CA–13379, June 30, 1976, after lengthy findings and discussion, Judge Schneider ordered the following:

1. National Football League Management Council, and each of the following named clubs of the National Football League, Atlanta Falcons, Baltimore Colts, Buffalo Bills, Chicago Bears, Cincinnati Bengals, Cleveland Browns, Dallas Cowboys, Denver Broncos, Detroit Lions, Green Bay Packers, Houston Oilers, Kansas City Chiefs, Los Angeles Rams, Miami Dolphins, Minnesota Vikings, New England Patriots, New Orleans Saints, New York Giants, New York Jets, Oakland Raiders, Philadelphia Eagles, Pittsburgh Steelers, St. Louis Cardinals, San Diego Chargers, San Francisco 49'ers, Washington Redskins shall:

A. Cease and desist from:

(1) Refusing to bargain collectively with National Football League Players Association by failing or refusing to provide the Association with the following information:

(a) The employment contract of Commissioner Pete Rozelle,

(b) Copies of all standard player contracts,

(c) The raw data relating to player injuries submitted by the NFL or any respondent club, or agents, to the Stanford Research Institute,

(d) A copy of each stadium lease executed between the respondent clubs and the particular stadia authorities,

(e) A listing by individual name and address of each of respondent clubs' doctors and trainers, including a description of each doctor's certified specialties and medical background, and each trainer's specialized training,

(f) Each respondent club's retired-reserve list, other than respondent Buffalo Bills,

(g) Any other information requested by the Players Association which is necessary for collective bargaining or for performance by the Players Association of its duties as collective-bargaining representative of the players.

(2) Unilaterally adopting or putting into effect increased wage scales for pre-season games, or any other increased compensation, without the prior consent of, or negotiation with, the collective-bargaining representative.

(3) In any like or related manner, interfering with, restraining or coercing employees in the exercise of rights guaranteed in Section 7 of the National Labor Relations Act.

B. Take the following affirmative action necessary to effectuate the policies of the Act:

(1) Provide the Players Association forthwith with' complete current infomation as to each of the items referred to above in paragraph 1, A, (1), (a)–(g) of this Order.

(2) Upon request bargain collectively with the Players Association and embody any agreement reached in a signed contract.

2. Respondents Houston Oilers, Philadelphia Eagles, and Pittsburgh Steelers, shall, additionally:

A. Cease and desist from:

(1) Trading, waiving, releasing or terminating employees because of their participation in union or concerted activities on behalf of, or as representatives of, the Players Association or any other labor organization.

(2) In any like or related manner interfering with, restraining or coercing employees in the exercise of rights guaranteed in Section 7 of the Act.

B. Take the following affirmative action necessary to effectuate the policies of the Act:

(1) Respondent Oilers shall offer to Bill Curry, Respondent Eagles shall offer to Kermit Alexander, and Respondent Steelers shall offer to Tom Keating, immediate and full reinstatement to his position on the club roster without prejudice to his seniority or other rights and privileges.

(2) Respondent Oilers shall make Bill Curry whole, Respondent Eagles shall make Kermit Alexander whole, and Respondent Steelers shall make Tom Keating whole, for any loss of earnings suffered by him by reason of the discrimination against him in accordance with the provisions of the remedy section, IV, above.

3. Respondents Miami Dolphins and San Diego Chargers shall, additionally, cease and desist from:

A. Demanding that players return bonuses paid to them for signing contracts because the players have gone on strike or have engaged in other union or concerted activities protected by the Act.

B. In any like or related manner interfering with, restraining or coercing employees in the exercise of rights guaranteed in Section 7 of the Act.

4. Respondent Dallas Cowboys shall, additionally, cease and desist from:

A. Threatening employees that they will be placed on waivers if they participate in strikes or in other protected concerted activities.

B. In any like or related manner interfering with, restraining or coercing employees in the exercise of rights guaranteed in Section 7 of the Act.

5. Respondent Houston Oilers shall, additionally, cease and desist from:

A. Threatening employees with fines, suspensions, or other reprisals if they attend or conduct meetings of the Players Association, discuss the Players Association, or give assistance or support to it.

B. In any like or related manner interfering with, restraining or coercing employees in the exercise of rights guaranteed in Section 7 of the Act.

6. Respondents Houston Oilers, Philadelphia Eagles, and Pittsburgh Steelers shall, in addition, preserve, and upon request, make available to the Board or its agents, for examination and copying all payroll records, social

security payment records, timecards, personnel records and reports, and all other records necessary to analyze the amount of backpay or other compensation due, and the right of reinstatement, under the terms of this Order.

7. Respondents shall, in addition:

A. Post at their places of business copies of the attached notice applicable to the particular respondents named therein. Copies of those notices, on forms provided by the Regional Director for Region 2, after being duly signed by Respondents' representatives, shall be maintained by Respondents for 60 consecutive days thereafter, in conspicuous places, including all places where notices to employees are customarily posted. Reasonable steps shall be taken by Respondents to insure that said notices are not altered, defaced, or covered by any other material.

B Notify the Regional Director for Region 2, in writing, within 20 days after receipt of this order, what steps Respondents have taken to comply herewith.

It is further recommended that the following allegation of the complaint alleging the commission of unfair labor practices be dismissed:

1. That the Respondents:

(a) Refused to supply the Players Association with (1) the names of players fined by the clubs, the amount of the fines, and the reasons therefor and, (2) the names of players whose insurance claims were denied.

(b) Put into effect an increased wage scale for pre-season games in order to undermine the representative status of the Players Association and to discourage union activities, in violation of Section 8(a)(3) and (1) of the Act.

(c) Unlawfully adopted the sudden death rule and unlawfully changed the punt rule.

2. That the respondent Atlanta Falcons traded Kenneth Reaves because he was a player representative and had engaged in concerted activities on behalf of the Players Association.

3. That the respondent Dallas Cowboys and respondent St. Louis Cardinals kept under surveillance the meeting places, meetings and activities of the Players Association and denied non-employee representatives of the Players Association access to pre-season training camps.

5.22 Enforcing the Robertson Settlement in the NBA

As the foregoing section emphasizes, labor relations in sports leagues are subject to monitoring. The National Basketball Association has additional constraints imposed on it resulting from the *Robertson* case and settlement in the mid-1970's. In *Robertson v. NBA,* 389 F. Supp. 867 (S.D.N.Y. 1975), the NBA players successfully thwarted attempts by the NBA to merge with the rival American Basketball Association. The players claimed that a merger would be anticompetitive, creating a monopoly and imperilling jobs.

As the ABA headed toward an almost certain demise, the players' stand softened. At length, in return for concessions gained in a new collective bargaining agreement, the NBA players agreed that the NBA could absorb the surviving ABA teams. This settlement had to be approved by the court hearing the *Robertson* case. The price paid by the NBA was that the court indicated it would retain jurisdiction in the case until 1987. Any perceived deviations from the terms of the *Robertson* settlement could be raised with the court or with a special master appointed by the court.

The result has been multiple instances in which actions by the league (and at times the union) have been felt to deviate from the language or spirit of the settlement. Between 1976 and 1981, when the league used a free agent compensation procedure that often found the NBA commissioner sitting as arbitrator to determine the compensation to be paid by a player's new club to his old, several rulings by the commissioner were contested by the players association as penalties. It was argued, successfully in a couple of cases involving free agents Marvin Webster and Bill Walton, that the commissioner's awards were so excessive that future free agents would be hampered by clubs' fears that the compensation assessed for signing a free agent would be unduly severe. (See *In re Robertson Class Plaintiffs,* 479 F. Supp. 657 [S.D.N.Y. 1979], *aff'd in part,* 625 F.2d 407 [2d Cir. 1980].) With the replacement of this process by a right of first refusal system in 1981, the appeal to the court or special master on these issues ended.

However, as the following discussions indicate, several other practices have been protested. The decisions are integral to the NBA's central operation.

In the Matter of Robertson Class Plaintiffs and National Basketball Players Association v. National Basketball Association, 70 Civ. 1526 (RLC), U.S. Dist. Ct., S.D.N.Y., Re: David Batton, February 12, 1981

This matter was initiated by the National Basketball Players Association (NBPA) on behalf of player Dave Batton against the National Basketball Association (NBA) and the New Jersey Nets. The NBPA sought a determination that Italian basketball teams and leagues are not professional within the meaning of Paragraph 2.A (2)(e) of the Robertson Settlement Agreement.

Paragraph 2.A. (1) of the Agreement recites that, under the NBA rules then in effect, an NBA team which drafted a player in the College Draft thereby obtained exclusive negotiating and contract-signing rights of indefinite duration. Paragraph 2.A.(2)(a)(b) and (c) provide that, beginning with the 1976 College Draft, the drafting team shall have exclusive rights to the player for only one year; that, if the player is not signed, at the end of that year, he is available to be drafted the subsequent year; and that if he is not then drafted, or is not signed in the second year, the player becomes a free agent, available to be signed by any NBA team.

These provisions are qualified, however, by Paragraph 2.A.(2)(e), which provides in substance that if a player, during the period in which an NBA team has drafted him and established exclusive rights, signs a contract with a non-NBA professional basketball team, the NBA team retains its exclusive rights until a year after the player is free from his non-NBA contract and announces his availability for NBA play. Paragraph 2.A(2)(e) reads, in pertinent part, as follows:

> If a player is drafted by an NBA team in either an initial or a subsequent draft and, during a period in which he may negotiate and sign a Player Contract with only the NBA team which drafted him, signs a Player Contract with a *professional basketball team not in the NBA* that covers at least the playing season immediately following said initial or subsequent draft, then such NBA team shall retain the exclusive NBA rights to negotiate with and sign the player for the period ending one year from the earlier of the following

two dates: (i) the date the player notifies the team that he is available to sign a Player Contract with such team immediately . . . or (ii) the date of the College Draft occurring in the twelve-month period from September 1 to August 30 in which the player notifies such NBA team of his availability and intention to play in the NBA playing season immediately following said twelve-month period, provided that such notice [in either (i) or (ii)] will not be effective until the player is under no contractual or other legal impediment to play with such team for such season. If during said one-year period the player signs a player contract with *a team in another professional basketball league* and (a) the player has not made a bona fide effort to negotiate a Player Contract with the NBA team with the exclusive NBA right to negotiate with and sign such player or (b) if such bona fide effort is made and such NBA team makes a bona fide offer of a Player Contract to such player, then such NBA team shall retain the exclusive NBA right to negotiate with and sign the player for additional one-year periods as measured in the preceding sentence; but if the player has made such bona fide effort and such NBA team fails to make a bona fide offer of a Player Contract to such player, then in no event shall said exclusive right be retained. . . . [Italics supplied].

David Batton, a third round draft choice of the Nets in 1978, rejected offers by the Nets and signed a contract with Pallacanestro Gabetti Cantu of the Federazione Italiana Pallacanestro (Italian League) for $45,000, plus bonuses. The Italian League is sanctioned by the International Amateur Basketball Association (FIBA), which governs eligibility for the Olympic games and other amateur competitions.

The FIBA defines an amateur as "one who plays . . . because he loves the game and who takes part in competitions without material gain of any kind." The testimony at the hearing tended to show that while the FIBA sanctioned the Italian League as an amateur league, the large salaries American players receive (some in excess of $100,000 per year) render the amateur classification a "mockery."

The NBPA argued that the Italian League is

recognized by International and American authorities as an amateur league. A decision by Special Master Telford Taylor that the Italian League is amateur would allow players to play two years in Italy, then return to the NBA as a free agent. The NBA, in arguing that the Italian League is indeed professional, was attempting to invoke the provisions of Paragraph 2.A.(2)(e) which would require a player returning to the NBA from Italy to negotiate with the club that drafted him.

The NBA relied heavily on the "common" or dictionary meaning of "professional." Taylor found that Batton and other players in Italy were professionals within that meaning of the term. But while the NBPA conceded that the players are professionals, the Association argued that Batton is a professional player in an amateur league. Taylor held that this argument was without force, in that it would be an absurdity to propose that an amateur team could be made up of professional players. Taylor also rejected the NBPA's argument that professional should be used as a term of art commonly used in the "basketball community" (i.e., if FIBA says the league is amateur, it cannot be professional). Taylor noted that the NBPA offered no evidence to controvert the fact that the FIBA and Olympic treatment of Italian League players as amateurs is in contradiction with and violative of their own standards.

The NBPA argued further that since the Italian League was in existence at the time of the Agreement, the distinction between professional leagues and amateur leagues was "well recognized within the basketball community." But Taylor ruled that there was no evidence that the parties intended to include the Italian League with bona fide amateur leagues.

The NBA argued that the intent of the parties in the Agreement was to insure that players would negotiate in good faith with the drafting team. The NBPA replied that the NBA was concerned only with leagues competing for fans and television contracts, not European leagues. The Special Master gave more weight to the NBA's argument, and accordingly, determined that the Italian League is a professional league within the meaning of Paragraph 2.A.(2)(e) of the Agreement.

In the Matter of Robertson Class Plaintiffs and National Basketball Players Association and National Basketball Association and Seattle Supersonics, No. 70 Civ. 1526 (RLC) Slip Opinion, Re: Gus Williams, May 6, 1982

Under the terms of the *Robertson* settlement agreement, compensation to a club for loss of a veteran free agent ended after the 1980–81 season, and in subsequent seasons, players with veteran free agent status have been able to negotiate and sign with any club, subject only to the prior team's right of first refusal. However, paragraph 2C(5) prevented players who became veteran free agents at the close of the 1979–80 season from sitting out during the 1980–81 season and then negotiating their services for the 1980–81 season under the right of first refusal. This paragraph specifically provided that the right of compensation rule would continue to apply if a player chose to sit out "despite having received an offer of a Player Contract (without an option clause) for only that season which specifies compensation payable to the player for the 1979–1980 NBA playing season and all other non-monetary terms contained in his Player contract for the 1979–1980 NBA playing season."

Gus Williams, who became a free agent at the end of the 1979–80 season, was evidently the only one affected by the above provision of the *Robertson* settlement agreement. Williams, through his agent and attorney Howard Slusher, had negotiated with Seattle and other clubs for his services. On September 30, 1980, Seattle offered by letter to sign Williams for a one-year contract for the 1980–81 season on the same terms and conditions as his contract for the 1979–80 season. There was no response to this letter until December 4, 1980, when Slusher wrote Alan Rothenburg, Seattle's representative, that Williams was unconditionally accepting the offer and would report on December 9.

On the advice of NBA counsel, Seattle decided

to treat the September 30 offer as still open. When Williams reported to Seattle on December 9, Seattle tendered to him a contract containing the following language:

> This contract is intended to comply with Article 2.C.(5) of the *Robertson* settlement agreement.
>
> Specifically, it is intended to provide for compensation for the 1980–81 playing season of 100 percent of the compensation payable to the player for the 1979–80 NBA playing season, and all non-monetary terms contained in the player contract for the 1979–80 NBA playing season. . .
>
> In the event there is any disparity between this contract and the terms and conditions required under the *Robertson* settlement agreement, the contract shall be deemed automatically amended to comply therewith.

Slusher asked Rothenberg to remove the above language, but Rothenberg refused. On the following day, this proceeding was instituted before the special master by the Players Association, and the NBA was joined as a respondent.

The special master filed his report on December 31, 1980, dismissing the action against the NBA and rejecting the claim that the issues posed no controversy within the meaning of Article III of the constitution. He held, however, that Seattle had not made a valid offer to Williams, because the September 30 letter was not accompanied by a player contract. Therefore, if Williams signed with another team after the 1980–81 playing season, Seattle would not be entitled to compensation.

The matter was subsequently brought before the U.S. District Court in May of 1981. The court stated that the review of the special master's proceeding and report was concerned solely with questions of law. The basic issues were whether under paragraph 2C(5) of the agreement, Seattle made an offer of a proper contract to Williams and whether Seattle would be entitled to compensation or the right of first refusal.

The court found these issues presented a proper case and controversy because the NBA season was in its final stages and negotiations for the following season were already underway.

The issues thus raised had ripened into an actual and concrete controversy between the parties, and it would be wasteful to postpone a decision until the season ended.

The parties themselves agreed that a valid offer of a contract may be made by letter without a player contract being appended. Apparently, the special master had concluded that because the NBA commissioner required the terms to be set out in a player contract before he would grant recognition to the contract, no valid offer existed. However, the court held that it would not accept the special master's interpretation, because it was clearly at variance with the parties' understanding and practice.

The court concluded that Seattle, by appending the language of paragraph 2C(5) with an explanation of its purpose, did not effectuate any modification in the money or nonmoney terms and conditions of the offered contract, or render it different from the contract which Williams and Seattle had just recently fulfilled.

Accordingly, Seattle tendered Williams a contract for the 1980–81 season at 100 percent of the compensation paid to him for his services in the prior season. Since Williams refused to sign this contract, he was therefore not entitled to negotiate in 1981–82 with other teams under the right of first-refusal provisions. Thus, any team other than Seattle that contracted with Williams for his services for 1981–82 had to compensate Seattle for loss of services as provided in paragraph 2C(1) of the *Robertson* settlement agreement.

In the Matter of Robertson Class Plaintiffs (NBPA) and National Basketball Association (Lawrence O'Brien), No. 70 Civ. 1526, U.S. Dist. Ct., S.D.N.Y., Taylor, Special Master, July 7, 1980.
Re: Junior Eligibles Rule

> This proceeding was initiated by a letter to me, dated May 7, 1979, from counsel for the National Basketball Players Association ("NBPA"), requesting, in substance, that the National Basketball Association ("NBA") be enjoined from putting into force and effect an amendment to the

NBA college draft rules, scheduled to be adopted that same day. . . .

The amendment was in fact adopted that day, but its effective date was postponed to the 1980 college draft. The rule in question is Section 6.03 of the By-Laws to the NBA Constitution, which provides as follows:

6.03 *Persons Eligible for Draft.* The following classes of persons shall be eligible for the annual draft:

　(a) Students in four year colleges whose classes are to be graduated during the June following the holding of the draft;

　(b) Students in four year colleges whose original classes have already been graduated, and who do not choose to exercise remaining college basketball eligibility;

　(c) Students in four year colleges whose original classes have already been graduated if such students have no remaining college eligibility;

　(d) Persons who become eligible pursuant to the provisions of Section 2.05 of these By-Laws.

Section 2.05 prohibits drafting players until four years after high school graduation, subject to the so-called "hardship" exception; this rule has now been replaced by Section 2.A. (2)(f) of the Settlement Agreement, making eligible to the draft a member of a graduating high school class "if he renounces his intercollegiate basketball eligibility by written notice to the NBA at least 45 days prior to such draft."

The amendment to the above rule, complained of here, is a resolution adopted by the NBA Board of Governors on May 7, 1979, which provides:

For purposes of Section 6.03(b) of the By-Laws, a student in a four-year college whose original class has graduated and who has remaining college basketball eligibility, shall be deemed to have chosen not to exercise such remaining eligibility only if he renounces such remaining eligibility by a written notice to the NBA at least 45 days prior to the draft for which he desires to become eligible. . . .

Since prior to the Robertson Settlement, most NBA players have been recruited from graduating students at four year colleges, and the NBA has had rules governing the annual "college draft." These rules were among the features of player-club relations attacked in the Robertson complaint, and the Settlement Agreement, in the introductory paragraph to Section 2, referred to the NBA College Draft Rules (together with the NBA rules on "option clauses" and "compensation between teams") as those "described in paragraphs A(1), B(1) and C(1) below which would be "modified and/or eliminated in the manner set forth in this . . . Settlement Agreement." Paragraph A(1) recites that under "present NBA rules" a drafted player may negotiate only with the drafting team, and that: "The present NBA rules place no time limitation on the duration of the exclusive right of an NBA team, obtained in the College Draft, to negotiate with such player."

It was a central, though not exclusive, purpose of Section 2 of the Settlement Agreement to limit the length of time that a drafting team would retain exclusive negotiating rights to the draftee. There is no need here to restate the rules in detail; their general pattern is that if a drafted player does not sign with the drafting team within a year, he falls back into the draft "pool" for the next year, and may then be drafted by any NBA team. If he is drafted again the second year, but does not sign a contract, then a year after that the player becomes a free agent. Accordingly, as a general matter it takes a player one year to "sit out" an initial draft, and two years to sit out his liability to draft and become a free agent. See *Robertson* v. *NBA,* 556 F. 2d 682, 686 n.5.

Although in the majority of cases student basketball players complete the four-year college course in four years, there are cases in which injury, illness, or other personal problems prevent this. Since a student is eligible under the NCAA rules for four years of college play, if the cause of failure to graduate has also kept the player off the basketball court for a year, he will have a year of eligibility left when the class with which he entered college graduates. . . .

It is common ground between the parties that, before and since the Settlement Agreement, NBA practice has not required students falling in category (b) to announce whether or not they intended to "exercise remaining college basketball eligibility." Thus it had been possible for such students to be drafted, but stay at college and play out their remaining year of eligibility. Under the Settlement Agreement (Section 2.A.(2) (a)), if such a player does not sign the contract tendered to him by the drafting team, he then becomes available for drafting by any team in the next year's draft. . . .

The change effected by the NBA resolution of May 7, 1979 requires the student in category (b), known to the trade as a "junior eligible," to renounce his college basketball eligibility if he wishes to attain draft eligibility. As viewed by both parties, the consequence is that a junior eligible may no longer both be drafted and play college basketball in the same year. . . .

The NBPA's basic argument is that NBA's May 7th resolution is a "unilateral change" in By-Law 6.03(b) which will "significantly impair the bargaining position" of the junior eligibles *vis-à-vis* the NBA clubs that draft them; NBPA concedes that the Settlement Agreement contains no specific language prohibiting such a change, but contends that the "clear meaning of paragraph 2 of the Settlement Agreement is that the old rules governing eligibility and other matters would continue except as to the extent specifically modified by the *Robertson* Settlement.". . .

As a policy matter, NBPA argues that the change "will eliminate entirely a junior eligible player's bargaining position," and thus serves an "anti-competitive" purpose, contrary to the "stated purpose of the Robertson Settlement to insure increased (rather than decreased) bargaining power for the players.". . . They point to the situation in 1978 regarding the well-known college player Larry Bird, a junior eligible who was drafted by the Boston Celtics, played out his remaining year of collegiate eligibility, and thus gave himself the option in 1979 of signing with the Celtics or going back to the draft pool. Under the amended rule Bird could not have been drafted without prior collegiate renunciation and then, if drafted, "would have had to choose between signing for a salary which he might consider inadequate or not playing basketball at all." In contrast, under the prior practice, Bird in 1979 had bargaining power in that he could turn down the Celtics' offer and go back into the draft pool. . . .

NBA, for its part, contends that the resolution of May 7th does not change the rule, but merely serves "to conform the practice of NBA teams to the language of the By-Law" . . . NBPA's claim, NBA contends, "seeks to have the Special Master read into the Settlement Agreement provisions that simply were not there," and thus beyond the Court's jurisdiction, "which is limited to enforcing the terms of the Settlement Agreement" . . . Acknowledging that NBA cannot alter "those rules which were mutually agreed upon," it is urged that nothing in the Agreement "imposes any restriction on NBA in making changes in its own pre-existing draft rules that were not modified by, or even referred to in, the Settlement Agreement. . . ."

The parties have devoted substantial portions of their memoranda to the question whether the May 7th amendment operates against the interests of junior eligibles. I find that NBPA has established that there may be situations in which the bargaining position of a junior eligible is worsened by putting him to an announced choice between draft eligibility and collegiate eligibility — a choice which he was not obliged to announce under the practice NBA has for some years tolerated under its By-Law 6.03(b). That fact (i.e., the disadvantage) is not irrelevant here, but its relevance is, I believe, tangential to more basic questions. . . .

As I read By-Law 6.03(b), the language cannot be rationally read as authorizing the practice which NBA has up to now been following, and which NBPA here seeks to perpetuate. The crucial words are "who do not choose to" etc. These words must signify a *formally disclosed* choice; they do not make sense if they are read to include an inner frame of mind, undisclosed to either college or club, or cover statements to friends or others that plainly are susceptible to a change of mind.

When President Calvin Coolidge stated publicly "I do not choose to run," the public read the words as meaning "I choose not to run." They were not read as meaning "I have not yet chosen whether to run or not." Yet that is exactly what the rule came to mean under the NBA's practice as NBA quite correctly states. . . . "In the past, despite the language of Section 6.03(b), NBA teams have drafted students whose original college classes had graduated but who had remaining college eligibility, without having received any indication from the student whether or not he intended to exercise his remaining college eligibility." I cannot accept that as a reasonable application of the rule; certainly its framers did not intend to confer draft eligibility on a state of *indecision* rather than one of announced choice.

The only argument the NBPA has made to the

contrary is not an interpretation of 6.03 but an invocation of past practice under it. In many circumstances such an argument might be weighty, if not persuasive. But in the present case, it must be recalled that the NBA practice developed before the Robertson Settlement at a time when, as recited in the Agreement itself (Section 2.A.(1)), "The present NBA rules place no time limit on the duration of the exclusive right of an NBA team, obtained in the College Draft, to negotiate with such player." Under these circumstances of contractual serfdom it did not much matter whether the junior eligible played out his remaining year or not. Once drafted, the collar of the drafting club was slipped on him indefinitely, and all he could do by playing out his collegiate eligibility was to postpone his indenture by a year.

The Settlement Agreement's time limitations on the drafting club's exclusive negotiating rights changed all that, and enabled the drafted junior eligible to serve his first year as a draftee on the college courts and thereby shake off the drafting club if he so desired. And under the continuing NBA practice, he could accomplish that by remaining silent and doing as he pleased.

The case of Larry Bird, so much relied on by the NBPA, is a good illustration. According to NBPA's uncontradicted account (pl. M. 3), "Bird had given no indication that he wanted to be drafted nor had he renounced his remaining year of collegiate eligibility." He played out that year and then "following negotiations, decided not to reenter the draft pool and instead, signed" with the Celtics, the drafting team.

It takes no more than a glance at the language of By-Law 6.03(b) to see that at no time was Bird draft-eligible under its terms. Prior to the draft, he was not one of those "who do not choose to exercise remaining collegiate basketball eligibility"; he was one who had chosen not to decide (or say) whether he would or would not do that. When the next collegiate basketball season opened (or sooner) Bird became one who had chosen *to* exercise his remaining collegiate eligibility, and thus was still plainly excluded from draft eligibility.

Thus the Bird case illustrates the total incompatibility of NBA practice with the terms of its own rule. . . .

Accordingly, I find that the NBA resolution of May 7th, complained of here, does not change, but rather reinstates, the rule of By-Law 6.03(b), and I deny NBPA's petition to prevent NBA from implementing that resolution.

O. Leon Wood, d/b/a Leon Wood v. NBA, 1984–2 Trade Cases, Paragraph 166, 262

Carter, D.J.: Leon Wood, a talented college basketball player, and a member of the United States Basketball team that won the gold medal in the Olympic games this past August in Los Angeles, has brought this action alleging that the National Basketball Association's ("NBA") college draft, maximum team salary rules and ban on player corporations constitute violation of section 1 of the Sherman Act, 15 U.S.C. sec. 1. Plaintiff seeks a preliminary injunction barring enforcement of the 1983 memorandum of understanding between the NBA and the NBA Players Association ("Players Association") pursuant to which the maximum team salary limitation was imposed, restraining defendants from refusing to deal with a corporation formed by plaintiff and outlawing the college draft as illegal restraints under the Sherman Act.

Plaintiff was selected by the Philadelphia 76ers Basketball Club ("Philadelphia") in the NBA annual college draft on June 19, 1984. Thereafter, Philadelphia and Wood's representative, Fred L. Slaughter, began negotiations. No agreement was reached, and plaintiff was offered a one year contract at $75,000. Patrick Williams, Vice President and General Manager of Philadelphia, states in his affidavit filed in this case that the contract was offered to Wood not because of the limitations of the 1983 memorandum agreement, but to preserve Philadelphia's exclusive right to negotiate with Wood pursuant to NBA regulations now operative in re rookie players. Williams asserts that Philadelphia was prepared to seek a way around the salary cap in order to negotiate a multi-year contract with Wood but could not get Slaughter to work out the terms.

Plaintiff has declined to accept the one year $75,000 offer. Plaintiff contends that he is suffering irreparable injury in being required either to sign a one year contract with Philadelphia at a level far below his value in an open market or forego playing basketball in the NBA for one season. He alleges that in signing at a salary not commensurate with his talents he would be exposing himself to a career ending injury. He urges the court to grant him preliminary relief requiring Philadelphia to negotiate with plaintiff unfettered by the restrictions the college draft, salary cap and bar on player corporations impose.

A brief summary of facts and transactions leading to the allegedly illegal NBA practices and procedures may help inform understanding. In 1970 a group of NBA players instituted an antitrust suit against the NBA challenging the reserve clause which gave one club the exclusive rights to the services of a player, the reserve compensation clause, college draft and other player allocation devices which the players alleged restricted competition. The litigation was pursued as a class action on behalf of all present NBA players and all those who would become NBA players prior to final judgment. The class plaintiffs were represented by the NBA Players Association, a defendant here.

On April 29, 1976, a settlement was reached after extensive arms-length negotiations between the NBA representatives, and representatives of the players which included the General Counsel of the Players Association and several named plaintiffs in the action. The settlement agreement eliminated the reserve clause, phased out the reserve compensation clause, modified the college draft, provided a $4.6 million settlement fund, and established machinery for judicial oversight of enforcement and implementation of the terms of the settlement. The settlement agreement was approved by this court and the Court of Appeals. *Robertson* v. *NBA* [1976–2 TRADE CASES para. 61,029], 72 F.R.D. 64 (S.D.N.Y. 1976) (Carter, J.), aff'd [1977–1 TRADE CASES para. 61,474], 556 F.2d 682 (2d Cir. 1977).

In 1983 the *Robertson agreement* was modified by a memorandum of understanding. Again, agreement was reached through intensive arms-length negotiations between representatives of the NBA and the Players Association. The agreement imposed a maximum and minimum team salary limitation. Each team is required through the 1986–87 playing seasons to pay in players' salaries and benefits at a minimum a certain percentage of overall NBA gross revenues projected for each upcoming playing season. Conversely, no team will be permitted to exceed in players' salaries and benefits a certain specified percentage of NBA annual gross revenues. In no case, however, will the salary cap be set below $3.6 million in the 1984–85 playing season, $3.8 million in 1985–86 playing season or $4.0 million in the 1986–87 playing season. The agreement allows for flexibility so that clubs who have reached the maximum salary limitations are able to exceed it to sign rookies, to replace retired or injured players and to sign veteran free agents. The memorandum of understanding was incorporated into a modification agreement pursuant to which the *Robertson* agreement remains in full effect except as expressly affected by the modification agreement. The modification agreement was presented to the court with a joint request by the NBA and the Players Association for court approval. On May 9, 1983, the court scheduled a hearing to determine whether the new agreement was fair, reasonable and adequate, and on June 13, 1983, filed a supplemental judgment in *Robertson* approving the agreement.

At the outset of our inquiry, it must be noted that the college draft as it now operates has been approved by this court and the Court of Appeals. The modification agreement with its maximum salary cap has been approved by this court. While the court's function when presented with a settlement of class action litigation is not to decide the merits of the controversy, *In re Traffic Executive Association-Eastern Railroad*, 627 F.2d 631, 633 (2d Cir. 1980), it must determine whether the settlement is fair, reasonable and adequate, *Weinberger* v. *Kendrick*, 698 F.2d 61, 73 (2d Cir. 1982), cert. denied, — U.S. —, 104 S.Ct. 77 (1983), and, moreover, must be satisfied that the settlement protects the rights and interest of absent members of the class. *Vulcan Society of Westchester County, Inc.* v. *Fire Department of the City of White Plains*, 505 F.Supp. 955, 961 (S.D.N.Y. 1981) (Sofaer, J.). That an agreement containing features that violated federal antitrust laws would be approved at two levels of the judiciary is exceedingly unlikely.

Mandatory Bargaining Subjects

The provisions under attack, the college draft and the maximum salary limitations, were, as indicated, the product of arms-length bargaining. The maximum team salary limitation clearly falls within the definition of terms and conditions of employment which are pursuant to sec.8(a) of the National Labor Relations Act, 29 U.S.C. sec. 158(d), mandatory subjects of collective bargaining. . . .

Similarly, the college draft constitutes a mandatory subject of collective bargaining since such rules determine the team which has exclusive rights to a player. In their original form in professional sports such rules severely circumscribed the movement of players from one team to another and operated to limit the leverage players might exert on owners to upgrade their salaries. See e.g., *Mackey* v. *National Football League*. . . .

The antitrust claim as to the college draft and the maximum salary limitation must fail. Both provisions affect only the parties to the collective bargaining agreement — the NBA and the players — involve mandatory subjects of bargaining as defined by federal labor laws, and are the result of bona fide arms-length negotiations. Both are proper subjects to concern by the Players Association. As such these provisions come under the protective shield of our national labor policy and are exempt from the reach of the Sherman Act. . . .

Plaintiff places great stress on the fact that he is a "non-veteran NBA player and was not within the bargaining unit represented by the defendant Players Association" (Plaintiff's Memorandum at 17). He argues that "any condition relating to the wages of an unrepresented non-union member cannot be a mandatory subject matter of collective bargaining." *Id.* at 19. What plaintiff is contending is that since he was not an NBA player when the union and owners reached agreement on the issues in contention here, that agreement cannot bind him. He cites no authority for that proposition, and indeed none can be found. To adopt plaintiff's principle would turn federal labor policy on its head. The Players Association is the recognized exclusive bargaining agent for NBA players. Art. XXIII of the October 10, 1980 Agreement. At the time an agreement is signed between the owners and the players' exclusive bargaining representative, all players within the bargaining unit and those who enter the bargaining unit during the life of the agreement are bound by its terms. *J.I. Case Co.* v. *NLRB*, 321 U.S. 332, 335 (1944) (when an employee is hired after the collective bargaining agreement has been made, "the terms of [his] employment already have been traded out"); *NLRB* v. *Laney and Duke Story Warehouse Co.*,

369 F.2d 859, 866 (5th Cir. 1966) ("[t]he duty to bargain is a continuing one, and a union may legitimately bargain over wages and conditions of employment which will affect employees who are to be hired in the future").

Indeed the law could be no other way. The aim of federal labor policy is to promote peace in labor-management relations, not chaos and turmoil which adoption of plaintiff's theory would produce. The Players Association has been acting as collective bargaining representative of NBA basketball players at least since the *Robertson* litigation commenced in 1970. It has bargained with owners on behalf of the players and has entered into a number of collective bargaining agreements binding the players including the agreement at issue here. The current agreement as to salary cap, college draft and ban on private player corporations is not due to expire until June 1, 1987. It is binding on plaintiff and all others now in the bargaining unit and all who hereafter enter the bargaining unit prior to the expiration date of the agreement — June 1, 1987.

Player Corporations

The ban on private corporations is a part of the collective bargaining agreement. The ban on player corporations was agreed to in the words of Players Association General Counsel, because "[t]hese individual corporations created administrative entanglements and accounting difficulties for the benefit plans established and administered by the Players Association and NBA." (Affidavit of Lawrence Fleisher at 13.) The ban arguably affects the terms and conditions of employment and could, therefore, fit the definition of mandatory subject of bargaining. Even if outside that definition, however, the ban presents no antitrust issues. It is a restriction agreed to in labor-management negotiations to simplify the union and NBA task of administering player benefits. Even though it may have an adverse impact on some individuals in the bargaining unit, *NLRB* v. *Allis-Chalmers Mfg. Co.*, 388 U.S. 175, reh. denied, 380 U.S. 892 (1967), it is not the proper subject of attack in proceedings seeking relief from antitrust violations. . . .

5.30 Labor Arbitration

Chapter 2 examined the background leading to the development of today's legal sports structure. The focus was on the contracts and the antitrust and labor cases that have been instrumental in this development. With Chapters 3 and 4 we began to see shifts in the types of legal precedents. We saw how extensive collective-bargaining-agreement provisions have caused change well beyond that dictated by the court decisions. Then arbitration decisions were added to the mix. We saw how arbitration has virtually replaced the role of the courts as a means of legal redress. This trend is still developing. A constant flow of grievances before labor arbitrators in all the sports leagues is reshaping the sports legal structure.

This section expands on the labor arbitration concept. It examines the types and procedures of arbitration utilized in the sports leagues (Section 5.31). Then important arbitration decisions are reviewed in Section 5.32. Because several arbitration awards have already been discussed in earlier chapters, no attempt is made here to catalog an exhaustive list. However, decisions such as those in the famous *Messersmith and McNally* (See *In re Twelve Clubs*, Section 5.32) arbitrations should be scrutinized in detail.

5.31 Types and Procedures

When players are involved in disputes with management, three general types of grievances occur. One is the injury grievance, which was examined in Section 4.32. Set forth at that point was the NFL's special injury grievance procedures. Not all leagues have two clearly delineated procedures — one for injury and the other for other types of player-club disputes. Even so, encased in their procedures in some fashion is a method of grieving over injuries.

The second type of labor arbitration in sports is a catch-all category designated in the NFL as the noninjury grievance. The jurisdiction conferred on the arbitration process is quite wide, basically encompassing all disputes that arise between player and management under the league's Collective Bargaining Agreement or Uniform Player Contract. Since we have earlier examined the NFL's injury grievance procedures, it is appropriate to stay with that league in an explication of its noninjury procedures. These are set forth below.

The third type of arbitration is special. This is salary arbitration, which occurs when a particular type of player cannot reach an agreement over salary with the club for the forthcoming year. These players are not free agents but still the "property" of the club, although collective bargaining has gained them some redress of salaries. The National Hockey League has a modified salary arbitration procedure. Major League Baseball, however, has the most extensive system. Annually, some 90 to 100 baseball players file for salary arbitration. While the numbers whose cases are actually heard is much smaller than that (in 1984 there were only ten), the salary arbitration system has been instrumental in reshaping baseball's overall salary structures. For example, in 1985, seven players who filed for arbitration submitted requests in excess of $1 million. Since baseball's salary arbitrations are limited for practical purposes to players who have between two and six years of major league service, the escalation in arbitration demands and awards has been significant.

National Football League Collective Bargaining Agreement, 1982

Article VII: Non-Injury Grievance

Section 1. Definition: any dispue (hereinafter referred to as a "grievance") involving the interpretation or application of, or compliance with, any provision of this Agreement, the Standard Player Contract, the NFL Player Contract, and any provision of the NFL Constitution and Bylaws pertaining to terms and conditions of employment of NFL Players, will be resolved exclusively in accordance with the procedure set forth in this Article; provided, however, that any dispute involving Section 1 of Article III, Section

11 of Article VII, Article VIII and Article IX of this Agreement, paragraph 8 of the Standard Player Contract and paragraph 3 of the NFL Player Contract will not be resolved under the procedure of this Article.

Section 2. Initiation: A grievance may be initiated by a player, a club, the Management Council, or the NFLPA. Except as provided otherwise in Article XV, Section 18, a grievance must be initiated within 45 days from the date of the occurrence or non-occurrence upon which the grievance is based, or within 45 days from the date on which the facts of the matter became known or reasonably should have been known to the party initiating the grievance, whichever is later. A player need not be under contract to an NFL club at the time a grievance relating to him arises or at the time such grievance is initiated or processed.

Section 3. Filing: Subject to the provisions of Section 2 above, a player or the NFLPA may initiate a grievance by filing a written notice by certified mail or TELEX with the Management Council. . . . The answer will set forth admissions or denials as to the facts alleged in the grievance. If the answer denies the grievance, the specific grounds for denial will be set forth. The answering party will provide a copy of the answer to the player(s) or club(s) involved and the NFLPA or NFLMC as may be applicable.

Section 4. Joint Fact Finding: Within ten days of the receipt of an answer, representatives of the NFLPA and the Management Council will meet in the appropriate team city to mutually determine the relevant facts of the grievance.

Section 5. Joint Fact Finding Report: The parties to any grievance will cooperate fully with the fact finding process by providing statements, witness identification, and production of relevant documents, all of which will be incorporated in and appended to a written report setting forth the facts not in dispute and, where appropriate, the facts in dispute. The report must be completed within fifteen (15) days after receipt of the answer and copies of the report will be provided to the grievant, the answering party, the NFLPA, the Management Council and the PCRC. The failure of either party to participate in the fact finding process may be immediately brought to the attention of the Notice Arbitrator who is authorized to issue an order directing prompt participation and cooperation in the fact finding process.

Section 6. Player-Club Relations Committee: If a grievance is not resolved after it has been filed and during the fact-finding process, it along with the answer and the fact finding report will be referred for disposition to the next mid-month conference of the Player-Club Relations Committee (PCRC), which will consist of one representative appointed by NFLPA and one representative appointed by the Management Council. The PCRC will confer once each midmonth to discuss and consider all pending grievances. Such conference may be had by telephone if both representatives agree, or otherwise in person. Meetings of the PCRC will alternate between Washington and New York. No evidence will be taken during the conference except by mutual consent. Discussions between the PCRC representatives will be privileged. If the PCRC resolves any grievance by mutual agreement between the NFLPA and Management Council representatives, such resolution will be made in writing and will constitute full, final and complete disposition of the grievance and will be binding upon the player(s) and club(s) and the parties to this Agreement.

Section 7. Appeal: If the PCRC has not considered a grievance within 30 days after it has been filed, regardless of the reason, or has failed to resolve a grievance within five days of its conference, either the player(s) or club(s) involved, or the NFLPA, or the Management Council may appeal such grievance by filing a written notice of appeal with the Notice Arbitrator and mailing copies thereof to the party or parties against whom such appeal is taken, and either the NFLPA or the Management Council as may be appropriate. If the grievance involves a suspension of a player by a club, the player or NFLPA will have the option to appeal it immediately upon filing to the Notice Arbitrator and a hearing will be held by an arbitrator designated by the Notice Arbitrator within seven (7) days of the filing of the grievance.

Section 8. Arbitration: The parties to this Agreement have designated Sam Kagel as the Notice Arbitrator. Within 30 days after execution of this Agreement, Mr. Kagel will submit to the parties a list of fifteen qualified and experienced arbitrators. Within 10 days thereafter, representatives of the parties will confer by conference call(s) with Mr. Kagel for the purpose of selecting three arbitrators from the list who, along with Mr. Kagel, will constitute the non-injury arbitration panel. If the parties are unable to select three arbitrators from the original list, the selection process outlined in this section will continue until three arbitrators are selected. In the event of a vacancy in the position of Notice Arbitrator, the senior arbitrator in terms of affiliation with this Agreement will succeed to the position of Notice Arbitrator, and the resultant vacancy on the panel will be filled according to the procedures of this section as well as any other vacancies occurring on the panel. The Notice Arbitrator will, so as to equalize the caseload of non-injury grievances between himself and the other arbitrators and without prior consultation with the NFLPA or the Management Council, designate himself or one of the other arbitrators to hear each case. Either party to this Agreement may discharge a member of the arbitration panel by serving written notice upon him and the other party to this Agreement between December 1 and 10 of each calendar year, but at no time will such discharges result in no arbitrators remaining on the panel.

Section 9. Hearing: Each arbitrator will designate a minimum of one hearing date each month for use by the parties to this Agreement. Upon being appointed, each arbitrator will, after consultation with the Notice Arbitrator, provide to the NFLPA and the Management Council specified hearing dates for each of the ensuing 12 months, which process will be repeated on an annual basis thereafter. The parties will notify each arbitrator 30 days in advance of which dates the following month are going to be used by the parties. The designated arbitrator will set the hearing on his next reserved date and, after consultation with the parties, designate a convenient place for hearing such grievance. If a grievance is set for hearing and the hearing date is then cancelled by a party within 30 days of the hearing date, the cancellation fee of the arbitrator will be borne by the cancelling party unless the arbitrator determines that the cancellation was for good cause. Should good cause be found, the parties will share any cancellation costs equally. If the arbitrator in question cannot reschedule the hearing within 30 days of the postponed date, the case may be reassigned by the Notice Arbitrator to another panel member who has a hearing date available within the 30 day period. At the hearing, the parties to the grievance and the NFLPA and Management Council will have the right to present, by testimony or otherwise, any evidence relevant to the grievance. All hearings will be transcribed. In cases which require one full hearing day or less, the transcript will be prepared on an expedited, daily copy basis. In such cases, if either party requests post-hearing briefs, the parties will prepare and simultaneously submit briefs to the arbitrator postmarked no later than twenty (20) days after receipt of the transcript. In cases requiring more than one full hearing day, the transcript may be prepared by ordinary means and the post-hearing briefs must be submitted to the arbitrator, postmarked no later than thirty (30) days after receipt of the last day's transcript.

Section 10. Arbitrator's Decision and Award: The arbitrator will, if at all possible considering the arbitrator's schedule and other commitments, issue a written decision within 30 days of the submission of briefs. The arbitrator may issue the decision after 30 days have passed from the date of receipt of the last day's transcript regardless of the failure of either party to submit a brief. The decision of the arbitrator will constitute full, final and complete disposition of the grievance, and will be binding upon the player(s) and club(s) involved and the parties to this Agreement; provided, however, that the arbitrator will not have the jurisdiction or authority: (a) to add to, subtract from, or alter in any way the provisions of this Agreement or any other applicable document; or (b) to grant any remedy whatsoever other than a money award, an order of reinstatement, suspension without pay, a stay of suspension pending decision, a cease and desist order, a credit or benefit award under the Bert Bell NFL Player Retirement Plan, an order of compliance with a specific term of this Agreement or any other applicable document, or an advisory opinion pursuant to Article XI, Section 9.

Section 11. Integrity and Public Confidence: In the event a matter filed as a grievance in accordance with the provisions of Section 3 above gives rise to issues involving the integrity of, or public confidence in, the game of professional football, the Commissioner may, at any stage of its processing, after consultation with the PCRC, order that the matter be withdrawn from such processing and thereafter be processed in accordance with the procedure provided in Article VIII of this Agreement on Commissioner Discipline.

Section 12. Time Limits: Each of the time limits

set forth in this Article may be extended by mutual written agreement of the parties involved. If any grievance is not processed or resolved in accordance with the prescribed time limits within any step, unless an extension of time has been mutually agreed upon in writing, either the player, the NFLPA, the club or the Management Council, as the case may be, after notifying the other party of its intent in writing, may proceed to the next step.

Section 13. Representation: In any hearing provided for in this Article, a player may be accompanied by counsel of his choice and/or a representative of the NFLPA. In any such hearing, a club representative may be accompanied by counsel of his choice and/or a representative of the Management Council.

Section 14. Costs: All costs of arbitration, including the fees and expenses of the arbitrator and the transcript costs, will be borne equally between the parties. When the arbitrator grants a money award, it will be paid within ten (10) days. Unless the arbitrator determines otherwise, each party will bear the cost of its own witnesses, counsel, and the like.

Baseball Basic Agreement, 1980, Article V

F. Salary Arbitration

Effective with the 1981 Championship Season the following salary arbitration procedure shall be applicable:

(1) *Eligibility.* The issue of a Player's salary may be submitted to final and binding arbitration by any Player or his club, provided the other party to the arbitration consents thereto. Any club, or any Player with a total of two years of Major League service however accumulated, but with less than six years of Major League service, may submit the issue of the Player's salary to final and binding arbitration without the consent of the other party (subject to the provisions of subparagraph (4) below).

(2) *Six Year Player — Club Consent to Arbitration.* Any Player with six or more years of Major League service, and who was not eligible to declare free agency under Article XVIII(B) at the close of the preceding championship season, may elect salary arbitration in the same manner and at the same time as other Players. Within ten days after receiving notice of such an election, the Player

Relations Committee shall advise the Players Association whether the Club will consent to salary arbitration. In the event the Club refuses to consent to salary arbitration, the Player may, within ten days thereafter, elect free agency . . .

(3) *Notice of Submission*

(a) *Player Submission.* Election of submission shall be communicated by telephone or any other method of communication by the Player to the Players Association. Written notice of submission shall then be given, within the specified time limits, by the Players Association on behalf of the Player to the designated representative of the Player Relations Committee. Within three days after the notice of submission has been given, the Players Association and the Player Relations Committee shall exchange salary figures . . .

(b) *Club Submission.* Written notice of submission by the Club shall be communicated to the Player by registered letter mailed between January 12 and January 22 . . .

Salary figures shall be exchanged by the Players Association and the Player Relations Committee as soon as practicable thereafter.

(4) *Withdrawal from Arbitration.* In the event the Club submits the matter to arbitration, the Player may within 7 days after receipt of the Club's salary arbitration figure notify the Club that he does not wish to arbitrate and the matter shall be deemed withdrawn from arbitration. In such event, or in the event that neither the Club nor the Player submit to arbitration the rights and obligations of the Club and Player shall be unchanged from those which existed prior to the adoption of this salary arbitration procedure. In the event the Club and Player reach agreement on salary before the arbitrator reaches his decision, the matter shall be deemed withdrawn from arbitration.

(5) *Timetable and Decision.* Submission may be made at any time between January 15 and January 25. In the event the offer of the Club is reduced on or subsequent to January 25, the Player's right to submit to arbitration shall be reinstated for a period of 7 days. Arbitration hearings shall be held as soon as possible after submission and, to the extent practicable, shall be scheduled to be held from February 1 to February 20. The arbitrator may render his decision on the day of the hearing, and shall make every effort to render it not later than 24 hours following the close of the hearing.

The arbitrator shall be limited to awarding only one or the other of the two figures submitted. There shall be no opinion and no release of the arbitration award by the arbitrator except to the Club, the Player, the Players Association and the Player Relations Committee. The arbitrator shall insert the figure awarded in paragraph 2 of the duplicate Uniform Player's Contracts delivered to him at the hearing and shall forward both copies to the League office of the Player and Club concerned.

(6) *Form of Submission.* The Player and the Club shall each submit to the arbitrator and exchange with each other in advance of the hearing single salary figures for the coming season (which need not be figures offered during the prior negotiations). At the hearing, the Player and Club shall deliver to the arbitrator a Uniform Player's Contract executed in duplicate, complete except for the salary figure to be inserted in Paragraph 2. Upon submission of a salary issue to arbitration by either Player or Club, the Player shall be regarded as a signed Player (unless the Player withdraws from arbitration as provided in subparagraph (4) above).

(7) *Selection of Arbitrator.* The Players Association and the Player Relations Committee shall annually select the arbitrators. In the event they are unable to agree by January 1 in any year, they jointly shall request that the American Arbitration Association furnish them lists of prominent, professional arbitrators convenient to the hearing sites. Upon receipt of such lists, the arbitrators shall be selected by alternately striking names from the lists. . . .

(9) *Conduct of Hearings.* The hearings shall be conducted on a private and confidential basis. Each of the parties to a case shall be limited to one hour for initial presentation and one-half hour for rebuttal and summation. The aforesaid time limitations may be extended by the arbitrator in the event of lengthy cross-examination of witnesses, or for other good cause. . . .

(11) *Hearing Costs.* The Player and Club shall divide equally the costs of the hearing, and each shall be responsible for his own expenses and those of his counsel or other representatives; provided, however, that the Club and Player shall divide equally the total of (a) the round trip air fare for one Club representative from the Club's home city to the arbitration site plus (b) the round trip air fare for the Player or one representative from the Player's residence to the arbitration site.

(12) *Criteria.* The criteria will be the quality of the Player's contribution to his Club during the past season (including but not limited to his overall performance, special qualities of leadership and public appeal), the length and consistency of his career contribution, the record of the Player's past compensation, comparative baseball salaries (see subparagraph (13) below for confidential salary data), the existence of any physical or mental defects on the part of the Player, and the recent performance record of the Club including but not limited to its League standing and attendance as an indication of public acceptance (subject to the exclusion stated in (a) below). Any evidence may be submitted which is relevant to the above criteria, and the arbitrator shall assign such weight to the evidence as shall to him appear appropriate under the circumstances. The following items, however, shall be excluded:

(a) The financial position of the Player and the Club.

(b) Press comments, testimonials or similar material bearing on the performance of either the Player or the Club, except that recognized annual Player awards for playing excellence shall not be excluded.

(c) Offers made by either Player or Club prior to arbitration.

(d) The cost to the parties of their representatives, attorneys, etc.

(e) Salaries in other sports or occupations.

(13) *Confidential Major League Salary Data.* For his own confidential use, as background information, the arbitrator will be given a tabulation showing the minimum salary in the Major Leagues and salaries for the preceding season of all Players on Major League rosters as of August 31, broken down by years of Major League service. The names and Clubs of the Players concerned will appear on the tabulation. In utilizing the salary tabulation, the arbitrator shall consider the salaries of all comparable Players and not merely the salary of a single Player or group of Players.

5.32   Arbitration on Vital Player-Owner Interests

Labor arbitrations have become the dominant means of dispute settlement between players and clubs in professional sports. Prior discussions, particularly in Chapter 4, have focused on the substantive interpretations given to contractual dealings between player and club. In most respects in this important area, arbitration has replaced litigation.

The cases which follow go one step beyond individual contract interpretation. These decisions involve questions striking at the heart of how leagues control players through various restrictive devices. The first case, involving pitchers Andy Messersmith and Dave McNally, has been called the baseball players' "emancipation proclamation." What could not be accomplished in 50 years of abortive antitrust litigation (see Chapter 2, Sections 2.22 and 2.24) was secured by this one arbitration decision. The reasoning by Arbitrator Seitz should be carefully noted, then compared with that of Arbitrator Luskin in the following decision, *NFLPA and NFLMC.*

The other arbitration decisions discussed in this section are of lesser impact, but their importance to the labor-management relations experienced in the various leagues make them noteworthy.

In re The Twelve Clubs Comprising National League of Professional Baseball Clubs and Twelve Clubs Comprising American League of Professional Baseball Clubs, Los Angeles and Montreal Clubs and Major League Baseball Players Association, Grievances Nos. 75–27 and 75–23, Seitz, Chairman of Arbitration Panel, December 23, 1975. Reported in 66 LA 101

. . . The Chairman understands the dispute in arbitration to be as follows:

The Association claims that the terms of the Uniform Player Contracts of Messersmith and McNally, respectively, having expired, the two players are at liberty to negotiate contract relationships with any of the other clubs in the leagues and that they are not to be regarded as having been "reserved" by the Los Angeles or the Montreal clubs, respectively, in such a manner as to inhibit other clubs from dealing with them.

The leagues and the clubs assert that the terms of the contracts of these players have not expired; that they are still under contract; and that, in any event, the grievants have been duly "reserved" by their respective clubs; and, accordingly, they are not free to deal with other clubs for the performance of services for the 1976 season; nor are such other clubs free to deal with them for that season excepting under circumstances and conditions not here obtaining. . . .

What has been set forth above refers to the "merits" involved in these disputes. The clubs and the leagues assert that the Panel need make no decision on the merits because the claims raised by the grievances are not properly before it for arbitration because Article XV of the collective agreement between the leagues and the Association (hereinafter referred to as Basic Agreement) denies to the Arbitration Panel authority to entertain arbitration proceedings with respect to the subject-matter in controversy.

It seems appropriate to investigate this "jurisdictional question" before consideration of the case "on the merits." In the discussion that follows, it should be appreciated that much relates to a consideration of the jurisdictional question also bears upon and spills over to the discussion on "the merits."

Jurisdictional Question

The cornerstone of the leagues' argument is Article XV — Reserve System. This provision in the Basic Agreement (1973) states:

Except as adjusted or modified hereby, this Agreement does not deal with the reserve system. The Parties have differing views as to the legality and as to the merits of such system as presently constituted. This Agreement shall in no way prejudice the position or legal rights of the Parties or of any Player regarding the reserve system.

During the term of this Agreement neither of the Parties will resort to any form of concerted action with respect to the issue of the reserve system, and there shall be no obligation to negotiate with respect to the reserve system. (Emphasis supplied.)

The matter to which Article XV of the extant Basic Agreement addresses itself was dealt with, previously, in the preceding Basic Agreement effective January 1, 1970. In that Agreement Article XIV (the counterpart and predecessor of current Article XV) was expressed as follows:

Regardless of any provision herein to the contrary, this Agreement does not deal with the reserve system. The parties have differing views as to the legality and as to the merits of such a system as presently constituted. This Agreement shall in no way prejudice the position or legal rights of the Parties or of any Player regarding the reserve system. (Emphasis supplied.)

It is agreed that until the final and unappealable adjudication (or voluntary discontinuance) of Flood v. Kuhn et al., now pending in the Federal District Court of the Southern District of New York, neither of the Parties will resort to any form of concerted action with respect to the issue of the reserve system, and there shall be no obligation to negotiate with respect to the reserve system. Upon the final and unappealable adjudication (or voluntary discontinuance) of Flood v. Kuhn et al., either party shall have the right to reopen the negotiations on the issue of the reserve system as follows: (Emphasis supplied.)

There follows the description of two conditions or events on the happening of which negotiations may be reopened on notice.

The leagues' position on "jurisdiction," very briefly stated, is that Article XV removes from the authority of the Panel any power to arbitrate these grievances because they ask for relief which is in derogation of those rights of the clubs provided for in the Major League Rules which it characterizes as the "core" of the Reserve System; that Rule 4(a) ("Reserve Lists"), Rule 3(g) ("Tampering"), part of the "core" of that System, interdict dealings and negotiations between a player on a club's reserve list with any other club in the leagues; that the Arbitration Panel derives its authority only from the provisions of the Basic Agreement, Article X of which defines an arbitrable "grievance" as a complaint which involves "the interpretation of or

compliance with, the provision of any agreement between the Association and the Clubs or any of them . . .; that Article XV expressly provides that "this Agreement does not deal with the reserve system"; and, accordingly, the grievances do not address themselves to disputes within the ambit of the Basic Agreement as to which the Arbitration Panel may exercise its authority.

The Reserve System of the league is nowhere defined in a sentence or a paragraph. Reference is commonly and frequently made in the press and by the news media to "Reserve Clause"; but there is no such single clause encompassing the subject matter. It seems fair to say, on the basis of what has been presented, that the "Reserve System" refers to a complex and a congeries of rules of the leagues (and provisions in the collective Basic Agreement and the Uniform Players Contract) related to the objective of retaining exclusive control over the service of their players in the interest of preserving discipline, preventing the enticement of players, maintaining financial stability and promoting a balance or a relative parity of competitive skills as among clubs. Such "exclusive control," it is said, is exercised by a Club placing the name of a player on its "reserve list" which is distributed to the other clubs in both leagues. A player on such a list, assert the leagues, cannot "play for or negotiate with any other Club until his contract has been assigned or he has been released" (Rule 4–A (a)) and may not be the subject of "tampering" as described in Rule 3 (g).

This system of reservation of exclusive control is historic in baseball and is traceable to the early days of the organized sport in the 19th century. Over the years, the scheme and structure of provisions designed to establish and maintain that control has been changed in expression. The leagues assert that the system was designed, initially, to combat the institutional chaos that resulted when players under contract with one club defected to another. In an effort to deal with the problem, it is represented, various versions of reserve clauses had been adopted. . . .

Clauses of this general character were the subject of considerable litigation and were attacked as unenforceable perpetual renewals not based upon mutuality of contract. Excepting for the Lajoie Case in 1902 (in which it appears the player left his club to play for another club *during* the first of three renewal seasons provided for in

his contract) the leagues were uniformly unsuccessful in obtaining injunctions against defecting
players based on these allegedly "perpetual
renewal clauses." They were so-called or characterized because it had been claimed that the
unilateral renewal by a club of a contract for the
period mentioned, renewed *all* of the terms of the
previously signed contract *including* the renewal
right; and consequently, at the end of the first
renewal period, the club could invoke the renewal
provision of the renewed contract to hold the
player for another renewal period — and so on,
indefinitely.

There were periods of time when standard
players contracts, for whatever the reason, did not
incorporate such renewal clauses. There were
periods, apparently, when there were no rival
leagues to which a player might "jump"; and the
clubs, apparently, did not anticipate the need for
applications for injunctive relief and were content
to rely on the various clauses making up the
traditional reserve system to afford the protection
of the interests they sought to maintain. . . .

The arguments of the parties on the jurisdictional question have revolved around the meaning
of Article XV. Broadly stated, the leagues contend
that Article XV removed the "core" of the reserve
system from the reach of the provisions in Article X
of the Basic Agreement which provide for grievance procedure and arbitration. The presentation
of the leagues has not been entirely consistent as to
what, precisely, is included in that "core." In the
main, it is said that the "core" is represented by
Major League Rules 4–A (Reserve Lists) and 3(g)
(No Tampering); but on several occasions the
"core" was described as including section 10(a) of
the Players Contract. . . .

The Leagues do *not* contend, with respect to
"peripheral" matters involving the reserve system,
that Article XV of the Basic Agreement removes
disputes from grievance and arbitration as provided in Article X of the Basic Agreement. They say
that it is "core" matters, exclusively, that are so
removed as to be beyond the authority of the Panel
in arbitration. Article XV, however, does not
distinguish, in its terms, between "core" and
"peripheral" provisions constituting the reserve
system. It states only that "this Agreement *does not
deal with the reserve system.*" (Emphasis supplied.) That system consists of *many* provisions in
the Basic Agreement, the Uniform Players Agree-

ment and the Major League Rules the purpose and
effect of which is to enable a club to reserve to its
own use, exclusively, the services of a player who
had signed a Uniform Players Contract. Literally,
there are a host of such provisions, some less
"peripheral" or more significant than others in the
kind or degree of exclusive control which may be
exercised over a player by a club. There would be
no utility in identifying here the host of such
provisions in the governing documents.

It seems clear that Section 10 (Renewal Clause)
of the Uniform Players Contract is not the most
insignificant of the restraints placed on a player to
achieve the objectives of the "reserve system."
Section 10 (a) enables a club, through contract
renewal, to "reserve," for its exclusive use, at least
during the renewal year, the performance and
skills of a player who had signed for a previous
year. Section 10(b) refers to the promise of the
Player "not to play otherwise than with the Club"
holding the renewed contract. If it were valid
to make a distinction between "core" and
"peripheral" matters in the reserve system (a
distinction not given expression in Article XV),
then it is difficult to regard Section 10 of the
Uniform Players Contract as anything other than a
"core" provision — as indeed, it has been
recognized to be, on occasion, by the Leagues, at
the hearings.

This leads the analyst of Article XV, at the
threshold, to the belief that, if the leagues'
explanation of the provisions be accepted, he is
confronted with a paradox or a contradiction. On
the one hand, *in stated terms,* Article XV declares
that "this Agreement *does not deal with the reserve
system*" (Emphasis supplied); and on the other
hand, Section 10 of the Players Contract clearly
provides for an important and exclusive reservation of rights by the Club of the Player's services as
against competing clubs in the leagues. As already
stated in a footnote, supra, under Article III of the
Basic Agreement, the Uniform Players Contract is
incorporated into that Basic Agreement "by
reference and made a part hereof." The consequence of pursuing the leagues' line of reasoning is to
say that notwithstanding that the parties agreed
that the 1973 Basic Agreement does *not* "deal"
with the reserve system, nevertheless, they continued to provide for a contract renewal clause
which is an important ingredient of or constituent
part and component of that reserve system.

Stated in the form of a question, the quandary and dilemma faced by the writer is this: What does it mean when the Basic Agreement professes not to "deal with the reserve system" if the Players Contract incorporated into and made a part of that Basic Agreement actually contains provisions which are components of that system? The quandary becomes even more perplexing when it is observed, from the Leagues' point of view, that the "guts" or "core" of the Reserve System is contained in the Major League Rules (4–A(a) and 3(g)); in the Uniform Players Contract (incorporated into and made a part of the Basic Agreement) the Player agrees "to accept, abide by and comply with all provisions of the . . . Major League Rules" (which establish the Reserve System) not inconsistent with the provisions of the Players Contract or the Basic Agreement (Players Contract Section 9(a)); and, Article XIII–Rule Changes, of the Basic Agreement itself, by providing for negotiations with respect to certain changes in Major League Rules, signifies that the Basic Agreement vests in the Players Association and the players certain rights and imposes upon them certain duties in respect of such Rules insofar as the reserve system is concerned.

In such a case, it is not easy to understand how the Basic Agreement could state that it does *not* "deal" with the Reserve System, when, at the same time, its own provisions and the provisions of the Players Contract and the Major League Rules which are absorbed into the Basic Agreement *patently* do "deal" with such rules.

This seeming contradiction is resolved and explained by the Association's argument addressed to the jurisdictional question. I shall not attempt to set forth here all the facets of that argument and will confine myself to the most important points. They are grounded upon a curious history of Article XV.

In advance of the 1968 Basic Agreement (the first made by the Association with the leagues), the Association made known its dissatisfaction with many aspects of the reserve system. The 1968 Basic Agreement provided for a "joint study" to be undertaken of the subject matter of their dispute. In 1970, the Flood Case was filed in the United States District Court for the Southern District of New York. The Association, in that case, supporting Flood, launched a broad-based attack upon the reserve system as constituting a combination in

unreasonable restraint of trade in violation of the antitrust laws. During the course of that litigation the parties negotiated their 1970 Agreement which contained an Article XIV, quoted, supra, the leading sentence of which provides: "Regardless of any provision herein to the contrary, this Agreement does not deal with the reserve system."

It is evident not only from a reading of the text of that Article XIV in the 1970 Basic Agreement, but, also, from the testimony presented, that the quoted language did not so much address itself to the question of what the Reserve System meant or what it *comprehended,* as to the impact and significance of pending litigation on the Reserve System. Clearly, from the time the Association came on the scene, it desired modifications in the kind and degree of exclusive future control which a club could exercise over a signed player. . . .

The Flood Case, as is commonly known, terminated in a decision of the Supreme Court of the United States holding that the antitrust laws have no application to the reserve system to organized baseball. When the parties were engaged in negotiating their 1973 Basic Agreement, the Association, despite the conclusions reached in the Flood Case, continued to apprehend the possibilities of litigation because of its reluctant acquiescence, in a labor agreement to be bound by the numerous provisions constituting a reserve system. It requested, and obtained from the Leagues, Article XV (quoted above) in the current agreement which, in all material respects, is identical with Article XIV in the 1970 Basic Agreement except as to its references to the already concluded Flood Case. In February, 1973 when the subject was under discussion, the Association asked for a letter from the leagues which would underline and give emphasis to its position under Article XV. Accordingly, on April 19, 1973 the following letter was sent to the Presidents of the Leagues by the Association:

The following will confirm our understandings with regard to Article XV of the Basic Agreement effective January 1, 1973:

1. Notwithstanding the above provision, it is hereby understood and agreed that the Clubs will not during the term of the Agreement, make any unilateral changes in the Reserve System which would affect player obligations or benefits.

2. It is hereby understood and agreed that during the term of the Agreement the Clubs will indemnify and save harmless the Players Association in any action based on the Reserve System brought against the Association as a party defendant.

This letter was "Confirmed" by signatures of the two League Presidents. It demonstrates that the Players Association considered the various provisions constituting the reserve system to be so much a part of its binding agreement with the leagues that it wanted assurance that the leagues, unilaterally, would make no changes in the system that might affect adversely the interests of the players. Such a position is wholly inconsistent with one that reads Article XV as excluding the reserve system, utterly, from the ambit and reach of the Basic Agreement, foreclosing the filing of a grievance claiming violation of the provisions on which that system is grounded.

These grievances are based, primarily and affirmatively, on Section 10(a) of the Players Uniform Contract, in that the Association claims that there is no longer a contractual relationship between the players and their clubs. Section 10(a), manifestly, to the extent that it reserves exclusive right to a player's performance, is part of the reserve system which the leagues have promulgated and to which the Association and the players it represents have agreed to adhere, during the term of the 1973 Basic Agreement. I find nothing in that Basic Agreement or in any other document evidencing the agreement of the parties, to exclude a dispute as to the interpretation or application of Section 10(a) of the Uniform Players Contract or the Major League Rules dealing with the Reserve System from the reach of the broad grievance and arbitration provisions in Article X.

The Merits

. . . Messersmith signed a one-year contract with the Los Angeles Dodgers in 1974. This contract was duly renewed by the Club for what is commonly called the "renewal year" of 1975. The renewal was effected under Section 10(a) of the Uniform Players Contract. . . .

The Players Association claims that Messersmith, having served out and completed his renewal year on September 29, 1975, was no longer under contract with the Los Angeles Club and,

accordingly, was a free agent to negotiate for the rendition of his services with any of the other clubs in the leagues; but that the clubs "have conspired to deny Mr. Messersmith that right and have maintained the position that the Los Angeles Club is still exclusively entitled to his services." (Joint Exhibit No. 1)

As an affirmative defense, it is the position of the leagues that, by virtue of having sent its reserve list on November 17, 1975 to the appropriate officials and the subsequent promulgation of that list by them, the Los Angeles Club has reserved Messersmith's services for its own use, exclusively, for the ensuing season. This position is based on Major League Rule 4-A(a) which provides:

(a) FILING. On or before November 20 in each year each Major league Club shall transmit to the Commissioner and to its League President a *list of not exceeding forty (40) active and eligible players, whom the club desires to reserve for the ensuing season* . . . On or before November 30 the League President shall transmit all of such lists to the Secretary-Treasurer of the Executive Council, who shall thereupon promulgate same, *and thereafter no player on any list shall be eligible to play for or negotiate with any other club until his contract has been assigned or he has been released* . . . (Emphasis supplied.) This Major League Rule is supported and supplemented by Major League Rule 3(g) which reads as follows:

(g) TAMPERING. To preserve discipline and competition and to prevent the enticement of players . . ., *there shall be no negotiations or dealings respecting employment, either present or prospective between any player . . . and any club other than the club with which he is under contract or acceptance of terms, or by which he is reserved* . . . unless the club or league with which he is connected shall have in writing, expressly authorized such negotiations or dealings prior to their commencement. (Emphasis supplied.)

Thus, it is the Los Angeles Club's position that Messersmith, having been duly placed on its reserve list in November, 1975, it has an exclusive right to his services in that ensuing season.

The Players Association does not contest that Messersmith was placed on the Club's Reserved List; but it disputes the effect of doing so. Stated in briefest compass, the dispute is whether the fact that the renewal year, which terminated in September, 1975 (as claimed by the Players Association) affected or destroyed the Club's right to reserve Messersmith for the ensuing year of 1976 and to place him on the Club's November 17, 1975 reserve list with the consequences spelled out in Major League Rules 4–A(a) and 3(g). This calls for a decision as to whether Messersmith is still under contract with the club; and then if not under contract, whether the provisions of Rule 4-A(a) and 3(g) of the Reserve System prohibit him and any other club from dealing with each other for the 1976 championship season.

This is the first time, since the advent of the Players Association in organized baseball, that this issue has been squarely presented to arbitration. In only one previous situation have similar facts been the subject of a grievance. That grievance had been withdrawn after the Player, at the end of the first renewal year, entered into a contract with his Club rendering the dispute moot.

I have reached the conclusion that, as a matter of contract construction, the position of the Players Association in the dispute has merit and deserves to be sustained.

Before stating some of the reasons for that conclusion I believe it to be appropriate and salutary to state how I approach this issue.

It would be a mistake to read this Opinion as a statement of the views of the writer either for or against a reserve system, or for that matter, the Reserve System presently in force. It is not my function to do so! The Arbitration Panel on which I sit has authority and power only to rule on grievances which involve the interpretation of, or compliance with the provisions of "any agreement" between the Players Association and the Clubs or between a Player and a Club (Article X of the Basic Agreement). . . .

It deserves emphasis that this decision strikes no blow emancipating players from claimed serfdom or involuntary servitude such as was alleged in the Flood Case. It does not condemn the Reserve System presently in force on constitutional or moral grounds. It does not counsel or require that the System be changed to suit the predilections or preferences of an arbitrator acting as a Philosopher-King intent upon imposing his own personal brand of injustice on the parties. It does no more than seek to interpret and apply provisions that are in the agreements of the parties. To go beyond this would be an act of quasi-judicial arrogance! . . .

Despite the broad attack on the system which it had launched in the Flood Case, the posture of the Players Association in *these* cases, as I understand it, is not to oppose a reserve system which accommodates the needs of the clubs with what it regards as the requirements of players in a society in which freedom to contract personal services is an important attribute. To that end, from time to time the Players Association has indicated to the leagues the manner in which it believes the reserve system might be modified or relaxed in some respects. . . .

No one challenges the right of a Club to renew a Player's contract with or without his consent under Section 10(a), "for the period of one [renewal] year." I read the record, however, as containing a contention by the leagues that when a Club renews a Player's contract for the renewal year, the contract in force during that year contains the "right of renewal" clause as one of its terms, entitling the Club to renew the contract in successive years, to perpetuity, perhaps, so long as the Player is alive and the Club has duly discharged all conditions required of it. This is challenged by the Players Association whose position it is that the contractual relationship between the Club and the Player terminates at the end of the first renewal year. Thus, it claims that there was no longer any contractual bond between Messersmith and the Los Angeles Club on September 29, 1975.

The League's argument is based on the language in Section 10(a) of the Player's Contract that the Club "may renew this contract for the period of one year *on the same terms*" (emphasis supplied); and that among those "terms" is the right to further contract renewal.

In the law of contract construction, as I know it, there is nothing to prevent parties from agreeing to successive renewals of the terms of their bargain (even to what has been described as "perpetuity"), provided the contract expresses that intention with explicit clarity and the right of subsequent renewals does not have to be implied. . . .

There is nothing in Section 10(a) which, explicitly, expresses agreement that the Players Contract can be renewed for any period beyond the first renewal year. The point the leagues present must be based upon the implication or assumption, that if the renewed contract is "on the same terms" as the contract for the preceding year (with the exception of the amount of compensation) the right to additional renewals must have been an integral part of the renewed contract. I find great difficulties, in so implying or assuming, in respect of a contract providing for the rendition of personal services in which one would expect a more explicit expression of intention. . . .

There are a number of other reasons which persuade to the same conclusions in the history of and the litigation in professional sports. In the interests of time and space I shall not discuss them, excepting for some observations with respect to basketball.

In the Barry Case (*Lemat Corporation* v. *Barry,* 80 California Reporter 240) and the Barnett Case (*Central New York Basketball, Inc.* v. *Barnett,* 181 N.E.2d 506) the California and Ohio Courts had before them provisions of basketball contracts with renewal clauses which, for present purposes, may be regarded as having the same effect as the renewal clause in Section 10(a) of the baseball Players Contract. In the Barnett Case, the contract which the Player had entered into with the club provided that the Club shall have the right "to renew this contract for the period of one year on the same terms" (emphasis supplied) except for the amount of compensation. In the Barry Case the contract provided that the tendered contract shall be "deemed renewed and extended for the period of one year *on the same terms and conditions in all respects as are provided herein.*" (Emphasis supplied.)

The California Court of Appeals in the Barry Case found that that case was almost on "all fours" with the Barnett Case. It stated that the Ohio Court's construction of Barnett's contract (that the Club "could renew that player's contract for an additional year") was a "reasonable practical construction of the renewal option" and that "so interpreted," "the renewal provision did not lack mutuality and was supported by sufficient consideration" — and it remarked that "the identical reasoning applies here.". . .

Thus in respect of the renewal clause in basketball which does not differ materially or significantly from Section 10(a) in the baseball Players Contract, the Courts construed the renewal clause as providing for an extension of the term of the contract only for the "renewal year"

without any option to exercise additional and successive renewals. (See also *Munchak Corporation* v. *Cunningham,* 457 F.2d 721, 724 (1972).) . . .

In this connection it is also pertinent to observe that the "no tampering rule" (which, in baseball, is contained in Major League Rule 3(g)), has its equivalent, in NBA basketball, in Section 35 of the NBA constitution. The prohibition there, however, applies to any player "who is *under contract* to any other member of the Association." (Emphasis supplied.) Thus, in the "reserve system" of NBA basketball, the player must have been under contract to be reserved; but in this case, the leagues argue that even if the contract be construed to have expired, the Player may be reserved.

In these circumstances I find that Section 10(a) falls short of reserving to a Club the right to renew a contract at the end of the renewal year. Accordingly, I find that Messersmith was not under contract when his renewal year came to an end.

We now turn to the Major League Rules, as to which it has already been stated that, by virtue of Section 9(a) of the Uniform Players Contract and Article XIII of the Basic Agreement, they are a part of the agreements of the parties if not inconsistent with the provisions of the Basic Agreement and the Players Contract.

The parties are in sharp conflict on this: The leagues claim that there is exclusive reservation of a player's services under Rule 4-A(a) regardless of the continued existence of any contractual relationship between the Club and the Player. . . . The Players Association, on the other hand, asserts that in the absence of a nexus or linkage of contract between the Player and the Club, there can be no exclusive reservation of the right to his future services.

In a manner of speaking, this conflict of positions reflects the difference between "status" and "contract" in identifying the rights and duties which persons owe to each other. Members of a family and citizens in a nation occupy a status which gives them rights and which imposes upon them duties which do not result from any formal consensual act in which they join. Obligations, in such cases, do not flow from a mutual coalescence of objectives and intentions with bargained benefits and detriments to one or the other, but from the status occupied in relation to the other person or institution. The classic ingredients of "contract," in such cases, are absent. The Major League Rules, said by the leagues to form the "core" (so-called) of the reserve system, existed long before contracts were negotiated by the leagues with the Players Association. With the advent of the Players Association and the bargaining-out of collective agreements, which included as part thereof the Players Contract and the Rules (to the extent that they were not inconsistent therewith), the relationship between players and their clubs may be described as having moved away from the "status" relationship which characterized earlier days towards a contract-type relationship. This is said with full knowledge of the fact that players, in the infancy of the organized sport, when they were not represented by an exclusive agent, signed players' contracts with their clubs.

An examination of the various rules which are components of the reserve system reveals inconsistency in identifying the situations in which they obtain. I shall not attempt an exhaustive survey of the variables in the provisions but will refer to a few which suggest that their application is not entirely divorced from the necessity that a player-club "contract" must be in existence. Thus, for example, Rule 2(a) provides for a club having "title" to not more than "forty (40) players contracts." This is the same number of "active and eligible players" which a club may place on its reserve lists "for an ensuing season" on or before November 20 of each year, pursuant to Rule 4-A(a). It strongly suggests that a player may not be placed on a reserve list unless he is under contract. A later provision in Rule 4-A(a) states that no player on any such list shall be eligible to play for or negotiate with any other club *"until his contract has been assigned or he has been released."* (Emphasis supplied.) Thus, a reading of Rule 2(a) and Rule 4-A(a) would seem to compel the conclusion that the contractual bond between player and club is a pre-condition for listing the player on the reserve list; and it is only *such* players who may be reserved until their contracts are assigned or released. The waiver provisions of Rule 8 (dealing with "unconditional release," surely an aspect of the reserve system) speak of the tender of an assignment of the Player's "contract" to all Major League clubs in accordance with waiver rules. Rule 9 provides that "A Club may assign to another club *an existing contract* with a player."....

These provisions and others in the very Rules which, allegedly, establish the kind of reservation of services for which the leagues contend, all subsume the existence of a *contractual relation.* The leagues would have it that it is only when there is a release or assignment that a contract must have been in existence; but even if there were no contract in existence (the players' contract having expired) a Club, by placing the name of a player on a list, can reserve exclusive rights to his services from year to year for an unstated and indefinite period in the future. I find this unpersuasive. It is like the claims of some nations that persons once its citizens, wherever they live and regardless of the passage of time, the swearing of to her allegiances and other circumstances, are still its own nationals and subject to the obligations that citizenship in the nation imposes. This "status" theory is incompatible with the doctrine or policy of freedom of contract in the economic and political society in which we live and of which the professional sport of baseball ("the national game") is a part....

Finally, on this point, it is evident that traditionally, the leagues have regarded the existence of a contract as a basis for the reservation of players. In Clubs' Exhibit No. 15 there is set forth the Cincinnati Peace Compact of the National and American Leagues, signed January 10, 1903 — probably the most important step in the evolution and development of the present Reserve System. In that document it is provided: "Second — *A reserve rule shall be recognized, by which each and every club may reserve players under contract,* and that a uniform contract for the use of each league shall be adopted." (Emphasis supplied.)

This emphasis on the existence of a contract for reservation of a player to be effective was perpetuated in the Major League Rules to some of which I have referred. It is even found in Rule 3(g) in which, however, it is referred to disjunctively along with acceptance of terms "or by which he was reserved." However, *even in Rule 3(g),* reading it analytically and construing it syntactically, one may reasonably reach the conclusion: — *no contract, no reservation.* . . .

Thus, I reach the conclusion that, absent a contractual connection between Messersmith and the Los Angles Club after September 28, 1975, the Club's action in reserving his services for the ensuing year by placing him on its reserve list was unavailable and ineffectual in prohibiting him from dealing with other clubs in the league and to prohibit such clubs from dealing with him.

In the case of McNally whom the Montreal Club had placed on its disqualified list, a similar conclusion has been reached.

I am not unmindful of the testimony of the Commissioner of Baseball and the Presidents of the National and American League given at the hearings as to the importance of maintaining the integrity of the Reserve System. It was represented to me that any decision of the Arbitration Panel sustaining the Messersmith and McNally grievances would have dire results, wreak great harm to the Reserve System and do serious damage to the sport of baseball.

Thus, for example, it was stated that a decision favoring these grievants would encourage many other players to elect to become free agents at the end of renewal years; that this would encourage clubs with the largest monetary resources to engage free agents, thus unsettling the competitive balance between clubs, so essential to the sport; that it would increase enormously the already high costs of training and seasoning young players to achieve the level of skills required in professional baseball and such investments would be sacrificed if they became free agents at the end of a renewal year; that driven by the compulsion to win, owners of franchises would over-extend themselves financially in improvident bidding for players in an economic climate in which, today, some clubs are strained, financially; that investors will be discouraged from putting money in franchises in which several of the star players on the club team will become free agents at the end of a renewal year and no continuing control over the players' services can be exercised; and that even the integrity of the sport may be placed in hazard under certain circumstances.

I do not purport to appraise these apprehensions. They are all based on speculations as to what may ensue. Some of the fears may be imaginary or exaggerated; but some may be reasonable, realistic and sound. After all, they were voiced by distinguished baseball officials with long experience in the sport and a background for judgment in such matters much superior to my own. However, as stated above, at length, it is not for the Panel (and especially the writer) to determine what, if anything, is good or bad about the reserve system. The Panel's sole duty is to interpret and apply the agreements and undertakings of the parties. . . .

In fact, on December 8, 1975, on my own initiative (but in my capacity as Chairman of the Arbitration Panel) I issued a statement to the parties in which I pointed out that, in a relatively short period of their relationship, due to a series of supervening circumstances, they had never accomplished full collective bargaining on their differences with respect to the historic reserve system that had long antedated that relationship; that these grievances in arbitration, important as they are, resulted from singular and special fact situations relating only to one aspect of a complicated system; that a composition and resolution by them of their larger differences as to the extent and impact of the reserve system was a matter of paramount importance; that it was more desirable that those differences (and the issues in the current litigation before the Panel) be resolved by the parties themselves, in collective bargaining, than by a quasi-judicial arbitration tribunal, such as the Panel, in adversary proceedings; and that I was concerned that a decision by this Arbitration Panel might even create new barriers to the accommodation of interests in full collective bargaining on the reserve system.

I pointed out to the parties that the fortuitous coincidence of the Panel's duty to decide these grievances and the fact that they were currently engaged in bargaining for a new contract, afforded them a unique opportunity to resolve their reserve system disputes as well as those involved in these grievances.

For whatever the reasons may have been, the parties, to the present, have not been successful in achieving the objectives I had in mind. The Panel is under a duty to "render a written decision as soon as practicable" following the conclusion of the hearings. However strong my conviction that the basic dispute should be determined by the parties, in collective bargaining rather than by an Arbitration Panel, that Panel could not justify any further delay, and the accompanying Award, accordingly, is being rendered. The parties are still in negotiations, however, and continue to have an opportunity to reach agreement on measures that will give assurance of a reserve system that will meet the needs of the clubs and protect them from the damage they fear this decision will cause, and, at the same time, meet the needs of the players. The clubs and the players have a mutual interest in the health and integrity of the sport and in its financial returns. With a will to do so, they are competent to fashion a reserve system to suit their requirements.

(The extensive footnotes in the opinion are omitted.)

NOTES _____

1. The baseball owners appealed the arbitration decision releasing Andy Messersmith and Dave McNally from their contractual obligations. Since a successful appeal of an arbitration decision is allowed only where there is a clear infidelity to the labor agreement, the court's refusal to reverse the decision was predictable. See *Kansas City Royals Baseball Corp.* v. *Major League Baseball Players Association* 532 F.2d 615 (8th Cir. 1976).

2. The foregoing decision involving Messersmith and McNally is also reported at 66 Labor Arbitrations and Dispute Settlements 101 (1975).

3. A comprehensive discussion of the foregoing arbitration decision and its appeal to the courts can be found in Berry and Gould, "A Long Deep Drive to Collective Bargaining: Of Players, Owners, Brawls and Strikes," 31 Case Western Law Review 685, 749–753 (1981).

In the Matter of Arbitration Between National Football League Players Association and National Football League Management Council, Luskin, Arb., May 14, 1980

On January 16, 1979, Edward R. Garvey, Executive Director of the NFLPA, wrote to Paul Sonnabend, Executive Director of the NFLMC, advising the Council that the NFLPA was filing a non-injury grievance against the council pursuant to Article VII of the Collective Bargaining Agreement. The letter stated that the grievance concerned the proper interpretation of the relevant sections of Article XV of the Collective Bargaining Agreement dealing with the re-signing of players who have played out their contracts and received a "qualifying offer" from their old team by February 1, ". . . but who have been forced to have re-signed with their old team under Section 17 for failure to generate an offer sheet from a new team" The letter further stated that it was the position of the

NFLPA that a player who was forced to re-sign with his old team under Section 17 and who signed a one-year contract under alternative (b) of that section, was free as of February 1 of the following year to pursue employment with any other team in the NFL without restriction. The letter described the existence of a "dispute" involving the interpretation or application of, or compliance with, provisions of the Agreement in view of the fact that representatives of the Management Council had taken the position that a player who has played for one year under alternative (b) of Section 17 is not free to pursue employment with other teams without restriction (as of February 1 of the following year), but was again made subject to all provisions of Article XV. . . .

The provisions of the Collective Bargaining Agreement cited by the parties as applicable in the instant dispute are hereinafter set forth as follows:. . .

ARTICLE XV
RIGHT OF FIRST REFUSAL/
COMPENSATION

Section 1. Applicability: Commencing with players who play out the options in their contracts or whose contracts otherwise expire (hereinafter referred to as "veteran free agents") in 1977, and with respect to veteran free agents through at least 1982, the following principles will apply:. . .

Section 17. Re-Signing: If a veteran free agent receives no offer to sign a contract or contracts with a new NFL club pursuant to this Article, and his old club advises him in writing by June 1 that it desires to resign him, the player may, at his option within 15 days, sign either (a) a contract or contracts with his old club at its last best written offer given on or before February 1 of that year, or (b) a one-year contract (with no option year) with his old club at 110% of the salary provided in his contract for the last preceding year (if the player has just played out the option year, the rate will be 120%). If the player's old club does not advise him in writing by June 1 that it desires to re-sign him, the player will be free on June 2 to negotiate and sign a contract or contracts with any NFL club, and any NFL club will be free to negotiate and sign a contract or contracts with such player, without any compensation between clubs or first refusal rights of any kind.

Section 18. Extreme Personal Hardship: In the event of alleged extreme personal hardship or an alleged violation of Article V, Section 1, of this Agreement, a veteran free agent may, within seven days after the February 1 expiration date of his contract, unless the condition arises after that date, file a non-injury grievance pursuant to Article VII of this Agreement. If the PCRC is unable to resolve the grievance, and should the outside arbitrator conclude that such extreme personal hardship objectively exists or that there has been a substantive violation of Article V, Section 1, then he may deny to the player's old club its right of first refusal. In the event a club's first refusal rights are denied under this Section because of extreme personal hardship, the club's last written contract offer to the player will constitute a "qualifying offer" for compensation pursuant to Section 11 of Article XV.

The Rozelle Rule was adopted in 1963. Prior to that change in the NFL constitution, a player who had played out his option was free to sign a contract with a different team. The Rozelle Rule in essence provided that any player whose contract had expired could sign a contract with a new club, but the new club was required to compensate the old club for the loss of that player's services. The two clubs could reach agreement, but in the absence of agreement, the amount of compensation would be determined by the Commissioner who could award compensation in the form of draft choices, money damages or the contract for the services of another player or players from the roster of the signing club. The Rozelle Rule continued in effect until it was suspended by the NFL in 1976 following the decision of the U.S. District Court in *Mackey* v. *National Football League.*

The first Collective Bargaining Agreement between the parties was negotiated in 1971 and was to expire by its terms in 1974. In 1972 the Players Association supported the institution of a suit in the U.S. District Court by its then President (Mackey). That suit (*Mackey* v. *National Football League*) charged that the Rozelle Rule constituted a *per se* violation of the anti-trust laws. . . .

In the latter part of December 1975, U.S. District Court Judge Larson issued his ruling in *Mackey* v. *National Football League.* He found that the Rozelle Rule was a *per se* violation of the anti-trust laws. In his opinion he stated that the freedom available to a player whose option year ends on May 1, "appears to be illusory." He referred to the fact that a club desiring the services of a player who had played out his option, could not sign that player without agreement in advance as to what compensation it would pay to the player's former club unless it was willing "to risk an unknown compensation award by Commissioner Rozelle. . . ." It was Judge Larson's opinion that in the four cases where Commissioner Rozelle had issued awards, the compensation had served to act "as an effective deterrent to clubs signing free agents without reaching a prior agreement on compensation with that player's former club." Judge Larson further found that because of the Rozelle Rule a player who had played out the option year of his contract and who became a free agent, was "not free to bargain with any other club.". . .

The Player's Association interpreted *Mackey* as completely supporting its prior position that it was not permissible to negotiate restrictions on player's movements. The NFL continued to insist that it needed some form of "system" for the long term continuation of professional football. It should be noted that in 1976, negotiations between the member clubs and individual players were conducted with the Rozelle Rule in a suspended state and with eligible players free to negotiate their player contracts without restrictions.

In March 1976, the NFLPA instituted a suit in the U.S. Federal Court, District of Minnesota. That suit was filed by Kermit Alexander who was then serving as President of the NFLPA. The suit was a class action by current and former NFL players against all NFL teams, asking for damages allegedly suffered as a result of the application (by the teams) of the Rozelle Rule. . . .

In October 1976, the Court of Appeals for the 8th Circuit issued its decision in *Mackey* v. *National Football League.* The Court rejected the lower court's finding that the Rozelle Rule was a *per se* violation of the anti-trust laws. It held that the Rozelle Rule was a violation of the anti-trust laws under the *"rule of reason test."* That decision rejected the lower court's holding that the reserve system was an impermissible subject of bargaining and, in fact, held that the reserve system was a mandatory subject for negotiations. It held that it was a labor exemption to the anti-trust laws for agreements reached as a result of *bona fide* bargaining. The court then concluded as follows:

> Our disposition of the antitrust issue does not mean that every restraint on competition for players' services would necessarily violate the antitrust laws. Also, since the Rozelle Rule, as implemened, concerns a mandatory subject of collective bargaining, any agreement as to inter-team compensation for free agents moving to other teams, reached through good faith collective bargaining, might very well be immune from antitrust liability under the nonstatutory labor exemption.
>
> It may be that some reasonable restrictions relating to player transfers are necessary for the successful operation of the NFL. The protection of mutual interests of both the players and the clubs may indeed require this.
>
> We encourage the parties to resolve this question through collective bargaining. The parties are far better situated to agreeably resolve what rules governing player transfers are best suited for their mutual interests than are the courts.

In *Smith* v. *Pro Football* the decision issued one month earlier by the District Court struck down the college draft. The decision, however, contained language which served to support the theory and concept of a "labor exemption."

Shortly after the Circuit Court of Appeals decision in *Mackey,* the parties engaged in an exchange of correspondence. Suggestions embodied in a letter from the NFLPA's Executive Director Garvey served to open the door to discussions concerning the development of a compensation plan that would prove to be acceptable to both parties. The Union indicated at that time that it could accept some form of restriction on player movement. The Garvey letter stated in part as follows:

> We have also suggested, as an alternative, that if there is a compensation plan, it be limited to the superstars. After all, you should be most concerned about the Bradshaw, Griese, Simpson, Kilmer type players, not the medium-range players. The union, on the other hand, has to be concerned primarily about raising the salaries and providing for protection of players earning between $15,000 and $75,000. The superstar takes care of himself. What then is wrong with saying that a player who is offered over $75,000 would be worth a draft choice?
>
> There are other solutions which we have suggested. My position is that you cannot unreasonably restrict player movement. The court and the Players Association in basketball accepted "first refusal." Maybe that, standing alone, would be a "reasonable" restriction. We are not inflexible.

Meetings were held shortly thereafter (November 1976) in New York, followed by meetings in December 1976, in Washington. There is evidence in the record that in Washington in December 1976, the Union's negotiators indicated that the Union might be willing to accept a system calling for compensation based upon salary levels that would cover a percentage of the top players, with the old club to retain a choice of either first refusal or compensation. That suggestion was conditioned, however, by a demand for the inclusion of a provision permitting the removal of a player from that system in instances where a contention of "racism" could be established or in instances where a player would be faced with "extreme personal hardship" if he was required to continue to play with a specific team. At a subsequent meeting in New York (December 28, 1976) there were discussions between the parties relating to specific forms of compensation. There was a suggestion that there be no right of first refusal nor compensation for an offer to a player that amounted to $40,000 or less. There were suggestions concerning the application of first refusal without compensation for offers falling within certain ranges, and various forms of compensation and rights of first refusal for offers of salaries in excess of $75,000.

In January, 1977, there were discussions between the parties in San Diego concerning the inclusion of arbitration procedures in non-injury cases. Management insisted that a precise limitation on remedies be established that would serve to preclude an outside arbitrator from declaring players to be free agents. Management indicated that it would insist on a provision of that nature in order to avoid an arbitration award which would have an impact similar to that generated by the baseball arbitration award of 1975 in the McNally-Messersmith decision. It would appear that there was agreement between the parties on that subject. . . .

The parties next met in New Orleans commencing on January 24, 1977. The Management Council's representatives again took the position that any agreement would have to include a "system" whereby a club could protect itself against the loss of its better players. . . .

In a meeting in Washington the parties agreed upon the non-injury arbitrators who would be named in the provision that subsequently appeared in the Agreement as Article VII, Section 6. The parties then met on February 14, 1977, in New York where they prepared a "first working draft." On February 16, 1977, a sliding scale of minimum salary levels (depending on the player's years of service) before restrictions on movement could become effective, was proposed. The parties reached a tentative agreement on those levels of salaries that would generate first refusal and those levels that would generate compensation. The Union negotiators insisted upon the inclusion of an "extreme personal hardship" provision, and tentative agreement was reached concerning a provision of that type. A number of negotiating sessions were held on February 22, 23 and 24, 1977, in Washington. Drafts were prepared, language was changed, agreements were reached, and a final draft was completed on February 28, 1977. The contract was signed on March 1, 1977.

The Agreement between the parties required a disposition of the *Alexander* class action. The parties appeared before District Court Judge Larson on March 4, 1977. Player representatives at that time requested that Judge Larson accept and retain jurisdiction over the Agreement and, in effect, to monitor the application of the controversial provisions of that Agreement, and most especially Article XV thereof. It would appear that Judge Larson expressed concern over that responsibility, but he did indicate at some point in time that he had "tentatively decided" to retain jurisdiction. At a later point in time Judge Larson expressed his regrets and indicated that he would not be in a position to retain jurisdiction. It was later contended by the Players Association that the failure of Judge Larson to accept the retention of jurisdiction led to the ultimate decision on the part of the Management Council to uniformly construe Article XV, Section 17, in a manner that led to the filing of the instant grievance.

The agreement was thereafter submitted to the players for ratification. Following the ratification of the Agreement a number of players intervened in the proceeding and filed objections to the proposed resolution of *Alexander*. The total class consisted of 5,700 persons. Eventually some twenty members of the class submitted objections. The settlement had been approved by the Union, by class representatives and class counsel, and by the NFL member clubs and the Management Council. After extensive hearings and after hearing objections to the proposed settlement, Judge Larson issued an order on July 27, 1977, approving the *Alexander* settlement. That settlement included the distribution of money damages in the amount of approximately $16,000,000 based upon a predetermined formula.

Judge Larson had found that the compensation/first refusal rule fundamentally revised the Rozelle Rule and had been established between the parties as a result of serious arms-length collective bargaining. He found that the new rule represented "a reasonable adjustment of player, club and league interests." Judge Larson's ruling encompassed forty-two specific findings with respect to "the modified player employment practices" in the Collective Bargaining Agreement. It included a review of Article XV. The Court made specific reference to the fact that Article XV did not grant complete free agent status to players. The court referred to the contentions advanced by the objectors to the effect that the compensation/first refusal rule would subject them "currently or in future years to collective bargaining limitations on their freedom of movement." The Court made specific reference to the requirement for compensation for talented veteran free agents and recognized the fact that although the new Collective Agreement was "less restrictive" than the Rozelle Rule, it was "more restrictive than an open market.". . .

The 8th Circuit affirmed Judge Larson's approval of the settlement in *Alexander* and it upheld the District Court's finding that the objectors' desire for complete unrestrained freedom of movement from club to club was not in the best interests of professional football, the owners, the players or the public that supported professional football. . . .

In May 1978, NFLPA Staff Counsel Berthelsen spoke with Karch, attorney for the Management Council, questioning a position adopted by the Los Angeles Rams when the Rams had informed a player (Tom Mack) that, although his Section 17 contract had expired on February 1, 1978, he could again go through the Article XV procedures. Karch responded by stating that he was "not surprised" since that was the position that all clubs had been advised they could take. Karch stated "that's the manner in which Article XV works, and we have so advised the Rams and all the clubs." There were discussions between Karch and Berthelsen concerning distinctions (if any) between contracts signed under Article XV, Section 17 (b) and those signed under Section 17(a). The evidence indicated that Berthelsen then informed Garvey of his conversation with Karch, and Garvey immediately called Rooney, who confirmed Karch's understanding that the clubs were interpreting Section 17 as a renewable option that was available to the teams. Garvey testified that Rooney responded that they (the clubs) had agreed to follow that principle at the Seattle owners' meeting in 1976 that had taken place before any preliminary understandings concerning the right of first refusal/compensation had been reached. Garvey testified in this proceeding that he had asked Rooney whether Rooney felt that he (Rooney) had a moral obligation to have disclosed that position in the subsequent hearings before Judge Larson at the time of the settlement of *Alexander*. Garvey testified that Rooney responded in the negative, after which Garvey expressed his outrage concerning that interpretation, "and I told him that I thought it was fraudulent conduct on their part."

Shortly thereafter and prior to the 8th Circuit Court of Appeals decision arising out of the settlement of *Alexander*, plaintiff class counsel Glennon suggested to the 8th Circuit that open issues existed as to the interpretation of the Bargaining Agreement that raised questions of good faith bargaining and fraud. Class counsel Glennon filed a motion for remand or, in the alternative, a stray of proceedings on appeal.

The 8th Circuit heard oral arguments concerning class counsel Glennon's contention that the improper interpretation of Section 17 of Article XV resulted in the establishment of a "perpetual option clause" that was more restrictive than the Rozelle Rule reserve clause that had formerly been in effect. He also charged bad faith collective bargaining, and he charged that a fraud had been committed upon the District Court. In its decision the 8th Circuit found the contentions advanced by class counsel to be "without merit." The 8th Circuit, in its decision, stated as follows:

> The only "new evidence" or "change in circumstances" is that the National Football League and its member clubs have interpreted the collective bargaining agreement in a manner different from that of the Players Association. This is precisely the kind of dispute to be resolved by arbitration and the normal channels of labor dispute resolution. Without deciding whether the plaintiff class followed the correct procedures in raising the issue, we hold that the District Court correctly refused to exercise supervisory jurisdiction over the collective bargaining agreement in this class action. The motion to remand or stay the appeal is denied.

Thereafter a motion was filed by class counsel Glennon before Judge Larson in the U. S. District Court to open the judgment pursuant to Rule 60(b). Affidavits were filed in support thereof charging bad faith and fraud. That motion was denied after Judge Larson indicated that he would neither re-open nor would he modify his earlier final judgment approving the *Alexander* settlement and the applicable provisions of the Collective Bargaining Agreement. He referred to the issue of "interpretation" as having been disposed of by the 8th Circuit's finding that differences in interpretation would constitute the kind of dispute to be resolved by arbitration. Judge Larson specifically referred to the Circuit Court of Appeals finding that the District Court (Judge Larson) had correctly refused to exercise supervisory jurisdiction over the Collective Bargaining Agreement "in this class action."

The Union offered testimony in support of its contention that the NFL had committed a fraud upon the Players Association when it had reached a secret agreement in Seattle to interpret any subsequent agreement relating to rights of compensation first refusal in a manner which would result in renewable options year after year. The Union contended that during all of the negotiation sessions that preceded the execution of the Agreement and during all of the Court proceedings before the District Court in *Alexander* and in the submission of briefs and in the oral arguments before the 8th Circuit Court of Appeals, Management Council representatives had never informed the Union negotiators nor had it informed the District Court or the 8th Circuit Court that it viewed Article XV, Section 17, as establishing a procedure whereby a renewable option existed for year after year, conditioned only by annual ten percent salary increases. The Union contended that clever deception or the act of deliberate fraud had resulted in permitting the NFL clubs to achieve an objective which they could not have achieved either in negotiations or in the proceeding before the District Court of Minnesota or the 8th Circuit Court of Appeals. The Union argued that the fraudulent procedure has proved to be effective for the NFL clubs for a period of three years and has resulted in the cynical destruction of the letter and spirit of the 1977 Collective Bargaining Agreement.

The Players Association argued that, if the parties had bargained a perpetually renewable option, the terms and conditions thereof would have been clearly spelled out. The Players Association argued that if Article XV, Section 17, is construed to provide for renewable options year after year, the provision is silent with respect to its length. Is it effective for five years or is it perpetual? The Union pointed to the absence of language concerning a salary scale of 130 percent the second time that Section 17 is exercised. The Union questioned the absence of language concerning bonuses or the applicability of performance bonuses where players change positions. The Union questioned the absence of language concerning option increases during periods of inflation and the effect upon players if a team moves from one city to another city. They pointed to the lack of language concerning procedures to be followed in non-football injuries and procedures to be followed where players are traded during succeeding option years.

The Players Association contended that the Union was informed of the Management's position with respect to its interpretation of Article XV, Section 17, only after Judge Larson had informed the parties that he had changed his mind and would not retain jurisdiction. The Union contended that, in view of the language of the Circuit

Court of Appeals in *Mackey* that restrictions must result from arms-length, bona fide collective bargaining, it could hardly be assumed that the Union would have reached agreement on a procedure that was more restrictive than the Rozelle Rule. The Union contended that if the parties had agreed to a renewable option, the Contract would have so stated. The Union contended that after a player goes through the entire procedure set forth in Article XV and completes a one-year contract with his old club pursuant to Section 17(b), that player is a free agent and is free to negotiate and sign with any team without restriction and without compensation to his former club.

The Players Association pointed to the fact that in the absence of contractual language that clearly provides a club with a perpetual option, a veteran free agent becomes free in every respect. The veteran free agent should be considered to be free to contract for his services with any other club without requiring compensation to his former club or without providing his former club with any right of first refusal. The Association pointed to a press release issued by the Management Council after the execution of the Agreement which described an "option playout" as the player for whom compensation exists. The Union argued that although that press release contained a "disclaimer," it was designed to explain the new Agreement for the news media.

The Players Association contended that if the Agreement was found to be ambiguous with respect to the status of players pursuant to Section 17(b), then and in that event the arbitrator would be empowered to issue an award finding that Article XV would have no application to players who had already played for one year under Section 17(b) and to direct the Management Council and the member clubs to "cease and desist" from any and all attempts to continue to apply the provisions of Article XV to those players.

The Union further contended that the arbitrator has the authority to issue an award finding that a fraud was committed upon the Players Association as a result of a conspiracy on the part of the NFL and that there was no meeting of the minds. The Union contended that, under those circumstances, the arbitrator would have the right and authority to issue an award finding that Article XV as it is currently being interpreted by the Management

Council cannot be considered to have contractual effect.

The Management Council contended that Article XV is clear and unambiguous and it serves to cover all players whose contracts in any way expire. The Management Council contended that the language of Article XV, Section 1, admits of no exception and there is no other provision of the Agreement which modifies Section 1 or otherwise creates a class of contracts removed from the provisions of Article XV. The Management Council contended that the language of Article XV, Section 17, cannot be read in a manner that would serve to permit a player to escape the first refusal/compensation provisions of Article XV by merely signing a contract under Section 17(b) at a ten percent increase in pay and thereafter wait for one year until that contract "expires." The Management Council contended that there is no language appearing in Section 17 that removes that section from the scope of Section 1.

The Management Council contended that the arbitrator is completely without authority to alter, modify or amend the clear and unambiguous language of Article XV in a manner which would result in the issuance of an award that would in effect sustain the Union's position in this case. The Management Council contended that in those instances where the Agreement serves to provide a player with "total freedom," it expressly provides for that eventuality. The Management Council pointed to the situations involving a player who does not receive a sufficient qualifying offer or a timely notice, as examples of instances whereby a player will achieve free agent status (no right of first refusal or compensation) in accordance with the precise language appearing in Article XV of the Collective Bargaining Agreement. The Management Council pointed to an additional exception in providing for circumstances under which a club can lose the right of first refusal pursuant to the language of Article XV, Section 18 (Extreme Personal Hardship — Race Discrimination). The Management Council contended that the history of the collective bargaining that preceded the execution of the Agreement indicated conclusively that the negotiators understood, discussed and agreed to the inclusion of the language that appears in Article XV of the current Agreement, and they knew and understood that Article XV, Section 17(b), would be applied in exactly the

manner in which the Council contends it was applied in the Dutton case.

Article VII provides for the filing of grievances arising out of a dispute "involving the interpretation or application of . . . provisions of this Agreement." The article permits the initiation of a grievance by a player, a club, the Management Council "or the NFLPA. . . ." In the instant case, the dispute that arose between the parties was significant in nature and involved a fundamental question that raised an arbitrable issue. . . .

The contention advanced by the NFLPA that the Management Council illegally conspired among themselves to establish a uniform and consistent interpretation of the provisions of Article XV in order to inhibit and prevent the submission of good faith offers to veteran free agents, cannot be sustained on the basis of the evidence in this record. The NFLPA argued that the "conspiracy" had its inception when Management Council representatives (in a meeting in Seattle in January 1977) agreed to a uniform interpretation of any subsequent agreement in a manner that would result in creating a system of perpetual options that would effectively prevent a veteran free agent from achieving total and complete freedom and the right to contract for his services without any restrictions including right of first refusal or compensation. It was the NFLPA's contention that the Management Council negotiators thereafter bargained in bad faith when it failed to disclose to the NFLPA negotiators that the Management Council would uniformly interpret the language of Article XV, Section 17, as providing the Management Council members with permanent options for the services of players who had completed their contracts and had become veteran free agents. The NFLPA also contended that the Management Council had committed a fraud upon the Court when it failed to disclose its position in the settlement proceedings before Judge Larson in *Alexander* and in the subsequent arguments advanced by the Management Council before the 8th Circuit Court of Appeals. . . .

During the entire period of the series of negotiating meetings that began with the New Orleans meetings in January 1977, and continued thereafter in Washington and New York, the Management Council negotiators did not state that they would construe the ultimately agreed-upon language in Article XV, Section 17, in a manner which would permit a team to exercise continuing options in accordance with the procedures set forth therein. The NFLPA did not, at any time, state to the Management Council negotiators that it would interpret the agreed-upon language in a manner which would provide a veteran free agent with complete and total freedom to contract with another team without being restricted by a right of first refusal or compensation in instances where a player had gone through the Section 17(b) procedures for a second time.

Both parties were represented by experienced, able and competent negotiators. The only conclusion that can be drawn is that both parties reached their own conclusions concerning the meaning of the language in question. The fact that neither party spelled out to each other the precise manner in which they would interpret the language that they agreed upon in Article XV, Section 17, would not mean that there was "no meeting of the minds."

The evidence would conclusively indicate that there was a meeting of the minds in almost every major respect. The parties did agree upon a system. They reached agreements based upon the views expressed by the 8th Circuit Court of Appeals in *Mackey*, when the Court referred to the fact that a reserve system was a mandatory subject for negotiations and that there was the need for reasonable restrictions relating to player transfers as "necessary for the successful operation of the NFL." The Court then proceeded to "encourage" the parties to resolve that question through collective bargaining since the parties were far better situated to agreeably resolve "what rules governing players' transfers are best suited for their mutual interests than are the courts." . . .

A difference of opinion between the parties to an agreement concerning the appropriate interpretation to be placed upon those words or provisions does not result in invalidating an Agreement or making that Agreement unenforcible. Ambiguities appearing in agreements are the subject of resolution by courts. Arbitrators are regularly concerned with the necessity for interpreting ambiguous langue where that language is susceptible of construction.

The parties to this Agreement had been negotiating under different circumstances and in different bargaining climates for approximately three years. They were at all times well aware of the agreements reached between the parties in baseball and basketball, and they were at all times aware of the arbitration awards in baseball. They were aware of the decisions of the Courts in the lawsuits that were filed that challenged the legality of the football draft, the standard players contract, the Rozelle Rule, and other forms of restrictions alleged to constitute violations of the anti-trust laws. Both parties were mindful of the need for meaningful movement away from previously fixed and rigid positions. The NFLPA demanded, negotiated and received substantial benefits upon the conclusion of the negotiations and the settlement of the pending litigation. There is evidence in this record that the settlement of the class action in *Alexander* involved the payment of approximately $16,000,000 by the NFL to the members of the class. The obligations assumed by the NFL for retroactive pension benefits and other forms of compensation involved costs to the NFL of in excess of $100,000,000. The member clubs obtained a "system" which they believed that they had to have and could live with. In return, the NFLPA obtained a contractual procedure whereby, under the established system, any player completing his contract would have the right to "test the market" and determine what his services might be worth to other clubs that would be willing to negotiate with that player. The fact that the system may not have worked as effectively as the NFLPA may have expected, would not necessarily indicate the existence of a conspiracy by the teams to engage in concerted action to refuse to make "offers" and to thereby nullify the system.

The primary issue in this proceeding must, therefore, turn on the interpretation to be placed upon the contractual language appearing in the applicable provisions of Article XV.

Article XV establishes certain precise procedures that must be followed by a team in order to retain its right of first refusal/compensation. A failure to follow those procedures could result in permitting a player to sign a contract with a new team without providing his former team with right of first refusal or compensation. In each instance, however, where that occurs, controlling contractual language is clear, precise and unambiguous. Under Article XV, Section 18 (Extreme Personal Hardship), the "outside arbitrator," under an established set of facts and circumstances, could find that there had been a substantive violation of

Article V, Section 1, or the existence of extreme personal hardship, in which event the arbitrator could deny to the player's old club its "right of first refusal." The parties have explicitly agreed that in the event first refusal rights are denied (under Section 18) because of extreme personal hardship, the club's last written contract offered to the player constitutes a "qualifying offer" for compensation pursuant to Article XV, Section 11. It should be noted that the last sentence of Article XV, Section 17 (Re-signing), permits a player to be free to negotiate and sign a contract or contracts with any NFL club without first refusal rights or compensation between clubs under circumstances where a player's old club does not advise him in writing by June 1st that it desires to re-sign him. That procedure appears in the Agreement immediately after that portion of Section 17(b) upon which the Union relies when it contends that a player becomes a free agent with a right to contract with any other team in the NFL without any provision for his old team to receive compensation or to have a right of first refusal. The language of Section 17 (b) does not serve to support the Union's contention in this case. The fact that provision is made for a salary of 110 percent of the salary provided in the last preceding year, or 120 percent if the player has played out the option year, does not necessarily mean that a team's contractual right to first refusal/compensation has ended at that point in time.

Article XV, Section 1 (Applicability), clearly and unambiguously concerns itself with players "who play out the options in their contracts or whose contracts otherwise expire . . . and with respect to veteran free agents through at least 1982 . . ." All of the sections of Article XV apply to those persons. The various sections establish precise procedures that are to be followed with respect to a team's right to exercise rights of first refusal or to receive compensation for the loss of the services of a veteran free agent based upon the timetables, the procedures and the salaries. Section 17 serves to define the rights and obligations of a veteran free agent who receives no offer to sign a contract with a different NFL club (pursuant to Article XV) and he is advised by his old club that the old club desires to resign him. The player has an option which he may exercise within fifteen days thereafter to sign a contract or contracts with his old club at its last best written offer or to sign a one-year contract (with no option year) with his old club at 110 percent of the salary provided in his contract for the last preceding year. There then follows a parenthetical provision which increases the salary to 120 percent if the player has just played out the option year. Nowhere within the language of Section 17(b) are there words or phrases which could be interpreted in a manner which places a limitation upon the option rights of a player's old club to one option or two options following the expiration of his contract or contracts.

It could very well be argued that the absence of language in Section 17 that specifically establishes a limitation upon the team's option rights or the absence of language that would provide annual options that a team may exercise by paying a player an additional ten percent each year that the option is exercised would create the existence of an ambiguity. Section 17(b) may not be a model of clarity, but the fact remains that Article XV, Section 1, becomes completely controlling since the general applicability of that provision has neither been modified nor amended by the language of Section 17(b).

In instances where the parties made provision for total free agent status, the contractual language explicitly provides for a team's loss of first refusal or compensaton rights. The last sentence of Article XV, Section 17, illustrates the procedures adopted by the parties throughout Article XV. In an instance where a team may lose its right of first refusal and retain its compensation rights, the language of Article XV, Section 18, is illustrative of that understanding. The arbitrator cannot infer from the absence of affirmative or negative language that the parties reached an agreement or understanding that would serve to confer total free agent status to a veteran player who had completed a year of service pursuant to a Section 17(b) contract. . . .

This arbitrator is fully aware of the extent of the authority vested in the arbitrator pursuant to the language appearing in Article V, Section 7. He is fully aware of the limitations thereof. He has weighed the massive amount of evidence submitted by the parties in this proceeding. In preparing the opinion and award in this case, he has been mindful of the fact that he does not have the jurisdiction or the authority "to add to, subtract from, or alter in any way the provisions of this agreement or any other applicable document. . . ."

The arbitrator has heretofore found that the NFLPA had the contractual right to file a grievance. He has found that the grievance filed on January 16, 1979, raised an arbitrable issue. . . .

The arbitrator has found that the Management Council did not engage in a conspiracy. It did not commit illegal acts nor did it perpetrate a fraud upon the NFLPA by the manner in which the teams uniformly interpreted Article XV, Sections 1 and 17. The arbitrator further found that the Management Council could not be charged with the commission of fraudulent acts when it affirmatively failed to specifically state to the NFLPA representatives (or to the Courts) that it had and it would construe Article XV, Section 17, in a manner which would provide a team with continuing options for the services of its players.

The arbitrator has found that the issues would have to turn upon the interpretation and application of the language appearing in Article XV, Sections 1 and 17 thereof. The arbitrator has further found that the controlling language in Article XV, Section 1, and the controlling language in Article XV, Section 17(b), are not ambiguous and the language is susceptible of interpretation. He has further found that the language of Article XV, Section 1, and Article XV, Section 17(b), does not lend itself to the construction advocated by the NFLPA. The arbitrator has further found that a team is not precluded from continuing to exercise the options available to a team after a veteran free agent has re-signed with his old team under Section 17 and thereafter re-signed with his old team under Section 17(b) under circumstances where the team has otherwise complied with the procedural steps set forth in the applicable portions of Article XV. . . .

In the Matter of Arbitration Between National Basketball Association (Indiana Pacers) and National Basketball Players Association (Darrell Elston), Seitz, Arbitrator, July 15, 1977

At issue was whether the impartial arbitrator had the authority to review the decision of a grievance panel.

Article XV of the Collective Bargaining Agreement outlines a comprehensive system of procedures for the settlement of disputes arising under the agreement or any player contracts. If a grievance is not resolved 30 days after its filing, the "Grievance shall . . . be referred to a Grievance Panel" unless the parties agree to submit the matter directly to the impartial arbitrator (Section 2[c] [1]). The NBA and the Players Association appoint an equal number of representatives to the panel and are also allowed two votes of their own at panel meetings. Section 2 (c) (4) declares that a resolution by majority vote or mutual agreement "shall constitute full, final and complete disposition of the Grievance, and shall be binding upon the player(s) and team(s) involved and the parties to this Agreement."

Elston had been placed on waivers by the Indiana Pacers while he was injured. The Pacers claimed that they did not release Elston for injury-related reasons. The association claimed that he was entitled to compensation for the balance of the year under his player contract.

The grievance panel heard all of the arguments, including the team's claim that Elston's grievance was not timely filed, and determined that the Pacers should pay Elston an additional $9,500.

Both parties to a dispute are represented on a grievance panel. The system aims for the settlement of disputes by mutual agreement. If the panel must resolve a dispute, its decision is final and binding. Seitz found that the CBA does not endow the arbitrator with the power to review a "full, final and complete disposition of (a) Grievance" by the grievance panel. He denied the Pacers' application for him to take jurisdiction and vacate the panel's decision and award

In the Matter of Arbitration Between National Basketball Association and National Basketball Players Association, Seitz, Arbitrator, Re: All-Star Game (Part I), (May 9, 1974)

On April 26, 1974, the NBA demanded immediate arbitration of the dispute involving alleged present and threatened violations of the 1972 Collective Bargaining Agreement by the NBA Players Association in reference to the proposed All-Star Game scheduled for May 18, 1974 in Providence, Rhode Island. Since both parties wanted a prompt decision, the award was issued two days after the hearing without the opinion (see Part II).

The Players Association had been planning and organizing the All-Star Game. Seitz found that provisions of the Uniform Player Contract, in the absence of written consent of the club, prohibit a player from participating in an All-Star Game. He found that the NBA did have standing to apply for and be granted the equitable relief of an injunction to prevent the Players Association from violating the Collective Bargaining Agreement.

The organization and planning of the All-Star Game by the Players Association and the participation or playing at the game by the players under Uniform Player Contracts without the written consent of their clubs constituted a violation and threatened violation of the Collective Agreement.

The Players Association was enjoined from particpating in the planning, organization, and administration of the game. All players under Uniform Player Contracts who did not have their club's written consent were enjoined from participating. Finally, the Players Association was enjoined from violating the agreements by failing to use its best efforts to prevent such players from playing or participating in the All-Star Game.

In the Matter of Arbitration Between National Basketball Association and National Basketball Players Association, Seitz, Arbitrator, Re: All-Star Game (Part II), May 15, 1974

The NBA claimed that it had the right to prevent the Players Association from planning and NBA players from participating in the 1974 ABA–NBA All-Star Game. At issue was whether the Uniform Player Contract and the Collective Agreement of November 15, 1972, actually conferred upon the NBA and the clubs the rights they asserted, and if so, whether they had relinquished those rights by their conduct or inaction.

For Seitz, the arbitrator, the meaning of the relevant provisions was clear. In paragraphs 5 and 17 of the Uniform Player Contract, players agreed not to play in exhibition games or for any other organization during the term of their contracts without the written consent of their clubs. In Article XV, section 2 of the Collective Bargaining Agreement, the Players Association agreed not to induce the breach or threat of breach of any contract between a player and the club.

According to the Players Association, the NBA was not entitled to relief because it had waived its rights, was estopped from seeking enforcement, and was barred by laches. Two similar All-Star Games were planned and played in 1971 and 1972. The association argued that the NBA had waived its rights to forbid players from playing in the 1974 game without club consent by not having exhausted legal remedies in 1971 and 1972. The NBA had merely issued protests and threats. It did not even take steps to collect the $3,000 in fines that Commissioner Kennedy imposed after the 1972 All-Star Game. Seitz disagreed. The self-restraint exercised in the NBA's pursuit of remedies and relief in 1971 and 1972 did not constitute a waiver of its contractual rights.

Seitz also found no merit in the estoppel or laches arguments. The NBA had never taken a position that such a game was permitted without written consent. And the 1974 game was the first game scheduled since the CBA of November 1972.

The Players Association argued that the NBA's action represented discriminatory enforcement of the CBA, since players have played in "hundreds" of summer league and benefit games without club consent and without club objection. Seitz, however, found several circumstances to support the NBA's view that the All-Star Game was in a different category and deserved different treatment. For example, (1) all proceeds from the other games went to designated charities, while part of the TV proceeds from the 1971, 1972, and proposed 1974 All-Star Games was to be distributed among player pension funds and players; (2) none of the unprotested games involved league confrontations; and (3) although the NBA had a $27-million, three-year contract with CBS, the TV arrangements for the 1974 All-Star Game were made with a rival network, which, the NBA claimed, would severely damage its business relations with television networks.

The Players Association also argued that an injunction should not issue because of the NBA's failure to show irreparable injury with inadequate remedy at law. But, an unusual provision in the Uniform Player Contract "covered the necessary bases." In paragraph 9, players agree that the loss of their services cannot be adequately compensated for in money damages and that a breach by a player will cause irreparable damage to the club. The provision also grants the club "the right to obtain from any court or arbitrator having jurisdiction, such equitable relief as may be appropriate, including a decree enjoining the player" from playing for any other person, firm, corporation or organization during the term of the contract. The parties had conferred upon the arbitrator the equitable powers necessary to enjoin the Players Association from planning and the NBA players from playing in the 1974 ABA–NBA All-Star Game.

In the Matter of Arbitration Between National Basketball Association and National Basketball Players Association, Seitz, Arbitrator Re: All-Star Game Break, April 4, 1977

Article XI, section 3 of the April 29, 1976, CBA states that "Players not invited to participate in the NBA All-Star Game shall have three days off during the All-Star Game break." In their grievance, the Players Association claimed that the Kansas City, Cleveland, Chicago, and Seattle clubs had violated this provision by scheduling practices during the three-day break for the February 13, 1977, All-Star Game.

The Cleveland club thought the grievance was "trivial" and "nitpicking." An arbitration hearing over a thing of such "microscopic magnitude," Cleveland argued, would tarnish the public image of the Players Association, the players, and the game of basketball. Seitz found the provision unambiguous and mandatory in form. The NBA and Players Association had considered it of sufficient magnitude to include it in the CBA. All of the other NBA clubs complied with the rule. Thus, Seitz was obliged to give the provision full force and effect. He was not authorized to pick and choose, to selectively rule on only "important" provisions.

The NBA argued that none of the clubs forced their players to practice. There were no threats of discipline. Those who participated did so voluntarily. Although no penalties were threatened, Seitz could not buy this justification argument for three reasons. First, the participation by the players was not necessarily voluntary. Seitz spoke of the disparity of power in the club-player relationship. Fearful of the risks involved, a player might be wary of challenging the perceived desires of the club. Second, Kansas City, Cleveland, Chicago, and Seattle stood to benefit by an advantage (extra practice) which other clubs, complying with the provision, did not enjoy. And third, no player has standing to waive any benefits or sacrifice any right provided in the CBA (see Article I, Section 3). Acceptance of the NBA's argument would open the door to an assertion that a player could waive any benefit or right stipulated in the CBA.

Seitz sustained the grievance, declaring that the clubs had violated the CBA. He declined, however, to award damages or to impose the fines ($10,000) which the Players Association sought. This was the first season in which the provision was operative. Also, players who practiced suffered no monetary loss or damage. Seitz felt that an arbitrator might have the authority to impose such fines only if a club, player, the NBA, or the Players Association repeatedly and deliberately violated the CBA.

NOTE _____

1. The foregoing cases are examples of arbitration imposed by terms of a collective bargaining agreement. Of less frequency, but of importance, are instances where

arbitration is agreed to in an individual contract. Courts normally enforce such provisions and do not permit the arbitration to be avoided by premature access to litigation.

For example, in *Erving* v. *Virginia Squires Basketball Club*, 468 F. 2d 1064 (2d Cir. 1972), Julius Erving signed a contract with the Virginia Squires of the American Basketball Association to play exclusively for the Squires for four years commencing October 1, 1971 for five hundred thousand dollars. After playing for the Squires for a season, Erving signed a contract to play for the Atlanta Hawks for over one and one-half million dollars. Erving brought suit against the Squires to have his contract set aside for fraud. Erving's contract, however, contained a provision that all disputes between the parties be settled by an arbitrator, and the District Court granted an injunction to the Squires preventing Erving from playing with any team other than the Squires pending the determination of the arbitration. The Circuit Court affirmed.

The court held that the arbitration clause did not lack mutuality and that the Squires had not waived this provision. The court rejected Erving's contention that the District Court had no power to direct the substitution of a neutral· arbitrator for the Commissioner of the ABA, who was disqualified because of the commissioner's association with a law firm which represented the Squires. Even though the arbitration provision provided that the Commissioner would act as arbitrator, the court held that, where disqualification occurred, a substitute should be selected.

The court also held that under the Federal Arbitration Act the issue of whether Erving was defrauded was for the arbitrator to decide. The Court rejected Erving's argument that the disputed contract was not a contract evidencing a transaction arising out of interstate commerce. The Court held that the Federal Arbitration Act applied to personal service contracts of any form of interstate exhibition other than baseball. It also rejected Erving's argument that basketball came under the Act's exclusionary clause, holding that these exceptions were limited to the transportation industry.

2. In *Livingston* v. *Shreveport-Texas League Baseball Corp.*, 128 F.Supp. 181, (W.D. La. 1955), a baseball manager sought contract damages from defendant baseball club which allegedly terminated his employment without cause. After unsuccessfully filing a claim with the league president, the plaintiff appealed to the President of the National Association pursuant to an official grievance rule. The Association refused to act. In sustaining defendant's motion to dismiss, the court held that the National Association had jurisdiction and that the manager's contract calling for arbitration by the National Association in the event of a dispute was binding.

In collective bargaining, an agreement is reached that attempts to provide for the best interests of management and of the majority of union members. In professional sports, more so than in the conventional industrial situation, individual employees may seek additional concessions. The

determination of what can be added to a player's contract, where more than the interests of the single player and his club are involved, becomes a complex inquiry.

5.40 Unresolved Issues Facing Sports Labor Unions

Sports labor unions are unique in that their membership experiences a 50 percent turnover every two to three years. In some sports, the membership shifts daily during the season as players are on and off the major league team rosters. Some members of the union earn from $20,000 to $40,000. Others earn $2 million. Some members have great bargaining leverage in negotiating the individual parts of their contracts; others have little. These dichotomies present formidable challenges to the sports union leadership. As can be seen in the first set of cases, tensions between a player's individual interest (as evidenced by the contract that is negotiated) and the union's perceived collective interest at times collide. The union finds itself contesting provisions in the individual contract. Or, even if that does not occur, and the union comes to the aid of the player in supporting the contract entered, the central question is still to what extent the union has bargained away the individual player's ability to negotiate a better deal.

The second area addressed, and one of growing sensitivity, is unauthorized and arguably illegal drug use by players. This issue has had to be addressed at all levels of professional and amateur sports, as stories of widespread use surface. The use may be one that is perceived necessary to attain greater strength, the better to compete. Or the use may be recreational, to fill in the long, boring hours on the road or to respond to the pressures of being a celebrity in a high-pressure business. Although reluctant to do so at first, sports unions have become involved in attempting to address the problems their members face. Both the NBA and Major League Baseball have forged agreements between management and the union. However, as some of the arbitration decisions reveal, the truce is an uneasy one, and there are questions as to what authority rests with the commissioner.

5.41 Individual versus Collective Interests

In the Matter of Arbitration Between Major Leagues of Professional Baseball Clubs (Atlanta Braves) and Major League Baseball Players Association (Alvin Moore), Dec. No. 32, Grievance No. 77–18, Porter, Impartial Arbitrator, September 7, 1977. Re: Moore

On April 1, 1977, a contract was entered into by the Atlanta Braves and Alvin E. Moore, which contained the following special covenant:

> The Atlanta Club and player Alvin Earl Moore agree that should player Moore not be satisfied with his playing time by June 15, 1977, that the Atlanta Club will initiate a trade that would not be consumated (sic) without the prior written consent of Alvin Moore. Notification of player Alvin Moore's dissatisfaction should be submitted in writing to the Atlanta Club prior to June 15, 1977.
>
> Should a trade not be consumated (sic) by the end of the 1977 championship baseball season Alvin Moore will become a free agent if he so desires.
>
> Should player Alvin Moore be satisfied with his playing time by June 15, 1977, this covenant of this contract will be declared null and void with all other aspects of this contract being in full force according to major league rules and the basic agreement.

On April 28, 1977, National League President Charles S. Feeney approved the contract but disapproved the special covenant in a letter to General Manager Bill Lucas of the Braves. The text of President Feeney's letter is as follows:

> The Special Covenants contained in Alvin Moore's contract is disapproved because it contains provisions inconsistent with the Reserve System Article of the new Basic Agreement.
>
> Please be sure that Player Moore receives a copy of this letter.

The present grievance was filed on June 7, 1977,

challenging the propriety of President Feeney's action in disapproving the covenant and requesting that the covenant "immediately be reinstated."

The Association's position is grounded in the recognition article, Article II of the Basic Agreement which provides:

> Article II — Recognition
>
> The Clubs recognize the Association as the sole and exclusive collective bargaining agent for all Major League Players, and individuals who may become Major League Players during the term of this Agreement, with regard to all terms and conditions of employment except (1) individual salaries over and above the minimum requirements established by this Agreement and (2) Special Covenants to be included in individual Uniform Player's Contracts, *which actually or potentially provide additional benefits to the Player*. (Emphasis added)

The Association argues that the special covenant in question clearly provides "actual or potential benefits" to player Moore and, hence, is a permissible subject for negotiation and agreement between Moore and his Club. . . .

According to the Association, there are only three valid reasons for a League President to disapprove a special covenant. He may do so: (1) if the covenant does not meet the test of Article II in that it does not "actually or potentially provide additional benefits to the Player"; (2) if the covenant violates an applicable law or is specifically prohibited by a Major League rule which is not inconsistent with the Basic Agreement, e.g., if the covenant provides for the giving of a bonus for playing, pitching or batting skill or a bonus contingent on the Club's standing, types of bonuses specifically prohibited by Major League Rule 3[a]; or (3) if the covenant purports to bind some third party whom the Club and the Player have no authority to bind (e.g. a covenant stating that, regardless of what a Player does on the field, an Umpire cannot eject him from a game or the League President or the Commissioner cannot discipline him). . . .

The Clubs reply that the Moore covenant strikes at the very heart of the reserve system which the parties negotiated following the Arbitration Panel's Decision No. 29, the so-called "Messersmith-McNally" case. In the wake of the Messersmith-McNally case, all players were theoretically free to play out their contracts and become free agents after an additional renewal year. Confronted by the impending collapse of the reserve system, the Clubs observe, the parties, for the first time, jointly negotiated a new reserve system and incorporated the new system in Article XVII of the 1976–1979 Basic Agreement. In the Clubs' view, Article II of the Basic Agreement does not provide authority for an individual Club and Player to negotiate what, in their opinion, is an entirely new reserve system, merely because such a system would provide a benefit to the Player. . . .

The Clubs concede that, in practice, the League Presidents have approved particular covenants which differ from and hence are arguably "inconsistent" with the provisions of the Basic Agreement. In its view, however, the inconsistencies in these approved covenants involved interests of the individual Clubs and Player, alone — e.g., covenants guaranteeing a player's salary for one or more years, covenants waiving a Club's rights regarding commercial endorsements, medical examinations, etc. They did not involve covenants, such as the Moore covenant, wherein the club and the Player sought to waive the interests of others — in this case the 25 other Clubs' interest in maintaining the kind of competitive balance among the various Clubs which the Reserve System of Article XVII was and is designed to provide.

The Moore covenant is said by the Clubs to contravene the scheme of Article XVII in three main respects. First, it grants to Moore, who presently has less than one year of Major League service, a conditional right to demand a trade, should he "not be satisfied with his playing time by June 15, 1977.". . .

Second, if a trade is not consummated by the end of the 1977 season, the Moore covenant renders Moore eligible to become a free agent, if he so desires, despite the fact that he will then have only a little more than a year's Major League service. . . .

Third, the Moore covenant does not expressly make him subject to the re-entry procedure, with its quota and compensation provisions. Under Article XVII, C, players who become free agents "pursuant to Section B" of Article XVII are subject to a negotiation rights selection procedure and a contracting procedure which provide among other things. . . .

The objective of this re-entry procedure, the Clubs contend, is to provide for an even and equitable distribution of players among all the Clubs and prevent a few of the richer Clubs from buying up a disproportionate share of the available free agent talent. To permit the Atlanta Club and Player Moore to by-pass the re-entry procedure would defeat this objective and allow the Atlanta Club to waive the rights which the other 25 Clubs have in maintaining the competitive balance which the re-entry procedure is designed to foster, the Clubs conclude. They ask, accordingly, that League President Feeney's disapproval of the Moore covenant be sustained by the Panel.

In the Chairman's judgment, both parties have advanced sound positions in support of their respective claims, but each has pushed his position to an unsound extreme. For reasons to be given more fully below, the Chairman is convinced the Moore covenant can be interpreted in a way which does not impinge upon the legitimate interests of the other Clubs and could and should have been approved on that basis. No reason appears why the Atlanta Club may not accord to Moore conditional rights to demand a trade and to become a free agent under Article XVII, B(2), despite the fact that he does not have the requisite years of Major League service to claim these rights unilaterally. The 5- and 6-year service requirements for Players seeking to exercise such rights unilaterally under Article XVII, D and B(2), respectively, are for the individual Club's benefit; and no persuasive evidence or argument has been presented to show why the benefit of long-term title and reservation rights to Moore's contract may not be waived by his club. But if Atlanta may waive the length of service requirements designed for its benefit, it may not waive the reentry procedure designed for the benefit of all 26 Clubs. Since the Moore covenant does not spell out the details of his free agency but simply states that he "will become a free agent if he so desires" upon the fulfillment of certain preconditions, and since the covenent is an integral part of a "Player Contract(s) Executed on or after August 9, 1976," it is reasonable to interpret the free agency as one arising under the terms of Article XVII, B(2) which governs the reemployment of Players who become free agents under contracts executed on and after the latter date. . . .

Negotiations between individual Clubs and Players are not, however, conducted in a vacuum.

To the contrary, and at the risk of belaboring the obvious, individual Player-Club negotiations are conducted not only within the framework of applicable law but within the framework of organized professional baseball and the attendant rules, agreements and regulations by which the sport or industry is governed and by which the Association on behalf of the Players and the Clubs comprising the two Major Leagues have agreed to be bound. Within the latter framework are innumerable matters affecting the interests and rights of all the Clubs and Players, such as the number of Player contracts to which each Club may have title and reservation rights, the number of Players each Club may retain on its active roster, the length of the intra or interleague trading periods, etc. Variations in any one of these provisions might give a Player "additional benefits" but are beyond the Club's power to make. Assuming, for argument's sake, that the 26 Clubs and the Association might agree to permit individual Clubs and Players to enter into Special Covenants varying these collective interests or rights, the Chairman believes stronger and more explicit language than Article II's bare "additional benefit" language is necessary to support the conclusion that such a result was intended.

To the extent the Association seeks to push its "additional benefit" argument to the point where the Moore covenant is to be interpreted as exempting Moore from the free agent quota system and other aspects of the reentry procedure designed to protect the interests of all 26 Clubs, the Chairman believes it presses its argument too far. . . .

The foregoing discussion foreshadows the Chairman's views of the Clubs' position in this matter, and no purpose would be served by repeating the discussion point by point. The Chairman has sustained the Clubs' basic argument that the "additional benefits" provisions of Article II does not authorize the Atlanta Club and Player Moore to by-pass the reentry procedure of Article XVII, since the latter procedure and its related quota provisions protect the interests of all 26 Clubs and cannot be waived by the Atlanta Club in the circumstances of this case. On the other hand, the Chairman has rejected the Clubs' claim that the Moore covenant is deficient because it contains a waiver of the length-of-service requirements which must be met before a Player has a unilateral right to

demand a trade under Article XVII, D or to elect free agency under Article XVII, B(2). The right to have title to and reserve Moore's contract for the number of years specified in Sections B(2) and (D) is a right of the Atlanta Club and may be waived by it as an additional benefit to Moore under Article II. This is the type of inconsistency with the Basic Agreement which is permissible because it bestows upon Moore a benefit which the Atanta Club may grant with damage to no one's interest but its own. . . .

In conclusion, it should be noted that nothing in this opinion is to be interpreted as expressing a view one way or another upon the merits of Moore's further claim that he was not satisfied with his playing time as of June 15, 1977. That issue is not before the Panel in this proceeding. . . .

In the Matter of Arbitration Between Major Leagues of Professional Baseball Clubs and Major League Baseball Players Association, Decision No. 35, Grievances Nos. 77–30, 77–31. Oct. 31, 1977. Re: Moore II

These grievances are sequels to Grievance No. 77–18, which involved the same parties and was the subject of Decision No. 32. In that decision, the arbitration panel held that the special convenant contained in the contract between Alvin E. Moore and the Atlanta Braves should be reinstated.

Moore played the bulk of the 1976 season with Richmond of the International League. In an effort to retain Moore's free agent status in the event that Moore was dissatisfied with his playing time with Atlanta in 1977, Moore's representative negotiated the following special covenant to the player's contract:

The Atlanta Club and player Alvin Earl Moore agree that should player Moore not be satisfied with his playing time by June 15, 1977, that the Atlanta Club will initiate a trade that would not be consummated [sic] without the prior written consent of Alvin Moore. Notification of player Alvin Moore's dissatisfaction should be submitted in writing to the Atlanta Club prior to June 15, 1977.

Should a trade not be consummated [sic] by the end of the 1977 championship baseball season Alvin Moore will *become a free agent if he so desires.* (Emphasis in original opinion.)

Should player Alvin Moore be satisfied with his playing time by June 15, 1977 this covenant of this contract will be declared null and void with all other aspects of this contract being in full force according to major league rules and the basic agreement.

On May 24, 1977, Moore's representative informed the Club that Moore was dissatisfied with his playing time and wished to be traded pursuant to the terms of the special convenant. The central question in these two grievances, one of which (No. 77–30) is brought by the Atlanta Club, and one of which is brought by the Association on behalf of Moore (No. 77–31), was whether or not Moore was entitled to become a free agent, since he declared his dissatisfaction with his playing time prior to June 15 and the Club failed to trade him.

The Club argued that where, as here, the satisfaction of a party to a contract is made the test, the party must act honestly and in good faith. The Club points out that although Moore played very little in the month of April, he was the starting third baseman for 18 of the 21 games played between May 1 and May 23. The three games Moore did not start in May were due to a medical problem (dilated eyes). For the entire period between April 8 and May 23, the Atlanta Club played a total of 41 games. Moore played the entire game in 18 games, did not play at all in 13 games, and played as a pinch hitter or pitch runner in 10 games.

The Association argued that Moore did in fact act in good faith in exercising his discretion under the contract's satisfaction clause. Moore claimed he was "really hurt" that he didn't play during the first few weeks of the season and that he deserved the chance to be a regular.

The Chairman of the Arbitration Panel, Alexander Porter, held that Moore's exercise of his discretion in invoking the terms of the special covenant could not be set aside on the ground that it was not reached in good faith. Porter noted that, although Moore played regularly in May, the fact is that he started less than half the games between April 8 and May 23. Further,

there was no assurance that the Club would continue to use Moore as the regular third baseman, Porter observed.

While reasonable men might differ as to whether or not a rookie player in Moore's situation should have been satisfied with his playing time, the Chairman pointed out that it was Moore's satisfaction — not the Club's or the Panel's opinion — that the Club contracted to meet. Porter rejected the Club's assertion that "a player in Moore's shoes could not in good faith be dissatisfied with starting less than half of the Club's games. . . ."

There was some dispute over conversations Moore had with Atlanta's Vice President, William D. Lucas. While Lucas claimed that Moore indicated verbally that he was satisfied with his playing time, Moore stated only that he was happy he was finally getting a chance to play. The chairman ruled that even if Moore had misled Lucas as to his satisfaction with his playing time, it cannot be claimed that Moore's assertion of dissatisfaction was reached in bad faith. Accordingly, Grievance No. 77–30, brought by the Atlanta Club, was denied, and Grievance No. 77–31, brought by the Association on behalf of Alvin E. Moore, was sustained.

In the Matter of Arbitration Between Major Leagues of Professional Baseball Clubs (Minnesota Twins) and Major League Baseball Players Association (Michael Grant Marshall), Decision No. 37, Grievance No. 37, October 25, 1978

The issue before the Panel was whether or not an individual club and player can waive the compensation provisions of the Free Agent Re-entry procedure, as set forth in Section C of Article XVII of the Basic Agreement. This type of waiver was contained in the contract between the Minnesota Twins and Michael Grant Marshall, which American League President Lee MacPhail refused to approve. Marshall, a Cy Young Award pitcher in 1974, had been plagued with injuries in the following seasons, and the Twins were reluctant to give him a high salary in 1978. The result was a one-year contract, with a relatively small salary, together with the provision waiving free agent compensation to the Twins. In this way, Marshall could become a free agent with as few restrictions as possible and could capitalize if his comeback was successful.

The provision in the contract contained the phrase that the parties intended and understood that Marshall's Free Agency status should be that which the Arbitration Panel approved in Decision #(*Moore I*). *Moore I* did not require compensation to be paid to the Atlanta Club for its loss of free agent Moore. The clubs, however, contended that that decision should be confined to the particular circumstances of the *Moore* case.

The Panel held that on the basis of *Moore I*, Marshall and the Minnesota club were entitled to draw the inference from the fact that no compensation was actually paid to Atlanta and from the Panel's silence on the compensation question that the article could be waived. However, in retrospect, Arbitrator Porter stated that he did not intend *Moore I's* silence to be taken as an affirmative holding. The Panel had concluded in *Moore I* that certain aspects of the reserve system and re-entry procedure, such as length of service, were designed for the benefit of individual clubs and could be waived. It was silent on the compensation issue, primarily because the parties had not addressed themselves to this issue and no detailed findings were made.

The Panel, after specifically addressing the issue in the present controversy, held that the cost to be paid by the Club which signs a free agent is a feature of the re-entry procedure, plainly designed to foster the interest of all 26 clubs in maintaining competitive balance. Thus compensation may not normally be waived by an individual Club or Player. Under this decision, Marshall and the Minnesota Twins were allowed to retain the waiver because of their reliance on the *Moore* decision, but subsequent parties could not.

In the Matter of Arbitration Between Major League Baseball Players Association (Richard Tidrow) and Major League Baseball Player Relations Committee, Inc. (Chicago Cubs), Panel Dec. No. 44, Grievance No. 80–18, Goetz, Impartial Arbitrator, November 4, 1980 (Revised January 17, 1981)

. . . The so-called "option clause" in question was set forth as follows in a footnote to the special covenants in Tidrow's Uniform Player's Contract dated April 17, 1978, covering the year 1980: "The Club reserves right to exercise option on Player's services at salary of $200,000 (Two Hundred Thousand Dollars) for year 1981 by December 20, 1980." This contract for 1980 had originally been entered into between Tidrow and the New York Yankees but was assigned to the Cubs on May 23, 1979, along with his contract covering the years 1977 through 1979, when Tidrow was traded.

The renewal option was exercised by a letter dated August 28, 1980, from Robert D. Kennedy, Executive Vice President of the Cubs, to Tidrow's attorney, Charles E. Stahl . . . .

Tidrow's 1977–1979 contract provided for salaries of $55,000, $65,000, and $75,000, respectively, for each of the three years, with $20,000 of the 1978 salary and $30,000 of the 1979 salary deferred and payable in $10,000 annual installments for five years commencing May 15, 1983. His contract for 1980 was entered into with the Yankees on April 17, 1978, as an extension of the 1977–1979 contract. It included special covenants, in addition to the disputed option clause, providing: (1) additional deferrals of 1978 and 1979 salaries under the existing contract; (2) $50,000 signing bonuses for 1978 and 1979, respectively, portions of which were to be deferred; and (3) a $150,000 salary for 1980, $90,000 of which was to be deferred. . . .

While the option clause of Tidrow's 1980 contract differs from the standard form of Uniform Player's Contract prescribed by Article III of the Basic Agreement, it nevertheless would be authorized under the second paragraph of Article III if it is "not inconsistent with" other provisions of the Basic Agreement. . . .

(a) Inconsistency with Article XVII B(2)

A threshold question on the merits therefore is whether there is any inconsistency between the option clause and Article XVII B(2) of the Basic Agreement. The Players Association takes the position that such an inconsistency necessarily results from the facts that: (i) the option clause (which has now been exercised) would have the effect of preventing Tidrow from becoming a free agent at the close of the 1980 season, whereas (ii) Article XVII B(2) of the Basic Agreement allows a Player to elect free agency after six or more years of Major League service – which Tidrow already has. Clearly these are two conflicting results. The Cubs, however, contend that Tidrow's case comes within the exception in Article XVII B(2) for a Player who has "executed a contract for the next succeeding season."

The weakness in this contention is that Tidrow's contract of April 17, 1978, containing the disputed option clause expressly states under Special Covenants: "This contract extends the contract dated January 25, 1977, and is *for the 1980 season*" (Emphasis added). In addition, the first sentence of paragraph 1 of this contract states that the Club employs the Player, "during the year(s) 1980." It is difficult to understand how a contract so definitely stating that it is for the 1980 season could possibly be deemed to be a contract executed for the 1981 season. The plain fact is that Tidrow has never executed a contract for 1981. . . .

That the parties did not intend a Player to forfeit his right to free agency upon a Club's exercise of an option such as this is further apparent from the bargaining history of Article XVII B(2). This provision represented a concession by the Players Association to the Clubs which had the effect of restricting the right to free agency after the end of the first contract renewal year that had been recognized in Panel Decision No. 29. In the 1976 negotiations, in which this provision was a major issue, the Clubs had proposed that free agency be available only after a specified period, plus an "option year" for which the Club could elect to retain the Player if it so desired. The rejection of that proposal is strong evidence that in agreeing to waive free agency for a Player who has "executed a contract" for the succeeding year, the Players Association was *not* agreeing to the elimination of free agency simply by the unilateral exercise by a Club of an option clause covering what otherwise would be the free agency year.

Thus, the plain meaning and purpose of Article XVII B(2) is that a Player relinquishes his right to elect free agency after six years of Major League service only in exchange for the full protection of a standard Uniform Player's Contract for the succeeding year. Since Tidrow had executed no such contract for 1981, and since the option clause of his 1980 contract would deprive him of the free agency opportunity afforded by Article XVII B(2), the option clause must be held to be inconsistent with that provision of the Basic Agreement.

(b) Actual or Potential Benefit to Tidrow

But even though the option clause in Tidrow's 1980 contract is inconsistent with Article XVII B(2) of the Basic Agreement, that fact does not automatically render the clause inoperative under Article III. Both parties seem to agree that under Panel Decision No. 32 (Chairman Porter) dated September 7, 1977, a special covenant in a Player's Contract may be inconsistent with a provision of the Basic Agreement dealing with the same subject, but still be authorized by Article II of the Basic Agreement, which provides:

> The Clubs recognize the Association as the sole and exclusive collective bargaining agent for all Major League Players, and individuals who may become Major League Players during the term of this Agreement, with regard to all terms and conditions of employment except (1) individual salaries over and above the minimum requirements established by this Agreement and (2) *Special Covenants to be included in individual Uniform Player's Contracts, which actually or potentially provide additional benefits to the Player*. (Emphasis added)

. . . In other words, the "inconsistency" provision of Article III of the Basic Agreement must be read together with the "additional benefit" provision of Article II to determine whether a particular special covenant is truly inconsistent with the entire Basic Agreement, so as to be ineffective. . . .

The Clubs urge that in applying this additional benefit test, all the special covenants in the contract of which the disputed clause is a part must be considered together as a "package," since that is the way they were negotiated. If that approach were to be followed here, there could be little doubt that Tidrow received substantial benefits over and above the typical Uniform Player's

Contract. By entering into his 1980 contract with the Yankees on April 17, 1978, Tidrow was assured that his salary for 1980 would be $150,000 as compared to $75,000 for 1979, that it would be payable on a "guaranteed" basis, that he would receive two $50,000 signing bonuses, that portions of his new compensation would be deferred, and that additional amounts of his 1978 and 1979 compensation would be deferred. Unquestionably, Tidrow was better off economically, on an overall basis, after signing this contract than he would have been under a standard contract for 1980. That is no doubt the reason he signed the contract so far in advance of the 1980 season.

The problem with this package approach to Article II is that it would virtually nullify the inconsistency restriction of Article III. This is because almost any detrimental special covenant inconsistent with the Basic Agreement could be made effective by the simple device of providing some offsetting additional benefit in another special covenant. . . .

For several reasons, it must be held that in this case the option clause in Tidrow's 1980 contract in itself potentially afforded him "additional benefits" within the meaning of Article II of the Basic Agreement, which as noted in Panel Decision No. 32 "should be liberally construed." These benefits consisted of the $200,000 salary, which — as things stood at the time of execution — was not only potentially more than he would have been certain of under the minimum salary reduction provisions of Article V B of the Basic Agreement, but also had inextricably linked to it the "guarantee" feature. Whether these two factors *actually* would provide additional benefits of course could not be determined at the time Tidrow's contract was executed in the Spring of 1978, since their operation was contingent upon future action by the Club in exercising the option and on other uncertainties. But as of the date of contract execution it would appear that they could *potentially* provide additional benefits, not only over the standard Uniform Player's Contract generally, but what is equally important, over the then indeterminate prospects of free agency for 1981 which they could supplant.

While the Club would not exercise the option for 1981 unless it seemed desirable to the Club, looking at the situation in 1978 there still would seem to have been at least a *possibility* that option terms at this level might be more beneficial to Tidrow than free agency. With hindsight, of course, that possibility is extremely remote, if not non-existent, but from the point of view of the parties at the time of contracting, it could not be presumed that these terms would necessarily be less advantageous than free agency. It simply was a speculation for both sides, the actual effect of which might never be known with certainty. In this regard, the option clause differed from a so-called "right of first refusal" clause, which could not possibly produce anything better than free agency.

This situation should also be distinguished from those in which a Club might provide a Player a token sum of money, or some other unrelated economic inducement, within the same covenant in which he would agree to forego free agency, solely to "buy off" the Player's collectively-bargained protection. . . .

Thus, in agreeing to the option clause, Tidrow was contingently substituting for free agency an otherwise bona fide alternative which at that time he could realistically deem in itself to be potentially better. This is not the case of a hapless rookie desperate to break into the Major Leagues at any price, whose naivete might be taken advantage of by a Club. Although not represented by legal counsel or an agent, Tidrow was a veteran Player, experienced in contract negotiations, who knowingly and willingly must have considered the option clause potentially preferable to free agency. Since in executing his two previous contracts he had foregone free agency, he surely was aware of that possibility resulting from the Club's exercise of the option for 1981. If he had any doubt about the propriety of that result, it should have occurred to him then to raise a question with the Player's Association at that point.

This, in turn, leads to a conclusive factor in this case. Whatever doubt might at one time have existed as to additional benefits under the option clause must now be resolved against Tidrow on the basis of the inconsistency between his own past conduct and his present position. By remaining silent until the latter part of 1979 and retaining $100,000 in bonuses for signing the contract he now seeks to overturn, Tidrow led the Cubs — who acquired his contract in apparent good faith — to act in reliance on his evident acceptance of all its terms. Under an established general principle of equity applicable to the law of contracts, he should be barred ("estopped") at this late date from disavowing the favorable initial assessment of the potential benefits of this covenant that can justifiably be attributed to him as a result of this prior inaction and the reliance it induced. The elements of this estoppel here are not just Tidrow's lack of diligence and the passage of time after accepting benefits under the contract, but also his actual or constructive knowledge that he might be foregoing free agency in a manner inconsistent with Article XVII of the Basic Agreement, plus the detrimental reliance his conduct induced in an initially uninvolved third party misled into assuming the option clause was valid. . . . In a sense, Tidrow seems to want to "have his cake and eat it.". . . [I]t should be emphasized that this is a narrow holding that is not to be construed as authorization for any and all option clauses under any and all circumstances. . . .

This decision therefore is strictly confined to the type of situation at issue here, in which a veteran Player: (a) in extending or renewing an existing Major League contract; (b) with full knowledge of the possible consequences for his free agency; (c) in the absence of any evidence of overreaching or effort by the Club systematically to nullify Article XVII of the Basic Agreement; (d) agrees to a significant potential additional benefit as an integral part of the terms of an optional renewal clause that could reasonably be viewed prospectively as a potentially advantageous alternative to free agency; and (e) fails to object to the clause until long after it has been relied on by an assignee Club. The Panel is expressing no opinion on cases in which any one of this unusual combination of factors might be absent. . . .

5.42   Drug Use by Players

Problems with athletes and drugs are not new. Incidents surfaced ten years ago and more, causing scandals at the time. However, after players were suspended or fined, the incidents were allowed to recede from the public's consciousness. In the 1980s, it is clear the problems will not go away.

Major infractions demand constant attention. By one account, over 40 incidents involving cocaine or marijuana use by those connected with sports commanded headlines between January 1, 1984, and June 1, 1985 (see San Diego Union, p. H–11, c. 3, June 23, 1985). Several more incidents occurred during the summer of 1985.

Three professional sports leagues have responded by instituting different types of programs. These should be briefly mentioned.

In Major League Baseball, players and management entered an agreement in 1984 establishing a voluntary drug treatment program. Any player who voluntarily seeks help is granted amnesty from disciplinary action. Players treated under the program may be placed on probation following treatment. During this time, they may be tested for drugs and required to seek further therapy.

Players not protected by the amnesty are those convicted of drug-related charges, those supplying other players, and repeat offenders. The commissioner is given certain discretion to impose penalties. As is seen below, excessive penalties will be challenged by the Players Association.

In early 1985, Commissioner Peter Ueberroth announced he was implementing his own drug testing program that would be applicable to all non-union personnel. Recognizing that union members were insulated by their collective bargaining agreements, Ueberroth nevertheless urged voluntary compliance. It was subsequently announced that baseball umpires would submit to the commissioner's testing program. The players' association remained adamant that the plan agreed to by management and the union in 1984 should control the players.

The National Basketball Association also devised a program for players through the collective bargaining process. Players who voluntarily seek treatment will be provided with same, at the club's expense and with no penalty imposed. If this occurs a second time, the player is suspended without pay during the treatment, but there is no further penalty. However, subsequent drug use, even if voluntarily disclosed, will result in a permanent disbarment. In addition, in the NBA, if a player is convicted of a crime involving the use of distribution of heroin or cocaine, or illegally uses these drugs, the player will be permanently barred from the league.

In the National Football League, management implemented a drug program that has the league and clubs giving educational instruction on drug abuse. The players' association has cooperated in this undertaking. Players can also seek treatment and will be aided in this by their teams. Drug testing is allowed at certain specified times, but random testing is not permitted. Although a player can seek rehabilitation a first time, repeaters can be disciplined.

Even with these guidelines, it is clear the leagues and the players' associations have a great challenge ahead. Where cases of drug abuse emerge, the tendency will be to take action to maintain a positive image for the league. This will inevitably lead to protests that the sanctions imposed are too harsh. Thus, the cases that have been handled so far must be consulted for future guidance as to what is permissible action and what is not.

In the Matter of Arbitration Between Major League Players Association (Ferguson Jenkins) and Major League Player Relations Committee (Commissioner Bowie Kuhn), Decision No. 41, Grievance No. 80–25 (1980)

Ferguson Jenkins, a pitcher for the Texas Rangers, was arrested by the Canadian police at Toronto Stadium on August 25, 1980, before the start of the baseball game between the Toronto Blue Jays and the Rangers. Jenkins was charged with possession of small amounts of marijuana, hashish, and cocaine, reportedly found in his luggage by customs officials. He was released on his written "promise to appear," which is the least restrictive form of release under Canadian law — that is, he was free to travel as he pleased, including outside Canada. At his appearance before the justice of the peace on August 27, Jenkins entered no plea, and a trial date was set for December 18, 1980.

After learning of Jenkins's arrest, Baseball Commissioner Bowie Kuhn contacted Jenkins's attorney, Edward Greenspan, and arranged for an investigatory interview on August 30, 1980. Henry Fitzgibbon, formerly with the FBI and then director of security for the commissioner's office, conducted the interview with Greenspan present. The line of questioning prepared by Fitzgibbon included questions designed to induce Jenkins to admit or deny the possession. On the advice of Greenspan, Jenkins did not respond. At the arbitration hearing, Greenspan testified that he had explained to Fitzgibbon at this time the nature of the charge and procedures under Canadian law.

Greenspan explained that Jenkins was charged with a summary conviction offense, one of the least serious criminal offenses in Canada, comparable to a misdemeanor in the United States and in the same category as impaired driving in Canada. If Jenkins was found guilty, the trial court judge had the discretion to order that the accused be discharged with no registration of the conviction, a procedure that is now pro forma on possession charges for first-time offenders. Finally, Greenspan explained that under the Canadian criminal code, the trial judge had the power to compel evidence obtained at the investigatory interview for use at the trial. Commissioner Kuhn testified that he received an oral summary of this information from an attorney from his office who was present at the interview.

In a letter dated September 8, 1980, Kuhn notified Jenkins that he was suspended, but promised to reconsider if Jenkins agreed to resume the interview. At the hearing, Kuhn testified that because Jenkins, when given the chance to explain, did not exonerate himself, Kuhn believed that not to suspend Jenkins would create serious public relations problems in maintaining the wholesome image of baseball.

The arbitration panel decided that the commissioner's authority to investigate and impose penalties on those who refused to cooperate was limited by the just cause standard of the Collective Bargaining Agreement. Accordingly, the primary issue was whether there had been just cause for the penalty imposed.

It was not entirely clear to the panel whether the cause of the suspension was Jenkins's arrest or his refusal to answer Fitzgibbon's questions, but the panel decided that neither was adequate to support the penalty. First, under the principles of United States and Canadian law, one is presumed innocent until proven guilty. However, an employee who is charged with a violent crime and whose fellow workers are unwilling to work with him or her, or whose employer is adversely affected by the publicity, might be barred from working pending the outcome of the proceedings.

In Jenkins's case, the first set of circumstances was not applicable; in fact, his teammates in all likelihood would prefer to have their leading pitcher with them. Further, given the light nature of the crime, the panel found it unlikely that a significant number of fans would withdraw their support if Jenkins were allowed to play before his day in court. The panel next found that Jenkins's refusal to answer the questions did not provide just cause for the penalty assessed, as Jenkins was justifiably concerned about the possible consequences of responding. The purpose of the interview seemed to be to enable the commissioner to make his own determination of Jenkins's guilt or innocence, which offends the moral values against self-incrimination. Likewise, the burden placed on Jenkins to prove his innocence or be subject to discipline was contrary to Anglo-American principles.

Finally, in the arbitration panel's opinion, the commissioner failed to give due consideration to Jenkins's past record: he had been in the Major Leagues since 1965 with no past record of misconduct or illegality and had been awarded the Order of Canada by the Candian government. The severe penalty of banishment was both humiliating and frustrating. On September 22, Chairman Raymond Goetz ordered the suspension revoked and Jenkins to return to active status with the Rangers.

In the Matter of Arbitration Between Bowie K. Kuhn, Commissioner of Baseball and Major League Baseball Players Association (Willie Wilson, Jerry Martin), Panel Decision No. 54, Gr. Nos 84–1 and 84–2, April 3, 1984

The issue in this case was whether Baseball Commissioner Bowie K. Kuhn had just cause for the suspensions and probation conditions imposed on Jerry Martin and Willie Wilson of the Kansas City Royals Club.

On October 13, 1983, Willie Wilson and Jerry Martin pleaded guilty to a charge of attempting to possess cocaine and were sentenced to one year in prison, with all but three months of the term suspended. Additionally, Wilson was fined $5,000, and Martin was fined $2,500. Each was placed on probation for two years commencing with release from prison.

On November 18 and December 2, Wilson and Martin were interviewed by a representative of the commissioner. During the interview, each acknowledged having used cocaine. Based on the players' criminal convictions and acknowledgment of the use of cocaine, Commissioner Kuhn, on December 15, 1983, imposed a one-year-without-pay suspension on each player. However, the commissioner added that the suspensions would be reviewed on May 15, 1984 "with a view to their reinstatement if . . . in his judgment warranted . . .". Further, the players were to remain on probation by Major League Baseball until the end of their court-imposed probationary period. The probationary period would contain "rehabilitation, aftercare, community service, testing procedures and the like, as may be appropriate to the individual case." During the term of the suspension, each player would be allowed to work out with his club but could not participate in the club's games.

Wilson and Martin filed grievances in January 1984, contending that the discipline imposed was violative of Article XI(A) of the Basic Agreement, as it failed to satisfy the requirements of "just cause." The association also contended that the commissioner had no authority to impose a probationary period.

Rule 21(f) of the Uniform Player Contract prohibits "practices or conduct not to be in the best interests of Baseball" and allows the commissioner to impose disciplinary action. The association argued that while the commissioner had a right to impose suspensions on the players upon showing of just cause, establishing a probationary period was not within the commissioner's authority. However, the arbitration panel concluded that the commissioner's authority was broad enough to impose a probationary period that seeks to "ensure abstinence and to educate both the afflicted player and others in the community as part of rehabilitation."

The Uniform Player Contract, Article XI(A), provides that a player may be subjected to discipline upon showing of "just cause." The Players Association argued that the commissioner had not proven "just cause" for the suspensions. The arbitration panel observed that "just cause" can be shown when, as in the instant case, the player's conduct damages the club's reputation and adversely affects the enterprise. While the panel recognized that clubs are not overseers of players' private lives, players' personal conduct may hurt a club's business to the extent that discipline is warranted. The panel ruled that the players' use of cocaine and criminal convictions were so serious as to their impact on baseball that the "just cause" standard was satisfied and discipline was warranted. In making such a ruling, the panel noted that the publicity surrounding the incident had a potentially damaging effect on the image of Major League Baseball.

The arbitration panel held that the two-pronged disciplinary action of suspension and probation is "responsive to both the misconduct and the potential medical implications of the players' involvement." However, the panel found the term "community service" overly vague, feeling its interpretations could lead to dispute. But in the instant case, both Wilson and Martin had begun community work "aggressively and voluntarily."

The panel found that the commissioner's decision to review the suspensions on May 15 with a "view to . . . reinstatement" offered no guidelines for criteria on which the decision or reinstatement would be made. Consequently, the panel ruled that the players' suspension beyond the May 15 date would be too severe in light of the "just cause" requirement. In ruling that the suspensions should end on May 15, assuming the players' good behavior, the panel cited three points in defense of Wilson and Martin: First, while both acknowledged some use of cocaine, there was no evidence that Wilson or Martin used cocaine on the job or that either became involved with criminal interests. Second, both Martin and Wilson cooperated fully and showed a sincere willingness to repair the damage that the commissioner believed the players had brought to the integrity of the game. Third, the magnitude of the penalties imposed on Martin and Wilson by the judicial system was extremely severe for the particular crime.

In the Matter of Arbitration Between Major League Baseball Players Association (Pascual Perez) and Bowie K. Kuhn, Commissioner of Baseball, Gr. No. 84–0, April 27, 1984

Pascual Perez, a pitcher for the Atlanta Braves, was arrested in January 1984 in the Dominican Republic for possession of 200 milligrams of cocaine. He was convicted, fined 1,000 pesos ($400), and released from prison on April 9. Baseball Commissioner Bowie K. Kuhn, having reviewed the court proceeding and interviewed Perez, suspended the pitcher without pay until May 15, 1984, for failing to conform to the "high standard of personal conduct" required by the Uniform Player Contract. This suspension led to the instant grievance.

On the day he was arrested, Perez was taken to police headquarters, stripped naked, and interrogated. At this point, Perez signed an incriminatory statement acknowledging his possession of the cocaine. Beyond this initial interrogation, Perez consistently challenged the accuracy of the written statements. There were serious questions of credibility of the police interrogator. Further, Perez contended that he was told that if he signed the statements, the police would help him. Even the Dominican court found that the police had violated the Code of Criminal Procedure by failing to mark, seal, or in any way identify what had been taken from Perez. The court, finding many other procedural errors on the part of the police, inexplicably convicted Perez of "possession" of 20 milligrams, rather than "distribution" or "pushing," which required a showing of possession of 200 milligrams or more. But even with his conviction on the lesser charge, there was virtually no evidence that what Perez had been carrying was cocaine.

On April 14, 1984, Perez was interviewed by Commissioner Kuhn's investigator. Perez denied consistently any wrongdoing. The commissioner based Perez's suspension on two factors: his conviction in the Dominican courts and his signed "confession." But the chairman of the arbitration panel, Richard I. Block, noted that since Perez was naked, scared, and unrepresented when he signed the "confession," the written statements fell short of proving the charge that Perez was carrying cocaine. Further, Block held that the Court proceeding was so flawed that Perez's conviction should be given no weight in the suspension proceeding.

The commissioner's office based its entire case on Perez's conviction and confession. No witness was present to testify against Perez at the commissioner's office. As Block points out, management bears the burden of proving the charge to justify the discipline. The panel held that management had not met this burden and that the suspension had to be lifted. In doing so, the arbitration panel ruled that while a conviction may be admitted as evidence for some purposes, the particulars of the instant case do not give rise to the conclusion that Perez was carrying cocaine.

The panel pointed out in its opinion that in no way should the ruling be read as an attempt to undercut the attempt of baseball management to deal with the drug problem. However, the panel found that a forceful and effective drug program

must proceed on a foundation of clear and competent evidence. The commissioner lacked the necessary evidence against Perez, and consequently, the grievance was granted.

In the Matter of Arbitration Between National Basketball Players Association (Bernard King) and National Basketball Association (Utah Jazz Basketball Club), Nicolau, Arb., (1980)

Bernard King, a basketball player under contract to the Utah Jazz, was arrested at his home on January 1, 1980, and charged with forceable sexual abuse and possible possession of cocaine. The following morning Frank Layden, the General Manager of the Jazz, after reading the police report and conferring with the owners, suspended King indefinitely without pay for "conduct detrimental to the Utah Jazz Basketball Club."

The validity of the suspension was brought before George Nicolau as Impartial Arbitration. The National Basketball Players Association, for King, contended first that King's guaranteed "no-cut" contract prohibited an indefinite suspension under any circumstances.

Under King's contract, a number of the standard provisions of the Uniform Player Contract which permit a club to suspend or terminate a player for various reasons were excised, and an addendum was attached. The addendum set forth the terms of the no-cut agreement and contained, in paragraph three, a clause which released a club from its obligation to pay bonuses if King was arrested and convicted for narcotics, theft, or any other felony charge. Left untouched in the Uniform Player Contract were paragraphs four and five which allowed a club to establish rules and impose penalties including suspension. The player agreed, among other things, to follow the rules and to conduct himself on and off the court according to the highest standards of morality, honesty and sportsmanship.

The NBPA maintained that paragraph three of the addendum meant that the parties contemplated the forfeiture of the bonuses as the exclusive means of providing the incentive for King to avoid criminal conduct. The arbitration held that the forfeiture provision dealt solely with bonuses and did not contradict or override the rights of the club under the uniform contract. The continued existence of paragraphs four and five in King's contract gave the right of suspension for just cause to the Club which held his contract.

The arbitrator agreed with the NBPA that the Club's action must be judged at the time it was taken and not in view of subsequent events. The Club made its decision solely on the information that he was arrested, without an independent investigation and without even speaking to King. Subsequent to the Club's decision, King was indicted, admitted his alcoholism and began treatment.

Additionally, the Club's decision must hold more than a mere surmise of harm to the employer's business; the connection beween the events and the effect on business must be "reasonable and discernible." The arbitrator noted that most of the cases which justified a suspension involved violent acts, such as armed robbery or manslaughter. This was not so in King's case. Nothing in the police reports suggested that his actions were violent or that he was a danger to society. In fact, he was released with no bond. Moreover, in the course of a basketball game, King did not come into contact with the public in a way which would lead the public to fear danger.

The arbitrator held that the Club's action could not be characterized as disciplinary according to paragraphs four and five of the Uniform Contract, since the Club was not prepared to prove King's guilt. The arbitrator further found no evidence that the Club's withholding of his salary was reasonably necessary to forestall economic retaliation by the fans. The Club could have protected itself by not playing King but continuing to pay him. By choosing to deprive him of his salary solely on the basis of alleged criminal conduct, the Club "engaged in unsustainable action."

The arbitrator did not decide whether, as the NBPA contended, King's actions were a result of his alcoholism. The NBPA argued that alcoholism was an illness covered by his "no-cut" contract, which required that he be paid when unavailable due to illness. The Club maintained that King's alleged alcoholism was not the basis for his suspension and that his alcoholism was contrived as a defense. The arbitrator held that the "nub" of the case was King's suspension because of the lodging of the criminal charges.

Because the balancing of interests was in King's favor, the arbitrator held the suspension was without just cause and ordered King's salary be repaid.

5.50   Strikes in Professional Sports

Until 1981, strikes had been more of a threat than an actual occurrence. There had been significant walkouts and lockouts in baseball, involving both players and umpires. The 1974 strike in football had been major, although admittedly a disastrous one for the players. But there had not been the all-out, no-holds barred walkout that would leave an entire sports season in disarray. In 1981, that changed. The baseball players walked in June and did not return until August. The season will forever be known as the "strike-shortened 1981" season. Records compiled for that year must carry an asterisk.

A similar occurrence befell football one year later. In September 1982, only a few weeks into the season, the NFL players went on strike. If anything, the strike was longer and more bitter than the baseball strike the year before. And, as in 1974, the football players fell short of their goals. It was not exactly a disaster repeated — solid gains were achieved — but it was hardly the victory concededly earned by the baseball players.

We cannot examine in this context the "why's," "wherefore's" and "who won's" of professional sports strikes. Other sources must be examined for such an analysis. What can be done is to consider some of the legal maneuverings, just before, during, and after a strike. One inevitable circumstance is that charges of unfair labor practices emanate from both sides. A more special circumstance, somewhat peculiar to sports, is that individual players may have bargained for what can almost be called strike protection. This led to extensive arbitrations in both baseball and football after the latest strikes. Summaries of the opinions appear in Section 5.52.

5.51   Unfair Labor Practices

In Section 5.21, we discussed charges of unfair labor practices in the context of collective bargaining. Enforcement mechanisms were examined that are used to remedy these practices where they are found to exist. As noted, the unfair labor charges are often part of the maneuvering by each side to gain advantage in the negotiation process. When an agreement is reached, the charges are often dropped as part of the settlement.

In certain instances the possible existence of unfair labor practices may be an impetus for a strike by players, who react to a feeling that management will not cooperate unless the strike weapon is deployed. In one case, however, the unfair labor charge was raised by a players' association in an attempt to forestall a strike. This occurred in baseball in 1981.

As we see from the decision by the court, the players' association's legal efforts were unsuccessful. Even so, the court's consideration of the charges raises important implications for labor relations in most sports leagues. In particular, the ability of a players union to gain access to the league's financial data, central to the charges levelled, has subsequently become a vital issue in all collective bargaining negotiations since 1981.

Silverman (NLRB) v. Major League Baseball Player Relations Committee, Inc., 516 F. Supp. 588 (S.D.N.Y. 1981)

Werker, District Judge.

There is an action brought by petitioner, the Regional Director of the Second Region of the National Labor Relations Board for and on behalf of the National Labor Relations Board (the "Board") seeking temporary injunctive relief pursuant to Section 10(j) of the National Labor Relations Act, as amended (the "Act"), 29 U.S.C. Sec. 160(j), pending the final disposition of matters presently before the Board. Respondents in this action are the Major League Baseball Player Relations Committee, Inc., ("PRC") and twenty-four of its constituent member clubs. . . .

FACTS

Since 1966 the Major League baseball players have been represented by the Players Association. During this time the respondent PRC has been the exclusive collective bargaining agent of twenty-six Major League clubs. The Board of Directors of the PRC is empowered to formulate labor relations policy for the clubs and direct all negotiations with the Players Association. C. Raymond Grebey, Director of Player Relations of PRC, has been designated by the PRC Board as the official spokesman for the PRC in all collective bargaining matters. To assist the PRC Board of Directors in dealing with the Players Association, the Board has designated a bargaining team, which includes Mr. Grebey, to conduct all negotiations.

The Players Association and the PRC bargain to establish an agreement on pensions, allowances and a variety of rules governing players' employment. Except as to a base salary, under the various agreements negotiated by the parties, the Players Association has waived its right to bargain with the PRC about individual player salaries. Thus, above a minimum salary, the subject has been left to each individual player to negotiate with his club.

Prior to 1975, when a Major League baseball player's employment contract expired, he was precluded from negotiating for employment with any other team except his own. In December 1975, as the result of grievances filed by the Players Association on behalf of John Messersmith and David McNally, an arbitrator found that Major League clubs could not reserve a player for more than one year ("option year") past the expiration of his contract. A player who completes the option year without signing a renewal contract with his team becomes a "free agent" who is able to negotiate with other clubs.

In 1976 the Players Association and the PRC

entered into a collective bargaining agreement, effective January 1, 1976 through December 31, 1979, which provided, *inter alia*, for "free agency" as established by the Messersmith-McNally decision. Pursuant to this agreement, however, a player was required to serve six years in the Major Leagues before becoming a "free agent." The agreement also provided for "compensation" in the form of an amateur player draft choice to each club which lost a "free agent" player selected by more than two clubs for negotiation rights. After four years of experimenting with this new system, the Players Association and the PRC commenced negotiations for a new collective bargaining agreement on November 11, 1979.

On January 16, 1980, the PRC presented a proposal which recognized the difference in quality, as measured by skill and ability, among the various players choosing to become "free agents." Under this proposal, as finally offered on May 12, 1980, a team losing a "free agent" selected by less than four clubs will not be afforded replacement player "compensation." If a player is selected for negotiation rights by four to seven clubs, the club signing a contract with the player must compensate the player's former club with an amateur draft choice, as before. However, if a player is selected by eight or more clubs, and meets certain minimum performance standards, the signing club must compensate the former club with not only an amateur draft choice, but also a professional player of the former club's choice from a list of unprotected players under contract with the signing club. In this third category, the player is referred to as a "ranking free agent" or "premium" player. Each club may retain 40 players under the contract. Depending upon the peformance level of the "free agent" signed, the signing team may protect from 15 to 18 of its 40 players.

The Players Association adamantly opposed this proposal as having a negative impact on player salaries. Since the proposal requires a club signing a "ranking free agent" to give up a professional player as well as an amateur draft choice, the Association predicts that the number of clubs willing to bid for a "premium" player and the salaries they would offer would be limited by the knowledge that they would be required to forfeit a player of perhaps comparable quality. Correspondingly, the player's present club could then offer him less to insure his remaining with the team.

As negotiations progressed, various matters were being resolved, but it became apparent that the issue of additional replacement player "compensation" was a significant impediment to settlement. Unable to reach agreement on the PRC's proposal, a strike deadline was established for May 23, 1980. On the eve of that deadline the PRC and the Players Association entered into a collective bargaining agreement ("basic agreement"), effective January 1, 1980 through December 31, 1983, establishing the terms and conditions of employment of Major League baseball players. As part of that agreement, a joint study committee was appointed to consider the unresolved matter of replacement player "compensation" for a club which loses a "free agent." The committee was to report to the PRC and the Players Association no later than January 1, 1981.

On December 8, 1980, Bowie Kuhn, Commissioner of Baseball, delivered a speech at the Annual Convention of Professional Baseball. Commenting on the financial difficulties facing the industry, Commissioner Kuhn expressed concern about escalating player salaries brought about by "free agency." He cited the companion problem of "compensation" as a threat to competitive balance in baseball and thus expressed a concern about adequate replacement talent for the loss of a "free agent." Sounding a clarion call to owners and players alike to recognize the need to correct the system of "free agency" which has given rise to these problems, he predicted further financial loss without cooperation between the two groups.

Meanwhile, the joint study committee met on several occasions between August 7, 1980 and January 22, 1981. At one of the meetings, Marvin Miller, the Executive Director of the Players Association, referring to the press reports of Commissioner Kuhn's statements at the Annual Baseball Convention on December 8, 1980, asserted that the clubs' "compensation" proposal was motivated by financial concerns and by a desire to reduce player salaries. Mr. Grebey rebutted these statements and clearly stated that reduction of player salaries was not a goal of the clubs' proposal and that no question of the clubs' ability to pay was relevant or was being raised on behalf of the clubs.

Failing to agree on a joint report, separate reports were issued by the PRC on February 17, 1981 and by the Players Association on February 19, 1981. The players' position, as reflected in its report, is that the additional compensation for a "ranking free agent" diminishes that "free agent's" bargaining position with the new team by the value of the player that the signing club expects to lose. The clubs repeated their position in the report submitted by its members, stating that its current approach is not designed to attack the subject of player salaries.

This impasse ended round one of negotiations over the PRC's proposal and set the stage for round two as provided for in Article XVIII, Section D(2) of the basic agreement:

Negotiations. Subsequent to receiving the report of the study committee, the parties shall promptly meet to commence negotiations on the subject of the study. If the parties are unable to reach agreement on the matter of player selection rights as compensation to a Club which loses a free agent player after receiving the report of the study committee and by February 15, 1981, the Clubs may thereafter but before February 20, 1981 unilaterally adopt and put into effect as part of the Basic Agreement the proposal on this matter . . . [see attachment 9] or a variation not less favorable to the Players Association. In the event the Clubs put such proposal into effect unilaterally, the Players Association may reopen the Basic Agreement with respect to the player selection rights provision put into effect by the Clubs and strike with respect thereto. . . .

On February 19, 1981, the parties having failed to reach an agreement on the "compensation" issue, the clubs invoked their option under the basic agreement and unilaterally adopted as part of that agreement their last proposal on the issue. On February 26, 1981, the Players Association likewise exercised one of its options under the agreement, reopening the basic agreement on the unresolved issue and setting a strike deadline of May 20, 1981. As a result of this reopener, the second round of negotiations began.

By letter of February 27, 1981, the Players Association requested the PRC to provide certain financial information for all members clubs. The Players Association premised the appropriateness of its request on Commissioner Kuhn's December 1980 speech which the Association interpreted as an affirmation of its belief that the "compensation" proposal was motivated by financial concerns.

Mr. Miller explained that the requested finan-

cial data was "necessary for the Players Association to properly discharge its duties and responsibilities . . . as the exclusive collective bargaining representative of all major league players, for purposes of preparation for and conduct of the ongoing negotiations."

On March 13, 1981, the PRC, through Mr. Grebey, refused to comply with the Association's request, repeating the PRC's position that its bargaining stance regarding "compensation" was not based on "economic incapacity or inability." By letters of April 7 and 20, 1981, the Players Association sought reconsideration of the PRC's decision not to comply with its request. Specifically, the association focused on the sharp increase in player salaries since the 1976 agreement. Noting a causal relationship between the "free agency" provisions of that agreement and the escalation of player salaries, the Association challenged the PRC to deny that its proposal is "designed to negatively impact upon the salaries of free agent players."

Grebey responded by letter of April 24, 1981, and again refused to comply with the Association's request. . . .

Meanwhile, during this second round of negotiations, various statements by club owners appeared in the media. These statements all reflect an expression of concern about the financial well-being of the baseball industry and/or the level of player salaries. Specifically, in an article appearing in *The Sporting News* on March 21, 1981, Ruly Carpenter, President of the Philadelphia Phillies, stated that "salaries have basically gotten to ridiculous proportions." Ray A. Kroc, Chairman of the Board of the San Diego Padres, made a statement which was quoted in *The Sporting News* magazine dated May 21, 1981, warning the players not to strike because there is a limit to the salaries they can be paid. He is also quoted as saying that only three or four clubs out of twelve in the National League are still making money.

On March 21, 1981, Toronto Blue Jays President, Peter Bavasi, predicted in a radio interview that the rise in salaries as a result of "free agency" would force the clubs into bankruptcy if the situation were not corrected. He further commented that cooperation from the players regarding the "compensation" proposal would be helpful in restraining clubs from expending large sums on "free agents" since they would have to give up a promising player as a price for signing a "premium" player.

On April 7, 1981, during a television interview, Ted Turner, President of the Atlanta Braves, similarly voiced concern about the financial state of the baseball industry due to salaries, as did Joseph Burke, in his capacity as Executive Vice President of the Kansas City Royals. Burke linked the rise in salaries to "free agency."

Believing that the PRC's bargaining position on the issue of player "compensation" was based at least in part on the financial difficulties of certain member clubs, on May 7, 1981, the Players Association filed an unfair labor practice charge with the Board alleging respondents' failure to bargain in good faith by refusing to comply with the Players Association's request for financial disclosure in violation of Sections 8(a)(1) and (5) of the Act, 29 U.S.C. Sec. 158(a)(1) and (5).

Following investigation and pursuant to Section 10(b) of the Act, 29 U.S.C. Sec. 160(b), the Board filed a complaint charging respondents with violating Sections 8(a)(1) and (5) of the Act. A hearing on this complaint before an administrative law judge of the Board is scheduled to commence on June 15, 1981.

The temporary injunctive relief sought by petitioner requires respondents to rescind their February 19, 1981, action by which they exercised their right under the 1980 basic agreement and unilaterally implemented their bargaining proposal regarding "compensation." This relief, if granted, would thus preclude the Players Association, under the terms of the basic agreement, from commencing a strike. Petitioner argues that if its request for relief is not granted, the Players Association and the baseball player-employees it represents will be forced to strike within forty-eight hours after this Court rules, or be bound through the end of 1983 by the PRC's proposal. Petitioner emphasizes that obvious irreparable harm to the players, owners and fans would flow from a decision by the Players Association to strike.

The Association contends that if petitioner should prevail in the proceedings presently before the administrative law judge, the Board would be unable to adequately remedy the PRC's alleged unfair labor practice by ordering the clubs to disclose the financial information which the Association seeks, since the Board cannot undo the effects of a strike which would ensue as a result of the denial of petitioner's instant request for relief.

Respondents vigorously oppose petitioner's application as a tactic by the Players Association to avoid the consequences of a contract freely bargained for and entered into by it.

DISCUSSION

To obtain a Section 10(j) injunction, petitioner must satisfy a two-fold test. First, this Court must find that there is reasonable cause to believe that an unfair labor practice has been committed. Second, the Court must determine whether the requested relief is just and proper. . . .

Unfair Labor Practice Claim

Section 7 of the Act provides that "[e]mployees shall have the right to . . . bargain collectively through representatives of their own choosing . . ." 29 U.S.C. sec. 157. Section 8(a)(5) of the Act implements this right by making it an unfair labor practice for an employer "to refuse to bargain collectively with the respresentatives of his employees. . . ." 29 U.S.C sec. 158(a)(5). Section 8(d) defines collective bargaining as, *inter alia,* "the mutual obligation of the employer and the representative of his employees to meet at reasonable times and confer in good faith with respect to wages, hours and other terms and conditions of employment. . . ." 29 U.S.C. sec. 158(d).

Information concerning subjects at issue in bargaining is presumed to be necessary and relevant to negotiations, and employers and unions alike must provide such information when requested in the course of bargaining. . . .

Since the Players Association exercised its option under the 1980 basic agreement on February 26, 1981, and reopened negotiations with regard to the PRC's "compensation" proposal, collective bargaining has been limited to one issue: the level of "compensation" to be paid to a club when a former player of the club, upon the expiration of his employment contract becomes a "free agent" and contracts with another club for employment.

The Board alleges in its petition that the public statements by club owners regarding claims of financial difficulties created a reasonable belief on the part of the Players Association that respondents' bargaining position during this second round of negotiations was based, "at least in part, on the present or prospective financial difficulties of certain of Respondents' member clubs." Although Marvin Miller has expressed some doubt as to club owners' inability to pay rising player salaries, he nevertheless takes the position that the Players Association must have the financial information it requests if it is to fulfill its duty of fair representation. If deprived of that information, the Association claims that it must blindly decide whether to press its demands and risk the loss of jobs for its members if the clubs cannot survive under the "compensation" terms proposed by the Association, or to recede from its position and accept the PRC's proposal without verifying owners' claims of financial distress caused by "free agency." Thus, the Association brought an unfair labor practice charge against the PRC for its failure to disclose the requested financial data after the clubs allegedly put into issue their inability to pay. . . .

Petitioner admits that at no time during bargaining sessions have respondents made a claim of inability to pay. Nevertheless, petitioner urges the Court to find that public statements made by several club owners as well as the Commissioner of Baseball about the financial condition of the industry are sufficient to support a finding of reasonable cause to believe that respondents have injected the inability to pay into the negotiations.

The cases cited by petitioner in support of its position are simply inapposite. In each case, inability to pay was put in issue at the bargaining table. . . .

Thus, Petitioner concedes, as it must, that the Board and courts have never found that an employer has injected financial condition into negotiations, absent statements or conduct by the employer at the bargaining table. Nevertheless, it urges this Court to find, on the basis of statements by Commissioner Kuhn and various owners, that the financial issue has become relevant to the negotiations regarding "compensation" because of the unique nature of collective bargaining in baseball. Mindful that this Court must be "hospitable" to the views of the Regional Director, however novel, *Danielson* v. *Joint Board*, 494 F.2d at 1244–45, I am nevertheless convinced that the Board's position is wrong, and thus will not "defer to the statutory construction urged by [it]." *Danielson* v. *International Organization of Masters*, 521 F.2d at 751.

It is the PRC Board of Directors which is charged with the *exclusive* authority to formulate the collective bargaining position of the clubs and to negotiate agreements with the Players Association. Indeed, Grebey, the official spokesman for the PRC in collective bargaining matters, has consistently denied that the clubs' financial status is at issue in the current negotiations.

Commissioner Kuhn's remarks in December 1980 at the convention cannot be imputed to the PRC as a statement of its bargaining position. First, petitioner's attempt to establish an agency relationship between the Commissioner and the PRC is unavailing. As Commissioner of Baseball, Kuhn presides at the regular joint meetings of the Major Leagues, but does not request nor preside at special meetings called by the PRC. Moreover, while Kuhn is responsible for disciplining players who may then file grievances against him in his capacity as Commissioner, he has likewise ordered the clubs to cease certain action when the interests of baseball warranted his intercession, as when he directed the clubs to open their training camps in the spring of 1976.

There can be little doubt that there is a correlation between "free agency" and the rise in player salaries. Commissioner Kuhn addressed this problem and expressed his concern about the high salaries negotiated between individual players and clubs. During his 1980 speech at the clubs' convention, he also voiced concern for a companion problem, and called for cooperation between the players and owners in combating the threat to competitive balance. He expressed optimism that a solution would be found by the joint study committee that was then considering the "compensation" issue. Fairly read, I cannot find that the Commissioner's speech supports the proposition that the clubs' bargaining position on the replacement player "compensation" proposal is motivated by financial inability. . . .

In a multi-employer bargaining unit as large and publicly visible as the Major League Baseball Clubs, it is inevitable that extraneous statements will be made by individuals affiliated in some way with the group which are inconsistent with the official position of the unit. This only underscores the necessity, recognized by the PRC, for centralized bargaining responsibility and authority. Clearly, individual expressions of opinion cannot serve to bind the entire bargaining unit in the absence of authority to speak for the group. *See Anderson Pharmacy,* 187 N.L.R.B. 301, 302 n.10 (1970).

Petitioner and the Association strain to emphasize the uniqueness of collective bargaining in the baseball industry to avoid the consequences of the established labor law regarding the inability to pay. However, this Court cannot accept "collective bargaining through the press" as a basis for a 10(j) injunction.

The Act has provided for collective bargaining between the parties through their authorized representatives. If this Court were to find that the several public statements by club officials and the Commissioner were sufficient to support a finding that the PRC and its negotiating team view the respondents' "compensation" proposal as related to the financial condition of the clubs, it would do violence to the intent and purpose of the Act which limits the jurisdiction of this Court. . . .

To accept petitioner's argument would permit disgruntled employers in a multi-employer unit who disagreed with the negotiation policies of their representatives to force negotiation issues into the courts . . . a result clearly contrary to the purpose of the Act. . . .

Moreover, the issue of salary, above a minimum rate, is not a subject of collective bargaining between the Players Association and the PRC. Rather, individual players negotiate independently with the clubs as to their salary. Indeed, it is the high player salaries which have resulted from the negotiation of individual contracts by players and clubs which Commissioner Kuhn addressed in his 1980 speech. Noting that player salaries are increasing at a more rapid rate than revenues, he opined that bargaining of individual contracts has led to this problem. He called upon players and owners to cooperate in this regard to arrest the trend and avoid loss to all, including the fans who will be required to pay higher ticket prices.

The evidence adduced at the hearing is insufficient to support a finding that the replacement player "compensation" proposal implemented by the PRC presents economic issues. Rather, the proposal is addressed to the inequities which flowed from the "compensation" for "free agents" as provided for in the 1976 agreement. Specifically, the proposal implemented by the PRC in February 1981, recognized the difference in skill and ability among "free agents" by the type of

compensation provided to a club losing the player. In addition, the proposal is designed to more adequately assist the clubs in replacing players lost in the "free agent" draft. Under the 1976 agreement, clubs were unable to replace lost players through the Minor League and amateur systems within a meaningful time period, if at all. . . .

The court is mindful that a strike may result from its denial of petitioner's request for a 10(j) injunction. Indeed, the industry has suffered a strike in the past. Nevertheless, in struggling with a temptation and even compulsion to prevent a strike in the public interest, I am bound by the law. The possibility of a strike, although a fact of life in labor relations, offers no occasion for this Court to distort the principles of law and equity. The resolution of the "compensation" issue is left to the parties through the negotiation process.

CONCLUSION

In accordance with the foregoing, I find there is no reasonable cause to believe that an unfair labor practice has been committed by respondents. The petition is therefore dismissed.

PLAY BALL!!!

SO ORDERED.

5.52 Salary Grievances Arising from Strikes

The dichotomy of interests between the union "rank and file" on the one hand and certain individual players on the other is nowhere better illustrated than the disputes that have arisen over a select number of players being paid during a players' strike. These occurred in connection with the baseball strike of 1981. Certain players had successfully negotiated salary guarantees into their contracts and now argued that these guarantees required their clubs to pay the players their salaries even when they were on strike. Several disputes over the rights to wages were grieved and are discussed below.

A different issue surfaced with the football strike of 1982. An arbitrator was called on to decide whether players on the disabled list were to be treated as on strike or were to be placed in a special category qualifying them for wages during the strike. This issue is also discussed below.

Arbitration Between Major League Players Association and Major League Baseball Players Relations Committee, Inc., Panel Decision No. 49, Goetz, Impartial Arbitrator, June 29, 1983

The issue in this case is to what extent, if any, are the players who were disabled at the commencement of the 1981 Major League Baseball Players' Strike entitled to a continuation of salary during the strike; and, if any such continuation is warranted, under what circumstances and for what period?

When this strike called by the Players Association started on June 12, 1981, a substantial number of contracted players were physically disabled and were receiving the salary specified in the individual Uniform Player Contract between the player and the club. Regulation 2 of the contract provides that a player injured within the scope of employment shall receive full salary for the remainder of the season or until able to play, whichever is shorter.

At the start of the 1981 strike, the clubs terminated salary payments to all players, including those on the disabled lists. Some of the disabled players filed default notices pursuant to paragraph 7(a) of the Uniform Player Contract, which provides for termination of a player's contract unless the club remedies the default within ten days. The clubs thereupon rescinded salary payments to the disabled players (the clubs never stopped paying medical and hospital expenses), and filed a grievance seeking reimbursement.

Some of the players were injured during the 1981 championship season; others were injured in spring training or during the 1980 season. While some players recovered from their disabilities during the series, none offered to, or were asked to, perform services for their clubs. (The arbitration panel included a lengthy history of the strike in the opinion.)

The Players Association relies heavily on the decision in *E. L. Wiegand Division, Emerson*

Electric Co. v. *National Labor Relations Board*, 650 F. 2d 463 (3rd Circ. 1981), cert. den. 102 S. Ct. 1429 (1982). The court upheld an NLRB decision that withholding disability payments to employees during a strike constituted an unfair labor practice in the circumstances of that case. The key determinant for whether an employee is entitled to disability payments is "whether they are due and payable on the date on which the employer denied them." However, arbitrator Raymond Goetz points out that in *Emerson*, disability payments were made on the basis of the employee's length of service. In other words, in *Emerson*, the rights to payments had "accrued" or become "vested" upon disability. Further, in *Emerson*, the employer attempted to coerce and restrain activity by threatening not to pay disabled employees during a strike. The question for interpretation in the instant case is whether the rights to disability payments had become fully vested at the time of the strike.

The clubs relied on four factors for their refusal to pay disabled players' salaries during the strike: (1) no players indicated they did not support the strike; (2) the Players Association authorized the strike as a unit; (3) the disability of players during the strike was purely a fortuitous circumstance; and (4) those who recovered did not offer their services to their clubs. The Players Association argued that the disabled players could not be on strike because they weren't in a position to opt not to play when the strike commenced.

The arbitration panel observed that payment to disabled players would in effect reward injury at the time of the strike. On his analysis of the question of accrual of rights, Goetz noted that these players would have had no rights to salary if not disabled. For these reasons, Goetz held that disabled players are not entitled to continuation of salaries during a Players Association strike. In doing so, Goetz notes that the "Player will be as well off economically as he would have been had he not been disabled."

The Players Association also argued that the clubs had been inconsistent by paying disabled players medical and hospital expenses but refusing to pay their salaries. However, Goetz held that the right to hospital and medical expenses are fully vested at the time of disability, and that the disabled players have no right to salaries during a strike.

The Players Association finally argued that the words in the Uniform Player Contract should be interpreted against the drafter (the clubs). But Goetz noted the well-established principles that this "interpret against the drafter" rule should only be applied as a last resort. When, as here, the contract can be interpreted and a result determined from the facts of the case, the "interpret against the drafter" rule plays no part.

Accordingly, the clubs' grievances against disabled players for salaries paid to them during the strike were sustained, and the players were ordered to promptly reimburse the clubs. The grievance of disabled players who had not been paid was denied. Chairman Goetz noted that this decision did not affect players with special covenants providing for "guaranteed" contracts.

Arbitration Between Major League Baseball Player Relations Committee, Inc. and Major League Baseball Players Association, Panel Decision No. 50A and 50B, Goetz, Impartial Arbitrator, Nov. 2, 1983

This was a consolidated case involving six clubs and eighteen players whose multiyear contracts in effect during the 1981 players' strike were "guaranteed contracts." The issue presented was whether the players were entitled to their salaries when the "guaranteed contracts" were silent on the issue of a strike.

With the advent of free agency in the 1970s, players began to request and receive what is known as "no-cut, guaranteed contracts." These contracts were guaranteed in that the player would receive a salary throughout the term of the contract even if the player was injured or no longer displayed sufficient skill at the professional level. The first of these contracts was signed by James ("Catfish") Hunter in 1975 with the New York Yankees. Hunter signed a five-year, "guaranteed contract." Without the

special covenants in Hunter's contract, the club would have had the right to terminate the contract at the end of each year.

At the beginning of the 1976 season, many free agents signed these long-term, "no-cut" contracts. The contract between Andy Messersmith and the Atlanta Braves provided for a three-year, "no-cut" contract. But unlike Hunter's contract, which specifically mentioned continuation of payment only when physically disabled, Messersmiths' contract also allowed for continuation of payment after death or in the event of a union strike. Also in 1976, agent Jerry Kapstein negotiated a five-year contract for Ken Holtzman with the New York Yankees. Kapstein devised a special covenant, which became known as the "Kapstein form," which provided in part as follows:

Club Agrees that This Entire Five-Year Contract Is A *"No-Cut Guaranteed Contract"*
The Club acknowledges, guarantees and agrees, that this entire contract is a "no-cut," guaranteed contract and that the payments due to the Player as basic compensation under Article 2 of this contract titled "Payment" as well as all payments guaranteed by the Club according to the payment schedule under Article I(d) of this Addendum, shall be payable by the Club to Player and shall remain in effect and shall be the obligation of the Club, despite the inability of the Player to perform the services provided for under the contract, and to be performed by him for the Club. Despite anything to the contrary recited herein, all payments of salary under Article I(d) of this Addendum, shall be payable by the Club to the Player despite the fact that Player's inability to so perform said services, is due either to a failure of Player to display sufficient professional skills or if the Player's inability to so perform said services, is due to a medical condition, including mental or physical handicap, or death of the Player. It matters not whether the Player suffers such disabilities on or off the baseball field or whether said disabilities are incurred during the "Championship Season" or during the "off-season." In the event of the death of the Player, all payments guaranteed under Article No. 2 of this contract and all payments required to be made in accordance to the schedule

set up under Article I(d) of this Addendum shall be payable by Club to Player's estate in full.

Section II of the contract provided exceptions to the "guaranteed contracts," which relieved the club from paying the player if the player were suspended or placed on a restricted list, if the player retired, or if there was a players' strike. Later, in 1976, Kapstein negotiated contracts for Rick Burleson, Fred Lynn, and Carlton Fisk with the Boston Red Sox. These contracts differed from Holtzman's in that they included an "Authorized and Unauthorized Activities" addendum. If a player was disabled while participating in an unauthorized activity, the club would be relieved of all liabilities and obligations to the players. Some of these activities included motorcycle racing, parachuting, skiing, and organized basketball. Kapstein negotiated many other contracts using a substantially identical form as the one used by the three Red Sox players.

A differently worded form of salary guarantee also came into use at the suggestion of Marvin J. Miller, executive director of the Players Association. The form stated:

> In order for the Player to be protected by a guarantee, the player's contract, in the section for "Special Covenants," should contain language such as the following: "Regardless of any provision herein to the contrary, all compensation and benefits payable to the Player hereunder shall be paid in any event, provided the Player does not abitrarily refuse to render his professional services. It is the intent and understanding of the parties that this entire Contract shall be a 'no-cut,' guaranteed contract despite any inability of the Player to exhibit sufficient skill or competitive ability, and despite any mental or physical handicap or injury or death."

The memorandum said nothing about specific exceptions to this guarantee beyond the "arbitrarily refuse" proviso. Although certain exceptions were added in a supplement, no provision for the possibility of a Players Association strike was made.

In 1977, Lamar Johnson signed a "guaranteed" contract with the Chicago White Sox. This contract provided for an exception of the guarantee in the event of a Players Association strike. Following the insistence of American League President Lee McPhail, most "guaranteed" contracts signed since 1977 contained a "strike exception." None of the contracts with specific "strike exceptions" were at issue in this arbitration.

California Angels and Frank Tanana, Panel Decision 50A

The Frank Tanana contract was negotiated by his agent, Tony Attanasio, with Harry Dalton, vice-president and general manager of the California Angels, in late 1976 and early 1977. After agreeing upon terms, Attanasio drafted an addendum to the Uniform Player Contract setting forth special covenants, including paragraph D, "Guaranteed No-Cut Contract":

> Regardless of the provisions contained in Section 5(b) and all of Section 7 of the Uniform Player Contract, and regardless of any other provision to the contrary in said Contract, other than the "prohibited activities" contained in the paragraph immediately above, all compensation and benefits payable to Player hereunder shall be paid in any event, provided the Player *does not arbitrarily refuse to render his professional services.* It is the intent, understanding and agreement of the club and the Player that this entire contract shall be a "no-cut" guaranteed contract despite any inability of the Player to exhibit sufficient skill or competitive ability, and despite any mental or physical handicap or injury or death, other than a disabling injury or death resulting from Player's participation in one or more of the "prohibited activities" as described above. Any assignment of this contract by the Club shall not affect in any manner whatsoever its obligation to make all payments owing to the Player hereunder. (Emphasis in original.)

With the exception of the reference to "prohibited activities," paragraph D tracked the guarantee recommended by the Players Association very closely.

During the negotiations, no mention was made either by Dalton or Attanasio of the possibility of a strike. The Tanana contract and the contract of Rod Carew were the only "guaranteed" contacts the Angels entered into with a "strike exception."

Before the start of the 1981 season, Tanana's contract was assigned to the Boston Red Sox. Tanana was with the Red Sox when the Players' strike began on June 12, 1981. A newspaper article in the *Boston Globe* quoted Tanana as saying he supported the strike.

Chairman Raymond Goetz of the arbitration panel began his opinion by emphasizing that as a general rule, an employer is not obligated to compensate employees while they are on strike. As one respected arbitrator put it in *The Carbon Limestone Company*, 66–3 ARB par. 8773 (Duff):

> It would be contrary to normal industrial experience if any economic benefits would be provided by an employer to employees who engage in a strike. In any event, if the continuation of any economic benefits is intended, *it should be set forth clearly* in the Agreement. (Emphasis added.)

Goetz pointed out that Tanana was seeking something highly unusual in labor-management relations. The opinion continued by finding that the provision that "all compensation and benefits payable to the Player hereunder shall be paid in any event" was inherently vague. Goetz found that there was "nothing in the discussions between Attanasio and Dalton to indicate that this imprecise wording was intended to create such an unusually open-ended salary obligation that it would be applicable when Tanana was withholding his services during a strike."

To begin with, the initial vagueness of the general statement that "*compensation . . . shall be paid in any event*" was limited by the immediately following clause: "provided the Player does not *arbitrarily* refuse to render his professional services." While this proviso was set up with the idea that the player who retired would not be paid, the clubs argued that a strike was included in this "arbitrarily refuse" to play clause. The Players Association argued that this clause did not apply to a strike since it was not within the player's individual control. Goetz rejected this argument, finding that strike action requires individuals acting in concert to withold services from their employer. Therefor, all players were responsible for the concerted activity (the strike) that they supported.

The Players Association also argued that Tanana's failure to perform during the strike was not an "arbitrary refusal" because it did not invoke any "*capricious* exercise of personal choice, without valid or rational reason" (emphasis theirs). However, Goetz found that "the proviso is worded broadly enough to *allow it to be read* as precluding the extraordinary requirement of compensation to an employee who is *willfully* withholding services because of participation in a strike."

Goetz also looked to the principal purpose of the parties in determining whether they intended to include compensation to the player during a players' strike as part of the guarantee. Goetz found the primary purpose of the "guaranteed" contract was to protect the player in the event of a physical disability or diminution of playing skills. Goetz held that the wording of the compensation provision in Tanana's contract could not properly be extended to guarantee payment in the strike situation because that would be totally unrelated to the parties' clearly ascertainable purpose of protecting the player against loss of ability to play due to disability or similar circumstances beyond one's control.

The Players Association then argued that since most "guaranteed" contracts have contained "strike exceptions," a player must be paid during the strike if the contract does not contain this strike exception. But Goetz held that the "strike exceptions" may be contained in other contracts for clarification purposes, to "eliminate any possible question." Players are mistaken, according to Goetz, when they argue that "strike exceptions" eliminate something that would otherwise be covered. In summary, the practice by the Angels and other clubs of obtaining express exceptions to *salary guarantees* falls far short of *establishing clear recognition* by the clubs that salary payments *had to be made* unless there was an express exception covering that contingency.

Goetz also invoked the rule of contract interpretation to interpret vagueness against the drafter of the contract. The term "arbitrarily refuse," which was part of the contract drafted by Attanasio, should be resolved against the player. Therefore, Goetz ruled that the clubs are covered during a players' strike by the "arbitrarily refuse" proviso.

Consequently, the arbitration panel found that any salary payment made to Tanana during the 1981 strike should be promptly refunded by Tanana.

Milwaukee Brewers and Larry Hisle, Panel Decision 50B

The special covenant in this case is similar to the one in the Tanana case, but the instant case presents two factors not present in the Tanana arbitration: (1) the subject of a strike was discussed during contract negotiations and (2) Hisle was disabled at the time the strike commenced.

The Hisle contract was negotiated by his agent, Richard Moss, with Bud Selig, president of the Brewers, and Richard Hoffman, vice-president in charge of finance, during the first three weeks of November 1977. By mid-November, Seliz and Moss had agreed upon a six-year, "guaranteed no-cut" contract at $250,000 per year, with a signing bonus of $615,000 and deferred compensation over 13 years. Moss sent the following addendum to Selig:

B. *Guaranty of Payment*

1. Regardless of any provision herein to the contrary, all compensation and benefits payable to Player shall be paid in any event, provided Player does not *arbitrarily refuse* to render his professional services. It is the intent and understanding of the parties that this entire Contract shall be a "no-cut," guaranteed contract despite any inability of Player to exhibit sufficient skill or competitive ability, and despite any mental or physical handicap or injury or death. In the event of Player's

death, all payments guaranteed under this Contract shall be payable by Club to Player's estate (or to a designee of Player if Player has so authorized in writing) in accordance with the schedule of payments specified herein. Should, during the six-year term of this Contract, Player arbitrarily refuse to render his professional services, Club shall be relieved of his obligation to make payments of salary (and a proportional share of deferred compensation) attributable to the period during which Player's arbitrary refusal continues.

This draft had no mention of the possibility of a players' strike. On November 15, Selig delegated to Hoffman the responsibility of negotiating all remaining noneconomic matters.

When Hoffman met with Moss on November 15, he had with him the special covenants to the contract between the club and Sal Bando. One of the covenants was an exception to the guaranteed contract for any strike by the Players Association. Hoffman asked Moss to include a "strike exception" in Hisle's contract, but Moss refused. Hoffman also requested an exception for retirement, but Moss told him that retirement was covered by the "arbitrarily refuse" proviso.

Moss prepared a supplement, which became attached to the contract and was signed by both parties on November 17 in the following form:

This letter shall constitute a Supplement to The Addendum to the Contract between Larry E. Hisle and the Milwaukee Brewers Baseball Club, dated November 17, 1977, and shall be deemed to supersede, amend and modify Section B of the Addendum to the extent it is inconsistent herewith.

It is hereby understood and agreed that the Club shall be relieved of its obligation to make payments of salary (and a proportional share of deferred compensation) attributable to the period during which Player Hisle is unable to render his professional services due to physical or mental incapacity:

   (a) Resulting from intentional self-injury, suicide or attempted suicide;
   (b) Resulting from sickness or disease attributable to drug abuse or alcoholism;
   (c) Resulting from activities or sports prohibited by Paragraph 5 of this Contract;
   (d) Resulting from his own felonious act.

When Hoffman told Selig of his inability to obtain a "strike exception," Selig replied that "it had to be included." When Hoffman told Moss of the necessity of a "strike exception," Moss replied that he had come there to execute the contract, not renegotiate it.

Moss and Hoffman then met with Selig to discuss the "strike exception." Testimony as to what was discussed in that meeting is conflicting. Both Hoffman and Selig testified that Moss had said that the possibility of a strike was covered by the "arbitrary refusal" proviso. However, Moss testified that he stated that the contract was silent on the issue of a strike and that he was willing to take his chances on the outcome of arbitration. Moss also denied telling Selig that the "strike exception" was covered by the "arbitrary refusal" proviso. Consequently, on November 17, the contract was signed by all parties with the addendum silent on the issue of a strike.

On August 6, 1979, Hoffman sent a letter to Moss requesting a formalization of terms regarding a "strike exception" among other things. Attached to the letter was a proposed supplement, part of which would relieve the club of salary obligations during a strike. On August 24, Moss responded by saying that he disagreed with "some of the contents" of the letter, but that he would discuss it with Hisle and then meet with Hoffman. The meeting never took place.

Hisle, who voted in favor of the strike, was on the disabled list when the strike began on June 12, 1981. He underwent surgery on June 23, and resumed play on September 1, 1981.

Goetz commenced his opinion by determining, as an issue of fact, that Moss's testimony regarding negotiations about a "strike exception" was more credible than that of Selig and Hoffman. The arbitrator held that while Moss never guaranteed that the club's salary obligations would be relieved in the event of a strike, the fact that the contract was silent on this issue did not necessarily mean that Hisle would have to be paid either.

The Players Association argued that since the club failed in its attempt to obtain the "strike exception," the club was fully liable to Hisle for his salary during the strike. But Goetz found that this was not the only inference to be drawn from the club's failure to obtain a strike exemption. As in the Tanana case, the addition of the "strike exception" would provide clarification to avoid *possible litigation*. Consequently, the silence of the contract on the possibility of a strike left room for argument on both sides.

While Goetz considered the role of the "interpret against the draftsman" rule, the arbitrator found the rule inapplicable in the instant case. Finding that there was no "meeting of the minds" — in fact, a genuine difference in opinion on the issue of a "strike exception" — Goetz held that the parties are equally responsible for the vagueness in the contract. However, instead of having to rule on an objective rule of reasonableness, Goetz avoided the difficult issue of ruling on the "strike exception" by resolving the case in favor of Hisle on the basis of his guarantee against physical disability.

The first point Goetz made was that Hisle's right to salary due to disability had accrued before the strike began. Goetz rejected the club's contention that Hisle had "arbitrarily refused" to play since he was physically unable to perform. Goetz felt that Hisle's failure to perform during the strike could not be seen as more of a "refusal" than before the strike. He upheld his side of the bargain by performing when he was physically able. His failure to perform when the strike started on June 12, 1981, was not due to the strike but due to circumstances beyond his control that prevented him from performing in any event.

Consequently, the arbitrator held that Hisle was entitled to his salary during the Players strike of 1981 due to the physical disability clause in his contract. The arbitrator made no ruling regarding the issue of the lack of a strike exception clause.

Arbitration Between Major League Baseball Player Relations Committee, Inc. and Major League Baseball Players Association, Panel Decision No. 50C, Goetz, Impartial Arbitrator, December 19, 1983

The issue here is whether Los Angeles Dodgers who signed long-term guaranteed contracts were entitled to salary payments for the period of the 1981 Players' Strike. The history of long-term guaranteed contracts was reviewed in Panel Decision 50A and will not be repeated here.

The six Dodger Players claiming salary continuation during the 1981 strike were Rick Monday, Steve Garvey, Reggie Smith, Terry Forster, Ron Cey, and Derrel Thomas. All six had contracts covering the 1981 season that included a special covenant concerning guaranteed salary either in the form recommended by the Players Association (quoted in Panel Decision 50A), or a slightly modified version thereof. None of the contracts contained express exceptions for a strike by the Players Association, nor was the topic of a strike discussed in any of the negotiations. (The opinion then detailed the history of the six negotiations, the Standard Players Association Addendum or a modification thereof was used, and the agent for all six players had never used a "strike exception" in negotiating their previous long-term contracts.)

Jerry Kapstein, drafter of the "Kapstein form" (see Panel Decision 50A), represented Steve Garvey in the negotiations. According to Kapstein, a form similar to the Players Association form was used for Steve Garvey at the request of Dodger President Peter O'Malley. But while Kapstein had previously provided a "strike exception" in his basic "Kapstein form," the "strike exception" was absent in Garvey's contract.

Beginning in 1979, the Dodgers added a strike exception to all long-term guaranteed contracts. However, all six players in this case signed contracts previous to 1979, and all six contracts extended at least until 1981 (the strike season).

The opinion, again authored by Chairman Goetz, held that this case was no different than the Tanana case (Panel Decision 50A). All six

used approximately the same vague language — "compensation . . . shall be paid in any event." Nothing in the negotiations indicated that the club intended such an open-ended agreement that would require compensation to a player on strike.

Goetz held that the "arbitrarily refuse" clause — which was contained in all six contracts in one form or another — could be read to preclude salary payment to a player who willfully witholds his services while on strike. Further, as in the Tanana case, Goetz found that the primary purpose of the parties here was to assure compensation despite lack of playing ability, disability, or death. These objectives were totally unrelated to the players' request to be paid during a strike.

The Players Association based its argument on the idea that since the Dodgers did not employ a "strike exception" until 1979, all guaranteed contracts without "strike exceptions" should require the club to compensate striking players. However, as in *Tanana*, Goetz observed that the club's inclusion of a "strike exception" simply could be "for purposes of clarification, *to eliminate any possible question* that the excepted situation is not within the general proviso" (emphasis in original) (50A, p. 30). Further, Goetz felt that the fact that the agents readily accepted the terms of the "strike exceptions" in later contracts pointed out that the agents did not expect the players to be compensated in the event of a strike anyway.

Finally, Goetz pointed out that when the Dodgers found out about the desirability of the inclusion of a strike exception, they insisted upon the use of the exception consistently, thereafter. The club points out, and Goetz agreed, that this change showed the Dodgers' desire to move toward more explicit expression in their contracts as the club obtained more professional outside legal advice.

Consequently, the arbitration panel ordered the players to return any salaries paid out to them for the strike period, and denied the grievances of those players who had not been paid.

New York Yankees and Tommy John, Panel Decision No. 50D

The New York Yankees signed free agent Tommy John to a three-year, guaranteed "no-cut" contract in January of 1979. While John's contract contained no "strike exception," this case differs from the case of the six Dodgers (Panel Decision 50C) in that the Yankees and John's agent, Robert Cohen, engaged in lengthy negotiations regarding the inclusion of a "strike exception."

Cohen negotiated an "agreement in principle" with Yankee President Al Rosen in November of 1978. The parties agreed on a three-year, guaranteed no-cut contract, with deferred compensation and life insurance provided for John. After several proposals and modifications, the parties agreed on the following addendum to the Uniform Player Contract:

> 5. Any other provision *to the contrary* notwithstanding and except as provided below in this paragraph *all compensation and benefits payable to the Player hereunder shall be paid in any event, provided the Player does not arbitrarily refuse to render his professional services.* Compensation and benefits do not have to be paid if Player becomes incapacitated or dies while on the Major League Player Roster of Club because of intentional self-injury, suicide, drugs, alcoholism, or because of participation in automobile or motorcycle racing, piloting of aircraft, fencing, parachuting or sky diving, boxing, wrestling, karate, judo, softball, football, basketball, soccer, skiing, hockey, "Superstar" or "Superteam" competition, and other activities prohibited by the Uniform Player Contract ("Contract"), paragraph 5(b).
>
> *It is the intent and understanding of the parties hereto that this entire Contract shall be a "no-cut," guaranteed contract, despite any inability of the Player to exhibit sufficient skill or competitive ability, and despite any mental or physical handicap or injury or death* except as provided in the previous paragraph. (Emphasis added.)

This contract form was signed by Yankee President George Steinbrenner on January 2, 1979. Shortly thereafter, Cohen received a phone call from Rosen informing him that the Yankees were having difficulty obtaining the full $500,000 face value of life insurance provisions as provided in the contract. Rosen requested that the club be permitted to provide $250,000 initially, and increase the amount gradually. Cohen, after discussing it with John, agreed to this modification. Soon after, Rosen called Cohen, explaining that owner Steinbrenner was furious that the contract contained no "strike exception." Cohen replied that he was aware that there was no strike exception, but that they had a signed contract and he saw no reason to change it. At the insistence of Rosen, who claimed he was under a great deal of pressure, Cohen agreed to speak with John about modification of the contract to include a "strike exception." After some further discussion with John, Cohen advised Rosen that John would be willing to give the Yankees a provision that he *would not* be paid in the event of a strike if (1) the Yankees *would return the life insurance* to the original face amount of $500,000 for the entire period until 2002 and (2) the club *would include a provision that John would* be paid in the event of a lockout by the clubs.

About a week later, Steinbrenner called Cohen demanding that the lockout provision be removed from the new contract. When Cohen and John refused, Steinbrenner said, according to Cohen's testimony, that "Maybe we should call the whole thing off." Cohen replied that would be fine and that he would negotiate with Kansas City instead. Cohen testified that Steinbrenner responded as follows:

> At that point in time, George said, "No, no, don't react so quickly." After a short conversation he said, "All right, you win, strike language is out, lock-out language is out, the insurance goes back to the way we wanted to put it originally, i.e., payable in 30 years," and that's it.

Cohen and John agreed to this final proposal, and the contract was signed the day before spring training. When the strike commenced on June 12, 1981, John had been on the disabled list for about a week. John acknowledged that he supported the strike.

Arbitrator Raymond Goetz held that like the Larry Hisle case (Panel Decision 50B), John would be entitled to compensation while disabled during the strike. As in the Hisle decision, Goetz recognized that "because such a vested benefit has already been earned, it cannot be cut off upon commencement of a strike. John was not in any position to "arbitrarily refuse" to perform since he was already physically unable to play. However, unlike Hisle, John was not disabled throughout the entire strike. While it may have been difficult to determine when John was able to play, this was unnecessary since Goetz held that due to the factual situation surrounding the "strike exception" negotiations, John was entitled to his full salary during the strike.

The Yankees made the same arguments as the Dodgers — that compensation to an employee while on strike is highly unusual, and that the "arbitrarily refuse" proviso encompasses a Players Association strike. While these arguments, based on earlier panel decisions, would seem to have considerable merit, Goetz held that the instant case is distinguishable from the decisions already rendered.

In applying a standard or reasonableness, the arbitrator found three key factors in holding for John: (1) the club's frantic efforts — after having agreed to special covenants — to add an express "strike exception"; (2) the grudging deletion of the "strike exception" by the club in order to give other concessions; (3) that when the club finally withdrew its demand for a strike "exception," the impression left John and Cohen to assume that the "Club was *giving up something of substance* it otherwise would have had." (Emphasis in original.) When Steinbrenner said "you win," the significance was that the club had made a great concession.

Further, Goetz took into account John's interpretation of the contract — that is, that he was guaranteed payment during a strike. While a party's unstated understandings of a contract are generally of little significance, the club, due to the lengthy negotiations, knew or should have known John's understanding of the contract. At most, Goetz notes, there was a mutual misunderstanding of the club's making.

Accordingly, the arbitrator held that John was entitled to his salary during the period of the 1981 strike.

Arbitration Between Major League Players Relations Committee, Inc. and Major League Baseball Players Association, Panel Decision No. 50F, Goetz, Impartial Arbitrator, February 27, 1984

This decision deals with claims made by three players under their contracts with the San Francisco Giants — John Montefusco, Gary Lavelle, and Randy Moffitt. A brief look at the history of long-term contracts was reviewed in Panel Decision 50A and will not be repeated here.

John Montefusco signed a five-year, guaranteed contract with the Giants on April 15, 1977. The salary guarantee in the special covenant read as follows:

> 2. The salary stipulated in 1977, 1978, 1979, 1980 and 1981 in Paragraph 2 on the face of this contract and $700,000.00 of deferred compensation in Paragraph 1 of the Special Covenants is guaranteed with the following exception: If the Player sustains a non-baseball injury off the field, then he shall be entitled to compensation in the amount of one-half (½) of the balance remaining for the years 1977, 1978, 1979, 1980 and 1981 prorated accordingly. *This clause only becomes effective in the event the club elects to release Player from the Club.* (Emphasis added in final contract.)

Also contained in the contract was a list of prohibited activities. If the players were injured participating in one of these prohibited activities, the club would be relieved of all financial liabilities and obligations.

Prior to any discussion about contract wording with Giants General Manager Spec Richardson, Montefusco had met with Giants President Bob Luri to negotiate compensation. Later, Montefusco told Lurie and Richardson that he wanted the contract to be "guaranteed no matter what." Lurie replied that would be "fine."

Montefusco testified that during these discussions, he "never even thought of a players strike." Montefusco's contract was assigned to the Atlanta Braves, and he was with Atlanta when the strike began on June 12, 1981. Montefusco openly supported the strike.

Arbitrator Ray Goetz noted that the instant case was similar to the Tanana case (Panel Decision 50A). The same rationale applied here: an employer is not usually expected to finance a strike against itself by compensating strikers for work not performed, and any claim to the contrary should be set out in the agreement.

The phraseology was more vague in Montefusco's contract than in that of Tanana's ("salary ... is guaranteed" as opposed to "compensation ... shall be paid in any event"). Looking at the negotiations, Goetz pointed out that all discussions centered on physical disability. The fact that Montefusco admitted that he never even thought about a strike was compelling evidence that a strike was not what he intended when he asked that his contract be guaranteed "no matter what."

The Players Association argued again that the subsequent inclusion of a "strike exception" in later contracts proved that the club believed it was liable to players who had no "strike exception" in the event of a strike. Goetz again rejected this argument:

> In the absence of any clarifying evidence of bargaining history, it is at least equally reasonable to infer that the specific exceptions were added in later contracts, as professional drafting assistance was called upon, *to eliminate any possible question* as to the scope of the guarantee. This was certainly true as to the express exception for retirement by the player included in many later contracts; there is no good reason why it could not have been equally true with respect to the strike exceptions.

Consequently, Montefusco's grievance for payment during the strike was denied.

The contract between Gary Lavelle and the Giants was identical in all relevant aspects to that of Montefusco. Goetz held that for the same reasons as the Montefusco decision, Lavelle must be denied his grievance.

The contract between Randy Moffitt and the Giants was substantially identical to that of Montefusco. However, the Players Association argued that a conversation between Moffitt and his agent, Ed Keating, distinguished this case from Monefusco's case. Moffitt's testimony was as follows:

> Q. Do you recall making any comment to Mr. Keating in Mr. Richardson's presence about a guarantee or the special covenants?

> A. I asked Mr. Keating, "You mean to tell me if I cannot render my services due to what is said in this contract, for any other reason, will I be paid in full?" Ed Keating said, "You will be paid for five consecutive years unless you do something which is stated in the contract."

Goetz held that this conversation was ineffective in proving that Moffit and the Giants had agreed that Moffitt should be paid in the event of a players' strike. While General Manager Richardson was present during the conversation in question, Goetz found that both Keating and Richardson "could reasonably have assumed Moffitt was asking about *disability* due to something other than unauthorized activities." Consequently, for reasons stated in Panel Decision 50A and the *Montefusco* decision, Moffitt was denied his grievance.

Arbitration Between Major League Baseball Player Relations Committee, Inc. and Major League Baseball Players Association, Panel Decision No. 50G

This is the fifth and final installment of Panel Decision 50, a consolidated case involving six clubs and 18 players. The instant case involves the grievances of San Francisco Giants Vide Blue and Darrel Evans, who claim entitlement to payment during the 1981 Baseball Players Strike under their guaranteed contracts.

On April 26, 1976, Giants General Manager Spec Richardson sent Blue's attorney Richard Sequeira a letter with several proposed clauses for Blue's contract. Included in the proposals was an express provision that relieved the club from liabilities and obligations in the event of a players' strike. Sequeira testified that in a May 9 meeting he discussed the "strike exception" with Richardson. Sequeira testified:

> I received these on the 27th and we had a meeting in my office on May 9th and we discussed a lot of things, one of which was the fact that we were not going to agree, under any condition, that the payment of compensation to this player be suspended for a strike or a lockout. I don't think I used those words "lockout," but if the owners wouldn't let them play.
>
> We talked about it, or I talked about it, in terms of the fact that I am not concerned with whose fault it would be in the event a strike occurred. Whether the owners wouldn't let them play or the players go on strike, that is of no concern to us. The man gets paid under the contract.

Both Giants President Bob Lurie and Richardson testified that Sequeira had never requested that Blue be paid in the event of a strike.

Between late May and mid-June, Sequeira and Richardson came to a basic agreement on the terms of the contract. On June 13, Sequeira sent to Giants attorney Jim Hunt a draft for the special covenants regarding guaranteed salary. This draft contained an "arbitrary refuse" provision in most guaranteed contracts. By July 26, Sequeira and Hunt had worked out an agreement on the terms that read as follows:

> III. *Guarantee.* Regardless of any provisions herein to the contrary, all compenation and benefits payable to the Player hereunder *shall be fully guaranteed, so long as the Player does not refuse to render his professional services.* It is the intent and understanding of the parties that this entire contract is a no-cut, guaranteed contract despite any inability of the Player to exhibit sufficient skill or competitive ability, and despite any mental or physical handicap or injury if such mental or physical handicap of injury makes it impossible or unreasonably difficult for Player to render the professional services required by this contract, or death, subject only to provisions of sub-paragraph a. hereunder and the provisions of Section IV. (Emphasis in original.)

There was no express mention of a "strike exception." One major difference between the

final draft and Sequeira's draft was the elimination of the word "arbitrarily." Hunt testified:

> Q. Did you discuss with him the reasons for your proposed counter language to the guarantee clause?
>
> A. I did.
>
> Q. In the course of those discussions, did the question of a players' strike come up?
>
> A. Well, I can't be certain of my precise words. *I can be sure that I used the example of a players' strike as one of the meanings of a refusal to render services.* I thought in the course of our negotiations, that was one of the less exotic ways that a refusal to render services could occur. I told Mr. Sequeira it could also occur, in my opinion, if a player refused to cross a picket line put up by another union. That that also would be a refusal to render services. (Emphasis in Original.)

According to Hunt, Sequeria made no response to Hunt's example of a strike as a situation whereby the player would refuse to render services. Also in the agreement was a "merger" clause:

> X. *Entire Agreement.* This instrument contains the entire agreement between the parties relating to the rights herein granted and the obligations herein assumed. Any oral representations or modifications concerning this instrument shall be of no force or effect excepting a subsequent modification in writing, signed by the party to be charged.

The Players Strike began on June 12, 1981. Blue openly supported the strike.

Arbitrator Raymond Goetz pointed out that if only the wording of the special covenants was considered, this case would be no different than that of Fred Tanana (Panel Decision 50A), and Blue's grievance would have to be denied. But the Players Association relied on Sequeira's claimed objection to the inclusion of a "strike exception" in the May 9 meeting, arguing that his objection at that time forced the Giants to eliminate the strike language from the final draft, and this entitled Blue to compensation during the strike. Goetz found several weaknesses to this argument.

First, regarding the testimony about the May 9 meeting, Goetz found the testimony of Lurie and Richardson, who denied Sequeira's claim that he insisted on the deletion of the "strike exception" to be more credible. Further, even if Sequeira did make such a demand, it is unlikely that Richardson or Lurie would have made no direct response. Goetz observes that, except under unusual circumstances not present here, silence cannot be construed as assent.

Second, whatever objections Sequeira had to Lurie and Richardson, he should have clarified them in his final negotiations with Hunt. Goetz found credible Hunt's assertion that he verbally included a strike as one way the player could "refuse to perform." If Sequeira disagreed, it was incumbent upon him to say so.

Finally, any reliance Sequeira placed on the May 9 conversation was misplaced in light of his acceptance of the "merger clause." The burden was on Sequeira to negotiate for specific language regarding compensation to the player in the event of a strike — Sequeira made no effort to fulfill this burden.

Goetz summarily dismissed the Players Association's argument that since the Giants had included a "strike exception" in subsequent contracts, contracts without "strike exceptions" were guaranteed in the event of a strike. Goetz noted, as in previous panel decisions, the club probably included the "strike exceptions" for purposes of explicit clarifications. Consequently, Blue's grievance was denied.

The contract for Darrel Evans, negotiated by Jerry Kapstein, used some of the special covenants known as the "Kapstein form" (see panel decision 50A), with the exception of the use of the language "willfully and intentionally refuses to render services," and the lack of an exception to the guarantee in the event of a players' strike. There was at no time any discussion of the possibility of a strike by Kapstein or the club.

Arbitrator Raymond Goetz denied the grievance for the reasons set out in *Tanana* (Panel Decision 50A).

In the Matter of Arbitration Between NFL Players Association and NFL Management Council, Kagel, Arbitrator, January 11, 1984

Re: Salary Payments for Players Injured and Unable to Play at Commencement of the 1982 Work Stoppage

On September 20, 1982, Players Association began a strike which ended on November 17, 1982. The players who were disabled as of the commencement of the work stoppage received no salary payments for the period September 21 through November 16, 1982. Because of this, the Players Association filed a grievance claiming that such players were entitled to such injury protection benefits as they would ordinarily be entitled to in the absence of a strike. Management responded to this grievance on January 4, 1983, claiming that the Players Association claim had been resolved in Article XXIII, Section 3, of the 1982 Collective Bargaining Agreement that both parties signed on December 11, 1982.

Management originally proposed Section 3 of Article XXIII at a meeting with the Players Association on November 15, 1982. At that time management negotiators explained to the Players Association negotiators that under this proposed section, all players injured or not would give up their salary for the period of the strike in exchange for the "money now" payments set out in Sections 1 and 2 of Article XXIII.

On November 18, 1982, the players presented to management a revised "money now" proposal in which Section 3 was changed to provide that it "shall not ban the filing or processing of any salary claims by any players who were injured prior to September 21, 1982." Management rejected this proposal. Alternatively, the union proposed in a November 30, 1982 meeting that injured players be given the option of "money now" payments or filing a grievance. This was also rejected by management.

On December 9, the Management Council submitted to the players a document that it called "The Complete Collective Bargaining

Agreement," which included Article XXIII, Section 3, unchanged from its earlier proposal, which in turn was incorporated into the December 11 agreement.

Arbitrator Sam Kagel held that players on NFL clubs' injury reserve and physically unable to perform lists were not entitled to salary payments for the period of the 1982 strike.

The Players Association argued that injury benefits were accrued payments that the players were entitled to for services rendered prior to the 1982 strike and were not "wages," i.e., payments due for services currently being rendered and thus under precedent in *Emerson Electric* were

entitled to such benefits. (See 650 F.2d 463 [3rd Cir. 1981].)

Kagel held, however, that even assuming this to be true, such provisions were modified by the adoption of Article XXIII, Section 3. Kagel found that this section was a valid provision of the Collective Bargaining Agreement, that management made it clear that this provision applied to injured players, and that this provision takes precedence over any alleged "accrued" salaries. Kagel found that there was no intention provided in any portion of the Collective Bargaining Agreement that injured players receive both "money now" and salary.

Chapter 6

MANAGEMENT PERSPECTIVES
ON SPORTS LEAGUES AND CLUBS

6.00 Legal Status of the Sports League

Until recent years, challenges as to how a sports league conducted its business came, if at all, from the outside. There were exceptions, such as when clubs occasionally challenged a ruling by the league commissioner. But such uprisings generally were handled internally and did not disrupt significantly the way the leagues did business. That scenario is changing.

The 1960s and 1970s have previously been noted for the challenges by players to league strictures on their freedom to move from one team or one league to another. Even more recently, owners have disputed the collective decisions. The legal focus has centered on the nature of a sports league. Is a league a joint venture among competitors? Or is it, in reality, one big enterprise, a so-called "single-business entity"? If it is the latter, so the reasoning goes, a league should be accorded the ability to act to order its affairs and strengthen its economic position without being deemed to have entered into combinations or conspiracies that violate the national antitrust laws.

A single-business entity could still be guilty of attempting to monopolize, under section 2 of the Sherman Antitrust Act, but it would largely be immune to a section 1 attack as an illegal combination acting in restraint of trade. If the argument for a single-business entity were to prevail, therefore, the leagues would clearly be free to dictate to their own clubs the terms of membership in the league. Other abilities to act collectively might also emanate.

In Chapter 1, we considered two bills that were introduced in the United States Senate in 1982 (see Section 1.22). The focus was on the testimony that was elicited both for and against these proposed bills. While neither bill was enacted into law, it was noted that similar attempts in Congress are ongoing. Now it is time to analyze in more detail various cases that precipitated the attempts in Congress to accord special status to sports leagues. While the ultimate verdict is perhaps still out, it appears that the judicial sentiment is not willing to acknowledge sports leagues as single-business entities. But the record is not clearly one-sided. As will be seen, depending on the context of the dispute, courts have vacillated somewhat in their assessment of a league's true nature. The significance of this becomes more apparent as we consider the many transactions or situations with which a league must deal. These are mentioned at this point and addressed more fully in the several subsections of this chapter.

The sale and movement of franchises are

primary concerns. Assuring financial stability of a club, and thus the league, avoiding unwanted antitrust complication, and responding to consumer complaints are constant problem areas. A league may want to expand by adding new franchises. The process by which the league makes this decision and then awards the franchises creates both business and legal concerns. Again, there may be antitrust implications, whereby a rival league may raise cries of attempts to monopolize. The league's own players, through their union, may seek involvement.

The history of professional sports is replete with the appearance of new leagues that challenge the existing order. Beginning with the 1880s in baseball, competing leagues have sought to gain a share of the action and profits. The legal problems engendered have been many, including blacklisting of players who jumped to a new league; challenges to the enforcement of a league's standard player contract; challenges to option and reserve clauses; charges of attempts by the old league to monopolize stadiums, the media, and other items essential to putting out a sports product; and alleged inducements of breach of contract.

If there are competing leagues, is a merger of the leagues far behind? This has been another recurring theme. It may not always be a merger, but something that gets the leagues to agree not to compete too vigorously against each other is likely to be proposed. The legal implications must be examined.

The rule-making authority of a league as to the operation of its business includes many facets. A traditional one has been the extent to which the authority is delegated to either a commissioner or to a special committee of owners. A more recent development has been the extent to which traditional rule-making procedures have been modified through collective bargaining agreements with the players. At issue are such questions as squad sizes, trade deadlines, waiver procedures, league and club discipline, free agency, and even rule changes in the game itself.

As noted in the foregoing, sports leagues must now cope with collective bargaining. In most circumstances, the clubs are members of a multiemployer collective bargaining unit. This does not indicate, however, just how clubs and leagues organize for collective bargaining purposes. Whether the league is actually a party to the negotiations or whether a separate entity such as a management council is the stand-in for the league varies from sport to sport. These considerations were covered, to an extent, in Chapter 5 and will not be repeated here. Even so, the league's role in collective bargaining, under whatever procedure, is an increasingly important function.

Leagues strive to maintain images that appeal to the public. Problems of violence, gambling, and drug abuse are constant concerns. The league may unilaterally institute policies to deal with these problems, or it may act in conjunction with the players' labor group. Either choice raises complications.

Leagues and clubs also have property interests to protect, residing in the names and logos under which they do business. The protection of these interests through numerous legal concepts must be analyzed.

From the foregoing, a brief look at the many dimensions of leagues, their delegates (such as a commissioner), and their constituent parts (the clubs) can be seen. The many sections that follow dissect many of these concerns, forcing a look at problems as they arise in the context of actual business dealings or legal disputes. We start with the case of *North American Soccer League* v. *National Football League*, a challenge by a relatively fledgling league to the NFL's rule that its owners cannot also have ownership interests in clubs in other leagues. Much of the focus is on whether the NFL as a league is a single-business entity. As noted, this theme is repeated in other important cases in this chapter.

North American Soccer League v. National Football League, 670 F.2d 1249 (2d Cir. 1982)

Mansfield, Circuit Judge

The North American Soccer League (NASL) and certain of its member soccer teams (collectively referred to herein as "the NASL") appeal from a judgment of the Southern District of New York, Charles S. Haight, Jr., *Judge*, dissolving a preliminary injunction and dismissing a complaint seeking a permanent injunction and treble damages for alleged violations of Section 1 of the Sherman Act, 15 U.S.C. Sec. 1, by the defendants, the National Football League ("NFL") and certain of its member football clubs. . . .

The central question in this case is whether an agreement between members of one league of professional sports teams (NFL) to prohibit its members from making or retaining any capital investment in any member of another league of professional sports teams (in this case NASL) violates the antitrust laws. . . .

The success of professional football as a business depends on several factors. The ultimate goal is to attract as many people as possible to pay money to attend games between members and to induce advertisers to sponsor TV broadcasts of such games, which results in box-office receipts from sale of tickets and revenues derived from network advertising, all based on public interest in viewing games. If adequate revenues are received, a team will operate at a profit after payment of expenses, including players' salaries, stadium costs, referees, travel, maintenance and the like. Toward this goal there must be a number of separate football teams, each dispersed in a location having local public fans willing to buy tickets to games or view them on TV; a group of highly skilled players on each team who are reasonably well-matched in playing ability with those of other teams; adequate capital to support the teams' operations; uniform rules of competition governing game play; home territory stadia available for the conduct of the games; referees; and an apparatus for the negotiation and sale of network TV and radio broadcast rights and distribution of broadcast revenues among members.

To perform these functions some sort of an economic joint venture is essential. No single owner could engage in professional football for profit without at least one other competing team.

Separate owners for each team are desirable in order to convince the public of the honesty of the competition. Moreover, to succeed in the marketplace by attracting fans the teams must be close in the caliber of their playing ability. . . .

Although specific team profit figures were not introduced at trial, the record is clear that the NFL and most of its members now generally enjoy financial success. The NFL divides pooled TV receipts equally among members. Pre-season gate receipts from each game are shared on a 50/50 basis between opposing teams, and regular season gate receipts are divided on the basis of 60% for the home team and 40% for the visiting team.

Although NFL members thus participate jointly in many of the operations conducted by it on their behalf, each member is a separately owned, discrete legal entity which does not share its expenses, capital expenditures or profits with other members. Each also derives separate revenues from certain lesser sources, which are not shared with other members, including revenues from local TV and radio, parking and concessions. A member's gate receipts from its home games varies from those of other members, depending on the size of the home city, the popularity of professional football in the area and competition for spectators offered by other entertainment, including professional soccer. As a result, profits vary from team to team. Indeed as recently as 1978, the last year for which we have records, 2 of the 28 NFL teams suffered losses. In 1977 12 teams experienced losses. Thus, in spite of sharing of some revenues, the financial performance of each team, while related to that of the others, does not, because of the variables in revenues and costs as between member teams, neccesarily rise or fall with that of the others. The NFL teams are separate economic entities engaged in a joint venture.

The National American Soccer League ("NASL") was founded in 1968 upon the merger of two pre-existing soccer Leagues. Like the NFL, the NASL is an unincorporated association of professional soccer teams whose members are separately owned and operated, and are financially independent. Its raison d'etre and the needs of its member teams are essentially the same as those of members of other major professional sports leagues, including the NFL. However, professional soccer is not as mature or lucrative as professional football. Just as was the case with NFL member teams a quarter of a century ago, NASL is struggling to achieve wider popularity and with it greater revenues. Consequently, the risk of investing in an NASL team is considerably greater than that of investing in the NFL.

Soccer was not a widely followed or popular sport when the NASL was founded, and several earlier attempts to put together a professional soccer league failed due to lack of fan interest. The NASL has been the most successful soccer league to date. The district court found that since the NASL was organized "professional soccer has experienced substantial and accelerated growth in fan interest, media following, paid attendance, number of franchises and geographic scope. . . . " 505 F.Supp. 659 at 666–67. With this success NASL teams have become increasingly more effective competitors of the NFL teams. The two sports are somewhat similar. Their seasons substantially overlap. The teams have franchises from their respective leagues in the same locations and frequently use the same stadia. An increasing, although small, percentage of the public are switching their interest as fans and TV viewers from professional football to professional soccer, threatening to reduce revenue which NFL teams derive from gate receipts and TV broadcast rights. Competition between NFL and NASL teams has not only increased on an inter-league basis but also between individual NFL and NASL teams. On the league front both organizations compete for a greater share of finite national and regional TV broadcast and advertising revenues. At the local level NFL teams compete against NASL teams for greater fan support, gate attendance, and local broadcast revenues.

In spite of its success relative to other leagues that have attempted to make soccer a viable competitor, the NASL and its member teams have been, to this point, financially unsuccessful. Last year the teams collectively lost approximately $30 million. Individual NASL franchises have been very unstable; for example, since the trial of this case 8 of the 24 NASL teams have folded. Thus the NASL is the weakest of the major professional sports leagues (the NFL, the NASL, the National Basketball Association, the National Hockey League, and Major League Baseball).

Because of the interdependence of professional sports league members and the unique nature of their business, the market for and availability of capital investment is limited. As the district court found, the economic success of each franchise is dependent on the quality of sports competition throughout the league and the economic strength and stability of other league members. Damage to or losses by any league member can adversely affect the stability, success and operations of other members. Aside from willingness to take the risk of investing in a member of a league in which members have for the most part not demonstrated a record of profits, the potential investor must be reasonably compatible with other members of the league, with a sufficient understanding of the nature of the business and the interdependence of ownership to support not only his newly-acquired team but the sports league of which it is a member. As the district court further noted, these conditions have tended to attract individuals or businesses with distinct characteristics as distinguished from the much larger number of financiers of the type prevailing in most business markets. Although, as the district court observed, the boundaries of this "sports ownership capital and skill" market are not as confined as NASL contends and not limited strictly to present major league sports owners, the sources of sports capital are limited by the foregoing conditions and existing sports league owners constitute a significant source. In short, while capital may be fungible in other businesses, it is not fungible in the business of producing major league professional sports. Regardless of the risk involved in the venture, which may vary greatly from league to league, league members look not merely for money but for a compatible fellow owner, preferably having entrepreneurial sports skill, with whom the other members can operate their joint business enterprise. League members recognize, for example, that if the owner of one team allowed it to deteriorate to the point where it usually lost every game, attendance at games in which that team was playing would fall precipitously, hurting not just that team, but every other team that played it during the season. In view of this business interdependence team owners, through their leagues, are careful about whom they allow to purchase a team in their league and leagues invariably require that the sale of a franchise be approved by a majority of team owners rather than by the selling owner alone.

For these reasons individuals with experience in owning and operating sports teams tend to be the most sought-after potential owners. Indeed, the NFL made clear that it values proven experience in a potential owner. When in1974 it expanded by 2 teams, 5 of the 8 prospective owners it considered seriously had professional sports team ownership experience; a sixth had experience in non-team sports. The two ownership groups to whom it awarded franchises included individuals with prior professional sports team ownership experience, and the NFL did not award the franchises to the highest bidder, a procedure that would have provided the most *immediate* financial reward to its owners.

The attractiveness of existing owners of major sports teams as sources of potential capital is further evidenced by the large number of members of major sports leagues who control or own substantial interests in members of other leagues. The record reveals some 110 instances of cross-ownership and some 238 individuals or corporations having a 10% or greater interest in other teams. Over the last 13 years there have been 16 cross-ownerships between NFL and NASL teams. Indeed, since the NASL was organized Lamar Hunt, the owner of the NFL's Kansas City Chiefs, has been involved as an NASL team owner, first of the Dallas Tornado team, then of the Tampa Bay team, and as a promoter of NASL.

Since 1975 Elizabeth Robbie, the wife of the NFL's Miami Dolphins owner Joseph Robbie, has been the majority owner of the NASL's Fort Lauderdale franchise. Mr. Robbie has apparently been the actual operator of the soccer team as well as the football team. . . .

Beginning in the 1950's NFL commissioners had a policy against a team owner maintaining a controlling interest in a team of a competing league. . . . In 1972 the NFL owners passed another resolution providing that NFL owners were not to acquire operating control of a team in a competing league. The participants agreed that any member holding such a controlling interest would make a "best effort" to dispose of it.

For the next five years the NFL members repeatedly passed the same resolution at meetings, except through inadvertence in 1975. During this period the NASL, which had come close to disbanding in 1968, grew more successful, due in no small part to the efforts of Hunt, who worked tirelessly to promote professional soccer and raise capital for it. NFL owners began to feel competi-

tion from the NASL. Leonard Tose, the owner of the Philadelphia Eagles, became one of the most vocal opponents of Hunt's soccer holdings. At approximately the same time the NASL Philadelphia Atoms were leading that league in attendance, and Tose's NFL football team, the Philadelphia Eagles, was losing money. (The Eagles lost money from at least 1969 to 1974, and in 1976 and 1977.) Tose became particularly incensed when Hunt began doing promotional work for the NASL. . . .

Tose was not the only NFL owner upset by competition from a soccer league team. Max Winter, the owner of the NFL's Minnesota Vikings, became concerned about competition from the Minnesota Kicks, an NASL member. . . .

Finally in 1978 the NFL owners moved to take strong action against Hunt and Robbie. An amendment to the NFL by-laws was proposed that would require both to divest their soccer holdings if they wished to continue to own an NFL team. The proposed amendment, which was to have been voted on at an October 1978 NFL owners' meeting, would also have prevented all majority owners, certain minority owners, officers and directors of NFL teams, and certain relatives of such persons from owning any interest in a team in a "major team sport." . . .

The first issue is whether Section 1 of the Sherman Act, which prohibits "[e]very contract, combination in the form of trust or otherwise, or conspiracy, in restraint of trade or commerce among the several States, or with foreign nations . . ." applies to the cross-ownership ban adopted by NFL and its members. The NFL contends, and the district court held, that Section 1 does not apply for the reason that the NFL acted as a "single economic entity" and not as a combination or conspiracy within the meaning of that law. We disagree. As the Supreme Court long ago recognized, the Sherman Act by its terms applies to "*every*" combination or agreement concerning trade, not just certain types. *Chicago Board of Trade* v. *United States,* 246 U.S. 231, 238, 38 S.Ct. 242, 244, 62 L.Ed. 683 (1918). The theory that a combination of actors can gain exemption from Section 1 of the Sherman Act by acting as a "joint venture" has repeatedly been rejected by the Supreme Court and the Sherman Act has been held applicable to professional sports teams by numerous lesser federal courts. . . .

The characterization of NFL as a single

economic entity does not exempt from the Sherman Act an agreement between its members to restrain competition. To tolerate such a loophole would permit league members to escape antitrust responsibility for any restraint entered into by them that would benefit their league or enhance their ability to compete even though the benefit would be outweighed by its anticompetitive effects. Moreover, the restraint might be one adopted more for the protection of individual league members from competition than to help the league. For instance, the cross-ownership ban in the present case is not aimed merely at protecting the NFL as a league or "single economic entity" from competition from the NASL as a league. Its objective also is to shield certain individual NFL member teams as discrete economic entities from competition in their respective home territories on the part of individual NASL teams that are gaining economic strength in those localities, threatening the revenues of such individual teams as the NFL Philadelphia Eagles, owned by Leonard Tose, because of competition by the NASL's Philadelphia team, and the revenues of the NFL Minnesota Vikings because of competition by the successful NASL Minnesota Kicks. The NFL members have combined to protect and restrain not only leagues but individual teams. The sound and more just procedure is to judge the legality of such restraints according to well-recognized standards of our antitrust laws rather than permit their exemption on the ground that since they in some measure strengthen the league competitively as a "single economic entity," the combination's anticompetitive effects must be disregarded.

Having concluded that Section 1 of the Sherman Act is applicable, we next must decide whether the NFL teams' cross-ownership ban violates that statute. The plaintiffs, characterizing the ban as a "group boycott" and "concerted refusal to deal," contend that the conduct is a species of the patently pernicious anticompetitive kind that must be condemned as *per se* unlawful without further proof. . . .

Combinations or agreements are *per se* violations of the Sherman Act only if they are so "plainly anticompetitive," *National Society of Professional Engineers* v. *United States*, 435 U.S. 679, 692, 98 S.Ct. 1355, 1365, 55 L.Ed.2d 637 (1978), and so lacking in any "redeeming virtue," *Northern Pac. R. Co.* v. *United States*, 356 U.S. 1,

5, 78 S.Ct. 514, 518, 2 L.Ed.2d 545 (1958), that "because of [their] unquestionably anticompetitive effects," *United States* v. *United States Gypsum Co.*, 438 U.S. 422, 440, 98 S.Ct. 2864, 2875, 57 L.Ed.2d 854 (1978), "they are conclusively presumed illegal without further examination under the rule of reason generally applied in Sherman Act cases," *Broadcast Music, Inc.* v. *CBS*, 441 U.S. 1, 8, 99 S.Ct. 1551, 1556, 60 L.Ed.2d 1 (1979). . . . As the arguments advanced by the NFL indicate, circumstances could exist that might justify a ban by a weak league as necessary to protect it against serious competitive harm by a cross-owner who threatened to misuse his position in that league to favor a stronger competing league and its members. Under those circumstances a ban "might survive scrutiny under the Rule of Reason even though [it] would be viewed as a violation of the Sherman Act in another context," . . .

Because agreements between members of a joint venture can under some circumstances have legitimate purposes as well as anticompetitive effects, they are subject to scrutiny under the rules of reason. . . .

In this case, the procompetitive effect claimed by the defendants for the cross-ownership ban is that the ban is necessary for the NFL owners to compete efficiently in the professional sports league market. On the other hand, the voluminous trial record discloses that the NFL's cross-ownership ban would foreclose NASL's teams from continued enjoyment of an access to a significant segment of the market supply of sports capital and skill thereby restraining at least some NASL teams from competing effectively against NFL teams for fan support and TV revenues. Any resulting restraint would benefit not merely the NFL as a league but those NFL teams that would be otherwise weakened individually and disproportionally (as compared with other NFL teams) by competing NASL teams. This evidence of the defendants' anticompetitive purpose is relevant in judging its potential anticompetitive effect.

. . . Because of the economic interdependence of major league team owners and the requirement that any sale be approved by a majority of the league members, an owner may in practice sell his franchise only to a relatively narrow group of eligible purchasers, not to any financier. The potential investor must measure up to a profile having certain characteristics. Moreover, on the supply side of the sports capital market the number of investors willing to purchase an interest in a franchise is sharply limited by the high risk, the need for active involvement in management, the significant exposure to publicity that may turn out to be negative and the dependence on the drawing power and financial success of the other members of the league. The record thus reveals a market which, while not limited to existing or potential major sports team owners, is relatively limited in scope and is only a small fraction of the total capital funds market. The evidence further reveals that in this sports capital and skill market owners of major professional sports teams constitute a significant portion. Indeed the existence of such a submarket and the importance of the function of existing team owners as sources of capital in that market are implicitly recognized by the defendants' proven intent in adopting the cross-ownership ban. If they believed, as NFL now argues, that all sources of capital were fungible substitutes for investment in NASL sports teams and that the ban would not significantly foreclose the supply of sports capital, they would hardly have gone to the trouble of adopting it. Unless the ban has procompetitive effects outweighing its clear restraint on competition, therefore, it is prohibited by Section 1 of the Sherman Act. . . .

NFL argues that the anticompetitive effects of the ban would be outweighed by various procompetitive effects. First it contends that the ban assures it of the undivided loyalty of its team owners in competing effectively against the NASL in the sale of tickets and broadcasting rights, and that cross-ownership might lead NFL cross-owners to soften their demands in favor of their NASL team interests. We do not question the importance of obtaining the loyalty of partners in promoting a common business venture, even if this may have some anticompetitive effect. But in the undisputed circumstances here the enormous financial success of the NFL league despite long-existing cross-ownership by some members of NASL teams demonstrates that there is no market necessity or threat of disloyalty by cross-owners which would justify the ban. . . .

For the same reasons we reject NFL's argument that the ban is necessary to prevent disclosure by NFL cross-owners of confidential information to NASL competitors. No evidence of the type of information characterized as "confidential" is supplied. Nor is there any showing that the NFL could not be protected against unauthorized disclosure by less restrictive means. . . .

Although there may be some merit in NFL's contentions that the ban would prevent dilution of the good will it has developed, that it would avoid any disruption of NFL operations because of disputes between its owners or cross-owners, or that it would prevent possible inter-league collusion in violation of the antitrust laws, these procompetitive effects are not substantial and are clearly outweighed by its anticompetitive purpose and effect. Its net effect is substantially to restrain competition, not merely competitors. It therefore violates the rule of reason. . . .

We reverse the order granting judgment of the NFL and remand with directions to enter a permanent injunction prohibiting the ban. Because the district court's decision made it unnecessary for it to consider the issue of damages, we remand for consideration of that issue. We affirm the dismissal of NFL's counterclaim requesting an injunction against cross-ownership.

NOTE

1. After the Second Circuit's decision in *North American Soccer League* v. *National Football League,* the NFL petitioned the U.S. Supreme Court for review under a writ of certiorari. The petition was denied, with Justice Rehnquist dissenting. Some of the justices' reasons should be noted (see 459 U.S. 1074 [1982]):

The NASL's complaint alleged that the cross-ownership rule excludes it from a substantial share of the market for "professional sports capital and entrepreneurial skill." The NFL contended that the relevant market was for capital generally, and that the rule does not exclude anyone from a significant share of the capital market. The District Court decided that the relevant market is in between — a market for "sports capital" — but did not define precisely the extent of this market. It then decided that any competition between the NFL and the NASL in that market is competition between two single economic entities. 505 F Supp 659 (SDNY 1980). It thus held that section 1 of the Sherman Act does not apply because the NFL is a single economic entity that cannot combine or conspire with itself. Id., at 689.

The Court of Appeals rejected this view. 670 F2d 1249 (CA2 1982). It thought "[t]he characterization of the NFL as a single economic entity does not exempt from the Sherman Act an agreement between its members to restrain competition." See *Perma Life Mufflers, Inc.* v. *International Parts Corp.,* 392 US 134, 141–142, 20 L Ed

2d 982, 88 S Ct 1981 (1968); *Timken Roller Bearing Co. v. United States,* 341 US 593, 598, 95 L Ed 1199, 71 S Ct 971 (1951). The Court of Appeals thought the objective of the cross-ownership rule is to protect individual teams as well as the league from competition.

At this point, the Court of Appeals had dealt with the District Court's entire holding. The District Court expressly declined to consider whether the cross-ownership rule violates the Rule of Reason. 505 F Supp, at 689. The application of the Rule of Reason is to be made by "the factfinder [who] weighs all of the circumstances of a case." *Continental T.V., Inc.,* v. *GTE Sylvania, Inc.,* 433 US 36, 49, 53 L Ed 2d 568, 97 S Ct 2549 (1977). See, e.g., *Berkey Photo, Inc.* v. *Eastman Kodak Co.,* 603 F2d 263, 302 (CA2 1979). The proper course for the Court of Appeals thus would have been to remand for findings by the District Court. However, it proceeded to decide the merits on its own.

The Court of Appeals first decided that there is a market for "sports capital and skill," which is a submarket of the capital market. "[A]n owner may in practice sell his franchise only to a relatively narrow group of eligible purchasers, not to any financier." It did not define this market except to say that it is "not limited to existing or potential major sports team owners," but "is relatively limited in scope and is only a small fraction of the total capital funds market." 670 F2d, at 1260. It is not clear whether the Court of Appeals was attempting to define the relevant market differently than did the District Court. If it was, it should have applied the clearly erroneous standard to the District Court's finding rather than substituting its own judgment. . . .

The Court of Appeals then proceeded to apply the Rule of Reason. There is no dispute as to the proper statement of the Rule. "The true test of legality is whether the restraint imposed is such as merely regulates and perhaps thereby promotes competition or whether it is such as may suppress or even destroy competition." *Chicago Board of Trade* v. *United States,* 246 US 231, 238, 62 L Ed 683, 38 S Ct 242 (1918).

On the basis of the facts as described by the Court of Appeals I seriously doubt whether the Rule of Reason was violated. The Court of Appeals held the cross-ownership rule is anticompetitive because it restricts the access of NASL teams to sports capital, and that this anticompetitive effect outweighs any procompetitive effects of the rule. It rejected the argument that the rule enables NFL owners to compete effectively in the entertainment market by assuring them of the undivided loyalty of fellow-owners.

I believe the Court of Appeals gave too little weight to the procompetitive features of the cross-ownership rule and engaged in excessive speculation as to its anticompetitive effect.

The NFL owners are joint venturers who produce a product, professional football, which competes with other sports and other forms of entertainment in the entertainment market. Although individual NFL teams compete with one another on the playing field, they rarely compete in the market place. The NFL negotiates its television contracts, for example, in a single block. The revenues from broadcast rights are pooled. Indeed, the only inter-team competition occurs when two teams are located in one major city, such as New York or Los Angeles. These teams compete with one another for home game attendance and local broadcast revenues. In all other respects, the league competes as a unit against other forms of entertainment. . . .

The cross-ownership rule, then, is a covenant by joint venturers who produce a single product not to compete with one another. The rule governing such agreements was set out over 80 years ago by Judge (later Chief Justice) Taft: A covenant not to compete is valid if "it is merely ancillary to the main purpose of a lawful contract, and necessary to protect the covenantee in the enjoyment of the legitimate fruits of the contract, or to protect him from the dangers of an unjust use of its fruits by the other party." *United States* v. *Addyston Pipe & Steel Co.,* 85 F 271, 282 (CCA6 1898), aff'd as modified, 175 US 211, 44 L Ed 136, 20 S Ct 96 (1899).

The cross-ownership rule seems to me to meet this test. Its purposes are to minimize disputes among the owners and to prevent some owners from using the benefits of their association with the joint venture to compete against it. Participation in the league gives the owner the benefit of detailed knowledge about market conditions for professional sports, the strength and weaknesses of the other teams in the league, and the methods his co-venturers use to compete in the market place. It is only reasonable that the owners would seek to prevent their fellows from giving these significant assets, which are in some respects analogous to trade secrets, to their competitors. . . .

The anti-competitive element of the restraint, as found by the Court of Appeals, is that competitors are denied access to "sports capital and skill." In defining this market, the Court of Appeals noted that although capital is fungible, the skills of successful sports entrepreneurs are not. This entrepreneurial skill, however, is precisely what each NFL owner, as co-venturer, contributes to every other owner.

The validity of covenants not to compete does not depend upon the availability to competing firms of similarly qualified individuals, but rests on the principle that competitors may seek to maintain their ability to compete effectively without running afoul of the antitrust laws. The Court of Appeals seems to me to have implicitly adopted the view that businesses must arrange their affairs so as to make it possible for would-be competitors to compete successfully. This Court has explicitly stated the contrary: . . .

The Court of Appeals also faulted the NFL for failing to show that its restriction was as narrow as possible.

Although the Court of Appeals did not cite any authority for this objection, it seems to be relying on the requirement of Addyston, supra, that the restraint be "necessary to protect the covenantee." 85 F, at 282. The Court of Appeals has taken this statement too far by adopting the least restrictive alternative analysis that is sometimes used in constitutional law. The antitrust laws impose a standard of reasonableness, not a standard of absolute necessity. . . .

It simply does not appear that the positive effects of the challenged restraint in helping the NFL to compete in the economic market place are outweighed by their negative effects on competition. The antitrust laws do not require the NFL to operate so as to make it easier for another league to compete against it. I fear that, under the decision below, the maxim that the antitrust laws exist to protect competition, not competitors, may be reduced to a dead letter.

I would grant certiorari.

6.10   Factors in Structuring a Sports Franchise

Before proceeding further with the examination of the nature of a sports league, particularly in the context of the league's many dealings with competing leagues and with its own constituencies, some consideration must be given to the factors involved in the constitution of a sports franchise. Involved is an exploration of the costs of obtaining a franchise, the capital assets of a club, the potentials for revenue, and the operations costs of various types of franchises. Much of this was discussed in Section 1.32, as it examined league and club profiles within the context of the economics of sports. The materials in this section shift the focus slightly.

Tax considerations in buying a club are discussed in Section 6.11. Section 6.12 examines disputes wherein the right to control the club is at issue. A third question relates to the right to own a franchise and the guidelines under which a league can decide whether or not to approve a transfer in ownership (Section 6.13). Finally, Section 6.14 contains the very important question of the right to move a franchise from one locale to another. Central to this theme is the dispute between the Oakland (Los Angeles) Raiders and the Los Angeles Memorial Col-

iseum on the one side and the NFL and most of its member clubs on the other. The implications, however, transcend the one case, and the analysis by the U.S. Court of Appeals must be closely scrutinized.

6.11   Tax Considerations

The possibility of favorable tax advantages has induced more than a few investors to take a plunge on a professional sports franchise. The big lure is that the Internal Revenue Service some years ago acquiesced to the notion that player contracts were depreciable assets. This set off a splurge of ever-escalating amounts claimed for purposes of depreciation. It at length also set in motion counterforces, namely challenges by the IRS to claimed depreciations and actions in Congress to amend the tax laws limiting the extent to which player contracts could be depreciated. Both types of challenges were successful, at least to a degree.

Following are key excerpts from sections 1056 and 1245 of the Internal Revenue Code. By these 1976 amendments, limits are placed on how much of a franchise cost can be allocated to player contracts. However, the limits are not finite, and there is still the problem of proof as to what the percentage should be. Thus, the *Laird* and *Selig* cases, though their facts predate the tax revision, are still important as guidelines in determining what courts consider in assessing whether the parties have accurately determined the amount of a purchase price to be allocated to player contracts. The stakes are high, as the desirability of a franchise depends in large part on the tax consequences.

Other tax problems facing franchises are briefly noted after the *Laird* and *Selig* decisions.

NOTE _____

1. The tax consequences arising out of the ownership of a sports franchise have evoked much scholarly and critical commentary. Sources to consult include the following:

(a) Weistart & Lowell, *The Law of Sports* (Indianapolis: Bobbs Merrill, 1979), pp. 840–932.

(b) "Amortization and Valuation of Intangibles: Tax Effects Upon Sports Franchises," 12 *Loyola Law Review* 159 (1978).

(c) Blum, M., "Valuing Intangibles: What Are the Choices for Valuing Professional Sports Teams?" 45 *Journal of Taxation* 286 (1976).

(d) Dickenson, C. and Z. Sutton, "The Effect of the 1976 Tax Reform Act on the Ownership of Professional Sports Franchises," 1 Comm/Ent 227 (1977).

(e) Horvitz, J. & T. Hoffman, "New Tax Developments in the Syndication of Sports Franchises," 54 *Taxes* 175 (1976).

(f) Jones, J., "Amortization and Nonamortization of Intangibles in the Sports World," 53 *Taxes* 777 (1975).

(g) Klinger, L., "Professional Sports Teams: Tax Factors in Buying, Owning and Selling Them," 39 *Journal of Taxation* 276 (1973).

(h) Lowell, C., "Deferred Compensation for Athletes," 10 *Tax Adviser* 68 (1979).

(i) "Professional Sports Franchising and the IRS," 14 *Washburn Law Journal* 321 (1975).

(j) "The Professional Sports Team as a Tax Shelter — A Case Study: The Utah Stars," 1974 *Utah Law Review* 556 (1974).

(k) "The Sale of Minor League Baseball Players During Liquidation—The Application of Corn Products to Depreciable Property," 45 *Temple Law Quarterly* 291 (1972).

(l) "Sports Franchises and the Treatment of League Expansion Proceeds," 57 *Taxes* 427 (1979).

(m) Strandell, V., "The Impact of the 1976 Tax Reform Act on the Owners of Professional Sports Teams," 4 *Journal of Contemporary Law* 219 (1978).

United States Code, Title 26, Section 1056. Basis Limitation for Player Contracts Transferred in Connection with the Sale of a Franchise

(a) General rule

If a franchise to conduct any sports enterprise is sold or exchanged, and if, in connection with such sale or exchange, there is a transfer of a contract for the services of an athlete, the basis of such contract in the hands of the transferee shall not exceed the sum of—

(1) the adjusted basis of such contract in the hands of the transferor immediately before the transfer, plus

(2) the gain (if any) recognized by the transferor on the transfer of such contract.

For purposes of this section, gain realized by the transferor on the transfer of such contract, but not recognized by reason of section 337(a), shall be treated as recognized to the extent recognized by the transferor's shareholders.

(b) Exceptions

Subsection (a) shall not apply—

(1) to an exchange described in section 1031 (relating to exchange of property held for productive use or investment), and

(2) to property in the hands of a person acquiring the property from a decedent or to whom the property passed from a decedent (within the meaning of section 1014(a)).

(c) Transferor required to furnish certain information

Under regulations prescribed by the Secretary, the transfer shall, at the times and in the manner provided in such regulations, furnish to the Secretary and to the transferee the following information:

(1) the amount which the transferor believes to be the adjusted basis referred to in paragraph (1) of subsection (a),

(2) the amount which the transferor believes to be the gain referred to in paragraph (2) of subsection (1), and

(3) any subsequent modification of either such amount.

To the extent provided in such regulations, the amounts furnished pursuant to the preceding sentence shall be binding on the transferor and on the transferee.

(d) Presumption as to amount allocable to player contracts

In the case of any sale or exchange described in subsection (1), it shall be presumed that not more than 50 percent of the consideration is allocable to contracts for the services of athletes unless it is established to the satisfaction of the Secretary that a specified amount in excess of 50 percent is properly allocable to such contracts. Nothing in the preceding sentence shall give rise to a presumption that an allocation of less than 50 percent of the consideration to contracts for the services of athletes is a proper allocation.

United States Code, Title 26, Section 1245. Gain from Dispositions of Certain Depreciable Property

(a) General rule

(1) Ordinary income

Except as otherwise provided in this section, if section 1245 property is disposed of during a taxable year beginning after December 31, 1962, the amount by which the lower of—

(A) the recomputed basis of the property, or

(B)(i) in the case of a sale, exchange, or involuntary conversion, the amount realized, or

(ii) in the case of any other disposition, the fair market value of such property, exceeds the adjusted basis of such property shall be treated as ordinary income. Such gain shall be recognized notwithstanding any other provision of this subtitle. . . .

(4) Special rule for player contracts

(A) In general

For purposes of this section, if a franchise to conduct any sports enterprise is sold or exchanged, and if, in connection with such sale or exchange, there is a transfer of any player contracts, the recomputed basis of such player contracts in the hands of the transferor shall be the adjusted basis of such contracts increased by the greater of—

(i) the previously unrecaptured depreciation with respect to player contracts acquired by the transferor at the time of acquisition of such franchise, or

(ii) the previously unrecaptured depreciation with respect to the player contracts involved in such transfer.

(B) Previously unrecaptured depreciation with respect to initial contracts

For purposes of subparagraph (A)(i), the term "previously unrecaptured depreciation" means the excess (if any) of—

(i) the sum of the deduction allowed or allowable to the taxpayer transferor for the depreciation of any player contracts acquired by him at the time of acquisition of such franchise, plus the deduction allowed or allowable for losses with respect to such player contracts acquired at the time of such acquisition, over

(ii) the aggregate of the amounts treated as ordinary income by reason of this section with respect to prior dispositions of such player contracts acquired upon acquisition of the franchise.

(C) Previously unrecaptured depreciation with respect to contracts transferred

For purposes of subparagraph (A)(ii), the term "previously unrecaptured depreciation" means—

(i) the amount of any deduction allowed or allowable to the taxpayer transferor for the depreciation of any contracts involved in such transfer, over

(ii) the aggregate of the amounts treated as ordinary income by reason of this section with respect to prior dispositions of such player contracts acquired upon acquisition of the franchise.

(D) Player contract

For purposes of this paragraph, the term "player contract" means any contract for the services of an athlete which, in the hands of the taxpayer, is of a character subject to the allowance for depreciation provided in section 167.

Laird v. United States, 556 F.2d 1224 (5th Cir. 1977)

This suit for refund of income taxes involved the tax treatment of the 1966 purchase of the Atlanta Falcons professional football team franchise. The Five Smiths, Inc. paid the NFL and its member clubs $8.5 million for the franchise and other assets including contracts for 42 veteran players. As part of the agreement, the Five Smiths was granted certain television rights and the right to share "equally with the NFL clubs in any Single Network television contracts." The three issues presented to the court of appeals were (1) whether intangible assets acquired by the Five Smiths were subject to depreciation; (2) whether the Five Smiths was entitled to a depreciation deduction for its rights to share proportionately in the television revenues produced by a four-year contract between the NFL and CBS; and (3) whether, assuming the purchaser was entitled to depreciate the player contracts, the district court's valuation was correct.

The response to the first issue, the government conceded that a 1971 revenue ruling (Rev. Rul. 71–137, 1971–1 C.B. 104), permitted the authorization of the acquisition costs of a professional football player, but maintained that the ruling was inapplicable unless a cost basis could be established. The government then advanced the bundle-of-rights theory: The five Smiths had purchased a bundle of inextricably intertwined assets whose values were so related that they were not capable of separate valuation. The court noted that the theory was basically a restatement of the Man Asset Rule, which contained a twofold test. Under this test, a deduction could be taken if the taxpayer could show that the asset had (1) an ascertainable value separate from goodwill, and (2) a limited useful life that could be ascertained with reasonable accuracy. The taxpayer had carried its burden of showing that the player contracts had a value separate and distinct from the franchise-goodwill value and that the contracts had a limited useful life of 5.25 years. Additionally, the court noted that *K Fox, Inc.* v. *United States*, 501 F.2d 1365 (Ct. Cl. 1975), which allowed a depreciation deduction for personal service contracts acquired in the purchase of a radio station, lent further support to the inapplicability of the mass asset theory.

The taxpayer had appealed the second issue and contended that the district court had erred in disallowing a deduction for the present value of its television rights under the four-year contract with CBS. The appeals court affirmed the trial court's holding that the deduction failed because the right to share proportionately had no definite useful life that could be ascertained with reasonable accuracy. The agreements showed that the television rights were to last as long as the Atlanta club remained a member of the NFL. Taxpayer also contended that after the four-year contract expired, teams were not under the obligation to continue their pooling arrangement, and thus the life of the contract was ascertainable. The court did not accept this argument because the pooling arrangement was of substantial economic benefit to the NFL teams and, in fact, had been the basis of the antitrust exemption of 15 USC, Sections 1291–1295. The court concluded: "Televised football

is by now a national tradition. We can be confident that Five Smiths' television rights will have substantial value as long as there remains an NFL and a television set in every living room."

The final issue involved the correctness of the district court's valuation of the players' contracts. The government contended as an alternative argument to its bundle-of-rights theory that the district court's method of valuation was arbitrary and unsupported by the evidence. The district court had accepted a compromise value submitted by the taxpayer, combining the qualitative judgments of Atlanta's first coach, Norbert Heckler, as to the relative contributions of college rookies and NFL veterans; the quantitative judgments of its experts, Texas E. Schramm and James Jinks; and the cost of acquiring rookies. The appeals court found that these comparisons between veteran and rookie players provided a reasonably reliable measure of the value of the expansion draftees; the higher cost of the college rookies showed the cost of substitute personnel, and the absence of a regular market for veteran players necessitated reference to prices in the college draft. Moreover, the court held that the valuations were of men, not machinery, and arriving at a compromise figure was an acceptable solution.

The valuation was reinforced by the 1976 tax legislation dealing with the transfer of players' contracts in connection with the sale of a sports franchise. Under section 212 of the Tax Reform Act of 1976 (codified at 26 U.S.C. sec. 1056 (a)), there is a presumption that not more than 50 percent of the total consideration is allocable to contracts for the services of athletes. While the December 31, 1975, purchase of the Falcons was not governed by the 1976 act, it indicated that the valuation was reasonable.

Finally, the government contested the district court's method of valuing the player contracts by subtracting from the total price the value of the other assets. It contended that the total of the individual asset values was greater than the lump sum purchase price. The appeals court, while rejecting the subtraction approach taken by the district, nevertheless concluded that the basis of the contracts could be calculated without valuing every right acquired by the Five Smiths. The court accordingly upheld the amortization of the value of the players' contracts at the sum of $3,035,000.

Selig v. United States, 565 F. Supp. 524 (E.D. Wisc. 1983)

The plaintiff taxpayer, a part-owner of the Milwaukee Brewers Baseball Club, Inc., sought a refund of income taxes that he paid under protest because the government had disallowed his share of the depreciation of certain baseball player contracts. The Brewers had obtained the player contracts in 1970 from the purchase of the assets of the Seattle Pilots and had allocated the purchase price as follows: $10.2 million to the 149 player contracts acquired; $100,000 to miscellaneous supplies and equipment.

The issue in this case was whether the allocation between the value of the player contracts and the value of the franchise was reasonable. The importance of this issue lies in the fact that the contracts were intangible assets that could be amortized over five years by a depreciation deduction under sec. 167(a) of the Internal Revenue Code. In contrast, no such deduction was allowed for the value of the franchise. Moreover, because the Brewers had elected to be treated as a Subchapter S corporation, these deductions for the depreciation of the player contracts could be passed through directly to the individual owners such as plaintiff.

The court upheld the allocation by the plaintiff and rejected the government's intimations that a conspiracy existed to deprive the government of its taxes. It also rejected the government's contention that the operation of a professional baseball team was not for a business purpose but, rather, gave "joy" to the owner, which could be valued and attributed to the value of the franchise. Finally, the court found the government's valuations of the player contracts unreliable.

In determining that the allocation between the player contracts and franchise value was reasonable, the court first found it necessary to distinguish the three markets in which the contracts were bought and sold. These are the "player market," where individual players are bought, sold, and traded by the clubs; the "free agent market," where the players rather than an assigning club negotiate for their contracts; and the "club market," where entire baseball clubs are bought and sold. The relevant market for allocation purposes was the club market, which is a free market. The government, however, had for the most part relied on the player market for its valuations, which was not a free market because it was restricted by the waiver and reserve rules that operated as price constraints.

After making these general observations, the court examined in detail the methods employed by the plaintiff and the government to allocate the purchase price. The plaintiff urged the court to assess the reasonableness of the $10.2 million allocation to player contracts by reference to five items: (1) the appraisals at the time of the sale, (2) the cost of player development, (3) the insurance on team's roster, (4) the small value of the franchise, and (5) the contracts of players who were free agents.

The court first found that the allocation was within the range of the appraised values performed for the Brewers in 1970. Two of the four appraisals were made by independent and knowledgeable appraisers, and the other two, while not independent, could be relied upon to confirm the appraisals. Another test of the reasonableness of the allocation was to analyze the costs of developing a major league player. The court agreed with the plaintiff's formula, which divided the average annual player development costs by the average number of players who move up from the minor leagues (between two to four players each year). Assuming this figure to be $350,000, then the 25-man roster would have a total fair market value of $8.7 million. In addition, the minor league contracts and other contracts acquired by the Brewers were worth at least $1.5 million, bringing the total to within the $10.2 million figure. The court rejected the government's method of calculation, which divided the player development costs per team by the number of minor league players, yielding a cost of only $30,000 per player. This method wrongly assumed that the cost of a player who moves into the major leagues is the same as the cost of any minor league player, and that the purpose of minor leagues is to give boys an opportunity to play baseball.

The fact that the total insurance coverage on the player contracts exceeded $11 million was further support for the reasonableness of the allocation. Additionally, the court compared the relatively small value of the franchise, stating that "The right to play baseball in Milwaukee is not worth much; everyone agrees on that." The evidence demonstrated that in 1973 Milwaukee was not viable as a baseball market. Finally, the court held that transactions which occur in the free agent market, typically a higher value than in the club market, supported the reasonableness of the Brewer's allocation.

The government used two approaches to prove the $10.2 million allocation was wrong. First, it tried to show that the value of the club was less than the $10.8 million that the Brewers paid and that the excess value should not be deducted. Second, it tried to show that the true value of the player contracts was at most $3.5 million.

The court rejected the government's first argument that the value was less than the $10.8 million paid. The government's expert had tried to show that the going concern value was between $6.7 million and $7.2 million by computing the discounted present value of the annual gross operating margins anticipated in the financial forecasts. The court stated that the value was the free market price — the price which was the result of an arm's-length transaction between a willing seller and a willing buyer. The price stood at $10.8 million.

The court also found the government's analysis of the value of the player contracts unreliable. Dr. Noll, the government's expert, relied on a regression analysis and an income-sensitivity analysis. In his regression analysis, Dr. Noll first developed a "salary equation," predicting player salaries based on performance statistics, then he developed a "transaction equation," which would predict the value of a player's contract from certain player statistics, the expected salary, and the difference between the actual salary and the expected salary. The court found this regression analysis unreliable since the equations were generated by using transactions in the player market instead of the club market where the contracts were purchased. Also, the data base was unreliable and incomplete, which further tainted the analysis.

Dr. Noll also used an income-sensitivity analysis, which was premised on the notion that revenues were sensitive to the quality of the team playing. The court found this analysis unpersuasive since it only looked at the marginal impact of team quality and ignored the minimum quality necessary to generate revenue. Further, income sensitivity bore no relationship to the fair market value of the player contracts.

The court also attached little weight to the government's production of other experts who testified as to the fair market value of the contracts. Finally, the government's attempt to compare the relative contract price and salary level of the Brewers to other American League clubs failed because the government again did not distinguish between the player market and the club market.

In conclusion, the court upheld the allocation of $10.2 million to player contracts and $500,000 to the franchise value. Because the Brewers were entitled to amortize the contracts over their useful lives and because of the nature of the Subchapter S status, plaintiff was entitled to take his proportionate share of the deductions. Therefore, plaintiff had overpaid his taxes and was entitled to a refund.

Selig v. United States, 740 F.2d 572 (7th Cir. 1984)

In a decision interspersed with history, highlights, and poetry about baseball, the court of appeals affirmed the allocation of $10.2 million of the $10.8 million purchase price of the Milwaukee Brewers baseball team to player contracts. The court noted that its review of the district court's findings was limited to determining whether the findings were clearly erroneous.

The court first found no error in the district court's market analysis. The government had argued it was unrealistic to value the players in the "free" club market when players in the future would be dealt in the player or free agent market containing restraints. However, the task of the district court was to allocate the purchase price among all the club's assets, not to assign specific values to individual players. Because the transaction occurred in the club market, the court correctly relied on data derived from that market in its analysis.

The government then attacked the admissibility of appraisals prepared several months after the Brewers started play. The appeals court found that these appraisals were sufficiently contemporaneous with the closing of the sale to constitute business records and were prepared in the regular course of business. Therefore, the appraisals qualified as hearsay exceptions under the Federal Rule of Evidence 803(a).

The appeals court then stated that, essentially, the government had simply failed to prove its case. The district court's ruling indicated that the plaintiff had carried his burden of proof. The district court had broad discretion on issues of credibility and assessing the weight of the evidence. Finally, the decision that the district court committed no clear error was supported by *Laird* v. *United States,* 556 F.2d 1224 (5th Cir. 1977), which stated that players are the primary assets of a football club: "Without them, there could not be a game." There was no significant difference in the 88 percent allocation approved in *Laird* from the 95 percent in the present case. After quoting a verse from "Casey at the Bat," the appeals court concluded that "there should be joy somewhere in Milwaukee — the district court's judgment is affirmed."

NOTE

1. As revenues accruing to sports franchises have grown, so has the interest shown in such revenues by state and local taxing authorities. The following are examples of additional tax problems that sports clubs increasingly face.

(a) In *Cincinnati Bengals, Inc.,* v. *Lindley,* 399 N.E. 2d 1257 (S.C. Ohio 1980), appellant Cincinnati Bengals sought a reversal of a decision by the tax commissioner, which held that 100 percent of the Bengals' payroll should be apportioned to Ohio in computing the Ohio franchise tax liability for the corporation. The Ohio Supreme Court affirmed the determination of the tax commissioner.

The Cincinnati Bengals, an Ohio Corporation with its principal place of business in Cincinnati, operates a football team in the National Football League. Between the years 1971 and 1974, the Bengals averaged 20 games per year (including exhibition games), 8 or 9 of which took place outside of the state of Ohio. The Bengals also employ scouts and other personnel who work primarily outside of Ohio. The tax commissioner determined that the entire compensation paid to the players should be apportioned to Ohio in accordance with R.C. 5733.05(B)(2)(b)(ii). The Bengals appealed to the board of tax appeals, which affirmed the commissioner's determination.

The Bengals' sole proposition of law was that compensation paid to players and scouts for games played and services performed outside of Ohio does not constitute compensation paid in Ohio for purposes of computing the franchise tax pursuant to R.C. 5733.05 (B)(2)(b). However, the Ohio Supreme Court noted that R.C. 5733.05(B)(2)(b)(ii) provided that "Compensation is paid in this state if: . . . (3) some of the service is performed within this state and either the base of operations, or if there is no base of operations, the place from which the service is directed or controlled is within the state . . ." The supreme court, in affirming the tax commissioner's determination, found that some of the serving, i.e., playing of some of the games is within Ohio. The court also held that the second prong of the test, that the base of operations must be in Ohio, had also been satisfied. Accordingly, the court held that the decision of the board of tax appeals, which determined that Ohio was the base of operations, was not unreasonable or unlawful, and should be therefore affirmed.

(b) In *City of Berkeley* v. *The Oakland Raiders,* 192 Cal. Rptr. 66 (Ct.App. 1983), the Oakland Raiders brought suit against the city of Berkeley, challenging the city's professional sports events license tax. The city ordinance required professional sports promoters to pay the city 10 percent of their gross receipts acquired from professional sports events.

The Raiders challenged the ordinance on both equal protection and due process grounds. The court held, however, that no equal protection rights are violated if the burden of a license tax falls equally upon all members of a class, even though other classes have lighter burdens or are exempt, so long as the classification is reasonable. The court held that a distinction between professional sports and amateur or school athletics is a reasonable classification.

The Raiders also objected to the inclusion of concession income in the calculation of gross receipts, but the court held that the ordinance encompassed such funds.

6.12   Control Considerations

Sports franchises are in many respects like other businesses. When more than one party is involved in the ownership, disputes are likely to occur. How the business has been structured may determine who prevails in an ensuing ownership battle. Thus, in addition to tax consequences, the considerations over control of the franchise may influence how the business is structured in the first place. Sports franchises are organized in one of four ways: (1) sole proprietorship, (2) regular corporation, (3) subchapter S corporation, or (4) partnership. None is guaranteed secure from legal problems, but some more than others invite potential difficulty. The following case explores the difficulty with the partnership.

JRY Corp. v. LeRoux, 18 Mass. App. Ct. 153 (1984)

At the core of this case was the complicated struggle for the control of the Boston Red Sox baseball team, which came to a peak in June 1983, and resulted in the filing of this action seeking an injunction. There were three legal issues: (1) the validity of certain amendments to the limited partnership agreement to alter the general mangement; (2) the involuntary dismissal of the amending partners; and (3) the effect of a letter expressing the exclusive right to negotiate for LeRoux's general partnership interest.

The Boston Red Sox is a limited partnership, consisting of the Boston Red Sox Baseball Club (BRS) and the New England Association (NEA). The three general partners are JRY Corporation (represented by Mrs. Yawkey through John Harrington), Haywood Sullivan, and Edward

LeRoux. The defendants were owners of a majority of the 30 units of the limited partnership: Curran, the former Red Sox counsel owned two units; Ball One and Strike One, corporations formed by J. Rodgers Badgett, held fourteen units; and LeRoux, who also had an equity interest in Strike One.

Badgett, while investing $5 million in the limited partnership, had very little to say about the control or management of the Red Sox. In October 1982, Badgett circulated a memorandum at a partnership meeting, which expressed his discontent with the management and placed a great deal of the blame on JRY and Mrs. Yawkey. He suggested that only one partner be designated as managing general partner, vested with all of the responsibility that the three general partners now shared. Relationships between the three general partners deteriorated rapidly. Mrs. Yawkey believed that LeRoux had substantially contributed to the memo, which she considered a personal insult.

In April 1983, LeRoux contacted David G. Mugar, who had earlier expressed a desire to become a general partner, to ascertain if he was still interested. After consulting with his "team" of attorneys, accountants, and consultants (including Carl Yastrzemski), Mugar decided he was interested. He drafted a letter addressed to Badgett and LeRoux, confirming that he had the exclusive right through May 31, 1983, to elect to purchase LeRoux's partnership interest at a price of $5 million and Badgett's limited partnership units at a price of $1 million for each unit. Both LeRoux and Badgett signed this letter.

JRY and Sullivan, however, immediately exercised their right of buy-out on the basis of this communication and sought to purchase LeRoux's share at the fair market price of $4 million, or at a price determined by a binding appraisal. LeRoux rejected this right of buy-out and stated that their demands were invalid.

At this point, Harrington and Sullivan asked Curran to resign as Red Sox general counsel because of a conflict of interest, since he held two limited partnership interests and also was personal counsel to LeRoux. Curran resigned, and LeRoux retained another lawyer, Samuel Adams. The court found that, because LeRoux did not have the authority to retain general counsel, this appointment was a nullity.

Badgett, increasingly disenchanted with his investment and the way the club was being operated, joined with Curran and LeRoux to seek changes in the operation of the club. Adams was asked to render his opinion as to whether an amendment altering the management would adversely affect the tax status of limited liability of the partnership. In the meantime, Richard H. O'Connell, discharged as general manager in 1977, was contacted about the possibility of becoming general manager again, this time under LeRoux.

LeRoux received favorable opinions from Adams on the amendments on June 6. These amendments were already signed by Curran and Badgett's duly authorized officer, and represented a majority of the limited partners. No meeting was called, nor was a vote taken on the amendments. LeRoux announced the change in management to a national press conference. The following day, the action by the plaintiffs seeking an injunction was filed.

First, the appeals court affirmed the trial court on the issue of the amendments altering the management structure, holding that the amendments were invalid on both procedural and substantive grounds. While the amending limited partners relied on section 5.8(b) of the partnership agreement as authority for their actions, the court held that the limitations set forth in section 5.8(c) precluded such action by the LeRoux group. Further, because the appointment of Adams was not approved by a majority of general partners as required by section 5.1(d), Adams's opinion letters failed to fulfill the obligatory requirements of section 5.8(c).

The court also held that section 5.8(a), which prohibits the limited partners from interfering with the operation of the business, takes precedence over section 5.8(b), which in some particular instances allows the limited partners to amend the partnership agreement. Further,

the court reasoned that in order to amend the partnership agreement, a unanimous vote of the limited partners (including Sullivan and Yawkey) would be required by section 5.8(d).

The appeals court reversed the trial court on the issue of involuntary withdrawal, holding that the actions of the limited partners were violative of section 5.8(a), and therefore invoked the rights of the general partners to buy out the limited partners.

While section 8.3(a) requires a unanimous vote among the general partners to effect an involuntary withdrawal of partners, the appeals court reversed the lower court by holding that LeRoux had forfeited his right to vote by violating his judiciary duty to the partnership. The court found that LeRoux's plans were to benefit himself and other limited partners, while destroying the rights of Yawkey and Sullivan. Since LeRoux could not be expected to vote objectively on the issue of withdrawal, the court found that his vote would not be counted.

The final issue the appeals court resolved was whether the "Mugar letter" constituted an "attempt to sell" and therefore entitled JRY and Sullivan to purchase LeRoux's general partnership share pursuant to section 7.4(b). While Yawkey and Sullivan argued that the "Mugar letter" conferred upon them the option to buy out LeRoux, the court held that LeRoux could investigate to find the market value of his general partnership without conferring a buy-out right in JRY or Sullivan. The court found that the "Mugar letter" was not an option contract, as contended by JRY and Sullivan, but merely an attempt by LeRoux to "test the water." Accordingly, the court held that the "Mugar letter" conferred no buy-out rights in Yawkey or Sullivan, but that the letter should be admitted as evidence of the fair market value of the general and limited partnership in any future proceedings or arbitration.

6.13 Right to Own a Club

An outsider's attempts to become an owner of a professional sports franchise can assume one of several scenarios. First is the extent to which current owners in a league can determine the suitability of the prospective owner, where an existing franchise is for sale and a transfer of ownership of the franchise is contemplated. A second circumstance is when an outsider demands the right to buy into a league through the creation of a new franchise.

A third possibility is a recent development, growing from the controversy surrounding the move by the NFL's Oakland Raiders to Los Angeles. The many legal ramifications of this move are explored in this section and in Section 6.14. The inquiry at this juncture is whether a city can acquire ownership of a sports franchise through eminent domain. The effort by the city of Oakland to proceed in this manner has inspired other localities to emulate Oakland's legal maneuver. For example, the city of Baltimore initiated similar legal action in an attempt to nullify the move of the Baltimore Colts to Indianapolis.

As the economic stakes involved in sports franchises rise, the legal battles over who can own franchises intensify.

Washington Professional Basketball Corp. v. NBA, 147 F. Supp. 154 (S.D.N.Y. 1956)

Sugarman, District Judge

The business of professional basketball, as conducted by The National Basketball League and its constituent teams on a multistate basis, *coupled with* the sale of rights to televise and broadcast the games for interstate transmission, is trade or commerce among the several States within the meaning of the Sherman Act, 15 U.S.C.A. sec. 1 et seq. The allegations of the complaint which, on these motions to dismiss must be deemed true, that plaintiff was denied participation therein by the defendants' alleged illegal conspiracy, states a claim upon which relief can be granted.

Plaintiff has standing to sue. Even though it never actually owned a playing team, the complaint alleges, which must on this motion be accepted as true, that plaintiff did everything required of it to acquire the remnants of the

defunct Baltimore Bullets and was prevented from completing that acquisition solely by the defendants' alleged illegal conspiracy complained of. The denial of a temporary injunction in a prior suit was based on "a very definite issue of fact as to whether, in fact, any binding contract was ever entered into" and "the absence of evidentiary proof that such contract was entered into" in the light of the defendants' denial there "that any such contract was entered into." That decision did not hold for all purposes that plaintiff was not a party aggrieved under the anti-trust laws.

The complaint seeks damages on a cause of action for an alleged illegal interference by defendants with plaintiff's claimed right to engage in the professional basketball business upon several *grounds*: federal anti-trust statute; common law tort; unlawful interference with a contract between plaintiff and another. Thus the case is one wherein this court has the right to decide all questions in the case even though it might ultimately decide the federal question adversely to the plaintiff.

Motions by defendants National Basketball Association, Podoloff, Madison Square Garden Corp., Inc. and Syracuse Professional Basketball Club, Inc. to dismiss the first claim and by defendants Boston Celtics Basketball Club, Inc., Zollner Machine Works, Inc. and Minneapolis Basketball, Inc. to dismiss the complaint are severally denied.

It is so ordered.

(Footnotes have been omitted.)

Levin v. NBA, 385 F. Supp. 149 (S.D. N.Y. 1974)

Plaintiffs, two businessmen, had an agreement to buy the Boston Celtics Basketball team. When plaintiffs applied to the NBA for a partnership that plaintiffs proposed to form, the NBA Board of Governors, which must approve all transfers of membership, rejected the application. Plaintiffs then brought an antitrust action against the league. Defendants moved for summary judgment dismissing the complaint; plaintiffs cross-moved for partial summary judgment on all issues except damages.

Plaintiffs contended that the reason for the rejection was their friendship and business associations with Sam Schulman, owner of the

Seattle Supersonics, who was an anathema to the other members of the league. Defendants, however, maintained that the reason for the rejection was that the business association between the plaintiffs and Schulman violated the "conflict of interest" provision of the NBA constitution, which reads "A member shall not exercise control, directly or indirectly, over any other member of the Association."

The court found that plaintiffs failed to establish that the conduct complained of constituted an antitrust violation. The court noted that although the antitrust laws apply to a professional athletic league, *Radovich* v. *NFL,* 352 U.S. 445 (1957), and that joint action by members of a league can have antitrust implications, *Denver Rockets* v. *All-Pro Management, Inc.,* 325 F. Supp. 1049 (C.D. Cal. 1971), this case involved plaintiffs who wanted to join with those unwilling to accept them, not to compete with them, but to be partners in the operation of a sports league for plaintiffs' profit. The court further found that the reason for the rejection was not an anticompetitive one, and that the exclusion of the plaintiffs from membership in the league did not have an anticompetitive effect nor an effect upon the public interest.

The decision noted that the law is well established that it is competition, and not individual competitors, that is protected by the antitrust laws. In addition, when the action under attack has neither anticompetitive intent nor effect, that conduct is not violative of the antitrust laws. The court relied on *Coniglio* v. *Highwood Services, Inc.,* 495 F.2d 1286, 1293 (2nd Cir. 1974), in which there was a "total failure to demonstrate any adverse effect on competition, actual or potential, an issue perfectly well suited to objected statistical analysis. In such instances, summary judgment is properly granted to lower the curtain on costly litigation where it is clear beyond cavil that one side simply has no support for its version of alleged facts." The court ruled that since in this case there was no exclusion of plaintiffs from competition with the alleged excluders, nor anticompetitive acts by them and no public injury occasioned thereby, the defendants' act did not constitute a violation of the antitrust laws. The court granted defendants' motion for summary judgment.

The Mid-South Grizzlies v. The National Football League, 720 F.2d 772 (3rd Cir., 1983)

The Mid-South Grizzlies (Grizzlies), a former member of the now-defunct World Football League (WFL), sued the National Football League (NFL) complaining that refusal of the NFL to grant membership to the Grizzlies violated the antitrust laws. The district court granted summary judgment, holding that the Grizzlies had shown no anticompetitive effects of their exclusion from the NFL. The court of appeals affirmed.

The court of appeals noted that the NFL arrived at its monopoly position in the relevant market of major league professional football with the aid of Congress. The 1966 Act of Congress, 15 U.S.C. Sec. 1291, permitted an exemption to the antitrust laws for the merger of two or more football leagues. The Grizzlies argued that this act not only permitted mergers, but also required the NFL to take affirmative steps to share its market power with others. However, the court of appeals rejected this argument, holding that the 1966 statute was not directed at preservation of competition in the market for professional football and cannot be construed as conferring any economic benefit on the class to which the Grizzlies belong.

The court also found that the Grizzlies' argument must fail because there was no injury to competition. While the plaintiffs argued that the NFL conspired to reject the Grizzlies' application in order to punish the Grizzlies for having competed against the NFL, the court held that even if this was so, the Grizzlies had proven no injury to competition. The court ruled that the effect of the rejection of the Memphis franchise was pro competitive in that it left the Grizzlies' franchise as a potential competitor in another league. The court also rejected the Grizzlies' contention that there was injury to intraleague competition, noting that the closest franchise to the Memphis area was the St. Louis club, which is 280 miles away from Memphis and would provide little or no competition for the spectators' money. Accordingly, the court of appeals affirmed the summary judgment for defendants.

NOTE _____

1. There are problems in determining who can be an "owner" in all aspects of professional sports. In instances such as horse and dog racing, racing commissions are usually established by the state. Often the commissions are deemed to have substantial discretion in setting rules for obtaining licenses to operate tracks (see, e.g., *Rodgers* v. *Southland Racing Commission*, 450 S.W.2d 3 [Ark. 1970]), but courts at times have held that a commission has acted arbitrarily when it did not follow required procedures (see, e.g., *Rose* v. *State Racing Commission*, 330 P.2d 701 [N.M. 1958]).

City of Oakland v. Oakland Raiders, 183 Cal. Rpt. 673 (Supp.Ct. 1982)

When contract negotiations for renewal of the licensing agreement for use of the Oakland-Alameda County Coliseum terminated, the owners of the Oakland Raiders announced their intention to move the football team to Los Angeles. To prevent this move, the city of Oakland instituted this action to acquire by eminent domain all of the property rights associated with the ownership of the franchise.

The trial court had granted the Raiders' motion for summary judgment on the grounds that the law of eminent domain did not permit the taking of intangible property not connected with realty and that the taking contemplated by the city was not within its authority to condemn for public use. The California Supreme Court, however, found a broad scope of property rights subject to a public taking under the recently revised eminent domain statutes (Code Civ. Proc., sec. 1230.010 et seq.), as well as numerous federal and state decisions expressly acknowledging that intangible assets such as patents, franchises, and contractual rights were subject to condemnation.

The court next discussed whether the city's attempt to take and operate the Raiders was a valid public use. The U.S. Supreme Court had established that public use may extend to matters of public recreation and enjoyment. The examples of municipality-owned and -operated stadiums in San Francisco and Anaheim demonstrated the accepted principle that providing access to spectator sports was an appropriate function of city government. The court found no substantial difference between owning the facility and owning the team which plays in the facility. Since public uses change over time, the operation of a sports franchise now may be considered to be an appropriate municipal function.

The Raiders' additional arguments were also summarily dismissed. Their first argument that the city could not condemn an established business was answered by the California statute which allowed a party to acquire a business unless expressly forbidden (Gov. Code sec. 37353[c]). Their second argument that the city's plan to promptly transfer the Raiders to private parties would vitiate the public use argument was answered by the Code of Civil Procedure sec. 1240.120(b), which allowed a transfer to protect a public purpose.

The California Supreme Court thus remanded the case to the trial court to determine whether the city's proposed exercise of its power of eminent domain was proper and reasonable. A separate opinion, written by Chief Justice Bird, expressed her fear that the majority did not consider the potentially dangerous consequences of its expansive decision. She questioned whether a city had the right to condemn a viable business and then sell it to another private party merely because the owner had announced his intention to move to another city and whether it was proper for a municipality to drastically invade personal property rights to further its policy interests. Despite her misgivings, Bird joined the judgment to permit a full hearing on all of the issues.

Note: After remand for trial on the merits, the trial court found against the city of Oakland. This was on appeal once again, as evidenced by the following.

City of Oakland v. Superior Court of Monterey County (Oakland Raiders et al., Real Parties in Interest), 179 Cal. Rptr. 729 (Ct. App. 1983)

In this proceeding, the city of Oakland petitioned the California Court of Appeals to issue a peremptory writ of mandate compelling vacation of judgment of the trial court which dismissed the city's complaint. The city argued that the judgment of the trial court was contrary to the law of the case established by the California Supreme Court in 32 Cal. 3d 60. The court of appeals agreed with the city's characterization of the judgment, and accordingly remanded the proceedings to the trial court.

The trial court gave five reasons for its conclusion that the city did not have the right to take the property in question. The trial court first held that the property was not located entirely within the boundaries of Oakland. The Raiders argued, and the trial court agreed, that because the Raiders played games outside Oakland, and that some players lived outside Oakland, that the Raiders were not entirely within the city boundaries. However, the court of appeals reversed the lower court on this issue, holding that the only possible site for the intangible property was the city of Oakland.

The court of appeals also overturned the lower court's determination that because there was no reasonable probability that the property would be devoted to a public use within seven years, no eminent domain action could be exercised. The trial court reasoned that, due to the probable legal disputes surrounding the action, the city would not have control of the Raiders within seven years. But the court of appeals held that the seven-year requirement does not include any delay caused by extraordinary litigation.

The court of appeals also determined that the trial court erred in concluding that the condemnation does not lie for the stated purpose. The court held that the Supreme Court had determined that the property sought to be taken was subject to acquisition for the stated purpose. The court of appeals also overturned the fourth objection sustained by the lower court. The court concluded that the trial court on remand was precluded from redetermining the effect of the city's late filing of the resolution of necessity and the late notice to the Raiders.

The final objection sustained by the trial court was that "the public interest and necessity do not require the proposed project, nor the acquisition of the Raiders." The court of appeals held that the trial court on remand was foreclosed from inquiring into this issue by the decision of the California Supreme Court.

Accordingly, the court of appeals remanded the proceeding to the trial court to rule on the remaining Raiders' objections. Further, the court directed the trial court to determine the issue of whether the stated purpose is a public use.

6.14 Right to Move a Franchise

The attempted move by the NFL Oakland Raiders to Los Angeles did more than precipitate the eminent domain suit discussed in the previous section. The move called into question the extent to which the majority of owners in a league can control other owners. The immediate question in the *Los Angeles Memorial Coliseum* suit relates to the right to move a franchise. The ultimate consequences extend far beyond and test a league's control over owners in most aspects of a club's operations.

We began the examination of the legal and business bases of a sports league in the discussion of *North American Soccer League* v. *National Football League* (see Section 6.00). In this section, we extend that discussion and contrast the traditional view of a sports league, as set forth in *San Francisco Seals, Ltd.* v. *National Hockey League*, with what we might term the new view in *Los Angeles Memorial Coliseum Commission* v. *National Football League*. Those intimately involved in sports feel that league operations may never be the same after the *Los Angeles* case.

San Francisco Seals, Ltd. v. NHL, 379 F. Supp. 966 (C.D. Cal. 1974)

Curtis, District Judge.

The plaintiff, San Francisco Seals, Ltd., is a professional hockey team affiliated with the National Hockey League. It brings this private anti-trust action against the National Hockey League and all other member clubs claiming that it has been unlawfully prevented from moving its franchise from San Francisco to Vancouver, B.C., which, plaintiff charges, constitutes a violation of both sections 1 and 2 of the Sherman Act (15 U.S.C. secs. 1, 2). The plaintiff has filed a motion for a partial summary judgment, while the defendants seek a summary judgment disposing of all issues. . . .

Each member owns and operates a professional ice hockey team franchised to play under the auspices of the National Hockey League with a designated home base. In this respect Section 4.1(c) of the constitution provides:

"Home Territory," with respect to any member, means: Each Member Club shall have exclusive territorial rights in the city in which it is located and within fifty miles of that city's corporate limits.

Section 4.2 provides:

Territorial Rights of League. The League shall have exclusive control of the playing of hockey games by member clubs in the home territory of each member, subject to the rights hereinafter granted to members. The members shall have the right to and agree to operate professional hockey clubs and play the league schedule in their respective cities or boroughs as indicated opposite their signatures hereto. No member shall transfer its club and franchise to a different city or borough. No additional cities or boroughs shall be added to the League circuit without the consent of three-fourths of all the members of the League. Any admission of new members with franchises to operate in any additional cities or boroughs shall be subject to the provisions of Section 4.3. . . .

On February 18, 1969, plaintiff made a formal application to exchange its San Francisco/Oakland franchise for one in Vancouver, B.C., to be issued to a new corporate entity in which the plaintiffs were to have an interest. The Board of Governors' denial of this request brought about the institution of this action. . . .

Before discussing the anti-trust aspects of this case it becomes important to clarify plaintiff's precise position. Although plaintiff claims to attack the general territorial scheme of the league, it apparently has no quarrel with that scheme insofar as it allocates to each team a "home territory" with certain exclusive rights within its limits. In fact, it is these exclusive rights that the plaintiff seeks to obtain for itself in an area of its own choosing.

The real thrust of plaintiff's complaint is that it is prohibited from transferring its franchise to Vancouver with all attendant territorial benefits and other league privileges. As previously pointed out "transfer" may not be a correct characterization of the transaction. An application for a new franchise at the new location may be a more accurate description of what has taken place. If so, plaintiff contends the refusal of the Board of Governors to grant such a franchise is a violation of section 1 of the Sherman Act. . . .

In applying either section 1 or section 2, inquiry must first be made as to the relevant market, and the court must determine whether the trade or commerce within that market is affected by the alleged restraints. . . .

. . . I find that the relevant product market with which we are here concerned is the production of professional hockey games before live audiences, and that the relevant geographical market is the United States and Canada.

Now let us examine plaintiff's relationship with the defendants within the relevant market. Plaintiff, of course, wishes to participate in this market, but not in competition with the defendants. It expects to maintain its league membership and to accept and enjoy all of the exclusive territorial benefits which the National Hockey League affords. As a member team, it will continue cooperating with the defendants in pursuit of its main purpose, ie., producing sporting events of uniformly high quality appropriately scheduled as to both time and location so as to assure all members of the league the best financial return. In this respect, the plaintiff and defendants are acting together as one single business enterprise, competing against other similarly organized professional leagues.

The main thrust of the Sherman Act is to prohibit some competitors from combining with other competitors to gain a competitive advantage over other competitors by creating impermissible restraints upon trade or commerce. It is fundamental in a section 1 violation that there must be at least two independent business entities accused of combining or conspiring to restrain trade. . . .

Within the relevant market in which we are here concerned, plaintiff and defendants are not competitors in the economic sense. It is of course true that the member teams compete among themselves athletically for championship honors, and they may even compete economically, to a greater or lesser degree, in some other market not relevant to our present inquiry. But, they are not competitors in the economic sense in this relevant market. They are, in fact, all members of a single unit competing as such with other similar professional leagues. Consequently, the organizational scheme of the National Hockey League, by which all its members are bound, imposes no restraint upon trade or commerce in this relevant market, but rather makes possible a segment of commercial activity which could hardly exist without it. . . .

Plaintiff relies upon *Blalock* v. *Ladies Professional Golf Association*, 359 F. Supp. 1260 (N.D.Ga.1973), as a case in point. Here the defendants were female professional golfers who were members of the Executive Board of the Ladies Professional Golf Association. As such they suspended another female professional golfer for a period of one year for cheating. The court pointed out that the plaintiff and the defendants were all individual competitors for prize money and that the suspension amounted to excluding the plaintiff from the market, since although suspended, she was still a member in good standing with the Ladies Professional Golf Association, and as such could not compete elsewhere. The court held that the defendants were acting completely within their unfettered subjective discretion and that each stood to gain financially by their actions. Under these circumstances the court held this to be a naked restraint of trade and hence a *per se* violation of section 1.

In *Blalock*, the plaintiff and defendants were actual competitors in the economic sense. . . . Within this market the actions of the defendants

had a direct effect upon competition within it, and the court quite properly held it to be a section 1 violation. Consequently, *Blalock* is clearly distinguishable, and for that reason is not persuasive.

I conclude, therefore, that as a matter of law and on the basis of the uncontroverted evidence before me, the actions of the Board of Governors pursuant to the constitution and bylaws of the National Hockey League do not violate section 1 of the Sherman Act, as they do not restrain trade or commerce within the relevant market. . . .

In claiming a section 2 violation of the Sherman Act, plaintiff charged the defendants with attempting to monopolize the business of major league hockey. It is urged that in order to dominate the market, the defendants have sought to keep out rival leagues by franchising more teams and locating them in areas where rival leagues might possibly succeed. Plaintiff urges that its request for an exchange was denied in order to keep it in San Francisco, thus discouraging the formation and growth of teams from rival leagues in that location. . . .

In the instant case, the area of the economy endangered by the defendants' alleged conspiracy to monopolize is that in which rival pro hockey leagues compete. The target of the defendants' alleged conspiracy is any rival league which might try to take over part of the National Hockey League's market. Plaintiff is not a rival hockey league, and the defendants' alleged actions to prevent the formation of rival leagues were not aimed at it. Actually, plaintiff does not claim to have been injured by the monopolistic practices of the National Hockey League as such, but that the monopolistic protection which affiliation with the National Hockey League can afford is being denied it at Vancouver. . . .

Los Angeles Memorial Coliseum Commission v. NFL, 727 F.2d 1381 (9th Cir. 1984)

J. Blaine Anderson, Circuit Judge:

These appeals involve the hotly contested move by the Oakland Raiders, Ltd. professional football team from Oakland, California, to Los Angeles, California. We review only the liability portion of the bifurcated trial; the damage phase was concluded in May 1983 and is on a separate appeal. After a thorough review of the record and the law, we affirm.

I. Facts

In 1978, the owner of the Los Angeles Rams, the late Carroll Rosenbloom, decided to locate his team in a new stadium, the "Big A," in Anaheim, California. That left the Los Angeles Coliseum without a major tenant. Officials of the Coliseum then began the search for a new National Football League occupant. They inquired of the League Commissioner, Pete Rozelle, whether an expansion franchise might be located there but were told that at the time it was not possible. They also negotiated with existing teams in the hope that one might leave its home and move to Los Angeles.

The L.A. Coliseum ran into a major obstacle in its attempts to convince a team to move. That obstacle was Rule 4.3 of Article IV of the NFL Constitution. In 1978, Rule 4.3 required unanimous approval of all the 28 teams of the League whenever a team (or in the parlance of the League, a "franchise") seeks to relocate in the home territory of another team. Home territory is defined in Rule 4.1 as

> the city in which [a] club is located and for which it holds a franchise and plays its home games, and includes the surrounding territory to the extent of 75 miles in every direction from the exterior corporate limits of such city. . . .

In this case, the L.A. Coliseum was still in the home territory of the Rams.

The Coliseum viewed Rule 4.3 as an unlawful restraint of trade in violation of section 1 of the Sherman Act, 15 U.S.C. sec. 1, and brought this action in September of 1978. The district court concluded, however, that no present justifiable controversy existed because no NFL team had committed to moving to Los Angeles. 468 F. Supp. 154 (C.D.Cal.1979).

The NFL nevertheless saw the Coliseum's suit as a sufficient threat to warrant amending Rule 4.3. In late 1978, the Executive Committee of the NFL, which is comprised of a voting member of each of the 28 teams, met and changed the rule to require only three-quarters approval by the members of the League for a move into another team's home territory.

Soon thereafter, Al Davis, managing general partner of the Oakland Raiders franchise, stepped into view. His lease with the Oakland Coliseum had expired in 1978. He believed the facility needed substantial improvement and he was unable to persuade the Oakland officials to agree to his terms. He instead turned to the Los Angeles Coliseum.

Davis and the L.A. Coliseum officials began to discuss the possibility of relocating the Raiders to Los Angeles in 1979. In January, 1980, the L.A. Coliseum believed an agreement with Davis was imminent and reactivated its lawsuit against the NFL, seeking a preliminary injunction to enjoin the League from preventing the Raiders' move. The district court granted the injunction, 484 F.Supp. 1274 (1980), but this court reversed, finding that an adequate probability of irreparable injury had not been shown. 634 F.2d 1197 (1980).

On March 1, 1980, Al Davis and the Coliseum signed a "memorandum of agreement" outlining the terms of the Raiders' relocation in Los Angeles. At an NFL meeting on March 3, 1980, Davis announced his intentions. In response, the League brought a contract action in state court, obtaining an injunction preventing the move. In the meantime, the City of Oakland brought its much-publicized eminent domain action against the Raiders in its effort to keep the team in its original home. The NFL contract action was stayed pending the outcome of this litigation, but the eminent domain action is still being prosecuted in the California courts.

Over Davis' objection that Rule 4.3 is illegal under the antitrust laws, the NFL teams voted on March 10, 1980, 22–0 against the move, with five teams abstaining. That vote did not meet the new Rule 4.3's requirement of three-quarters approval.

The Los Angeles Memorial Coliseum Commission then renewed its action against the NFL and each member club. The Oakland-Alameda County Coliseum, Inc., was permitted to intervene. The Oakland Raiders cross-claimed against the NFL and is currently aligned as a party plaintiff.

The action was first tried in 1981, but resulted in a hung jury and mistrial. A second trial was conducted, with strict constraints on trial time. The court was asked to determine if the NFL was a "single business entity" and as such incapable of combining or conspiring in restraint of trade. Referring to the reasoning in its opinion written for the first trial, 519 F.Supp. 581, 585 (1981), the court concluded the League was not a "single entity.". . .

The district court denied the NFL's motions for

change of venue, but did employ a detailed voir dire of the jury pool and of the jurors eventually empaneled. The trial was bifurcated so the jury could first determine liability. In the liability portion, counsel were limited to 40 hours of trial time per side in an effort to narrow the matters presented.

The trial was conducted and witnesses called, including owners of various NFL member teams and the League Commissioner, Pete Rozelle. The jury was instructed on the antitrust liability issues and sent out May 6, 1982. On May 7, 1982, the jury returned a verdict in favor of the Los Angeles Memorial Coliseum Commission and the Oakland Raiders on the antitrust claim and for the Raiders on their claim of breach of the implied promise of good faith and fair dealing. The court then continued the case to September 20, 1982, to begin the damages trial.

On June 14, 1982, the court issued its judgment on the liability issues, permanently enjoining the NFL and its member clubs from interfering with the transfer of the Oakland Raiders' NFL franchise from the Oakland Coliseum to the Los Angeles Memorial Coliseum. The court determined, in addition, that there was "no just reason for delay in entering this final judgment on plaintiff's and cross-claimant's claim for declaratory and equitable relief, and . . . expressly direct[ed] this final judgment be entered." Vol. 16 Clerk's Record # 2090. The NFL and its original clubs immediately appealed the permanent injunction (No. 82–5572); the original clubs of the American Football League also appealed (No. 82–5573), as did the Los Angeles Rams Football Co. (No. 82–5574) and the Oakland-Alameda County Coliseum (No. 82–5664). The Oakland Raiders cross-appealed challenging six orders entered by the court in 1981 and 1982 (Nos. 82–5665 and 83–5398). The NFL and Oakland Coliseum have also appealed the failure of the district court to grant their post-trial motions. (Nos. 83–5714 and 83–5732.)

The damages trial was completed in May 1983 with the jury returning a verdict awarding the Raiders $11.55 million and the Los Angeles Coliseum $4.86 million. These awards were trebled by the district court pursuant to 15 U.S.C. § 15. The NFL and the other defendants have appealed. (Nos. 83–5907, 83–5908 and 83–5909.) This panel will hear and decide the damage appeals. But, because these appeals were expe-

dited, the damage appeals will be decided in a later opinion after briefing, possible argument, and submission.

II. SHERMAN ACT SEC. 1

The jury found that Rule 4.3 violates sec. 1 of the Sherman Act, 15 U.S.C. sec. 1. . . .

. . .The NFL, however, raises two arguments against the lower court's judgment finding section 1 liability. First, the NFL contends that it is a single entity incapable of conspiring to restrain trade under section 1. Second, it insists that Rule 4.3 is not an unreasonable restraint of trade under section 1.

A. *Single Entity*

The NFL contends the league structure is in essence a single entity, akin to a partnership or joint venture, precluding application of Sherman Act section 1 which prevents only contracts, combinations or conspiracies in restraint of trade. The Los Angeles Coliseum and Raiders reject this position and assert the League is composed of 28 separate legal entities which act independently.

The district court directed a verdict for plaintiffs on this issue and as a preliminary matter the NFL states the jury should have been allowed to decide the question. A directed verdict may be granted pursuant to Fed.R.Civ.P 50(a) when, viewing the evidence in a light most favorable to the nonmoving party, the testimony and all the inferences that the jury could justifiably draw therefrom are insufficient to support any other finding. *Independent Iron Works, Inc.* v. *United States Steel Corp.*, 322 F.2d 656, 661 (9th Cir.), *cert. denied*, 375 U.S. 922, 84 S.Ct. 267, 11 L.Ed.2d 165 (1963). When there is no substantial evidence to support a claim, i.e., only one conclusion can be drawn, the court must direct a verdict, even in an antitrust case. *Cleary* v. *Nat'l Distillers and Chemical Corp.*, 505 F.2d 695, 696 (9th Cir.1974). Our review is *de novo*. *Santa Clara Valley Distributing Co.* v. *Pabst Brewing Co.*, 556 F.2d 942, 944 (9th Cir.1977).

It is true, as the NFL contends, that the nature of an entity and its ability to combine or conspire in violation of sec. 1 is a fact question. *Murray* v. *Toyota Motor Distributors, Inc.*, 664 F.2d 1377, 1379 (9th Cir.), *cert. denied*, 457 U.S. 1106, 102 S.Ct. 2905, 73 L.Ed.2d 1314 (1982). It would be reversible error, then, to take the issue from the jury if reasonable minds could differ as to its resolution. *Id.* Here, however, the material facts are undisputed. How the NFL is organized and the nature and extent of cooperation among the member clubs is a matter of record; the NFL Constitution and Bylaws contain the agreement. Based on the undisputed facts and the law on this subject, the district court correctly decided this issue.

The district court cited three reasons for rejecting the NFL's theory. Initially, the court recognized the logical extension of this argument was to make the League incapable of violating Sherman Act section 1 in every other subject restriction — yet courts have held the League violated section 1 in other areas. 519 F.Supp. at 583. Secondly, other organizations have been found to violate section 1 though their product was "just as unitary . . . and requires the same kind of cooperation from the organization's members." *Id.* Finally, the district court considered the argument to be based upon the false premise that the individual NFL "clubs are not separate business entities whose products have an independent value." 519 F.Supp. at 584. We agree with this reasoning.

NFL rules have been found to violate section 1 in other contexts. Most recently, the Second Circuit analyzed the NFL's rule preventing its member-owners from having ownership interests in other professional sports clubs. *North American Soccer League* v. *National Football League,* 670 F.2d 1249, 1257–1259 (2d Cir.), *cert. denied,* 459 U.S. 1074, 103 S.Ct. 499, 74 L.Ed.2d 639 (1982). It recognized the cooperation necessary among league members, even characterizing the NFL as a joint venture, but nonetheless applied rule of reason analysis and found the cross-ownership rule violated section 1. . . .

Cases applying the single entity or joint venture theory in other business areas also contradict the NFL's argument. As stated by the Supreme Court:

> Nor do we find any support in reason or authority for the proposition that agreements between legally separate persons and companies to suppress competition among themselves and others can be justified by labeling the project a "joint venture." Perhaps every agreement and combination in restraint of trade could be so labeled.

Timken Roller Bearing Co. v. *United States,* 341 U.S. 593, 598, 71 S.Ct. 971, 974, 95 L.Ed. 1199, 1206 (1951). *Timken* involved an allegation of territorial division among three companies that shared partial common ownership. In *Perma Life Mufflers, Inc.* v. *International Parts Corp.,* 392 U.S. 134, 141–142, 88 S.Ct. 1981, 1985–1986, 20 L.Ed.2d 982, 992 (1968), the Court reiterated that common ownership will not suffice to preclude the application of section 1. . . .

In recognition of that a broad application of *Timken* and *Perma Life* could subvert legitimate pro-competitive business associations, this circuit has found the threshold requirement of concerted activity missing among "multiple corporations operated as a single entity" when "corporate policies are set by one individual or by a parent corporation." . . . The facts make it clear the NFL does not fit within this exception. While the NFL clubs have certain common purposes, they do not operate as a single entity. NFL policies are not set by one individual or parent corporation, but by the separate teams acting jointly.

It is true the NFL clubs must cooperate to a large extent in their endeavor in producing a "product" — the NFL season culminating in the Super Bowl. The necessity that otherwise independent businesses cooperate has not, however, sufficed to preclude scrutiny under section 1 of the Sherman Act. In *Associated Press* v. *United States,* 326 U.S. 1, 65 S.Ct. 1416, 89 L.Ed. 2013 (1945), the Supreme Court rejected the assertion that the AP was immune from section 1 because it was a necessary cooperative of independent newspapers which produced a product its individual members could not. *Id.* at 26, 65 S.Ct. at 1427, 89 L.Ed. at 2034 (Frankfurter, J., concurring). More recently, the Court found the cooperation required among ostensible competitors in arranging blanket licensing of copyrighted songs precluded only a finding of per se illegality; instead, rule of reason analysis was the proper method to determine the legality of the arrangement. *Broadcast Music, Inc.* v. *Columbia Broadcast System, Inc.,* 441 U.S. 1. . . .

The case of *United States* v. *Sealy, Inc.,* 388 U.S. 350, 87 S.Ct. 1847, 18 L.Ed.2d 1238 (1967), is closely on point. Sealy licensed manufacturers to sell bedding products under the Sealy name and allocated territories to the licensees. The facts showed, however, that this arrangement was not vertical but horizontal; the 30 licensees, owning all of the stock of Sealy, controlled all its operations. 388 U.S. at 352–353, 87 S.Ct. at 1849–1850, 18 L.Ed.2d at 1242. Describing the Sealy organization as a joint venture, the Court nonetheless found it a per se violation of the Sherman Act. . . .

The NFL structure is very similar to that in *Sealy*. The League itself is only in very limited respects an identity separate from the individual teams. It is an unincorporated, not-for-profit, "association." It has a New York office run by the Commissioner, Pete Rozelle, who makes day-to-day decisions regarding League operations. Its primary functions are in the areas of scheduling, resolving disputes among players and franchises, supervising officials, discipline and public relations. The decision involved here on territorial divisions is made by the NFL Executive Committee which is comprised of a representative of each club. Even though the individual clubs often act for the common good of the NFL, we must not lose sight of the purpose of the NFL as stated in Article I of its constitution, which is to "promote and foster the primary business of League members." Although the business interests of League members will often coincide with those of the NFL as an entity in itself, that communality of interest exists in every cartel. . . .

Our inquiry discloses an association of teams sufficiently independent and competitive with one another to warrant rule of reason scrutiny under section 1 of the Sherman Act. The NFL clubs are, in the words of the district court, "separate business entities whose products have an independent value." 519 F.Supp. at 584. The member clubs are all independently owned. Most are corporations, some are partnerships, and apparently a few are sole proprietorships. Although a large portion of League revenue, approximately 90%, is divided equally among the teams, profits and losses are not shared, a feature common to partnerships or other "single entities." In fact, profits vary widely despite the sharing of revenue. The disparity in profits can be attributed to independent management policies regarding coaches, players, management personnel, ticket prices, concessions, luxury box seats, as well as franchise location, all of which contribute to fan support and other income sources.

In addition to being independent business entities, the NFL clubs do compete with one another off the field as well as on to acquire players, coaches, and management personnel. In certain areas of the country where two teams operate in close proximity, there is also competition for fan support, local television and local radio revenues, and media space.

These attributes operate to make each team an entity in large part distinct from the NFL. It is true that cooperation is necessary to produce a football game. However, as the district court concluded, this does not mean, "that each club can produce football games only as an *NFL* member." 519 F.Supp. at 584. This is especially evident in light of the emergence of the United States Football League.

For the foregoing reasons, we affirm the district court's rejection of the NFL's single entity defense. . . .

B. *Rule of Reason*

In *Chicago Board of Trade* v. *United States*, 246 U.S. 231, 238, 38 S.Ct. 242, 244, 62 L.Ed. 683, 687 (1918), Justice Brandeis announced what has become the classic approach used in rule of reason analysis:

> The true test of legality is whether the restraint imposed is such as merely regulates and perhaps thereby promotes competition, or whether it is such as may suppress or even destroy competition. . . .

. . . To establish a cause of action, plaintiff must prove these elements: "(1) An agreement among two or more persons or distinct business entities; (2) Which is intended to harm or unreasonably restrain competition; (3) And which actually causes injury to competition." *Kaplan* v. *Burroughs Corp.*, 611 F.2d 286, 290 (9th Cir. 1979). . . .

Our rejection of the NFL's single entity defense implicitly recognized the existence of the first element — the 28 member clubs have entered an agreement in the form of the NFL Constitution and Bylaws. As will be developed in more detail, we have no doubt the plaintiffs also met their burden of proving the existence of the second element. Rule 4.3 is on its face an agreement to control, if not prevent, competition among the NFL teams through territorial divisions. The third element is more troublesome. It is in this context that we discuss the NFL's ancillary restraint argument.

Also, a showing of injury to competition requires "[p]roof that the defendant's activities had an impact upon competition in a relevant market," *Kaplan,* 611 F.2d at 291, proof that "is an absolutely essential element of a rule of reason case." . . .

In a quite general sense, the case presents the competing considerations of whether a group of businessmen can enforce an agreement with one of their co-contractors to the detriment of that co-contractor's right to do business where he pleases. More specifically, this lawsuit requires us to engage in the difficult task of analyzing the negative and positive effects of a business practice in an industry which does not readily fit into the antitrust context. Section 1 of the Sherman Act was designed to prevent agreements among competitors which eliminate or reduce competition and thereby harm consumers. Yet, as we discussed in the context of the single entity issue, the NFL teams are not true competitors, nor can they be.

The NFL's structure has both horizontal and vertical attributes. . . . On the one hand, it can be viewed simply as an organization of 28 competitors, an example of a simple horizontal arrangement. On the other, and to the extent the NFL can be considered an entity separate from the team owners, a vertical relationship is disclosed. In this sense the owners are distributors of the NFL product, each with its own territorial division. In this context it is clear that the owners have a legitimate interest in protecting the integrity of the League itself. Collective action in areas such as League divisions, scheduling and rules must be allowed, as should other activity that aids in producing the most marketable product attainable. Nevertheless, legitimate collective action should not be construed to allow the owners to extract excess profits. In such a situation the owners would be acting as a classic cartel. Agreements among competitors, i.e., cartels, to fix prices or divide market territories are presumed illegal under sec. 1 because they give competitors the ability to charge unreasonable and arbitrary prices instead of setting prices by virtue of free market forces. . . .

On its face, Rule 4.3 divides markets among the 28 teams, a practice presumed illegal, but, as we have noted, the unique structure of the NFL precludes application of the per se rule. *North American Soccer League,* 670 F.2d at 1258–1259.

. . . Instead, we must examine Rule 4.3 to determine whether it reasonably serves the legitimate collective concerns of the owners or instead permits them to reap excess profits at the expense of the consuming public.

1. Relevant Market

The NFL contends it is entitled to judgment because plaintiffs failed to prove an adverse impact on competition in a relevant market. The NFL's claim that it is entitled to judgment notwithstanding the verdict is governed by the same standards as a motion for directed verdict, discussed above. The court is not permitted to account for witness credibility, weigh the evidence or reach a different result it finds more reasonable as long as, viewing the evidence in a light most favorable to the nonmoving party, the jury's verdict is supported by substantial evidence.

In the antitrust context the relevant market has two components: the product market and the geographic market. Product market definition involves the

> process of describing those groups of producers which, because of the similarity of their products, have the ability — actual or potential — to take significant amounts of business away from each other. A market definition must look at all relevant sources of supply, either actual rivals or eager potential entrants to the market.

Kaplan, 611 F.2d at 292 (quoting *SmithK-line Corp.* v. *Eli Lilly & Co.,* 575 F.2d 1056, 1063 (3d Cir.), *cert. denied,* 439 U.S. 838, 99 S.Ct. 123, 58 L.Ed.2d 134 (1978)). Two related tests are used in arriving at the product market: first, reasonable interchangeability for the same or similar uses; and second, cross-elasticity of demand, an economic term describing the responsiveness of sales of one product to price changes in another. . . .

The claims of the Raiders and the L.A. Coliseum, respectively, present somewhat different market considerations. The Raiders attempted to prove the relevant market consists of NFL football (the product market) in the Southern California area (the geographic market). The NFL argues it competes with all forms of entertainment within the United States, not just Southern California. The L.A. Coliseum claims the relevant market is stadia offering their facilities to NFL teams (the product market) in the United States (the geographic market). The NFL agrees with this geographic market, but argues the product market involves cities competing for all forms of stadium entertainment, including NFL football teams.

That NFL football has limited substitutes from a consumer standpoint is seen from evidence that the Oakland Coliseum sold out for 10 consecutive years despite having some of the highest ticket prices in the League. A similar conclusion can be drawn from the extraordinary number of television viewers — over 100 million people — that watched the 1982 Super Bowl, the ultimate NFL product. NFL football's importance to the television networks is evidenced by the approximately $2 billion they agreed to pay the League for the right to televise the games from 1982–1986. This contract reflects the networks' anticipation that the high number of television viewers who had watched NFL football in the past would continue to do so in the future.

To some extent, the NFL itself narrowly defined the relevant market by emphasizing that NFL football is a unique product which can be produced only through the joint efforts of the 28 teams. Don Shula, coach of the Miami Dolphins, underscored this point when he stated that NFL football has a different set of fans than college football.

The evidence from which the jury could have found a narrow pro football product market was balanced, however, with other evidence which tended to show the NFL competes in the first instance with other professional sports, especially those with seasons that overlap with the NFL's. On a broader level, witnesses such as Pete Rozelle and Georgia Frontierre (owner of the L.A. Rams) testified that NFL football competes with other television offerings for network business, as well as other local entertainment for attendance at the games.

In terms of the relevant geographic market, witnesses testified, in particular Al Davis, that NFL teams compete with one another off the field for fan support in those areas where teams operate in close proximity such as New York City-New Jersey, Washington, D.C.-Baltimore, and formerly San Francisco-Oakland. Davis, of course, had firsthand knowledge of this when his team was located in Oakland. Also, the San Francisco Forty-Niners and the New York Giants were paid

$18 million because of the potential for harm from competing with the Oakland Raiders and the New York Jets, respectively, once those teams joined the NFL as a result of the merger with the American Football League. Al Davis also testified at length regarding the potential for competition for fan support between the Raiders and the Los Angeles Rams once his team relocated in Los Angeles.

Testimony also adequately described the parameters of the stadia market. On one level, stadia do compete with one another for the tenancy of NFL teams. Such competition is shown by the Rams' move to Anaheim. Carroll Rosenbloom was offered what he considered to be a more lucrative situation at the Big A Stadium, so he left the L.A. Coliseum. In turn, the L.A. Coliseum sought to lure existing NFL teams to Los Angeles. Competition between the L.A. Coliseum and the Oakland Coliseum for the tenancy of the Raiders resulted.

It is true, as the NFL argues, that competition among stadia for the tenancy of professional football teams is presently limited. It is limited, however, because of the operation of Rule 4.3. Prior to this lawsuit, most teams were allowed to relocate only within their home territory. That is why Carroll Rosenbloom could move his team to Anaheim. This is not to say the *potential* for competition did not previously exist. There was evidence to the effect that the NFL in the past remained expressly noncommitted on the question of team movement. This was done to give owners a bargaining edge when they were renegotiating leases with their respective stadia. The owner could threaten a move if the lease terms were not made more favorable.

The NFL claims that it is places, not particular stadia, that compete for NFL teams. This is true to a point because the NFL grants franchises to locales (generally a city and a 75 mile radius extending from its boundary). It is the individual stadia, however, which are most directly impacted by the restrictions on team movement. A stadium is a distinct economic entity and a territory is not.

It is also undoubtedly true, as the NFL contends, that stadia attempt to contract with a variety of forms of entertainment for exhibition in their facilities. In the case of the L.A. Coliseum, this includes college football, concerts, motorcycle races and the like. An NFL football team, however, is an especially desirable tenant. The L.A. Coliseum, for example, had received the highest rent from the Rams when they played there. We find that this evidence taken as a whole provided the jury with an adequate basis on which to judge the reasonableness of Rule 4.3 both as it affected competition among NFL teams and among stadia.

We conclude with one additional observation. In the context of this case in particular, we believe that market evidence, while important, should not become an end in itself. Here the exceptional nature of the industry makes precise market definition especially difficult. To a large extent the market is determined by how one defines the entity: Is the NFL a single entity or partnership which creates a product that competes with other entertainment products for the consumer (e.g. television and fans) dollar? Or is it 28 individual entities which compete with one another both on and off the field for the support of the consumers of the more narrow football product? Of course, the NFL has attributes of both examples and a variety of evidence was presented on both views. In fact, because of the exceptional structure of the League, it was not necessary for the jury to accept absolutely either the NFL's or the plaintiff's market definitions. Instead, the critical question is whether the jury could have determined that Rule 4.3 reasonably served the NFL's interest in producing and promoting its product, i.e., competing in the entertainment market, or whether Rule 4.3 harmed competiton among the 28 teams to such an extent that any benefits to the League as a whole were outweighed. As we find below, there was ample evidence for the jury to reach the latter conclusion.

2. The History and Purpose of Rule 4.3

The NFL has awarded franchises exclusive territories since the 1930's. In the early days of professional football, numerous franchises failed and many changed location in the hope of achieving economic success. League members saw exclusive territories as a means to aid stability, ensuring the owner who was attempting to establish an NFL team in a particular city that another would not move into the same area, potentially ruining them both.

Rule 4.3 is the result of that concern. Prior to its amendment in 1978, it required unanimous League approval for a move into another team's home territory. That, of course, gave each owner

an exclusive territory and he could vote against a move into his territory solely because he was afraid the competition might reduce his revenue. Notably, however, the League constitution required only three-quarters approval for all other moves. The 1978 amendment removed the double-standard, and currently three-quarters approval is required for all moves.

That the purpose of Rule 4.3 was to restrain competition among the 28 teams may seem obvious and it is not surprising the NFL admitted as much at trial. It instead argues that Rule 4.3 serves a variety of legitimate League needs, including ensuring franchise stability. We must keep in mind, however, that the Supreme Court has long rejected the notion that "ruinous competition" can be a defense to a restraint of trade. *United States* v. *Socony-Vacuum Oil Co.,* 310 U.S. 150, 221. . .

3. Ancillary Restraint and the Reasonableness of Rule 4.3

The NFL's primary argument is that it is entitled to judgment notwithstanding the verdict because under the facts and the law, Rule 4.3 is reasonable under the doctrine of ancillary restraints. The NFL's argument is inventive and perhaps it will breathe new life into this little used area of antitrust law, but we reject it for the following reasons.

The common-law ancillary restraint doctrine was, in effect, incorporated into Sherman Act section 1 analysis by Justice Taft in *United States* v. *Addyston Pipe & Steel Co.,* 85 F. 271 (6th Cir.1898), *aff'd as modified,* 175 U.S. 211, . . . Most often discussed in the area of covenants not to compete, the doctrine teaches that some agreements which restrain competition may be valid if they are "subordinate and collateral to another legitimate transaction and necessary to make that transaction effective." *Id.* at 797–798; *see Addyston Pipe,* 85 F. at 281–82; *Lektro-Vend,* 660 F.2d at 265.

Generally, the effect of a finding of ancillarity is to "remove the *per se* label from restraints otherwise falling within that category." R. Bork, *Ancillary Restraints and the Sherman Act,* 15 Antitrust L.J. 211, 212 (1959). We assume, with no reason to doubt, that the agreement creating the NFL is valid and the territorial divisions therein are ancillary to its main purpose of producing NFL football. The ancillary restraint must then be tested under the rule of reason, *id.*, the relevance of ancillarity being it "increases the probability that the restraint will be found reasonable." *Aydin Corp.* v. *Loral Corp.*, 718 F.2d 897, 901 (9th Cir.1983). As we have already noted, the rule of reason inquiry requires us to consider the harms and benefits to competition caused by the restraint and whether the putative benefits can be achieved by less restrictive means.

The competitive harms of Rule 4.3 are plain. Exclusive territories insulate each team from competition within the NFL market, in essence allowing them to set monopoly prices to the detriment of the consuming public. The rule also effectively foreclosed free competition among stadia such as the Los Angeles Coliseum that wish to secure NFL tenants. *See Smith* v. *Pro Football, Inc.*, 593 F.2d at 1185. The harm from Rule 4.3 is especially acute in this case because it prevents a move by a team into another existing team's market. If the transfer is upheld, direct competition between the Rams and Raiders would presumably ensue to the benefit of all who consume the NFL product in the Los Angeles area.

The NFL argues, however, that territorial allocations are *inherent* in an agreement among joint venturers to produce a product. This inherent nature, the NFL asserts, flows from the need to protect each joint venturer in the "legitimate fruits of the contract, or to protect him from the dangers of an unjust use of those fruits by the other party." *Addyston Pipe & Steel*, 85 F. at 282. We agree that the nature of NFL football requires some territorial restrictions in order both to encourage participation in the venture and to secure each venturer the legitimate fruits of that participation.

Rule 4.3 aids the League, the NFL claims, in determining its overall geographical scope, regional balance and coverage of major and minor markets. Exclusive territories aid new franchises in achieving financial stability, which protects the large initial investment an owner must make to start up a football team. Stability arguably helps ensure no one team has an undue advantage on the field. Territories foster fan loyalty which in turn promotes traditional rivalries between teams, each contributing to attendance at games and television viewing.

Joint marketing decisions are surely legitimate because of the importance of television. Title 15, U.S.C. sec. 1291 grants the NFL an exemption from antitrust liability, if any, that might arise out of its collective negotiation of television rights with the networks. To effectuate this right, the League must be allowed to have some control over the placement of teams to ensure NFL football is popular in a diverse group of markets.

Last, there is some legitimacy to the NFL's argument that it has an interest in preventing transfers from areas before local governments, which have made a substantial investment in stadia and other facilities, can recover their expenditures. In such a situation, local confidence in the NFL is eroded, possibly resulting in a decline in interest. All these factors considered, we nevertheless are not persuaded the jury should have concluded that Rule 4.3 is a reasonable restraint of trade. The same goals can be achieved in a variety of ways which are less harmful to competition.

. . . Because there was substantial evidence going to the existence of such alternatives, we find that the jury could have reasonably concluded that the NFL should have designed its "ancillary restraint" in a manner that served its needs but did not so foreclose competition.

The NFL argues that the requirement of Rule 4.3 that three-quarters of the owners approve a franchise move is reasonable because it deters unwise team transfers. While the rule does indeed protect an owner's investment in a football franchise, no standards or durational limits are incorporated into the voting requirement to make sure that concern is satisfied. Nor are factors such as fan loyalty and team rivalries necessarily considered.

The NFL claims that its marketing and other objectives are indirectly accounted for in the voting process because the team owners vote to maximize their profits. Since the owners are guided by the desire to increase profits, they will necessarily make reasonable decisions, the NFL asserts, on such issues of whether the new location can support two teams, whether marketing needs will be adversely affected, etc. Under the present Rule 4.3, however, an owner need muster only seven friendly votes to prevent three-quarters approval for the sole reason of preventing another team from entering its market, regardless of whether the market could sustain two franchises. A basic premise of the Sherman Act is that regulation of private profit is best left to the marketplace rather than private agreement. *See United States* v. *Trenton Potteries*, 273 U.S. 392, 47 S.Ct. 377, 71 L.Ed. 700 (1927). The present case is in fact a good example of how the market itself will deter unwise moves, since a team will not lightly give up an established base of support to confront another team in its home market. . . .

Finally, the NFL made no showing that the transfer of the Raiders to Los Angeles would have any harmful effect on the League. Los Angeles is a market large enough for the successful operation of two teams, there would be no scheduling difficulties, facilities at the L.A. Coliseum are more than adequate, and no loss of future television revenue was foreseen. Also, the NFL offered no evidence that its interest in maintaining regional balance would be adversely affected by a move of a northern California team to southern California.

It is true, as the NFL claims, that the antitrust laws are primarily concerned with the promotion of *interbrand* competition. *Continental T.V., Inc.* v. *GTE Sylvania Inc.*, 433 U.S. 36, 51, 97 S.Ct. 2549, 2558, 53 L.Ed.2d 568, 581, n. 19 (1977). To the extent the NFL is a product which competes with other forms of entertainment, including other sports, its rules governing territorial division can be said to promote interbrand competition. Under this analysis, the territorial allocations most directly suppress intrabrand, that is, NFL team versus NFL team, competition. A more direct impact on intrabrand competition does not mean, however, the restraint is reasonable. The finder of fact must still balance the gain to interbrand competition against the loss of intrabrand competition. *See id.*, at 51–56, 97 S.Ct. at 2558–2560. Here, the jury could have found that the rules restricting team movement do not sufficiently promote interbrand competition to justify the negative impact on intrabrand competition.

To withstand antitrust scrutiny, restrictions on team movement should be more closely tailored to serve the needs inherent in producing the NFL "product" and competing with other forms of entertainment. . . .

Some sort of procedural mechanism to ensure consideration of all the above factors may also be necessary, including an opportunity for the team proposing the move to present its case. . . .

Substantial evidence existed for the jury to find that the restraint imposed by Rule 4.3 was not reasonably necessary to the production and sale of the NFL product. Therefore, the NFL is not entitled to judgment notwithstanding the verdict.

III. JURY INSTRUCTIONS

The NFL also claims it is entitled to a new trial because of error in the jury instructions. In particular, the NFL argues that the instructions lacked the specificity required in a complex lawsuit such as this, that certain of its legal theories should have been presented to the jury, and that the instructions failed to articulate all the requirements of the law for finding an unlawful restraint of trade. The L.A. Coliseum and the Raiders respond by stating that the instructions as given were entirely adequate and the NFL simply attempted to have the jury charged with a partisan and erroneous view of the law. . . .

The NFL first contends the instructions failed to emphasize the unique nature of the business of producing NFL football, a business, it argues, most aptly characterized as a joint venture. The trial court's rule of reason instruction, however, told the jury it should consider the "nature of" and "facts peculiar to" the industry and that "one factor you may consider is the degree of mutual cooperation inherent among the member clubs of a professional sports league and the extent to which professional sports leagues differ from ordinary kinds of businesses." . . .

IV. VENUE

Oakland Coliseum, intervenor joined by the NFL, argues that the trial court abused its discretion by denying a change of venue motion made pursuant to 28 U.S.C. section 1404(a). In relevant portion, section 1404(a) allows a district court to change venue "in the interest of justice." Oakland Coliseum claims justice would have best been served by moving the case because it was impossible to secure an impartial jury in the Central District of California due to pretrial publicity and the economic interest of the prospective jurors in the outcome of the lawsuit. Prior to voir dire, the district court made a thoughtful and thorough analysis of Oakland's contentions in its memorandum and order denying the change of venue motion. 89 F.R.D. 497 (1981).

We will find an abuse of discretion warranting reversal only if Oakland Coliseum shows "that the setting of the trial was inherently prejudicial or that the jury selection process permits an inference of actual prejudice.". . .

We assume, with some basis, that the Raiders' proposed move and this lawsuit generated a large amount of publicity in the Los Angeles area. That in itself, however, is insufficient to compel a finding that the defendants were denied an impartial jury. . . . Only in those situations which are "utterly corrupted by press coverage" will we indulge in a presumption of actual prejudice on the part of any or all of the jurors. . . . No such showing has been made out here. The trial court used a very thorough voir dire process to ensure the jury panel members were not influenced by the publicity prior to trial, including administering a 48-page questionnaire prepared by the NFL to all prospective jurors, giving each side ten peremptory challenges instead of the normal three, and dismissing jurors for cause if even the slightest doubt of prejudice was raised. During the trial, the court admonished the jurors each day to refrain from exposure to any type of media coverage of the trial. In fact, one juror was excused because he admitted reading an unscreened newspaper, even though he adamantly denied reading anything but the Ann Landers column, the comics and the "Family Weekly" section. 23 T.R.2d at 4705–4706, 4920. In view of the trial court's thorough cautionary actions, we cannot say either that he abused his discretion in denying a change of venue or that defendants received an unfair trial because of the publicity. . . .

The other arguments made by Oakland on this issue, such as the one claiming it was denied a representative jury because the jury had no football fans, lack merit. Parties are not entitled to jurors of a particular bent or persuasion. They are entitled only to jurors as fair and impartial as all human circumstances and an evenhanded selection process permits. Nor do we believe the "cumulative" effect of the publicity, economic interests and the like show a sufficient likelihood of actual bias. Without more, we are compelled to affirm the denial of the change of venue motion and conclude that the defendants received a fair trial by an impartial jury.

V. CONCLUSION

The NFL is an unique business organization to which it is difficult to apply antitrust rules which were developed in the context of arrangements between actual competitors. This does not mean that the trial court and jury were incapable of meeting the task, however. The lower court correctly applied and described the law. The reasonableness of a restraint is a "paradigm fact question," *Betaseed, Inc.* v. *U and I Inc.*, 681 F.2d 1203, 1228 (9th Cir. 1982), and our review of the record convinces us the jury had adequate evidence to answer that question.

We believe antitrust principles are sufficiently flexible to account for the NFL's structure. To the extent the NFL finds the law inadequate, it must look to Congress for relief.

The judgment finding the NFL liable to the Los Angeles Coliseum and the Raiders, and enjoining the NFL from preventing the Raiders from relocating in Los Angeles, is affirmed.

Spencer Williams, District Judge, Sitting by Designation, concurring in part, dissenting in part. . . .

I respectfully dissent from the majority's opinion, insofar as it affirms the district judge's directed verdict that the N.F.L. was not a single entity as a matter of law.

The dispositive issue before this Court is whether the NFL's invocation of Rule 4.3 to block the Raiders' move to Los Angeles violates the letter and spirit of section 1 of the Sherman Act, 15 USC sec. 1. I conclude that the NFL is, as a matter of law, a single entity insofar as this aspect of its operations is concerned, and not subject to the strictures of Sherman Act section 1. . . .

Of particular importance to our analysis is the fact that the NFL Constitution provides for coordination of business activities and revenue sharing to an overwhelming degree. For example, the money derived from lucrative national broadcasting contracts is shared among league members according to agreed upon formulae, and this revenue makes up a large part of the revenue of each team. As to gate receipts for regularly scheduled contests between member clubs, there is a prearranged equation splitting gate admissions between the "home" and "visiting" clubs. Thus, each team relies, to a significant degree, on revenue jointly generated. It is not surprising that, concomitant with this virtual "partnership" arrangement, of which the above-mentioned revenue sharing is most significant, other operating decisions which would normally be made by the owners of a single franchise are subordinated to specified consent of the other clubs. For example, establishment of a new franchise is submitted for approval to all NFL owners before any expansion is permitted. Agreements among owners regarding who shall have the right to employ certain athletes occur every year at an annual "draft" of available players.

At issue here is one aspect of the relationship among the member clubs of the NFL as to when a member franchise club may be relocated to a city other than its original home. It is quite relevant to disposition of this instant suit that those challenging the legality of Rule 4.3 are the Raiders, presently a member club, and the L.A. Coliseum, a stadium seeking an NFL tenant. . . .

The only realistic manner in which to define what constitutes a single entity for antitrust review is to focus upon the purpose the definition is to serve. "Single entity" taken in a functional sense begins and ends with an analysis of formal organizational and operational aspects of an enterprise, reconciled with the realities of the economic competition in the marketplace. If the aim of the Sherman Act section 1 is consumer-dictated supply, unfettered by conspiracy between competing producers — and, I submit that it is — extreme caution is warranted in defining precisely what competitive units exist in the marketplace. It is equally as important to permit collaboration and concerted action among branches of a single economic entity in the marketplace with impunity from the Sherman Act section 1, as it is to police conspiracies between economic competitive entities. Nonetheless, all economic units remain susceptible to challenge under the antitrust laws from those external entities injured by acts violative of section 1, or competitive entities injured as result of monopoly, or attempted monopoly, in an industry under Sherman Act section 2 tenets.

Resolving whether the NFL is a single entity requires consideration of many factors, including formalistic aspects of operations such as ownership, overlapping directorates, joint marketing or manufacturing, legal identity, corporate law autonomy, and substantive aspects such as *de facto* autonomy of member clubs, chains of command over policy decisions, public perception and economic interdependency rendering otherwise independent member clubs subordinate to the integrated whole. When the entities in question are to be evaluated under the antitrust laws, the crucial criterion is whether the formally distinct member clubs compete in any economically meaningful sense in the marketplace. . . .

The majority's attempt to reconcile its decision with that of *General Business Systems, supra,* is misleading and inaccurate. The text of the majority's opinion implies that corporate policies *must* be unitary for a business organization to be found a single entity. In *General Business Systems, supra,* at 980–81, the Circuit concluded that in any case in which the relationship between the two or more formal entities did "not fall clearly at either of these extremes"; *i.e.,* "where corporate policies are set by one individual or a parent corporation" or where "jointly owned corporations that compete in the marketplace, hold themselves out to the public as competing organizations, and set policy independently. . . " (*id.* at 980), the case must be sent to the jury. This admonition was disregarded in this case — a paradigm case testing the functional "single entity" concept.

The district court placed an unwarranted emphasis upon the formalistic aspects of the relationship of the NFL and the member clubs, ignoring the subtle, but yet more significant interdependency of the member clubs and the indivisibility of the clubs with the NFL. 519 F.Supp. 581, 582–83. For example, the district court makes much of two such formal organizational characteristics: separate incorporation and management. *Id.* But, when viewed from the mundane perspective of daily operations, emphasis upon these legal formalisms obscures the reality of life in the NFL. Only the athletic strategems are autonomous — albeit tightly constrained by league guidelines on eligibility, medical and physical condition and exploitation of player talent. The NFL cannot truly be separated from its member clubs, which are simultaneously franchisees and franchisors. The Raiders did not, and do not now, seek to compete with the other clubs in any sense other than in their win/loss standings; they do not challenge the plethora of other ancillary regulations attendant to the league structure, including the draft, regulation and scheduling of meetings between teams, and the system of pooled and shared revenues among the clubs because they wish to remain within its beneficial ambit.

As the majority opinion correctly points out:

> this lawsuit requires us to engage in the difficult task of analyzing the negative and positive effects of a business practice in an industry which does not readily fit into the antitrust context. Section 1 of the Sherman Act was designed to prevent agreement among competitors which eliminate or reduce competition and thereby harm consumers. Yet, ... the NFL teams *are not true competitors, nor can they be.*

Majority opinion, at 1391, *emphasis added.* Yet, the majority's analysis falters in a similar manner. It is the commonality of, or necessary cooperation in, the means of production, not the formal structure of the ownership of the NFL infrastructure which should be determinative of the classification of this enterprise.

The profound interdependency of the NFL and member clubs in the daily operation and strategic marketing of professional football belies the district court's conclusion that each member club is an individual and economically meaningful competitor. The dispositive factor in determining whether the member clubs are capable of conspiring to restrain competition — the *sine qua non* of the Sherman Act section 1 — by reason of Rule 4.3, is the extent, if any, of their competition in an economic sense. Virtually every court to consider this question has concluded that NFL member clubs do *not* compete with each other in the economic sense. See *North American Soccer League v. NFL,* 670 F.2d 1249, 1251 (2d Cir.1982); *Smith v. Pro Football, Inc.,* 593 F.2d 1173, 1179 (D.C.Cir.1978); *Mackey v. NFL,* 543 F.2d 606, 619 (8th Cir.1976); *Mid-South Grizzlies v. NFL.,* 550 F. Supp. 558, 562 (E.D.Pa. 1982); *U.S. v. NFL,* 116 F. Supp. 319, 323–324 (E.D.Pa.1953). . . .

What these courts have all recognized, and what ultimately persuades me, is that functionally distinct units that cannot produce separate, individual goods or services absent coordination are inextricably bound in an economic sense, and must adopt certain intra-league instrumentalities to regulate the whole's "downstream output." In the case of the member clubs, this "downstream output" is professional football, and the organ of regulation is the unincorporated, not-for-profit, association commonly known as the NFL. There is virtually no practical distinction between the League, administered by the appointed Commissioner, *per se,* and the member clubs; the NFL represents to all clubs, including the Raiders, the least-costly and most efficient manner of reaching day-to-day decisions regarding the production of their main, and collectively produced, product. . . .

390 F.Supp. 73, 81–82 (N.D.Cal.1974), *appeal vacated,* 586 F.2d 644 (9th Cir.1978), *cert. denied,* 441 U.S. 907, 99 S.Ct. 1996, 60 L.Ed.2d 375 (1979) ("(a) conceivable effect of the "ransom" or "Rozelle" rule) would be to *perpetually* restrain a player from pursuing his occupation among the clubs of a league that holds a virtual monopoly of professional football employment in the United States," which "goes far beyond any possible need for fair protection . . . and imposes upon the player-employers or the purposes of the NFL such undue hardship as to be an unreasonable restraint . . . ."); *cf., North American Soccer League, et al. v. NFL., et al., supra,* (NFL ban on cross-ownership of professional football and soccer league clubs violative of Sherman Act section 1).

The paradox to which I return, as the root of why the NFL, as well as other sports leagues, must be regarded as a "single entity" is that the keener the on-field competition becomes, the more successful their off-the-field, and ultimately legally relevant, collaboration. The formal entities, including the member clubs — including the Raiders — which the district court ruled to be competitors cannot compete, because the only product or service which is in their separate interests to produce can only result as a fruit of their joint efforts. This systemic cooperation trickles down to all members of the league, regardless of their on-the-field record, at least to the extent of the shared revenues. . . .

A ruling that the NFL cannot enforce Rule 4.3 is effectively ruling that it may not enforce any collective decision of its member clubs over the dissent of a club member, although this is precisely what each owner has contractually bargained for in joining the enterprise. Without power to reach collective decisions, the NFL structure becomes superfluous, and professional sports, without a cost-effective policing mechanism such as the league, will dissolve in the face of uncontrollable free-riding and loss of economies of scale. . . .

NOTES

1. From the foregoing majority decision, footnote 4 of the opinion should be mentioned:

> One district court case has reached the opposite conclusion in a somewhat similar context. In *San Francisco Seals, Ltd.* v. *National Hockey League*, 379 F.Supp. 966 (C.D.Cal.1974), the court upheld the NHL's right to preclude the Seals' proposed move to Vancouver. The court found both that the NHL is a single entity incapable of conspiring in violation of sec. 1 of the Sherman Act and that the denial of the move had no anticompetitive effect. A recent law review article argues that the court in *Seals* correctly decided the single entity issue. M. Grauer, *Recognition of the National Football League as a Single Entity under Section 1 of the Sherman Act: Implications of the Consumer Welfare Model*, 82, Mich.L.Rev. 1 (1983). Although *Seals* and this article offer persuasive reasons for recognizing the NFL as a single entity, we do not find these reasons so compelling that existing precedent can be ignored or that we should grant this association of 28 independent businesses blanket immunity from attack under sec. 1 of the Sherman Act. The unitary nature of the NFL can be accounted for by analyzing the competitive harms and benefits of Rule 4.3 under the rule of reason, without impinging on Congress' authority to decide whether a specific industry deserves an exemption from the antitrust laws.

2. In addition to the Grauer article, cited in note 1 above, several other legal scholars have explored the implications of the *Los Angeles Memorial Coliseum* case, including the following:

(a) Kurlantzick, "Thoughts on Professional Sports and the Antitrust Laws: *Los Angeles Memorial Coliseum Commission* v. *National Football League*," 15 *Connecticut Law Review* 183 (1983).

(b) Glick, "Professional Sports Franchise Movements and the Sherman Act: When and Where Teams Should Be Able to Move," 23 *Santa Clara Law Review* 55 (1983).

(c) Kempf, "The Misapplication of Antitrust Law to Professional Sports Leagues," 32 *DePaul Law Review* 625 (1983).

(d) Lazaroff, "The Antitrust Implications of Franchise Relocation Restrictions in Professional Sports," 53 *Fordham Law Review* 157 (1984).

(e) Weistart, "League Control of Market Opportunities: A Perspective on Competition and Cooperation in the Sports Industry," 1984 *Duke Law Journal* 1013.

(f) Roberts, "Sports Leagues and the Sherman Act: The Use and Abuse of Section 1 to Regulate Restraints on Intraleague Rivalry," 32 *UCLA Law Review* 219 (1984).

(g) Note, "Antitrust Analysis in Professional Sports Management Cases: The Public Cries 'Foul'," 25 *Arizona Law Review* 995 (1983).

3. An attempt was made to block a franchise movement through invocation of state antitrust laws. This action was unsuccessful. In *State of Wisconsin* v. *Milwaukee Braves, Inc.*, 144 N.W. 2d 1 (Wisc. Sup. Ct. 1966), the Wisconsin Supreme Court held that its state antitrust laws were preempted in this instance by the Commerce Clause, even though baseball was not covered under the federal antitrust laws. Later cases in differing circumstances have also held that state antitrust statutes cannot control professional sports activities. See, *e.g.*, *Matuszak* v. *Houston Oilers, Inc.*, 515 S.W. 2d 725 (Tex. Civ. App. 1974), *Robertson* v. *NBA*, 389 F. Supp. 867 (S.D.N.Y. 1975), *HMC Management* v. *New Orleans Basketball Club*, 375 So. 2d 700 (La. App. 1979), and *Partee* v. *San Diego Chargers Football Co.*, 194 Cal. Rptr, 367 (Cal. Sup. Ct. 1983).

6.20 Competing Leagues and Ensuing Problems

The legal problems arising from competing leagues have already been explored in a variety of contexts. One of the major battlegrounds has been a league's attempts to bind players to clubs in the league for lengthy periods of time through reserve and option clauses. The legal consequences of these clauses were considered in Chapter 2, Sections 2.42 and 2.43. Several decisions effectively curtailed a league's ability to control the player market in the manner it had in prior times. Players, however, are only one possible area of control that a new league may wish to wrest from the established league. At the beginning of this chapter we presented *NASL* v. *NFL*, to illustrate attempted control of the "owner market."

Without repeating earlier considerations, this section introduces challenges to other control mechanisms. These include geographical markets, additional player control mechanisms and stadium and arena controls. The materials conclude with the complaint issued in the case of *USFL* v. *NFL*, the latest in the challenges by a new league to the established order. While the USFL's attack on NFL alleged predatory practices is a broad one, special note is made of the USFL's emphasis on attempts by the NFL to control the access to network television. Yet another control mechanism is brought to the fore in this complaint.

6.21 Control of Geographic Markets

A new league which wishes to compete with an established league must concern itself with several problems. One important consideration is where to locate the new league's franchises. A question is whether any new franchise can successfully compete in a locality that already has a professional team in the same sport. The answer is often no, although this is not invariably the case. Larger markets may be viewed as capable of sustaining an additional team and as essential to a new league's obtaining the needed television contracts and resulting exposure. The result may be that a new league locates some teams in existing markets and some in open areas.

The established league does not view the creation of a new league with equanimity. The old league's owners undoubtedly foresee fights over signing players and other forms of competition that will increase expenses. The old owners may also be concerned about a new league gaining an insurmountable advantage in certain markets that are currently open. If a resultant move is made by both the old and new leagues to enter the open area, a legal battle is inevitable.

American Football League v. Nationall Football League, 323 F.2d 124 (4th Cir. 1963)

Haynsworth, Circuit Judge.

The American Football League and owners of its franchises are contending against the National Football League and the owners of its franchises for victory in the courts. The American Football League and the owners of its franchises lost in the Court below, when the District Court held that there had been no violation of Sections 1, 2 or 3 of the Sherman Act by the National Football League and the owners of its franchises. We affirm. . . .

In 1959, the National Football League operated with twelve teams located in eleven cities. There were two teams in Chicago and one each in Cleveland, New York, Philadelphia, Pittsburgh, Washington, Baltimore, Detroit, Los Angeles, San Francisco, and Green Bay, Wisconsin. In 1960, two additional franchises were placed, one in Dallas and one in Minneapolis-St. Paul, the Dallas team beginning play in 1960 and the Minneapolis-St. Paul team in 1961. In 1961, one of the Chicago teams, the Cardinals, was transferred to St. Louis.

The American Football League was organized in 1959, and began with a full schedule of games in 1960. Affiliated with it were eight teams located in eight cities, Boston, Buffalo, Houston, New York, Dallas, Denver, Los Angeles and Oakland. After the 1960 season, the Los Angeles team was moved to San Diego.

In the first half of the 1952 season, a team operated under a National League franchise in Dallas. It failed and was replaced by a team located in another city, but a few years later there was substantial interest in Texas as a fruitful area for professional football.

Many of the National League owners were interested in expanding the league. Halas, owner of the Chicago Bears, was the earliest and most ardent advocate of expansion. Early in 1956, he predicted that National would expand from twelve to sixteen teams during the period of 1960–1965. In July 1957, Bert Bell, National's Commissioner, predicted some expansion by 1960, and at National's annual meeting in January 1958, an expansion committee was appointed composed of Halas and Rooney, owner of the Pittsburgh Steelers. Marshall, of the Washington Redskins, was an implacable foe of expansion, but the District Court found, with reason, that by 1959 a majority of the owners were in favor of expansion to sixteen teams and the granting of four additional franchises, two at a time.

As the National League contemplated expansion, the interest of the owners centered on Houston, Dallas, and two or three other cities. The weather in the Southwest was particularly favorable, and, with the improvement of the financial condition of the National League teams and the increasing revenues they received from television, it was thought that Houston and Dallas, with their natural rivalry, could each support a team. Those two cities were considered by National's owners as the most likely prospects for expansion with Minneapolis-St. Paul, Buffalo and Miami close behind.

Meanwhile, there were people actively interested in acquiring franchises to operate National League teams in Houston and Dallas. Clint Murchison, Jr. and his father, of Dallas, had sought to purchase the San Francisco 49'ers, the Washington Redskins and the Chicago Cardinals, intending, if successful in acquiring one of those teams, to move it to Dallas. In 1957 and 1958, Lamar Hunt, of Dallas, and the Houston Sports Association applied to National for franchises to operate teams in those two cities. Hunt also sought to acquire the Chicago Cardinals and move that team to Dallas. Early in 1959, Murchison and Hunt (Dallas) and Cullinan, Kirksey and Adams (Houston Sports Association) were all actively seeking National League franchises. They were given encouragement by Bell, Halas and Rooney, all of whom were talking in terms of expansion into Houston and Dallas about 1961.

In February and April 1959, Halas held press conferences to stimulate sales of tickets to a preseason game between the Chicago Bears and the Pittsburgh Steelers, scheduled to be played in Houston in August. In those press conferences, he discussed expansion plans, predicting that expansion would begin about 1960, and that the most likely cities were Houston, Dallas, Miami and Buffalo. Upon inquiry by Murchison, Halas suggested that he plan to make a formal application for a Dallas franchise to be considered at National's annual meeting in January 1960.

Meanwhile, in the spring of 1959, Hunt, of Dallas, decided that a new league was feasible and could be successfully organized. He had been told by Bell that he might submit a formal application for the Dallas franchise at the January 1960 annual meeting. However, he was either unsure of National's expansion into Dallas, of when it would occur, or of his chances of obtaining the franchise in competition with Murchison.

The remainder of 1959 was very eventful. Hunt proceeded actively with his plan to organize a new league. In July, he disclosed his intention to Commissioner Bell. On July 28, Bell, with Hunt's permission, told a congressional committee of Hunt's plans, and stated that the National League owners favored organization of the new league. Early in August, Hunt and Adams publicly announced the formation of the new league, with teams owned by them to be located, respectively, in Dallas and Houston. Hunt and his associates were actively in touch with interested persons in a number of other cities. On August 22, representatives from Los Angeles, Dallas, Houston, New York, Minneapolis and Denver signed articles of association. Representatives from many other cities had been in touch with Hunt. Wilson, of Detroit, sought an American franchise for Miami, and later for Buffalo, and the Buffalo franchise was formally granted in October. In November, an application for a franchise to be placed in Boston was approved. Thus in late November, American had tentative arrangements for teams in Houston, Dallas, Minneapolis, New York, Boston, Denver, Buffalo and Los Angeles.

In the meanwhile, Murchison, of Dallas, and Cullinan and Kirksey, who had been associated with Adams in efforts to obtain a National franchise for Houston, continued their efforts to obtain National franchises for those two cities. In late August, at their insistence, Halas, with the approval of a number of National owners, publicly announced that National's expansion committee would recommend to the 1960 meeting franchises for Dallas and Houston to begin play in 1961, the Houston franchise to be conditioned upon the availability of an adequate stadium. Construction of a new stadium in Houston was in contemplation, and there was hope that a National League team might obtain use of the Rice University Stadium until a new municipal stadium was constructed and available. Just after the death of Commissioner Bell on October 11, 1959, the National League owners met informally and agreed to adopt the announced recommendation of the expansion committee. This was followed by a widely publicized press release announcing that the National League would grant two new franchises in 1960, one of them to go to Dallas and the other to Houston if an adequate stadium was made available in Houston.

In October, however, it became known that the Rice University Stadium would not be made available for use by a National League team, and all further consideration of a National League franchise in Houston was then abandoned.

A number of people in Minnesota had been seeking a National League football team, but after Hunt's plans for a new league had been disclosed to them, Winter, Boyer and Skoglund, of Minneapolis, entered into American's Articles of Association, which were executed in August 1959. Winter, however, remained in touch with representatives of the National League, as did Johnson, an influential Minneapolis newspaperman. Johnson and Winter preferred a National League team to an American League team, but, on August 22, 1959, they had no assurance that the National League would place a franchise in Minnnesota at any reasonably foreseeable date. They must have retained some hope their preference for the National League might be realized, however, when National's announcements of its intention to place a team in Houston were conditioned upon the availability of an appropriate stadium, coupled with prominent mention of Minneapolis in connection with National's later expansion to sixteen teams. When it became known that an appropriate stadium in Houston was not available, Johnson and Winter sought definite commitments from the National League. They obtained telegraphic commitments in November. Winter, Skoglund and Boyer failed to deposit the performance bond of $100,000, which was required of American League members in November, but, thereafter, Skoglund and Boyer sought to obtain leases from the Minneapolis Stadium Commission for an American League team.The Commission refused to enter into such lease arrangements until the placement of a National League team in Minneapolis-St. Paul was settled.

In January 1960, Winter, of Minneapolis, and Haugsrud, of Duluth, formally applied to the National League for a franchise. Boyer joined in its presentation, stating that he had withdrawn from the American League and had obtained a complete release and a return of the $25,000 deposit, which he, Winter and Skoglund had made. At National's annual meeting on January 28, 1960, franchises were granted to Dallas and Minneapolis-St. Paul, the grant to Minneapolis-St. Paul being conditioned upon the enlargement of the Minneapolis stadium and the sale of 25,000 season tickets for the 1961 season when play was to commence. The Dallas franchise, however, permitted it to operate in 1960, for Murchison was very anxious that his National League team commence play in Dallas in the same year Hunt's American League team commenced play there.

On the next day, the American League had its annual meeting, during which it granted a franchise to Oakland, which took the place of Minneapolis-St. Paul. The American League owners preferred Oakland to other applicants, because they wanted a second team on the West Coast and because they regarded the Oakland area as promising.

It thus came to pass that in the 1960 season, teams of the two leagues were in direct competition in New York, Dallas, Los Angeles, and in the San Francisco-Oakland area. Each league had teams in other cities in which there was no direct competition between the leagues. The two leagues were competing on a national basis for television coverage, outstanding players and coaches, and the games of each league competed for spectators with the televised broadcast of a game of the other.

The first and most important question on appeal, therefore, is a review of the District Court's determination of the relevant market. The District Court recognized that the two leagues and their member teams competed with each other in several ways, and that the relevant market with respect to one aspect of their competition would not necessarily be the relevant market with respect to another. Since each league recruited players and coaches throughout the nation, he concluded that the relevant market with respect to their competition in recruiting was nationwide. He necessarily found that their competition for nationwide television coverage, with a blackout only of the area in which the televised game was played, was nationwide. As for the competition for spectators, he found the relevant market to be those thirty-one metropolitan areas in the United States having a population of more than 700,000 people according to the 1960 census. This determination was based upon testimony that a metropolitan area of that size might be expected to support a major league professional football team. Indeed, Hunt, of the American League, had testified that a metropolitan area of 500,000 might support such a team. The District Court's determination was influenced by American's contention that the bare existence of the National League and its member teams foreclosed certain markets to it and limited its capacity to operate successfully. It is reinforced by the evidence of many applications from other cities which were actively pressed upon American, some of which, at least, were thought worthy of real consideration.

In addition to those cities in which American actually placed franchises, Hunt testified that there was substantial interest in a franchise in Vancouver, Seattle, Kansas City, Louisville, Cincinnati, Philadelphia, Jacksonville, Miami, Atlanta, St. Louis and Milwaukee. The eighth franchise was placed in Oakland only after consideration of the "strong case" made by Atlanta. In short, it abundantly appears that cities throughout the United States and one Canadian city were actively competing for league franchises, there being many more applicants than available franchises.

In this Court, the plaintiffs contend that the relevant market is composed of those seventeen cities in which National now either has operating franchises, or which it seriously considered in connection with its expansion plans in 1959.

. . . They include in the relevant market all of the closed cities in which there is a National League team, but no American League team, but exclude from the relevant market all of those closed cities in which there is an American League team but no National League team, and all of those other cities in which there is now no major league professional football team, but which would be hospitable to a franchise and which have a potential for adequate support of a professional football team. They advance the unquestioned principle that the relevant market should be geographically limited to the area in which the defendants operate, or the area in which there is effective competition between the parties.

In very different contexts, the relevant market has been found to be a single city, a group of cities, a state, or several states. In considering an attempt to monopolize, it, of course, is appropriate to limit the relevant geographic market to the area which the defendant sought to appropriate to itself, and, if monopoly power has been acquired in a separably identifiable and normally competitive market, it is irrelevant that the defendant did not possess the same monopoly power in an unrelated market elsewhere.

Plaintiff's contention here, however, is a simple fractionalization of a truly national market. Each league has teams franchised to cities on the Atlantic, on the Pacific and in the midlands. Each team in each league travels back and forth across the country to play before many different audiences in many different cities. Most of the official season games are played in a city in which there is a franchised team, but that is not invariable, and most of the preseason exhibition games are played in cities in which there is no franchised team. In locating franchises, neither league has restricted itself to any geographic section of the country or limited itself to any particular group of cities. In American's brief history, it has moved one team from Los Angeles to San Diego, and the many changes which have occurred in National's franchises belie any notion of geographic limitation.

Though we may concentrate our attention upon competition between the leagues for franchise locations and lay aside for the moment clearly national aspects of their competition for players, coaches and television coverage, *location of the franchise is only a selection of a desirable site in a much broader, geographically unlimited market*. It is not unlike the choice a chain store company makes when it selects a particular corner lot as the location of a new store. It preempts that lot when it acquires it for that purpose, but, as long as there are other desirable locations for similar stores in a much broader area, it cannot be said to have monopolized the area, or, in a legal sense, the lot or its immediate vicinity.

The National League was first upon the scene. In 1959, it had franchises in eleven cities, the two Chicago teams being in direct competition with each other. It now has franchises in fourteen cities, some of which the District Court found capable of supporting more than one professional football team. Obviously, the American League was of that opinion, for it placed teams in New York, Los Angeles, and the San Francisco-Oakland area, where National, at the time, had well established teams. Most of the other cities in which each league operates, however, are incapable of supporting more than one professional football team. In such a city, a professional football team, once located there, enjoys a natural monopoly, whether it be affiliated with the National or American League, but the fact that National had teams located in such cities before American's advent does not mean that National had the power to prevent or impede the formation of a new league, or that National's closed cities should be included in the relevant market if American's closed cities are to be excluded. The fact is that the two leagues are in direct competition for regular season spectators only in New York, Dallas, and the San Francisco-Oakland area, and, during the 1960 season, in Los Angeles. If the relevant market is not to be limited to those cities, it must be, geographically, at least as broad as the United States, including Hawaii and portions of Canada.

Though there may be in the nation no more than some thirty desirable sites for the location of professional football teams, those sites, scattered throughout the United States, do not constitute the relevant market. The relevant market is nation-wide, though the fact that there are a limited number of desirable sites for team locations bears upon the question of National's power to mono-polize the national market.

The District Court's finding that National did not have the power to monopolize the relevant market appears plainly correct. In 1959, it occupied eleven of the thirty-one apparently desirable sites for team locations, but its occu-pancy of some of them as New York and San Francisco-Oakland was not exclusive, for those metropolitan areas were capable of supporting more than one team. Twenty of the thirty-one potentially desirable sites were entirely open to American. Indeed, the fact that the American League was successfully launched, could stage a full schedule of games in 1960, has competed very successfully for outstanding players, and has obtained advantageous contracts for a national television coverage strongly supports the District Court's finding that National did not have the power to prevent, or impede, the formation of the new league. Indeed, at the close of the 1960 season, representatives of the American League declared that the League's success was unprecedented.

American advances a theory, however, that, since the National League won Minneapolis-St. Paul in competition with American, National could have taken several other cities away from American had it undertaken to do so. This is only a theory, however, unsupported by evidence. It ignores the fact that American won Houston over National's competition, and that each league has won one and lost one in their direct competition for franchise locations. It ignores the fact that National was committed to expansion from twelve to sixteen teams in two separate steps, two teams at a time, so that it had but two franchises to place at the time American was being organized. American questions the finding that sixteen teams is a maximum that one league can efficiently accommodate, but the finding is based upon evidence and was not clearly erroneous. In short, there is no basis for a contention that the evidence required a finding that National, had it wished, could have placed a team in every location sought by American, or in a sufficient number of them to have destroyed the league.

American complains that National, the first

upon the scene, had occupied the more desirable of the thirty-one potential sites for team locations. Its occupancy of New York and San Francisco-Oakland was not exclusive, however, and the fact that its teams in other locations, such as Baltimore and Washington, enjoyed *a natural monopoly does not occasion a violation of the antitrust laws unless the natural monopoly power of those teams was misused to gain a competitive advantage for teams located in other cities, or for the league as a whole.* It frequently happens that a first competitor in the field will acquire sites which a latecomer may think more desirable than the remaining available sites, but the firstcomer is not required to surrender any, or all, of its desirable sites to the latecomer simply to enable the latecomer to compete more effectively with it. . . .

American also charges the defendants with an attempt to monopolize. They say that National offered franchises to be located in Dallas and Houston, and later to Minneapolis-St. Paul in substitution for Houston, for the sole purpose of preventing organization of the American League. It relies upon certain statements made by Marshall, of the National League Washington Redskins, and it discounts all of National's earlier discussion of its expansion plans as froth designed to influence congressional action upon a pending bill granting certain exemptions from the antitrust laws to professional football.

It is true that a lobbyist for the Sports Bill had informed the National League owners that expan-sion of the National League, or plans for its expansion, would be helpful in developing con-gressional support for the bill, particularly among Congressmen from the areas affected by the expansion. It is also true that after National's absorption of three teams from the All American Conference in 1950, there was little talk in the National League of expansion until after the Supreme Court's decision in *Radovich* in 1957. Early in 1956, however, Halas had predicted that National would expand from twelve to sixteen teams during the period, 1960–1965. Later, as indicated above, there was much discussion of it and much of it public. The remaining years of the 50's were consistently referred to as a period of consolidation, while the early years of the 60's were to witness the expansion of the league from twelve to sixteen teams in two separate steps. These declarations had gone so far and had become so specific that National would have greatly embarrassed itself if it had not undertaken their execution, though American had never appeared upon the scene. Moreover, the District Court found that there was substantial business and economic reasons for advocacy by National League owners of the planned expansion. The statement attributed to Marshall, of the Washington Redskins, that he had heard of no reason for expansion except to prevent formation of the American League, the District Judge found to be untrue, for Marshall had been present when business and economic reasons for the expansion had been discussed. Marshall, himself, consistently opposed expansion, though at the 1960 meeting, after some personal differences with Murchison and some of Murchison's associates had been adjusted, he acquiesced in the granting of franchises to Dallas and Minneapolis-St. Paul. Marshall may have made the statement attributed to him, but, in light of his opposition to expansion and the evidence of business considerations which induced other National League owners to advocate expansion, the District Court was not required to find that Marshall's statement was true. On the contrary, the District Court's finding is abundantly supported by the evidence, particularly in light of the fact that what the National League did in 1959 and 1960 was simply to implement on schedule the plans it had announced much earlier.

The plaintiffs also charge as conspiratorial acts certain suggestions which were considered by some of the owners of each league during the late summer and autumn of 1959.

Both Hunt and Murchison, of Dallas, were naturally concerned about the impending direct competition between the two Dallas teams. The Pauleys, of the National League's Los Angeles Rams, and Hilton, of the American League's Los Angeles Chargers, were similarly concerned about their direct competition in Los Angeles. Hunt and Murchison, both well-known businessmen of Dallas, were well acquainted with each other, while the Pauleys and Hilton were friends and business associates in Los Angeles, and, naturally, they discussed the problem among themselves. Hunt also travelled about the country to meet in New York with Rosenbloom, the owner of National's Baltimore Colts, with Halas in Pasadena, California, and, later, in Chicago and with others. There were also conversations between Anderson, the owner of National's Detroit Lions and Wilson, a resident of Detroit, a friend of Anderson's and a stockholder of the Lions, who was also the owner of American's Buffalo Bills. Murchison attended some of the conversations in which Hunt participated with others.

During these several conversations, the first of which was held upon arrangements made during a telephone call placed by Hunt to Murchison, Murchison expressed a willingness to let Hunt join him as a co-owner of the National League team in Dallas. Later, Murchison indicated to Hunt that he would be willing to step aside entirely, so that Hunt might become the sole owner of the National League team in Dallas, but costly competition in Dallas was not so easily avoided, for Hunt declined such suggestions on the ground that he felt committed to other American League owners. This led to some suggestions that the ambitions of other American League owners might be met by their becoming owners of National League teams. In light of National's planned expansion to sixteen teams, the suggestion was made that Adams, of Houston, might be a participant in a National League team in that city and the two remaining franchises would go to Minneapolis-St. Paul and to Wilson for a team to be placed in Buffalo or Miami. Nothing came of any such suggestions, however, for no National League owner-participant in the discussions was willing to consider a franchise for Denver, nor were they willing to consider enlargement of their expansion plans to include more than sixteen National League teams. At one time it was suggested that a fifth American League owner might be able to purchase the Chicago Cardinals and thus realize his ambition to become the owner of a major league football team, but, as the District Court found, there was never any indication that the National League would consider incorporating more than four new teams.

The District Court found that these conversations were not conspiratorial acts by National League owners. The evidence supports the finding. They grew out of informal talks among friends and business associates about their mutual problems, particularly in Dallas and Los Angeles. . . . In light of the previously existing relationships between Murchison and Hunt, the Pauleys and Hilton, and Anderson and Wilson, it would have been very surprising if some such informal discussions had not taken place between them. . . .

We conclude, therefore, that the District Court properly held that the plaintiffs have shown no monopolization by the National League, or its owners, of the relevant market, and no attempt or conspiracy by them, or any of them, to monopolize it or any part of it. No violation of the Sherman Act having been established, the judgment of the District Court is affirmed.

Portland Baseball Club, Inc. v. Kuhn, 491 F. 2d 1101 (9th Cir. 1974)

Per Curiam:

This case grew out of the effort during the late Sixties to bring major league baseball to Seattle and San Diego. The plaintiff, Portland Baseball Club, Inc., formerly owned the Pacific Coast League franchise in Portland. The advent of major league baseball in Seattle would have substantially reduced the value of the plaintiff's franchise.

Organized baseball has a procedure by which compensation is provided to owners of minor league franchises for such injury to their territories, the heart of which is Rule 1(a) of the Professional Baseball Rules. . . .

Following timely notice in 1968 by the recently formed Seattle Pilots and San Diego Padres of their intention to operate in Pacific Coast League territory, negotiations to fix the compensation required by Rule 1(a) between the Pacific Coast League and the Pilots and the Padres were unsuccessful. As provided by the Professional Baseball Rules, the matter was submitted to arbitration, the result of which was an award to the Pacific Coast League of three hundred thousand dollars for the loss of the Seattle territory and two hundred and forty thousand dollars for the loss of the San Diego territory. The plaintiff in due course received its proper share of these amounts. These awards were incorporated into a settlement agreement in which the Pacific Coast League "for itself and member clubs" acknowledged that the "execution of this Agreement constitutes full satisfaction of all claims, causes of action, interests and rights to indemnify whether arising at law, in equity or pursuant to Professional Baseball Rule 1(a) or any other baseball rule or regulation.". . .

Not satisfied with these awards and perhaps distressed by the fact that, while the Padres paid the National League ten million dollars for League membership and the Pilots $5,535,000 to the American League for similar rights, neither major league paid a cent to the Pacific Coast League and its member clubs, the plaintiff brought this suit against the Commissioner of Baseball, the two major leagues, the individual major league clubs, other than Seattle and San Diego, the president of the Pacific Coast League and individual member clubs of the Pacific Coast League.

The plaintiff's theory of recovery appears to be that there has been no compliance with Rule 1(a) because at the time of the negotiations and arbitration the Pilots and the Padres were not "Major League Clubs" inasmuch as neither at that time had fielded a team. The negotiations and arbitration consequently did not fulfill the obligation of the "Major League or Major League Club" to provide compensation. . . .

Judge Solomon heard the case and in a thorough opinion, D.C., 368 F. Supp. 1004 (1974), found that jurisdiction existed. He then held that the plaintiff was not the real party in interest under Rule 17(a), F.R.Civ.P., but that even if it were, it was bound by the arbitration. Judge Solomon properly concluded that the Padres and Pilots became major league clubs when their membership agreements with the major leagues were signed in 1968. The plaintiff's theory thus collapses. We can do no better than to adopt Judge Solomon's opinion as our own. This we do. Finally, the plaintiff's claim for relief under the antitrust laws was properly dismissed. *Flood* v. *Kuhn*, 407 U.S. 258, 92 S.Ct. 2099, 32 L.Ed. 2d 728 (1972).

6.22 Control Over Player Markets

When competing leagues exist, players become prized objects. Consumers pay to watch the players. Owners strive to keep their own players and to obtain others currently playing in the rival league.

We previously considered the legality of several player control devices in Chapter 2, Sections 2.42 and 2.43. Other examples of ways in which owners gain advantage in the player market are considered in this section and later in this chapter in Section 6.61. This section concentrates on the antitrust problems over control of player markets, and Section 6.61

explores the tort concepts of interference with a contractual or business relationship.

American Basketball Association Players Ass'n. v. **National Basketball Ass'n., 404 F. Supp. 832 (S.D.N.Y. 1975)**

Carter, District Judge

. . . The National Basketball Association (NBA) is charged with effectuating an unlawful conspiracy and combination to violate Sections 1 and 2 of the Sherman Act, 15 U.S.C. secs. 1 and 2. The major thrust of the complaint is that the NBA is seeking a monopoly of professional basketball by eliminating the American Basketball Association (ABA) as a viable and effective rival in the field.

Plaintiffs now move for a preliminary injunction to bar the NBA from holding a special draft of Moses Malone, Shep Wise, Mel Bennett, Mark Olberding and Charles Jordan who are currently players in the ABA. . . .

The evidentiary hearing disclosed that Lawrence O'Brien, Commissioner of the NBA, and Simon P. Gourdine, Deputy Commissioner, in October or November, 1975, aware that some of the ABA clubs were going out of business, discussed the possibility that some of the players under contract to an ABA club might desire to negotiate with an NBA club. O'Brien and Gourdine canvassed the roster of ABA players and determined that, for NBA purposes, the ABA players fell into three categories: (1) those with whom an NBA club already held NBA rights to negotiate pursuant to an NBA annual player draft; (2) those eligible for NBA draft but not drafted by any NBA club; and (3) those who had not been eligible for NBA draft at its last annual draft, but had since become eligible. Those in the first category interested in playing in the NBA would be required to negotiate with the NBA club holding their draft rights. Those in the second category would be free to negotiate with any NBA club they wished and vice versa. Those in the third category were the five players who are the subject of the instant motion. As to those players it was determined that a special draft would be held. A telegram setting forth the above was sent out to NBA owners on or about November 18th. In early December, Malone's attorney advised the NBA Commissioner that

Malone was free to negotiate with an NBA club or clubs and inquired with what club or clubs Malone could negotiate.

O'Brien and Gourdine decided that if no procedure was available for Malone to negotiate with NBA clubs when he wanted to, then the NBA might be violating this court's injunction which bars the NBA from refusing to negotiate with players from the rival league. They decided that it was necessary that the special draft for the NBA rights to the five players be set for an early date. December 9th was the date chosen and on December 4th they notified the owners to that effect. The NBA also issued a public statement which was widely disseminated announcing the special draft. . . .

It is clear that the NBA will suffer no injury if the special draft is postponed since the stated reason for holding it now is to maintain a posture of compliance with the previous order of this court. If it has no mechanism for dealing with Malone and others because of this court's order in the instant motion, the NBA obviously cannot be held to have violated the court's earlier mandate. If that were the only consideration, plaintiff's motion would be granted since the special NBA draft and its attendant publicity will certainly not enhance the ABA's public image, and could conceivably further erode the chances of the league for survival. Unfortunately for plaintiff's purposes, no credible evidence supporting either of these propositions was proffered at the evidentiary hearing. The burden is on the party seeking a preliminary injunction affirmatively to show its entitlement to relief. *Stark* v. *New York Stock Exchange,* 466 F.2d 743, 744 (2d Cir. 1972).

The yardstick determinative on a motion for preliminary injunction is a showing of irreparable injury and the likelihood of success on the merits, or sufficiently serious questions going to the merits to make them a fair ground for litigation and the balance of hardship tipping decidedly in favor of the party requesting preliminary relief. . . .

I should make clear at the outset what issue is being explored. Part of the plaintiff's presentation indicates that its counsel may view the issue to be the lawfulness of the NBA draft of ABA players. As I understand the proof submitted, the NBA annually holds a draft of all eligible basketball players, and those clubs to whom NBA draft rights to players are assigned have the exclusive right to negotiate for the services of those particular players. Some of these players drafted by the NBA actually sign with an ABA club. The ABA follows a similar procedure, and some of the players to whom ABA clubs have draft rights sign with the NBA. While my tentative view, that the demise of the NBA's college draft as condemned by the Sherman Act is all but certain, is a matter of record, *see Robertson* v. *NBA*, 389 F. Supp. 867, 895 (S.D. N.Y.1975), it is clear that a full and final evaluation of the draft and other NBA practices must await trial on the merits, which is set for June 1st next. Thus, the basic lawfulness of the NBA draft procedure is not a consideration on this motion.

The critical issue on which plaintiffs' motion turns is the nature of its proof that the NBA has conspired to eliminate the ABA as a rival league and that the decision to hold the special draft of Malone and company and the public announcement of the plans for that event were part of that conspiracy to violate the antitrust laws.

There has been no credible evidence establishing any such scheme or conspiracy by the NBA to eliminate the ABA. There has been no proof that the troubles of ABA clubs can be attributed to any action by the NBA or any of its clubs or owners. Nor has any credible evidence been submitted that the applications for admission to the NBA taken by two ABA franchises resulted from NBA initiative. Moreover, there is not a scintilla of credible evidence that either the decision to hold a special draft of the five players in question now, or to announce that draft publicly was part of any conspiracy to weaken or remove the ABA as a competitive force in professional basketball. While the probability is that holding the special draft now may inflict further wounds on the ABA, the NBA is not required to refrain from action which may be hurtful to a competitor. A conspiracy within the meaning of the Sherman Act must be established. *See Checker Motors Corp.* v. *Chrysler Corp.*, 283 F.Supp. 876, 885 (S.D.N.Y.1968), *aff'd* 405 F.2d 319 (2d Cir.), *cert. denied* 394 U.S. 999, 89 S.Ct. 1595, 22 L.Ed. 777 (1969).

Therefore, even under the lesser serious-questions standard, entitlement to the requested relief has not been established. Accordingly, the motion for preliminary injunction is denied. . .

Washington State Bowling Proprietors Ass'n v. Pacific Lanes, 356 F. 2d 371 (9th Cir. 1966)

The District Court for the Western District of Washington entered judgment upon a jury verdict finding defendants guilty of violating sections 1 and 2 of the Sherman Act. Plaintiff, the owner-operator of a Tacoma, Washington, bowling establishment, had brought suit against several other Tacoma bowling establishments and against the state and local trade associations of the bowling proprietors. Defendants had been charged with engaging in an unlawful combination and conspiracy whose purpose, as framed by the pretrial order, was to monopolize the bowling industry, to wit:

1. The enforcement of so-called "eligibility rules" whereby defendants conducted bowling tournaments limited to persons who restricted their league and tournament bowling to establishments which were members of three bowling proprietors associations;

2. The limitation of the number and size of bowling establishments by dissuading others from building and by convincing suppliers and manufacturers not to deal with such persons;

3. The fixing and stabilizing of the cost of bowling, and thus the reduction of competition except as against nonmember establishments; and

4. The regulation and control of the number, size, and conditions of bowling establishments throughout the U.S., thus eliminating competition.

The jury answered special interrogatories, finding (1) that all defendants had conspired to restrain trade in violation of section 1 of the Sherman Act; (2) that all defendants had conspired to monopolize commerce in violation of section 2 of the act; (3) that such unlawful acts had substantially affected the interstate commerce portion of plaintiff's and others' business; and (4) that such acts had caused loss to plaintiff's business in the amount of $35,000.

The district court denied defendants' motions for judgment N.O.V. and a new trial, and entered judgment on the verdict of treble damages of $105,000, plus attorney's fees and costs of $22,500.

Defendants appealed. They raised several points which the Ninth Circuit handled *seriatim,* affirming the district court's decision.

Defendants also asserted error in the district judge's charge that a group boycott was a *per se* violation of the Sherman Act. Defendants urged a "Rule of Reason" approach, whereby a group boycott could be deemed a reasonable regulation of competition rather than a restraint of trade. Here, for example, defendants contended that they had the right to place restrictions on their business (even though such restrictions might restrict commerce) to prevent cheating and other abuses. Defendants contended that only commercial boycots (those directed against "other traders" and not, like a group boycott, against consumers) were a *per se* violation of the act. The Ninth Circuit, however, held that a group boycott was a *per se* violation, and hence the abuses which allegedly existed in the bowling industry did not justify restraints, however "reasonable," on interstate commerce.

Defendants contended, also, that there had been no proof of the specific intent to monopolize. The Ninth Circuit found the proof adequate, citing the jury's affirmative answer to the interrogatory about section 2 violations (see (b) of para. 2, *supra*).

Defendants also alleged the evidence insufficient to show that a connection existed between defendants' various programs (i.e., eligibility rule, "overbuilding," and price fixing) and thus insufficient to show that the conspiracy was interstate in nature. The court found the record "replete" with evidence showing the conspiratorial activities of the national association (to which all local proprietors belonged) and of the two local associations. As such, there was a reasonable inference, which the jury could and did draw, that the various programs were part of the same conspiracy. Thus, plaintiff's allegation of a national conspiracy was supported by the evidence.

Heldman v. United States Lawn Tennis Ass'n., 354 F. Supp. 1241 (S.D.N.Y. 1973)

Plaintiff Gladys Heldman, organizer and promoter of the Virginia Slims circuit for women professional tennis players, and plaintiff-intervenor Billie Jean King, then ranked the world's number one female tennis player, sought to enjoin the United States Lawn Tennis Association (USLTA), who sanctions tournaments such as the U.S. Nationals, from interfering with their respective business opportunities. Heldman, who had obtained the commitments of 65 of the top women players and key sponsors for the 18-game circuit, claimed the defendants, by barring or threatening to bar the women who participated in events not sanctioned by the USLTA, would cause her signed players to decline in popularity and talent, which would harm her business opportunities as a promotee. King alleged that because of the threatened suspension, she was unable to make timely career plans and estimated losses around $40,000 if she was ineligible to play in the U.S. Nationals.

Of the three requisites necessary for the issuance of a preliminary injunction, the court concluded that the plaintiffs failed on two accounts: showing irreparable injury and showing that the balance of equities tipped in their favor. Given these conclusions, the court found it unnecessary to evaluate the strength of the merits of plaintiff's case and called the legal issues too close and too complex to predict the outcome.

The court first held that the record did not warrant the cries of distress from the plaintiff and intervenor since it was the plaintiff's circuit that was fully financed and operating. The eligibility problems could have been avoided if Heldman had simply applied for the readily available USLTA sanctions. Additionally, it was only speculative that the USLTA would bar plaintiff's players from national tournaments. Likewise, King's contention that unless there was an injunction, she could not decide how to plan her events was not an irreparable injury.

These talks of threats and allegations of tortious conduct were not credibly supported and did not warrant injunctive relief.

As for the balancing of equities, the court held that to enjoin the USLTA, a 90 year-old, nonprofit organization fostering the development and integrity of tennis, would unduly damage its prestige and could impair the functioning of its sanctioning system. Additionally, the evidence gave substantial indication that the plaintiff violated her fiduciary duties of good faith and fair dealing with the USLTA, invoking the "clean-hands" doctrine to support the denial of the injunction.

The court thus denied the motion for a preliminary injunction, and, reiterating its position that it would be a close and complex trial on the merits, set a trial date.

6.23   Control over Stadiums

In many localities, only one facility exists that can accommodate contests on a major league level in a particular sport. If an existing club already uses the facility, it will hardly welcome a competitor into the same arena. Indeed, the established club may own the facility or may have obtained a provision in its lease with the facility owner that gives the club an exclusive as to the sport in which the club participates.

As the *Hecht* case indicates, there are limits to which a club can eliminate competition by exclusive control of the playing arena. The "essential facilities" doctrine may preclude obtaining a monopoly in this fashion.

Hecht v. Pro-Football, Inc., 570 F. 2d 982 (D.C.Cir. 1977)

A private antitrust action was brought by a group of promoters, who in 1965 unsuccessfully sought to obtain an American Football League (AFL) franchise for Washington D.C., against Pro-Football, Inc., operator of the Washington Redskins, and the D.C. Armory Board, which operates RFK Stadium. The Armory Board leased RFK to the Redskins.

Plaintiff contended that RFK is the only stadium in the Washington area suitable for pro football; that a restrictive covenant prevented his obtaining use of the stadium; and his inability to obtain such use prevented his submission of an acceptable AFL franchise application. Plaintiff's complaint alleged that the restrictive covenant constitutes a contract in restraint of trade in violation of Sections 1 and 3 of the Sherman Act, and that the Redskins by obtaining the covenant and refusing to waive it monopolized professional football in the D.C. area in violation of Section 2 of the Sherman Act. The jury verdict for defendants was reversed, and the case remanded for a new trial.

In 1965, the AFL decided to add two new franchises, one to a city with an existing NFL franchise, one to a city without. Hecht and his group sent an application form to the AFL and followed this with a meeting with AFL Commissioner Foss. They discussed application details, the need to bolster the group's financial position and the feasibility of leasing RFK Stadium.

Hecht persuaded additional investors to join his group, and he met with the Secretary of the Interior as to the legality of the restrictive covenant in the Redskins' RFK lease. In the summer of 1965, Hecht's application was considered by the AFL owners. Conflicting evidence was presented as to the Hecht group's chances of being approved if it had gotten use of the Stadium.

On September 7, 1965, Hecht submitted a written proposal to the Armory Board for use of RFK Stadium. He was informed no such lease was possible due to the restrictive covenant in the Redskins' lease. The Board further stated they would consider a sharing of the Stadium should the Redskins waive the covenant.

On October 4, 1965, a memorandum from the Interior Department expressed the opinion that the restrictive covenant violated antitrust laws. Hecht was caught in the middle — the Redskins would not seriously negotiate for the stadium absent an AFL franchise for Hecht, and the AFL would not seriously consider his application without a stadium. In August 1966 the Redskins broke off negotiations. In October, Hecht filed his original complaint.

Section 4 of the Clayton Act confers standing to sue on "any person injured in his business or property by reason of anything forbidden in the antitrust laws . . ." This requires that plaintiff establish an injury in fact to his business or property and that there is shown to be a causal connection between that injury and defendant's acts. The Redskins contended that Hecht had shown neither.

The Redskins asserted that Hecht never was actually engaged in a business. The courts, however, have generally not insisted that plaintiff actually be presently engaged in a business to have antitrust standing. It is sufficient if he has manifested the intention and preparedness necessary to do so. Next, the Redskins alleged Hecht failed to show the requisite causal connection between his injury and the restrictive lease convenant. This was a question of fact for the jury.

Suits brought under the Sherman Act must be assessed in relation to the market affected, in this case indisputedly the business of professional football. The trial judge's instruction that the relevant geographic market was the nation as a whole was clearly erroneous as a matter of law. The relevant geographic area is "the area of effective competition in which the seller operates and to which the purchaser can practically turn for supplies." Courts have regularly identified single cities or towns as relevant geographic areas covered by the Act.

In the instant case, Hecht sought to enter the Washington D.C. professional football market. He argued he was frustrated by the Redskins denying his use of RFK Stadium, which use was a condition precedent to a successful franchise application. The "seller operates" and the customer can "practically turn" for his supply of professional football within the D.C. area. This is the relevant geographical market. The area of effective competition between Hecht and the Redskins would have been the nation's capital.

The trial judge erred in failing to instruct the jury that the relevant area was Washington D.C., the area in which Hecht and the Redskins would have competed for customers.

The offense of "monopolization" under Section 2 of the Sherman Act implicates both monopoly possession and an element of willfulness and intent. The intent element is satisfied if it can be inferred that defendant maintains his power by conscious and willful business policies, however legal, that inevitably result in exclusion or limitation of competition. Hecht requested a jury instruction to the effect that monopolistic intent could be found if the Redskins had consciously engaged in acts that maintained and protected the Washington football monopoly. The trial judge, in denying the instruction, did so because Hecht did not show the Washington area could support two teams. This instruction was in error.

The trial judge found that a natural monopolist does not violate Section 2 unless he acquired or maintained power by using means which are exclusionary, unfair, or predatory. He instructed the jury that, if it found the Redskins to have a natural monopoly, this does not violate the antitrust laws unless acquired by the previously stated means.

The trial judge further instructed the jury that Hecht had the burden of proving the Redskins did not have a natural monopoly. The trial judge instructed the jury to find a natural monopoly in a particular city, if the city was unable to support two professional teams under existing circumstances. This was erroneous. Once plaintiff has shown defendant's maintenance of monopoly power through conscious means, a presumption is raised which defendant can defeat only by showing that its power derives from superior skill, foresight and industry, or from the advantages of natural monopoly conditions. When a defendant seeks to avoid a charge of monopolization, asserting a natural monopoly owing to the market's inability to support two competitors, the defendant bears the burden of proof in that area.

The district court erred in failing to give plaintiff's requested instruction concerning the "essential facility doctrine," which states that where facilities cannot practicably be duplicated, those in possession of them must allow them to be shared on fair terms. To be essential, a facility must be economically infeasible to duplicate and denial of its use must inflict a severe handicap on potential market entrants. Such a facility need not be shared if sharing would be impractical or inhibit defendant's ability adequately to serve its customers.

Hecht showed RFK to be the only D.C. area stadium suitable for professional football games. He further showed that a sharing of the stadium could be made both practical and convenient. He requested an instruction that if the jury found (1) the use of RFK was essential to a professional football operation in Washington, (2) that stadium facilities could not practicably be duplicated, (3) that another team could use RFK without interferring with the Redskins' use and (4) that the restrictive covenant prevented equitable sharing by potential competitors, the jury must find the restrictive covenant an unreasonable restraint of trade in violation of Sections 1 and 3 of the Sherman Act. The instruction requested was correct and failure to give it was prejudicial error.

Section 4 of the Clayton Act grants plaintiff standing to complain of an antitrust infraction only if he has been "injured in his business or property" by defendant's acts. The trial judge should have instructed the jury it need only find plaintiffs sustained injury to their business *or* their property.

Because the trial judge erred in at least four important jury instructions and in the admission of two important pieces of evidence, the judgment was reversed and remanded for a new trial.

6.24   Control of Television Markets

A league's ability to obtain television contracts, both national and local, is considered crucial to the league's long-term financial prospects. These contracts are particularly important for a new league to compete with an established league.

When the desired television contracts are not forthcoming, the accusations begin.

The United States Football League struggled through two seasons of play in 1983 and 1984 under a contract with ABC that did little to offset the league's substantial operating losses. The USFL owners decided to stick to a spring schedule in 1985 (which also proved to be financially burdensome) and to switch to a fall schedule in 1986. None of the three major networks offered the league a contract for the 1986 fall season. The networks' failure to deal, along with other perceived background maneuverings by the rival NFL, led the USFL to file a $1.3 billion lawsuit against the NFL. Later, the USFL also filed directly against the networks.

The *USFL* v. *NFL* complaint, summarized below, illustrates the breadth of dealings involved when rival leagues compete. As one league appears to be gaining the ultimate advantage, it is likely the other will claim the advantages are the result of anticompetitive practices.

United States Football League v. National Football League, No. 84 Civ. 7484, U.S. District Court, Southern Dist. of New York, complaint filed October 17, 1984

The United States Football League (USFL) filed suit against the National Football League (NFL) on October 17, 1984. The action was brought following the announcement in August 1984 that the USFL would be shifting the playing season from the spring to the fall, thus competing directly against the NFL.

The USFL charged the NFL, each individual NFL club, and NFL Commissioner Alvin R. (Pete) Rozelle with violating section 2 of the Sherman Act by willfully and unlawfully monopolizing, attempting to monopolize, and conspiring to monopolize the business of major league professional football in the United States. The USFL also charged with respect to section 2 of the Sherman Act that there was a conspiracy among the defendants and the involuntary co-conspirators (NBC, CBS, and ABC) to eliminate the USFL Member Clubs as competitors of the defendant NFL clubs (Complaint, p. 18). In respect to section 1 of the Sherman Act, the USFL charged that the NFL, with the involuntary cooperation of the major television networks, has engaged in a continuing combination and conspiracy in unreasonable restraint of interstate commerce and trade, which has effectively foreclosed the USFL from competing against the NFL in the business of major league professional football in the United States (Complaint, p. 57).

The USFL prayed for the following:

1. That the court award actual damages of $440,000,000 ($1,320,000,000 when trebled in accordance with 15 U.S.C. sec. 13);
2. that the NFL be permanently enjoined from (a) making efforts to impede the USFL's attempts to obtain national network television coverage; (b) increasing player rosters, which will affect the USFL's ability to negotiate with talented players; (c) negotiating with or making offers to players currently under USFL contracts; (d) making exclusive service contracts with game officials; (e) taking actions that will impede the USFL's efforts to engage professional football coaches; (f) making disparaging statements about the USFL; and (g) making exclusive stadium contracts.

Also, the USFL prayed for the restructuring of the NFL in a fashion that would permit the USFL to compete in the market of professional football. The USFL also prayed for the costs and attorney's fees incurred in prosecuting this action (Complaint, p. 59).

The bulk of the USFL's complaint focused on the NFL's influence over the major television networks. The USFL charged that the defendants, by entering into highly profitable, long-term television contracts with each network, has made it impossible for the USFL to compete effectively in the business of professional football (Complaint, p. 25). Further, the USFL

charged that the NFL has either expressly or impliedly threatened the three major networks (NBC, CBS, and ABC) with discontinuance or reduction of the sale of the "extremely valuable NFL television rights to any network which enters into a meaningful future television contract with the USFL" (Complaint, p. 30). ABC has, as a result of the defendants' influence, refused to cooperate with the USFL in the promotion of the plaintiff's league (Complaint, p. 28).

6.30   Role of the Commissioner

The idea of a commissioner vested with substantial powers came about in the aftermath of the Chicago "Black Sox" scandal in 1919. The baseball owners believed a strong hand was needed to make certain that such damaging events did not recur. Judge Kenesaw Mountain Landis was chosen to be the first commissioner. The tradition has continued, largely adopted by all sports leagues.

The duties and powers of the commissioner are many, as evidenced by the excerpts from the NFL constitution and by-laws, set forth in Section 6.31. The major concentration in the following subsections is on the commissioner's role in the discipline of players and owners, in the regulation of interclub dealings, and as arbitrator for certain types of disputes.

6.31   General Powers

The basic source detailing a commissioner's powers is usually the league's constitution and bylaws. However, the league's collective bargaining agreements with players and umpires or referees may also specify certain duties and responsibilities of the commissioner. These culminate in both a conferral of and a limitation on the commissioner's powers. The collective bargaining agreement, under labor law principles, takes precedence if there is any conflict (see Chapter 3, Section 3.00).

In all likelihood, there is no direct conflict between a league's bylaws and its collective bargaining agreements. The more likely occurrence is that the collective agreement places limitations on what would otherwise be a broad and relatively unrestricted grant of authority to the commissioner.

The powers of the NFL's commissioner, typical of those accorded most leagues' commissioners, should be analyzed in the framework of both the bylaws, as set forth below, and the league's collective agreement with its players.

Constitution and Bylaws, National Football League

ARTICLE VIII: Commissioner

Employment

8.1 The League shall select and employ a person of unquestioned integrity to serve as Commissioner of the League, and shall determine the period and fix the compensation of his employment except:

(a) Pete Rozelle is hereby appointed as Commissioner of the League upon terms and conditions heretofore approved by the League in an employment contract with Pete Rozelle.

(b) Until June 1, 1976 any successor to Pete Rozelle as Commissioner must be approved by no less than twelve (12) of the fifteen (15) clubs which were members of the National Football League in 1966 in addition to the requirements set forth in subparagraph (c) below.

(c) Any extension or modification of the existing contract or any new contract beween the League and Pete Rozelle as Commissioner shall be approved by the affirmative vote of not less than two-thirds or 18, whichever is greater, of the members of the League.

All other voting requirements and procedures for the selection of or successor to the office of Commissioner shall be determined by the affirmative vote of not less than two-thirds or 18, whichever is greater, of the members of the League.

Independence

8.2 The Commissioner shall have no financial interest, direct or indirect, in any professional sport.

Jurisdiction to Resolve Disputes

8.3 The Commissioner shall have full, complete, and final jurisdiction and authority to arbitrate:

(a) Any dispute involving two or more members of the League, or involving two or more holders of an ownership interest in a member club of the League, certified to him by any of the disputants.

(b) Any dispute between any player, coach and/or other employee of any member of the League (or any combination thereof) and any member club or clubs.

(c) Any dispute between or among players, coaches, and/or other employees of any member club or clubs of the League, other than disputes unrelated to and outside the course and scope of the employment of such disputants within the League.

(d) Any dispute between a player and any official of the League.

(e) Any dispute involving a member or members in the League, or any players or employees of the members or the League, or any combination thereof, that in the opinion of the Commissioner constitutes conduct detrimental to the best interests of the League or professional football.

Financial and Other Authority

8.4 (A) The Commissioner, on behalf of the League, may incur any expense which, in his sole discretion, is necessary to conduct and transact the ordinary business of the League, including but not limited to, the leasing of office space and the hiring of employees, and other assistance or services; provided, however, that the Commissioner shall not have authority to incur any expense for any extraordinary obligations, or make any capital investment on behalf of the League without prior approval by the Executive Committee.

(B) The Commissioner shall: (a) preside at all meetings of the League and the Executive Committee; (b) be the principal executive officer of the League, and shall have general supervision of its business and affairs, (c) approve for payment all proper charges.

Policy and Procedure

8.5 The Commissioner shall interpret and from

time to time establish policy and procedure in respect to the provisions of the Constitution and By-Laws and any enforcement thereof.

Detrimental Conduct

8.6 The Commissioner is authorized, at the expense of the League, to hire legal counsel and take or adopt appropriate legal action or such other steps or procedures as he deems necessary and proper in the best interests of either the League or professional football, whenever any party or organization not a member of, employed by, or connected with the League or any member thereof, is guilty of any conduct detrimental either to the League, its member clubs or employees, or to professional football.

Game Officials

8.7 The Commissioner shall select and employ a Supervisor of League Game Officials and shall further select and approve all game officials for all pre-season, regular season, and post-season games. All fees and traveling expenses of game officials shall be paid by the League after approval by the Commissioner. It shall be the duty of each member to accept as game officials for any game such game officials as the Commissioner shall assign to such game.

Public Relations Department

8.8 The Commissioner shall have authority to establish a Public Relations Department for the League, and such department shall be under his exclusive control and direction. He may employ persons to staff said department and shall fix and determine the compensation therefor.

Broadcasts and Television

8.9 Subject to the provisions of Article X hereof, the Commissioner shall have the exclusive authority to arrange for and sell all broadcasting and television rights to the Conference Championship Games and the World Championship Game.

League Contracts

8.10 The Commissioner shall have authority to arrange for and negotiate contracts on behalf of the League with other persons, firms, leagues, or

associations; provided, however, that except in instances where the Commissioner is otherwise specifically authorized herein, any contract involving a substantial commitment by the League or its members shall not be binding unless first approved by the affirmative vote of not less than three-fourths or 20, whichever is greater, of the members of the League.

Reports

8.11. The Commissioner shall render an annual report to the League members at each Annual Meeting.

Bond

8.12 The Commissioner shall file and maintain in effect a surety bond with the League in the sum of Fifty Thousand Dollars ($50,000); said bond shall be conditioned upon faithful performance by the Commissioner of his duties and shall name the League as obligee. The expenses for such bond shall be paid by the League.

Disciplinary Powers of Commissioner

8.13 (A) Whenever the Commissioner, after notice and hearing decides that an owner, shareholder, partner or holder of an interest in a member club, or any player, coach, officer, director or employee thereof, or an officer, employee or official of the League has either violated the Constitution or By-Laws of the League, or has been or is guilty of conduct detrimental to the welfare of the League or professional football, then the Commissioner shall have complete authority to:

(1) Suspend and/or fine such person in an amount not in excess of five thousand dollars ($5,000), and/or

(2) Cancel any contract or agreement of such person with the League or with any member thereof.

(3) In cases involving a violation of the prohibitions against tampering and set forth in Sections 9.1(C), 10 and 11, 9.2. and 12.1 (B) hereof, award or transfer selection choices and/or deprive the offending club of a selection choice or choices.

(4) In cases involving a violation affecting the competitive aspects of the game, award or

transfer players and/or selection choices, and/or deprive the offending club of a selection choice or choices, and/or cancel any contract or agreement of such person with the League or with any member thereof, and/or fine the offending club in an amount not in excess of twenty-five thousand dollars ($25,000) despite the provisions of subsection (1) herein.

(B) Whenever the Commissioner determines that any punishment which the Commissioner has the power to impose pursuant to Section 8.13 (A), is not adequate or sufficient, considering the nature and gravity of the offense involved, he may refer the matter to the Executive Committee, with a recommendation that all or any part of the following additional or increased punishments or discipline be imposed:

(1) Cancellation or forfeiture of the franchise in the League of any member club involved or implicated; if such occurs, the affected franchise shall be sold and disposed of under the provisions of Section 3.8(B) hereof.

(2) Cancellation or forfeiture of the interest in a member club, or in the franchise thereof, owned by a person involved or implicated therein; if such occurs, the interest held by any person so implicated, shall be sold and disposed of under the provisions of Section 3.8 (B) hereof.

(3) Declare one or more players of the offending club to be a free agent or that one or more players, and the contracts thereon held by the offending club, be assigned to another club or clubs.

(4) Assignment to another club or a nominee of the League, of the lease on any stadium or playing field held for or owned by the offending club or any person owning any interest therein.

(5) Assignment to one or more clubs of players on the Selection or Reserve Lists of the offending club.

(6) Require the sale of any stock or interest in a member club of such offending person by the method and under the procedure specified in Section 3.8 (B) hereof.

(7) Make any other recommendation he deems appropriate.

The Executive Committee may impose such other or additional discipline or punishment as it may decide.

Any such ruling or decision by the Commissioner under the circumstances referred to in this sub-paragraph 8.13 (B) of Article VIII, after approval or ratification by the affirmative vote of no less than three-fourths or 20, whichever is greater, of the members of the League, as aforesaid, shall be final, conclusive, and unappealable; any party involved in or affected by any such decision agrees to release and waive any and all claims that such party may now or hereafter have or possess arising out of or connected with such decision against the Commissioner, individually and in his official capacity, as well as against the League and any officer or employee thereof, and every member club therein and against any director, officer, shareholder or partner thereof, or the holder of any interest therein, whether for damages or for any other remedy or relief. . . .

(C) Whenever the Commissioner, after notice and hearing determines that a person employed by or connected with the league or any member club thereof, has bet money or any other thing of value on the outcome or score of any game or games played in the League, or has had knowledge of or has received an offer, directly or indirectly, to control, fix or bet money or other consideration on the outcome or score of a professional football game, and has failed to report the same in the manner hereinafter prescribed, then such Commissioner shall have complete and unrestricted authority to enforce any or all of the following penalties:

(1) Suspend such person indefinitely or for a prescribed period of time.

(2) Bar such person from the League for life.

(3) Cancel or terminate the contract of such person in the League or any member club thereof.

(4) Require the sale of any stock, or other interest of such offending person in any member club by the method and under the procedure specified in Section 3.8 (B) hereof.

(5) Fine such person in an amount not in excess of Five Thousand Dollars ($5,000).

(6) Cancel or declare to be forfeited any interest in a member club, or in the franchise thereof, owned by any person so involved; in such event, any interest of the offending person so implicated in the club or any stock owned by such person in any member club shall be sold under the procedure provided in Section 3.8 (B) hereof.

(7) Assign to another club or a member of

the League the lease on any stadium or playing field held for or owned by the offending club or by any person owning any interest therein.

(8) Assign to one or more other clubs players on the Selection or Reserve Lists of the offending club.

(9) Impose such other or additional punishment or discipline as the Commissioner may decide. . .

(D) Whenever the Commissioner finds, in his sole and exclusive discretion, that any peson whether or not connected or affiliated with the League, or a member club therein, is guilty of conduct detrimental to the best interest of the League or professional football, then in addition to his other powers prescribed in the Constitution and By-Laws of the League, the Commissioner shall have the right to bar and prohibit such person from entry to any stadium or park used by the League, or its member clubs or affiliates for the practice or exhibition of professional football.

(E) The Commissoner shall have authority to change, reduce, modify, remit, or suspend any fine, suspension, or other discipline imposed by the Commissioner and not requiring approval of the member clubs.

Miscellaneous Powers of Commissioner

8.14 (A) The Commissioner shall have the power, without a hearing, to disapprove contracts between a player and a club, if such a contract has been executed in violation of or contrary to the Constitution and By-Laws of the League, or, if either or both of the parties to such contract have been or are guilty of an act or conduct which is or may be detrimental to the League or to the sport of professional football. Any such disapproval of a contract between a player and a club shall be exercised by the Commissioner upon the written notice to the contracting parties within ten (10) days after such contracts are filed with the Commissioner. The Commissioner shall also have the power to disapprove any contract between any club and a player or any other person, at any time pursuant to and in accordance with the provisions of Section 8.13 (A) of the Constitution and by-Laws.

(B) The Commissioner shall have the power to hear and determine disputes between clubs in respect to any matter certified to by him by either or both of the clubs; he shall also have the power to settle and determine any controversy between two clubs which, in the opinion of the Commissioner, involves or affects League policy.

(C) The Commissioner shall have the right to propose amendments or modifications in the Constitution and By-Laws of the League by submitting such amendments or modifications in writing to the League no less than fifteen (15) days prior to the holding of any Annual Meeting of the League or recessed session thereof.

6.32   Discipline

A league's commissioner is granted certain disciplinary powers. In the previous section, certain details of the NFL commissioner's disciplinary powers were specified in 8.13 of the league's constitution and bylaws. As noted in the introduction to the previous section, these must be considered in conjunction with provisions of the league's collective bargaining agreement with the players association, insofar as the disciplinary powers pertain to players. Consequently, 8.13 of the bylaws must be considered with Article VIII of the NFL collective agreement, set forth below.

The Commissioner is normally extended disciplinary powers that apply to all parties involved in the league and club operations. At times, even club owners feel the sting of the commissioner's powers, as the cases discussed below illustrate.

National Football League, 1982 Collective Bargaining Agreement

ARTICLE VIII: Commissioner Discipline

Section 1. Commissioner Discipline: Notwithstanding anything stated in Article VII of this Agreement, Non-Injury Grievance, all disputes involving a fine or suspension imposed upon a player by the Commissioner for conduct on the playing field, or involving action taken against a player by the Commissioner for conduct detrimental to the integrity of, or public confidence in, the game of professional football, will be processed exclusively as follows: the Commissioner will promptly send written notice of his action to the player, with a copy to the NFLPA. Within 20 days following written notification of the Commissioner's action, the player affected thereby or the NFLPA, with the approval of the player involved, may appeal in writing to the Commissioner. The Commissoner will designate a time and place for hearing, which will be commenced within 10 days following his receipt of the notice of appeal. As soon as practicable following the conclusion of such hearing, the Commissioner will render a written decision, which decision will constitute full, final, and complete disposition of the dispute, and will be binding upon the player(s) and club(s) involved and the parties to this Agreement with respect to that dispute.

Section 2. Time Limits: Each of the time limits set forth in this Article may be extended by mutual agreement of the Commissioner and the player(s) and the club(s) involved.

Section 3. Representation: In any hearing provided for in this Article, a player may be accompanied by counsel of his choice. A representative of the NFLPA may also participate in such hearing and represent the player. In any such hearing, a club representative may be accompanied by counsel of his choice. A representative of the Management Council may also participate in such hearing and represent the club.

Section 4. Costs: Unless the Commissioner determines otherwise, each party will bear the cost of its own witnesses, counsel and the like.

Section 5. One Penalty: The Commissioner and a Club will not discipline a player for the same act or conduct. The Commissioner's disciplinary action will preclude or supersede disciplinary action by any club for the same act or conduct.

Section 6. Fine Money: Any fine money collected pursuant to this Article will be contributed to the Brian Piccolo Cancer Fund or the Vincent T. Lombardi Cancer Research Center, as the player shall choose.

NOTE

1. See Section 4.34 for examples of disputes over player discipline, whether initiated by the club or by the commissioner. See also Sections 5.21 and 5.43.

Riko Enterprises, Inc. v. Seattle Supersonics, 357 F.Supp. 521 (S.D.N.Y. 1973)

Tenney, District Judge

. . . Philadelphia and Seattle are member teams of the National Basketball Association (hereinafter "NBA") and signatories to its constitution. As members of the NBA they are eligible to participate in its annual college draft by which each team is allowed to select, on a rotating basis, those college players with whom they desire to negotiate contracts of employment. Under the NBA constitution, once a player is selected by a team as a draft choice, that team, and only that team, has the right to negotiate for his services.

In 1969, John Brisker became eligible for the NBA college draft. No NBA member team, however, selected him as one of its choices at the draft meetings. In July 1969, Philadelphia asked that Brisker be placed on its supplemental draft list. Brisker, however, signed a contract to play for the Pittsburgh team of the rival American Basketball Association. In the spring of 1972, the Pittsburgh team became insolvent and Brisker was again free to negotiate with NBA teams. Brisker's attorney contacted the Seattle team and indicated his desire to play in the NBA.

At this point, petitioner and respondent disagree with respect to the action taken by Seattle. Petitioner claims that Seattle continued to negotiate with Brisker even after being informed by NBA Commissioner Kennedy that Philadelphia possessed sole negotiating rights. Seattle, on the other hand, claims that it directed Brisker's attorney to negotiate with Philadelphia and continued to do so until Kennedy informed Brisker's attorney, by letter on June 19, 1972, that Brisker was a "free agent." On August 7, 1972, Brisker signed a contract to play for Seattle. On August 14, 1972, Philadelphia filed formal charges with the Commissioner against Seattle, claiming that Seattle had wilfully violated the NBA's constitution and by-laws by negotiating with Brisker while he was still on Philadelphia's draft list. On August 15, 1972, Commissioner Kennedy approved Brisker's contract with Seattle.

The matter was brought before the NBA Board of Governors (hereinafter the "Board") at a meeting held on September 20, 1972. At that meeting the Board voted to table the charges brought by Philadelphia under paragraphs 13 and

14 of the constitution and refer the matter to the Commissioner under paragraph 24 for disposition. On November 16, 1972, the Commissioner issued his decision finding that Seattle had violated the NBA constitution (*i.e.,* "violated the simple principle of fair play"), fining them $10,000 and awarding Seattle's first round draft pick in the 1973 college draft to Philadelphia. On March 28, 1973, Philadelphia filed the instant petition for an order confirming the Commissioner's award. Seattle, by order to show cause returnable April 11, 1973, moved to vacate the award. The NBA college draft is scheduled to be held on April 16, 1973. . . .

The NBA constitution is a contract between the member teams of the NBA. Consequently, the terms of that contract define the jurisdiction of any arbitration; pursuant to it Philadelphia brought its charges against Seattle under paragraphs 13 and 14 of the constitution asking that its membership be terminated. Paragraph 13 provides in pertinent part:

> 13. The membership of a member . . . shall be suspended or terminated . . . by a vote of two-thirds of the Board of Governors if the member . . . shall do or suffer the following:
> (a) Willfully violate any of the provisions of the Constitution or By-Laws of the Association.

Philadelphia's action was brought pursuant to paragraph 13(a). Paragraph 14, in great detail, describes the procedures to be followed in determining charges brought under paragraph 13. That procedure includes the filing of formal charges with the Commissioner, the filing of a formal answer to the charges, the convening of a special meeting of the Board to hear the charges, the right to appear by counsel and submit evidence, and a vote of the Board on the question of the charges. A two-thirds vote is required to sustain the charges. A *second* two-thirds vote is required to suspend or terminate membership. Paragraph 15 allows the Board, *in its discretion,* to levy a fine or to order forfeiture of a draft choice in lieu of termination or suspension.

The instant case followed the prescribed procedure up to the point of presenting the charges to the Board. At that point, all of the members of the Board, including petitioner's and respondent's representative voted to table the paragraphs 13 and 14 charges and to refer the matter to the Commissioner under paragraph 24. Paragraph 24, in pertinent part, provides:

> (k) All actions duly taken by the Commissioner pursuant to this paragraph 24 or pursuant to any other Section of the Constitution, *which is not specifically referable to the Board of Governors,* shall be final, binding and conclusive, as an award in arbitration, and enforceable in a court of competent jurisdiction in accordance with the laws of the State of New York. (Emphasis added.)

It is this provision which petitioner asserts as the basis for its application for an order confirming the award. The Court, however, finds that in ordering the forfeiture of Seattle's draft rights under paragraph 24(k), the Commissioner exceeded his powers as an arbitrator under the constitution.

Paragraph 24(k) clearly excludes actions which are referable specifically to the Board. There can be no question that charges brought pursuant to paragraph 13(a) are to be determined *only* by the Board and then only in accordance with the procedures outlined in paragraph 14. It is obvious that the remedies of termination of membership or forfeiture of draft rights were considered so drastic that a two-thirds vote of the Board was required to employ them. . . .

There remains the question of the validity of the $10,000 fine. It is the opinion of the Court that since the action was commenced under paragraph 13(a) even the penalty of a fine in lieu of termination of membership was within the sole discretion of the Board. Paragraph 15 reads, in pertinent part:

Fine As Alternative to Expulsion

> 15. If a charge that a member or person has committed any of the offenses described in paragraph 13 is sustained, *two-thirds of all the Governors may in lieu of compelling the divestiture of the owner or suspending or terminating the membership of such member or person, direct that the divestiture of the ownership of such a member or person be suspended or terminated only if the member or person fails to pay a stated fine* in a stipulated manner and by a stipulated date, which fine may be required to be paid, in whole or in part, to any other member or members as compensa-

tion to such member or members for damages sustained by it or them by reason of such act or acts of omission or commission by such offending member or person. . . . *Moreover, the Board of Governors, may in its discretion, either in addition to, or in lieu of such fine, direct the forfeiture of the offending member's draft rights.* (Emphasis added.)

It is evident from a reading of paragraphs 14 and 15 that in order to impose a fine for a charge of violating paragraphs 13(a) a two-thirds vote of the Board is required, both to sustain the charges and then to impose the fine.

It may be argued, however, that the parties, at least in respect to the imposition of a fine, consented to the jurisdiction of the Commissioner when they, too, voted to refer the matter to the Commissioner under paragraph 24. It is at this point that the Court will turn to respondent's second claim that the arbitration was procedurally defective.

Paragraph 24(k) provides that the action of the Commissioner shall be enforceable as an award in arbitration under the laws of New York. New York CPLR section 7506(b) provides that "[t]he arbitrator *shall* appoint a time and place for the hearing. . . ." (Emphasis added.) Section 7506(c) provides that "[t]he parties are *entitled* to be heard, to present evidence and to cross-examine witnesses." (Emphasis added.) The papers and testimony before this Court show that Commissioner Kennedy conducted no hearing and did not allow Seattle to submit any evidence to rebut the charges. Moreover, the NBA constitution makes no provision for a hearing or other due process in actions taken by the Commissioner under paragraph 24. No court, state or federal, should affix its imprimatur to any such "award." Cf., *Fuentes* v. *Shevin*, 407 U.S. 67, 92 S.Ct. 1983, 32 L.Ed.2d 556 (1972). This is a clear violation of New York law and, standing alone, is reason enough to vacate the award of both the forfeiture of the draft right and the levying of the fine under 9 U.S.C. section 10(c) (1970). . . .

Finally, Seattle has moved to preliminarily enjoin Philadelphia from exercising Seattle's first round draft choice in the NBA college draft scheduled to be held on April 16, 1973. However, the NBA is not a party to the present proceeding. A temporary injunction against Philadelphia would not, absent NBA approval, restore Seattle's first

round draft choice but would merely invite confusion. The requested relief must accordingly be denied.

The "award" of the Commissioner dated November 16, 1972, is hereby vacated.

So ordered.

Atlanta National League Baseball Club, Inc. and Turner v. Kuhn, 432 F.Supp. 1213 (N.D. Ga. 1977)

Edenfield, District Judge.

Plaintiffs brought this diversity action pursuant to 28 U.S.C. sec 1331 seeking to enjoin defendant from imposing certain sanctions against plaintiffs. Both sides have filed motions for summary judgment and the court deferred ruling on such motions pending a trial on the merits. The case was heard on April 25 and 26, 1977, and the court is now prepared to rule on the merits.

Factual Background

Plaintiff Turner is Chief Executive Officer of plaintiff Atlanta National League Baseball Club ("Atlanta Club"). The Atlanta Club, together with 25 other teams, is a signatory to an agreement known as the Major League Agreement. That agreement, the latest version of which was executed on January 1, 1975, constitutes a contract between the two baseball league associations, the American League of Professional Baseball Clubs and the National League of Professional Baseball Clubs, of which the Atlanta Club is a member. The Agreement establishes the office of the defendant, the Commissioner of Baseball, and defines his authority, powers and responsibilities.

The origin of the instant controversy can be traced to the changes that were made in baseball's reserve system in 1976. . . .

An agreement was reached in July, 1976 which established a special reentry draft to be conducted in November of each year for those players who had become free agents at the end of a baseball season. Procedures were established for the November draft whereby negotiation rights with each free agent could be drafted by up to twelve teams, each of which were then given negotiation rights for that player. Between the end of the season and three days prior to the draft, however, only the club of record, the team for which the prospective free agent was playing out his option, had negotiation rights with that player. With the advent of this new reserve system there was concern on the part of the clubs and the Commissioner that the clubs of record have the maximum opportunity to retain their prospective free agents in an effort to preserve a competitive balance among the clubs in professional baseball. Accordingly, during the post-season period in which the club of record has exclusive negotiating rights with a free agent, other clubs were allowed to talk with the free agent or his representative about the merits of contracting with a particular team, *"provided, however, that the Club and the free agent shall not negotiate terms of contract with each other."* Collective Bargaining Agreement, Art. VII, 3(a). To help ensure that this provision was observed and that tampering was avoided, both the Executive Council, established by the Major League Agreement, and the Player Relations Committee encouraged the Commissioner to issue warnings that tampering violations would not be tolerated, and to make every effort to deter such violations.

On August 27, 1976 the Commissioner issued the first in a series of warnings in the form of a teletyped notice to each major league club. . . .

A second warning was issued on September 28, 1976 which specified that both direct and indirect dealings were prohibited prior to the end of the season. . . .

The third warning, issued on October 5, 1976, emphasized that the tampering rule would be enforced and stated that "Possible penalties will include fines, loss of rights under [amateur free agent] and re-entry drafts and suspension of those responsible.". . .

On September 24, 1976 the Commissioner held a hearing on certain alleged tampering violations committed by John Alevizos, then Executive Vice President and General Manager of the Atlanta Club, in communicating with Gary Matthews, who was then completing his option year with the San Francisco club. The Commissioner found that Alevizos had violated 3(g) and fined the Atlanta Club $5,000 for each of two violations and ruled that the Atlanta Club would be denied a selection in the first round of the amateur player draft to be held in January 1977. In his October 5 decision, the Commissioner indicated that he had considered suspending Alevizos, but Alevizos' employment with the Atlanta club had already been terminated.

On October 20, 1976 Turner attended a cocktail party in New York City sponsored by the New York Yankees Club, and there engaged in a conversation with Robert Lurie, co-owner of the San Francisco club. In the presence of several media representatives, Turner told Lurie that he would do anything to get Gary Matthews and that he would go as high as he had to. *See* Commission's decision of December 30, 1976. Turner's comments were reported by a few San Francisco newspapers. On October 25, 1976, Lurie filed a complaint concerning these statements with the Commissioner. . . .

The draft was conducted on November 4, and twelve teams drafted negotiation rights with Matthews by the fifth round. The same day a formal hearing was held in which Turner admitted making the above comments, claiming that they were made in jest but denied that there had been any direct or indirect negotiations of contract terms with Matthews or his agent. Matthews testified by way of affidavit that there had been no direct or indirect contacts with the Atlanta club as to contract terms.

> On December 30, the Commissioner announced his decision in the Turner matter. He concluded that Turner's statements were in clear violation of the prohibitions of the directives . . . These statements clearly had the effect of subverting the collective bargaining agreement and the re-entry draft procedures adopted pursuant to it. I am therefore compelled to find that they were not in the best interests of Baseball within the meaning of Section 3, Article I of the Major League Agreement.

December 30 decision at 2. In considering appropriate sanctions, the Commissioner decided not to disapprove Matthews' contract with the Atlanta Club which had been signed on November 17. This decision was based on the urgings of Turner and upon the Commissioner's conclusion that Matthews had not engaged in any improper contact. Instead, the Commissioner decided to suspend Turner from baseball for one year, reasoning that (1) Turner had suggested that such a sanction would be appropriate, (2) this was the second Atlanta tampering violation, and (3) the Commissioner had warned in one of his directives that suspensions might be imposed. As a further sanction, the Commissioner decided that the Atlanta Club would not be entitled to exercise its first round draft choice in the June, 1977 amateur free agent draft. . . .

Extent of Judicial Review

Defendant first claims that plaintiffs are barred from bringing this action, having waived their access to the courts under the Major League Agreement. Article VII, section 2, of that agreement provides:

> The Major Leagues and their constituent clubs, severally agree to be bound by the decisions of the Commissioner, and the discipline imposed by him under the provisions of this Agreement, and severally waive such right of recourse to the courts as would otherwise have existed in their favor.

Plaintiffs contend that this provision is unenforceable in that it violates public policy.

When faced with the same waiver provision in *Finley & Co., v. Kuhn*, No. 76C–2358 (N.D.Ill., September 7, 1976), the court rejected the Commissioner's argument that the waiver of recourse to the courts deprived the court of subject-matter jurisdiction.

> Simply stated, defendants' legal theory, if accepted, would entitle him to render a decision on any question dealing with baseball no matter how unauthorized or arbitrary that decision might be. This is an untenable position. The extent of defendant Kuhn's contractual power is a question for the court. Indeed, whether the Commissioner's decision in issue here is the type of decision to which the parties agreed they would be bound is itself at issue. Accordingly, jurisdiction is not lacking. . . .

In a further attempt to limit the extent of judicial review, defendant argues that the Commissioner acted as an arbitrator herein, and the parties agreed under the Major League Agreement to be bound by such arbitration. *See* Article VII, section 1. Pursuant to the United States Arbitration Act, 9 U.S.C. section 1, *et seq.,* such arbitration agreements are enforceable, and in reviewing an arbitration decision, the court is limited to four narrow questions: Whether (1) the decision is the result of fraud; (2) there is evidence of bias on the

part of the arbitrators; (3) the arbitrator was guilty of misconduct; and (4) the arbitrator exceeded his powers. 9 U.S.C. section 10(a)–(d). . . .

Although the Commissioner is designated as an arbitrator in Article VII, section 1, his task in that capacity is to resolve "[a]ll disputes and controversies related in any way to professional baseball *between* clubs (including their officers, directors, employees and players)." (Emphasis added.) Plaintiffs argue that this section is inapplicable to the instant situation because this was not a dispute between parties as referred to in sec. 1. The initial telegram from Kuhn to Turner on October 28, 1976 stated—

> The San Francisco Club has filed with this office allegations from which it appears that the Atlanta Club may have violated [Rule 3(g), the Collective Bargaining Agreement and the Guidelines].

However, in Kuhn's October 5, 1976 telegram warning that tampering violations would not be tolerated, the Commissioner encouraged "clubs and club personnel to submit to this office any information in their possession regarding possible instances of tampering" and designated Alexander Hadden to serve as "clearinghouse" for this information. Thus, Lurie's complaint was, in a sense, solicited by the Commissioner.

In this respect, and bearing in mind that it was the Commissioner's own directive that he was claiming to enforce, the instant case is similar to *Professional Sports, Ltd.* v. *Virginia Squires Basketball*, 373 F.Supp. 946 (W.D.Tex.1974), wherein the court found an agreement to be bound by the Commissioner of Basketball's arbitration decision inapplicable where the dispute was one generated by the Commissioner himself. 373 F.Supp. at 950. . . .

That the Commissioner did not act as an arbitrator herein is supported by the sanctions imposed. Typically in an arbitration dispute the arbitrator adjudicates the rights as between two parties and accords relief to one of them. Here, the Commissioner was not deciding Lurie's rights vis á vis Turner, and granting relief to Lurie; rather, a punishment was imposed which would primarily affect only Turner and the Atlanta Club.

The court is inclined to view the Commissioner's authority as deriving not from the arbitration clause of the Major League Agreement, but from Article I, sec. 2, where he is given the power to "INVESTIGATE, either upon complaint or upon his own initiative, any act . . . alleged or suspected to be not in the best interests of the national game of Baseball," and "TO DETERMINE, after investigation, what punitive action is appropriate . . ."

The Sanctions

Viewing the evidence concerning punishment here, a casual, nonlegalistic observer might say that this case represents a comedy of strange tactical errors on both sides. Both at the hearing before the Commissioner and afterward, but before decision, Turner asked for "suspension" as his punishment in lieu of cancellation of the Matthews contract, which he feared. The Commissioner also did some inexplicable things: He approved Atlanta's signing of Matthews, apparently the only tangible mischief resulting from Turner's remarks, but having approved the act of signing he then punished Turner for publicly suggesting in advance he intended to do it. He also forbade Turner the right to manage his business or to even go on his own property except as a paying customer. The Atlanta Baseball Club is called the "Atlanta Braves"; and considering the severity of this punishment, the same casual observer might call this an Indian massacre in reverse. In their encounter with the Commissioner the Braves took "nary" a scalp, but lived to see their own dangling from the lodgepole of the Commissioner, apparently only as a grisly warning to others. At about the same time and for an identical offense, though perhaps not as flagrant, the venerable owner of the St. Louis Cardinals was fined $5,000. All of which adds nothing to the *legal* power of this court to extricate plaintiffs from a suspension which they invited and to which they assented, both orally and contractually.

Plaintiffs say, however, that the suspension of Turner here amounted to an abuse of discretion. It has been suggested that an "abuse of discretion" is the virtual equivalent of an error of law. Other cases say that the exercise of an honest judgment, however erroneous it may appear to be, is not an abuse of discretion, especially where there are a large number of facts and "the facts themselves largely define the wisdom of the discretion. . . ." *Weeks* v. *Bareco Oil Co.,* 125 F.2d 84, 93 (7th

Cir.1941); *In re A. Roth Co., Inc.,* 125 F.2d 396, 398 (7th Cir. 1942).

Here the Commissioner could properly conclude that this was the second instance of improper conduct with respect to one player. He could also consider that Turner's comments were made after six warning directives had been issued, one of which cautioned that suspensions would follow from tampering violations. None of these aggravating circumstances were present in the St. Louis case. With these differences present, honest minds could, and indeed do, disagree as to what is an appropriate punishment. The court, therefore, simply cannot say the Commissioner abused his discretion. In Article VII, sec. 2, of the Major League Agreement the clubs explicitly agreed to be bound by the discipline imposed by the Commissioner and obviously intended to give him a certain amount of leeway to choose the appropriate sanction. Judicial review of every sanction imposed by the Commissioner would produce an unworkable system that the Major League Agreement endeavors to prevent. Here, Turner was warned of the suspension, he asked for the suspension, the contract specifically authorized it, and he got it.

The denial of the June draft choice, however, stands on a somewhat different legal footing. Under the best interests of baseball clause, Article I, sec. 2, the Commissioner is given the authority to "determine, after investigation, what *preventive, remedial or punitive action* is appropriate in the premises." (Emphasis added.) Those punitive measures which the Commissioner may take are explicitly enumerated in Article I, sec. 3:

> In the case of conduct by Major Leagues, Major League Clubs, officers, employees or players which is deemed by the Commissioner not to be in the best interests of Baseball, action by the Commissioner for each offense may include any one or more of the following: (a) a reprimand; (b) deprivation of a Major League Club of representation in joint meetings; (c) suspension or removal of any officer or employee of a Major League or a Major League Club; (d) temporary or permanent ineligibility of a player; and (e) a fine, not to exceed Five Thousand Dollars ($5,000.00) in the case of a Major League Club and not to exceed Five Hundred Dollars ($500.00) in the case of any officer, employee or player.

Denial of a draft choice is simply not among the penalties authorized for this offense.

Defendant argues, however, that the list of sanctions enumerated in this section is intended to be only illustrative rather than definitive, as indicated by use of the language that penalties "*may* include any one or more of the following." (Emphasis added.) Thus he says that the listing of specific sanctions in sec. 3 does not preclude the Commissioner from imposing other sanctions that he deems appropriate. He says that *Milwaukee American Ass'n.* v. *Landis, supra*, so holds. The court does not perceive *Landis* as going that far. In *Landis,* the Commissioner had found that the owner of the St. Louis Club, in his handling of a player under contract to that club, had engaged in conduct claimed to be not in the best interests of baseball. As a sanction, the Commissioner declared the player to be a free agent. The St. Louis Club argued that the Commissioner lacked authority to impose the sanction since it was not specifically listed in Article I, sec. 3. Although the court affirmed the action of the Commissioner and in doing so noted his wide range of powers, the question raised by the St. Louis Club in *Landis* and by the plaintiffs herein was left unanswered:

> [W]hether there is given to the commissioner the power in so many words to declare Bennett a free agent is immaterial, since the agreements and rules grant to the commissioner jurisdiction to refuse to approve Bennett's assignment by St. Louis to Milwaukee, and to declare him absolved from the burdens of the same and of his contract with St. Louis.

49 F.2d at 302. Since the Commissioner had the explicit authority to accomplish the same result by simply refusing to approve the contract, thereby automatically making Bennett a free agent (now under Rule 12(a) of the Major League Rules), there was no need to expand the sanctions listed in sec. 3 to include this measure.

The recent case of *Finley & Co.* v. *Kuhn,* 76C–2358 (N.D.Ill.1977), also did not decide the question of whether the sanctions listed in sec. 3 are exclusive, although defendant would suggest otherwise. The issue in *Finley* was again the Commissioner's authority to disapprove certain assignment as not being in the best interests of baseball. Although the court noted that the power to set aside assignments of players was not explicitly listed in the Commissioner's powers under sec. 3, it stated that

> Section 3 does not say that the Commissioner shall have *only* the power to act in the enumerated ways, though that could have been said if it was intended. The section says that the Commissioner *may* act in one of the enumerated ways, without expressly limiting him.

Judgment Order at 4. Although this language tends to support the Commissioner's argument, the court does not end its analysis there. The court continues:

> The question arises whether this enumeration of sanctions which the Commissioner might impose invokes the established rules of construction that the specific controls the general, and that the expression of a type or types of authority operates to exclude the conclusion that other and different types of authority were intended to be conferred.

The court goes on to observe that the enumerated sanctions are "punitive" in nature, and although the Commissioner is empowered under sec. 2 to take what remedial, preventive or punitive measures he deems appropriate, there is no comparable list of "remedial" or "preventive" actions he is empowered to take. "Obviously such a list would be impossible to draw in the face of the unpredictability of the problems which might arise." Judgment Order at 4–5. In concluding that the Commissoner did have the authority to cancel certain assignments, the court seems to imply that whether or not the Commissioner is limited in the punitive sanctions he may impose, he is not similarly limited in the preventive or remedial measures available to him.

Other provisions of the Major League Agreement and the Major League Rules support plaintiffs' position that the Commissioner is limited in his authority to take punitive measures. For example, Article I, sec. 2(a), gives the Commissioner the authority "to summon persons and to order the production of documents, and, in the case of refusal to appear or produce, to impose such *penalties* as are hereinafter provided." The reference in sec. 2(a) to "penalties" presumably refers to those enumerated sanctions in sec. 3, since there is no further reference in the agreement to penalties for failure to appear or produce. In addition, Rule 50, "Enforcement of Major League Rules," provides in relevant part:

> (a) PENALTIES. In case the Commissioner shall determine that a league or club has violated any of the foregoing Rules, *as to which penalty provisions are not otherwise set forth in the Major League Agreement or Major League Rules,* the Commissioner may impose a fine or, in case of a club, may suspend the benefit of any or all of these Rules as to such club for a period not exceeding thirty (30) days. [Emphasis added.]

The implication of this provision is that the sum total of punitive sanctions available to the Commissioner are those specifically itemized in the Major League Agreement, Article I, sec. 3, or under the Major League Rules such as Rule 50.

[10, 11] Thus, the language of the Major League Agreement and Major League Rules seems to imply that the list of sanctions in sec. 3 is exclusive, and basic rules of contract construction support this conclusion. Prior to the original Major League Agreement, there were no presumed powers vested in a Commissioner. The 1921 agreement created the office of the Commissioner and defined his powers out of whole cloth. In such a situation, the maxim *"Expressio unius est exclusio alterius"* is particularly applicable, *Dorris* v. *Center,* 284 Ill.App. 344, 1 N.E.2d 794, 795 (1936). Moreover, in light of the fact that this contract purports to authorize the imposition of a penalty or forfeiture, it must be strictly construed, 17A *Corpus Juris,* 2d sec. 320.

Set against this background are numerous instances where the Commissioner has taken action that was not listed in sec. 3, and testimony on the part of certain parties to the Major League Agreement which indicates that the intention of sec. 3 was to provide an illustrative list of sanctions available to the Commissioner. The court has little trouble with the numerous instances defendant cites where a Commissioner has declared a player to be a free agent. While the Commissioner may have believed that he was acting pursuant to an unlimited sanction authority, he nevertheless had the explicit authority to disapprove contracts and therefore render players free agents. *See Milwaukee American Ass'n.* v. *Landis, supra,* 49 F.2d at 304; Rule 12(a) of the Major League Rules.

In other instances, however, the Commissioner has taken action which falls outside the enumerated sanctions and which did not involve the disapproval of contracts. Plaintiffs would argue that in these instances, the Commissioner was acting pursuant to his remedial and preventive powers, whereas here he was utilizing his punitive powers. However, at times the distinction between what is remedial and preventive and what is punitive is difficult to decipher, since a remedial action in favor of one party will often serve as a punishment to another. Defendant argues that in the instant situation, the deprivation of a draft choice was also a remedial measure which reduced an unfair competitive advantage that Atlanta gained in signing Matthews. The trouble with this argument is that unlike most remedial situations where relief is afforded to the party injured by the wrongful conduct, here the only party which may have been injured, the San Francisco club, received no relief at all.

In any event, the court need not decide whether the Commissioner acted within his authority in those instances which are not now before the court. That the Commissioner's authority in those cases went unchallenged does not persuade this court of the Commissioner's unlimited punitive powers in light of contractual language and established rules of construction to the contrary. . . . If the Commissioner is to have the unlimited punitive authority as he says is needed to deal with new and changing situations, the agreement should be changed to expressly grant the Commissioner that power. The deprivation of a draft choice was first and foremost a punitive sanction, and a sanction that is not specifically enumerated under sec. 3. Accordingly, the court concludes that the Commissioner was without the authority to impose that sanction, and its imposition is therefore void. . . .

Tortious Interference

In light of the foregoing conclusions, the court must finally consider whether the Commissioner's actions constituted tortious interference with plaintiffs' business. An intentional interference with existing contractual relations of another is usually considered prima facie sufficient for liability, the burden shifting to the defendant to show that such interference was privileged or justified. *Prosser, The Law of Torts* (4th ed. 1971) at 942. The court has little trouble concluding that, with the exception of the deprivation of the draft choice, defendant's conduct was justified. The defendant acted within the scope of his authority, and indeed, was executing his assigned duties as Commissioner. Defendant's liability in tort for the draft choice sanction is slightly more difficult since the imposition of that sanction was ultra vires. However, inasmuch as the June draft has yet to be held, and plaintiffs' draft choice is being restored by order of this court, it now appears that plaintiffs have suffered no injury with respect to this sanction. . . .

Summary

In summary, the Commissioner's decision to deprive plaintiffs of their first round draft choice in the June, 1977 amateur draft is hereby HELD to be ultra vires and therefore VOID. With respect to the balance of plaintiffs' claims, the court CONCLUDES that the Commissioner acted within the scope of his authority and hereby AWARDS judgment in favor of defendant. Each party is to bear its own costs in this action.

6.33   Interclub Dealings

Clubs deal with other clubs in a variety of contexts that go beyond the actual contest on the field. A principal area of dealing is obtaining players from other clubs through trades, sales, waivers, or free agent signings. The commissioner's office has the primary responsibility to insure that rules relating to a club's control, assignment or waiver of its players are handled according to league rules.

When a commissioner determines that the rules have been broken and moves to remedy the breach, the club owners at times respond by challenging the commissioner's authority. The cases indicate that, while the commissioner's powers are broad, they are not absolute.

Milwaukee American Ass'n. v. Landis, 49 F. 2d 298 (N.D. Ill. 1931)

This suit was brought by Milwaukee American Association and others against Kenesaw M. Landis, the commissioner of baseball, seeking to enjoin Landis from disallowing option contract between two baseball clubs concerning the status of one Bennet. Bennet intervened on the behalf of the commissioner and insisted, because of plaintiff's actions, he should be relieved of his contract relationship with them.

The facts leading to this action were the following: One person, Mr. Bell, owned several baseball clubs. Over a two-year period, without disclosing this control over several clubs, Bell sold, transferred, and assigned Bennet to many of the clubs under his control, not allowing other teams an opportunity to claim Bennet. The question for the court was whether, under the code governing baseball, the commissioner may disallow such secret sales agreements.

The baseball code, whose rules are binding on all major league clubs and on agreements between major and minor league clubs, is for the mutual protection of players and owners and is designed to promote competition. The rule involved here stated that before assigning a player to a minor league club, each of the other major league clubs must be given an opportunity to claim the player, and only when there is no refusal to waive such an opportunity may that player be sent to the minor leagues. The exception to that rule is by an option agreement approved by the commissioner. After two years of manipulation, Bell attempted to assign Bennet to Milwaukee with an option agreement. The commissioner disapproved. An analysis of other code provisions made it clear that the commissioner was endowed with the powers of a benevolent despot. He can act upon anything "detrimental to baseball" and determine what preventive, remedial, or punitive action is appropriate. It was held that plaintiff's actions were a violation of the clear intent of the code. To manipulate control by transferring players under the form of deceptive sales and purchases irrespective of a player's right is wrong.

The injunction was denied, and Bennet was freed of his contractual obligations.

Charles O. Finley Co. v. Kuhn, 569 F.2d 537 (7th Cir. 1978)

Two major issues involving the power of the commissioner of baseball were raised by Finley & Company's appeal: (1) whether the commissioner is contractually authorized to disapprove player assignments that he finds to be "not in the best interests of baseball," and (2) whether the waiver-of-recourse clause in the major league agreement is valid and enforceable.

Shortly before the June trading deadline in 1976, the Oakland athletics negotiated agreements to sell their contract rights for Joe Rudi and Rollie Fingers to the Boston Red Sox and for Vida Blue to the New York Yankees. On June 18, Commissioner Bowie Kuhn disapproved the assignments "as inconsistent with the best interests of baseball, the integrity of the game and the maintenance of public confidnce in it." Kuhn was concerned about Finley's decimation of his own club, the lessening of the competitive balance in professional baseball via the buying of success, and the unsettled circumstances of baseball's reserve system.

Finley's suit alleged that Kuhn acted arbitrarily and capriciously beyond the scope of his authority, violated Oakland's procedural constitutional rights, and violated antitrust laws by conspiring to eliminate Oakland from baseball. Finley sought specific performance of its contracts of assignment with Boston and New York. The district court granted Kuhn's motion for summary judgment on the antitrust and constitutional counts. On March 17, 1977, the trial court ruled in Kuhn's favor on the remaining counts. On August 29, 1977, the district court granted Kuhn's counterclaim for a declaratory judgment that the waiver-of-recourse clause was valid and enforceable. The court of appeals affirmed those decisions.

I. *Commissioner's Authority.* In reaching its conclusions about the broad discretionary power afforded the commissioner, the "umpire and governor of professional baseball," the court examined the numerous exercises of broad authority under the best-interests' clause by past commissioners. It also examined the 1964 amendments to the agreement, which expanded the commissioner's authority, and the express language of the agreement itself.

Article I, Section 2(a) and (b) of the agreement provides that

> the functions of the Commissioner shall be to investigate . . . any act, transaction or practice not in the best interests of the national game of baseball" and "to determine what preventive, remedial or punitive action is appropriate . . . and to take such action. . .

Oakland argued that the commissioner's authority under the best-interests clause was limited to situations involving a rules' violation or moral turpitude. Oakland relied on Major League Rule 21, which lists examples of unsportsmanlike conduct, as an indication of the limits of what is "not in the best interests" of baseball.

Rule 21, however, goes on to state that "nothing herein contained shall be construed as exclusively defining or otherwise limiting acts, transactions, practices or conduct not to be in the best interests of baseball. . . ." Moreover, Rule 12(a) provides that "no. . . (assignment of players) shall be recognized as valid unless . . . approved by the Commissioner." The court held that this exercise of the commissioner's authority was not limited to situations involving Major League rules or moral turpitude.

Article I, Section 3 of the agreement enumerates sanctions that the commissioner "may" impose for conduct deemed not in the best interests of baseball. Oakland claimed that this provision limits the commissioner's authority since the power to disapprove assignments of players is not included. The court found that the list does not purport to be exclusive and held that the commissioner was vested with authority to take whatever preventive or remedial action deemed appropriate when the commissioner determined that an act, transaction, or practice was not in the best interests of baseball.

Oakland argued that Kuhn's action was

procedurally unfair since clubs were given no notice that assignments, permissible under the rules, could be disapproved. The court found that anyone who signed the agreement was on notice that such an exercise of authority was possible and that the action was neither an abrupt departure nor a change in policy in view of the contemporaneous developments and changes in the reserve system. Oakland also accused Kuhn of acting with malice. The court concluded that Kuhn had acted in good faith, after investigation, consultation, and deliberation. Moreover, "(w)hether he was right or wrong is beyond the competence and the jurisdiction of this court to decide."

II. *Antitrust.* The district court had said that "Baseball, an anomaly of the antitrust law, is not subject to the provisions of that Act." On appeal, Oakland argued that baseball's exemption applied only to the reserve system. The court found it clear from the three baseball cases (*Federal Baseball* v. *National League; Toolson* v. *N.Y. Yankees*; and *Flood* v. *Kuhn*) and from language in *Radovich* v. *National Football League* that the Supreme Court intended to exempt the entire business of baseball, not just a particular facet, from the federal antitrust laws.

III. *Waiver of Recourse Clause.* Article VII, Section 2 provides:

> The Major Leagues and their constituent clubs, severally agree to be bound by the decisions of the Commissioner, and the discipline imposed by him under the provisions of the Agreement, and severally waive such right of recourse to the courts as would otherwise have existed in their favor.

The court held this "covenant not to sue" valid and binding on the parties and the courts.

In this federal diversity action, the conflict-of-law rules of Illinois, the state of locus, controlled. Illinois rules dictate that the place of making governs the construction and obligations of a contract to be performed in more than one state. The court looked to the laws of Illinois, since the original Major League Agreement was made in Chicago in 1921.

Illinois courts will generally not intervene in questions involving the enforcement of bylaws and matters of discipline in voluntary associations. Illinois also allows contracting parties to require that all disputes be resolved by arbitration. The court held that the waiver-of-recourse clause was valid and enforceable when viewed as requiring binding arbitration by the commissioner for disputes between clubs.

Aside from these considerations, the court refused to find the clause invalid as against public policy because the waiver was voluntary, knowing, and intelligent and was fairly negotiated by parties occupying equal bargaining positions.

In the Matter of Boston Celtics and Houston Rockets (Johnson Contract assignment), 1977, Commissioner O'Brien, Arbitrator

The dispute before the National Basketball Association Commissioner Lawrence O'Brien involved the assignment of John H. Johnson's two-year, "no-cut" contract with the Houston Rockets to the Boston Celtics, in return for the Celtics' second-round draft picks in each of the 1977 and 1978 seasons. Red Auerbach of the Celtics, who negotiated the trade, testified that he was told by the Houston representative Ray Patterson prior to June 9, 1977, that Johnson's contract called for only $150,000 for each of its remaining two years and was not a no-cut contract. On June 9, Auerbach, Patterson, and Russ Granik, the NBA representative, apparently completed a conference call as required by the NBA rules, confirming the trade. However, no one stated his version of the terms of Johnson's contract during this phone conversation.

When Auerbach received Johnson's contract and assignment forms in October 1977, he learned that the terms required annual payments of $300,000 and that the contract was a no-cut. Boston immediately attempted to cancel the contract and urged that Johnson should be returned to Houston, that the two draft choices should be returned to Boston, and that Houston should receive an additional penalty for its reprehensible conduct.

Patterson, for his part, testified that he had at least two telephone conversations with Auerbach prior to the conference call and had correctly detailed the terms. Houston argued that Auerbach knew of the terms, but disavowed the transaction when it was decided in October that Johnson did not fit into Boston's plans. Houston further argued that the rule requiring conference calls to finalize trades would be undermined if a club could nullify a contract by claiming it was not told of its terms.

The commissioner found that the only innocent party was Johnson, who had not played for two weeks because of the dispute. O'Brien then made the following additional observations and findings:

I am also compelled to say that the deference that should be accorded to Mr. Auerbach for his almost 30 years' of service to the Celtics does not excuse his apparent disregard for the seriousness with which a conference call formalizing one of the most important types of transactions in which a team can engage should be approached. It is unacceptable to have a general manager — any general manager — testify that he paid little or no attention to the details of a conference call because of his determination to rely upon discussions that took place prior to that call. Having generously apportioned the blame for the situation in which we now find ourselves, I make the following findings which are, I believe, dispositive of the contentions raised by the parties:

1. I find that Houston did not willfully misrepresent the terms of the Johnson contract to Boston. I not only reject the assertion of fraud and the request for some additional penalty to be assessed on Houston, but I also note that I specifically reject Boston's attempt to somehow color Mr. Patterson's conduct here by vague references to a prior Milwaukee transaction, never spelled out in adequate detail at a time when Mr. Patterson was president of the NBA's Milwaukee team.

2. I do find, nevertheless, that whether or not Mr. Patterson attempted to advise Mr. Auerbach of the details of the Johnson contract, Mr. Auerbach, at the time the transaction was consummated, did not believe that he was agreeing to assume a "no-cut contract" and that, to borrow a lawyer's phrase, there was not a "meeting of the minds" on this aspect of the transaction.

3. As much as I would like to embrace Houston's argument that the conference call of any transaction should be dispositive, I find that the memorandum of the conference call in this case, and the NBA practices pursuant to which that memorandum was created, are inadequate to reach that result. Thus, although I can assure all concerned parties that those procedures will promptly be strengthened by measures designed to ensure that there will be no recurrence of disputes such as the instant one, I am unable to give the memorandum in this case the dispositive effect which it should and *will*, in the future, have in all player transactions.

4. I find that although Boston did not agree to assume a $300,000 "no cut" contract for Mr. Johnson, its representative contributed greatly to the confusion in which the parties now find themselves engulfed. I also find that Boston was willing to pay two draft choices for the privilege of "taking a look" at Mr. Johnson on the assumption that Mr. Johnson's contract was not a "no-cut" contract; and that even though Mr. Johnson's contract turned out to be different from what Boston thought it was, Boston did, prior to disaffirming that contract, have the opportunity to evaluate Mr. Johnson and has decided that it is not interested in having Mr. Johnson perform for its team at any price.

Accordingly, based upon the above findings, the facts set forth in this opinion and award and the entire record before me, I rule that Boston's request that the trade be nullified be granted only to the extent that the Johnson contract be ruled the obligation of Houston, but that Boston's request for the return to it of its second-round draft picks (or their equivalent) be denied. Mr. Johnson should report immediately to the Houston team and Houston is directed to honor all of the obligations under its contract with Mr. Johnson.

6.34 Arbitration

When arbitration first became prevalent in professional sports, the league commissioner was normally the one designated as arbitrator, either by the owners or, later, per terms of the collective bargaining agreement. Substantial dissatisfaction with the commissioner as arbitrator was expressed by the players, however, and at length this function, when it related to player-club disputes, was largely removed from a commissioner's perview. The appointment of one or more impartial arbitrators became the norm.

The commissioner in most sports has continued to act as arbitrator for certain types of disputes, mainly involving one club against another, but at times pertaining to player discipline. The foregoing dispute over the trade of J. J. Johnson from the Houston Rockets to the Boston Celtics is one example where interclub disputes will be handled by commissioner arbitration. Examples of player discipline, resulting in appeal to a commissioner, can be found in such as Section 4.34, Section 5.21 and Section 5.43. Even so, within the broad category of discipline, one must consult both a league's constitution and bylaws and a league's collective bargaining agreement to determine if the commissioner still retains the ultimate arbitration power.

In addition to these examples in which the commissioner acts as arbitrator, the following examples pertain to game protests in which the commissioner played an arbitrator role.

In the Matter of New Jersey Nets and Philadelphia '76ers, Re: Game Protest, Commissioner O'Brien, Arbitrator, Nov. 22, 1978

New Jersey protested the result of a game it lost in double overtime (137–133) at Philadelphia on Nov. 8, 1978 (the "Game"). After receiving two technical fouls, a player or coach is automatically expelled from a game. Referee Powers assessed third technical fouls against New Jersey player, Bernard King, and Coach Kevin Loughery. King had kicked a chair in an outburst following his ejection. Loughery had failed to leave the court promptly following his ejection.

New Jersey wanted to be declared the winner, claiming it could have won in regulation if any one of three disputed technical fouls had not been called. They argued that the first technical foul called on Loughery was improper because he had entered upon the playing court to prevent a fight, a permissible action. O'Brien found this argument without merit, since the purpose for Loughery's action was a matter of judgment for the officials at the game.

New Jersey also argued that NBA rules and practices do not authorize a referee to assess more than two technical fouls on any one person. Philadelphia cited the "elastic clause" in support of its response that such action should be permissible when an ejected player or coach refuses to leave the court. Rule 2, section III:

> The referees shall have power to make decisions on any point not specifically covered in the rules. The Commissioner will be advised of all such decisions at the earliest possible moment.

Although there is no specific prohibition of third technicals, Rule 12A, Section VI b lists the penalties for technical fouls for unsportsmanlike conduct: first infraction — technical foul and $75 fine; second — technical foul, $150 fine, and ejection from the game. The clear implication is that an ejected player or coach is no longer a participant and cannot logically receive any further technical fouls. Moreover, referees were taught the two-technical-foul rule at officials' training camp.

Powers had substituted his view for a long-standing and widely understood interpretation of the NBA rules. O'Brien found that Powers was without authority to assess the third technicals on King and Loughery. Either of the converted technical foul shots could have affected the final outcome of the game. O'Brien sustained New Jersey's protest but refused to award them the victory. Philadelphia was blameless and might have altered its strategy if the technical foul shots had not been converted.

O'Brien ordered the game replayed from the point at which the first improper call was made — the third technical against King. The game was to resume with five minutes, 50 seconds remaining in the third quarter, the score at

84–81, and Philadelphia in possession of the ball.

In the Matter of Kansas City Kings and New York Knickerbockers, 1979, Re: Game Protest, Commissioner O'Brien, Arbitrator

The final quarter of the basketball game between the Kansas City Kings and the New York Knickerbockers on December 30, 1978, was played in only 11 minutes instead of the regulation 12 minutes. Kansas City, the loser of the game by four points, lodged a protest to the NBA commissioner, Lawrence O'Brien, requesting that the game be resounded in the fourth quarter and replayed from the point at which the clock inadvertently malfunctioned.

O'Brien, however, held that the result of the game should stand. Neither team was aware of the error when it occurred with over ten minutes remaining, and the timing mistake impacted equally on both sides since both teams guided their play according to the time as they perceived it. In O'Brien's opinion, to comply with the technical requirement by forcing the teams to meet for one additional minute would disregard the reality that the action in the closing minutes was greatly influenced by the time shown. It was equally unfair to resume the game with 11 minutes left, as it would ignore the 10 minutes during which New York was able to overcome a 4-point deficit and assume the lead. Cautioning that his decision was strictly limited to the facts of this case, O'Brien denied Kansas City's protest.

6.40   League Controls Over Its Product

Leagues and clubs have property interests in their names, logos, and images. They must constantly be on guard against encroachment, whether it be by commercial intrusions or, at times, by perceived governmental interference. The track record in defending against misappropriation is much better against commercial ventures than against a government, as the

following cases illustrate. However, even the former present substantial legal problems to a league or a club; and the principles on which one can proceed must be thoroughly understood. As the *ABA* v. *AMF Voit* case illustrates, there is not always a protectable interest. The legal concepts are technical, and care must be taken in attempting to utilize them.

6.41   Commercial Interference

Two types of cases are analyzed in this section. The first series of cases examine the types of property rights that leagues and clubs have in their names, logos and even perhaps the distinctive equipment used in league play. The existence of protectable trademarks is a central inquiry, but there are other legal bases for asserting property rights which must be considered.

The second concern is a league's ability to set requirements for the type of equipment or other paraphernalia used in league play. When standards are set, adversely affected players and manufacturers will protest.

American Basketball Ass'n. v. AMF Voit, Inc., 358 F. Supp. 981 (S.D.N.Y. 1973)

Duffy, District Judge

This is a motion for a preliminary injunction to prevent the alleged infringement of an alleged trademark owned by the plaintiff. Various claims of unfair competition are also charged. . . .

When the ABA was formed, its first Commissioner, George Mikan, determined that the new league would have to have a "gimmick" to differentiate it from the older established National Basketball Association. Among other things, it was decided that a multicolored basketball could be one such "gimmick."

Until this time, all official basketball games, whether professional or scholastic, had been played with a leather ball consisting of eight tan leather panels affixed to an underlying bladder in a particular sequence. The ABA did not change the size of the ball or the shape of the leather panels but proposed that the uniformly tan panels be changed by dyeing the leather to produce a red-white-blue-white-red-white-blue-white combination. It was thought that this would be more appealing to women and more attractive on color television. . . .

As a "promotional stunt," the various teams of the ABA, at the inception of the league, had "ball nights" wherein a patron who attended the league game on a particular night would receive a promotional red, white and blue basketball as a souvenir. These promotional balls were originally supplied by Wilson Sporting Goods Company ("Wilson"). These balls were purchased by the teams· through the league office and were apparently made of inferior "rubber" or vinyl. These promotional balls also showed the ABA logo along with the Wilson logo. The Wilson promotional basketballs apparently were not suited to playground use and would bulge out of shape. After a couple of years, the ABA dropped this source of supply for promotional balls.

During this period, the league teams apparently were experiencing some difficulty in obtaining these balls. For example, the New York Nets, an ABA team, had manufactued for promotional purposes a red, white and blue ball identical to the league's game ball, which bore only the logo of the New York Nets.

In any event, it is clear that after the advent of the ABA, many companies began selling red, white and blue basketballs without the ABA logo but carrying the logo of the manufacturer and/or distributor. These companies included Hutch Athletic Goods Company, Regent Sporting Goods Company, Pennsylvania Rubber Company, Mac-Gregor Co. and Spalding Co.

When the ABA originally used its red, white and blue ball, Commissioner George Mikan asked a patent lawyer to take steps to assert a design patent right over the coloration. Apparently nothing came of this approach. The ABA thereupon applied for a copyright for the coloration of the basketball. This application was rejected.

On March 15, 1971, an application for the trademark in question in this action was filed with the Patent Office by the plaintiff. Almost a year later, on February 22, 1972, the trademark was published in the Official Gazette of the United States Patent Office. Subsequently, four separate oppositions to registration of the trademark were filed, including one by the defendants, AMF.

On its part, AMF points out that it felt competitive forces and pressures from its sales force which led to its manufacturing and marketing and then distributing red, white and blue basketballs starting in about November 1970. This ball was catalogued by AMF as "WBR" ball. In the initial Research and Development Order and in the initial Production Order, the officials of AMF referred specifically to a "Red, White and Blue ABA Ball" and to the production of an "ABA Basketball." It should be noted that the red and the blue of the WBR ball are more vibrant than those used in the official ABA basketball.

Initially, in advertising the introduction of the WBR basketball, AMF referred to its basketball as an "ABA Type Basketball." It is undisputed that many other manufacturers and retail outlets of red, white and blue basketballs have described them in the media as "ABA Style" basketballs and in fact do so to the present time. However, AMF stopped such references some time ago. Indeed, at least once, when the defendants' WBR basketball was so referred to by an AMF customer the defendant notified the retailer that it did not produce an "official" ABA basketball. Such references at the retail level were stopped thereafter.

Recognizing a trend toward multicolored sports goods, AMF has started production of other types of multicolored balls, e.g., green, gold and white basketballs. These other multicolored basketballs are displayed with the red, white and blue basketball, both in the defendants' catalogues and in retail dealer displays. . . .

The plaintiff claims that the red, white and blue panels and the arrangement thereof on its official game ball constitute a valid trademark. . . .

The plaintiff further contends that even if at the outset the coloration of its official basketball was not such as to be a trademark, it has achieved that status by a "secondary meaning" or the subsequent association by the public of the coloration of the ball with the league. . . .

The ABA charges, first, that the defendants infringed on its claimed trademark by selling basketballs of a coloration similar to that of the claimed trademark; second, that they have engaged in unfair competition by selling such basketballs of inferior quality; and last, that they diluted the plaintiff's trademark by the display in retail outlets and media advertising of the red, white and blue basketballs with other multicolored basketballs. . . .

Cutting through the claims and contentions of the parties, it is this Court's finding that the mere coloration of the various panels of the ordinary basketball is not sufficiently distinctive to be the subject of a statutory trademark. The basketball used by the plaintiff is of the same configuration as an ordinary basketball except that the colors of the particular panels are different. I find that the colors are merely a decoration or embellishment. . . .

The use of colors on sports equipment started some time ago. An early example was the adornment of white tennis socks with a red, white and blue band. This was held *not* to be a protected design under either the law of trademark or otherwise. *Cf.* In re David Crystal, Inc., 296 F.2d 771, 49 C.C.P.A. 775 (1961).

On all of the basketballs produced at the hearing herein, there was a logo of the manufacturer of the basketball alone save for those which were authorized by the ABA (or the National Basketball Association) which also contained the logo of the professional league. These logos were the truly distinctive features of the various basketballs, not the colors of the panels.

While conceding that color used merely as decoration may not be the subject of a valid trademark plaintiff claims that its coloration of the basketball forms a distinctive design. Distinctive designs, whether colored or not, may be protected as trademarks. In re Swift & Co., 223 F.2d 950, 42 C.C.P.A. 1048 (1955); *The Barbasol Co.* v. *Jacobs,* 160 F.2d 336 (7th Cir. 1947). Far from adopting a distinctive design, however, plaintiff has merely added coloring to the panels of a standard basketball. This change in coloration of the tan panels of previous basketballs was merely decorative or ornamental. Ex parte Hall, 73 U.S.P.Q. 8 (F.T.C.1947); *Radio Corp. of America* v. *Decca Records, Inc.,* 51 F.Supp. 493 (S.D.N.Y.1943). Therefore, I cannot find that the dyeing of the standard panels in red, white and blue constituted a valid trademark at its inception. In re Burgess Battery Co., 112 F.2d 820, 27 C.C.P.A. 1297 (1940).

We come then to the question of "secondary meaning," which is an entirely different problem for this Court to resolve. A design which lacks sufficient distinction to qualify as a valid trademark may nonetheless become a good mark if it acquires "secondary meaning." . . .

Basically, "secondary meaning" within the trademark laws is equivalent to an association between the "trademark" and the supposed source of the goods such that an ordinary man would immediately associate the goods with their source. *Continental Motors Corp.* v. *Continental Aviation Corp.,* 375 F.2d 857 (5th Cir. 1967).

Here the basic question is whether the red, white and blue basketball is so identified with the plaintiff that an ordinary man would find that any red, white and blue basketball was the symbol or trademark of the ABA and that the ABA was its source.

To support its claim of trademark due to this secondary meaning, the plaintiff requested the Roper organization to conduct a pilot survey of the market for multicolored basketballs. At the hearing, the results of this survey were received in evidence over the objection of the defendants. This pilot survey, although admittedly incomplete, showed that at best, only 61 per cent of the persons surveyed associated the red, white and blue basketball with the ABA. When considered with the control group which showed a 18 per cent "guess" factor, it would appear that approximately 42 per cent of the people interviewed knowingly associated the ABA with the red, white and blue basketball. This survey was further deficient in that: it was set up so that no logo showed on the red, white and blue basketball; it was limited to a universe of males between the ages of 12 and 23; and it was limited to those who had played basketball within the last year. No attempt was made to contract those who would actually purchase basketballs. For this reason alone, I find the "universe" to be too narrow to allow the survey to be given any substantial weight. . . .

More difficult on the question of secondary meaning is the use by the defendants of the terms "ABA ball" or "ABA type" basketball in the intercompany memorandum and in the advertising of some of its retailers. This is particularly disturbing since the defendants' ball bears the word "Official." To the trade the designation "official" means of an official weight and size. Since it is known to the trade what the word means, I believe that no unfair competition with the plaintiff occurred. Furthermore, at the time that AMF used these terms in its interoffice memoranda and its advertising, there were a large number of others manufacturing red, white and blue basketballs, each labelled with the logo of the manufacturer. There could be no confusion as to the source of the basketballs. I find that the use of the terms was merely a shorthand way of saying "similar to" the red, white and blue basketballs used by the ABA. . . .

Accordingly, I find that the affixation of red, white and blue panels to an ordinary basketball is not sufficient to create a trademark, and that no "secondary meaning" entitled to the protection of a trademark has been established.

For the reasons cited above, this Court grants the motion by plaintiff to consolidate the hearing of the motion for a preliminary injunction with the trial of the case for a permanent injunction pursuant to F.R.Civ.P. Rule 65(a)(2) and adjudges that the plaintiff's demand for a preliminary and permanent injunction must be denied.

Settle order on notice.

National Football League Properties, Inc. v. Consumer Enterprises, Inc., 327 N.E.2d 242 (Ill. App. Ct. 1975)

Defendant Consumer Enterprises appealed from an order granting a preliminary injunction to plaintiff, the exclusive licensing agent for member clubs of the National Football league. The defendant was in the business of manufacturing and selling embroidered cloth emblems and had made and sold duplications of plaintiff's marks without authorization.

The appeals court initially held that plaintiff had a property right entitled to protection. The symbols of the NFL and its clubs had acquired a strong secondary meaning and had perpetuated the goodwill of the clubs. The court rejected defendant's contention that it was merely copying the marks and selling them as decorative products, an activity which did not perform the trademark function of source identification.

Defendant had maintained that under the *Sears* and *Compco* doctrine (*Sears, Roebuck & Co. v. Shffu Company*, 376 U.S. 225 [1963]; *Compco Corp. v. Day Brite Lighting, Inc.*, 376 US 234 [1963]), no state could prohibit the copying of U.S. patented products or trademarks. The court found defendant's inter-

pretation overbroad, and because of the strong association of the mark with the sponsorship of the NFL, copying of the plaintiff's mark was not permitted.

Defendant also had relied on *Boston Professional Hockey Ass'n., Inc. v. Dallas Cap & Emblem Manufacturing, Inc.*, 360 F. Supp. 459 (N.D. Tex. 1973) in which the court had held that symbols of the National Hockey League could be copies as long as a disclaimer was attached. The court noted that the efforts of the NFL and plaintiff had clearly established a secondary meaning, and a disclaimer would not adequately protect the property rights. More importantly, great difficulty existed in framing an effective disclaimer.

Finally, the court noted that a likelihood of confusion as to the source of defendant's emblems existed, and plaintiff would also succeed under the broader theory of unfair competition. Concluding that plaintiff had shown a probability of ultimate relief from trademark infringement, unfair competition, and deceptive practices, the appeals court upheld the trial court's order, which enjoined the manufacture and sale by defendant of its emblems bearing the trademark of the NFL teams.

National Football League Properties, Inc. v. Dallas Cap & Emblem Mfg., Inc., 327 N.E.2d 247 (Ill. App. Ct. 1975)

In a suit almost identical to the *Consumer Enterprises* suit also brought by National Football League Properties, the court of appeals held that plaintiff was entitled to complete preliminary injunctive relief. This modified the trial court's order that defendants could manufacture and sell emblems bearing the marks of the NFL clubs with an appropriate disclaimer on the face of each emblem indicating that the emblem was not sponsored by or originated from plaintiff or any NFL club.

The appeals court heard testimony concerning the effect of a clear and legible disclaimer, but concluded that for the reasons set forth in the

NFLP v. *Consumer Enterprises* opinion, plaintiff had shown a property right to be protected and a probability of success on the merits, entitling the plaintiff to complete preliminary injunctive relief.

NFL Properties, Inc. v. Wichita Falls Sportswear, Inc., 532 F. Supp. 651 (W.D. Wash. 1982)

The controversy between the parties concerns Wichita's manufacture of "NFL football jersey replicas." An NFL football jersey replica is a football style shirt bearing large numerals, colors corresponding to an NFL team, sleeve design, and either the full team name (i.e. "Seattle Seahawks"), the team nickname (i.e. "Seahawks"), the "home" city name or regional designation of the respective NFL team (i.e., "Seattle") or the name of a team player (i.e., "Jim Zorn"). . . .

Plaintiffs seek to enjoin Wichita from manufacturing or selling NFL football jersey replicas. They allege that such activity constitutes: (1) infringement of the federally registered service marks of the member clubs in violation of section 32(1) of the Lanham Act, 15 U.S.C. sec. 1114(1); (2) infringement of the common law trademarks of the member clubs; (3) false designation of the origin and sponsorship of Wichita's goods, in violation of section 43(a) of the Lanham Act, 15 U.S.C. sec. 1125(a); (4) unfair competition and misappropriation of the commercial properties of the member clubs, in violation of the common law; (5) infringement of the registered trademarks of the Seattle Club, in violation of RCW sec. 19.77.140; (6) deceptive business practices, in violation of RCW sec. 19.86.020; (7) misappropriation of the rights of publicity of the member clubs, in violation of the common law right of publicity; and (8) tortious interference with the business relationships of NFLP, its licensees and the consuming public, in violation of the common law. . . .

NFLP was created by the member clubs of the NFL in 1963. Each member club grants an exclusive license, either directly or through a trust, to NFLP to act as licensing representative for the trademarks and other commercial identifications of the member clubs. NFLP then authorizes manufacturers to produce merchandise bearing the NFL member club's marks. An NFLP licensee is required to pay to NFLP a royalty fee of 6.5% of all net sales of licensed products. Royalties paid by licensees are the sole source of funding for a charitable foundation known as NFL Charities. Since 1971, NFLP has donated almost five million dollars to NFL Charities, including the United Way and the National Negro College Fund.

NFLP conducts a nationwide comprehensive program of trademark protection on behalf of the member clubs. It has investigators in each city with a franchise club to investigate claims of trademark infringement. Complaints are received from a variety of sources, including retailers, licensees and consumers. In every instance, appropriate action to protect the trademarks is taken. The vast majority of these matters are settled amicably. NFLP has, however, gone to court to defend its trademark rights. . . .

NFLP also maintains a quality control program to monitor the quality and appearance of its licensees' merchandise. This program is in addition to whatever quality control the individual licensees maintain.

Wichita was founded by its president Leo Cooke in 1976. It began as a manufacturer of softball uniforms for local area teams. Defendant began the manufacture of NFL football jersey replicas in 1977.

NFLP became aware of defendant's activities in 1978. In accordance with its standard procedures, NFLP sent defendant a "cease and desist" letter. The matter seemed to have been resolved amicably in 1979. In the spring of 1980, however, NFLP again received evidence of defendant's allegedly infringing activity. After Wichita declined to cease and desist, plaintiffs commenced the present action.

A preliminary injunction was granted by Judge Rothstein on October 3, 1980. Defendant was enjoined from producing shirts bearing "large numerals and the team colors, strip configuration, and the team name and/or the 'home' city name or regional designation of the respective Member Clubs." . . . The preliminary injunction was modified on March 13, 1981. In lieu of a full injunction, defendant was ordered to place a disclaimer label on each of its NFL football jersey replicas which read "Not authorized or sponsored by the NFL." Although less restrictive in impact, the order was expanded in scope to include jerseys bearing the name of any player of a member club.

A contempt hearing was held before Judge

Rothstein on November 21, 1981. Wichita was found in contempt for selling jerseys with team nicknames before the injunction was modified. . . .

Plaintiffs seek reinstatement of the original injunction with an inclusion of player names. Defendant responds that it is legally competing in the NFL football jersey replica market and cannot be restrained.

Trademark Infringement — Common Law and Section 43(a)

An NFL football jersey replica consists of four separate elements: First, the shirt must bear official team colors of an NFL member club. Second, it must bear a large numeral. Third, an NFL football jersey replica usually has some sleeve design. Finally, it must have a descriptive term which relates the shirt to an NFL team. This term can be an NFL full team name, a team nickname, a city or regional designation or the name of a team player. It is this fourth element, the descriptive term, that the actual controversy is about. Absent this fourth element, the NFLP has disclaimed any interest in the shirts of other manufacturers. The issue then is whether plaintiffs have trademark rights in these descriptive terms when presented with the other three elements or a colorable imitation thereof.

Plaintiffs' federal cause of action is premised on section 43(a) of the Lanham Act, 15 U.S.C. sec. 1125(a). The statute provides in part:

> Any person who shall affix, apply, or annex, or use in connection with any goods or services, or any container or containers for goods, a false designation of origin, or any false description or representation, . . . and shall cause such goods or services to enter into commerce, . . . shall be liable to a civil action . . . by any person who believes that he is or is likely to be damaged by the use of any such false description or representation.

In order to sue under the statute, it is not necessary for a mark or trademark to be registered. *New West Corp.* v. *NYM Co. of California, Inc.,* 595 F.2d 1194, 1198 (9th Cir. 1979). Whether the theory is section 43(a) of the Lanham Act or state unfair competition law, the ultimate test is whether the public is likely to be deceived or confused by the similarity of the marks. *Id.* at 1201. The burden on plaintiffs is twofold: First, plaintiffs must establish secondary meaning in their use of the descriptive terms in the football context. Second, defendant's activities must be shown to have created a likelihood of confusion.

To meet their burden, plaintiffs prepared a nationwide probability survey. Since it would be impossible to bring every potentially confused consumer into court and have him or her testify, a survey can be highly probative on the issues of secondary meaning and likelihood of confusion. . . .

Defendant did not seek to introduce a survey of its own. Instead, Wichita challenged plaintiffs' survey as to the universe selected, the relevancy of the questions and the potentially slanted formulation of the questions.

The first step in designing a survey is to determine the relevant "universe." "The universe is that segment of the population whose characteristics are relevant to the mental associations at issue." *McCarthy,* section 32:47 at 500. A survey of the wrong universe is of little probative value. The universe selected by plaintiffs was the entire population of the continental United States between the ages of thirteen and sixty-five.

Defendant argues that the only relevant universe is likely purchasers of NFL football jersey replicas. Plaintiffs respond, with some authority, that the relevant universe is the entire population. The last word by the Ninth Circuit would indicate the relevant universe is potential purchasers. . . .

The Court does not reach the issue, however, because plaintiffs' survey is separately projectable for the universe defendant claims is legally relevant. Separate data is available for prior purchasers of NFL football jersey replicas, "fans" and "fans plus" of NFL member clubs. . . .

In general, the Court is impressed with the steps plaintiffs took to insure the reliability of the survey. It was well-designed, meticulously executed and involved some of the best experts available. The Court was not persuaded by defendant's efforts to challenge plaintiffs' survey. In view of the fact that defendant offered no survey data of its own, plaintiffs' survey results were essentially uncontroverted.

Secondary Meaning

Secondary meaning has been defined as association, nothing more. *Carter-Wallace, Inc.* v. *Proctor & Gamble Co.,* 434 F.2d 794, 802 (9th Cir.

1970). The basic element of secondary meaning is a mental recognition in buyers' and potential buyers' minds that products connected with the symbol or device emanate from or are associated with the same source. *Levi Strauss & Co. v. Blue Bell, Inc.*, 632 F.2d 817, 200 U.S.P.Q. 713, 716 (9th Cir. 1980). The public does not have to know the specific corporate identity of the single source as long as the public associates the product bearing the mark with a single, though anonymous source. . . .

In order to establish secondary meaning, plaintiffs' survey was directed toward answering this question: When presented with football replica jerseys do people associate such jerseys with the National Football League or its franchised team? The data indicates a significantly high association in the public's mind between the jerseys and the NFL or member clubs. The association level varied from 55–80% depending upon the descriptive term employed (nickname, city name or player name).

The level of association between the shirt and the NFL is not surprising. Evidence was introduced that the descriptive terms are often used in the parlance to refer to specific NFL member clubs. More significantly, Wichita's own pleadings admit that it designed its jerseys to capitalize on the market of those people who want to associate themselves with an NFL team. . . .

Defendant argues, however, that the relevant inquiry for secondary meaning in this context is not whether the public associates the products bearing the marks in question with the NFL or a member club but whether the mark primarily denotes to the consumer that the jersey replica was produced, sponsored or endorsed by the NFL member club. That is, because plaintiffs do not manufacture the products in question (but, instead, license the right to manufacture the jerseys with the marks to a number of producers), there is no single though anonymous source of the product.

Trademark law does not just protect the producers of products. The creation of confusion as to sponsorship or products is also actionable. . . .

The correct standard should be reachable deductively. There is a symmetry between the concepts of secondary meaning and likelihood of confusion. Secondary meaning requires an examination of the non-infringing party's mark and product, and tests the connection in the buyers' mind between the product bearing the mark and its source. Likelihood of confusion in a sponsorship context focuses on the product bearing the allegedly infringing marks and asks whether the public believes the product bearing the marks originate with or is somehow endorsed or authorized by the plaintiff. . . . Just as the relevant inquiry for the establishment of likelihood of confusion in a sponsorship context is the belief that sponsorship or authorization was granted, the inquiry should be the same in order to establish secondary meaning.

Plaintiffs' survey has data directed toward the inquiry above. One question in the survey asked people who had only seen "official" jerseys (that is, exact copies of jerseys plaintiffs' licensees sell) whether they thought the company that had made the jersey had "to get authorization or sponsorship, that is permission, to make it?" If the interviewee responded that authorization was required, he was asked from whom was the authorization obtained.

Of the interviewees who were exposed to the official NFL football jersey replica, 45.3% of the general public who saw jerseys with a city name/regional designation descriptive term, 55.5% of those who saw the player name and 44.8% of the interviewees who saw the team name on the shirt, believed that the manufacturer was required to obtain authorization from the NFL or one of the member clubs in order to manufacture the jerseys. The overall belief level was around 50%. For those interviewees within the class of potential purchasers (prior purchasers, fans and fans plus) the belief levels were even higher.

After considering the survey results, the testimony of the witnesses and the other evidence presented, the Court is satisfied that plaintiffs have made a sufficient showing of secondary meaning in their marks.

Likelihood of Confusion

Likelihood of confusion is the keystone to any trademark infringement action. Despite the levels of secondary meaning established, absent a showing of likelihood of confusion there is no actionable wrong. The stronger the evidence of secondary meaning, however, the stronger the mark and the more likely in confusion.

A strong mark is inherently distinctive and will be afforded the widest ambit of protection from infringing uses. *AMF Inc.* v. *Sleekcraft Boats,* 599 F.2d 341, 349 (9th Cir. 1979). The more arbitrary and fanciful the mark, the more distinctive. Focusing on the descriptive terms in a football context, the team nicknames seem extremely fanciful. Why one team is a bear and another a lion is anyone's guess. As for the city name/regional designations, these marks are inherently nondistinctive as they describe the geographic location of the team. By establishing secondary meaning in the city names/regional designations in a football context, plaintiffs nonetheless may be entitled to trademark protection.

. . . . A similar showing of secondary meaning was made for player names. Moreover, even if plaintiffs' marks are "weak," they still would be entitled to limited protection. Plaintiffs do not seek a monopoly over the word "Seattle," for example, but only use of the term as it relates to NFL football jersey replicas. . . .

The court is struck with the physical similarity between the "official" NFL football jersey replicas and Wichita's product. There is some variation in design and striping and color, but the differences are not significant. Indeed, Wichita's product, when considered with the testimony of defendant's witnesses, is a calculated effort to create distinctions in the products which will have no real meaning in the minds of consumers. Moreover, the strong correlation in survey data between those responding to questions after having seen the "official" jerseys and those answering after having seen the defendant's product, supports the conclusion of similarity. . . .

The next factor is the likelihood of confusion. Actual confusion is not a necessary finding in order to establish likelihood of confusion. *See Fleischmann Distilling Corp.* v. *Maier Brewing Co.,* 314 F.2d 149, 159 (9th Cir. 1963). Evidence that defendant's use has already led to confusion is a persuasive factor, however, that future confusion is likely. *AMF Inc.* v. *Sleekcraft Boats,* 599 F.2d 341, 352 (9th Cir. 1979).

The evidence of actual confusion concerns the testimony of a retail purchaser of defendant's products and the survey itself. The purchaser assumed defendant's product (shirts bearing the word "Chargers" on them) were licensed. In the survey, interviewees confronted with identical copies of defendant's jersey were asked if they felt authorization was required in order to manufacture the jersey. Depending on the descriptive term employed on the jersey, 41.8% of the general public who saw shirts with the city name/regional designation, 53.6% of the interviewees who were shown jerseys with a player's name on the front and 47.8% of those shown shirts with the team nickname felt that authorization from the NFL or the member club was required. The results were higher for people in the potential purchaser category.

The final factor is the intent of the defendant. Although a plaintiff need not prove that defendant intended to exploit the good will and reputation associated with a mark, where such intent is shown, the inference of likelihood of confusion is readily drawn. *HMH Publishing Co.* v. *Brincat,* 504 F.2d 713, 720 (9th Cir. 1974). There is some authority that a showing of intent shifts the burden to the defendant to prove that his efforts have been unsuccessful.

The Court finds that defendant intended to create confusion as to authorization or sponsorship. Several factors are relevant in the Court's determination of intent. Wichita's overall conduct in these proceedings has been questionable at best. Judge Rothstein found defendant in contempt of the preliminary injunction by its continued sales of jerseys with team nicknames. Even though defendant "knew" it was not allowed to sell the jerseys, it continued to do so. More illuminating was Wichita's activities with regard to the disclaimer requirement of the modified injunction. Judge Rothstein ordered defendant to place the phrase "Not authorized or sponsored by the NFL" on the label of any jersey manufactured or sold by Wichita. In compliance with this order, defendant had some of the disclaimers placed on the back of labels where they would not be seen by consumers. Others were designed so that the disclaimer would lie well under the throat of the jersey, hidden from the eye of consumers. On another batch of jerseys defendant, without Court approval, modified the phrasing of the disclaimers. In the Court's mind, defendant's conduct is evidence of its intent to place the disclaimers where they could not be seen or understood. This is direct evidence of defendant's intent to create confusion as to sponsorship since the very purpose of the disclaimers was to rectify any sponsorship confusion.

An important factor in the Court's determination of intent was the demeanor of the witnesses for the defendant. The Court had the opportunity to listen to Wichita's president, Leo Cooke, on the stand. At one point he testified that Wichita did not intend to sell Los Angeles Rams shirts when it sold jerseys bearing the word "Rams" to the Los Angles area. These shirts were allegedly meant for Irvine High School students. The unfortunate fact, however, was that the nickname for Irvine High School was not the "Rams" but "Vacaros." At another point in his testimony Mr. Cooke stated that many of the shirts sold were not intended to be NFL football jersey replicas, but were intended to service high schools which incidentally shared a nickname with an NFL member club. Again, problems arose as the evidence indicated that the large bulk of these orders were in infant and toddler sizes. Mr. Cooke then suggested that the toddler and infant sizes may have been for the children of the high school students.

Finally, there is the general intent of the defendant. There is no question that Wichita intended to manufacture its products to resemble NFL football jersey replicas. Mr. Cooke testified that he sold shirts with city names and team nicknames to NFL fans who wished to support a particular member club. Moreover, defendant continued to manufacture its product after being informed by NFLP that such conduct was, in their view, infringing activity. Defendant intended to appropriate the good will and reputation of the NFL. This reflects on Wichita's intent to confuse the public as to sponsorship.

After considering the overall conduct of the defendant, its specific conduct with regard to the disclaimers, and the demeanor of its witnesses, the Court finds that Wichita intended to create confusion as to authorization or sponsorship. . . .

Bars to Recovery

Defendant asserts three "defenses" to the charge of trademark infringement. First, Wichita argues that the marks are functional and therefore not subject to trademark status. Second, granting plaintiffs trademark rights is said to constitute a product monopoly in violation of the doctrine of *Sears, Roebuck & Co.* v. *Stiffel Co.,* 376 U.S. 225, 84 S.Ct. 784, 11 L.Ed.2d 661 (1964), and *Compco Corp.* v. *Day-Brite Lighting, Inc.,* 376 U.S. 234, 84 S.Ct. 779, 11 L.Ed.2d 669 (1964) (hereinafter referred to as "*Sears-Compco*"). Finally, the marks are claimed to be generic.

Trademark law does not prevent a person from copying the functional features of a product. *Job's Daughters,* 633 F.2d 912, 917 (9th Cir. 1980). Functional features constitute the actual benefit that the consumer wishes to purchase, as distinguished from an assurance that a particular entity made, sponsored or endorsed a product. *Id.* Functionality is not, however, limited to tangible items which "work" (such as a chair or a doorknob) but includes features which are aesthetically pleasing.

The Ninth Circuit case of *Pagliero* v. *Wallace China Co.,* 198 F.2d 339 (9th Cir. 1952), well illustrates the concept of aesthetic functionality. The issue in *Pagliero* was whether defendant's copying of plaintiff's floral pattern design for china constituted trademark infringement. The Court found no trademark infringement because the design served primarily as a functional part of the product. . . .

Wichita asserts that the descriptive terms in the context of an NFL football jersey replica are crucial ingredients in the commercial success of plaintiff's licensing program. In other words, no consumer who wishes to purchase an NFL football jersey replica would buy a jersey unless it has the descriptive term which relates the jersey to a member club. . . .

Even assuming the marks are functional does not, however, preclude trademark protection. A functional feature may additionally serve as a trademark and be protected as such. As the Court stated in *Job's Daughters:*

> Our holding does not mean that a name or emblem could not serve simultaneously as a functional component of a product and a trademark. That is, even if the Job's Daughters' name and emblem, when inscribed on Lindeburg's jewelry, served primarily a functional purpose, it is possible that they could serve secondarily as trademarks if the typical customer not only purchased the jewelry for its intrinsic functional use and aesthetic appeal but also inferred from the insignia that the jewelry was produced, sponsored or endorsed by Job's Daughters.

633 F.2d at 919. It is exactly this showing of trademark significance that plaintiffs made in their

demonstration of secondary meaning and likelihood of confusion.

Defendant's next argument is that trademark protection would constitute an impermissible product monopoly under the doctrine of *Sears-Compco*. Assuming the applicability of *Sears-Compco* to plaintiffs' cause of action, Wichita's argument misses the point. *Sears-Compco* concerned the prohibition of copying a product not protected by a federal patent or copyright. Plaintiffs do not seek to prohibit the manufacture of jerseys, only jerseys which bear their marks. The jerseys are the product and not the marks. . . .

Trademarks always grant "product monopolies" in that they allow exclusive use of features which connote origin or sponsorship. Adopting Wichita's definition of "product" would subsume all trademark law.

Defendant's final defense is the genericness doctrine. In other words, defendant contends that the marks are generic for NFL football jersey replicas. "The genericness doctrine in trademark law is designed to prevent . . . anti-competitive misuse of trademarks. At its simplest, the doctrine states that when a trademark primarily denotes a product, not the product's producer, the trademark is lost." *Anti-Monopoly, Inc.* v. *General Mills Fun Group*, 611 F.2d 296, 301 (9th Cir. 1979.) A generic mark no longer serves a trademark function. Considering plaintiffs' establishment of secondary meaning and likelihood of confusion, the Court finds that the primary significance of the marks is source identification. Defendant is a trademark infringer of plaintiffs' marks and has violated sec. 43(a) of the Lanham Act. . . .

Remedy

. . . The scope of the injunction in this case has been influenced by the relative equities between the parties and the efficacy of less extensive relief. Plaintiffs have fairly represented themselves in this matter. Their claim has not been overbroad nor their demands excessive. The Court is mindful of the fact that the funds collected by NFLP from its licensing program are used for charitable purposes.

The conduct of defendant, on the other hand, has been far from laudable. Wichita was openly contemptuous of Judge Rothstein's preliminary injunction. Defendant sold a significant number of jerseys in direct violation of the order. Even when defendant had obtained a modified injunction, its conduct, perhaps within the strict letter of the injunction, was violative of the intent of the order. The disclaimers used by defendant were small, often incorrectly phrased, sometimes placed on the back of a label and generally situated in such a way that they could not be seen by the consumer. More significantly, the testimony of defendant's president, Leo Cooke, at times strained credulity.

Defendant has shown itself unwilling to comply with the order of the Court in the past. Anything less than a full injunction would provide Wichita an opportunity to circumvent the order. . . .

The Court concludes that the scope of the injunction must include not only jerseys in the full official colors of an NFL member club but also jerseys which use the dominant team color of an NFL member club. A jersey with the dominant team color is substantially similar to one with the full official colors and would be likely to confuse. There is no evidence, however, that use of a nondominant team color on the jersey would create a likelihood of confusion.

The injunction should also permit Wichita to use team colors and certain descriptive terms for non-NFL football jersey replicas. In other words, throughout the country there are non-NFL teams and organizations such as high schools, colleges and Pop Warner Leagues (hereinafter referred to as "non-NFL entities") which share a nickname with an NFL member club and have either the full team colors or the dominant team color of such NFL member club. Defendant should be able to service these non-NFL entities. Direct sales to these organizations or to stores (within a limited geographic area) which service these organizations are permitted. Wichita has the option, moreover, to differentiate its non-NFL entity jerseys from NFL football jersey replicas by placing the name or designation of the non-NFL entity on the jersey in sufficient size and proximity that it may be seen and understood.

Pursuant to the above stated reasons, defendant's use of the marks is found to create a likelihood of confusion and to violate section 43(a) of the Lanham Act. Plaintiffs are entitled to full injunctive relief. The injunction, as well as findings of fact and conclusions of law, accompany this memorandum opinion. Should this opinion contain findings of fact or conclusions of law not separately set forth in the appropriate section, they shall be treated as so set forth and are to be incorporated therein.

Gunter Harz Sports, Inc. v. United States Tennis Association, Inc., 511 F. Supp 1103 (D. Neb. 1981)

This case grew out of the decision of the United States Tennis Asssociation (USTA) in 1977 to honor a temporary ban imposed by the International Tennis Federation (ITF) on the use of "double-strung" tennis rackets and the subsequent adoption of a new rule defining a racket, which permanently prohibited their use. The plaintiff, in the business of manufacturing and distributing tennis equipment, alleged that the USTA's action constituted a group boycott of the double-strung rackets, with the effect of restraining competition in the sale of tennis rackets and stringing systems in violation of section 1 of the Sherman Act.

The Court first found that because the USTA, as a nonprofit sanctioning organization, did not compete at any level with plaintiff-manufacturer, the standard of "per se" unreasonableness could not be applied to the USTA's form of group boycott. Instead, when the purpose of the boycott has been to protect fair competition in a self-regulated industry, courts have utilized the rule of reason. The Supreme Court's analysis of *Silver* v. *New York Stock Exchange,* 373 U.S. 341 (1963), provided a framework for the court's inquiry into the USTA's actions.

The first question was whether the collective action was intended to accomplish an end consistent with the policy justifying self-regulation. The court specifically was to preserve the essential character and integrity of the game, which was consistent with their roles.

Second, the court found that the actions of the USTA were reasonably related to those goals. The ITF, in a study of the double-strung racket, had found that the racket imparted excessive amounts of topspin, which resulted in almost exclusive use of topspin, extreme difficulty in returning serves, and appreciably less play at the net. Viewing all of the evidence, the court found that the USTA and ITF could reasonably have concluded that the rule and the ban were necessary to preserve the character of the game as it had traditionally been played.

In the face of players' strikes and walkouts occasioned by the use of the double-strung rackets, the court then concluded that the actions were not more extensive than necessary.

In sum, the court found any effect the USTA's actions had on plaintiff's ability to compete was incidental to the USTA's primary purpose in promoting tennis competition.

NOTE ————————————————

1. In *STP Corp.* v. *U.S. Auto Club*, 286 F. Supp. 146 (S.D.Ind. 1968), a race car owner sought an injunction and damages against a racing association. The plaintiff alleged the defendant had wrongfully amended technical specifications for race car eligibility with the intent to exclude plaintiff's turbine engine racers from competition. The court held it was reasonable to amend engine specifications to provide competitive equivalency between piston powered and turbine powered race cars. Relief was denied.

6.42   Government Interference

Sports events are enormously popular and followed by such large numbers of the population that outsiders constantly maneuver to capitalize on the popularity. Even governments succumb to this temptation and consider ways by which sports events can generate state revenue beyond the obvious excise and entertainment taxes. Using the outcomes of sports events as the basis for legalized gambling is one approach.

Sports leagues have long tried to disassociate themselves from any ties to gambling. Even when it is a government that is controlling the action, a league predictably will object. The NFL's attempts to prevent the state of Delaware from running a football lottery are discussed below. The Delaware lottery eventually collapsed, not from the lawsuit, but because of its own internal problems. The threat to leagues has not disappeared, however.

In 1984, the national government of Canada instituted a sports lottery. The then Commissioner of Baseball, Bowie Kuhn, instituted suit against the Canadian government. In 1985, the suit was still pending. This and other possible intrusions in the future make the analysis in *NFL v. Delaware* timely and highly relevant.

National Football League v. Delaware, 435 F. Supp. 1372 (D. Del. 1977)

Plaintiffs, the National Football League and its 28 member clubs, brought an action against the state of Delaware seeking injunctive relief barring the state's use of a lottery scheme based on games of the NFL. Plaintiffs claimed they were being harmed by forced association with gambling and claimed misappropriation, violation of trademark and unfair competition laws, violation of Delaware Trademark Act, and violation of the Delaware Lottery Law.

The state of Delaware had devised a football lottery called "Scoreboard," which included three different games. One game, "Football Bonus," consisted of two, seven-game pools, the object of which was to select all the correct winners. Prizes were awarded on a pari-mutual basis as a function of the total amount of money bet. "Touchdown I" and "Touchdown II" consisted of 12 games with point spreads. The object was to beat the spread. "Touchdown I" also awarded prizes on a pari-mutual basis but was discontinued in favor of "Touchdown II," which utilized fixed payoffs, the amount dependant upon the number of games bet. Tickets to the lottery were available at authorized agents, and the games were listed by the city names of the NFL clubs, not by team nicknames.

The court examined each of the NFL claims individually:

Misappropriation. This claim was based on the contention that Delaware was unfairly capitalizing on the success and popularity of the NFL. Plaintiffs claimed that their schedules and scores were a tangible product and could not be used without their approval. They further claimed that the use of this "tangible product" for gambling purposes was harmful to their image. The court felt that since schedules and scores were widely disseminated, and since gambling in Nevada existed without harm to the NFL's reputation, there was no misappropriation.

Trademark and Unfair Competition. The court noted that one cannot create the impression that a connection exists between services offered and the holder of a registered trademark. If there is confusion as to this, there is an affirmative duty on the party to eliminate the confusion. The court noted the lottery tickets in question bore no NFL insignia, and the state truthfully told the public what service they performed. However, the plaintiffs were able to show that confusion existed among the public as to whether the NFL was directly associated with the lottery. Therefore, the court stipulated that the lottery tickets must explicitly declare that the NFL was in no way connected.

Delaware Trademark Act. The suit was pending before the act was passed, and the court did not deem it applicable.

Delaware Lottery law. The constitution of the state of Delaware prohibited gambling but not lotteries. Plaintiffs claimed that the schemes in question were really not a lottery but constituted gambling. They based their claim on the theory that a lottery was pure chance. Since an element of skill was involved in betting on football games, the state was really running a gambling operation. However, the court held that chance only had to be the "dominant factor" in a lottery. They noted that so-called experts such as Jimmy the Greek were often wrong in their predictions and that, although some knowledge of teams would be helpful, chance was still the dominant factor in the lottery.

The Delaware Lottery Law also determined the amount of revenue to be paid out and the amount to be kept by the state. At each drawing, not less than 45 percent of the total proceeds were to be given as prizes, and not less than 30 percent was to be kept by the state. The court found "Touchdown II" to be in violation of the provision, since in one week almost no prizes might be awarded, while in another week almost everyone might win. The court declared "Touchdown II" to be in violation of 29 Delaware Code Sections 4085 (a)(11) and 4815.

In conclusion, the court ruled that a clear and conspicuous statement that "Scoreboard" was not associated with or authorized by the NFL must be given on all materials and that "Touchdown II" was in violation of the law. All other requests for relief were denied. The court found no merit in defendants' counterclaim that the NFL was barred from bringing suit against them because the NFL had not brought suit against other betting schemes based on NFL Games (as in Nevada).

6.50   Sports and Related Industries

The sports industries deal with other industries on a constant basis. In order to get the product to the public, any number of business institutions in other fields must be utilized, including banks, insurance, concessionaires, and governmental bodies. Of great importance is a sports league's working relationship with the media — print, radio, and television. This vital subject is covered as a separate topic in Volume II, Chapter 6. It is noted here because it falls so squarely under management concerns.

Of particular concern to sports leagues is the ability to deal on a leaguewide basis with television and radio networks. Reference is again made to Chapter 6 for full explication of the basis of this ability, but note should here be made of the principal legislation enabling this to happen (15 U.S.C. secs. 1291–1295), and the two cases establishing parameters on a league's ability to control dissemination of its product over the air (see *U.S. v. NFL*, 118 F.Supp. 319 [E.D.Pa. 1953], and *U.S. v. NFL*, 196 F.Supp. 445 [1961]).

6.60   Operational Concerns at the Club Level

The variety of business and legal problems faced by a sports club is so substantial that no attempt is made to explore in detail how a club should proceed. What is presented here is an outline of these concerns (Exhibit 6–1). Four important areas are then analyzed: interferences with contractual relations (Section 6.61); dealing with consumer interests (Section 6.62); stadium leases (Section 6.63); and concessions contracts (Section 6.64). Even in discussing these topics, only highlights of the types of legal dispute likely to arise are covered; but one can derive from these some sense of the complexities involved.

Omitted from the discussions in this section are problems of tort liabilities. Reference is made to Volume II, Chapter 4 for a thorough consideration of this topic, as it impacts on both professional and amateur sports.

6.61   Interferences with Contractual Relations

The temptation to sign a player or coach already under contract to another club is at times too much to resist. In Chapter 2, Sections 2.10–2.14, we examined the possible remedies to be invoked against the defecting player or coach. The negative injunction was a principal focus of the discussion.

This section examines the legal basis for proceeding against the party who is attempting to lure away the player or coach. The cases examine both the extent of the ability to assert an interference with contract and the remedies available, both injunctive relief and damages.

American League Baseball Club of New York, Inc. v. Pasquel, 63 N.Y.S.2d 537 (Sup.Ct. 1946)

This was an action by the New York Yankees against Jorge Pasquel and the Mexican Baseball League seeking a temporary injunction restraining the defendants from attempting to induce Yankee players to repudiate their contracts with the club.

Exhibit 6-1   Operational Concerns of a Sports Club

A. Player Selection and Control
  1. The Draft
  2. Options and Reserve
  3. Free Agents
B. Player and Coaches Contracts
  1. Negotiation Considerations
      a. Present Costs and Immediate Tax Liabilities
      b. Long-Run Costs and Ultimate Tax Liabilities
      c. Club Morale
      d. Problems With Individual Concessions
  2. Responding to Breach: Negative Injunctions
      a. The Early Developments: Concern for Mutuality
      b. The Standards to Be Met
      c. Raising the Implication of Injunctory Relief
  3. Damages as an Alternative Remedy
      a. Use of Liquidated Damages Clauses
      b. Measuring Damages in the Absence of a Liquidated Damages Clause
  4. Arbitration In Contracts Disputes
C. Dealings With Other Clubs
  1. Trades
  2. Free Agent Compensation
  3. Other Disputes
D. The Media
  1. Local TV and Radio Contracts
  2. Dealings With Members of the Print and Broadcast Media
E. Stadiums, Arenas, Concessions and Parking: Contracts and Leases
F. Consumer Relations
  1. Ticket Sales
  2. Television Blackouts
  3. Relocating the Franchise
G. Tort Liabilities
  1. Responsibility for Player Actions
  2. General Responsibility for Arena Safety
  3. Alleged Negligent Medical Treatment of Players
  4. Defamation
H. Disciplining Players
I. Dealings with the League

Pasquel, the vice-president of the Mexican League, attempted to sign Phil Rizutto and other Yankees to contracts even though he undoubtedly knew of the existence of present contracts prior to making his offer. Pasquel said he would continue to entice players to go to the Mexican league.

The court ruled that such attempts were malicious, wrongful, and illegal. Though Pasquel argued that the contracts between plaintiff and the players were unenforceable because they were inequitable and monopolistic in character, the court said that made no difference in that malicious attempts to induce employees to leave their employer were illegal even if there was no contract for a definite term or even if the contract was terminable at will. An employee has a manifest interest in the freedom to exercise judgment; an unjustified interference by a third party is actionable. Plaintiff could enjoin strangers from attempting to induce players voluntarily performing their agreement with plaintiff to discontinue doing so.

In answer to defendant's claim that injunctive relief should be denied when a contract is contrary to public policy and monopolistic, the court said there was no real proof that organized baseball is an illegal monopoly. Defendants only showed that an individual ballplayer's freedom to contract is limited. Baseball is a *rendition of services* and therefore, even if it is a monopoly, there is no restraint of trade. The injunction was granted.

World Football League v. Dallas Cowboys Football Club, Inc., 513 S.W. 2d 102 (Tex. Civ. App. 1974)

Bateman, Justice

This is an interlocutory appeal from a temporary injunction. Although numerous defendants were named in the petition, the temporary injunction was ordered only against the appellant World Football League ("WFL"), and it was temporarily enjoined "from [1] directly or indirectly entering into any oral or written contracts with any football players now under contract with the [appellee] Dallas Cowboys Football Club, Inc. [the "Club"]

to perform services as football players in the World Football League, or [2] from inducing or attempting to induce any such football players under contract with the Dallas Cowboys Football Club, Inc. to engage in promotional, commercial or advertising activities for the World Football League or anyone acting in its behalf."

The Club owns a professional football team known as the Dallas Cowboys. It alleged that it had contracted for and owned the services of certain professional football players and that WFL had induced and would continue to induce some of those players to breach their contracts with the Club by entering contracts to play professional football for teams franchised by WFL after the expiration of their contracts with the Club. The Club also alleged that WFL had induced and would continue to induce certain Cowboy players to engage in promotional activities for WFL while under contract with the Club.

By its fifth point of error WFL says the trial court erred in granting appellee temporary injunctive relief because there is no evidence, or in any event insufficient evidence, to support a finding that the Club has a probable right to injunctive relief or will suffer probable harm unless a temporary injunction is issued. The ultimate question in reviewing an order granting a temporary injunction is whether the trial court abused its discretion in granting it. *Texas Foundries, Inc.* v. *International Molders & Foundry Workers' Union,* 151 Tex. 239, 248 S.W.2d 460, 462 (1952).

The cause of action alleged by the Club was one sounding in tort; i.e., engaging in a concerted program and course of conduct to obtain players for WFL by directly, intentionally and tortiously interfering with the contractual relationships existing between the Club and its players, and also in encouraging, soliciting and inducing players under binding contracts with the Club to breach those contracts and sign contracts with WFL, and to engage in promotional activities for WFL prior to the expiration of their contracts with the Club. We have searched the statement of facts carefully and find no evidence therein that WFL has been guilty of, or has threatened, any of the tortious conduct alleged in the club's pleadings.

It appears from the undisputed evidence that WFL is a newly organized professional football league, issuing franchises to local professional football teams in approximately twelve places in the United States and Canada. The "Club" is franchised by the National Football League. Calvin Hill, Craig Morton and Mike Montgomery have for several years been among the better players of the Club. Each of them had a separate written contract by which he agreed to play professional football for the club for certain designated compensations and for a certain period, usually of two years, with an option to the Club to renew for an additional period of one year at a rate of compensation equal to ninety percent of the "base salary" specified in the contract. This latter year is known as "the option year." Each contract year is from May 1 until the following April 30. Hill, Morton and Montgomery are in the "option years" of their respective contracts, that is, in each case, the year beginning May 1, 1974. Each of these three players, in the month of April 1974, signed a written contract to play for one of the franchised teams of WFL. The Club complains bitterly of this so-called "raiding" of its ranks of good players.

In December 1973 or January 1974, a form of letter was written on the letterhead of WFL, signed R. Steven Arnold, "W.F.L. Organizer," and addressed to and received by a substantial number of the Club's players, substantially as follows:

Dear Player:

The World Football League will begin play in 1974 with franchises in twelve areas, including New York, Chicago, Detroit, Toronto, New England, Southern California, Hawaii, and Florida. The remaining franchises will be awarded from some twenty applications for membership under consideration.

It is the intention of the World Football League to be "Major League" in every way, particularly in signing the top professional players available. We feel strongly that every player should honor his present contractual obligation. However, we would very much like to talk with you about the possibility of joining our League at the expiration of your present contract.

In order for us to know your status and to contact you, please fill out and return the enclosed post card as soon as possible.

Wishing you a Merry Christmas and a Happy and Prosperous New Year!

Enclosed with that letter in each instance was a post card addressed by rubber stamp to Steve Arnold Enterprises, and containing on the other side spaces which could be filled in by the player giving his name, the name of his team, his off-season address, the number of years his present contract has to run, not including the option year, and whether he would be interested in hearing an offer from the WFL. Some of the Club's players filled out and returned these cards and others did not.

WFL also published a brochure, apparently for public distribution giving certain information concerning the organization of WFL, its organizers and owners and pointing out, among other things, that players were available for the new league, including current professional players as well as graduating college seniors.

The Club argues that WFL is guilty of "pirating" its players and that unless enjoined it will continue to do so, but the only evidence of any contact whatever between WFL and the Club's players is the above quoted letter and the post card enclosed therewith. These writings do not suggest an unlawful "raiding scheme." The letter plainly states that the player should honor his existing contractual obligations and inquires only about the possibility of the player's interest in joining one of the WFL teams after the expiration of his present contract. There was no evidence of legal malice or deceitful means used by WFL or any motive or effort on its part to interfere with the contractual relations between the Club and its players.

The Club also contends that WFL arranged for, and induced three players to participate in, press conferences and various publicity activities surrounding the signing of contracts with WFL teams by Hill, Norton and Montgomery, thus causing a breach of the contracts between said players and the Club. In each of those contracts the player agrees "that during the term of this contract he will play football and engage in activities related to football only for the Club . . ."

The Club's principal contention is that the signing of the Cowboy players by WFL teams for services to be rendered after expiration of their present contracts is an unlawful inteference with the Club's present contractual relations with its players, as defined by the above provision of its contracts, because the players so signing will not use their best efforts for the team under their current contracts, the morale of the entire team will suffer, the enthusiasm of the fans will wane, and the new employers will reap the benefits of any favorable publicity for outstanding performance of the players so signing. The Club argues further that publicity resulting from the signing of such contracts for future services is a breach of the present obligations which the players owe to the Club.

These facts, even if true, do not present grounds for equitable relief. We must consider the freedom of contract of the individual players as well as the rights of the Club under its present contracts. Bargaining for future services is a matter of economics. The Club can assure itself of the continued services and loyalty of its players by offering them long-term contracts and other financial inducements. If it chooses not to do so for economic reasons, it has no legal ground to complain if the players look elsewhere for their future careers and enter into contracts for services to be performed when their present contracts with the Club expire. Signing such contract is neither a breach of the contract by the players nor a tortious interference by the future employers, and the threat to enter into such contracts affords no ground for equitable relief. Neither does the publicity necessarily attendant upon the signing of contracts with well-known players constitute a tort. An injunction restraining the signing of such contracts because of the attendant publicity would be an unreasonable restraint on the freedom of contract of the players and their prospective employers.

We should not be understood, however, as holding that other promotional and publicity activities for the benefit of future employers would not be subject to restraint as "activities relating to football," which the players are bound by their present contracts to reserve for the Club. No such limited equitable relief was sought either in the trial court or in this court. The Club has cast its entire case for injunctive relief on its contention that the signing of contracts for future services would in itself be a tortious interference with the players' performance of their obligations under their present contracts with the Club. Since the injunction cannot be sustained on that ground, it must be dissolved. . . .

Cincinnati Bengals, Inc. v. Bergey, 453 F. Supp. 129 (S.D. Ohio 1974)

The Cincinnati Bengals of the National Football League brought an action for a preliminary and permanent injunction against its linebacker Bill Bergey, who signed a lucrative contract in 1974 for his future personal services with the Virginia Ambassadors of the new World Football League, effective after his contract with Cincinnati expired. At the heart of plaintiff's complaint was its claim that its right to full performance from Bergey had been undermined.

On the basis of testimony from coaches in the NFL, the court concluded that football, more so than other professional sports, is a team sport in which coaches develop the players to become cohesive units. However, the court found the Bengals' claim that the WFL contract would impair Bergey's performance and would have a divisive influence on his teammates was essentially speculative and unsubstantiated. In contrast, the court found that the WFL would be greatly harmed if enjoined in its promotional efforts. The evidence established that the WFL's motive for signing NFL players was not to cause any harm to the NFL teams but to create credibility in the new league by guaranteeing the college players as well as the public that the league was stable. If precluded from this promotional effort, those who have invested vast sums of money into the WFL could be hurt.

The court then discussed in great detail two sports cases which bore directly on the issue of future service contracts. The court held that the cases stood for the proposition that it is not illegal for either the player or the sports organization, at the time when the player is under a valid contract to one team, to negotiate and enter into a contract with a different, competing team and league and agree to render services at the expiration of the current contract (see *Washington Capitols Basketball Club* v. *Barry*, 419 F.2d 472 [9th Cir. 1969]; *Munchak Corporation* v. *Cunningham*, 457 F.2d 721 [4th Cir. 1972]).

The plaintiff also failed to carry its burden to satisfy the four essential criteria that must be met before an injunction is issued. The court first found that it was unlikely that the plaintiff would prevail on the merits, since it found no evidence of maliciousness, necessary to show tortious interference with a contract, and no evidence of any breach. The court next found no harm to the public interest since the threatened harm was due to competition and any injunction which would stifle competition would not be in the public interest. Neither could the plaintiff demonstrate an absence of harm to the WFL if the injunction were issued or that it would suffer irreparable harm to itself. The fact that the Bengals might have to pay more for future services was not evidence of irreparable injury but only that the NFL now had a competitor.

The court did find, and it took into account, that if five or six key Bengals were under contract for future services, it was reasonably certain that the effect would be adverse to the Bengals. The court concluded, however, that in the present case the plaintiffs did not meet its heavy burden, and thus denied the motion for an injunction.

New England Patriots Football Club, Inc. v. University of Colorado, 592 F.2d 1196 (1st Cir. 1979)

Aldrich, Senior Circuit Judge.

In 1973 one Charles L. Fairbanks contracted with plaintiff New England Patriots Club, a professional football organization and member of the National Football League, to act as its manager and head coach. By later agreement the employment was to continue until January, 1983. The contract contained a provision that Fairbanks was not to provide services connected with football to any entity other than plaintiff, or to perform services of any kind for anyone without plaintiff's permission during the period of employment. In November, 1978, Fairbanks was approached by various persons, defendants herein, some of whom were officially, and some sentimentally, attached to the University of Colorado. Defendants' objective was to persuade Fairbanks to quit the Patriots and become head football coach at the University. Their successful initiation of this endeavor, at first behind the Patriots' back, and later, over its vigorous opposition, resulted in the present action where, following a hearing, the district court entered a preliminary injunction enjoining defendant regents, defendant president, defendant athletic director, and defendant Vickers, a Colorado football fan and angel, from causing the University to employ Fairbanks as the University's coach. Fairbanks is not a party to the suit, and has not been enjoined.

Defendants appeal. In connection with the appeal, they moved for a stay pending resolution. This we denied. At the same time, in response to the representation by counsel for defendants that time was of the essence because of the nature of the employment, we agreed to expedite the hearing. We also acceded to Fairbanks' request, tendered through counsel for defendants, to file an amicus brief.*

Although this is not our first experience with the athletic milieu's response to legal embroilment engendered by contract jumping, we set out the factual contentions in some detail in order to get in the mood. For this opportunity we are primarily indebted to the Fairbanks amicus brief.*

The extension of the contract to January 26, 1983 was agreed to on June 6, 1977. The briefs are silent as to this date, an understandable reticence in view of the fact that by that time Fairbanks had, apparently, already decided he might not keep his word.

> For a number of years, Fairbanks was extremely unhappy with remaining in professional football [and] with his present location .... Fairbanks believed the health of his family, and a reassessment of career objectives, *mandated a change*. Accordingly, for a number of years, he had been investigating business opportunities outside football, as well as coaching at the college level, ... (Amicus br. 8) (Emphasis suppl.)

---

* In granting permission we had assumed, wrongly, it proved, that counsel knew what an amicus is, namely, one who, "not as parties, ... but, just as any stranger might," *Martin* v. *Tapley*, 1875, 119 Mass. 116, 120, "for the assistance of the court gives information of some matter of law in regard to which the court is doubtful or mistaken," 1 Bouvier's Law Dictionary 188 (3d ed. 1914), rather than one who gives a highly partisan, ("eloquent," according to defendants) account of the facts.

This justification for nonperformance so satisfied Fairbanks that it was followed by a footnote expressing indignation at the court's refusal to recognize it.

Nor was this the only mantle of protection. Because in 1973 the Patriots allegedly had lured Fairbanks from the University of Oklahoma, inducing him to break his contract there, defendants conclude that the Patriots are barred from relief by the doctrine of unclean hands. We disagree.

Both parties may have done the University of Oklahoma dirt, but that does not mean unclean hands with respect to "the controversy in issue. . . ." The precedential effect of a court's extending this doctrine to cover circumstances such as this staggers the imagination. In all fairness, Fairbanks was not concerning himself, perhaps, with a commercial transaction; in fact, he seems put out that anyone should suppose he had to.

It was only *noblesse oblige* that caused him to speak to the Patriot's owner, William Sullivan, at all.

> The purpose for this meeting was that Fairbanks felt he owed a personal responsibility to Sullivan to tell him the reasons for his leaving. (Amicus br. 9)

Finally, he was misrepresented; crass materialism had nothing to do with it.

> The impression that the Patriots attempt to make — that Fairbanks was induced to leave for money — simply is not true. (Amicus br. 9–10).

Money does create some problems, however, quite apart from inducing Fairbanks to sign for an engagement that he had little intention of keeping. If ascertainable money damages could fully compensate the Patriots, under familiar principles there would be no basis for injunctive relief. The district court, however, found that ascertainment would be difficult. It further found that Fairbanks' services were unique, and that, accordingly, the loss of his services would occasion the Patriots irreparable harm.

Fairbanks was insufficiently modest to dispute this last. However, the cause was taken up by the defendants. They dispute both findings, offering reasons which, to put the matter in its kindest light, we may be too unsophisticated to understand. Then, in a turnabout for which, perhaps apprehending our shortcomings, no reasons are even offered, defendants state,

> In contract, the continuation of the preliminary injunction which prevents Fairbanks from signing with Colorado does irreparably harm the University. (Defendants br. 40)

While we are attempting to reconcile these conclusions, there comes the final drive.

> Fairbanks' departure may have no effect or, even possibly a beneficial effect, on the Patriots' performance and attendance in the future. (Defendants br. 42)

The injunction is an ungracious, even an ungrateful act.

Somehow it seems as if there were an extra man on the field.

Whatever may be thought rules elsewhere, the legal rules are clear. A contract is not avoided by crossed fingers behind one's back on signing, nor by unsupported, and at once inconsistently self-deprecating and self-serving protests that the breach was to the other party's benefit. Equally, we are not taken by Fairbanks' claim that because, when he told Sullivan that he was leaving at the end of the season and Sullivan responded that he was "suspended," it was Sullivan who broke the contract.

> The simple fact is that Fairbanks was fired. (Amicus br. 11)

Whatever may be thought the meaning in the trade of suspension, as distinguished from its commonly understood meaning, it is a novel concept that a contract-breaker had the option to require the other party to accept his choice of dates. At least until Fairbanks withdrew his unlawful announcement, the Patriots had a right not to accept the services of an unfaithful servant, or, as Sullivan put it to him at the time, one who had "his body in Foxboro and his heart in Colorado."

In this circumstance defendants are reduced to three claims; that they are protected from suit by the Eleventh Amendment of the Constitution; that the court lacks jurisdiction because Fairbanks, who has not joined, is an indispensable party; and that the injunction should not be granted, both because it is an indirect way of avoiding the rule that a personal service contract cannot be specifically enforced, and in any event, because Fairbanks, by employment at the college level, would not be engaging in competition with the Patriots. Because the injunctive issue flows naturally as part of the factual recitation we have just interrupted, we will treat it first.

At the hearing Fairbanks testified that although the contract read "services directly connected with football . . . [or for] another entity not connected with football," this meant, simply, activities competitively connected with the Patriots. Apparently he has no more regard for the parole evidence rule forbidding the contradiction of unambiguous language than for other rules foisted upon him by legalisms. Parenthetically, having in mind, as sometimes helpless dialspinners, that professional and prominent college football teams compete for TV viewers, and hence, presumably, for the advertising dollar, we may wonder whether we have to accept at face value the protestation of no competitive activity here. In any event, there is ample authority contradicting both aspects of defendants' legal position. Indeed, some courts have gone even further, and have enjoined the defaulting athlete himself from noncompetitive sport . . . We would not distinguish between an athlete and a coach. To enjoin tortious interference by a third party, whether or not competitive, would seem a lesser step . . .

While there is contrary authority, in this circumstance we need only refer to the familiar principle that at the preliminary injunction stage an appellate court will not reverse if there is a supportable legal basis for the district court's action even if, on final analysis, it may prove to be mistaken . . .

We comment briefly on the self-serving statement in Fairbanks' amicus brief that he is "through with professional football." There is no such finding in the record, and even though that may now be the conventional wisdom, neither the Patriots nor the court are bound to accept it. At this stage Fairbanks could be expected to say no less. Defendants' constant stress that the injunction is unproductive, and nothing but "punishment" in light of the fact that a position with the University "is the only game in town," is a total nonsequitur that cuts the other way. If there may, in part, be a punitive effect, we could not avoid wondering how

great a miscarriage that would be with respect to one who, on his own testimony, promised a longer term than he intended to keep, not only to afford himself sanctuary while he looked around, but, again on his own testimony, putting himself in line for higher pay meanwhile, and whose seeming only defense to his announced total breach is a claim that the Patriots grabbed the gun.

This same principle that we need not finally resolve all possibly debatable questions of law is fully sufficient to dispose of defendants' claim that Fairbanks is an indispensable party, F.R.Civ.P. 19(a) and (b). The standard steps which here lead us to the ultimate question of fairness are too familiar to require repeating. What is fair is, basically, a subjective question. Some courts in inducing-breach-of-contract cases have regarded the question as too insubstantial to require comment, and have allowed the case to proceed without the other contracting party in silence . . . Indeed, defendants cite no persuasive authority the other way. It is to be borne in mind that any issue of fairness is only fairness to Fairbanks; defendants can suggest no unfairness to themselves resulting from his absence. They do say that it would be unfair to Fairbanks if, due to possibly divergent interests, they omitted points he might have made. Having been exposed, through his amicus brief, to the points that Fairbanks might personally make here, it might be difficult to be moved by this contention even if, in the abstract, it were a valid one. More important, on the single issue in this case, we perceive no different interests. On the broader questions, general rights of Fairbanks and the Patriots under the contract, the decision will have no effect because Fairbanks is not a party, and for the further reason that it could not seemingly affect them even if he were.

It is a conceded fact that in a pending judicial proceeding brought by Fairbanks in the state of Colorado in which the Patriots is a defendant, Fairbanks has been ordered to respect the contract provision and arbitrate his dispute before the Commissioner of the National Football League. This seems a complete answer to defendants' claim that by plaintiff's failure to join Fairbanks as a party, plaintiff is engaging in "piecemeal litigation." Rather, plaintiff appears to have no justiciable claim against him in a court of law. We reject the claim that Fairbanks is an indispensable party.

NOTES _____

1. The topic of interference with a contractual relationship has been frequently explored both in cases dealing in the sports and entertainment fields and in scholarly articles. The following should be noted:

(a) Weistart & Lowell, *The Law of Sports*, sec. 4.14, pp. 397–408.

2. Additional cases include the following:

(a) *City of New York* v. *New York Jets Football Club*, 429 F. Supp. 987 (1977).

(b) *Hennessy* v. *National Collegiate Athletic Ass'n.*, 564 F.2d 1136.

(c) *Munchak Corporation* v. *Cunningham*, 457 F.2d 721 (1972), *Washington Capitols Basketball Club, Inc.* v. *Barry*, 419 F.2d 472 (1969).

3. Related cases in entertainment field include the following:

(a) *Lumley* v. *Gye*, 2 El & Bl 216, 118 Eng.Rep. 749 (1853).

(b) *Show Management* v. *Hearst Publishing Co.*, 196 Cal. App.2d 606 (1961).

(c) *Shaw* v. *Merrick*, 401 N.Y.S.2d 508 (1978).

(d) *Smith* v. *American Guild of Variety Artists*, 349 F.2d 975 (1965), vacated 384 U.S. 30 (1966), *cert. denied* 387 U.S. 931 (1967).

(e) *Potter's Photographic Applications Co.* v. *Ealing Corp.*, 292 F.Supp. 92 (1968).

(f) *Roulette Records, Inc.* v. *Princess Production Corp.*, 224 N.Y.S.2d 204 (1962), aff'd. 12 N.Y.2d 815 (1962).

(g) *Warner Bros. Pictures, Inc.* v. *Simon*, 251 N.Y.S.2d 70 (1964), aff'd. 15 N.Y.2d 836 (1965).

(h) *Uptown Enterprises* v. *Strand*, 195 Cal.App.2d 45 (1961).

6.62 Dealing with Consumer Interests

A sports club must balance carefully its economic potentials and the effects that the implementation of certain policies will have on the goodwill the club seeks to maintain with its consumers. At times, the business decisions of a club draw adverse reactions. The fans can always stay away, of course, but consumer boycotts in sports have not proved effective.

Occasionally there are sports consumers who feel sufficiently aggrieved to seek legal redress. Among many circumstances likely to incur consumer ire, none has been more volatile than a club's decision to "encourage" preseason ticket sales by aligning these sales to regular season ticket packages.

Pfeiffer v. New England Patriots Football Club, Inc., U.S. Dist. Ct., E.D. Mass., No.72–2501–G, July 25, 1972.

Leo T. Pfeiffer, a season ticket holder for football games of the 1971 and 1972 New England Patriots, brought this action on behalf of himself and members of the same class for a permanent injunction to prohibit the defendant, New England Patriots, from selling the three-game preseason tickets and for treble damages as well as costs of bringing the suit. The district court awarded summary judgment to the defendant.

The plaintiff alleged that he and fellow members of his same class were injured by being forced to purchase the three-game preseason tickets along with the seven-game season tickets as an illegal tying arrangement in violation of the Sherman Act, 15 U.S.C. sec. 1. Plaintiff further alleged that such an illegal tying arrangement was an abuse of the monopoly position of the New England Patriots and as such is a violation of section 2 of that act, 15 U.S.C. sec. 2.

The facts of the case are that the plaintiff purchased two season tickets (seven season games and three preseason games) on March 31, 1971 for $80.00 per ticket. It is not clear from the record whether plaintiff had other options in ticket plans available as defendant asserts. Between April 29, 1971 and December 20, 1971 the New England Patriots and the attorney general of Massachusetts agreed upon various alternate ticket purchasing plans for buyers of tickets. These plans, which defendant asserts represent the plans available to plaintiff for the 1971 and 1972 seasons, are: (1) ten-game plan (which plaintiff purchased), whereby the three preseason, exhibition games and the seven regular season games were combined; (2) seven-game plan, whereby tickets only to the seven regular season games were sold; (3) seven-game plan plus one or two preseason games; (4) any combination of games from one to ten. The price for each individual game would remain the same under all plans.

Though plaintiff did not state in his complaint, it appeared from defendant's responses filed in the form of affidavits from Mr. William Sullivan, President of the New England Patriots, that priority of seating arrangement was accorded to purchasers of the largest packets of tickets. Those purchasers who took the ten-game plan would have seating priority over those who purchased the seven-game plan. It does appear that the value of the ten-game ticket packet was in its seating preference priority, which it granted the holder, as the price of each game was the same. Those fans having the least preference of seats were those who chose the combinations of one to ten game tickets. All these respective ticket holder's preferences were subject to those ticket holders who had purchased that same combination of tickets in prior seasons. A purchaser who held a complete season ticket plan in 1969 would have seating priority over the plaintiff (a 1971 season ticket purchaser). These practices of the defendant both to the ticket package options available and the seating priority arrangement were continued for the 1972 football season.

Plaintiff alleged that the forcing of the season ticket purchaser to buy the three preseason game tickets was a combination (tying) of a nondesired, unequal product with the desired product (the regular season game ticket). Plaintiff further alleged in his complaint that this illegal tying of the preseason game ticket to the season game ticket forced the buyer to pay a higher price for the preseason games. The exhibition game tickets were the same price as the season game tickets. That this selling arrangement was an illegal abuse of the monopoly position held by the defendant as the only professional football team in the New England region was asserted by plaintiff. Pfeiffer finally alleged that due to this illegal abuse of defendant's monopoly position, plaintiff and members of his class were coerced to attend football games wherein the physical facilities were inadequate.

Defendant asserted as shown above that plaintiff and members of his same class were not forced to purchase the three preseason game tickets but rather were offered four differing plans. Defendant further attempted at great length to prove that the preseason game tickets were as valuable and desirable to the fan as a regular season game ticket. Defendant denied that it held a monopoly position in professional sports as it competed for viewer time and support with professional baseball (Boston Red Sox), professional basketball (Boston Celtics), professional hockey (Boston Bruins), and college and high school football.

The district court judge held that since the single-game tickets were available to the plaintiff, he was not forced to purchase the ten-game plan, and there existed no restraint of trade in the form of an illegal tying arrangement and that summary judgment would be awarded defendant. As to the preferred seat location policy of the defendant, the court found that the policy of granting preference "to purchasers of more comprehensive season ticket plans is a reasonable and good business practice." The evaluation of whether the exhibition games were of the same quality as the regular season games was determined to be "out of our (the court's) league."

NOTE _____

1. A synopsis of the *Pfeiffer* opinion appears in 1973 Trade Cases ¶ 74,267.

Coniglio v. Highwood Services, Inc., 495 F.2d 1286 (2d Cir. 1974)

This action was brought by former season ticket holder for professional football games charging violations of Sherman Act predicated on an alleged tying arrangement whereby season ticket holders were required to purchase tickets for exhibition games. The district court dismissed the complaint, and the plaintiff appealed.

Plaintiff Coniglio, an avid football fan of the Buffalo Bills football team, had been a season ticket holder of the team since 1964. In 1966, the Bills altered its season ticket sale policy by requiring the purchaser of a season ticket to also buy a ticket for an exhibition game. Also in that year, the American Football League and the older National Football League tentatively agreed to merge into one league, provided congressional approval, obviating a possible antitrust violation, could be obtained. In 1968, the Bills increased the number of exhibition games included in the season ticket package to two. And two years later the season ticket holders were required to purchase tickets for three exhibition games. Plaintiff Coniglio did not renew his season ticket subscription for the 1971 season, and instead purchased individual tickets for five of the seven regular season home games played by the Bills.

Coniglio commenced an antitrust action against Highwood, the NFL, and its commissioner, Pete Rozelle, claiming that for the period 1966–1970 Highwood's policy of conditioning the purchase of season tickets, to a requirement to buy exhibition game tickets, constituted an unlawful tying arrangement in violation of section 1 of the Sherman Act, 15 U.S.C sec. 1. Moreover, Coniglio charged that it also constituted an abuse of the Bills' monopoly power over professional football in the Buffalo area, in breach of section 2 of the Sherman Act, 15 U.S.C. sec. 2. In addition, Coniglio alleged that the unlawful tie beween season tickets and exhibition game tickets was the product of a conspiracy between Highwood, the NFL, and Rozelle, and that such conspiracy was a further violation of section 1 of the Sherman Act.

The court of appeals relied heavily for its decision on *Northern Pacific Railway Co.* v. *United States*, 356 U.S. 1 (1958). In that case the court defined a tying arrangement as "an agreement by a party to seal one product but only on the condition that the buyer also purchase a different [or tied] product" *Northern Pacific Railway Co.* v. *United States*, 356 U.S. at 5. The court in that case further described the basis upon which a tying arrangement would be found violative of section 1 of the Sherman Act. "[Tying arrangements] are unreasonable [restraints of trade and commence] in and of themselves whenever a party has sufficient

economic power with respect to the tying product to appreciably restrain free competition in the market for the tied product and a 'not insubstantial' amount of interstate commerce is affected" *Northern Pacific Railway Co.* v. *United States*, 356 U.S. at 6. Utilizing the *Northern Pacific* analysis, the court of appeals identified four factors essential in determining whether a particular sales practice constitutes an illicit tying arrangement: (1) two separate and distinct products — a tying product and a tied product; (2) sufficient economic power in the tying market to coerce purchase of the tied product; (3) anticompetitive effects in the tied market; and (4) involvement of a "not insubstantial" amount of interstate commerce in the tied market.

The court held the fourth factor to be satisfied since in 1970 alone the total value of the tied exhibition game tickets was appoximately $483,000. As to the second requirement, the court noted that the buyer was not "free to take either product (season ticket or exhibition game ticket) by itself"; indeed, a season ticket could not be purchased unless a certain number of exhibition game tickets, three in 1970, were purchased as well. In view of the advantages obtained through the purchase of a season ticket, principally the preferential seat selection accorded the season ticket holder, and the large amount of such tickets purchased, the court found that there was sufficient evidence of the desirability of the tickets to make the existence of the requisite economic power a triable issue of fact.

As to the first factor, the court found that the distinction between exhibition and regular season contests was sufficiently sharp at the very least to render the factual determination of product separability more appropriate for a trial rather than for summary judgment.

However, the court held that plaintiff Coniglio failed to satisfy the third factor; it ruled that Coniglio failed, as a matter at law, to demonstrate an anticompetitive effect in the tied (exhibition football game) market. The court reasoned that just as the Bills had a monopoly over the presentation of regular season professional football games in the relevant geographic market, Buffalo, it also had a monopoly over the presentation at exhibition football games — the tied product. Thus the court held that Highwood was not using its economic power in the tying (season ticket) market to "restrain free competition in the market for the tied product, it being undisputed that there were neither actual nor potential competitors to the Bills in the professional football market." Accordingly, the tying arrangement attacked by Coniglio was ruled not to fall within the realm of contacts in restraint of trade or commerce proscribed by section 1 of the Sherman Act, 15 U.S.C. sec. 1.

The court held that the propriety of summary judgment in the case rested on "Coniglio's total failure to demonstrate any adverse effect on competition, actual or potential, an issue perfectly well-suited to objective, statistical analysis. In such instances, summary judgment is properly granted to lower the curtain on costly litigation where it is clear beyond cavil that one side simply has no support for its version of the alleged facts."

As to Coniglio's argument regarding section 2 of the Sherman Act, the court held that since Highwood did not use the tying arrangement either to prevent competition or destroy it, its ticket sale practice did not represent an unlawful abuse of its monopoly power.

Decision of district court dismissing complaint was affirmed.

NOTES _____

1. In *Broder* v. *Pfizer, Inc.,* 1973 Trade Cases Paragraph 74, 268, a class action was instituted, alleging that a professional football team violated the Sherman Act, Section 2 by requiring season ticket holders also to purchase exhibition game tickets. The trial court dismissed the action and held that plaintiffs were not coerced into buying exhibition game tickets. Single game tickets were available for every regular season home game. In its business judgment, a club could allocate preferred seating to package buyers of both preseason and regular season tickets.

2. In *Driskill* v. *Dallas Cowboys Football Club, Inc.,* 498 F. 2d 321 (5th Cir. 1974), a season ticket holder alleged that the defendant club engaged in an illegal tying arrangement by

requiring the purchase of preseason tickets and low-interest stadium bonds as a condition for the purchase of regular season tickets. The U.S. Court of Appeals affirmed the trial court's summary judgment for defendant. Plaintiff did not plead that the tying of season tickets to preseason tickets and stadium bonds had an anticompetitive effect, a necessary element in proving an illegal tying arrangement. The court held that since the Cowboys had a complete monopoly in the relevant market, there could be no adverse effect on competititors. Also, since preseason and regular season games are the same product, there is no tying. The court also noted that tickets were available for regular season games; thus, there was no coercion.

Shayne v. Madison Square Garden Corp., 1974 Trade Cases, Paragraph 74,920

Plaintiff sued on behalf of himself and others similarly situated to recover treble damages allegedly sustained from defendant's sale of seating tickets for the New York Knickerbocker basketball and New York Ranger hockey games at Madison Square Garden. Defendant had various plans for its season ticket subscription sale consisting of combinations of regular season and preseason games and other special sports and entertainment events. Plaintiff charged that these plans were inherently coercive in that they exploited more desirable events and more desirable seat locations to sell tickets to the less popular events and to fill poor seats.

The court, however, did not view this as an illegal "tying" arrangement, as there was no identifiable alternative to which access was denied to the season subscriber. The special events were separately available products rather than tied products.

One clearcut legal issue that did emerge was whether subscription selling was ever valid when the subscription embraced differentiable products. The court found this issue a "shapeless concern" with whether or not a set of plans such as the defendant's was an unfair set of practices in commerce, distinct from any specifiable antitrust violations or steps toward violation.

The court, however, could not find the existence of a class in order to maintain the action as a class action. While unanimity of view was not a requisite, the controversy must essentially be one between the defendant and the class as a whole. The facts of this case suggested that many season subscribers would advance their differing interest in the validation of the plan and the controversy was thus a tripartite type. Accordingly, the court denied the plaintiff's motion for an order determining that the action be maintained as a class action.

NOTE _____

1. The lower court's denial of plaintiff's motion to grant class action status was upheld on appeal. See *Shayne v. Madison Square Garden Corp.*, 491 F. 2d 397 (2d Cir. 1974).

Strauss v. Long Island Sports, Inc., 394 N.Y.S. 2d 341 (Sup. Ct. 1977)

Plaintiff purchased four season tickets for the New York Nets basketball team's 1976–77 season. He purchased the tickets after a large media campaign by the Nets to sell the tickets, using superstar Julius Erving ("Dr. J") as the main enticement. Soon after plaintiff bought his season tickets, Dr. J was sold to the Philadelphia '76ers. Plaintiff claimed that he and others purchased tickets "in the reasonable expectation that Julius Erving would play unless injured." Plaintiff claimed that the absence of Dr. J deprived season ticket holders of the principal reason for their purchases.

After several suits similar to plaintiffs were filed, the New York State Attorney-General instituted an investigation to determine if any consumer protection laws were violated by the Nets. Defendant agreed to give a 10 percent rebate to those who purchased the tickets before the sale of Dr. J. Any person who received the rebate waived his right to further relief against the Nets.

The Nets moved to consolidate three other lawsuits with the instant case. Plaintiff Strauss opposed this motion and moved for an order determining his suit to be maintained as a class action. After discussing the requirements for a class action, the court held that plaintiff's action should proceed as a class action. While defendant claimed that each plaintiff should have to

prove his or her reliance on Dr. J appearing in a Nets uniform, the court held that the presence of individual questions of reliance did not preclude a class action. Accordingly, the court entered an order that this action should proceed as a class action.

NOTE _____

1. Clubs and other proprietors of sporting events may deem it necessary to exclude certain patrons. The reasons for the actions taken vary. The people excluded may be alleged ticket scalpers, have records of disorderly conduct, or have committed other acts contrary to the proprietor's policies. If the grounds for exclusion are clearly set forth, the actions by the proprietors will normally be upheld. For example, see the following:

(a) In *Tamello v. New Hampshire Jockey Club*, 163 A. 2d 10 (N.H. Sup Ct. 1960), the court ruled that a private enterprise may discriminate as to those admitted onto the premises, so long as the decisions are not made in a capricious, arbitrary, or unreasonable manner. Since there was no finding as to the basis of dismissal, the case was remanded.

(b) In *Toms v. Tiger Lanes, Inc.*, 313 So. 2d 852 (La. App. 1975), plaintiff's disturbing threats and unprovoked attack on another patron justified defendant's expelling plaintiff from the premises.

(c) In *Levine v. Brooklyn National League Baseball Club, Inc.*, 36 N.Y.S. 2d 474 (Sup. Ct. 1942), ticket speculators sought to enjoin the defendant ball club from denying admission to individuals who purchased tickets from plaintiffs. The court denied the injunction, holding that a recitation on the ticket that it was nontransferrable and could not be resold was valid.

(d) In *People v. Licata*, 320 N.Y.S. 2d 53 (Ct. App. 1971), defendant's conviction for criminal trespass was affirmed, despite his purchasing an admission ticket, where defendant had previously been served with a written noice that stated he was barred from entering the race track premises.

(e) *Mandel v. Brooklyn National League Baseball Club Inc.*, 372 N.Y.S. 2d 152 (Sup. Ct. 1942), followed *Levine*, above, in denying injunction sought by plaintiff to prevent club from denying admission to persons who had purchased tickets from her.

6.63   Stadium Leases

A club has many concerns over the arena or stadium in which it plays its home games. Most professional sports teams do not own the arena in which they perform. This requires the club to lease from the stadium owner, who may be a private party or municipal authority.

The leases entered are often complex, long-term instruments. Future events are not always adequately contemplated. Among the greatest causes for dispute are when a club later decides to move to another locale. The spurned stadium owner will seek every legal redress at its disposal.

HMC Management Corporation v. New Orleans Basketball Club, 375 So. 2d 700 (La. App. 1979)

HMC Management Corporation (HMC), a business corporation operating the Louisiana Superdome facility, the Louisiana Stadium and Exposition District (LSED), a body politic of the state of Louisiana, the attorney general of Louisiana, and the state of Louisiana brought suit against the New Orleans Basketball Club (Jazz) and its individual partners, as well as against the National Basketball Association (NBA) and its individual team members. The plaintiffs brought their suits on two counts: (1) in contract, alleging that the Jazz, by moving the club to Utah, had breached a 1975 lease with LSED which would require the Jazz to play their home games in the Superdome for five years; and (2) under Louisiana's antitrust laws, alleging that the NBA and Jazz, by monopolizing professional basketball in Louisiana, had caused the Jazz to move to Utah as a result of their antitrust activities.

The plaintiffs sought a preliminary injunction to prevent the Jazz from conducting any business in Utah. The issue was further complicated by the question of whether the original lease of 1975 between the Jazz and the LSED had been superseded by a later lease between the Jazz and HMC. The trial judge held that the only legal contract was the later lease, and consequently held that the LSED and the state had no right of action. The court of appeal reversed on this issue, holding that the 1975 lease was still valid, and that LSED and the state of Louisiana had an actual interest in the action brought.

The plaintiffs alleged that the NBA had created a monopoly on nationwide professional basketball, that it uses this monopoly to restrict the services of its players, to restrict the granting of additional franchises, to fix prices charged patrons for its games and that it engages in several other violations of the Louisiana antitrust laws. The plaintiffs further alleged that the illegal activities of this monopoly had caused the Jazz to move from the Superdome in violation of the lease between the plaintiffs and the Jazz, causing loss of rent and profits and preventing the plaintiffs from contracting with another team to play in the Superdome. The defendants argued, and the court of appeals agreed, that since the NBA is involved in interstate commerce, the federal antitrust laws would be applicable and thus preempt most of the Louisiana antitrust claims. However, the court held that in terms of the breach of contract, the plaintiffs had a right of action to seek the additional remedy of damages under the Louisiana antitrust laws. But the court of appeals upheld the defendants' exception, which claimed that the plaintiffs had not been specific enough to state a cause of action. Accordingly, the court of appeals permitted the plaintiffs to amend their complaint.

The city of New Orleans and its mayor attempted to enter the suit as third-party beneficiaries of the lease contracts. The court of appeals, in affirming the lower court, noted that a third-party beneficiary can only sue on a contract if the contract manifests an intention to confer a benefit on that third party. The court held that the contract between LSED and the Jazz was clearly not intended to confer a benefit on the city. The court also dismissed the city's attempts to intervene on theories of mutual intent to contract or quasi-contract.

The court of appeals finally addressed the issue of the plaintiffs' attempt for a preliminary injunction, which would stop the Jazz from conducting business in Utah. The court affirmed the trial court, ruling that the request for an injunction must be denied. The court, noting that the injury to defendants, by requiring the Jazz and all other NBA teams to alter their schedules, would be greater than that of the plaintiffs. Accordingly, the writ for a preliminary injunction was dismissed.

6.64 Concessions

Among the many concerns involved in the operation of its business, a club must even fret over the legal problems relating to the hot dogs and beer sold at its games. Concessions are generally the province of a separate business enterprise. Thus, a contract must be entered to supply those "indispensables" to any sports action. The contract between the concessionaire and either the stadium owner or club can create legal problems as wide-ranging as with any other commercial venture.

Twin City Sportservice, Inc. v. Charles O. Finley & Co., 512 F.2d 1264 (9th Cir. 1975)

When Charles O. Finley, the new owner of the Athletics baseball team moved the team to Oakland, California, in 1968, he insisted that he was not bound by the 1950 contract between his predecessor and Sportservice, a concession franchise, which permitted the concession to follow the team. Sportservice instituted a suit on the breach of contract, and Finley counterclaimed with an antitrust action. The trial court found for Finley on the antitrust claim, and this appeal followed.

In order to determine whether a party has a monopoly power in an antitrust action, it was essential first to determine the relevant market. The court of appeals disagreed with the trial court's premise that the concessionaire is the seller of concession services to the stadium owner. Instead, the appeals court held that a concessionaire sells its services to spectators and buys its franchise from the stadium owner. The court of appeals found this a threshold issue and remanded it to determine the relevant market. In doing so, it set forth its observations as guidelines for the trial court. The court cautioned that the relevant market could not be limited to those offered for sale by major league baseball teams since there was a high degree of substitutionality, and concessionaires can serve more than one leisure activity.

Because the court remanded the case, it found it unnecessary to determine what percentage of the market amounts to a showing of a monopoly, but reminded the court that a 50 percent share is often inadequate to establish a monopoly. It also found it unnecessary to determine whether the length of the agreement constituted an exclusive dealing unreasonably restraining competition, but doubted whether the follow-the-franchise provision had anticompetitive effects in view of the highly mobile professional sports franchises. Finally, the court disapproved of the trial court's decision that certain loan agreements in the 1950 contract constituted an illegal tying arrangement, since the requirement of two separate products was lacking.

TABLE OF CASES

Alabama Football, Inc. v. Greenwood, 4.29: 283*

Alabama Football, Inc. v. Stabler, 4.29: 283*

Alabama Football, Inc. v. Wright, 4.29: 285

Allen v. Commissioner of Internal Revenue, 4.23: 239*

Allen Bradley Co. v. Local Union No. 3, 2.41: 112*

Ali v. Playgirl, Inc., 4.53: 333*

Ali v. State Atheltic Com. of New York, 4.60: 345*

All-Pro Management, Denver Rockets v., 2.42, 4.71: 130, 354*

American Basketball Players Ass'n. v. National Basketball Ass'n., 6.22: 504*

American Basketball Ass'n. v. AMF Voit, Inc., 6.41: 528*

American Football League v. National Football League, 6.21: 497*

American League Baseball Club of Chicago v. Chase, 2.22: 93*

American League Baseball Club of New York v. Pasquel, 6.61: 540*

American League of Professional Baseball Clubs, 2.24, 2.30: 100, 108*

AMF Voit, American Basketball Ass'n. v., 6.41: 528*

Atlanta National League Baseball Club and Turner v. Kuhn, 6.32: 517*

Argovitz, Detroit Lions & Billy Sims, 4.11: 202*

Ashe v. Pepsico, Inc., 4.53: 339*

Baltimore Colts, Dutton v., 4.34: 307

Barnett, Central New York Basketball, Inc., v., 1.16, 2.12: 19, 79

Barry, Lemat Corporation v., 2.14: 88

Barry, Washington Capitols Basketball Corp. v., 2.13: 85

Basksi v. Wallman, 4.11: 208

Bergey, Cincinatti Bengals, 6.61: 544

Binderup v. Pathe Exchange, 223: 98

Blalock v. LPGA, 4.72: 367*

Boise Baseball Club, Inc., v. Kuhn, 2.24: 107

Borge v. Com. of Internal Revenue, 4.32: 243

Boris v. United States Football League, 4.71: 362*

Boston Celtics and Houston Rockets, 6.33: 525*

Boston Professional Hockey Ass'n. v. Cheevers, 2.42: 122

Bowman v. National Football League, 4.71: 3.62

Brooklyn National League Baseball Club, Levine v., 6.62: 552

Brooklyn National League Baseball Club, Mandel v., 6.62: 552

California Sports, Inc. and Wilton N. Chamberlain, 4.28: 269*

California Sports, Inc., McCourt v., 2.43: 134*

Cannon v. Los Angeles Rams, 4.25: 254*

Cepeda v. Swift & Co., 4.53: 340*

Central New York Basketball Inc. v. Barnett, 1.16, 2.12: 19, 79*

Chamberlain, Wilton N, California Sports Inc. and, 4.28: 269*

Chandler, Corbett v. 2.22: 97

Chandler, Gardella v. 2.22: 95*

Chandler, Kowalski, v., 2.22: 97

Chargers Football Club, Hennigan v., 4.32: 295*

Charles O. Finley, Hunter and, 4.29: 277*

Charles O. Finley & Co., v. Kuhn, 1.13, 2.24, 6.33: 11, 107, 524*

---

* Asterisk indicates full text of case given.

Chase, American League Baseball Club of Chicago v., 2.22: 93*

Cheevers, Boston Professional Hockey Ass'n. v., 2.42: 122

Chuy v. Philadelphia Eagles, 4.26: 258*

Cincinnati Bengals, Inc. v. Bergey, 6.61: 544

Cincinnati Exhibition Co. v. Marsans, 2.12: 73*

City of Berkeley v. Oakland Raiders, 6.11: 475

City of Oakland v. Oakland Raiders, 6.13: 480*

City of Oakland v. Superior Court of Monterey County, 6.13: 481*

Commissioner of Internal Revenue, Allen v., 4.23: 239*

Commissioner of Internal Revenue, Borge v., 4.32: 243

Commissioner of Internal Revenue, Frost v., 4.23: 237*

Commissioner of Internal Revenue, Heidel, 4.23: 236*

Commissioner of Internal Revenue, Hundley, v., 4.23: 238*

Commissioner of Internal Revenue, Kurt Frings Agency v., 4.23: 243

Commissioner of Internal Revenue v. Laughton, 4.32: 243

Commissioner of Internal Revenue, Patterson v., 4.23: 242

Commissioner of Internal Revenue, Robinson v., 4.23: 241

Commissioner of Internal Revenue, Wills v., 4.23: 235

Community Sports, Inc. v. Denver Ringsby Rockets, 4.28: 268*

Coniglio v. Highwood Services, 6.62: 549*

Connecticut Professional Sports Corp. v. Heyman, 2.11, *2.12: 73, 75*

Connell Construction Co. v. Plumbers & Steamfitters Local Union 100, 2.41: 116

Constituent Member Clubs of the National Football League, and their agent, National Football League Management Council, and NFLPA, 5.21: 386*

Consumer Enterprises, Inc., National Football League Properties v., 6.41: 531*

Cooga Mooga, Inc., In re: 322

Corbott v. Chandler, 2.22: 97

Crescent Amusement Co., United States v. 2.23: 98

C. Schmidt & Sons, Sharman v., 4.53: 341*

Cunningham, Munchak Corp. v., 2.13: 87

Dallas Cap & Emblem Co., National Football League Properties v., 6.41: 531*

Dallas Cowboys Football Club, Inc., Driskill v., 6.62: 551

Dallas Cowboys Football Club, Inc. v. Harris, 2.12: 77*

Dallas Cowboys Football Club, Inc., World Football League v., 6.61: 542

Daly v. Smith, 2.11: 68*

Deesen v. Professional Golfers Ass'n., 4.71: 349*

Delaware, National Football League v., 6.42: 539*

Del Puente, Mapleson v., 2.11: 68

Denver Ringsby Rockets, Community Sports, Inc. v., 4.28: 268*

Denver Rockets v. All-Pro Management, 2.42, 4.71: 130, 354*

Detroit Football Club v. Robinson, 4.25: 254*

Detroit Lions and Billy Sims v. Argovitz, 4.11: 202*

Detroit Lions and Mitchell Hoopes, 4.31: 287*

Dillon, Webster v., 2.11: 68

Driskill v. Dallas Cowboys Football Club, 6.62: 551

Drysdale v. Florida Team Tennis, Inc., 2.42: 130

Dutton v. Baltimore Colts, 4.34: 307*

Eckles v. Sharman, 4.25: 255*

Ellis v. Rocky Mountain Empire Sports, Inc., 4.32: 303*

Erving v. Virginia Squires Basketball Club, 1.16, 5.32: 19, 428*

Ettore v. Philco Television Broadcasting Corp., 4.53: 342

Ewing, Metropolitan Exhibition Co. v., 2.11: 69*

Federal Baseball Club of Baltimore, Inc. v. National League of Professional Baseball Clubs, 2.22, 3.49, 4.70: 94*

Flockton, Montague v., 2.11: 68

Flood v. Kuhn (U.S. Supreme Court), 1.16, 2.24: 17, 101*

Flood v. Kuhn (U.S. Dist. Ct.), 2.42: 118*

Florida Team Tennis, Drysdale v., 2.42: 130

Floyd, Houston Oilers, v., 4.32: 296

Foreman, George Foreman Associates v., 4.11: 208

Freeman and Locklear, Winnipeg Rugby Football Club v., 2.12: 74

Frost v. Commissioner of Internal Revenue, 4.23: 237*

Galento, Zwirn, v., 4.11: 207

Gardella v. Chandler, 2.22: 95*

George Foreman Associates v. Foreman, 4.11: 208

Gotham Football Club, Sample v., 4.26: 257*

Greenwood, Alabama Football Inc. v., 4.29: 283*

Griffith, United States v., 223: 98

Gunter Harz Sports, Inc. v. U.S. Tennis Ass'n., 6.41: 538*

Haelon Laboratories, Inc. v. Topps Chewing Gum, 4.53: 327*

Hallman, Philadelphia Ball Club v., 2.11: 70

Hampson, Nassau Sports v., 2.42: 122

Harrington v. New Orleans Saints, 4.32: 305*

Harris, Dallas Cowboys Football Club v., 2.12: 77*

Haywood v. National Basketball Association, 2.24: 104

Hecht v. Pro-Football, Inc., 6.23: 507*

Heidel v. Commissioner of Internal Revenue, 4.23: 236*

Heldman v. United States Lawn Tennis Ass'n., 6.22: 506*

Hennigan v. Chargers Football Co., 4.32: 295*

Henricksen, Uhlaender v., 4.53: 328*

Heyman, Connecticut Professional Sports Corp. v., 2.11, 2.12: 73, 75*

Highwood Services, Coniglio v., 6.62: 549

Hirsch v. S.C. Johnson & Son, Inc., 4.53: 329*

HMC Management Corp. v. New Orleans Basketball Club, 6.63: 553*

Hoopes, Mitchell, Detroit Lions and, 4.31: 287*

Houston Oilers v. Floyd, 4.32: 296

Houston Oilers, Inc. v. Neely, 2.13: 82*

Houston Oilers, Spain v., 4.32: 294

Houston Rockets, Boston Celtics and, 6.33: 525*

Hudson, Minnesota Muskies v., 2.13: 84*

Hundley v. Commissioner of Internal Revenue, 4.23: 238*

Hunter, James v. Charles O. Finley, 4.29: 277*

Internal Boxing Club of New York, United States v., 2.23, 2.24; 98, 103

Interstate Circuit v. United States, 2.23: 98

Jeffra, Rosenfeld v., 4.11: 207

Jewel Tea, Local No. 189, Amalgamated Cutters v., 2.41: 112*

Johansson, Machen v., 2.14: 88*

Johnson v. United States, 4.23: 242

Johnston v. Time, Inc., 4.53: 344*

JRV Corp. v. LeRoux, 6.12: 476*

Julian Messner Co., Spahn v., 4.53: 344

Kansas City Kings and New York Knicks, 6.34: 528*

Kansas City Royals Baseball Corp. v. Major League Baseball Players Association, 5.32: 416

Kapp v. National Football League, 2.42, 4.70: 125, 349*

Killifer, Weegham v., 2.11, 2.13: 73, 81*

Kowalski v. Chandler, 2.22: 97

Kuhn, Atlanta Baseball Club and Turner v., 6.32: 517*

Kuhn, Boise Baseball Club, Inc. v., 2.24: 107

Kuhn, Charles O. Finley & Co. v., 1.13, 2.24, 6.63: 11, 107, 524*

Kuhn, Commissioner of Baseball, and MLBPA (Willie Wilson and Jerry Martin), 5.42: 438*

Kuhn, Flood v. (U.S. Supreme Court), 1.16, 2.24: 17, 101*

Kuhn, Flood v. (U.S. District Court), 2.42: 118*

Kuhn, Portland Baseball Club v., 2.24, 6.21: 107, 503

Kurt Frings Agency v. Commissioner of Internal Revenue, 4.23: 243

Ladies Professional Golf Ass'n., Blalock v., 4.72: 367*

Lafkovsky, Safro v., 2.12: 76

Laird v. United States, 6.11: 471*

Lajoie, Philadelphia Base Ball Club, Ltd. v. (Ohio), 2.11: 73

Lajoie, Philadelphia Base Ball Club Ltd., v. (Pennsylvania), 2.11: 71*

Landis, Milwaukee American Assocation v., 6.33: 523*

Laughton, Commissioner of Internal Revenue v., 4.32: 243

Lemat Corporation v. Barry, 2.14: 88*

LeRoux, JRV Corp. v., 6.12: 476*

Levin v. National Basketball Association, 6.13: 478*

Levine v. Brooklyn National League Baseball Club, 6.62: 552

Linseman v. World Hockey Association, 4.71: 359*

Livingston v. Shreveport-Texas League Baseball Corp., 5.32: 428

Local No. 3, Allen Bradley Co. v., 2.41: 112

Local Union No. 189, Amalgamated Cutters, and Butcher Workmen of North America v. Jewel Tea Co., 2.41: 112*

Long Island American Ass'n. Football Club v. Manrodt, 2.12: 78*

Long Island Sports, Inc., Strauss v., 6.62: 552

Los Angeles Dons, Schultz v., 4.32: 296

Los Angeles Chargers, New York Footbacll Giants v., 2.13: 81*

Los Angeles Memorial Coliseum Commission v. National Football League, 1.20, 6.14: 20, 483*

Los Angeles Rams v. Cannon, 4.25: 254*

Lumley v. Gye, 2.11: 69

Lumley v. Wagner, 2.11: 68, 69

Machen v. Johansson, 2.14: 88*

Mackey v. National Football League, 2.42, 4.70: 122, 349*

Madison Square Garden, Inc. v. Muhammed Ali, 4.29: 285*

Madison Square Garden, Inc., Shayne v., 6.62: 551*

Major Indoor Soccer League and Professional Soccer Players Ass'n. (PROSPA) and MISL Players Ass'n., 5.13: 378*

Major League Baseball Player Relations Committee (Atlanta Braves) and Major League Baseball Players Ass'n. (Robert Horner), 4.28: 270*

MLB Player Relations Com., Silverman (NLRB) and, 5.51: 442*

Major League Baseball Players Ass'n. and Major League Baseball Players Relations Committee:
Panel Decision, No. 49, 5.52: 447*
Panel Decision No. 50A and 50B, 5.52: 449*
Panel Decision No. 50C, 5.52: 454*
Panel Decision No. 50D, 5.52: 455*
Panel Decision No. 50F, 5.52: 456*
Panel Decision No. 50G, 5.52: 457*

Major League Baseball Players Ass'n. (Carlton Fisk) and Major League Baseball Player Relations Com. (Boston Red Sox), 4.28: 273*

Major League Baseball Players Ass'n. (Ferguson Jenkins) and MLB Player Relations Com., 5.41: 437*

Major League Baseball Players Ass'n., Kansas City Royals v., 5.32: 416

Major League Baseball Players Ass'n. (Richard Tidrow) and MLB Player Relations Com., 5.41: 433*

Major League Baseball Players Ass'n. (Pascual Perez) and Bowie K. Kuhn, Commissioner of Baseball, 5.42: 439*

MLB Players Association (Willie Wilson and Jerry Martin), Kuhn and, 5.42: 438*

Major Leagues of Professional Baseball Clubs (Atlanta Braves) and MLBPA (Alvin Moore: I), 5.41: 429*

Major Leagues of Professional Baseball Clubs (Atlanta Braves) and MLBPA (Alvin Moore: II), 5.41: 431*

Major Leagues of Professional Baseball Clubs (Cleveland Indians) and MLBPA (James Bibby), 4.29: 279*

Major Leagues of Professional Baseball Clubs Minnesota Twins) and MLBPA (Michael Grant Marshall), 5.41: 432*

Mandel v. Brooklyn National League Baseball Club, 6.62: 552

Manok v. Southeast District Bowling Ass'n., 4.72: 366*

Manrodt, Long Island American Ass'n. Football Club v., 2.12: 74*

Mapleson v. Del Puente, 2.11: 68

Marsans, Cincinnati Exhibition Co. v., 2.12: 73*

Martin v. National League Baseball Club, 2.22: 97

McCourt v. California Sports, Inc., 2.43: 134*

Metropolitan Exhibition Co. v. Ewing, 2.11: 69*

Metropolitan Exhibition Co. v. Ward, 2.11: 69*

Mid-South Grizzlies v. National Football League, 6.13: 479*

Milton, Spencer v., 2.12: 74*

Milwaukee American Ass'n. v. Landis, 6.33: 523

Milwaukee Braves, State of Wisconsin v., 2.24, 6.14: 100, 496

Minnesota Muskies v. Hudson, 2.13: 84*

Minnesota Vikings, Alan Page and, 4.24: 252*

Molinas v. National Basketball Ass'n., 4.72: 364*

Molinas v. Podoloff, 4.72: 366

Montague v. Flockton, 2.11: 68

Morgan, Trammel v., 4.11: 207

Morio v. North American Soccer League, 1.14, 5.12: 14, 374*

Motschenbacher v. R.J. Reynolds Tobacco Co., 4.53: 337*

Muhammed Ali, Madison Square Garden v., 4.29: 285

Munchak Corp. v. Cunningham, 2.13: 87

Namath v. Sports Illustrated, 4.53: 342*

Nassau Sports v. Hampson, 2.42: 122

Nassau Sports v. Peters, 2.42: 122

National Basketball Ass'n., American Basketball Players Ass'n. v., 6.22: 504*

National Basketball Association, Haywood v., 2.24: 104

National Basketball Association, Levin v., 6.13: 478*

National Basketball Association, Molinas v., 4.72: 364*

National Basketball Association, O. Leon Wood v., 5.22: 399*

National Basketball Ass'n., Robertson Class Plaintiffs v., 5.22: 395*

National Basketball Association, Roberston v., 1.11, 2.23, 4.70: 5, 100, 349

National Basketball Ass'n., Washington Professional Basketball Corp., 6.13: 478*

National Basketball Ass'n. and National Basketball Players Ass'n. (All-Star Game: Part I), 5.32: 425*

National Basketball Ass'n. and NBPA (All-Star Game: Part II), 5.32: 426*

National Basketball Ass'n. and NBPA (All-Star Game Break), 5.32: 427*

National Basketball Ass'n. (Atlanta Hawks) and NBPA (Bill Willoughby), 4.34: 307*

National Basketball Ass'n. (Atlanta Hawks) and NBPA (Ken Charles), 4.31: 288*

National Basketball Ass'n. (Atlanta Hawks) and NBPA (Michael Sojourner), 4.32: 300*

National Basketball Ass'n.(Chicago Bulls) and NBPA (Robert Love), 4.35: 308*

National Basketball Ass'n. (Cleveland Cavaliers) and NBPA (Ronald Cox), 4.21: 230*

National Basketball Ass'n. (Denver Nuggets) and NBPA (Rudy Hackett), 4.27: 261*

National Basketball Ass'n. (Detroit Pistons) and NBPA (Ben Poquette), 4.37: 312*

National Basketball Ass'n. (Golden State Warriors) and NBPA (Charles Johnson), 4.27: 262*

National Basketball Ass'n. (Houston Rockets) and NBPA (John Vallely), 4.27: 261*

National Basketball Ass'n. (Indiana Pacers) and NBPA (Darrell Elston), 5.32: 425*

National Basketball Ass'n. (New Jersey Nets) and NBPA (Robert Love), 4.27: 263*

National Basketball Ass'n. (New Orleans Jazz) and NBPA (Toby Kimball), 4.32: 301*

National Basketball Ass'n (Portland Trail Blazers) and NBPA (Bob Davis), 4.32: 292*

National Basketball Ass'n. (Seattle Supersonics) and NBPA (Gerald Edwards), 4.32: 301*

National Basketball Players Ass'n. (Bernard King) and NBA (Utah Jazz), 5.42: 440*

National Football League Management Council and . . . NFL, and NFLPA, 5.21: 391*

NFL Management Council (Tampa Bay Buccaneers) and NFLPA (Jim Peterson), 4.32: 293*

NFL Management Council v. John Hannah & Leon Grey, 4.35: 310*

National Football League Players Association (NFLPA) and Russ Bolinger v. Detroit Lions, 4.24: 253*

NFL Players Ass'n. (Bob Lee) v. Minnesota Vikings, 4.27: 267*

NFL Players Ass'n. (Dante Pastorini) and NFLMC Oakland Raiders), 4.27: 263*

NFL Players Ass'n. (Dick Cunningham) and NFLMC (Philadelphia Eagles), 4.34: 306*

NFL Players Ass'n. (Ed Sharockman) and NFLMC (Minnesota Vikings), 4.31: 289*

NFL Players Ass'n. (Elvin Bethea) and NFLMC (Houston Oilers), 4.41: 314*

NFL Players Ass'n. (Eric Harris) and NFLMC (St. Louis Cardinals and New Orleans Saints), 4.32: 297*

NFL Players Ass'n. (Henry Childs) and NFLMC (New Orleans Saints and Washington Redskins), 4.33: 305*

NFL Players Ass'n. (Keith Lewis and Ezekial Moore) and NFLMC (Houston Oilers), 4.32: 298*

NFL Players Ass'n. (Rickie Harris) and New England Patriots, 4.36: 312*

NFL Players Ass'n. (Steven Manstedt) and NFLMC (New Orleans Saints), 4.32: 299*

NFL Players Ass'n. (William Stanfill) and NFLMC (Miami Dolphins), 4.32: 294*

NFL Players Ass'n. v. National Labor Relations Board, 5.21: 384*

National Football League, American Football League v., 6.21: 497*

National Football League, Bowman v., 4.71: 362

National Football League v. Delaware, 6.42: 539*

National Football League, Kapp v., 2.42, 4.70: 125, 349*

National Football League, Los Angeles Memorial Coliseum Committee v., 1.20, 6.14: 20, 483*

National Football League, Mackey v., 2.42, 4.70: 122, 349*

National Football League, Mid-South Grizzlies v., 6.13: 479*

National Football League, North American Soccer League v., 1.12, 5.11, 6.00: 7, 372, 527*

National Football League, Radovich v., 2.43: 131*

National Football League, United States Football League v., 6.24: 509*

National Football League Properties, Inc. v. Consumer Enterprises, 6.41: 531*

National Football League Properties, Inc. v. Dallas Cap and Emblem Mfg., 6.41: 531*

National Football League Properties, Inc. v. Wichita Falls Sportswear, Inc., 6.41: 532*

National Hockey League, Neeld v., 4.71: 363*

National Hockey League, San Francisco Seals Ltd. v., 6.14: 482*

National League Baseball Club, Martin v., 2.22: 97*

National League of Professional Baseball Clubs, Federal Baseball Club of Baltimore v., 2.22, 4.70: 94, 349*

Neeld v. National Hockey League, 4.71: 363*

Neely, Houston Oilers v., 2.13: 82*

Neff v. Time, Inc., 4.53: 344*

New England Patriots Football Club, Pfeiffer v., 6.62: 548*

New England Patriots Football Club v. University of Colorado, 6.61: 545*

New Hampshire Jockey Club, Tamello v., 6.62: 552*

New Jersey Nets and Philadelphia 76s, 6.34: 527*
New Orleans Basketball Club, HMC Corp. v., 6.63: 553*
New Orleans Saints, Harrington v., 4.32: 305*
New Orleans Saints, Tillman v., 4.32: 294*
Nilon v. Philadelphia Section of the Professional
    Golfers Ass'n., 4.71: 353*
New York Football Giants, Inc. v. Los Angeles Chargers,
    2.13: 81*
New York Knicks, Kansas City Kings and, 6.34: 528*
New York Yankees, Sielicki v., 4.32: 304*
New York Yankees, Toolson v., 2.22: 97*
North American Soccer League v. National Football
    League, 1.12, 5.11, 6.00: 7, 372, 527*
North American Soccer League, Morio v., 1.14, 5.12:
    14, 374*

Oakland Raiders, City of Berkeley v., 6.11: 475
Oakland Raiders, City of Oakland v., 6.13: 480*
O'Brien v. Pabst Sales Co., 4.53: 331*

Pabst Sales Co., O'Brien v., 4.53: 331
Pacific Lanes, Washington State Bowling Proprietors v.,
    6.22: 505
Page, Alan, and Minnesota Vikings, 4.24: 252*
Palmer v. Schonhorn Enterprises, Inc., 4.53: 333*
Paramount Famous Lasky Corporation v. United States,
    2.23: 98
Paramount Pictures, United States v., 2.23: 98
Parrish, Zinn v., 1.15, 4.11: 15, 202, 208*
Pasquel, American League Baseball Club of New York v.,
    6.61: 540*
Pathe Exchange, Binderup v., 2.23: 98
Patterson v. Commissioner of Internal Revenue, 4.23:
    242
Pennington, United Mine Workers of America v., 2.41:
    112*
People v. Sorkin, 4.11: 209
Pepsico, Ashe v., 4.53: 339*
Peters, Nassau Sports v., 2.42: 122
Pfeiffer v. New England Patriots Football Club, 6.62:
    548*
Philadelphia Ball Club v. Hallman, 2.11: 70
Philadelphia Ball Club, Ltd. v. Lajoie (Ohio), 2.11: 73
Philadelphia Ball Club, Ltd. v. Lajoie (Pennsylvania),
    2.11: 71*
Philadelphia Eagles, Chuy v., 4.26: 528*
Philadelphia Section of PGA, Nilon v., 4.71: 353*

Philadelphia World Hockey Club, Inc. v. Philadelphia
    Hockey Club, Inc., 1.11, 2.23, 2.40, 4.70: 4, 100, 119,
    349*
Philco Television Broadcasting Corporation, Ettore v.,
    4.53: 342
Playgirl, Inc., Ali v., 4.53: 333*
Podoloff, Molinas v., 4.72: 366
Portland Baseball Club, Inc. v. Kuhn, 2.24, 6.21: 107, 503
Professional Golf Association, Deesen v., 4.71: 349
Pro-Football, Inc., Hecht v., 6.23: 507
Pro-Football, Inc., Smith v., 2.42, 4.70: 127, 129, 349

Radovich v. National Football League, 2.23, 2.24, 4.70:
    98, 104, 349*
Reynolds v. National Football League, 2.43: 131*
Riko Enterprises v. Seattle Supersonics, 6.32: 515*
R.J. Reynolds Tobacco Co., Motschenbacher v., 4.53:
    337*
Rocky Mountain Empire Sports, Inc., Ellis v., 4.32: 303*
Robertson Class Plaintiffs and NBPA v. NBA, 5.22:
    394*
Robertson Class Plaintiffs and NBPA v. NBA and
    Seattle (Gus Williams), 5.22: 395*
Robertson Class Plaintiffs, In re, 5.22: 393
Robertson Class Plaintiffs (NBPA), and NBA (Junior
    Eligibles Rule), 5.22: 396*
Robertson v. National Basketball Association, 1.11,
    2.23, 4.70: 5, 100, 349*
Robinson v. Com. of Internal Revenue, 4.23: 241
Robinson, Detroit Football Club v., 4.25: 254*
Rosenfeld v. Jeffra, 4.11: 207

Safro v. Lakofsky, 2.12: 76
Sample v. Gotham Football Club, 4.26: 257*
San Francisco Seals, Ltd. v. National Hockey League,
    6.14: 482*
Schonhorn Enterprises, Palmer v., 4.53: 333*
Schultz v. Los Angeles Dons, 4.32: 296
S.C. Johnson & Co., Hirsch v., 4.53: 329*
Scripps-Howard Broadcasting Co., Zacchini v., 4.53:
    344
Seattle Supersonics, Riko Enterprises v., 6.32: 515*
Selig v. United States, 6.11: 473, 474*
Sharman v. C. Schmidt & Sons, Inc., 4.53: 341
Sharman, Eckles v., 4.25: 255*
Shayne v. Madison Square Garden Corp., 6.62: 551*
Shreveport-Texas Baseball Corp., Livingston, 5.32: 428

Shubert Theatres, United States v., 2.23, 2.24: 98, 103
Sielicki v. New York Yankees, 4.32: 304*
Silverman (NLRB) and Major League Baseball Player Relations Committee, 5.51: 442*
Smith, Daly v., 2.11: 68
Smith v. Pro-Football, Inc., 2.42, 4.70: 127, 129, 349*
Sorking, People v. 411: 209
Southeast District Bowling Association, Manok v., 4.72: 366*
Spahn v. Julian Messner Co., 4.53: 344
Spain v. Houston Oilers, Inc., 4.32: 294
Spencer v. Milton, 2.12: 74*
Sports Illustrated, Namath v., 4.53: 342*
Stabler, Alabama Football, Inc. v., 4.29: 283*
State Athletic Commission of New York, Ali v., 4.60: 345*
State of Wisconsin v. Milwaukee Braves, 2.24, 6.14: 100, 496
STP Corporation v. U.S. Auto Club, 6.41: 538
Strauss v. Long Island Sports, Inc., 6.62: 552
Superior Court of Monterey County, City of Oakland v., 6.13: 481*
Swift & Co., Cepeda v., 4.53: 340*

Tamello v. New Hampshire Jockey Club, 6.62: 552
Tiger Lanes, Inc., Toms v., 6.62: 552
Tillman v. New Orleans Saints Football Club, 4.32: 294
Time Inc., Johnston v., 4.53: 344*
Time Inc., Neff v., 4.53: 344
Time Inc., Virgil v., 4.53: 344
Toms v. Tiger Lanes, Inc., 6.62: 552
Toolson v. New York Yankees, 2.22: 97*
Tops Chewing Gum Co., Haelon Laboratories v., 4.53: 327
Trammel v. Morgan, 4.11: 207
Twin City Sportservice, Inc. v. Charles O. Finley & Co., 2.24, 6.64: 107, 554*
Twelve Clubs Comprising National League . . . and Twelve Clubs Comprising American League . . . and Major League Baseball Players Ass'n., 5.32: 407*

Uhlaender v. Henricksen, 4.53: 328*
United Mine Workers of America v. Pennington, 2.41: 112*
United States v. Crescent Amusement Co., 2.23: 98
United States v. Griffith, 2.23: 98
United States, Johnson v. 4.23: 242

United States v. International Boxing Club of New York Inc., 2.23, 2.24: 98, 103
United States, Laird v., 6.11: 471
United States, Paramount Famous Lasky Co., 2.23: 98
United States v. Paramount Pictures, Inc., 2.23: 98
United States, Selig v., 6.11: 473, 474
United States v. Shubert, 2.23, 2.24: 98, 103
United States Football League, Boris v., 4.71: 362*
United States Football League v. National Football League, 6.24: 509*
U.S. Auto Club, STP Corporation v., 6.41: 538
U.S. Lawn Tennis Association, Heldman v., 6.22: 506*
U.S. Tennis Association, Gunter Harz Sports, Inc. v., 6.41: 538*
University of Colorado, New England Patriots Football Club v., 6.61: 545*

Virgil v. Time Inc., 4.53: 344
Virginia Squires Basketball Club, Erving v., 1.16, 5.32: 19, 428*

Wallman, Baksi v., 4.11: 208
Ward, Metropolitan Exhibition Co. v., 2.11: 69*
Washington Capitals Basketball Club v. Barry, 2.13: 85*
Washington Professional Basketball Corp. v. National Basketball Ass'n., 6.13: 478*
Washington State Bowling Proprietors Ass'n. v. Pacific Lanes, 6.22: 505
Webster v. Dillon, 2.11: 68
Weegham v. Killefer, 2.11, 2.13: 73, 81*
Wichita Falls Sportswear, Inc., National Football League Properties v., 6.41: 532*
Willis v. Com. of Internal Revenue, 4.23: 235*
Winnipeg Rugby Football Club v. Freeman and Locklear, 2.12: 74*
Wood (O. Leon) v. National Basketball Association, 5.22: 399*
World Football League v. Dallas Cowboys Football Club, 6.61: 542*
World Hockey Association, Linseman v., 4.71: 359*
Wright, Alabama Football, Inc. v., 4.29: 285

Zacchini v. Scripps-Howard Broadcasting Co., 4.53: 344
Zinn v. Parrish, 1.15, 4.11: 15, 202, 208*
Zwirn v. Galento, 4.11: 207

INDEX

Agents (*see* Attorneys/Agents)

All-American Football Conference (AAFC), 67

American Association (baseball) (AA), 65, 67

American Bar Association, code of professional responsibility, 214–215

American Basketball Ass'n. (ABA), 4, 5, 19, 20, 45, 67, 84–85, 87–88, 255–256, 393, 528–531

American Basketball League (ABL), 67

American Football League (AFL), 27, 45, 67, 77, 81–83, 126, 497–503

American Hockey League (AHL), 4

American League (baseball) (AL) (*see* Major League Baseball)

Antitrust
 application of, 41, 66, 92–107, 118–119, 349, 496, 503, 525
 baseball exemption (*see* Major League Baseball)
 basketball (*see* National Basketball Association)
 boxing (*see* Boxing)
 boycotts, 359–364
 cartel aspects, 37–38
 Clayton Act, 90–92, 98, 123, 127
 eligibility rules, 349–364
 entertainment industries, 98
 essential facilities doctrine, 507–510
 football (*see* National Football League)
 franchises
  cross-ownership of, 463–469
  movement of, 481–496
  right to own, 478–481 (*see also,* Franchises)
 geographic markets, 497–503
 golf (*see* Golf)
 hockey (*see* National Hockey League)
 labor exemption, 91, 111–134, 399–402
 mergers (*see* Mergers)
 monopoly, 497–510
 player draft, 125–130
 player markets, control of, 503–507
 player restraints, 93–107, 116–138, 349–369, 399–402
 refusals to deal, 5, 349–369, 478–480, 538
 reserve clause, 5, 100–107
 Rozelle rule, 122–126, 128–129, 131–134
 rule of reason, 124, 125, 128, 129, 130–134
 Sherman Act, 90–92, 94–96, 98–100, 106, 112, 119–124, 127, 131
 settlements, 131–134, 482–483
 single entity theory, 38, 463–469, 481–496
 state law applications of, 93–94, 496
 suspensions, 364–369
 territorial rights, 483–496
 tying arrangements, 548–552
 writings about, 496

Arbitration
 collective bargaining provisions for, 290–292, 402–406
 types of disputes heard
  all-star games, 425–427
  bonus clauses, 252–253, 279–283
  discipline, 300–301, 306–308
  drug use by players, 437–441
  duties after breach, 277–283
  extra benefits, 313–315
  free agency, 407–425, 429–436
  game protests, 527–528
  guaranteed contracts, 261–268
  injuries, 292–295, 297–303
  loans to players, 311–312
  option clauses, 269–277, 433–436
  powers of panels, 425

renegotiation of contracts, 308–311
reserve system, 407–416
salaries during strikes, 448–460
salary reduction, 312–313
special covenants, 429–433
termination, economic reasons for, 288–289
termination, because of injury, 292–295, 297–303
termination, because of lack of skill, 287–288
termination, for retirement, 289
trades, 305–306, 525–526
waiver of liability, 230, 232
Arenas (*see* Stadiums and Arenas)
Ass'n. of Representatives of Professional Athletes
(ARPA), form contract, 226–227
Attendance, 41, 54, 56, 59 (*see also,* NBA, NFL, NHL)
Attorneys/agents
agreements with players, 15–17, 223–228
ARPA form, 226–227
compensation, 15–17
duration, 16
NFLPA form, 224–225
criticism, of, 202, 209
establishing player relationship, 202–228
ethical constraints, 213–217
ABA code provisions, 214–215
NCAA provisions, 215–217
fraud by, 209–213
functions, 109–202, 228–234, 321–345
counseling, 200
managing, 200, 321–345
marketing, 200, 208, 321–345
negotiating, 199, 228–234
planning, 201
resolving disputes, 201
regulation of
federal laws, 208–209
players associations, 217–223
state certification laws, 202–208
writings about, 228
Auto racing
antitrust, 538
right of publicity and privacy, 337–339

Bargaining subjects (*see* Collective Bargaining)
Bargaining units (*see* Labor Law and Relations)
Baseball (*see* AA, Federal, MLB, MLBPA, Mexican,
Players, and Union Leagues or Associations)
Basketball (*see* ABA, ABL, EPBL, FIBA, Italian League,
NBA, and NBPA)

Bell, Bert, statement of, 13
Body surfer, right of privacy, 344
Bonus clauses, 243–253
disputes over, 248–253, 279–283
types of, 244–248
awards or honors, 247–248
other contingencies, 248
statistical performance, 245–246
status, 245
volume of play, 246–247
Bowling
exclusion of patrons, 552
suspensions and blacklists, 366–367
Boxing
anticipatory breach, 285–287
antitrust, 98
equal protection, 354–359
injunctions, 76–77, 88–90
licensing of managers, 207–208
rights of publicity & privacy, 333–335, 342
tax problems, 241, 242
Broadcasting
league-wide agreements, 540
markets, control of, 33, 509–510
revenues, 3, 26, 36, 57–64

California, regulation of agents in, 202–208
Cartels (*see* Antitrust; Leagues)
Central Hockey League, 4
Clayton Act (*see* Antitrust)
Clubs (*see* Franchises)
Collective bargaining (*see also,* Labor law and relations)
enforcement mechanisms, 383–401
forcing of, 374–378
provisions
agent's approval, 194–195
assignment of contracts, 172
benefits, 174–175, 196–197
deferred compensation, 165, 197
discipline, 176–177
draft, 178–181, 195
drug treatment program, 436
endorsements, 322
free agency, 182–185, 196
free agency, compensation for, 190–196
grievance procedures, 196, 290–292, 402–406
injury protection, 170–172
options, 181–182, 195
right of first refusal, 185–190, 195

salaries, 163–165, 194
salary arbitration, 405–406
salary cap, 165–169
severance pay, 165
standard form, requirement of, 162
termination pay, 169–170, 194
termination notice, 174
waivers, 173
Commissioners
arbitration, 526–528
discipline by, 514–523
general powers, 511–514
interclub dealings, 523–526
role of, 11–13
voiding contracts, 523–526
Concessions, stadium, 554
Congress (*see* Legislation)
Constitutional Law, (*see* Equal protection)
Constitutions and by-laws (*see* Leagues)
Consumers (fans)
exclusion of, 552
protective laws, 552
season tickets
false representation, 552
tie-in with preseason, 548–552
Contracts, attorneys/agents' (*see* Attorneys/agents)
Contracts, foreign leagues, 318–321
Contracts, player
assignments (trades), 305–306
breach of
by player, 19, 20, 68–89, 93–94
damages for, 68, 255–256
discipline, 306–307
endorsements, 321–322
enforcement of, 67–89
formation of, 254–255
guarantees, 152, 263–268, 448–460
injunctions, 68–89
injuries, 170, 292–305
length of, 257–260
negotiation of (*see* Attorneys/agents)
options, 181, 195, 269–277, 433–436
physical condition, 144–145, 156
renegotiation of, 310–311
salaries, 42–52, 448–460
skill representation, 145, 157–158
termination of, 287–289
waivers of liability, 230–232
Cosell, Howard, statement of, 31–34
Cunningham, David, statement of, 34–35

Davis, Al, statement of, 27–28
Deferred compensation (*see* Taxation: Players)
Discipline, players
arbitration of, 300–301, 306–308
collective bargaining provisions, 176–177
players contracts, 306–307
Draft, player, 5, 125–130, 354
collective bargaining provisions, 178–181, 195
Drugs
arbitration over, 437–441
treatment programs, 436

Eastern Hockey League, 4
Eastern Professional Basketball League, 75
Eligibility rules
juniors eligible (NBA), 396–399
litigation over, 349–364
Eminent domain, 480–481
Endorsement contracts
FTC regulations, 322, 326
league provisions, 321–322
sample form, 323–326
Equal Protection Clause, 345–349
Equitable relief (*see* Injunctions)

Federal Communications Commission, 34
Federal League, 67
Federal Trade Commission, 322, 326
Fehr, Donald, statement of, 37–38
Fines (*see* Discipline; Suspensions)
Flaherty, Colin, statement of, 38–40
Football (*see* AAFC, AFL, NFL, NFLPA, USFL, and WFL)
Foreign leagues, 318–321
Franchises
control struggles for, 476–477
cross-ownership of, 10, 463–469
eminent domain, taking by, 480–481
movement of, 6, 20, 21, 25–35, 481–496
operational concerns (outline), 541
owners, 7, 8, 9, 11, 19, 478–480
right to own, 478–481
taxation of (*see* Taxation: Franchise)
values of, 4, 9, 59, 60
Free agency, 9, 11, 270–283, 395–396, 407–425, 429–436

Garvey, Ed, statement of, 35–37

Golf
    antitrust issues, 349–354, 367–369
    disciplinary actions, 367–369
    right of publicity & privacy, 333
Grievances, (*see* Arbitration)

History (*see* Leagues)
Hockey (*see* AHL, EHL, CHL, IHL, NHL, WHA, and WHL
Horse Racing, exclusion of patrons, 552

Income Averaging (*see* Taxation: Player)
Injunctions, Player Contracts, 68–90
    basic standards, 68–73
    indefiniteness, 69, 70
    lack of mutuality, 70, 72–73, 73–80
    unclean hands, 80–87
    undue harshness, 87–90
    uniqueness, 72, 73–80
Injuries,
    arbitration over, 292–295, 297–303
    collective bargaining provisions, 170–172
    contract provisions disputes, 292–305
International Amateur Basketball Association (FIBA), 394–395
International Hockey League, 4
Italian Basketball League, 394–395
    sample contract, 318–321

Labor exemption (*see* Antitrust)
Labor law and relations
    arbitration
        binding nature of, 416, 425, 428
        grievance procedures (NFL), 290–292, 402–405
        salary (baseball), 405–406
        types of disputes (*see* Arbitration)
    drug abuse, 436–441
    individual versus collective, 429–436
    injunction under 10(j), 374–378
    jurisdiction, 708–111
    mandatory bargaining, 400–401
    MISLPA, 378–383
    multiemployer unit, 372–374
    NASLPA, 14, 372
    NLRB, 108–111, 384–393, 442–447
    player corporations, 401

Robertson settlement, 383, 393–401
    strikes, 441–460
    strikes, salaries during, 447–460
    unfair labor practice, 374–-378, 383–393, 442–447
    union certification, 372–374
    union membership, 378–383
    union organizers, 378–383
    unit, 371–383
Leagues
    attendance figures, 41
    budgets, 52
    cartel aspects of, 37–38
    commissioners of (*see* Commissioners)
    constitution and bylaws, 21–23, 134–138, 140–141, 150–151
    expansion, 36, 497–503
    expenditures, 40, 52–53, 57–58
    functions, 7
    governance, 4
    history of, 1–3, 17–18, 65–67, 463–464
    interleague rivalries, 7–9, 65–67, 496–510
    legal status, 461–469, 485–492
    membership rights, 477–496
    rules of, 12, 233, 244
    single entity theory, 38, 463–469, 481–496
Libel, 34–345
Legislation 25–40
    hearings over, 23–25
    proposed in Congress, 23–25
Loans to players, 311–312
Lockouts (*see* Labor law and relations, strikes)

Major Indoor Soccer League (MISL), 36, 244, 378, 384
Major Indoor Soccer League Players Ass'n., 378–383
Major League Baseball (MLB), agreement of, 12, 13
    antitrust, application of 41, 92–97, 100–107, 118–119, 349, 496, 503, 525
    bonus clauses, 244, 246–247, 248, 279–283
    cartel aspects, 37–38
    collective bargaining provisions
        agent's approval, 194–195
        assignment of contracts, 172
        benefits, 174–175, 196–197
        deferred compensation, 197
        drug treatment program, 436
        free agency, 182–185, 196
        free agency, compensation for, 193–194, 196
        injuiry protection, 170

salaries, 163–165, 194
  salary arbitration, 196, 405–406
  termination pay, 169–170, 194
  waivers, 173
commissioner of, 11–13
  disciplinary power, 517–523
  voiding contracts, 523
  voiding trades, 524–525
concessions contracts, 554
constitution and bylaws, 140–141
consumers, exclusion of, 552
drug abuse, 436–441
expenditures, 40
franchises
  movement of, 31–32
  values, 60
free agency, 9, 270–283, 407–416, 429–436
history of, 1, 17–18, 65, 67
injunctions, player contracts, 69–75, 81
labor, NLRB jurisdiction, 108–111
leagues, budgets, 52
MLBPA, 407–416
options, 270–277, 433–436
owners, 8, 11, 476–477
reserve system, 407–416
revenues
  broadcast, 61, 62, 63
  general, 36, 40
  sharing of, 3
right of publicity and privacy, 327–329, 340–341
rules of, 12, 233, 244
salaries
  during strikes, 448–459
  player's individual, 43, 48, 49, 50
  team total, 51
standard player contract provisions
  assignments, 159
  endorsements, 321–322
  physical condition, 156
  skill representation, 157–158
tampering, 411, 517–523
taxation, players, 235–240
taxation, teams, 473–475
tortious conduct, 540, 542
Major League Baseball Players Association (MLBPA),
    407–416
  Fehr, Donald, statement of, 37–38
Mergers
  ABA-NBA, 5

AFL-NFL, 27
  legal sanctions for, 91–92
Mexican League, 67
Minor Leagues (hockey), 4, 5
Monopoly (*see* Antitrust)

National Basketball Association
  all-star games, 425–427
  antitrust
    application of, 100, 349
    boycotts, 5, 354–359
    eligibility, 354–359
    labor exemption, 399–402
    player markets, 504–506
    refusals to deal, 5
    suspensions and blacklists, 364–366
    tying arrangements, 551–552
  attendance figures, 41, 54
  bonuses, 244, 246, 247
  collective bargaining provisions
    benefits, 176
    deferred compensation, 165
    draft, 179–181
    drug treatment program, 436
    free agency, 182
    options, 181–182
    right of first refusal, 185–190
    salary cap, 165–169
  commissioner
    disciplinary powers, 515–517
    voiding trades, 525–526
  constitution and by-laws, 150–151
  consumer protection, 552
  draft, 5, 354
  expenditures, 52–53
  eligibility rules, 396–399
  franchises
    movement of, 21, 28–29
    values, 60
  free agency, 9, 11, 395–396
  history of, 1
  injunctions, player contracts, 79–80, 84–87, 88
  libel, 344–345
  merger with ABA, 5
  NBPA, 394
  options, 269–270
  owners, 8, 9, 19, 478–479
  player contracts

discipline, 300–301, 307–308
formation of, 255–256
guarantees, 261–263
injuries, 292–293, 300–303
renegotiation of, 308–310
salary reduction, 312–313
termination of, 288–289
reserve clause, 5
revenues
broadcast, 3, 61, 62
gate, 55, 56
general, 40
sharing of, 3
right of publicity or privacy, 341–342
Robertson settlement, 383, 393–401
salaries
player's individual, 43–45
team total, 51
salary cap, 391–402
stadium leases, 553–554
standard player contract
allowable amendments, 142, 152–155
assignments, 145–146
bonuses, 146
complete form, 143–151
options, 155
physical condition, 144–145
proper attire, 142
publicity, 152
skill representation, 145
salary guarantees, 28–29
Stern, David, commissioner, 28–29
taxation, players, 242
waiver of liability, 230, 232
National Basketball Players Ass'n. (NBPA), 394
National Collegiate Athletic Ass'n., constitution and
by-laws, 215–217
National Football League (NFL)
antitrust
application of, 98–100, 349
boycotts, 362–363
eligibility rules, 362–363
franchises, cross-ownersip, 463–469
franchises, movement of, 483–496
franchises, right to own, 479–481
labor exemption, 122–134
player markets, 497–503
settlements, 131–134
single entity theory, 483–496
territorial rights, 483–496

tying arrangements, 548–551
attendance, 56, 59
attorneys/agents
functions of, 208–209
regulation of, 217–223
Bell, Bert, statement of, 13
bonus clauses, 244, 246–253
collective bargaining provisions,
benefits, 175–176
Davis, Al, statement of, 27–28
discipline, 176–177
draft, 178–179
endorsements, 322
free agency, 182
free agency, compensation for, 190–192
injury grievance, 290–292
injury protection, 170–172
options, 181
non-injury grievance, 402–405
right of first refusal, 185–186
salaries, 163
severance pay, 169
standard form, requirement of, 162
termination notice, 174
termination pay, 169
waivers, 173
commissioner
discipline, 514–515
powers of, 511–514
competition with other leagues, 9
constitution and by-laws, 21–23, 134–138
draft, 125–130
drug abuse, 437
franchises
eminent domain, taking by, 480–481
expansion, 36
movement of, 20–21, 27–28, 29–30, 31, 34–35,
482–496
values, 60
free agency, 9, 416–425
history of, 1
injunctions, player contracts, 74, 77–78, 81–84
leagues, functions, 7
loans to players, 311–312
merger, with ALF, 27
options, 126, 277
owners, 8, 479–480
player contracts, 15–16
discipline, 306–307
extra benefits, 314–315

formation of, 254–255
guarantees, 263–268
injuries, 293–299, 303–305
length of, 257–260
renegotiation of, 310–311
termination of, 287–289
trades, 305–306
revenues
broadcast, 3, 26, 36, 57–64
gate, 56–60
general, 26, 27, 29, 36, 37, 40, 41, 57–60
sharing of, 3, 26, 36, 56
right of publicity or privacy, 329–330, 342–344
Rozelle, Pete, statement of, 25–27
Rozelle Rule, 122–126, 128–129, 131–134
salaries
during strikes, 459–460
players' individual, 43, 45–47, 208
team total, 46–47
standard player contract
assignments, 159
bonuses, 158
bribery, 158
extension of, 161
physical condition, 155–156
skill representation, 157
termination pay, 160
tampering, 126
taxation
players, 236–237
teams, 471–473, 475–476
television, 33, 509–510, 540
tortious conduct, 257–260, 542–547
trademark protection, 531–540
National Footbal League Players Ass'n. (NFLPA)
contract advisor form, 224–225
Garvey, Ed, statement of, 35–37
regulation of agents, 217–223
National Hockey League (NHL)
antitrust
application of, 100, 349
boycotts, 359–362, 363–364
eligibility, 359–364
labor exemption, 119–122
settlements, 482–483
attendance figures, 41
bonuses, 244, 246
collective bargaining provisions
draft, 195
endorsements, 322

free agency, compensation for, 195
options, 195
right of first refusal, 195
franchises
movement of, 29, 30, 482–483
values, 60
league governance, 4
minor league affiliates, 4, 5
options, 195
owners, 8
revenues
broadcast, 3, 61, 62
general, 40
sharing of, 3, 30–31
salaries
player's individual, 42–45, 51–52
standard player contract
bonuses, 158
physical condition, 156
skill representation, 157
termination, 160
Ziegler, John, statement of, 30–31
National Labor Relations Board (NLRB), 384–393,
442–447
jurisdiction of, 107–111
Negative Covenants (*see* Injuctions)
No-Cut Contracts (*see* Contracts, Players; Standard
Player Contracts)
North American Soccer League (NASL)
cross-ownership problems, 463–469
franchise organization, 7, 9
history of, 463–464
labor relations, 372–378
league functions, 7, 14–15
owners, 8, 465
revenues, 9
North American Soccer League Players Association
(NASLPA), 14, 372

Option Clauses, 126, 195, 269–270, 277
Owners (*see* Franchises)

Partnerships, control of, 476–477
Player Contracts (*see* Contracts, Player)
Player Draft (*see* Draft, Player)
Player Salaries (*see* Salaries, Player)
Players Associations, 13–15 (*see also* MISLPA, MLBPA,
NBPA, NFLPA, NASLPA)
Players League, 65, 67
Privacy, Right of

libel, compared with, 344–345
publicity, compared with, 331–339
relinquishment of, 340–342
trademark, compared with, 339–340
yielding to news, 342–344
Prize-fighting (*see* Boxing)
Professional athlete, definition of, 394–395
Publicity, right of
libel, compared with, 344–345
privacy, compared with, 331–339
recognition of, 327–331
relinquishment of, 340–342
trademark, compared with, 339–340
yielding to news, 342–344

Racing commissions, 480
Reserve system, 5, 69–73, 93–94, 101–107, 407–416
Restraint of trade (*see* Antitrust)
Revenues, leagues and clubs,
broadcast, 3, 26, 36, 57–64
gate, 55–60
general, 26, 27, 29, 36, 37, 40, 41, 57–60
sharing of, 3, 26, 30–31, 36, 56
Right of privacy (*see* Privacy)
Right of publicity (*see* Publicity)
Robertson settlement (NBA), 383, 393–401
Rozelle, Pete, statement of, 25–27
Rozelle Rule, 122–126, 128–129, 131–134

Salaries, player
during strikes, 448–460
player's individual, 42–52, 208
team total, 46–47, 51
Salary Cap (NBA), 165–169, 391–402
Schwartz, Louis, statement of, 38
Sherman Act (*see* Antitrust)
Soccer (*see* MISL, MISLPA, NASL, NASLPA)
Stadiums and arenas, 38–40, 552–554
Standard Player Contract Provisions
allowable amendments (NBA), 142, 152–155
assignments, 145–146, 159
bonuses, 146, 158
bribery, 158
complete form (NBA), 143–151
extension of, 161
options, 155
physical condition, 144–145, 155–156
skill representation, 145, 157
proper attire, 142

publicity, 152
salary guarantees, 152
termination pay, 160
Stern, David, statement of, 28–29
Strikes (*see* Labor Law and Relations)
Suspensions, 364–369

Tampering, 126, 411, 517–523
Taxation: Franchise
license tax, 475–476
sale of team, treatment of players contracts, 470–475
state income tax, 475
writings about, 469–470
Taxation: Player
deductions, 235–236
deferred compensation
contractual, 240–241
pension plans, 241–242
income averaging, 236–238
income splitting, 238–240
personal corporations, 242–243
Television (*see* Broadcasting)
Tennis
antitrust, 130, 506–507, 538
contract form, 315–318
trademark, 339–340
Territorial rights (*see* Antitrust)
Tortious conduct, mental infliction, 257–260
Tortious interference, 255–256, 522–523, 540, 542–548
Trademark, 339–340, 528–540
Trade name, 329–330

Unfair Labor Practices (*see* Labor Law and Relations)
United States Football League, 40, 43, 45, 47–48, 60–61, 63, 66, 209–213, 244, 277, 509–510
Union Association, 65, 67
Unions (*see* Labor Law and Relations; Players Associations)

Waiver of Liability, 230–232
Waivers (*see* Collective Bargaining)
Wilson, Lionel, statement of, 29–30
Western Hockey League (WHL), 4
Workers Compensation, 303–305
World Football League (WFL), 283–285
World Hockey Association (WHA), 4, 45

Ziegler, John, statement of, 30–31